# Social Psychology

W • W • Norton & Company • New York • London

# Social Psychology

**Thomas Gilovich**
CORNELL UNIVERSITY

**Dacher Keltner**
UNIVERSITY OF CALIFORNIA AT BERKELEY

**Richard E. Nisbett**
UNIVERSITY OF MICHIGAN

W. W. Norton & Company has been independent since its founding in 1923, when William Warder Norton and Mary D. Herter Norton first published lectures delivered at the People's Institute, the adult education division of New York City's Cooper Union. The Nortons soon expanded their program beyond the Institute, publishing books by celebrated academics from America and abroad. By mid-century, the two major pillars of Norton's publishing program—trade books and college texts—were firmly established. In the 1950s, the Norton family transferred control of the company to its employees, and today—with a staff of four hundred and a comparable number of trade, college, and professional titles published each year—W. W. Norton & Company stands as the largest and oldest publishing house owned wholly by its employees.

Editor: Jon Durbin
Developmental Editor: Sandy Lifland
Managing Editor, College: Marian Johnson
Editorial Assistant: Kelly Rolf
Director of Manufacturing, College: Roy Tedoff
Book Design and Graphics: Antonina Krass
Cover Design: Debra Morton Hoyt
Cover Art and All Chapter Opener Illustrations: John S. Dykes (www.jsdykes.com)
Photo Research: Neil Hoos, Kelly Mitchell, Kelly Rolf
Composition and Page Layout: Carole Desnoes
Offset Prep: Jay's Publishers Services
Art Studio: ElectraGraphics
Manufacturing: R.R. Donnelley

Library of Congress Cataloging-in-Publication Data

Gilovich, Thomas
    Social psychology / Thomas Gilovich, Dacher Keltner, Richard E. Nisbett.
        p. cm.
    Includes bibliographical references and index.
    **ISBN 0-393-97875-3**
    1. Social psychology.  I. Keltner, Dacher. II. Nisbett, Richard E. III. Title.

HM1033.G52 2005
302—dc22                                                                    2005053946

W. W. Norton & Company, Inc. 500 Fifth Avenue, New York, NY 10110
                         www.wwnorton.com
W. W. Norton & Company Ltd., Castle House, 75/76 Wells Street, London W1T 3QT

1 2 3 4 5 6 7 8 9 0

# ABOUT THE AUTHORS

**THOMAS GILOVICH** is Professor of Psychology and Co-Director of the Center for Behavioral Economics and Decision Research at Cornell University. His research focuses on how people evaluate the evidence of their everyday experience to make judgments, form beliefs, and decide on courses of action. He is the recipient of the Russell Distinguished Teaching Award and is a fellow of the American Psychological Society, the American Psychological Association, and the Committee for the Scientific Investigation of the Claims of the Paranormal. His other books include *How We Know What Isn't So: The Fallibility of Human Reason in Everyday Life*, *Why Smart People Make Big Money Mistakes—and How to Correct Them* (with Gary Belsky), and *Heuristics and Biases: The Psychology of Intuitive Judgment* (with Dale Griffin and Daniel Kahneman).

**DACHER KELTNER** is Professor of Psychology and the Director of the Center for the Development of Peace and Well-Being at the University of California at Berkeley. His research focuses on the pro-social emotions, such as love, sympathy and gratitude, morality, and power. He is the recipient of the Western Psychological Association's award for outstanding contribution to research, the Positive Psychology Prize for excellence in research, the Distinguished Teaching Award for Letters and Sciences, and the Distinguished Mentoring Award at UC Berkeley, and is a fellow of the American Psychological Association and the Society for Personality and Social Psychology. His other book is *Understanding Emotions* (with Keith Oatley and Jennifer Jenkins).

**RICHARD E. NISBETT** is Theodore M. Newcomb Distinguished University Professor of Psychology at the University of Michigan, Senior Research Scientist at Michigan's Institute for Social Research, and Co-Director of the University's Culture and Cognition Program. His research focuses on how people from different cultures think, perceive, feel, and act in different ways. He is the recipient of the Distinguished Scientific Contribution Award of the American Psychological Association and the William James Fellow Award of the American Psychological Society, and is a member of the National Academy of Science and the American Academy of Arts and Sciences. His other books include *The Geography of Thought: How Asians and Westerners Think Differently...and Why*, *Human Inference: Strategies and Shortcomings of Social Judgment* (with Lee Ross), *The Person and the Situation* (with Lee Ross), and *Culture of Honor: The Psychology of Violence in the South* (with Dov Cohen).

## We dedicate this book to

Karen, Ilana, and Rebecca Dashiff Gilovich

Mollie McNeil and Natalie and Serafina Keltner-McNeil

Sarah Nisbett

# Contents in Brief

# Contents

PART ONE    Connecting to Others  45

CHAPTER 2    Groups  46

CHAPTER 3   Attraction 86

CHAPTER 4   Relationships 128

CHAPTER 5    The Social Self 168

# PART TWO    Influencing Others 211

## CHAPTER 6    Social Influence 212

## CHAPTER 7    Attitudes and Persuasion 256

CHAPTER 8  Attitudes and Behavior  296

PART THREE Social Thought 335

CHAPTER 9 Causal Attribution 336

CHAPTER 10 Social Judgment 380

CHAPTER 11    # Stereotyping, Prejudice, and Discrimination 428

PART FOUR  Social Sentiments 471

CHAPTER 12  Emotion 472

CHAPTER 13  Aggression and Altruism 512

CHAPTER 14  Morality, Justice, and Cooperation 552

# Featured Topics in Social Psychology

# Preface

As we were putting the finishing touches on this book, a series of events unfolded in New Orleans, Louisiana, that raised all sorts of social psychological questions and reinforced the importance of studying and understanding social psychological phenomena. Hurricane Katrina wreaked havoc on the city, causing billions of dollars in damage and dismantling most of the communications infrastructure that is essential to an effective emergency response. Partly because of failing communications, but also because of difficult weather conditions, bureaucratic delays, and the fact that some emergency helicopters were shot at by angry residents stranded in the city without food and water, efforts to deal with the unfolding humanitarian crisis were slow to develop. Without a sufficient presence by the police, the National Guard, and emergency medical personnel, parts of the city descended into a Hobbesian world in which gangs of armed thugs raped and assaulted people seeking shelter, including stranded tourists.

The frightening events in New Orleans revealed how much of everyday life depends on invisible norms and social structures that few people can identify or articulate, but that nonetheless guide harmonious human interaction. The chaos that engulfed the city also raises numerous questions about how norms and social structures function, and how people act both within and outside these structures. Why weren't more effective relief efforts planned in advance, especially since it was known several days beforehand that a hurricane would probably strike the city? What concoction of anger, hostility, frustration, and alienation would lead individuals to shoot at rescue helicopters? What inspired some residents to lead frightened tourists to safety and led others to take advantage of their vulnerability? The whole nation was asking these sorts of questions, including the community of scholars who call themselves social psychologists. Indeed, social psychologists spend their professional lives studying questions such as: Why do people make the decisions that they do? Why can groups be prone to such disturbing conflict and yet so quickly reconcile? How can we best curtail people's selfish impulses and foster cooperation? This book is our attempt to summarize and integrate the very best attempts to come to grips with such questions.

The time for such an integration, we believe, could not be better. Social psychology has been undergoing exciting changes in recent times, with important contributions being made by cultural psychologists, evolutionary psychologists, neuroscientists, and researchers who are exploring the interplay between deliberate and automatic mental processes. We wanted to capture the excitement of this new work, to highlight what we believe are its most important contributions, and to integrate it with the discipline's enduring themes.

What are the enduring themes of social psychology? One of them is the extraordinary power that situations can have over people's behavior. Time and time again, social psychologists have been able to illuminate how subtle changes in the social context or prevailing circumstances dramatically alter people's actions. This message is profoundly counterintuitive because we are raised in Western society to think that individuals should and do control their own actions, and so getting this message across is one of the most important contributions we can offer undergraduate students, whatever their field of study. The message is also, we believe, profoundly optimistic, as it points to effective situational interventions and discourages an outlook in which one is quick to condemn people for not always being able to discern the path to the most effective or admirable action.

A second lasting theme of social psychology involves the role of a person's construal of stimuli and prevailing situations—that is, the degree to which a person's understanding of the world is an interpretation that might or might not be shared by others. Time and time again, social psychologists have been able to illuminate how it is the person's interpretation of events or circumstances that influences behavior, not the objective events or circumstances themselves. This basic insight dates back to some of the founding figures in social psychology, such as Solomon Asch, and in many ways set the stage for the cognitive revolution in psychology.

Many of the classic studies in social psychology illustrate both of these central themes. Stanley Milgram's study of obedience is the quintessential example. Our treatment of Milgram's research is therefore largely dedicated to demonstrating both the extraordinary power of the situation that Milgram created and the extent to which subtle determinants of the construal of the situation make escape difficult for the participant.

Two additional themes have become more and more prominent in social science research in the past decade: (1) the evolutionary context of human behavior, and (2) the remarkable evidence about the differences among cultures in behavior previously assumed to be universal. Although people sometimes think evolutionary and cultural approaches are at odds with one another, our treatment of them is based on the premise that they provide invaluable, *complementary* insights into everyday social behavior. To this end, we try to show how an evolutionary theorist would think about some of the basic phenomena of social psychology, often reporting on animal behavior that is analogous to what we see in humans, and discussing how behavior that is uniquely human is understandable in terms of the early challenges to survival and reproduction faced by our ancestors. We also discuss how adaptation to different conditions, however, may have taken some universal tendencies in different directions based on culture.

We take a particularly close look at two quite different ways of being human (and all sorts of blends and variants in between these two). One of these is the Western way (studied almost exclusively by psychologists for the first 100 years that psychology could be called a science), in which relationships are seen as informal, role relations as relatively unscripted, and the self as existing independently of groups. The other is the Eastern way (probably more characteristic of most of the world's people), in which relationships and role constraints are seen as more structured, and the self as fundamentally enmeshed in groups. We spend a great deal of time attempting to convince the student that there really are two such very different ways of being human, and we explore many of the social, perceptual, and cognitive consequences of these different ways of being.

There are several other themes in recent research that we emphasize because they are so far-reaching in their implications. Foremost among these is the research on automatic versus consciously mediated behavior, which makes clear that much of human thought, emotion, and action is instigated by causes that lie outside of awareness. This fact is essential to understanding both of our major themes. Situations have the power that they do because we often cannot see crucial aspects of them that influence us. Construal is far more important than we realize because we often lack the tools to see how it is carried out or even that it is being carried out.

Robert Abelson has said that the best studies in social psychology can be read as parables: the parable of the individual who felt trapped into harming another person in the name of science, the parable of the clergyman who did not help someone in need because he was in a hurry, the parable of the group that went along with a poor decision in order to save everyone's face. In our teaching, we find that students are captivated by such narratives, and we deliberately treat studies as parables in this text. We also begin chapters with a parable or conundrum whose solution requires understanding the material the student is about to read. We find both types of narratives to be excellent ways to help students grasp and retain central issues in social psychology.

The text is designed as a series of narratives in another sense as well. Where there is a line of research that involves puzzles that are addressed by the next study, which in turn creates another puzzle to be solved, we present the research as a sleuthing operation. We feel this is an excellent way of holding students' interest and ensuring that they retain the most important material.

The sleuthing perspective is also used to demonstrate to the student how research is conducted from a methodological standpoint. "To show," as Woodrow Wilson put it while he was still a professor at Princeton, "the manner of a scholar." Because the methodology is highlighted in much of the work we discuss, we do not have a separate chapter on the topic. We believe that students learn methodology much better when it is presented in the context of a line of research than when presented in abstract, decontextualized fashion. We have tried to make sure that all of our field's varied methods—for example, archival analyses, semantic and affective priming, neuroimaging, and participant observation—are discussed in sufficient depth to give the reader an understanding of how they work and what their strengths and weaknesses are. The bulk of that discussion is embedded within the individual, substantive chapters, with each methodological point brought up in the context of a particular research example to which it is most germane. Nevertheless, a separate section at the end of the Introduction acquaints the student with the methodological basics, such as the crucial distinction between correlational and experimental research. This section also serves as a glossary of terms describing different kinds of methods. Beyond that, the content of the text itself does the job of illustrating the methods social psychologists use when they go about their business of trying to expand the understanding of human social behavior.

Aside from not having a separate chapter on methods, our text differs from most others in that it has chapters dealing with four emerging bodies of knowledge. Studies of different cultures and inquiries about how we have evolved have led to new insights about the self, about our relationships, about the nature and function of our emotional experience, and about our moral judgments. These developments have inspired new literatures—and separate chapters in our textbook. Our text attempts to integrate the classic studies with these emergent trends in our discipline and to weave them around the twin themes of the power of the situation and construal.

Our organization is different from most current social psychology textbooks. We think it is important to begin with the most fundamentally social topics. Thus, after a broad overview chapter sketching the major themes of the text, we begin with four chapters that deal with how we relate to one another—how we act in groups, how we come to like and pursue some individuals and dislike and avoid others, the varied nature of our relationships, and how our sense of self is constructed in our interactions with others. We continue with three chapters on social influence—influence that is largely face-to-face, influence that largely has its source in the mass media, and the mutual influence that attitudes and behavior have on one another. We then pursue the importance of construal directly, with three chapters that deal with everyday thought and how our thoughts shape our actions. The book ends with three chapters focusing on feelings—on the basics of emotion, on how our passions inspire acts of altruism and bouts of aggression, and how they infuse our sense of morality and justice and our desire to cooperate.

We chose this organization because we have found in teaching our courses that the content of these early chapters comes closest to what our students had in mind when they opted to enroll in something called Introduction to Social Psychology. The material in these chapters is particularly fascinating to them and draws them into the later topics. But one of us has taught an introductory social psychology course every year for over two decades and has never covered the topics in the textbook in the order in which they are presented in this text. It should come as no surprise, then, that we have written every chapter with an eye toward modularity. Each chapter stands on its own and can be assigned and read before or after any of the others—after the Introduction, of course.

## ANCILLARIES

Our book comes with a full range of ancillary materials created by a talented group of social psychology instructors. There is an Instructor's Manual, as well as Powerpoint Lecture Slides, by Todd Nelson from California State University, Stanislaus. The Instructor's Manual includes Tom Gilovich and Dennis Regan's lecture notes from their jointly taught social psychology course at Cornell University. The Powerpoint Lecture Slides and the art from the book are also available on the Norton Media Library CD-Rom. Jane Richards from the University of Texas, Austin, has written the Test-Item file, which includes 1,000 questions. Connie Wolfe from Muhlenberg College has created the Study Guide and contributed content for the Student Website—wwnorton.com/socialpsych. This includes the Norton Gradebook—wwnorton.com/web/gradebook—which allows students and instructors to store and track their online quiz results effectively. The Norton Social Psychology DVD containing video clips focusing on real-world research in action is also available to adopters of our book. Finally, all of the instructor's materials are also available online and ready for downloading for WebCT and Blackboard courses at the Norton Resource Library—ww norton.com/nrl.

## ACKNOWLEDGMENTS

No book is written in a vacuum. Many people have helped us in the course of writing this text, starting with our families. Karen Dashiff Gilovich was her usual bundle of utterly lovable qualities that make the sharing of lives so enjoyable— and the difficulties of authorship so tolerable. Mollie McNeil was a steady source of kindness, enthusiasm, and critical eye and ear. Sarah and Susan Nisbett were sounding boards and life support systems.

Mikki Hebl, Dennis Regan, and Tomi-Ann Roberts went well beyond the call of collegial duty by reading every chapter and providing us with useful commentary. In addition to giving us the considerable benefit of their good judgment and good taste, they also pointed out a few of our blind spots and saved us from an occasional embarrassing error.

We are also grateful to Jon Durbin, Vanessa Drake-Johnson, and Paul Rozin for bringing us together on this project and getting it all started. We have had a great deal of fun working together and have enjoyed the opportunity to think and write about the broad discipline that is social psychology. Thanks. We would also like to extend our gratitude to Jon for his energy, for his encouragement, and for his interest and openness to creating a new kind of social psychology text, one that we hope captures cutting-edge trends while returning to a more close-up, in-depth style of presentation.

And what would we have done without Sandy Lifland? Between us, there are at least 1.5 obsessive-compulsives, and yet Sandy's attention to detail outdid our collective obsessiveness by a factor of ten. We shudder to think of the number of errors that might have found their way into the book if it were not for her. But Sandy was not just a mistake-detector, she helped us to unify (or at least harmonize) our three voices, and she had many good ideas about how to solve the difficult problems that came up in the effort to present a field as vast as social psychology in a single book. Our thanks to Neil Hoos, Kelly Mitchell, and Kelly Rolf for doing such a good job locating photos for the text, and for putting up with our firm, yet nonetheless sometimes changing, opinions on these matters. We are also grateful to Antonina Krass and Carole Desnoes for teaching us more than a few things about design and for giving our book a look we are enthusiastic about.

Laura Reynolds and Carol Traynor also helped in innumerable ways in preparation of the book, and the students in the Culture and Cognition Program at the University of Michigan were stimulating colleagues and helpful critics.

Our thanks to the following reviewers and consultants for their helpful suggestions and close reading of earlier drafts of various chapters in the book:

## CONSULTANTS

| | |
|---|---|
| Mikki Hebl | *Rice University* |
| Dennis Regan | *Cornell University* |
| Tomi-Ann Roberts | *Colorado College* |

## REVIEWERS

| | |
|---|---|
| Glenn Adams | *University of Toronto* |
| Craig Anderson | *Iowa State University* |
| Elliott Beaton | *McMaster University* |
| Susan Boon | *Calgary University* |
| Tim Brock | *Ohio State University* |
| Susan Cross | *Iowa State University* |
| George Cvetkovich | *Western Washington University* |
| Dan Dolderman | *University of Toronto* |
| Richard Eibach | *Yale University* |
| Eli Finkel | *Northwestern University* |
| Marcia Finkelstein | *University of South Florida* |
| Azenett Garza-Caballero | *Weber State University* |
| Jon Haidt | *University of Virginia* |
| Lora Haynes | *University of Louisville* |
| Steve Heine | *University of British Columbia* |
| Andy Karpinski | *Temple University* |
| Marc Kiviniem | *University of Nebraska, Lincoln* |
| Ziva Kunda (deceased) | *Waterloo University* |
| Marianne LaFrance | *Yale University* |
| Alan Lambert | *Washington University* |
| Jeff Larsen | *Texas Tech University* |
| Norman Li | *University of Texas, Austin* |
| Doug McCann | *York University* |
| Daniel Molden | *Northwestern University* |
| Gerrod Parrott | *Georgetown University* |
| Ashby Plant | *Florida State University* |
| Deborah Prentice | *Princeton University* |
| Jane Richards | *University of Texas, Austin* |
| Jennifer Richeson | *Northwestern University* |
| Alex Rothman | *University of Minnesota, Twin Cities Campus* |
| Darcy Santor | *Dalhousie University* |
| Jeff Sherman | *Northwestern University* |
| Colleen Sinclair | *University of Missouri, Columbia* |
| Jeff Stone | *University of Arizona* |
| Warren Thorngate | *Carleton University* |

Zakary Tormala    *Indiana University, Bloomington*
David Wilder    *Rutgers University*
Connie Wolfe    *Muhlenberg College*
Joseph Vandallo    *University of South Florida*
Leigh Ann Vaughn    *Ithaca College*
Randy Young    *Bridgewater State University*
Jennifer Yanowitz    *University of Minnesota, Twin Cities Campus*

T.G.
D.K.
R.E.N.
September 2005

# Social Psychology

# Chapter Outline

# CHAPTER 1

# Introduction

In April 2004, more than a year after the start of the war in Iraq, CBS broadcast a story on *60 Minutes II* that exposed American atrocities against Iraqi prisoners in the Abu Ghraib prison near Baghdad. CBS showed photos of naked prisoners with plastic bags over their heads, stacked up in a pyramid and surrounded by jeering and laughing male and female American soldiers. Other photos showed hooded prisoners who were standing on narrow pedestals with their arms stretched out and electric wires attached to their bodies. CBS also reported that prisoners had been required to simulate sexual acts.

Most Americans were appalled at the acts and ashamed of the behavior of the U.S. soldiers. The reaction on the part of many Iraqis and others in the Arab world was to regard the acts as evidence that the United States had malevolent intentions toward Arabs (Hauser, 2004). The United States dropped yet further in the esteem of the world.

The assumption—or hope—of many Americans was that the soldiers who had perpetrated these acts were rotten apples—exceptions to a rule of common decency prevailing in the military. But social psychologists were not so quick to reach such a conclusion.

Thirty years before the atrocities at Abu Ghraib, Philip Zimbardo and his colleagues paid twenty-four Stanford University undergraduate men, chosen for their good character and mental health, to be participants in a study of a simulated prison (Haney, Banks, & Zimbardo, 1973). By the flip of a coin it was determined who would be a "guard" and who would be a "prisoner." The guards wore green fatigue uniforms and reflective sunglasses. The prisoners wore tunics with nylon stocking caps and had a chain locked around one ankle. The "prison" was set up in the basement of the psychology department, and the researchers planned that the study would last for two weeks. But the guards quickly turned to verbal abuse and physical humiliation, requiring the prisoners to wear bags over their heads, stripping them naked, and requiring them to engage in simulated sex acts. The study had to be terminated after six days because the behavior of the guards produced extreme stress reactions in several of the prisoners.

Zimbardo today maintains that the balance of power in prisons is so unequal that they tend to be brutal places unless heavy constraints are applied to curb the guards' worst impulses. Thus, both in Abu Ghraib and at Stanford, it can be said that "It's not that we put bad apples in a good barrel. We put good apples in a bad barrel. The barrel corrupts anything that it touches" (quoted in Schwartz, 2004).

It might be objected that the soldiers in Iraq were only following orders and that, left to their own devices, they would not have chosen to behave as they did. This may be the case, but it only pushes the question back one step: Why did they follow such orders? Social psychologists seek to find answers to just such questions.

In this chapter, we explain what social psychology is and what social psychologists study. We also present some of the basic concepts of social psychology, especially the surprising degree to which social situations can influence behavior, the role of "construal," or the interpretive processes people use to

**Prison Situations and Intimidation**
(A) Military guards at the Abu Ghraib prison in Iraq used torture, humiliation, and intimidation to try to obtain information from the prisoners. This included stripping them and making them lie naked in the prison corridors, as shown here, or stacking them naked in a pyramid, as in the image shown on *60 Minutes II.* Such degradation echoes what happened in the Zimbardo prison study, as shown in (B) a photo of a "guard" seeking to humiliate one of his prisoners at the simulated prison.

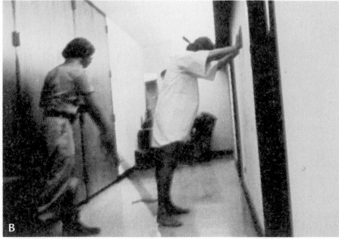

understand situations, and how two different kinds of thinking—one rapid, intuitive, and unconscious, and the other slower, more analytic, and conscious—contribute in tandem to understanding what is happening in social situations. We also describe some recent developments in social psychology that are beginning to change the field—namely, the application of evolutionary concepts to human behavior and the discovery of some great differences in human cultures that frequently lead people in different societies to respond to the "same" situation in very different ways.

# CHARACTERIZING SOCIAL PSYCHOLOGY

People have long sought explanations for human behavior. They have wondered about such things as the brutality of guards toward prisoners, as at Abu Ghraib, why people are inclined to stereotype members of different groups, why people risk their lives to help others, and why crowds can turn into violent mobs. Stories and parables have attempted to explain human behavior for millennia. Folk wisdom has been passed from generation to generation through folklore, jokes, and admonitions, explaining why people do what they do and prescribing behaviors to avoid or to follow. Social psychologists go beyond folk wisdom and try to establish a scientific basis for understanding human behavior by conducting studies and setting up experiments. As such, **social psychology** can be defined as the scientific study of the feelings, thoughts, and behaviors of individuals in social situations.

> **social psychology** The scientific study of the feelings, thoughts, and behaviors of individuals in social situations.

## EXPLAINING BEHAVIOR

The actions at Abu Ghraib can be studied from many points of view, but social psychologists are particularly inclined to study it as an instance of social influence, asking how the individual guards were affected by the actions of one another, and the orders, explicit and implied, of people whose opinions they valued. "The elixir of power, the elixir of believing that you're helping the CIA, for God's sake, when you're from a small town in Virginia, that's intoxicating," said Gary Myers, the attorney for one of the guards charged with abusing the prisoners in Abu Ghraib. "And so, good guys sometimes do things believing that they are being of assistance and helping a just cause. . . . And helping people they view as important."

Social psychologists study situations in which people (real and imagined, encountered today or in the past, face to face or through television or the Internet) exert social influence, and how people respond to influence attempts of various kinds. Social psychologists are also greatly concerned with how people make sense of their world—how they decide what and whom to believe, how they make inferences about the motives, personalities, and abilities of other people, and how they reach conclusions about the causes of events. Social psychologists address questions like the following: Why might people assigned to play the role of guards abuse those who are assigned to be prisoners? Why do roles like prison guard, football fan, or class clown exert such powerful influences on social behavior? Does the presence of others affect how people perceive a situation or their ability to solve a difficult problem? What is the best way to persuade others to

**Explaining Situations**    Social psychologists seek to understand how individuals act in relation to others in social situations. Why might some people on the line seek to ignore everyone else (and be left alone by everyone), and others seek to talk to anyone who will listen to them? Are they more willing to wait because they are with other people? Does their behavior change based on the number of people present or the length of the wait?

change their opinions or to do something they might not do under normal conditions? When people are led to say something they don't believe, do their beliefs normally move in the direction of what they've said, or do they more typically become even more firmly entrenched in their initial beliefs?

These sorts of questions lie at the heart of social psychology. There are answers to all of them—answers hard won by research. Some of the answers surprised even the social psychologists who conducted the research, because they commonly have the same sorts of expectations that nonpsychologists have, based on "folk" theories about human behavior. Such findings are counterintuitive. The results are not what most people think would happen. For example, we would not expect ordinary undergraduates to treat people badly just by virtue of being assigned to be a prison guard. On the other hand, some folk theories are right on the money. For example, we tend to like people who like us, and the people we like generally have interests that are similar to ours. When experimental findings reflect what our intuitions and folk wisdom say will happen, social psychologists elaborate that folk wisdom—they seek to discover when it applies and what lies behind the phenomenon in question. Yet, we will demonstrate numerous times in this book that many of our most strongly held folk theories or intuitions fail to give complete answers to many important questions. And others are just plain wrong. Thus, social psychologists need to test intuitions by devising studies and crafting experiments that successfully isolate the causes of behavior in social situations.

We are convinced that much of what social psychologists know about human behavior is invaluable. Social psychology now forms a significant part of the curriculum in many schools of business, public health, social work, education, law, and medicine. Social psychological research on such topics as judgment and decision making, social influence, and how people function in groups are relevant to all those fields. Social psychologists apply their knowledge to important questions regarding individuals and society at large, studying how to reduce stereotyping and prejudice in the classroom and workplace, how to make eyewitness testimony more reliable, how physicians can best make use of diverse sources of information to make a correct diagnosis, what goes wrong in airplane cockpits when there is an accident or a near-accident, and how decisions by businesses, governments and individuals can be improved.

Research by social psychologists regularly influences government policy. For example, research on the effects of different kinds of welfare programs is used in shaping government-assistance policies. Research also affects decisions by the courts. The landmark 1954 *Brown* v. *Board of Education* ruling that struck down school segregation in the United States drew heavily on social psychological research, which had indicated that segregated schools were inherently unequal in their effects (and thus unconstitutional). By the time you have finished this book, you will have a great deal of the knowledge drawn on by educators, business-people, and the government. We hope and believe that this knowledge will change your understanding of yourself and others, and make you more effective and satisfied in your personal and professional lives.

## COMPARING SOCIAL PSYCHOLOGY TO RELATED DISCIPLINES

The events at Abu Ghraib, like so many other telling social events, can be studied from many viewpoints, including those of politicians, criminologists, sociologists, and personality psychologists. Each takes a different approach to what happened and offers different kinds of explanations.

Personality psychology is a close cousin of social psychology, but it stresses individual differences in behavior. Whereas social psychologists look at how individuals react "on average" in social situations, personality psychologists look at the effects of individual traits and characteristics on their reactions. Thus, social psychologists would examine the general situation at Abu Ghraib, in which orders were not clear but pressures were brought to bear on the guards to "soften up" the prisoners to get information about other insurgents and upcoming attacks. Personality psychologists would instead look at whether certain traits and dispositions—for example, sadism or hostility—predict cruel behavior across a range of situations. Personality psychologists try to find coherence in the way individuals behave across situations, such that they can reasonably be described as having a position on a trait dimension. For example, everyone has a location on the dimension of extraversion (outgoingness) to introversion (shyness). Some people can be shown to behave more or less consistently in an extraverted or introverted fashion across a wide range of situations. Others—the great majority, actually—are harder to predict, and consistency typically comes in the form of situation-specific consistency: in situation X they behave in extraverted fashion; in situation Y, in more introverted fashion (Mischel, 2004; Mischel, Shoda, & Mendoza-Denton, 2002).

Social psychology is also related to cognitive psychology, the study of how people perceive, think about, and remember aspects of the world. In fact, many psychologists call themselves cognitive social psychologists. They differ from cognitive psychologists primarily in that the topics studied are usually social—perceptions and beliefs about other human beings. Cognitive psychologists would be more likely to study categorization or memory for words or objects.

Sociology is the study of behavior of people in the aggregate. Sociologists study institutions, subgroups, bureaucracies, mass movements, and change in demographic characteristics (for example, age, gender, socioeconomic status) of populations. Sociologists might ask about the religious and social backgrounds of the insurgents in Iraq, whether they are part of a mass movement, and whether imprisonment and torture of insurgents would be a successful strategy to stop further attacks against American forces and the new Iraqi government and police force. Social psychologists sometimes do sociological work themselves, although they are likely to bring an interest in individual behavior to the study of aggregates. A sociologist might study economic or government policy influences on marriage and divorce rates in a population, whereas a social psychologist would be more likely to study why *individuals* fall in love, get married, and sometimes get divorced.

## PROXIMAL AND DISTAL INFLUENCES IN SOCIAL PSYCHOLOGY

Fifteen years ago, social psychologists would have said that their field deals primarily with the "proximal" factors influencing behavior—that is, factors that exist in the here-and-now or that immediately precede what the individual does. This would include the situation itself, how the individual perceives the situation, and the processes—conscious and unconscious—of perceiving and reacting to situations. But things have changed. In recent times, two important "distal" factors—that is, factors that are more removed in time from a given context or episode—have greatly influenced the field of social psychology. One such distal factor is evolution. Psychologists can apply evolutionary theory to an understanding of human behavior. Using the evolutionary approach, psychologists seek primarily to understand the ways in which all, or nearly all, humans behave in similar fashion, and they try to explain these commonalities in terms of adaptation. Another distal factor is culture. Using the cultural approach, psychologists attempt to understand the deep cultural differences that exist between different societies and how they lead people to behave quite differently in situations that on the surface appear to be the same.

Social psychology (and psychology as a whole) differs from all other social science fields, including anthropology, political science, and economics, in that its chief investigative tool is the experiment. We will now discuss some of the most important influences on social behavior and how social psychologists use research—typically *experimental* research—to gain greater understanding about what is happening in social situations. We begin our discussion of important influences on social behavior by considering the proximal factors.

## THE POWER OF THE SITUATION

Are we all capable of acts of evil or brutality? The philosopher Hannah Arendt in 1963 suggested as much in her controversial book *Eichmann in Jerusalem.* In her book, Arendt described the trial of Adolf Eichmann, the notorious architect of Hitler's plan to exterminate the Jews in Nazi-occupied Europe. Advancing a very controversial thesis, Arendt described Eichmann as little more than a bureaucrat doing his job. While not condoning his actions (Arendt was herself Jewish), Arendt argued that Eichmann was not the demented, sadistic personality one expected (and that the prosecutor claimed), but instead he was a boring, unimaginative, uncaring cog in a machine that he served, not with glee, but with a resigned (if nevertheless perverse) sense of duty. Perhaps even more disturbingly, the logical conclusion of Arendt's theory is that any one of us is capable of performing acts of brutality. Look at the person sitting closest to you right now. Do you think that he or she is capable of atrocities? Do you think that any situation could be so powerful that even you or the person next to you could act as Eichmann did in Nazi Germany or as the prison guards behaved at Abu Ghraib?

**The Person or the Situation?**
Adolf Eichmann was apprehended in
Argentina, where he had escaped
after the end of World War II, and
taken to Israel to stand trial for the
murder of 6 million Jews. Here he
stands with Israeli police in a bullet-
proof glass cage during his trial. Was
Eichmann a brutal murderer or simply
a bureaucrat following the orders of
his superiors?

Arendt's book created a firestorm of indignant protests, and abuse was heaped
on her for what many regarded as her attempted exoneration of a monster. But
as we will see, research has provided support for Arendt's heretical views. To see
how this could be so, we will examine this research and ask another question,
one that is central to the study of social psychology: How does the situation that
people find themselves in affect their behavior?

The founder of modern social psychology was Kurt Lewin, a Jewish Berliner
who fled Nazi Germany in the 1930s and became a professor at the University of
Iowa and then at MIT. Lewin was a physicist before he became a psychologist,
and he applied a powerful physical intuition to an understanding of psychological existence. He believed that the behavior of people, like the behavior of
objects, is always a function of the *field of forces* in which they find themselves
(Lewin, 1935). To understand how fast a solid object will travel through a
medium, for example, one must know such things as the viscosity of the
medium, the force of gravity, and any initial force applied to the object. In the
case of people, the forces are psychological as well as physical. The person's own
attributes are also important determiners of behavior, of course, but these attributes always interact with the situation to produce the resulting behavior.

The social equivalent of Lewin's concept of the field of forces is the role of the
situation, especially the social situation, in guiding behavior. The main situational influences on our behavior, influences that we often misjudge or fail to see
altogether, are the actions—sometimes just the mere presence—of other people.
Friends, romantic partners, even total strangers can cause us to be kinder or
meaner, smarter or dumber, lazier or more hard working, bolder or more cautious. They can produce drastic changes in our beliefs and behavior by what they
tell us, by modeling through their actions what we should think and do, by subtly implying that our acceptability as a friend or group member depends on

**Kurt Lewin** A pioneer of modern
social psychology, Lewin stressed the
importance of the field of forces,
including the social situation, in
affecting a person's behavior.

adopting their views or behaving as they do, or even by making us feel that our freedom is being encroached upon by their influence attempts, which may lead us to actually move in the opposite direction. We rely on other people to define for us what emotions to feel in various situations, and even to define who we are as individuals. All this has been shown in studies that have demonstrated the power of the situation.

## THE MILGRAM EXPERIMENT

In the same year as the publication of Arendt's book, Stanley Milgram (1963, 1974) published the results of a now-classic experiment on social influence. Milgram advertised in the local newspaper for men to participate in a study on learning and memory at Yale University in exchange for a modest amount of money. (In subsequent experiments, women also participated, with similar results.) When the volunteers—a mix of laborers, middle-class individuals, and professionals ranging in age from their twenties to their fifties—arrived at the laboratory, a man in a white lab coat told them that they would be participating in a study of the effects of punishment on learning. There would be a "teacher" and a "learner," with the learner trying to memorize word pairs such as "wild/duck." The volunteer and another man, a somewhat heavy-set, pleasant-looking man in his late forties, drew slips of paper to determine who would play which role. But things were not as they seemed: the pleasant-looking man was actually an accomplice of the experimenter, and the drawing was rigged so that he was always the learner.

We will describe Milgram's study in more detail in Chapter 6. For now, suffice it to say that the "teacher" was instructed to administer shocks—from 15 to 450 volts—to the learner each time he made an error. Labels under the shock switches ranged from "slight shock" through "danger: severe shock" to "XXX." The experimenter explained that the first time the learner made an error, the teacher was to administer a shock of 15 volts; the next time the learner made an error, 30 volts, and so on, in ascending 15-volt magnitudes. The teacher was given a 45-volt shock so that he would have an idea of how painful the shocks would be. What he didn't know was that the learner, who was in another room, was not actually being shocked.

Despite groans, pleas, screams, and eventually silence from the learner as the intensity of the shocks increased, 80 percent of the participants continued past

**The Milgram Study** To examine the role of social influence, Stanley Milgram set up a study in which participants believed they were testing a learner (actually a confederate) and punishing him with shocks when he gave wrong answers. (A) Milgram's "shock machine, and (B) the participant and experimenter attaching electrodes to the learner before the start of the testing.

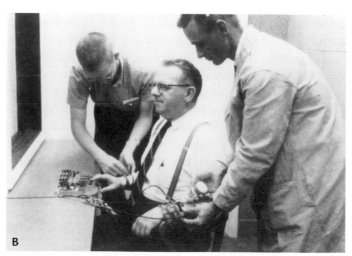

the 150-volt level (at which point the "learner" had mentioned that he had a heart condition and had screamed, "Let me out of here"). Most participants became concerned as the shock levels increased and turned to the experimenter to ask what should be done. But the experimenter insisted they go on. The first time the teachers expressed reservations, they were told, "Please continue." If the teacher balked, the experimenter said, "The experiment requires that you continue." If the teacher continued to be recalcitrant, the experimenter said, "It's absolutely essential that you continue." If necessary, the experimenter escalated to, "You have no other choice. You must go on." If the participant asked if the learner was liable to suffer permanent physical injury, the experimenter said, "Although the shocks may be painful, there is no permanent tissue damage, so please go on."

In the end, 62.5 percent of the participants went all the way to the 450-volt level, delivering everything the shock generator could produce. The *average* amount of shock given was 360 volts, *after* the point at which the learner let out an agonized scream and became hysterical. Milgram and other experts did not expect so many participants to continue to administer shocks as long as they did (a panel of thirty-nine psychiatrists predicted that only 20 percent of the participants would continue past the 150-volt level and that only 1 percent would continue past the 330-volt level; they believed that only a tiny proportion of participants would continue to the 450-volt level).

At first, some researchers expressed suspicion as to whether Milgram's participants really believed that they were shocking the learner. To prevent the scientific community from having to rely on his own assertions about whether his participants took the situation seriously, Milgram invited social scientists to observe his experiments from behind a one-way mirror. The observers could scarcely believe what they were seeing. One of them reported:

> I observed a mature and initially poised businessman enter the laboratory smiling and confident. Within twenty minutes he was reduced to a twitching, stuttering wreck, who was rapidly approaching a point of nervous collapse. He constantly pulled on his earlobe and twisted his hands. At one point he pushed his fist into his forehead and muttered: "Oh God, let's stop it." And yet he continued to respond to every word of the experimenter and obeyed to the end. (Milgram, 1963, p. 377)

What made the participants in Milgram's study engage in behavior that they had every reason to believe might seriously harm another person? Milgram's participants were not monsters. Instead, the situation was extraordinarily effective in getting them to do something that most people would predict only heartless fiends would do. For example, the experiment was presented as a scientific investigation—an unfamiliar situation for most participants. In all probability, the participants had never been in a psychology experiment, no one had ever placed them in a situation in which they were possibly doing serious physical damage to another human being, and they had no means by which they could readily step out of the vaguely defined role the experimenter had placed them in. The experimenter explicitly took responsibility for what happened (a frequent pledge by Adolf Hitler during the years he marched his nation over a precipice). Moreover, participants could not at the outset have guessed what the experiment involved, so they were unprepared to have to resist anyone's demands. And, as Milgram stressed, the step-by-step nature of the procedure was undoubtedly crucial. If the participant didn't quit at 225 volts, then why quit at 255? If not at 420, then why at 435?

"Evil is obvious only in retrospect."

—GLORIA STEINEM

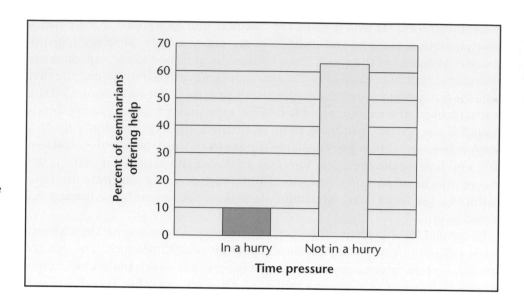

**Figure 1.1  The Power of the Situation and Helping**   The bars show the percentage of seminarians offering help to the man in the doorway as a function of being on time or not. Seminarians who were in a hurry were much less likely to help the man than were seminarians who were not in a hurry. (Source: Adapted from Darley & Batson, 1973)

## SEMINARIANS AS SAMARITANS

A classic experiment by John Darley and Daniel Batson (1973) shows the importance of the situation in even simpler fashion. These investigators asked students at the Princeton University Theological Seminary about the basis of their religious calling to determine whether particular students were primarily concerned with religion as a means toward personal gains or were more concerned with religion for its moral and spiritual values. After determining the basis of their religious concerns, the psychologists asked each young seminarian to go to another building to deliver a short sermon. The seminarians were told what route to follow in order to get there most easily. Some were told that they had plenty of time to get to the building where they were to deliver the sermon, and some were told that they were already late and should hurry. On the way to deliver their sermon—on the topic of the Good Samaritan, by the way—each of the seminarians passed a man who was sitting in a doorway and had his head down while he was coughing and groaning. It turned out that the nature of religious orientation was of no use in predicting whether or not the seminarians would help. But, as can be seen in Figure 1.1, whether seminarians were in a hurry or not was a very powerful predictor. The seminarians, it turned out, were pretty good Samaritans as a group—but only so long as they were not in a rush.

## CHANNEL FACTORS

**channel factors** Certain situational circumstances that appear unimportant on the surface but that can have great consequences for behavior, either facilitating or blocking it or guiding behavior in a particular direction.

Kurt Lewin (1952) introduced the concept of **channel factors** to help explain why certain circumstances that appear unimportant on the surface can have great consequences for behavior, either facilitating or blocking it. The term is also meant to reflect the fact that such circumstances can sometimes guide behavior in a very particular direction by means of making it easier to follow one path rather than another. Consider a study by Howard Leventhal and others on how to motivate people to take advantage of health facilities' offerings of preventive care (Leventhal, Singer, & Jones, 1965). They attempted to persuade Yale seniors to get tetanus inoculations. To convince them that this was in their best interest, they had them read scary materials about the number of ways one could get tetanus (in addition to the proverbial rusty nail you undoubtedly know about).

To make sure they had the students' attention, they showed them photos of people in the last stages of lockjaw. But not to worry—they could avoid this fate simply by going to the student health service at any time and getting a free inoculation. Interviews showed that most participants formed the intention to get an inoculation. But only 3 percent did so. Other participants were given a map of the Yale campus with a circle around the health center and were asked to review their weekly schedules and decide on a convenient time to visit the center and the route they would take to get there. Bear in mind that these were seniors who knew perfectly well where the health center was. So one might assume that this condescending treatment would produce little more than annoyance. In fact, it increased the percentage of students getting an inoculation ninefold, to 28 percent.

The channel factor in this case was the requirement to shape a vague intention into a concrete plan. A similar channel factor accounts for the use of public health services more generally. Attitudes about health, personality tests, and demographic variables such as age, gender, and socioeconomic status, and other individual differences don't do a very good job of predicting who will use them. The most powerful determinant of usage yet discovered is the mere distance to the closest service (Van Dort & Moos, 1976).

## THE FUNDAMENTAL ATTRIBUTION ERROR

People are thus governed by situational factors—such as the subtle social pressure that one person can apply to another or whether or not they are late—more than they tend to assume. You are likely to be surprised by many of the findings reported in this book because most people's intuitions about how people are likely to behave in a given situation are based on an underestimation of the power of external forces that operate on the person and a ready, but often mistaken, assumption that the causes of behavior can be found mostly within the person.

Psychologists call internal factors **dispositions**—that is, beliefs, values, personality traits, or abilities, real or imagined. People tend to think of dispositions as the underlying causes of behavior. Seeing a prison guard humiliating a prisoner, we may assume that the guard is a cruel person. Seeing a stranger in the street behave in an angry way, we are likely to infer that the person has a disposition that is aggressive or ill-tempered. Seeing an acquaintance engaged in a helpful action, we may think of the person as kinder than we had realized. Such judgments are valid far less often than we tend to think. Seeing an acquaintance give a dollar to a beggar may prompt us to assume that the person is quite generous, but subsequent observations of the person in different situations are almost as likely as not to disconfirm such an inference.

The failure to recognize the importance of situational influences on behavior, together with the tendency to overemphasize the importance of dispositions or traits, was labeled the **fundamental attribution error** by Lee Ross (1977). Many of the findings in social psychology can be viewed as a warning to look for situational factors that might be affecting someone's behavior and to hesitate before assuming that the person has dispositions that match the behavior. We hope and expect that as you read this book you will become more attuned to situational factors and less inclined to assume that behavior can be fully explained by characteristics inherent in the individual. To paraphrase the wisdom of the oft-quoted American Indian adage, one should exercise extreme caution in judging another person unless one has walked a mile in that person's moccasins—and hence attained a clear understanding of the situational forces compelling one action or another. The ultimate lesson of social psychology, we believe, is thus a

**dispositions** Internal factors, such as beliefs, values, personality traits, or abilities that guide a person's behavior.

**fundamental attribution error** The failure to recognize the importance of situational influences on behavior, together with the tendency to overemphasize the importance of dispositions or traits on behavior.

compassionate one. It encourages people to look to another person's situation—to try to understand the complex field of forces acting on the individual—to fully understand the person's behavior. What to think and how to act effectively and in moral fashion in everyday social life can be difficult to discern, but the study of social psychology instills an appreciation of that difficulty.

On the basis of long experience teaching about the Milgram experiment, we doubt that we've convinced you that the person who sits next to you in class would have delivered a lot of shock; we're confident we haven't convinced you that *you* would have. We hope, however, that by the time you complete this course you will regard it as a serious possibility that you might have acted as Milgram's participants did, recognizing that situations can be extraordinarily powerful, and character can sometimes be of little use in predicting what people will do.

**LOOKING BACK,** we have seen that situations are often more powerful in their influence on behavior than we realize. Whether people are kind to others or not, whether they take action in their own best interest or not, can be dependent on subtle aspects of situations. Such situational factors are often overlooked when trying to understand our own behavior or that of others, and behavior is often mistakenly attributed to presumed traits or dispositions (the fundamental attribution error). The cognitive processes that we use to understand situations and behavior are the topic of the next section.

## THE ROLE OF CONSTRUAL

In the Zimbardo study, "prisoners" were "arrested" at their homes and dragged off to the police station, where they were fingerprinted and booked. From there, they were sent to "prison," where they were stripped of their clothes, given prison uniforms and numbers, and thereby divested of their individual identities. Guards wore uniforms, sunglasses, and no identifying name tags, and freely exercised their authority by humiliating the prisoners. How the prisoners and guards were dressed strongly affected how they interpreted the situation and their roles within it, which in turn affected their behavior. Thus, Zimbardo's study shows how our understanding of people's behavior and the situations they find themselves in is subject to our **construal** of the behavior or situation—that is, it is subject to a great deal of interpretation and inference, much of which we are unaware of. Whether we regard people as freedom fighters or as terrorists, as guards or interrogators, will affect our perceptions of their actions.

### INTERPRETING REALITY

Look at Figure 1.2. Do you see a white triangle? Most people do. But in fact there is no white triangle. We construct a triangle in our minds out of the *gaps* in the picture. The gaps are located just where they would be if a triangle were laid over a black-outlined triangle and a portion of each of three circles. That makes a good, clear image, but it's entirely a creation of our perceptual apparatus and our background assumptions about the visual world. These assumptions are automatic and unconscious, and they can be almost impossible to override. Now that you know the triangle is in your mind's eye and not on the page, do you still see it? Now look at a painting by surrealist painter Salvador Dalí (see Figure 1.3). Dalí

**construal** Interpretation and inference about the stimuli or situations we confront.

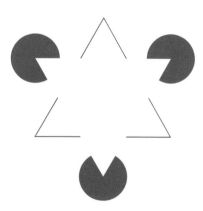

**Figure 1.2 Gestalt Principles and Perception**   When viewing the above figure, known as the Kanisza Triangle, we fill in the empty spaces in our mind and perceive a triangle.

**Figure 1.3 Gestalt Principles in Art**
In his *Slave Market with Disappearing Bust of Voltaire*, Salvador Dalí confronts the viewer in the center of the painting with the bust of the French philosopher Voltaire. But on closer inspection, the bust is largely the product of the gap in the wall behind the two merchants. Their faces form Voltaire's eyes, and their collars form his nose and cheeks. The same Gestalt principles are also at work in a less celebrated portion of the painting. Notice the sloping hill off to the right, and how it forms the pear in the fruit dish sitting on the table in which the woman in the foreground (Dalí's wife Gala) is sitting.

was an acknowledged master at using the mind's tendency to construct meaningful figures from the gaps in an image. As such, he created a number of well-known double images—paintings that could be seen, alternately, in one of two ways, as in this painting.

Our perceptions normally bear a resemblance to what the world is really like, but perception requires substantial interpretation on our part and is subject to significant error under certain conditions. German psychologists in the early part of the twentieth century convincingly argued for this view in the case of visual perception. The theoretical orientation of those psychologists centered on the concept of *Gestalt*. The word "Gestalt" is German for "form" or "figure." The basic idea of **Gestalt psychology** is that objects are perceived, not by means of some automatic registering device, but by active, usually unconscious, interpretation of what the object represents (as when we see a triangle from the gaps in a picture, or a bust of Voltaire from the gaps between the two merchants in Dalí's painting). What we see is not necessarily what is actually there but what is plausible—what makes a good, predictable "figure" in light of stored representations we have of the world, and what makes sense in light of the context in which we encounter something.

What's true for perception is even more true for judgments about the social world. Judgments and beliefs are constructed from perceptions and thoughts, and they are not simple readouts of reality. A study conducted by Liberman, Samuels, and Ross (2002) showed in a concrete way how construal could operate to define a situation and dictate behavior. The investigators asked Stanford University dormitory resident assistants to nominate students in their dorms whom they thought were particularly cooperative or competitive. Both types of students were then recruited to participate in a psychology experiment in which they would play a game that offered them the opportunity to pursue either a competitive or a cooperative strategy.

The game they used is called the **prisoner's dilemma** (which we will discuss in greater detail in Chapter 14). The game gets its name from the dilemma that

**Gestalt psychology** Based on the German word, *Gestalt*, meaning "form" or "figure," this approach stresses the fact that objects are perceived not by means of some automatic registering device but by active, usually unconscious, interpretation of what the object represents as a whole.

**prisoner's dilemma** A situation involving payoffs to two people in which trust and cooperation lead to higher joint payoffs than mistrust and defection. The game gets its name from the dilemma that would confront two criminals who were together involved in a crime and who are being held and questioned separately. Each must decide whether to "cooperate" and stick with a prearranged alibi, or "defect" and confess to the crime in the hope of lenient treatment.

would confront two criminals who were together involved in a crime, were apprehended, and were being held and questioned separately. Each prisoner could behave in one of two ways: confess the crime hoping to get lenient treatment by the prosecutor, or deny the crime hoping that the prosecutor would not bring charges or would fail to persuade a jury of their guilt. But of course the outcome that would result from the prisoner's choice would be dependent on the other prisoner's behavior. If both denied the crime—a "cooperative strategy"—both would stand a good chance of going free. If one denied the crime and the other admitted it—a "defecting strategy"—the prisoner who admitted the crime would get treated leniently, and the denying prisoner would get the book thrown at him. If both admitted the crime, then both would go to prison.

It is possible to play the game with monetary payoffs rather than prison time. The particular payoffs that Liberman and his colleagues used are shown in the matrix in Table 1.1. If both cooperate (deny the crime) on a given trial, they both make some money; if both defect (admit the crime), neither gets anything. If one defects and the other doesn't, the defector wins big and the cooperator loses a small amount. As we'll discuss in greater detail in Chapter 14, each player does better by defecting, no matter what the other player does (win 80¢ rather than 40¢ if the other player cooperates, get nothing rather than lose 20¢ if the other defects). And yet if each player follows the logic of defecting, and acts accordingly, both players are worse off (they each get nothing) than if they had both cooperated (they each would have gotten 40¢).

The researchers employed two experimental conditions that differed from each other in a way that seems trivial on the surface: for half the participants the game was described as "the Wall Street game," and for the other half as "the community game." Figure 1.4 shows how construal affected the results: the majority of students who played the Wall Street game played it in a competitive fashion; the majority who played the community game played it in a cooperative fashion. It seems reasonable to infer that the terminology that was used prompted different construals: the name "Wall Street" conjures up images of competitors struggling against one another for monetary advantage. The word "community" stirs up thoughts of sharing and cooperation. Whether the participants' resident assistants had thought they were highly competitive or highly cooperative was of no

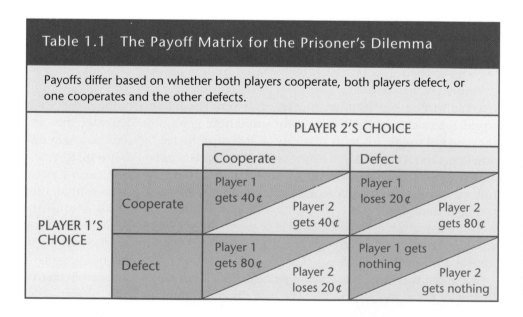

**Table 1.1   The Payoff Matrix for the Prisoner's Dilemma**

Payoffs differ based on whether both players cooperate, both players defect, or one cooperates and the other defects.

|  |  | PLAYER 2'S CHOICE | |
|---|---|---|---|
|  |  | Cooperate | Defect |
| PLAYER 1'S CHOICE | Cooperate | Player 1 gets 40¢ / Player 2 gets 40¢ | Player 1 loses 20¢ / Player 2 gets 80¢ |
|  | Defect | Player 1 gets 80¢ / Player 2 loses 20¢ | Player 1 gets nothing / Player 2 gets nothing |

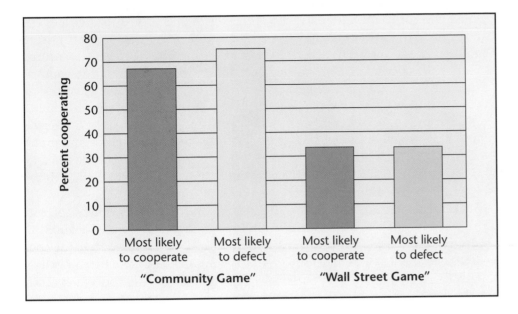

**Figure 1.4 Construal and the Prisoner's Dilemma**  Percentage of Stanford University students who cooperated given that they played the "Wall Street game" versus the "community game" and given that their resident adviser either picked them as most likely to cooperate or most likely to defect (compete). (Source: Liberman, Samuels, & Roth, 2002)

use in predicting behavior. The situation exerted its influence through its effect on the way participants interpreted the meaning of the activity they were performing. And once again the presumed dispositions of people were of no use in predicting behavior.

## SCHEMAS

How do we know how to behave in different kinds of situations? For example, if we are riding on an uncrowded train or subway, and someone asks us to give up our seat so he or she can sit, what is it that prompts us to respond in a particular way? For that matter, how do we know how to behave even in the most ordinary and common situations, such as sitting in a college seminar? Although it usually seems as if we understand social situations immediately and directly, a great deal of research shows that we depend on elaborate stores of systematized knowledge to understand even the simplest and most "obvious" situation. These knowledge stores are called **schemas**—generalized knowledge about the physical and social world, such as what kind of behavior to expect when we are dealing with a minister, a sales clerk, a professor, or a panhandler, and how to behave in a seminar, at a funeral, or when eating at a McDonald's or at a four-star restaurant, or when riding on a crowded or empty subway. There is even a schema—alleged to be universal—for falling in love.

Schemas capture the regularities of life and lead us to have certain expectations we can rely on so that we don't have to invent the world anew all the time. We have a schema for "a party," for example. We expect people to act cheerful, excited, and maybe a little silly, and, if it is a party consisting of young people, there may be loud music, dancing, and a certain amount of rowdiness. (We miss those parties ourselves; our most frequently activated party schema now centers on standing around with a drink trying to remember the name of the person we're talking to.)

An early experiment by Solomon Asch (1940), another of the great German founders of social psychology who immigrated to the United States in the 1930s, shows that schemas can sometimes operate very subtly to influence judgments. Asch asked two groups of undergraduate students to rank various professions in terms of their prestige or status. One of the professions was "politician." Before

**schemas** Generalized knowledge about the physical and social world and how to behave in particular situations and with different kinds of people.

**Schemas** Our schemas are generalized knowledge about the physical and social world that help us to know what is expected of us and how to behave in particular situations. (A) Our schema of a pizza shop leads us to order at a counter, wait for the pizza to be ready, and then either take it to a bare table or home to eat. (B) But our schema of a high-end restaurant leads us to be seated at a table with silverware, glasses, and a tablecloth, to choose what we want from a menu, to order at the table, and to be served food and wine by a waiter.

they gave their own ratings, participants were told that a sample of fellow students had previously ranked politicians near the top in prestige, whereas another group of participants was told that their fellow students had ranked politicians near the bottom. This manipulation affected the participants' judgments substantially, but not because it changed their minds about politicians or because they were trying to conform. Asch was able to show that participants in the first group took the term "politician" to refer to statesmen of the caliber of Thomas Jefferson and Franklin D. Roosevelt. Participants in the second group were rating something closer to corrupt political hacks. It wasn't that the participants were blindly going along with the ratings of their peers, but rather that their peers' ratings served to define just what it was that was being judged via the different schemas that their ratings suggested. Many of the persuasion attempts we are exposed to in the media have the goal not so much of "changing the judgment of the object" but rather of "changing the object of judgment." Pro-abortion advocates try to call up schemas related to *freedom*, and anti-abortion activists try to activate schemas related to *murder*. Pro–affirmative action advocates encourage schemas related to *diversity*, and anti–affirmative action advocates try to activate schemas related to *fairness*.

## STEREOTYPES

**stereotypes** Schemas that we have for people of various kinds that can be applied and misapplied so as to facilitate, and sometimes derail, the course of interaction.

Much work in social psychology has been dedicated to the study of **stereotypes**—schemas that we have for people of various kinds. Research on stereotyping examines the content of these person schemas and how they are applied and misapplied so as to facilitate, and sometimes derail, the course of interaction. We tend to judge a person based on particular person schemas that we have—stereotypes about a person's nationality, gender, religion, occupation, neighborhood, or sorority. Such summaries may be necessary in order to function efficiently and effectively. But they can be wrong, they can be applied in the wrong way and to the wrong people, and they can be given too much weight in relation to more specific information we have about a particular person (or would have if we didn't assume the stereotype is all we need to know). The frequently pernicious role of stereotypes is the subject of an entire chapter of this book (Chapter 11).

**Stereotypes and Construal** How observers interpret reality affects their reaction to what is going on. These Iraqi boys look at the wall paintings showing the U.S. Statue of Liberty administering shock to an Iraqi prisoner. Their stereotypes about Americans as occupiers rather than rescuers are most likely reinforced through such paintings and affect how they regard Americans.

**LOOKING BACK,** we have seen that although it often seems as though our understanding of situations is the result of a direct, unmediated registration of meaning, our comprehension even of the simplest physical stimulus is the result of construal processes that make use of well-developed knowledge structures. Such structures are called schemas when they summarize commonly encountered situations and stereotypes when they describe different types of people. Next we consider just how accessible to consciousness our construal processes usually are.

## AUTOMATIC AND CONTROLLED PROCESSING

How would you initially react if you saw a stranger at an airport carrying a backpack, looking agitated, and sweating profusely? In the post-9/11 world, you might fear that such a person might be carrying a bomb and that you could become a victim of a terrorist attack. The mind processes information in two different ways when you encounter a social situation: one is automatic and unconscious, often based on emotional factors, and the other is conscious and systematic, and more likely to be controlled by careful thought. Often emotional reactions to people occur before conscious thought takes over. Thus, your fearful reaction to the person with the backpack might automatically kick in without any special thought on your part. But when you start thinking systematically, you might realize that he might have just come in from the summer heat, that he might be agitated because he is late for his plane, and that there is no reason to suspect that he might be carrying a bomb or threatening your safety in any other way.

Research by Patricia Devine and her colleagues shows how automatic and controlled processing can result in incompatible attitudes in the same person toward members of outgroups (Devine, 1989a, 1989b; Devine, Monteith, Zuwerink, & Elliot, 1991; Devine, Plant, Amodio, Harmon-Jones, & Vance, 2002). People with low expressed prejudice toward an outgroup may nevertheless show feelings toward people in the outgroup that are almost as prejudiced as those of people who confess to explicit disliking of the group—when feelings are gauged by auto-

**Automatic Processing** People often react quickly to frightening situations so that they can take immediate actions to save themselves from danger if necessary. The boy is touching the snake under the supervision of his teacher, but an automatic reaction is still visible. If the boy were to come across a snake in the grass, he would likely have a stronger automatic fear reaction.

matic or "implicit" measures. For example, when white participants read words reminiscent of African Americans and then were asked to make judgments about whether a particular individual whom they read about was hostile or not, they were more likely to report that the individual was hostile than if they hadn't read such words. And this was true whether they were willing to express anti-black attitudes in a questionnaire or not. The judgments of the "unprejudiced people" could thus be shown to be prejudiced when studied by a technique that examines nonconscious processing of information. Furthermore, Anthony Greenwald and his colleagues showed that the great majority of white people take longer to classify black faces with pleasant stimuli than to classify white faces with pleasant stimuli (Greenwald, McGhee, & Schwartz, 1998). This was true even for participants who showed no overt prejudice when asked about their attitudes.

## TYPES OF UNCONSCIOUS PROCESSING

The unconscious mind plays an important role in producing beliefs and behaviors even when there is no motive to hide what is going on in our minds. There are two major types of unconscious processing that have been identified. The great psychologist William James identified one type that has given rise to the study of what is called "skill acquisition." If you have ever driven a car and realized that you haven't a clue as to what you have been doing—even what you have seen—for the last few minutes, you know about this type of automaticity. As skills are learned and then overlearned, they can be carried out without awareness. They also can be performed without distracting us from other, conscious thoughts and processing.

The other type of automaticity (associated with the name of Sigmund Freud, but with roots extending well back into the nineteenth century) concerns the production of beliefs and behaviors without awareness of the cognitive processes that have generated them. Sometimes in solving problems we are well aware of the relevant factors that we are dealing with, and the procedures we are using to solve them. This is often true when we solve mathematical problems—for example, "Take half the base, multiply it by the height and. . . ." But these

**William James** One of the founding fathers of the field of psychology, James wrote about attention, memory, and consciousness, asking how unconscious processing affects behavior.

sorts of cognitive processes—where most of what is going on is visible to our consciousness—are rarer than you might think. For many cognitive processes, it seems, we cannot accurately describe what is going on in our heads (Nisbett & Wilson, 1977; Wegner & Bargh, 1998; Wilson, 2002). This applies to our guesses about how we go about making judgments about other people, to our understanding of how we go about making causal attributions for physical and social events, and even to how we come to choose one applicant versus another for a job (or one romantic partner over another). Often we cannot even consciously identify some of the crucially important factors that have affected our beliefs and behavior. We know this in part from experiments that present visual stimuli so rapidly that people cannot even report having seen them, and yet their beliefs and behavior are affected by them.

## FUNCTIONS OF UNCONSCIOUS PROCESSING

Why are our minds designed so that so much takes place outside of awareness? It is because conscious processes are generally slow and can run only serially— one step or one problem at a time. Automatic processes are typically much faster and can operate in parallel. When one recognizes a face as belonging to a fourth-grade classmate, one has done so by processing numerous features (forehead, eyes, chin, coloring, and so on) at the same time. Doing all of this one step at a time would leave us hopelessly mired in computation. And it's quite handy to be able to drive on autopilot while carrying on an interesting conversation or enjoying the scenery.

Because much of what goes on in our heads is not available to us consciously, we are unable to figure out exactly what factors influence us, and to what degree, and we experience the world as being manifested to us as it is, without any real cognitive work on our part. This is one reason why scientific research on human behavior is so essential. We can't simply ask people what caused them to behave as they did, because often they do not know. Instead, social psychologists must craft experiments to isolate the true causes of people's behavior.

Some examples should make these points clearer. When a person encounters novel stimuli while the arm is flexed (bent back toward the shoulder), attitudes toward the stimuli tend to be favorable (Cacioppo, Priester, & Berntson, 1993). When a person encounters novel stimuli while the arm is extended away from the body, the person tends to form more negative attitudes. This is because the muscular feedback from the arm positions gives "information" about whether the object is desirable or undesirable (based on a lifetime's experience embracing positive stimuli and pushing away negative stimuli). But people are quite unaware that they have incorporated this bodily information into their judgments (and in many experiments of this type become annoyed when they are asked if such "irrelevant" information played any role in their judgments!).

Or consider social category membership. Easily discriminable personal features, such as gender, race, and age, tend to trigger stereotypes that play a role in producing judgments about people, even when the individual is unaware that these social categories have influenced the judgment in question (Blair, Judd, & Fallman, 2004; Brewer, 1988; McRae, Stangor, & Milne, 1994). And the same is true even of behavior. Bargh, Chen, and Burrows (1996) have found that just mentioning words that call to mind the elderly ("cane," "Florida") causes college students to walk down a hall more slowly. Others have found that activating the concept of "professor" actually makes students do better on a trivia test (Dijksterhuis & van Knippenberg, 1998)!

The concepts of automaticity and preconscious processing of information help us to understand why we are often blind to the role of many important situational factors and why the processes underlying construal may be hidden from us. We will refer often to these concepts throughout the book, and we will repeatedly distinguish those social behaviors that appear to be the result of effortful, deliberate, and conscious processing from those that appear to be the result of effortless, automatic, and nonconscious processing.

**LOOKING BACK,** we have seen that much behavior and many kinds of construal processes are carried out without awareness, sometimes without awareness even of the factors we are responding to. We overestimate the degree to which our mental processes are accessible to consciousness. In the next two sections, we will examine the distal influences on behavior—our evolutionary history and the cultural circumstances in which we find ourselves.

## EVOLUTION AND HUMAN BEHAVIOR: HOW WE ARE THE SAME

**natural selection** An evolutionary process that operates to mold animals and plants such that traits that enhance the probability of survival and reproduction are passed on to subsequent generations.

Why do human beings generally live in family groupings, assign roles to people on the basis of age, adorn their bodies, classify flora and fauna, and have rites of passage, narratives, and myths? Evolution may serve as an explanation for such behaviors.

Evolutionary theory has been around for about 150 years, ever since Charles Darwin's famous voyage to the Galápagos Islands and the discoveries he made about the modifications in animal and plant characteristics that had occurred over time. The theory has proved invaluable in understanding why (and how) organisms of all kinds have the traits and properties they do. The key notion is that a process of **natural selection** operates to mold animals and plants so that traits that enhance the probability of survival and reproduction are passed on to

subsequent generations. Organisms that die before they reproduce have either had bad luck or possess characteristics that are less than optimal in the environments in which they find themselves. And organisms that don't reproduce don't pass on their characteristics (through their genes) to a new generation. Those that do reproduce give their genes a chance to live on in their offspring, with the possibility that their characteristics will be represented in at least one more generation. Disadvantageous characteristics are selected against; characteristics better adapted for the environment are selected for.

Darwin himself assumed that natural selection is important for behavioral propensities just as it is for physical characteristics like size, coloring, or susceptibility to parasites. And the number and importance of things that are universally true about humans is certainly consistent with the idea that much of what we share is the result of natural selection and is encoded in our genes. These ideas were generally accepted by scientists until the 1920s. But the approach fell into disrepute because of misplaced and unfounded claims that Darwin's ideas could be applied to the behavior of human beings struggling for supremacy over one another, with might justifying right. The movement approvingly espoused "the survival of the fittest"—which was incorrectly taken to mean the survival of one human group over another. This movement, called Social Darwinism, was a distorted application of Darwin's theory, but it drew adherents nevertheless. A rogue version of Darwin's theory was also used by some to justify fascism and the ruthless domination of the weak by the strong. Some in the scientific community overreacted to these misappropriations by rejecting the notion that evolution has played a role in shaping human behavior. Not wishing to fight the strong emotional reactions of these people, other scientists simply dropped the subject. But toward the end of the twentieth century, developments in evolutionary theory and comparative biology, anthropological findings, and studies by psychologists convinced many that the theory can be quite helpful in explaining why people behave as they do.

## HUMAN UNIVERSALS

One theme that emerges from evolutionary theory is that many human behaviors and institutions are universal, or very nearly so. This would follow clearly from evolutionary reasoning. In the process of human evolution, we have acquired basic behavioral propensities—much as we have acquired physical features like bipedalism—which help us adapt to the physical and social environment. Table 1.2 contains a list of these reputed universals. Two things should be noted about the practices and institutions in Table 1.2, aside from their alleged universality. One is that we share some of these practices with animals, especially the higher primates. These include facial expressions (almost all of which we share with chimpanzees and with some other animals), dominance and submission, food sharing, group living (true of all primates except orangutans), greater aggressiveness on the part of males (true of almost all mammals), preference for own kin (true of almost all animals), and wariness around snakes (true of all the large primates, including humans). The other, even more striking aspect of Table 1.2 is that the number of universals we share with other animals is (so far as we know) quite small. The bulk of Table 1.2 represents a large number of behaviors and institutions that would appear to be effective adaptations for highly intelligent, group-living, upright-walking, language-using animals that are capable of living in almost any kind of ecology. These latter universals are compatible with both an evolutionary interpretation (we are a particular

> "There is grandeur in this view of life . . . and that, whilst this planet has gone cycling on according to the fixed law of gravity, from so simple a beginning endless forms most beautiful and most wonderful have been, and are being, evolved."
> —CHARLES DARWIN

**Universal Facial Expressions** Chimpanzees and humans express dominance and submission, anger and fear, through similar facial expressions. (A) The screaming chimp and (B) basketball coach Bobby Knight yelling during a game both have their mouths open and show their teeth in an aggressive display of dominance.

## Table 1.2  Universal Behaviors, Reactions, and Institutions

A sampling of some of the behaviors and characteristics that anthropologists believe hold for all human cultures, grouped into categories to show general areas of commonality.

### SEX, GENDER, AND THE FAMILY

| | | |
|---|---|---|
| Copulation normally conducted privately | Rape | Rape proscribed |
| Live in family (or household) | Sex differences in spatial cognition | Sexual jealousy |
| Husband usually older than wife | Sexual modesty | Sexual regulation |
| Males dominate public realm | Division of labor by gender | Males more aggressive |
| Males more prone to lethal violence | Females do more child care | Marriage |
| Mother-son incest unthinkable | Incest prevention and avoidance | Preference for own kin |

### SOCIAL DIFFERENTIATION

| | | |
|---|---|---|
| Age statuses | Classification of kin | Ingroup distinguished from outgroup |
| Division of labor by age | Leaders | |

### SOCIAL CUSTOMS

| | | |
|---|---|---|
| Baby talk | Pretend play | Group living |
| Dance | Rites of passage | Law (rights and obligations) |
| Dominance/submission | Tabooed foods | Magic to win love |
| Feasting | Toys | Practice to improve skills |
| Gossip | Body adornment | Property |
| Hygienic care | Death rites | Rituals |
| Magic to increase and sustain life | Etiquette | Tabooed utterances |
| Non-bodily decorative art | Food sharing | |

### EMOTION

| | | |
|---|---|---|
| Childhood fear of strangers | Wariness around snakes | Rhythm |
| Facial expressions of fear, anger, disgust, happiness, sadness, and surprise | Envy | Melody |

### COGNITION

| | | |
|---|---|---|
| Aesthetics | Anthropomorphism of animals | Myths |
| Belief in supernatural, religion | Medicine | Taxonomy |
| Classification of flora | Language | |
| Classification of fauna | Narrative | |

Source: Compiled by Donald Brown, 1991, appearing in Pinker, 2002.

kind of creature qualitatively different from any other, with many adaptations so effective that they have become wired into our biology) and an interpretation based on the idea that these practices are simply the result of our species' super-high intelligence (we have figured out that incest is a bad idea and that classification of flora is useful).

## GROUP LIVING, LANGUAGE, AND THEORY OF MIND

Evolution has prepared humans to live cooperatively in cohesive social groups. Group living contributed to survival in ages past, as groups provided protection from predators, greater success in finding foraging areas, access to mates, and other adaptive functions. The ability to produce and understand language has facilitated the ability to live in groups and to convey not only emotions and intentions to others, but also beliefs and attitudes and complex thoughts. The claim is made that infants are born pre-wired to acquire language, perhaps because of its importance to humans living together in groups (Pinker, 1994). Languages are learned by all normal children, at developmental stages that are almost identical from one culture to another. All infants are born with the full range of possible sounds (phonemes) that exist in the totality of languages spoken anywhere on earth, and they babble these sounds in the crib. Language acquisition consists of dropping all the "wrong" phonemes that are not used by the child's particular language. Thus, children can learn to speak any language, depending on where they grow up; they can learn to speak their native language perfectly well even if they grow up with deaf parents who never speak at all; and twins can sometimes develop their own unique languages in the crib, which follow rules of grammar in the same way as formally recognized languages (Pinker, 1994, 2002). In short, while there are not separate language "modules" (special-purpose cognitive systems) for specific languages, there are general, inherited propensities to develop grammatical language.

Just as evolution has prepared humans to live together in groups and to be able to communicate to promote survival and reproduction, it also may have provided humans with a **theory of mind**—the understanding that other people have beliefs and desires. The implications of this for group living are profound, as it may prevent misunderstandings that could lead to aggression and even possible death. Children recognize before the age of two that the way to understand other people's behavior is to recognize what their beliefs and desires are (Asch, 1952; Kuhlmeier, Wynn, & Bloom, 2003; Leslie, 2000). People do what they do because they want to achieve some goal and because they believe that the behavior in question will produce the desired result. By the age of two, an infant can recognize "pretend" games, as when the mother holds a banana to her ear and pretends it's a telephone. By the age of three or four, children's theories of mind are sophisticated enough that they can recognize when other people's beliefs are false (Wellman, 1990). It seems highly unlikely to some psychologists that these very sophisticated theories have been learned. Instead, like theories about the physical world, it seems plausible that evolution has provided us with information that is too universally essential to leave to chance or laborious trial-and-error learning. Given the importance of accurate understanding of others' beliefs and intentions, why not have a theory of mind pre-wired?

Some of the most powerful evidence for a theory of mind comes from the study of people who, through a genetic defect or physical or chemical trauma before or after birth, seem not to have one, or to have only a weak version of one. Such a claim has been made about people with *autism*. Individuals with autism

**theory of mind** The understanding that other people have beliefs and desires.

**Theory of Mind** Because autistic children lack a theory of mind, they do not recognize or understand the beliefs and desires of others. Because of this deficit, they have difficulty communicating and interacting with other people, as shown by the boy who is ignoring the man who is working with him.

have deeply disordered abilities to interact and communicate with others. They do not seem to be able to comprehend the beliefs or understand the desires of others, including the false beliefs of others. This contrasts with the abilities of most children, who by the age of four are able to understand that other people can have false beliefs (Perner, Frith, Leslie, & Leekam, 1989).

The standard method of showing that most children can recognize false beliefs is to show them a candy box and ask them what is in it. Naturally, the children say that candy is in it. The children are then shown that pencils or some other objects are in the box. In other words, the children are shown that their former belief was false. Then the box is sealed up, and the children are told that a friend of theirs is about to come in and will be asked what is in the box. Children are asked to predict what the friend will say. In one study, almost all normal children with a mental age of four correctly said that the friend would guess that candy was in the box, showing that they were aware the friend would be misled by the box and would assume that the kind of box accurately indicated what its contents were. In contrast, only a small minority of children with autism (including those with a much higher mental age) correctly guessed that the friend would have a false belief. Such children can solve problems about the physical world at a very high level, but understanding the beliefs and desires of other people is extremely difficult for them. The evidence that theories of mind are universal among nonimpaired children comes from the study of children very different from the Western ones usually studied. Avis and Harris (1991), for example, studied theory of mind in BaAka children. The BaAka are a pygmy people who live in the rain forests of Cameroon. They are hunter-gatherers who are not literate. Using a task conceptually the same as that used with Western children (Perner, Leekam, & Wimmer, 1987), Avis and Harris found that BaAka children typically learned by the age of four or five to predict a person's behavior on the basis of the person's beliefs.

## PARENTAL INVESTMENT

Why do men so often choose to marry younger women? Why do women often look for husbands who will be able to support them and their children? The evolutionary approach provides a possible answer to these questions in its theory of **parental investment**. In almost all mammalian species, the two sexes typically have different costs and benefits associated with the nurturing of offspring. This has to do with the fact that the number of offspring a female can have over the course of her lifetime is highly limited. The value of each child to her is therefore relatively high, and it is very much in the interest of her genes to see to it that each infant grows to maturity. For males, however, a nearly unlimited number of offspring is theoretically possible because so little energy is involved in creating them. A male can walk away from copulation and never see his mate or offspring again. Indeed, this is just what the males of many mammalian species do (as well as some individual human beings). Even if the male stays with the female and their offspring, however, his investment in the offspring is less than that of the female. As we will see in the chapter on attraction (Chapter 3), many apparent differences between males and females are consistent with the implications that follow from this asymmetry. Evolution thus provides one possible way of looking at many seemingly universal tendencies toward certain human behaviors related to sex, gender, and child rearing.

## AVOIDING THE NATURALISTIC FALLACY

Evolutionary theory as applied to human behavior is controversial—sometimes for sound reasons and sometimes for reasons that are less so. The claim that there are substantial, biologically based differences between men and women in behaviors related directly or indirectly to mate choice is particularly objectionable to some people. Such claims are controversial in part because they follow a long and embarrassing history of faulty assertions about biological differences that have been used to legitimize and perpetuate male privilege (Bem, 1993). Even more objectionable, evolutionary theory has been invoked as justification for assuming that the different human races are different almost at the level of separate subspecies. But the fact that a theory can be misused is no reason to reject the theory itself in all its aspects.

Claims about biological shaping of human behavior can also be controversial because of a mistaken tendency for people to think that evolutionary claims mean that biology is destiny—that is, to assume that what we are biologically predisposed to do is what we inevitably *will* do, and perhaps even *should* do. Not so. There are many things we are predisposed to do that we readily overcome. The tendency for eyesight to fail with advancing age is genetically determined, but it is easily dealt with by corrective lenses. The tendency for people to lash out when they are frustrated is (less easily) dealt with by teaching children that aggression is not an appropriate response to frustration. The claim that the way things *are* is the way they *should be* is known as the **naturalistic fallacy**, and it has no logical foundation. Civilization can be regarded as the never-ceasing attempt to modify what comes naturally. With some notable and depressing exceptions, it has been highly successful in reducing the extent to which human life is "nasty, poor, brutish, and short."

Nevertheless, people frequently commit the naturalistic fallacy, and so we might expect pundits and politicians to excuse personal habits or advocate social policies that are consistent with evolutionary claims about the basis of observed gender differences. And indeed, one hears increasing amounts of nonsense from armchair evolutionists about these and other alleged biologically determined aspects of human behavior. That being the case, we must take care to separate the wheat from the chaff. We must be sure that any such claims about inherited

**parental investment** The evolutionary principle that since males and females have different costs and benefits associated with reproduction and the nurturing of offspring, one sex will value and invest more in each child than will the other.

**naturalistic fallacy** The claim that the way things *are* is the way they *should be*.

behavior and preferences rest on a solid scientific foundation. Caution about evolutionary claims is called for. What is not called for, however, is a rejection of evolutionary ideas out of hand.

**LOOKING BACK,** we have seen that evolutionary theory informs our understanding of human behavior just as it does our understanding of the physical characteristics of plants and animals. The many universals of human behavior suggest that these behaviors are in some sense wired in. Of great relevance in this respect are language and theory of mind. We have noted that differential parental investment of males and females may help us to understand certain differences between men and women. Nonetheless, we have also warned against the naturalistic fallacy, or the assumption that the way things *are* are the way they *should* be. As we are about to see, the most important legacy of evolution for human beings is the great flexibility it allows for adaptation to distinctive circumstances.

## CULTURE AND HUMAN BEHAVIOR: HOW WE ARE DIFFERENT

Despite the existence of universal human tendencies to have various emotions, customs, and forms of social organization, there is great flexibility among humans in the particular expression of these tendencies. The enormous behavioral flexibility of humans is tied to the fact that—together with rats—we are the most successful of all the mammals in our ability to live in virtually every type of ecology. Our adaptability and the range of environments we have evolved in have resulted in extraordinarily great differences between human groups and cultures. Based on the prevailing culture, humans may be more or less likely to cooperate with each other, to divide the roles of men and women, or to try to distinguish themselves as individuals.

### CULTURAL DIFFERENCES IN SELF-DEFINITION

Until recently, psychologists regarded cultural differences as being limited primarily to differences in beliefs, preferences, and values. Some cultures regard the world as having been created by a supernatural force, some by impersonal natural forces, some don't ponder the question much at all. The French like to eat extremely fatty goose liver, the Chinese like to eat chicken feet, and the Americans like to eat cotton candy—tastes that each finds incomprehensible in the others. These differences, while interesting, are not the sort of thing that would make anyone suspect that fundamentally different psychological theories are needed to account for the behavior of people in different societies.

But recent work shows that cultural differences go far deeper than beliefs and values. In fact, they extend all the way to the level of fundamental forms of social existence and self-conceptions, and even to the perceptual and cognitive processes used to develop new thoughts and beliefs. We will be discussing many of these differences throughout the book, but one set of inter-related dimensions is particularly central, and so we introduce it at some length here. Before you begin reading about these dimensions, however, take a pencil and paper and

**Collectivism versus Individualism**
Collectivist or interdependent cultures emphasize the group and family, while individualist or independent cultures emphasize the individual.
(A) The collectivist emphasis on the group extends even to exercise, as shown by these Mitsubishi salesmen in Japan who are exercising together before the showroom opens. (B) The individualist emphasis of the independent culture can be seen as this American inline skater exercises alone while listening to music rather than in the company of other people.

write down ten things that describe who you are. No, really do this. You'll get much more out of the following section if you do.

How plausible do you find the following propositions?

- People have substantial control over their life outcomes, and they much prefer situations in which they have choice and control to those in which they do not.
- People want to achieve personal success. They find that relationships with other people can sometimes make it harder to attain their goals.
- People want to be unique, to be different from other people in significant respects.
- People want to feel good about themselves. Excelling in some ways and being assured of their good qualities by other people are important to personal well-being.
- People like their relations with others to be on a basis of mutuality and equality, but if some people have more power than others, their preference is to be in the superior position.
- People believe the same rules should apply to everyone—individuals should not be singled out for special treatment because of their personal attributes or connections to important people. Justice is—or should be—blind.

There are hundreds of millions of people who are reasonably well described by those propositions, but they tend to be found in particular parts of the world, namely Europe and many of the present and former nations of the British Commonwealth, including the United States, Canada, and Australia. Westerners are highly **individualistic** or **independent** (Fiske, Kitayama, Markus, & Nisbett, 1998; Hofstede, 1980; Hsu, 1953; Markus & Kitayama, 1991; Triandis, 1995). They think of themselves as distinct social entities, tied to each other by bonds of affection and organizational memberships to be sure, but essentially separate from other people and having attributes that exist in the absence of any connection to others. They tend to see their associations with other people, even their own family members, as voluntary and subject to termination once they become sufficiently troublesome or unproductive (see Table 1.3).

**individualistic (independent) cultures** Cultures in which people tend to think of themselves as distinct social entities, tied to each other by voluntary bonds of affection and organizational memberships but essentially separate from other people and having attributes that exist in the absence of any connection to others.

## Table 1.3 Independent versus Interdependent Societies

People in independent (individualistic) cultures have different characteristics than do people from interdependent (collectivistic) cultures, as shown by the difference in their emphases on the individual and on the group.

| INDEPENDENT SOCIETIES | INTERDEPENDENT SOCIETIES |
| --- | --- |
| Conception of the self as distinct from others, with attributes that are constant. | Conception of the self as inextricably linked to others, with attributes depending on the situation. |
| Insistence on ability to act on one's own. | Preference for collective action. |
| Need for individual distinctiveness. | Desire for harmonious relations within group. |
| Preference for egalitarianism and achieved status based on accomplishments. | Acceptance of hierarchy and ascribed status based on age, group membership, and so on. |
| Conviction that rules governing behavior should apply to everyone. | Preference for rules that take context and particular relationships into account. |

But these characterizations describe other peoples less well. In fact, they provide a poor description of most of the world's people, particularly the citizens of most East Asian countries, such as the Chinese (Triandis, McCusker, & Hui, 1990), the Japanese (Bond & Cheung, 1983), the Koreans (Rhee, Uleman, Lee, & Roman, 1995), people from other Asian countries such as India (Dhawan, Roseman, Naidu, Thapa, & Rettek, 1995) and Malaysia (Bochner, 1994), and people from many Latin American countries. People in these societies are more **collectivistic** or **interdependent** in their orientation than are Westerners (see Table 1.3). They do not have as much freedom or personal control over their lives, and they do not necessarily want or need these things (Sastry & Ross, 1998). Figure 1.5 is

**Figure 1.5 Self, Ingroup, and Outgroup in Interdependent and Independent Cultures** People in independent cultures feel that they have a distinct existence apart from any ingroups, and they do not treat people in outgroups as differently from ingroup members as do people in interdependent cultures. People in interdependent societies feel that the ingroup is part of who they are and that those in outgroups (acquaintances, strangers) are very different from themselves and need not be treated the same as ingroup members. East Asians, for example, describe themselves as more similar to ingroup members (family, circle of friends, coworkers) than do Westerners, but as more different from outgroup members. (Source: Nisbett, 2003)

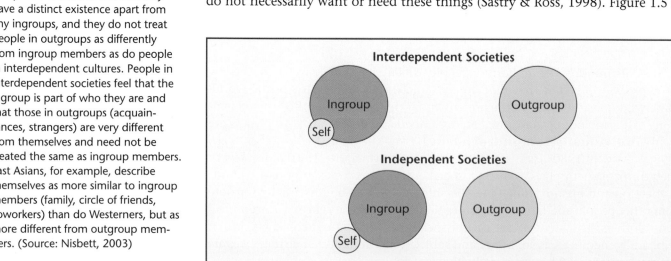

designed to illustrate this fundamental difference between people in independent and interdependent societies.

This difference in self-definition among people in independent and interdependent societies has important implications for the nature of their personal goals and strivings, values and beliefs (see Table 1.4). Success is important for East Asians, but in good part it generally matters to them as it brings credit to the family and other groups to which they belong rather than merely as a reflection of personal merit. Personal uniqueness is not very important to interdependent peoples and may in fact even be undesirable. In a clever experiment by Kim and Markus (1999), Korean and American participants were offered a pen as a gift for being in a study. Several of the pens were of one color and one pen was of another color. Americans tended to choose the unique color and Koreans the common color. There is a saying frequently heard in East Asia that, "the nail that stands out is hammered down." Being better than others is not such a necessity in order for interdependent people to feel good about themselves, and feeling good about themselves is in itself not so terribly important a goal as it is for Westerners and other independent peoples (Heine, Lehman, Markus, & Kitayama, 1999). Interdependent people tend not to expect or even value mutuality and equality in relationships; on the contrary, they are likely to expect hierarchical relations to be the rule (Hsu, 1953; Triandis, 1989, 1995). They tend not to be universalists in their understanding of social norms; instead, they believe in different strokes for different folks. Justice should keep her eyes wide open, paying attention to the particular circumstances of each case that comes before her.

> **collectivistic (interdependent) cultures** Cultures in which people tend to define themselves as part of a collective, inextricably tied to others in their group, and in which they have relatively little individual freedom or personal control over their lives but do not necessarily want or need these things.

## Table 1.4  Values and Beliefs of Individualist and Collectivist Cultures

People in individualistic (independent) and collectivist (interdependent) cultures tend to have different values and beliefs, as can be seen below in what people in individualist cultures tend to want and believe and what people in collectivist cultures tend to want and believe.

| INDIVIDUALIST CULTURES | COLLECTIVIST CULTURES |
| --- | --- |
| Want to get the recognition they deserve when they do a good job. | Want the employer to have a major responsibility for their health and welfare. |
| Want to have considerable freedom to adopt their own approach to the job. | Want to work in a congenial and friendly atmosphere. |
| Want to fully use their skills and abilities on the job. | Want to be completely loyal to their company. |
| Want to work in a department that is run efficiently. | Believe that knowing influential people is more important than ability. |
| Believe that decisions made by individuals are better than those made by groups. | Believe that the better managers are those who have been with the company the longest time. |

Source: Hofstede, 1980.

## INDIVIDUALISM VERSUS COLLECTIVISM IN THE WORKPLACE

The distinction between independence and interdependence as cultural predilections is so important that we develop it throughout this book, but we will present some representative findings now so that the concept will be well grounded at the outset. One of the first social scientists to measure the dimension of independence (or individualism) versus interdependence (or collectivism) was Geert Hofstede (1980), who surveyed the values of tens of thousands of IBM employees around the world. Table 1.4 on p. 31 shows the sorts of values and beliefs that Hofstede examined and the differences he observed in individualist versus collectivist cultures. Figure 1.6 displays these results geographically, showing the degree of interdependence expressed on average by the citizens of sixty-seven countries. You can see that the countries of British heritage are the most independent, followed by the countries of continental Europe, South Asia, Asia Minor, and Latin America.

Although Hofstede himself studied few East Asian societies, we now have a great deal of evidence about them. The research to date indicates that those cultures are turning out to be very different from the Western cultures. In a survey similar to that of Hofstede, two professors in a business school in the Netherlands, Charles Hampden-Turner and Alfons Trompenaars, examined independence and interdependence among 15,000 middle managers from the United States, Canada, Great Britain, Australia, Sweden, the Netherlands, Belgium, Germany, France, Italy, Japan, Singapore, and Korea (Hampden-Turner & Trompenaars, 1993). They presented these managers, who were attending seminars conducted by the investigators, with dilemmas in which independent values were pitted against interdependent values. In line with Hofstede's results, they found that managers from East Asia valued interdependence, managers from British and former British colonies valued independence, and managers from

**Figure 1.6 Individualism and Collectivism**   The map shows the degree of individualism and collectivism among IBM employees around the world, indicating greater individualism in Great Britain and in the United States, Canada, Australia, and New Zealand, all former British colonies. People in the countries represented by the tan color were not surveyed by the researchers. (Source: Sabini, 1995, p. 261; based on data from Hofstede, 1980)

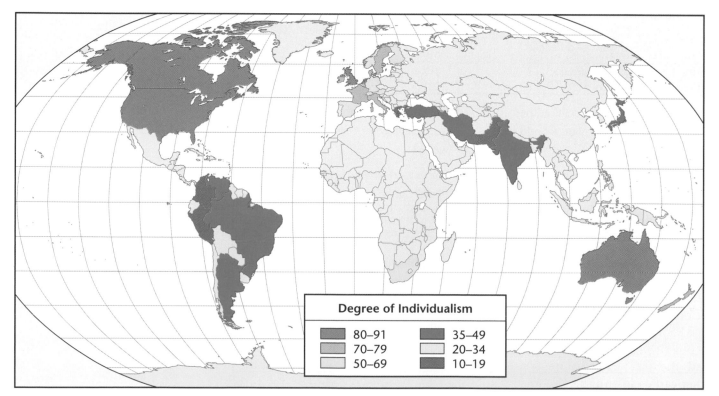

Degree of Individualism

80–91   35–49
70–79   20–34
50–69   10–19

Box 1.1   FOCUS ON CULTURE

# Individualism or Collectivism in Business Managers

Charles Hampden-Turner and Alfons Trompenaars (1993) studied individualism versus collectivism in thousands of business managers. To examine the value placed on individual distinctiveness and accomplishment versus harmonious relations within the group, they asked the business managers in their seminars whether business managers preferred

**jobs in which personal initiatives are encouraged and individual initiatives are achieved**

or

**jobs in which no one is singled out for personal honor, but in which everyone works together.**

To examine the acceptance of ascribed status (for example, age, family, religious background) as a basis for rewarding employees, Hampden-Turner and Trompenaars asked the business managers whether they agreed with the following sentiment:

**It is important for a manager to be older than his subordinates. Older people should be more respected than younger people.**

To see whether their respondents felt there should be universal rules governing employer-employee relations, or whether instead circumstances and specific situations should be taken into account, the investigators asked the business managers how they thought one should deal with an employee who had performed well for fifteen years, but had recently become unproductive. If circumstances indicate it's unlikely that performance will improve, should the employee be dismissed on the grounds that

**job performance should remain the grounds for dismissal, regardless of the age of the person and his previous record.**

or

**[it is] wrong to disregard the fifteen years the employee has been working for the company. One has to take into account the company's responsibility for his life.**

The cultures studied fell into three major clusters. The East Asian managers were by far the most interdependent or collectivistic in their expressed values, the managers from the British and former Commonwealth nations were the most independent or individualistic (with the United States and Canada being the most extremely independent), and the managers from continental Europe were in between. There was also an interesting difference within Europe. The researchers found that the people from the northwestern European nations of Sweden, the Netherlands, and Belgium were more independent than the people from the more southern European nations of France, Italy, and Germany.

continental European nations valued a mix of independence and dependence. Examples of the researchers' questions can be seen in Box 1.1.

## DICK AND JANE, DENG AND JANXING

The first page of a reader for American children from the 1930s shows a little boy running with his dog. "See Dick run," the primer reads. "See Dick run and play." "See Spot run." The first page of a Chinese reader from the same era shows a little boy sitting on the shoulders of a bigger boy. "Big Brother loves Little Brother" reads the text. "Little Brother loves Big Brother." The difference between what the American child and the Chinese child of the 1930s were exposed to on the first

九　好朋友

小強是一個可愛的男孩子，
他是我的好朋友。
我們常常一同讀書，
一同玩耍，
大家很快樂。

的 [322]　ノ ／ イ 竹 自 自 的 的 的　　同 [囘]　丨 冂 冋 冋 同 同

**A** Dick

See Dick.

See Dick run.

1

**B**

**Attention to Action versus Relationships** (A) The Dick and Jane readers of the United States emphasize action and individualism, as shown on this page with the drawing of Dick running and the words, "See Dick. See Dick run." (B) Japanese and Chinese readers are more likely to emphasize relationships, as seen in this Chinese reader in which two boys walk down the street with their arms around each other. The text says, "Xiao Zhiang is a very nice boy. He is my best friend. We always study together and play together. We have a lot of fun together."

"Culture is an inherited habit."
—FRANCIS FUKUYAMA

day of class says much about the differences between the worlds of children from the two cultures. The American child is taught to orient toward action and to be prepared to live in a world where control and individual choice are possible. The Chinese child is more likely to be taught to be attuned to relationships. To the Westerner, it makes sense to speak of the existence of the person apart from any group. To East Asians (for example, Chinese, Japanese, and Koreans) and to many of the world's other peoples, the person really exists only as a member of a larger collective—family, friends, village, corporation. People are related to one another like ropes in a net—completely interconnected and having no real existence without the connections (Munro, 1985).

## WHO ARE YOU?

Westerners' belief that they are self-contained is revealed by simply asking them to describe themselves. Kuhn and McPartland (1954) invented a simple "Who Am I" test that asks people to list twenty statements that describe who they are. (We asked you to list ten statements that describe who you are at the beginning of this section.) Americans' self-descriptions tend to be context-free answers referring to personality traits ("I'm friendly," "hard-working," "shy") and personal preferences ("I like camping"). When more interdependent participants respond to this little test, however, their answers tend to refer to a relationship with some other person or group ("I am Jan's friend") and are often qualified by context ("I am serious at work," "I am fun-loving with my friends") (Cousins, 1989; Ip & Bond, 1995; Markus & Kitayama, 1991). You might want to look back at your answers on the ten-question "Who Am I" test you took at the beginning of this section and see what type of characterizations you emphasized.

Social psychologists Vaunne Ma and Thomas Schoeneman (1997) administered the "Who Am I" test to American university students and to four different groups living in Kenya—university students, workers in Nairobi (the capital city), and traditional Masai and Samburu herding peoples. Kenya was for decades a colony of Great Britain, and city dwellers, especially those who are educated, have had a great deal of exposure to Western culture. Kenyan students have been exposed still more to Western culture and are being educated in a Western tradition. In contrast, traditional African tribespeople are reputed to have little sense of themselves as individuals. Rather, their sense of self is defined by family, property, and position in the community. Tribespeople are constantly made aware of their roles and status in relation to family and other groups (Mwaniki, 1973).

Figure 1.7 shows how differently these four African groups view themselves. Traditional Masai and Samburu characterize themselves in terms of roles and group memberships, whereas Kenyan students are far more likely to mention personal characteristics. Kenyan students, in fact, differ only slightly from American students. Workers in Nairobi are in between the tribespeople and the students. This pattern of evidence, when considered in relation to the very large differences typically found between East Asian and Western students, suggests that modernization by itself does not produce substantial differences in self-conceptions. Rather, it is a Western orientation that seems essential to an independent conception of the self.

> Among traditional Kenyan tribespeople, the individualist is "looked upon with suspicion. . . . There is no really individual affair, for everything has a moral and social influence."
>
> —JOMO KENYATTA (1938), FIRST PRESIDENT OF INDEPENDENT KENYA

## SOME QUALIFICATIONS

Societies differ in many ways, and it's not possible to put each society entirely in one box or the other and say that some are independent in all respects and others are interdependent in all respects. Moreover there are regional and subcultural differences within any large society, such as that of the United States. The U.S. South, for example, is more interdependent and collectivist than much of the rest of the country in the sense that family connections and community ties tend to be more important (Vandello & Cohen, 1999). On the other hand, the South has been described as more tolerant of character quirks and various kinds of social deviance than other regions of the country—individualistic tendencies more characteristic of independent societies (Reed, 1990).

Moreover, the socialization within a given society of particular individuals or particular types of individuals may be oriented more toward independence or more toward interdependence. Gender socialization in our society is a good

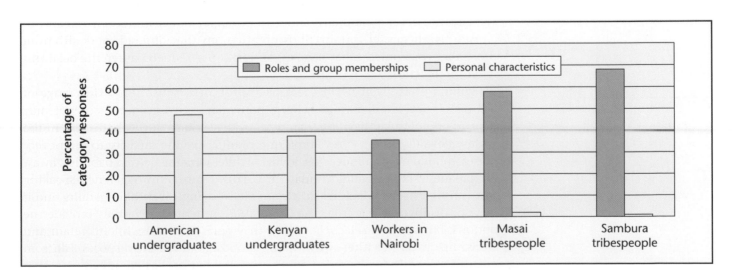

**Figure 1.7 Self-Characterization** The graph shows the percentage of "role and group membership" and "personal characteristics" responses on the "Who Am I" test by American undergraduates, Kenyan undergraduates, workers in Nairobi, Masai tribespeople, and Sambura tribespeople. (Source: Ma & Schoeneman, 1997)

example of this (Kashima et al., 1995). While Dick is depicted in children's readers as running and playing (being independent), Jane is often shown caring for her dolls and cooking for others (being interdependent). So there are individual differences within each culture. In addition, the same person can have a relatively independent orientation in some situations (for example, competing in a debate tournament) and a relatively interdependent orientation in others (for example, singing in a choir) (Gardner, Gabriel, & Lee, 1999; Kühnen & Oyserman, 2002; Trafimow, Triandis, & Goto, 1991).

Nevertheless, the broad generalizations we have made about different cultures hold fairly well, as you will see in later chapters. Some cultures are much more concerned than others with issues of individuality, freedom, personal achievement, and universally applicable rules. Others are more concerned with harmony within the group, achievement as it serves collective goals, and social rules that take particular relationships and context into account. Many of the most important findings in social psychology turn out to have a different character when examined in one sort of culture rather than the other, as we will have occasion to note repeatedly in this book.

## CULTURE AND EVOLUTION AS TOOLS FOR UNDERSTANDING SITUATIONS

As we have seen, both culture and evolution affect how people see the world and behave within it. It may be useful to look at both culture and evolution as ways of understanding extremely broad situations and how people process and react to those broad situations. The situations confronting humans for their first several hundred thousand years concerned the necessities of surviving, reproducing, and nourishing their young in a fundamentally social environment. Within such an environment, humans had to learn to deal with competition, social influence, and dominance relations. Such challenges may have resulted in the evolution of pre-wired inclinations to formulate theories and schemas and to behave in certain ways in reaction to certain social situations. But such inclinations were tools that could be applied flexibly, or not at all, and many, if not most of these tools, were highly modifiable by culture (Sperber, 1996). Indeed, they *required* culture of some sort to develop naturally. Different ecologies and economies led people to constantly encounter certain kinds of situations that differed markedly from those that confronted other peoples, and in turn produced different social systems and practices.

Evolution has given us all the capacity for an astonishingly wide range of behaviors. But whether we develop a particular pre-wired option or not may depend on how adaptive the behavior is for the circumstances that confront the society (Sperber, 1996). For example, all infants have the capacity to utter every known phoneme, and indeed they do so while lying in the crib babbling away. But Japanese-speaking adults find it hard to distinguish *r* from *l*, French-speaking adults find it hard to distinguish *te* from *the*, and English-speaking adults find it hard to distinguish *dew* from the German *dü*. Inherited potentials provide the options, but societies select those that they consider worthwhile to retain and allow the others to wither away. Nature proposes but culture disposes. Far from making us rigidly programmed automatons, evolution has equipped us with a large repertoire of tools for dealing with the enormous range of circumstances that humans confront. Cultural circumstances and general intelligence determine which tools we develop and which tendencies we try to override.

**LOOKING BACK,** we have seen that people in Western societies tend to be individualistic or independent, whereas people in other societies are more likely to be collectivistic or interdependent. Westerners tend to define themselves as having attributes that exist apart from their relations with other people. Non-Westerners tend to define themselves in terms of their relations with others. These differences have important implications for many of the most important phenomena of social psychology. We have also seen that both evolution and culture make important contributions to understanding human social behavior, with evolution predisposing us to certain behaviors, but culture determining which behaviors are likely to be developed in particular situations.

## DOING RESEARCH

Given the enormous range of influences on how people respond to social situations, how is it that social psychologists go about investigating various situations and people's reactions to them? One way they do so is to study social phenomena in natural settings. This might mean observing how people react to natural disasters like hurricanes or floods or manmade disasters like wars or lynch mobs. Another way is to set up controlled experiments in a laboratory. Kurt Lewin, the founder of modern social psychology, showed that social psychology could be an experimental science in the same way that chemistry and cognitive psychology are. He demonstrated that even such complicated and multifaceted phenomena as authoritarian versus democratic leadership styles and group influence could be studied in the laboratory. Following Lewin's lead, social psychologists have taken the position that no social phenomenon is beyond empirical investigation, and many can be studied in controlled laboratory settings.

> "The real purpose of [the] scientific method is to make sure Nature hasn't misled you into thinking you know something you actually don't know."
> —ROBERT PIRSIG, ZEN AND THE ART OF MOTORCYCLE MAINTENANCE

### THEORIES AND HYPOTHESES

Where do testable theories about human behavior come from? They come from just about anywhere: from folk theories, from plays and novels, from observation of social enigmas, from stray comments overheard on a plane or subway, or from other published research. Milgram was planning to compare the obedience of people in different societies, and he set up an experiment to make that comparison. To his credit, he realized that no story about national differences could match the importance of the remarkable degree of obedience he found in his fellow Americans, and he began to examine factors affecting homegrown American obedience. Moreover, much of the initial social psychological research on persuasion was motivated by the desire to understand what was thought to be the great effectiveness of Nazi propaganda during World War II. And much of the research on prejudice and discrimination has received its impetus from everyday observation of intergroup enmity and violence.

### CORRELATIONAL AND EXPERIMENTAL RESEARCH

The most important distinction in types of methods you should be aware of—both for purposes of science and for those of daily life—is that between correlational and experimental research. In **correlational research**, there is not random assignment to different situations or conditions, and psychologists

**correlational research**
Research in which there is not random assignment to different situations or conditions, and from which psychologists can just see whether or not there is a relationship between the variables.

simply determine whether or not there is a relationship between two or more variables. In **experimental research**, people are randomly assigned to different situations (or conditions), and it is possible to make very strong inferences about how these different situations or conditions affect people's behavior. In the Darley and Batson study, seminary students were randomly assigned to be either in the "late" condition or the control condition. Because participants in the two conditions were, on average, the same kind of people, one can be sure that something having to do with being late is what caused such a large proportion of seminarians in the "late" condition to fail to help the apparent victim.

*Correlational Research*    The other social sciences are normally only able to make use of correlational data, in which the natural association between two or more variables is examined. In correlational research, where by definition there is no manipulation of variables, one can never be sure about causality. Does variable A causally influence variable B, or is it the other way around? Or is it some third variable that influences both? For example, *Time* magazine (February, 2004) published a cover story devoted to the proposition that love and sex are good for physical and mental health. The magazine was able to quote statistics such as one showing that married people are happier than unmarried people. But this leaves open large questions that should cause us to be skeptical of the magazine's causal claims. Happier people may be more appealing to others, and more likely to be married for that reason. Or perhaps good physical and mental health lead both to greater likelihood of marriage and greater likelihood of being happy. It is possible to approach such questions with what are called "natural experiments" or "quasi-experiments." For example, people's happiness could be assessed at some point prior to marriage and at some point after marriage. If most people reported greater happiness after marriage than before, this would strengthen *Time*'s position on causality.

In correlational research, one looks at the degree of relationship between two or more variables. Strength of relationship can range from 0, meaning there is no relationship at all between the variables, to 1.0, meaning that the covariation is perfect—the higher the level on one variable the higher the level on the other—without exception. By convention, a correlation of .2 would indicate a very slight relationship, a correlation of .4 a moderately strong relationship, and a correlation of .6 or higher a very strong relationship.

Correlational studies can be very helpful in alerting us to various possibilities for valid causal hypotheses about the nature of the world, but they don't tell us about the direction of causality, and they don't tell us whether some "external" variable is driving the association between the two variables of interest. Consider some examples.

1. *People who watch the 11:00 local news—with its murders, fires, and other newsworthy mayhem—see more danger in the world than people who do not.* The most obvious explanation is that watching dangers on TV makes people feel more at risk. But mightn't it be the case that people who are anxious watch local TV in order to justify their fearfulness? Or is it some third variable: for example, elderly people may have more anxiety about their lives and may have more time to watch TV? Note that we can refine this study and potentially rule out the latter hypothesis. For example, it may not in fact be the case that the elderly are more likely to watch TV than younger people, and/or it may be the case that they are no more anxious about their lives in general than are

> **experimental research**
> Research in which people are randomly assigned to different situations (or conditions), and from which it is possible to make very strong inferences about how these different situations or conditions affect people's behavior.

younger people. This still leaves a myriad of as yet unimagined factors that might produce the relationship. Nevertheless, as we will see later, clever analysis of correlational data can sometimes be quite persuasive about the meaning of the relationship.

2. *People who watched a great deal of violent TV when they were eight years old are more likely to be incarcerated for violence and other criminal behavior in adolescence and adulthood.* At first blush, it seems obvious that watching violent TV would tend to make people more violent. On the other hand, it also seems obvious that people with more violent temperaments would be more likely to want to watch violent TV when younger and more likely to engage in criminal behavior when older. Note, however, that such a **longitudinal** study rules out the opposite direction of causality: nothing that happens when a person is thirty can affect anything the person did when younger. And again, clever analysis of data such as these can make some interpretations much less plausible than others.

The problem with correlational research is that it suffers from **self-selection**—that is, the investigator has no control over which participants have a given level on a given variable. For example, the investigator does not choose which eight-year-olds watch a lot of television and which watch a little. The child in effect chooses the level of TV watching, and the investigator can't know what other qualities the child brings with high or low TV watching. Experiments avoid the self-selection problem altogether.

*Experimental Research*    In experimental research, there is an **independent variable** (usually defined as the variable about which a prediction is made and that is manipulated) and a **dependent variable** (the variable that is presumed to be affected by the independent variable manipulation and that is measured). In experiments, the researcher determines what will be the independent variable and what levels there will be for that variable. In the Darley and Batson experiment, there were actually three levels of hurry: none, some, and substantial. But they might have had only the two we described or many degrees of hurry. The dependent variable is measured in some way—by verbal reports, behavior (helping or not; getting an inoculation or not), or physiological measures. The great power of experiments comes from the fact that participants are allotted their positions on the independent variable by **random assignment**. This means that participants are as likely to be assigned to one condition as to another, and that, on average, except for the manipulation of the independent variable, there should be no differences across experimental groups. For example, it is possible to expose young children to violent TV for a couple of hours (or, in a **control group**, which does not receive the experimental manipulation, to some innocuous programs) and see whether they behave in a more violent fashion subsequently. They do indeed, which buttresses the hypothesis that violent TV leads to violence in later life (see Chapter 13).

In general, experimental research can sometimes answer, or at least speak to, the causality questions that are left unclear in purely correlational research. Sometimes it cannot, however, because of logistical or moral impediments, and in these cases we are left merely with correlational findings that we must supplement with theory or common sense to make them meaningful. In our view, findings such as that happier people have better marriages are not very valuable. Too many plausible interpretations exist supporting all kinds of causal hypotheses.

**longitudinal studies** Studies conducted over a long period of time with the same population, which is periodically assessed regarding particular behaviors.

**self-selection** A problem that arises when the participant, rather than the investigator, selects his or her level on each variable, bringing with this value unknown other properties that make causal interpretation of a relationship difficult.

**independent variable** The variable about which a prediction is made and that is manipulated in experimental research.

**dependent variable** The variable that is presumed to be affected by the independent variable manipulation and that is measured in experimental research.

**random assignment** Assigning participants in experimental research to different groups randomly, such that they are as likely to be assigned to one condition as to another.

**control group** The group of participants that does not receive the experimental manipulation.

And of course it's not possible to marry people off and see if they get happier, and it is difficult at the very least to make people happy somehow and see if their marriages get better. However, it is possible, as we noted earlier, to take advantage of **natural experiments**—for example, to look at people's happiness before and after they get married. And indeed, it turns out that people are happier after marriage than they were before (Argyle, 1999). This is scarcely decisive, but it is strongly suggestive of the direction of causality.

We will see many illustrations of the difference in power between correlational and experimental studies in this book and of the clever ways that people have managed to circumvent the problems characteristic of correlational research.

*Validity*    We should note that often there are weaknesses in experimental studies as well. Sometimes experiments are a bit sterile and so removed from everyday life events that it can be hard to know just how to interpret them (Aronson, Ellsworth, Carlsmith, & Gonzalez, 1990). This is sometimes called poor **external validity**—that is, weakness in knowing how to relate the stimulus situation in the experiment to elements of real-life situations. Poor external validity is certainly not always fatal—in fact, investigators sometimes deliberately strip down a situation to its bare essentials to make a theoretical point that would be hard to make with real-world materials. We will discuss in greater detail the issue of when external validity is essential and when it is not in Chapter 2. For now, it is sufficient to note that when the purpose of the research is to generalize the *results* of an experiment directly to the outside world, external validity is critical. But when the purpose of the research is to clarify a general idea or theory, and then apply that sharpened idea to the outside world, external validity is much less essential.

*Reliability*    **Reliability** concerns the degree to which the particular way one measures a given variable—a pencil-and-paper IQ test, judges' ratings of a person's "charisma"—is likely to yield consistent results. If you take an IQ test twice, do you get roughly the same score? Do people tend to be seen as equally charismatic on different occasions? Reliability is typically measured by correlations on a 0–1 scale.

*Statistical Significance*    A finding is only a finding if it has **statistical significance**, meaning that the probability of obtaining the result by chance is less than some quantity. By convention, this quantity is usually set at 1 in 20 (or .05), but probabilities can of course go much lower than that, sometimes by orders of magnitude. Statistical significance is primarily a matter of the size of the difference between groups—or of a relationship between variables—and the number of cases the finding is based on. The bigger the difference or relationship, and the larger the number of cases, the greater the statistical significance. We will not mention the concept of statistical significance again because all of the findings we report in this book are statistically significant (though not all are based on large effects).

## OTHER KINDS OF RESEARCH

Social psychologists sometimes carry out research that is not necessarily either correlational or experimental in nature. These include demonstrations, observational studies, surveys, and field experiments.

---

**natural experiments**  Naturally occurring events or phenomena having somewhat different conditions that can be compared with almost as much rigor as in experiments where the investigator manipulates the conditions.

**external validity**  An experimental setup that closely resembles real-life situations.

**reliability**  The degree to which the particular way one measures a given variable is likely to yield consistent results.

**statistical significance**  A measure of the probability of a given result occurring by chance.

*Demonstrations*    Some of the most important research in psychology correlates no variable with any other variable and manipulates nothing. Perhaps the best-known and certainly one of the most important **demonstration studies** in the history of social psychology is Milgram's "mere" demonstration of astonishing obedience in a setting drawing on many real-world elements. The prison study by Zimbardo and colleagues is another "mere" demonstration. In a sense, though, these studies do have "control groups." Can you think what they might be?

*Observational Studies*    **Observational studies** are more characteristic of the sort of research done by anthropologists than by psychologists. Such studies involve observation of—and usually participation in—the lives of people in some group or situation with the intention of studying aspects of group beliefs, values, or behavior. Nonetheless, social psychologists sometimes do use observational studies as a means of learning about a topic before they study it more formally through experimental studies.

*Surveys*    **Surveys** involve asking questions of people, sometimes students in laboratories and sometimes citizens in the community. Surveys can ask any sort of question at all. Often there is an intent to correlate variables—for example, to see whether there are gender, race, socioeconomic, or regional differences in preferences for various kinds of social policy. Surveys can even be vehicles for experiments, telling some respondents one thing and other respondents another before asking them about important target questions. You will see several examples of this sort of experiment-within-a survey.

*Field Experiments*    **Field experiments** are conceptually like laboratory experiments except that they occur in the real world, usually under circumstances in which participants are not aware that they are in a study of any kind. An example would be an experiment studying people's responses to different kinds of advertisements in magazines or on TV, or an experiment in which researchers would study the reactions of people who were asked to do something like giving up their seats on an uncrowded bus or train or subway.

Finally, it should be noted that findings of real importance are usually studied by means of many of the techniques discussed, providing triangulation that could not be produced by any number of replications using the same sort of procedure.

**demonstration studies** Research in which no variable is correlated with any other variable and in which nothing is manipulated.

**observational studies** Research involving observation of and often participation in the lives of people in some group or situation with the intention of studying aspects of group beliefs, values, or behavior.

**surveys** A series of questions asked of people, sometimes students in laboratories and sometimes citizens in the community, to ascertain their attitudes or beliefs.

**field experiments** Experiments that are set up in the real world, usually under circumstances in which participants are not aware that they are in a study of any kind.

**LOOKING BACK,** we have seen that research consists of formulating theories and hypotheses and then conducting correlational or experimental research to determine whether these hypotheses accurately account for what is happening. Correlational research can establish if two variables are related to each other, either positively or negatively or not at all, but it cannot establish causality. Experimental research aims to determine causality by manipulating an independent variable to see how such a manipulation will affect the dependent variable. In doing research, psychologists are often, though not always, concerned with external validity—that is, whether the experimental setting captures real-life situations and is readily generalizable to them. Other forms of research include demonstrations, observational studies, surveys, and field experiments.

# SUMMARY

1. *Social psychology* is the scientific study of the feelings, thoughts, and behaviors of individuals in social situations.

2. Social psychology emphasizes the influence of *situations* on behavior. People often find it difficult to see the role that powerful situations play in producing their own and others' behavior, and they are inclined to overemphasize the importance of personal dispositions in producing behavior. The two tendencies together are called the *fundamental attribution error*.

3. Social psychology also focuses on the role of *construal* in understanding situations. People often feel that their comprehension of situations is direct, without much mediating thought. In fact, even the perception of the simplest objects rests on substantial inference and the existence of complex cognitive structures for carrying it out.

4. The primary tool people use for understanding social situations, and physical stimuli for that matter, is the schema. *Schemas* are the stored representations of numberless repetitions of highly similar stimuli and situations. They tell us how to interpret situations and how to behave in them. *Stereotypes* are schemas for people of various kinds—police officers, Hispanics, yuppies. Stereotypes serve to guide interpretation and behavior, but they can often be mistaken or misapplied, and they can lead to damaging interactions and unjust actions.

5. People's construals of situations are often largely *automatic and unconscious* and, as a consequence, people are sometimes in the dark about how they reached a particular conclusion or behaved in a particular way.

6. The *evolutionary perspective* focuses on practices and understandings that are universal and that seem to be indispensable to social life. This leads to the suspicion that we are pre-wired to engage in those practices. Some evolutionary theorists have argued that differences between males and females may be explained by the fact that the two sexes have reason for differential *parental investment*. They also talk about other universal characteristics that are more cognitive in nature, including *language*, which appears in almost identical fashion, at almost identical rates of development, in people in all cultures, as well as a *theory of mind*, which also apparently appears very early in normal people in all cultures.

7. There is a great range of behaviors and meanings that can differ dramatically across cultures. Many of these differences involve the degree to which a society is *interdependent* in its characteristic social relations (that is, having relationships of different kinds with many people of a highly prescribed nature) versus *independent* (that is, having fewer relationships of a looser sort). These differences influence conceptions of the self, understandings of the nature of human relationships, and even basic cognitive and perceptual processes.

8. Social psychologists use research to systematically examine various *hypotheses* about behavior in the social world. There is an important distinction between *correlational research,* in which it is possible to measure only variables whose relations are being studied, and more powerful *experimental research,* in which it is possible to be certain that something about the *independent variable* has had an effect on the *dependent variable.*

# CRITICAL THINKING ABOUT BASIC PRINCIPLES

1. It's a serious problem for expensive restaurants in Manhattan when reservation holders don't show up. The restaurants lose a considerable amount of overhead for each no-show. Many restaurants have made it a custom to ask patrons to "Please call us if you won't be able to make it." Recently, some restaurants have started asking instead, "Will you call us if you're not able to make it?" Would you think this would be more effective than the standard request, or less? Why?

2. Suppose you are making "get out the vote" calls for a political party the night before the election. What would you say to increase the likelihood that voters would actually make it to the polls?

3. Aristotle's moral philosophy was based on what has come to be called "virtue ethics." He encouraged people to strive to develop all the character traits of a virtuous person. Do you see limits to how much can be achieved by such a moral philosophy? How could it be profitably supplemented?

## KEY TERMS

channel factors (p. 12)

collectivistic (interdependent) culture (p. 30)

construal (p. 14)

control group (p. 39)

correlational research (p. 37)

dependent variable (p. 39)

demonstration studies (p. 41)

dispositions (p. 13)

experimental research (p. 38)

external validity (p. 40)

field experiments (p. 41)

fundamental attribution error (p. 13)

Gestalt psychology (p. 15)

independent variable (p. 39)

individualistic (independent) culture (p. 29)

longitudinal studies (p. 39)

natural experiments (p. 40)

naturalistic fallacy (p. 27)

natural selection (p. 22)

observational studies (p. 41)

parental investment (p. 27)

prisoner's dilemma (p. 15)

random assignment (p. 39)

reliability (p. 40)

schemas (p. 17)

self-selection (p. 39)

social psychology (p. 5)

statistical significance (p. 40)

stereotypes (p. 18)

surveys (p. 41)

theory of mind (p. 25)

## FURTHER READING

Darley, J. M., & Batson, C. D. (1973). From Jerusalem to Jericho: A study of situational and dispositional variables in helping behavior. *Journal of Personality and Social Psychology, 27*, 100–119.

Doris, J. M. (2002). *Lack of character: Personality and moral behavior.* New York: Cambridge University Press.

Liberman, V., Samuels, S. M., & Ross, L. (2002). The name of the game: Predictive power of reputations vs. situational labels in determining Prisoner's Dilemma game moves. *Personality and Social Psychology Bulletin, 30*, 1175–1185.

Milgram, S. (1974). *Obedience to authority.* New York: Harper & Row.

Ross, L., & Nisbett, R. E. (1991). *The person and the situation: Perspectives of social psychology.* New York: McGraw-Hill.

# PART ONE

# Connecting to Others

SOCIAL PSYCHOLOGY IS THE ONE BRANCH OF PSYCHOLOGY THAT DEALS primarily with the important fact that we live our lives connected to others. We originate in families, we seek out friendship and romance, and we spend a great deal of our waking moments in groups of various sorts—in classes, on the job, in a place of worship, or with those who share our hobbies and enthusiasms. In our opening section, we therefore explore a number of factors that set our connections to others in motion, and we also examine a number of consequences of our social connectedness. In Chapter 2, we consider how life in groups can influence performance and alter decisions, and we illustrate how certain types of behavior emerge only in groups. Chapter 3 proceeds from the (happy) observation that our connections to others are not always externally imposed. We have some choice as to whom we spend our time with, and so in this chapter we discuss some of the most important determinants of why we are more attracted to some people than to others. Chapter 4 takes the investigation a step further. We form relationships with those to whom we are attracted—and, alas, often with those to whom we aren't attracted as well. In this chapter, we explore many of the different types of human relationships and a number of variables that determine whether or not they go well. Chapter 5 ends this section of the book. In this chapter, we cover a topic that may seem outside the theme of social connectedness—the self. But as social psychologists have discovered, the self is forged in our interactions with others, and we will therefore explore many of the causes and consequences of the fundamentally social nature of the self.

# Chapter Outline

# CHAPTER 2

# GROUPS

Arizona Senator John McCain was a thirty-one-year-old Navy pilot when, on October 26, 1967, he took off for his twenty-third bombing run over North Vietnam. His target was a power plant located on the edge of a small lake in the center of Hanoi, the capital of North Vietnam. Diving at 550 miles per hour, his radar detection alarm sounded, indicating that a surface-to-air-missile was locked onto his plane and rapidly approaching. He waited just long enough to release his bombs before beginning evasive maneuvers. It was too late. The missile blew off his right wing, and his jet plummeted to earth.

As he ejected from his aircraft, he struck part of the plane, breaking both arms and one leg. He landed in the middle of the lake near his target and was immediately set upon by an angry mob. Dragging him from the lake, they broke his shoulder with a rifle butt and stabbed him with a bayonet in his ankle and groin. Before the mob could finish with him, a Vietnamese army truck arrived, and soldiers took him to the infamous "Hanoi Hilton" where a great many American prisoners spent the duration of the war.

During his captivity, McCain was savagely beaten, some-times for refusing to divulge information, other times for refusing an offer of early release because he was the son of Admiral Jack McCain, commander of U.S. forces in the Pacific. (The soldiers' code of conduct stipulates that prisoners of war should be released in the order in which they were captured.) Before his ordeal was over, McCain spent five and a half years as a prisoner of war, two in solitary confinement.

In interviews afterwards, McCain has consistently maintained that, despite his severe injuries, despite all the beatings, despite imprisonment in "a filthy room, about twenty feet by twenty feet, lousy with mosquitoes and rats," the hardest part of his ordeal was the experience of solitary confinement—being cut off from his fellow human beings. "What part of my time as a POW was more difficult, physical mistreatment or solitary confinement? It was without question being held captive in solitary confinement . . . taking this interaction away is a tremendous torture to the spirit" (McCain, 1999, 2003).

The importance of companionship and of living in groups is taken as a given in social psychology. With this in mind, our focus in this chapter is life in groups and the ways people are influenced by the presence and actions of those around them. We examine how the presence of others influences our performance on tasks, how groups sometimes morph into unruly mobs, and how and why group decisions sometimes differ from those made by individuals.

**Group Bonds**   (A) John McCain (lower right) and other U.S. Navy pilots during the Vietnam War. (B) In October 1967 during a bombing raid over North Vietnam, McCain was shot down and taken prisoner by the enemy. He remained a prisoner of war for five and a half years, during which time he suffered great hardship and torture but bonded with his fellow prisoners.

## THE NATURE AND PURPOSE OF GROUP LIVING

McCain's experience, and his reaction to it, speaks to the fundamentally social nature of human beings. Humans are creatures who live in groups. One can ask *why* humans live in groups, or, to push the question back one step further: Why

do all the large primates except the orangutan live in groups? The answer, surely, is that group life offers large primates some not-well-understood advantages in the struggle for survival. The advantages are not well understood because both solitary and group lifestyles have been successfully pursued by different mammal species. Wolves live in groups but bears do not, and neither appear any worse off for the particular lifestyle they have pursued.

Still, it is generally maintained that life with others offered our human ancestors protection from predators, efficiency in food acquisition, assistance with child rearing, and defense against human aggressors—benefits that we are less equipped to do without than are, say, bears or orangutans. It is also generally maintained that these benefits are so crucial to survival that we have a psychological need to be with others and belong to groups (Baumeister & Leary, 1995). When isolated from others, people typically become extremely upset. Hermits frequently succumb to *acedia*—becoming listless and alienated and eventually unresponsive to impinging stimuli. McCain's experience reflects the difficulty of being kept in solitary confinement. Many who are kept socially isolated for a sufficiently long time literally lose their minds. And young humans, even those old enough to have the skills necessary to provide for themselves materially, have great difficulty surviving without being in a group. The same is true of young gorillas and chimps.

Before examining how groups influence individual performance, reactions, and decisions, we should first consider the question: What, exactly, is a group? This is not an easy question, as there are so many different types of groups, and the different types don't always share many features. The members of a baseball team are clearly a group, but are the members of a large lecture course a group? Most people would say that the individuals riding together in an elevator are not a group. But suppose the elevator breaks down, and those inside must figure out how to escape or summon help? Most people would say that the individuals in the elevator now seem more like a real group. But why would this be so?

One definition that captures these intuitions is that of Cartwright and Zander, who maintained that a group is "a collection of individuals who have relations to one another that make them interdependent to some significant degree" (Cartwright & Zander, 1968, p. 46). Thus, the people in the functioning elevator do not make up a group because they are not very interdependent. But once the elevator breaks down and they must decide on joint action (or whether to take joint action), they become interdependent, and hence more of a group. Note that interdependence varies along a continuum and, therefore, by this definition, so should whether or not a collection of people constitutes a group (McGrath, 1984). And to most people this seems right. The members of a family are more of a "real" group than are the participants in a seminar, and they in turn are more of a group than are the students in a large lecture course. By this reasoning, a nation's citizens make up something of a group, but they are less of a group than are the members of a tribe or band, who interact with one another more frequently and are more directly dependent on one another.

Let us now examine the psychological impact of different types of groups that vary along this continuum. First, we consider the impact of other people—be they strangers who happen by or members of a tight-knit group—on how well we perform. Second, we examine how and why we sometimes act more impulsively when we get "lost" in a crowd. Finally, we examine how the decisions made by groups—typically intact, highly cohesive groups—differ from those made by individuals.

> "No man is an island, entire of itself; every man is a piece of the continent, a part of the main."
> — JOHN DONNE

# SOCIAL FACILITATION

What effect does the presence of other people have on human performance? That is, does the presence of others typically help or hinder performance, or does it exert no effect at all? To address this question, let's consider it in more personal and vivid terms. Suppose you are off by yourself trying to perfect a skill—practicing the piano, developing a top-spin lob for your tennis game, or working through the intricacies of conjugating Latin verbs. You feel you are making acceptable progress when along comes, say, Jack Nicholson or Reese Witherspoon, or maybe your mother or a perfect stranger, who takes a seat nearby and proceeds to observe. What does this other person's presence do to your performance? Does it provide you with the energy and focus necessary to bring your performance to new heights? Or do you become so nervous and distracted that your performance suffers?

## INITIAL RESEARCH

Norman Triplett was the first person to experimentally examine this question. Triplett was something of a bicycling enthusiast (or "wheelman" as they were known at the time). After reviewing speed records put out by the Racing Board of the League of American Wheelmen, Triplett noticed that the fastest times were recorded when cyclists competed directly against one another on the same track at the same time. Much slower speed records were obtained when cyclists raced alone against the clock. Thus, Triplett believed that the presence of others tended to facilitate human performance.

Triplett realized, however, that the cycling records were not the best test of his hypothesis. For one thing, different cyclists performed in the different events: one cyclist might race only against the clock, another only against another cyclist. Thus, the superior times recorded under direct competition might not be due to the competition itself, but to something about the kind of people who chose to compete against one another rather than against the clock. As we discussed in Chapter 1, psychologists refer to this as the problem of self-selection: the variable of interest (in this case, the racing condition) is intertwined, or confounded, with the type of person who chooses the condition. The unfortunate result is that it is impossible to tell which is causing the observed effect—the conditions themselves or the type of people who choose to perform in those conditions. As you will remember, psychologists overcome this problem by conducting controlled experiments in which people are randomly assigned to the different conditions of the experiment, thus ensuring (within the bounds of probability) that, on average, an equivalent mix of different kinds of people are present in each.

To overcome this problem of self-selection, Triplett (1898) conducted what is widely regarded as social psychology's first experiment. He invited a group of forty children to his laboratory and had them reel in fishing lines as fast as they could. Each child did so on six trials with rest periods between. On three trials the child was alone, and on three trials there was another child alongside doing the same thing. What Triplett found under these more controlled conditions matched what he had seen in his analysis of cycling times. The children tended to reel in fishing line faster when in the presence of another child engaged in the same activity. The presence of others appeared to facilitate human performance. Research on this subject thus came to be known as research on **social facilitation.**

A number of subsequent experiments reinforced Triplett's findings and

> "The bodily presence of another rider is a stimulus to the racer in arousing the competitive instinct; that another can thus be the means of releasing or freeing nervous energy for him that he cannot of himself release."
>
> —NORMAN TRIPLETT

**social facilitation**  Initially a term for enhanced performance in the presence of others; now a broader term for the effect—positive or negative—of the presence of others on performance.

**Social Facilitation and Competition**
Performance is typically enhanced in the presence of others when the activity is well learned. Here Lance Armstrong is energized by the presence and cheering of the spectators as he competes in the 2004 Tour de France.

extended them in two important ways. First, the same effects were obtained when the others present were not doing the same thing (that is, not "co-acting"), but were merely present as an audience of passive observers (Gates, 1924; Travis, 1925). Second, the same effect was also observed in a vast number of animal species, indicating that the phenomenon is really quite general and fundamental. For example, animals as diverse as dogs, fish, armadillos, opossums, and frogs have been shown to eat more when in the presence of other members of the same species than when alone (Ross & Ross, 1949; Uematsu, 1970; Platt, Yaksh, & Darby, 1967; Platt & James, 1966; Boice, Quanty, & Williams, 1974). It has also been shown that ants dig more earth (Chen, 1937), drosophila do more preening (Connolly, 1968), and centipedes run faster through mazes (Hosey, Wood, Thompson, & Druck, 1985) when together than when alone. For both humans and animals, then, much of the research on this topic indicates that the presence of others facilitates performance.

Unfortunately, not all of the relevant findings conform to this pattern. Numerous exceptions emerged soon after Triplett's original findings. Floyd Allport (1920), for example, asked students at Harvard and Radcliffe to refute philosophical arguments as best they could in a five-minute period. The students provided higher-quality refutations when working alone than when working in the presence of another student. The presence of others has also been shown to inhibit performance on arithmetic problems, memory tasks, and maze learning (Dashiell, 1930; Pessin, 1933; Pessin & Husband, 1933). And the presence of other members of the same species has also been found to sometimes inhibit the performance of animals (Allee & Masure, 1936; Shelley, 1965; Strobel, 1972).

## RESOLVING THE CONTRADICTIONS

Putting all of these findings together, it seemed for a time that the best answer to the question "What is the effect of the presence of others on performance?" was that it sometimes helps and sometimes hurts. That is not a terribly satisfying answer, of course. It is as helpful as a political pundit saying that the Democrats will capture the White House in the next election, . . . but then again they might not. You would certainly ask for more from any political forecaster, and you could legitimately ask for more from those who study the effects of the presence of others on human performance.

***Zajonc's Theory***    Fortunately, a more satisfying understanding was eventually obtained. After a period of approximately twenty-five years in which the field largely became discouraged by the lack of progress on this topic and moved on to other issues, social psychologist Robert Zajonc (rhymes with "science") proposed an unusually elegant theory to account for all of the divergent findings on this topic. Zajonc (1965) argued that the presence of others, indeed the *mere* presence of others, tends to facilitate performance on simple or well-learned tasks, but to hinder performance on difficult or novel tasks. Even more important, Zajonc's theory explained *why* the presence of others has these effects.

Zajonc's theory has three components. First, the mere presence of others makes a person more aroused. (More generally, the mere presence of another member of the same species tends to arouse any organism, but we will focus on people for now.) People are dynamic and unpredictable stimuli, capable of doing almost anything at any time. We thus need to be alert or aroused in their presence in order to be able to react to what they might do.

Second, arousal tends to make a person more "rigid," in the sense that the person becomes even more inclined to do what he or she is already inclined to do. In the language Zajonc used, arousal makes a person more likely to make a **dominant response** (see Box 2.1). Think of it this way: In any situation, there are a variety of responses you can make, and these responses can be arranged in a hierarchy according to their likelihood of occurrence. Whatever you are most

> **dominant response** In a hierarchy of responses, the response you are most likely to make.

## Box 2.1    FOCUS ON DAILY LIFE

# Social Facilitation of Prejudice

One potential manifestation of the facilitation of dominant response tendencies runs counter to most people's intuitions. That is, it is generally believed that prejudiced individuals are less likely to show their prejudice in most public settings. To do so is to risk others' disapproval. But if some forms of prejudice represent dominant response tendencies, they should be facilitated in the presence of others— even when those others disapprove of prejudice. In one study that examined this idea, students were seated in front of a computer and shown, very briefly, pairs of images—a black or white face followed by a picture of a gun or a hand tool. The students were asked to respond as quickly as possible as to whether the second image was a gun or a hand tool. If they didn't respond within a half second, they were informed that they did not respond quickly enough. This procedure was repeated over and over again, and the experimenters recorded, as a measure of prejudice, the number of mistakes participants made. In particular, they were interested in how often a hand tool was mistakenly identified as a gun when it was preceded by a black face compared to when it was preceded by a white face.

Some participants did this task alone, not expecting to have to interact with anyone in the experiment. Others did the task expecting to share their responses with others after they were finished. What the investigators found was that participants made 13 percent more errors (calling a tool a gun if it was preceded by a black face) when they expected to interact with others than when they did not (Lambert, Payne, Jacoby, Shaffer, Chasteen, & Khan, 2003).

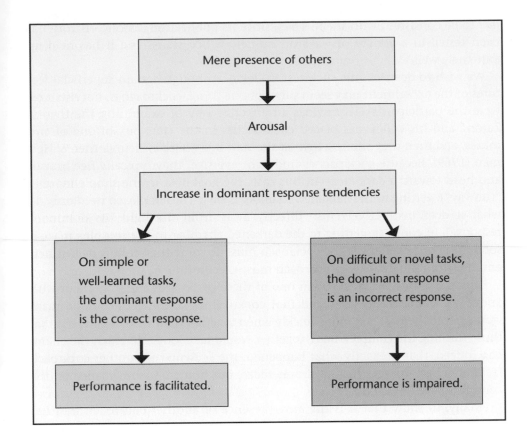

**Figure 2.1 Zajonc's Model of Social Facilitation**   The presence of others (indeed, their *mere* presence) increases arousal and facilitates dominant response tendencies. This facilitates performance on easy or well-learned tasks, but hinders performance on difficult or novel tasks.

inclined to do in that situation is at the top of the hierarchy and is thus the "dominant response." Suppose, for example, that you are typing a memo, and you wish to type the letter "d." You would most likely do so correctly by pressing down on the middle finger of your left hand. As we all know from experience, however, we sometimes make mistakes, and our mistakes are not random. If you don't press the correct key, you are likely to press the "s" key next to it or the "c" just below. All possible responses can be ordered in a hierarchy according to the likelihood that you will make them. When aroused, Zajonc argued, people are even more inclined to make the response that is at the top of their hierarchy.

The third component of Zajonc's theory links the increase in dominant response tendencies to the facilitation of simple tasks and the inhibition of complex tasks. For easy or well-learned tasks, the dominant response is the correct response. Indeed, that is tantamount to what it means for a task to be easy or well learned. Your reflexive response is the correct response. Thus, the presence of other people, by facilitating your dominant response, facilitates the correct response and improves performance. In contrast, for difficult or novel tasks, the dominant response is unlikely to be the correct response. Again, that is what it means for a task to be difficult or novel. Your reflexive response is not the correct response. Thus, the presence of others facilitates an *incorrect* response and hinders performance. This is shown schematically in Figure 2.1.

*Testing the Theory*   Zajonc's theory brought much-needed clarity to this field by providing a remarkably accurate summary of the diverse findings that existed at the time. Like any theory, however, Zajonc's formulation needed to be subjected to more stringent tests. The existing findings did not offer a sufficiently rigorous test; after all, the theory was based on the existing findings and therefore *had* to be consistent with them. Thus, since its publication, Zajonc's theory has been tested in a variety of ways on numerous occasions, and it has held up extremely well.

We wish to describe one such test in detail. Although certain superficial features of the experiment may seem silly (for one thing, cockroaches, not humans, were the participants), it provides an effective way of examining the theory. Zajonc and his colleagues placed cockroaches in the start box of one of two mazes, and then they shone a light at the start box (Zajonc, Heingartner, & Herman, 1969). Because cockroaches find light aversive, they typically flee from it and head toward a dark area—in this case, the goal box. In the simple maze (a "runway"), getting to the darkened chamber is easy. The cockroach need only do what it does instinctively: run directly away from the light (its dominant response). In contrast, getting to the darkened chamber in the complex maze is something of a challenge. The cockroach must do more than follow its instincts and flee from the light. The cockroach must execute a turn.

Zajonc had his cockroaches run one of these two mazes either alone or with another cockroach. He predicted that cockroaches running the simple maze would get to the goal box more quickly when together than when alone, but that those running the complex maze together would take longer to reach the chamber. Indeed, that is exactly what happened: the presence of another cockroach facilitated performance on the simple maze, but hindered performance on the complex maze (Figure 2.2A).

Finally, to show that it is the *mere* presence of another cockroach that has these effects—as opposed to competition or some other more complex factor than the presence of conspecifics (others of the same species)—Zajonc added a condition in which the cockroach ran the maze, not with another cockroach running alongside, but with other cockroaches merely present as a passive "audience." To accomplish this, Zajonc built a set of plexiglass boxes, or "grand-

**Figure 2.2 Social Facilitation on Simple and Complex Tasks**
(A) Average time (in seconds) taken by cockroaches to negotiate simple or complex mazes when alone or alongside another cockroach. (B) Average time to negotiate simple or complex mazes when alone or in the presence of an audience. The cockroaches take less time to run simple mazes when they are in the presence of others but more time to run complex mazes with others present. (Source: Zajonc, Heingartner, & Herman, 1969)

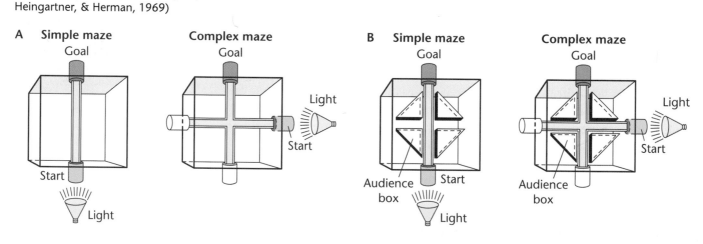

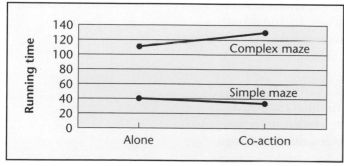

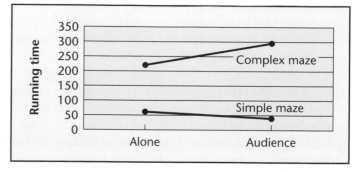

stands," that flanked the two mazes and filled them with observer cockroaches. Here, too, he predicted that the presence of the observing cockroaches would facilitate performance on the simple maze, but inhibit performance on the complex maze. And indeed, as Figure 2.2B indicates, the results were exactly as predicted. The presence of a passive audience helped performance on the simple task but interfered with performance on the difficult task.

*A Methodological Aside: External Validity and Theory Testing*   You may question whether these results have any external validity—that is, if they can be generalized to the real world and therefore tell us something about real, everyday social interaction. The findings were obtained in an artificial situation that could not occur in the real world (cockroaches would not naturally sit in grandstands observing other cockroaches running in mazes). Nonetheless, the results show what happens in a controlled situation in which contaminating factors cannot play a role.

To test theories, it turns out, it is often more important to know what *can* happen, even under bizarre circumstances, than to know what typically *does* happen under natural conditions (Mook, 1983). One is not always interested in generalizing experimental *findings* directly to conditions in the real world. Instead, one is concerned with testing or validating a theory, and it is the improved understanding of the *theory* that is then applied to the real world and allows the investigator to predict real-life phenomena with greater precision.

An example from the physical sciences may be helpful. At first glance, most people find it hard to accept physicists' contention that, absent any wind resistance, light objects (for example, feathers) fall to the ground with the same speed as heavy objects (for example, cannonballs). After all, in any real-world environment, they do not. A cannonball is better able to overcome wind resistance and hence falls more quickly to the ground than a feather. To correct our faulty intuitions, the physicist could drop a feather and a cannonball in a perfect vacuum, and we would see quite readily that, in fact, they do fall at the same rate. Note that no one would squawk, "But the study has no external validity! There are no perfect vacuums to be found out in the real world!" It doesn't matter that there aren't. The physicist's claim entails a prediction about what would happen without wind resistance, and the only way to properly test the claim is to see what would happen in an admittedly artificial environment, a vacuum. The physicist is testing a theoretical understanding, and the best way to do so is to observe what *can* happen, even in the most artificial environment. And what is true for the physicist is equally true for the experimental social psychologist.

In similar fashion, the very artificiality of Zajonc's experiment was what permitted the most stringent test of his ideas. First, in this artificial context we need not guess at what the dominant response might be. Because cockroaches invariably run from light, it is clear that that is their dominant response. Second, it is possible in this context to construct two different conditions, one in which the dominant response leads to the goal and one in which it does not. Zajonc's theory predicted that the presence of a passive cockroach audience would facilitate performance in one condition and hinder it in the other. That was exactly what was found.

**RUBES®**                              **By Leigh Rubin**

*Why cockroaches give lousy surprise parties*

Now, having validated Zajonc's theory, we can apply it to the real world by making more precise predictions than we could before about what ought to happen in everyday life. A clever experiment conducted in a university pool hall represents just such a real-world extension (Michaels, Blommel, Brocato, Linkous, & Rowe, 1982). Students playing recreational pool were unobtrusively observed and deemed skilled or unskilled based on their performance. Zajonc's theory, again, predicted that the presence of an audience would make the skilled players perform better (for them, the task is easy or well-learned) but make the unskilled players perform worse (for them, the task is difficult or novel). To test this prediction, the experimenters walked up to the pool tables and watched. As expected, the good players did even better than before, and the poor players did even worse.

## MERE PRESENCE OR EVALUATION APPREHENSION?

Zajonc's theory remains to this day the most compelling and widely accepted account of social facilitation effects. Few theorists question Zajonc's contention that the presence of others increases arousal, and virtually no one disputes the claim that the presence of others tends to facilitate performance on easy tasks and to hinder performance on difficult tasks (Geen, 1989; Guerin, 1993; Sanna, 1992; Thomas, Skitka, Christen, & Jurgena, 2002). There is one element of Zajonc's theory, however, that is disputed—whether it is the *mere* presence of other people that increases arousal. When most people reflect on why they would be aroused in the presence of others, it is not the mere presence of others that seems decisive. Instead, it seems to be a matter of **evaluation apprehension**— a concern about looking bad in the eyes of others, about being evaluated, that is important (Blascovich, Mendes, Hunter, Salomon, 1999; Cottrell, Wack, Sekerak, & Rittle, 1968; Seta & Seta, 1992).

> **evaluation apprehension**
> A concern about how one appears in the eyes of others— that is, about being evaluated.

*Testing for Evaluation Apprehension*     A number of social psychologists have argued that evaluation apprehension is the critical element underlying social facilitation effects. To evaluate this contention experimentally, there must be three conditions: one with the subject performing alone, one with the subject performing in front of an evaluative audience, and one with the subject performing in front of an audience that cannot evaluate the subject's performance. In one such experiment, the investigators cleverly built "from scratch" a response hierarchy in their participants so that they would know exactly what the dominant and subordinate responses were (Cottrell, Wack, Sekerak, & Rittle, 1968). The participants were given a list of ten nonsense words such as "nansoma," "paritaf," or "zabulon." The participants were asked to pronounce two of the ten words once, two words twice, two words five times, two words ten times, and two words twenty-five times. They were thus much more familiar with some of the words than with others. After this initial training phase of the experiment, the test phase began. Now the participants were told that these same words would be flashed on a screen very briefly (some so briefly they might not be visible), and their task would be to identify each word as it was shown. If they could not identify a word, they should guess. Unbeknownst to the participants, none of the target words was actually shown, and they were reduced to guessing on every trial (this task is thus known as a "pseudo-recognition" test).

The participants performed this task either: (1) alone, (2) in the presence of two fellow students who watched the proceedings attentively, or (3) in the presence of blindfolded "observers." The blindfolds in the latter, "mere presence," condi-

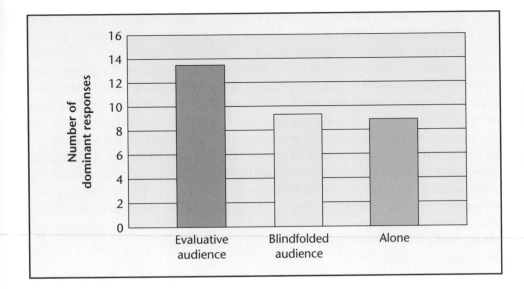

**Figure 2.3 Evaluation Apprehension and Social Facilitation**   Average number of dominant responses made by participants who were responding alone, next to a blindfolded audience (who therefore couldn't monitor or evaluate their performance), or next to an attentive audience (who could evaluate their performance). (Source: Cottrell, Wack, Sekerak, & Rittle, 1968)

tion were supposedly to prepare the individuals for a subsequent experiment in perception, but in reality they were there to prevent any evaluation of the participants' performance. The researchers were interested in how often the participants guessed a "dominant" word (those they had pronounced twenty-five times), and how this varied across the three conditions. The results, shown in Figure 2.3, highlight the importance of evaluation apprehension. Individuals performing in front of an evaluative audience made more dominant responses than those performing alone; those performing in front of a blindfolded audience did not. Thus, the audience that could not evaluate the participants' performance had no effect on performance. This experiment seems to demonstrate conclusively that it is the concern about others as a source of evaluation, not their mere presence, that produces the standard social facilitation effects. But maybe (as is sometimes the case) there is less to this demonstration than meets the eye.

*Testing for Mere Presence*    Recall that to distinguish between the mere presence and evaluation apprehension accounts of social facilitation, three conditions are necessary: an alone condition, a condition with another person merely present, and a condition with a potentially evaluative person present. The previous experiment appears to have these three conditions, but appearances can be deceiving. Although participants in the alone condition in that experiment were alone in an objective sense (no one else was physically present), they may not have been psychologically or phenomenologically alone. After all, they were in an experiment, one in which they were asked to perform a strange task. It seems likely they would feel apprehensive about performing, and about the prospect of their performance being somehow surreptitiously recorded (which it was!). Thus, the alone condition used in this study may not have been a "true" alone condition. Participants may have felt the presence of the experimenter even when the experimenter was not physically present.

Note that this would artificially raise the dominant response rate in the alone condition, so that it would not be significantly different from the mere presence condition. Of course, this still leaves a substantial difference between the mere presence and evaluation conditions (see Figure 2.3), but that is not a problem for Zajonc's theory. His theory states that the mere presence of another person is *sufficient* to induce arousal. It does not rule out the possibility that arousal could be increased still further by factors such as evaluation apprehension. To adequately test Zajonc's theory, then, it is essential to create a condition in which participants feel truly alone.

An ingenious experiment by Hazel Markus (1978) managed to create a true alone condition. When participants arrived individually for the experiment, they were told to go into an adjoining room to wait for the other participants to arrive. While there, they were required to put on the necessary attire for the experiment. In particular, they were required to: (1) take off their own shoes, (2) put on a pair of lab socks over their own socks, (3) put on a pair of oversized lab shoes, and (4) put on a similarly oversized lab coat. The participants did all this and waited, in vain, for the "other participants" to arrive. In reality, there were no other participants. After ten minutes, the experimenter reappeared and stated that the other participants were apparently not coming, and the experiment would have to be scratched. The participants were then instructed to change back into their own clothes.

Unbeknownst to the participants, all of this changing of clothes was surreptitiously observed and timed through a one-way mirror. Markus was interested in how quickly participants could perform the novel tasks of putting on and taking off the unfamiliar lab coat, socks, and shoes, as well as how quickly they could perform the well-learned tasks of taking off and putting on their own, very familiar, shoes. Participants did this either alone, with another person watching attentively, or in the mere presence of a repairman working on a piece of apparatus with his back to the subject.

Notice how the alone condition in this experiment improves upon those used in previous studies. Not only is the subject physically alone, but there is no reason to worry about being observed or evaluated. From the subject's perspective, the experiment has yet to begin. He or she is *not doing anything,* and therefore there is no cause for evaluation apprehension. The subject is both physically and psychologically alone.

Even though the participants did not think they were "performing," Zajonc's theory predicts that they should change their own clothes faster and the novel clothes more slowly when in the mere presence of another person. As shown in Table 2.1, that is exactly what happened. Participants took off and put on their

## Table 2.1  Social Facilitation and the Effect of an Audience

The amount of time, in seconds, participants took to change each item of clothing varied based on whether they were changing their own clothing or novel, lab clothing, and whether they were alone or in the presence of another person who was ignoring them (merely present) or evaluating them (attentive audience).

|  | ALONE | MERELY PRESENT AUDIENCE | ATTENTIVE AUDIENCE |
|---|---|---|---|
| Well-learned tasks (own shoes) | 16.5 | 13.5 | 11.7 |
| Novel tasks (lab shoes, socks, and coat) | 28.8 | 32.7 | 33.9 |

Source: Markus, 1978.

own shoes more quickly, and the experimenter's shoes, socks, and coat more slowly, when in the presence of another person—even when the other person had his back turned and was unable to observe. Thus, when a true alone condition is included, an effect of the *mere* presence of another person can be observed. Note again that the effects were stronger for an attentive audience than for a merely present audience, but that is not a problem for the theory. It just means that evaluation apprehension can add to a person's arousal, and thus compound the effect of mere presence. Overall, these results strongly support Zajonc's theory.

## CURRENT PERSPECTIVES

On the basis of Markus's experiment and similar investigations (Rajecki, Ickes, Corcoran, & Lenerz, 1977; Schmitt, Gilovich, Goore, & Joseph, 1986), it seems safe to say that the mere presence of others is sufficient to increase arousal and thus facilitate performance on well-learned tasks and inhibit performance on novel tasks. At the same time, there continues to be an interesting and healthy debate about *why* the mere presence of others has such effects, or even *what it means* when we say "mere presence." The term has always been defined negatively: it is what is "left over" when all other effects (such as evaluation apprehension) have been removed. A more positive definition would be useful. A positive definition might allow us to make productive use of the obvious fact that the mere presence of another person does not *always* affect performance. A presence that is undetected, for example, is unlikely to alter performance. An *awareness* of the mere presence of another person is necessary. In what ways would our understanding of social facilitation effects be influenced by altering Zajonc's theory to state that it is the *awareness* of the mere presence of others that is sufficient to increase arousal?

Some social psychologists have argued, in fact, that it is not the mere presence of another person that has these effects, but something that always accompanies the awareness of the mere presence of another. They have put forward a **distraction-conflict theory** of social facilitation effects that is based on the idea that being aware of another person's presence creates a conflict between attending to that person and attending to the task at hand. They believe that it is this attentional conflict that is arousing, and that it is *this* arousal that supposedly underlies the standard social facilitation effects (Baron, 1986; Baron, Moore, & Sanders, 1978; Groff, Baron, & Moore, 1983; Huguet, Galvaing, Monteil, & Dumas, 1999; Sanders, 1981). Thus far, not enough supportive data have been collected to settle the issue in favor either of this account or Zajonc's formulation (Guerin, 1993). But, intriguingly, researchers have shown that nonsocial distractions (for example, being required to perform two tasks simultaneously) can generate effects reminiscent of the standard social facilitation effects (Sanders & Baron, 1975).

One hundred years of research on social facilitation have also made it clear that people are complex stimuli, and that their presence can have a variety of effects that often overlay the more basic, "mere presence," effects we have focused on here. As we have seen, people are often quite concerned about making a good impression on others, and this evaluation apprehension can intensify arousal and lead to more pronounced social facilitation effects. There are occasions, however, in which the presence of others can mask the typical effects. If those who are present belittle effort and devalue accomplishment, then performance will be inhibited even on simple tasks. In many work settings, for

**distraction-conflict theory**
A theory based on the idea that being aware of another person's presence creates a conflict between attending to that person and attending to the task at hand and that it is this attentional conflict that is arousing and that produces social facilitation effects.

example, there are powerful norms against working too hard, and "rate busters" are made to feel the wrath of the group, with output suffering on even the simplest tasks (Homans, 1965). Similarly, African-American students sometimes put out less effort—and hence perform less well—in the presence of other African Americans in order to avoid "acting white" (Ogbu, 1991; Ogbu & Davis, 2003). And consider Erving Goffman's rather charming example of adolescent boys riding a carousel. When others are present, the boys engage in a variety of behaviors designed to convey "role distance," or disinterest, in the carousel (Goffman, 1961). If such a desire to maintain role distance were to emerge in any performance setting, it would surely impede output, regardless of how energizing the presence of others might be.

Perhaps the most common pattern of responses that runs counter to the social facilitation effects we have discussed is what social psychologists call **social loafing**, or the tendency to exert less effort when working on a group task in which individual contributions cannot be monitored (Hoeksema-van Orden, Gaillard, & Buunk, 1998; Karau & Williams, 1995; Latané, Williams, & Harkins, 1979; Shepperd, 1995; Shepperd & Taylor, 1999; Williams, Harkins, & Latané, 1981). If you and your friends have to move a heavy refrigerator up a flight of stairs, for example, you might be tempted to "coast" a bit and hope that the more vigorous efforts of your friends will get the job done. In these situations, people often loaf because their contributions are not seen as crucial to the success of the effort, and because their individual contributions—and hence they themselves—cannot be assessed.

**social loafing** The tendency to exert less effort when working on a group task in which individual contributions cannot be monitored.

## PRACTICAL APPLICATIONS

The basic pattern of facilitation of simple tasks and inhibition of complex tasks is reliable enough to warrant some practical advice. Of greatest relevance to student life, perhaps, is the obvious recommendation for how to study. Study alone. When the material is complex or unfamiliar and must be committed to memory, it is best to do so without the arousal and distraction brought on by the presence of others. Study groups may be helpful for reviewing or for dividing up and summarizing vast amounts of material, and groups can be invaluable when some members have information or approaches that the others do not, but the hard work of absorbing and integrating new ideas should be done alone. Then, once the material is assimilated, sitting cheek-by-jowl with the other students in the examination room should aid performance.

**Dominant Responses and Social Facilitation** People tend to do better on well-learned tasks but worse on difficult or poorly mastered tasks in the presence of others. Presumably the children who know the material well will do better on these standardized tests in the presence of other test takers because their dominant responses will be the correct responses. But children who don't know the material well will be more likely to give the incorrect answers in the presence of others, since these will be their dominant responses.

Another potentially important practical application involves the way workspaces should be designed. If the tasks to be accomplished in the workplace are simple or repetitive (and the workforce is highly motivated), then the work setting should be arranged so that people are in contact with one another. Such a design reaps the benefits of social facilitation of simple tasks. If the tasks to be performed are challenging and ever-changing, however, then it may be wise to give everyone the luxury of privacy. Such a design avoids the costs of social inhibition of performance on complex tasks.

**LOOKING BACK,** we have seen how even the most minimal group situations—the mere presence of a single other person—can influence performance. The presence of others is arousing, and arousal accentuates a person's existing performance tendencies. Easy tasks are made easier, and difficult tasks are made more difficult. The presence of a great many people, of course, is typically even more arousing, and can affect our behavior beyond its influence on performance. We therefore turn to the impact of large groups of people—crowds—on social behavior, and the question of why crowds sometimes turn into mobs.

# DEINDIVIDUATION AND
# THE PSYCHOLOGY OF MOBS

Consider the following very similar reactions to two very different events in San Francisco. The first event involves the tragic circumstances surrounding the murders of Mayor George Moscone and Supervisor Harvey Milk in 1978. In early November of that year, Milk's political rival Dan White resigned his seat on the Board of Supervisors, citing the difficulty of raising a family on a supervisor's meager salary. Shortly afterwards, White had a change of heart and informed Mayor Moscone that he wanted to reclaim his seat. Moscone refused, and on November 27 he was prepared to name a successor to White on the Board. That day, however, White entered City Hall with a .38 caliber revolver, tracked down the mayor in his office, and shot him four times at point-blank range. White then left the mayor's office through a back door. Reloading his revolver in the hallway, he walked across the building to the supervisors' offices. There he found Milk, San Francisco's first openly gay supervisor, and killed him with a fusillade of five shots. White then fled City Hall, but turned himself in to police a little over an hour later.

In a rather swift trial, White's lawyers argued that he was minimally responsible for his deeds because of the severe depression he was experiencing as a result of financial pressures and his decision to resign his seat on the Board of Supervisors. His lawyers claimed that his depression led him to subsist on a junk-food diet, which further "diminished his capacity" to distinguish right from wrong and to understand the implications of his actions. These tactics were ridiculed in the press as the now-infamous "Twinkie defense." Ridiculous or not, it was effective. Instead of the first-degree murder conviction that prosecutors sought, White was found guilty of the lesser charge of voluntary manslaughter. Rather than the death penalty or life imprisonment, White faced a maximum sentence of eight years. With good behavior, he would be eligible for parole in less than five years. (White ended up serving a little over five years, but twenty-two months after his release from prison, he committed suicide.)

The verdict was anathema to members of San Francisco's gay community. Many thought the verdict would have been more severe if a supervisor other than Harvey Milk had been slain. The evening of the verdict, gay activists organized a peaceful protest march, but events quickly got out of hand. It began with several demonstrators smashing the glass windows and doors of City Hall. Over the pleas of rally organizers urging calm, the crowd began to chant, "Kill Dan White! Get Dan White!" The vandalism and violence soon intensified. When police moved in to quell the disturbance, a battle ensued. The demonstrators threw rocks and bottles at police, set fire to numerous police cars, and looted nearby stores. In the

62

**The Psychology of Mobs**
(A) Upon learning of the killing of Harvey Milk and George Moscone by Dan White, a mob of demonstrators gathered to mourn their passing. (B) When Dan White was given a light sentence in his trial for their murder, demonstrators again took to the streets, rioting and setting cars on fire in protest of what they considered a travesty of justice.

end, twelve police cars were gutted by fire, twenty police officers were injured, and seventy demonstrators needed medical attention. Eight people were arrested.

As unfortunate and destructive as the rioting was, it nevertheless strikes most people as "rational"—it fits with the average person's conception of human nature. The riots were a lashing out against a system that the protesters thought had failed. When frustrated, people aggress.

Now consider the striking similarity to events that erupted in the same city three years later in response to a much less "rational" cause. The stimulus, believe it or not, was the San Francisco 49ers' *victory* over the Cincinnati Bengals in Super Bowl XVI, a victory that earned the city its first professional championship in any sport. Within minutes of the game's conclusion, giddy fans poured out of homes and bars and into the streets to celebrate. Initially, it was all harmless, celebratory stuff—horns blared, beer was chugged, champagne was sprayed. As the evening wore on, however, events took a more sinister turn, eventually echoing what had transpired in the aftermath of the Dan White verdict. Bonfires were started in an intersection and atop a car. When police tried to restore order, a veritable riot ensued as they were met with a barrage of stones, bricks, and bottles. Before the streets were cleared, 8 police officers and 100 others were treated for injuries, and seventy arrests were made.

## EMERGENT PROPERTIES OF GROUPS

These two events in San Francisco's history, and many others like them around the world, challenge us to come to grips with the question of how large groups of people are sometimes transformed into unruly mobs. How is it that peaceful gatherings can spin out of control and become violent? How is it that when submerged in a crowd, law-abiding citizens engage in acts of destruction they would never commit alone? How can we understand, in other words, the psychology of "the mob"?

Social psychologists have addressed this question in the context of examining the **emergent properties of groups**, or those behaviors that only surface ("emerge") when people are in groups. People do things in groups that they would never do alone. Indeed, we often hear people say that the group has "a mind of its own." As a result, the behavior of large groups of people is more than the sum of the behavioral propensities of its individual members.

**emergent properties of groups**
Those behaviors that only surface ("emerge") when people are in groups.

A simple thought experiment is instructive. Imagine you have won a contest in which first prize is a free ticket to a U2 concert at your local arena. Being something of a U2 fan, you do not hesitate to attend. What sort of behavior do you observe or engage in at the concert? Chances are you and the rest of the crowd are quite boisterous. There is dancing in the aisles, "air guitar" imitations of The Edge, and frequent shouts of "Bono!," "With or without you," or "Achtung baby!"

Now contrast that experience with winning a slightly different contest. In this case, first prize entitles you to your own *personal* U2 concert. The band comes to your school and gives a concert just for you in the biggest amphitheater on campus. How do you behave? No doubt you would still have an enjoyable time, but we suspect you would not dance much, your talent at air guitar would not be displayed, and you wouldn't scream out requested songs with the same gusto. We do things in group settings that we do not do alone.

It should be noted at the outset that the psychology of the mob and other emergent properties are extremely difficult to study—much more difficult, certainly, than studying the effect of the presence of others on human performance. Indeed, the previous topic, social facilitation, is almost ideally suited for experimental investigation. First, people are more than willing to perform in laboratory settings, and they are motivated to do well. Second, it is easy to create a performance setting in the laboratory in which an audience is either present or absent, providing ready manipulation of the independent variable (the variable that the experiment *controls*). Finally, there are countless objective measures of the quality and quantity of human performance, taking care of the dependent variable as well (the variable that the experimenter *measures*).

Studying the impulsive and often destructive behavior of the mob presents more of a challenge. People are on their best behavior when they enter a scientific laboratory, and therefore it is difficult to create a laboratory situation in which they will "act out." Also, there are ethical constraints against putting people in situations in which aggressiveness and acts of destruction are likely. The psychology of the mob is thus difficult to re-create in a laboratory. Therefore, as we shall see, some of the most informative research on the subject takes place out in the real world and not in the laboratory.

**Emergent Properties of Groups**
Some behaviors only surface when people are part of a group and submerge their individual identities into the group. The people in this flash mob converged at this store after receiving e-mails telling them the time and place at which to gather. Their screams and raised arms reflect the fact that they are in a group and would be highly unlikely if each were there alone.

## DEINDIVIDUATION AND THE GROUP MIND

One of the first people to offer an extensive analysis of the psychology of the mob was not an experimental social psychologist, but a French sociologist, Gustav LeBon (1895). LeBon thought that people tended to lose their higher mental faculties of reason and deliberation when they were in large groups. "By the mere fact that he forms part of an organised crowd, a man descends several rungs in the ladder of civilization." For LeBon, this descent stems from the collection of individual, rational minds giving way to a less reflective "group mind."

Social psychologists have expanded LeBon's ideas by examining how the thought patterns of individuals change when they come together in large

"Whoever be the individuals that compose it, however like or unlike be their mode of life, . . . their character, or their intelligence, the fact that they have been transformed into a crowd puts them in possession of a sort of collective mind."
—GUSTAV LEBON (1895)

**Deindividuation and Rioting**
When people are in a group and angry, they may let go of self-control and give in to impulses to wreak havoc. Normally law-abiding citizens merge into this crowd and break windows and smash cars with little thought to personal responsibility or the law.

**deindividuation** The reduced sense of individual identity accompanied by diminished self-regulation that comes over a person when he or she is in a large group.

groups, and how these changes make them more susceptible to group influence. In other words, they ask: What general orientation to the world do people typically maintain when they are alone, and how does that orientation change when they are in a group? How does a collection of individual minds evolve into a group mind? A number of social psychologists have cited the importance of a sense of **deindividuation**—that is, the loss of individual identity accompanied by diminished self-regulation—that comes over a person when he or she is in a large group (Diener, 1980; Festinger, Pepitone, & Newcomb, 1952; Prentice-Dunn & Rogers, 1989; Singer, Brush, & Lublin, 1965; Zimbardo, 1970). Most of the time, we feel individuated—that is, we feel individually identifiable by others, we consider ourselves individually responsible for our actions, and we are concerned with the propriety and future consequences of our behavior. When in large crowds, however, we sometimes feel deindividuated—that is, we feel "lost in the crowd," responsibility for our actions is diffused, and we are caught up in what is happening in the moment.

*A Model of Deindividuation*    Philip Zimbardo (1970) proposed a theoretical model of deindividuation that specifies how certain antecedent conditions create the kind of psychological state that enables the impulsive and often destructive behaviors found in mobs (see Figure 2.4). Perhaps the most important of these antecedent conditions are the anonymity one enjoys by blending in with a large group and the diffusion of responsibility that occurs when there are many people to share the blame. (It is often easier to mete out a stiff penalty to an individual than to everyone in a large group.) These antecedents, along with the arousal, heightened activity, and sensory overload that often accompany immersion in a large group, lead to the internal state of deindividuation. The deindividuated state is characterized by diminished self-observation and self-evaluation, and a lessened concern with how one looks and is evaluated by others. Thus, a deindividuated person is less aware of the self, more focused on others and the immediate environment, and hence more responsive to behavioral cues—for good or for bad. Being in a deindividuated state lowers the threshold for exhibiting behavior that is typically inhibited. People are more likely to engage in a host of impulsive behaviors, both because there is more of a "push" to do so (because of increased arousal and many impulsive others to imitate) and

| ANTECEDENT CONDITIONS | INTERNAL STATE (DEINDIVIDUATION) | BEHAVIORAL EFFECTS |
|---|---|---|
| • anonymity<br>• diffusion of responsibility<br>• energizing effect of others<br>• stimulus overload | • lessened self-observation and self-evaluation<br>• lessened concern with the evaluations of others<br>• weakening of internal controls (lessened concern with shame, guilt, fear, commitment) | • impulsivity<br>• irrationality<br>• emotionality<br>• antisocial activity |

**Figure 2.4 A Theoretical Model of Deindividuation and Related Phenomena** Certain antecedent conditions lead to an internal state of deindividuation, which in turn leads to behavioral effects that in other situations would be kept under control. (Source: Zimbardo, 1970)

because the constraints that usually "pull" them back from such actions are weakened (because of a lessened sense of evaluation and responsibility).

What emerges is the kind of impulsive, irrational, emotional, and occasionally destructive behavior that we think of as characteristic of mobs. This kind of behavior often creates its own momentum and is less responsive to stimuli that might otherwise bring it under control. It can be difficult to terminate. Thus, Zimbardo's model of deindividuation is not an account of mob violence per se. Instead, it is a theoretical analysis of crowd-induced *impulsive* behavior—behavior that because of its very impulsivity often turns violent (Spivey & Prentice-Dunn, 1990).

One element that is not explicitly spelled out in the model but that is a very important part of the thinking behind it is that people often find the impulsivity that accompanies deindividuation to be liberating. Zimbardo argues that people go through much of their lives in a straitjacket of cognitive control. Living under such constraints can be tiresome and stifling, and so people sometimes yearn to break free of the straitjacket and act in a more spontaneous, impulsive fashion. In support of this idea, Zimbardo notes that virtually all societies try to safely channel the expression of this need by scheduled occasions in which people are encouraged to "let loose." We can see this in the form of harvest rites in agrarian cultures, carnivals in religious societies, galas and festivals throughout history, and, perhaps, in the mosh pits and use of intoxicants at modern rock concerts.

**Deindividuation and Impulsive Behavior** During carnivals and festivals, people tend to let loose their usual control over their behavior. These women unleash their inhibitions during a Mardi Gras parade in New Orleans.

***Testing the Model*** It is probably safe to say that this model sounds plausible to most readers. It also fits media accounts of events that have transpired in various riots and other episodes of mass antisocial actions. The key question, then, is how well does the model stand up to systematic empirical test? Our intuitive sense of what is plausible is not an infallible guide to what is actually true, and media accounts cannot always be accepted at face value.

As we said earlier, most of the best empiri-

cal work on this subject takes place, not in the laboratory, but in the real world (for exceptions, see Lea, Spears, & de Groot, 2001; Postmes & Spears, 1998). Note also that this work involves very few controlled experiments (neither in the real world nor in a laboratory setting). Instead, most of the work involves the examination of archives—data originally gathered with no thought to its relevance to deindividuation. These records are used to search for predicted correlations between the various antecedent conditions and resultant behaviors.

Because these empirical tests are not controlled experiments, they do not "control for" or rule out various alternative interpretations of the results. Indeed, we trust that many readers will be able to think of other explanations having nothing to do with deindividuation for some of the empirical results we report below. Nevertheless, it is important to ask whether these alternative interpretations can account for *all* of the relevant findings. One result may be flawed in one way and thus be open to a particular alternative interpretation, while a second result may be flawed in a very different way that takes care of the first objection. If each finding requires a *different* alternative explanation, but all fit the model of deindividuation, we have reason to prefer the deindividuation account.

Of course, the most nagging interpretive problem with any correlational result is the inability to establish causality. As most readers have heard many times, "correlation does not imply causation." Diffusion of responsibility may indeed be correlated with acts of senseless violence, but that does not mean that it causes the violence. There is always the possibility that a third variable has caused both, creating a "spurious," or misleading, correlation between the two. Only by conducting an experiment in which the influence of such third variables are controlled can the causal connection between two variables be established. As a result, one can think of alternative interpretations of almost any correlational finding. (In fact, trying to identify such hidden mechanisms can be an engaging challenge and a useful intellectual exercise.) With these interpretative cautions in mind, let us examine the existing evidence.

*Suicide Baiting*     Imagine that on your way to class, you notice a disturbance ahead. When you get closer, you find that everyone, with neck craned, is looking up at one of the top floors of a high-rise dormitory. It appears that a student, clearly upset, is halfway out an open window and is threatening to jump. What do you do?

Most of you would no doubt think about what you could do to stop the poor soul from jumping, or whom you might summon to try to deal with the situation. But not everyone is so beneficent. Hard as it may be to believe, people occasionally engage in **suicide baiting**—that is, they urge the individual to jump. Are instances of suicide baiting more likely when there are a great many individuals gathered below and they form a mob? Are people more likely to engage in suicide baiting when they are deindividuated?

To answer these questions, researchers examined fifteen years of newspaper accounts of suicidal jumps and averted jumps (Mann, 1981). They found twenty-one instances of attempted suicide, with suicide baiting occurring in ten of them. They then analyzed the data to determine whether two variables associated with deindividuation, the cover of darkness and the presence of a large group of onlookers, were present when suicide baiting occurred and absent when it did not occur. As shown in Figure 2.5, both variables were indeed associated with suicide baiting. Suicide baiting was more than twice as likely when the crowd size exceeded 300 than when it was smaller. Also, suicide baiting was more than four times as likely if the episode took place after 6 p.m. than if it took place earlier in

**suicide baiting** Urging a person who is on the verge of committing suicide to take his life.

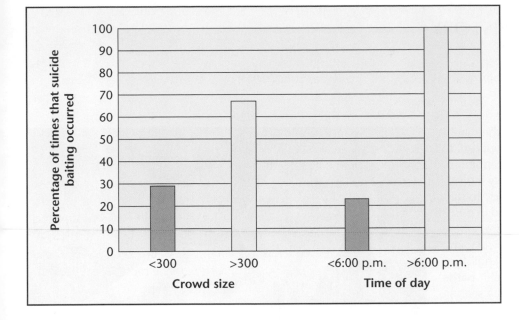

**Figure 2.5 Deindividuation and Suicide Baiting** When prevailing conditions are likely to increase individuals' anonymity, suicide baiting tends to increase. The rate of suicide baiting goes up, both when there is a crowd of onlookers (more than 300 people) and under cover of darkness (after 6:00 p.m.). (Source: Adapted from Mann, 1981)

the day. As people feel more anonymous, either by being lost in a large crowd or under the cloak of darkness, they are more inclined to taunt and egg on a potential suicide.

Although it is possible to question some of the details of these analyses (for example, why were the cutoffs set at 300 people and 6 p.m.?) and to suggest alternative interpretations (the larger the group, the more likely it is to contain a psychopath who starts the taunting), the data are nevertheless consistent with the idea that variables that lead to deindividuation also lead to antisocial behavior.

*The Conduct of War* Wars have always been a part of what English novelist and scientist C. P. Snow calls the "long and gloomy history of man." The conduct of warfare, however, has varied enormously from culture to culture and epoch to epoch. Warfare practices vary in their ferocity, for example. At the "high" end of the ferocity scale we find head-hunting, ritualistic torture, and "saturation bombing" of civilian targets such as the Allied bombing of Dresden during World War II. At the very low end would be what Tom Wolfe (1979) has described as "single-combat" warfare: the David and Goliath battles in which the warring parties select a single warrior to do battle with each other. The losing side pays a price in territory or some other form of wealth, but less damage is done to both groups.

Is the brutality of warfare related to deindividuation? The theory predicts that it should be. It should be easier for people to "let go" of the usual prohibitions against barbarity when they feel anonymous and unaccountable for their actions. To determine whether such a relationship does in

**Warfare and Deindividuation** Two knights covered with armor fight especially ferociously, with the armor both protecting them and masking their identities, in this painting by Eugene Delacroix titled *A Fight between Knights.*

Box 2.2   FOCUS ON HISTORY

# Celts and Warfare

The ancient Romans were terrified of the Gauls, who fought savagely and with little thought to self-preservation. Depending on your point of view, Gallic fighters were either extremely individuated or extremely deindividuated: They fought naked! The Romans eventually succeeded in pushing them to the far corners of the empire, where they became Bretons, Welsh, Irish, and Scots, and in modern times have been known in English as Celts. The Scots painted their faces blue in battle for many centuries (which you may have seen in the film *Braveheart*), and they were regarded as ferocious fighters. Their descendants, the so-called Scotch Irish (some Scottish, some Irish, and some Scots who had settled in Northern Ireland), were the main settlers of Appalachia and the U.S. South. Body paint was no longer required for them to maintain their reputations as fearsome fighters, first against the Native Americans, and then in the Civil War, when they

**Fierce Gallic Fighters**   Roman statue of "The Dying Gaul."

out-generaled and out-soldiered the North. The tradition has continued into the twentieth century. Southerners are heavily over-represented in the U.S. military.

fact exist, the warfare practices of twenty-three non-Western cultures were investigated (Watson, 1973). Each culture was examined for whether its warriors were deindividuated before battle (that is, whether they wore masks or war paint), and for how aggressively they waged war (that is, did they torture the enemy, did they fight to the death in all battles?). As predicted, there was a strong correlation between deindividuation and aggressiveness in warfare. Among those cultures in which warriors changed their appearance before battle, 80 percent were deemed particularly aggressive; among those cultures in which warriors did not change their appearance, only 13 percent were deemed especially aggressive. When warriors are disguised in battle, they fight more ferociously (see Box 2.2).

*Halloween Mayhem*   To American readers, one of the most familiar occasions for uninhibited and impulsive behavior is Halloween night. The destructive acts that are perpetrated on that holiday range from mild episodes of egg throwing to much more serious hooliganism. One group of social psychologists decided to take advantage of the Halloween atmosphere to conduct an ambitious test of the role of deindividuation in antisocial behavior (Diener, Fraser, Beaman, & Kelem, 1976). They set up research stations in twenty-seven homes throughout the city of Seattle and monitored the behavior of over one thousand trick-or-treaters. At each participating house, the children were told that they could take one piece of candy from a large bowl sitting on a table in the entrance to the house. Next to

## Table 2.2  Deindividuation and Transgression

The percentage of trick-or-treaters who transgressed was affected by whether they had been asked to give their name (individuated condition) or not (anonymous condition) and whether they were alone or in a group.

|  | INDIVIDUATED | ANONYMOUS |
|---|---|---|
| Alone | 7.5% | 21.4% |
| In groups | 20.8% | 57.2% |

Source: Diener, Fraser, Beaman, & Kelem, 1976.

the bowl of candy was a bowl filled with coins. To assess antisocial behavior, the experimenter excused herself from the scene and covertly monitored the children's actions. Would the children take just their allotted single piece of candy, or would they take more—perhaps even some coins?

The investigators examined the influence of two variables connected to deindividuation. First, the children arrived individually or in groups, and the investigators expected that those in groups would feel more anonymous and therefore be more likely to transgress. Second, the experimenter purposely "individuated" a random sample of children arriving both alone and in groups. In particular, the experimenter asked each child his or her name and address, and then repeated this information aloud for emphasis. Individuating the children—that is, identifying them by name so they would no longer feel anonymous—was predicted to inhibit any temptation to transgress.

As can be seen in Table 2.2, both variables had the anticipated effect. The children who arrived in groups were much more likely to transgress than those who were alone, regardless of whether they were anonymous or not. Children who were anonymous were much more likely to transgress than those who were individuated, regardless of whether they were alone or in groups. Putting these two findings together, the children in anonymous groups were the most likely to transgress.

*Summary of the Evidence*   The strength of each of the studies mentioned thus far lies in the "realness" and significance of the dependent variables—suicide baiting, warfare practices, and stealing. Unfortunately, with but one exception, all of the results are correlational findings, and so we cannot be sure of the direction of causality. The one exception is the Halloween study. Part of the study was correlational: some participants showed up alone, and others arrived in groups. Perhaps being in a group does indeed cause a person to feel deindividuated and therefore to be more likely to act out, but perhaps it is just that rowdier people prefer to trick-or-treat with others. The other half of the study, however, is a true experiment and does not suffer from this interpretive problem. Children were randomly assigned to the anonymous and individuated conditions, and so we can be sure that *on average* the two groups consisted of the same type of people. The tendency of anonymous children to act out can therefore confidently be attributed to anonymity per se, and not to the kind of people who seek out anonymity.

## SELF-AWARENESS AND INDIVIDUATION

If "losing oneself" in a crowd and becoming deindividuated make a person more likely to behave impulsively, it stands to reason that being especially self-conscious would have the opposite effect. Anything that focuses attention on the self, such as being in front of a camera, seeing oneself in a mirror, or wearing a name tag, may lead to **individuation** and make one particularly inclined to act carefully and deliberately and in accordance with one's sense of propriety. This is just what **self-awareness theory** predicts. When people focus their attention inward on themselves, they become concerned with self-evaluation and how their current behavior conforms to their internal standards and values (Duval & Wicklund, 1972).

*Studies of Self-Awareness*   Numerous experiments have shown that people do indeed act in ways that are more consistent with their enduring attitudes and values when they have been made self-conscious by being placed in front of a mirror or an attentive audience (Beaman, Klentz, Diener, & Svanum, 1979; Carver, 1974; Carver & Scheier, 1981; Duval & Lalwani, 1999; Froming, Walker, & Lopyan, 1982; Gibbons, 1978; Scheier, Fenigstein, & Buss, 1974). In one study, students were asked to solve a series of anagrams and told to stop when a bell sounded. In a control condition, nearly three-quarters of them fudged a bit by continuing to work beyond the bell. But in a condition in which participants were made self-aware by working in front of a mirror, less than 10 percent cheated (Diener & Wallbom, 1976). Although most students *say* that cheating is a bad thing, it appears to take a bit of self-awareness to get them to act on that belief. Note that because being in a state of self-awareness is the flip side of feeling deindividuated, all of these experiments that support self-awareness theory also provide support for the model of deindividuation.

**Individuation and Self-Awareness** Anything that focuses attention on the self and individual identity is likely to lead to heightened concern with self-control and propriety. Name tags on these people at a business conference lead to individuation and restrained behavior.

*Self-Consciousness and the Spotlight Effect*   The negative relationship between self-consciousness and deindividuation raises the question of how self-conscious people typically are in the normal course of events. There are pronounced individual differences, of course, in the degree to which people are focused on themselves and the degree to which they think others are focused on them as well (Fenigstein, Scheier, & Buss, 1975). But there is also reason to believe that the typical level of self-consciousness, at least when other people are around, is fairly high. This was implied by our earlier discussion of institutionalized rituals such as carnivals, galas, and festivals that encourage deindividuation. People participate in such events so they can "let go" and get a respite from their usual self-conscious state. Roy Baumeister (1991) takes this a step further and argues that such disparate actions as alcoholism, binge eating, masochism, and even suicide are ways of escaping self-consciousness and not attending to the self.

The evidence is clear that alcoholism has precisely this effect (Hull, Levenson, Young, & Scher, 1983; Hull & Young, 1983; Hull, Young, & Jouriles, 1986). In one telling study, college students who were given gin and tonics or just tonic water were asked to give an extemporaneous speech. Those who had consumed alcohol

**individuation** Emphasizing individual identity by focusing attention on the self, which will generally lead a person to act carefully and deliberately and in accordance with his or her sense of propriety and values.

**self-awareness theory** A theory that predicts that when people focus their attention inward on themselves, they become concerned with self-evaluation and how their current behavior conforms to their internal standards and values.

delivered speeches with significantly fewer first-person pronouns—"I," "me," or "myself" (Hull, Levenson, Young, & Scher, 1983). Thus, when people say they "lose themselves to the bottle," they mean it. It is noteworthy in this regard that recovering alcoholics who score high on measures of self-consciousness are nearly twice as likely to relapse as those who score low (Hull, Young, & Jouriles, 1986). The escape from the self-consciousness that alcohol provides these individuals appears to be too appealing for them to live without.

Further evidence for the claim that the typical level of self-consciousness in social situations is rather high comes from research on the **spotlight effect**, or people's conviction that other people are attending to them—to their appearance and behavior—more than is actually the case. People who make an insightful comment in a group discussion, for example, believe that others will notice and remember their contributions more than others actually do. Skiers who ski near the chairlifts are convinced that people riding the lifts are carefully scrutinizing their form. Yet, when riding the lifts themselves, they claim to rarely scrutinize anyone else. And people who suffer an embarrassing mishap such as triggering an alarm in a public building or falling down while entering a lecture hall think they will be judged more harshly by others than is actually the case (Epley, Savitsky, & Gilovich, 2002; Gilovich, Kruger, & Medvec, 2002; Gilovich, Medvec, & Savitsky, 2000; Savitsky, Epley, & Gilovich, 2001).

In one of the clearest demonstrations of the spotlight effect, participants who arrived (individually) for an experiment were asked to put on a T-shirt sporting a picture of the pop singer Barry Manilow. Despite obvious signs of displeasure, everyone did so. They then reported to another room down the hall where, upon entering, they found a group of fellow students filling out questionnaires. After leaving the room moments later, the participants were asked to estimate the percentage of those other students who would be able to recall the person pictured on the T-shirt. As predicted, the participants overestimated how much they had stood out in their new shirt. They estimated that 46 percent of the other students would be able to identify that it was Barry Manilow pictured on their shirt when, in fact, only 23 percent were able to do so (Gilovich, Medvec, & Savitsky, 2000).

> **spotlight effect**  People's conviction that other people are attending to them—to their appearance and behavior—more than is actually the case.

**LOOKING BACK,** we have seen that social psychologists have examined the relationship between self-consciousness and behavior from two directions. Research on deindividuation has shown that the diminished sense of self-awareness that sometimes occurs when people are immersed in large groups makes them get "caught up" in ongoing events and encourages impulsive—and sometimes destructive—actions. Research on the spotlight effect and self-awareness has shown how carefully we typically monitor our own behavior with an eye toward what others might think, and how the awareness of self encourages people to act with a greater sense of propriety. A concern with what others might think about us also plays a role when we come together with others to make group decisions, the topic to which we now turn.

## GROUP DECISION MAKING

When people come together in groups, one of the most important things they do is make decisions. Groups that cannot decide what to do or how to act do not function well. They wallow, bicker, and often split apart. It should come as no surprise, then, that social psychologists have spent considerable energy studying how—and how well—groups make decisions (Hinsz, Tindale, & Vollrath, 1997; Kerr, MacCoun, & Kramer, 1996; Levine & Moreland, 1990, 1998).

Much of this research on group decision making was guided by the assumption that decisions made by groups are typically better than those made by individuals. Many heads are better than one. And indeed, when groups and individuals are presented with problems for which there is a precise, factual answer, groups are more likely to arrive at the solution than the average individual (Laughlin, 1988; Laughlin & Ellis, 1986). Take the following problem as an example:

> A man bought a horse for $60 and then sold it for $70. He then repurchased the horse for $80 and then, changing his mind yet again, sold it again for $90. How much money did he make on his series of transactions? (Answer is on p. 75)

Yet, there are many contexts in which group decisions are no better than those rendered by individuals. The key to understanding such contexts is to recognize that, although arriving at a best possible solution to a problem may be the *group's* most important goal, it may not be the most important goal to any of the individual group members. Individuals may be more concerned with how they will be judged by everyone else, how they can avoid hurting someone's feelings, how they can dodge responsibility if things go wrong, and so on. To understand this, consider a parallel you often witness in the classroom: Although a question-and-answer session is nominally devoted to clarifying uncertainties, many of those who speak up craft their questions as much to show off as to obtain information. Similarly, when people get together to make group decisions, often a number of predictable social psychological processes unfold that can subvert the stated goal of arriving at the best possible choice.

## GROUPTHINK

Among peer groups and in informal social settings in which social harmony is all-important and the costs of rendering an incorrect decision are not so great, it is hardly surprising that defective decision making sometimes results from group pressures to reach a unanimous decision. But what about those contexts in which life and death are literally at stake and the incentives to "get it right" are high? Surely people wouldn't go along with faulty reasoning in such contexts merely to preserve group harmony or to avoid embarrassment, would they? Yes, they would—and they do.

Irving Janis carefully analyzed a number of decisions made at the very highest levels of government and found evidence of just this sort of calamitous group decision making (Janis, 1972, 1982; see also Esser, 1998). Among the "fiascos" Janis looked at were: (1) The Kennedy administration's attempt to foster the overthrow of Fidel Castro's regime by depositing a group of Cuban refugees trained by the CIA on the beaches of Cuba's Bay of Pigs but failing to provide air cover. (The refugees were captured in short order, thus humiliating the United States internationally, both for its role in trying to undermine a sovereign nation and for initially denying its involvement in the affair.) (2) The Johnson administration's decision to increase the number of U.S. soldiers fighting in Vietnam. (This policy failed to advance U.S. objectives in the region and substantially increased the number of lives lost.) (3) The conclusion by the U.S. naval high command that there was no need to take extra precautions at Pearl Harbor in response to warnings of an imminent attack by the Japanese. (This course of action had severe

> When people "come together . . . they may surpass, collectively and as a body, the quality of the few best. . . . When there are many who contribute to the process of deliberation, each can bring his share of goodness and moral prudence."
>
> —ARISTOTLE

Box 2.3   FOCUS ON GOVERNMENT

# Groupthink in the Bush Administration

Groupthink seems to have played a role in the miscalculations that plagued the Bush administration's decision to invade Iraq in 2003. A report by the U.S. Senate Intelligence Committee identified groupthink as one factor that led the Bush administration to err so badly in its claim that Iraq possessed weapons of mass destruction (WMD). Specifically, the report concluded that many of the groups involved in assessing the threat posed by Iraq ". . . demonstrated several aspects of groupthink: examining few alternatives, selective gathering of information, pressure to conform within the group or withhold criticism, and collective rationalization" (Select Committee on Intelligence, 2004). The committee also found fault with administration analysts for failing to put in place common safeguards against groupthink. They stated that ". . . the presumption that Iraq had active WMD programs was so strong that formalized . . . mechanisms established to challenge assumptions and 'groupthink,' such as . . . 'devil's advocacy,' and other types of alternative or competitive analysis, were not utilized."

Unfortunately, this tendency on the part of policy-making groups to seek support for existing views rather than subject them to critical scrutiny is not confined to this particular administration or to the deliberations about whether to invade Iraq. It is sufficiently common that the U.S. military has its own name for the phenomenon—"incestuous amplification," which is defined by *Jane's Defense Weekly* as "a condition in warfare where one only listens to those who are already in lock-step agreement, reinforcing set beliefs and creating a situation ripe for miscalculation."

---

repercussions on December 7, 1941, the "day of infamy," when U.S. ships at the Pearl Harbor naval base were destroyed in a surprise attack by the Japanese.) Janis argues that these calamitous decisions were made because of **groupthink**, a kind of faulty thinking on the part of highly cohesive groups in which the critical scrutiny that should be devoted to the issues at hand is subverted by social pressures to reach consensus (see Box 2.3). Other investigators have made the same claim about other disasters, such as the ill-fated launch of the *Challenger* space shuttle (Esser & Lindoerfer, 1989).

> **groupthink** A kind of faulty thinking on the part of highly cohesive groups in which the critical scrutiny that should be devoted to the issues at hand is subverted by social pressures to reach consensus.

***Symptoms and Sources of Groupthink***   According to Janis, groupthink is a sort of psychological diminishment characterized by a shallow examination of information, a narrow consideration of alternatives, and a sense of invulnerability and moral superiority (see Figure 2.6). In his words, "Groupthink refers to a deterioration of mental efficiency, reality testing, and moral judgment that results from ingroup pressures" (Janis, 1972, p. 9). Thus, victims of groupthink, often under the direction of a strong leader, ignore or reject alternative viewpoints, discourage others from coming forward with other ideas and assessments, and end up believing in the wisdom and moral correctness of their proposed solutions. Thus, the very source of a group's potentially superior decision making—the airing of divergent opinions and the presentation of varied facts and perspectives—never comes into play.

It is clear from the historical record that social psychological forces have had a hand in numerous instances of faulty decision making—faulty decision making with the most disastrous consequences. What is less clear, however, is whether these psychological processes cluster together to produce a recognizable condi-

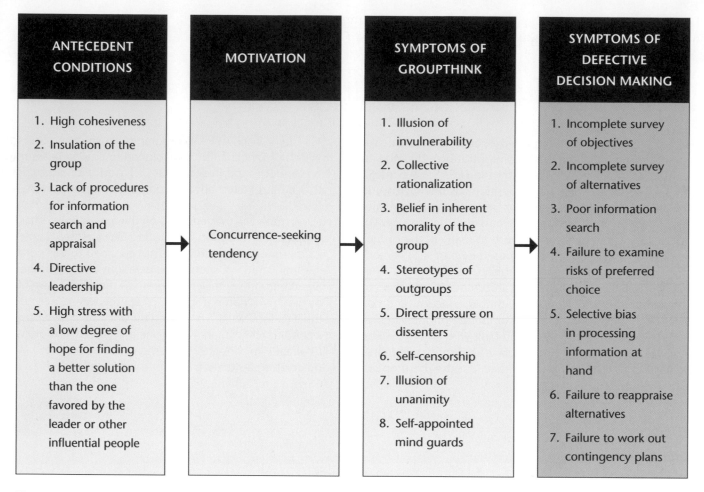

| ANTECEDENT CONDITIONS | MOTIVATION | SYMPTOMS OF GROUPTHINK | SYMPTOMS OF DEFECTIVE DECISION MAKING |
|---|---|---|---|
| 1. High cohesiveness<br>2. Insulation of the group<br>3. Lack of procedures for information search and appraisal<br>4. Directive leadership<br>5. High stress with a low degree of hope for finding a better solution than the one favored by the leader or other influential people | Concurrence-seeking tendency | 1. Illusion of invulnerability<br>2. Collective rationalization<br>3. Belief in inherent morality of the group<br>4. Stereotypes of outgroups<br>5. Direct pressure on dissenters<br>6. Self-censorship<br>7. Illusion of unanimity<br>8. Self-appointed mind guards | 1. Incomplete survey of objectives<br>2. Incomplete survey of alternatives<br>3. Poor information search<br>4. Failure to examine risks of preferred choice<br>5. Selective bias in processing information at hand<br>6. Failure to reappraise alternatives<br>7. Failure to work out contingency plans |

**Figure 2.6 Essential Elements of Janis's Groupthink Hypothesis**
Specifiable prevailing conditions lead decision-making groups to be excessively concerned with seeking consensus, which detracts from a full, rational analysis of the existing problem (Source: Adapted from Janis & Mann, 1977, p. 132)

**self-censorship** The decision to withhold information or opinions in group discussions.

tion of groupthink (Turner & Pratkanis, 1998). Do the factors cited by Janis run together, or are they best considered as individual social psychological processes that tend to inhibit effective decision making? And are the various sources and symptoms of groupthink *essential* ingredients of this sort of faulty decision making? Is group cohesiveness, for example, a necessary element of groupthink? Questions such as these have not been adequately resolved and the evidence gathered to test Janis's thesis has been mixed at best (Aldag & Fuller, 1993; Longley & Pruitt, 1980; McCauley, 1989; Tetlock, Peterson, McGuire, Chang, & Feld, 1992). Nonetheless, his observations have been useful in identifying social factors that can lead to calamitous decisions, as well as factors that can improve group decision making.

For example, strong, directive leaders who make their preferences known sometimes intimidate even the most accomplished group members and stifle vigorous discussion (McCauley, 1998). Also, just as Janis contends, there are times when the issue that must be decided is so stressful that groups seek the reassurance and comfort of premature or illusory consensus. And both strong leaders and the drive to find consensus breed **self-censorship**, or the decision to withhold information or opinions. As one example, Janis notes that Arthur Schlesinger, a member of President Kennedy's inner circle during the Bay of Pigs deliberations, was ever afterwards haunted ". . . for having kept so silent during those crucial discussions in the Cabinet Room . . . I can only explain my failure to do more than raise a few timid questions by reporting that one's impulse to blow the whistle on this nonsense was simply undone by the circumstances of the discussion" (Janis, 1982, p. 39). Some of the participants in that fiasco have written that the pressures to agree with the unsound plan were so great because the group was a newly created one, and the participants were reluctant to step on one another's toes. People did not want to risk their own prestige by putting that of others on the line. In contrast, by the time they came together to deliberate over subsequent crises, they had been around the block with one another and were more willing to offer and accept criticism without worrying so much about threatening their relationship to the group.

*Preventing Groupthink*    Even though the theory may be less than precise, Janis's suggestions for how to improve group deliberations (or, in his terms, to prevent groupthink) have considerable merit. Freer, more vigorous discussion is likely to take place, for example, if the leader refrains from making his or her opinions or preferences known at the beginning. Just as scientists make sure that their data are collected and coded by "blind" observers who are in the dark about the investigator's favored outcome, policymakers are wise to install analogous procedures to ensure that the boss's views do not affect the comments and opinions of everyone else. Groups can also avoid the kind of tunnel vision and illusory consensus (the false belief that everyone agrees) that Janis describes by making sure the group is not cut off from outside input. Individuals who have not been privy to the early portions of a discussion can provide a healthy freshness of perspective as well as put the brakes on any rash actions that might otherwise develop too much momentum to be stopped. Finally, a similar safeguard against rash action and unsound argumentation can be provided by designating one person in the group to play devil's advocate—to be given every incentive to name any weaknesses in the group's proposed plan of action. Again, just as scientists are taught to evaluate their pet theories by trying to find their weakest elements and by specifying how alternative theories could explain the very same data, policymakers would be wise to install procedures that encourage the identification of every plan's Achilles' heel.

In addition to his analysis of foreign-policy fiascos, Janis also examined a number of highly successful decisions—for example, the Marshall Plan to rebuild Europe after World War II, and the Kennedy administration's handling of the Cuban Missile Crisis—and claimed that the deliberations leading to these decisions were not marked by the same symptoms of groupthink.

In the case of the Cuban Missile Crisis, Janis reviewed the historical record of the crisis and discovered how John Kennedy and his advisers sought to avoid another fiasco after the Bay of Pigs incident early in his administration. Severely embarrassed by that event, both by the woeful outcome and the shoddy decision processes it revealed, Kennedy took steps to ensure that all policies would be evaluated more thoroughly from then on. When faced with a wrenching decision as to what to do about Soviet missiles in Cuba, for example, Kennedy took a number of steps that could have been crafted by Irving Janis himself. Kennedy frequently excused himself from the group so as not to constrain the discussion. He also brought in outside experts to critique his advisers' analysis and tentative plans, and he appointed specific individuals (his brother, Robert Kennedy, and Theodore Sorensen) to act as devil's advocates. These safeguards seem to have paid off, as the negotiations that kept Soviet missiles out of Cuba were one of the enduring highlights of the tragically short Kennedy administration.

Janis's investigation of disastrous group decision making and of successful group decision making led him to very strong conclusions about the need to carefully deliberate and to avoid self censorship. His message is clear: Fall victim to

Answer to horse transaction problem: $20.

**Preventing Groupthink**   Kennedy's cabinet met during the Cuban Missile Crisis to try to resolve the impasse with the Soviets over Soviet missiles in Cuba. They took steps to avoid groupthink by encouraging vigorous debate and making recommendations based on unbiased analysis.

groupthink and open the door to disaster; avoid groupthink and the likelihood of a satisfactory decision increases substantially.

*Groupthink in Other Cultures*    Groupthink is a problem that can look different in non-Western cultures than in Western ones. The drive toward harmony is greater, for example, in East Asian cultures such as Japan than in Western cultures such as the United States (Nisbett, 2003). Groupthink in places like Japan can be so great, in fact, that even at scientific meetings there is rarely true debate or any other exchange that might appear confrontational and that might cause anyone to "lose face." Japanese scientists who are familiar with Western norms of scientific discourse believe that their science suffers as a consequence of not giving ideas a public airing. In fact, there is evidence that Japanese science is underperforming given the amount spent on scientific research in that country (French, 2001). Still, Japanese corporations are in general highly effective, and in some industries they are the most competitive in the world. How is this possible if open and free debate does not take place? Japanese managers have meetings at which policy issues are discussed, but they may only appear on the surface to be like Western meetings. Nothing is really debated; instead, participants simply nod their approval of the proposal that is brought to them. This sounds like a recipe for disasters like the Bay of Pigs, but it turns out that managers typically discuss matters with everyone individually before the meeting to find out their views. The frank exchange goes on prior to the meeting, consensus is achieved as a result of these individual encounters, and the larger meeting is then little more than a rubber stamp. This procedure of one-on-one discussion and consensus finding is different from procedures to improve group decision making in Western organizations, but it appears to also be helpful in preventing groupthink.

## GROUP DECISIONS: RISKY OR CONSERVATIVE?

Implicit in all the concern over avoiding groupthink is the suspicion that groups are often too rash—that decisions made by groups are often riskier and less thoroughly thought out than those made by individuals. But note that popular culture tends to hold precisely the opposite belief—namely, that groups abhor risk and tend to adopt middle-of-the-road solutions. Thus, in the United States at least, we tend to celebrate the swashbuckling CEO or politician who breaks free of institutional inertia and "takes chances" and "gets things done." So which is it? Do groups tend to make riskier or more risk-averse decisions than individuals? What type of error do we invite—risky or conservative—when we turn over a difficult decision to a group?

An MIT graduate student by the name of James Stoner put this very question to the test in 1961 by having participants make decisions about various choice dilemmas—that is, they had to render advice to a set of hypothetical individuals considering various risky courses of action. In one scenario, for example, an engineer had to decide whether to stay in his current job that paid a moderate salary or take a position with a new firm in which, if successful, he could earn a great deal more money. Should he stick with the security of his current firm, or take a gamble on the new job? Here is this particular choice dilemma:

> Mr. A., an electrical engineer, who is married and has one child, has been working for a large electronics corporation since graduating from college five years ago. He is assured of a lifetime job with a modest, though adequate, salary, and liberal pension benefits upon retirement. On the other hand, it is very unlikely that his salary will increase much before he retires. While attending a convention, Mr. A. is offered a job with a small, newly founded company that has a highly uncertain future. The new job would pay more to start and would offer the possibility of a share in the ownership if the company survived the competition of the larger firms. (Adapted from Stoner, 1961)

> Imagine that you are advising Mr. A. Listed below are several probabilities or odds of the new company's proving financially sound.

> *Please check the lowest probability that you would consider acceptable to make it worthwhile for Mr. A to take the new job.*
> _____ The chances are 1 in 10 that the company will prove financially sound.
> _____ The chances are 3 in 10 that the company will prove financially sound.
> _____ The chances are 5 in 10 that the company will prove financially sound.
> _____ The chances are 7 in 10 that the company will prove financially sound.
> _____ The chances are 9 in 10 that the company will prove financially sound.
> _____ Place a check here if you think Mr. A should *not* take the new job no matter what the probabilities.

As you can see, participants were asked to give their advice by specifying the likelihood of success that would be necessary for the engineer to decide to take the job with the new company. If the new company was sure to succeed, clearly the engineer should take it because it would pay more money; if it was sure to fail, the engineer should stay put. Participants had to decide what the new firm's chances had to be to make the switch worthwhile.

Stoner's participants rendered such decisions for twelve different choice dilemmas. They did so first individually, and then they met with other participants to discuss each dilemma and arrive at a consensus answer. Stoner then compared the consensus or group odds with the average odds specified by each individual. He expected the group to insist on higher odds of success (that is, a more conservative recommendation) than the average odds specified individually by each group member. What he found was just the opposite. The groups tended to recommend riskier courses of action than did the individual group members. Stoner,

*"It's agreed, then, that we move forward on the philodendron."*

and many after him, concluded that groups tend to make riskier decisions than individuals, a pattern that came to be known as the **risky shift** (Stoner, 1961; Wallach, Kogan, & Bem, 1962). And the group members weren't just feigning boldness to appear courageous to everyone else. When participants were subsequently asked to render new *individual* decisions, the group discussion had left its mark. These later individual recommendations tended to be riskier than what these same individuals had recommended originally.

But as was the case with the findings on social facilitation, the initial, clear picture as to whether groups make riskier decisions than individuals soon became murky. Several follow-ups to Stoner's work found decisions made by groups that were more cautious or "risk averse" than those made by individuals. Groups sometimes insist on greater odds of success, in other words, before they are willing to recommend a risky course of action. Indeed, such a result was even found on two of Stoner's twelve original choice dilemmas. But the notion that groups sometimes make riskier decisions than individuals and sometimes make less risky decisions is hardly satisfying. Can't social psychologists tell us *when* groups tend to be risky and *when* they tend to be more cautious? Have they been able to discern some higher-order clarity to the mixed pattern of results as they did for the mixed results from experiments on social facilitation?

The key to discovering whether there is any higher-order clarity is to examine, in detail, the kind of issues that tend to elicit conservative group decisions and the kind that tend to induce risky decisions. We've already seen an example of an issue for which group discussion tends to make everyone riskier. Now consider a choice dilemma for which group discussion tends to make everyone more cautious:

> Mr. C., a married man with a seven-year-old son, can provide his family with all the necessities of life, but few of the luxuries. Mr. C.'s mother recently died, leaving his son (that is, her grandson) a small inheritance she had accumulated by scrimping and saving, making regular donations to a savings account at her local bank. Mr. C. would like to invest his son's inheritance in the stock market. He is thinking about investing in a group of "blue-chip" stocks and bonds that should

earn a 6 percent return on investment with reasonable certainty. However, he recently received a reliable tip about a new biotech company that has excited all the venture capitalists. If things go as well as predicted, he could more than quadruple his son's investment in the company within the first year; if things do not go well, however, he could lose the money and join the long list of those who have been burned by investing in high-tech start-ups. (Adapted from Stoner, 1961)

How does this example differ from the earlier one? One thing that many people report is that their first reaction to the two scenarios is very different. In the first, stay-or-switch-jobs dilemma, they find themselves thinking "Go for it. Don't be stuck in a dead-end job all your life; you'll regret it later." In contrast, when reading the second scenario, they find themselves thinking, "Not so fast! You shouldn't put your son's (and his grandmother's) legacy at risk."

## GROUP POLARIZATION

Researchers hypothesized that what group discussion does is make people more inclined to go in the direction in which they are already predisposed to go. If the issue is one that prompts most people to be inclined toward risk, talking it over with other members of a group may make everyone even more risk seeking. If the issue is one that prompts most people to be reluctant to take a chance, talking it over may make everyone even more conservative. And that's just what the research literature has shown. There is no overall risky shift; groups do not always make riskier choices than individuals. Rather, there is a **group polarization** effect—that is, group decisions tend to be more *extreme* than those made by individuals. Whatever way the individuals are leaning, group discussion tends to make them lean further in that direction (Moscovici & Zavalloni, 1969; Myers & Bishop, 1971; Zuber, Crott, & Werner, 1992).

If that is so, it implies that the same result should hold true even when groups discuss issues other than "choice dilemmas"—issues that have nothing to do with risk. And it does. In one study, for example, French students expressed their opinions about General Charles DeGaulle and about Americans, first individually and then again after having discussed them in groups. The results? Their initially positive sentiments toward DeGaulle became even more positive, and their initially negative sentiments toward Americans became even more negative (Moscovici & Zavalloni, 1969). It appears that one is more likely to hear the term "ugly American" from a group of foreigners than from a collection of individual foreigners.

But why does group discussion lead to more extreme inclinations on the part of group members? Why don't the individuals in the group simply conform to the group average, with the result that group discussion does not tend to move the group in one direction or the other? Subsequent research has led to a consensus opinion that there are two causes that work in concert to produce group polarization. One involves the force of the precise information brought up during group discussion; the other involves the tendency of people to try to claim the "right" position in the distribution of opinions within the group. Let's consider each explanation in turn.

*The "Persuasive Arguments" Account*    When trying to decide whether to pursue a risky or conservative course of action, people consider the different arguments in favor of each course. It stands to reason that, on those dilemmas for

> **group polarization**  The tendency for group decisions to be more extreme than those made by individuals; whatever way the individuals are leaning, group discussion tends to make them lean further in that direction.

which people are predisposed to take chances, they can think of more and better arguments in favor of risk. On those dilemmas for which people are predisposed to play it safe, they can think of more and better arguments that favor caution. But any one person is unlikely to think of *all* the arguments in favor of one alternative or the other. Thus, when the issue is put to the group, each person is likely to be exposed to new arguments. This expanded pool of arguments, in turn, is likely to be skewed toward arguments in favor of risk when the issue is one for which people are already predisposed toward risk (otherwise, where would the initial inclination come from?) and likely to be skewed toward arguments in favor of caution when the issue is one for which people are already predisposed to play it safe (otherwise, . . . you get the picture).

The net result, then, is that group discussion tends to expose the average person to even more arguments in favor of the position that the average person was already inclined to take. This only serves to strengthen those initial inclinations, and group polarization is the inevitable result. This suggests that rich, personal, face-to-face discussion is not necessary to produce group polarization. All that should be required is exposure to the pool of arguments that true group discussion tends to elicit. Several studies have tested this idea by having participants read other arguments in private so that they are exposed to the arguments without knowing who in the group might have advanced them. In support of the persuasive arguments interpretation, these studies have tended to show that this is sufficient to produce group polarization (Burnstein & Vinokur, 1973; Burnstein, Vinokur, & Trope, 1973; Clark, Crockett, & Archer, 1971).

*The "Social Comparison" Interpretation*    Although exposure to the full pool of arguments is sufficient to induce group polarization, it is not all there is to this effect. There are other social psychological processes at work that give rise to the same outcome. Foremost among them is the very human tendency to compare oneself with everyone else. We all want to know how we stack up against others. "Am I as smart as most people here?" "Does everyone else drive a better car than I do?" "Am I getting as much out of life as the average Joe?"

Leon Festinger developed his highly influential **social comparison theory** to account for the ubiquity of such comparisons. Festinger (1954) argued that people use objective means to evaluate themselves and comprehend their world whenever objective means are available. The way to determine if one has the ability to dunk a basketball is simply to give it a try. But for many questions—"How is one supposed to act here?" "Am I a kind person?"—there is no objective standard, and so we must compare how we stand in relation to others. How is everyone else acting? Do others act kindly more often than I? These sorts of comparisons are not only common, but research inspired by Festinger's theory has shown that they have important consequences (Stapel & Blanton, 2004; Suls & Wheeler, 2000; Wood, 1989).

For our present purposes, however, consider how these comparisons might lead to group polarization. When considering an issue for which people are inclined to take risks (a career choice early in life), it is likely that most people will tend to think that they are more tolerant of risk than the average person. In this case, riskiness is valued, and people like to think of themselves as having more than an average amount of a valued trait. When considering an issue for which people are inclined to be cautious (investing money that belongs to a beloved relative), however, it is likely, for the same reason, that most people will think they are more risk averse than the average person. People tend to think, in other

**social comparison theory**
A theory that maintains that when there is not an objective standard of evaluation or comprehension, people evaluate their opinions and abilities by comparing themselves to others.

But what happens when they discuss an issue with others who are inclined to
make the same choice and are also inclined to think of themselves as on the outer
edge of the correct side of the opinion distribution? Many will find, inevitably,
that they do not occupy as desirable a location on the opinion distribution as
they thought. This leads to an attempt on the part of some individuals to reclaim
the "right" position. The group as a whole, then, becomes a bit riskier on those
issues for which a somewhat risky approach initially seemed warranted, and a bit
more conservative on those issues for which a somewhat cautious approach
seemed warranted. In other words, the desire to be a bit different from others, but
in the right direction—that is, to be "better" than others—leads quite predictably
to the group polarization effect.

The way to test this interpretation, of course, is to do just the opposite of what
was done to test the persuasive arguments account. There it was necessary to
expose people to a pool of arguments without conveying any information about
the positions endorsed by everyone else. Here it is necessary to expose people to
everyone else's positions without conveying the content of any of the arguments
for or against one position or another. And, as predicted, when people are told
only about others' positions and not the basis of those positions, the group polarization effect is observed (Teger & Pruitt, 1967). Interestingly, the group polarization effect in this experiment was weaker than usual, which is also just what
one should expect if both the persuasive arguments and social comparison interpretations are valid and contribute to the effect.

*Valuing Risk*    There is one more piece of the puzzle to be explained. Social psychologists have provided perfectly satisfactory accounts of why group discussion
tends to intensify group members' initial leanings. But why do group members
tend to lean so often in the risky direction? Recall that in Stoner's original investigation, a shift toward greater risk was observed on ten of the twelve scenarios,
a predisposition toward risk that has been replicated in countless subsequent
studies. Why?

The logic of both the persuasive arguments and social comparison interpretations leads to the inescapable inference that people—at least the American college students who have made up the bulk of the participants in these
studies—must typically value risk taking over caution. This would explain why
arguments in favor of a relatively risky course of action resonate so effectively
with the participants in these studies (the persuasive arguments account) and
why people try to stake out the risky end of the opinion distribution (the social
comparison account). It is not hard to show that this is the case. When participants read descriptions of people, some of whom come across as risk takers and
others of whom do not, they assume that the risk takers possess a variety of
favorable traits such as intelligence, confidence, and creativity as well (Jellison &
Riskind, 1970). Also, when participants are asked to specify the level of risk with
which they are comfortable in a given situation, the level of risk with which the
average person is comfortable, and the level of risk with which the person they
*most admire* is comfortable, the latter is assumed to be comfortable with the greatest risk (Levinger & Schneider, 1969). Clearly, risk is valued.

The high value placed on risk, by U.S. participants at least, is typically attributed to the broader culture in which they live. The hard-edged capitalism that
is such an integral feature of U.S. life requires an active encouragement of risk

and a willingness to take on the possibility of failure. (Note that two-thirds of all new businesses in the United States go under within a year.) Thus, we celebrate the stories of people like J. C. Penney, who went bankrupt twice before making his fortune, or Ted Turner, who bet the ranch on his vision of a global, twenty-four-hour television news service. Some have even argued (in what we consider to be a very shaky contention) that the American love affair with risk is part of our biological makeup. Because America is a nation of immigrants, the argument goes, we inherited the genes of those who took a chance on life in the new world—a gamble that was not taken by those who had a cautious outlook (Farley, 1986).

Regardless of the cause of the high value Americans place on derring-do, it implies that a shift toward greater riskiness after group discussion should occur more often among U.S. participants than among participants in other cultures that do not value risk as highly. And that is indeed the case. In studies conducted in Uganda and Liberia, the recommendations made by participants in response to the Choice Dilemma Questionnaire scenarios tended to be more cautious than those made by U.S. participants. In addition, the recommendations made by participants in these two African countries tended not to become more risky—as they did among U.S. participants—after group discussion compared to recommendations made individually before the group discussion (Carlson & Davis, 1971; Gologor, 1977).

## POLARIZATION IN MODERN LIFE

How do the phenomena we've just discussed affect group decision making on controversial issues in modern life? What would a group of university administrators concerned about declining support for affirmative action think about affirmative action policies after a group discussion? How would those alarmed about the rise of radical Islam feel about the proper policies to combat Islamic terrorism after they had had a chance to talk things over with others within their group?

Note that these issues are unlike those typically studied in the research literature on group polarization. They are not the sort for which people "generally" lean in the same direction. They are, after all, contentious public-policy questions, which means there are strong advocates of all sides on each issue. The movement toward the extremes that we saw in the group polarization literature depends on there being a general direction in which most people lean—toward riskiness on one issue, caution on another; pro–Charles DeGaulle on one hand, anti-American on the other. It might seem, then, that there is no basis for predicting what effect discussion might have on the group members' attitudes.

But here the appearance is deceiving. Although the issues under discussion are indeed subject to contentious public-policy debate, the people most likely to meet in a group to discuss them are those who share the same general perspective, concerns, and general preferences. Thus, they would be homogeneous groups, and they would tend to lean in the same direction on the issues. The lessons of group polarization therefore would indeed apply. When homogeneous groups come together, their discussions are likely to lead to even stronger attitudes than the ones the group members came in with (Schulz-Hardt, Frey, Luthgens, & Moscovici, 2000).

Is this a problem? At the very least, group homogeneity robs the group of one of its greatest potential strengths—the give and take of *different* perspectives and sources of information that allow the best course of action to be discerned. Heterogeneous groups tend to outperform homogeneous groups when it comes to making the most effective decisions. (Note, however, that this effect is not as strong as one might suppose, in part because of a tendency for group members to talk about information they *share*—information that is often easier to talk about and that leads to more congenial discussion—rather than information unique to one person or another; Kelly & Karau, 1999; Postmes, Spears, & Cihangir, 2001; Stasser, 1999; Stasser & Titus, 1985). This effect was anticipated by the founding fathers of the United States, who spoke passionately about the evils of opinion homogeneity and took steps (the much-praised "checks and balances") to guard against the tyranny of the majority. Their view, strongly validated by subsequent social psychological research, was that deliberative bodies function best when they provide for the airing of competing views.

To the modern mind, group polarization may be particularly troubling because of the possibility that contemporary life may encourage dialogue among primarily like-minded individuals. At one level, society is more heterogeneous and multicultural than it has ever been, and there are many more voices to be heard in public debate. But at the same time, it has become easier and easier for people to screen their inputs to hear only those voices they want to hear. Not everyone watches one of the three general nightly news programs. Instead, there is a cacophony of niche programming (geared toward those with conservative views or liberal views) being broadcast, and it is ever easier to select those offering opinions one already holds. Rather than reading a metropolitan newspaper serving the diverse interests of a broad community, the Internet makes it possible for individuals to carefully tailor their media input—the information and opinions they receive—to fit their preexisting preferences. And rather than coming together to discuss the issues of the day with a broad spectrum of the general public, one can sit at home and discuss them with a set of like-minded individuals who are all signed up to the same Internet chat group (McKenna & Bargh, 1998).

This would be problem enough if such a restricted range of inputs served only to reinforce people's preexisting beliefs. But the literature on group polarization makes it clear that more than this happens. Group discussion among like-minded individuals does not just reinforce existing opinion; it makes it more extreme. Thus, modern communication technologies such as the Internet may incubate extremism. The various hate groups that make extensive use of Internet communication were certainly not created by the Internet. Nevertheless, this mode of communication, and the group polarization tendencies it abets, might very well feed their extremist views.

> "The differences of opinion, and the jarrings of parties . . . promote deliberation and circumspection; and serve to check the excesses of the majority."
> —ALEXANDER HAMILTON, *THE FEDERALIST*

**LOOKING BACK,** we have seen how groupthink can lead to defective decision making, as people in highly cohesive groups may self-censor their own ideas and assessments, ignore or reject alternative viewpoints, and succumb to ingroup pressures. To avoid this, the group should encourage the airing of all viewpoints, the leader should refrain from stating his opinions at the outset, and someone should be designated to play devil's advocate. We have also seen how group decision making can lead to group polarization, in which group decisions tend to be more extreme than those made by individuals because of both the force of persuasive arguments and social comparison. To avoid the growing polarization in the modern world and to promote well-reasoned decisions, it is important to have a dialogue among diverse groups of people to air a full range of opinions.

# SUMMARY

1. Human beings, like all large primates except the orangutan, are group-living animals who influence and must get along with others.

2. The presence of other people sometimes facilitates human performance and sometimes hinders it, but in predictable ways. Research in the area of *social facilitation* has shown that the presence of others is arousing, and that arousal increases people's tendencies to do what they are already predisposed to do. On easy tasks, people are predisposed to respond correctly, and so increasing this tendency facilitates performance. In contrast, on novel or difficult tasks, people are not predisposed to respond correctly, and so arousal hinders performance by making it more likely that they will respond incorrectly.

3. A number of clever experiments have indicated that it is the *mere presence* of others that leads to social facilitation effects, although other factors, including *evaluation apprehension*, can intensify them. Moreover, *distraction-conflict theory* explains social facilitation by noting that awareness of another person can distract an individual and create a conflict between attending to the other person and to the task at hand, a conflict that is itself arousing.

4. *Social loafing* is the tendency to exert less effort on a group task when individual contributions cannot be monitored.

5. There is a tendency for large groups of people to sometimes transform into unruly mobs. This may happen because the anonymity and diffusion of responsibility that are often felt in large groups can lead to a mental state of *deindividuation* in which one is less concerned with the future, with normal societal constraints on behavior, and with the consequences of one's actions.

6. The deindividuated state of "getting lost in the crowd" stands in marked contrast to how people normally feel, which is quite individually identifiable. *Self-awareness theory* maintains that focusing attention on the self will lead to *individuation* and, in turn, careful deliberation and concern with how well one's actions conform to internal moral standards.

7. Most people overestimate how much they personally stand out and are identifiable to others, a phenomenon known as the *spotlight effect*.

8. *Groupthink* is the tendency for members of cohesive groups to deal with the stress of making highly consequential decisions by pursuing consensus more vigorously than a critical analysis of all available information. Groupthink has been implicated in the faulty decision making that has led to a number of policy fiascos.

9. Group decision making is affected by how cohesive a group is, how directive its leader is, and ingroup pressures that can lead to *self-censorship*, or the tendency for people to refrain from expressing their true feelings or reservations in the face of apparent consensus on the part of the other group members and to ignore or reject alternative viewpoints.

10. Exchanging views with fellow group members can lead to more extreme decisions and make people more extreme in their attitudes. When groups make riskier decisions than individuals, the *risky shift* has occurred.

11. Group discussion tends to create *group polarization*, whereby initial leanings in a risky direction tend to be made more risky by discussion and initial leanings in a conservative direction tend to be made more conservative.

12. Group polarization is produced through *persuasive arguments*, in that a larger pool of information and arguments are made available to all group members. It is also produced through *social comparison* whereby people compare their opinions and arguments to those of other people when there are not objective standards of evaluation.

13. People from cultures that place a high value on risk are more likely to make risky decisions after group discussion than people from cultures that do not value risk as highly.

14. Polarization is a particularly common outcome in homogeneous groups, something we noted may be a particular problem in the modern world, as people are likely to read newspapers and watch news programs that fit their preexisting views. This polarization may be further reinforced through communication on the Internet, which makes it increasingly easy for people to find like-minded others and to exchange information solely with those who share their opinions.

# CRITICAL THINKING ABOUT BASIC PRINCIPLES

1. What experiments can you think of from this chapter that: (a) lack external validity, and this lack represents a serious shortcoming of the research; (b) lack external validity, but this lack does not represent a shortcoming at all; and (c) do not lack external validity?

2. In light of what you've learned about the presence of others on performance, what activities can you think of that (a) are typically performed with people working side-by-side but would be better performed by people working alone, and (b) are typically performed by people working alone but would be better performed by people working side-by-side?

3. Research on the spotlight effect indicates that people tend to overestimate the extent to which others take note of them and their behavior. But as with nearly all psychological phenomena, there are exceptions. Can you think of any examples of circumstances or instances in which people systematically *under*estimate the extent to which others take note of them?

4. Copy the "Mr. A., the electrical engineer" example from page 77 and give it to four of your friends. Have them render a decision individually and then bring them together and have them discuss the case and arrive at a consensus opinion. Finally, compare the joint opinion with the average individual recommendation. Is the group's recommendation riskier than the average individual recommendation?

# KEY TERMS

deindividuation (p. 64)
distraction-conflict theory (p. 59)
dominant response (p. 52)
emergent properties of groups
 (p. 62)
evaluation apprehension (p. 56)

group polarization (p. 79)
groupthink (p. 73)
individuation (p. 70)
risky shift (p. 78)
self-awareness theory (p. 70)
self-censorship (p. 74)

social comparison theory (p. 80)
social facilitation (p. 50)
social loafing (p. 60)
spotlight effect (p. 71)
suicide baiting (p. 66)

# FURTHER READING

Hogg, M. A., & Abrams, D. (1993). *Group motivation: Social psychological perspectives.* New York: Harvester Wheatsheaf.

Janis, I. L. (1983). *Groupthink: Psychological studies of policy decisions and fiascoes.* Boston: Houghton-Mifflin.

Levine, J. M. (1998). Small groups. In D. T. Gilbert, S. T. Fiske, & G. Lindzey (Eds.), *Handbook of social psychology* (4th ed., Vol. 2, pp. 415–469). New York: McGraw-Hill.

Sunstein, C. R. (2003). *Why societies need dissent.* Cambridge, MA: Harvard University Press.

# Chapter Outline

# CHAPTER 3

# Attraction

Many aspects of the 1992 U.S. presidential election made it interesting to students of politics, such as the third-party candidacy of Ross Perot that may have tipped the election away from George H. W. Bush and in favor of Bill Clinton. But there was also one feature of the election that made it particularly interesting to psychologists. The managers of the Clinton and Bush campaigns—James Carville for Clinton and Mary Matalin for Bush—were lovers during the campaign, and they married shortly after the election.

This fact led many people to assume that Carville and Matalin had no deep ideological connections to the political campaigns they oversaw. They were just "hired guns" who would say and do whatever it took to get their candidates elected. After all, how could two people with such apparently different political orientations truly be in love?

The love story of James Carville and Mary Matalin speaks to the mysterious nature of interpersonal attraction. It is sometimes hard to figure out why two people are drawn to each other and get along so well. Sometimes it's even hard to figure out why we ourselves are attracted to certain people. Although we typically know whether or not we like someone, we are often at a loss to explain why. To be sure, we know that we like people who are nice to us, make us laugh, share our values, and so on. But these obvious influences notwithstanding, it is also abundantly clear that sometimes we are drawn to some people and repulsed by others in ways we cannot describe with precision. "We just hit it off." "He rubs me the wrong way." "We share a certain chemistry."

The goal of this chapter is to unravel these mysteries. What are the most powerful determinants of whether you will like someone? What is the underlying basis of good or bad "chemistry"? Our discussion of these questions will be broadly based—that is, we will examine what makes people like one another in all sorts of ways and contexts, but with an emphasis on romantic attraction. As we will see, many of the same determinants of attraction influence those we choose as friends and those to whom we are drawn as romantic partners.

We will organize our discussion by considering the effects of three particularly potent determinants of attraction—physical proximity, similarity, and physical attractiveness. We will then examine efforts to integrate these different determinants of who is attracted to whom into one overarching theory.

## STUDYING ATTRACTION

Interpersonal attraction exists between acquaintances, coworkers, friends, mentors, lovers, as well as countless others. It can be based on sexual arousal, intellectual stimulation, or respect for another's actions or beliefs. Attraction to others can also be conscious or preconscious, based on well-thought-out beliefs or on automatic "gut feelings." Because each of these facts is already known to most people, some have argued that there is little to gain by studying attraction. We already know the important stuff, it has been said, and scientific investigation is unlikely to take us much further.

But note that people have also made essentially the *opposite* argument—that the causes of attraction, far from being widely known, are unlikely to yield to empirical investigation. Indeed, some have argued that a satisfying analysis of interpersonal attraction not only cannot be achieved, it *should not* be attempted. Doing so would rob us of some of the appeal of this delightful aspect of human experience. As Keats put it, "Do not all charms fly at the mere touch of cold philosophy?" Or consider the comments of former Wisconsin Senator William Proxmire, a longtime critic of government funding of basic research, particularly basic research in the behavioral sciences: "If scientists could understand, weigh, measure, and calculate love, there'd be a lot less of it going on. I love the mystery" (Stewart, 1988, pp. 56–61). In Proxmire's view, more knowledge would bring less enjoyment.

But surely such an anti-intellectual stance can be readily dismissed. Try to think of a single example in which knowing more about how something works has made you appreciate it less. You probably can't. Knowing that a rainbow is the result of light refracted through droplets of water does not render it less beautiful. Knowing that all living things have been sculpted by evolution does not

"I do not like thee, Dr. Fell.
The reason why I cannot tell.
But this I know, and know full well,
I do not like thee, Dr. Fell."
—MOTHER GOOSE
NURSERY RHYME

**Interpersonal Attraction**   While Mary Matalin was a Republican who worked to elect George H. W. Bush, and James Carville was a Democrat who worked to elect Bill Clinton, they nonetheless were attracted to and eventually married each other. Their mutual attraction was surprising to many observers because of a widespread—and generally valid—conviction that people tend to like those who are similar to themselves on important dimensions such as political philosophy.

diminish the wonder of existence. If anything, a deeper understanding typically results in a richer, not a diminished, experience.

So there is no reason to believe that psychologists should refrain from unraveling the mysteries of interpersonal attraction. But can they do so successfully? Have those who have worked in this area discovered any "secrets" of liking and loving that most people do not already know? You be the judge. At the end of this chapter, you can decide for yourself whether you understand the underpinnings of attraction better than you did beforehand. To foreshadow just a bit, the scientific study of interpersonal attraction has indeed yielded a few surprises. It has demonstrated an impact of certain variables that few people would suspect to play any role at all in who likes whom. More often, however, the relevant research has shown that our intuitions in this area are pretty good. Many of the variables that the average person would expect to have an influence on our affections do indeed have an effect—but sometimes a *much* more powerful effect than almost anyone would guess. The surprises, in other words, lie not in the discovery of new and unanticipated causes of attraction, but in demonstrations of how powerful certain "unsurprising" causes can be.

# PROPINQUITY

Something that everyone realizes *has* to influence whether people become friends or lovers is simple physical proximity, or **propinquity**. You cannot come to like someone you never encounter (although not all encounters need to be face-to-face). This is particularly easy to illustrate in a college environment. Who are your best friends on campus? Are they the people who were on your hall freshman year? Are they the ones you encountered often in the same classes? Are they your peers on the track team, drama club, or debate society? The most enduring friendships are forged between people whose paths cross frequently. Out of numerous chance encounters comes a sense of comfort and familiarity that often gives rise to something deeper and long lasting.

> **propinquity** Physical proximity.

## STUDIES OF PROPINQUITY AND ATTRACTION

A number of studies have demonstrated the effects of propinquity on who becomes friends and romantic partners. Remember that these studies are important, not so much because they demonstrate *that* a relationship between propinquity and attraction exists (most people would guess that anyway), but because they demonstrate how *strong* the relationship is. As one person put it, "Cherished notions about romantic love notwithstanding, the chances are about 50–50 that the 'one and only' lives within walking distance" (Eckland, 1968).

One study of propinquity was conducted in the 1940s in a married student housing project at MIT known as Westgate West (Festinger, Schachter, & Back, 1950). The project was built to house American servicemen (and their families) who had returned from World War II and wished to begin or resume their college education with financial assistance provided by the GI bill. The housing project consisted of seventeen ten-unit apartment buildings that were isolated from other residential areas of the city. The incoming students were randomly assigned to their residences, and few of them knew one another beforehand. Friendships

> "Despite the fact that a person can pick and choose from a vast number of people to make friends with, such things as the placement of a stoop or the direction of a street often have more to do with determining who is friends with whom."
>
> —WILLIAM WHYTE, JR.,
> *THE ORGANIZATION MAN*

sociometric survey A survey
that attempts to measure the
interpersonal relationships in a
group of people.

functional distance An architectural layout's propensity to
encourage or inhibit certain
activities, like contact between
people.

were sure to develop among many of the residents, and the question was how much of an impact proximity would have on who befriended whom.

To find out, the investigators conducted a **sociometric survey**—that is, they asked each resident to name the people (three in this case) they saw socially most often in the entire housing project. The effect of propinquity was striking: two-thirds of those listed as friends lived in the same building as the respondent, even though those in the same building represented only 5 percent of the residents of Westgate West. More striking still was the pattern of friendships *within* each building. Figure 3.1 shows the layout of the Westgate West apartment houses. Note that the physical distance between each apartment was quite small—19 feet between the doorways of adjacent apartments and 89 feet between those at the end of each corridor. Nevertheless, even within such a confined space, greater proximity led to more friendships. Forty-one percent of those living in adjacent apartments listed one another as friends, compared to only 10 percent of those living at opposite ends of the apartment building.

Proximity presumably leads to friendship because it facilitates chance encounters. If so, then pure physical distance should matter less than what one might call **functional distance**, or an architectural layout's propensity to encourage contact between certain people and discourage it between others. The MIT study shows just how important functional distance is. As Figure 3.1 indicates, the stairs are positioned such that upstairs residents will encounter the occupants of apartments 1 and 5 much more often than the occupants of the middle apartments. And, in fact, the residents of apartments 1 and 5 formed twice as many friendships with their upstairs neighbors as did those living in the middle apartments. Note also that the residents of apartments 1 and 6, and apartments 2 and 7, are equally distant from one another physically. They reside directly above one another. But the stairs that pass the door of apartment 1 make it and apartment 6 vastly closer from a functional perspective. Are the residents of apartments 1 and 6 more likely to become friends than the residents of apartments 2 and 7? Absolutely. The residents of apartments 1 and 6 were two-and-a-half times more likely to become friends than were the residents of apartments 2 and 7. Thus, it is functional distance, more than physical distance, that is decisive. Propinquity promotes friendship because it (literally) brings people together.

The effect of propinquity on friendship formation was also nicely demonstrated in an investigation of the social organization of the Training Academy of the Maryland State Police (Segal, 1974). The aspiring police officers were assigned alphabetically to their dormitory rooms and classroom seats. Thus, Cadet Aronson should have found himself cheek-by-jowl with future officer Asch, as should Cadets Zajonc and Zimbardo. Did these frequent encounters lead to friendship? They did indeed, and Figure 3.2 shows how strongly. Both axes of Figure 3.2 represent the alphabetical position of each of the forty-five trainees (from, say, Aron-

**Figure 3.1 Propinquity** Schematic diagram of an MIT apartment complex. (Source: Festinger, Schachter, & Back, 1950)

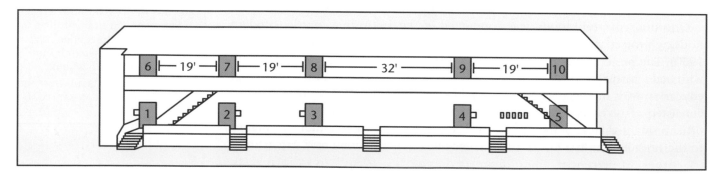

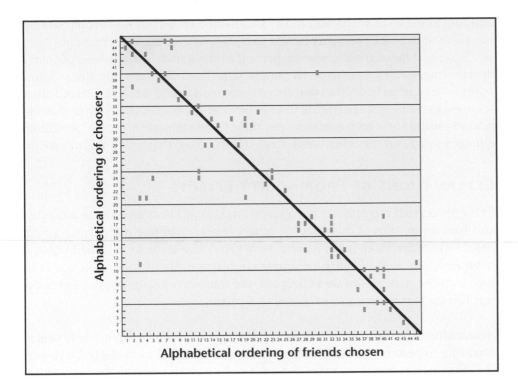

Figure 3.2 **Propinquity and Friendship Formation**    Friendship choices among trainees at the Maryland State Police Training Academy. Numbers across the bottom indicate place in alphabetical ordering of friends chosen. Numbers down the left margin indicate place in the alphabetical ordering of choosers. (Source: Segal, 1974)

son to Zimbardo). Each point in the diagram thus represents the alphabetical position of those people named as friends (the horizontal axis) by trainees with a particular alphabetical position themselves (the vertical axis). Notice that nearly all of the points lie close to the diagonal line. This means that Aronson and Asch tended to become friends with one another, and not with Zajonc and Zimbardo.

Once again, simple physical proximity was found to exert a much more powerful effect than one would imagine on who befriends whom by encouraging some contacts and discouraging others. This effect, mind you, was obtained in a situation in which *all* of the forty-five trainees lived and studied together rather closely. It was not as if the Aronsons and Zimbardos were assigned to different campuses. Minor differences in proximity produced profound effects on patterns of friendship. The correlation between the alphabetical position of each person and the average alphabetical position of those people he named as friends was .9.

But are any cautions in order? You may be wondering about the diversity of the populations examined in both the MIT and Police Academy studies. Perhaps propinquity has a powerful effect on friendship formation in homogeneous groups, but not in diversified groups in which it must "compete" with other determinants of who befriends whom—such as similarity of age, race, ethnicity, or religion. Indeed, the populations in both studies were notably lacking in diversity (all of the trainees in the Police Academy, for example, were young males, and all but one were white).

The effect of proximity on friendship formation has been examined in more diverse populations, with its biggest effects found on friendships that develop between people of *different* races, ages, or social classes. One study, for example, examined the patterns of friendships in a Manhattan housing project in which half the residents were black, one-third were white, and the rest were Puerto Rican (Nahemow & Lawton, 1975). Each ethnic group contained people of all ages. Both proximity and similarity had strong effects on who befriended whom. Eighty-eight percent of those designated as a "best friend" lived in the same building as the respondent, and nearly half lived on the same floor. Interestingly, the effect of proximity was particularly pronounced in friendships that developed *across* age and racial groups. Seventy percent of the friendships between people of different ages and races involved people who lived on the same floor as one another, compared to only 40 percent of the same-age and same-race friendships. It appears that people are willing to look beyond the immediate environment to find friends of their own age and race; their friendships with people of a different age or race, on the other hand, tended to be those that fell in their laps.

## EXPLANATIONS OF PROPINQUITY EFFECTS

So it appears that propinquity has a surprisingly large effect on acquaintanceship and friendship. Why is this effect so much greater than one might have anticipated? There are three main reasons why proximity leads to friendship. As we have seen, one is availability, or simple contact. Another is our tendency to be nice to those with whom we expect to have frequent encounters. A third is the comfort created by repeated exposure to a person.

*Availability and Propinquity*    You must establish contact with another person if you are to become friends, and proximity makes contact more likely. Of course, the same is true for people you *dis*like: proximity can bring about the kind of unpleasant encounters with others that earn your antipathy. Indeed, there is evidence that the people one dislikes the most tend to live nearby as well (see Box 3.1).

But proximity does not simply make friendship *possible,* it also *encourages* it. And that makes the relationship between proximity and liking much stronger than the relationship between proximity and loathing. Proximity brings about the kind of "passive contacts" between people from which friendships grow—the first "hello" in the hallway; the first discussion of the weather near the mailbox. Without these encounters friendships fail to develop, and without proximity these encounters often fail to occur.

*The Effect of Anticipating Interaction*    People tend to give others with whom they expect to interact the benefit of the doubt. Simply knowing that we will interact with someone makes us like that person more. In one demonstration of this effect, women at the University of Minnesota were given information about the personalities of two fellow students—one who would later join them in a discussion of student dating habits, and the other with whom they would have no future contact (Darley & Berscheid, 1967). The two personality profiles were made equivalent through **counterbalancing**—half the participants were told they would meet one student (say, Student A rather than Student B); the other half were told they would meet the *other* student (say, Student B rather than Student A). Thus, on average, the person with whom the participants expected to interact was, objectively speaking, no more or less appealing than the person they would not meet. Nevertheless, participants liked the person they expected to meet significantly more.

This initial positive stance toward others is likely to create a positive cycle in which the favorable expectations of each partner are reinforced by the positive behavior of the other. The powerful effects of proximity on friendship are one result. Because we know we must occasionally interact with those next door or down the hall, we make an effort to

**counterbalancing** A methodological procedure whereby an investigator makes sure that any extraneous variable (for example, a stimulus person's name) that might influence the dependent measure (for example, liking) is distributed equally often across the different levels of the independent variable (for example, the stimulus person a participant expects to meet and the stimulus person the participant does not expect to meet).

**THE FAR SIDE®** By GARY LARSON

**And so it went, night after night, year after year. In fact, the Hansens had been in a living hell ever since that fateful day the neighbor's "For Sale" sign had come down and a family of howler monkeys had moved in.**

Box 3.1 FOCUS ON DAILY LIFE

# Liking, Disliking, and Propinquity

Whom do you dislike the most on campus? Is it your neighbor next door or the person downstairs who blasts the stereo whenever you try to study, the speakers sending bass notes your way with such intensity that they shake the very desk at which you try to work? Is it the person who leaves discarded dental floss, half-eaten pizza slices, and soiled laundry in the hallway, the bathroom, or the lobby? What about the person who always seems to commandeer the adjacent table in the dining hall, such that his or her grating voice, bombastic boasts, and offensive jokes are impossible to ignore?

It seems that we most dislike those who do the most to annoy us. It also seems that it is typically easier to be annoyed by someone who is close at hand. This has been empirically demonstrated by Ebbe B. Ebbesen and his colleagues (Ebbesen, Kjos, & Konecni, 1976). Ebbeson thought that not only do our friends tend to come from those who live close to us, but our enemies do as well. Only those nearby can readily spoil our environment and thereby earn our wrath.

Ebbesen asked residents of a large suburban condominium complex in southern California to list the three people in the complex they liked the most and the three people they disliked the most. Proximity was related to both. Sixty-three percent of those named as "most liked" lived in the same cluster within the complex as the respondent. The effect was even stronger for those named as "most disliked," as 73 percent were from the same cluster. Furthermore, the average distance between the respondents and those they named as most liked was 236 feet, but the average distance between the respondents and those they most disliked was 151 feet.

The effects of proximity on liking and disliking stem in part from a common mechanism. Proximity provides the opportunity for both. But the causes of each are also different. Proximity promotes liking by facilitating the frequency of encounters; it engenders disliking by allowing a person's environment to be spoiled by others. When the respondents were asked why they liked and disliked the people they did, their answers were quite different. The most common reason they gave for liking someone was a characteristic of the person named; the most common reason for disliking someone was something he or she did to ruin the local environment.

That disliking is even more tightly connected to propinquity should not be surprising. After all, one can always travel to find friends, but who would do so to find enemies?

have our initial encounters go well. Therefore, most interactions should be rewarding and serve to advance friendships. This was demonstrated in a simple but telling experiment in which previously unacquainted participants arrived in threes. Person A had a get-acquainted conversation with Person B, and Person B had a get-acquainted conversation with Person C. A and C never interacted, although they did witness each other's interaction with B. Afterwards, everyone rated how much they liked everyone else, and the consistent result was that A and C liked one another the least (Insko & Wilson, 1977). Interactions tend to be rewarding.

***The Mere Exposure Effect*** You may remember Robert Zajonc for his research on how the mere presence of another person helps or hinders performance (see Chapter 2). Zajonc has conducted another important line of research on **mere exposure**, which helps to explain our reactions to those we frequently encounter.

Zajonc contends that the "mere repeated exposure of the individual to a stimulus is a sufficient condition for the enhancement of his [or her] attitude toward it" (Zajonc, 1968, p. 93). Less formally, the more you are exposed to something, the more you tend to like it. Things that you already like become more likable; things you find it hard to tolerate become a bit more tolerable. This may strike you

> **mere exposure effect** The finding that repeated exposure to a stimulus (for example, an object or person) leads to greater liking of the stimulus.

as implausible. After all, what about all those pop tunes that seem to become more irritating each time they are played on the radio? Or what about the wisdom captured in such sayings as "familiarity breeds contempt" and "absence makes the heart grow fonder?" Zajonc's claim does not seem to square with intuition.

Upon reflection, however, the claim is less perverse than it first appears. You may indeed become increasingly irritated by a song that is played by station after station on the radio—at first! But what happens long after the song has fallen from favor and you hear it again as part of some "golden oldies" retrospective? Chances are that you end up liking the song more than you would have had you not been exposed to it so many times before (remember, these are bad songs we're talking about!). Baby boomers all over the country can recall despising such insipid songs as Three Dog Night's "Jeremiah Was a Bullfrog," only to experience—quite reluctantly—a nostalgic acceptance of its "virtues" when it was thrust upon them once again in films such as *The Big Chill*. Familiarity seems to breed, not contempt, but approval.

Researchers have collected a massive amount of empirical support for the claim that mere repeated exposure facilitates liking (Bornstein, 1989; Moreland & Beach, 1992; Zajonc, 1968). Some of the most striking (albeit less convincing) evidence is correlational. For instance, there is a remarkable correlation between the frequency with which people are exposed to various items in a given domain and how much they like those items. As one example, people report that they like those flowers that are mentioned frequently in our language more than those that are mentioned less frequently. Lilies and violets are liked more than geraniums and hyacinths, and they appear roughly six times as often in written texts. The same is true of people's preferences for trees, fruits, and vegetables. People like pines more than birches, apples more than grapefruits, and broccoli more than leeks, and, in each case, the former appears roughly six times as often in print. Moving beyond things that grow in the ground, the same relationship is found among countries of the world and U.S. cities. Americans prefer the frequently encountered Venezuela to the less frequently encountered Honduras, and the commonly mentioned Chicago to the less commonly mentioned Omaha.

**The Influence of Mere Exposure on Liking**    It may seem hard to believe, but many now-revered landmarks elicited anything but reverence initially. (A) When the Eiffel Tower was completed in Paris, France, in 1889, to commemorate the French Revolution's centennial, a group of artists and intellectuals, including Alexandre Dumas, Guy de Maupassant, and Emile Zola, signed a petition calling it "useless and monstrous" and "a disgraceful column of bolts." (B) San Francisco's TransAmerica building likewise elicited negative reactions initially, with noted *San Francisco Chronicle* columnist Herb Caen angrily suggesting knitting a giant tea cozy to cover the spire.

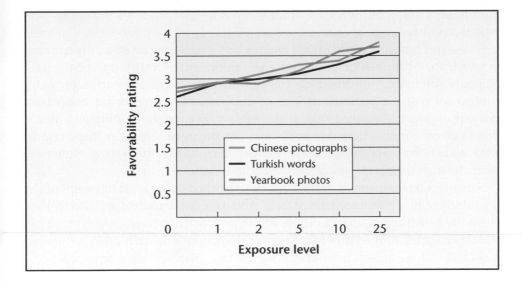

**Figure 3.3  The Mere Exposure Effect**    Positivity of subjects' reactions to yearbook pictures, Chinese pictographs, and nonsense words as a function of frequency of exposure. (Source: Zajonc, 1968)

Zajonc would like to argue that all of these relationships exist partly because the more often people are exposed to something, whether it be a fruit, vegetable, or U.S. city, the more they tend to like it. He readily acknowledges, however, that it could just as easily be the opposite. Rather than liking roses because they are often written about, people might write about them because they like them. In certain domains, however, this alternative explanation is less compelling. For example, there is a strong correlation between people's preference for various letters in the English alphabet and how often they appear in the language (Alluisi & Adams, 1962). It is hard to imagine that there are so many "e's" or "r's" in the English language because people like those letters. It's more plausible that people like them because they are exposed to them so often. Each of us also tends to be disproportionately exposed to the letters in our own names, and so it is no surprise that we tend to be disproportionately fond of them, although there are other explanations of this effect as well—for example, that we like them because they're "ours" (Hoorens, Nuttin, Herman, & Pavakanun, 1990; Nuttin, 1987).

Ultimately, of course, the true test of this or any other hypothesis is how well it fares in experimental tests. To set up one such test, Zajonc (1968) created a stimulus set of Turkish words that were utterly unfamiliar to his participants—for example, *kadirga, afworbu,* and *lokanta*. Different words within this set were then shown to his participants 0, 1, 2, 5, 10, or 25 times. Afterwards, the participants were asked to indicate the extent to which they thought each word referred to something good or bad. As shown in Figure 3.3, the more times participants saw a given word, the more they assumed it referred to something good. Zajonc has replicated this experiment with Chinese pictographs (symbols used in Chinese writing) and college yearbook pictures as stimuli (in the latter case, subjects judged how much they thought they would like the person). As shown in Figure 3.3, the mere exposure effect was obtained each time.

A critic might be concerned about a possible alternative interpretation of these results, however. Note that the context in which they took place was rather pleasant. The surroundings were agreeable, the atmosphere congenial, and the experimenters endeavored to make the participants feel relaxed. Perhaps the positive feelings induced by this atmosphere "rubbed off" on the stimuli that were presented, leaving them with a favorable impression of those that were presented most often. Thus, perhaps it was not mere exposure that produced the results, but repeated positive associations.

To test this interpretation, Zajonc and his colleagues conducted an experiment in which the manipulation of exposure was sufficiently subtle to escape the participants' attention, and in which the stimuli were associated with a pleasant context for half the participants and an unpleasant context for the other half (Saegert, Swap, & Zajonc, 1973). If the same effects could be obtained under these two conditions, then one could rule out the possibility that they are due either to positive associations or to the efforts of compliant subjects who guessed what the hypothesis was and responded accordingly.

Female undergraduates from the University of Michigan arrived in groups of six for a study of the "psychophysics of taste" and were led to individual cubicles and given their instructions. The purpose of the experiment was ostensibly to study their "perception of the tastes of substances that differ from each other in specific ways and which you will taste in different orders." Each cubicle contained a different substance, which participants were to rate in terms of taste. Participants were sent back and forth between cubicles according to a carefully arranged schedule to make their ratings. The schedule was crafted such that each participant occupied the same cubicle as another participant, with no conversation allowed, either 10, 5, 2, 1, or 0 times. The six participants were thus "merely exposed" to one another a different number of times, without the manipulation of exposure being a salient feature of the experiment. In addition, for half the participants the substances being tasted were pleasant (three flavors of Kool-Aid) and for the other half unpleasant (weak solutions of vinegar, quinine, and citric acid).

After the taste tests were completed, the participants were asked to indicate how likable they thought each of their fellow participants was. The results were clear-cut: whether encountered while tasting pleasant or unpleasant stimuli, those who were encountered most often were the most liked. It appears that *mere repeated exposure* is sufficient to increase liking.

Two other experiments on the mere exposure effect are particularly noteworthy. The first rests on the observation that the image each of us has of our own face is not the same as the image our friends have of us. Because we typically see ourselves in the mirror, the image we have of ourselves is a mirror image, whereas our friends typically see our "true" image. Thus, if simple exposure induces liking, we should prefer our mirror image, and our friends should prefer our true image. And, when an experiment showing participants mirror-image and true-image photographs was conducted, that was exactly what happened (Mita, Dermer, & Knight, 1977).

Perhaps the most intriguing test of the mere exposure effect was done with albino rats as the subjects (Cross, Halcomb, & Matter, 1967). One group of rats was raised for the first fifty-two days of life in an environment in which selections of Mozart's music were played for twelve hours each day (specifically, *The Magic Flute*, Symphonies 40 and 41, and the Violin Concerto No. 5). A second group was exposed to an analogous schedule of music by Schoenberg (specifically, *Pierrot Lunaire, A Survivor from Warsaw, Verklarte Nachte, Kol Nidre,* and

**The Mere Exposure Effect and Self-Image**   People see themselves when they look in the mirror, which means that they are familiar with a reverse image of themselves—and this is the image they generally prefer. Others see them as they truly are, and usually prefer this true image to a mirror image. (A) George W. Bush's mirror image, and (B) his normal image. Which image do you prefer?

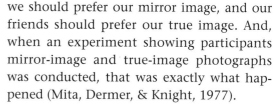

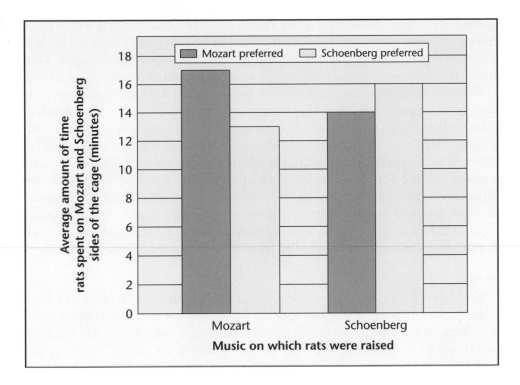

**Figure 3.4 Mere Exposure and Musical Preferences** The bars show the musical preferences of rats raised on a musical diet of Mozart or Schoenberg. The height of the bars represents the average number of minutes the rats who had earlier been exposed either to the music of Mozart or Schoenberg chose to inhabit a side of their cages that led to Mozart or Schoenberg being played. (Source: Cross, Halcomb, & Matter, 1967)

Chamber Symphonies Nos. 1 and 2). The rats were then placed individually in a test cage that was rigged such that the rat's presence on one side of the cage would trip a switch that caused previously unheard selections of Mozart to be played, whereas the rat's presence on the other side would generate new selections of Schoenberg. The rats were thus able to "vote with their feet" and express a preference for the quintessentially classical music of Mozart or the modern, atonal compositions of Schoenberg. The results support the mere exposure effect: rats raised on a musical diet of Mozart moved significantly more often to the side of the cage that led to Mozart being played, whereas those raised on a diet of Schoenberg moved to the side that led to Schoenberg's music being played (see Figure 3.4). (In case you were wondering, rats run in a control condition with no initial exposure to music later exhibited a preference for the music of Mozart.)

But *why* does mere repeated exposure lead to liking? As he did with his account of mere presence and social facilitation (see Chapter 2), Zajonc provided a compelling explanation that draws upon fundamental psychological principles. In this case, Zajonc hypothesized that repeated exposure leads to liking through classical conditioning. Recall from your introductory psychology class Pavlov's famous dogs, who would salivate (an "unconditioned response") when presented with food (an "unconditioned stimulus"). When a bell (the "conditioned stimulus") was repeatedly presented along with the food, the dogs soon began to salivate (the "conditioned response") merely upon hearing the bell. The dogs, in other words, learned to associate the bell with the food and hence responded to the bell in some of the same ways they responded to the food. In the case of repeated exposure, the stimulus is likewise paired with something very rewarding—the *absence* of any aversive consequence. One therefore learns to associate the stimulus with the absence of anything negative, and a comfortable, pleasant attachment to the stimulus is formed. Mere repeated exposure thus leads to attraction because it is reinforcing. More broadly, this conditioning process helps organisms distinguish stimuli that are "safe" from those that are not, and to develop tendencies to approach the former and avoid the latter (Zajonc, 2001).

The sheer weight of Zajonc's analysis and all of the correlational and experimental evidence marshaled to support it lead to one irresistible conclusion: the more often people are exposed to something, the more they tend to like it. This mere exposure effect is surely one of the most important elements of successful advertising. It is the warm, comfortable feeling about a product to which we have been frequently exposed that often leads us to reach for one brand rather than another on the supermarket shelf, or to vote for one political candidate over another. To be sure, advertisers often do not rely on the effect of *mere* repeated exposure alone. Rather, the product is typically presented along with a persuasive message or some positive stimulus—such as an attractive face or body—that the consumer might come to associate with the product itself. Still, one has to wonder how much of the success of any good ad campaign is due, not to specific arguments and symbols, but to mere repeated exposure. The more we see or hear of a product, the more we tend to like it.

**LOOKING BACK,** we have seen that proximity is a potent determinant of who ends up being friends, lovers, and spouses. Proximity not only enables such relationships, it encourages them. Proximity to others means that we tend to encounter them more, and the more often we encounter people, the more we tend, through mere exposure, to like them. Also, when people know they will interact frequently with each other, they often assume the best of one another and typically do their best to make sure their interactions go smoothly. Another factor that tends to make interactions go smoothly—and that likewise facilitates attraction—is similarity, a subject to which we now turn.

## SIMILARITY

We began this chapter by discussing James Carville and Mary Matalin, who are married to one another despite being on opposite ends of the political spectrum. Carville works mainly for Democratic politicians and Matalin provides assistance to Republican candidates and office holders. Many people wonder how these two can get along, a reaction that nicely illustrates a second important determinant of attraction—**similarity**. People tend to like other people who are similar to themselves (Berscheid & Reis, 1998; Byrne, 1961; Byrne, Clore, & Smeaton, 1986; Caspi & Herbener, 1990; Locke & Horowitz, 1990; Ptacek & Dodge, 1995; Rosenblatt & Greenberg, 1988). And everyone knows this, as everyone knows that "birds of a feather flock together." Not that friends agree about everything, of course. If Carville and Matalin did not root for the same baseball team or could not agree about the best musical groups of the 1990s, no one would have been puzzled. But disagreement on core political values is rather mystifying. It is hard to fathom how two people with such different political views could be drawn to each other. Perhaps Carville and Matalin shared similar beliefs about other things that mattered greatly to them but that were not clear to others.

### STUDIES OF SIMILARITY AND ATTRACTION

One of the early demonstrations of the importance of similarity in attraction comes from a study that, coincidentally, also testifies to the importance of the variable we just discussed—propinquity. In his 1956 classic *The Organization Man,*

"To like and dislike the same things, that is indeed true friendship."

—SALLUST,
*THE WAR WITH CATILINE*

William Whyte presented data on various social gatherings that took place in the Chicago suburb of Park Forest (Whyte, 1956). Figure 3.5 is a modified version of one of his charts. Color coding indicates that the residents of particular houses participated in the social event described in the legend. Note the extensive evidence of the power of proximity. Those invited to the surprise baby shower all lived next to or across the street from one another, as did those attending the Valentine's Day costume party, the picnic at the forest preserve, and the two New Year's Eve parties. Note also, however, that there are exceptions to the rule of proximity. People with shared interests sometimes went beyond their immediate neighborhood to find one another and establish an interaction. This was true, for example, of those in the gourmet society and those in the Saturday night bridge group. Similarity of interests, like proximity, can lead to interaction and to liking.

The impact of similarity on attraction has been demonstrated in many ways. First, a number of investigators have found that people who intend to marry are quite similar to one another on an extremely wide range of characteristics. In one study, the members of 1,000 engaged couples—850 of whom eventually married—were asked to provide information about themselves on eighty-eight characteristics (Burgess & Wallin, 1953). The average similarity of the couples was then compared to the similarity of random "couples" created by pairing individual members of one couple with individual members of *another* couple. This analysis revealed that members of engaged couples were significantly more similar to one another than members of random couples on sixty-six of the eighty-eight characteristics. Furthermore, for none of the characteristics were the

**Figure 3.5  Similarity of Interests and Liking**   Layout of shared activities in the Park Forest housing tract. (Source: Adapted from Whyte, 1956)

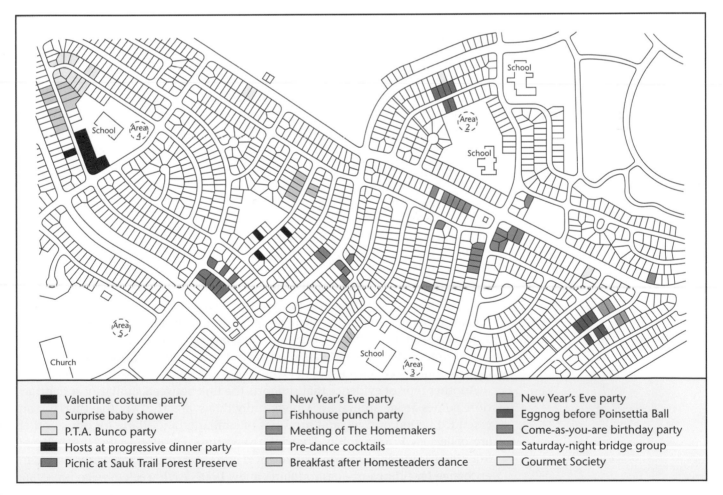

| | | |
|---|---|---|
| ■ Valentine costume party | ■ New Year's Eve party | ■ New Year's Eve party |
| □ Surprise baby shower | □ Fishhouse punch party | ■ Eggnog before Poinsettia Ball |
| □ P.T.A. Bunco party | ■ Meeting of The Homemakers | ■ Come-as-you-are birthday party |
| ■ Hosts at progressive dinner party | ■ Pre-dance cocktails | ■ Saturday-night bridge group |
| ■ Picnic at Sauk Trail Forest Preserve | □ Breakfast after Homesteaders dance | □ Gourmet Society |

Box 3.2    FOCUS ON DAILY LIFE

# Do Couples Look More Alike over Time?

Many people claim that not only do the two people in a couple tend to look like each other, but they look more alike the longer they have been together. There are many reasons why this might be so. People who live together may adopt similar styles of dress and grooming. They doubtless have similar diets, which may make them look more alike over time. They obviously live in the same regions of the country, and because of climatic factors they may acquire the same suntan and the same number of wrinkles.

Perhaps most interesting from a psychological perspective, couples also experience many of the same emotions. The death of a child devastates both parents; winning the lottery brings elation to both. More generally, a downbeat household is typically one in which both members are unhappy; an upbeat household is one in which both are happy. Eventually, a lifetime of experiencing the same emotions may have similar effects on the face and physical bearing of each member of the couple. As someone once said, "After age forty, we all have the faces we deserve." A happy lifetime tends to produce "crow's feet" around the eyes; an unhappy one tends to leave creases around the outside of the mouth. Thus, people who live together and experience the same emotions may converge in facial appearance.

Is there truth to this idea? Our old friend Robert Zajonc and his colleagues have collected evidence indicating that there is indeed (Zajonc, Adelmann, Murphy, & Niedenthal,

1987). They enlisted the help of twelve married couples to see whether they came to look more alike over time. The members of each couple were fifty to sixty years old, and they provided both current pictures of themselves and pictures taken during their first year of marriage, approximately twenty-five years earlier. The pictures were cropped and reproduced so that extraneous identifying information such as style of dress and type of film was eliminated. Judges who were unaware of who was married to whom were then asked to assess how much each of the men resembled each of the women (for both the current and older photos).

To check for the possibility that older people as a whole are simply more alike, Zajonc and his colleagues established a set of control couples by pairing members of different couples with one another and then assessing the similarity of these "random" couples. Contrary to the notion that older people are generally more homogeneous in appearance, there was no tendency for these random couples to converge in appearance over time. This set them apart from the actual couples, who looked significantly more alike roughly twenty-five years into their marriages than they did as newlyweds. Thus, not only do we seek mates who are similar to ourselves, we become even more similar in appearance over time. Birds of a feather not only flock together, but being in the same flock can make the feathers still harder to distinguish.

members of engaged couples more *dissimilar* to another than one would expect by chance. The similarity of engaged couples was strongest for demographic characteristics (for example, social class, religion) and physical characteristics (for example, health, physical attractiveness; see Box 3.2), and was less strong—but still present—for personality characteristics (for example, leadership, sensitivity). Subsequent research that has focused on personality per se has also shown that married couples exhibit considerable similarity in the behaviors indicative of such core personality characteristics as extraversion and genuineness (Buss, 1984).

Another type of evidence that supports the link between similarity and attraction comes from studies in which individuals are thrown together for an extended period of time, and measures of similarity and liking for one another are collected. In one study, Theodore Newcomb recruited male University of Michigan transfer students to live for a year, rent-free, in a large house in exchange for filling out questionnaires a few hours each week (Newcomb, 1956,

1961). Newcomb made sure that none of the students knew one another beforehand. Among the questionnaires they filled out were several that asked them to indicate how much they liked each of their housemates. To an increasing degree over the course of the fifteen-week study, as students got to know one another and their attitudes and values better and better, the students' liking of one another was predictable from how similar they were. Interestingly, although this was true of similarity in values and attitudes, it was *most* true in terms of shared opinions about the other house members. Bob and Dennis were more likely to hit it off if both detested Rick than if they differed in their evaluations of Rick's merits (see also Griffitt & Veitch, 1974).

**Physical Similarity** Over time, the members of a couple tend to look like each other, perhaps because of initial physical similarities, but also because of shared diet, living conditions, and emotional experiences.

The third type of evidence that supports the proposition that people are attracted to those who are similar to themselves comes from the "bogus stranger" paradigm (Byrne, 1961; Byrne, Clore, & Smeaton, 1986; Byrne, Griffitt, & Stefaniak, 1967; Byrne & Nelson, 1965; Griffitt & Veitch, 1971; Tan & Singh, 1995). In these experiments, participants are given the responses to attitude or personality questionnaires supposedly filled out by someone else. In reality, the responses are constructed by the experimenter to create a given level of similarity to the participants' own responses—which, to avoid suspicion, are typically assessed much earlier in a classroom setting. The experiment is described as a study of "the accuracy of interpersonal judgments based on limited information." After reading the responses of the bogus stranger, the participants are asked to rate the bogus stranger on a number of dimensions, including how likely it is that they would like the person in question. In study after study of this type, the more similar the stranger is to the participant, the more the participant likes him or her.

## BUT DON'T "OPPOSITES ATTRACT"?

Although most people accept the idea that similarity fosters attraction, they also endorse the counter-theory of **complementarity**—that opposites attract. The idea is that individuals with divergent characteristics should complement each other nicely and thus get along well. Children are taught the role of complementarity through the Mother Goose nursery rhyme of Jack Sprat: "Jack Sprat could eat no fat. His wife could eat no lean. And so between them both you see, they licked the platter clean."

**complementarity** The tendency for people to seek out others with characteristics that are different from and that complement their own.

Heterosexuality, of course, is a prime example of complementarity in attraction. But the notion seems like it applies beyond heterosexuality. It seems that a dependent person might profit from being with someone who is nurturant, or that a person who is quiet might get along with someone who likes to talk. The yin and yang of two divergent personalities ought to create a successful unity.

But is there any evidence (beyond heterosexuality) to support this complementarity hypothesis? The first thing to note in answer to this question is that complementarity, if it exists, is surely more limited in scope than the widespread impact of similarity on attraction. Unlike similarity, for example, there is no reason to expect that complementarity of attitudes, beliefs, or physical characteristics will lead to attraction. People with different attitudes or beliefs tend to quarrel over them, and people with different physical attributes often come from different geographical regions (and thus have to overcome a lack of propinquity and the absence of a shared culture).

Complementarity should thus only be found, if at all, in people's personality traits. And not even in all personality traits at that. The hypothesis really only makes sense for those traits for which one person's needs can be met by the other (Levinger, 1964). Someone who is dependent can have his or her needs taken care of by a partner who is nurturant. But someone who is a hard worker would be unlikely to want to be with someone who is lazy, and someone who values honesty would be unlikely to associate with someone who is a habitual liar. Thus, one might reasonably expect to find complementarity in such traits as dependence-nurturance or introversion-extroversion, but not in such traits as honesty, optimism, or conscientiousness.

What about this restricted set of personality characteristics? Is there any evidence for complementarity among them? Although a few studies have been offered in support of the complementarity hypothesis (Wagner, 1975; Winch, 1955; Winch, Ktanes, & Ktanes, 1954, 1955), many of them have been criticized on methodological grounds (Katz, Glucksberg, & Krauss, 1960), and there are many more studies that have failed to provide evidence for the hypothesis (Antill, 1983; Boyden, Carroll, & Maier, 1984; Levinger, Senn, & Jorgensen, 1970; Meyer & Pepper, 1977; Neimeyer & Mitchell, 1988).

Thus, similarity appears to be the rule, and complementarity the exception. And, in the final analysis, that should not be terribly surprising. For one thing, complementarity conflicts with (and thus is masked by) the more powerful effect of similarity on attraction. Second, to the extent that complementarity exists, it exists sporadically. Even two people who seem to represent a perfect example of complementarity are likely to complement one another on only one or two features of their personalities. All of their other characteristics are likely to be similar or unrelated. An examination of such a couple would thus reveal considerable evidence of similarity and only a little support for complementarity.

## WHY DOES SIMILARITY PROMOTE ATTRACTION?

Interactions with people who share our beliefs, values, and personal characteristics tend to be rewarding, which tends to increase our attraction toward them. All told, similarity leads to attraction for at least four reasons.

*Similar Others Validate Our Beliefs and Orientations*    People who share our beliefs validate our beliefs. People who endorse our values reinforce our values. In short, it is often a pleasure to interact with similar others because they reinforce rather than challenge our beliefs, outlooks, ideologies, and personal strivings. This is perhaps easiest to appreciate by considering our interactions with people who do *not* share our beliefs and attitudes. As those who have had contentious political discussions surely know, interactions with those who challenge our beliefs and assumptions can be unsettling, and this often leads us to dislike the person associated with such unsettling feelings. An experiment in which people's physiological reactions were monitored by a polygraph machine makes this point nicely (Clore & Gormly, 1974). The participants were confronted by a confederate who either agreed or disagreed with their attitudes. Not surprisingly, the participants tended to like the confederate who agreed with their views more than the confederate who disagreed with them. More important, the amount of arousal the participants experienced while listening to the confederate predicted the strength of their affective reactions. The more aroused they were while hearing the confederate agree with them, the more they liked the confederate; the more aroused they were while hearing the confederate disagree with them, the more they disliked the confederate. Validation is comforting, and it can lead to liking for those who provide it; contradiction can be aversive, and it can lead to antipathy for those who provide it.

***Similarity Facilitates Smooth Interactions***  Interactions with similar others are often rewarding because they tend to go smoothly. Two people who share a religious faith, for example, will often find common ground when they watch a movie, listen to the news, or take a vacation together. Two atheists would tend to do likewise. But if the believer and the atheist were paired, their views would often clash, putting their enjoyment of the movie, the news, or the vacation at risk. Those who share similar views and beliefs and orientations with us enable us to interact without conflict over our views.

One study contrasted an attitude's overall importance with its importance to interactions (Davis, 1981). The logic was as follows. Some of your beliefs and attitudes, such as your view of human nature or political orientation, are extremely important to you. Other characteristics, such as your food preferences or tastes in music, are often less important, but they may nonetheless have more impact on your day-to-day interactions with another person. For which characteristics should similarity to another person make the most difference? In other words, who are you more drawn to, someone with whom you share qualities that manifest themselves in everyday interaction, or someone with whom you share more important but less manifest characteristics?

To answer this question, the researchers asked participants how much they liked people who agreed or disagreed with them on various attitudes. They also rated each attitude for both overall importance and importance in day-to-day

*"We are so in synch. I was just about to ask you for a divorce."*

interaction. The results showed clearly that similarity on attitudes of relevance to everyday interaction had more influence on the participants' sentiments than similarity on attitudes of overall importance. Thus, similarity fosters attraction because it encourages smooth interaction.

*We Expect Similar Others to Like Us*    Someone who is similar to us on many dimensions can be counted on to see the world the way we do, including that part of the world that is most important to us—ourselves. There surely are few psychological phenomena more basic than our tendency to like people who like us (Condon & Crano, 1988; Curtis & Miller, 1986; Kenny & LaVoie, 1982; Kenny & Nasby, 1980). Part of the reason we like similar others, then, stems from our basic narcissism.

*Similar Others Have Qualities We Like*    We tend to think that most of our beliefs and attitudes have merit. We think of them as *reasoned* positions derived from careful review of relevant information. In short, we tend to think that most of our beliefs, values, tastes, and habits are the "right" ones to have. To a certain extent, we also think that most of our personality characteristics are the appropriate ones to have. Although we may grant that we have a few personal foibles, we nonetheless strive to be the best that we can be on those characteristics we deem most important.

The logical consequence of such an orientation is that we tend to think that people who are similar to ourselves have the right qualities just as we do. Or, stated another way, if we believe that our views and characteristics are largely the product of reason, someone who disagrees with us will strike us as "unreasonable." Similar others should thus be favored over dissimilar others. After all, who wouldn't prefer a reasonable person to an unreasonable one?

**LOOKING BACK**, we have seen that, all else being equal, people are more inclined to like those who are similar to themselves than people who are dissimilar to themselves. Similar others validate our beliefs and values, they have qualities we like, and our interactions with them tend to be less marred by conflict. So birds of a feather do flock together. Having established the importance of propinquity and similarity on attraction, we now turn to the effect of physical attractiveness on attraction.

## PHYSICAL ATTRACTIVENESS

It is hardly surprising to learn that one of the most powerful determinants of interpersonal attraction is physical attractiveness—that is, whether another person is "good looking." After all, who receives the most attention at health clubs, at parties, and at a host of other social gatherings? Attractive people have an advantage in winning others' attention and affection. This advantage is certainly more important initially than later on in a relationship, but it rarely disappears altogether. Even if it did, its initial effect would still be considerable. As your parents may have told you, you never get a second chance to make a first impression.

Empirical research on the impact of physical attractiveness indicates that, if anything, a person's looks play an even more important role in interpersonal attraction than intuition might suggest. Physical features also exert a powerful

"There are many more obscure, miserable and impoverished geniuses in the world than underappreciated beauties."
—JERRY ADLER, *NEWSWEEK*

influence on attraction surprisingly early in life and in a considerable number of different domains.

Before reviewing these potentially distressing findings, however, it is worthwhile to consider (and keep in mind) some important caveats that offer hope to those of us (that is, most of us) who don't have beauty-queen or movie-star looks. First, although there are certain constellations of features that are deemed attractive by most people, there is nonetheless considerable variability in what individual people find attractive. The prospect of requited love is by no means limited to those regarded as physically attractive by most people. Second, although people are predisposed to like those who are physically attractive, the reverse is also true. We tend to find people we like more attractive than those we don't like (Kniffin & Wilson, 2004). More heartening still, perhaps, is that happy couples tend to idealize one another's physical attractiveness—that is, they perceive each other as physically attractive, even if they are not seen that way by others (Murray & Holmes, 1997; Murray, Holmes, & Griffin, 1996). Finally, although some people are considered good looking throughout their lives, physical attractiveness is less static or stable than we often think (Zebrowitz, 1997; Zebrowitz, Olson, & Hoffman, 1993). People who are unattractive in their teens sometimes bloom in young adulthood, while the looks of the kings and queens of the high school prom may fade. In a long life, most of us have our moments in the sun and shade.

## IMPACT OF PHYSICAL ATTRACTIVENESS

What have social psychologists discovered about the impact of physical attractiveness in everyday life? The most frequently documented finding—and possibly the least surprising—is that attractive individuals are much more popular with members of the opposite sex than are their less attractive counterparts. This has been shown in studies in which indices of popularity such as dating frequency and friendship ratings are correlated with physical attractiveness (Berscheid, Dion, Walster, & Walster, 1971; Curran & Lippold, 1975; Feingold, 1984; Reis, Nezlek, & Wheeler, 1980); in investigations in which blind dates are asked afterwards how attracted they are to their partners (Brislin & Lewis, 1968; Curran & Lippold, 1975; Walster, Aronson, Abrahams, & Rottman, 1966); and in studies of video dating services in which participants indicate how attracted they are to individuals shown on videotape (Riggio & Woll, 1984; Woll, 1986). In all of these situations, attractive individuals are sought out more than their less attractive peers.

But attractive individuals benefit in other areas as well. For those interested in getting good grades, note that an essay supposedly written by an attractive author is typically evaluated more favorably than one attributed to an unattractive author (Anderson & Nida, 1978; Cash & Trimer, 1984; Landy & Sigall, 1974; Maruyama & Miller, 1980). For those interested in earning money, studies have shown that each one-point increase (on a five-point scale) in physical attractiveness is worth approximately $2,000 in additional annual salary (closer to $3,000 in inflation-adjusted dollars; Frieze, Olson, & Russell, 1991; Roszell, Kennedy, & Grabb, 1989; see also Cash & Kilcullen, 1985). For those worried about receiving help in an hour of need, consider that men are more likely to come to the aid of an injured female experimenter if she is good looking (West & Brown, 1975). For those tempted to commit a crime, note that attractive defendants are often given a break by jurors (Efran, 1974). When convicted, attractive criminals receive lighter sentences by judges (Stewart, 1980). In one study, for example, participants recommended prison sentences that were 86 percent longer for unattractive defendants than for attractive defendants (Sigall & Ostrove, 1975). Crime may not pay, but the wages are clearly better for those who are good looking.

**halo effect** The common belief—accurate or not—that attractive individuals possess a host of positive qualities beyond their physical appearance.

*The Halo Effect*    Attractive individuals benefit from a **halo effect**, the common belief—accurate or not—that attractive individuals possess a host of positive qualities beyond their physical appearance. Thus, people may endeavor to date, mate, and affiliate with the physically attractive, not only because of their looks, but also because of numerous other attributes attractive people are thought to offer. In experiments in which people were asked to make inferences about individuals depicted in photographs, good-looking men and women were judged to be happier, more intelligent, and more popular, and to have more desirable personalities, higher incomes, and more professional success (Bar-Tal & Saxe, 1976; Dion, Berscheid, & Walster, 1972; Eagly, Ashmore, Makhijani, & Longo, 1991; Feingold, 1992b; Moore, Graziano, & Millar, 1987). The only consistently negative inferences about them were that they were often perceived as immodest and as less likely to be good parents (Bar-Tal & Saxe, 1976; Dion, Berscheid, & Walster, 1972; Wheeler & Kim, 1997). Moreover, attractive women were sometimes also seen as vain and materialistic (Cash & Duncan, 1984; Dermer & Theil, 1975; Podratz, Halverson, & Dipboye, 2004).

The halo effect appears to vary in predictable ways across different cultures. In individualistic cultures such as the United States, physically attractive individuals are assumed to be more dominant and assertive than their less attractive counterparts. In contrast, in collectivist cultures such as Korea, attractive individuals are thought to be more generous, sensitive, and empathetic than unattractive individuals. Note that in both collectivist and individualist cultures, attractive individuals are thought to be smarter, better adjusted, and more sociable than less attractive individuals (Wheeler & Kim, 1997).

Is there any validity to these beliefs? Given the preferential treatment that physically attractive people often receive, it would be surprising if there were not some impact on their development. Indeed, there is evidence that physically attractive individuals do have more winning personalities. The effects are not large, but they are present on the very personality dimensions one might expect. Physically attractive people are not above average in intelligence, for example (Sparacino & Hansell, 1979). Nonetheless, they do seem to be somewhat happier, less stressed, and more satisfied with their lives, and they perceive themselves as having greater control over what happens to them (Diener, Wolsic, & Fujita, 1995; Umberson & Hughes, 1987).

Some of the personality correlates of physical attractiveness were revealed in an experiment in which participants had five-minute telephone conversations with members of the opposite sex. The experimenters rated all participants for physical attractiveness. Because the conversations took place over the phone, however, the participants themselves did not know what the person they were talking to looked like. Nevertheless, when the participants rated their partners afterwards on a number of personality dimensions, the participants rated the individuals who had been deemed attractive by the experimenters as more likable and socially skilled than their less attractive counterparts (Goldman & Lewis, 1977). A lifetime of easier, rewarding social encounters appears to instill in attractive individuals the confidence and social skills that bring about still more rewarding interactions in the future (Langlois et al., 2000; Reis et al., 1982).

But what happens when the attractiveness of the conversation partner is known? Because much of the population is so taken with physical beauty and because those who are physically attractive are thought to possess a host of other desirable characteristics, people may make a greater effort when dealing with someone who is good looking. They may listen better, be more responsive, more energetic, and more willing to express agreement with an attractive person. The net result is that attractive people may be given an advantage that makes it easier to come across as socially skilled—even when that is not the case. The physical attractiveness stereotype may give rise to a **self-fulfilling prophecy**—that is, a tendency for people to act in ways that elicit confirmation of a belief that they hold (see Chapters 10 and 11). In this case, believing that an attractive person possesses certain desirable characteristics, people may act in ways that elicit those very characteristics.

> **self-fulfilling prophecy** The tendency for people to act in ways that elicit confirmation of a belief that they hold.

This was demonstrated in a clever experiment in which undergraduate men were asked to have a get-acquainted conversation with an undergraduate woman over the telephone. Each of the male participants was given a photograph supposedly taken of his conversation partner. In reality, the photos were chosen to be quite attractive for half the participants and unattractive for the others (their actual conversation partners, of course, represented the full range of attractiveness). The conversations were tape-recorded, and the critical analysis involved ratings of how warm and socially adept the woman was. When just the woman's comments—and *only* the women's comments—were played to *other* participants who were not shown the woman's photo and thus had no preconceptions about her appearance, a rather stunning result emerged. They rated the woman who had talked to someone who thought she was attractive as warmer and more socially poised than the woman who had talked to someone who thought she was unattractive (Snyder, Tanke, & Berscheid, 1977). Once again the deck is stacked in favor of the physically attractive: people talk to them in ways that bring out their warmth and confidence, thereby confirming the stereotype that they are socially skilled.

*Early Effects of Physical Attractiveness*    Perhaps the most remarkable aspect of the impact of physical attractiveness is how early in life it has an effect. Attractive infants receive more affectionate and playful attention from their mothers than do less attractive infants, and this occurs even before leaving the hospital in which they were born (Langlois, Ritter, Casey, & Sawin, 1995). Their good fortune continues in nursery school, where they are more popular with their peers than are unattractive children (Dion, 1973; Dion & Berscheid, 1974). Furthermore, nursery school and elementary school teachers tend to assume that attractive pupils are more intelligent and better behaved than their less attractive classmates (Adams, 1978; Adams & Crane, 1980; Clifford & Walster, 1973; Martinek, 1981). Even more disturbing are the findings of an experiment in which college students were given a written report that described a transgression committed by a seven-year-old child. Attached to the report was a photograph of the child. Half the time the child was attractive, and half the time he or she was unattractive. When asked to evaluate the episode, those who thought the transgression was committed by an attractive child viewed it as less serious. They also thought the attractive child was less likely to act out similarly in the future, and they considered him or her to be more honest and pleasant (Dion, 1972). What could be less fair?

Studies such as these demonstrate that even very young children are the objects of discrimination based on physical appearance. Research has also shown that children—infants, in fact!—are the perpetrators of such discrimination as well. In these experiments, infants as young as three months were shown slides of two human faces side by side. One of the faces was previously judged by adults as attractive, and the other as unattractive. The slides were typically shown to the infant for ten seconds, and the amount of time the infant spent looking at each one was recorded by someone who was unaware of which slide, the one on the left or right, was the attractive one. (The infant's eye movements were video-taped, and the scoring was done from the videotape so that the stimulus slides were beyond the judge's field of vision.) Looking time was interpreted as an index of the infant's preference. In several studies, infants showed a clear preference for attractive over unattractive faces (Langlois et al., 1987; Langlois, Ritter, Roggman, & Vaughn, 1991; Samuels & Ewy, 1985). This was true even though the attractive and unattractive faces were not extreme (the attractive faces were not the *most* attractive faces the investigators could find, nor were the unattractive faces the least attractive), and the preference held true for male faces, female faces, and even faces of other infants (Langlois, Ritter, Roggman, & Vaughn, 1991). Thus, the prejudice in favor of physically attractive people is exhibited extremely early in life and may even be present at birth. Moreover, by the end of the first year, when infants' behavioral repertoires are more advanced, they have been shown to be more inclined to play contentedly with an adult stranger if the adult is attractive than if the adult is unattractive. The infants, for example, turned or moved away from an unattractive stranger more than three times as often as they did from an attractive stranger (Langlois, Roggman, & Rieser-Danner, 1990).

*Gender and the Impact of Physical Attractiveness*   It's important to note that physical attractiveness has a different impact on men than on women. One glance at the newsstand, even by a visitor from Mars, would reveal that attractive women's faces and bodies predominate in the visual media. We are bombarded with images of the "ideal woman." The world tends to take in and evaluate women's attractiveness more than men's.

It should come as no surprise, then, that attractiveness is more important in determining women's life outcomes than men's. Obesity, for example, negatively affects women's, but not men's, social mobility. Overweight girls are less likely to be accepted to college than their average or thin peers (Wooley & Wooley, 1980). Women deemed unattractive at work experience more negative outcomes than men (Bar-Tal & Saxe, 1976). And physical attractiveness matters more in terms of popularity, dating prospects, and even marriage opportunities for women than for men (Margolin & White, 1987).

So beauty can translate into power for women. It functions as a kind of currency that women can use in obtaining financial and social resources. Barbara Fredrickson and Tomi-Ann Roberts (1997) have argued that these kinds of external rewards encourage women's preoccupation with their own attractiveness, even coaxing them to adopt a kind of outsider's point of view on their physical selves. What Freud called women's "vanity" may be more appropriately viewed as a survival tactic in a world that so heavily emphasizes women's physical attractiveness.

## WHY DOES PHYSICAL ATTRACTIVENESS HAVE SUCH IMPACT?

Having established the importance of physical appearance in attraction, we now turn to the important question of why. Why is physical attractiveness so important in everyday social life? There are at least three reasons.

*Immediacy*    A person's physical appearance often trumps other characteristics such as intelligence, ambition, moral character, and personality because it is so visible—and visible so *immediately*. It affects our immediate, "gut" reaction to someone we meet for the first time. A person's keen intelligence and strong moral fiber can be demonstrated, but it usually takes time. Beauty is manifest right away. We might think that intelligence, for example, ought to matter more than beauty in our interactions with others. But let anyone who thinks so ". . . show up at a trendy restaurant like Indochine at 9:30 on a Friday night and try to get a table on the strength of his IQ" (Adler, 1994). Perhaps this is why a sperm bank established to sell the genes of Nobel Prize winners was a complete flop: would-be parents opted for beauty over brains virtually every time (Nobel gene biz bombs, 1985).

*Prestige*    Imagine that you are returning to your high school for your five-year reunion with your current boyfriend or girlfriend, whom you met in college. How much do you care about your boyfriend's or girlfriend's appearance?

Now imagine that you are returning to your high school for a sentimental visit. You will be visiting after hours when no one—certainly none of your old high school friends—is likely to be around. Again, your boyfriend or girlfriend agrees to go with you. Now how much do you care about your partner's appearance?

Most people will confess to being more concerned about their partner's appearance at the reunion than during the clandestine visit. A partner's looks often matter more in public than in private. To be sure, good looks are partly valued in and of themselves, with no thought of what effect they may have on others. A person "consumes" the good looks of his or her partner through such direct effects as aesthetic appreciation and sexual excitement. But, in addition, there are substantial indirect effects of having an attractive partner: other people may evaluate you more highly because you are able to attract such a desired "commodity." Knowing this can increase the motivation to seek out a physically attractive boyfriend or girlfriend.

Experimental research bears this out. In one study, each participant entered a waiting room and was seated across from two fellow students, one male and one female, who were confederates of the experimenter (Sigall & Landy, 1973). The man was described as a fellow participant in an experiment on perception, and he was made up to look completely average in appearance. The status and appearance of the woman was varied across experimental conditions. To half the participants, she came across as physically attractive: her clothes and makeup were chosen to accentuate her natural good looks. To the other half of the participants, she came across as unattractive: she "wore an unbecoming wig, no makeup, and unflattering clothes" (Sigall & Landy, 1973, p. 219). In addition, half the time she was described as the girlfriend of the male confederate, and half the time she was introduced as someone waiting to see another professor.

After this brief introductory scene, the participant was led to a separate cubicle and asked to give his first impressions of the other "participant" as part of an experiment on the perception of people. As predicted, participants' impressions of the male confederate were influenced by whether or not he was thought to be the boyfriend of an attractive or unattractive woman. Participants thought the confederate was more likable, friendly, and confident when his "girlfriend" was attractive than when she was unattractive. The attractiveness of the female confederate had no such effect when she was thought to be merely waiting to see someone else.

Subsequent research has reinforced this general finding while simultaneously qualifying it in predictable ways (Bar-Tal & Saxe, 1976; Hebl & Mannix, 2003).

**Immediacy and Attractiveness**
Queen Nefertiti of pre-biblical times was considered physically attractive in her time and in ours. Her clear skin, widely spaced and large eyes, small nose and chin, full lips, and high eyebrows are features deemed attractive in all eras.

For instance, the effect is much stronger for impressions of males than impressions of females in heterosexual relationships: being with an attractive woman boosts a man's image more than being with an attractive man boosts a woman's image. Perhaps this is why most of the famous "mismatches" on physical appearance involve a stunning woman with an accomplished, but less attractive man—Julia Roberts and Lyle Lovett, Christie Brinkley and Billy Joel, or Angelina Jolie and Billy Bob Thornton. In addition, the effect is rather fine-grained: being with an attractive woman boosts a man's presumed intelligence, income, and occupational status more than his presumed personality, popularity, or happiness.

*Biology*    Before we can discuss the third reason why so many people are drawn to those who are physically attractive, we must consider *what* it is that people find attractive. What do people who are considered attractive look like? What features set them apart from everyone else?

It might seem that there could be no clear answer to this question. After all, doesn't it depend on who is doing the judging—on one's unique preferences as well as the more general tastes of the culture or historical era to which one belongs? In short, doesn't the assessment of what is attractive vary enormously from person to person, culture to culture, and era to era?

To be sure, there is considerable variation from person to person as to specific preferences (Beck, Ward-Hull, & McLear, 1976; Wiggins, Wiggins, & Conger, 1968). Some are attracted to blond men with Nordic features; others are drawn to those with a more Mediterranean look. Some prefer sultry women; others opt for a more "pixie-ish" type. There is also substantial variation in preferences between cultures and subcultures, and across historical periods, particularly in terms of preferences for different skin colors, body weights, amount of body hair, and various ornamentation practices such as nose rings, teeth filing, and hairstyles (Darwin, 1871; Fallon, 1990; Ford & Beach, 1951; Hebl & Heatherton, 1997; see Box 3.3).

But such variation across people, cultures, and historical periods does not

**Preferred Body Types**    In the United States today most women wish to be thin, but in the past there was a preference for women with a heavier body type and more curves, as shown in the paintings of Peter Paul Rubens in the early seventeenth century and Auguste Renoir in the early twentieth century. (A) Rubens's *Venus before a Mirror* (1614–1615), and (B) Renoir's *Blond Bather* (1919).

## Box 3.3  FOCUS ON HEALTH

# The Flight to Thinness

Anyone who has seen the paintings of Renoir or Rubens is aware of the marked variability over time in what is considered the ideal weight for women. This has received a great deal of media attention in recent years because much of the world, the United States in particular, is in the midst of an obsession with thinness. And it may be an unhealthy fad at that, having been blamed for the alarming increase in such eating disorders as bulimia and anorexia nervosa in young women (Brumberg, 1997). Society's current preference for thin women is something of an anomaly, given a historical preference for heavier physiques. The trend toward thinness has been documented in a number of ways. Photographs of women appearing in *Vogue* and *Ladies' Home Journal* were examined over the course of the twentieth century, and the researchers computed the relative size of the women's busts and waists. The bust-to-waist ratio declined markedly across this time span, indicating a turning away from a more voluptuous standard of female beauty (Silverstein, Perdue, Peterson, & Kelly, 1986). Analyses of *Playboy* centerfolds and Miss America contestants over the latter half of the twentieth century have revealed a similar trend toward slenderness (Garner, Garfinkel, Schwartz, & Thompson, 1980; Wiseman, Gray, Mosimann, & Ahrens, 1992). This trend is captured more vividly, perhaps, by the reaction of one of today's recognized beauties, Elizabeth Hurley, at an exhibition of the clothes worn by a sex symbol of another era: "I've always thought Marilyn Monroe looked fabulous, but I'd kill myself if I was that fat" (*Allure* magazine, January 2000).

Recent cross-cultural findings may help to make sense both of the historical norm and the current deviation. Judith Anderson and her colleagues examined the preferred female body type in fifty-four cultures and related these preferences to the reliability of the food supply in each (Anderson, Crawford, Nadeau, & Lindberg, 1992). What they found was that in cultures with a relatively uncertain food supply, moderate to heavyset women were considered more desirable. But in cultures with very reliable supplies of food, a relatively thin body type tended to be preferred. And it is hard to imagine a culture with a more stable food supply and a more pronounced infatuation with slender bodies than that of the contemporary United States.

And get this! What Anderson found cross-culturally over long time periods has also been found across individuals over much shorter time periods. Leif Nelson and Evan Morrison asked male students who were entering a cafeteria (and were presumably hungry) to indicate what body weight they "personally consider ideal in a member of the opposite sex." The hungry participants entering the cafeteria expressed a preference for a significantly heavier female body type than did the sated participants leaving the cafeteria (Nelson & Morrison, 2005).

The current obsession with thinness also appears to be characterized by some unfortunate misperceptions. In one telling study, for example, male and female undergraduates were shown a series of nine drawings of body types ranging from very thin to very heavy (Fallon & Rozin, 1985). The participants were asked to identify the body types along a continuum that represented: (1) their own current body type, (2) the body type they would most want to have, (3) the body type they thought would be most attractive to the opposite sex, and (4) the body type of the opposite sex that they personally found most attractive (this time, of course, on a set of line drawings of the opposite sex). The male students, on average, thought their current body type was precisely as heavy as the ideal body type. Moreover, they also believed that their body type was most attractive to female University of Pennsylvania students (although in actuality the women preferred a more slender male physique than the men anticipated). The results were quite different for the female students. The women judged themselves to be considerably heavier than their own ideal, and considerably heavier than what they thought would be most attractive to men. Perhaps the most disturbing finding is that the women in this study thought that what was most attractive to men was a body type considerably more slender than what the men actually preferred. An unfortunate pair of "thought bubbles" spring immediately to mind: A women standing next to a man worrying that "I'd feel more comfortable around him if only I lost a few pounds," while the man is simultaneously thinking, "She looks great, but she would look even better if she'd gain a few pounds."

But why would women think that men are more attracted to slender physiques than they actually are? Most explanations center on the mass media, which confront women with images of rail-thin supermodels, actresses, and newscasters. There is doubtless considerable truth to this claim, but it begs an additional question: Why would the media perpetuate an image of an ideal body type that neither men nor women truly think is ideal? One explanation places the blame on the fashion industry. Designers want their clothes to take center stage, not the models who wear them, and a curvaceous figure more often than not "spoils the line." Stated differently, many clothes look better (or at least top fashion designers believe they look better) on lanky women. The net result is the current madness in which society is quite literally making itself sick (through excessive dieting or anorexia or bulimia) in the service of the narrow interests of the fashion industry.

mean that all determinants of physical attractiveness are arbitrary or subject to the whims of fashion. In fact, there is reason to believe that there *have* to be some features of the human face and body that have universal appeal. For one thing, there is widespread agreement among Western judges as to who is and who is not attractive (Cross & Cross, 1971; Iliffe, 1960; Langlois et al., 2000). Individuals may not always be able to articulate *why* they find someone physically attractive, but they do tend to agree with one another. What was true for Supreme Court Justice Potter Stewart with respect to pornography appears to be true for a great many of us with respect to physical attractiveness: We may not be able to define it, but we "know it when we see it."

There is also widespread agreement among people from different cultures and subcultures as to who is generally considered attractive (Cunningham, Roberts, Barbee, Druen, & Wu, 1995; Langlois et al., 2000; Rhodes et al., 2001). Asians, blacks, and whites, for example, share roughly the same opinions of which Asian, black, and white faces they find attractive (Bernstein, Lin, & McClellan, 1982; Maret, 1983; Maret & Harling, 1985; Perrett, May, & Yoshikawa, 1994; Thakerar & Iwawaki, 1979). Moreover, as we discussed earlier, infants prefer to look at faces that adults consider attractive more than at faces that adults consider unattractive. Thus, before receiving much exposure to cultural conceptions of beauty, infants possess some (possibly innate) notion of what constitutes physical attractiveness (Langlois et al., 1987; Langlois, Ritter, Roggman, & Vaughn, 1991; Samuels & Ewy, 1985).

But what is the basis of this widespread agreement among infants and adults, both within and across different cultures? What features characterize the physically attractive? Most attempts to address this question have been guided by biological, or evolutionary, theorizing. The central idea is that we have evolved to have a preference, or "taste," for people possessing physical features that signify health or, more generally, **reproductive fitness**. Reproductive fitness refers to the capacity to get one's genes passed on to subsequent generations. By mating with reproductively fit individuals, people maximize the chances of their own genes being passed on. They increase their chances, in other words, for their genes' long-term evolutionary survival.

> **reproductive fitness** The capacity to get one's genes passed on to subsequent generations.

**Universal Agreement on Attractiveness** Most people in all cultures and subcultures would find the facial features of the women in this Miss World contest to be attractive, whether they are Asian, black, or white.

Consider a person from our deep evolutionary past who had a powerful, inherited attraction to individuals with features characteristic of ill health—say, unusually blotchy skin or skeletal features badly out of proportion. Mating with someone with such afflictions may be—from a narrow, biological perspective only—a losing proposition. The ill health that may underlie such physical symptoms may prevent a woman from carrying a fetus to term or render a man unable to provide much assistance to the child and mother. Furthermore, if these afflictions are genetic they may be passed on to any offspring who do survive, which may place them at risk of failing to make it to reproductive age. Either way, a strong sexual attraction to individuals with signs of ill health puts one at risk of an evolutionary dead end. People with such passions are likely to leave relatively few offspring in subsequent generations, and so there are few people around today who have such passions.

It may strike you as odd that such a fundamentally cognitive product—a *judgment* about whether a person is attractive—could be inherited and shaped by evolution. It may make sense that biological traits like height, brain size, and hair color are inherited, but it may seem implausible that psychological assessments and inclinations might have similar biological roots. It may also seem like a rather strange thesis because you are doubtless unaware of assessing someone's reproductive fitness when deciding (quite quickly and automatically) whether you find that person attractive.

Such reservations, although understandable, can be put to rest. Numerous tastes are inherited. Note, for example, that there is nothing inherently pleasing about sugar or salt. Their good taste resides not in their chemical structures, but in our senses. Sugar and salt taste good to us because of the taste receptors that evolution has bequeathed to us. Earlier organisms that lacked these receptors did not seek out the most advantageous foods, and thus they did less well in the evolutionary struggle for survival.

Note also that our appetite for nutritious food is anything but deliberate. We do not seek out sugar, salt, or fat because we think it is healthy for us. In fact, we often try to *avoid* such foods because we think they are *un*healthy. (They are considered unhealthy mainly because they contribute to "old age" diseases like cancer and arterial sclerosis that typically occur after peak reproductive age. The critical point here is that *getting* to reproductive age might be enhanced by consuming such foods, whereas life beyond peak reproductive age may be diminished by their consumption.) Nonetheless, the benefits to survival that these foods provide have given us the cravings that we have, and it is these cravings—not their evolutionary significance—that drive our behavior.

If evolution has given us a taste for sugar and salt, what features of the human face and body has it made us find attractive? Following the evolutionary thesis, we should be attracted to people with features that signify reproductive fitness, and not to people with features that might indicate disease or reproductive problems. Thus, we might expect people to steer clear of facial features that are too anomalous—for example, eyes placed so close together that the person looks like a cyclops, or so far apart that the person looks like E.T. At the extremes, such features could be a reflection of genetic problems or an indication that something has gone wrong during early development—both of which could make the person's offspring poor evolutionary prospects.

There is evidence that people do indeed find anomalous facial features unattractive and that they are drawn to "average" faces. Through either photographic or computer technology, one can make a composite face out of any number of individual faces (Galton, 1878; Langlois & Roggman, 1990). Such composite (or average) faces of both men and women are typically considered more attractive than the individual faces from which they were constructed, and this effect is stronger the more individual faces are put into the composite. To a significant extent, then, the more average or typical a face is, the more attractive it is. (Perhaps, then, we should not be envious of those who are physically attractive because, after all, they are "just average"!) Notice that this preference for average faces connects to the common intuition that there are fewer "types" of attractive people than unattractive people. Those near the average will, as Tolstoy so famously said of happy families, tend to be largely the same, but there are many ways to depart from average.

> "Happy families are all alike; every unhappy family is unhappy in its own way."
> —LEO TOLSTOY, *ANNA KARENINA*

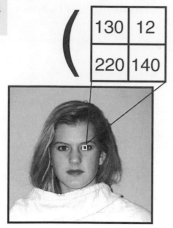

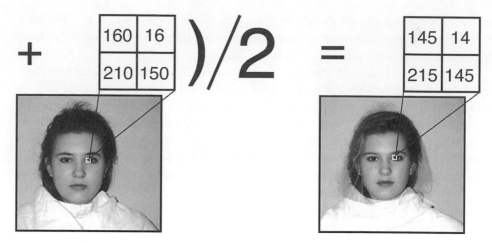

Individual Face 1

Individual Face 2

Averaged Configuration of
Face 1 and Face 2

**Attraction to Average Faces**
To test the hypothesis that people are attracted to average faces, Langlois and Roggman (1990) created an average face by dividing each individual face into small squares (as shown by one square pictured on each of the individual photos) and assigned to each square a number based on a shade of gray. They then averaged the shades of gray across the two photos to create an averaged configuration of the two individual photos, and continued by averaging even more individual faces with the newly created face. Participants found the average faces to be more attractive than the individual faces from which they had been constructed.

This does not mean that averageness is all there is to attractiveness. Far from it. It just means that averageness is an important component of perceived facial beauty. Beyond overall facial configuration, you no doubt can think of many people who are attractive precisely *because* of something extreme about them. The "bee sting" lips of supermodels depart from the norm, and people with strikingly colored eyes are thought to be especially attractive by most people.

Indeed, there is evidence that averageness is not the be-all and end-all of attractiveness. A study using composite faces made this point using three types of composites: (1) an *average* composite that was constructed by averaging all the faces from a pool of sixty photographs, (2) an *attractive* composite formed by averaging only the photographs of the fifteen faces previously judged to be most attractive, and (3) an *attractive +50 percent* composite that was created by calculating the point-by-point differences between the average and attractive composites and then exaggerating these differences by 50 percent (Perrett, May, & Yoshikawa, 1994).

If averageness were all there was to attractiveness, then the average composite should be the most attractive because it was created by averaging a greater number of faces. In addition, any composite that is exaggerated away from the average should be perceived as less attractive than an average face. Yet neither of these results was obtained. Instead, the attractive composite was considered by both British and Japanese judges to be significantly more attractive than the average composite, and the attractive +50 percent composite was judged to be even more attractive than an average face. Both the attractive and attractive +50 percent composite faces had higher cheekbones, a thinner jaw, and larger eyes than the purely average composite.

Another feature of the face and body that might signal physical health and therefore play an important role in judgments of physical attractiveness is bilateral symmetry. Humans and most other animals tend to be bilaterally symmetrical: an eye or limb on one side of the body is paired with an eye or limb in the same spot on the other side. Nonetheless, few of us are perfectly symmetrical. That is why, for example, it is possible for us to prefer mirror-image photographs of ourselves, but for our friends to prefer regular photographs (consult photos on p. 96). If we were perfectly symmetrical there would be no difference between the two photographs. Thus, bilateral symmetry is a matter of degree.

Biologists believe that departures from symmetry typically result from injuries

to the organism *in utero,* particularly injuries caused by exposure to parasites. This has been empirically documented in numerous animal species (Hubschman & Stack, 1992; Moller, 1992b; Polak, 1993). Moreover, the degree of body asymmetry in human infants has been shown to be correlated with the number of infectious diseases experienced by the mother during pregnancy (Livshits & Kobyliansky, 1991). Because parasitic infections during development lead to departures from perfect symmetry, bilateral symmetry serves as a signal of an organism's ability to resist disease. Therefore, according to evolutionary theory, individuals who are bilaterally symmetrical should be sought out by potential mates. Disease resistance is obviously an advantageous trait, and so organisms that possess it should be in demand.

And they are. Bilaterally symmetrical individuals have been shown to have an advantage in sexual competition in a variety of animal species (Manning & Hartley, 1991; Markow & Ricker, 1992; Moller, 1992a). More important for our purposes, this also appears to be true for humans. Facial attractiveness is correlated with the degree of facial bilateral symmetry (Thornhill & Gangestad, 1993).

Thus, two features that signal health and reproductive fitness—averageness and bilateral symmetry—are important determinants of perceived attractiveness. Each of these effects, by the way, exists independently of the other: averageness affects attractiveness ratings when symmetry is statistically controlled, and vice versa. This is important to establish because a face that is "average" in configuration will also be highly symmetrical. These findings testify to the value of a biological approach to attraction, one that examines the reproductive significance of potential cues to attractiveness.

## SEX DIFFERENCES IN MATE PREFERENCES AND PERCEIVED ATTRACTIVENESS

Do men and women differ in what they consider attractive in someone of the opposite sex? Many people believe that they do, and the differences have been ascribed to both evolution and cultural upbringing. Because the evolutionary interpretation has proven to be so controversial and has received so much attention in the popular press, we will discuss it at length. The controversy surrounds the claims that there are inherited, biologically based differences between men and women in how much physical attractiveness matters in selecting a mate, as well as biologically based differences in what is considered the most desirable age in a partner. We begin our discussion of this perspective with a presentation of

**Sex Differences in Mate Preferences**
Evolutionary psychologists contend that issues of reproductive fitness lead men to prefer young, beautiful women who are likely to produce healthy offspring, and women to prefer men with material resources and power who will be good providers. Larry King and his wife, Shawn Southwick-King, epitomize these differences in mate preferences.

**intrasex competition** Direct competition among two or more males or among two or more females for access to members of the opposite sex.

**intersex attraction** The interest in and attraction toward a member of one sex on the part of a member of the opposite sex.

the core ideas laid out by evolutionary psychologists and some of the evidence they offer to advance their claims. We then provide an extensive critique of this evolutionary approach and the evidence so frequently cited to support it, a critique that, among other things, involves a consideration of an alternative, sociocultural perspective.

*Investment in Offspring*    The core idea, once again, is that evolution has instilled in everyone—males and females—certain desires that provide reproductive advantage. Evolutionary psychologists also claim that evolution favors fundamentally different preferences in women and men. The basis of these predicted differences lies mainly in the differences between men and women in the amount they typically *invest in their offspring*. Women tend to invest much more, a difference in investment that starts even before the child's conception. Men contribute infinitesimally small spermatazoa, which merely contain genetic material for the potential zygote; women provide a much larger ovum, which contains both genetic material and nutrients the zygote needs in the initial stages of life. Because of this difference, ova are much more "expensive" to produce, and so the average woman will produce only 200 to 250 mature ova in her lifetime, compared to the millions of sperm the average man produces each *day*. After conception, of course, in utero development takes place entirely within the woman, taxing her physiologically and preventing her from conceiving another child for at least nine months (during which time her male partner is free—biologically—to conceive a large army). After the child is born, an extended period of nursing further taxes the woman and drastically reduces her fertility, thus lengthening the period during which no additional offspring can typically be produced. The burden of bringing a child into the world is not equally shared.

But how do differences between men and women in parental investment lead to systematic differences in what is considered attractive in a potential mate? Biologists have observed throughout the animal kingdom that the sex that invests the most in the offspring is almost always more "selective" in choosing a mate than the sex that invests less. Because males typically invest less than females, they must compete more vigorously among themselves for access to "choosy" females. As a result of their direct competition with one another (**intrasex competition**), evolution has favored those with greater size. That is why males are bigger than females in so many species. (Females tend to be larger than males in those species—such as the hyena—in which it is the *male* that invests more heavily in the offspring.) Part of this competition is the quest for females' attention and affection (**intersex attraction**). This is why it is typically the male who is the louder, gaudier member of the species—he tends to have the more colorful plumage, the more elaborate mating dance, the more intricate song. (Note, of course, that humans are something of an exception in this regard. Although in some societies men have been the more extensively adorned sex, in many they have not—including those most likely to spring to your mind.)

Thus, one of the most straightforward predictions from evolutionary psychology is that women ought to be more selective in their choice of mates, or, stated the other way, men should be more indiscriminate than women. This hypothesis conforms to both the historical record and to everyday observation: in virtually all societies in which this has been systematically studied, the average man appears ready to jump into bed much more quickly and with a much wider range of potential partners than the average female. Note that the world's oldest profession, prostitution, is one in which it is nearly always a man making the payment. A number of studies make this point empirically, with the most ambitious being a cross-cultural study with over 16,000 participants from societies all over the globe. Men and women in this study were asked: "Ideally, how many different sexual partners would you like to have" over different time intervals, ranging from one month to the rest of their lives. Across every time interval and in all regions of the world, men expressed a desire for a greater number of sexual partners (Schmitt, 2003).

If women are indeed more discriminating than men, what do women find attractive in a potential mate? And although men may be less discriminating, what do they find attractive in a mate? Evolutionary psychologists contend that the difference between men and women in parental investment should give rise to different criteria for what each considers desirable. Consider the situation for men. If they are to reproduce successfully, they need to find mates who are fertile. Those who seek out mates who are less fertile tend to leave fewer offspring. The genes of men with such a predilection would have been less likely to make it to the present day. But how does one spot a fertile woman? There are no direct cues, of course. Nevertheless, because women experience a relatively narrow window of lifetime fertility (witness the much-discussed "biological clock"), there is at least one reasonably good indirect cue—youth. Past a certain age, women are no longer capable of reproducing, and so men (who, like women, have evolved to pursue their reproductive interests), should be drawn to youth and the cues associated with youth—smooth skin, lustrous hair, full lips, and a figure in which the waist is much narrower than the hips (Singh, 1993). Being attracted to women who possess such characteristics, the argument goes, should increase the chances of mating with a woman who is fertile, and therefore it should increase the likelihood of getting one's genes represented in subsequent generations.

The key reproductive facts confronting women are much different. A man's biological clock is set to a much more leisurely pace—men typically continue to be fertile throughout life. Thus, there is no evolutionary pressure for women to develop an equally strong attraction to men with youthful characteristics. Instead, given the demands of nine months of gestation and years of breastfeeding, a critical task confronting women in our ancestral past was to acquire a

**Sex Differences in Perceived Attractiveness**   These two cartoons were run in newspapers in college towns to spoof the asymmetry in what many women and men are thought to be looking for in a date or mate. The cartoon on the left appeared in *The Cornell Sun*, while the one on the right (set up to look like a personal ad) appeared in *The Michigan Daily*.

ONE SECOND BEFORE THE BLIND DATE

Young LSA female seeks young engineering, pre-law, or pre-med male who plans on graduating with honors.  He must enjoy long protests in the diag, occasional romps in the stacks and taking road trips in his spacious and comfortable luxury car. Art students, philosophy majors or general studies majors need not apply.

Please send stock portfolio synopsis and GPA transcripts.

Young college male seeks young college female:

Send photo

mate who had resources and who could be counted on to invest them in their children. According to evolutionary psychologists, then, women should be attracted to men who either possess material resources or possess characteristics associated with acquiring them in our ancestral past—physical strength, industriousness, and social status.

Taken together, these considerations have led evolutionary psychologists to predict that men ought to be more interested than women in finding mates who are physically attractive and who have a youthful appearance. In contrast, women should be more interested than men in finding mates who can and will provide material resources. Former Colorado Congresswoman Pat Schroeder expressed this hypothesized sex difference memorably by noting that a middle-aged congresswoman does not appear to exert the same animal magnetism on the opposite sex that a middle-aged congressman does (Wright, 1995). You no doubt have noticed just such a pattern of apparent preferences in everyday life. It is not uncommon on college campuses, or anywhere else, for men to date women who are younger than they are. Women date younger men less often, and when they do it is often with a little extra deliberation ("Is this okay?") and a little extra explanation to others ("He's very mature for his age.").

This asymmetry in what is desired in a mate has been examined systematically in studies of personal ads in the United States, Canada, and India (Harrison & Saeed, 1977; Kenrick & Keefe, 1992; Rajecki, Bledsoe, & Rasmussen, 1991). What was found was an overwhelming tendency for men to seek youth and beauty and to offer material resources, but for women to seek resources and accomplishment and to offer youth and beauty. The result is so reliable—and so unsurprising—that even rather elliptical references to the phenomenon (see accompanying cartoons) can be counted on to elicit knowing reactions (for more extensive evidence, see Feingold, 1990, 1992a).

This hypothesis has also been tested cross-culturally, in a study involving over 10,000 participants in thirty-seven diverse cultures across the globe (Buss, 1989, 1994a). Among those surveyed were respondents from the West (Germany, the Netherlands, Israel, and Brazil), from industrialized regions in non-Western countries (Shanghai, China, and Tehran, Iran), and from more rural societies (the Gujarati Indians and South African Zulus). It is noteworthy (and heartening) that when asked what they desire in a mate, both men and women in *all* cultures rated kindness and intelligence more highly than either physical attractiveness or earning potential. Nevertheless, just as evolutionary psychologists would predict, men in nearly every culture rated physical attractiveness as more desirable in a mate than women did (see Figure 3.6A). And in *every* culture, men preferred marriage partners who were younger than they were (see Figure 3.6B). The magnitude of the preferred age difference varied from less than a year in Finland to over seven years in Zambia (the mean difference was 2.7 years). At the same time, women consistently preferred partners who were older than they were. They also consistently assigned greater importance than men did to various indices of a potential mate's ability to provide material resources, such as having "good financial prospects," "social status," and "ambition-industriousness" (see Figure 3.6C).

***Critique of Evolutionary Theorizing on Sex Differences in Attraction*** We doubt that the empirical evidence we have presented on sex differences in attraction comes as much of a surprise. One cannot fail to notice that, for better or worse, men tend (and we emphasize *tend*) to value youth and appearance in a mate more than women do, and women tend to value accomplishment and social sta-

> "It is a truth universally acknowledged, that a single man in possession of a good fortune, must be in want of a wife."
>
> —JANE AUSTEN,
> *PRIDE AND PREJUDICE*

> "Friendly young busty brunette seeks financially secure gentleman."
>
> "White male, 50, looking for female to be spoiled and pampered in palatial home. Please be 21–34 and have extremely sexy figure."
>
> "Blond bombshell 5'7" slender grad student seeking friend/companion/lover. You must be confident, financially secure, mature, and willing to please."
>
> —PERSONAL ADS FROM
> *THE VILLAGE VOICE*

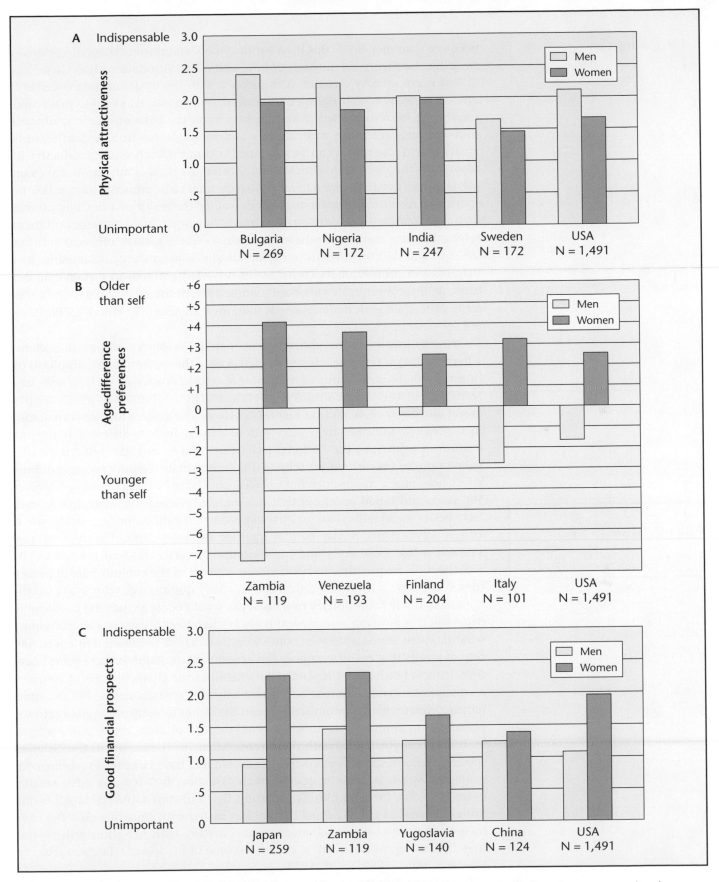

**Figure 3.6 Asymmetry of Male and Female Mating Preferences** The bars show representative findings from a cross-cultural survey of mating preferences. (The importance of physical attractiveness and good financial prospects was rated on a four-point scale ranging from "indispensable" to "unimportant." Age-difference preferences are simply the respondents' average preferred age difference between self and spouse.) (Source: Buss, 1989)

tus more than men do. Is this then a triumph of evolutionary theorizing? Should we judge the theory on the basis of how well it fits with data such as these?

This is not an easy question. Consistency with the available data is certainly one criterion by which theories are judged. Yet, nearly all of these predictions could have been made by the average person on the basis of everyday observation—without reference to evolution and reproductive fitness. Furthermore, nearly all of these results can be explained without reference to reproductive fitness or any inherited male-female differences in the basis of attraction. For example, the tendency for women in all known cultures to be attracted to men bearing status and material resources might very well be the result of a flexible, nonbiological adaptation to an environment in which women in all cultures find themselves. Because men everywhere have, on average, greater physical size and strength and do not suffer from the handicaps of pregnancy and nursing, men may have disproportionate control over material resources in virtually all cultures. Being economically vulnerable, women might therefore quite rationally be more concerned with material needs than men are (Eagly & Wood, 1999; Wood & Eagly, 2002).

One implication of this difference in material resources is that, in societies where the two sexes have relatively equal power, the greater female emphasis on finding a mate with status and economic resources should be lessened. In a reanalysis of the cross-cultural data collected by evolutionary psychologists, Wood and Eagly (2002) found just this pattern. The greater the gender equality in a society (as indicated by United Nations data on income differential, the proportion of women in the national legislature, and so on), the less importance women placed on earning capacity in a potential mate. Gender equality did not affect how much importance men placed on women's attractiveness, however. Yet, Eagly and Wood point out that it is widely believed that attractive women have better social skills than unattractive women (Eagly, Ashmore, Makhijani, & Longo, 1991). Thus, it may be that men are seeking potential mates with presumably better social skills, and commensurately better child-raising skills.

If the most frequently cited evidence in support of the evolutionary approach to sex differences in attraction can be so easily questioned, why buy into the approach at all? Evolutionary psychologists would counter that the best way to deal with this problem is the way it is always handled in science—by examining what happens across a range of conditions in an effort to obtain a nuanced pattern of results that no other theory can accommodate. Thus, broad evolutionary theorizing is bolstered by research that examines the characteristics of different species that inhabit different social and physical environments. For example, female primates vary in promiscuity, from the rather monogamous gibbon to the philandering chimpanzee. As it happens, the size of male testes across all primates is highly correlated with the extent of female promiscuity in the different species. Males in species with promiscuous females have large testes (chimps, for example), whereas those in species with "trustworthy" females have smaller testes (gibbons, for example). This pattern fits, and thus supports, broad evolutionary ideas. If a male's sexual partner has mated with someone else, the male increases his reproductive chances by also mating with her shortly thereafter, thereby besting his rival with the sheer volume of his sperm (Harcourt, Harvey, Larson & Short, 1980; Short, 1979).

Or consider those species such as the Panamanian poison-arrow frog in which it is the *male* who invests more in the offspring. Does the typical pattern of behavioral sex differences found so widely in the animal kingdom reverse in such species? Absolutely. The females in these species are typically larger than their male coun-

> "The mind is not sex-typed."
> —MARGARET MEAD

terparts, and they compete with one another more fiercely for the favors of the relatively choosy males (Trivers, 1985). Once again, the broader evolutionary theory is strengthened by the exception that "proves" (that is, tests) the rule.

To examine what happens across a broad range of conditions was, of course, precisely the point of the ambitious cross-cultural studies described earlier (Buss, 1989; Schmitt, 2003). The guiding logic has surface appeal: if the same sex differences show up in culture after culture, it is unlikely that they are the result of socialization practices (which, for many practices and institutions, vary so widely from culture to culture). But as we have just discussed, it is not clear how rigorous this logic is. The uniformity across cultures may be the indirect result of relatively simple differences between men and women in size and strength, and in gestation and lactation, that ultimately result in certain behavioral patterns—not the direct result of genetically inherited behavioral tendencies. In the end, cross-cultural studies like the ones described cannot overcome the problems they were designed to address. Ultimately, they never overcome the problem of resting on a sample size of one—the human species.

A second problem with the evolutionary account of sex differences in human mating behavior is that not all of the most celebrated findings can, in fact, be rigorously derived from evolutionary theory. Consider the prediction that men should value a potential mate's physical attractiveness more than women do. Unlike the prediction that men should emphasize youth more than women do (which is a straightforward derivation from male and female differences in length of lifetime fertility), this prediction is, if anything, *easier* to derive from everyday observation than from the theory of evolution. Stripped of its relationship with youth, physical attractiveness is simply not much of a cue to fertility. There may be some correlation between physical attractiveness and fertility, but it is mainly the result of the extremes at the lower end of both variables—certain gross physical pathologies lead to both an unpleasant appearance and reduced fertility. But shouldn't a tendency to avoid mating with such a person be at least as important to females as to males? After all, females have historically mated with fewer partners than men have, and so being tethered to an infertile partner is reproductively more catastrophic for women.

What, then, would count as truly unambiguous support for the evolutionary framework? The answer is simple: any empirical result that one would not discover without the guidance of evolutionary theory and that all other accounts would have difficulty explaining. There are some findings that may fit the bill. Recall our earlier discussion of bilateral symmetry and its relationship to physical attractiveness. Symmetrical individuals are sought out, the argument goes, because symmetry is a sign of "good genes," and combining a sexual partner's good genes with one's own increases the chances that one's own genes will survive and be passed on in future generations. This logic has led investigators to propose that symmetry ought to be particularly preferred in potential mates when the probability of conception is relatively high (the only time, after all, when issues of genetic transmission are relevant). Thus, in one study, women who were at various phases of their menstrual cycles were asked (we're not kidding) to sniff a number of T-shirts that had earlier been worn by a group of men who varied in their degree of bilateral symmetry. As the investigators anticipated, the T-shirts of the symmetrical men were judged to have a better aroma than those of less symmetrical men—but only by those women who were close to the ovulation phase of their menstrual cycle (Gangestad & Thornhill, 1998; Thornhill & Gangestad, 1999). It is unclear, of course, whether symmetrical men actually have a more appealing scent (to ovulating women, at least), or whether women simply associate such a scent with more attractive men. Either way, it is unlikely that anyone, without the help of evolutionary theory, would ever have predicted or sought to test such a relationship.

It has also been argued that the "strong jaw" of a particularly masculine-looking male face is also a sign of good genes. So, do women actually find such masculinized faces attractive? Not typically. In general, women rate slightly *feminized* faces as most attractive (Perrett et al., 1998). But when women are ovulating and the chances of conception following intercourse are highest, their preferences tend to shift toward more masculinized faces (Penton-Voak et al., 1999). This pattern, too, is one that would have been hard to anticipate without the guidance of the evolutionary perspective. Further studies along these lines have shown that women during the ovulatory phase of their menstrual cycle can more quickly recognize male faces as male (but not female faces as female) than during other times of the month, and that females during the ovulatory phase prefer men who pursue more confident, assertive, and competitive tactics of self-presentation (Gangestad, Simpson, Cousins, Garvar-Apgar, & Christensen, 2004; Macrae, Alnwick, Milne, & Schloerscheidt, 2002).

To our minds, studies such as these, which assess changes in judgments of attractiveness across biologically meaningful conditions, provide the strongest support for the evolutionary approach to human attraction. The field awaits further studies of this sort that go beyond simply documenting the male and female differences that most people have observed in their daily lives. Meanwhile, it is important to bear in mind that the broader theory of evolution is unsurpassed in its ability to explain many of the complicated behavioral patterns observed throughout the animal kingdom. Biological accounts of human behavior will always spark controversy, and one should remain skeptical of glib, overreaching accounts (Bem, 1993). Nonetheless, it would be hard to maintain that evolution has shaped the behavioral tendencies of every plant and animal on earth but not those of humans! History has not been kind to those who have argued that humans are "special," or fundamentally different from all other life on earth. Therefore, rather than simply dismissing evolutionary accounts of human behavioral tendencies (sex differences included), such accounts should be critically examined, and modified when necessary, to contribute to a fuller understanding of the origins of human behavior.

**LOOKING BACK,** we have seen that one of the most powerful determinants of interpersonal attraction is physical attractiveness. Physically attractive individuals are more popular with the opposite sex than are less attractive people, are evaluated more positively than less attractive people, and tend to have somewhat better social skills than less attractive individuals. The effects of physical attractiveness arise as early as infancy, are especially important for women's life outcomes, and appear to be based in part on biological predispositions, as certain elements of physical attractiveness may indicate reproductive fitness.

## THEORETICAL INTEGRATION

Thus far, we have examined three important causes of interpersonal attraction—proximity, similarity, and physical attractiveness. That each of these variables is related to attraction is not in itself surprising. Most of you have observed for yourselves that people often want to befriend physically attractive others who share their values and live nearby. The lessons to be learned—the *surprise,* if you will—is how *much* of an impact each of these variables has. This is perhaps particularly true of proximity: people typically abhor the thought that even their most cherished relationships could be so powerfully influenced by something that is often beyond their control.

In order for knowledge of interpersonal attraction to advance, however, social psychologists must do more than expand everyday intuitions about attraction. They must also integrate these determinants into a coherent conceptual framework or theory.

## THE REWARD PERSPECTIVE ON INTERPERSONAL ATTRACTION

One of the most widely accepted theories of interpersonal attraction has the virtue of simplicity: people tend to like those who provide them with rewards. The rewards need not be tangible, they need not be immediate, and they need not come from direct interaction. But according to this reward framework, we tend to like those who make us feel good (Clore & Byrne, 1974; Lott & Lott, 1974).

Here is a test: Think of all your friends and ask yourself whether the reward framework helps to explain your liking for them. Some of the rewards are easy to identify. Your friendship with one person, for example, may give you access to a clique to which you would otherwise not belong. You may like another person because she is hilarious, and because you have fun when you are around her. For many of your friends, however, the rewards may be more indirect and immaterial. Indeed, the very best friends are those whose rewards may be the most indirect of all: they are the ones who make you feel good about yourself when you are around them.

The reward framework certainly fits with the three influences we have discussed in this chapter. Being with physically attractive others can bring rewards by pleasing our senses or by boosting our status in the eyes of others. Being with similar others is rewarding because they validate our views, they can be counted on to like us, and interactions with them tend to go smoothly. Evolutionary accounts of heterosexual attraction likewise fit this theory: we tend to be attracted to those who seem likely to increase our reproductive fitness and thus bring about the ultimate reward of passing our genes on to future generations. The evolutionary perspective is a specific variant of the reward perspective.

The reward framework applies less well to the impact of proximity on attraction, but even here there is a connection. Because we know we will often encounter those who live nearby, we make sure to be on our best behavior as we approach each encounter with them. As a consequence, the interactions tend to go well, and we walk away pleased (and therefore rewarded) by the other person.

The reward framework also helps in identifying other potential influences on interpersonal attraction. Indeed, the reward perspective can provide a basis for answering that most practical of questions: What can you do to get others to like you? From what we have discussed thus far, it would seem wise to get an apartment near the mailbox, steer clear of anomalous opinions, and wash your hair regularly. The reward perspective goes further. If you want people to like you, reward them. Make other people feel good about themselves when they are around you. This is reminiscent of the advice given by Dale Carnegie in his phenomenally popular book *How to Win Friends and Influence People*: To win friends you should, "Dole out praise lavishly."

It might seem that such a strategy would backfire. People surely see through

William Gladstone and Benjamin Disraeli alternated being Prime Minister of Britain in the latter half of the nineteenth century. An English gentlewoman once reported that, a few weeks before, she had been seated next to Gladstone at dinner and felt that he was the most interesting man in London. Shortly thereafter, she was seated next to Disraeli and felt that she was the most interesting woman in London. Who do you think was the better politician—Gladstone or Disraeli?

most efforts at ingratiation and resent the attempt to influence them. Wealthy individuals, for example, are surely alert to the existence of "gold diggers" who feign affection in an effort to get them to part with their money. Nevertheless, there probably wouldn't be a term "gold digger" if a considerable number were not successful in their quest. This suggests that ingratiation may be more effective than perhaps it "should" be. Flattery may get you pretty far after all (Jones, 1964; Vonk, 2002).

The reward theory of interpersonal attraction is not without its critics. For example, studies have shown that we are not always most enamored of those who reward us the most. Someone who consistently sings our praises is not always liked more than someone who is initially less positive and then comes around to see our virtues (Aronson & Linder, 1965; Mettee, Taylor, & Friedman, 1973; but see also Berscheid, Brothen, & Graziano, 1976). This finding does not fit with a straightforward derivation of the reward framework because the person who liked us from the beginning has provided us with more rewards and therefore should earn more of our affection.

But note that such findings are not really at variance with reward theory once a broader perspective on rewards is adopted. The person who is initially cool to us but then warms up, for example, might very well provide us with the most rewards because we experience the additional pleasure of getting such a person to come around to our side. In addition, it can be more gratifying to earn the affections of someone who is discerning than someone who doles out praise indiscriminately.

## THE SOCIAL EXCHANGE PERSPECTIVE ON INTERPERSONAL ATTRACTION

The reward perspective on interpersonal attraction is really just one variant of a broader class of theories that view much of human interaction as manifestations of **social exchange**. These theories start from the very economic assumption that people's preeminent motivation is to maximize their own utility (or feeling of satisfaction). People seek out rewards in their interactions with others, and they are willing to pay certain costs in order to obtain them. Typically, people desire interactions or relationships in which the rewards exceed the costs. Such interactions yield a net gain in utility. If rewarding interactions are not available, however, an individual is likely to seek out those interactions in which the costs exceed the rewards by the smallest amount. More generally, social exchange theories posit that people tend to pursue those interactions that yield the most favorable difference between rewards and costs. (Note however, that too large a discrepancy between rewards and costs can sometimes be aversive. Indeed, **equity theory** maintains that people are also motivated to pursue fairness, or equity, in which rewards and costs are shared equally among individuals.)

Although it can be a bit jarring to view our inter-

---

"We always do believe in praise of ourselves. Even when we know it is not disinterested, we think it is deserved."

—DAVID LODGE, *THINKS*

**social exchange theory** A theory based on the fact that there are costs and rewards in all relationships, and that how people feel about a relationship depends on their assessments of its costs and rewards, and the costs and rewards available to them in other relationships.

**equity theory** A theory that maintains that people are motivated to pursue fairness, or equity, in their relationships, with rewards and costs shared roughly equally among individuals.

*"Will he ever be able to produce revenue again!"*

actions with others in such harsh economic terms, the central notion that people are mindful of costs and benefits has been stressed by many observers of the human condition. This notion has been expressed, for example, by individuals as varied as the seventeenth-century French writer François de La Rochefoucauld ("Friendship is a scheme for the mutual exchange of personal advantages and favors.") to the twentieth-century American economist Thomas Schelling ("Aside from everything else that it is, marriage in this country is a voluntary contractual arrangement between people who are free to shop around."). The notion of "shopping around" is key to the social exchange perspective: people are seen by social exchange theorists as shopping around for the interactions that yield the most favorable trade-offs of costs and benefits.

**LOOKING BACK,** we have seen that the reward perspective on interpersonal attraction maintains that people tend to like those who provide them with rewards, including both immediate and deferred rewards, tangible and intangible rewards. The social exchange perspective maintains that people are motivated to maximize their own utility (satisfaction) and generally desire interactions in which rewards exceed costs, whereas equity theory maintains that people seek equity, or equally shared rewards and costs. When applied to the subject of interpersonal attraction, the social exchange perspective implies that people will be most attracted to those who provide the most rewards at the least cost. But because costs and benefits are exchanged in the context of a relationship that unfolds over time, the role of exchange in attraction is really just one facet of the broader issue of the role of exchange in relationships, the topic to which we turn in the next chapter.

> "A proposal of marriage in our society tends to be a way in which a man sums up his social attributes and suggests to a woman that hers are not so much better as to preclude a merger or a partnership in these matters."
>
> —ERVING GOFFMAN

> "Love is often nothing but a favorable exchange between two people who get the most of what they can expect, considering their value on the . . . market."
>
> —ERICH FROMM

## SUMMARY

1. A major determinant of who we end up being attracted to is *propinquity*, or sheer closeness of contact with potential targets of attraction. To a remarkable extent, the people one knows, and likes, and even loves, are those with whom one comes in contact most frequently in neighborhoods, on the job, and in recreational settings.

2. Three reasons for the power of propinquity are: (a) sheer *availability*: one has to come into contact with others to have a chance to know and like them, (b) *anticipation of interaction:* people tend to put their best foot forward for those they know they will see again, and (c) the *mere exposure effect*: simply encountering a person or object, even under negative circumstances, makes us like the target more.

3. A second major source of attraction is *similarity*. Engaged couples are more similar to one another than are randomly paired men and women. Studies using the *bogus stranger* paradigm invariably find that people like individuals who resemble them more than individuals who do not. There is scant evidence that "opposites attract."

4. Four reasons for the effect of similarity on attraction are: (a) similar others validate our beliefs and values, (b) similarity facilitates smooth interactions, (c) we expect similar others to like us (which is rewarding), and (d) similar others have qualities we like.

5. *Physical attractiveness* is another major source of attraction. Physically attractive people are much more popular with the opposite sex. Attractive peo-

ple are given higher grades for their work. People who are physically attractive earn more money in the workplace, and they even receive lower sentences for crimes. In short, they benefit from a halo effect, in that they are believed to have many positive qualities that go beyond their physical appearance.

6. Attractiveness has an impact even in infancy and childhood: attractive infants receive more attention from their mothers, and attractive children are believed to be more intelligent by their teachers. People think a transgression by a child is less serious if the child is attractive. Moreover, even three-month-olds will look longer at an attractive face than at an unattractive one.

7. *Gender* is an important variable when it comes to attractiveness, with physical appearance affecting the lives of women more than men. Women deemed unattractive at work suffer worse outcomes than men who are considered unattractive.

8. Physical attractiveness has such impact because: (a) it has immediacy—you see it before any other virtues or faults, (b) the attractiveness of one's friends and partner affects one's prestige, and (c) biology plays a role—that is, we are wired to appreciate some kinds of physical appearance more than others.

9. Evolutionary psychologists argue that our biology prompts an attraction to features that signify *reproductive fitness*—that is, the capacity to perpetuate our genes in future generations if we were to mate and have children with a person who possesses those features. These include physical characteristics that signal vitality, fertility, and likely reproductive success.

10. Evolutionary psychologists also claim that there are biologically based differences between men and women in the importance placed on attractiveness and in the determinants of attractiveness.

11. In species in which parental investment is greater for the female, the males must compete vigorously among themselves (*intrasex competition*) for access to choosy females. The males also must compete for the females' attention (*intersex attraction*) and, as such, they are typically the louder and gaudier of the species.

12. In the human species, say the evolutionary psychologists, differential parental investment on the part of men and women leads women to prefer fewer sexual partners than men. It leads men to prefer women whose physical appearance gives the impression that they will be fertile—for example, features such as smooth skin and a waist that is narrow in relation to hips. Women are attracted to men who can be expected to provide for them and for their children—men who are strong, industrious, and have social status.

13. Though much evidence from the animal kingdom and from the study of humans supports the hypotheses of the evolutionists, most of the human findings can be explained without resort to an evolutionary explanation. The strongest support for the evolutionary approach to attractiveness in humans comes from studies showing that women increase their preference for attractive (or at least symmetrical) and masculine men during the ovulatory phase of their menstrual cycles, when they have a relatively higher probability of conceiving.

14. The notion of *reward* can explain most of the reasons we like people—we tend to like those who provide us with the greatest rewards (broadly construed).

15. Another way to understand attraction is in terms of *social exchange*. This theory holds that people pursue those interactions that provide the most favorable difference between rewards and costs.

## CRITICAL THINKING ABOUT BASIC PRINCIPLES

1. Most (but by no means all) evolutionary psychologists are male. How do you think an evolutionary approach to attraction might be different if it were taken up by many more female researchers? What predictions might we see advanced and tested that are different from those we see now? Are there any "twists" on currently advanced claims that might be made?

2. In the run-up to the 2004 U.S. presidential election, many households put up "Bush Must Go" signs in their front yards. The motive, clearly, was to influence undecided voters to vote against the incumbent president, George W. Bush. Do any of the ideas presented in this chapter give one reason to believe that the effort might have backfired, and actually *increased* support for Bush?

3. Evolutionary psychology is the idea that behavioral predispositions, in the same way as anatomy and physiology, are determined by genes and passed on from generation to generation. This idea has been derided by some as "just so" theorizing because its advocates provide evolutionary explanations that fit (like Rudyard Kipling's "just so" stories) the behavior patterns we observe "just so." Can you think of any examples for which this criticism seems valid? Can you think of any for which it is invalid?

## KEY TERMS

complementarity (p. 101)

counterbalancing (p. 92)

equity theory (p. 124)

functional distance (p. 90)

halo effect (p. 106)

intersex attraction (p. 116)

intrasex competition (p. 116)

mere exposure effect (p. 93)

propinquity (p. 89)

reproductive fitness (p. 112)

self-fulfilling prophecy (p. 107)

social exchange theory (p. 124)

sociometric survey (p. 90)

## FURTHER READING

Cash, T. F., & Pruzinsky, T. (Eds.). (1990). *Body images: Development, deviance, and change.* New York: Guilford Press.

Etcoff, N. L. (1999). *Survival of the prettiest: The science of beauty.* New York: Doubleday.

Fredrickson, B. L., & Roberts, T. (1997). Objectification theory: Toward understanding women's lived experiences and mental health risks. *Psychology of Women Quarterly, 21,* 173–206.

Miller, G. (2000). *The mating mind: How sexual choice shaped the evolution of human nature.* New York: Doubleday.

Regan, P. C., & Berscheid, E. (1999). *Lust: What we know about human sexual desire.* Thousand Oaks, CA: Sage.

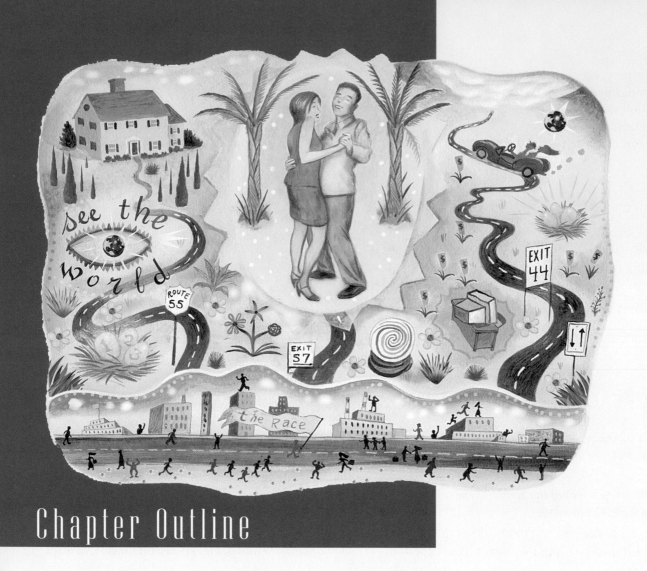

# Chapter Outline

# CHAPTER 4

# Relationships

O n a chilly January morning in 1800, a filthy, stark-naked, twelve-year-old boy, scampering around on all fours, was spotted digging for potatoes in the fields of the French village of Saint Sernin. He had survived for years on his own in the forest scavenging for acorns and hunting small animals. The owner of the field captured the wild-eyed, frightened boy, and took him home.

The boy, soon to be named Victor, had many difficulties living inside the owner's house. He prowled restlessly on all fours, and refused to wear clothes. He defecated in public without shame, and rejected all food except acorns and potatoes. His communication was restricted to grunts, howls, and bursts of wild laughter. He was unresponsive to human language, but would turn quickly at the sounds of nuts being cracked. He showed no interest in humans, except fear, and never smiled, cried, or met the gaze of other people.

Eventually, Jean Itard, a twenty-six-year-old doctor from the Paris Deaf-Mute Institute, took Victor, known as the "Wild Boy of Aveyron," into his custody, and devoted five years to teaching Victor language and human ways. Victor could learn only a few words, but he did learn to wear clothes, sleep in beds, eat at a table, and take baths. He came to feel real affection for Jean Itard, but he never learned much in the way of human decorum. At a dinner party at a wealthy socialite's home, where Dr. Itard hoped to show off Victor's progress, Victor wolfed down his food, stuffed desserts into his pockets, stripped to his underwear, and leaped through the trees like a squirrel. Victor eventually died in his forties, house trained but wild, fearful, and virtually mute (Itard, 1801/1962).

There are over thirty-five documented cases of feral (wild) children like Victor, who grew up in the wild on their own. They have long provoked the human imagination, for they promise an answer to an age-old question: What is human nature, stripped of all the influences of society and civilization? Without parents or other adults to raise them, cut off from human family, friends, and groups, such children do not develop language, morals, or manners; they remain largely unresponsive to other people and cannot function in social settings; they show no sexual interest in the opposite sex; and they lack self-awareness. Their lives highlight the core theme of this chapter: relationships are central to human functioning. And, in fact, relationships help to create human nature.

In contrast to the impoverished bonds between Victor and other humans were the strong bonds forged between six young German-Jewish Holocaust survivors whose parents had died in gas chambers. When they were between the ages of six and twelve months, these children had all been sent to Terezin, a concentration camp in Czechoslovakia. While they were cared for in the camp by fellow inmates, they did not develop relationships with their caregivers, since these adults were likely to disappear quickly from their lives, but they did form strong attachments to each other. After the war, the children were taken to England, and they continued to maintain the strong bonds they had forged with each other, fearing separation, clinging to each other, and helping each other to adjust to their new circumstances (Freud & Dann, 1951). These children learned to speak, learned manners and morals, and eventually learned to forge positive relations with adults. The relationships that they had with each other saved them from the fate of Victor and other feral children like him.

What, then, does social psychology have to say about relationships? This chapter moves beyond the topic of attraction, which we discussed in the last chapter, to the question of how attraction and other variables make themselves felt in ongoing personal relationships. We start the chapter by characterizing what relationships are and then consider how central they are to our functioning. We review evidence for the claim that humans have a basic need for relationships, and then ask how relationships affect our sense of self, our social cognition, and our emotions. We then turn to a theory—attachment theory—that seeks answers to a difficult question: What are the origins of our patterns of relating to others? We will discover that our early attachment style, established

**Feral Children and Social Deficits**
Victor, the Wild Boy of Aveyron, was a feral child who grew up alone in the woods, without human contact, until he was about twelve years old. Although he eventually learned to wear clothes, to eat at a table, and to say some words, he was never comfortable in highly socialized settings, he never developed complex language skills, and he did not develop strong attachments with people. His lack of early relationships with other humans affected his social functioning for his entire life.

in our relations with our parents, lays an important foundation for our romantic relations and personal difficulties later in life. We then examine the different ways of relating to others, and how these are affected by our underlying assumptions about the basis of the relationship. We discuss communal, family-like relationships, and exchange, equity-based relationships. Then we continue with a discussion of power and hierarchical relationships. We conclude with a discussion of perhaps the most mysterious and compelling relationship, the romantic bond. We examine the romantic relationship, asking which relationships will flourish and which will languish. We consider the causes of divorce and marital dissatisfaction, as well as what makes for fulfilling romantic relations.

## CHARACTERIZING RELATIONSHIPS

While we discussed attraction and first impressions in Chapter 3, in this chapter we discuss **interpersonal relationships**, attachments in which bonds of family or friendship or love or respect or hierarchy tie together two or more individuals over an extended period of time. Relationships are generally characterized by an interdependence in which the individuals think about, influence, and engage in joint activities or have joint memories of shared experiences.

> **interpersonal relationships**
> Attachments in which bonds of family or friendship or love or respect or hierarchy tie together two or more individuals over an extended period of time.

Within social psychology, the study of relationships is relatively recent (Duck, 1997; Hartup & Stevens, 1997). The problems in studying relationships are different from those that we will encounter elsewhere in the book (Bradbury & Karney, 1993; Gonzalez & Griffin, 1997; Karney & Bradbury, 1995). Many of the studies we will review in this chapter are not true experiments with random assignment of participants to different conditions. Instead, these studies look at the dynamics of relationships that have already formed. This kind of research faces a challenging methodological problem called self-selection. You will recall that this occurs whenever investigators do not have control over assignment of participants to the conditions that are to be compared. When participants "select" their own condition, we can never know in what ways—other than the particular condition they are in—they may differ from other participants. In the case of Victor and other feral children, it seems reasonable to assume that their profound isolation led them to develop in abnormal ways. Yet, we have to ask ourselves: Why exactly were these children abandoned by their parents? Were they strange, unusually difficult and fussy, or unresponsive to others? Were their parents themselves unbalanced?

We would reach very different conclusions depending on the answers to these questions. Lacking the ability to perform an actual experiment—randomly assigning some children to a "grow up alone" condition—we cannot know for sure if we are seeing the effects of severe social deprivation or some other set of factors. As it happens, Harry Harlow (1959) performed a classic series of experiments with baby rhesus monkeys that give us reason to think that the evidence about feral children means what it seems to—that they suffer from the severe effects of social deprivation. Some monkeys were raised without contact with other rhesus monkeys but with access to two "mother surrogates"—props vaguely resembling monkeys. One was a wire contraption that gave the infant food; the other was covered with terry cloth. The monkeys spent most of their time cling-

**Reactions to Early Social Isolation**
Infant rhesus monkeys raised without contact with other monkeys crave contact but have difficulty interacting once they do encounter others of their kind. (A) As infants, they prefer a terry-cloth "mother" to a wire "mother" with a bottle that feeds them, as they want contact comfort. (B) Later, in situations with other monkeys, they show extreme fear, inappropriate social behavior, and an inability to interact as other monkeys do.

ing to the terry-cloth mother, and when they were frightened they rushed to the terry-cloth mother for comfort.

Much like feral children, monkeys raised in isolation were in no way normal when they reached adolescence. As adolescents, they were highly fearful, could not interact with their peers, and engaged in inappropriate sexual behaviors—for example, attacking potential mates or failing to display typical sexual positions during copulation.

It is not just monkeys and people who require social interaction to be fully functioning members of their species. A natural experiment with elephants makes a similar point. You will recall that a natural experiment involves an accidentally produced set of conditions (rather than conditions created by an experimenter) that largely avoids self-selection problems. Elephants in some areas of Africa have been slaughtered for the ivory in their tusks, leaving young elephants to grow up on their own, much like the wild boy of Aveyron or Harlow's rhesus monkeys. These adolescent elephants are quite antisocial and aggressive, not only toward their own species but toward others as well, killing rhinoceroses for sport, for example. African gamekeepers have solved the problem of the wild elephants by importing adult elephants to show them how to be elephants. Even elephants have a culture that has to be learned if they are to be proper members of their species.

## THE IMPORTANCE OF RELATIONSHIPS

Most Westerners believe in the sanctity of the individual. People from Western cultures often seek to find out who they are in solitary rites of passage—for example, while backpacking in the woods or engaging in quiet contemplation. While these ideas and practices are no doubt appealing, they ignore a deeper truth: human nature is profoundly social and is shaped by our relationships. In the first section of the chapter, we will examine how this is so. We will see that humans have what appears to be a biological need to belong in relationships. We will discover that our sense of self, which for many, particularly those from individualist backgrounds, seems autonomous and separate from others, is in fact continually shaped by our past relationships. In addition, we will look at evidence showing that our basic cognitive processes and our emotions and well-being are also shaped by our relationships.

> "We are all in this together, by ourselves."
> —LILY TOMLIN

## THE NEED TO BELONG

It is self-evident that humans have biologically based needs for food, oxygen, warmth, and safety. Without these needs, we cannot survive. Roy Baumeister and Mark Leary claim that the same is true for relationships: we have a need to be embedded in healthy relationships, sharing bonds with family members, romantic partners, friends, and fellow group members. This was certainly apparent in the studies of feral children and Harlow's monkeys. In collectivist cultures, as we shall see throughout this book, the sense of self is deeply rooted in connection to others. Yet, even in individualistic cultures, people derive their sense of self in part from the reactions of significant others. How do we evaluate whether humans do have a need to belong? Baumeister and Leary (1995) propose five criteria, which will help guide our discussion of relationships throughout this chapter.

First, there should be an *evolutionary basis* for our most important relationships (Simpson & Kenrick, 1998). Relationships help individuals and offspring survive, thus contributing to the increased likelihood of the replication of the individual's genes. Long-term romantic bonds evolved, to a large extent, in order to facilitate reproduction and to raise human offspring, who are especially vulnerable and dependent for many years (Ellis, 1992; Ellis & Malamuth, 2000; Emlen, 1997; Fisher, 1992; Hrdy, 1999). Parent-offspring attachments ensure that infants and children have sufficient protection to survive until they can function independently (Bowlby, 1969/1982; Buss, 1994b; Daly, Salmon, & Wilson, 1997). Friendships evolved as a means for nonkin to cooperate and to avoid the costs and

**The Need to Belong** There is an evolutionary basis for the need to belong. (A) Not only do elephant parents feed and protect young elephants, but they teach them appropriate social behavior that enables them to live in groups. If the young elephants grow up without adults, they are likely to become anti-social and aggressive and have difficulty living in groups. (B) Primates have a need to belong, as evidenced in this photo showing a friendship between a female (left) and male olive baboon. They groom each other frequently, rest together, and enhance each other's reproductive fitness.

perils of competition and aggression (Dunn & Herrera, 1997; Fehr, 1996; Palombit, Seyfarth, & Cheney, 1997; Smuts, 1985; Trivers, 1971).

Second, if relationships have an evolutionary basis and there is a basic need to belong, then they should also be *universal*. We should see similar kinds of dynamics between romantic partners, parents and children, siblings, friends, and group members in different cultures around the world. In the chapter on attraction, for example, we saw that in different cultures women assign greater weight to a potential mate's resources than men do, whereas men more heavily value the beauty of a potential mate than women do, although there is considerable cultural variation in what resources are of value and who is considered beautiful (see Chapter 3). In other sections of this chapter, we will consider universality and cultural variation in relationships.

Third, if the need to belong is the product of millions of years of evolution, it should *guide social cognition*, just as hunger momentarily heightens our sensitivity to the odors and sights that promise food. The motivation to form and maintain healthy relationships with family members, romantic partners, friends, and group members should govern how we construe people, situations, and events. Social psychologists have been quite active in assessing this thesis. Relationships do, in fact, exert a powerful influence upon how we define our selves, what we remember, and the attributions we make (Baldwin, 1992; Karney & Coombs, 2000; Reis & Downey, 1999).

Fourth, the need to belong should be *satiable*. Thus, in specific relationships, it should motivate thoughts and behaviors, much as thirst and hunger do, until the need is satisfied. Consider one kind of relationship that is important to us all—friendship. In Western European cultures, college students tend to restrict their intimate, meaningful interactions to, on average, about six friends (Wheeler & Nezlek, 1977). It seems that we satisfy our need for frequent, stable, and meaningful friendships with a limited number of close friends, and once that is satisfied, we no longer seek it in other contacts. But if the need to belong is no longer satisfied in existing relationships, individuals will be motivated to seek to satisfy that need in other relationships. Observational studies in prisons, for example, find that prisoners suffer great anguish at the loss of contact with their family. As a result, they often form substitute families based on kinship-like ties with other prisoners (Burkhart, 1973).

Finally, if the need to belong is chronically unmet, as we saw with feral children and Harlow's monkeys, the individual should *suffer profound negative consequences*. Here the evidence is robust, supporting the assertion that relationships

> "No more fiendish punishment could be devised, were such a thing physically possible, than that one should be turned loose in society and remain absolutely unnoticed by all the members thereof."
>
> —WILLIAM JAMES

**Universality of Relationships**
Siblings in different cultures all play, support, and fight with each other, although the specific kinds of play, support, and conflict may vary according to the culture.

are essential to our physical and mental well-being (Myers, 2000b). In the chapter on emotion, we will see that having healthy relationships is a major determinant of how happy people are (see Chapter 12). Later in this chapter, we will cite other findings showing that friendship and happy marriages promote well-being and longer life. For the moment, consider the following findings: Numerous studies find that mortality rates are higher for divorced, unmarried, and widowed individuals (Lynch, 1979). Being integrated into a rich web of friendships and groups, on the other hand, is associated with lower mortality rates (Berkman, 1995). In one study in Alameda County, California, people who lacked ties to others were 1.9 to 3.1 times more likely to have died nine years later, depending on the gender and background of the individual (Berkman & Syme, 1979). Admissions to hospitals for psychological problems are three to twenty-three times higher for divorced than for married individuals, depending on the study and nature of the psychological problems in question (Bloom, White, & Asher, 1979). Suicide rates are higher for single and divorced individuals (Rothberg & Jones, 1987). So, too, are crime rates (Baumeister &

*"Ezra, I'm not inviting you to my birthday party, because our relationship is no longer satisfying to my needs."*

Leary, 1995). Breast cancer patients who participated in weekly sessions of emotionally supportive group therapy survived eighteen months longer than women in a nonintervention control group (Spiegel, Bloom, Kraemer & Gottheil, 1989). More generally, having a lot of support from others strengthens our cardiovascular, immune, and endocrine systems (Oxman & Hull, 1997; Uchino, Cacioppo, & Kiecolt-Glaser, 1996).

It would seem, then, that humans have a basic need to belong, to connect, to be embedded in a rich network of relationships. Relationships seem to have an evolutionary basis, and thus they are a universal part of human nature. They motivate thoughts and behaviors until satisfied, and without them, we suffer both physically and psychologically. Let's now take a closer look at how our relationships shape our sense of self.

## RELATIONSHIPS AND THE SENSE OF SELF

You may have had the experience of interacting with someone who reminds you of an old friend, your brother or sister, your mother or father, or an old love interest. Such an encounter might take you back to a different sense of self and a different set of emotions that you hadn't felt for some time. In the presence of someone who reminds you of a grammar school bully, for example, you might feel anxious, weak, and persecuted for no seemingly rational reason. Our past relationships shape our current interactions.

Susan Andersen and Serena Chen have offered a fascinating account called **relational self theory**, which examines how prior relationships shape our current beliefs, feelings, and interactions (Andersen & Chen, 2002). They argue that an important part of the self-concept is the **relational self**, which refers to the beliefs, feelings, and expectations about our selves that derive from our relation-

**relational self theory** A theory that examines how prior relationships shape our current beliefs, feelings, and interactions vis-à-vis people who remind us of significant others from our past.

**relational self** The beliefs, feelings, and expectations about our selves that derive from our relationships with significant others in our lives.

ships with significant others in our lives. There are likely to be different relational selves that derive from our relationships with our parents, our romantic partners, our friends, and authority figures. When we encounter someone who reminds us of a significant other, a specific relational self is activated, as are the associated feelings, beliefs, and self-evaluations, which then shape our interactions with that new individual, often without our awareness. Your mom might have thought that you were incorrigibly lazy, and she might have been critical of your accomplishments and efforts. Around her, you might have felt mild shame and inadequacy. When you encounter someone who resembles your mom, say a professor or a traffic court judge, Andersen and Chen contend that these beliefs, feelings, and interaction patterns will likely be transferred to that person, and they will shape the content of the new relationship.

To document that past relationships shape our current beliefs, feelings, and interactions, Andersen and her colleagues developed the following experimental technique. In a pretest session, participants first write down fourteen descriptive sentences about a positive significant other—namely, someone they like and feel close to—and a negative significant other—namely, someone they don't like and want to avoid. Participants typically write about parents, siblings, and friends. Two weeks later, participants engage in a study of acquaintanceship with another participant, who actually does not exist, but is purported to be in another room. Participants are given a description of this other person that either resembles the participant's own positive or negative significant other, or, in a control condition, the positive or negative significant other of another participant. To what extent do our relationships with significant others transfer to new people who resemble that person? A great deal, as we will see.

First of all, interacting with someone who resembles a significant other alters our working self-concept—that is, how we think about ourselves in the current moment. In one study, after describing a significant other, participants wrote down twenty sentences that described what they were like with that person (Hinkley & Andersen, 1996). Two weeks later, participants were exposed to descriptions of a new person who resembled their significant other or someone else's, and they then listed fourteen statements describing themselves. Participants exposed to a new person reminiscent of their significant other were more likely to describe themselves in terms that resembled what they are like with that significant other than were participants in the control condition. For example, if a participant listed traits like "silly" and "irreverent" when describing what she was like with her father, these traits were more likely to appear in her self-description two weeks later after encountering someone who reminded her of her father. Thus, encountering people who remind us of significant others alters how we think about ourselves in the current situation, often at an automatic level, shaping the more immediate, accessible thoughts we have about ourselves in any particular context.

Encountering people who remind us of significant others also shapes our emotional lives. To examine this claim, Andersen and her colleagues assessed participants' facial expressions as they were exposed to information about a new person who resembled either a positive or a negative significant other (Andersen, Reznik, & Manzella, 1996). Those participants who read about someone who resembled a positive significant other as compared to a negative significant other expressed more positive emotion as judged by their facial expressions, and they liked the new person more. This may account for the common experience of just feeling good about someone, or feeling bad about someone who, for no explicable reason, gives you the creeps. Perhaps the new person resembles a significant other in your life, good or bad, and you transfer your feelings about your significant other onto the new person. Our leaders are not immune to these transference phenomena. President Harry S Truman is said to have trusted Joseph Stalin at first because, although Truman knew him to be a wicked man in many respects, he reminded Truman of "Boss Pendergast" of the Missouri Democratic machine—a man who was thoroughly corrupt but always aboveboard in his dealings with Truman.

The relational self not only activates specific self-beliefs and emotions, it also shapes our current interactions. In one illustrative study, participants, whom we'll call perceivers, interacted with another participant, whom we'll call the target (Berk & Andersen, 2000). In the usual fashion, the experimenter manipulated whether the target resembled a positive or negative significant other of the perceiver. Participants liked a new person who resembled a positive significant other more than a person who resembled a negative significant other or other people's significant others, and the well-liked new person was more likely to show positive emotion toward the participant, as you can see in Figure 4.1. The process seems to be: (1) the target reminds me of good old X, (2) I therefore like the target, (3) so I express positive affect toward the target, and (4) as a consequence, the target expresses positive affect toward me.

Clearly one message from this research on the relational self is that we should try to surround ourselves with people who remind us of positive individuals in our lives. We should also be wary of our immediate, gut dislikes of people, for those reactions may have more to do with previous relationships than with the new person in our life. The broader lesson is that our relationships with significant others can shape our emotions, our self-evaluations, and our behavior in new relationships.

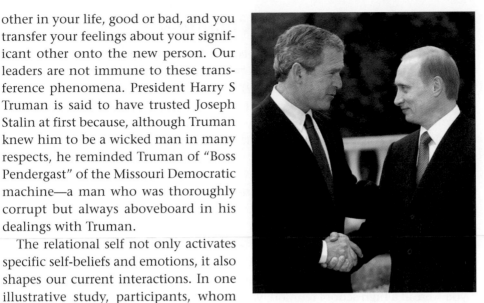

**Relational Self Theory and Transference Phenomena** Sometimes a new person resembles a significant other from our past, which affects how we react to him or her. When George W. Push met Vladimir Putin for the first time, he reported that he looked into Putin's eyes and saw he could trust him. Is it possible that Bush saw in Putin a reminder of some person who was generally seen as threatening but was personally reasonable in his dealings with Bush?

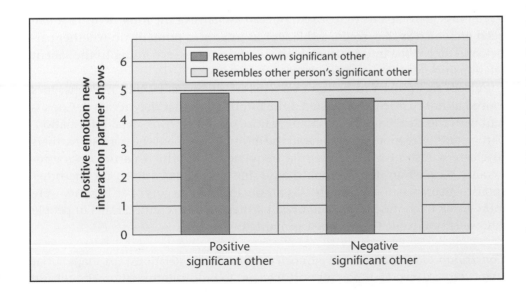

**Figure 4.1 The Relational Self and Interactions with Others** New interaction partners are more likely to express positive emotion toward us when they remind us of positive significant others. In this study, Berk and Andersen had participants interact with someone who reminded them of a positive or negative significant other in their own lives, or someone else's significant other. The researchers then coded those interactions for the amount of positive emotion showed by the new interaction partner. As you can see, the new interaction partner expressed more positive emotion toward the participant when he or she reminded the participant of a positive significant other. (Source: Adapted from Berk & Andersen, 2000)

## RELATIONSHIPS AND SOCIAL COGNITION

Andersen and Chen's relational self theory offers an enduring insight: how we construe our social worlds is often shaped by our long-standing personal relationships (see also Baldwin, 1992, 1999). Let's look more specifically at this general claim by considering three recent discoveries: (1) relationships influence important categories that help organize how we construe social information, (2) we construe close others as we construe ourselves, and (3) we share social construals with close others.

***Relationships as Organizing Categories***    When you encounter situations or people, you can rely on many different categories to organize and remember the wealth of information. You could rely on physical categories (that person has enormous ears), culture-related categories (she's from the South), or even moral categories (he's lying yet again). Relationships likewise can be categories that help us to process, store, and recall social information (Fiske, 1992). For example, if you were at a high school reunion, you might selectively attend to the complex stream of interactions in terms of relationships ("hey, my old friends are all laughing," "the popular girls are still snubbing everyone," "all my old rivals have lost their hair").

To test the hypothesis that relationships act as important, organizing categories, Constantine Sedikides and his colleagues presented participants with five pieces of information about eight different people, half of whom were female and half of whom were male (Sedikides, Olsen, & Reis, 1993). For example, the participants read the following about Eric: "is blond," "favorite actor is Robert De Niro," "is a member of the Rotary Club," and "has never traveled outside of Wisconsin." The participants read the following information about Rose: "takes vacations at Daytona Beach," "wakes up at 5 a.m. every day," "favorite TV show is *L.A. Law*," and "is fascinated by modern art." In all conditions, a male was paired with a female (for example, Eric was listed right above Rose). In one condition, participants were told that the four female-male dyads were married, and the members of each couple were identified. In the other condition, participants were told that the targets were married to an unspecified other. Thus, in one condition, participants read the items about Eric and Rose and believed that they were a married couple; in the other condition, they read the same information but did not believe that Eric and Rose were married to each other. After a 2.5-minute distracter task, participants were asked to recall as many of the forty items that had been presented as they could. Sedikides was interested primarily in whether participants stored the information about the eight people according to the salient relationship category—namely, married partners.

Indeed, this proved to be the case. First of all, Sedikides and his colleagues looked at how participants clustered the information that they recalled. Consistent with the idea that relationships organize our memory of social information, participants were more likely to recall the information about the married partners in clusters. Also of interest was the frequency with which participants erroneously recalled an item for one spouse that was actually given for the other spouse. Again relationships acted as an organizing category: participants were more likely to confuse traits in married partners than to confuse traits in people who were not explicitly described as married.

***Construing Close Others as We Construe Ourselves***    Relationships shape social cognition in a second important way: we tend to process information about close

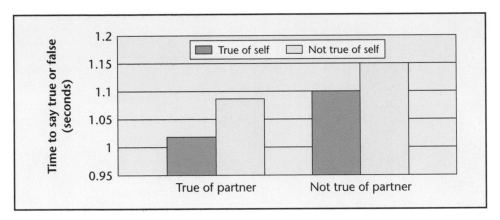

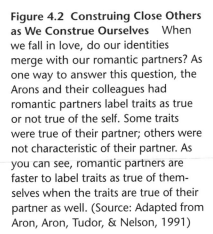

**Figure 4.2 Construing Close Others as We Construe Ourselves**   When we fall in love, do our identities merge with our romantic partners? As one way to answer this question, the Arons and their colleagues had romantic partners label traits as true or not true of the self. Some traits were true of their partner; others were not characteristic of their partner. As you can see, romantic partners are faster to label traits as true of themselves when the traits are true of their partner as well. (Source: Adapted from Aron, Aron, Tudor, & Nelson, 1991)

others much as we process information about ourselves. In estimating the likelihood of future events, we are unrealistically optimistic about the bright futures of our close friends, much as we are optimistic about our own future (Perloff & Fetzer, 1986). In explaining close others' behaviors, we are prone to the same biases that we have when explaining our own behavior. Thus, for the self and close others, in Western European cultures and other cultures as well, we attribute successes to dispositional factors, and failures to situational factors (Fincham & Bradbury, 1993). For example, when a close friend fails to hand in a paper on time, you might find yourself coming up with the same explanations that you would use to justify your own actions. You might think of a sickness in the family or a very rare computer malfunction as opposed to the possibility that he's just lazy or uninterested.

Aron and Aron have integrated these findings into a **self-expansion account of relationships**, which holds that people enter into and remain in close relationships to expand the self by including resources, perspectives, experiences, and characteristics of the other as part of their own self-concept (Aron, Aron, & Allen, 1989; Aron & Aron, 1997). We enter into relationships, in effect, to create a more complete self. One implication of this perspective is that, in the course of relationships, our self and our representation of close others should merge (Aron & Fraley, 1999).

In one relevant study, married couples first rated ninety trait adjectives for how accurately they described themselves and their spouse (Aron, Aron, Tudor, & Nelson, 1991). After a brief distracter task, participants viewed each trait on a computer screen and were asked to indicate as quickly as possible whether the trait was "like me" or "not like me." As you can see in Figure 4.2, participants were faster in identifying traits on which they were similar to their spouse. Participants were slower to ascribe traits to themselves that their partner did not possess.

*Sharing Social Construals with Close Others*   When a loved one dies, the survivor literally feels as though part of his or her mind is gone (Bonanno & Kaltman, 1999). Survivors often have the debilitating sense that they can no longer remember parts of their lives, that they can't make their way to familiar places, and that they no longer understand their current lives as they once did. This sort of phenomenon was captured experimentally by Dan Wegner and colleagues in their study of a kind of "distributed cognition" that they call **transactive memory**, the knowledge that people in relationships have about their partner's encoding, storage, and retrieval of information (Wegner, 1986; Wegner, Erber, & Raymond, 1991). After years together, most friends, romantic partners, and family members know what their relationship partners are likely to attend to and

**self-expansion account of relationships**  A theory that holds that people enter into and remain in close relationships to expand the self by including resources, perspectives, experiences, and characteristics of the other as part of their own self-concept.

**transactive memory**  The tendency for people in relationships to share information processing of events based on their knowledge of their partner's encoding, storage, and retrieval of information.

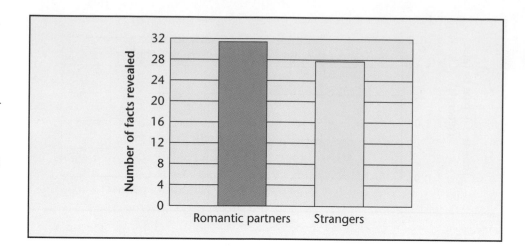

**Figure 4.3 Shared Construal and Transactive Memory** Romantic partners are often observed to collaborate in telling the stories of their lives, to the point of finishing each other's sentences. Do they also collaborate in storing and remembering information? It appears so. In this study, Wegner and colleagues presented romantic partners or randomly paired partners with 64 facts embedded in sentences, and then later asked these individuals to recall as many of the 64 facts as possible. Romantic partners were better able to recall facts than randomly paired strangers. (Source: Adapted from Wegner, Erber, & Raymond, 1991)

remember about any particular context. Thus, if asked to remember a story or body of knowledge or list of information, relationship partners are likely to remember more information than two randomly paired individuals. This is because the relationship partners should know what their partners will focus on, and thus they should be able to allocate their attention to different items of information. This will enable them to remember more, as a team, than individuals who have to remember everything on their own.

To test this intriguing possibility, Wegner and colleagues had fifty-nine heterosexual dating couples complete a memory task. They gave the partners sixty-four sentences, each of which contained an underlined word from a specific area of expertise, such as food, science, television, or culture. For example, participants might read that "Yeasts reproduce by budding" or that "Midori is a Japanese melon liqueur." The experimental manipulation was quite simple. In half of the conditions, participants were given the sentences and asked to remember them with their romantic partner. In the other half of the conditions, participants were asked to try to remember the items with a member of another couple—that is, with a stranger. After a five-minute filler task, participants were separated and asked to write down as many of the underlined items as possible. In Figure 4.3, we present the number of items that either member of each dyad could accurately recall. As you can see, romantic partners together recalled significantly more of the items than strangers recalled together.

## RELATIONSHIPS AND AFFECTIVE LIFE

It is clear that our relationships profoundly influence our emotional lives (Berscheid & Reis, 1998). Furthermore, certain emotions are intensified in particular relationships. Take the intriguing case of laughter. When asked to draw pictures of each other's face with crayons, pairs of friends were more likely than pairs of strangers to share mutual laughter—that is, to laugh at the same time—thus signaling that they were sharing the pleasure of the task (Smoski & Bachorowski, 2003). As we shall see in the emotion chapter (Chapter 12), many emotions—for example, love, jealousy, anger, or embarrassment—have evolved to help us form and maintain important relationships (Keltner & Haidt, 2001).

Relationships also exert a profound effect on our moods and sense of well-being. One way to study this effect is to use **experience-sampling studies**, in which researchers provide participants with beepers, and randomly signal them during the day to provide information about what they are doing and how they

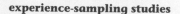

**experience-sampling studies** Studies in which researchers provide participants with beepers and randomly signal them throughout the day so that the participants will provide information about what they are doing and how they are feeling at that precise moment.

are feeling at that precise moment (Bolger, Davis, & Rafaeli, 2003). People experience more positive emotions when they are around other people as opposed to when they are alone (Berscheid & Reis, 1998). This is especially true when people are having more intimate interactions with close friends and romantic partners (Delespaul, Reis, & deVries, 1996; Diener, Larsen, & Emmons, 1984).

The literature on loneliness further attests to the importance of relationships to our emotional well-being (Peplau & Perlman, 1982). Lonely people, who report a chronic shortage of close contact with others, suffer in various ways. They are more likely to report elevated levels of anxiety and depression, for example. It should be noted, however, that this research is particularly prone to the problem of self-selection. Anxious, depressed people are not much fun to be around, and they may be lonely because they're not happy rather than not being happy because they're lonely (Barnett & Gotlib, 1988; Gotlib, 1992). Both directions of causality seem plausible, but all we can know from the research is that anxiety and depression are associated with a lack of contact with others.

Experimental research likewise attests to the powerful influence that significant others have on how we feel (Baldwin, 1994; Baldwin & Holmes, 1987; Collins & Read, 1994). In a clever series of studies, Mark Baldwin and colleagues examined whether unconscious exposure to important authority figures would influence participants' self-evaluations (Baldwin, Carrell, & Lopez, 1990). Baldwin and his colleagues had University of Michigan graduate students in psychology write about three of their latest research ideas. After writing about each idea, participants were then presented subliminally (that is, below the threshold of conscious detection) with a photograph of a powerful authority figure at the University of Michigan, Robert Zajonc. In this photo, Zajonc looked stern and disapproving, as shown by his furrowed brow and pursed lips. Other participants were presented subliminally with a photo of another local researcher, who was smiling and looking happy. Graduate students evaluated their research ideas much less positively after being exposed to the picture of Robert Zajonc frowning than after being exposed to the photo of the local scholar smiling.

> "Sticks in a bundle are unbreakable."
> —KENYAN PROVERB

**LOOKING BACK,** we have seen that relationships exert a powerful, and often underappreciated, influence on our thoughts and feelings. Our need to belong in relationships is an evolved, universal motive that shapes our thoughts and actions. If not satisfied, it can have highly negative consequences for our well-being. Most profoundly, relationships shape how we construe our social worlds, both as individuals and as couples, and they sway our emotional lives both positively and negatively. We next consider the effects that the very earliest relationships have on our later lives.

## THE ORIGINS OF HOW WE RELATE TO OTHERS

The studies that we have just reviewed may have left you wondering about your own relationships. Do you have a consistent way of relating to your friends, family, and romantic partners? If so, what are the origins of this style of relating to others? Does it have to do with your early experience with your parents, or did it develop more from your interactions with your peers? These are fundamental questions that have motivated the influential theory of human attachment.

## ATTACHMENT THEORY

**Attachment theory** was first advanced by John Bowlby, a seminal theorist in the study of relationships, and one of the early advocates of evolutionary accounts of human behavior (Bowlby, 1969/1982; Hazan & Shaver, 1994; Mikulincer & Shaver, 2003; Simpson & Rholes, 1998). The central thesis of Bowlby's theory is that our early attachments with our parents shape our relationships for the remainder of our lives.

Unlike many mammals, human infants are born with few developed survival skills. They cannot flee predators, find food or feed themselves, or locate shelter. They survive, Bowlby reasons, by forming intensely close attachments to parents or parental figures. Evolution has led to infants having a variety of traits that promote parent-offspring attachments, including the capacity to smile, to make evocative vocalizations like coos, and baby-faced features that evoke love and devotion (Berry & McArthur, 1986; McArthur & Baron, 1983). These features, including large head and large eyes, also evoke attachment for other mammals toward their offspring. In fact, their babies pull at our own heart-strings. Likewise, evolution has led to a variety of parental traits that promote attachment—most notably, strong feelings of filial love and protective instincts toward their infants (Fehr, 1994; Fehr & Russell, 1991; Hazan & Shaver, 1987, 1994; Hrdy, 1999).

Early in development, children rely on their parents for a sense of security, which allows them to explore the environment and to learn. A child's confidence in the secure base that the parents provide derives in part from the parent's availability and responsiveness to the child. This is evident in the literature on depressed mothers. Depressed mothers are less responsive to their children's actions, and their children in turn tend to feel less secure and more anxious (Field, 1995). Of course, there are alternative accounts of this finding. Researchers have learned that depression and anxiety are inherited, and that they tend to be found together. In light of this, it is possible that depressed mothers are transmitting to their children genes that predispose them to depression and anxiety, rather than producing anxiety through their own behavior.

As children form attachments to parents, they develop **working models** of how relationships function (Baldwin, Keelan, Fehr, Enns, & Koh-Rangarajoo,

---

**attachment theory** A theory about how our early attachments with our parents shape our relationships for the remainder of our lives.

**working models of relationships** Conceptual models of relationships with current others based on the other person's availability, warmth, and ability to provide security as derived from children's experience with how available and how warm their parents were.

---

**Traits That Evoke Attachment**
Evolution has led infants to have traits that evoke attachment, so that primary caregivers, most typically parents, will feed, shelter, and protect them until they are able to do so themselves. Thus, the chimp, kitten, and seal pup have such features as large eyes, which evoke positive emotion and attachment—even from members of other species, such as humans. Similar features in human infants, as well as smiles and coos, also promote attachment of parents to infants, and lead the adults to protect the infants from harm.

1996; Collins & Read, 1994; Pietromonaco & Feldman-Barrett, 2000). These models are based on children's experience with how available their parents are, and the extent to which they do or do not provide a sense of security. A working model of relationships, then, is the individual's collection of beliefs about another's availability, warmth, and ability to provide security. These working models, Bowlby claimed, originate early in life and shape our relationships from "cradle to grave."

Inspired by Bowlby's theorizing, Mary Ainsworth classified the attachment patterns of infants according to how the children responded to separations and reunions with their caregivers, both in the laboratory and in the home (Ainsworth, 1993; Ainsworth, Blehar, Waters, & Wall, 1978). Using an experimental procedure that came to be known as the **strange situation**, Ainsworth had the infants and their caregivers enter an unfamiliar room containing a large number of interesting toys. As the infant explored the room and began to play with some of the toys, a stranger walked in. The stranger remained in the room, and the caregiver quietly left. Returning after three minutes, the caregiver greeted and comforted the infant if he or she was upset. The separation typically caused infants to be distressed. Infants whose caregivers responded quickly and reliably to their distress cries were typically securely attached. Such infants were comfortable in moving away from their caregivers to explore a novel environment—with the occasional glance back at the caregiver to make sure that things were okay. The child felt safe even though she was not in contact with the caregiver. Caregivers who were not so reliable in their responses to their infants—sometimes intruding on the child's activities and sometimes rejecting the child—tended to have infants who showed anxious attachment and were likely to cry or show anger when placed in novel environments. They were less comforted by contact with their caregiver when it occurred. Caregivers who rejected their infants frequently tended to produce children with avoidant attachment. In a strange situation, the avoidant child might not seek out the caregiver and might even reject attention when it was offered.

## ATTACHMENT STYLES

To classify adults' attachment styles, researchers have developed different self-report measures (for example, Bartholomew & Horowitz, 1991; Brennan, Clark, & Shaver, 1998: Hazan & Shaver, 1987). One such approach is presented in Table 4.1. Read each of the three paragraphs and decide which one best describes your feelings toward close others in your life. In classifying the attachment patterns of infants and adults, researchers have concentrated on three specific styles. Individuals with a **secure attachment style** feel secure in relationships, and they are thus comfortable with intimacy and desire to be close to others during times

**The Strange Situation** Mary Ainsworth set up an experimental situation in which she was able to measure infants' attachment to their caregiver. (A) A mother and child would enter an unfamiliar room with many interesting toys. The infant would explore the room and play with the toys. In the meantime, a stranger would enter the room and then the mother would leave. (B) When the mother returned to the room, she would pick up the infant and comfort him if he was upset that she had left the room. (C) The mother would then put down the infant, who would be free to return to playing with the toys or might react by crying and protesting the separation.

---

**strange situation** An experimental situation designed to assess attachment to caregivers: an infant is observed after her caregiver has left her alone in an unfamiliar room with a stranger and then reacts to reunion with the caregiver upon her return to the room.

**secure attachment style** An attachment style characterized by feelings of security in relationships; individuals with this style are comfortable with intimacy and desire to be close to others during times of threat and uncertainty.

### Table 4.1  Measuring Attachment Styles

Researchers present participants with paragraphs like those below in order to assess their attachment styles. In this method, participants are asked to select the paragraph that best describes how they relate to other people.

| ATTACHMENT STYLE | DESCRIPTION |
| --- | --- |
| Secure Style | I find it relatively easy to get close to others and am comfortable depending on them and having them depend on me. I don't often worry about being abandoned or about someone getting too close. |
| Avoidant Style | I am somewhat uncomfortable being close. I find it difficult to trust completely, difficult to allow myself to depend on anyone. I am nervous when anyone gets close, and often, romantic partners want me to be more intimate than I feel comfortable being. |
| Anxious Style | I find that others are reluctant to get as close as I would like. I often worry that my partner doesn't really love me or won't stay with me. I want to merge completely with another person, and this desire sometimes scares people away. |

Source: Adapted from Hazan & Shaver, 1987.

**avoidant attachment style**
An attachment style characterized by feelings of insecurity in relationships; individuals with this style are prone to exhibit compulsive self-reliance, prefer distance from others, and during conditions of threat and uncertainty are dismissive and detached.

**anxious attachment style**
An attachment style characterized by feelings of insecurity in relationships; individuals with this style compulsively seek closeness, express continual worries about relationships, and during situations of threat and uncertainty excessively try to get closer to others.

of threat and uncertainty. Individuals with an **avoidant attachment style** feel insecure in relationships, and they are prone to exhibit compulsive self-reliance, prefer distance from others, and during conditions of threat and uncertainty are dismissive and detached. Individuals with an **anxious attachment style** also lack feelings of security in relationships, but they respond differently than do avoidant individuals. Anxious individuals compulsively seek closeness, express continual worries about relationships, and during situations of threat and uncertainty make excessive attempts to get closer to others. Such anxious individuals are often the proverbial high-maintenance romantic partners that some of your friends might bemoan.

A central claim of attachment theory is that these attachment styles are stable across life—that is, the attachments you form early in life shape how you relate as an adult to your romantic partners, your children, and your friends. Evidence supports this provocative thesis. Individuals classified as secure, avoidant, or anxious at age one tend to be similarly classified in early adulthood (Fraley & Spieker, 2003; see Box 4.1). A four-year longitudinal study of adults found that 70 percent of adults reported the same attachment style across all four years of the study (Kirkpatrick & Hazan, 1994). Secure individuals were particularly likely to remain secure (83.3 percent remained secure across the four years). Nonetheless, other researchers have found some change in people's attachment styles (Baldwin, Keelan, Fehr, Ens, & Koh-Rangarajoo, 1996; Baldwin & Fehr, 1995).

Important early life events are also associated with later attachment styles.

Box 4.1   FOCUS ON CULTURE

# Building an Independent Baby in the Bedroom

If you are a white, middle-class North American, odds are you slept by yourself in your own bedroom from infancy on. And that probably seems perfectly normal to you. Normal maybe, common definitely not. There are few cultures in the world where such a sleeping arrangement is customary. In an article entitled "Who Sleeps with Whom Revisited," Shweder, Jensen, and Goldstein (1995) describe the sleeping arrangements of people in many of the world's cultures. The sleeping arrangements predict fairly well how independent and individualistic a given culture is. In Japan, most children sleep with their parents until they are adolescents. In the non-Western, nonindustrial world, it is virtually unheard of for a very young child not to sleep with his or her parents, and such a practice would be regarded as a form of child abuse. Even in the United States, 55 percent of African-American children less than one year of age sleep with a parent every night, and 25 percent of African-American children one to five years old sleep with a parent. In a white, predominantly blue-collar community in Appalachian Kentucky, 71 percent of children between the ages of two months and two years were found to sleep with their parents, as well as 47 percent of children between two years and four years of age.

This study reveals the extent to which interdependent and independent self-construals permeate social behavior. In more interdependent cultures, young children are much more likely to sleep side by side with their parents than in independent cultures. While we can only speculate about the effects these patterns of sleep have on attachment patterns, one might expect secure attachments in the independent cultures to be defined by greater independence and autonomy than secure patterns in interdependent cultures.

Brennan and Shaver (1993) found that anxious individuals were more likely to have experienced parents who divorced, the death of a parent, and abuse during childhood. In a forty-year longitudinal study of women who graduated from Mills College in Oakland, California, in 1960, Klohnen and Bera (1998) found that women who classified themselves as avoidant at age fifty-two had also reported greater conflict in the home thirty years earlier at age twenty-one.

Attachment styles exert important influences upon people's behavior within intimate relationships (Collins & Feeney, 2000; Feeney & Collins, 2001; Rholes, Simpson, & Orina, 1999; Simpson, Ickes, & Grich, 1999; Simpson, Rholes, & Phillips, 1996). In one imaginative study, Chris Fraley and Phil Shaver (1998) surreptitiously observed romantic partners as they said good-bye in airports. Afterwards, they had the romantic partners fill out attachment questionnaires. Avoidant partners sought less physical contact and engaged in fewer embraces and less hand-holding as they departed from one another. Anxious individuals, on the other hand, expressed greater fear and sadness.

"O.K., step away from the laptop and hold up your end of the conversation."

In self-report studies, secure individuals were more likely to report that their partners and friends were more forthcoming in offering support than did anxious and avoidant individuals (Florian, Mikulincer, & Bucholtz,

**Anxious Attachment** Attachment styles influence how people behave with intimate others. Whereas avoidant partners are likely to avoid physical contact and leave each other quickly, anxious partners may be more likely to touch each other and to stretch out the moment of leave taking, as here where the woman continues to wave goodbye to her partner who has already turned and walked away.

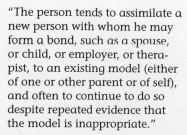

"The person tends to assimilate a new person with whom he may form a bond, such as a spouse, or child, or employer, or therapist, to an existing model (either of one or other parent or of self), and often to continue to do so despite repeated evidence that the model is inappropriate."

—JOHN BOWLBY

1995). Secure individuals also tended to interpret their partners' negative behavior—for example, criticism or insensitivity— in a more positive fashion than did either anxious or avoidant individuals (Collins, 1996).

In light of the preceding findings, you might expect that a secure attachment style would predict more positive life outcomes. And indeed, you would receive empirical support for this assumption from several studies (for example, Cooper, Shaver, & Collins, 1998). Compared to those with different attachment styles, secure individuals report the greatest relationship satisfaction (Shaver & Brennan, 1992). In the four-year longitudinal study we described earlier, secure individuals were less likely to have experienced a romantic breakup (25.6 percent) over the four-year period under study than avoidant individuals (52.2 percent) or anxious individuals (43.6 percent). In the Mills College study, secure individuals were more likely to be married at age fifty-two than were avoidant individuals (82 percent versus 50 percent), and to report fewer marital tensions. Moreover, several studies have uncovered more general life problems associated with an anxious attachment style (Mikulincer & Shaver, 2003). Anxiously attached individuals are more likely to interpret life events in pessimistic, threatening fashion, which increases the chances of depression. They are also more likely to suffer from eating disorders, maladaptive drinking, and substance abuse, in part to reduce their distress and anxiety.

Finally, experimental evidence indicates that when people are made to think about secure attachments when they are in threatening situations, this opens them up to be more trusting in relationships in general. Mario Mikulincer of Bar-Ilan University in Israel and his colleagues have presented participants with words related to secure attachments—for example, "hug" and "love." These security-related words, even when presented below the participants' awareness, led the participants to be less prejudicial toward outgroups after threat (Mikulincer & Florian, 2000) and to be more altruistic toward others (Mikulincer, Gillath, & Shaver, 2002).

**LOOKING BACK,** we have seen that our way of relating to our intimate others has origins in our early bonds with our parents. This attachment exerts considerable effects on our current relationships, on how we act toward others and appraise events within our relationships, and on our personal well-being. The more secure our attachment style, the healthier our relationships and lives tend to be.

## DIFFERENT WAYS OF RELATING TO OTHERS

Do relationships with different kinds of people influence our thoughts and feelings in different ways? Relational self theory largely focused on how positive and negative relationships with significant others (be they parents, friends, or siblings) affect our relationships with those who resemble them. Attachment theory maintains that working models established early in life, in interactions with parents, shape our romantic lives years later. These theories have less to say about other types of common bonds, such as those between close friends, members of a social hierarchy, or individuals at work. As we shall now see, our assumptions and beliefs about the basis of different kinds of relationships affect how we think, act, and feel, even what we consider right and wrong.

## BASIS OF DIFFERENT KINDS OF RELATIONSHIPS

In his **relational models theory**, Alan Fiske offers a far-reaching account of four qualitatively different ways that humans relate to one another (Fiske, 1991b, 1992). These different social relations are characterized by highly distinct ways of defining the self and others, allocating resources and work, making moral judgments, and punishing transgressions. This rich theory derives from an extensive reading of the anthropological and sociological literatures on relationships, and from Fiske's own fieldwork among the Moose (prounounced "Moh-say") of Burkina Faso in West Africa.

A **communal sharing relationship** is based on the belief that membership in the group transcends the concerns of the individual. A prototypical example of this kind of relationship is the family. Another is a group of extremely close friends. For communal sharing bonds, work is determined according to what the individual can offer; justice and fairness are assessed according to evaluations of the individual's need; and moral judgment is based on caring, compassion, and benevolence.

An **authority ranking relationship** is based on hierarchy, status, and a linear ordering of people within a group. Prototypical examples of this kind of relationship include those in the military, bureaucracies, modern corporations, and tribal groups governed by a chieftain. In these groups, individuals are aware of status differences and social hierarchy. Who works, who does what, and who gets which rewards are determined by a top-down process dictated by superiors. Justice is based on power: what is fair is what those in power deem to be fair. Moral judgments are guided by principles of obedience and respect and what authority figures deem to be right and wrong.

An **equality matching relationship** is based on equality, reciprocity, and balance. Prototypical examples of this relationship include those between dorm roommates, members of a carpool, and most (but not all) friendships. Work is governed by the principle of sameness: each person contributes the same. Justice is governed by equality, which holds that each person should receive equal resources. And moral judgment is also guided by the principle of equality—that all individuals should be granted similar rights and freedoms based on what is fair.

---

**relational models theory**
A theory that there are four qualitatively different kinds of relationships (communal sharing, authority ranking, equality matching, and market pricing), each characterized by highly distinct ways of defining the self and others, allocating resources and work, making moral judgments, and punishing transgressions.

**communal sharing relationship** A relationship based on a sense of sameness and kinship. Resources are generated by those in the group capable of doing so, and resources go to those in need.

**authority ranking relationship** A relationship based on hierarchy, status, and a linear ordering of people within a group.

**equality matching relationship** A relationship based on equality, reciprocity, and balance.

*"O.K., who else has experienced the best-friend relationship as inadequate?"*

A **market pricing relationship** is based on a sense of proportion, and is a relationship in which people are concerned with ensuring that their inputs to the relationship correspond to what they get out of the relationship. A prototypical example of this relationship is that between a boss and employee, or between an investor and a corporation. In this relationship, rewards are proportionate to one's contributions. Justice is based on the principle of equity—that is, one's rewards should correspond to one's inputs. And morality is governed by concerns over efficiency and utility: the rightness of any act is evaluated according to the extent to which it maximizes positive outcomes and minimizes negative outcomes for the greater good.

As you consider these four ways of relating to others, keep in mind that we can relate to the same person in the four different ways. For example, married spouses feel bonded together as a communal unit; they occasionally feel dominant or submissive toward one another; they may often feel like equals; and on occasion, perhaps regrettably, they may feel like employer and employee.

What sort of research has relational models theory inspired? Most of the relevant studies have shown that people rely on these four ways of relating to other people to interpret and remember social events (Fiske, 1992; Haslam, 1994; Haslam & Fiske, 1992). For example, in one study, Fiske asked whether people are more likely to make social mistakes with people from the same relationship category than with people across relationship categories. To find out, Fiske had people from four different countries keep track of their social mistakes in a diary and then classify the individuals involved into one of the four relational categories (A. Fiske, 1993). Social mistakes occur when you confuse the identity of one person with another. You make a phone call expecting one friend, but another friend answers the phone. You buy a birthday present for one sister, but it turns out it's your other sister's birthday. The social mistakes participants most commonly reported included misnaming and "misactions," where an action, such as a phone call or gift, was directed at the wrong person. Fiske found that people from the four countries were more likely to confuse the identities of individuals within each of the four relational categories than across the four categories. Our actions toward others, both right and wrong, are governed by these four relational categories. Perhaps the most dramatic mistake was made by a Vai woman from Liberia, who introduced the current president of Liberia with the name of the former president whom the current president had assassinated!

Cross-cultural similarities in the social mistake study support Fiske's claim that his four relationship types are universal. Fiske claims that all societies employ all of the relationship types (with the exception of a few preliterate societies that don't use market pricing). Fiske also claims, however, that different cultures emphasize different relationship categories and use them for different purposes (Fiske, 1992). Thus, for example, modern Western society tends to rely heavily on market pricing as a way of organizing relationships, whereas traditional hunter-gatherer societies emphasize communal sharing. Chinese society is very much based on authority ranking as a means of exerting social control, whereas Japanese society emphasizes equality matching or peer control. For example, control in the Chinese classroom is exerted by the teacher, whereas in the Japanese classroom control is achieved in part by peer pressure from fellow students. Similarly, a given society may emphasize equality matching for distribution of social benefits that another society may be more inclined to allocate according to market pricing principles. Sweden, with its long tradition of equality, is an example of the former type in its social welfare policies, and the United States is an example of the latter.

> **market pricing relationship**
> A relationship based on a sense of proportion, trade, and equity, in which people are concerned with ensuring that their inputs to a relationship correspond to what they get out of the relationship.

Taken together, the evidence indicates that individuals construe other people according to Fiske's four relational models. In the chapter on morality and justice (Chapter 14), we will review evidence that addresses Fiske's claim that a person's ideas about justice and morality are shaped by the type of relationship the person is in. Let's now rely upon Fiske's classification to look at what is known about other kinds of relationships.

## EXCHANGE AND COMMUNAL RELATIONSHIPS

Two other influential social psychologists, Margaret Clark and Judson Mills, have carved up the world of relationships in a different fashion, though one that is largely compatible with Fiske's approach (Clark, 1992; Clark and Mills, 1979, 1993). They argue that there are two fundamentally different types of relationships—exchange relationships and communal relationships—that arise in different contexts and are governed by different norms. **Exchange relationships** tend to be short-term relationships in which the individuals feel no responsibility toward one another. In exchange relationships, giving and receiving are governed by concerns about equity and reciprocity. Examples of exchange relationships include interactions between strangers, new acquaintances, or a student working for a professor. These relationships closely resemble the market pricing relationships that Fiske described.

**Communal relationships**, on the other hand, tend to be based on long-term bonds in which the individuals feel a special responsibility for one another. In communal relationships, individuals give and receive according to the principle of need. Examples of exchange relationships are relations between family members and close friends. Children who take care of their elderly parents do so simply because their parents need help, not because they expect a benefit in return (although those who anticipate a sizable inheritance may do so more diligently than those who do not!). This kind of relationship is similar to the notion of communal sharing described by Fiske.

Clark and Mills have relied on two different methods to show how exchange and communal relationships differ. In one method, they compared the behavior of friends (who are more likely to have a communal relationship) with those of mere acquaintances (who are more likely to approach one another with an exchange orientation). With the other method, they experimentally manipulated the communal versus exchange status of the relationship by varying the motives of the individuals in their experiments. In the communal condition, participants hear about another participant in the study (the target person), who is described as a new transfer student who has signed up for the experiment in the hope of meeting people. This is designed to make the participants want a communal relationship with the target person. In the exchange condition, participants are told that the target person has been at the university for two years and signed up for the experiment because it was a convenient time for her husband to pick her up afterward. This is designed to encourage the participants to keep things on an exchange basis with the target person.

With these two methods, Clark and Mills have documented that communal and exchange relationships operate according to much different principles and dynamics. In communal relationships, people are more likely to keep track of each other's needs. Thus, in one study, one participant completed a task in which she formed four-letter words out of letters provided by the experimenter while another participant (actually an accomplice of the experimenter) worked on a similar but more difficult task in an adjacent room (Clark, Mills, & Powell, 1986).

> **exchange relationships** Relationships in which the individuals feel little responsibility toward one another and in which giving and receiving are governed by concerns about equity and reciprocity; such relationships are often short term.
>
> **communal relationships** Relationships in which the individuals feel a special responsibility for one another and give according to the principle of ability and receive according to the principle of need; such relationships are often long term.

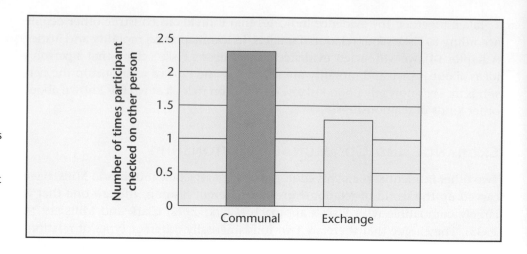

**Figure 4.4  Sensitivity to Others' Needs in Exchange and Communal Relationships**    Participants completed a word-formation task with another individual (the experimenter's accomplice) who was in another room, and who signaled difficulties with the task by turning on a red light that flashed behind the back of the real participant. When the individual signaling distress had earlier expressed an interest in forming a friendship with the participant (the communal condition), the participant was much more likely to turn around and see whether the individual in the other room was having trouble. (Source: Clark, Mills, & Powell, 1986)

When the task was too difficult for the participant (the accomplice) next door, she was to signal her need for help to the real participant by turning on a red light, which the participant needed to turn around to see. As you can see in Figure 4.4, participants in the communal condition turned around to check in on the other "participant" almost twice as often as participants in the exchange condition.

In communal relationships, individuals are more sensitive to one another's needs. In exchange relationships, people are more concerned about their own and the other person's inputs. This would make sense if people in exchange relationships were concerned with equity; they would want to make sure that their inputs corresponded to the outputs they received. Since individuals in communal relationships are governed by considerations of need, they should be less concerned with their own and their partner's respective contributions. Exploring this thesis, Clark and Mills told their participants that they would take part in a visual-search task, in which they and another participant (the accomplice) would search a large matrix of numbers for specified sequences and circle them. They would receive a reward based on the number of sequences they each circled. After doing an experimental manipulation designed to activate communal or exchange orientations, researchers gave the participant the matrix with several numbers circled by the other "participant" in the other room. The dependent measure of interest was whether the real participant would choose a pen having the same color ink or one having a different color to circle numbers. As expected, in the exchange condition, participants were much more likely to choose a different color ink, to ensure that their unique contribution would be known and rewarded (Clark, 1984; Clark, Mills, & Powell, 1986).

The difference between communal and exchange approaches to relationships is fundamental to an understanding of cultural differences. First, societies differ a great deal in terms of which approach they prefer in general. People in East Asian and Latin American societies are inclined to take a communal approach to many questions to which people in European and Commonwealth countries would be inclined to take an exchange approach. Recall from Chapter 1 the question as to how businesspeople would treat an employee who had put in fifteen good years of service, but over the past year had fallen down on the job and showed little chance of recovering from the injury (see Box 1.1). East Asians tended to feel that there was a company obligation to treat the employee as family and to keep him on the payroll. Western businesspeople were more likely to feel that the relationship was a purely contractual or exchange-based one and that the employee should be let go. Once again, there are differences among

Western nations, however, with people from Catholic countries being more likely to take a communal stance on this and other questions than people from Protestant countries.

## POWER AND HIERARCHICAL RELATIONSHIPS

Starting as early as age two, people arrange themselves into social hierarchies, with some individuals occupying higher positions than others. Within a day or so, young adults within groups agree with one another about who has high status and who has low status (Anderson, John, Keltner, & Kring, 2001). In fact, power concerns are evident in most kinds of relationships, including intimate bonds like the marital relationship or the parent-child relationship (Bugental & Lewis, 1999).

Power affects almost all facets of social life. Power can influence the way we speak: low-power individuals generally speak politely, making requests indirectly or by asking vague questions, whereas high-power individuals generally speak forcefully and directly, asking pointed questions and making commands (Brown & Levinson, 1987). Power even influences how we look at each other (Dovidio, Brown, Heltman, Ellyson, & Keating, 1988; Dovidio, Ellyson, Keating, Heltman, & Brown, 1988). A clear indicator of power is the following pattern of gaze: high-power individuals look at listeners when speaking and are looked at when speaking, whereas low-power individuals look away when speaking but look at others when listening (Ellyson & Dovidio, 1985). Power even shapes the way we dress. For example, it is a common practice for more senior medical doctors to wear longer white lab coats than more junior doctors.

So far we have characterized power in general terms, but now we need to deal with three fundamental questions concerning power and hierarchical relations: What is power? Where does it come from? And how does power influence behavior?

*What Is Power?*   **Power** is typically defined according to two attributes: the ability to control one's own outcomes and those of others, and the freedom to act (S. Fiske, 1993; Kelley & Thibaut, 1978). Power is related to status, authority, and dominance, but it is not synonymous with them. **Status** is the outcome of an evaluation of attributes that produces differences in respect and prominence, which in part determines an individual's power within a group (French & Raven, 1959; Kemper, 1991). But it is possible to have power without status (for example, the corrupt politician) and status without relative power (for example, a religious leader in an interminably long line at the Department of Motor Vehicles). **Authority** is power that derives from institutionalized roles or arrangements (Weber, 1947). Nonetheless, power can exist in the absence of formal roles (for example, within informal groups). **Dominance** is behavior that has the acquisition or demonstration of power as its goal. Yet, power can be attained without performing acts of dominance (for example, leaders who attain their positions through their cooperative and fair-minded style).

*Where Does Power Come From?*   How do people attain their positions within social hierarchies? This question may be of interest to you, particularly in light of the many advantages that people in the upper echelons enjoy—for example, reduced depression and anxiety, improved health, and even greater life expectancy (Adler et al., 1994; Williams & Collins, 1995). As it turns out, the sources of power vary in complex ways, which may account for why you might feel powerful in certain contexts and relatively weak in others.

> "The fundamental concept in social science is Power, in the same sense that Energy is the fundamental concept in physics. . . . The laws of social dynamics are laws which can only be stated in terms of power."
>
> —BERTRAND RUSSELL

> "You see what power is—holding someone else's fear in your hand and showing it to them!"
>
> —AMY TAN

**power** The ability to control one's own outcomes and those of others, and the freedom to act.

**status** The outcome of an evaluation of attributes that produces differences in respect and prominence, which in part determines an individual's power within a group.

**authority** Power that derives from institutionalized roles or arrangements.

**dominance** Behavior that has the acquisition or demonstration of power as its goal.

Certain individual difference factors relate to how much power people might enjoy (Anderson, John, Keltner, & Kring, 2001; Coats & Feldman, 1996; Mueller & Mazur, 1997; Savin-Williams, 1977). For example, extraverted people—that is, those who are gregarious, energetic, and prone to positive emotion—often attain elevated levels of power within natural social groups. People with superb social skills are more likely to rise in social hierarchies. And even appearance matters. People who are physically attractive, males who are taller and have large muscle mass, and even males with large, square jaws often attain higher positions in social hierarchies.

At the interpersonal level, power can originate in five different sources (French & Raven, 1959). Power can derive from *authority* based on roles within groups. This is true in formal hierarchies, such as the workplace, as well as in informal hierarchies, such as family structures in cultures that have historically given older siblings elevated power vis-à-vis younger siblings (Sulloway, 1996). Power can derive from *expertise* based on knowledge. A medical doctor wields power over her patients because of her specialized knowledge and experience. Power can derive from *coercion* based on the ability to use force and aggression. Power can stem from the ability to provide *rewards* to others. This helps explain why members of elevated socioeconomic status often wield power over those of lower socioeconomic status (Domhoff, 1998). It explains why majority group members are generally more powerful than minority group members (Brewer, 1979; Ng, 1980). And it explains why ethnic and gender background matter in terms of the power of white men over black men and the power of men over women (Sidanius, 1993). Finally, power derives from the ability to serve as a role model, which is known as *reference power*. This is likely to contribute to the power resident assistants generally have over the students they oversee in college dormitories.

***How Does Power Influence Behavior?***     Thus far, we have defined power, and considered its myriad and complex sources. Let's now consider how power influences our behavior. Sayings related to this question abound and are one source of the hypotheses about the effects of power: "Power corrupts." "Money [a source of power] is the root of all evil." A recent theoretical formulation known as the approach/inhibition theory of power, suggests that we might be wary of those with power (Keltner, Gruenfeld, & Anderson, 2003). Elevated power is defined by control over others, freedom to do whatever you wish, and the lack of social constraint. As a consequence, the theory goes, elevated power should make you a little bit less concerned about the evaluations and actions of others, and therefore

**Power and Intimidation**  High-power individuals often feel less constrained by social rules about appropriate behavior than do low-power individuals. Lyndon Johnson approaches Senator Theodore Green more closely than is socially acceptable, touches his arm, and leans in close to his face as he seeks to intimidate him into voting the way Johnson wants him to.

less careful or more automatic in your social thought. Less constrained by others, you should also act in more disinhibited ways when you enjoy elevated power. In general, with elevated power you should be inclined to approach-related behavior, moving toward satisfying your goals. In contrast, reduced power is associated with increased threat from others, punishment, and social constraint. As a result, being in reduced power or lower positions in social hierarchies should tend to make you more vigilant and careful in social judgment and more inhibited in social behavior.

A first hypothesis based on the approach/inhibition theory of power is that high-power individuals should be a little less systematic and careful in how they judge the social world (Brauer, Chambres, Niedenthal, & Chatard-Pannetier, 2004; S. Fiske, 1993; Vescio, Snyder, & Butz, 2003). One result is that high-power individuals should be more likely to thoughtlessly stereotype others, rather than carefully attending to and relying on individuating information (Fiske, 1993a; Neuberg & Fiske, 1987). Several studies have tested this hypothesis and found that participants given power in an experiment are indeed less likely to attend to individuating information and more likely to rely on stereotypes (Goodwin, Gubin, Fiske, & Yzerbyt, 2000; see also Vescio, Snyder, & Butz, 2003).

Members of powerful groups have an increased tendency to stereotype as well. Sidanius and Pratto have found that **social dominance orientation**—the desire to see one's own group dominate other groups—is more strongly endorsed by individuals associated with more powerful groups (Pratto, 1996; Sidanius, 1993). These include men as compared with women, European Americans compared to African Americans, and individuals in hierarchy-enhancing careers (for example, the police) as opposed to hierarchy-attenuating careers (for example, social workers). Measures of social dominance, in turn, correlate with increased stereotyping and prejudice. Just being a member of a more powerful group, it would seem, predisposes you to stereotype others.

> **social dominance orientation**
> The desire to see one's own group dominate other groups.

Predisposed to construe others in broad strokes and to rely on stereotypes, high-power individuals should tend to judge others' attitudes, interests, and needs in more simplistic, less accurate fashion. A study of the attitudes and judgments of more powerful, tenured college professors and their less powerful, untenured colleagues confirmed this prediction (Keltner & Robinson, 1996, 1997). The high-power professors judged the attitudes of the less powerful, untenured colleagues less accurately than did the low-power professors. In a similar vein, power differences may account for the tendency of males to be slightly less accurate than females in judging expressive behavior (Henley & LaFrance, 1984; LaFrance, Henley, Hall, & Halberstadt, 1997; but see also Hall, 1984). Power may even be at work in the striking finding that younger siblings, who experience reduced power vis-à-vis older siblings, outperform their older siblings on theory-of-mind tasks, which assess the ability to construe correctly the intentions and beliefs of others (Jenkins & Asington, 1996; Perner, Ruffman, & Leekam, 1994; see Chapter 1).

Power even seems to prompt less careful thought in individuals who experience a tremendous incentive to demonstrate sophisticated reasoning—Supreme Court justices. A study compared the decisions of U.S. Supreme Court justices when they wrote opinions endorsing the positions of coalitions of different sizes (Gruenfeld & Kim, 1998). In some cases, justices wrote on behalf of a minority, typically equated with low power in democratic decision groups that use a "majority wins" rule (Davis, 1973; Jost, 1998). In other cases, justices wrote on behalf of the victorious majority. As you might have expected, justices writing from positions of power crafted less complex arguments in their opinions than

Box 4.2  FOCUS ON BUSINESS

# Power, Profligacy, and Accountability

In 2001 and 2002, Enron, the energy trading company based in Houston, Texas, collapsed in spectacular fashion. Once one of the most lauded companies in the world, it proceeded to lose billions of dollars in stockholders' assets, and had to lay off thousands of workers, in large part due to fraudulent accounting practices. Most emblematic of the Enron managers who exhibited corruption, greed, and immorality was Jeffrey Skilling.

Fresh from earning an MBA from Harvard University, Skilling was hired at Enron and saw himself as the company visionary, specializing in creating energy markets. He was aggressive, brash, and out of control. He would shout profanities at financial analysts who questioned his proposals. He took his favorite employees on outrageous vacations—in one, he and his friends trashed expensive SUVs in the Australian outback. He frequented Enron parties with strippers, and eventually divorced his wife to marry his secretary, whom he quickly promoted to a new job with an annual salary of $600,000. He had difficulties with alcohol. Eventually it was his reckless, deceptive business practices that fueled the Enron demise.

One way to understand the Enron collapse is to think about the context that gave rise to its reckless culture and often illegal investment style. It is a lesson about the perils of unchecked power. This story fits what we have learned about the disinhibiting effects of power. Another approach is to think about how people who actively seek out, desire, and express their power might be more likely to act in such out-of-control fashion. This has been the tack taken by David Winter and his colleagues. They have investigated the correlates of the need for power, which is measured from people's interpretations of the ambiguous social situations portrayed in Thematic Apperception Test scenes (Winter, 1973, 1988; Winter & Barenbaum, 1985). They find that college students who need a lot of power are more likely to hold offices in their dorms, fraternities, and university organizations; they are more likely to seek high-power careers—for example, in the law; and they are more likely to engage in profligate, disinhibited behaviors reminiscent of Jeffrey Skilling's reckless actions. They are more likely to gamble, drink, and seek one-night stands.

Winter and his colleagues have also documented an important factor that constrains the disinhibiting effects of power: accountability. Accountability refers to the condition in which one individual feels responsible to others. When individuals who have a high need for power experience accountability-enhancing life events—for example, having children—they are less likely to engage in profligate behaviors like gambling or drinking.

---

did those writing from low-power positions (for similar results see Gruenfeld, 1995; Janis, 1972; Janis & Mann, 1991; Nemeth, 1986).

The theory's second hypothesis is that power should make disinhibited (less constrained) social behavior more likely, even when it is inappropriate or unethical (see Box 4.2). Support for this hypothesis is found in numerous studies. High-power individuals are more likely to touch others and to approach them closely physically (Goffman, 1967; Henley, 1977; Heslin & Boss, 1980). People given power in an experiment are more likely to feel attraction to a random stranger (Bargh, Raymond, Prior, & Strack, 1995), to turn off an annoying fan in the room where the experiment is being conducted (Galinsky, Gruenfeld, & Magee, 2003), and to flirt in overly direct ways (Gonzaga, Keltner, & Ward, 2003; see also Rudman & Borgida, 1995). In the flirting study, a male and a female were paired with each other, and either the male or the female was given the power to evaluate his or her partner's performance on a pronunciation task. In a subsequent, rather informal, interaction, the high-power partner was more likely to flirt in direct

> "Power is the ultimate aphrodisiac."
>
> —HENRY KISSINGER

fashion, by touching the other person and gazing into the other person's eyes for unusually long periods of time. Consistent with an earlier point we made, the high-power participant was also more inaccurate in estimating his or her partner's emotions, assuming, perhaps dangerously, that the partner felt more positive emotion and less anxiety than was actually the case (Gonzaga, Keltner, & Ward, 2003).

In contrast, low-power individuals show inhibition of a wide variety of behaviors (for example, Guinote, Judd, & Brauer, 2002). Individuals with little power often constrict their posture (Ellyson & Dovidio, 1985), inhibit their speech (Holtgraves & Lasky, 1999; Hosman, 1989) and facial expressions (Keltner, Young, Heerey, Oemig, & Monarch, 1998), and clam up and withdraw in group interactions (Moreland & Levine, 1989).

Perhaps most unsettling are studies showing that elevated power makes antisocial communication and behavior more likely. For example, high-power individuals are more likely to violate politeness-related communication norms: they are more likely to talk more, to interrupt more, and to speak out of turn more (DePaulo & Friedman, 1998). They are also more likely to behave rudely at work (Pearson & Porath, 1999). Now consider a study in which two low-power fraternity members and two high-power members were brought to the laboratory and asked to tease each other by making up nicknames and telling amusing stories about one another (see Figure 4.5). High-power fraternity members teased low-power targets by making up nasty nicknames and telling more humiliating stories than did low-power fraternity members (Keltner, Young, Heerey, Oemig, & Monarch, 1998). This finding is consistent with other studies showing that, across a wide variety of contexts (for example, school playgrounds, hospital settings, summer camps), high-power individuals are more likely to tease in hostile fashion (Keltner, Capps, Kring, Young, & Heerey, 2001).

Power disinhibits more harmful forms of aggression as well, leading to violent behavior against low-power individuals. For example, power asymmetries predict the increased likelihood of sexual harassment (Studd, 1996). Moreover, across cultures and historical periods, the prevalence of rape rises with the cultural acceptance of male dominance and the subordination of females (Reeves-Sanday, 1997). Furthermore, Green, Wong, and Strolovitch (1996) found that the incidence of hate crimes against disliked minority groups (that is, nonwhites) was highest when the proportion of demographic majority members (that is, whites) in a particular neighborhood was largest relative to the proportion of minority members.

We have not portrayed power in a flattering light. High-power individuals tend to act in overly direct, impulsive, and even aggressive fashion. This may

**Figure 4.5 An Approach/Inhibition Theory of Power and the Dynamics of Teasing** The approach/inhibition theory of power holds that high-power individuals are more impulsive in their behavior, whereas low-power individuals are more likely to inhibit their behavior, and shift it according to social context. In this study, high- and low-power fraternity members teased each other in groups of four by making up nicknames about each other. Consistent with the approach/inhibition theory of power, high-power fraternity members teased in more hostile fashion than low-power members, whereas low-power members showed greater variation in their teasing according to whom they were teasing. (Source: Keltner, Young, Heerey, Oemig, & Monarch, 1998)

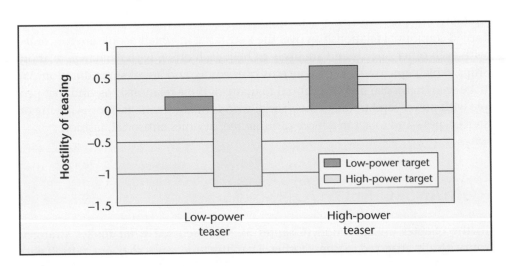

help shed light on certain disturbing trends in society—the child abuse perpetrated by some Catholic priests, the excessive personal expenditures of some CEOs at the company's expense even while the company is going down the tubes. Such tendencies are all the more alarming when we consider the scrutiny to which people in power are subject, and the influence they have over our lives.

What are we to do? Research suggests that we should be careful about who gains power, for power seems to allow individuals to express their true inclinations, both good and bad. If the person is inclined toward malevolent or competitive behavior, power will only make him or her more so inclined. If, on the other hand, the person is more benevolent or good natured, power will amplify the expression of those tendencies. In a study that nicely illustrates this claim, Chen and colleagues identified and preselected participants who were either more self-interested and exchange-oriented, or more compassionate and communal-oriented (Chen, Lee-Chai, & Bargh, 2001). Each participant was then randomly assigned to a high-power or low-power position in a clever, subtle manner: high-power individuals were seated in a snazzy leather professorial chair during the experiment; low-power individuals were seated in a plain chair typical of psychology experiments. Participants were then asked to volunteer to complete a packet of questionnaires with the help of another participant, who was late. Consistent with the idea that power amplifies the expression of preexisting tendencies, the communal-oriented participants with high power took on the lion's share of filling out the questionnaires. In contrast, the exchange-oriented participants with high power acted in more self-serving fashion, leaving more of the task for the other participant. The effects of power, then, depend quite dramatically on who is in power.

*"I'm not a machine, Deborah, I can't just turn my greed on and off."*

**LOOKING BACK,** we now see that our assumptions and beliefs about the basis of different kinds of relationships affect how we think, act, and feel, even what we consider right and wrong. Fiske's relational models theory posits that there are four different kinds of relational styles—communal sharing, authority ranking, equality matching, and market pricing—which determine our judgments of justice and morality, and our construal and memory of social events. Clark and Mills have contrasted communal relationships over the long term, in which people are concerned with each other's needs and are likely to help each other, with exchange relationships, which are governed by concerns over equity and are of short duration. We have seen that social power is central to many of these relationships, and that people with power tend to judge their social worlds in automatic fashion—relying on stereotypes—and to act in a more disinhibited, at times antisocial, fashion.

## ROMANTIC RELATIONSHIPS

In the chapter on attraction (Chapter 3), we discussed what makes strangers romantically attracted to one another. That literature tends to concern itself with relationships up until the initial moment of romantic interest. What happens after? That is the topic of this last section in our chapter on relationships.

As everyone knows, romantic relationships are based on love. But they vary based on the strength of the love, trust, and dependence felt by each of the partners toward the other. Romantic relationships involve intimacy between the partners, and they generally include a physical expression of this intimacy. According to Robert Sternberg's **triangular theory of love**, the three major components of love are intimacy, passion, and commitment, which can be combined in different ways (Sternberg, 1986). For example, intimacy and passion combine to form romantic love, often known as passionate love, which is characterized by feelings of sexual arousal and generally culminates in sexual intimacy. Intimacy and commitment combine to form companionate love, which involves intimacy without sexual arousal. Intimacy, passion, and commitment combine to form consummate love, which Sternberg considers the ultimate form of love.

> **triangular theory of love**
> A theory that states that there are three major components of love—intimacy, passion, and commitment—which can be combined in different ways.

There are two facts that seem undeniable about romantic bonds. The first is that they are such an important part of our social life. Almost all of us enter into a romantic relationship at some point in our lives. Although people are delaying the age at which they marry, 90 percent of Americans and Canadians still marry, and it is unusual to never enter into an intimate, romantic relationship with another person.

The second important fact is that romantic relationships are important to our well-being (Myers, 2000a). As we shall see in the chapter on emotion (Chapter 12), one of the strongest predictors of whether people are satisfied with life is whether they are in a satisfying romantic relationship. Married people are happier with life than divorced and single people. Moreover, healthy romantic bonds are also conducive to good physical health (Berscheid & Reis, 1998).

If marriage can lead to a happier, longer life, then why do so many marriages end in divorce? What are the predictors of problems that may lead to unhappy romantic relationships? And what makes for more satisfying romantic relationships? Researchers on marital dissatisfaction and satisfaction have attempted to uncover the factors that weaken or strengthen romantic bonds (Bradbury, 1998; Fincham, 2003; Hill & Peplau, 1998).

## MARITAL DISSATISFACTION

Regrettably, something seems to be going wrong with the institution of marriage—at least in North America. Current estimates are that approximately one-half of first marriages now end in separation or divorce (Martin & Bumpass, 1989; Myers, 2000a). Studies of people's reports of marital satisfaction indicate that marriages seem to be less satisfying today than they were thirty years ago (Glenn, 1991; Myers, 2000a). Marital conflict stimulates adrenal and pituitary stress responses, which are known to cause cardiac problems and inhibit immune responses (Kiecolt-Glaser, Malarkey, Cacioppo, & Glaser, 1994). And now we are learning that there is a legacy of unhappy marriages. Children of divorced parents can experience greater difficulties, both during childhood and later in adulthood (Amato & Keith, 1991; Wallerstein, Lewis, & Blakeslee, 2000). As we saw in the section on attachment, early divorce of parents is associated with an anxious attachment style in the child—a style that is associated with romantic and personal difficulties.

Given that romantic dissastisfaction seems so widespread and has such far-reaching effects, we will examine the factors that are likely to predict romantic dissatisfaction and divorce. Understanding what these factors are will help us to get our romantic relationships right, so that they will be less likely to end in the loosening of romantic bonds and in divorce.

***Demographic Predictors of Marital Dissatisfaction and Divorce***    One way to understand unhappy romantic bonds is to ask whether certain kinds of people or certain circumstances make marital dissatisfaction or divorce more likely. To answer this question, researchers typically ask romantic partners to fill out questionnaires dealing with their satisfaction with their relationships (see Table 4.2). They then relate the participants' responses to measures of the personalities and backgrounds of their partners.

What we have learned is the following: First, personality matters. Neurotic people, who tend to be anxious, tense, emotionally volatile, and plaintive, have less happy romantic relationships and are more likely to divorce (Karney & Bradbury, 1997; Karney, Bradbury, Fincham, & Sullivan, 1994; Kurdek, 1993). Highly neurotic individuals are more likely to experience negative emotion, to experience health problems (Watson & Pennebaker, 1989), and to react strongly to interpersonal conflict (Bolger & Schilling, 1991). All of these tendencies are likely

---

### Table 4.2  Measuring the Elements of the Commitment Model of Romantic Relationships

To assess how strong the bonds between romantic partners are, researchers ask the partners to respond to statements that reveal possible alternative romantic partners, investment in the relationship, commitment to the relationship, and satisfaction with the relationship.

| ELEMENT OF MODEL | SAMPLE ITEM |
| --- | --- |
| Alternatives | "All things considered, how attractive are the people other than your partner with whom you could become involved?" |
| Rewards | "Are there special activities associated with your relationship that you would in some sense lose or that would be more difficult to obtain if the relationship were to end (for example, shared friends, child rearing, recreational activities, job)?" |
| Investments | "Have you devoted your time and effort and money to buying and improving the home you share, cultivating friendships, rearing children, or building a business together, which would be lost or damaged if the relationship were to end?" |
| Commitment | "For how much longer do you want your relationship to last?" |
| Satisfaction | "All things considered, to what degree do you feel satisfied with your relationship?" |

Source: Adapted from Rusbult, 1980.

to reduce the satisfaction derived from romantic bonds. For similar reasons, people who are highly sensitive to rejection have greater difficulties in intimate relationships (Downey & Feldman, 1996; Downey, Freistas, Michaelis, & Khouri, 1998; see also Murray, Holmes, MacDonald, & Ellsworth, 1998). Moreover, romantic partners and friends sensitive to rejection respond with greater hostility when feeling rejected by intimate others (Ayduk, Downey, Testa, Yen, & Shoda, 1999; Downey, Feldman, & Ayduk, 2000). In middle school, peers who are sensitive to rejection are more lonely (Downey, Lebolt, Rincon, & Freitas, 1998). And relationships in which both partners are sensitive to rejection are more likely to end sooner (Downey, Freitas, Michaelis, & Khouri, 1998).

Certain demographic factors also predict problems in romantic relationships. Most notably, individuals from lower socioeconomic (SES) backgrounds are more likely to divorce (Williams & Collins, 1995). Being from a lower SES background is more likely to introduce into the relationship financial and work-related problems, which are some of the primary reasons why marriages break up (Berscheid & Reis, 1998). Moreover, people who marry at younger ages are more likely to divorce. There are several possible explanations of this finding. It may be that younger people are not as effective at being partners in long-term romantic relations. Or people who marry young may not be as effective at choosing the right romantic partners. (It might be worth noting that, although some species of penguins eventually "get married" to a lifetime partner, they are quite fickle when young, bouncing from one relationship to another with abandon!)

*The Interaction Dynamics of Unhappy Partners*   A second way of thinking about what makes romantic partners unhappy is to think about the specific behaviors that lead to difficulties or happiness. Are there telltale signs that a couple will be headed for divorce, or that a couple will remain happy together for the rest of their lives? John Gottman and Robert Levenson are pioneers in what is known as the **interaction dynamics approach**, and they have documented remarkably powerful predictors of dissatisfaction and divorce (Levenson & Gottman, 1983; Gottman & Levenson, 1992).

Gottman and Levenson have studied married partners engaged in intense conversations, which are videotaped in the laboratory and then studied carefully for the telltale signs of romantic problems. In a conflict discussion task, partners talk for fifteen minutes about an issue that they both recognize is a source of intense conflict in their relationship, and they try their best to resolve it. For example, partners might talk about unsatisfying sex, the husband's inability to get better-paying work, or their child's difficulties in high school. Participants also engage in other conversations about the events of the day and about something pleasant in the relationship. Gottman and Levenson then code the interactions for several negative behaviors, including anger, criticism, defensiveness, contempt, sadness, and fear. They also code the interactions for several positive behaviors, including affection, enthusiasm, interest, and humor.

In one long-term study, starting in 1983 and continuing to this day, Gottman and Levenson have followed the marriages of seventy-nine couples from Bloomington, Indiana. Based on their observations, they have identified "the Four Horsemen of the Apocalypse"—that is, the negative behaviors that are most harmful to relationships. One is *criticism*. A robust finding in the marriage literature is that, as one would expect, more-critical

**interaction dynamics approach** A methodological approach to the study of the behaviors and conversations of couples, with a focus on negative behaviors such as anger, criticism, defensiveness, contempt, sadness, and fear, and positive behaviors such as affection, enthusiasm, interest, and humor.

*"I hope when I grow up I'll have an amicable divorce."*

partners who continually carp and find fault with their partners have less satisfying marriages. Partners who can deliver criticism in a lighthearted, playful fashion, on the other hand, tended to be happier (Keltner, Young, Heerey, Oemig, & Monarch, 1998).

The next two predictors of dissatisfaction and divorce are *defensiveness* and *stonewalling* (resisting dealing with problems). When romantic partners are unable to talk openly and freely about their difficulties without being defensive, they are in trouble. This is especially true of men. To the extent that the male partner stonewalls, withdraws, denies, and rejects the issues the female partner brings up, there is great dissatisfaction in the relationship. In contrast, the more people disclose to one another, the more they tend to like each other (Collins & Miller, 1994).

Finally, there is one emotion that is particularly toxic to romantic bonds, and that is *contempt*. Contempt is the emotion felt when one person looks down on another. It has to do with rejection and feelings of superiority. You might feel contempt when you hear a person bragging to a group of friends, and you know that what he is saying is not true. In Gottman and Levenson's work, a wife's expression of contempt is especially predictive of dissatisfaction and divorce. For example, in Figure 4.6 we present the frequency that contempt was observed in a discussion about a topic of conflict for couples who eventually divorced, and for those who did not (Gottman & Levenson, 1999). The couples who eventually divorced expressed more than twice as much contempt as the couples who stayed together.

It should be noted that the Gottman and Levenson studies are susceptible to a version of the self-selection problem: Do married couples get divorced because they express contempt and other unpleasant emotions, or do they express these emotions because their relationship is on rocky ground? If the former is the case, then the lesson would be very clear: be pleasant or face the consequences. If the latter is the case, there wouldn't be much of a lesson at all—just the sad recognition that when things are going badly in a relationship the partners are going to express unpleasant affect. Two additional findings by Gottman and Levenson, however, suggest that negative affect may in fact make a direct contribution to relationship stability.

In the study of seventy-nine couples from Indiana, Gottman and Levenson used measures of the four toxic behaviors (criticism, defensiveness, stonewalling, and contempt) to predict who would stay together and who would be divorced fourteen years later. Quite remarkably, they could predict who would stay married and who

**Figure 4.6 Contempt and Marital Dissatisfaction** A particularly toxic emotion in romantic bonds is contempt. In this study, Gottman and Levenson coded facial expressions of contempt from a fifteen-minute conversation. Married partners who expressed more contempt were more likely to be divorced fourteen years later than married partners who expressed less contempt. (Source: Gottman & Levenson, 1999)

would divorce with 93 percent accuracy based on these four measures gathered from a fifteen-minute conversation (Gottman & Levenson, 2000). This finding suggests, though it does not prove, that affect plays a role in causing the breakup.

For the couples who eventually divorced, it was possible to predict which couples would do so earlier and which couples would stay in the marriage somewhat longer. For early divorcing couples, who were divorced on average 7.4 years after they were married, negative affect—for example contempt and anger—was especially predictive of the demise of the marriage. For later-divorcing couples, who divorced on average 13.9 years after they were married, it was the absence of positive emotions like humor and interest that predicted the end of their bond.

*Dangerous Attributions*    Thus far, we have seen that divorce and dissatisfaction are more likely to befall romantic partners from certain backgrounds and romantic partners who are especially prone to criticize, to be defensive and stonewall, and to express certain kinds of negative emotion. In light of a central theme of this book, one would also expect certain construal tendencies to be problematic in maintaining romantic bonds. One robust construal tendency associated with dissatisfaction and dissolution is *blame*. In a review of twenty-three studies, Bradbury and Fincham (1990) looked at the relationship between romantic partners' causal attributions and their relationship satisfaction. The researchers studied the partners' attributions in different ways. In some studies, partners' attributions were coded from their conversations with one another. For example, a participant might spontaneously attribute a partner's insensitivity and rudeness at an important social gathering either to situational factors—the noise and drunkenness of the crowd—or to dispositional factors—the partner's enduring boorishness and arrogance. In other studies that contributed to the review, romantic partners were asked to make attributions for hypothetical things their partners might do. In still other studies, partners made attributions for the most negative and the most positive event that had occurred that day in their relationship.

What is clear from these studies is that dissatisfied, distressed couples make attributions that cast their partner and their relationship in a negative light (Karney & Bradbury, 2000; McNulty & Karney, 2001). Distressed couples attribute positive events in their relationships to unstable causes that are specific, unintended, and selfish. For example, a distressed partner might interpret a partner's unexpected gift of flowers as the result of some whim, particular to that day, which would no doubt be followed by some selfish request. Happier couples tend to attribute the same unexpected gift of flowers to stable causes that are general, intended, and selfless. A satisfied romantic partner would thus attribute the gift of flowers to the partner's enduring kindness and thoughtfulness. In terms of negative events in the relationship, we see a complementary pattern of results. Happier partners attribute negative events—the forgotten anniversary or sarcastic comment—to specific and unintended causes, whereas distressed partners attribute the same kinds of negative events to stable and global causes and see their partners as blameworthy and selfish. Before we move on to what makes for a stronger romantic relationship, let's be mindful of the "Four Horsemen of the Apocalypse." By identifying their presence sooner rather than later, you might be able to keep your own marriage from becoming a negative statistic.

## CREATING STRONGER ROMANTIC BONDS

Thus far, we have painted a somewhat bleak picture of the demise of romantic relationships. Let's now turn to the kinds of things you can do to build more intimate, healthy, and satisfying bonds. The literature we have just reviewed provides some clues. You might be wise to marry when a bit older; to avoid highly anxious, rejection-sensitive, neurotic individuals when choosing a partner; to minimize the criticism, defensiveness, stonewalling, and contempt in your interactions; and to try to interpret your partner's actions in a more flattering light. Moreover, your relationships will be more satisfying, we shall now see, if you are more committed to your partner, if you idealize your partner, and if you keep doing exciting, exhilarating things together.

*The Investment Model of Relationship Commitment*    One of the most challenging dimensions to a relationship has to do with the dreaded "C" word, commitment. All relationships face the difficult commitment problem: How do you know that your partner will remain committed to you in the face of so many alternatives, and how will you remain committed for the long haul as well? This is an especially difficult problem in independent cultures that value freedom and the pursuit of individual self-interest. In today's Western world in which one is free to leave a relationship—even a marital relationship—with relatively little social censure or pang of conscience, the difficulties of remaining committed are particularly acute.

Caryl Rusbult has developed an **investment model of interpersonal relationships**, which helps us to understand how we might remain committed and happy in romantic relationships (Rusbult, 1980, 1983). A flowchart of the investment model is presented in Figure 4.7. Three things make partners more committed to one another: rewards, alternatives, and investment in the relationship. The first and most obvious determinant of commitment is *rewards*. Time after time, in questionnaires that ask romantic partners to rate the rewards they receive from their relationship as well as what they give, one of the strongest determinants of romantic satisfaction is how much they get out of the relationship (Cate, Lloyd, Henton, & Larson, 1982).

Simple rewards, however, are not enough. Whether or not there are *alternative partners* also is a strong contributor to the commitment a partner feels. The fewer alternatives a romantic partner has, the more committed, and the more likely the partner will remain in the relationship. For example, in questionnaire studies, romantic partners who report few alternatives are less likely to break up later on (White & Booth, 1991). A person may stick with a relationship that is not terribly satisfying if it is the only game in town. In contrast, people sometimes leave gratifying relationships in pursuit of others that appear to be even more promising. (Think of the multiple marriages of the gorgeous movie star or the wealthy entrepreneur.)

The third determinant of commitment in Rusbult's investment model is the

---

**investment model of interpersonal relationships** A model of interpersonal relationships that maintains that three things make partners more committed to one another: rewards, alternatives, and investments in the relationship.

---

**Figure 4.7 Rusbult's Investment Model of Romantic Commitment** According to Rusbult's model, three factors determine how committed romantic partners are: how many rewards they derive from the relationship, the available romantic alternatives, and how much they have invested in the relationship. More committed partners, in turn, are more likely to engage in pro-social behavior, like forgiveness, and they are more likely to feel trust and satisfaction in the bond.

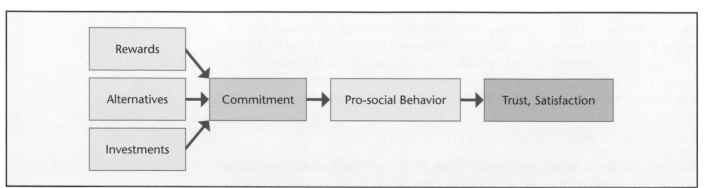

# Investment and the Return of the Battered Woman

One of the most telling studies of the predictive power of the investment model is one in which it was used to predict whether women who had sought shelter from abusive husbands would return to them (Rusbult & Martz, 1995). Some of the women returned to their husbands right away (defined as within three months), some only after an extended period (between three months and a year), and some never returned. Rusbult was interested in whether the investments these women had made in their relationships and the quality of the alternatives that were available to them would predict whether they would reconcile with their husbands. (Satisfaction level was anticipated to have little impact in this case, because, given the severity of the abuse these women had experienced, there was unlikely to be much satisfaction left for any of them.) As part of the standard admissions procedure in a battered women's shelter, the women were asked a number of questions that could serve as measures of investments (for example, duration of relationship, number of children) and alternatives (for example, independent income source, transportation available). Consistent with the investment model, measures of each of these constructs were related to whether and when the women returned to their abusive husbands. Women who were heavily invested in their relationship and who had limited opportunities for alternative arrangements were most likely to return.

one that gives it its name: the *investments* that one has put into the relationship. Satisfaction and possible alternatives aside, a person is more likely to remain in a relationship if he or she has invested heavily in it in the past. A person's investments can be direct, such as the time, effort, caring, and love that he or she has given to the relationship. Or they can be indirect, such as the shared memories, mutual friends, or shared possessions that are part of the relationship.

Most empirical tests of Rusbult's investment model have examined dating couples and married partners over time, using self-report questionnaire measures administered every six months or so for a couple of years (Berg & McQuinn, 1986; Rusbult, 1983; Simpson, 1987). Partners report on the three determinants of their commitment (rewards, alternatives, and investments), their level of commitment, and how satisfied they are in their relationship (see Table 4.2 on p. 158 for sample items). By using these measures and studying couples over time, Rusbult and colleagues have begun to paint a picture of how commitment promotes positive behavior, trust, and satisfaction.

Knowing how people evaluate their relationship in terms of the variables specified in the investment model allows one to predict which relationships will endure with much greater accuracy than if the predictions were made blindly. Furthermore, each of three determinants of commitment—rewards, alternative possibilities, and investments—has been shown to be important. Each one increases the ability to predict a couple's decision to stay or leave (see Box 4.3).

Other studies by Rusbult and colleagues have shown how commitment promotes more satisfying and stable bonds. More-committed partners tend to represent their life with their partner in more interdependent, intertwined terms (Agnew, Van Lange, Rusbult, & Langston, 1998). When asked to describe their relationship, more-committed partners are more likely to use plural pronouns ("we"), and they are more likely to represent their own identity and that of their partner as overlapping. If you hear a new romantic interest of yours use phrases like "What are we doing this weekend?" or "When will we apply to graduate school?," it is safe to assume that he or she feels committed to you. Commitment promotes a sense of merged identity.

In other research, highly committed partners were found to be more likely to engage in pro-social behaviors, like self-sacrifice and accommodation, rather than retaliation, in the face of demands on the part of their partner (Wieselquist, Rusbult, Agnew, & Foster, 1999). For example, a more-committed married partner, in adjusting to the demands of the arrival of a first child, would be more likely to adjust his or her personal life, sacrificing regular exercise at the gym, poker night with the boys, or two movies a week, so that the family thrives. Such accommodating behaviors would promote increased trust in the other partner at later points in the relationship, thus motivating the individual's increased commitment to the relationship.

And finally, commitment promotes forgiveness (Finkel, Rusbult, Kumashiro, & Hannon, 2002). For example, in one study, romantic partners filled out a daily diary in which they reported their partner's betrayals. These included inappropriate flirtations, disclosures of personal information, and even infidelity—the kind of problems that can rapidly break a romantic bond. More-committed partners were more likely to forgive their partner for these kinds of transgressions.

***Illusions and Idealization in Romantic Relationships***   One of the most striking qualities of love is its delirious irrationality. We describe love as sickness, madness, or fever. We call the person we love a deity, a treasure, a person of unimaginable beauty and virtue. Perhaps this irrationality has some benefit for the relationship. In terms of Rusbult's investment model, to the extent that we idealize our partner, we are likely to feel his or her actions are all the more rewarding and that there are no comparable alternatives. The end result of our irrational constructions is enhanced commitment.

Sandra Murray and her colleagues have collected compelling evidence that suggests that the idealization of romantic partners is an important ingredient in satisfying intimate bonds (Murray & Holmes, 1993, 1997; Murray, Holmes, Dolderman, & Griffin, 2000; Neff & Karney, 2002). In one study, married couples and dating partners rated themselves and their partner on twenty-one traits related to virtues (for example, understanding, patient), desirable attributes within romantic relationships (for example, easygoing, witty), and faults (for example, complaining, distant) (Murray, Holmes, & Griffin, 1996). Murray and her colleagues also gathered measures of the romantic partners' relationship satisfaction. They then compared the participants' ratings of their partner's virtues and faults to their ratings of their satisfaction in the relationship.

What do you think would predict satisfaction in the relationship: knowing the truth about your partner's virtues, faults, and traits, or idealizing your partner? Idealization was captured in the tendency for participants to overestimate their partner's virtues and underestimate their faults when compared with the partner's own self-ratings. Two findings suggest that Blake's poem about the beneficial blindness of love stands the test of time. Individuals who idealized their romantic partners were more satisfied in their relationship. Individuals also reported greater relationship satisfaction when they themselves were idealized by their partners.

In other studies, Murray and Holmes (1999) have examined how people idealize their romantic partners. In one study, people were asked to write about their partner's greatest fault. Satisfied partners engaged in two forms of idealization, as

> "Love to faults is always blind,
> Always is to joy inclined,
> Lawless, winged, and unconfined,
> And breaks all chains from
>     every mind."
>
> —WILLIAM BLAKE

coded from the descriptions of their partner's greatest fault. First, they saw virtue in their partner's faults. For example, an individual might write that his or her partner was melancholy, but that melancholy gave the partner a depth of character that was incomparably rewarding. Second, satisfied partners were more likely to offer "yes, but" refutations of the fault. For example, a satisfied partner might write that her husband did not like to hold down a steady job, but at least that gave him more time to help out at home.

Work by Hawkins, Carrere, and Gottman (2002) suggests that more satisfied couples also idealize their partner's emotions. In this study, ninety-six couples from the Seattle, Washington, area completed the conflict discussion task that we described earlier (see p. 159). They then returned to the lab and viewed their interaction on videotape, using a rating dial to provide continuous ratings of how much positive and negative affect their partner expressed during the interaction. These self-report measures were compared with judges' ratings of the partner's positive behavior (humor, affection) and negative behavior (anger, contempt). More-satisfied romantic partners overestimated how much positive affect their partner was showing compared to judges' ratings, and they underestimated their partners' negative emotion. Several other studies have shown that happier couples interpret their spontaneous interactions in a more positive light than do outside observers (Robinson & Price, 1980).

*Novel and Arousing Activities*    One of the most robust findings in the literature on romantic satisfaction has to do with the effects of having children on the quality of the relationship (Myers, 2000a). Although having children makes people happy, and their personal satisfaction remains what it was prior to parenthood, the arrival of children has a devastating effect on marital satisfaction. In fact, married partners typically only return to their previous level of satisfaction once the children leave the home. (This reminds us of the discussion among the priest, the rabbi, and the minister on the topic of when life begins. The priest asserted it occurred at conception, the rabbi at birth, and the minister as being when the dog dies and the last child goes away to college.) One obvious reason that children place a burden on the marriage is that married partners, in the course of their relationship, have less time to devote just to each other. Whereas courtship and the early phases of a relationship include late-night dancing, candlelit exchanges of poetry, weekend getaways, and other exhilarating activities, the later stages of a relationship, especially when children are involved, become oriented around diaper changing, bottle cleaning, sibling conflict, and chauffeuring to soccer practices and piano lessons.

One obvious recommendation, then, is to buck this trend and commit to engaging in novel and exhilarating activities. That is just what Art Aron and his colleagues have found. They conducted a study in which spouses who had been married for several years engaged in one of two tasks (Aron, Norman, Aron, McKenna, & Heyman, 2000). In the novel, arousing condition, partners were tied together at the knees and wrists with velcro straps, and they were required to move a soft ball positioned between their heads across a long mat. This unusual activity was a source of amusement. In the other condition, each partner had to push a ball on his or her own to the middle of the mat with a stick. Just as much exercise was involved, but not as much novelty or engagement with the partner. Spouses reported significantly higher marital satisfaction after engaging in the novel, arousing task, both compared to the participants in the other condition, and compared to an earlier assessed baseline (see also Gable, Reis, Impett, & Asher, 2004). The moral: Keep trying new and pleasurable things.

**LOOKING BACK,** we have seen that romantic relationships are an important part of most people's social lives and that they are important to people's psychological and physical well-being. Nonetheless, many marriages do not provide satisfaction, and many end in separation and divorce. Personality and demographic factors can predict unhappiness in marriage. Negative interactions, particularly the expression of toxic behaviors like criticism, defensiveness, stonewalling, and contempt, are more likely to lead to unhappy marriages, while positive interactions, including the expression of affection, enthusiasm, interest, and humor, are more likely to lead to happy marriages. Finally, relationships in which the partners are committed are likely to be stable and possibly grow.

## SUMMARY

1. There is a biologically based *need to belong,* evident in the evolutionary benefits and universality of different relationships and in the negative consequences that accompany the absence of relationships, as shown by the deficits in feral children.

2. Relationships shape the sense of self and how social events are remembered and explained. People all have certain *relational selves,* or beliefs, feelings, and expectations that derive from their relationships with particular other people. When one of these is activated by a particular person, the person is seen in the light of the relevant relational self.

3. John Bowlby's *attachment theory* holds that, early in development, children rely on their parents for a sense of security. Some children are luckier in these formative relationships than others. People having a *secure attachment style* are comfortable with intimacy and wish to be close to other people when they are stressed. People having an *avoidant attachment style* feel insecure in relationships and distance themselves from others. People who have an *anxious attachment style* are also insecure in relationships but respond to this insecurity by compulsively seeking closeness and by obsessing about the quality of their relations with others.

4. Researchers have discovered that attachment styles are quite stable over the lifespan. Secure, anxious, and avoidant individuals live quite different lives, enjoying different levels of relationship satisfaction (securely attached individuals are the most satisfied and the least likely to break up) and suffering different kinds of difficulties (anxiously attached individuals are particularly prone to psychological problems).

5. Fiske's relational models theory posits that there are four different kinds of relational styles: (a) the *communal sharing*, family-like, relationship style, in which members of the group receive what they need and give what they can; (b) the *authority ranking* relationship style characteristic of corporations and tribal groups headed by chiefs, in which power flows from a head to those lower and resources are distributed as the head sees fit; (c) the *equality matching* relationship style governed by the principles of reciprocity and sameness, which is typified by friendships; and (d) the *market pricing* relationship style governed by the principle of benefits in proportion to inputs and characteristic of companies that reward individuals in proportion to their contributions. All of these relationship styles are practiced by all societies (with the exception of market pricing for some), but different cultures apply different styles in different domains.

6. Clark and Mills have contrasted *communal relationships* over the long term with *exchange relationships* of short duration that are governed by concerns of equity.

7. Power is based on *status, authority,* and *dominance relations*. According to the approach/inhibition theory of power, elevated power makes people look at things in more simplistic fashion, and act in the social world in more disinhibited ways.

8. The most mysterious and compelling relationship is the romantic bond. Romantic relationships are an

important part of our social life, and they are important to our satisfaction with our lives and even our physical health.

9. Divorce and marital dissatisfaction are often caused by *marrying young, criticism, defensiveness, stonewalling*, and *contempt*.

10. Happy romantic relations are affected by *commitment*, which is a function of rewards in the relationship, *alternatives* to the relationship, and *investments* in the relationhip. Happy couples have more *positive illusions* about their partners, and they are likely to pursue novel but arousing activities together.

## CRITICAL THINKING ABOUT BASIC PRINCIPLES

1. A central theme of this chapter is that our relationships influence how we construe our social worlds. Can you think of how our relationships influence: (a) our self-concept; (b) how we attend to and remember social information; and (c) the explanations we offer for our own and others' behavior?

2. Imagine that you are working in a preschool near your college, and each day you are present when the parents drop off their children. One child, upon being dropped off, expresses extreme distress and anger when his parents leave. How would you classify this child's attachment style? As the child matures into adulthood, what would you expect of his relationships with others and the particular difficulties he might encounter?

3. If you were on a radio show and were asked to provide ten tips for avoiding divorce and having a satisfying marriage, what advice would you give? More specifically, what five things would you encourage people thinking about marrying to do to avoid marital problems? And what five things would you recommend to bring greater pleasure and joy to their relationship?

## KEY TERMS

anxious attachment style (p. 144)
attachment theory (p. 142)
authority (p. 151)
authority ranking relationship
   (p. 147)
avoidant attachment style (p. 144)
communal relationships (p. 149)
communal sharing relationship
   (p. 147)
dominance (p. 151)
equality matching relationship
   (p. 147)

exchange relationships (p. 149)
experience-sampling studies (p. 140)
interaction dynamics approach
   (p. 159)
interpersonal relationships (p. 131)
investment model of interpersonal
   relationships (p. 162)
market pricing relationship (p. 148)
power (p. 151)
relational models theory (p. 147)
relational self (p. 135)
relational self theory (p. 135)

secure attachment style (p. 143)
self-expansion account of
   relationships (p. 139)
social dominance orientation
   (p. 153)
status (p. 151)
strange situation (p. 143)
transactive memory (p. 139)
triangular theory of love (p. 157)
working models of relationships
   (p. 142)

## FURTHER READING

Bowlby, J. (1969/1982). *Attachment and loss: Vol. 1. Attachment* (2nd ed.). New York: Basic Books.

Duck, S. (1997). *Handbook of personal relationships: Theory, research, and interventions* (2nd ed.). Chichester, England: Wiley.

Fiske, A. P. (1992). Four elementary forms of sociality: Framework for a unified theory of social relations. *Psychological Review, 99,* 689–723.

Keltner, D., Gruenfeld, D., & Anderson, C. A. (2003). Power, approach, and inhibition, *Psychological Review, 110,* 265–284.

Mikulincer, M., & Shaver, P. R. (2003). The attachment behavioral system in adulthood: Activation, psychodynamics, and interpersonal processes. In M. P. Zanna (Ed.), *Advances in experimental social psychology* (Vol. 35, pp. 53–152). New York: Academic Press.

# Chapter Outline

# CHAPTER 5

# The Social Self

In his treatment of patients suffering from various neurological disorders, Oliver Sacks worked with one fascinating patient, William Thompson, who suffered from Korsakoff's syndrome (Sacks, 1985). Often the result of long years of alcohol abuse, Korsakoff's syndrome destroys memory structures in the brain, resulting in amnesia, intellectual deterioration, and the loss of some sensation. William was unable to remember things for more than a second or two. As a result, he had no stable sense of self. He lived in an eternal and at times inexplicable present. Each new interaction required that William create a new identity, a new social reality, both for himself and for those with whom he was interacting. Here is one illustrative exchange, in which William attributes a variety of identities to Oliver Sacks:

> "What'll it be today?" he says, rubbing his hands. "Half a pound of Virginia, a nice piece of Nova?"
>
> (Evidently he saw me as a customer—he often would pick up the phone on the ward, and say "Thompson's Delicatessen.")
>
> "Oh Mr. Thompson!" I exclaim. "And who do you think I am?"

"Good heavens, the light's bad—I took you for a customer. As if it isn't my old friend Tom Pitkins. . . . Me and Tom" (he whispers in an aside to the nurse) "was always going to the races together."

"Mr. Thompson, you are mistaken again."

"So I am," he rejoins, not put out for a moment. "Why would you be wearing a white coat if you were Tom? You're Hymie, the kosher butcher next door. No bloodstains on your coat though. Business bad today? You'll look like a slaughterhouse by the end of the week!" (Sacks, 1985, p. 108)

During this interaction, Sacks felt swept away by William's continually shifting identities and assumptions, saying "He would whirl, fluently, from one guess, one hypothesis, one belief, to the next, without any appearance of uncertainty at any point—he never knew who I was, or what or where *he* was, an ex-grocer, with severe Korsakov's, in a neurological institution. . . . such a patient *must literally make himself (and his world) up every moment*" (Sacks, 1985, pp. 109–110). Sacks writes: ". . . other people excite and rattle him, force him into an endless, frenzied, social chatter, a veritable delirium of identity-making and -seeking" (Sacks, 1985, p. 115).

William's condition—his life without a stable sense of self—brings into focus the four themes of this chapter on the social self. First, it is clear from William's frenzied "identity making" that the self has deep roots, tied to our relations with others, which William's neurological condition has destroyed. The self has enduring foundations that guide us as we move through different social interactions. In this chapter, we will detail how biologically based dispositions, our family, our current and historical social context, our cultural origin, and our gender all contribute to our sense of self.

William's shifting sense of self points to a second insight of this chapter: the power of self-knowledge—that is, our beliefs about ourselves. William approaches each new situation, each new person, with no preexisting self-knowledge, as that has been lost in the deteriorated memory structures of his brain. While it might seem desirable to approach each new situation without bias or preconception, William's condition leads to a different conclusion: our self-knowledge gives coherence and order to our social perception and behavior. In our treatment of self-knowledge, we will examine the forms and functions of self-knowledge and how it varies dramatically in different cultures.

Our third interest in this chapter is to illuminate the nature of self-evaluation—our assessments of our virtues and flaws. We will focus in particular on self-esteem—the value we place on ourselves. We will discuss the various determinants of self-esteem, how self-esteem varies in different cultures, and the potential risks of having too much self-esteem. Can someone like William, who lacks a stable sense of self, maintain positive self-regard?

Finally, one cannot help but be impressed by the drama of William's interac-

> "A man has as many social selves as there are individuals who recognize him. As many different social selves as there are distinct groups about whose opinions he cares."
> —WILLIAM JAMES

tions. He quickly falls into different characters, just as an actor might take on different personae with different mannerisms, accents, and costumes. William sweeps up other individuals in his rapidly changing dramas. Part of the self is a dramatic performance. This notion, so nicely illustrated by William's characters, will guide the last section of this chapter, which will focus on self-presentation and the different facets of the public self that are realized in the drama of social life.

## FOUNDATIONS OF THE SELF-CONCEPT

The development of the **self-concept**—that is, understanding of the existence and properties of a separate self and its characteristics—is one of the most regular developmental achievements (Harter, 1983). At about nine months of age, children start to differentiate self from other, and by fifteen to eighteen months of age, they clearly have a sense of their individual self. Typical year-and-a-half-old children will touch rouge on their noses upon seeing themselves in a mirror, revealing a sense of self-awareness. Children of the same age will react more strongly to photos of themselves than to photos of other people.

**Self-Awareness** Most eighteen-month-old children have a sense of self-awareness, recognizing themselves as individuals. They recognize that the image they are staring at in a mirror is their own self. When they see rouge on the nose of the image in the mirror, they touch the spot on their own nose.

This nascent sense of self expands dramatically into a complex web of beliefs, images, goals, and feelings. Where do these aspects of the self come from? Where do you think *your* core self comes from? One basis of the self-concept derives from biologically based traits that we in part inherit from our parents.

### BIOLOGICAL DISPOSITIONS

When asked to describe themselves, people from a wide range of different cultures do so in terms of traits. You yourself might say you are calm, warm, modest, and outgoing. These are all **traits**, which refer to the consistent ways that people think, feel, and act across classes of situations. Traits are an important part of how you understand yourself, and how others understand who you are.

Researchers have identified five traits (openness, conscientiousness, extraversion, agreeableness, and neuroticism) that lie at the core of our self-definitions and that collectively are known as the **Five-Factor Model** of personality, or the **Big Five** (Costa & McCrae, 1995; John, 1990; John & Srivastava, 1999). Table 5.1 presents descriptors of these traits, which go by the helpful acronym OCEAN. People who are *open to experience* are imaginative, curious, and artistic. Highly *conscientious* people are efficient, achievement-oriented, and organized. *Extraverts* are sociable, energetic, and enthusiastic. *Agreeable* people are warm, friendly, and kind. And *neurotic* people are anxious, tense, and emotionally volatile.

Decades of research indicate that people think of their own personalities in terms of these traits (John, 1990; McCrae, 1982). People also describe other people in terms of these traits, and these judgments are often accurate, in the sense that they correspond, to some degree, to the way people describe themselves (Funder, 1995; Funder & Colvin, 1988; John & Robins, 1993; Kenny, 1991; Watson, 1989).

Several lines of evidence indicate that these five traits are partially inherited, biologically based dispositions. First, these five traits appear to be *universal*. When researchers have asked people in various countries—including China, the Philip-

**self-concept** An understanding of the existence and properties of a separate self and its characteristics.

**traits** Consistent ways that people think, feel, and act across classes of situations.

**Five-Factor Model (Big Five)** Five personality traits (openness, conscientiousness, extraversion, agreeableness, and neuroticism) that psychologists believe are the basic building blocks of personality.

## Table 5.1   Descriptors of the Five-Factor Model of Personality

Five traits are believed to lie at the core of self-definitions. The Five-Factor Model of Personality is based on whether people are high or low on each of these "Big Five" personality traits.

| TRAIT | HIGH | LOW |
| --- | --- | --- |
| Openness to experience | Wide interests, imaginative, intelligent | Narrow interests, simple, commonplace |
| Conscientiousness | Organized, thorough, planful | Careless, disorderly, irresponsible |
| Extraversion | Sociable, assertive, active | Reserved, shy, withdrawn |
| Agreeableness | Sympathetic, appreciative, affectionate | Cold, unfriendly, quarrelsome |
| Neuroticism | Tense, anxious, moody | Stable, calm, unemotional |

pines, Japan, Germany, and Spain, for example—to describe themselves and other people, they do so with terms related to these five traits (John & Srivastava, 1999). These five dimensions seem to be part of universal human nature. This suggests that these dimensions have some evolutionary basis and evolved genetic underpinnings (Buss, 1999).

Second, people's levels of openness to experience, conscientiousness, extraversion, agreeableness, and neuroticism are partly *heritable*—that is, these traits in part depend on tendencies inherited from parents (Loehlin, 1992; Plomin & Caspi, 1998). To determine the **heritability** of personality traits—that is, the degree to which they are determined by genes—researchers have assessed the personalities of identical and fraternal twins, who are raised in the same family environment but differ in their genetic similarity. Identical, or **monozygotic**, twins originate from a single fertilized egg that splits into two exact replicas that then develop into two genetically identical individuals. Fraternal, or **dizygotic**, twins arise when two different eggs in the female reproductive tract are fertilized by different sperm cells. Fraternal twins, like ordinary siblings, share on average half of their genes. Studies consistently find that the personalities of identical twins tend to be more similar than the personalities of fraternal twins, suggesting that personality traits have a genetic component (Plomin & Caspi, 1999). For example, across 23,000 pairs of twins, the correlation between monozygotic twins' self-reports of extraversion (outgoingness) was .51—much higher than the .18 correlation for dizygotic twins (Loehlin, 1992). The correlation for neuroticism was .48 for monozygotic twins and .20 for dizygotic twins (see Figure 5.1).

Interestingly, the correlations for trait similarity between identical twins raised apart are actually slightly higher than for those raised together. This may be because twins raised together (or their families) attempt to create distinct personality "niches" for themselves in the family, which may lead them to move away from tendencies that come naturally to them (see our discussion of niches

**heritability** The degree to which traits or physical characteristics are determined by genes, and hence inherited from parents.

**monozygotic (identical) twins** Twins who originate from a single fertilized egg that splits into two exact replicas that then develop into two genetically identical individuals.

**dizygotic (fraternal) twins** Twins who originate from two different eggs fertilized by different sperm cells; like ordinary siblings, they share on average half of their genes.

**Heritability in Monozygotic Twins**
Identical twins raised apart typically share many basic personality traits and also often have in common many unusual habits and interests. Jim Springer (left) and Jim Lewis (right) are identical twins who were adopted into different families when they were four weeks old and did not see each other again for thirty-nine years. When they rediscovered each other, they found that they enjoyed the same cigarettes (Salems), beer (Miller Lite), cars (blue Chevrolets), hobbies (woodworking), and interests (stock-car racing). They both stood the same way, held their hands the same way, suffered from migraine headaches and slightly high blood pressure. Both had built circular benches around trees in their back yards, had had first wives named Linda, second wives named Betty, a son named James (James Alan and James Allan), and a dog named Toy. Moreover, when given personality tests, their scores on measures of tolerance, conformity, flexibility, self-control, and sociability were almost identical.

for siblings of different birth order below). Taken together, these results suggest that personalities in part stem from biological dispositions—for example, the tendency to be shy or outgoing—that we inherit from our parents.

Finally, there are *specific biological processes*, starting quite early in life, that are associated with the different personality dimensions and that account, in part, for who you are. Take shyness or introversion, for example, the other end of the extraversion dimension. In his longitudinal studies of shy children, Jerome Kagan has found that shy children can be identified at about nine months of age. Early in life, these children have elevated levels of the stress hormone cortisol, which makes fearful responses more likely (Kagan, 1989). Another trait, neuroticism, is associated with heightened sympathetic autonomic nervous system activity, which is involved in elevated stress and tension (Zuckerman, 1996, 1998). And other evidence has linked extraversion to elevated levels of the neurotransmitter dopamine, which is associated with approach-related behavior, enthusiasm, and receptiveness to rewards (DePue, 1995).

Taken together, studies of the universality, heritability, and biological basis of

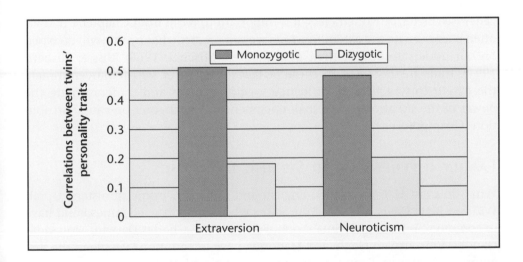

**Figure 5.1 Heritability of Traits**
Monozygotic, genetically identical twins resemble each other more in their extraversion and neuroticism than dizygotic twins, who share half of their genes. (Source: Adapted from Loehlin, 1992)

Box 5.1   FOCUS ON BIOLOGY

# Genes Matter in the Right Environment

Advances in the study of genetics make up some of the most exciting scientific discoveries in the history of science. Scientists have mapped the human genome. They are seeking ways of modifying genes related to various diseases—for example, cancer. And there are many researchers who are looking for genes related to psychological maladies—for example, schizophrenia or depression or autism.

These are exciting developments, and they might leave you with the sense that to a large extent who you are, your social self, is a product of your genes. Recent work by Avshalom Caspi, Terrie Moffitt, and their colleagues, however, suggests that genes alone do not shape the self. Rather, certain genes require specific environmental conditions in order to shape behavior—yet another confirmation of the power of the situation.

In one important study, Caspi, Moffitt, and colleagues tested for the two forms of the Monoamine oxidase A (MAOA) gene (Caspi et al., 2002). Monoamine oxidase is an enzyme that metabolizes different neurotransmitters in the brain, and it allows for smooth communication between neurons. Humans and nonhumans with a defective MAOA gene have been shown to be more violent. Caspi and colleagues identified men with this defective gene and those without it, and they also identified men who had or had not been maltreated by their parents as children—a common precursor of violence in adulthood. Overall, the defective MAOA gene alone did not have an effect on whether the boys committed violent crimes—for example, rape, assault, robbery—by the age of twenty-six. Boys who had the defective gene *and* who were mistreated as children, however, were three times as likely to have been convicted of a violent crime by age twenty-six as the boys who had the defective gene but who had not been mistreated. Although those with the gene for low MAOA activity who had also suffered maltreatment were only 12 percent of the population of boys in the cohort, they were responsible for 44 percent of the cohort's convictions for violent crime. Eight-five percent of the boys with the low MAOA gene who were severely maltreated developed some form of antisocial behavior.

the Big Five suggest that our sense of self in part derives from the biological dispositions we inherit from our parents. These dispositions are likely to be evident from the first day of birth, and they play a significant role in how people develop more complex identities (Malatesta, 1990). So, part of the self originates in the genes (see Box 5.1). Nonetheless, it is important to recall from Chapter 1 that we often overestimate the extent to which we can predict what people will do based on our understanding of their personalities (Mischel, 1968; Ross & Nisbett, 1991). Traits are quite real. As social perceivers, however, we often overestimate the extent to which traits influence specific actions and underestimate the power of the situation, as we shall document in the chapter on causal attribution (Chapter 9).

## FAMILY INFLUENCE AND SIBLING DYNAMICS

What do most U.S. presidents, English and Canadian prime ministers, Oprah Winfrey, Bette Davis, and all of the actors who have portrayed James Bond have in common? What do Virginia Woolf, Ben Franklin, Charles Darwin, Mohandas Gandhi, Vincent Van Gogh, and Madonna have in common? People in the first group are firstborns. People in the second group are later borns.

What does birth order have to do with our sense of self? According to Frank Sulloway (1996, 2001), a great deal. Sulloway has looked at sibling dynamics from an evolutionary perspective, and arrived at his "Born to Rebel" hypothesis. His theory goes as follows. Across species, sibling conflict—particularly when resources are scarce—is frequent, widespread, and on occasion, deadly. We can show this with a few extreme examples. Sand sharks devour one another prior to birth in the oviducts of the mother, until one well-fed shark emerges. Once a blue-footed boobie drops below 80 percent of its body weight, its siblings exclude it from the nest, or worse, peck it to death. Infant hyenas are born with large canine teeth, which they often turn to deadly effect upon their newly born siblings. Even in humans, observational studies reveal that young siblings engage in frequent conflict, up to

**Shared Genes and Environments in Families** Genes and environment interact to create dispositions and interests. The Kennedy men were charming, charismatic, competitive, and adventurous (sometimes to the point of foolhardiness). (A) Joe Kennedy, Sr., surrounded by sons Joe, Jr. (left) and Jack (right). (B) The next generation of Kennedys also shared good looks, charm, and a competitive streak that led many of them into positions of power. Pictured here is Jack's son, John F. Kennedy, Jr.

**Sibling Conflict** Sibling conflict is frequent and widespread and based on competition over resources such as food, space, and parental attention. (A) Blue-footed booby chicks fight with each other, and (B) a spotted hyena bites its sibling.

diversification A principle that maintains that siblings develop into quite different people so that they can peacefully occupy different niches within the family environment.

**Sibling Dynamics** First-borns like Prince William (right) are often more responsible and likely to support the status quo than younger siblings like Prince Harry (left) who often are more mischievous, open to novel experiences, and more likely to rebel against authority.

one conflict every five minutes (Dunn & Munn, 1985), often to the chagrin of parents a bit too tired to mediate yet another struggle. (You may remember long car trips in which the chief entertainment was sibling baiting.)

Humans have evolved adaptations or solutions to threats to survival, and one such adaptation involves a resolution of sibling conflict. According to the principle of **diversification**, siblings develop into quite different people so that they can peacefully occupy different niches within the family environment. Just as different plant species will coexist alongside one another in different areas of a creek-bed ecosystem, siblings diversify by developing different traits, abilities, and preferences, thereby occupying different identities within the family.

So what identities do older and younger siblings take on? Throughout most of development, older siblings are bigger, more powerful, and often act as surrogate parents. They are invested in the status quo, which, not coincidentally, benefits them. ("Things were fine until you came along.") In contrast, younger siblings, with the "establishment" niche already occupied by their older sibling, are born to rebel. They develop in ways that make them inclined to challenge the family status quo. In a review of 196 studies with 120,800 participants, Sulloway found that older siblings tend to be more assertive and dominant—two components of extraversion—and more achievement-oriented and conscientious. This is consistent with their more assertive, powerful role in the family. In contrast, younger siblings tend to be more agreeable, and they are likely to be more open to novel ideas and experiences. This personality profile emerges, presumably, as younger siblings learn to coexist with their more dominant older siblings—which accounts for their elevated agreeableness—and as they think of imaginative ways to carve out their own niche in the world—which maps onto their increased openness to experience.

To further test his hypotheses regarding birth order and personality, Sulloway examined the personalities and lives of 3,400 different scientists across human history, looking at twenty-eight scientific revolutions. Who do you think would be more open to revolutionary scientific ideas, such as Copernicus's thesis that the earth revolves around the sun, or Darwin's theory of evolution, which argued that humans were not designed by God but instead evolved through a gradual process of natural selection? The answer is younger siblings, which is consistent with the personality finding that they are more open to novel ideas. For example, after Darwin published *On the Origin of Species* in 1859, 100 percent of the younger-sibling scientists in Sulloway's sample endorsed the theory, whereas only 50 percent of the older-sibling scientists did. Before you younger siblings start taunting your older kin about their narrow-minded and outdated ideas, however, take note: younger siblings are also more likely, given their openness to experience, to endorse radical but misguided pseudoscientific ideas—for example, phrenology, a theory of how personality types relate to bumps on the head.

Also consistent with the notion that younger siblings are more open to novel ideas, later-born scientists were more likely than firstborns to excel in numerous scientific disciplines. And younger-sibling scientists were more likely to travel to faraway lands, often risking their own lives, in the pursuit of novel ideas. Charles Darwin may be the best case study of Sulloway's hypothesis. The fifth of six children, Darwin developed perhaps the most revolutionary scientific theory in human history, one that challenged religious ideas about the creation of life on Earth. He excelled in five scientific areas: geographic exploration, geology, zoology, botany, and psychology. And he circumnavigated the globe on the ship *The Beagle*, often facing great dangers as he collected evidence that led to his original, paradigm-shifting theory of evolution.

## CONTEXT AND THE SENSE OF SELF

In the film *Zelig*, Woody Allen played a character beset by the remarkable ability to take on the appearance of the people around him. Surrounded by a group of African Americans he begins to look black; in the presence of a group of elderly Greeks he takes on their Mediterranean appearance. The humor of this premise stems from how it makes light of a deeper truth: that our sense of self shifts dramatically according to the specific context in which we find ourselves. Outspoken among our best friends, we become shy and inhibited in a large group of new acquaintances. Students who are rebellious and free-spirited in the dorm will shift to a more sober and conventional demeanor around parents or professors.

*Social Context*   The notion that our self-concept changes in different contexts is consistent with the idea of situationism, as well as with empirical evidence. We have seen in the chapter on relationships (Chapter 4) that our sense of self changes when we interact with people who remind us of different significant others, such as a best friend or parent. In interactions with subordinates, we will act and feel quite dominant, but we will shift behavior dramatically when interacting with equal-status peers (Moskowitz, 1994). Fall into a dark mood and the more peripheral aspects of your self—that is, the parts of your self that are not central to your identity, will seem more negative (Sedikides, 1995). Moreover, momentary failures—for example on single exams or interpersonal tasks—increase our feelings of self-criticism and self-doubt (Brown, 1998).

*Distinctiveness*   William McGuire and Alice Padawer-Singer (1978) have proposed a more general explanation of the effects of context on self-definition. According to their **distinctiveness hypothesis**, we identify what makes us unique in each particular context, and we highlight that in our self-definition. To test this hypothesis, sixth graders at different schools were asked to spend seven minutes describing themselves. On average, children wrote 11.8 statements, and these statements referred to their recreational activities, attitudes, friends, and school activities. (The children, incidentally, were more likely to refer to their dog when defining themselves than to all other family members combined!)

> **distinctiveness hypothesis**   The hypothesis that we identify what makes us unique in each particular context, and we highlight that in our self-definition.

**Context and the Sense of Self**   In *Zelig,* Woody Allen takes on the appearance of those with whom he interacts, providing a dramatic illustration of how we often express different traits and characteristics when in different social contexts. (A) Zelig looks Chinese when he is next to the Chinese man, and (B) Zelig takes on African-American features when he stands between the two African-American men.

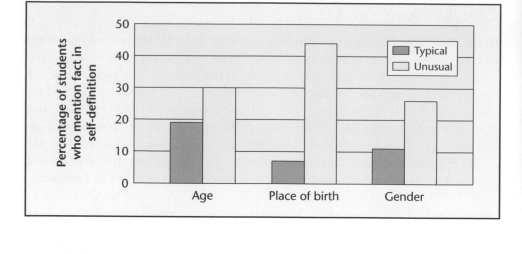

**Figure 5.2 Distinctiveness and the Sense of Self** When asked to write down who they are, American children define themselves according to how they are unique and different from their classmates. (Source: Adapted from McGuire & Padawer-Singer, 1978).

**social comparison theory** The hypothesis that we compare ourselves to other people in order to evaluate our opinions, abilities, and internal states.

"It is not enough to succeed. Others must fail."

—GORE VIDAL

McGuire and Padawer-Singer examined these descriptions to see whether children defined themselves according to how they differed from their classmates. Indeed, they did (see Figure 5.2). Thirty percent of children who were especially young or old (that is, six months from the modal age of their classmates) mentioned their age in their self-definition, whereas only 19 percent of the other children did so. Forty-four percent of children who were born outside of the United States mentioned this biographical fact, whereas only 7 percent of those born in the United States mentioned it. Twenty-six percent of children in the minority gender in their class mentioned their gender as part of their self-definition compared to 11 percent of children in the majority gender (see also Cota & Dion, 1986). Would you expect more interdependent peoples, such as East Asian students, to be likely to highlight the distinctive aspects of the self? How they might have behaved in McGuire and Padawer-Singer's study can be inferred from influential studies of culture and the self (see below).

*Social Comparison* In 1954, Leon Festinger proposed a highly influential account, which he called **social comparison theory**, about the way we make use of other people to define ourselves (Festinger, 1954; see also Suls & Wheeler, 2000; Wood, 1996). The essence of the theory is that, when people have no objective standard that they can use to learn about their own abilities and attitudes and personality traits, they do so in large part by comparing themselves to others. How would you know how good you are at tennis or physics, or how conscientious you are, without comparing yourself to other relevant people? Festinger noted, however, that there is no point in comparing yourself to a Serena Williams or an Albert Einstein, nor is it very helpful to compare yourself to total novices. To get a sense of how good you are at something you must compare yourself to people who have approximately your level of skill. But we like to feel good about ourselves, so we tend to prefer to compare ourselves with people who are slightly less able than ourselves. All of this is a bit ironic because, according to the theory, it leaves us in the position of saying, "Compared to people who are about as good at tennis as I am, I'm pretty darn good!" or "Compared to people who are about as conscientious as I am, I'm pretty darn conscientious!" But such *downward social comparison* does help us to define ourselves, as well as being ego-enhancing (Aspinwall & Taylor, 1993; Helgeson & Mickelson, 1995; Lockwood, 2002). Sometimes *upward social comparison* is also useful in defining ourselves, even if it means losing some self-esteem. We do this if we aspire to be substantially better at some skill, or if we wish to have a better personality (Blanton, Pelham, De Hart & Kuyper, 1999). Whether we seek to compare ourselves with people who are superior to us or inferior, however, we are relying on them for defining a part of the self.

## CULTURE AND THE SELF-CONCEPT

The American Declaration of Independence and the *Analects* of the Chinese philosopher Confucius have shaped the lives of billions of people. Yet, they reflect radically different ideas about the self and the place of the individual in society. The Declaration of Independence prioritized the rights and freedoms of the individual, and it protected the individual from having those rights and liberties infringed on by others. Confucius emphasized the importance of knowing one's place in society, of honoring traditions and social roles, and of thinking of others before the self.

These texts reflect broad and deep cultural differences in views of the self, produced by the most powerful kind of context effects—those produced by the cultures we inhabit. In Western societies, people are concerned about their individuality, about self-actualizing, about the importance of freedom and self-expression. Cultural adages reflect this: "The squeaky wheel gets the grease." "If you've got it, flaunt it." In Asian cultures, the homilies and folk wisdom encourage a different view of the self: "The empty wagon makes the most noise." "The nail that stands up is pounded down."

The anthropologist Edward Hall (1976) characterized interdependent societies as being "high-context" cultures and independent societies as being "low-context" cultures. In high-context cultures, the social relationship you have with the person you are dealing with is crucial in determining proper behavior toward the person. You are literally a different person in relation to your teacher than in relation to your mother, and in relation to your friend than in relation to an acquaintance. In low-context societies, particular role relations matter less. To the independent person, it makes sense to speak of having attributes—preferences, beliefs, abilities—that are characteristic of the person across situations. The self is not bounded or defined by the relationship or context. To the interdependent person, the attributes of the self are dependent on the particular relationship the person has with the individual with whom he or she is dealing (see Figure 5.3).

Some aspects of Eastern language capture the interdependent or high-context nature of their societies. In Chinese culture, *jên*, or politeness to others, is considered a supreme virtue. In Japanese, the word for "I"—meaning the person

> "We hold these truths to be self-evident, that all men are created equal, that they are endowed by their Creator with certain inalienable rights, that among these are Life, Liberty, and the pursuit of Happiness."
> —DECLARATION OF INDEPENDENCE

> "A person of humanity wishing to establish his own character, also establishes the character of others."
> —CONFUCIUS

**Figure 5.3 Conceptual Representations of the Self** The two schematics show: (A) independent construal, and (B) interdependent construal. The independent self is construed as consisting of fixed, distinctive attributes that exist across situations and relationships. The interdependent self is construed as consisting of more fluid attributes that exist partly in relation to other people. (Source: Markus & Kitayama, 1991, p. 226)

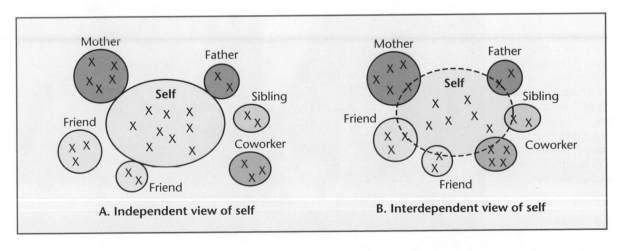

A. Independent view of self   B. Interdependent view of self

who is the same across situations and in relation to everyone—is almost never used. Instead, a Japanese man would use different words for "I" when talking with a colleague (*watashi*), his child (*tochan*), old college pals (*ore*), and close female friends (*boku*). Sometimes when referring to themselves the Japanese use the word *jibun*, which originally meant "my portion"—reflecting the sense of self as a part of the whole—and which now would be translated "shared life space." A Korean woman must use different words for "you" and for "dinner," depending on whether she is inviting a professor or a student. These rules are not arbitrary conventions. They reflect the fact that Easterners' self-conceptions change, depending on whom they are interacting with.

In one of the most influential recent developments in psychology, psychologists such as Hazel Markus, Shinobu Kitayama, and Harry Triandis have offered rich, far-reaching theories about how culture-based self-conceptions shape the emotions we feel, our basic motivations, and our ways of perceiving the social world (Markus & Kitayama, 1991; Triandis, 1989, 1994, 1995). This theorizing highlights the differences between independent and interdependent self-construals. The independent self is widespread throughout much of the West, including especially Northern Europe and North America. Within cultures with independent self-construal, the self is an autonomous entity that is distinct and separate from others. The imperative is to assert uniqueness and independence, as seen in the research on the distinctiveness hypothesis. The focus is on internal causes of behavior. Together, these forces lead to a conception of the self in terms of traits that are stable across time and social context. Table 5.2 shows that even the insults that a culture prefers reflect the degree to which the self is embedded in relationships.

In contrast, for people having interdependent self-construals, the self is fundamentally connected to, even intermixed with, other people. The imperative is for a person to find his or her status and roles within the community and other collectives—for example, within families and organizations. The focus is on how the social context and the situation influence current behavior. And together these forces lead to a self-conception in which the self is embedded within social

**Culture and Self-Concept** In interdependent cultures, the social relationships you have with other people are crucial in determining how you behave toward them. These Japanese businessmen want to fit in with Western business associates. They attend a smile workshop to learn how to smile and to behave as Western businessmen would expect, so that their reactions will not be misconstrued by their Western associates.

## Table 5.2 Insults in Independent and Interdependent Cultures

Noting that southern Italy is more collectivist or interdependent than northern Italy, Semin and Rubini asked people from both regions to list insults that they knew. They found that insults in northern Italy tended to be directed toward the individual, whereas insults in southern Italy were much more likely to be directed at people with whom the person had relationships.

| INDIVIDUALISTIC INSULTS | RELATIONAL INSULTS |
| --- | --- |
| **Negative physical features**<br>*Bruttone.*<br>(You are incredibly ugly.) | **Relational sexual insults**<br>*Vaffanculo te a 36 dei tuoi parente.*<br>($#@% you and 36 of your relatives.) |
| **Ill omens**<br>*Che ti venga un cancro.*<br>(I wish you a cancer.) | *Tua madré puttana.*<br>(Your mother is a whore.) |
| **Animal analogies**<br>*Porco.*<br>(Swine.) | **Relatives equated with animals**<br>*Figlio di troia.*<br>(Your mother is a breeding sow.) |
| **References to excretia**<br>*Stronzo.*<br>(Pile of shit.) | **Bad wishes to target's relative**<br>*A li mortacci tuoi.*<br>(Go to your @#$! dead relatives.) |
| **Individual sexual insults**<br>*Segaiolo.*<br>(Male organ.) | |

Source: Semin & Rubini (1990).

relationships, roles, and duties. As we emphasized in Chapter 1, this kind of self-construal is prevalent in many Asian cultures, as well as in many Mediterranean, African, and South American cultures.

In the remaining sections of this chapter, we will consider some of the ways in which culture shapes self-knowledge, self-evaluation, and concerns about how we present ourselves in public. Many of these studies have been conducted with Western participants only, but for some phenomena we have evidence for other cultures as well. It is striking how much that evidence forces revision of generalizations previously held to be universally applicable.

## GENDER AND THE SELF-CONCEPT

As you read about culture and independent and interdependent self-construals, you may have wondered about the relationship between gender and the self-concept. If so, you would join many others who have also thought about this. In their review of the literature on the self-concept and gender, Susan Cross and Laura Madson (1997) showed that women in the United States tend to construe the self in interdependent terms—that is, in terms of connection to others. In contrast, men in the United States tend to construe the self in more independent terms—that is, by prioritizing difference and uniqueness. The same gender differences are found among Japanese (Kashima, Siegal, Tanaka, & Kashima, 1992).

The evidence for these basic differences in self-construal is manifold. When women define themselves, they are more likely than men to refer to social characteristics and relationships (Maccoby & Jacklin, 1974). When asked to show photographs that are revealing of the self, women are more likely to reveal photos that include other people, such as friends and family members (Clancy & Dollinger, 1993). In social interactions, women report more thoughts about their partners (Ickes, Robertson, Tooke, & Teng, 1986), and in general women tend to be more empathetic and better judges of others' personalities and emotions (Ambady, Hallahan, & Rosenthal, 1995; Bernieri, Zuckerman, Koestner, & Rosenthal, 1994; Davis, 1980; Davis & Franzoi, 1991; Eisenberg & Lennon, 1983; Hall, 1984). Men tend to be more attuned to their own internal responses, such as increases in heart rate, whereas women are more attuned to situational cues, such as others' reactions (Pennebaker & Roberts, 1992; Roberts & Pennebaker, 1995).

Throughout this text, you will encounter evidence that is consistent with these gender differences in self-construal. Women tend to be better judges of others' emotions (see Chapter 12). They are less aggressive (see Chapter 13). And they emphasize community more in their moral judgments (see Chapter 14).

Where do these gender-related differences in self-construal come from? Clearly there are many agents of socialization that guide women and men into these differing self-construals. We shall see in the chapter on attitudes and persuasion (Chapter 7) that the media portray women and men differently, more typically portraying men in positions of power and agency. Cultural stereotypes lead teachers to have different expectations of women and men, as we shall see in Chapter 11. Our family context plays a role as well. Parents raise girls and boys differently. For example, parents tend to talk with girls more about emotions and being sensitive to others (Fivush, 1989, 1992). The friendships and groups we form from the earliest ages also affect gender differences in self-construal. Starting at age three, and continuing through the primary school years, girls and boys tend to play in gender-segregated groups that reinforce and amplify the differences in self-construals (Maccoby, 1990). Girls' groups tend to focus on cooperative games that play out different relationships (for example, mother and child). Boys' groups tend to emphasize competition, hierarchy, and distinctions among one another. As adults, gender-specific roles further amplify these differences. For example, even today, women take on most of the responsibilities of raising children, which calls upon interdependent tendencies.

**LOOKING BACK,** we have seen that our social self has several foundations. One foundation consists of the biologically based traits that are present early in life and that have been genetically transmitted from our parents. Another foundation consists of our position in our family: firstborns tend to be more assertive and achievement-oriented; later-borns tend to be more agreeable and open to new, and at times, radical ideas. A third foundation is context, as our sense of self shifts from one situation to another. Finally, culture and gender also serve as foundations, and they matter a great deal—a theme that we will return to again and again. People from Western European cultures—in particular, men—define the self in independent terms, emphasizing uniqueness and autonomy, whereas people from East Asian cultures, and women, define the self in interdependent terms, emphasizing connection to others. We shall see the effects of these independent and interdependent self-construals throughout the remainder of the chapter, starting in our next section on self-knowledge.

## SELF-KNOWLEDGE

The search for self-knowledge—our understanding of our thoughts, feelings, preferences, and beliefs—has deep roots. Socrates exhorted Athenians to examine the self, to find its essential and distinctive characteristics. Buddhist thought counsels us to still the self, to transcend the material self and its desires, illusions, and frustrations.

Our self-knowledge has many forms, including specific beliefs, images, networks of memories and associations, and rich novelistic narratives or stories (Brown, 1998; Kihlstrom & Cantor, 1984; McAdams, 1996). There are also different perspectives of the self. In William James's terminology, the "I" self is like an observer of ourselves; it is the self that looks upon the individual and his or her actions. The "me" self is what the "I" self observes; it is the collection of attributes, preferences, and actions that the "I" self beholds.

Our self-beliefs are one aspect of our self-knowledge, and they can be organized at several levels of analysis (Brewer & Gardner, 1996; Deaux, Reid, Mizrahi, & Ethier, 1995). Personal beliefs refer to our personality traits, our unique abilities and attributes, and our idiosyncratic preferences, tastes, and talents. Our **social beliefs** concern the roles, duties, and obligations we assume in groups—for example, in work organizations or on recreational sports teams. **Relational self-beliefs** refer to our identities in specific relationships—for example, as doting husband, black sheep of the family, or outraged neighbor. Finally, we have beliefs about the **collective self**, which refer to the social categories to which we belong—for example, Irish Canadian, Freemason, Libertarian, Phishhead, weekend trainspotter, or member of Red Sox Nation. Let's begin our discussion of self-knowledge and self-beliefs by considering some of the functions they serve.

*"I don't know anybody here but the hostess—and, of course, in a deeper sense, myself."*

**social beliefs** Beliefs about the roles, duties, and obligations we assume in groups.

**relational self-beliefs** Beliefs about our identities in specific relationships.

**collective self** Our identity and beliefs as they relate to the social categories to which we belong.

### THE ORGANIZATIONAL FUNCTION OF SELF-KNOWLEDGE

In an influential essay, Anthony Greenwald characterized self-knowledge as a "totalitarian ego" (Greenwald, 1980). Totalitarian political regimes, like those in the former Soviet Union or in Mussolini's fascist Italy, suppress dissent, rewrite history to fit political ideologies, and tolerate little or no contradiction. Self-knowledge, Greenwald contends, operates in a similar fashion, construing current situations and revising our personal histories to fit our preexisting beliefs about the self. This characterization of self-knowledge aptly summarizes years of research on how self-knowledge organizes our construal of information (see also Chapter 7 on perceptual biases and resistance to persuasion).

*Memory and the Self-Reference Effect*    Our self-knowledge improves our memory of information that we encounter. The tendency to elaborate upon and recall information that is integrated into our self-knowledge is called the

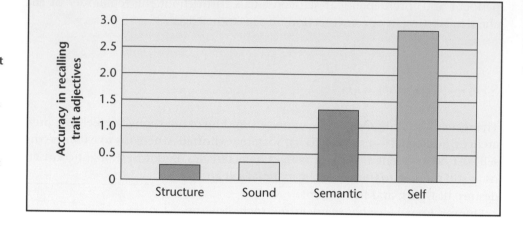

**Figure 5.4 The Self-Reference Effect** People are more accurate in recalling trait adjectives when they consider whether a word applies to themselves (the column on the far right) than when they process the words according to their font style (structure), sound, or semantic meaning. (Source: Adapted from Rogers, Kuiper, & Kirker, 1977)

**self-reference effect** The tendency to elaborate upon and recall information that is integrated into our self-knowledge.

**self-schemas** Knowledge-based summaries of our feelings and actions and how we understand others' views about the self.

**self-reference effect** (Klein & Kihlstrom, 1986; Klein & Loftus, 1988). It is explained by a powerful principle in the study of memory: information that is integrated into preexisting knowledge structures, such as the beliefs that we have about ourselves, is more readily recalled.

In a first study to document the self-reference effect, participants were presented with forty different trait adjectives (Rogers, Kuiper, & Kirker, 1977). For ten adjectives, participants answered structural questions about the words—for example, whether the font was big or small. For ten adjectives, participants answered phonemic questions, addressing whether a given adjective rhymed with a target adjective. For ten adjectives, participants answered a semantic question, addressing whether each adjective was a synonym or an antonym of a target word. And finally, for still another ten adjectives, participants answered yes or no as to whether the word described the self, thus integrating the adjective into their self-knowledge. An hour later, after a few filler tasks, participants were asked to recall the original forty traits.

Figure 5.4 presents the results. When information is integrated into our self-knowledge, we remember it better—the self-reference effect. Other findings illustrate that our self-knowledge is detailed, complex, and elaborate. For example, in the study of trait adjectives, it took participants more time to assess whether a trait was like or not like the self than it took to answer the questions about structure, sounds, or semantics, which suggests that people were using more elaborate knowledge structures to answer the question related to the self-concept. Studies of the self-reference effect suggest that to the extent that you personalize your perception of events and objects in the environment—scenes of sunsets, statements by political leaders, outcomes of athletic competitions, passing remarks made by some authority figure—you will be more likely to think about and remember that information. Self-knowledge shapes what we remember.

*Self-Schemas and Self-Understanding*    Self-knowledge also shapes what we selectively attend to in our social environment—a thesis explored by Hazel Markus (1977). Her particular concern was **self-schemas**, which she defined as knowledge-based summaries of our feelings and actions and how we understand others' views about the self. Markus argued that people with specific self-schemas—for example, self-schemas about extraversion or independence—should process information in that domain more quickly, retrieve evidence consistent with that self-description more rapidly, and more strongly resist information that contradicts that self-schema.

To test these hypotheses, Markus identified participants who labeled themselves as either quite dependent or quite independent, whom we will call "schematic" participants. She also identified "aschematic" participants; these were participants for whom dependence/independence was not important to their self-definition. All participants returned to the laboratory three to four weeks later and responded to a series of traits presented on a computer screen. The schematic participants judged schema-relevant traits as true or not true of themselves much more quickly than aschematic participants, suggesting that we are particularly attuned to information that maps onto important elements of our self-concept. The schematic participants generated many more behaviors for the schema-relevant traits, suggesting that past actions and experiences supporting the self-concept come readily to mind. And the schematic participants were more likely to quickly refute feedback from a personality test that gave them counter-schematic information—for example, refuting feedback that told the independent participants that the results of the test indicated that they were actually dependent.

Let's apply these studies of the self-reference effect and self-schemas to one of the most important properties of the self: its stability—that is, the fact that it is quite similar over time (Caspi & Roberts, 2001; Roberts & DelVecchio, 2000). Shy, inhibited children identified as such as early as age two tend to be more hesitant to enter into social interactions at age eight (Kagan, 1989), and they take more time to enter into marriage and intimate bonds later in life (Caspi, Elder, & Bem, 1988). Explosive children identified by the severity of their temper tantrums at age eight have greater difficulties in school and in the workforce, and they are twice as likely to divorce (Caspi, Elder, & Bem, 1987). What we are like early in life—whether we are kind, outgoing, impulsive, or demure—tends to resemble what we are like later in life.

Studies of the self-reference effect and of self-schemas point to likely sources of the stability of the self. Once we form beliefs about ourselves, probably quite early in life, we are likely to remember information that is consistent with those self-beliefs. Our self-beliefs lead us to attend to events and experiences that confirm our prior beliefs. They lead us to look back upon the past in ways that support our current self-concept (Ross, 1989). And they lead us to resist information that might reveal some new, surprising facet to the self.

***Culture and Self-Beliefs***    Our self-concept is affected by the culture in which we grow up. Culture affects what we think about the world, what we think is important, and how we organize our beliefs about ourselves and our place in the world. Thus, our beliefs about the self vary dramatically according to our cultural background, and in ways that are consistent with cultural differences in self-construal in general (Dhawan, Roseman, Naidu, Thapa, & Rettek, 1995; Heine et al., 2001; Kitayama, Markus, Matsumoto, & Norasakkunkit, 1997). In one illustrative study, Japanese and American college students first completed the Twenty Statements Test, listing twenty open-ended responses to the statement, "I am . . ." (Cousins, 1989; see Chapter 1). American college students defined themselves primarily in terms of personal attributes (traits), consistent with an independent self-construal. Japanese students, on the other hand, were three times more likely than American students to define themselves in terms of social roles, consistent with an interdependent self-construal.

Is it that Japanese students simply don't think of themselves in trait terms? Not really. Instead, it looks as though Japanese students think of their traits in more situation-specific terms. In another condition, Cousins asked participants to define themselves in particular social contexts—for example, at home, at school, or with close others. In this condition, Japanese students were much more likely to list personal attributes than in the context-free format. This finding is consistent with the notion that the interdependent self is highly context-specific and tied to particular relationships. Thus, our cultural context affects what we attend to and how we organize the world, just as self-schemas do.

## THE MOTIVATIONAL FUNCTION OF SELF-KNOWLEDGE

Self-knowledge serves a second general function: it helps motivate action (Carver & Scheier, 1982; Higgins, 1999; Scheier & Carver, 1977; Sedikides & Skowronski, 1997; Wicklund, 1975). Our self-knowledge includes possible selves, which refer to the kinds of people we hope or expect to be in the future (Cross & Markus, 1991; Markus & Nurius, 1986). For example, you might imagine yourself ten years from now as a celebrated writer or as a lawyer seeking to redress injustice. Such aspirations motivate present actions—writing late into the night, or studying for the LSATs—that will help us get closer to our possible selves.

In his **self-discrepancy theory**, Tory Higgins has detailed how different forms of self-knowledge embody important cultural and moral standards and produce emotions like guilt and shame, which motivate morally appropriate behavior (Higgins, 1987). In addition to our **actual self**—that is, who we truly believe ourselves to be—Higgins proposes that we compare our actual selves to two other selves, and that these comparisons have important motivational implications (Higgins, 1999). The first is an **ideal self**, which represents the wishes and aspirations we and other people maintain about ourselves. When primed (subtly reminded, often out of awareness) to think about our ideal self, we experience what Higgins calls a **promotion focus**, which includes a sensitivity to positive outcomes, approach-related behavior, and cheerful emotions if we are living up to our ideals and aspirations.

The second is the **ought self**, which refers to the duties, obligations, and the external demands we feel we are compelled to honor. When primed to think about our ought self, we experience a **prevention focus**, which involves a sensitivity to negative outcomes, an avoidance motivation, and agitated emotions such as guilt or anxiety when we fail to live up to our sense of what we ought to do.

The experimental evidence consistently supports Higgins's account of how our self-knowledge has differing motivational consequences. When people are subtly induced to think about how they might approximate their ideal selves, they generally show elevated cheerful affect (Higgins, Shah, & Friedman, 1997; Shah & Higgins, 2001), approach-related behavior, and heightened sensitivity to positive outcomes (Brendl, Higgins, & Lemm, 1995). But if they think they will never become their ideal self, they will experience dejection-related emotions such as depression and shame and will show reduced physiological arousal. Similarly, a prevention focus, triggered by associations regarding the "ought" self and their deviation from it, will activate agitated affect (guilt, anxiety, terror, panic) and elevated physiological arousal, avoidant behavior, and sensitivity to negative outcomes (Strauman & Higgins, 1987).

## THE SELF AS A STANDARD IN SOCIAL PERCEPTION

We have seen that the beliefs we maintain about ourselves—our self-knowledge—are more than mere abstractions. They organize our construal of the social environment and motivate appropriate action by evoking emotions like shame and

**self-discrepancy theory** A theory that appropriate behavior is motivated by cultural and moral standards regarding the ideal self and the ought self. Violations of those standards produce emotions like guilt and shame when they are not adhered to.

**actual self** The self we truly believe ourselves to be.

**ideal self** The self that embodies the wishes and aspirations we and other people maintain about ourselves.

**promotion focus** A focus on positive outcomes, approach-related behavior, and cheerful emotions that help us live up to our ideals and aspirations.

**ought self** The self that is concerned with the duties, obligations, and external demands we feel we are compelled to honor.

**prevention focus** A sensitivity to negative outcomes often motivated by a desire to live up to our ought self and to avoid the guilt or anxiety that results when we fail to live up to our sense of what we ought to do.

guilt. Let's now address how we use our self-knowledge to judge other people. Several early findings suggest that we use our self-knowledge as a standard. We have a lot of information about ourselves; it is quite vivid and accessible; and, not surprisingly, we appear to use it when judging others.

For example, the **self-image bias** refers to the tendency to judge others' personalities according to their similarity or dissimilarity to our own personality (Lewicki, 1983). Lewicki had participants rate their true selves on twenty different adjectives such as "popular," "warm," "demanding," "fearful," "impractical," and "intelligent." Participants also rated the personalities of twenty other individuals on the same items, including family members (mother, father), a best friend, the most unusual person ever met, and even a most disliked teacher. For each participant, Lewicki created two measures. The first was how desirable the participant considered each dimension (in this case, each trait) to be. The second was how central, or important, the dimension was in participants' judgments of the personalities of the twenty other individuals. In the critical analysis, Lewicki found that the dimensions that participants rated themselves most positively on were also the most central or important in their judgments of other people. For example, if you have an extremely positive assessment of your warmth, this trait is the most salient in how you judge your friends and foes. If you value your practicality or your bravery, you will judge others according to their practicality (or lack of it) and their tendency to be fearful or brave. Thus, your most valued aspects of yourself guide your construction of others' personalities.

Research by David Dunning and his colleagues suggests that people use the self even more generally as a standard in defining traits, abilities, and other social concepts (Dunning, Meyerowitz, & Holzberg, 1989; Dunning, Perie, & Story, 1991). You may have noticed this tendency in yourself. You may have the tendency to be, say, spontaneous and impulsive, and—not coincidentally—define your ideal romantic partner or political leader as someone who prioritizes spontaneity and the true expression of the self over abiding by conventions and traditions. In Dunning's terms, people have egocentric construals of social categories and attributes.

In one study of egocentric social construal, participants first reported on their own SAT scores, how many hours a week they studied, and their weekly athletic activity (Dunning & Cohen, 1992). Several weeks later, in the context of another experiment, participants indicated the kind of performance that they thought would define studiousness and athleticism. What defines a smart, studious, or athletic individual? Not surprisingly, how smart, studious, or athletic you yourself are. The higher your own SAT score, the more you study each week, and the more athletic activity you engage in, the higher your standard for calling someone smart, studious, or athletic.

Thus far, the evidence we have reviewed suggests that people use their self-knowledge in an egocentric fashion as a guide in judging other people and in judging important abilities. But should we expect people who construe themselves in interdependent terms to use the self as a standard? Probably not. Embedded within the interdependent self-construal is a greater focus on others, on fitting into relationships and groups, and on fulfilling others' expectations. In light of these tendencies, one might expect people from interdependent cultures to rely upon other people, rather than the self, as a standard for social judgment.

To understand what is happening when judging others, you should consider the following questions. Is Cincinnati similar to Chicago, or is Chicago similar to Cincinnati? Is Belgium similar to France, or is France similar to Belgium? Though it might seem that any object A must be as similar to object B as object B is to

**self-image bias** The tendency to judge others' personalities according to their similarity or dissimilarity to our own personality.

object A, for any actual concrete judgment, one object—usually the more "important" or salient—is implicitly the standard against which the other object is compared (Tversky, 1977). Thus, large, salient Chicago is the implicit standard against which any smaller city would be compared, and the larger France would be the standard against which the smaller Belgium would be compared.

This asymmetry in similarity judgments applies to people, too. For example, is Rosalind Carter similar to Laura Bush, or is Laura Bush similar to Rosalind Carter? You would probably say that the person currently in the news (Laura Bush) would be the person to whom someone who is no longer in the news (Rosalind Carter) would be compared. Taking this one step further, we can ask what the standard of comparison is when people are comparing themselves to other people. When asked to make such a comparison, university students in the United States consistently say that other people are more similar to themselves than they are to other people (Markus & Kitayama, 1991; see also Satterwhite, Feldman, Catrambone, & Dai, 2000). Thus, for the typical independent U.S. college student, the self is salient and is the standard of comparison. But Asian students are more likely to say that they are more similar to other people than that other people are similar to them. In their construal, the other person is the standard of comparison, and the self is compared to that standard.

Dov Cohen and Alex Gunz (2002) conducted a study indicating that Asian self-knowledge reflects the perspective of other people. They asked Canadian and Asian students (a potpourri of students from Hong Kong, China, Taiwan, Korea, and various South and Southeast Asian countries) to recall specific instances of ten different situations in which they were the center of attention—for example, "being embarrassed." Canadians were more likely than Asians to reproduce the scene from their original point of view, looking outward from their own perspective. Asians were more likely to imagine the scene as an observer might, describing it from a third-person perspective. In recalling their embarrassing acts, Asians took on the perspective of others. You might say that Westerners are the heroes of their autobiographical novels; Easterners are members of the cast in a movie touching on their lives (see also Chua, Leu, & Nisbett, 2005).

## ILLUSIONS AND BIASES ABOUT THE SELF

While self-knowledge affects what we attend to and remember, our emotions, behaviors, and judgments, it can also affect our sense of personal well-being. Our self-knowledge can include illusions about ourselves—for example, that we are funnier, smarter, or warmer than we really are. Shelley Taylor and Jonathon Brown have proposed the controversial hypothesis that illusions about the self, far from being detrimental, actually enhance personal well-being (Taylor & Brown, 1988, 1994; see also Taylor, 1989). You might think it is important to recognize the truth about yourself, warts and all, and you would not be alone. Many therapies and important developments in psychology, like the humanistic movement of Abraham Maslow and Carl Rogers, encourage us to accept our many weaknesses, foibles, and flaws. Yet, dozens of studies, carried out with Europeans and North Americans, find that people who are well adjusted are more prone to various illusions about the self than those suffering from low self-esteem and dysphoria (unhappiness).

More specifically, well-being seems to be positively correlated with *unrealistically positive views about the self*. Thus, people who are well adjusted tend to believe that positive personality traits describe themselves better than negative traits. Moreover, they falsely assume consensus (universality) when it comes to their negative traits and actions: "Look, everyone cheats on their income taxes." And they assume uniqueness for their positive traits: "Unlike most people, I try to express gratitude whenever someone does me a favor."

Second, people who are happy and well adjusted have *exaggerated perceptions of control*. If you're playing dice and need to throw a small number, you're likely to throw the dice in a constrained, quiet, and gentle fashion; if you need to throw a large number, you'll probably throw with larger motions and fire the dice against the green felt. People think they can control events that they, in fact, can't influence. A well-known study by Ellen Langer examined the illusion of control of participants who were entered in a lottery (Langer, 1975). They were either given a ticket (from a set of 227 tickets, each with the photograph and name of a different famous football player) or they chose their own ticket from the batch of cards. When asked if they would be willing to sell back their ticket, those who were given the ticket asked for $1.96 on average, whereas those who had "had control" and chosen their own ticket held out for close to $9! So does anyone understand that they don't have control over events such as lotteries? It turns out that depressed people do. In general, depressed people tend to have more accurate appraisals of their control of environmental events than do other people (Abramson, Metalsky, & Alloy, 1989).

Finally, *optimism*—the sense that the future offers the promise of happiness and success—is a hallmark of well-being (Aspinwall & Brunhart, 1996; Scheier & Carver, 1987; Seligman, 1991). Many people from Western backgrounds are prone to unrealistic optimism. When asked to indicate the likelihood that various positive events or negative events will happen to them and to other college students, most college students think that positive events are more likely to happen to them than to others, and negative events are less likely to happen to them than to others (Weinstein, 1980; see Table 5.3). Of course, unusually positive and problem-free futures are not going to be enjoyed by more than half of all participants. More recent work by Justin Kruger has shown that although such comparative optimism is common, it is not inevitable, and predictable instances of comparative *pessimism* occur as well. Kruger's work indicates that comparative optimism stems from people's egocentrism—their tendency to focus on themselves (and whether an event is likely or unlikely to happen to them) and to simply ignore what happens to comparison "others" (Kruger & Burrus, 2004). This results in people being overly optimistic about common positive events ("yep, that'll happen to me") and rare negative events ("no way"). But it also results in overly *pessimistic* assessments about rare positive events ("I'll never be that lucky") and common negative events ("there's no escaping it"). Nonetheless, evidence of the more pervasive optimism described by earlier researchers has been obtained when people's assessments of what is likely or unlikely to happen to them is compared to what actually transpires (Buehler, Griffin, & Ross, 1994; Hoch, 1985; Shepperd, Ouellette, & Fernandez, 1996).

Taylor and Brown believe that unrealistically positive views of the self, exaggerated perceptions of control, and unrealistic optimism promote elevated well-being in three ways: (1) these illusions about the self elevate positive mood and reduce negative mood, (2) the illusions foster healthier social bonds by making people more altruistic and magnanimous, and (3) viewing oneself in such positive terms promotes goal-directed behavior. Sensing that one is highly able and in control, and expecting positive outcomes, one is more likely to persist in pursuing goals central to life—at work, at play, or in love.

Taylor and Brown's controversial thesis has been critiqued on several grounds (Colvin & Block, 1994). Consider research on narcissists, who are prone to

> "Lord, I thank thee that I judge not—as others do."
> —PURITAN PRAYER

## Table 5.3  Evidence of Unrealistic Optimism

Researchers asked college students to indicate the likelihood that various positive and negative events would happen to them and to others. Positive scores indicated that they believed that their own chances of the event were greater than those of others; negative scores indicated the belief that others were more likely to experience the event. Estimates were made on the following scale: 0 = won't happen; 100 = absolutely certain will happen. Most Western students thought that positive events are more likely to happen to them than to others, but that negative events are more likely to happen to others than to themselves.

| LIFE EVENT | COMPARATIVE JUDGMENT OF OWN VERSUS OTHERS' CHANCES |
|---|---|
| Like post-graduation job | 50.2 |
| Own your own home | 44.3 |
| Travel to Europe | 35.3 |
| Work recognized with award | 12.6 |
| Live past 80 | 11.3 |
| Have a mentally gifted child | 6.2 |
| Weight constant for 10 years | 2.0 |
| Have drinking problem | −58.3 |
| Attempt suicide | −55.9 |
| Divorce after a few years of marriage | −48.7 |
| Heart attack before age 40 | −38.4 |
| Contract venereal disease | −37.4 |
| Become sterile | −31.2 |
| Develop gum problems | −12.4 |

Source: Weinstein (1980).

"There is no human problem which could not be solved if people would simply do as I advise."

—GORE VIDAL

extreme versions of these self-enhancing illusions (John & Robins, 1994; Raskin & Terry, 1988). True narcissists, for example, have no trouble endorsing a self-report item that the world would be a better place if they were in charge. Narcissists have been shown to make good first impressions, but to be rather unpopular in the long run (Paulhus, 1998). People are charmed by narcissists' charisma initially, but eventually tire of their self-promotion. Thus, it's hard to argue that such a tendency is ultimately beneficial.

In addition, recent longitudinal evidence has documented the downside of one particular kind of self-enhancement: the overestimation of academic talents (Robins & Beer, 2001). College students who at the start of their college careers overestimated their academic abilities exhibited deteriorating academic performance over time, became disengaged with school, and experienced drops in their self-esteem. Thus, self-enhancement may prove detrimental, at least in certain domains (Colvin, Block, & Funder, 1995).

Perhaps the greatest challenge to Taylor and Brown's thesis about the benefits of self-illusions comes from recent cross-cultural research. This work strongly suggests that East Asians are less likely to endorse positive illusions about the self than are Westerners (Heine, Lehman, Markus, & Kitayama, 1999; Kitayama,

Markus, Matsumoto, & Norasakkunkit, 1997). For example, Japanese college students are less likely to assume that they are better than average, as American college students do, in important abilities like academic talent (Markus & Kitayama, 1991). Students in Japan are also less likely to show evidence of unrealistic optimism than students in Canada (Heine & Lehman, 1995; Heine, Kitayama, Lehman, Takata, & Ide, 2002).

A survey of people in forty-two nations analyzed by Sastry and Ross (1998) found that non-Asians, as compared to Asians, were more likely to feel that they had "completely free choice and control over their lives" as opposed to feeling that what they did "has no effect on what happens to them." People in countries heavily influenced by Northern and Western European culture, such as Sweden, Finland, Canada, and the United States, were particularly likely to have a strong sense of personal control. Most important, although a low sense of personal control was associated with depression and anxiety for non-Asians, this was not true for Asians. In societies that do not value personal control, the lack of a sense of control is not a barrier to a positive sense of well-being.

The cultural evidence suggests that self-illusions do not automatically promote elevated well-being. They often do so for Westerners because a positive view of the self, sense of control, and optimism, are cherished values. In contrast, personal well-being for East Asians should be more closely tied to interdependent values. Interestingly, research by Mark Suh, Ed Diener, and colleagues is consistent with this possibility. They have found that the well-being of East Asians is more dependent on fulfilling social roles and expectations, consistent with an interdependent self-construal (Suh, Diener, Oishi, & Triandis, 1998).

**LOOKING BACK,** we have seen that self-knowledge serves as an important basis for organizing, understanding, and acting in the social world. The self-reference effect leads us to remember information that is integrated into our self-knowledge. Self-knowledge also affects what we attend to in our social environment. Our self-schemas—knowledge-based summaries of our traits, abilities, feelings, and others' views of us—guide our understanding of ourselves and others. There are several possible selves, including our "actual selves," our "ideal selves," and our "ought selves," and they affect our thoughts, feelings, and behavior. For Westerners, the self normally serves as a standard in judgments about other people. For East Asians and others from interdependent cultures, other people serve as the standard for social judgment. In the next section, we will see that Westerners also tend to hold themselves in higher esteem than do non-Westerners.

## SELF-EVALUATION

In 1987, California Governor George Deukmejian signed Assembly bill 3659 into law. This bill allocated an annual budget of $245,000 for a self-esteem task force, whose charges were to understand the effects of self-esteem upon social ills like drug use, teenage pregnancy, and high-school dropout rates, and to elevate schoolchildren's self-esteem. The initiative was banking on the assumption that elevating self-esteem would help to cure society's ills. Several findings might be interpreted as offering support for this assumption. People with low self-esteem are less satisfied with life, more hopeless, and more depressed (Crocker & Wolfe, 2001), and they are less able to cope with life challenges such as loneliness at col-

**Elevated Self-Esteem** People in the self-esteem movement feel that it is important that all children have high self-esteem so that they will be happy and healthy. They have encouraged teachers to make every child a VIP for a day and coaches to award trophies to every child who plays on a team, whether the team wins or loses. Here we see every child on this ice hockey team holding a trophy.

lege (Cutrona, 1982). They tend to disengage from tasks following failure (Brockner, 1979), and they are more prone to antisocial behavior and delinquency (Donnellan, Trzesniewski, Robins, Moffitt, & Caspi, 2005). Raising self-esteem might produce healthier, happier, more robust children.

By now, such a legislative act should strike you as something that could only happen in a Western culture, or perhaps California more specifically. Indeed, later in this section, we will examine the rather pronounced cultural differences in self-esteem. For the moment, however, let's fully consider the premise of the California task force—that elevating self-esteem is an important mission likely to yield numerous benefits. To do so, we need to know what self-esteem is and where it comes from.

## TRAIT AND STATE SELF-ESTEEM

**self-esteem** The positive or negative overall evaluation you have of yourself.

**trait self-esteem** The enduring level of confidence and affection that people have for their defining abilities and characteristics across time.

**state self-esteem** The dynamic, changeable self-evaluations that are experienced as momentary feelings about the self.

**Self-esteem** refers to the positive or negative overall evaluation you have of yourself. Researchers usually measure self-esteem with simple self-report measures like that in Table 5.4. As you can see from this scale, self-esteem concerns how you feel about your attributes and qualities, your successes and failures, your sense of self-worth. People with high self-esteem feel quite good about themselves. People with low self-esteem feel ambivalent about themselves; they feel they have both positive and negative attributes. People who truly dislike themselves are extremely rare and are typically found in specific clinical populations such as severely depressed individuals.

**Trait self-esteem** is the enduring level of confidence and affection that people have for their defining abilities and characteristics (for example, kindness, generosity, wittiness) across time. Studies indicate that trait self-esteem is fairly stable: those who exhibit high trait self-esteem at one point in time tend to exhibit high trait self-esteem even many years later; those who exhibit low trait self-esteem tend to exhibit low trait self-esteem many years later (Block & Robins, 1993).

There is also **state self-esteem**, the dynamic, changeable self-evaluations that are experienced as momentary feelings about the self (Heatherton & Polivy, 1991). State self-esteem rises and falls, for example, during different stages of development. As males move from early adolescence (age fourteen) to early adult-

## Table 5.4    Self-Esteem Scale

Indicate your level of agreement with each of the following statements by using the scale below.

| 0 | 1 | 2 | 3 |
|---|---|---|---|
| STRONGLY DISAGREE | DISAGREE | AGREE | STRONGLY AGREE |

\_\_\_\_\_  1. At times I think I am no good at all.

\_\_\_\_\_  2. I take a positive view of myself.

\_\_\_\_\_  3. All in all, I am inclined to feel that I am a failure.

\_\_\_\_\_  4. I wish I could have more respect for myself.

\_\_\_\_\_  5. I certainly feel useless at times.

\_\_\_\_\_  6. I feel that I am a person of worth, at least on an equal plane with others.

\_\_\_\_\_  7. On the whole, I am satisfied with myself.

\_\_\_\_\_  8. I feel I do not have much to be proud of.

\_\_\_\_\_  9. I feel that I have a number of good qualities.

\_\_\_\_\_10. I am able to do things as well as most other people.

To determine your score, first reverse the scoring for the five negatively worded items (1,3,4,5, & 8) as follows: 0 = 3, 1 = 2, 2 = 1, 3 = 0. Then, add up your scores across the 10 items. Your total score should fall between 0 and 30. Higher numbers indicate higher self-esteem.

Source: Rosenberg (1965).

hood (age twenty-three), self-esteem tends to rise. During the same period, females' self-esteem tends to fall (Block & Robins, 1993).

Self-esteem also fluctuates according to momentary context. For example, current moods, both positive and negative, move self-esteem in a positive or negative direction, respectively (Brown, 1998). When people experience a temporary setback—especially those with low self-esteem to begin with—their self-esteem frequently takes a temporary dive (Brown & Dutton, 1995). When college students watch their beloved college football team lose, their feelings of personal competence often drop (Hirt, Zillman, Erickson, & Kennedy, 1992). When children of average intelligence are in classrooms with academically talented children rather than with children who have lower academic abilities, research has shown that their self-esteem is generally lower (Marsh & Parker, 1984).

## CONTINGENCIES OF SELF-WORTH

Self-esteem is also closely connected to the domains of our lives that are particularly important to us. Some of you may rest your feelings of self-worth and self-esteem on your academic achievements. For others, your self-esteem may be more closely tied to your athletic prowess, sense of humor, talent for bringing people together at parties, or religious values.

To account for the diverse sources of self-esteem, Jennifer Crocker and Connie

Wolfe have proposed a **contingencies of self-worth** account of self-esteem (Crocker & Wolfe, 2001; Crocker & Park, 2003). Their model is based on the premise that self-esteem is contingent on—that is, rises and falls with—successes and failures in domains upon which a person has based his or her self-worth.

They have focused on several possible domains (among many others) that account for fluctuations in college students' self-esteem: approval, appearance, God's love or what might be called religious identity, family support, school competence, competition, and virtue (see also Crocker, Luhtanen, Cooper, & Bouvrette, 2003). A sample item measuring the domain of academic competence is "My self-esteem gets a boost when I get a good grade on an exam or paper." An item measuring the domain of others' approval is "I can't respect myself if others don't respect me." People vary in their responses according to which of these domains is most important to their self-esteem. Similarly, cultures and subcultures also vary as to which domains are considered most important. For example, the experience of God's love is much more important to the self-esteem of African Americans than to the self-esteem of either European Americans or Asian Americans. Crocker and Wolfe suggest that, to the extent that we can create environments that allow us to pursue and satisfy our specific contingencies of self-worth, we will enjoy elevated self-esteem and its numerous benefits.

We are also in a sense hostages to our contingencies of self-esteem. If things are going well in domains that are important to us, our self-esteem will be high, but if they are going badly in these domains then our self-esteem will plummet. Crocker, Samuel Sommers, and Riia Luhtanen (2002) studied the self-esteem of University of Michigan students who had applied to graduate school. The researchers created a Web page that contained an online questionnaire measuring self-esteem. They asked students to go to the Web site and fill out the questionnaire every day that they received a communication from a graduate school—either an acceptance or a rejection. Needless to say, students in general had higher self-esteem on days when they received an acceptance and lower self-esteem on days when they received a rejection, but these effects were much larger for those students whose self-esteem was more contingent on academic competence than for those for whom self-esteem was less contingent on academic competence. Keeping such findings in mind, we can see the value of deriving self-esteem from multiple domains. The more that we are able to derive our sense of self-worth from multiple domains that are in part separate from one another, the more likely we are to avoid feeling devastated by any particular setback or failure in one domain (Linville, 1987; Showers, 1992).

**contingencies of self-worth**
An account of self-esteem maintaining that self-esteem is contingent on successes and failures in domains upon which a person has based his or her self-worth.

**sociometer hypothesis**
A hypothesis that maintains that self-esteem is an internal, subjective index or marker of the extent to which we are included or looked on favorably by others.

## SOCIAL ACCEPTANCE AND SELF-ESTEEM

Thus far, we have defined self-esteem as the feeling of affection one has for oneself. Can we say more about where self-esteem comes from? One answer is that self-esteem reflects our standing with others—a thesis that Mark Leary developed in his **sociometer hypothesis**. According to this view, self-esteem is an internal, subjective index or marker of the extent to which we are included or excluded by others (Leary, Tambor, Terdal, & Downs, 1995). His argument is an evolutionary one, in that it assumes that we are social animals and that we thrive when we are in healthy social relationships. Our feelings of state self-esteem provide rapid, attention-grabbing information about the health of our social bonds. Elevated self-esteem indicates that we are thriving in our relationships, which are so crucial to our survival. In contrast, depressed self-esteem suggests that we are having interpersonal difficulties—or are in danger of having difficulties. Thus, low self-esteem is not something to be avoided at all costs; rather, it is something to be carefully attended to and acted upon.

In one study, Leary and his colleagues led participants to believe that they were to engage in a group task (Leary, Tambor, Terdal, & Downs, 1995). Prior to the task, they had written essays about "what it means to be me" and "the kind of person I would most like to be." These quite revealing, if not embarrassing, essays were given to other participants (who were in another location), and they made selections as to who they would like to work with in the group setting. The experimenter ignored these choices and randomly assigned some participants to a condition in which they had supposedly been passed over by others and had to work alone, and other participants to a condition in which they worked with a group. Participants in the work-alone condition, who believed they had been excluded, reported lower levels of self-esteem than those included by the group. Our momentary feelings strongly track the extent to which others approve of us and include us (Baumeister, Twenge, & Nuss, 2002).

> **self-evaluation maintenance model**  A model that maintains that we are motivated to view ourselves in a favorable light, and that we do so through two processes: reflection and social comparison.

## MOTIVES FOR SELF-EVALUATION

We frequently engage in self-evaluation, a process that is steered by two powerful motives. We are motivated to find out the truth about ourselves so that we have a stable sense of who we are and what we are capable of doing. But we also want to feel good about ourselves.

***The Motive to Elevate Self-Esteem***    Having elevated self-esteem is a high priority in Western cultures. So much so, in fact, that the desire to maintain high self-esteem shapes our friendships. According to Abraham Tesser's **self-evaluation maintenance model**, we are motivated to view ourselves in a favorable light, and interpersonally we do so through two processes: reflection and social comparison (Tesser, 1988). First, through *reflection*, we flatter ourselves by association with others' accomplishments. When our college football team wins, for example, we are more likely to wear school colors the following Monday and to use the pronoun "we" when describing the game-winning drive or decisive goal-line stand, presumably because our association with our team reflects favorably upon the self (Cialdini et al., 1976). Basking in the reflected glory of another's accomplishments is especially likely to boost our self-esteem when the other person is close to us and the person's success is in a domain that is *not* important to our own self-esteem.

*"So, when he says, 'What a good boy am I,' Jack is really reinforcing his self-esteem."*

Second, we flatter ourselves through *social comparison*, strategically noting how our own performance compares favorably to that of others, especially when the domain is relevant to our self-concept. Putting reflection and social comparison together, Tesser maintains that we will tend to select friends who are not our equal in domains that matter to us, but we will seek out people who excel in domains that are not our own.

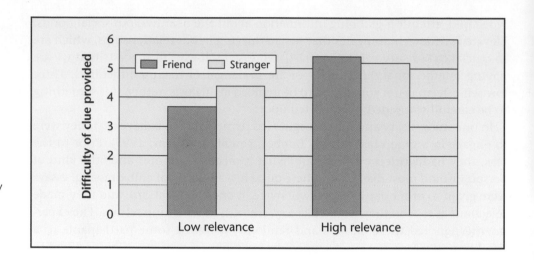

**Figure 5.5 Comparison and Self-Esteem** Friends enhance the performance of their friends more than that of strangers when the task is described as a playful game and therefore not relevant to self-definition. Friends undermine their friends' performance as much as they undermine the performance of strangers when the task is described as an assessment of verbal skills and thus relevant to self-definition. (Source: Adapted from Tesser & Smith, 1980)

"Every time a friend succeeds, I die a little."

—GORE VIDAL

In one study of reflection and social comparison, Tesser and Smith documented the ways friends aid or undermine each other in the service of maintaining their self-esteem (Tesser & Smith, 1980). Two pairs of friends, seated in four individual booths, played a word game with one another. Each participant had to guess four different words based on clues provided by the three other participants. The participants each chose clues from a list of ten clues clearly marked in terms of level of difficulty, and these clues were conveyed by the experimenter, which prevented participants from knowing the source of the clue. In the high-relevance condition, the task was described as a measure of verbal skills. In the low-relevance condition, the task was presented as a playful game. Thus, in the high-relevance condition, participants would presumably be a bit worried by their friend's possible success, to which they might compare their own performance unfavorably, and thus they might give harder clues. In the low-relevance condition, a friend's success would reflect positively upon the participant, and presumably would motivate the participant to provide easier clues.

As you can see in Figure 5.5, when the word game was not relevant to the self (that is, it was described as a playful game), participants provided easier clues to a friend than to a stranger, presumably to elevate their friend's performance, and by association, their own self-regard. (Of course, participants may have provided easier answers to make their friend feel good.) Matters were quite different, however, when the word game was relevant to participants' self-concept. In this condition, participants provided clues to a friend that were as hard as the clues they provided to a stranger! They did so, the theory goes, out of fear that a stellar performance on the part of the friend would reflect badly upon themselves.

Recall the key implication of Tesser's theory—that we should choose friends whom we outperform in domains relevant to our self-concept but who are talented in domains that are not relevant to the self. To test this hypothesis, Tesser and his colleagues had 270 fifth and sixth graders identify their closest friends, the most and least important activities relevant to their self-concept (for example, sports, art, math), and their friends' performance in those domains (Tesser, Campbell, & Smith, 1984). As evidence of self-enhancing comparison processes, students rated their own performance as better than that of their friends in the self-defining activities. Evidence of reflection processes was also observed: students rated their friends' performance as equal to their own in the least important domain. For example, if a student greatly valued athletics and had little interest in art, his closest friends tended not to be as good at athletics but to be skilled in art.

Teachers' ratings further revealed how self-enhancement shapes friendships. Students overestimated their performance relative to teachers' ratings on their most important activities, and they overestimated their friends' performance, again relative to the teacher's ratings, in the least important domain.

The tendency to remain close to people whom we outperform in domains relevant to the self holds within families as well. For example, eminent scientists reported feeling closer to fathers who pursued different occupations from their own than did scientists whose fathers were engaged in similar occupations (Tesser, 1980). Participants who are within three years of age of a sibling feel closer to that sibling when they feel they outperform the sibling in self-relevant domains, but less close to the sibling when they feel the sibling outperforms them. These kinds of comparison processes are another reason why siblings could be expected to develop different talents, abilities, and traits within the same family setting—a theme we explored in discussing Frank Sulloway's research on the Born to Rebel hypothesis.

*The Motive to Find Out the Truth about the Self*    Thus far, we have seen the far-reaching influence of self-enhancement. But we do not seek to look at ourselves solely through rose-colored glasses. The truth also matters. **Self-verification theory** holds that we strive for stable, accurate beliefs about the self, because such beliefs give us a sense of coherence (Cooley, 1902; Mead, 1934; Swann, 1992), and make us more predictable to ourselves and others (Goffman, 1959). Accuracy also tells us which endeavors to pursue (because success is likely) and which to avoid (because failure is likely).

We gather truthful information about ourselves in two general ways. First, we selectively attend to and recall information that is consistent with our self-views, even when that information is not flattering. People with negative self-views, for example, spend more time studying negative rather than positive feedback about themselves, they remember negative feedback better, and they prefer to interact with other people who are likely to provide negative rather than positive feedback (Swann & Read, 1981; Swann, Wenzlaff, Krull, & Pelham, 1992).

Second, we create self-confirmatory social environments through our behavior. Our **identity cues**, such as our customary facial expressions, our posture,

> **self-verification theory** A theory that holds that we strive for stable, accurate beliefs about the self because such beliefs give us a sense of coherence.
>
> **identity cues** Customary facial expressions, posture, gait, clothes, haircuts, and bodily decorations, which signal to others important facets of our identity, and by implication, how we are to be treated and construed by others.

**Identity Cues and Self-Construal**
We create self-confirmatory social environments through the clothes we wear, hairstyles, jewelry, tattoos, and other identity cues. (A) These people with Mohawks identify with other punks, and (B) these students and Sean Combs wear T-shirts showing their identification with others who believe in the importance of getting out the vote for the 2004 presidential election.

gait, clothes, haircuts, body decorations, signal to others important facets of our identity, and by implication, how we are to be treated and construed by others.

Wearing a simple T-shirt conveys information about our political affiliations, our music preferences, the clubs we belong to, the holidays we take, our university, and even our sexual attitudes. As another example, college students' dorm rooms—including the way that clothes are folded (or not, as the case may be) and books arranged, and what is hanging on the walls—convey valid information about individuals' personalities (Gosling, Ko, Mannarelli, & Morris, 2002), and likewise they provide clues about their preferred kinds of interactions and exchanges.

As many novels so convincingly portray, people also choose to enter into relations that maintain consistent views of the self, even when those views are dark, ruinous, and tragic. We are attracted to similar people, as we saw in the attraction chapter (Chapter 3). These sorts of preferences guarantee that our personal lives will likely confirm our views of the self. In a study of intimate bonds, romantic partners who viewed each other in a congruent fashion—that is, whose perceptions of each other were in agreement—reported more commitment to the relationship, even when one partner viewed the other in a negative light (Swann, De La Ronde, & Hixon, 1994).

How might we integrate the self-enhancement and self-verification perspectives on self-knowledge? One answer is that these two motives guide different processes related to self-knowledge and self-evaluation. Self-enhancement seems to be most relevant to our emotional responses to feedback about the self, whereas self-verification determines our more cognitive assessment of the validity of the feedback (Swann, Griffin, Predmore, & Gaines, 1987). To test this hypothesis, Swann and colleagues gave participants with negative or positive self-beliefs negative or positive feedback. In terms of participants' evaluations of the accuracy and competence of the feedback—that is, the quality of the information—truth prevailed. Namely, participants with negative self-beliefs found the negative feedback most diagnostic and accurate, whereas participants with positive beliefs rated the positive feedback higher on these dimensions. All participants, however, felt good about the positive feedback and disliked the negative feedback. Our quest for truth, then, guides our assessment of the validity of self-relevant information. Our desire to think favorably about ourselves guides our emotional reactions to the same information.

## CULTURE AND SELF-ESTEEM

East Asian languages have no term meant to capture the idea of feeling good about oneself. The Japanese have a term now, but like the Japanese rendering for baseball—namely, *beisoboru*—the term for self-esteem is simply borrowed from English: *serufu esutiimu*. That it was Westerners who invented the term "self-esteem" reflects a long-standing concern in North America with the uniqueness of the individual and self-esteem. In the early nineteenth century, New England "transcendentalist" writers, including Ralph Waldo Emerson, Henry David Thoreau, and Margaret Fuller, were reacting against what they felt was the failure of established religions to provide for people's spiritual needs. The transcendentalists emphasized the dignity of the individual's activities, the power of the individual to affect society, and the unity of the individual with nature and with God. Paradoxically, these individualist concerns were present along with many collectivist concerns, and transcendentalists were associated with early radical political movements, such as the women's suffrage movement.

Anecdotally, then, it seems that self-esteem is more important in Western cul-

"Whoso would be a man must be a nonconformist. Hitch your wagon to a star. Insist on yourself; never imitate. The individual is the world."
—RALPH WALDO EMERSON

"Independence is happiness."
—SUSAN B. ANTHONY

tures—perhaps particularly in North American culture—than in other parts of the world. Do people in Western, independent cultures report higher levels of self-esteem than people from interdependent cultures? Indeed, they do. As compared to the world's more interdependent peoples—from Japan to Malaysia to India to Kenya—Westerners consistently report higher self-esteem and a more pronounced concern with evaluating the self (Dhawan, Roseman, Naidu, Thapa, & Rettek, 1995; Markus & Kitayama, 1991).

Several studies suggest that people from Western cultures create social contexts and interactions that enhance individuals' self-esteem, as we saw in Tesser's work on self-enhancement. For example, a great deal of people's emotional energy in the West is directed toward saying and doing things intended to enhance their own and others' self-esteem. In ordinary conversation, Americans make many more spontaneous comments favorable to themselves than do Japanese individuals. Moreover, when Americans and Canadians are asked to rate themselves on various dimensions, they insist they have more positive traits than other people do and fewer negative ones (Holmberg, Markus, Herzog, & Franks, 1997).

People in different cultures also structure their daily lives in ways that give rise to differences in self-esteem. Situations described by Japanese as common in their country are regarded as less enhancing of self-esteem—by both Japanese and Americans—than situations common in the United States (Kitayama, Markus, Matsumoto, & Norasakkunkit, 1997). For example, Japanese are much more often encouraged to engage in "assisted" self-criticism than are Americans. Situations reported by Americans as common in their country are regarded by both Americans and Japanese as more esteem-enhancing than situations common in Japan. For example, Americans are much more often praised for their achievements than are Japanese. Thus, the social environment would seem to promote high self-esteem more for Americans than for Japanese.

It's important to realize that Asians and other non-Westerners don't generally feel bad about themselves. Rather than wanting personal distinctiveness or superiority, most non-Westerners are more likely to be concerned with other ways of being a good person—for example, they are motivated toward self-improvement or commitment to collective goals (Heine, 2005; Crocker & Park, 2004; Pyszczynski, Greenberg, Solomon, Arndt, & Schimel, 2004). In this more abstract sense of wanting to be a good member of one's culture, there is no reason to assume that cultures differ (Norenzayan & Heine, 2004).

Instead of tooting one's own horn, in East Asian cultures, especially in Japan, a form of self-criticism is practiced that produces social harmony and improves specific skills. Japanese math teachers and sushi chefs are appraised by their colleagues throughout their careers. They are encouraged to critique themselves in sessions with their peers—not the sort of activities that would operate to build self-esteem, however beneficial they might be to skill development.

Steven Heine and his colleagues have shown that the cultural difference in orientation toward promoting self-esteem versus working to improve the self has important consequences for what sorts of activities people seek out (Heine et al., 2001). They asked Canadian and Japanese students to take a so-called "creativity test," and then gave them false feedback about their performance. Some were told they had performed very well, and others were told they had performed very badly. The experimenter then gave the participants the opportunity to work on a similar task. The Canadians worked longer on the task if they had succeeded on it; the Japanese worked longer if they had failed. Canadians thus avoided being reminded of failure, and Japanese used the occasion to improve. Note that these findings suggest some interesting consequences. We might expect West-

> "America is a vast conspiracy to make you happy".
> —JOHN UPDIKE

erners to become specialists, getting ever better on a relatively small set of things they do well; East Asians might be more likely to become Jacks and Jills of all trades.

## CULTURE CHANGE AND SELF-ESTEEM

It is easy to think about cultural differences as if they were engraved in stone. In fact, however, cultures are dynamic, ever in flux. Although people in the West have generally been more concerned with individual distinctiveness and merit than have people in other parts of the world, this has not been true for people in all sectors of a given society at all times (see Figure 5.6). It seems unlikely that European peasants in the Middle Ages were much more concerned with their individuality than peasants in China or India at the time. And there have been periods in Chinese history when the intelligentsia, at least, were quite interested in individual differences and in standing out as being unique.

At some point between the end of the Middle Ages and the beginning of the Enlightenment in the seventeenth century, however, people in Western Europe began to become ever more independent and individualistic. The trend accelerated, if anything, in the late twentieth century (Baumeister, 1987; Seligman, 1988, Twenge, 2002). Whereas American parents in the 1940s right after World War II placed great importance on obedience in their children, by the 1970s American parents, especially middle-class parents, were more concerned that their children be independent and have good judgment (Remley, 1988). In addition, there has been a corresponding increase in the United States in parents' concerns about the self-esteem of their children. Between 1968 and 1984, American college students increased greatly in their reported self-esteem (Twenge & Campbell, 2001).

> "Men resemble the times more than they resemble their fathers."
>
> —ARAB PROVERB

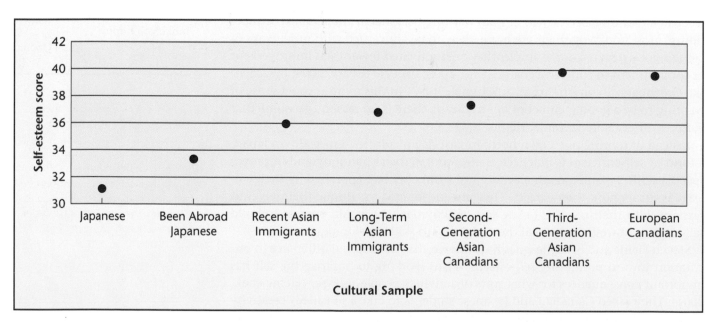

**Figure 5.6  Cultural Change and Shifts in Self-Esteem**   Self-esteem in Asians increases as a function of the degree of their exposure to North American culture. The figure shows self-esteem for Japanese who live in Japan; for Been Abroad Japanese—that is, those who have spent time in a Western culture; for Recent Asian Immigrants—that is, those who have moved to Canada within the last 7 years; for Long-Term Asian Immigrants—that is, those who have lived in Canada for more than 7 years; for Second-Generation Asian Canadians— that is, those who were born in Canada but whose parents were born in Asia; for Third-Generation Asian Canadians—that is, those who were born in Canada, whose parents were born in Canada, but whose grandparents were born in Asia; and for European Canadians— Canadians whose ancestors were Europeans. (Source: Adapted from Heine & Lehman, 2003)

One might imagine that as cultures gain greater exposure to Western concepts about individuality, freedom, and self-expression—and to situations that promote them—we might see shifts in self-esteem. That indeed is what Steven Heine and Darrin Lehman (2003) have documented. As you can see in Figure 5.6, as Asian individuals experience more and more contact with Canada, they become more and more like Canadians with respect to self-esteem.

## POSSIBLE DANGERS OF HIGH SELF-ESTEEM

The considerations above suggest that self-esteem is becoming an increasingly central part of personal identity in many parts of the world. Is this a good thing? Maybe not. Roy Baumeister and his colleagues have highlighted some specific and compelling dangers of elevated self-esteem (Baumeister, Smart, & Boden, 1996). A person who has such elevated self-esteem may think he is superior, but he may be especially sensitive to threats, insults, and challenges. This may be because his high self-esteem is actually inflated egotism. He may be very volatile, and he may use violent action to reassert his superiority and to dominate those who challenge him. Thus, elevated self-esteem mixed with threats to the ego may lead to violence.

The evidence for this thesis is robust, and it challenges the widespread assumption that depressed self-esteem is the cause of violence. In self-report studies, people who report elevated self-esteem and grandiosity also report greater aggressive tendencies (Wink, 1991). Hare (1993) has observed that psychopaths, who he estimates might be responsible for 50 percent of serious crimes, have grossly inflated views of their self-worth, and at the same time they are highly sensitive to insults and threats. Alcohol tends to elevate people's self-esteem and to increase the likelihood of aggression (Banaji & Steele, 1989). Interview and questionnaire studies of murderers, bullies, and rapists find that they are not depressed and insecure; instead, they tend to have inflated views of themselves. Members of violent youth gangs tend to be assertive, defiant, and narcissistic, and violence often occurs when they are disrespected or threatened. Baumeister and his colleagues even go so far as to suggest, drawing upon historical scholarship, that slavery, terrorism, and genocide are products of the dangerous mixture of feelings of superiority and threats to the ego.

**Dangers of High Self-Esteem**
Gang members identify with the group and wear similar clothing (shown here by their bandanas) to promote group cohesion and, ultimately, to elevate self-esteem. They compare themselves to members of other gangs and are likely to engage in violence if they feel other gangs or individuals have insulted or disrespected them.

Baumeister and his colleagues' provocative thesis serves as a caveat for the faith that Westerners place on raising people's self-esteem. Certainly, there are many benefits to modesty and humility, and there appear to be clear possible risks associated with attempting to raise self-esteem.

**LOOKING BACK,** we have seen that self-esteem concerns how people feel about their traits and abilities, successes and failures, and overall self-worth. Trait self-esteem is fairly stable, generally enduring from childhood into adulthood. In contrast, state self-esteem is changeable, fluctuating across different stages of development and according to context. We have seen that people have different contingencies of self-worth, with some more invested in intellectual ability, others in religious orientation, still others in sociability. Our moods and state self-esteem go up and down as we meet with success and failure in the domains most relevant to the ego. We seek to maintain and elevate self-esteem, both through basking in reflected glory and comparing ourselves with others. We are also motivated to gather truthful information about ourselves, paying attention to information consistent with our self-views and creating self-confirmatory social environments. We have discussed how culture affects self-esteem: people of non-Western cultures are less concerned with feeling positive about their attributes than are modern Westerners, and non-Westerners are more likely to seek out opportunities for self-criticism. Though high self-esteem is probably beneficial for the most part, it appears that there is such a thing as too much of it. We next consider how people present themselves to others in the service of creating the impressions that they desire.

## SELF-PRESENTATION

Thus far, we have largely emphasized the interior side of the self, focusing on studies of self-knowledge and self-evaluation. But there is a much more public self, one that we actively create in our social interactions and that is shaped by the perceptions of other people (Baumeister, 1982; Mead, 1934; Schlenker, 1980; Shrauger & Schoeneman, 1979). This public self is concerned with **self-presentation**—that is, presenting who we actually are, or who we would like others to believe we are. Another term for this is **impression management**, which refers to how we attempt to control the beliefs other people have of us.

Consider the fascinating life of Alexi Santana, who entered Princeton Univer-

**Self-Presentation**   James Hogue attended Princeton University on an academic scholarship under the assumed name of Alexi Santana. He constructed a false identity for himself at Princeton, and everyone believed that he was the self-educated eighteen-year-old from Utah that he presented himself as. He was a member of Princeton University's track team and was admitted to the most selective of Princeton's private eating clubs. In a documentary called *Con Man,* Jessie Moss showed that Hogue had had a pattern of assuming false identities. Hogue is shown (A) competing for Palo Alto High School under another assumed name, and (B) under arrest for forgery, wrongful impersonation, and falsifying records at Princeton.

**Public and Private Face**    People may present themselves differently in public and private. (A) Nick Nolte is not showing a carefully constructed public face when he is arrested on suspicion of driving under the influence, but (B) he does present such a public face when he arrives at a screening of one of his movies.

sity as a member of the class of 1993. He quickly excelled in his classes, was a star member of the track team, was admitted to one of Princeton's most exclusive eating clubs, and was soon heralded in local newspapers. He dazzled his dorm mates with his exploits, his tales of being raised on a sheep farm in the wild canyons of southern Utah, and by his striking habits—for example, he arose at dawn (this is striking to most college students, at least) and preferred to sleep on the floor. He was quite a presence. The only trouble was that his was a completely made-up identity. In actuality, Santana was James Hogue, a thirty-four-year-old drifter and former track star from Kansas City, who had been convicted and served time for various crimes, including forged checks and bicycle theft. He had gotten into Princeton thanks to a fraudulent application and had won the intense admiration of his peers based on a completely fictitious identity.

The sociologist Erving Goffman has offered the most far-reaching account of how we construct our identities in the public realm, something Hogue had mastered. Goffman has argued that the claims people make about their social selves govern much of their public behavior. He built his theory from naturalistic observation. Rather than doing controlled experiments, he studied how people behave in public settings. He would carefully observe the ritualistic behavior of gamblers in casinos, the odd greeting rituals of patients in mental institutions, and the habitual cries, such as "oops," when people commit social gaffes.

From these observations, he arrived at the view that public life allows us the opportunity for strategic self-presentation, by which we attempt to create and maintain an impression of ourselves in the minds of others (Baumeister, 1982; Brown, 1998; Goffman, 1959; Leary & Kowalski, 1990; Schlenker & Leary, 1982). In Goffman's terms, **face** refers to who we want others to think we are. We may want others to think we are gifted but temperamental artists, that we are recovering alcoholics who will drink no more, that we have intellectual gifts that allow us to excel without studying, or that we are the object of many romantic interests. Social interactions are the stage on which we play out these kinds of claims, regardless of how true they are. Much like a play, the social drama of self-presentation is highly collaborative. We depend on others to honor our desired social identities, and others likewise depend upon us to honor their face claims. Goffman's insights have shaped the study of the self in several lasting ways.

**self-presentation**    Presenting who we actually are, or who we would like others to believe we are.

**impression management**    Attempting to control the beliefs other people have of us.

**face**    Who we want others to think we are.

**Self-Monitoring**   During their first presidential debate on September 30, 2004, John Kerry and George W. Bush debated at the University of Miami. The television networks used close-ups on a split screen to show Bush reacting to statements that Kerry was making. Bush was not self-monitoring his expressions, as he believed that the cameras were only on Kerry.

**public self-consciousness**  Our awareness of what other people think about us—our public identity.

**private self-consciousness**  Our awareness of our interior lives—our private thoughts, feelings, and sensations.

**self-monitoring**  The tendency for people to monitor their behavior in such a way that it fits the demands of the current situation.

## IDEAS ABOUT THE PUBLIC SELF

Other researchers have continued to explore what Goffman called the public self. Thanks in part to Goffman's theorizing, researchers now differentiate between public and private self-consciousness (Fenigstein, Scheier, & Buss, 1975). **Public self-consciousness** refers to our awareness of what other people think about our selves—very much akin to Goffman's concept of face, or public identity. **Private self-consciousness** refers to our awareness of our interior lives—our private thoughts, feelings, and sensations. Researchers measure these two facets of the self with self-report questionnaires. In general, people who attend a great deal to their public self, or who are high in public self-consciousness, overestimate the extent to which others attend to them (Fenigstein, 1984), and they define their identity more in terms of social attributes, such as popularity and attractiveness. In contrast, people who attend more to their private self define their identity more in terms of personal feelings.

The concept of **self-monitoring** also derives in part from Goffman's analysis of strategic self-presentation (Gangestad & Snyder, 2000; Snyder, 1974, 1979). Self-monitoring refers to the tendency for people to monitor their behavior in such a way that it fits the demands of the current situation. High self-monitors carefully scrutinize situations, and they shift their self-presentation and behavior to fit the prevailing context. Low self-monitors act in accordance with their internal inclinations, impulses, and dispositions, independent of the social context. High self-monitors are like actors, changing their behavior according to those they are with. In contrast, low self-monitors are more likely to behave in accordance with their own traits and preferences. Patients in a psychiatric hospital scored low on a self-monitoring scale, consistent with Goffman's thesis that effective social functioning requires that we participate in strategic self-presentation (Snyder, 1974).

## SELF-HANDICAPPING: PROTECTING YOUR OWN FACE

Goffman's ideas about face have likewise inspired studies of how face concerns shape social behavior (see Box 5.2). Because how we appear to others is so important to us, we will on occasion act in self-destructive ways to protect our own claims about the self (Arkin & Baumgardner, 1985; Deppe & Harackiewicz, 1996). One such behavior is **self-handicapping**, which refers to the tendency to engage in self-defeating behaviors in order to prevent others from drawing unwanted attributions from poor performance. People self-handicap in innumerable and often imaginative ways. People avoid studying for exams or training to the fullest extent for an athletic competition. They show up late for interviews, and they say inappropriate things on first dates. These self-destructive behaviors serve an important purpose: they provide an explanation for possible failure, thus maintaining the desired public self. If you don't perform as well as expected on an exam that you didn't prepare for, there is no threat to the claims you would like to make about your academic talents. Of course, people sometimes claim "self-handicaps" they have not experienced. You yourself may have sometimes encouraged people to believe you studied less for an exam than you actually did! The phenomenon is so common that students on at least one campus, Dartmouth College, have given the people who do it a name—"sneaky bookers."

In one of the first studies of self-handicapping, male participants were led to believe either that they were going to succeed or have difficulty on a test that they were scheduled to take (Berglas & Jones, 1978). In the next part of the experiment, participants were given the chance to ingest one of two drugs: the first would enhance their test performance; the second would impair it. Participants who felt they were likely to fail the test preferred the performance-inhibiting drug, even though it would seem to diminish their chances of success. Apparently, people would rather fail and have a good reason for it than to go for success and have no excuse for their failure.

> **self-handicapping** The tendency to engage in self-defeating behaviors in order to prevent others from drawing unwanted attributions about the self as a result of poor performance.

## Box 5.2   FOCUS ON HEALTH

# Dying to Present a Favorable Self

Thus far, you might be led to conclude that self-presentation is a good thing. Erving Goffman himself wrote often about how our strategic self-presentation and how we honor others' public claims are essential ingredients of harmonious communities. But our worries about our public image, and the means by which we are guided by self-presentational concerns, may be dangerous to our health (Leary, Tchividjian, & Kraxberger, 1994). Many practices that promote health are awkward or embarrassing and pose problems for our public identity. As a consequence, we avoid them. We sacrifice physical health to maintain a public identity defined by composure and aplomb. For example, between 30 and 65 percent of respondents reported embarrassment when buying condoms (Hanna, 1989). This embarrassment may deter sexually active teenagers from buying and using condoms, which of course increases their risk of sexually transmitted diseases and unwanted pregnancies. Similarly, the fear of embarrassment at times prevents obese individuals from pursuing physical exercise programs (Bain, Wilson, & Chaikind, 1989).

In other instances, we engage in risky behavior to enhance our public image and identity. Concerns about others' impressions and our own physical appearance are good predictors of excessive sunbathing, which increases the likelihood of skin cancer (Leary & Jones, 1993). Moreover, adolescents typically cite social approval as one of the most important reasons for why they start to drink alcohol and smoke (Farber, Khavari, & Douglass, 1980). The same need for a desired public image motivates many cosmetic surgeries, which carry several health risks.

**Self-Handicapping** In the animal kingdom, self-handicapping behaviors or traits may signal superior genes to potential mates. (A) The peacock's tail makes quick flight difficult, and (B) the stag's antlers also make some movements difficult.

One view of self-destructive behaviors, then, is that they protect our public identity in the event of failure. An evolutionary theory of self-handicapping contends that such behaviors sometimes signal superior genes to potential mates (Zahavi & Zahavi, 1997). In numerous species, males have evolved physical traits that handicap survival-related behavior. Male peacocks have elaborate tails that make quick flight difficult. Certain male swallows have unusually long tails that hinder flight. Adult male orangutans have fleshy pads surrounding their eyes that narrow their field of vision, and significantly restrict sight—no doubt a hindrance in aggressive encounters. The heavily branched antlers of some male deer prevent certain physical movements, and have been shown to be maladaptive in combat. All of these physical traits expend valuable energy and resources, and they often hinder the very actions important to survival. At the same time, these traits have important signal value to potential rivals and mates: only an individual with superior genes can afford them. Thus, any success a handicapped organism enjoys must be the product of great talent and genes—the same thing you hope your friends will think when you get an A after (allegedly) not having cracked a book.

## SELF-PRESENTATION AND LANGUAGE

In many parts of the world, honesty is a virtue. We encourage it in our children and cherish it in our intimate relationships. And yet in Goffman's world of strategic self-presentation, honesty can be downright dangerous; it can threaten other people's desired public identities. Imagine that a friend asks you for your evaluation of a really odd haircut or new love interest of hers who gets on your nerves. If you hope to remain friends, it is sometimes best to avoid the unvarnished truth, and to artfully phrase your response in a way that preserves your friend's desired image.

These examples reveal how Goffman's analysis of face concerns and self-presentation shape social communication. Inspired by Goffman's theorizing, linguists like Brown and Levinson (1987) have pointed to two levels of communication. **On-record communication** refers to the statements we make that we intend to be taken literally. On-record communication tends to follow the rules of honest communication; it is direct, relevant, and delivered in sincere, straightforward fashion (Clark, 1996; Grice, 1975). When you shout "fire" dur-

**on-record communication**
The statements we make that we intend to be taken literally.

ing a fire, you hope that people will take it as an on-record claim, with no ambiguity, and no other meaning. **Off-record communication** is indirect and ambiguous; it allows you to hint at ideas and meanings that are not explicit in the words you utter. Off-record communication violates the rules of direct, honest communication with a variety of tactics, such as exaggeration, understatement, metaphor, and rhetorical statements, suggesting that nonliteral interpretations are possible (Brown & Levinson, 1987). With off-record communication, you might communicate your disapproval of your friend's haircut with hints ("Have you thought about going to my hair stylist?"), obvious exaggeration ("No, don't worry about your hair, it's the best haircut I've ever seen"), vagueness ("Your haircut makes you look interesting, sort of country and western"), or metaphors ("Don't worry about it. Your hair is a blast"). Our concern over preserving other people's face claims motivates the use of off-record communication.

> **off-record communication**
> Indirect and ambiguous communication that allows us to hint at ideas and meanings that are not explicit in the words we utter.

Let's look at two surprising ways in which we use off-record communication to protect others' face claims, often to the benefit of our relationships. A first is teasing. Our claim that teasing is a polite, off-record form of communication may surprise you. There no doubt is a dark side to teasing. At times the wrong kind of teasing can humiliate in offensive and damaging ways (Georgeson, Harris, Milich, & Young, 1999). Yet, very often people rely on teasing as a playful, indirect way of noting how others have acted inappropriately, thus allowing them to correct and avoid similar mistakes in the future (Keltner, Capps, Kring, Young, & Heerey, 2001). You may be interested to know that couples who resort to lighthearted teasing rather than direct, honest criticism, tend to negotiate conflicts in more cooperative fashion, and that people (including children) who have many warm relationships tend to be very skilled at playful teasing (Keltner, Young, Heerey, Oemig, & Monarch, 1998).

Now consider flirting and courtship. Think of the last time you expressed your initial attraction to someone. We suspect you were not as forward in expressing your romantic preferences and inclinations as participants on reality dating shows. You probably did not declare "I am very attracted to you, more than to the other people in this room, could envision a long-term relationship with you because of your keen wit, kindness, and beauty, and would like to go home with you tonight." Such a direct expression of affection is fraught with possibilities of embarrassment for everyone—the speaker, the recipient, and anyone within earshot of such an unlikely proclamation. Instead, we flirt, express our affection, and court in indirect and off-record ways. For example, we often express our initial interest in the form of teasing ("I'd never go out with someone who dresses like you"). Here our words say one thing that is on-record, but what is implied or off-record is actually the opposite—that we would like to go out with the person. Many of the nonverbal actions of flirtation have the strategic indirectness that so interested Goffman. For example, studies find that people who are flirting are engaging in behaviors that on the surface seem silly and absurd, but that actually allow them to explore romantic interest. These include the "accidental" touch to the shoulder, playful wrestling, the keep-away games—all are ways in which we can come into physical contact with one another without laying it on the line (Grammer, 1990; Moore, 1985).

**LOOKING BACK**, we have examined how we present ourselves to others, or self-presentation. Researchers have distinguished between public self-consciousness, which refers to our awareness of what others think of us, and private self-consciousness, which refers to our private thoughts, feelings, and sensations. Some people are high self-monitors, and they change their behavior based on the situation in which they find themselves. Others are low self-monitors, and they attend more to their own preferences and dispositions, with little regard for the situation or what others think. People may self-handicap, or engage in self-defeating behaviors, in order to "save face" for possible failures. They may also engage in off-record communication, so that they hint at disagreement or disapproval to avoid possible censure or rejection by the group.

## SUMMARY

1. There are several different foundations of the sense of self, or *self-concept*. The self originates in part from biologically based dispositions inherited from parents, as well as from family birth order. Firstborns tend to be more assertive and achievement-oriented; later borns tend be more open to experience and cooperative.

2. The self is shaped by the social context, with people using *social comparison* to learn about their own abilities, attitudes, and personal traits.

3. According to the *distinctiveness hypothesis*, people in Western cultures tend to define themselves according to what is unique about themselves compared to others in the social context.

4. The self is profoundly shaped by whether people live in independent or interdependent cultures.

5. Gender also affects how people define themselves, with women generally emphasizing their relationships and defining themselves in an interdependent way, and men generally emphasizing their uniqueness and construing themselves in an independent way.

6. There are several forms and functions of *self-knowledge*. Self-knowledge can take the form of beliefs, images, memories, and stories we tell about our lives. This self-knowledge helps guide construal of social information, through memories and self-schemas, typically reinforcing preexisting beliefs about the self.

7. Self-knowledge embodies cultural and moral standards, and it motivates appropriate behavior. *Self-*

*discrepancy theory* investigates how people compare their actual selves to both their ideal and ought selves.

8. Self-knowledge varies across cultures. In independent cultures, people use their self-knowledge as standards in judging others. They tend to have unrealistically positive beliefs about themselves, an illusion of control, and unrealistic optimism, which all enhance their sense of well-being. In interdependent cultures, other people rather than the self serve as standards for social judgment, and there is less evidence of self-illusions.

9. There are two kinds of self-esteem: *trait self-esteem*, which tends to be a stable part of identity, and *state self-esteem*, which changes according to different contextual factors, such as personal failure or the loss of a beloved sports team.

10. The motivation to have elevated self-esteem guides the formation of friendships that allow one to engage in favorable social comparisons and esteem-enhancing pride taken in the friend's successes.

11. Self-esteem is more important and elevated in Western than in East Asian cultures.

12. There are perils of high self-esteem, and studies have linked various forms of antisocial behavior with narcissistic levels of self-esteem.

13. *Self-presentation theory* considers the self to be a dramatic performer in the public realm. People seek to create and maintain a favorable public impression of themselves. *Face* refers to what people want others to think they are.

14. Researchers now distinguish between *private* and *public self-consciousness*. They have shown that people engage in *self-monitoring* to ensure that their behavior fits the demands of the social context.

15. People protect their public self through *self-handicapping behaviors*, which are self-defeating behaviors that can explain away possible failure.

16. Face concerns and self-presentation shape social communication. *On-record communication* is direct; *off-record communication* like joking and teasing is indirect and subtle.

## CRITICAL THINKING ABOUT BASIC PRINCIPLES

1. What are some different ways in which the self is a product of the situation?

2. Consider some situation bearing both potential for success and possibilities of failure. What aspect of self-understanding would be called upon in each case?

3. Independent peoples are motivated to move their actual selves into line with their "ideal selves." What kinds of motivations do you suppose serve a similar function for changing the self for interdependent peoples?

4. Do you think interdependent people would be more likely than independent people to be high self-monitors or low self-monitors? Why?

## KEY TERMS

actual self (p. 186)
collective self (p. 183)
contingencies of self-worth (p. 194)
distinctiveness hypothesis (p. 177)
diversification (p. 176)
dizygotic (fraternal) twins (p. 172)
face (p. 203)
Five-Factor Model (Big Five) (p. 171)
heritability (p. 172)
ideal self (p. 186)
identity cues (p. 197)
impression management (p. 203)
monozygotic (identical) twins (p. 172)

off-record communication (p. 207)
on-record communication (p. 206)
ought self (p. 186)
prevention focus (p. 186)
private self-consciousness (p. 204)
promotion focus (p. 186)
public self-consciousness (p. 204)
relational self-beliefs (p. 183)
self-concept (p. 171)
self-discrepancy theory (p. 186)
self-esteem (p. 192)
self-evaluation maintenance model (p. 195)
self-handicapping (p. 205)

self-image bias (p. 187)
self-monitoring (p. 204)
self-presentation (p. 203)
self-reference effect (p. 184)
self-schemas (p. 184)
self-verification theory (p. 197)
social beliefs (p. 183)
social comparison theory (p. 178)
sociometer hypothesis (p. 194)
state self-esteem (p. 192)
traits (p. 171)
trait self-esteem (p. 192)

## FURTHER READING AND FILMS

Allen, W. (1983). *Zelig.* "Human chameleon" Leonard Zelig (Woody Allen) soars to celebrity in the 1920s and 1930s with his unexplained ability to transform himself into anyone he meets. Allen's "mockumentary" finds Zelig in the unlikeliest of places—from the intensity of a New York Yankees dugout to the frenzy of a Nazi rally.

Dennis, N. F. (2002). *Cards of identity.* Normal, Il: Dalkey Archive Press (originally published 1955). A very entertaining novel about a group of people (psychologists?) who find individuals with identities that are making them miserable and change their identities by surrounding them with people and evidence supporting the new identity. If you're confident that couldn't happen to you, finish this text before reading Dennis's book.

Higgins, E. T. (1987). Self discrepancy: A theory relating self and affect. *Psychological Review*, 94, 319–340. A classic paper showing how the "ought self" and the "ideal self" are different not only from the "actual self" but from each other.

Taylor, S. E. (1989). *Positive illusions: Creative self-deception and the healthy mind*. New York: Basic Books. A recounting of the ways in which psychologically healthy people hold various illusions about themselves and the nature of the world. Who says wishful thinking is dangerous? (Actually, several of the author's critics—but she has interesting answers.)

# PART TWO

# Influencing Others

THE PREVIOUS SECTION EXPLORED OUR CONNECTION TO OTHERS and examined some of the implications of our fundamentally social existence. This section expands on the implications of our social nature. Our relationships with one another are not passive. We constantly influence one another, and this section examines the most important types of social influence. In Chapter 6, we discuss how conformity pressures sometimes lead us to think and act alike, why people sometimes give in to the commands of authority, even a malevolent authority, and some of the most effective tactics for getting people to comply with requests. In Chapter 7, we examine social influence more broadly, with a review of the research on what makes some persuasive messages, especially those presented through the mass media, more effective than others. In Chapter 8, we take note of the fact that people's attitudes and behavior often match, and we investigate how much of this is the result of attitudes influencing behavior and how much is the result of behavior influencing attitudes.

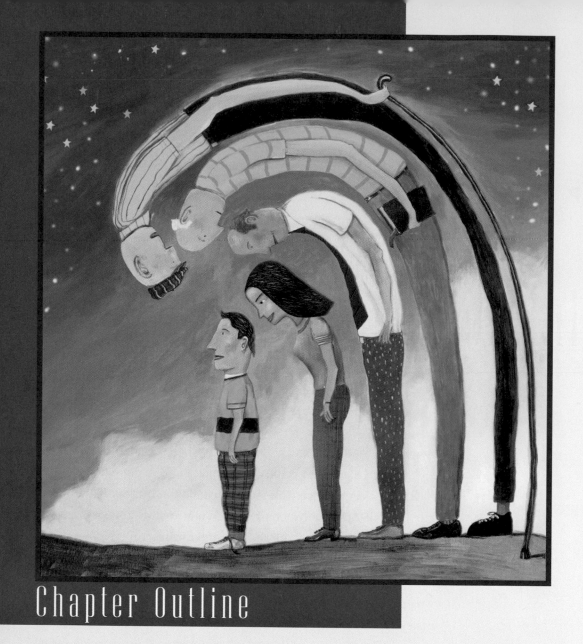

# Chapter Outline

# CHAPTER 6

# Social Influence

In the fall of 1992, over 500 experimental social psychologists (your three textbook authors among them) gathered in San Antonio, Texas, for the field's annual conference. Like nearly everyone who visits the city, most of us paid a visit to the area's most prominent tourist attraction, the Alamo.

An eighteenth-century Franciscan mission, the Alamo was the scene of an episode of epic bravery in Texas's war for independence from Mexico. Settlers from the United States had formed a provisional government and an army with the intention of separating from Mexico. In 1836, a group of fewer than 200 Texan soldiers were garrisoned at the Alamo when word was received that 4,000 Mexican troops under the command of General Antonio López de Santa Anna were approaching to take back the fort. The commander of the Alamo, Lieutenant Colonel William Travis, offered each soldier the opportunity to leave before the battle began. And he apparently did so in dramatic fashion, using his saber to draw a line in the sand and inviting all who were interested in advancing the cause of Texas's independence to cross the line and join him in the defense of the Alamo. All of them did, and all of them were killed trying to hold off Santa Anna's forces.

It is a moving story, not only because they all chose to stay and face their deaths, but also because they fought fiercely and heroically, holding off Santa Anna's forces for twelve days, a period of time that historians contend was crucial to Texas's efforts to organize an effective army under the command of Sam Houston. Indeed, six weeks after the taking of the Alamo by the Mexican army, Houston's forces defeated Santa Anna at San Jacinto, and Texas's independence from Mexico was secured. At least one commander is believed to have rallied his troops during the decisive battle with the cry, "Remember the Alamo!"

There is no denying the heroism of those 200 men. They gave (in Lincoln's words about another historic battlefield) their "last full measure of devotion" to the cause. But there is something about experiencing the Alamo in the presence of so many social psychologists—of so many people attuned to the importance of the tiniest situational details—that made it hard to imagine that the event actually occurred in such a storybook fashion. If one summons all that one knows about human behavior, it is unlikely that all 200 individuals, as the usual version of the story implies, enthusiastically crossed the line to join Travis. Instead, it is much more likely that the most devoted did so, and then a few more crossed the line so as not to be outdone, and then others only reluctantly did so, after thinking to themselves, "Oh #@!$%, everyone's staying! What am I going to do?"

**Social Influence and the Situation**
At the Battle of the Alamo in 1836, Texan defenders were all killed trying to prevent the Mexican army from retaking the fort. Each individual's decision to stay and fight to the death likely resulted from his sense of duty and conviction but also from social influence.

One of the great lessons of social psychology is that many seemingly subtle details of a given situation—the possibility of embarrassment, the presence of a few other people, the violation of routines—can have a powerful impact on people's behavior. As a result, the study of social psychology changes forever the way one views human behavior, whether it be the behavior of bona fide heroes like those who defended the Alamo or, at the other end of the benevolence-malevolence spectrum, those who participated in acts of genocide like the Holocaust in World War II Europe or the Sudanese massacres in this decade. Nowhere is this lesson more pointedly demonstrated than in the discussion of social influence.

In examining this topic, we will discuss a number of "situationist classics" in social psychology. By that, we mean experiments that have become well known—both inside psychology and out in the broader culture—for revealing how seemingly inconsequential elements of the social situation can have a surprisingly powerful effect on people's behavior. The results of these experiments have surprised and intrigued generations of students, forcing them to rethink some of their basic assumptions about human nature. We will begin by defining social influence and then discuss the factors that produce conformity to peers, obedience to authorities, and compliance with requests.

## WHAT IS SOCIAL INFLUENCE?

**Social influence**, broadly speaking, refers to the myriad ways that people affect one another. It involves the changes in attitudes, beliefs, feelings, and behavior that result from the comments, actions, or even the mere presence of others. Social influence is a subject to which everyone can relate. We are frequently the targets of other people's influence attempts—whether it be a friend's pressure to go out drinking; Madison Avenue's efforts to get us to buy into the latest fashion trends; a charity's request for us to donate our time or money; or a parent's, politician's, or priest's attempts to shape our moral, political, or religious values. We are also often the agents of social influence, as when we unconsciously smile at someone for actions we like and frown at someone for actions we dislike, or when we deliberately try to coax a friend into dating Janice in order to reduce the competition for Jane. Doing well in the world demands that we know when to yield to the influence attempts of others and when—and how—to resist. It also demands that we exercise some skill in our attempts to influence others.

Social psychologists distinguish among several types of social influence. The one most familiar to the average person is **conformity**, which social psychologists define as changing one's behavior or beliefs in response to some real (or imagined) pressure from others. Pressures to conform can be implicit, as when one decides to toss out one's loose-fitting jeans in favor of those with a tighter cut (or vice versa) simply because other people have done so. But conformity pressure can also be rather explicit, as when members of a peer group pointedly encourage one another to smoke cigarettes, try new drugs, or push the envelope on some new extreme sport. This latter, explicit conformity pressure shades into another type of social influence, **compliance**, which social psychologists define as responding favorably to an explicit request by another person. Compliance attempts can come from people with some power over you, as when your boss or professor asks you to run an errand or baby-sit her kids, or from "equal power" sources, as when a peer asks to borrow your notes. Compliance attempts of the former variety are often not as nuanced and sophisticated as the latter because they don't have to be (note how much easier it would be for your professor to get you to agree to loan him $20 than it would be for the person sitting next to you in the classroom). Finally, another type of social influence, which social psychologists refer to as **obedience**, occurs when the power relationship is unequal and the more powerful person issues a command rather than a request, to which the less powerful person submits.

Is a tendency to go along with others a good thing or a bad thing? In today's Western society, which prizes autonomy and individual initiative, the term "conformity" connotes something bad to most people. If someone called you a conformist, for instance, you probably wouldn't like it. And some types of conformity *are* bad. Going along with a crowd to perpetrate a hurtful prank, to try a dangerous new drug, or to drive a vehicle while intoxicated are good examples. Other types of conformity are neither good nor bad, as when we conform to the norm to wear athletic shorts very short (1970s) or very long (1990s). Still

---

**social influence** The myriad ways that people impact one another, including changes in attitudes, beliefs, feelings, and behavior, that result from the comments, actions, or even the mere presence of others.

**conformity** Changing one's behavior or beliefs in response to explicit or implicit (whether real or imagined) pressure from others.

**compliance** Responding favorably to an explicit request by another person.

**obedience** Social influence in which the less powerful person in an unequal power relationship submits to the demands of the more powerful person.

other types are clearly beneficial, both to ourselves (because we don't have to deliberate about every possible action) and to others (because it eliminates potential conflict and makes human interaction so much smoother). Conformity plays a big part, for example, in getting many people to inhibit anger; to pay taxes; to form lines at the theater, museum, and grocery store; and to step to the right of oncoming pedestrians. Would any of us really want to do away with those conformist tendencies? Indeed, evolutionary psychologists and anthropologists have argued that a tendency to conform is generally beneficial. We should probably do what others are doing in the same situation unless we have good reasons not to (Boyd & Richerson, 1985; Henrich & Boyd, 1998).

## CONFORMITY

**Conformity Pressures and Fashion**
Social influence may affect what we do and say and even what we wear. Millions of people bought Hush Puppies when they became fashionable, in an effort to be seen as "cool."

Hush Puppies, the formerly popular suede shoes with the eraser-like soles, were on their way to being phased out in 1994. No one was buying them. But just before Wolverine, the shoe's manufacturer, pulled the plug on the shoe, two of its executives heard that some kids were wearing them in some of the fashionable clubs of Manhattan. The few pairs that were available were being snapped up at any odd retail outpost that was still carrying them. Fashion designers, always attuned to the latest trends in such style incubators as New York City, soon started incorporating this classic American shoe in their collections. Sales took off, and plans to terminate the shoe were shelved. Whereas only 30,000 pairs were sold in 1994, that number swelled to 430,000 in 1995 and to over a million and a half in 1996, the year Hush Puppies won the Council of Fashion Designers' prize for the "best accessory" (Gladwell, 2000).

The rebirth of Hush Puppies is a compelling demonstration of the power of conformity. After all, the million-plus people who bought Hush Puppies in 1996 did not suddenly all detect the product's virtues on their own. They influenced each other. Doubtless the influence was sometimes purely implicit ("Look at the cool shoes those guys are wearing"), and other times it was a bit more explicit ("Check out these new shoes I got; aren't they cool?"). The same is true when prison guards abuse inmates (see Chapter 1), or when individuals fail to stop a bully. Sometimes the conformity pressures from the people around them are explicit, and sometimes they are implicit. We will try to understand the forces that elicit this type of social influence by exploring the full range of the implicit-explicit continuum.

### AUTOMATIC MIMICRY AND THE CHAMELEON EFFECT

As the cartoon on the next page illustrates, sometimes we mindlessly imitate others' behavior. It is often said that yawning and laughter are contagious, but a lot of other behavior is as well. Like it or not, we are often subconscious copycats.

But why would we mindlessly copy others' behavior? William James (1890) provided part of an explanation by proposing his principle of **ideomotor action**, whereby merely thinking about a behavior makes its actual performance more likely (for example, merely thinking about eating a bowl of Haagen Dazs ice

**ideomotor action** The phenomenon whereby merely thinking about a behavior makes its actual performance more likely.

**Ideomotor Action and Conformity**
When we see others behave in a particular way, we may unconsciously mimic their postures, facial expressions, and even their behaviors. Before the signing of the 1995 Mideast Peace Accord, Bill Clinton, Israeli Prime Minister Yitzhak Rabin, Egyptian President Hosni Mubarak, and King Hussein of Jordan all adjusted their ties, as Yasser Arafat, who was not wearing a tie, looked on.

cream makes it more likely that we will actually open the freezer, take out the ice cream, and indulge). When we see others behave in a particular way, the idea of that behavior is brought to mind (consciously or otherwise) and, through the process of ideomotor action, we are more likely to behave that way ourselves. Tanya Chartrand and John Bargh experimentally tested this idea in a study of what they termed the **chameleon effect**, or the "nonconscious mimicry of the postures, mannerisms, facial expressions, and other behaviors of one's interaction partners" (Chartrand & Bargh, 1999, p. 893).

Undergraduates at New York University took part in two ten-minute sessions in which they, along with another participant, were asked to describe various photographs from popular magazines such as *Newsweek* and *Time*. The other participant was, in reality, a confederate of the experimenter, and there was a different confederate in each of the two sessions. The confederate in one session frequently rubbed his or her face, whereas the confederate in the other session continuously shook his or her foot. As the participant and confederate went about their business of describing the various photographs, the participant was surreptitiously videotaped. This allowed Chartrand and Bargh to determine whether participants tended to rub their face in the presence of the face-rubbing confederate and shake their feet in the presence of the foot-shaking confederate. The videotapes, it is important to note, were taken of the participant only—the confederate was not visible on the tape. This ensured that those timing how long each participant rubbed his face or shook her foot were unaffected by knowledge of what the confederate was doing.

As predicted, the participants tended to mimic (or conform to) the behavior exhibited by the confederate. They shook their feet more often when in the presence of a foot-shaking confederate and rubbed their face more often when in the

**chameleon effect** The nonconscious mimicry of the expressions, mannerisms, movements, and other behaviors of those with whom one is interacting.

*"I don't know why. I just suddenly felt like calling."*

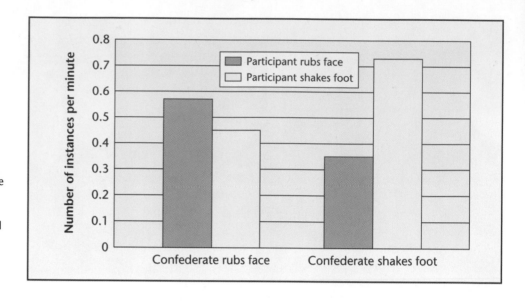

**Figure 6.1 Unconscious Mimicry** Average number of times per minute participants performed an action (face rubbing, foot shaking) while in the presence of a someone performing that action or not. (Source: Chartrand & Bargh, 1999)

**autokinetic illusion** The apparent motion of a stationary point of light in a completely darkened environment.

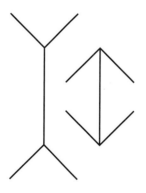

**Figure 6.2 The Müller-Lyer Illusion** In the Müller-Lyer illusion, the framing of the vertical lines by the arrows affects the perception of their lengths, just as social perception is affected by frames of reference. Even though the two vertical lines are exactly the same length, the vertical line on the left appears longer than the vertical line on the right because of its outward-pointing "fins" at the top and bottom, as opposed to the inward-pointing "fins" at the top and bottom of the line on the right.

presence of a face-rubbing confederate (see Figure 6.1). A follow-up study revealed that this tendency to mimic others is particularly strong among people who have an empathic orientation toward others or who have a need to affiliate with others (Chartrand & Bargh, 1999; Lakin & Chartrand, 2003). Even more intriguing, additional follow-up studies have looked at the consequences of behavioral mimicry and found that people tend to like those who mimic them more than those who do not (Chartrand & Bargh, 1999), and that individuals who have been mimicked tend to engage in more pro-social behavior immediately afterwards—such as donating money to a good cause or leaving large tips to the person who mimicked them (van Baaren, Holland, Kawakami, & van Knippenberg, 2004; van Baaren, Holland, Steenaert, & van Knippenberg, 2003).

## INFORMATIONAL SOCIAL INFLUENCE AND SHERIF'S CONFORMITY EXPERIMENT

A much earlier conformity experiment by Muzafer Sherif (1936) dealt with a type of conformity that lies further along the implicit/explicit continuum—conformity that is less automatic and reflexive. Sherif was interested in how groups influence the behavior of individuals by shaping how reality is perceived. He noted that even our most basic perceptions are not direct, but are influenced by prevailing frames of reference. In the well-known Müller-Lyer illusion reproduced here, one horizontal line appears longer than the other because of how the lines are "framed" by the two sets of arrows (see Figure 6.2). Sherif designed his experiment to examine the circumstances in which other people serve as a *social* frame of reference.

Sherif's experiment was built around the **autokinetic illusion**, or the tendency of a stationary point of light in a completely darkened environment to appear to move. The phenomenon was noted by ancient astronomers and stems from the fact that with complete darkness there are no other stimuli to anchor one's sense of the light's location. Perhaps, Sherif thought, other people would fill the void and serve as a frame of reference against which one's perceptions of the light's movement would be assessed. To begin, Sherif put individual participants in a darkened room, presented them with a stationary point of light on trial after trial, and had them estimate how far it "moved" each time. What he found was that some people thought, on average, it moved very little on each trial (say, two inches), and others thought it moved a good deal more (say, five inches).

Sherif's next step was to bring several participants into the room together and have them call out their estimates for each to hear. He found that people's estimates tended to converge over time. Those who individually had thought the light had moved a fair amount soon lowered their estimates; those who individually had thought it had moved very little soon raised theirs (see Figure 6.3). Sherif argued that everyone's individual judgments quickly fused into a group norm, and the norm influenced how far the light was seen to move. His interpretation was reinforced by a follow-up experiment that found that when participants were brought back for individual testing up to one year later, their judgments still showed the influence of their group's earlier responses (Rohrer, Baron, Hoffman, & Swander, 1954).

The behavior of Sherif's participants is typically interpreted as the result of **informational social influence**, or the use of other people—their comments and their actions—as a source of information about what's likely to be right, proper, or effective (Deutsch & Gerard, 1955). We want to be right, and the opinions of other people are a useful source of information we can draw upon to "get it right." Although we shouldn't mindlessly go along with what other people think all the time, we shouldn't simply ignore others' opinions either. Indeed, we do so at our peril. The tendency to use others as a source of information is particularly pronounced when we are uncertain of the right answer. We are more likely to conform to others' views about the appropriate macroeconomic policy to follow than about the relative quality of the climate in Buffalo versus Honolulu. New York City residents were doubtless more inclined to follow the behavior of others right after the attack on the World Trade Center than they were on a typical autumn day. Note that the task Sherif asked his participants to perform is about as ambiguous as it gets, and so informational social influence is at its peak. The light, in fact, doesn't move it all; it just appears to. And that appearance, being so uncertain and ambiguous, is readily influenced by the expressed judgments of others (see also Baron, Vandello, & Brunsman, 1996; Levine, Higgins, & Choi, 2000; Tesser, Campbell, & Mickler, 1983).

> **informational social influence** The influence of other people that results from taking their comments or actions as a source of information as to what is correct, proper, or efficacious.

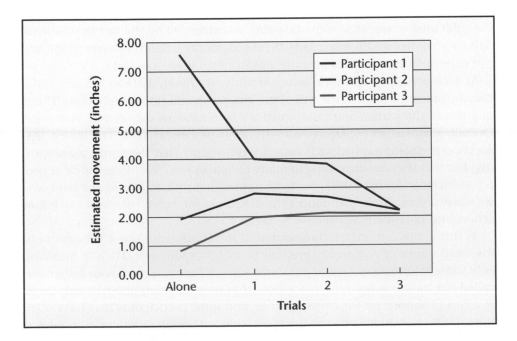

**Figure 6.3 Informational Social Influence** Sherif's conformity experiment used the autokinetic effect to assess group influence. Participants estimated how far the point of light appeared to move, first when they were alone, and later in the presence of other people. (Source: Sherif, 1936)

## NORMATIVE SOCIAL INFLUENCE AND ASCH'S CONFORMITY EXPERIMENT

You may be thinking to yourself, "What's the big deal here? Why *wouldn't* participants conform to one another's judgments? After all, the task was impossible, and no one could have felt confident in his or her own judgment. Why not rely on others?" If you were entertaining such thoughts, you were pursuing a line of reasoning advanced by another pioneer of conformity research, Solomon Asch. Asch thought that Sherif's experiment, although informative about a certain type of conformity, did not speak to those situations in which there is a clear conflict between one's own judgment and that of the group. It does not apply, for example, to the experience of knowing that one has consumed too much alcohol to drive an automobile safely while being urged to do so by one's peers ("Come on. Don't be a wimp, you'll be fine."). Asch predicted that when there is a clear conflict between one's own judgment and the judgments advanced by the group, there would be far less conformity than that observed by Sherif. He was right. But the reduced rate of conformity was not what made his experiment the second most famous in the history of social psychology (and one of the most famous in all of psychology). What made his study so well known was how often participants *did* conform, even when they thought the group was out of its collective mind.

You may already be familiar with Asch's procedure (Asch, 1956). A group of individuals were gathered together by the experimenter to perform a simple perceptual task—to determine which of three lines was the same length as a target line (see Figure 6.4). Each individual called out his judgment publicly, one at a time. The task was sufficiently easy that the experience was uneventful—at first.

On the third trial, however, one individual found that his private judgment was at odds with the expressed opinions of everyone else in the group. That one individual was the one true participant in the experiment; the seven others were confederates instructed by Asch to respond incorrectly. The confederates responded incorrectly on eleven more occasions before the experiment was over, and the question was how often the participant would forsake what he knew to be the correct answer in order to conform to the incorrect judgment rendered by everyone else. Here there was no ambiguity, as there was in Sherif's experiment; the right answer was clear to participants, as evidenced by the fact that individuals in a control group who made these judgments when they were alone and not experiencing any social pressure almost never made a mistake.

As Asch predicted, there was less conformity in this study than in Sherif's, but the rate of capitulation to the will of the group was still surprisingly high. Three-quarters of the participants conformed to the erroneous majority at least once. Overall, participants conformed on a third of the critical trials. The reason that Asch's experiment has had such impact is not simply that the results are surprising, but that they are disturbing to many people as well. We like to think of people as sticking to what they know to be right rather than following the herd, and we worry about people abandoning the dictates of their own conscience to follow others into potentially destructive behavior.

As this discussion implies, informational social influence is not thought to be the main source of conformity pressure in Asch's experiment. There is undoubtedly some informational social influence at work here (the erroneous judgments called out by the majority were for lines that were between one-half and three-quarters of an inch off the correct answer, and some participants may have questioned their own judgment and therefore regarded the confederates' responses as

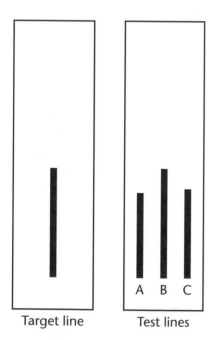

**Solomon Asch** A pioneer of conformity research, Asch studied the effect of normative social influence.

**Figure 6.4 Normative Social Influence** Individuals in a group had to compare test lines to a target line and say publicly which test line was the same length as the target line. To avoid the disapproval of the group, many participants conformed to the judgments of the majority rather than expressing their own judgment. (Source: Asch, 1956)

Target line    Test lines
A  B  C

Box 6.1   FOCUS ON HEALTH

# Bulimia and Social Influence

Why do young women engage in binge eating and then purging by vomiting or using laxatives? The phenomenon is relatively new. Such behavior, known as bulimia, was virtually unheard of until roughly thirty years ago. Does it exist because the fashion industry and media have persuaded women to want to be thinner than it is natural for them to be (see Chapter 3)? Is it because depression and anxiety have increased in recent decades? Is it because body image and self-esteem have worsened?

**Thinness and Social Influence**
These models do whatever they can to maintain their slim bodies.

All of these factors may play a role in the current epidemic of bulimia, but another factor is social influence. Christian Crandall (1988) studied sorority women at a large midwestern university and found that the more bulimic a woman's friends were, the more bulimic she was likely to be. This was not because bulimic women discovered each other and became friends while nonbulimic women sought out peers who preferred to keep their food down. Early in the school year, when women had known each other only for a short while, there was no association between the level of a woman's engagement in bulimic activity and the level of her friends' engagement in such activity. But over the course of the year, women in now-established friendship groups (not a *new* group of friends) came to have similar levels of bulimia.

Crandall studied two different sororities and found two slightly different patterns of influence. In one sorority, women who differed in their level of bulimic activity from the average level in the sorority were less likely to be popular. Crandall inferred from this that there was an "appropriate" or normative level of bulimia in that sorority, and deviations from it *in either direction* were punished by rejection. In the other sorority, more binge eating (up to a fairly large amount) was associated with more popularity. In that sorority, Crandall concluded, there was pressure toward considerable binge eating, and those most inclined to binge were rewarded with popularity.

*"Call the Ford agency—another supermodel just blew away."*

informative). But the primary reason people conformed was to avoid standing out, negatively, in the eyes of everyone else (see Box 6.1). Social psychologists refer to this as **normative social influence**, or the desire to avoid the disapproval, harsh judgments, and other social sanctions (barbs, ostracism) that others might deliver (Deutsch & Gerard, 1955). People are typically loathe to depart from the norms of society, or at least the norms of those subgroups they most care about, because of a fear of the likely social consequences (Cialdini, Kallgren, & Reno, 1991). The normative social pressures in Asch's experiment are sufficiently intense that the participants found themselves in a wrenching dilemma

> **normative social influence**
> The influence of other people that comes from the desire to avoid their disapproval, harsh judgments, and other social sanctions (for example, barbs, ostracism).

222

**Normative Social Influence** One true participant (the man in the middle) and seven confederates were asked to say which of three lines was the same length as the target line. (A) The participants listened to the experimenter's instructions. (B) When the confederates unanimously responded incorrectly, the true participant leaned forward to take another look at the lines. (C) The true participant conformed to the erroneous majority on some of the trials, but after twelve trials he said that "he has to call them as he sees them."

(see photo above). "Should I say what I truly think it is? But what would everyone else think? They all agree, and they all seem so confident. Will they think I'm nuts? Will they interpret my disagreement as a slap in the face? But what kind of person am I if I go along with them? What the #@!$% should I do?"

To get an idea of the intensity of their dilemma, imagine the following scenario. As part of a discussion of Asch's experiment, your social psychology professor shows an overhead of the target line and the three test lines, and reports that although the right answer is line B, the confederates all say it's C. As your professor attempts to move on from the basics of Asch's experiment, one student raises his hand firmly and announces with conviction, "But the right answer *is* C!"

What would happen? Doubtless everyone would chuckle, making the charitable assumption that the student was trying to be funny. But if the student insisted that the confederates' answer was correct, the chuckles would turn to awkward, nervous laughter, and everyone would turn toward the professor in an implicit plea to "make this awkward situation go away." On subsequent lectures, most people would avoid sitting by the individual in question, and a buffer of empty seats would surround him. (And, of course, lunch invitations, dating opportunities, offers to join a fraternity or other social club would diminish as well.) *That* is the fate that Asch's participants felt they risked if they departed from the majority's response. It is no great surprise that they so often chose not to take the risk (Janes & Olson, 2000; Kruglanski & Webster, 1991; Levine, 1989; Schachter, 1951). Let's now consider the factors that influence the potency of these conformity pressures.

## FACTORS AFFECTING CONFORMITY PRESSURES

Several generations of researchers have conducted research that examines the characteristics of the group and the characteristics of the task or situation that influence the tendency to conform. We review the highlights of that research to gain a clearer understanding of when the tendency to conform will be particularly strong and when it will not. Central to our review is the distinction between informational and normative social influence. As we shall see, as either source of influence intensifies, so does the rate of conformity.

*Group Size* It is surely no surprise to learn that conformity increases as the size of the group increases. Larger groups exert both more normative influence (better to be disliked or shunned by a few than by many) and more informational social influence than smaller groups (all things being equal, a position advanced by many is more likely to be correct than a position advanced by a few). What is more surprising, perhaps, is that the effect of group size levels off pretty quickly (see Figure 6.5). Research using Asch's paradigm, for example, has shown an increase in con-

*THE FAR SIDE*® BY GARY LARSON

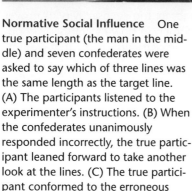

© 1984 FarWorks, Inc. All Rights Reserved/Dist. by Creators Syndicate    Larson

The Far Side® by Gary Larson © 1984 FarWorks, Inc. All Rights Reserved. Used with permission.

**Laboratory peer pressure**

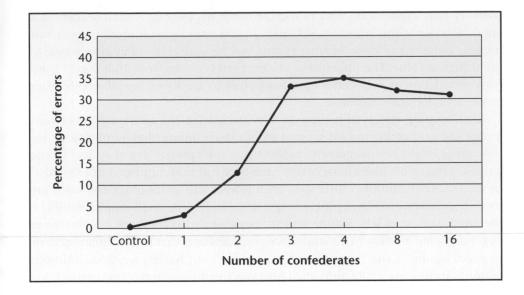

**Figure 6.5  The Effect of Group Size on Conformity**  As the number of individuals reporting an incorrect answer increases, conformity increases—but only up to a point. As group size reaches four people, conformity rates level off. (Source: Asch, 1951)

formity as the size of the group increases, but only to a group size of four or five; after that, the amount of conformity levels off (Campbell & Fairey, 1989; Gerard, Wilhemy, & Conolley, 1968; Insko, Smith, Alicke, Wade, & Taylor, 1985; Rosenberg, 1961).

This makes sense, of course, from the standpoint of both informational and normative social influence. The larger the number of people who venture a particular opinion, the more likely it has merit. But only to a certain point. After a while, the opinions offered are unlikely to be independent of one another, and thus they do not offer any real information. Also, as the number of people increases, the fear of being judged harshly increases. But here, too, only to a point. There is only so much embarrassment one can feel, and the difference between being viewed as odd, foolish, or difficult by two versus four people is psychologically much more powerful than the difference between being viewed that way by, say, six versus eight, or twelve versus fourteen.

*Group Unanimity*    One of the more powerful effects observed in Asch's original studies was what happened when the unanimity of the group was broken. Recall that in the basic paradigm, when all group members but the one true participant reported an incorrect answer, the participant went along and reported the wrong answer a third of the time. That figure dropped to 5 percent when the true participant had an ally—that is, when just one other member of the group deviated from the majority. This effect occurs because the presence of an ally weakens both informational social influence ("Maybe I'm not crazy after all") and normative social influence ("At least I've got someone to commiserate with"). This effect also suggests a powerful tool for protecting independence of thought and action. If one expects to be pressured to conform and wants to remain true to one's own beliefs, bring along an ally.

Note that the other individual who breaks the group's unanimity need not offer the correct answer, just one that departs from the group's answer. Suppose the right answer is the shortest of the three lines, and the majority claims it's the longest. If the "ally" states that it's the middle line, the ally reduces the rate of conformity, even though the participant's own view of the matter has not been reinforced. What matters is the break in unanimity. This fact has important free speech implications. It suggests that we might want to tolerate loathsome and

> "'The way to get along,' I was told when I entered Congress, 'is to go along.'"
>
> —JOHN F. KENNEDY

> "It takes a great deal of bravery to stand up to our enemies, but just as much to stand up to our friends."
>
> —ALBUS DUMBLEDORE, *HARRY POTTER AND THE SORCERER'S STONE*

patently false expression ("The Holocaust never happened." "The President is a child molester." "The World Trade Center attacks were a government hoax."), not because there is any value in what is said, but because it liberates *other people* to say things of value. The presence of voices, even bizarre voices, that depart from conventional opinion liberates the body politic to speak out, and thus can foster productive political discourse.

The liberating effects of having an ally, along with the relationship between group size and conformity discussed earlier, have interesting implications for how juries might best be constructed. What is the optimal size of a jury? In the United States, most juries have twelve members, but that number is not specified in the U.S. Constitution. Other sizes are allowed, and juries of six and eight are used in some states. From a purely pragmatic standpoint, smaller juries would be preferred (they cost less in time and money), provided they are as effective as larger ones. But are they? One important consideration that legal scholars urge us to guard against is the "tyranny of the majority"—of having a near-unanimous majority intimidate a sole individual into swallowing his or her true convictions and caving in to the majority.

On these grounds, the conformity research makes it clear that twelve-person juries are to be preferred to smaller ones. Because conformity pressures level off at four or five members, twelve-person juries may be no more "tyrannical" than, say, six-person juries. Note that on purely statistical grounds, however, someone who dissents from the majority is more likely to have an ally—a bracing partner in dissent—in a group of twelve than in a group of six. Thus, if a fair trial is to include the possibility of a minority viewpoint swaying all other jury members or, more likely, creating a "hung jury" (that is, one that cannot reach unanimity), then fairness is best achieved by a twelve-person jury than by a smaller one (Valenti & Downing, 1975).

*Expertise and Status*  Imagine that you were a participant in Asch's experiment and that the other participants who were inexplicably calling out what you thought was the wrong answer were all former Major League batting champions. On the assumption that one can't lead the league in hitting without exceptional eyesight, it is likely that you would grant the group considerable authority and go along with their opinion. Alternatively, if the rest of the group were all wearing Coke-bottle glasses, it's unlikely you would take their opinions seriously.

As this thought experiment illustrates, the expertise and status of the group powerfully influence the rate of conformity. Expertise and status are often correlated, of course, as those with special expertise are granted greater status, and those with high status are often assumed (not always correctly) to have considerable expertise. To the extent that they are separable, however, expertise primarily affects informational social influence. Experts are more likely to be right, and so their opinions are taken more seriously. Status, in contrast, mainly affects normative social influence. The disapproval of high-status individuals can hurt more than the disapproval of people one cares less about.

The effect of expertise and status has been demonstrated in numerous studies (Cialdini & Trost, 1998; Crano, 1970; Ettinger, Marino, Endler, Geller, & Natziuk, 1971). One of our favorites was one of the earliest, and used a paradigm that is quite different from Asch's. Torrance (1955) gave the members of Navy bombing crews— pilot, navigator, and gunner—a number of reasoning problems such

> "If there is any principle of the Constitution that more imperatively calls for attachment than any other it is the principle of free thought—not free thought for those who agree with us but freedom for the thought that we hate."
>
> —OLIVER WENDELL HOLMES

**Expertise, Status, and Social Influence**  When the United States was preparing to invade Iraq to unseat Saddam Hussein and secure his weapons of mass destruction in March 2003, the U.S. administration sent Secretary of State Colin Powell to speak to the delegates of the United Nations because he had great credibility. Powell presented what he believed were the facts about Iraq's weapons of mass destruction and hoped to convince the delegates of the need to invade Iraq.

as the "horse-trading" problem discussed in Chapter 2 (see page 72). He then asked the crews to report one answer for the whole group. Torrance monitored the group's deliberations and found that if the pilot originally came up with the correct solution, the group eventually reported it as their answer 91 percent of the time. If the navigator offered the correct answer, the group reported it 80 percent of the time. But if the lowly gunner offered the correct answer, the group offered it up only 63 percent of the time. The opinions of higher-status individuals often carry more weight with the group as a whole (Foushee, 1984).

*Culture*    We have emphasized throughout this book that people from interdependent cultures are much more concerned about their relations to others and about fitting into the broader social context than are people from independent cultures. With such a different orientation toward the collective versus the individual self, one might expect people from interdependent cultures to conform more than those from independent cultures. People reared in interdependent cultures are likely to be more susceptible to both informational social influence (the actions and opinions of others are likely to be considered more telling) and normative social influence (the high regard of others is likely to be considered more important).

Evidence supports this contention. In one early test of cross-cultural differences in conformity, Stanley Milgram (1961) conducted experiments using Asch's paradigm in Norway and France. Milgram maintained that Norwegians emphasize group cohesiveness more than the French and, just as he expected, he found that the Norwegian participants conformed more than the French participants.

But why study Norway and France (other than that both are delightful places to visit and conduct research)? As we have discussed independent versus interdependent cultures throughout this book, France and Norway have not loomed large in the discussion. What about the greater independent/interdependent divide that exists between a broader sample of the world's regions? A more systematic analysis of the results of the Asch procedure as used in 133 different studies in seventeen countries found that conformity does indeed tend to be greater in interdependent countries than in independent countries (Bond & Smith, 1996). The individualism that is highly valued in American and Western European societies has given individuals in those societies a greater willingness to stand apart from the majority. Note also that the willingness to resist the influence of the majority may be increasing. More recent conformity experiments in the United States and Great Britain using Asch's procedure have tended to find lower rates of conformity (Bond & Smith, 1996; Perrin & Spencer, 1981).

*Gender*    To grow up as a boy or girl in a given society is to grow up in a slightly different culture. Societies differ tremendously in how they socialize boys and girls, but all societies sex-type to some degree. Thus, if there are cultural differences in conformity, might we not expect gender differences as well? Perhaps. Women are raised to value interdependence and to nurture important social relationships more than men are, whereas men are raised to value and strive for autonomy and independence more than women are. One might therefore expect women to be more subject to social influence, and hence to conform more than men.

But as we shall soon see, people are more likely to conform when they are confused by the events unfolding around them. And if women are taught to attend to relationships, and hence are more likely to be the "experts" on human relationships, their greater sophistication about relationships may give them the confidence necessary to resist the influence of the majority.

**Gender and Conformity**    Girls are socialized to value social relationships and as such may be more likely than boys to form cliques and to conform. In the 2004 film *Mean Girls,* a clique of four popular girls exerted an influence on how the other girls in the school dressed and acted.

**internalization** Private acceptance of a proposition, orientation, or ideology.

**public compliance** Agreeing with someone or advancing a position in public but continuing to believe something else in private.

The research findings are what you might expect given these two opposing considerations. Overall reviews of the literature on gender differences in conformity have shown that women tend to conform a bit more than men—but only a bit (Eagly, 1987; Eagly & Carli, 1981). The difference tends to be biggest when the conformity situation is of the face-to-face type like that in Asch's original study. But the difference also seems to be very strongly influenced by the specific content of the issue at hand. To illustrate, would you be more likely to conform to other people when they assert that the atomic number of beryllium is 62, or when they assert that the most important ingredient in a good sandwich is horseradish? If you're like most people, you know more about sandwiches than about the periodic table, and so you would be more likely to stand your ground on matters related to lunchtime meals. Analyses of the specific contexts in which men and women differ in the tendency to conform reveal just this effect (Sistrunk & McDavid, 1971). Thus, women tend to conform more about "male" issues or in "male" domains (for example, about geography or the periodic table), whereas men tend to conform more about "female" issues or in "female" domains (for example, about how to make a good dessert or how to raise a child). It should therefore come as no surprise that, overall, there is a difference in conformity between men and women, but it is only a small one. Women are socialized to nurture relationships more than men are, and so they are more subject to social influence. But their greater comfort with relationships and knowledge about relationships may also give them a more solid foundation from which they can resist social influence attempts.

*Difficulty (or Ambiguity) of the Task*    Comparing the Asch and Sherif experiments points out the importance of how challenging the task is and hence how difficult it is to arrive at a confident answer oneself. When the judgment at hand is unambiguous and easy to make, informational social influence is virtually eliminated. Only normative social influence is at work, and resistance to the group is stronger (Allen, 1965; Baron, Vandello, & Brunsman, 1996). Imagine, for example, that you are visiting a foreign country and you are uncertain about what is called for in a given situation. Would you be decisive and assertive? Certainly not. When the "right" thing to do is unclear, we are particularly inclined to rely on others for guidance.

*Anonymity*    While an easy task eliminates informational social influence, the ability to respond anonymously eliminates normative social influence. When everyone else is unaware of one's judgment, there is no need to fear the group's disapproval. This highlights an important distinction between the impact of informational and normative social influence. Informational social influence, by influencing how we come to see the issues or stimuli before us, tends to influence our **internalization**, or private acceptance of the position advanced by the majority (Kelman, 1958). We don't just ape a particular response, we adopt the group's perspective. We see it their way or tend to assume they've got things right. Normative social influence, in contrast, often has a greater impact on **public compliance** than on private acceptance. To avoid disapproval, we sometimes do or say one thing but continue to believe another.

*The Interpretative Context of Disagreement*   One feature of Asch's experiment that makes his results particularly surprising to many people is that the participants conformed to the erroneous judgments of a group of strangers. Why would the participants care so much about what these other people think of them, people whom they have never seen before and likely will never see again? If people conform this much to the questionable judgment of strangers, surely they would conform even more to the judgments of those they know, care about, and must deal with in the future (Lott & Lott, 1961; Wolf, 1985).

How can we explain this curious feature of Asch's experiment? What is responsible for such high rates of conformity when the social pressures to conform might seem rather weak? The key to resolving this question is to note that participants in Asch's experiment face a double whammy. First, they must confront the fact that everyone else sees things differently than they do. Second, they have no basis for understanding *why* everyone else sees things differently. ("Could I be mistaken? No, it's plain as day. Could they be mistaken? I don't see how because they're not any farther away than I am and it's so clear. Are they any different than I am? No, they don't look different from anyone else.")

Knowing why our opinions are different ("They don't see the lines the way I do because they're wearing distorting glasses.") can embolden us to hold our ground because it can lessen both informational and normative social influence. Informational social influence is lessened because the explanation can diminish the group's impact as a source of information ("They're biased."). Normative social influence is lessened because we can assume that those in the majority are aware of why we differ from them. For instance, if we have different views on affirmative action because we are members of different ethnic groups, those in the majority might think we're biased, afraid, or have different values, but at least they won't think we're crazy. In Asch's situation, in contrast, the participants faced the reasonable fear that if they departed from everyone else's judgment, their behavior would look truly bizarre and everyone would think they were nuts.

Lee Ross and his colleagues sought to examine this interpretation of Asch's experiment by replicating his results in one condition and adding another condition in which participants *could* explain to themselves why their own judgments differed from those of the majority (Ross, Bierbrauer, & Hoffman, 1976). The participants in this study were asked to judge not the length of lines but the duration of tones. First one tone was played and then another, and the participant's task was to state which was longer in duration. Participants earned points for each correct response, according to the payoff matrix depicted in the left-hand portion of Table 6.1. The matrix shows that participants were to receive 10 points for each correct response (saying "1" when it really was 1, and saying "2" when it really was 2) and nothing for an incorrect response.

But in the novel, "different payoffs" condition of the experiment, participants learned that the other three participants (who in reality were confederates of the experimenters) would be operating under a different payoff scheme, depicted in the right-hand portion of Table 6.1. The experiment unfolded just like Asch's: most trials were uneventful, with the confederates calling out what the true participant knew to be the correct answer. No problem. But on a select number of trials, the confederates all called out "2" when the true participant knew it was 1. How to respond?

Note that in the condition that replicates Asch's experiment, or the one in which the basic payoff matrix (shown on the left of Table 6.1) is in effect for everyone, the participant has no explanation for why everyone else is responding

## Table 6.1  Explanations Affect Conformity

Payoff matrices in a conformity experiment in which participants either have no explanation for why opinions differ (basic matrix), or they have an explanation (alternative matrix). Values indicate the number of points to be awarded participants for every combination of (a) the participant's response, and (b) the correct answer.

| | | BASIC MATRIX | | | ALTERNATIVE MATRIX | |
|---|---|---|---|---|---|---|
| | | P's response | | | P's response | |
| | | 1 | 2 | | 1 | 2 |
| True Answer | 1 | 10 | 0 | 1 | 10 | 0 |
| | 2 | 0 | 10 | 2 | 0 | 100 |

Source: Ross, Bierbrauer, & Hoffman (1976).

incorrectly. Baffled, these participants ought to conform at roughly the same level as that observed in Asch's study. But those in the "different payoffs" condition do have an explanation: everyone else is being seduced by the posssibility of a big 100-point payoff and calling out "2" as something of a long shot. This understanding ought to embolden participants and reduce how much they conformed.

As Figure 6.6 illustrates, that is exactly what happened. Participants in the Asch-like condition called out the incorrect response (that is, they conformed) much more often than did those in the different-payoffs condition—and much more often than those in a control condition who called out their responses when they were alone (a condition included to verify that the correct response really was easy for participants to discern).

The lesson here is that it is difficult to act independently when one doesn't know what to make of things. It is hard to be assertive when one is puzzled by everything going on. It is easier to stand one's ground, in other words, when one

**Figure 6.6  Interpretive Context and Conformity**   Rates of conformity when the majority's response "makes sense" or not. (Source: Ross, Bierbrauer, & Hoffman, 1976)

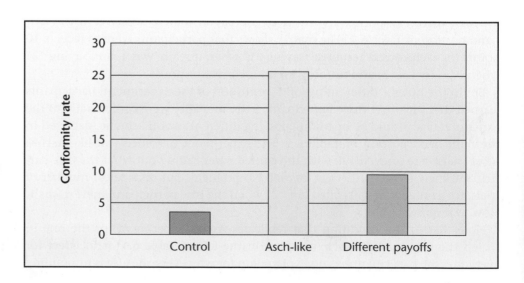

has a clear understanding of what might cause others to make erroneous judgments. This lesson will also prove crucial to an adequate understanding of our next topic, obedience. Before we get to that, however, we must take note of the fact that small minorities sometimes sway the opinion of entire societies, and examine when and how minority viewpoints have their greatest impact.

## THE INFLUENCE OF MINORITY OPINION ON THE MAJORITY

There was a time in the United States when people owned slaves, when women were not allowed to vote, and when children worked long hours for scandalously low pay in unhealthy conditions. Small groups of abolitionists, suffragettes, and child welfare advocates, we now recognize, saw things more clearly than their peers and worked tirelessly to change public opinion about each of these issues. And they succeeded. The views of the broader public were changed in each case, and important rectifying legislation was passed. Minority opinion became the opinion of the majority.

Examples such as these remind us that, as powerful as conformity pressures can be, majority opinion does not always prevail. Not only can conformity pressure be resisted, but minority voices can be heard sufficiently clearly that the prevailing majority opinion can be changed. How do minority opinions come to influence the majority? Are the sources of influence the same as those that majorities bring to bear on minorities?

In the first experimental examination of these questions, Serge Moscovici and his colleagues had participants call out in a group setting whether a color was green or blue (Moscovici, Lage, & Naffrechoux, 1969). The border between blue and green, of course, is not always clear, but the critical stimuli they showed their participants were ones that the participants, when tested alone, nearly always thought were blue. They showed their participants these stimuli in the presence of a minority of respondents (confederates of the experimenters) who responded "green" and recorded how the participants responded.

When the minority responded with "green" consistently, the true participants responded likewise 8 percent of the time. When the minority varied their responses randomly between "green" and "blue," the participants did so only

> "Give me a firm place to stand and I will move the world."
> —ARCHIMEDES OF SYRACUSE

**Minority Influence on the Majority**
Minority opinions can exert social influence on the prevailing majority opinion through consistent and clear messages that persuade the majority to systematically examine and reevaluate its opinions. (A) British suffragette Emmaline Pankhurst presented her views in favor of women's right to vote to an American crowd in 1918. (B) Rosa Parks refused to give up her seat at the front of a bus in Montgomery, Alabama, in December 1955. Her actions resulted in a city-wide bus boycott that eventually led the U.S. Supreme Court to declare that segregation was illegal on the city bus system.

1 percent of the time, about the same as when they responded alone. But that was not the only effect the minority had. At this point, when the participants thought the experiment was over, the experimenter introduced them to a second experimenter who, they were told, was also interested in color vision. This second experimenter showed participants a series of blue-green colors and noted where each of them, individually, thought "blue" left off and "green" began. What Moscovici and his colleagues found was that participants who had earlier been exposed to a consistent minority identified more of these stimuli as green—their sense of the border between blue and green had shifted. Thus, the consistent minority opinion had both a direct effect on participants' responses in the public setting, and a "latent" effect on their subsequent, private judgments.

Further investigation of minority influence in paradigms like Moscovici's has shown that minorities have their effect primarily through informational social influence (Moscovici, 1985; Nemeth, 1986, Wood, Lundgren, Ouellette, Busceme, & Blackstone, 1994). People in the majority are typically not terribly concerned about the social costs of stating their opinion out loud—they have the majority on their side, and normative social influence is minimized. Their thoughts on the matter are often of the automatic sort. But they might wonder why the minority keeps stating its divergent opinion. This can lead them to consider the stimulus more carefully, leading to a level of scrutiny and more systematic thought that can lead to a genuine change in attitude or belief. Thus, majorities typically elicit more conformity, but it is often of the public compliance sort. In contrast, minorities typically influence fewer people, but the nature of the influence is often deeper, resulting in true private acceptance (Maass & Clark, 1983).

**LOOKING BACK,** we have seen that conformity can occur in response to implicit or explicit social pressures and can be the result of either informational social influence or normative social influence. We have seen that group size is important for normative influence, but that it appears to reach maximum effect at around four people. Unanimity also is crucial in conformity: a single ally can help an individual hold out against the group. We have seen that people from more interdependent cultures conform more than do people from more independent cultures, and that women conform slightly more than men. More difficult tasks create more conformity, and plausible explanations for why others might hold views different from our own tend to reduce conformity. Conformity pressures notwithstanding, minorities often do have an influence, primarily through informational social influence. We next consider the pernicious consequences of a particular type of conformity—obedience to the orders of a person in authority.

## OBEDIENCE TO AUTHORITY

The study of when and why people obey the commands of someone in authority has been dominated by the one set of social psychological experiments more famous than Asch's—those of Stanley Milgram. Milgram's experiments constitute what is arguably the most widely known research program in all of psychology. Milgram's experiments are sufficiently well known, in fact, that ". . . they have become part of our society's shared intellectual legacy—that small body of historical incidents, biblical parables, and classic literature that serious thinkers feel free to draw on when they debate about human nature or contemplate human history" (Ross, 1988).

## THE SETUP OF THE MILGRAM EXPERIMENTS

Milgram's research on obedience began as an investigation of conformity. He was intrigued by Asch's findings but wondered about their limitations in much the same way that Asch had wondered about the limitations of Sherif's findings. Recall that Asch thought it only natural that people would readily conform to others' responses when they didn't have a firm opinion themselves. But what would happen, he wondered, if there was a clear conflict between the individual's personal convictions and the responses of the group? Asch found considerable conformity even then, which surprised him. Milgram's findings surprised Milgram even more.

Milgram was interested in whether the kind of conformity pressures observed in Asch's paradigm were sufficiently powerful to lead people to do something far more significant than report an incorrect line length. He wondered what would happen if he had a confederate perform a line-judging task like Asch's, or some other task, and asked participants to deliver electric shock whenever the confederate responded incorrectly. Would participants conform here, when doing so involved hurting another human being?

**Stanley Milgram**    Using a "shock generator" that looked real but was actually just a prop, Milgram studied whether participants would continue to obey instructions and shock a learner even after believing that the learner was in grave distress as a result of the shocks.

This is an interesting question, but Milgram never pursued it. The reason is that he realized that he first needed to obtain data from a control group to see how willing participants would be to deliver electric shock in the absence of any conformity pressure (Evans, 1980). And that is where he received his experimental surprise, one that changed his research program entirely.

We described the details of Milgram's basic procedure (his intended "control group") on pp. 10–11 in Chapter 1, so we will describe them only briefly here before turning our attention to a number of important variations. Responding to an ad in a New Haven newspaper, participants in Milgram's study reported for an experiment on learning. A "random" draw was rigged so that the participants always became the "teacher" and the confederate always became the "learner." The teacher's job was to administer electric shock every time the learner—a genial, middle-aged man who was strapped into a chair with his arm on a shock-delivery apparatus—made a mistake and reported the wrong word from a list of word pairs presented at the beginning of the study (for example, glove-book, grill-detergent, anvil-pope). Teachers were briefly strapped to the chair and given a 45-volt shock so that they would know that the shocks were painful. The teachers then started off delivering 15 volts after the learner's first mistake and increased the shock in 15-volt increments after each subsequent mistake. As the mistakes accumulated, participants found themselves required to deliver 255, 300, 330—all the way up to 450—volts of electricity. (In reality, no electric shock was actually delivered.) If the participant expressed reservations or tried to terminate the experiment, the experimenter would respond with a carefully scripted set of responses—"please continue," "the experiment requires that you con-

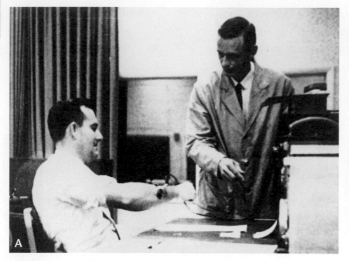
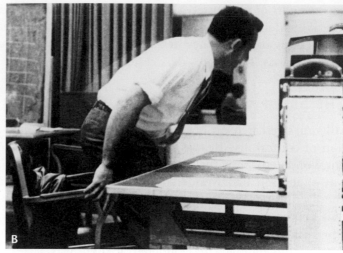

**The Milgram Experiment** Participants were led to believe that the shock generator had thirty levels of shock, ranging from "slight shock" to "danger: severe shock" to "XXX." (A) The participant was given a sample shock of 45 volts (this was the only real shock in the experiment), and (B) the participant stood up to ask the experimenter if he could stop the experiment when he thought that the learner had passed out from the shocks.

tinue," "it is absolutely essential that you continue," "you have no other choice, you must go on."

The great surprise in these studies was that people continued to obey the experimenter's orders and to shock the confederate. In the "remote feedback" condition in which the learner was in an adjoining room and could not be heard except when he vigorously pounded on the wall after a shock of 300 volts, 66 percent of the participants continued the learning experiment and delivered the maximum shock of 450 volts. In the "voice feedback" condition, the participants could hear a series of increasingly desperate pleas by the learner—including screaming that he had a heart condition—until finally, and ominously, he became silent. Despite these cues indicating that the learner was suffering, 62.5 percent of the participants delivered the maximum shock (Milgram, 1965, 1974).

## OPPOSING FORCES

Milgram's participants found themselves in an agonizing conflict, caught between two opposing sets of forces. On one hand were the forces compelling them to complete the experiment and to continue delivering shock. Among these was a sense of "fair play"—they had agreed to serve as participants, they had already received payment for having done so, and they felt that they now had to fulfill their part of the bargain. Some participants were also likely motivated by the reason they had agreed to be participants in the first place—to advance science and the understanding of human behavior. Another important motivating factor was normative social influence—in this case, the desire to avoid the disapproval of the experimenter or of anyone else associated with the experiment whom they imagined they might encounter on their way out. Closely related to this concern was the very human desire to avoid "making a scene" and not upsetting others (Goffman, 1966; R. Miller, 1996).

On the other hand, there were several powerful forces compelling the participants to want to terminate the experiment. Foremost among these was the moral imperative to stop the suffering of the learner. This could have been both a concrete desire not to see this particular individual hurt, as well as a more abstract injunction against hurting others (and the implication of what the abandonment of this abstract principle would say about the kind of people they were). Some participants were also likely to be concerned about what would happen if something went wrong. "What if he dies or is permanently injured?" "Will there be a lawsuit?" Still others may have wondered about the prospect of having to walk out with the learner after everything was over and the embarrassment (even retaliation) it might bring. And how could the participants be sure that the roles wouldn't be reversed? At the moment, they occupied the teacher role, but could they be certain that there wouldn't be a new round in which *they* were strapped into the shock machine?

*"Tuning in" the Learner*   By specifying the opposing forces acting on participants, we can gain an understanding of why they responded the way they did and why the whole experience was so stressful. We can also gain some insight into how the rate of obedience might be altered by modifying the strength of these opposing forces (Blass, 2000, 2004; A. Miller, 1986). This is exactly what Milgram did in a comprehensive series of studies. First, he tried to increase the forces that compel people to terminate the experiment. These were all triggered by an awareness of the learner's suffering, and so Milgram attempted to increase these forces by increasing the prominence of the learner. He called this "tuning in the learner" (and noted that participants spontaneously tried to do the opposite: to deal with their own discomfort by tuning

out the learner—by, say, literally turning away from him in their chairs). In the "remote feedback" condition, the learner could neither be seen nor heard (except for one episode of vigorous pounding). In the "voice feedback" condition, the learner still could not be seen, but he and his vigorous protests could be heard very clearly, which made the teacher constantly aware of him. In a "proximity" condition, the learner received his shock in the same room in which the participant delivered it, from only 1.5 feet away. Finally, in the "touch proximity" condition, the participant was required to force the learner's hand onto the shock plate (using a sheet of insulation so that the participant would not also be shocked). Figure 6.7 shows the effect of these manipulations. As the learner became more and more present and "real," it became more difficult for the teachers to deliver the shocks, and obedience rates diminished.

**Tuning in the Learner**   In a "touch proximity" condition, participants were required to force the learner's hand onto the shock plate, which dramatically reduced the participants' obedience rates.

**Figure 6.7 Tuning in the Learner**
The effect of experimental manipulations that make the learner more and more salient on (A) mean level of shock participants delivered, and (B) the percentage of participants who delivered the maximum amount of shock. (Source: Milgram, 1965)

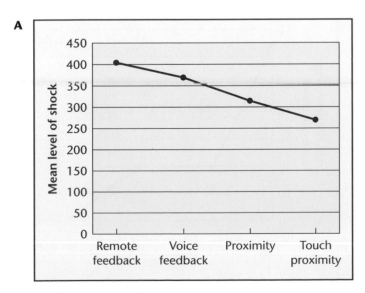

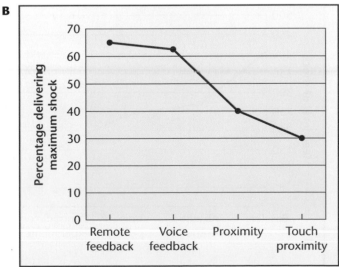

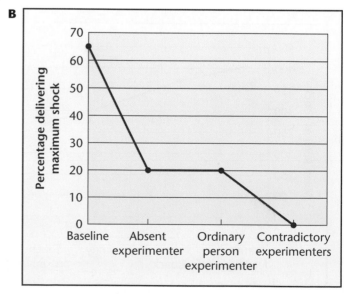

One lesson to be drawn from this is chilling. The more removed we are from others, the easier it is to hurt them. And the technology that societies have developed to inflict harm allows perpetrators to inflict it from a great distance. Combat is often no longer hand-to-hand. Rather, lethal weapon systems can be activated by a mere push of a button, guiding a predator drone to a target or firing a missile from an underground silo a continent away. The remoteness of the victims in such cases makes the harm done to them abstract, so that it has less of an effect on the perpetrators.

**Tuning out the Victim** When missiles are fired from a ship at sea, the victims of the target cannot be seen, which makes the harm more abstract. Orders to fire such weapons are not likely to be questioned.

*"Tuning out" the Experimenter* Another way to influence obedience in Milgram's paradigm is to strengthen or weaken the "signal" coming from the experimenter, and thus strengthen or weaken the forces acting on participants to complete the experiment. Milgram conducted a number of variations on this theme as well. In the standard version of the study, the experimenter was present in the same room, right next to the participant. In an "experimenter absent" condition, the experimenter gave the initial instructions alongside the participant but then left the room and issued his orders over the telephone. In so doing, the power of the experimenter was diminished by removing him physically from the scene.

Another way to alter the experimenter's power is to alter his authority. In one version, for example, an "ordinary person" (ostensibly another participant, but in reality a confederate) was the one who delivered the orders to increase the shock level each time the learner made a mistake. In still another version, there were two experimenters who initially instructed the participant to shock the victim. At one point, however, one of the two experimenters announced that he found the proceedings objectionable and argued with the other experimenter, who continued to urge the participant to complete the experiment.

Figure 6.8 shows the results of these manipulations. As the experimenter became less of a force of authority in the participant's mind, it became easier for the participant to defy the experimenter, and so the rate of obedience declined.

**Figure 6.8 Tuning out the Experimenter** The effect of experimental manipulations that make the experimenter less and less salient on (A) mean level of shock participants delivered, and (B) the percentage of participants who delivered the maximum amount of shock. (Source: Milgram, 1965)

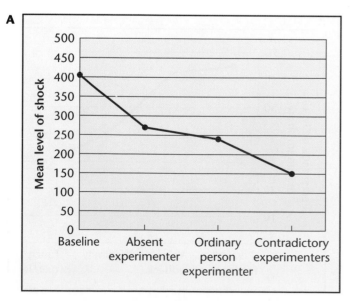

Note that this series of experimental variations had a more pronounced effect than the earlier series (that is, compare Figures 6.7 and 6.8). This tells us that making it *easier* for participants to disobey can be more effective than increasing their *desire* to disobey. As we shall see, this provides an important clue to a true understanding of the surprising levels of obedience observed in Milgram's experiments.

## WOULD YOU HAVE OBEYED?

As we mentioned in Chapter 1, no one anticipated such widespread obedience. A group of psychiatrists predicted that fewer than 1 percent of all participants—a pathological fringe—would continue until they delivered the maximum amount of shock. This failure of prediction is matched by an equally noteworthy failure of after-the-fact insight—almost no one believes, even after hearing the basic results and all the experimental variations, that he or she would deliver very high levels of shock. Thus, although the variations give us some understanding of when and why people engage in such surprising behavior, they do not give us a fully satisfying explanation of this phenomenon. As one social psychologist put it, they do not pass a critical "empathy test" (Ross, 1988). They do not lead us to empathize fully with the obedient participants and take seriously the possibility that *we* would also obey to the end—as most participants did. A truly satisfying explanation might not convince us that we would *surely* do so, but it should at least convince us that we *might* act that way.

Are there elements of Milgram's studies, and any explanations based on them, that *do* satisfy the empathy test? There are, and we present them below. And when appropriate, we present them alongside a discussion of the real-world relevance of Milgram's research. Milgram's work is often taken to speak to the question of how large segments of a population can obey the directives of a malevolent government and commit hideous crimes against humanity such as those witnessed during the Holocaust in Nazi Germany, in the "ethnic cleansing" in Bosnia, or in the tribal massacres in Rwanda. Explanations of such incomprehensible cruelties vary along an "exceptionalist"/"normalist" continuum. The exceptionalist thesis is that such crimes are perpetrated only by "exceptional" people—that is, exceptionally sadistic, desperate, or ethnocentric people. Many Germans were virulent anti-Semites. The Serbs had long-standing hatreds and resentments against the Bosnians. The Rwandan Hutus had scores to settle with the Tutsi. The normalist thesis, in contrast, is that the capacity for such destructive obedience lies in all of us and thus, given the right circumstances, can be perpetrated by almost anyone. Milgram's research, of course, is typically taken to support the normalist position. Milgram himself certainly took this position. When asked by Morley Safer on the CBS show *Sixty Minutes* whether he thought something like the Holocaust could happen in the United States, Milgram offered this opinion:

> I would say, on the basis of having observed a thousand people in the experiment and having my own intuition shaped and informed by these experiments, that if a system of death camps were set up in the United States of the sort we had seen in Nazi Germany, one would be able to find sufficient personnel for those camps in any medium-sized American town. (Quoted in Blass, 1999, p. 955)

Let's take a closer look.

*They Tried but Failed*    One of the reasons people think they would never behave the way the average participant in Milgram's experiments behaved is that they misunderstand exactly how the average participant acted (Ross, 1988). People conjure up images of participants blithely going along with the experimenter's commands, increasing the shock level from trial to trial, being relatively inattentive to the learner's situation. Indeed, Milgram's experiments have often been described as a demonstration of "blind" obedience.

But that's not what happened. Participants did not mindlessly obey. Nearly all tried to disobey in one form or another. Nearly everyone called the experimenter's attention to the learner's suffering in an implicit plea to stop the proceedings. Many stated explicitly that they refused to continue (but nonetheless went on with the experiment). Some got out of their chairs in defiance, only to sit back down moments later. The participants tried to disobey, but they just weren't particularly good at it. As Lee Ross (1988) put it, "the Milgram experiments have less to say about 'destructive obedience' than about ineffective and indecisive *dis*obedience."

This distinction is critical in giving all of us the sense, however reluctant, that, yes, perhaps we would have delivered about as much shock as the average participant. We know that we wouldn't *intend* to be obedient, and we wouldn't ignore the learner's suffering. But most of us have had the experience of having good intentions but being unable to translate those intentions into effective action. We've *wanted* to speak up more forcefully and effectively against racist or sexist remarks, but we were too slow to respond or the words didn't come out right. Or we've *wanted* to reach out to those who are ignored at social gatherings, but we got distracted by all that was going on and our own social needs. Most of us can relate to being good-hearted but ineffective, but not to being uncaring.

A chilling parallel to the behavior of Milgram's participants can be found in the behavior of some (we emphasize the *some*) of the German soldiers called upon to execute Polish Jews during World War II (Browning, 1992). Members of German Reserve Police Battalion 101, for example, were mostly individuals who hoped to avoid the inevitable violence of the war by volunteering for police duty in the German city of Hamburg. After the invasion of Poland, however, they were removed from Hamburg and made to serve as military police in occupied Poland. Most of what they were called upon to do was innocuous, routine police work. But on July 13, 1942, they were roused from their barracks before dawn and taken to the outskirts of the village of Jozefow, where they were given their gruesome orders—to round up all the Jewish men, women, and children from the village, send all able-bodied young men to a work camp, and shoot the rest.

Most were shocked by their orders and found them abhorrent. Many resisted. But their resistance, like that of Milgram's participants, was feeble. Some occupied themselves with petty errands or moved to the back of the battalion, hoping they wouldn't be called upon to take part. Others took part in the roundup, but then refrained from shooting if no one was watching. Still others fired but missed intentionally. What they *didn't* do was assertively state that they wouldn't participate, that what they were being asked to do was wrong. They tried to find an easy way to disobey, but there was no easy way.

In the case of Milgram's experiments, the difficulty participants experienced in trying to halt the proceedings was partly due to the fact that the experimenter was not playing by the normal rules of social life. The participants offered *reasons* why the experiments should be stopped, but the experimenter largely ignored those reasons, coming back with minimally responsive statements such as "the experiment requires that you continue." Participants could be forgiven for being a bit confused and uncertain about how to act. And, as we saw in the discussion of conformity, people are unlikely to act decisively when they do not have a solid grasp of the events transpiring around them. What is one to do when charged with administering electric shock in order to "teach" someone who is no longer trying to learn anything, at the insistence of an authority figure who seems unconcerned about the learner's predicament? How does one respond when events have stopped making sense?

This has important implications for the ways in which Milgram's experiments generalize to those real-world instances of destructive obedience with which one should be most concerned. Many of the most hideous episodes of genocide in human history have occurred right after large-scale social upheavals. With the social order so drastically altered, the confidence required for decisive action to stop such atrocities is hard to come by. Those who would want to stop such actions—and would rein them in under normal circumstances—may be unusually uncertain and indecisive about how to do so.

*Release from Responsibility*    Participants' ineffectiveness in stopping the experiment meant that they were trapped in a situation of terrible conflict and stress. They knew that what was happening shouldn't continue, and yet they were unable to bring it to an end. They were, therefore, desperate for anything that would reduce their stress. Fortunately for the participants (but unfortunately for the learner had he really been receiving electric shock), the experimenter provided something to reduce their stress in the form of "cover" or justification for their actions. The experimenter took responsibility for what was happening. When participants asked, as many did, "Who is responsible for what happens here?," the experimenter responded, "I am responsible." Participants seized upon this as a justification for their actions, and the stress they were experiencing was, to a significant degree, reduced.

This, too, should make us consider the possibility that we might, after all, have delivered quite a bit of electric shock ourselves. We have all been in stressful situations that have been confusing and in which we've wanted the stress and confusion to end. "All of my friends are making me uncomfortable by savagely teasing that guy in our English class, and they'll disapprove if I speak out." "Everyone's popping those pills as if they weren't harmful, and they'll think I'm a wimp if I don't too." It is always tempting in such situations to grab at anything that would make the dilemma "go away." "Maybe the guy in our class really does deserve it, and I'm being too sensitive." "Maybe the pills really are harmless, and I'm blowing things out of proportion."

Of course, the cover the experimenter provided in Milgram's experiments only worked because the person taking responsibility was perceived to be a legitimate authority. People wouldn't allow just anyone to take responsibility and then assume that everything was okay. If you were approached by a strange character on campus who said, "Quick, help me set fire to the Psychology Building. I'll take full responsibility," you would surely reject the idea that the responsibility could legitimately be transferred to this individual, and you would, we trust, refrain from pitching in. In Milgram's experiments, participants believed that they could legitimately transfer responsibility to the experimenter. He was a representative of science, a respected enterprise, and, in nearly all variations of Milgram's paradigm, he was affiliated with Yale University, a respected institution (although obedience was still high in a condition in which the experimenter operated out of a storefront in downtown Bridgeport). These facts made it easier for partici-

**Legitimacy of Experiment** To see how participants would react if the experiment were not conducted at Yale and the authority seemed less legitimate, Milgram had the participants report to "Research Associates of Bridgeport," above a storefront in downtown Bridgeport (A), and inside a seedy office (B). Obedience rates declined somewhat but remained high even under such conditions.

pants to reduce their own stress over what was happening by assuming the experimenter knew better and was ultimately responsible for what happened.

The cover provided by authorities perceived to be legitimate likewise has implications for acts of destructive obedience that are part of civilization's historical record. In Nazi Germany, in the Balkans, in Rwanda, and in all historical instances of genocide, the call to arms has been issued by authority figures who either explicitly assumed responsibility or whose position supported an assumption of responsibility. And the claim of responsibility has nearly always been legitimized by some overarching ideology. Whether it be nationalism, religious ideology, or ethnic identity, all appeals to genocide are draped in a legitimizing ideology that seeks to transform otherwise hideous actions into what is seen as morally appropriate behavior (Staub, 1989; Zajonc, 2002).

**A Step to Genocide** Anti-Jewish laws included the 1941 decree that all Jews had to display the Star of David badge in public to identify themselves as Jews.

***Step-by-Step Involvement*** Another way to make it seem more plausible that we ourselves might have acted like the average participant is to recognize that participants did not deliver 450 volts of electricity out of the blue. We hear the level of the terminal shock and think to ourselves, "No way would I do that." And we wouldn't—not right off the bat. But that is not what Milgram's participants were asked to do.

Recall that each participant first had to administer only 15 volts to the learner. Who wouldn't do that? That's feedback, not punishment. Then 30 volts. No problem there either. Then 45, 60, 75—each step is a small one. Once one has started down this path (and who wouldn't start?), it's hard to get off; one slides down a slippery slope that leads to more shock. Indeed, the increments are so small that if a certain level of shock seems "too much," why wouldn't the previous level have been too much as well (Gilbert, 1981)?

Recognizing the importance of the step-by-step nature of participants' obedience also helps us pass the "empathy test." Most of us have had the experience of gradually getting in over our heads in this fashion. We may tell a very innocuous "white" lie—one that sets in motion a cascade of events that requires more and more deception. Or we may "dig in our heels" over a small matter in a dispute—which leads to more recalcitrance and the inability to ever make an appropriate concession. Our behavior often creates its own momentum, and it is hard to know in advance where it will lead. Milgram's participants can certainly be forgiven for not foreseeing how everything would unfold. Would we have seen it any more clearly?

The parallels between this element of Milgram's procedure and what happened in Nazi Germany are striking. German citizens were not asked, out of the blue, to

Box 6.2   FOCUS ON HISTORY

# Step-by-Step to Genocide

Anti-Jewish laws and policies of the German government before and during World War II. Note the gradual nature of anti-Jewish statutes and policies.

**1. April 1, 1933**
Boycott of Jewish businesses is declared.

**2. April 7, 1933**
Law for the Restoration of the Professional Civil Service authorizes the dismissal of non-Aryan (especially those with Jewish parents or grandparents) civil servants (except for those who had held that status since 8/1/14, who had fought at the front for Germany in World War I, or whose father or son had been killed in action in World War I).

**3. September 22, 1933**
Reestablishment of Reich Chamber of Culture leads to the removal of non-Aryans from organizations and enterprises related to literature, the press, broadcasting, music, and art.

**4. September 15, 1935**
Reich Citizenship Law defines citizens of the Reich as only those who are of German or kindred blood.

**5. September 16, 1935**
Law for the Protection of German Blood and German Honor forbids marriage between Jews and nationals of German or kindred blood and declares marriages conducted in defiance of this law void, forbids relations outside of marriage between Jews and nationals of German or kindred blood, forbids Jews from employing in their household female nationals of German or kindred blood who are under age forty-five.

**6. November 16, 1936**
Jews are prohibited from obtaining passports or traveling abroad, except in special cases.

**7. April 1938**
Jews are forced to register with the government all property valued at 5,000 marks or more.

**8. July 25, 1938**
Fourth Decree of the Reich Citizenship Law terminates the licenses of Jewish physicians as of September 30, 1938.

**9. September 27, 1938**
Fifth Decree of the Reich Citizenship Law allows Jewish legal advisers to attend professionally only to the legal affairs of Jews.

**10. October 5, 1938**
Jewish passports and ration cards are marked with a J.

**11. January 1, 1939**
All Jews are required to carry a special ID card.

**12. July 1940**
Purchases by Jews are restricted to certain hours and stores; telephones are taken away from Jews.

**13. September 19, 1941**
Jews are forced to display the Jewish badge prominently on their clothing and with few exceptions are not allowed to use public transportation.

**14. October 14, 1941**
Massive deportation of German Jews to concentration camps begins.

**15. October 23, 1941**
Jewish emigration is prohibited.

**16. January 20, 1942 (The Wansee Conference)**
Nazi leaders decide that 11 million Jews (every Jew in Europe) are to be killed.

---

assist with or condone the deportation of Jews, Gypsies, homosexuals, and communists to the death camps. Instead, the rights of these groups were gradually stripped away. First, certain business practices were restricted, then travel constraints were imposed, then citizenship was narrowed, and only after some time were people loaded into boxcars and sent to the death camps (see Box 6.2). The Nazis would doubtless have had a much harder time had they started with the

> "It is easier to resist at the beginning than at the end."
> —LEONARDO DA VINCI

last step. Their own citizens would likely have been less cooperative; their various victims would likely have resisted more actively. It is telling in this regard that the most vigorous defiance of the Nazis' genocide plans tended to take place not in Germany, but in the countries Germany overran. There are many reasons for this, of course, but one of them may well be that the pace of Germany's implementation of the "final solution" was much more rapid in the conquered countries than in Germany itself.

**LOOKING BACK,** we have tried to shed some light on the mystery of people's willingness to obey leaders who demand immoral behavior. We focused on several elements of the situation that make obedience easier to understand, including the fact that a person's attempts to disobey are often blocked, responsibility for what happens is frequently taken by the person in authority, and once the obedience begins there is typically no obvious point at which to stop. But when the circumstances lead the individual to be "tuned in" to the victim, obedience is substantially reduced. When the circumstances lead the individual to "tune out" the person in authority, obedience is also greatly reduced. In Milgram's experiments, the person making the demands was always an authority. What happens when we are asked to do something by someone who is not in a position of authority? To answer this question, we turn to our next topic, compliance.

## COMPLIANCE

Milgram's research teaches us how common it is for people to obey the insistent commands of someone who occupies a position of authority—and about why they so commonly do so. But attempts to influence behavior often come from people without any special authority or status. Charities urge us to give money. Con men try to induce us to go along with their schemes. Salespeople want us to buy their products. And friends ask us for favors. If you want to get someone to do something, and you have no power over the person or no special status to trumpet and only your wits to help you, what approach should you take? Conversely, if you're worried about being taken advantage of by those who have their own (and not your) best interests at heart, what techniques should you watch out for? Social psychologists have studied different strategies for eliciting compliance, and their research gives us some clues about how (and how effectively) these strategies work.

Compliance attempts come in (roughly) two types: those directed at the mind and those directed at the heart. People can be led to do things because they come to see that there are good reasons for doing so, or because their feelings guide them to do so. Of course, the heart and mind are not so neatly separable, and thus many compliance attempts represent a blend of the two approaches. If we want to do something, for example, we work hard to find sufficient reason for doing it (Chapter 8). Similarly, if our head tells us about the wisdom of a particular course of action, our heart often follows. Still, it is useful for understanding the techniques of compliance to recognize that some are primarily reason based and others primarily feeling based (see Box 6.3).

Box 6.3  FOCUS ON DAILY LIFE

# Mindless Compliance

As we saw earlier in the discussion of the "chameleon effect," a fair amount of social behavior is rather mindless—for example, we often copy the mannerisms and speech patterns of others without being aware that we are doing so. Spend an afternoon around someone who says "like" three times per sentence and soon you too will be saying, "I was, like, trying to, like, go to class when, like, this huge. . . ." The extent to which we operate on automatic pilot is further illustrated by the occasions in which we run into someone we know who says, "How's it goin?," and, instead of answering, we respond, "How ya doin?" The remarkable aspect of such exchanges is that both parties are satisfied. Neither question has been answered, but no one cares. The proper *form* of the interaction has been met: Person A says something, and B responds.

This rather pervasive mindlessness suggests that even reason-based compliance attempts can be rather mindless and still effective. The reasons we consent to comply, in other words, may not hold up to inspection—but we don't always inspect, and if the form of the request is right, we may comply anyway. The mindlessness of some everyday compliant actions was illustrated in an experiment in which Ellen Langer, Arthur Blank, and Benzion Chanowitz (1978) approached individuals who were about to use the library copy machine and asked if they could "cut in" and use it

first. Some participants were asked this question point blank, with no explanation given. Others were given a reason—"Excuse me . . . May I use the Xerox machine, because I'm in a rush?" Finally, a third group was offered a nonsensical reason that could only be effective if the participants processed the request mindlessly—"Excuse me . . . May I use the Xerox machine, because I have to make copies?"

Langer and her colleagues reasoned that if the request was a large one—the experimenter was cutting in to make a lot of copies—the participants would pay attention and comply with the request only if a real reason was given, not a nonsensical reason. But if the request was small—only a few copies were to be made—the request would be processed mindlessly, and even a nonsensical reason would do. So, for each of the three requests (no reason, real reason, nonsense reason), half the participants were asked if the experimenter could cut in to make twenty copies, and half were asked if the experimenter could cut in to make five copies. As you can see from the data below, participants tended to respond as predicted. The nonsensical request was typically turned down if the request was large, but it was honored if the request was small. Sometimes our seemingly thoughtful actions are not thoughtful at all. The reasons behind reason-based compliance attempts can sometimes be quite weak.

| REQUEST | NO REASON | NONSENSE REASON | REAL REASON |
|---------|-----------|-----------------|-------------|
| 5 copies | 60% | 93% | 94% |
| 20 copies | 24% | 24% | 42% |

## REASON-BASED APPROACHES

We often feel most compelled to comply with a request from someone when that person has previously done something for us. All societies that have ever been studied possess a powerful **norm of reciprocity**, according to which people should benefit those who benefit them (Gouldner, 1960). The norm also exists in many bird and mammal species. For example, when one monkey removes para-

**norm of reciprocity**  A norm dictating that people should provide benefits to those who benefit them.

sites from another's back, the latter typically returns the favor, which helps to cement the social bond between the two.

When someone does us a favor, it creates an obligation to agree to any reasonable request he or she might make in turn. To fail to respond is to violate a powerful social norm and to run the risk of social sanction (Cotterell, Eisenberger, & Speicher, 1992). Indeed, the English vocabulary is rich in derogatory terms for those who do not uphold their end of the norm of reciprocity: *sponge, moocher, deadbeat, ingrate, parasite, bloodsucker, leech.* If you do a favor for someone, that person is likely to look favorably on a reasonable request you subsequently make because of the fear of being seen as a sponge, moocher, and so on. Perhaps that is why restaurant customers often leave larger tips when they are given a piece of candy by the wait staff (Strohmetz, Rind, Fisher, & Lynn, 2002).

The influence of the norm of reciprocity in eliciting compliance was demonstrated with great clarity in a simple experiment in which two individuals were asked to rate a number of paintings, ostensibly as part of an experiment on "aesthetics" (D. Regan, 1971; see also Whatley, Webster, Smith, & Rhodes, 1999). One of the individuals was a real participant; the other was a confederate of the experimenter. In one condition, the confederate returned from a break in the procedure with two sodas and proceeded to offer one to the real participant. "I asked (the experimenter) if I could get myself a Coke, and he said it was OK, so I bought one for you, too." In another condition, the confederate returned empty-handed. Afterwards, during another pause in the experiment, the confederate asked the participant for a favor. He explained that he was selling raffle tickets for which the prize was a new car and that he stood to win a $50 prize if he sold the most raffle tickets. He then proceeded to ask if the participant was willing to buy any raffle tickets, which cost 25¢ apiece: "Any would help, the more the better." (To make sure all participants had the means to purchase some tickets, they had already been paid—in quarters!—for their participation in the study.)

In a testament to the power of the norm of reciprocity, participants who were earlier given a Coke by the confederate bought twice as many raffle tickets as those who were not given a Coke (or were given a Coke by the *experimenter,* to

**Reciprocity and Compliance** The norm of reciprocity leads people to want to comply with a request from someone who has done them a favor. This candidate hands out daffodils at the market when she is campaigning for office, which may lead people to want to reciprocate the favor by voting for her in the election.

control for the possibility that simply receiving a Coke may have put participants in a good mood and that it was *that,* and not the compulsion to reciprocate, that had increased compliance). Thus, doing a favor for someone creates an uninvited debt that the recipient is obligated to repay. Solicitors often try to take advantage of this pressure by preceding their request with a small gift. Insurance sales agents give out calendars or return-address labels. Pollsters who want you to complete a survey send it along with a dollar. Cult members offer a flower before giving their pitch. Our hearts sink when we see these gifts coming, and we often go to great lengths to avoid them—and the obligations they bring.

*The Reciprocal Concessions or the Door-in-the-Face Technique* Robert Cialdini, social psychology's most innovative contributor to the literature on compliance, has explored a novel application of the norm of reciprocity. The inspiration for his decision to conduct research on the technique is best introduced in his own words:

> I was walking down the street when I was approached by an eleven- or twelve-year-old boy. He introduced himself and said that he was selling tickets to the annual Boy Scouts circus to be held on the upcoming Saturday night. He asked if I wished to buy any at five dollars apiece. Since one of the last places I wanted to spend Saturday evening was with the Boy Scouts, I declined. "Well," he said, "if you don't want to buy any tickets, how about buying some of our big chocolate bars? They're only a dollar each." I bought a couple and, right away, realized that something noteworthy had happened. I knew that to be the case because: (a) I do not like chocolate bars; (b) I do like dollars; (c) I was standing there with two of his chocolate bars; and (d) he was walking away with two of my dollars. (Cialdini, 1984, p. 47)

Cialdini's experience with the Boy Scout led him to articulate a general compliance technique in which people feel compelled to respond to a concession with one of their own, thus making reciprocal concessions (Cialdini et al., 1975; Reeves, Baker, Boyd, & Cialdini, 1991). First, you ask someone for a very large favor that he or she will certainly refuse, and then you follow that request with one for a more modest favor that you are really interested in receiving. The idea is that the drop in the size of the request will be seen as a concession, a concession that the target of the request must match to honor the norm of reciprocity. The most available concession is to comply with the second request. Another way of looking at this **reciprocal concessions technique** is that the first favor is so large and unreasonable that it is inevitably refused, slamming the door in the face to that request but then opening it just a crack to the subsequent, smaller request. The combination of a large request followed immediately by a smaller request is hence also known as the **door-in-the-face technique**.

Cialdini demonstrated the power of this reciprocal concessions, or door-in-the-face, technique in a field study in which students were approached on the Arizona State University campus by members of Cialdini's research team posing as representatives of the "County Youth Counseling Program" and asked if they would be willing to chaperone a group of juvenile delinquents on a day trip to the zoo. Not surprisingly, the overwhelming majority, 83 percent, refused. But the experience—and the response rate—was much different for another group of students who had first encountered a much larger request. They were first asked whether they would be willing to counsel juvenile delinquents for two hours a

> "There is no duty more indispensable than that of returning a kindness."
> —CICERO

**door-in-the-face technique (reciprocal concessions technique)** Asking someone for a very large favor that he or she will certainly refuse, and then following that request with one for a more modest favor (that tends to be seen as a concession that the target will feel compelled to honor).

week for a minimum of the next two years. All of them refused, at which point they were asked about chaperoning the trip to the zoo. Now 50 percent of the students agreed to chaperone—triple the rate of the other group (Cialdini et al., 1975). A series of carefully crafted follow-up studies revealed that it was the pressure to respond to what was perceived as a concession that was responsible for the dramatic increase in compliance. For example, this technique does not work when the two requests are made by different individuals. In that case, the second, smaller request is not seen as a concession, and hence it does not create the same obligation.

Do you want to put this technique to good use in your own lives? Then consider an experiment in which professors were asked if they would be willing to meet for "fifteen to twenty minutes" to discuss a topic of interest to a student. When faced with this request by itself, 57 percent agreed. Yet, 78 percent agreed to the request when it was preceded by another request—to spend "two hours a week for the rest of the semester" with the student (Harari, Mohr, & Hosey, 1980).

*The That's-Not-All Technique*    Another technique that uses the norm of reciprocity in a similar way, the **that's-not-all technique**, may be more familiar to you. Suppose you're at a consumer electronics store and have asked about a widescreen plasma TV you've been wanting. You're told it costs $1,999 and comes with a three-year warranty. After a moment in which you say nothing, the salesperson says, "And that's not all; it also comes with a free DVD player!" This add-on can strike people as something of a gift from the store or the salesperson, creating some pressure to reciprocate. If so, this pressure can result in increased sales.

Jerry Burger has demonstrated the effectiveness of this technique. At an arts fair on the Santa Clara University campus, individuals who approached the booth of the Psychology Club bake sale were told that the cupcakes on display cost 75¢ each. Before the potential customers could respond, half of them were also told that the price included two medium-sized cookies. This nearly doubled sales, from 40 to 73 percent (Burger, 1986; Burger, Reed, DeCesare, Rauner, & Rozolis, 1999).

*The Foot-in-the-Door Technique*    All of us perform certain actions because they are consistent with our self-image. Environmentalists take the time to recycle (even when sorely tempted to toss a bottle or can into the trash) because that's part of what it means to be an environmentalist. Skiers will rise early to tackle fresh snow (even when they really want to sleep in) because that's what real skiing enthusiasts do. This suggests that if requests can be crafted to appeal to a person's self-image, the likelihood of compliance can be increased.

One very general way to do so is to employ what's known as the **foot-in-the-door technique**. It complements the door-in-the-face technique because it starts with a small request to which everyone complies (which allows the person making the request to get a foot in the door) and then follows up with a larger request involving the real behavior of interest. The idea is that the initial agreement with the small request will lead to a change in the individual's self-image as someone who does this sort of thing or who contributes to such causes. The person

**that's-not-all technique**
Adding something to an original offer, which is likely to create some pressure to reciprocate.

**foot-in-the-door technique**
A compliance technique in which one makes an initial small request to which nearly everyone complies, followed by a larger request involving the real behavior of interest.

**Foot-in-Door Technique**    After the beauty consultant succeeds in getting the potential customer to agree to sit down for the application of makeup, it may then be easier for her to get the customer to agree to a second request to purchase some makeup.

then has a reason for agreeing with the subsequent, larger request: "It's just who I am."

In the first systematic examination of the foot-in-the-door technique, the investigators knocked on doors in a California neighborhood and asked home-owners whether they would be willing to have a large billboard sign bearing the slogan "Drive Carefully" installed on their lawn for one week (Freedman & Fraser, 1966). One group of residents was shown a picture of the sign and how large and unattractive it was, and so it is not surprising that only 17 percent agreed to the request. Another group of residents had first been asked two weeks earlier to comply with a much smaller request—to display in a window of their home a three-inch-square sign bearing the words "Be a safe driver." Virtually all of them agreed to do so. When they were later asked to display the billboard on their lawn, a staggering 76 percent of them agreed to do so. To examine the breadth of this effect, the investigators ran another condition in which the first request was of a very different sort (signing a petition) than the second and involved a very different issue (keeping California beautiful). Even with these differences in the two requests, however, asking the first led nearly half the respondents to agree to the second, larger request. Perhaps we should be even more careful than we already are about agreeing to the requests that others make of us. Performing the most trivial favors can set us up to give in to much more substantial requests (Burger, 1999; Schwartzwald, Bizman, & Raz, 1983).

You may have noticed the similarity between the effectiveness of the foot-in-the-door technique and the impact of the step-by-step nature of the requests made by Milgram in his study of obedience. In both studies, eliciting compliance to a small and unobjectionable action (signing a petition, administering 30 volts of electricity) paves the way to much more serious behavior. The similarity between the two experiments also shows that taking away a reason for *not* doing something can be as powerful as providing a reason for doing it. Having admin-istered, say, 160 volts of electricity takes away a reason for refusing to administer 175 volts. After all, what's so different about the two levels of shock? And con-senting to an earlier request like displaying a small sign takes away a reason for refusing to put up a much larger sign ("No thanks, I don't do that sort of thing.")

Another technique that works in precisely this way involves legitimizing the tiniest imaginable contribution. Charities might solicit money, for example, by ending their request with the words, "even a penny would help." Such a request invalidates the thought that "I can't really afford to give." Furthermore, once the decision to give is made, there are a host of reasons why most people would be reluctant to make a truly small donation. Indeed, research on the effectiveness of this technique shows that such "even a penny" appeals substantially increase the percentage of individuals who donate, but do not lower the amount that is typi-cally given (Brockner, Guzzi, Kane, Levine, & Shaplen, 1984; Cialdini & Schroeder, 1976; Reeves, Macolini, & Martin, 1987; Weyant, 1984). The net result is that such appeals increase overall charitable giving.

## EMOTION-BASED APPROACHES

Cognitive, or reason-based, appeals can be effective in obtaining compliance, but so can affective, or emotion-based, approaches.

*Positive Mood*   Suppose you want to ask your dad for a new computer, a new amplifier for your guitar, or simply to borrow the family car for a road trip. When would you ask? When he's just come home from work in a foul mood, cursing his boss and his suffocating job? Or after he's just landed a promotion and a big raise? It does not take an advanced degree in affective science to know that it's better to ask when he's in a good mood. When people are in a good mood, they feel expansive, charitable, and affirmative, and they are therefore more likely to agree to such requests. There is no clearer example of the power of emotion-based compliance appeals than this. Even little children know to ask someone for a favor when that person is in a good mood.

The wisdom of this approach has been verified in countless experiments. In one study, participants received a telephone call from someone who claimed to have spent her last dime on this very ("misdialed") call, and who asked if the participant would dial the intended number and relay a message (Isen, Clark, & Schwartz, 1976). In one condition, no more than twenty minutes before receiving the call, participants had been given a free sample of stationery to put them in a positive mood. In another condition, participants did not receive a free sample before receiving the call. When the request was made of individuals who had not earlier been given the free sample, only 10 percent complied. But the compliance rate shot up dramatically among participants who received the request a few minutes after having been given the gift (see Figure 6.9), and then it declined gradually the longer the delay between the gift and the request.

Feeling good quite clearly makes people more likely to agree to requests and, more generally, to help others. This has been shown to hold true in experiments that have lifted participants' moods by telling them they did well on a test, having them think happy thoughts, giving them cookies, and playing cheerful music, and that confronted them with requests to make change, donate to charity, help with experiments, give blood, and tutor students (Carlson, Charlin, & Miller, 1988; Isen, 1999). Positive moods tend to increase compliance for two main reasons. First, our moods color how we interpret events. Requests for favors are more likely to be perceived as less intrusive and threatening when we are in a good mood. Giving others the benefit of the doubt, we may look upon someone who asks to borrow our notes not as an irresponsible or lazy individual who doesn't deserve to be bailed out, but as a victim of circumstance who could get

**Figure 6.9  Positive Mood and Compliance**   Percentage of respondents who agreed to help a stranger by making a telephone call and relaying a message one to twenty minutes after receiving a small gift. (Source: Isen, Clark, & Schwartz, 1976)

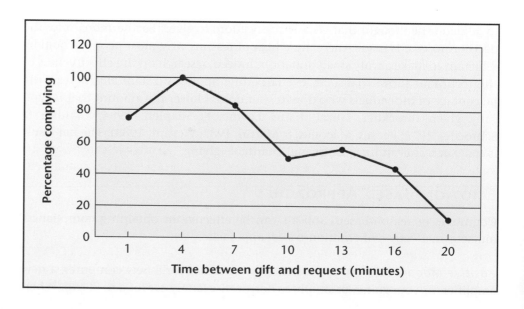

**Positive Mood and Requests**
When people are in a good mood, they are often more likely to agree to requests. People at this charity ball in Monaco are dancing and having a good time, and as such are more likely to donate money to the Princess Grace Foundation.

back on track with a little assistance (Carlson, Charlin, & Miller, 1988; Forgas, 1998a, 1998b; Forgas & Bower, 1987).

Another reason good moods increase compliance involves what is known as mood maintenance. Pardon the tautology, but it feels good to feel good, and we typically want the feeling to last as long as possible (Clark & Isen, 1982; Wegener & Petty, 1994). And one way to sustain a good mood is to do something for another person. Or stated differntly, one way to wreck a good mood is to turn down a request and invite all sorts of self-recrimination ("What kind of heartless person am I?") that pollutes and erodes a positive mental state. Several studies implicate mood maintenance as an important component of the impact of positive moods on compliance. In one study, participants were first either given cookies (which put them in a good mood) or not given cookies. They were then asked (by someone other than the person who provided the cookies) if they would be willing to assist with an experiment by serving as a confederate. Half the participants were told the job of confederate would involve *helping* the "true" participant in the experiment; the other half were told it would involve *hindering* the participant. Having received a cookie (and being in a good mood) increased the compliance rate when the task involved helping the participant, but not when it involved hindering the participant (Isen & Levin, 1972). Helping another person promotes feeling good; hurting someone does not.

*Negative Mood*    If a good mood increases compliance, symmetry might lead us to expect a bad mood to decrease it. It can, but even the slightest introspection reveals that certain types of bad moods are likely to *increase* compliance, not decrease it. And people know this, and use it to their advantage. Suppose, for example, that your boyfriend or girlfriend was excessively flirtatious with a member of the opposite sex (alas, not you, or it wouldn't be excessive), and you point out the offense. Would that be a good time to ask your partner for something? You bet it would! When people feel guilty, they are often motivated to do what they can to get rid of that awful feeling. So one type of bad mood at least, that associated with feeling guilty, should enhance compliance.

Social psychologists have demonstrated a strong link between guilt and compliance (more of the former leads to more of the latter) in numerous experiments in which participants have been led to feel guilty by being induced to lie, to break a camera, to knock over stacks of carefully arranged index cards, or to injure an adorable laboratory rat (Carlsmith & Gross, 1969; Darlington & Macker, 1966; J. Regan, 1971; D. Regan, Williams, & Sparling, 1972). In a particularly clever test of the effect of guilt on compliance, researchers asked Catholics to donate to the March of Dimes either when they were on their way into church for confession or on their way out. The presumption was that those on their way in were rehearsing their sins and thus feeling guilty; those on their way out had expiated their sins and hence were no longer plagued by guilt. As the investigators predicted, those solicited on the way in gave more money than those solicited on the way out (Harris, Benson, & Hall, 1975).

The desire for expiation is only one reason that guilt is likely to increase compliance, however, and the other reasons make it clear that other negative emotions can lead to increased compliance as well. This was suggested by the results of an experiment in which participants were recruited to assist with a study of "growth and development" (J. Regan, 1971). The study was described as having been running for six weeks, and the participant's task was to monitor a voltage meter (located to the participant's left) to make sure the stimulation delivered to a two-month-old albino rat (located to the participant's right) "stayed at the predetermined mild level." Meanwhile, the experimenter was stationed in an adjoining room, ostensibly to measure the rat's pulse, but from where the participant's every move could be surreptitiously monitored. As the experiment got underway, all participants performed their assigned task—for a while. But because the voltage meter registered the same 109 to 110 volts moment by monotonous moment, pretty soon all participants turned their attention to the rat itself. When they did, the experimenter delivered an intense shock through the floor of the rat's cage, causing the rat to jump and squeal in pain, and the voltage meter to shoot up from 110 to 140 volts. The experimenter then called out from the adjoining room, "Something's wrong . . . his pulse is wild . . . [with a tone of frustration] Six weeks!" The experimenter then proceeded to terminate the experiment and sent the participant to the department secretary to receive the promised payment. While at the secretary's office, the participant received an appeal to donate to a charitable cause.

The unsettling experience with the rat, of course, was designed to make participants feel guilty (because their inattentiveness to the assigned task apparently caused the rat to receive too much shock and thus jeopardized the experiment). It also permitted an examination of whether their guilt would increase the amount they gave to the charitable cause. It did. Participants who thought their actions had led to the fiasco donated nearly three times as much money as participants who went through the procedure uneventfully, with nothing bad happening to the rat. Once again, guilt increased compliance.

But another condition of the experiment yielded a telling result. Participants in this condition also witnessed the rat jump and squeal, but at a random moment, not right after they had turned their attention away from their assigned task. And they heard the experimenter yell from the adjoining room, "There has been a short circuit in here. . . . This isn't your fault at all." These participants, then, had no reason to feel guilty over what had happened, and yet they ended up donating just as much as the guilty participants. Apparently, *witnessing* harm is enough to enhance the impulse to "do good"; one needn't be the cause of the

harm. Thus, simply feeling upset, or even sad, can lead to an increase in people's willingness to comply with requests.

These results point to an underlying powerful determinant of the effect of bad moods on compliance, what has come to be known as the **negative state relief hypothesis** (Cialdini, Darby, & Vincent, 1973; Cialdini & Fultz, 1990; Cialdini, Schaller, Houlihan, Arps, Fultz, & Beaman, 1987). We don't want to feel bad, and so we jump at the opportunity to do something to brighten our mood. Doing something for someone else, especially when it's done for a good cause, is one way to make us feel better. We help others, in other words, largely to help ourselves.

The effect of bad moods on compliance has been linked to a quest for negative state relief as a result of experiments like the following (Cialdini, Darby, & Vincent, 1973). Participants were greeted individually and told that the study was part of the experimenter's undergraduate research methods course and would be conducted in the office of a graduate student who had offered it for use. In one condition, the experimenter gestured for the participant to have a seat at a table. Things were arranged so that when the participant sat down as instructed, three boxes of computer cards crashed to the floor (computer cards are relics of the days when computers could not accept data typed on a keyboard). The experimenter then exclaimed, "Oh no! I think it's the data from Tom's master's thesis. . . . They seem to be hopelessly mixed up. I guess we should clean up the mess as best we can and go on with the experiment." The experimenter then left the room, ostensibly to get materials needed for the study. While the experimenter was away, a second experimenter appeared and explained:

> . . . she [the first experimenter] said it would be alright if I asked her subjects to help me out with my class project. I'm interested in surveying undergraduate study habits, and I need some people who would be willing to call students on the phone and administer a 10-min interview concerning their study habits. I can't give you any experimental credit for doing this, but I would appreciate your help. Would you

> **negative state relief hypothesis** The idea that people engage in certain actions, such as agreeing to a request, in order to relieve negative feelings and to feel better about themselves.

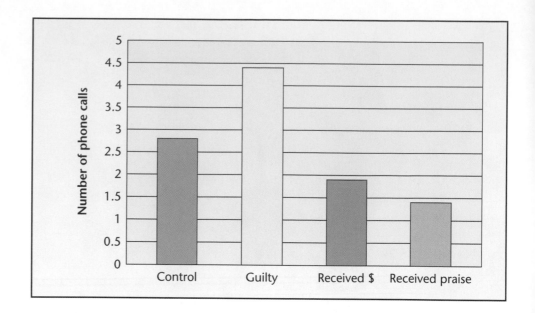

**Figure 6.10 Test of the Negative State Relief Hypothesis** Number of phone calls participants agreed to make, depending on experimental condition. (Source: Cialdini, Darby, & Vincent, 1973)

make some interview calls for me? Any number of calls up to 15 would help. (Cialdini, Darby, & Vincent, 1973, p. 507)

The spilling of the computer cards, of course, was choreographed to make the participant feel guilty, and the request to make phone calls was the means to assess whether their guilt increased their compliance. It did. As Figure 6.10 indicates, guilty participants volunteered to make an average of 4.4 calls, compared to an average of 2.8 on the part of control participants who hadn't previously spilled the boxes of cards. But here's the telling part. Participants in two additional conditions had an experience between the time they knocked over the computer cards and the time the second experimenter made her request, and this experience was designed to rid them of the negative state they were experiencing. One group of participants was given an unexpected sum of money for completing an innocuous task; participants in the other group were lavishly praised for their performance on an innocuous task. The investigators reasoned that if it is the specific emotion of guilt that motivates people to comply, the compliance rate among these two groups should be just like that in the "guilty" condition. After all, these participants may be in a better mood overall, but they are every bit as guilty as they were before their unexpected, mood-lifting experience. In contrast, if it is the simple desire to get rid of a bad mood that increases compliance, the compliance rate among these two groups should be just like that in the control group. They no longer feel bad, so they no longer need to seek out a means to lift their mood.

As Figure 6.10 illustrates, the results strongly support the negative state relief hypothesis. Participants in these two conditions offered to make significantly fewer phone calls than did participants who were made to feel guilty but who did not enjoy a mood-lifting experience. It appears that the primary reason that people are motivated to comply with requests when they are in a bad mood is to get into a better frame of mind.

Does this mean that all there is to the link between bad moods and increased compliance is the desire for negative state relief? Almost certainly not. Although the desire to improve our mood is likely to be the most consistent and powerful motive at play, there are other considerations as well. Even if we desire relief from guilt, sadness, and embarrassment equally, the behaviors we are willing to engage in to achieve that relief may be different for some of these emotions. Guilt and sadness can both lead to withdrawal—which can interfere with compliance—but the circumstances that elicit withdrawal are likely to be very different for the two states. When sad, you might be reluctant to be around those who are happy; when feeling guilty, you might want to avoid anyone or anything that reminds you of your transgression. And another type of bad mood, that produced by anger, is likely to be another story entirely. People sometimes revel in their anger and hence, at least for a time, may be less interested in seeking relief from it. So, although all sorts of bad moods increase compliance because doing someone a favor promises relief from a negative state, the precise profile of the relationship between mood and compliance is likely to be different for different types of bad moods. Historically, social psychologists who have studied compliance have focused on the effects of the rather pronounced difference between being in a good or a bad mood. But research that distinguishes between the different varieties of good and bad moods is proving to be informative in related areas of social psychology, and the field of compliance awaits the results of similar, more fine-grained investigations (Lerner, Gonzalez, Small, & Fischhoff, 2003; Lerner, Small, & Loewenstein, 2004; Tiedens & Linton, 2001).

**LOOKING BACK,** we have seen that reason-based approaches induce compliance by providing good reasons for people to comply with a request. One of these reasons is the norm of reciprocity, by which people feel compelled to benefit those who have benefited them. In the door-in-the-face, or reciprocal concessions technique, people who have refused a large request are induced to then agree to a smaller request. In the that's-not-all technique, people are induced to buy an expensive product because a gift has been added to the deal. In the foot-in-the-door technique, people comply with a small request and then are induced to grant a larger request. Emotion-based approaches also can lead to compliance. People who are in a positive mood are more likely to comply with a request in order to maintain their good mood. On the other hand, according to the negative state relief hypothesis, people who feel guilty or sad are also likely to comply with a request in order to feel better. With all these ways to be influenced, it is comforting to know that there are some tested ways of avoiding social influence.

## RESISTING SOCIAL INFLUENCE

Our analysis of when and why people conform, comply, and obey should lead the way to a better understanding of how people can be encouraged to resist social influence. Sometimes people are pressured to do destructive things—either to themselves or to others—so it is important to identify some principles that might help people to resist that pressure.

The first thing to note is that, although we have emphasized in this chapter the very common tendency to give in to social pressure, people do not always do so. In fact, there is a tendency for people to resist attempts by others to restrict their freedom to act or think as they wish. According to **reactance theory**, people experience an unpleasant state of arousal when they believe their freedoms are threatened, and people often act to reduce this unpleasant arousal by reasserting their prerogatives (Brehm, 1956). If your parents tell you that you cannot, under

**reactance theory** Reasserting prerogatives in response to the unpleasant state of arousal experienced by people when they believe their freedoms are threatened.

> "I'd rather be a free man in my grave
> Than living as a puppet or a slave."
> —REGGAE LEGEND JIMMY CLIFF

any circumstances, dye your hair, is your desire to have it dyed diminished or increased? If your college administration were to issue an edict banning portable MP3 players on campus, would your desire to have your portable music player with you at all times go up or down? Reactance theory predicts that the moment you feel your freedom is being taken away, the freedoms become more precious, and your desire to maintain them is increased.

But how effectively would you act to reassert your freedom, or what factors might increase your ability to resist such blatant social influence attempts? One important variable is practice. We saw in Milgram's experiments that many of the participants wanted to disobey and even tried to do so, but they weren't very good at it. Maybe if they had been trained to disobey when the situation called for it, they would have done a better job. The common bumper sticker, "Question Authority," may be effective in this regard. By frequently questioning authority, we become practiced in doing so, and so it becomes easier and easier with each opportunity. It is interesting in this regard that there is evidence that the Christians who tried to save Jews during the Holocaust tended to be people who had a history of helping others, either as part of their job or as volunteers. Thus, those who helped were often not any more predisposed to like Jews than those who did not help. As one Catholic resistance group described it, "Our feelings toward the Jews have not changed. We continue to deem them political, economic and ideological enemies of Poland . . . This fact, however, does not release us from the duty of damnation of murder" (Tec, 1986, p. 87). They were more likely to help, in other words, not because their attitudes were more favorable; they were just more practiced at helping.

**Resisting Social Influence**  The women pictured on this cover of *Time* magazine all refused to go along with those who were knowingly covering up wrongdoing. Cynthia Cooper (left) was a vice president of the internal audit department of WorldCom who discovered an accounting fraud and confronted the company's controller with her findings. Coleen Rowley (center) was an FBI agent who told her superiors prior to 9/11 that the flight training of known suspects may have constituted a terrorist threat. Sherron Watkins (right) was a vice president of corporate development at Enron who identified fraud at the company and wrote a letter to her boss detailing her suspicions rather than pretending that nothing was wrong.

Another way to increase the ability to resist social influence is to have an ally. We saw in Asch's experiments that just having one additional person depart from the majority was sufficient to produce a drastic reduction in conformity. If you know in advance that your friend, your employee, or your child is likely to be subject to intense social pressure, make sure he or she is with a friend or colleague. The presence of one other person dramatically reduces normative social influence.

We also saw in Milgram's experiments that the stepwise nature of the procedure likely played an important role in the surprising levels of obedience observed in those studies. This suggests that we all need to be wary of potentially slippery slopes. We would be well served to look ahead and ask ourselves, "If I'm going along with this because it's just one . . . [drink, fib, concession], will I be in a better position to resist once I've given in to this first step, or will I be in a worse position?" It's often easiest to resist influence from the start, rather than giving in and hoping to put a halt to things later on. We are rationalizing creatures (see Chapter 8), and so once we've taken a step down a path to problematic or immoral action, it's fairly easy to rationalize that step. Having done so, it then becomes easy to rationalize the next step. And then the next one, and the next one.

We saw in our discussion of compliance that many influence attempts are based on appeals to our emotions. A particularly effective strategy for dealing with these types of appeals is simply to put off a response—to delay. If there is a "first law" of emotional experience, it would have to be that emotional states fade. What is felt strongly now is likely to be felt less strongly later. Therefore, the compulsion to give in because one is caught up in a particular emotion can be diminished by simply waiting to respond. The advice, "better sleep on it," is wise, not because any greater insight is likely to be achieved overnight, but because an initial emotional compulsion is likely to dissipate, and the question of whether to comply with a request can then be evaluated on the merits of the idea, not on the basis of an intense emotional state.

> "Avoid the near occasion of sin."
> —ROMAN CATHOLIC TEACHING

**LOOKING BACK,** we have seen that there are ways that people can resist social influence, especially social influence to do things that are morally suspect. People may resist influence if they have some experience in questioning authority and helping others rather than turning their backs on people in need. They may find an ally, who can help them to resist social pressure to conform. They may look ahead to see if small actions may lead to large, immoral actions. And finally, they may delay making a decision or taking an action to see if they feel the same way with time and further thought.

## SUMMARY

1. There are three types of social influence. *Conformity* involves a change in a person's attitudes or behavior in response to (often implicit) pressure from others. *Compliance* involves going along with explicit requests made by others. Finally, *obedience* involves giving in to the commands of an authority.

2. There are three sources of conformity. Sometimes people conform mindlessly and automatically, when the very perception of someone else's behavior makes them more likely to behave that way themselves (the principle of *ideomotor action*). Other times, people conform because of *informational social influence*—that is, they look upon the actions of others as information about what is best to do. Still other times people conform because of *normative social influence*—that is, out of concern for the social consequences of their actions.

3. Several characteristics of the group affect conformity pressure. The larger the *group size*, the greater its influence—but only up to a size of about four people. *Unanimous groups* are far more effective than those with even a single other dissenter. Moreover, the greater the *expertise* and *status* of group members, the greater their influence.

4. Culture and gender affect conformity. People from more interdependent cultures are more likely to conform than people from independent cultures. Women are somewhat more likely to conform than men. But both men and women conform more in domains in which they are less knowledgeable.

5. Several task factors affect conformity pressure. The more *difficult* and *ambiguous* the task is, as with the autokinetic experiment, the greater the conformity. When people's responses are *anonymous*, they are less affected by others' responses. Finally, when people have *satisfying explanations* of others' judgments, such as monetary gain, they are less affected by others' responses.

6. The direction of influence is not always from the majority to the minority. Sometimes *minority influence* can be substantial, especially when it is a consistent minority.

7. The study of obedience has been dominated by the experiments of Stanley Milgram, who documented that most people go along with seemingly harmful commands of an authority.

8. Participants in obedience experiments are caught in a conflict between two opposing forces: *normative*

*social influence* and *moral imperatives*. The balance between these forces shifts toward the former when participants tune out the learner and tune in the experimenter.

9. Although Milgram's results strike nearly everyone as wildly counterintuitive, they can be rendered less surprising by considering the *stepwise nature* of his commands, the *attempts to terminate* the experiment made by most participants, and the ability of participants to place the onus of *responsibility* on the experimenter, not themselves.

10. Compliance with the requests of others may be elicited through both *reason-based techniques* and *emotion-based techniques*.

11. Powerful reason-based approaches include invoking the *norm of reciprocity* by, say, doing a favor for someone or making a concession (the *door-in-the-face technique*), and starting up a *foot-in-the-door process* by first getting someone to agree to a small request before making the more substantial request in which one is really interested.

12. Powerful emotion-based approaches include getting the targeted person in a good mood, which is likely to increase compliance because of *mood maintenance*.

13. Compliance may also result from a desire for *negative state relief*, as an act of compliance may reduce guilt or sadness.

14. Sometimes attempts to influence us backfire, as when would-be influencers generate *reactance*. Our attempts to resist influence are aided by simple practice at it, by having an ally, by being wary of slippery slopes, and by avoiding action in the face of an emotional influence attempt by "sleeping on" the request.

## CRITICAL THINKING ABOUT BASIC PRINCIPLES

1. The "foot-in-the-door" and the "door in the face" compliance techniques sound similar, but they can be better understood by comparing and contrasting them. What psychological processes are responsible for each? What conditions need to be met (that is, who must make the request, what must the nature of the request be) for each to be effective?

2. Your mother (bless her heart) does not believe that you would flip the higher voltage switches if you participated in one of Milgram's experiments and were commanded to do so. What could you tell your mother about the Milgram situation that could get her to believe—really, truly believe—that maybe her child would act like the other participants after all?

3. It has been reported that Milgram became interested in studying the power of various politeness norms after witnessing the extent to which participants in his obedience experiments went along with the experimenter's commands out of a sense of propriety. This led Milgram to instruct his graduate students to, for example, get on an uncrowded bus with plenty of empty seats for all to see, and ask someone to give up his or her seat. Everyone given this task reported that it was difficult to do; some simply couldn't do it. To get a firsthand look at how powerfully such norms affect our behavior, try doing what Milgram asked his graduate students to do. Can you?

## KEY TERMS

autokinetic illusion (p. 218)
chameleon effect (p. 217)
compliance (p. 215}
conformity (p. 215)
door-in-the-face technique (p. 243)
foot-in-the-door technique (p. 244)
ideomotor action (p. 216)

informational social influence
   (p. 219)
internalization (p. 226)
negative state relief hypothesis
   (p. 249)
normative social influence (p. 221)
norm of reciprocity (p. 241)

obedience (p. 215)
public compliance (p. 226)
reactance theory (p. 251)
reciprocal concessions technique
   (p. 243)
social influence (p. 215)
that's-not-all technique (p. 244)

# FURTHER READING

Blass, T. (2004). *The man who shocked the world: The life and legacy of Stanley Milgram.* New York: Basic Books.

Cialdini, R. B. (2000). *Influence: Science and practice* (4th ed.). Boston: Allyn & Bacon.

Gladwell, M. (2000). *The tipping point: How little things can make a big difference.* Boston: Little, Brown.

Ross, L. (1988). Situationist perspectives on the obedience experiments. *Contemporary Psychology, 33,* 101–104.

# Chapter Outline

# CHAPTER 7

# Attitudes and Persuasion

S ince the 1964 Surgeon General's Report on Smoking and Health detailed a scientifically established relationship between smoking tobacco and lung cancer, we have witnessed one of the great persuasion battles of our time. The U.S. Government has spent billions of dollars on public service announcements on television, in print, and on the airwaves portraying the perils of smoking. And the tobacco industry has spent billions of dollars extolling the pleasures of smoking. The battle between those supporting smoking and those opposing it has been expensive and passionate. Meanwhile, millions of lives have been lost, and millions of people have begun or continued to smoke.

The public service ads that try to persuade people to stop smoking are graphic, powerful, and backed by highly credible, prestigious, and expert sources, from medical associations to the U.S. Government. These ads have made people aware of the high risks of smoking, including the facts that one out of every three cancer-related deaths is related to smoking, that smoking causes between 400,000 and 500,000 premature deaths each year in the United States, that smoking increases the chances of early impotence in men, and that women who smoke are four times as likely to have seri-

**Advertising and Smoking** (A) In 1985, the R. J. Reynolds Company introduced an advertising campaign for Camel cigarettes that featured the "cool" cartoon character "Joe Camel." The ads appealed to children and led to a huge increase in the sales of cigarettes to children and teenagers. The Federal Trade Commission successfully sued R. J. Reynolds for targeting underage children and forced the company to end the Joe Camel campaign. (B) Public service ads were created to persuade people to stop smoking. This Cancer Country ad parodies the Marlboro cigarette ads in which cowboys are smoking cigarettes and looking rugged and manly, and instead stresses the connection between smoking and cancer.

"The object of oratory alone is not truth, but persuasion."
—THOMAS BABINGTON MACAULAY

"Men are not governed by justice, but by law or persuasion. When they refuse to be governed by law or persuasion, they have to be governed by force or fraud, or both."
—GEORGE BERNARD SHAW

ous side effects from birth control pills, and to suffer from fertility problems. The results of these public service ads have been remarkable. In the 1950s, about half of all Americans smoked. Today, just a little over 30 percent of Americans smoke.

But what about the remaining 30 percent who continue to smoke, despite being fully aware of the significant health risks of doing so? The $3 billion that the tobacco industry spends each year on advertising is no doubt partially responsible for the large number of people who still smoke. One especially effective campaign promoting smoking was the "Joe Camel" campaign in which Joe Camel, a cartoon mascot of Camel cigarettes, appeared on billboards, in magazines, and on promotional items, such as T-shirts. Soon after the start of the campaign, Camel's market share among underage smokers rose from 0.5 to 32.8 percent! Another successful campaign increased sales of Virginia Slims cigarettes. Their slogan, "You've come a long way, baby," was specifically targeted at women and linked smoking Virginia Slims cigarettes to women's quest for success, independence, and thinness. After the introduction of the Virginia Slims campaign, smoking by twelve-year-old girls increased by 110 percent.

This story about the battle over smoking, about the millions of people who have kicked the addictive habit, as well as the large numbers of people who continue to smoke, reveals the two overarching themes of this chapter: susceptibility and resistance to persuasion. People can be remarkably susceptible to persuasion. Charismatic leaders like Nelson Mandela, Martin Luther King, Jr., or Mohandas (Mahatma) Gandhi can stir masses to bring about radical social change in the absence of significant institutional power or money. Approximately one in ten young adults who spend a weekend retreat with the Moonies—that is, followers of the Reverend Sun Myung Moon and his Unification Church, which many think of as a religious cult—will become a full-fledged member, often abandoning family and friends forever (Galanter, 1989). President George W. Bush's constant references to Saddam Hussein while discussing the 9/11 terrorist attacks led 69 percent of Americans to believe that

Iraq's former leader was involved in the attacks, even though there had never been any evidence that supported this contention (Milbank & Deane, 2003).

Nonetheless, people can also be remarkably resistant to persuasion. Some researchers estimate that only 1 percent of POWs in the Korean War altered their political beliefs to any significant degree, even though they were tortured and indoctrinated in the most extreme ways (Zimbardo & Leippe, 1991). Many well-financed and skillfully designed campaigns to encourage people to practice safe sex have failed (Aronson, Fried, & Stone, 1991). Often people are stubbornly resistant to changing their minds, even when it affects their health or their economic well-being.

We will organize this chapter around a fascinating tension: Why is it that in response to attempts at persuasion, from political indoctrination to door-to-door religious proselytizing, people sometimes change their minds, whereas other times they do not? What are the mechanics of attitude change? How do persuasive messages change people's attitudes, often in lasting and significant ways? And how do people resist attitude change? Moreover, what does this resistance to persuasion reveal about people's attitudes and convictions? But before we consider why attitudes change, and why they do not, we first must consider what attitudes are, how they are measured, and why people have them in the first place.

> "The receptive ability of the masses is very limited, their understanding small; on the other hand, they have a great power of forgetting. This being so, all effective propaganda must be confined to a very few points which must be brought out in the form of slogans until the very last man is enabled to comprehend what is meant by any slogan. If this principle is sacrificed by the desire to be many sided, it will dissipate the effectual working of the propaganda, for the people will be unable to digest or retain the material that is offered them."
>
> —ADOLF HITLER

## THE BASICS OF ATTITUDES

What exactly is an attitude? In the most general sense, we define an **attitude** as an evaluation of an object in a positive or negative fashion. Let's break this definition down a bit more. Most theorists assume that attitudes include three different elements: affect, cognitions, and behavior (Breckler, 1984; Eagly & Chaiken, 1998; Zimbardo & Leippe, 1991). And how do we know what people's attitudes are? We can see how they act, or we can attempt to measure their attitudes directly. Let's first examine the three components.

> **attitude** An evaluation of an object in a positive or negative fashion that includes the three elements of affect, cognitions, and behavior.

### THE THREE COMPONENTS OF ATITUDES

At their core, attitudes involve *affect*—that is, emotional reactions to the object (Breckler, 1984; Zanna & Rempel, 1988). Attitudes have to do with how much we like or dislike an object, be it a politician, a landscape, the latest athletic shoe, laundry detergent, or ourselves. In fact, almost all objects trigger some degree of positive or negative emotion, and this is the affective component of attitudes (Bargh, Chaiken, Raymond, & Hymes, 1996; Cacioppo & Bernston, 1994; Fazio, Jackson, Dunton, & Williams, 1995; Fazio, Sanbonmatsu, Powell, & Kardes, 1986; see Box 7.1).

Attitudes also involve *cognitions*. These include knowledge about the object, as well as beliefs, ideas, memories, and images. If you have a positive attitude toward a beloved sports team, for example, you may also possess esoteric knowl-

## Box 7.1 FOCUS ON NEUROSCIENCE

# Is the Bad Stronger than the Good?

At the very core of our attitudes is a positive or negative response to an attitude object, whether it is an old friend's voice, a roommate's messy pile of dishes, or the smell of freshly cut grass. Pioneering research by neuroscientist Joseph LeDoux has found that one part of the brain—the amygdala—is central to the initial affective evaluation that lies at the core of our attitudes (LeDoux, 1989, 1993, 1996). This almond-shaped region of the brain receives sensory information about a stimulus from the thalamus and then provides information about the positive or negative valence, or value, of the object. This evaluation occurs, remarkably, before the mind has categorized the object. Thus, before we even know what an object is, we have a gut feeling about it. Moreover, when scientists recorded individual neurons in the amygdala, they discovered that it was particularly sensitive to emotional stimuli—for example, faces. When the amygdala is damaged, various animals no longer have appropriate evaluations of objects: they eat feces, attempt to copulate with members of other species, and show no fear of threatening stimuli such as snakes or dominant animals. In our chapter on emotion, we will consider further implications of this important research, describing how our minds are designed to form very rapid, even unconscious preferences (see Chapter 12).

LeDoux's research raises another interesting question: Are our initial positive and negative evaluations of stimuli comparable? Reviews by Shelley Taylor (1991), Paul Rozin and Edward Royzman (2001), Roy Baumeister and his colleagues (Baumeister, Bratslavsky, Finkenauer, & Vohs, 2001), and John Cacioppo and Wendy Gardner (1999) provide a seemingly conclusive, perhaps unsettling answer: negative evaluations are stronger than positive evaluations. It would certainly make evolutionary sense for an organism to be more vigilant and responsive to pain than to pleasure, to danger than to safety. Without such a bias, the chances of survival would seem to be diminished.

Consider a few generalizations that support the conclusion that the bad is stronger than the good. Negative stimuli, such as frightening sounds or noxious smells, bring about more rapid and stronger physiological responses than positive stimuli, such as delicious tastes. Losing $10 seems more painful than gaining $10 is pleasurable. Negative trauma, such as the death of a loved one or sexual abuse, can change the individual for a lifetime; there don't appear to be equivalent effects from positive events. Or consider Paul Rozin's ideas about contamination. Brief contact with a cockroach will spoil a delicious meal (the negative stimulus contaminates the positive stimulus). The inverse—making a pile of cockroaches delicious by touching it with your favorite food—is unimaginable (Rozin & Royzman, 2001).

In important work directly addressing the claim that our negative evaluations are more potent than our positive evaluations, Tiffany Ito, John Cacioppo, and their colleagues presented participants with positively valenced pictures—for example, photographs of pizza or of a bowl of chocolate ice cream—and negatively valenced slides—for example, photographs of a mutilated face or of a dead cat (Ito, Larsen, Smith, & Cacioppo, 1998). They carefully recorded participants' electrocortical activity on the scalp and studied one region of the brain that is known to be involved in the evaluative response to stimuli. In several studies like this, they discovered a clear negativity bias in evaluation: the negative stimuli generated greater brain activity than the positive or neutral stimuli. It seems, alas, that the bad is indeed stronger than the good.

**Contamination**  A cockroach on food spoils a delicious meal.

edge about the team's strengths and weaknesses, its players' virtues and vices, and memories of the team's most exhilarating or tragic seasons.

Finally, attitudes are associated with specific *behaviors* (Fishbein & Ajzen, 1975). When our attitudes are primed—that is, brought to mind, even unconsciously—we are more likely to act in ways consistent with the attitude (Bargh, Chen, & Burrows, 1996). Recent studies in neuroscience even suggest that our attitudes activate a region in the brain—the motor cortex—that supports specific actions (Preston & de Waal, 2002). You see a young child crying or a delicious-looking hot fudge sundae, and your mind prepares your body for action. Thus, attitudes are associated with specific intentions and actions.

This analysis of attitudes helps us understand issues to which we will turn shortly. How might you change another person's attitudes? It is clear that there are several inputs to attitudes, implying that there are several possible sources of change. Prompting someone to behave in a particular way can do the trick. Providing compelling information can also lead to attitude change, as can changing the emotion the person feels in the presence of the attitude object. These ideas will inspire our discussion in this chapter and the next about the most effective routes to attitude change.

Our analysis reveals just as readily why it can be so hard to change another person's attitudes. To do so requires that you overhaul a rich association of emotions, thoughts, and behaviors, both past and present. It's not always easy. But before moving to a discussion of attitude change, let's consider how we measure attitudes.

## MEASURING ATTITUDES

Attitude questionnaires may be the most widely used methodology in social psychology. Researchers routinely ask how participants feel about members of other groups, their romantic partners, themselves, the president, and so on. The simple approach to measuring attitudes is to have participants rate an attitude object on a **Likert scale**, named after Rensis Likert, its inventor. The Likert scale lists a set of possible answers, with anchors on each extreme—for example, 1 = never, 7 = always. To determine your attitudes toward the use of cell phones while driving, you might be asked to respond on a 1 to 7 scale, with 1 being the least favorable answer ("it's never acceptable") and 7 being the opposite anchor ("it's always acceptable"). You've probably responded to many of these kinds of queries yourself. Yet, when it comes to the study of complex attitudes—for example, your attitudes toward abortion or a politician—researchers have had to develop more sophisticated techniques.

To understand why, answer the following questions: How much do you value freedom? How strongly do you feel about the reduction of discrimination? How important to you is a less polluted environment? If an investigator asked these questions of a random selection of individuals—especially a random selection of university students—odds are that most would provide strong positive responses. But surely people must vary in their real attitudes toward these issues. How, then, do we capture people's real attitudes if traditional Likert scales sometimes fail to differentiate people with stronger and weaker attitudes?

One approach, developed by Russell Fazio, is to measure the *accessibility* of the attitude—that is, the degree to which the attitude is ready to become active in the individual's mind, guiding thought and behavior (Fazio, 1995; Fazio & Williams, 1986). Fazio and his colleagues measure the accessibility of attitudes by simply assessing the time it takes the individual to respond to the attitude question,

**Likert scale** A scale used to assess people's attitudes that includes a set of possible answers and that has anchors on each extreme.

which is known as a **response latency**. A person who takes 750 milliseconds to respond affirmatively to the question, "Do you approve of the president's policy toward Iraq?," would presumably possess stronger attitudes in this realm than the individual who takes several seconds. This, indeed, is what Fazio and colleagues have found. For example, in a study conducted five months before Ronald Reagan and Walter Mondale squared off in the 1984 presidential election, Fazio and Williams (1986) measured how long it took participants to answer how good a president the opposing candidates would make. The time it took participants to respond to this question was a strong predictor of who they felt won the first debate between the two candidates, and more importantly, it predicted the candidate they voted for six months later. Attitude accessibility, then, is one way to refine our measurement of strong, meaningful attitudes.

A second approach to assessing attitude strength is to determine the *centrality* of the attitude to the individual's belief system (Krosnick & Petty, 1995). To assess centrality, researchers measure a variety of attitudes within a domain and calculate the extent to which a particular attitude is linked to the other attitudes. For example, in a study of social and political attitudes, a researcher might ask you your attitudes toward the death penalty, affirmative action, abortion, stem cell research, gay marriage, sex education in high school, alternative energy sources, drug legalization, and taxation. To the extent that an attitude is really important to you, it should be centrally located in your wider network of social-political attitudes, and highly correlated with your attitudes toward other issues. For example, if abortion is a defining social issue for you as it is for many, and you care passionately about it, then your attitude toward abortion is likely to guide your attitudes toward other social issues, such as stem cell research or sex education in high school.

There are several other ways of measuring attitudes. One makes use of *scenarios*—that is, situations involving actions and reactions. Participants read stories setting up scenarios, and then they express their attitudes by indicating what kind of action or response is appropriate on the part of the protagonist in the scenario. Another method is *content analysis*. Using this method, researchers intensively code participants' spontaneous speech or writings to infer the presence and intensity of various attitudes.

**LOOKING BACK,** we have seen that attitudes have many elements—affect, cognitions, and behaviors—and we have delved briefly into how to measure attitudes. But why do people have attitudes in the first place?

## FUNCTIONS OF ATTITUDES

What purposes do attitudes serve? One answer is that they guide behavior. As we will see in the next chapter, this intuition—that attitudes guide behavior—is certainly valid, but attitudes guide behavior less powerfully than most people suspect.

Researchers have, however, highlighted four other functions of attitudes (Pratkanis, Breckler, & Greenwald, 1989; Eagly & Chaiken, 1998). As we discuss these different functions, we will cast our net broadly, reviewing research that attests to the importance of attitudes in topics as wide-ranging as food preferences and the fear of death.

# THE UTILITARIAN FUNCTION OF ATTITUDES

Attitudes serve what has been called a **utilitarian function**—that is, they alert us to rewarding objects and situations we should approach and to costly or punishing objects or situations we should avoid. When you become aware of an attitude you hold, say, toward the smell of popcorn or the sight of your new boss, you are by definition aware of positive and negative information about the attitude object.

In numerous studies researchers have shown that attitudes toward fairly neutral objects can be modified by pairing that object with a stimulus that generates a strong positive or negative reaction (Petty & Wegener, 1998). People's attitudes toward political slogans, consumer products, persuasive messages, and other people can be changed when paired with emotionally arousing stimuli such as pleasing odors, electric shock, harsh sounds, or pleasant pictures (Gresham & Shimp, 1985; Janis, Kaye, & Kirschner, 1965, Razran, 1940; Staats & Staats, 1958; Zanna, Kiesler, & Pilkonis, 1970). In these instances, the attitude toward one object becomes associated with a new object—a principle that advertisers have long exploited. Ads that use animals, babies, or sexually alluring young women and men are more likely to sell products than those that use less intrinsically rewarding objects, like cartoons or historical figures (Pratkanis & Aronson, 2000).

> **utilitarian function** An attitudinal function that serves to alert us to rewarding objects and situations we should approach, and costly or punishing objects or situations we should avoid.

Food preferences also illustrate the utilitarian function of attitudes. Here our dietary likes and dislikes help us to eat foods that are beneficial to survival and to avoid foods that are potentially dangerous. The typical human has 10,000 taste buds devoted to sweet, sour, salty, and bitter tastes. Each taste bud has receptor cells with fifty short hair-like structures that, when stimulated by food particles, send a signal to the medulla, the thalamus, and the cortex, which convert that electrochemical signal to our experience of taste. The preference for sweet foods—no doubt one of our strongest positive attitudes—helps us identify foods of nutritional value, such as foods that provide Vitamin C, which humans, unlike many mammals, do not synthesize in their body.

**Attitudes and Associations**   Our attitudes alert us to rewarding objects—or threatening or neutral ones. A positive attitude toward a beautiful woman may help to sell a car if an association is created between the woman and the car. Here a Chinese model poses next to a sports car, thereby pairing the emotionally arousing stimulus of the beautiful woman with the car.

Foods also contain toxic compounds to ward off predators. These toxins are bitter-tasting, pungent-smelling, and often released by plants when threatened by a predator (for example, the proverbial onion that releases toxins when it is cut). When you eat a turnip or cabbage, you are getting a sublethal dose of these toxins. Our strong distaste, or dislike, for bitter foods helps us avoid these toxins (Profet, 1992; Rozin & Kalat, 1971). Interestingly, women are particularly sensitive to bitter tastes and smells during the first trimester of pregnancy. They often experience this sometimes overwhelming negative attitude toward tastes and smells as the nausea of pregnancy sickness, which prevents them from eating these foods and thus protects the fetus from being exposed to dangerous toxins at a particularly vulnerable stage of development (Profet, 1992).

Consider another preference domain where our attitudes

*"It's broccoli, dear."*
*"I say it's spinach, and I say the hell with it."*

**Survival and Preferred Landscapes**
Some evolutionary psychologists claim that people have evolved a preference for landscapes that have water, semi-open space, ground cover, and distant views to the horizon, since these environments provided survival advantages to our ancestors. This view of El Capitan and the Yosemite Valley shows such preferred characteristics.

signal survival-related information about rewards and threats in our environment. Evolutionary psychologists have made interesting claims about why we prefer certain landscapes over others (Orians & Heerwagen, 1992). They assert that people prefer landscapes that have water, semi-open space, even ground cover, and distant views to the horizon. These kinds of environments offered our ancestors reliable sources of water, opportunities for hunting animals and gathering food, shelter, and the means to detect and hide from predators. We still prefer these kinds of environments today, the argument goes, because of the evolutionary advantages these attitudes conferred upon those who possessed and acted upon them.

## THE EGO-DEFENSIVE FUNCTION OF ATTITUDES

In addition to signaling rewards and threats, attitudes also serve an **ego-defensive function**, protecting us from awareness of unpleasant facts, including knowledge of our own unseemly attributes and impulses. We develop certain attitudes, this reasoning holds, to maintain cherished beliefs about ourselves.

One influential ego-defensive account of select attitudes is the **terror management theory** of Greenberg, Pyszczynski, Solomon, and their colleagues (Arndt, Greenberg, & Cook, 2002; Greenberg et al., 1990; Greenberg, Pyszczynski, Solomon, Simon, & Breus, 1994). These theorists argue that the human condition is defined by an existential dilemma. On the one hand, we have a deeply rooted instinct for self-preservation. On the other hand, we are self-aware organisms, and we are acutely conscious of the certainty of our own eventual death. Our most basic desire for life will be thwarted and taken from us, and often in an unpredictable, horrifying fashion.

To ward off the anxiety we feel when contemplating our own demise, we adopt

**ego-defensive function**
An attitudinal function that enables us to maintain cherished beliefs about ourselves by protecting us from awareness of our negative attributes and impulses or from facts that contradict our cherished beliefs or desires.

**terror management theory**
A theory positing that to ward off the anxiety we feel when contemplating our own demise, we cling to cultural worldviews and strongly held values out of a belief that by doing so part of us will survive death.

death-denying attitudes, motivated by the belief that a part of us will survive death. We develop religious systems, which often guarantee a place in the after-life. We live our lives within cultural worldviews and historical narratives that give us the feeling that we are valuable members of something permanent and bigger than our individual selves. We participate in cultural traditions that have lasted hundreds, even thousands of years, such as communion in the Catholic Church. And we create literature and art, in part, the theory goes, to reassure our-selves with the sense of symbolic immortality. According to terror management theory, many attitudes—from religious convictions to the love of literature—are defensive reactions that push fears of mortality out of consciousness. You may recall the tremendous amount of flag display after the attack on the World Trade Center and the Pentagon. Terror management theory holds that such an abun-dant display of patriotic symbols helps to ward off Americans' fear of death.

One of the most thoroughly tested hypotheses derived from terror manage-ment theory is that making people aware of their own mortality should increase their expression of death-denying attitudes. In over seventy-five exper-iments, Pyszczynski, Greenberg, Solomon, and colleagues have made people's mortality salient in a number of ways. Students have had to write about their

**Terror Management and Flag Display** After the attacks on the World Trade Center and the Pentagon on 9/11, Americans displayed patri-otic symbols to show their identifica-tion with something larger than themselves—their nation—a reaction some psychologists have attributed to an effort to ward off anxiety about possible future attacks. (A) Rescue workers erected the U.S. flag at Ground Zero in New York City two days after the attacks, and (B) throughout the city, street vendors did a brisk business selling "I Love America" T-shirts and red, white, and blue ribbons.

own death—for example, answering the question, "What will happen to you as you physically die?" In other studies, participants were interviewed as they passed a mortuary. Compared to control participants, people made aware of their own mortality expressed more positive evaluations of their own group, greater patriotism, increased religious conviction, greater conformity to cultural standards, and a greater inclination to punish moral transgressors. Death is one of life's few certainties, and a source of many of our strongest attitudes and deepest values. Reminders of our inevitable death increase the salience and importance of such attitudes and values.

## THE VALUE-EXPRESSIVE FUNCTION OF ATTITUDES

In the late 1970s and early 1980s, sociologist Kristin Luker spent hundreds of hours interviewing a select group of housewives in their living rooms. These women met regularly and eventually created the seeds of the pro-life movement (Luker, 1984). They did so to reaffirm cherished attitudes—that women can take pride in being mothers and homemakers first and foremost—which they felt were denigrated by the women's movement and the *Roe* v. *Wade* decision that legalized abortion.

This group dynamic reveals a third function of attitudes, their **value-expressive function**, by which attitudes help us express our most cherished values—usually in groups where they can be supported and reinforced. If you were to predict which first-year students at your college would join various groups on your campus—the Korean Christian group, the Young Republicans, the Students for Diversity, Take Back the Night, and so on—surely those students' social attitudes would be a big help in making predictions. We typically choose to express our social and political attitudes in groups, and this is an important factor in motivating us to identify with different groups. These are our **reference groups**—that is, groups whose opinions matter to us and that affect our opinions and beliefs.

The value-expressive function of attitudes accounts for a variety of phenomena. For example, children in the United States express an early allegiance to the Democratic or Republican party, in part to express the values of a very important group, the family (Niemi & Jennings, 1991). People who are deeply committed to having low prejudice are more likely to associate with groups that promote those attitudes, and they feel guilt and shame when their actions contradict their attitudes toward minority groups (Devine, Monteith, Zuwerink, & Elliot, 1991;

**value-expressive function**  An attitudinal function whereby attitudes help us express our most cherished values—usually in groups in which they can be supported and reinforced.

**reference groups**  Groups whose opinions matter to us and that affect our opinions and beliefs.

**Value Expression and Reference Groups**  We express our values through our membership in different reference groups in which we can freely espouse our attitudes with like-minded others. (A) People who like to ride motorcycles and who don't want the government to interfere with their liberties may join biker groups and attend rallies like this one in Sturgis, South Dakota. (B) Young people who enjoy politics and believe in the value of legislative solutions may campaign for political candidates or join youth legislatures like this one in Montgomery, Alabama.

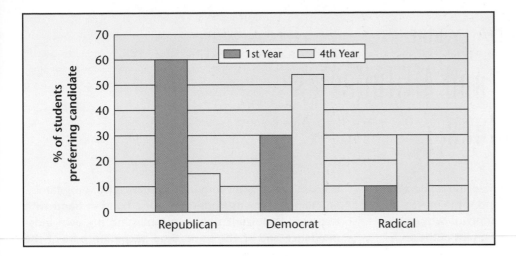

**Figure 7.1  The Value-Expressive Function of Attitudes**    Bennington students' candidate preferences became more liberal over their time at college. (Source: Newcomb, 1958)

Devine, Plant, Amodio, Harmon-Jones, & Vance, 2002; Plant & Devine, 1998). Conservative political groups, it is thought, attract individuals committed to economic freedom and social constraint; liberal political groups attract individuals committed to economic equality and social freedom (Hunter, 1991). And within political groups, it has been found, people tend to overestimate the similarity between their own attitudes and the attitudes of their leaders (Judd, Kenny, & Krosnick, 1983).

Theodore Newcomb's study of student attitudes at Bennington College richly illustrates the value-expressive function of attitudes (Newcomb, 1958). Newcomb studied all 600 students who attended Bennington, an isolated, experimental liberal arts college in pastoral Vermont—brand new at the time of Newcomb's study in the mid-1930s. The school was left-leaning in its politics, and it was run by charismatic, liberal professors. The students, on the other hand, were largely from upper-class, Protestant, staunchly Republican families. The question is: Would the students' conservative background or the liberal context in which they were immersed for several years prevail in shaping their political attitudes?

As it turns out, it was the experience at Bennington College that shaped the students' political attitudes profoundly, and in a lasting fashion (which may, in part, account for your parents' ambivalence about your departure to college!). In a four-year period, most students' political conservatism dropped dramatically. This attitude change played out in their voting preferences, as you can see in Figure 7.1. First-year students were much more likely to prefer the Republican candidate; fourth-year students the Democratic or radical left-wing candidate. And in a follow-up study of 129 students, about twenty-five years later, 60 percent of these students voted for the more liberal presidential candidate, John F. Kennedy, in his election against Richard Nixon, suggesting that the changes these women underwent during college stayed with them throughout their lives.

Other findings attest to the value-expressive function of holding liberal attitudes at Bennington College. Most notably, more liberal students tended to garner greater respect from their Bennington peers and to be better integrated into college groups than the conservative students. The conservative students, in contrast, were less likely to be leaders in the eyes of their peers, and they felt more alienated at the college and were likely to spend more time at home. Whether students became liberals or remained conservatives, their attitudes reflected a deep value-expressive function (see Box 7.2).

Box 7.2   FOCUS ON DAILY LIFE

# Reference Groups and Attitudes as Expressions of Values

Some Bennington students shifted markedly in a liberal or radical direction while at Bennington, and some moved little or not at all. Newcomb's explanation of why some changed and some did not has become a part of the social science vocabulary (Newcomb, 1958). Students who changed tended to treat the college, faculty, and/or fellow students as reference groups—that is, as groups whose opinions mattered to them and whose members were attractive to them. Often, independence from family was cited by such students as a motive for identifying with one or more of the college groups:

> I think my change of opinions has given me intellectual and social self-respect at the same time. . . . As I gradually became more successful in my work and made more friends, I came to feel that it didn't matter so much whether I agreed with my parents. It's all part of the feeling that I really belong here.

> Social security is the focus of it all with me. I became steadily less conservative as long as I was needing to gain in personal security both with students and with faculty.

> Of course there's social pressure here to give up your conservatism. I'm glad of it, because for me this became

the vehicle for achieving independence from my family. So changing my attitudes has gone hand in hand with two very important things: establishing my own independence and at the same time becoming part of the college organism.

In contrast, students who managed to maintain their conservative orientation were likely to be the ones for whom the family remained the reference group or who actively rejected students and faculty at the college as possible reference groups:

> Probably the feeling that my instructors didn't accept me led me to reject their opinions.

> I wanted to disagree with all the noisy liberals, but I was afraid and I couldn't. So I built up a wall inside me against what they said. I found I couldn't compete, so I decided to stick to my father's ideas. For at least two years I've been insulated against all college influences.

> [From a student who had decided early on that she had little chance of social success.] It hurt me at first, but now I don't give a damn. The things I really care about are mostly outside the college.

---

**knowledge function** An attitudinal function whereby attitudes help organize our understanding of the world, guiding how we attend to, store, and retrieve information.

## THE KNOWLEDGE FUNCTION OF ATTITUDES

A fourth and final function of attitudes is the **knowledge function**, by which attitudes help organize our understanding of the world. Our attitudes guide how we attend to, store, and retrieve information, making us more efficient, and on occasion more biased, social perceivers. Most typically, we pay attention to and recall information that is consistent with our preexisting attitudes (Eagly & Chaiken, 1998).

For example, in one illustrative study by Lepper, Ross, Vallone & Keavney supporters of Jimmy Carter and Ronald Reagan, as well as undecided voters, watched a videotape of a debate between the two candidates during the 1980 presidential campaign. Members of these three groups answered a simple question: Who won the debate? As you can see in Figure 7.2, students' preexisting attitudes led parti-

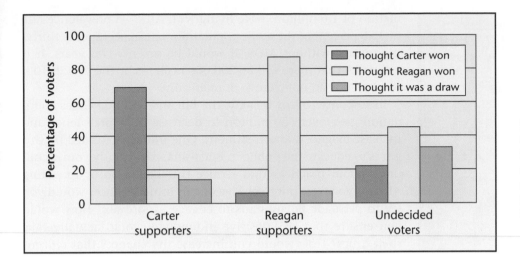

**Figure 7.2 The Knowledge Function of Attitudes** After viewing a video-tape of a presidential debate, Carter and Reagan supporters think their own candidate won the debate. (Source: Lepper, Ross, Vallone & Keavney, unpublished data)

sans to much different conclusions about who emerged victorious. Carter supporters thought Carter had won. Reagan supporters were more strongly convinced that Reagan had won. And the undecided voters were intermediate, although more of them concluded that Reagan had prevailed.

This theme, that our attitudes lead us to seek out and selectively attend to information that bolsters our preexisting attitudes, is a robust one in social psychology, and has motivated several lines of research. We will develop these ideas in different chapters, but it is worth a bit of foreshadowing here. Our attitudes toward ourselves will lead us to recall selectively past experiences that are consistent with those self-evaluations (Greenwald, 1980; Markus, 1977; see Chapter 5). Prejudicial attitudes toward different outgroups lead us to selectively interpret the actions of members of those groups in ways that are consistent with our prejudices (Hamilton & Trolier, 1986; see Chapter 11). We like physically attractive individuals, and we interpret their actions more favorably (Dion, Berscheid, & Walster, 1972; see Chapter 3).

Clearly there is a bit of irony at work here. Our attitudes are built upon our experiences and our acquisition of knowledge. Yet, eventually our attitudes become entrenched, and they bias us toward inferring that new information supports our attitudes. In the service of efficiency, our attitudes can sometimes sacrifice open-minded inquiry.

**LOOKING BACK**, we have seen that our attitudes are vital to our daily living. They help us identify rewarding and threatening objects and contexts. They help us avoid unpleasant realities about life and who we are. They are part of why we belong to different groups. And they are powerful guides to our construal of the social world. Changing them, we shall now see, is no trivial matter. The question of how to do so has led to the enduring study of persuasion.

## PERSUASION AND ATTITUDE CHANGE

The small country of Botswana, Africa, has been one of the most devastated by the AIDS epidemic. In 2004, it was estimated that 260,000 people, out of a pop-

**Attitude Change and AIDS Prevention**   With the goal of stopping the spread of AIDS in Africa, public health officials have initiated campaigns to raise public awareness, to change sexual practices, and to increase diagnosis and treatment. This billboard stresses prevention, care, and openness so that the AIDS virus will no longer ravage the population and leave behind orphans without parents to care for them.

ulation of 1.6 million, were living with AIDS—a prevalence rate of 36.5 percent of the adult population. Life expectancy is thirty-nine years; without AIDS, it would be seventy-two years. It is estimated that there will be 200,000 orphans by the year 2010 if these trends do not change dramatically.

In response to this tragedy, the Bill and Melinda Gates Foundation gave over $50 million to decrease AIDS prevalence and increase diagnosis and treatment. One initiative funded by this gift is to educate the public in Botswana, particularly young children, about practices that reduce the likelihood of spreading AIDS. If you were put in charge of this initiative, how would you try to persuade Botswanans to engage in safe sex? How would you ensure that HIV-positive individuals would actually take their drugs? How would you increase the chances that citizens would volunteer for HIV tests, which are given as a routine part of health checkups?

The barriers to these kinds of attitude change are significant. There is a certain stigma in many parts of Africa associated with the use of condoms. The same is true of admitting to having AIDS. It is hard to change centuries-old sexual attitudes and practices. If the spread of AIDS is the most significant health crisis facing the world today, this campaign may well be one of the most ambitious and challenging persuasion efforts ever undertaken. The literature we are about to review suggests that there are no simple, one-solution-fits-all, sources of persuasion. In fact, there are multiple routes to persuasion, and our success in persuasion depends critically upon whom we are trying to persuade.

## A TWO-PROCESS APPROACH TO PERSUASION

**Elaboration Likelihood Model**
A model of persuasion that maintains that there are two different routes of persuasion: the central route and the peripheral route.

**heuristic-systematic model of persuasion**   A model of persuasion that maintains that there are two different routes of persuasion: the systematic route and the heuristic route.

**central (systematic) route of persuasion**   A persuasive route wherein people think carefully and deliberately about the content of a message, attending to its logic, cogency, and arguments, as well as to related evidence and principles.

Two important theoretical accounts were developed in the 1980s to explain how people change their attitudes in response to persuasive messages. The two accounts, Shelly Chaiken's **heuristic-systematic model** of persuasion (Chaiken, 1980; Chaiken, Liberman, & Eagly, 1989) and Richard Petty and John Cacioppo's **Elaboration Likelihood Model** of persuasion (Petty & Cacioppo, 1979, 1984, 1986) were developed independently and employ different vocabularies. But in their essentials they are quite similar (see Figure 7.3). For the sake of convenience, our discussion is organized around the Elaboration Likelihood Model (ELM).

The ELM starts from the assumption that there are two routes to persuasion. Through the **central route** (known as the **systematic route** in Chaiken's model), people think carefully and deliberately about the content of the message. They attend to the logic and cogency of the arguments contained in the message, as well as to the evidence and principles that are cited, and they retrieve relevant experiences, memories, and images. All of this elaborate thinking can lead the individual to change an attitude or not, based on a sifting of the arguments and the evidence.

Through the **peripheral route** (known as the **heuristic route** in Chaiken's model), the individual primarily attends to superficial aspects of the message that are tangential to its substance. Here the individual might consider how long the message is or how expert the communicator seems. Using the peripheral route, the individual relies upon relatively simple, sometimes implicit or unconscious cues such as communication heuristics, or rules of thumb, which justify attitude change. Thus, the person might change an attitude because "a lot of people seem to be following this course of action" or "because there are a lot of arguments here." Or peripheral cues might change the individual's basic emotional reaction to the attitude object. An attractive communicator, for example, might make the receiver feel more positively toward the attitude object simply by eliciting general feelings of liking or attraction.

What determines whether we will go through the central or peripheral route in responding to a persuasive message? One factor is our *motivation* to devote time and energy to a message. When the message has personal consequences for us, for example, we are more likely to go through the central route. A second factor is our *ability* to process the message in depth. When the message is clear, and we have time, we are able to process it deeply. When we have little motivation and little ability to process the message, we instead attend to the peripheral cues associated with the message—for example, the appearance and credentials of the communicator.

In more concrete terms, three factors make the central route to persuasion more likely: (1) the *personal relevance* of the message—that is, whether it bears upon our goals, concerns, and well-being; (2) our *knowledge* about the issue—the more we know, the more likely we are to scrutinize the message with care and thoughtfulness; and (3) whether the message makes us feel *responsible* for some action or outcome—for example, when we have to explain the message to others. In contrast, peripheral processing is triggered by factors that (1) reduce our motivation, or (2) interfere with our ability to attend to the message carefully (Eagly & Chaiken, 1993; Petty & Cacioppo, 1986; Petty & Wegener, 1998). Thus, when people are distracted—for example, if they are carrying out some other task—they will be more likely to attend primarily to the peripheral cues of the message. This is also true of people who are tired, or who are in an uncomfortable posture, or who are given messages that are incomplete or hard to comprehend (Kiesler & Mathog, 1968; Petty & Wegener, 1998).

> **peripheral (heuristic) route of persuasion** A persuasive route wherein people attend to relatively simple, superficial cues related to the message, such as the length of the message or the expertise or attractiveness of the communicator.

> "Of the modes of persuasion furnished by the spoken word there are three kinds. The first kind depends on the personal character of the speaker; the second on putting the audience into a certain frame of mind; the third on the proof, provided by the words of the speech itself."
>
> —ARISTOTLE

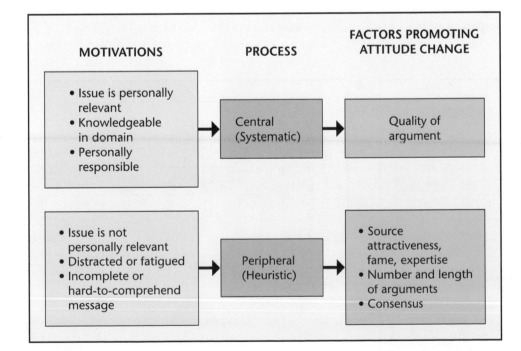

**Figure 7.3  A Two-Process Approach to Persuasion**  According to Petty and Cacioppo's Elaboration Likelihood Model, there are two routes to persuasion: a central route and a peripheral route, which are engaged by different motivations and which promote attitude change by different factors. Chaiken's model refers to these two processes as the systematic and heuristic routes.

To test the ELM approach to persuasion, researchers typically first generate strong and weak arguments related to an issue—for example, establishing mandatory senior exams at a university. They then present these strong and weak arguments as part of a message. They also vary the potency of various peripheral cues associated with the message, such as the number of arguments offered or the communicator's fame. Finally, they typically vary some factor, such as the personal relevance of the issue, to manipulate the likelihood that the individual will process the message "centrally" or "peripherally." If participants process the message via the central route to persuasion, they should be influenced mainly by the strong and not the weak arguments. The strength of the arguments should be less important for individuals who are attending only to the peripheral cues of the message, however, as these participants should be more affected by such things as the number of arguments and the attractiveness of the communicator.

Consider one study that varied the strength of the arguments, the relevance of the issue, and a peripheral cue, the source expertise. In this study, participants either read eight weak arguments in support of a comprehensive exam to be implemented at their school, or eight strong arguments (Petty, Cacioppo, & Goldman, 1981). Personal relevance was manipulated by notifying the participants that this exam would be initiated either the following year, which would mean the participants would have to take the exam, or in ten years, after the students' graduation (presumably!). Finally, source expertise was varied: half of the participants were told the arguments were generated by a local high school class, and half were told that the arguments were generated by the "Carnegie Commission on Higher Education" chaired by a Princeton University professor.

Take a close look at Figure 7.4. You can see that when the message was not relevant to the students—that is, when the exam was to be implemented ten years later—the expertise of the source mattered but the strength of the argument did not. The participants with scant motivation to attend to the message gave little thought to the quality of the arguments, but they were moved by whether the arguments were produced by a high school class or a professorial committee. The results differed for participants who would have to take the exam, for whom the message was clearly relevant. They were more persuaded by strong than by weak arguments, but they were not influenced by whether the communicator was an expert or not.

**Figure 7.4 Central or Peripheral Route to Persuasion** (A) Strong arguments lead to attitude change for participants for whom the issue is personally relevant more than for those for whom the issue is not relevant. (B) The expertise of the source of the communication, in contrast, matters more for participants for whom the issue is not personally relevant, suggesting they mainly attend to peripheral aspects of the message. (Source: Adapted from Petty & Cacioppo, 1986, p. 154).

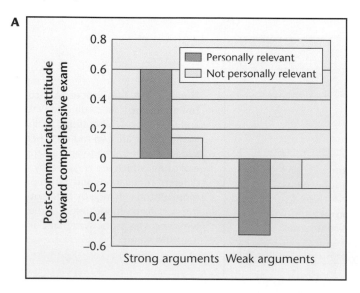

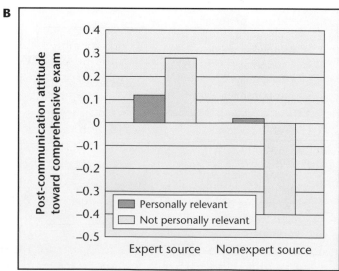

The routes to persuasion, then, are twofold. Some messages persuade by prompting us to thoughtfully integrate new arguments and evidence into our belief systems, thus prompting change. Other messages persuade with more superficial cues—the beauty or charm of the communicator, for example—or even with subliminal cues (see Box 7.3). If you're interested in more enduring attitude change, however, your best bet is to convince people through the central route. With the central route, people attend to the message more carefully, and its effects are more pronounced. The central compared to the peripheral route of persuasion is thought to bring about attitude change that is more enduring, more resistant to persuasion, and more predictive of behavior (Eagly & Chaiken, 1993; Mackie, 1987; Petty, Haugtvedt, & Smith, 1995).

## THE WHO, WHAT, AND WHOM OF PERSUASION

Now that you have a better sense of how persuasive messages work, let's look at some more specific investigations of how—and how well—persuasion works. Many of these studies were inspired by an influential approach to attitude change developed by Carl Hovland and his colleagues at Yale University, starting in the 1940s and 1950s (Hovland, Janis, & Kelley, 1953). Their Yale School approach, which was derived from their work on mass communication for the army during World War II, highlighted the rational, deliberative processes involved in attitude change. These processes included attending to the message, comprehending it, integrating it into preexisting knowledge and beliefs, accepting it, and remembering it. In the course of studying attitude change, Hovland and his colleagues also analyzed and studied the different components making up the persuasive message that was designed to bring about the attitude change. They broke down the persuasive message into three components: (1) the who, or source, of the message, (2) the what, or content, of the message, and (3) the whom, or target of the message.

> **source characteristics** Characteristics of the person who delivers the message, including the person's attractiveness, credibility, and expertise.

*Source Characteristics*  Are we more likely to buy cereal heartily eaten and advertised by Tiger Woods or by Joe Average? Are we more likely to buy a brand of aspirin recommended by the American Medical Association or by the League of Women Voters? Are we more likely to buy cars advertised by young, beautiful women or by middle-aged, average-looking accountants? Some corporations think that star athletes, expert associations, and beautiful models help to sell products, as shown by the large number of endorsements by Tiger Woods, who is making scores of millions of dollars every year ($62 million in 2002) for promoting various products. Advertisers believe that *who* delivers the message, or what we'll call **source characteristics**, is an important part of a persuasive message. These source characteristics are independent of the actual content of the message, and they can be powerful peripheral means for changing people's attitudes.

A first source characteristic is the *attractiveness* of the communicator. Beautiful movie stars like Catherine Zeta-Jones make millions of dollars advertising consumer products, from cell phones to investment houses. They appear regularly in public service announcements—for example, urging teens to read, stay in school, or avoid drugs and cigarettes. From one perspective, this makes no sense, for beauty (or celebrity) has

**Persuasion and Celebrity Endorsements**  Advertisers often use celebrities to endorse and advertise their products, believing that who delivers the message is an important factor in convincing people to buy their product. Canon has made Maria Sharapova, the Russian tennis star and 2004 women's Wimbledon champion, its global spokesperson.

## Box 7.3 FOCUS ON POPULAR CULTURE

# A Subliminal Route to Persuasion?

In 1990, the rock band Judas Priest was tried for contributing to the suicide deaths of Ray Belknap and James Vance. Prosecutors alleged that the men had been led down the path to suicide by the subliminal message, "Do it," that the band had embedded into one of its songs. Can subliminal messages have such powerful effects? Might subliminal messages be a third, implicit or unconscious route to persuasion?

We will see numerous times in this book that subliminally presented stimuli can activate certain concepts, and even shape people's everyday thoughts, feelings, and actions (Dijksterhuis, Aarts, & Smith, 2005). Consider a pair of laboratory experiments that suggest that subliminal persuasion attempts may be effective. In one, pictures of a target person were shown to participants immediately after a subliminal presentation of either a pleasant image (for example, a child playing with a doll) or an unpleasant one (for example, a bloody shark). When later asked to evaluate the target person, those for whom the target was paired with positive subliminal images provided more favorable evaluations than those exposed to negative images (Krosnick, Betz, Jussim, & Lynn, 1992). In a study that directly examined the impact of subliminal messages on behavior, participants were told not to drink anything for three hours before arriving at the experiment (Strahan, Spencer, & Zanna, 2002). Upon arrival, half the participants were allowed to quench their thirst and half were kept thirsty. Participants were then subliminally primed, some with words related to thirst (thirst, dry) and some with neutral words (pirate, won). They were then allowed to drink as much as they wanted of each of two beverages. Thirsty participants who were primed with thirst-related words drank significantly more than thirsty participants primed with neutral words. A follow-up study using the same procedure found that subliminal messages can even influence a person's *choice* of beverage. Specifically, the two beverages that participants were offered were described as sports drinks, with one labeled Super-Quencher and the other Power-Pro. When asked at the end of the experiment how many discount coupons for the two drinks they would like, thirsty participants who were exposed to thirst-related subliminal messages requested 24 percent more of the Super-Quencher coupons than thirsty participants exposed to neutral subliminal messages.

Should we be alarmed that advertisers, political campaign managers, or rock bands might try to alter our behavior by bombarding us with messages we can't see and hence can't defend ourselves against? Not so fast. There are a number of important differences between the outside world and the laboratory environment in these experiments that make it less likely that these effects could be obtained in daily life. The target of the persuasion attempt in these studies is typically something about which one has no firm opinion, such as a new sports drink. It's one thing to shift attitudes and behavior with respect to neutral stimuli; it is another thing entirely to do so with respect to more familiar, psychologically significant stimuli—for example, to get Republicans to vote for a Democratic candidate or to induce Coke drinkers to switch to Pepsi. In addition, in the laboratory the subliminal message is presented right before the target attitude or behavior is assessed, and the individual encounters no competing messages in the interim. That's rarely, if ever, the case in the real world. A subliminal command to "Drink Coke" could conceivably motivate people to leave their seats to get a drink but, once in the lobby, with advertisements of all sorts of merchandise screaming at them, they might be as likely to drink Pepsi as Coke, or even to order a candy bar instead of a beverage.

In fact, there has never been a demonstration, nor is there any reason to believe that there ever would be a demonstration, of subliminal stimuli inducing people to do something that they are opposed to doing. There is no reason to believe that being subliminally primed with the words "do it" would lead anyone not already comfortable with the idea of homicide to kill another person. Nor is there any reason to believe that Democrats can be subliminally induced to vote for Republican candidates, Apple enthusiasts to buy a Dell Computer, or clean-cut adolescents to join a cult.

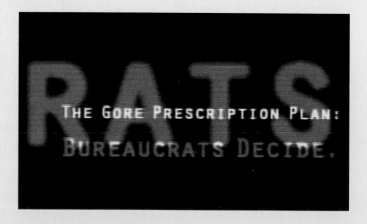

**Subliminal Advertising**  In a television ad run by the Republicans during the 2000 presidential election, the word "RATS" was quickly flashed on the screen in a subliminal attack on Al Gore, the Democratic candidate, and his Medicare plan.

**Credibility and Persuasion** If people believe that a communicator is sincere, knowledgeable, and trustworthy, they will be more likely to believe his message. Martin Luther King, Jr., is pictured here at the Lincoln Memorial during the March on Washington in August 1963, as he is about to give his "I Have a Dream" speech. His actions in the months leading up to the rally, as well as his strong and poetic words and dramatic presentation, contributed to his credibility and ability to persuade.

no logical connection to the trustworthiness of an opinion about a consumer product or risky behavior. Here the ELM helps. Attractive communicators promote attitude change through the peripheral route of persuasion. We like and trust physically attractive people (see Chapter 3), and thus we are more likely to endorse the attitudes they communicate.

In general, attractive communicators appear to be more persuasive than less attractive communicators (Petty & Cacioppo, 1986). More attractive communicators are particularly persuasive to people for whom the message is not terribly pressing and who have little knowledge in the domain, both of which are circumstances that make people more likely to attend to the message's peripheral cues (Chaiken, 1980; Petty, Cacioppo, & Schumann, 1983; Wood & Kallgren, 1988).

A second influential source characteristic is the *credibility* of the communicator. Credibility refers to the expertise and trustworthiness of the communicator. Credible individuals often have a certain style of speaking: they speak with little hesitation, and they make eye contact, express emotion, use dramatic gestures, and avoid signs of nervousness, such as face touches (Mehrabian & Williams, 1969; Riggio & Friedman, 1983). Next time you watch a presidential debate, or a newscaster broadcasting the evening news, watch for these clues to credibility and notice how the communicator is probably doing everything possible to avoid showing signs of insincerity.

Advertisers try to use credibility to their advantage. Ads for toothpaste and aspirin cite the testimonials from medical professionals who endorse the product. Actors who play doctors on television, and who have no obvious knowledge about medicine, have even been brought in to endorse health-related products. Is this an effective tactic? What would the ELM predict? As we hope you anticipated, such communicators produce more attitude change in circumstances that promote the peripheral route to persuasion—namely, when the individual is less motivated and has reduced ability to attend to the message. Thus, commu-

> "Every time a message seems to grab us, and we think, 'I just might try it,' we are at the nexus of choice and persuasion that is advertising."
>
> —ANDREW HACKER

nicators perceived to be high in credibility produce more persuasion when the topic is of little personal relevance to the target are when the target is distracted, since such a target would not be paying much attention to the message itself (Petty, Cacioppo, & Goldman, 1981; Kiesler & Mathog, 1968; Rhine & Severance, 1970).

What about all the noncredible communicators who crowd the airwaves these days? The crackpots moralizing about AIDS, blathering about the problems in the Middle East, or maintaining that the Holocaust never happened. Do these messages fall on deaf ears?

An early study by Hovland and Weiss (1951) suggests otherwise. In this study, participants first rated the likelihood that a nuclear submarine would be built in the near future (at the time they did not exist). Five days later, participants read an essay about the imminence of nuclear submarines, written either by the highly credible physicist Robert Oppenheimer, the "father of the atomic bomb," or by a noncredible journalist who worked for *Pravda*, the propaganda newspaper of the former Soviet Union. As one might expect, the Oppenheimer essay led to greater attitude change than the essay by the less credible *Pravda* writer, even though the content of the essay was exactly the same.

Much more surprising, however, were the results observed in the measures gathered four weeks later. Here, participants who had read the essay by the *Pravda* writer, although unmoved initially, actually shifted their attitudes toward the position he advocated. This latter effect came to be known as the **sleeper effect**—that is, messages from unreliable sources exert little influence initially, but over time they have the potential to shift people's attitudes. Careful research by Anthony Pratkanis, Tony Greenwald, and their colleagues has identified how the sleeper effect works. It seems that, over time, people dissociate the source of the message from the message itself. You hear some loose cannon on talk radio arguing forcibly against the evidence for global warming or arguing excitedly that sexual behavior is not a cause of AIDS. Initially you discount his message because of his lack of credibility. But over time, the message has the chance to influence your views because you dissociate the source of the message from its content. Importantly, when cues that discount the noncredible source *precede* the message—for example, when the trustworthiness of the communicator is called into question at the get-go—the sleeper effect does not occur (Pratkanis, Greenwald, Leippe, & Baumgardner, 1988). In this case, people develop a negative reaction to the ensuing message and counterargue against it, thus reducing its impact.

*Message Characteristics* Since Aristotle, philosophers have sought to elucidate the principles of persuasive messages. You can take courses on rhetoric that are devoted to this very issue. What are the **message characteristics** that make a communication persuasive? If you were hired by an aspiring political candidate to head up her ad campaign, what strategies would you employ? By now you should anticipate what the ELM might say: that it depends on the audience's motivation and ability to process the message.

As we saw in Figure 7.3, *high-quality messages* are more persuasive in general, and are especially so for people who find the message relevant, who have knowledge in the domain, and who feel responsible for the issue. What, then, makes for high-quality messages? In general, higher-quality messages have certain attributes. They refer to desirable yet novel consequences of taking action in response to the message (Burnstein & Vinokur, 1973). They often appeal to core values of

**sleeper effect** An effect that occurs when messages from unreliable sources initially exert little influence but later cause individuals' attitudes to shift.

**message characteristics** Aspects of the message itself, including the quality of the evidence and the explicitness of its conclusions.

the audience (Cacioppo, Petty, & Sidera, 1982). Not surprisingly, messages presented in overly complex, confusing, illogical, or garbled or technical language bring about less attitude change than clearer, more straightforward messages (Chaiken & Eagly, 1976; Leippe & Elkin, 1987).

What are other elements of high-quality messages? In general, you will produce more attitude change if you make your conclusions explicit (Hovland, Lumsdaine, & Sheffield, 1949). Yet, with more knowledgeable audiences, it often is better to make more implicit arguments, and to let the audience reach their own conclusions (Stayman & Kardes, 1992). You will also be more persuasive if you explicitly refute the opposition, thereby giving the receiver of the message material with which to counterargue against subsequent opposing messages (Hass & Linder, 1972). This is true, at any rate, for informed and relatively intelligent audiences (Petty & Wegener, 1998). And you will be more persuasive if you argue against your own self-interest. For example, Walster, Aronson, and Abrahams (1966) found that a message delivered by a prison inmate advocating longer prison sentences was more persuasive than a message in which the same prisoner argued for shorter sentences. When someone argues in a direction contrary to obvious self-interest, the source of the message is perceived to be more sincere.

What about the truth of persuasive messages? Do facts stand a chance when pitted against vivid, but unrepresentative statements? Research by Hamill, Wilson, and Nisbett (1980) suggests that *vivid information* embedded in a personal narrative with emotional appeal can be more persuasive than statistical facts that are objectively more informative. In their study, the researchers first assessed participants' attitudes toward welfare. In one condition, participants read a vivid, gripping story about a woman who was a lifetime welfare recipient. This mirrored a story Ronald Reagan told to great effect about a "welfare queen," a lifetime recipient of welfare who exploited the system to enjoy a life of comfort and leisure. In another condition, participants were given facts about welfare: that the average stay was two years, and that only 10 percent of welfare recipients receive welfare for four years or more. In a third condition, participants were given both types of information. In this condition, it should have been clear that the case they read about was quite atypical of welfare recipients in general. Which message do you think would lead to more attitude change: the vivid but unrepresentative story, or the plain facts? You no doubt are anticipating our punch line: students were much more likely to change their attitudes after hearing the vivid story—even when they also had the cold statistics. The facts did little to alter their attitudes.

Vivid images abound in the media, and apparently to great effect. Anti-abortion messages often include enlarged pictures of aborted fetuses. The nightly news highlights the single murder, kidnapping, or fire in its local coverage. More generally, a common phenomenon that speaks to the power of vivid images is the **identifiable victim effect**. When "Baby Jessica" McClure was trapped inside a well for fifty-eight hours in 1987, her plight tugged at the hearts of the entire nation and galvanized the efforts of people from all over. Meanwhile, countless children of the same age were dying of preventable childhood diseases, child abuse, and neglect. If similar resources were spent on preventive medicine, hundreds of lives could be saved. Such abstract, "statistical" lives, however, seldom compete successfully with the vivid, flesh-and-blood life of an identifiable victim (Collins, Taylor, Wood, & Thompson, 1988; Shedler & Manis, 1986; Taylor & Thompson, 1982).

**Arguing against Self-Interest**
Patrick Reynolds, the grandson and heir of the late R. J. Reynolds (founder of the R. J. Reynolds Tobacco Company, the second-largest tobacco company in the United States and manufacturer of such brands as Camel, Kool, Winston, and Salem cigarettes), is shown speaking to students about the dangers of smoking. He watched his father and older brother both die of emphysema and lung cancer brought on by cigarette smoking and decided to devote his life to anti-smoking advocacy. His anti-smoking speeches and support for a smoke-free society have high credibility given his family history and the fact that his arguments, if effective, would have the effect of reducing his inheritance.

**identifiable victim effect** The tendency to be more moved by the plight of a single, vivid individual than by a more abstract aggregate of individuals.

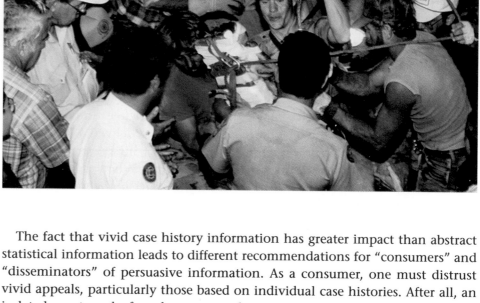

**The Identifiable Victim Effect**    Vivid images in the media can profoundly shape people's attitudes and sense of what is important. The media reported to the nation that an eighteen-month-old baby, Jessica McClure, fell into a narrow backyard well in Midland, Texas, and was trapped there for fifty-eight hours in 1987. Television cameras recorded every move of the rescue workers who struggled to free her from the eight-inch-wide pipe in which she was trapped. The workers are shown here with Jessica just after they rescued her. People care about the plight of identifiable victims much more than they do about abstract victims.

> "The death of a single Russian soldier is a tragedy. The death of a million soldiers is a statistic."
> —JOSEPH STALIN

The fact that vivid case history information has greater impact than abstract statistical information leads to different recommendations for "consumers" and "disseminators" of persuasive information. As a consumer, one must distrust vivid appeals, particularly those based on individual case histories. After all, an isolated event can be found to support almost any position. Although individual episodes can be riveting, they might not be representative of the general state of affairs. Consumer beware! As a presenter of information, on the other hand, the recommendation is the opposite. If cold statistics indicate that one's claims are valid, then the presentation of those statistics should be leavened with anecdotes aplenty. Their power to capture attention should be employed for one's own and the audience's benefit.

Let's return to our hypothetical question about running an AIDS education campaign in Botswana. In designing a public service announcement or pamphlet to hand out in schools, you might be inclined to scare the daylights out of your audience. Should you show them pictures of AIDS victims as they waste away, or pictures of orphaned eight-year-olds raising their one- and two-year-old siblings? The ELM would offer somewhat competing notions regarding fear and persuasion. On the one hand, intense fear could disrupt the careful, thoughtful processing of the message, thus reducing the chances of persuasion. On the other hand, the right kind of fear might heighten the participant's motivation to attend to the message, thus increasing the likelihood of attitude change.

What does the evidence say? In general, it is advisable to make health ad campaigns frightening, and to also provide information about how to act on the fear that is created (Boster & Mongeau, 1984). In a study that first lent support to this recommendation, Howard Leventhal and his colleagues tried to change the smoking habits of participants in one of three ways. Some participants were shown a graphic film of the effects of lung cancer, which included footage of a lung operation in which the blackened lung of a smoker was removed. Other participants were given a pamphlet with suggestions about how to quit smoking. A third group was shown the film and given the pamphlet (Leventhal, Watts, & Pagano, 1967). Participants who saw the scary film reduced their smoking more

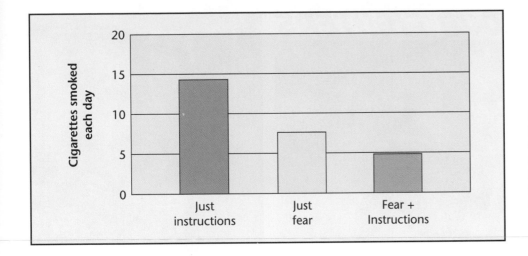

**Figure 7.5  Fear and Persuasive Messages**   Inducing fear about something by showing vivid images reduced smoking substantially more than simply providing instructions about quitting. Fear plus instructions was the most effective treatment.

than did those who just read the pamphlet (and thus would not have had their motivation to quit increased by a fear induction). Fear by itself can be persuasive. But participants who both saw the film and read the pamphlet decreased their smoking the most, as you can see in Figure 7.5, which presents participants' self-reports of their daily smoking behavior one month after the intervention. In general, persuasive messages that provide information that can be acted upon can be highly effective (Leventhal, 1970; Leventhal, Watts, & Pagano, 1967; Robberson & Rogers, 1988). On the other hand, it is possible to frighten people so much that they will choose to deny the danger rather than act to combat it, especially if there is no clear recommendation about how to deal with the threat (Becker & Josephs, 1988; Job, 1988; Rogers & Mewborn, 1976).

Not only do vividness and fear matter in a persuasive message, but how a message is targeted to a particular cultural group also matters. Thus, a substantial difference exists in the sort of message content that one finds in the media of independent and interdependent societies. Marketing experts Sang-pil Han and Sharon Shavitt analyzed the advertisements in American and Korean news magazines and women's magazines (Han & Shavitt, 1994). They found that the American ads emphasized benefits to the individual ("Make your way through the crowd" or "Alive with pleasure"), whereas Korean ads focused on benefits to collectives ("We have a way of bringing people closer together" or "Ringing out the news of business friendships that really work"). Han and Shavitt also conducted experiments in which they manipulated the content of advertisements and measured their effectiveness. They found that the individual-oriented ads were more effective with American participants and that the collective-oriented ads were more effective with Korean participants.

*Receiver Characteristics*   Communication by its very nature always involves both a communicator and someone who receives the message. We have seen throughout this section that the receiver, or target, matters. Consistent with the postulates of the ELM, receivers who are more personally involved, knowledgeable, and responsible respond to messages quite differently than do those who are less motivated. More generally, are certain people more vulnerable or amenable to persuasion? We will now see that **receiver characteristics** such as personality, mood, and age can matter, often in surprising and significant ways.

**receiver characteristics**  Characteristics of the person who receives the message, including age, mood, and motivation to attend to the message.

**Message Characteristics and Targeting**   Messages may differ based on the times and culture. Messages are often targeted to collective concerns in interdependent societies and to individual concerns in independent societies. Similarly, messages may vary based on the times in the same society. (A) During World War II, U.S. army posters stressed collective concerns. (B) In recent times, with the advent of the volunteer army, U.S. army recruitment posters have used the slogan "an army of one" and have stressed how the army can bring out the best in the individual.

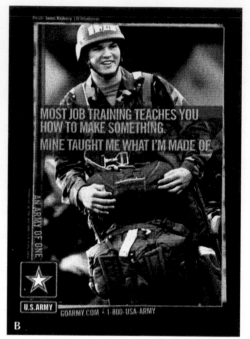

One facet of personality that influences the likelihood of attitude change is called the *need for cognition* (Cacioppo, Petty, Feinstein, & Jarvis, 1996). This refers to the degree to which people like to think deeply about issues. People high in the need for cognition like to think, to puzzle, to ponder, and to consider multiple perspectives on issues. This is the kind of person who passes her time on the subway reading *Scientific American* or completing complex puzzles. People low in the need for cognition don't find thought and contemplation to be that much fun. How does the need for cognition influence persuasion? As you might imagine, people with a high need for cognition are more persuaded by high-quality arguments, and they are relatively unmoved by peripheral cues of persuasion (Cacioppo, Petty, & Morris, 1983; Haugtvedt & Petty, 1992).

A second important audience characteristic is *mood*. People who are good at communication go to great lengths to create particular moods in their audience. Ronald Reagan, known as "the great communicator," was famous for his disarming, infectious humor during his speeches and press conferences. Hitler staged enormous rallies, surrounded by bold, Nazi banners, awesome displays of military strength, and thousands of supporters signaling in unison, for his most important speeches. His intent was to stir the emotions of his audience to make them more receptive to his ideas.

Early studies found that people who were exposed to persuasive messages while eating or listening to beautiful music were more likely to change their attitudes (McGuire, 1985). More recent work by Duane Wegener and Richard Petty is starting to clarify which messages are more persuasive for people in different moods. In general, the recommendation is for the message content to match the goals and content of the mood. Thus, more pessimistic, counter-attitudinal messages tend to prompt greater message processing in sad or depressed people, whereas uplifting, optimistic, pro-attitudinal messages prompt greater message processing in happy people (Bless et al., 1996; Mackie & Worth, 1989; Wegener & Petty, 1994; Wegener, Petty, & Smith, 1995).

Finally, what about the *age* of the audience? Researchers consistently find that younger people are more susceptible to persuasive messages than are adults or the elderly (Sears, 1986). This finding has great real-world significance. One problem is the reliability of children as witnesses in legal cases. To what extent should we take seriously the testimony of young children—for example, in child abuse cases—if their attitudes can be so readily altered by motivated attorneys and misleading questions (see work by Elizabeth Loftus to discover the extent to which such manipulations are possible; Loftus, 1993, 2003)? Another problem concerns the extent of advertising directed at young children. Given that advertising, and the media more generally, can shape people's attitudes (see next section), perhaps we should worry about the immense amount of advertising that is directed at children aged sixteen and younger.

David Sears has drawn upon this link between age and susceptibility to persuasion as part of a broader critique of the persuasion literature (Sears, 1986). Most studies of attitude change involve participants who are students in their first couple of years in college. These individuals are at a developmental stage that is very dynamic, as we saw in the Bennington College study, and they are particularly prone to attitude change. As people age, their attitudes become less malleable. Sears poses a thorny question: Does the literature on attitude change that we have reviewed generalize to other age groups? It is likely, he concludes, that the persuasion literature overestimates the extent to which we change our attitudes. In the final section of this chapter, we will elaborate on this theme and consider instances in which people resist attitude change.

Let's now return to your hypothetical job in Botswana, where you must take on the daunting task of increasing AIDS awareness and safe-sex practices. How might the literature on persuasion help you? Perhaps the most important lesson is to tailor your message according to whether the audience is likely to go through the central or peripheral route to persuasion. Certain Botswanans are likely to go through the central route. These are individuals for whom AIDS is personally relevant, who know quite a bit about AIDS, and who feel a sense of personal responsibility to stop its spread. Think of parents who are trying to teach their children to engage in safe-sex practices. For people like this, there is no substitute for high-quality messages, ones that are logical and clear, that make subtle rather than heavy-handed recommendations, and that appeal to clear consequences and values.

**Persuasion and Mood** The mood of an audience can affect whether a message will lead to attitude change. (A) In Germany in the 1930s, Adolf Hitler staged rallies like this one of Hitler Youth to create a mood of strength and unity that would encourage people to support his ideas. (B) In Poland in the 1980s, emboldened and energized by the election of a Polish pope (John Paul II) and his visit to the land of his birth, demonstrators marched in the streets with a banner for Solidarnosc ("Solidarity"), the first Polish trade union, despite the government's ban of the union.

For many other people, and in many contexts, the peripheral route to persuasion is likely to be a better bet. This is likely to be true for younger audiences, those who know less about AIDS, or for people who don't think that AIDS is relevant to them. In contexts where people do not have the time to think carefully—for example, in reading a placard on a public bus—the peripheral route is likely to be more effective. In these situations, you'd best design messages that use attractive and credible communicators, that have clear conclusions, and that have the weight of various communication heuristics working in your favor.

**LOOKING BACK,** we have seen how the Elaboration Likelihood Model spells out two ways of processing persuasive messages. In the central route to processing, it is primarily the quality of the arguments that is attended to. In the peripheral route, such factors as the sheer number of arguments and communicator attractiveness are likely to be more important. Messages tend to be more effective if they are clearly laid out, if they refute opposing messages, and if they are vivid. Recipients of a message who have a high need for cognition are more likely to process messages through the central route. Moreover, recipients who are in a good mood are more persuadable than those who are not, and younger people are more persuadable than older people. We next consider how these and other factors are used by the media in their attempts to persuade us.

## THE MEDIA AND PERSUASION

The mass communication media make up a $200-billion-a-year industry. Each year the average American watches 1,550 hours of television, or about 3 to 4 hours a day, listens to almost 1,200 hours of radio, and spends about 180 hours reading newspapers. Each day the average American sees about 100 ads on television and is exposed to another 100 to 300 ads in newsprint and the radio (Pratkanis & Aronson, 2000). All told, half of Americans' waking hours are spent in contact with the media, which significantly exceeds the time they spend in face-to-face social interaction with friends and family.

Given our media-saturated lives, it's easy to imagine that almost all of our attitudes are shaped by mass communications. Decisions to buy Dockers or Khakis from the Gap, or a Dell or an Apple laptop, could be guided by commercials recently seen on TV or heard on the radio. Which candidate we choose in the voting booth could be guided by recent political ads. Many conspiracy theories capitalize on this notion: according to these accounts, daily life is controlled by

**The Media and Persuasion** In the 1964 presidential campaign, Lyndon Johnson ran a television ad in which a little girl stood in a field pulling off the petals of a daisy as a voice counted down, culminating in a nuclear explosion. The ad was an emotional attack on Barry Goldwater, the Republican presidential candidate, indirectly portraying him as too ready to use nuclear weapons. The ad only ran once, but it may well have contributed to the defeat of Goldwater and the election of Johnson as president.

all-pervasive media organizations, owned and operated by a hidden and nefarious elite. But does everyone believe this is so?

Most people believe that other people are profoundly susceptible to the media. Moreover, in what is known as the **third-person effect**, most people assume that "other people" are more prone to being influenced by persuasive campaigns than they themselves are (Duck & Mullin, 1995; Hoorens & Ruiter, 1996; Perloff, 1993; Vallone, Ross & Lepper, 1985). They do so because they assume that others do not share their powers of rational analysis and restraint. In one study of this third-person effect, participants judged the likely impact of three media presentations on themselves and on other respondents (Innes & Zeitz, 1988). For all three presentations—a political ad campaign, a depiction of media violence, and a campaign designed to deter people from associating with individuals who drink and drive—participants rated others as more likely to be influenced than themselves.

So how powerful are the media in actually shaping our attitudes? Documenting the effects of the media upon people's attitudes is no simple task. To do so, researchers have done some experiments, but more typically they have relied on survey methodologies in which people report which programs and ads they have seen. Retrospective self-reports, however, are notoriously fallible. If participants say they have seen some ad, how can we be sure? How can we be certain that viewers saw the ad under the same conditions? And once again, what about self-selection effects? For example, highly motivated citizens are more likely to tune in to political ads than less motivated citizens (Iyengar, 2004). Any effect of the ad campaign is confounded by these differences in political motivation.

Notwithstanding these difficulties, many studies attest to the power of the media, and in different parts of this book we will consider these studies. For example, in our chapter on aggression and altruism we will see that violence in the media and video games does indeed make people more aggressive (see Chapter 13). But the effects of the media are not always as robust as you might imagine. Let's study a few examples of how the media sometimes produce surprisingly little attitude change. This review will serve as a platform for considering how people resist persuasive attempts.

> **third-person effect** The assumption by most people that "other people" are more prone to being influenced by persuasive messages (such as those in media campaigns) than they themselves are.

## THE SURPRISINGLY WEAK EFFECTS OF THE MEDIA

William McGuire reviewed the evidence regarding the effects of intensive media campaigns on fairly specific behaviors and found remarkably small, sometimes nonexistent, effects (McGuire, 1985, 1986). His conclusions have for the most part stood the test of time. People are often quite independent minded in the face of the media glut. Let's look at three specific cases in which the media have had counterintuitively weak or nonexistent effects.

*Consumer Advertising*    First, what about consumer advertising? Advertising in the United States is a multibillion-dollar industry. Do the captivating Nike or Abercrombie and Fitch commercials make you go out and buy their products? McGuire claims they don't. When one looks carefully at the correlation between the ad budget of a product and its market share—that is, the proportion of consumers who buy a product—one finds a very weak or nonsignificant correlation. Even when such effects do occur, they are usually short-lived, typically lasting less than one year (Bird, 2002; Landes & Rosenfield, 1994). How much a company spends on a product may have little direct effect upon whether people buy it or not. Ads do have other effects, however, that may indirectly influence purchasing behavior. Ads have been shown to increase product loyalty, product awareness, and warm or excited feelings about the product, all of which may in turn influence purchasing behavior (McGuire, 1986).

*Political Advertising*    What about political ads? As elections draw near, our TVs become filled with dramatic and, at times, controversial political ads. Here numerous studies by political scientists have challenged conventional wisdom: most studies document no significant correlation between the amount a candidate spends on an election and success in the election (Jacobson, 1978; Levitt, 1994). While a study of the 1976 Democratic presidential primaries did find a correlation between a candidate's expenditures and the number of votes obtained, this was only true during the early stages of the campaign. Other variables, such as the candidate's previous success, were more important in predicting the candidate's ultimate success (Grush, 1980). Turning to the effects of political ads, relevant studies indicate that they have very small effects upon voting behavior (Kaid, 1981). They mainly influence late-deciding voters, and they are as likely to influence voters against as for the advertised candidate. Work by Ansolabehere and Iyengar (1995) suggests that certain kinds of ads, most notably negative ads that aggressively critique the opponent, may turn potential voters off from voting. As support for this claim, they note the historical rise in negative ads, and the drop in voter turnout in presidential elections: in 1960, voter turnout for the presidential election was 62 percent; by 1988, it had slipped to 50 percent (although it did rise to just under 60 percent in the 2004 presidential election). In a careful study of the 1992 Senate campaigns, Ansolabehere and Iyengar divided campaigns into negative ones, defined by attack advertisements, and positive ones, defined by ads offering reasons to vote for a given candidate. The positive Senate campaigns averaged a higher voter turnout (57 percent) than the negative campaigns (49.7 percent).

**Political Advertising**    As elections draw near, political ads on the radio, television, and billboards try to persuade voters how to vote. (A) In the 2004 presidential campaign, George Bush ran an ad showing John Kerry, the Democratic candidate, windsurfing, with the claim that he shifts his views "whichever way the wind blows." (B) This ad on a truck in New York City on the last night of the Republican Convention expressed dissatisfaction with Bush as president with the words "George W. Bush, 'You're fired!'"

*Public Service Announcements*    Public service announcements (PSAs) are inserted into television breaks and urge the public to follow beneficial health or social practices. They provide compelling arguments against taking drugs or smoking cigarettes or engaging in unsafe sex practices. Other PSAs encourage parents to read to their children, to play with them, and to praise them. Do these have much effect upon later behavior? Again, the answer appears to be no

(Tyler, 1984). Careful studies have found that well-designed, heavily exposed campaigns against drug abuse, for example, have had little impact upon children's knowledge about the dangers of drugs, or, more importantly, their drug-taking behavior (Schanie & Sundel, 1978). This includes the D.A.R.E. campaign that you may have participated in as a junior high school student. D.A.R.E. is an extremely expensive and widely used program to discourage drug use. A recent longitudinal study, however, found that children who participated in the D.A.R.E. program in sixth grade did not use drugs more or less, either initially, immediately after the program, or ten years later, than children who did not participate in D.A.R.E. (Lynam et al., 1999).

Though standard mass communication efforts are often ineffective, there have been novel methods of persuasion that have proven effective. For example, when adolescents are taught by use of scenarios how to turn away requests for unprotected sex, reports of unprotected sex and rates of sexually transmitted diseases (STDs) go down (Jemmott, Jemmott, & Fong, 1998; Jemmott, Jemmott, Braverman, & Fong, 2005).

## THE MEDIA AND CONCEPTIONS OF SOCIAL REALITY

How do we respond to McGuire's claim of low media impact? One angle is to argue that McGuire has focused on the wrong type of influence. Perhaps it is unrealistic to expect specific ads to affect specific behaviors. Our behaviors, after all—whether we buy Crest or Pepsodent, whether we engage in safe sex or not—are determined by a complex combination of different forces. It seems unlikely that, out of the white noise of the competing messages from the media that bombard us each day, one message in particular would prompt us to take specific action.

Another response is to argue that the media have an even more unsettling influence: they shape our very conception of social reality. Specific advertisements may not lead us to buy specific products, but they might lead us to have an unlimited desire for shopping, or a conviction that personal happiness is to be found in materialistic pursuits. Political ads may not lead us to vote for a particular candidate, but they may lead us to conclude that the country is going downhill (Eibach, Libby, & Gilovich, 2003).

Political scientist Shanto Iyengar refers to this effect of the media as **agenda control**. The media might not directly influence your moment-by-moment behavior, but it does shape what you think about and what you think is important and true. For example, the prominence of issues in the news media—fear of crime or concern about traffic congestion or worry about the condition of the economy—is correlated with the public's perception that those issues are important (Dearing & Rogers, 1996; Iyengar & Kinder, 1987). In one experiment, viewers saw a series of newscasts. In one condition, they saw three stories dealing with U.S. dependence on foreign energy sources; in another, six such stories; and in a final condition, no stories like this. When exposed to no news about dependence on foreign energy, 24 percent of the viewers cited energy as one of the three most important problems facing the country. This percentage rose to 50 percent for the participants who saw three stories on the subject, and 65 percent for the participants who saw six stories (Iyengar & Kinder, 1987). So a politician in office

**Public Service Ads** Public service ads try to persuade people to avoid drugs or alcohol or cigarettes or unsafe sex and to instead engage in healthy and productive behaviors. This anti-drug ad was part of a campaign to encourage kids to choose not to take drugs.

**agenda control** Efforts of the media to select certain events and topics to emphasize, and thereby shape what issues and events we think of as important.

should hope that news reports focus on things that are going well at the time, and a politician who wishes to defeat the incumbent should wish that the media focus on things that are not going well (see Box 7.4). It is no wonder that during the 2004 election Kerry was hoping that the media would dwell on Iraq and the economy, where Bush was considered weak, and not on terrorism or moral values, where Bush was considered strong.

George Gerbner and his colleagues have shown that the media shape our broader conceptions of social reality (Gerbner, Gross, Morgan, & Signorielli, 1986). These researchers have laboriously coded the content of television programs, and they have found that the world depicted on TV scarcely resembles social reality. On prime-time programs, for example, males outnumber females by a factor of 3 to 1. Ethnic minorities, young children, and the elderly are substantially underrepresented. Many jobs, such as those in the service industry or the blue-collar world, are likewise underrepresented. Crime is wildly more prevalent per unit of time on prime-time television than in the average U.S. citizen's real life.

In careful assessments of the television viewing habits of individuals, Gerbner and his colleagues have documented that heavy television viewers—namely those who watch five hours or more per day—construe social reality much like the reality they view on television. Heavy television viewers tend to endorse more racially

## Box 7.4    FOCUS ON THE MEDIA

# The Hostile Media Phenomenon

President George W. Bush likes to refer to the media as "the filter," expressing the conviction that the mainstream media have reported on his presidency through a biased political lens that reflects badly on his views and agenda. He is not alone in seeing the media as biased. Former presidents expressed similar doubts about the objectivity of the media—Richard Nixon felt that the media were run by an elite Jewish clique. The thesis that the media are ideologically biased has produced two runaway best-sellers—Ann Coulter's *Slander* and Bernard Goldberg's *Bias*—that accuse the media of being liberal. They point to such "evidence" as the more frequent use of the term "far right wing" than "far left wing" in publications like the *New York Times*, and they note the left-wing views of prominent people in the media like Dan Rather and Bill Moyers. Journalist Eric Alterman provides counterarguments to these assertions in his book *What Liberal Media?*, as does liberal humorist Al Franken in his book *Lies and the Lying Liars Who Tell Them*. And an entire organization, Fairness and Accuracy in

Reporting (FAIR; www.fair.org) is devoted to documenting bias in the media (for example, showing that conservatives are more likely to appear as experts on news shows like *Nightline*). Where does the truth lie?

One answer is in "the mind of the media consumer." Robert Vallone, Lee Ross, and Mark Lepper (1985) have documented the hostile media phenomenon, which refers to the tendency for partisans in social disputes to perceive the media as biased, and in particular, as favoring the other side. For example, in one telephone survey, conducted three days prior to the 1980 presidential election, among Jimmy Carter supporters who felt that the media had favored one candidate in its coverage, 83 percent thought that it favored Reagan. In contrast, for Reagan supporters who felt the media had been biased, 96 percent felt that the media had favored Carter. Vallone and his colleagues reason that this assumption of hostile media flows from the belief that we see the world objectively and that anyone who begs to differ, to present another side, must be biased.

prejudiced attitudes. They assume that women have more limited abilities than men. They overestimate the prevalence of violent crime and assume that the world is quite dangerous and sinister. And they overestimate the number of physicians and lawyers in the population. Of course, you should be worried about the possibility of self-selection effects producing these results. Perhaps more-prejudiced, cynical people watch more television in the first place, and it is these individual differences that produce the aforementioned results, and not television viewing. Nevertheless, Gerbner and his colleagues advance a provocative thesis: pervasive media exposure may very well determine our most basic assumptions about the world we live in, about the groups that make up our society, about how we derive satisfaction and well-being, and about human nature.

**LOOKING BACK,** we have seen that media persuasion effects—at any rate, advertising effects—are weaker than we might assume, even though most people believe that the media are quite effective, at least for other people! It seems that the greatest effects of the media involve influencing our conceptions of reality and exerting agenda control—that is, making us feel that some issues are particularly important. In the next section, we examine some of the reasons that people might be less susceptible to persuasion and thus better able to resist it than we might assume.

## RESISTANCE TO PERSUASION

Although the media may have their biggest effects indirectly in shaping our most basic assumptions about social reality, we must still explain why they do not have more powerful direct effects. If McGuire is right that media effects are generally small and even nonexistent, how can we explain why this is so? As we will now see, part of the answer lies in the fact that many of the important principles of social psychology—the power of our perceptual biases, of preexisting commitments, and of prior knowledge—serve as sources of independent thought and significant forces of resistance in the face of persuasive attempts.

### ATTENTIONAL BIASES AND RESISTANCE

When the office of the Surgeon General issued its 1964 report linking smoking to lung cancer, it would seem to have provided incontrovertible evidence requiring smokers and nonsmokers alike to shift their attitudes toward smoking. The report, after all, represented the carefully weighed opinion and near-unanimous consensus of the scientific community. And yet, after the release of the report, 40 percent of smokers found the report flawed compared to 10 percent of nonsmokers. We would like to think that we can absorb data and information in relatively unbiased fashion, updating our attitudes accordingly (Pronin, Gilovich, & Ross, 2004), and that if we learned that a habit was dangerous to our health, we would alter our attitudes toward that habit accordingly. But as we have seen, our minds sometimes go about their business very differently, responding selectively to information in a way that maintains our original attitudes.

Let's break this assertion down a bit. First, several studies indicate that people

are inclined to *attend selectively* to information that confirms their original attitudes (Eagly & Chaiken, 1998; Sweeney & Gruber, 1984). That is, we tune in to information that reinforces our attitudes, and we tune out information that contradicts them. In one study, students who either supported the legalization of marijuana or opposed it listened to a message that advocated legalization (Kleinhesselink & Edwards, 1975). The message contained fourteen arguments: seven that were strong and difficult to refute (and clearly appealing to the pro-marijuana students) and seven that were silly and easy to refute (and very attractive to the anti-legalization students). The students heard the message over earphones accompanied by a continual static buzz. To combat this problem, students were allowed to press a button to eliminate the buzz for five seconds. This allowed the researchers to determine the information to which the students preferred to attend—arguments that were consistent with their attitudes or that opposed their position.

As you might have anticipated, the pro-legalization students pushed the button more often when the speaker was delivering the strong arguments in favor of legalization—wanting to hear the information that would reinforce their preexisting attitudes. The anti-legalization students, in contrast, were more likely to push the button while the speaker offered up the easy-to-refute arguments in favor of legalization, the very information that would reinforce their position. In a similar study, students who were asked to write essays about federal funding for abortion or the use of nuclear energy tended to select as reference material for their essays magazine articles that supported their opinion (McPherson, 1983). You yourself might find that you turn to select magazines or radio programs to clarify important opinions—for example, about the Iraq war or about a political candidate—and to obtain information that supports your preexisting attitudes (see Chapter 2).

Not only do we selectively attend to and seek out information that supports our attitudes, we also *selectively evaluate* the information we take in. Specifically, we are prone to look favorably upon information that supports our attitudes, and especially critically upon information that contradicts our attitudes. For example, in one study, Ziva Kunda (1990) had female and male students read a story presented as a *New York Times* article that detailed how caffeine consumption in females is associated with an increased risk of fibrocystic disease. Half of the participants were high-caffeine users—fans of lattes, cappuccinos, and the occasional diet Coke or Mountain Dew. The other half of the participants were low-caffeine users. The article, of course, should be most threatening to the female high-caffeine users, and thus it should be greeted with the greatest skepticism by that group. As you can see in Figure 7.6, this proved to be the case. Independent of caffeine-use habits, the male participants found the article fairly convincing, as did the females who used little caffeine. It was the high-caffeine-using females who were less convinced by and more critical of the article.

Kunda's study raises an interesting question: How do partisans of an issue respond to the mixed scientific evidence that so often characterizes the state of knowledge regarding complex social problems? Is capital punishment an effective deterrent to murder? Will tax cuts targeted to the rich produce "trickle

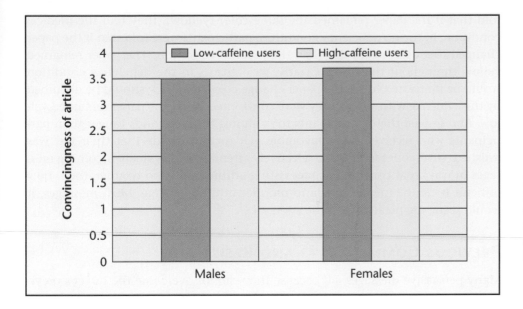

**Figure 7.6 Selective Evaluation**
Female high-caffeine users find an article about the dangers of caffeine use for women less convincing than do men or women who don't drink a lot of coffee. (Source: Kunda, 1990)

down" benefits to all? Do generous welfare benefits discourage significant segments of society from joining the workforce? One possible result—the one that as citizens we would hope for—is that mixed evidence would lead partisans to a more moderate position. In this scenario, partisans consider the facts in support of their own position and that of the other side, and they integrate this information into a more balanced, moderate position if that is what the facts call for. An alternative view, the belief polarization hypothesis, holds that people will dismiss evidence that contradicts their initial views, and derive support from evidence that is consistent with their views.

To test this hypothesis, Lord, Ross, and Lepper (1979) had death penalty opponents and proponents read two different studies that examined the deterrent effects of capital punishment. One study suggested that the death penalty had a deterrent effect, reducing murder rates in the states in which it was implemented. The other study suggested that murder rates were actually higher in states with capital punishment. As in Kunda's study of caffeine consumers, both sides found the study that supported their views to be the more rigorously conducted. And both sides were highly critical of the design and details of the study that contradicted their position. As a result of reading the two studies, the two sides' differences were actually *greater* at the end of the study. Thus, when we encounter mixed evidence on an issue of importance to us, we often become even more firmly entrenched in our attitudes. It is no wonder that we are resistant to so many persuasive communications.

In related research, Peter Ditto and colleagues have shown that people are more critical of evidence that violates cherished beliefs about their personal health (Ditto & Lopez, 1992). Patients who receive diagnoses indicating that they are unhealthy are more likely to downplay the seriousness of the diagnosis and the validity of the test that produced the diagnosis (Ditto, Jemmott, & Darley, 1988). In a clever extension of this work, Ditto and Lopez (1992) gave undergraduates a test of a fictitious medical condition called "TAA deficiency" that was supposedly associated with pancreatic disorders later in life. The test was simple: to put saliva on a piece of yellow paper, and observe whether it would change color in the next twenty seconds. In the deficiency condition, participants were

> "The human understanding when it has once adopted an opinion draws all things else to support and agree with it. And though there be a greater number or weight of instances to be found on the other side, yet these it either neglects and despises, or else by some distinction sets aside and rejects, in order that by this great and pernicious predetermination the authority of its former conclusion may remain inviolate."
>
> —FRANCIS BACON

told that if the paper remained the same color (yellow), they had the medical condition; in the no deficiency condition, participants were told that if the paper changed to a dark green, they had the medical condition. The paper remained yellow throughout the study. Clearly, participants in the deficiency condition would be motivated to see the paper change color, and they should be disturbed by the evidence with which they were confronted—that the paper remained yellow. And indeed these participants took almost thirty seconds longer than participants who received more favorable evidence to decide that their test was finished. Given our tendency to selectively attend to and evaluate incoming messages in ways that confirm our preexisting attitudes, it is no wonder, then, how difficult it can be for the media to produce attitude change. Most messages, it would seem, are preaching to the choir.

## PREVIOUS COMMITMENTS AND RESISTANCE

Many persuasive messages fail because they cannot overcome the target's previous commitments. For example, empirical studies show that political allegiances are often passed from parent to child (see Box 7.5). Such allegiances may be rooted in an individual's upbringing and family background, and they may be deeply intertwined with the individual's social identity (McGuire, 1985). Political ads that try to convince potential voters to shift their political allegiances must, in effect, convince voters to abandon these deep commitments—not a likely outcome. Similarly, anti-drug campaigns are designed to reduce the drug-taking behavior of individuals who may be engaging in a habitual act that is embedded in a way of life and a community of friends.

You'll recall that in Asch's line judgment studies of social influence, public commitment reduced the likelihood of conformity (see Chapter 6). The same is

## Box 7.5   FOCUS ON HEREDITY

# The Genetic Basis of Attitudes

One of the deepest sources of our commitment to important attitudes, and our resistance to persuasive messages, is our genes. Work by Abraham Tesser (1993) of the University of Georgia suggests that our attitudes are in part inherited. To support this claim, Tesser examined the attitudes of monozygotic, or identical twins, who share 100 percent of their genes, and the attitudes of dizygotic, or fraternal twins, who share 50 percent of their genes. For most attitudes surveyed, there was a greater similarity in the attitudes of identical than of fraternal twins. This was true, for example, for attitudes about the death penalty, jazz, cen-

sorship, divorce, and socialism. Moreover, researchers found that the more-heritable attitudes were also more accessible, less susceptible to persuasion, and more predictive of feelings of attraction to a stranger who shares those attitudes.

Of course, there is no gene for attitudes toward censorship or socialism; the hereditary transmission must be via some other element of temperament, such as a fear of novelty (which might make you dislike jazz but be more tolerant of censorship), impulsivity, or a preference for risk taking.

true in the attitude change literature. Relevant social psychological evidence indicates that public commitments make people resistant to attitude change. In this work, participants are asked to make public statements regarding their attitudes (Kiesler, 1971; Pallak, Mueller, Dollar, & Pallak, 1972). When participants make public commitments to their attitudes—as people do every day when they discuss politics and social issues with their friends—they are more resistant to subsequent counter-attitudinal messages than are control participants.

Why might public commitments increase our resistance to persuasive communications? The most obvious reason is that it is hard to back down from a public commitment, even when evidence is presented against the position we took. Another reason is not so obvious: public commitments engage us in more extended thought about a particular issue, which tends to produce more extreme, entrenched attitudes. This is supported by Abraham Tesser's **thought polarization hypothesis**. To test his hypothesis, Tesser measured participants' attitudes toward social issues, such as legalizing prostitution (Tesser & Conlee, 1975). He then had the participants think for a few moments about the issue. When they stated their attitudes toward the same issue a second time, they routinely gave stronger ratings: opponents and proponents polarized. The repeated expression of attitudes has led to more extreme attitudes in a variety of domains, including attitudes toward people, artwork, fashions, and football strategies (Downing, Judd, & Brauer, 1992; Judd, Drake, Downing, & Krosnick, 1991; Tesser, Martin, & Mendolia, 1995). A caveat is in order here, however. Increased thought about an attitude object can lead to more moderate attitudes for people who have previously had little motivation to think about the issue or little preexisting knowledge vis-à-vis the issue (Judd & Lusk, 1984).

> **thought polarization hypothesis** The hypothesis that more extended thought about a particular issue tends to produce more extreme, entrenched attitudes.

## KNOWLEDGE AND RESISTANCE

In our review of the ELM approach to attitude change, we saw that prior knowledge makes people scrutinize messages much more carefully. People with a great deal of knowledge are more resistant to persuasion. Such people have more beliefs, emotions, and habits tied up with their attitudes, which should make attitude change for more knowledgeable individuals less likely. This intuition has been borne out in the experimental literature (Haugtvedt & Petty, 1992; Krosnick, 1988; Lydon, Zanna, & Ross, 1988; Zuwerink & Devine, 1996). For example, in one study of individuals' attitudes toward environmental preservation, Wendy Wood (1982) divided students into two groups: those who were pro-preservation and who knew a lot about the issue, and those who were pro-preservation but who were less knowledgeable about the subject. In a second session, she exposed these two groups of students to a message opposed to environmental preservation. The students with a great deal of knowledge about the environment moved only a little in their attitudes, and they counterargued a great deal in response to the message, relying upon what they already knew and strongly believed about the issue. The less knowledgeable students, however, shifted their attitudes in the direction of the anti-preservation message, for they had less knowledge to rely upon to counterargue against the message.

## ATTITUDE INOCULATION

Thus far, we have examined how people's belief systems—their biases, commitments, and preexisting knowledge—make them resistant to attitude change. This is due to the more general tendency to selectively attend to, and favorably evaluate, evidence that supports preexisting attitudes. There are also techniques that can be used to further these tendencies to resist persuasion—or to instill them in people with less commitment, knowledge, and confidence in their opinions.

William McGuire has developed such a technique that finds inspiration in a rather unusual source: the inoculations we receive against viruses. When we receive an inoculation, we are exposed to a weak dose of the virus. Exposure to this small dose of the virus stimulates our immune system, which then is prepared to defend against exposure to larger doses of the virus. McGuire believed that resistance to persuasion could be encouraged in a similar fashion, by **attitude inoculation**—small attacks upon our beliefs that would engage our attitudes, prior commitments, and knowledge structures, and thereby counteract the larger attack (McGuire & Papageorgis, 1961).

In studies that attest to the efficacy of attitude inoculation, McGuire first assessed participants' endorsements of different cultural truisms, such as "It's a good idea to brush your teeth after every meal if at all possible" or "The effects of penicillin have been, almost without exception, of great benefit to mankind" (McGuire & Papageorgis, 1961). More than 75 percent of the participants checked 15 on a 15-point scale to indicate their agreement with truisms like these.

Now comes the intervention. McGuire and Papageorgis exposed participants to a small attack upon their belief in the truism. For example, in the tooth-brushing example, the participants might read, "Too frequent brushing tends to damage the gums and expose the vulnerable parts of the teeth to decay." In some conditions, the researchers asked the participants to refute that attack by offering arguments against it; this was the attitude inoculation. In other conditions, the researchers asked the participants to consider arguments in support of the truism. Then, some time between one hour and seven days later, the researchers asked the participants to read a three-paragraph-long, full-scale attack on the truism.

In Figure 7.7, we present data that attest to the immunizing effectiveness of attitude inoculation. As you can see in the first column, prior to the attack participants strongly endorsed the truism. The subsequent, forceful attack did indeed reduce the belief in the truism for those people who faced no initial attack (the second column). But having earlier refuted a mild attack against the truism

**attitude inoculation** Small attacks upon our beliefs that engage our attitudes, prior commitments, and knowledge structures, enabling us to counteract a subsequent larger attack and be resistant to persuasion.

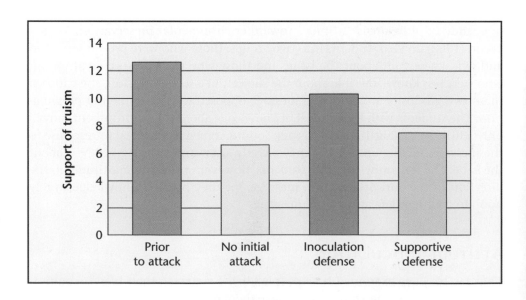

**Figure 7.7 Attitude Inoculation**
Attitude inoculation, in which people use preexisting attitudes, commitments, and knowledge to come up with counterarguments, makes people more resistant to attitude change. (Source: McGuire & Papageorgis, 1961)

led people to substantially resist the subsequent stronger attack (Column 3). Furthermore, counterarguing against the initial attack was clearly more effective than generating arguments that supported the truism (Column 4).

Think how useful attitude inoculation might be. For example, in smoking-prevention programs, adolescents might be presented with pro-smoking arguments likely to be advanced by peers and advertisements (for example, "smoking is about freedom and maturity") and then encouraged to counterargue against these pressures—a clear example of attitude inoculation.

**LOOKING BACK**, we have seen that media efforts and attempts by others to change people's attitudes are not as effective as people commonly believe. People often selectively attend to and evaluate information that confirms their original attitudes and beliefs, and they ignore or criticize information that disconfirms them. We have also seen that preexisting commitments to political ideologies or values increases resistance to counter-attitudinal messages and persuasion. Finally, we have shown how attitude inoculation, or small attacks upon beliefs, can make people resistant to attitude change, as the small attacks give people the chance to muster arguments that they can use when faced with stronger attacks on their beliefs and attitudes.

## SUMMARY

1. *Attitudes* are dispositions to evaluate objects in a negative or positive light. Attitudes include three different elements: *affective evaluations* (emotions), *cognitions* (thoughts and knowledge), and *action tendencies*.

2. Attitudes can be measured with self-report *Likert scales*, with response latencies that capture *attitude accessibility* (the degree to which the attitude is ready to become active in an individual's mind), and with attitude linkage measures that gauge *attitude centrality* (the extent to which an attitude is correlated to attitudes about other issues).

3. Attitudes serve several functions. They serve a *utilitarian function*, signaling rewards and punishments. They serve an *ego-defensive function*, protecting people from undesirable beliefs about themselves—for example, the recognition that their lives will inevitably end. They serve a *value-expressive function*, reflecting values that people want others, especially

their *reference groups*, to acknowledge. And attitudes serve a *knowledge function*, organizing how people construe the social world and guiding how people attend to, store, and retrieve information.

4. Both the *heuristic-systematic model* of persuasion and the *Elaboration Likelihood Model* of persuasion hypothesize that there are two routes to persuasion. Factors that determine which route is used include motivation, or how important the message is to the person, and ability to process the message.

5. When using the *central (systematic) route* to persuasion, people attend carefully to the message, and they consider relevant evidence and underlying logic in detail. People are especially likely to go through this route when the message is relevant to them, when they have knowledge in the domain, and when the message evokes a sense of personal responsibility. When going through the central route, people are more persuaded by high-quality messages.

6. In the *peripheral (heuristic) route to persuasion*, people attend to superficial aspects of the message. They use this route when they have little motivation or time or ability to attend to its deeper meaning. In this route, people are persuaded by source characteristics, such as attractiveness and credibility of the communicator, and message characteristics, such as how many arguments there are and whether the conclusions are explicit.

7. The elements of the persuasive process can be broken into three components: the *source* of the message, the *content* of the message, and the *target* of the message.

8. A noncredible source is unlikely to induce immediate attitude change, but with time, a *sleeper effect* may occur. This is when attitude change occurs after time has passed and the message has become dissociated from its source.

9. Vivid communications, including images of *identifiable victims*, are usually more effective than more pallid ones, and fear-evoking communications that provide fear-reducing courses of action produce more attitude change than either non-fear-evoking communications or fear-evoking communications that do not provide fear-reducing courses of action.

10. Message content often varies in independent and interdependent societies, with ads in independent cultures emphasizing the individual and ads in interdependent societies emphasizing the collective.

11. The target, or audience, of a message also affects whether a particular message is effective and whether attitude change occurs. Audience, or *receiver characteristics,* include the need for cognition (that is, how deeply people like to think about issues), mood, and age.

12. According to the *third-person effect,* most people believe that other people are more likely to be influenced by the media than they are. But in fact the media have surprisingly weak effects on most people. This is true in the case of consumer advertising (which rarely leads to long-lived effects), political advertising (which has small effects on most voters and mainly affects late-deciding voters), and public service announcements (which are unlikely to have a lasting impact on behavior unless they are also accompanied by specific suggestions and practice in avoiding negative behaviors).

13. The media are most effective in *agenda control*—that is, in shaping what people think about. They do so through the number of stories and discussions they present on various issues, like terrorism, moral values, war, the environment, or the economy, and therefore are likely to be present in people's minds.

14. People can be resistant to persuasion because of pre-existing biases, commitments, and knowledge. People selectively attend to and evaluate information in accordance with their original attitudes, tuning in information that supports their preexisting attitudes and beliefs, and tuning out information that contradicts them.

15. Public commitment to a position helps people to resist persuasion. Just thinking about an attitude object can produce *thought polarization,* or movement toward extreme views that can be hard for a communicator to alter.

16. People with more knowledge are more resistant to persuasion because they are able to counterargue against messages that take an opposite position to what they know and believe.

17. Resistance to persuasion can be encouraged through *attitude inoculation*, or exposing a person to weak arguments against a person's position and allowing the person to generate arguments against it.

## CRITICAL THINKING ABOUT BASIC PRINCIPLES

1. Gordon Allport, one of the founders of social psychology, argued that the attitude is the central construct in our discipline. The four important functions that attitudes serve bolster this claim. For each of the four functions of attitudes that we covered in this chapter, discuss a finding from another chapter you have read so far that illustrates the function.

2. Imagine that you have been put in charge of a political ad campaign for a young candidate running for office. She has given you the charge of appealing to two sectors of the population who have been showing low rates of voter turnout—young voters aged eighteen to twenty and busy women who have children and full-time careers. What sort of audience-specific campaigns would you propose, based on

what you have learned from the dual-process approach to persuasion?

3. Imagine you were designing an anti-drug campaign for children aged nine to twelve, who are particularly vulnerable to pressure to take drugs. What sort of techniques would you use to encourage them to resist this kind of persuasion?

## KEY TERMS

agenda control (p. 285)
attitude (p. 259)
attitude inoculation (p. 292)
central route of persuasion (p. 270)
ego-defensive function (p. 264)
Elaboration Likelihood Model (p. 270)
heuristic route of persuasion (p. 271)
heuristic-systematic model (p. 270)
identifiable victim effect (p. 277)

knowledge function (p. 268)
Likert scale (p. 261)
message characteristics (p. 276)
peripheral route of persuasion (p. 271)
receiver characteristics (p. 279)
reference groups (p. 266)
response latency (p. 262)
sleeper effect (p. 276)
source characteristics (p. 273)

systematic route of persuasion (p. 270)
terror management theory (p. 264)
third-person effect (p. 283)
thought polarization hypothesis (p. 291)
utilitarian function (p. 263)
value-expressive function (p. 266)

## FURTHER READING AND FILMS

Eagly, A. H., & Chaiken, S. (1993). *The psychology of attitudes*. Fort Worth, TX: Harcourt Brace & Company.

Orwell, G. (1990). *1984*. New York: Signet (originally published in 1945). How a fictitious society controls the thoughts and beliefs of its members.

Pratkanis, A. R., & Aronson, E. (2000). *Age of propaganda*. New York: Freeman.

Reifenstahl, L. (1934). *Triumph of the will*. Documentary of the Nazi Party rally at Nuremberg in 1934, showing Adolf Hitler's persuasive power as an orator as he whips a large number of people into an emotional state.

Zimbardo, P. G., & Leippe, M. R. (1991). *The psychology of attitude change and social influence*. New York: McGraw-Hill.

# Chapter Outline

# CHAPTER 8

# Attitudes and Behavior

hroughout the United States' long and painful military involvement in Vietnam—a conflict that split the nation into "hawks" and "doves," consumed the energies of three administrations, and ultimately cost the lives of 58,000 U.S. soldiers—the government put a positive spin on the enterprise. It maintained that there was "light at the end of the tunnel," that Communist North Vietnam would soon be vanquished, that a satisfactory deal would soon be struck, or that the South Vietnamese regime the U.S. was supporting would soon become sufficiently strong to conduct its own defense. But these positive pronouncements notwithstanding, throughout the war many government officials developed doubts about the U.S. effort in Vietnam and the prospects for success. These doubts often surfaced as key decisions needed to be made, such as whether to increase the number of U.S. soldiers stationed in South Vietnam or whether to initiate a bombing campaign against North Vietnam.

Lyndon Johnson, the U.S. president responsible for the biggest buildup of American troops in Vietnam, employed an interesting tactic to deal with those in his administration

**Public Advocacy and Private Acceptance**   Despite the continuing problems in fighting the Vietnam War, U.S. President Lyndon Johnson publicly declared that the war was going well and insisted that his advisers and cabinet members also publicly express their support and confidence. (A) Defense Secretary Robert McNamara had reservations about the war that may have been alleviated to a degree by the constant necessity of defending it. Here he is shown briefing the press on U.S. air attacks. (B) To bolster morale, Johnson himself spoke to U.S. troops in South Vietnam, while U.S. General William Westmoreland, South Vietnamese General Nguyen Van Thieu, South Vietnamese Premier Nguyen Cao Ky, and U.S. Secretary of State Dean Rusk looked on.

**Behavior Can Influence Attitudes**
Although he considers himself an environmentalist, Arnold Schwarzenegger drives a gas-guzzling Hummer and his actions have helped to promote the car as a civilian vehicle. Driving a Hummer may lead people who are concerned about the environment to rationalize their actions and come to believe that the vehicle is actually not having a negative impact on the environment.

who began privately to express such doubts and to waver from the administration's policy on the war (Halberstam, 1969). Johnson would send those with doubts about the war on a "fact-finding" mission to Vietnam, nearly always with a group of reporters in tow. One might think this a rather risky move on Johnson's part because if any of these less-than-staunch supporters expressed their doubts to the press, the administration's policies would be undermined. But Johnson knew they would not express their doubts publicly, preferring to try to influence administration policy from the inside. Unable to express their doubts out of loyalty, and confronted by criticism of the war effort by reporters, the doubters would be thrust into the position of publicly *defending* administration policy. This public advocacy, Johnson reasoned, would serve to lessen their doubts and help turn the skeptics in his administration into advocates.

Johnson's strategy speaks to the issue of the consistency between attitudes and behavior, and whether the consistency between the two is the result of attitudes influencing behavior or behavior influencing attitudes. We know that both types of influence exist. Those who have strong pro-environment attitudes are more likely to vote Green or Democratic than Republican. Attitudes influence behavior. But we also know that people rationalize, and so behavior influences attitudes as well. Environmentally minded individuals who drive gas-guzzling SUVs tend to convince themselves that their choice of vehicles is not so harmful to the environment after all.

The behavior of driving an SUV leads them to change their attitudes about an SUV's impact on the environment.

The relative strength of these two effects is worth pondering. Which is stronger: the effect of attitudes on behavior, or the effect of behavior on attitudes? It is a question that is difficult to answer, but what *is* clear from decades of research on the topic is that the influence of attitudes on behavior is a bit weaker than most people would suspect and that the influence of behavior on attitudes is much stronger than most would suspect. Thus, Johnson was right: get people to behave in a particular way and their attitudes will typically follow.

In this chapter, we will examine what social psychologists have learned about the consistency between attitudes and behavior, first by reviewing research that has tracked how well attitudes predict behavior. This research highlights the fact that attitudes are often a surprisingly poor predictor of behavior, but also specifies the circumstances under which they predict behavior most powerfully. We will then examine several "consistency theories" that lay out the reasons why people tend to maintain consistency among their attitudes and between their attitudes and behavior. The research inspired by these theories has shown how powerfully people's behavior influences their attitudes.

## PREDICTING BEHAVIOR FROM ATTITUDES

Most academic discussions of how well attitudes predict behavior begin with a remarkable study conducted by Richard LaPiere in the early 1930s (LaPiere, 1934). LaPiere spent two years touring the country with a young Chinese couple, visiting numerous hotels, auto camps, restaurants, and cafes. Although prejudice and discrimination against Chinese individuals were common at the time, it is reassuring to learn that LaPiere and his traveling companions were denied service by only one of the 250 establishments they visited. Maybe anti-Chinese prejudice wasn't so strong after all.

To find out, LaPiere wrote to all of the establishments they had visited and asked whether their policy was to serve "Orientals." Approximately 90 percent of those who responded said they would not, a response rate that is stunningly inconsistent with what LaPiere actually observed during his earlier tour of the country. This was unfortunate in human terms because it indicated that anti-Chinese prejudice was indeed rather robust. And to many social psychologists of that era it was unfortunate in scientific terms because it suggested that attitudes do not seem to predict behavior very well. To a scientific discipline that had treated attitudes as powerful determinants of people's behavior, this was truly surprising—and rather unsettling—news.

**Attitudes Do Not Always Predict Behavior** This store in Elk City, Idaho, displays a sign declaring "No Earth Firster or Sympathizer Allowed." The store owners may indeed intend to bar environmentalists from the store, but can they always recognize an environmentalist? And if an identifiable environmentalist were to walk in, would they live up to their claim and refuse the business?

Note that this was not some fluke associated with the particularities of LaPiere's study. Numerous experiments conducted over the next several decades yielded similar results. Indeed, a much-cited review in the 1960s of the existing literature on attitudes and behavior concluded that, "The present review provides little evidence to support the postulated existence of stable, underlying attitudes within the individual which influence both his verbal expressions and his actions" (Wicker, 1969, p. 75).

Most people find this result surprising. Why? Why do we think that people's attitudes are strong predictors of their behavior if careful empirical studies of the issue reveal that they are not? Part of the reason there is such a rift between belief and reality stems from a sampling problem (combined with a bit of a failure of logic). Every day, we see plenty of evidence of attitudes and behavior that go together. People who picket abortion clinics have attitudes opposed to abortion. People who show up at the local bowling alley have positive attitudes toward the sport. Families with a large litter of kids (usually) have positive attitudes about children. Evidence of a tight connection between attitudes and behavior is all around us. But note that this evidence only tells us that if one behaves a certain way, one is likely to have a positive attitude toward that behavior. Logically, such a relationship does not entail its complement (which is really the critical issue): that people with a positive attitude toward a given behavior are likely to behave in a manner consistent with their attitude. What is not so salient in everyday life are the more numerous instances of people with positive attitudes toward bowling who do not bowl much or people with positive attitudes toward kids who do not have children.

There are, after all, many reasons why people may fail to act on their attitudes. If we pursue this point more deeply and consider all the reasons why people may not act in a manner consistent with their attitudes, two consequences follow. First, the finding that attitudes so often fail to predict behavior with much accuracy may no longer be so surprising. Second, and more important, we may be able to specify *when* attitudes are likely to be highly predictive of behavior and when they are not. So let us consider various reasons why people may act at variance with their underlying attitudes.

## ATTITUDES SOMETIMES CONFLICT WITH OTHER POWERFUL DETERMINANTS OF BEHAVIOR

Suppose you were asked to predict the strength of the relationship between (1) people's attitudes toward dieting, and (2) actual, successful dieting. Would you expect a strong relationship? Certainly not. Although people who like the idea of dieting may cut back on food consumption more than those who don't like the idea, the relationship is unlikely to be strong because cutting back is determined by so many things other than the person's attitude about dieting, including eating habits, individual physiology, and whether a roommate is pigging out or dieting as well. Attitudes toward dieting thus compete with a lot of other determinants of behavior.

What is true about attitudes toward dieting is true about attitudes in general. They all compete with other determinants of behavior. The situationist message of social psychology (and of this book) necessarily entails that attitudes will not always win out over these other determinants, and hence attitudes will not always be so tightly connected to behavior.

One particularly potent determinant of a person's actions that can weaken the

**Attitudes and Norms** An individual's attitudes can compete with social norms of appropriate behavior. The man on the cell phone may believe that he should be able to talk on his cell phone no matter where he is, but the attitudes of others in the theater may lead him to quickly end his conversation and refrain from future cell phone conversations in a theater, lecture hall, train, or library.

relationship between attitudes and behavior is an individual's understanding of the prevailing norms of appropriate behavior. You might relish the idea of talking in animated fashion with the person next to you in the movie theater or lecture hall, but let's hope you refrain from doing so out of the recognition that it just isn't done. Others would disapprove. Similarly, the hotel and restaurant owners in LaPiere's study may have wanted to turn away the Chinese couple, but they refrained from doing so out of concern about how it would look and the scene it might cause.

The importance of other people's approval in determining behavior is captured in an influential account of how people choose to act, an account known as the **theory of reasoned action** (Ajzen & Fishbein, 1980). The theory is one of "reasoned" action because it assumes that people quite consciously and deliberately choose to act in certain ways. As can be seen in Figure 8.1A, people's attitudes toward a given course of action combine with their **subjective norms**—that is, their sense of whether others will (or will not) approve of that course of action—to create an intention to behave in a particular fashion. The intention, in turn, leads to that very behavior unless various constraints or impediments get in the way.

In one test of the theory of reasoned action, expectant mothers were asked about their attitudes toward breast-feeding and their assessments of what others might think of their decision to breast-feed or not (Manstead, Profitt, & Smart, 1983). Their attitudes were assessed by asking what they thought of certain consequences of breast-feeding versus bottle-feeding, such as "Breast-feeding estab-

**theory of reasoned action**  A theory that maintains that people's deliberate behavior can be accurately predicted by knowing their attitudes toward specific behaviors and their subjective norms.

**subjective norms**  People's beliefs about whether others are likely to approve of a course of action.

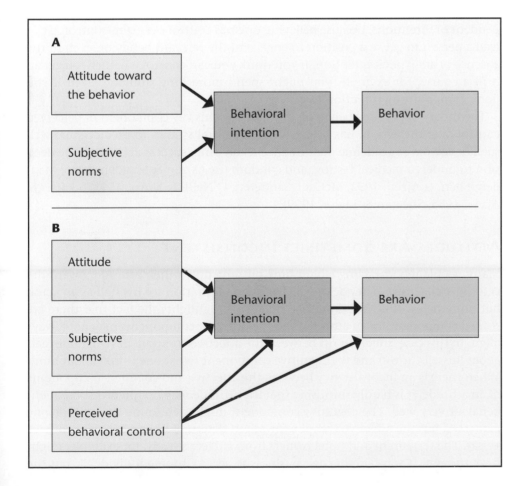

**Figure 8.1 Theories of How Attitudes Guide Behavior**   (A) The theory of reasoned action, and (B) the theory of planned behavior. (Source: Madden, Ellen, & Ajzen, 1992)

**theory of planned behavior**
The successor to the theory of reasoned action that maintains that the best predictors of deliberate behavior are people's attitudes toward specific behaviors, their subjective norms, and their beliefs about whether they can successfully perform the behavior in question.

lishes a close bond between mother and baby." Subjective norms were assessed by asking how they thought various individuals (for example, the baby's father, a close friend) would view breast-feeding and how much they cared about those individuals' views. Six weeks after their babies were born, the mothers were recontacted and asked about how their babies were being fed. As the theory of reasoned action predicts, the mothers' attitudes were significant predictors of their initial intentions to breast-feed or bottle-feed their babies, and of their subsequent decisions to breast-feed or not. The mothers' subjective norms were also significant predictors of their initial intentions and subsequent actions. Importantly, however, their subsequent actions were best predicted by a combination of their attitudes and subjective norms, just as the theory predicts.

That is all well and good for behavior such as breast-feeding or bottle-feeding, for which the intention to act in a particular way almost guarantees that very action because all that is required is the simple decision to act accordingly. But what about those things like successful dieting, getting a good grade, or forming a successful rock-and-roll band? Intending to do these things does not automatically make them happen, and so the connection between attitudes (and subjective norms) and behavior is unlikely to be as strong. To account for this, the architects of the theory of reasoned action have supplanted it with the **theory of planned behavior** (Ajzen, 1985, 1996). As can be seen in Figure 8.1B, the key change is the addition of people's beliefs about whether they can successfully perform the given behavior. You may be favorably disposed toward being a stand-up comic, but unless you believe you can make a roomful of strangers laugh, you're unlikely to try it. Thus, perceived control has an effect on a person's intention to perform a given behavior, which in turn has a strong effect on whether it is performed. Perceived control also has a direct effect on the behavior itself, independent of intentions, because believing one has control over some outcome can lead a person to get in a position to engage in the relevant behavior, even in the absence of an explicit intention. If you think you can control whether you get an A in a course, for example, you might spend more time studying, even if you don't form a strong intention to get an A.

The theory of planned behavior, by including this key component of perceived control over the action, has been shown in several studies to predict quite well such behaviors as academic performance, exercising, success at dieting, the decision to undergo medical testing, and condom use (Ajzen & Madden, 1986; Madden, Ellen, & Ajzen, 1992; McCaul, Sandgren, O'Neill, & Hinsz, 1993; Schifter & Ajzen, 1985; Sheeran & Taylor, 1999).

## ATTITUDES ARE SOMETIMES INCONSISTENT

Many people report having a hard time pinning down their attitude toward the actor Russell Crowe. They acknowledge great admiration for his skill as an actor, but nonetheless they just don't like him. This highlights the fact that there are several components of an attitude, and the different components may not always align. In this case, there is a rift between the affective component (what one feels about Russell Crowe) and the cognitive component (what one thinks about him). When there is an inconsistency between the affective and cognitive components of an attitude, it is hardly surprising that the attitude may not predict subsequent behavior very well. The cognitive component might determine the attitude one expresses, but the affective component might determine one's behavior (or vice versa). The restaurant and hotel owners from LaPiere's study, for example, might have thought it was bad for their business to serve Chinese individuals, but the feelings aroused by a living, breathing Chinese couple may have made it hard to deny them service.

*Inconsistency between Affective and Cognitive Components of Attitudes*    Evidence supports the idea that attitudes tend to be poor predictors of behavior when there is an inconsistency between the affective and cognitive components. In one study, students indicated both their thoughts and their feelings about participating in psychology experiments (Norman, 1975). The students were then ranked in terms of how positively they *felt* about participating, and how positively they *thought* about participating (for example, whether they thought participating would advance their goals). This permitted each student to be scored for affective-cognitive consistency. Those who ranked high on both thoughts and feelings about participating in psychology experiments were deemed consistent, as were those who ranked low in both. Those who ranked high on one but low on the other were deemed inconsistent. Three weeks later, a different experimenter asked the students if they would participate in a psychology experiment. Those who ranked high on both thoughts and feelings tended to say yes, and those who ranked low on both tended to say no. The behavior of students who were affectively and cognitively consistent, in other words, was predictable. The behavior of the inconsistent students was not. Among these students, neither their thoughts nor their feelings about participating in psychology experiments were very good predictors of whether they actually agreed to participate (Chaiken & Baldwin, 1981).

*Introspecting about the Reasons for Our Attitudes*    The inconsistency we sometimes experience between our thoughts and feelings about something has important implications for what we are likely to get out of introspecting about the reasons we like or dislike it. Consider your attitude toward a person to whom you are attracted. Why are you attracted to that person? If you put this question to yourself, a number of factors are likely to spring to mind: "He's cute." "She's ambitious." "She's not at all demanding."

But many times it's not so easy to know exactly why we like someone. It may not be because of specific, readily identifiable attributes; we may simply share some indescribable chemistry. When introspecting about such cases, however, we may focus on what is easy to identify, easy to justify, and easy to capture in words—and thus miss out on the real reasons for our attraction. Timothy Wilson and his colleagues put this idea to empirical test by asking students about the person they were dating. Participants in one group were simply asked for an overall evaluation of their relationship. Those in another group were first asked to list why they felt the way they did and then to give an overall evaluation of their relationship. The researchers recontacted the participants nearly nine months later and asked about the status of their relationship. The attitudes of participants in the first group were much more accurate predictors of the current status of the relationship than were those of participants who had introspected about their reasons for liking their partners (Wilson, Dunn, Bybee, Hyman, & Rotondo, 1984). Thinking about why we like someone can sometimes lead to confusion about how much we like that person.

Wilson has shown that this effect applies far beyond our attitudes toward romantic partners and that introspecting about the reasons for our attitudes about all sorts of objects can undermine how well those attitudes guide our behavior. The cause in all cases is the same: introspection may lead us to focus on the easiest-to-identify reasons for liking or disliking something at the expense of

**Inconsistent Attitudes**    There is often a disconnect between attitudes and behavior when a person's attitudes have inconsistent components. William Bennett, who served as Secretary of Education under Ronald Reagan and drug czar under George H. W. Bush, advocated high standards and moral behavior and wrote the best-selling *The Book of Virtues*. Yet, Bennett's attitudes toward moral behavior were seemingly at odds with his high-stakes gambling (he lost millions of dollars). Was there an inconsistency between what he thought and felt about morality, or did gambling not fit his prototype of immoral behavior?

the *real* reasons for our likes and dislikes. When people are induced to think carefully about the reasons they prefer one product over another (as opposed to simply stating a preference), their choices are less likely to correspond to the "true" value of the product as determined by experts (Wilson & Schooler, 1991). Also, when people reflect on their reasons before making a choice (again, as opposed to simply choosing), they are more likely to subsequently regret their choice (Wilson et al., 1993).

Does this mean that introspection is always (or even typically) harmful, and so we should dispense with careful analysis and always go with our gut? Not at all. In deciding whether to launch a military campaign, for example, it is imperative that no analytic stone goes unturned and that the reasons for and against the idea have been exhaustively considered from all angles. More generally, there are many occasions when the real reasons for our attitudes are perfectly easy to identify and articulate, and so introspection will produce no rift between the variables we think are guiding our attitudes and those that actually are. The contaminating effect of introspection is limited to those circumstances in which the true sources of our attitudes are hard to pin down. This happens most often when the basis of our attitudes is largely affective, so that a cognitive analysis of reasons for a particular attitude is likely to seize upon seemingly plausible but misleading cognitive reasons. When the basis of our attitudes is largely cognitive, in contrast, the search for reasons is more likely to yield the real reasons, and introspection is unlikely to diminish the relationship between attitudes and behavior (Millar & Tesser, 1986; Wilson & Dunn, 1986). Thus, introspecting about the reasons why you like a certain artist may create a rift between your expressed attitudes and your subsequent behavior, but introspecting about why you would prefer one digital camera over another is unlikely to create such a rift.

## ATTITUDES ARE SOMETIMES BASED ON SECONDHAND INFORMATION

What is your attitude toward Fiji? Connecticut Senator Joseph Lieberman? The Moonies? Chances are you have attitudes about all three, perhaps even very strong ones. Yet, you've probably never been to Fiji, have never met Senator Lieberman, and have never (knowingly) encountered any actual Moonies—that is, members of Reverend Sun Myung Moon's Unification Church. This creates the possibility that your attitude may be a bit off the mark, and thus may not match how you would behave if you actually went to Fiji, met Senator Lieberman, or were confronted by a member of the Unification Church. Similarly, the hoteliers and restaurateurs in LaPiere's study may have had precious little exposure to Chinese individuals, and so what they imagined "Orientals" were like may not have matched the actual Chinese couple they encountered. Their abstract attitude toward "Orientals" thus did not predict the behavioral response elicited by this particular Chinese couple.

Numerous experiments have shown that attitudes based on direct (or firsthand) experience predict subsequent behavior much better than those derived indirectly (or secondhand). In one of the earliest studies, Dennis Regan and Russ Fazio (1977) measured Cornell University students' attitudes about a housing shortage that caused some freshman students to spend the first month or two of the year sleeping on a cot in a dormitory lounge. Some of the students had firsthand experience with the housing crisis because they were the ones forced to sleep on the cots; others had merely heard about the crisis or read about it in the student newspaper. The students expressed their attitudes on such questions as how much they thought the affected students had suffered as a result of the crisis, how concerned they thought the administration was about the shortage, and what priority the administration should assign to solving the crisis. The students were also given an opportunity to act on their attitudes—to sign a petition demanding that the administration take steps to solve the crisis, write a letter that the researchers would take to the administration, and sign up to join a committee to make recommendations about the housing situation.

Clearly, the students who were directly affected by the crisis were more likely to take action, but that was not the focus of the study. Instead, Regan and Fazio were interested in whether the *correlation* between the students' attitudes and their overt behavior was higher among the directly affected students than among the others. It was. Among the directly affected students, those with strong attitudes about the crisis were much more likely to take relevant action than those with less strong opinions. Among students who were not directly affected, this relationship was much weaker.

Additional studies have shown this to be a very reliable effect. Attitudes about participating in psychological research predict actual participation much more strongly among those who have previously taken part in research (Fazio & Zanna, 1978). Attitudes about solving intellectual puzzles predict more strongly who will attempt to solve them among those who have previously tried their hands at such puzzles (Regan & Fazio, 1977). And attitudes about flu shots predict whether one gets inoculated more strongly among those have received flu shots in the past (Davidson, Yantis, Norwood, & Montano, 1985). When the attitudes we have about some object or event are based on firsthand experience, our attitudes turn out to be rather telling guides to our subsequent actions after all.

## MISMATCHED ATTITUDES AND ACTUAL ATTITUDE TARGETS

Closely related to the previous point is the possibility that our attitude may not match the attitude "target" we confront. Typically, in fact, the attitudes we express are about general classes of things—the environment, pushy people, French cooking, or global trade. But the attitude-relevant behavior that is typically assessed deals with a particular instance of that class—donating to Greenpeace, reacting to a specific insistent individual, ordering *foie gras*, or picketing a meeting of the World Trade Organization. Because of such a vast mismatch in the level of specificity between general attitudes and specific instances of real behavior, it is no wonder that attitudes do not always predict behavior particularly well.

Several studies have shown that attitude-behavior consistency is higher when the attitude and behavior are at the same level of specificity. Highly specific attitudes typically do a better job of predicting specific behaviors, and rather general attitudes typically do a better job of predicting how one behaves "in general" across a number of different manifestations of, say, environmentalism, political activism, or xenophobia (Ajzen, 1987).

In one study that illustrates this point nicely, 244 married women were asked a number of questions about their attitudes toward birth control pills (Davidson & Jaccard, 1979). The questions varied from the general (what they thought about birth control) to the specific (what they thought about using birth control *pills* during the next two years). The investigators then waited two years before recontacting the respondents, at which time they asked them whether they had used birth control pills at any point since the initial survey. What the investigators discovered was that the women's general attitudes toward birth control were

**General Attitudes and Specific Targets** A person who dislikes and complains about global free trade may not demonstrate against the World Trade Organization (WTO). Yet, someone who holds very strong attitudes against the WTO specifically may engage in a protest against it, as here in Seattle, Washington, in 1999.

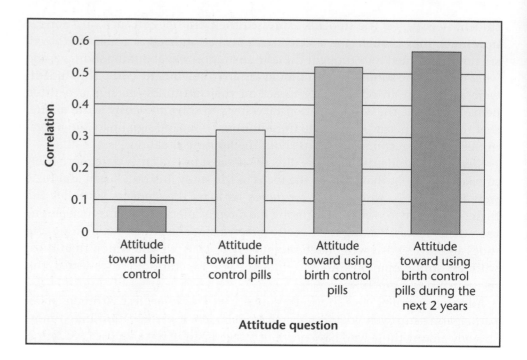

**Figure 8.2 Attitude Specificity and the Ability of Attitudes to Predict Behavior** The correlation between whether or not a sample of women used birth control pills during a two-year period and their responses to a number of different attitude questions. (Source: Davidson & Jaccard, 1979)

unrelated to whether they used birth control pills during the period of the study. But their more specific attitudes about using birth control pills in the near future were strongly predictive of whether they actually used them (see Figure 8.2).

These findings may also help to explain LaPiere's results. The attitudes expressed by the various merchants LaPiere surveyed were rather general—whether they would serve "Orientals." But the behavior, of course, involved one specific Chinese couple with a specific demeanor and bearing, and dressed in a specific fashion. Perhaps the results would have been different if LaPiere had asked the merchants whether they would serve a well-dressed Chinese couple of impeccable demeanor. If you want to predict a specific behavior accurately, you have to measure people's attitudes toward that specific behavior.

The broader point here is that what we usually think of as attitudes toward different classes of people, places, things, and events are often expressions of our attitude toward a prototype of a given category. But if we encounter a specific situation or person who doesn't fit the prototype, it's likely that our behavior in this situation or toward the person in question will not reflect our stated attitudes. Consider the findings of a study by Charles Lord, Mark Lepper, and Diane Mackie (1984) in which they asked male college students about their attitudes toward gay men. The researchers also elicited from each student his stereotype of the "typical" gay man. Approximately two months later, the students were approached by a different experimenter and asked if they would be willing to show some visiting students around campus. One of the visitors, "John B.," was described in such a way that the participants would think he was gay. For half the participants, the rest of the description of "John B" was crafted to fit their own, individualized stereotype of a male homosexual; for the other half, it was not. What the investigators found was that the students' willingness to show "John B." around campus was strongly predicted by their attitudes toward gay men (those with positive attitudes said they were willing; those with negative attitudes said they were not), but only if "John B." matched their prototype of a gay individual (Lord, Lepper, & Mackie, 1984; see also Lord, Desforges, Ramsey, Trezza, & Lepper, 1991).

# "Automatic" Behavior That Bypasses Conscious Attitudes

When most people think of attitudes influencing behavior, they think of a person reflecting on her attitude and then choosing to behave in line with it (or not). The influence of the attitude on behavior is conscious and deliberate. The theory of reasoned action certainly reflects this view, and the success of that theory indicates that there are many times when our attitudes influence our behavior in exactly this way. But many times our behavior is more reflexive than reflective, and the prevailing situational stimuli may elicit behavior automatically.

To be sure, sometimes our automatic behavior is consistent with—indeed caused by—our attitudes. In fact, that's one of the purposes of attitudes: they allow us to respond quickly, without having to do much weighing of pros and cons. We go with our gut feeling. But some types of automatic behavior bypass our attitudes altogether, as when we jump away from something that looks like a snake in the grass. When such actions are elicited directly and mindlessly from the surrounding context, the connection between attitudes and behavior will necessarily be weak. One of the strongest and most influential research trends in social psychology over the past decade has been uncovering more and more instances in which our behavior is automatically elicited by stimuli present in the environment. Let's consider some noteworthy examples.

In an experiment described as an investigation of "language proficiency," participants were asked to perform a sentence-completion task. They were given thirty sets of 5 words each and were asked to form a grammatical English sentence using four of them. For half the participants, embedded within these 150 words were many that are stereotypically associated with the elderly—gray, wrinkle, Florida, bingo, and so on. This was designed to **prime** (mentally activate) the concept of the elderly among these participants. The remaining participants were exposed to neutral words that are not associated with the elderly, and hence their concept of the elderly was not "primed." The experimenter then thanked the participants for their efforts, and the study, from the participants' perspective, was over.

But it had only begun. A second experimenter covertly timed how long it took each participant to walk from the threshold of the laboratory to the elevator down the hall. The investigators had predicted that merely activating the concept of the elderly for some of the participants would make them automatically mimic how they habitually behave around the elderly, and thus walk more slowly down the hallway. Amazingly, it did. Participants who had performed the sentence-completion task using numerous words associated with the elderly took 13 percent longer to walk to the elevator (Bargh, Chen, & Burrows, 1996).

Social psychologists of late have been remarkably successful in demonstrating numerous instances of this sort of automatic behavior. The activation of different mental contents—traits, stereotypes, and goals—often directly elicits behavior dictated by those mental contents without any awareness on the part of the individuals so affected. Activating the traits of rudeness or intelligence, for example, has been shown to make people behave more assertively or to perform better on tests of general knowledge (Bargh, Chen, & Burrows, 1996; Dijksterhuis & van Knippenberg, 1998). Activating the goal of achievement has been shown to lead people to persevere longer at difficult tasks (Bargh, Gollwitzer, Lee-Chai, Barndollar, & Trotschel, 2001). In possibly the most remarkable set of demonstrations, Dutch social psychologists Ap Dijksterhuis and Ad van Knippenberg

> "Civilization advances by extending the number of operations we can perform without thinking about them."
> —Alfred North Whitehead

**prime** A stimulus (typically a word or image) presented to mentally activate a concept, and hence make it accessible.

**Priming** Activating general categories like professor or supermodel may lead people to construe themselves along the lines of that category and to act as they think someone in that category would act. Activating a specific instance of that category, however, such as (A) Albert Einstein, or (B) Claudia Schiffer, may have the opposite effect, leading people to act inconsistently with the category stereotype, as people may compare themselves to these specific people and feel that they aren't like them much at all.

primed students either with a social category associated with intellectual accomplishment (professors) or with a social category not noted for refined habits of mind (soccer hooligans). Those primed with the professor cues subsequently performed better on a test of general knowledge than those primed with cues associated with soccer hooligans (Dijksterhuis & van Knippenberg, 1998).

More remarkably still, Dijksterhuis, van Knippenberg, and their colleagues demonstrated that activating the category of professor or supermodel led participants to perform in a manner *consistent* with the category, but activating a specific instance (example) of the category (for example, Albert Einstein, Claudia Schiffer) led participants to perform in a manner *inconsistent* with the category stereotype. That is, they performed worse on the general-knowledge test when primed with Einstein and better when primed with Claudia Schiffer (Dijksterhuis et al., 1998). These results fit the general tendency for the activation of *categories* to produce behavior in line with the category in question because it affects construal. People think of themselves as (and act!) more intelligent when viewing themselves—however implicitly—through the "lens" of a professor than they do when viewing themselves through the lens of a model. The activation of *instances* of a category, in contrast, tends to yield behavior that contrasts with the category in question (Herr, 1986; Schwarz & Bless, 1992; Stapel, Koomen, & van der Plight, 1997). This is because instances tend to serve as standards of judgment—in this case, Einstein serves as a very high standard (making people feel unintelligent), and Claudia Schiffer serves as a relatively low standard (making people feel smart).

Much of this recent work on the automatic nature of everyday social behavior provides another reason why there is often a limit to how well attitudes predict behavior. Those types of automatic behavior that bypass our conscious attitudes are, by definition, beyond the influence of our stated attitudes.

**LOOKING BACK,** we have seen that attitudes can be surprisingly weak predictors of behavior. This occurs because attitudes sometimes conflict with social norms about appropriate behavior, because general attitudes sometimes do not correspond to the specific action that is required in a given situation, because the affective and cognitive components of an attitude may not be in sync, and because some behavior is automatic and bypasses conscious thought altogether. In the next section, we will see that behavior often influences attitudes to a marked degree.

# PREDICTING ATTITUDES FROM BEHAVIOR

Many young people have chafed at being sent to church, temple, or mosque, often with the complaint, "Why do I have to go? I don't believe any of this stuff." And many of them have been told, "It doesn't matter if you believe it. What's important is that you continue with your studies and your prayers." Some resist to the very end, and abandon the endeavor the minute their parents give them permission. But a remarkable number stick with it and, after doing so, find themselves genuinely holding some of the very religious convictions and sentiments they originally resisted. Over time, mere outward behavior can give way to genuine inner conviction.

This illustrates the second part of our story on the connection between attitudes and behavior. We just learned that attitudes can predict behavior, but not as strongly as most people would suspect. That is one part of the story. The second part of the story is how powerfully behavior can influence attitudes. Social psychological research over the past half century has documented time and time again the surprising extent to which people tend to bring their attitudes in line with their actions. This urge reflects the powerful tendency to justify or rationalize our behavior and to minimize any inconsistencies between our attitudes and actions.

> "Well done is better than well said."
> —BENJAMIN FRANKLIN

**balance theory** A theory that people try to maintain balance among their beliefs, cognitions, and sentiments.

## COGNITIVE CONSISTENCY THEORIES

Why does our behavior have such a powerful influence on our attitudes? A number of influential theories have been put forward to explain this relationship. As a group, they are referred to as "cognitive consistency" theories, and they attempt to account for some of the most common sources of rationalization that we use to bring our attitudes in line with our actions.

*Balance Theory*    The earliest social psychological consistency theory was Fritz Heider's **balance theory**. Heider (1946) claimed that people try to maintain balance among their beliefs, cognitions, and sentiments. If your two friends like each other, everything is fine and balanced. But if your two friends detest each other, you've got a problem: you have an imbalanced set of relationships on your hands. According to Heider, you will exert psychological energy to achieve or restore balance in this set of relationships. You may, for example, decide you like one friend less, or conclude that their dislike of each other is a misunderstanding based on a relatively trivial issue.

In a threesome (or triad), things are balanced if the product of the three sentiments (+ for liking, − for disliking) is positive. If my enemy (−) is disliked by a particular person (−), balance is achieved by

**Balance Theory**    People like to maintain balance between what their heroes like and what they like. When LeBron James of the Cleveland Cavaliers endorses Nike Air Zoom Generation sneakers, his fans may be inclined to buy those sneakers to maintain balance between their support for James, the products he likes, and the products that they themselves like.

**Balanced Relationships**  It's easier to remember that Jerry, George, Elaine, and Kramer from *Seinfeld* like each other than that Kramer likes Jerry and Newman, but Jerry and Newman detest each other.

my liking that person (+): (−) × (−) × (+) = +. You'll recognize that advertisers take advantage of this desire for balance. They'll have a beloved celebrity (+) say positive things (+) about a burger establishment or brand of basketball shoe, which puts psychological pressure on you to like that type of burger or shoe [(+) × (+) × (+) = +].

Support for Heider's balance theory comes from studies that either establish two relationships in a triad and then elicit people's inferences about the third, or present various balanced and imbalanced relationships and then examine how well people remember them or how favorably they rate them. People "fill in" unspecified relations by assuming balance, and they both remember balanced relationships better and rate them more favorably (Hummert, Crockett, & Kemper, 1990; Insko, 1984). It's easier to remember that *Seinfeld's* Jerry, George, and Elaine all like each other than that Kramer likes Jerry and Newman, who can't stand each other. And if you know the president likes his vice-president and likes to watch pro football, you'll be tempted to conclude that the vice-president likes to watch football too.

*Cognitive Dissonance Theory*  By far the most influential consistency theory, and possibly the most influential theory in the entire field of social psychology, is Leon Festinger's **cognitive dissonance theory** (Festinger, 1957). Like Heider, Festinger argued that people are troubled by inconsistency between their thoughts, sentiments, and actions, and that they will expend psychological energy to restore consistency. More specifically, Festinger thought that an aversive emotional state—dissonance—is aroused whenever people experience an inconsistency between two cognitions. Because the cognitions can be about their own behavior (for example, "I just failed to live up to my vow"), the theory posits that people are troubled by inconsistency between their cognitions and their behavior as well. This unpleasant emotional state motivates behavior to restore consistency.

What counts as cognitive inconsistency and how do people get rid of it? According to Festinger, people try to eliminate or reduce inconsistency by changing one or more of the discrepant cognitions to make them consistent. No controversy there. But his views about what exactly constitutes inconsistency have been modified by the tremendous amount of research that his theory inspired. Festinger argued that we experience inconsistency (and dissonance) whenever the opposite of one cognition follows from the other. If you think Friends of the Earth is a more worthy charity than the American Society for the Prevention of Cruelty to Animals (ASPCA), you'll experience some dissonance if you give your money to the ASPCA instead of Friends of the Earth. As we shall see, this definition of inconsistency doesn't quite work, both because it's vague (it's not always clear what the opposite of a given cognition might be) and because it predicts more dissonance than people actually experience (if you claim you don't like surprises and yet you find yourself delighted by a surprise birthday party, you are unlikely to be troubled by the inconsistency). Although Festinger may have been a bit off the mark in this regard, the overall theory has proven to be very insightful and productive, and subsequent efforts to specify what exactly constitutes

**cognitive dissonance theory**
The theory that inconsistencies among a person's thoughts, sentiments, and actions create an aversive emotional state (dissonance) that leads to efforts to restore consistency.

**Leon Festinger**  Studying how people evaluate themselves and their actions, as well as how they bring their attitudes in line with their behavior, Leon Festinger developed both social comparison theory and cognitive dissonance theory.

psychological inconsistency have done a great deal to further our understanding of psychological conflict and rationalization.

## EXPERIENCING AND REDUCING DISSONANCE

To develop some sense of the kinds of inconsistency that people find troubling, and to get a flavor for the diverse phenomena that can be explained by the theory of cognitive dissonance, let's take a look at some of the classic experiments on the subject—experiments that have excited generations of students of social psychology.

*Decisions and Dissonance*   Even a moment's reflection tells us that all hard decisions arouse some dissonance. Because the decision is hard, there must be some desirable features of the rejected alternative, some undesirable features of the chosen alternative, or both. All are inconsistent with the choice that was made, and hence they produce dissonance (Brehm, 1956). If you move to Los Angeles from a small town in the Midwest in pursuit of good weather, you'll enjoy the sun, but the dirty air and hours spent in traffic will likely arouse dissonance. According to Festinger, once you've made an irrevocable decision to move to L.A., you'll exert mental effort to reduce this dissonance. You'll rationalize. You'll maintain that the lack of visibility is mainly due to haze, not smog, and you'll tell your friends about how much you've learned from the "books on tape" you listen to on your long commute.

Numerous experiments have documented this tendency for people to rationalize their decisions. In one study, the investigators interviewed bettors at a racetrack, some just before and some just after placing their bets on a particular horse (Knox & Inkster, 1968). The investigators reasoned that the act of placing a bet and making an irrevocable choice of a particular horse would cause the bettors to reduce the dissonance associated with all the negative features of the chosen horse (doesn't do well on a wet track) and all the positive features of the competing horses (the perfect distance for one horse, the best jockey on another). Dissonance reduction

**Rationalizing Decisions to Reduce Dissonance**   After placing a bet at the track, as here at the Kentucky Derby, people are likely to concentrate on the positive features of the horse they bet on and to downplay any negative features. This rationalization process gives them greater confidence in the choice they made.

should be reflected in greater confidence on the part of those interviewed right *after* placing their bets. That is exactly what the investigators found. Those who were interviewed as they waited in line to place their bets gave their horses, on average, a "fair" chance of winning the race; those who were interviewed after they had placed their bets and were leaving the ticket window gave their horses, on average, a "good" chance to win. One participant provided some extra commentary that serves as something of a window on the process of dissonance reduction. This participant had been interviewed while waiting in line (that is, before placing his bet) but then, emerging from the ticket window, he approached another member of the research team and said, "Are you working with that other fellow there? Well, I just told

him that my horse had a fair chance of winning. Will you have him change that to a good chance? No, by God, make that an excellent chance." Making hard decisions triggers dissonance, which in turn triggers processes of rationalization that make us more comfortable with our choices. Similar findings have been observed in elections: voters express greater confidence in their candidates when they are interviewed after they have voted and are leaving the polling station than when they are interviewed approaching it (Frenkel & Doob, 1976; Regan & Kilduff, 1988).

Festinger argued that dissonance-reduction processes only arise after an irrevocable decision has been made. He maintained, for example, that:

> One may regard the theoretical question as settled. There is a clear and undeniable difference between the cognitive processes that occur during the period of making a decision and those that occur after the decision has been made. Reevaluation of alternatives in the direction of favoring the chosen or disfavoring the rejected alternative . . . is a post-decision phenomenon. (Festinger, 1964, p. 30)

**effort justification** The tendency to reduce dissonance by finding reasons for why a person has devoted time, effort, or money for something that turned out to be unpleasant or disappointing to the person.

The evidence from the betting and election studies we have just reviewed seems to support Festinger's contention. But this claim is an odd one in light of other things we know about people. One of humankind's distinguishing characteristics is the ability to anticipate the future. If, in the process of making a decision, one sees that there are blemishes associated with what is emerging as one's favorite option, why not start the process of rationalization beforehand so that dissonance is minimized or eliminated altogether (Wilson, Wheatley, Kurtz, Dunn, & Gilbert, 2004)?

Indeed, during the past decade, research has established that the same sorts of rationalization and distortion that dissonance experiments have documented after decisions have been made also subconsciously take place *before* they are made. This research has shown that, whether choosing restaurants, vacation spots, consumer goods, or political candidates, once people develop a slight preference for one option over the others they distort subsequent information to support their initial preference (Brownstein, 2003; Russo, Medvec, & Meloy, 1996; Russo, Meloy, & Medvec, 1998; Simon, Krawczyk, & Holyoak, 2004; Simon, Pham, Le, & Holyoak, 2001). Thus, the small size of a French restaurant tends to be rated as a plus by those leaning toward French food ("nice and intimate"), but as a minus by those leaning toward Thai food ("we won't be able to talk without everyone overhearing us"). It appears, then, that Festinger was right that decisions evoke dissonance and dissonance reduction, but these processes occur more often and more broadly than he anticipated—they can occur both before and after decisions are made.

**Effort Justification**   This college freshman is undergoing a hazing ritual as he runs down a gauntlet of upperclassmen who are swinging paddles at him. To justify the painful and humiliating experience, he may come to value the group that he is trying to join even more.

*Effort Justification*   The element of dissonance theory that rings most true to many people is the idea that if you pay a high price for something—in dollars, time, or effort, it doesn't matter which—and it turns out to be disappointing, you're likely to experience dissonance. As a result, you're likely to devote mental energy to justifying your effort. The most salient example of **effort justification** on campus, perhaps, is fraternity hazing. Someone who undergoes a painful or humiliating initiation ritual will have a need to believe it was all worthwhile, and one way to do that is to extol the virtues of being in that particular fraternity. The Greek system, in other words, capitalizes on cognitive dissonance. The same dynamics exist elsewhere, of course. Those who don't own pets often suspect that pet lovers exaggerate the pleasure they get from their animals in order to offset all the early-morning walking, poop scooping, and furniture wrecking. And those who choose not to have children suspect that homebound, sleep-deprived, overtaxed parents are fooling themselves when they say that nothing in life brings greater pleasure.

The role of dissonance reduction in such situations was explored in an early study by Aronson and Mills (1959). The female undergraduate participants in their study signed up for an experiment thinking it involved joining an ongoing discussion group about sex. When they arrived, however, they were told that not everyone can speak freely and comfortably about such a topic, and so potential participants needed to pass a screening test in order to join the group. Those assigned to a control condition simply read aloud a list of innocuous words to the male experimenter. Those assigned to the mild initiation condition read aloud a list of mildly embarrassing words—for example, "prostitute," "petting," "virgin." Finally, those assigned to the severe initiation group had to read aloud a list of quite obscene words and a passage from a novel describing sexual intercourse.

All participants were then told they had passed their screening test and could join the discussion group. The group was meeting that very day, but because everyone else had been given a reading assignment beforehand, the participant was told that it was best if she just listened in on this session. Then, over head-phones in a nearby cubicle, the participant heard a stultifyingly boring discussion of the sex life of invertebrates. Not only was the topic not what the participants had in mind when they signed up for a discussion group about sex, but the members of the discussion group " . . . contradicted themselves and one another, mumbled several non sequiturs, started sentences that they never finished, hemmed, hawed, and in general conducted one of the most worthless and unin-teresting discussions imaginable" (Aronson & Mills, 1959, p. 179).

Aronson and Mills argued that the discussion was boring and disappointing to all the participants but it produced dissonance only for those who had under-gone a severe initiation to join the group. The cognition "I suffered to get into this group" is inconsistent with the realization that "this group is worthless and boring." One way for the participants in the severe initiation condition to reduce dissonance would be to convince themselves that the group and the discussion were not so boring after all. And that's just what they did. When the experi-menters asked participants at the end of the study to rate the quality of the dis-cussion on a number of scales, those in the severe initiation condition rated it more favorably than those in the other two conditions (see Figure 8.3).

This sort of *sweet lemons rationalization* ("it's really not so bad") is fairly com-mon and can often be seen in everyday life. One particularly noteworthy mani-festation was explored by Joel Cooper, who wondered about the role of effort justification in psychotherapy. Students in clinical psychology programs are often warned about giving in to the impulse to treat certain clients free of charge. Payment is viewed as an extra incentive for the client to do the hard work nec-essary for the therapy to succeed. All that we have seen thus far suggests that clients will indeed tend to work harder to justify paying the therapist's rather large fee. But this invites the question of how much of a client's improvement is due to the specifics of a particular therapy and how much of it is due to trying to prevent or reduce cognitive dissonance. Effort justification may arise not only because of the high fee, but also because of the hard work involved in therapy.

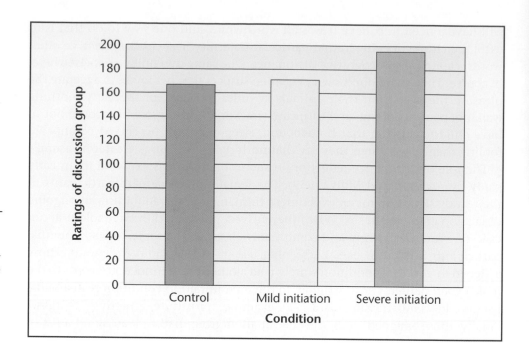

**Figure 8.3 Group Initiation and Liking for the Group**    Ratings of a discussion group by participants who experienced no initiation, a mild initiation, or a severe initiation to join the group. (Source: Adapted from Aronson & Mills, 1959)

**Effort Justification in Psychotherapy**
Psychotherapy may work both because of the therapist and her treatment, but also because the patient feels the need to justify the hard work and high cost of the therapy sessions.

Clients must dredge up traumatic episodes, confess to embarrassing personal shortcomings, and go over troublesome issues from childhood—all of which may need to be justified to avoid the dissonance that would result if the effort was (or was thought to be) unsuccessful.

Cooper (1980) pursued this question by comparing the effectiveness of standard treatments of specific psychopathological conditions with a bogus therapy that consists of nothing more than hard work. Does the effort to justify the hard work involved in the bogus therapy make it as successful as legitimate therapies? In one study, Cooper had students who suffered from an inability to be assertive engage either in an accepted treatment procedure or forty minutes of strenuous physical exercise. The standard treatment was behavioral rehearsal, in which the person thinks of stressful situations in which assertiveness is called for and imagines acting assertively. The exercise therapy was "sold" to participants as effective because increased physical activity increases social sensitivity, which in turn has "an inhibiting effect on fear of assertiveness or, to put it another way, it may help you to become assertive."

Participants in both conditions were told before they received their "treatment" that they would receive $2 for participating in this clinical study. When they finished with the study, however, they were sent to a receptionist who paid them, without comment, only $1. The key test of the effectiveness of the therapy was whether participants asked for, and perhaps even insisted on, the other dollar. Someone who has trouble being assertive, after all, is unlikely to summon what it takes to demand the full payment. What Cooper found (see Figure 8.4) was that both "therapies" were effective: participants in each of these two conditions were more insistent on receiving the extra $1 than participants in a control condition. But the standard therapy was not signifi-

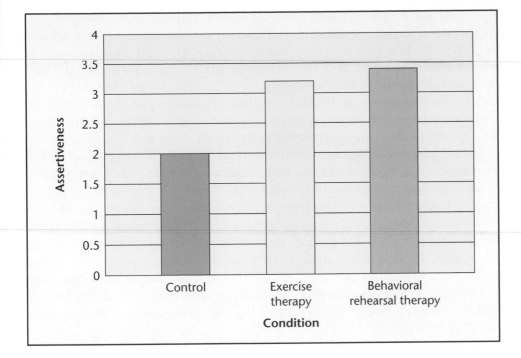

**Figure 8.4 Effort Justification and the Effectiveness of Psychotherapy** The amount of assertiveness exhibited by unassertive individuals who received either no special treatment, a standard psychotherapeutic intervention (behavioral rehearsal), or a novel effort-only treatment (physical exercise). The dependent measure (as represented by the numbers on the y-axis) refers to how assertively the participant reacted to being given less than the promised amount for participating in the study. (Source: Cooper, 1980)

cantly more effective than Cooper's bogus exercise therapy. The need to justify the high price (in money, effort, and unpleasantness) that one pays in psychotherapy appears to be an important component of its success—or, at any rate, of people's evaluations of its success.

*Induced Compliance and Attitude Change* Dissonance theory can also explain what often happens as a result of **induced (forced) compliance**—that is, as a result of inducing individuals to behave in a manner that is inconsistent with their beliefs, attitudes, or values. Most people will feel some discomfort with the mismatch between their behavior and their attitudes. One way to deal with the inconsistency—the easiest and most likely way, given that the behavior cannot be taken back—is for people to change their original attitudes or values. This was the core idea behind Lyndon Johnson's stratagem, described in the opening to this chapter: by having doubters in his administration give press conferences in which they publicly defended the administration's position, the inconsistency between their private doubts and their public comments led them to dispel their doubts.

Numerous experiments have demonstrated how powerfully induced compliance can shift a person's original attitudes. In the very first experiment that demonstrated such an effect, Leon Festinger and Merrill Carlsmith (1959) had participants engage in what can only be described as experimental drudgery for an hour (loading spools on a tray over and over, turning pegs on a pegboard one quarter turn at a time). Participants in the control condition were sent immediately afterwards to see someone from the Psychology Department who would interview them about their experiences as research volunteers. When asked how much they enjoyed the experiment, they gave quite low ratings. No surprise there.

Participants in two other conditions were told that the experiment was about how people's performance on a task is influenced by their expectations about it beforehand. These participants were led to believe that they were in a control, "no expectation" condition, but that other subjects were told beforehand that

**induced (forced) compliance** Subtly compelling individuals to behave in a manner that is inconsistent with their beliefs, attitudes, or values, which typically leads to dissonance and often to a change in their original attitudes or values in order to reduce their dissonance.

the study was either very interesting or boring. Looking rather sheepish, the experimenter explained that the next participant was about to show up and needed to be told that the study was interesting. This was usually done, the experimenter explained, by a confederate posing as a participant. But the confederate was absent, putting the experimenter in a bit of a jam. Would you, the experimenter asked the participant, play the role usually played by the confederate and tell the next participant that the experiment is interesting? The experimenter offered the participant either $1 or $20 for doing so.

In this "play within a play," the true participant thinks he's a confederate and believes the other person (the real confederate) is the next participant. What is most important to the experiment, and what is readily apparent to the participant, is that he has just lied (nearly every participant agreed to the request) and said that a mind-numbingly boring study is interesting. Festinger and Carlsmith argued that this act would produce dissonance for those participants who were given only $1 for the assignment. Their words were inconsistent with their beliefs, and $1 was not enough to justify the lie. Those given $20 could at least tell themselves that, yes, they did lie, but they were justified in doing so (and nearly anyone else would do so) because the pay was so good and the lie was of little consequence.

Festinger and Carlsmith predicted that participants in the $1 condition would rationalize their behavior—that is, they would reduce their dissonance—by changing their attitude about the tasks they had performed. By convincing themselves that the task was not uninteresting after all, their lie would not really be a lie. When later asked by the person from the Psychology Department to evaluate their experience, these participants would rate the task more favorably. As Figure 8.5 indicates, that is exactly what they did. Only the participants in the $1 condition rated the activities above the neutral point.

Note that there is a broad and very important lesson here about how best to influence someone else's attitudes, a lesson that has important implications for child rearing, among other things. If you want to get people to do something (take school seriously, take care of the environment, avoid foul language), and

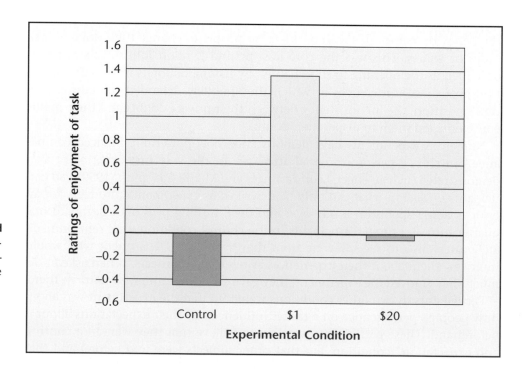

**Figure 8.5 Induced Compliance and Attitude Change** Ratings by participants in the control, $1, and $20 conditions of how much they enjoyed the boring experimental task after telling another student it was interesting. (Source: Festinger & Carlsmith, 1959)

you want them to internalize the broader message or value behind what you have gotten them to do, then use the smallest amount of incentive or coercion necessary to get them to do it. In other words, don't go overboard with the incentives. If the inducements are too substantial, people will justify their behavior by the inducements (like the $20 condition of Festinger and Carlsmith's study), and they will not need to rationalize their behavior by coming to believe in the broader purpose or philosophy behind it. But if the inducements are just barely sufficient (as in the $1 condition), people's need to rationalize will tend to produce deep-seated attitude change in line with their behavior. Thus, for example, if you're going to pay your children for doing their homework, be sure you pay them the least amount necessary to get them to do it.

Evidence in support of this idea—and of its potential role in child rearing—comes from experiments using what is known as the "forbidden toy" paradigm (Aronson & Carlsmith, 1963; Freedman, 1965; Lepper, 1973). In one experiment of this type, an experimenter showed nursery school children a set of five toys and asked the children to tell him how much they liked each one. The experimenter then explained that he would have to leave the room for a while, but that he would be back soon. In the meantime, the child was free to play with any of the toys, except for the child's second favorite. Half the children were told not to play with the forbidden toy and that the experimenter would "be annoyed" if they did. This was the *mild threat* condition. In the *severe threat* condition, the children were told that if they played with the forbidden toy the experimenter "would be very angry" and "would have to take all of my toys and go home and never come back again."

While the experimenter was gone, each child was covertly observed, and none played with the forbidden toy. Aronson and Carlsmith predicted that this restraint from playing with the forbidden toy would produce dissonance, but only for the children in the mild threat condition. For them, the desirability of the toy would be inconsistent with their not playing with it, an inconsistency that Aronson and Carlsmith predicted the children would resolve by derogating the toy—by convincing themselves that it wasn't such a great toy after all. Those who received the severe threat should experience no such dissonance because not playing with it was justified by the threat they received. Thus, nothing would cause them to derogate the toy. To find out if their predictions were correct, Aronson and Carlsmith had the children reevaluate all five toys when the experimenter returned. As expected, the children in the severe threat condition either did not change their opinion of the forbidden toy or they liked it even more than beforehand (see Figure 8.6). In contrast, many of those in the mild threat condition viewed it less favorably, and none viewed it more favorably. Thus, the threat of severe punishment will keep children from doing something you don't want them to do, but they will still, later on, want to do it. The threat of mild punishment—if it's just enough of a threat to keep them from doing it—can bring about psychological change, such that they will no longer even be tempted to do what you don't want them to do.

In a subsequent experiment using this paradigm, Freedman (1965) found that children were still derogating the forbidden toy six weeks later. Thus, the psychological changes wrought by induced compliance can be quite enduring. They can also be quite pervasive. Mark Lepper (1973) conducted a forbidden toy experiment and found that being induced, under minimal constraint, to refrain from playing with an attractive toy can lead to substantial changes in a person's more general self-concept. In particular, three weeks after participating in a forbidden toy experiment, a group of children participated in another experiment in which

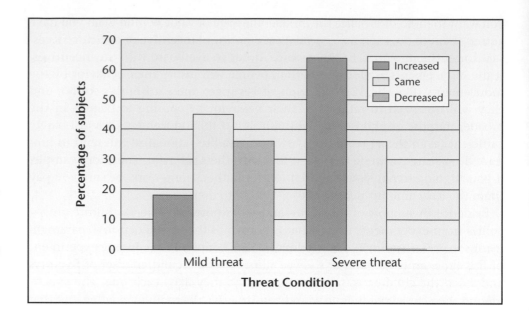

**Figure 8.6 Derogation of the Forbidden Toy** The percentage of children in the mild and severe threat conditions whose opinion of the forbidden toy increased, stayed the same, or decreased. (Source: Aronson & Carlsmith, 1963)

they faced a strong temptation to cheat, without (they thought) their actions being monitored. The remarkable result was that children who had been in the mild threat condition of the forbidden toy paradigm were significantly less likely to give in to the temptation to cheat three weeks later. They apparently resolved the dissonance surrounding their earlier decision not to play with the attractive toy by playing up their moral virtues—by concluding something like "I'm a good kid, I do what I'm told, and I don't cheat."

## WHEN DOES INCONSISTENCY PRODUCE DISSONANCE?

We saw earlier that there is some trouble with Festinger's original statement of when people will experience dissonance. Festinger thought that people would experience dissonance whenever they held two inconsistent cognitions. But what constitutes inconsistency? Is it really inconsistent to refrain from playing with an attractive toy if an authority figure asks you not to? Apparently it is, given the results obtained by Aronson and Carlsmith (and subsequent investigators). But what's so jarringly inconsistent about such behavior? There are many things we refrain from doing that we know we would find enjoyable, even when we have no compelling reason (like a severe threat) to refrain from doing them. Which of these are likely to induce dissonance and which are not? After a very healthy start, the development of cognitive dissonance theory became bogged down over the lack of a clear answer to this question. For some time, the answer that experimental social psychologists gave to the question of whether two cognitions were psychologically inconsistent was, "Ask Festinger." This is not the sort of clarity and precision on which productive theories are based.

One of the earliest and most significant contributors to our understanding of cognitive dissonance, Eliot Aronson, took this problem to heart and offered a solution. The key to understanding whether a particular inconsistency will arouse dissonance, Aronson argued, is whether it implicates one's core sense of self (Aronson, 1969). People like to think of themselves as rational, morally upright, worthy individuals, and anything that challenges such assessments is likely to arouse dissonance. Thus, expending great effort to join a boring group calls into question one's wisdom and rationality; telling another student that a boring task is interesting challenges one's integrity. It is cognitions and behaviors that are inconsistent with one's sense of self that produce dissonance (Sherman & Gorkin, 1980).

To understand the sorts of cognitions that are likely to challenge a person's sense of judgment and personal character, it is useful to think about when *someone else's* actions lead us to question *that person's* character. Or better still, it is useful to think of the justifications others could offer that would *prevent* us from questioning the person's judgment or moral fiber. First, we are unlikely to draw negative inferences about others when they can offer an excuse that indicates they could hardly have acted otherwise. If a computer-savvy friend doesn't drop by to help with a pressing computer problem because his boss wouldn't let him off work, we would not be justified in thinking ill of him. He had no choice. Second, we are unlikely to draw negative inferences about others when they offer, not an excuse, but a justification for their actions (see Chapter 9). Justifications carry an implicit acknowledgment that one could have behaved otherwise, but to do so would not have been the best course of action. Thus, we wouldn't think ill of a friend who did not help with a pressing computer problem because he had to console a distraught roommate. Third, we are likely to judge others harshly in rough proportion to the magnitude of harm they have done. We would (justifiably) think worse of a friend whose failure to help with a computer problem caused his friend to fail a course as opposed to just being unable to turn in an assignment early. Finally, we are unlikely to judge other people as harshly if the harm they caused was unforeseen. If a friend had no way of knowing how critical his help would have been, we would not feel justified in questioning his character.

This analysis of when we hold people responsible for their actions provides some insight into when people will hold *themselves* responsible for their actions, and thus experience dissonance as a result of those actions. This analysis suggests, in other words, that people ought to experience dissonance whenever they act in ways that are inconsistent with their core values and beliefs and (1) the behavior was freely chosen, (2) the behavior was not sufficiently justified, (3) the behavior had negative consequences, and (4) the negative consequences were foreseeable.

*Free Choice*  The critical role of freedom of choice has been apparent since the very earliest dissonance experiments and has been demonstrated most often and most clearly in the induced-compliance paradigm. In the first demonstration of this kind, students at Duke University were offered either $.50 or $2.50 to write an essay in favor of a state law banning Communists from speaking on college campuses. (This experiment was done in the mid-1960s and both payments may now seem low; for comparable amounts today, it would be reasonable to multiply these amounts by a factor of 6–8.) Because the law was at variance with the U.S. Constitution's guarantee of freedom of speech, nearly all students were opposed to it, and their essays thus conflicted with their true beliefs. For half the participants, their freedom to accept or decline the offer to write such an essay was stressed. For the other half, it was not. There was no dissonance effect among these latter participants. Indeed, those paid $2.50 later expressed attitudes more in favor of the ban than did those paid $.50 (presumably because writing the essay was associated with the good feelings that accompany the larger reward). In the free-choice group, however, the standard dissonance effect was obtained: those paid $.50 changed their attitude more than those paid $2.50 (Linder, Cooper, & Jones, 1967).

*Insufficient Justification*  This last experiment, like all of the induced-compliance studies, also demonstrates the importance of insufficient justification to the experience of cognitive dissonance. If a person's behavior is justified by the existing incentives, even behavior that is dramatically in conflict with the person's beliefs and values will not produce dissonance—and the rationalizations that arise to combat it. Those paid $2.50 for writing an essay that was inconsistent with their true beliefs felt no pressure to change their attitudes because their behavior was psychologically justified by the large cash payment. Those paid only $.50 had no such justification, and thus they felt the full weight of their inconsistency. Thus, it appears that most of us are willing to sell our souls for money, and if the money is good enough, it doesn't even seem necessary to justify the sale.

*Negative Consequences*    If nothing of consequence results from acting at variance with our attitudes and values, it is easy to dismiss it as a trivial matter. This suggests that people will only experience dissonance if their behavior results in harm of some sort. In one study that examined this idea, participants were paid either $.50 or $5.00 to write an essay favoring the legalization of marijuana, a proposal the participants initially opposed (Nel, Helmreich, & Aronson, 1969). Some participants were told their essays would be shown to groups of people who were already locked into their positions on the issue, either for or against. Others were told their essays would be shown to groups of undecided individuals. As predicted, the standard dissonance effect (more pro-legalization attitudes afterwards on the part of those paid a mere $.50 to write the essay) was found only among those who thought their essays were to be shown to an undecided audience.

The importance of perceived negative consequences has also been demonstrated in the paradigm pioneered by Festinger and Carlsmith (and described earlier). Specifically, participants were induced to tell someone (a confederate) who they thought was about to take part in a boring experiment that it was really very interesting. The participants were provided with either a small or large incentive for doing so. Half the time the confederate seemed convinced that the boring task really was going to be interesting, and half of the time the confederate clearly remained unconvinced ("Well, you're entitled to your own opinion, but I don't think that I have ever enjoyed an experiment, and I don't think that I will find this one much fun."). Note that there were no negative consequences when the person appeared unconvinced: no one was deceived. Thus, if negative consequences are necessary for the arousal of cognitive dissonance, the standard dissonance effect should only occur when the person is convinced. That is exactly what was found: the boring task was rated more favorably only by those participants who were offered little incentive to lie to another person and that person appeared to believe the lie (Cooper & Worchel, 1970).

*Foreseeability*    We typically do not hold people responsible for harm they have done if the harm is not foreseeable. If a dinner guest who is allergic to peanuts becomes ill after eating an entrée with a mild peanut sauce, we do not hold the host responsible if the guest never informed the host of the allergy. This suggests that it may be the *foreseeable* negative consequences of one's actions that generate cognitive dissonance. Negative consequences that are not foreseeable do not threaten one's self-image as a moral and decent person, and thus they may not arouse dissonance.

This hypothesis has been verified in experiments in which participants were induced to write an essay in favor of a position they personally disagreed with (for example, that the size of the freshman class at their university should be doubled). If any negative consequences of such an action (for example, the essays are to be shown to a university committee charged with deciding whether to implement the policy) are made known to the participants after the fact, there is no dissonance and hence no attitude change in the direction of the essay they wrote. But if the negative consequences were either foreseen (participants knew beforehand that their letters would be shown to the committee) or foreseeable (participants knew beforehand that their letters *might* be shown to such a committee), the standard dissonance effect was obtained (Cooper, 1971; Goethals, Cooper, & Naficy, 1979).

## SELF-AFFIRMATION AND DISSONANCE

If dissonance results from challenges or threats to people's sense of themselves as rational, competent, and moral, then it follows that they can ward off dissonance not only by dealing directly with the specific threat itself, but also indirectly by taking stock of their other qualities and core values. Claude Steele has argued that this sort of **self-affirmation** is a common way that people cope with threats to their self-esteem. "Sure, I might have violated a friend's confidence, but I am very empathetic when other people are having difficulties." "I know I drive an SUV, but no one attends church services more regularly than I do." By bolstering oneself in one area, one can tolerate a bigger hit in another.

In one of the cleverest demonstrations of the effects of self-affirmation, Steele (1988) asked science majors and business majors at the University of Washington to participate in an experiment using the standard free-choice paradigm. In a control condition, both groups showed the usual dissonance effect of finding hidden attractions in the chosen alternative and hidden flaws in the unchosen alternative. But in another condition, the experimenters had the business and science majors put on white lab coats before rendering their final evaluations. Steele predicted that wearing a lab coat would affirm an important identity for the science majors, but not for the business majors. The results supported his predictions. The business majors reduced dissonance just as much as participants in the control condition; the science majors did not. If you feel good about yourself, you don't have to sweat the small stuff like minor decisions.

## IS DISSONANCE UNIVERSAL?

We have been discussing cognitive dissonance as if it were a cross-culturally universal phenomenon. Is it? There is substantial evidence on the question, reveal-

> **self-affirmation** Taking stock of one's good qualities and core values, which can help a person cope with threats to self-esteem.

ing quite an interesting answer. Heine and Lehman (1997) used the free-choice, self-affirmation paradigm in which all participants were asked to choose between two objects (CDs in this case), but some were first provided self-affirmation in the form of positive feedback on a personality test. Heine and Lehman's participants were Japanese and Canadian, and the researchers wanted to see if the dissonance effect was the same in people from these two different cultures. They found the usual result for the Canadians: (1) they showed a substantial dissonance effect in the control condition, finding previously unnoticed attractions in the chosen CD and previously unnoticed flaws in the unchosen one, but (2) they showed no dissonance effect if they were given positive feedback about their personalities. The Japanese participants, in contrast, were unaffected by the self-affirmation manipulation. More striking still, they showed no dissonance effect in either condition, which led Heine and Lehman to conclude that cognitive dissonance might be a phenomenon unique to Westerners. But Sakai (1981), using an induced-compliance paradigm in which participants were persuaded to do something they didn't want to do, found dissonance effects for Japanese participants—if they were led to think that other students were observing their behavior.

So does this imply that East Asians may experience dissonance in the induced-compliance paradigm but not in the free-choice paradigm? That would be messy, and fortunately that is not the correct resolution of the conflict between the two sets of results. Throughout this book, we have emphasized that East Asians, along with many other people in the world, are more attuned to other people and their reactions than are Westerners. If Sakai found dissonance effects in the induced-compliance paradigm because Japanese can be made to question their actions and be made uncomfortable by them if others are observing them, then it ought to be possible to show that East Asians will also exhibit dissonance effects in the free-choice paradigm—if they are led to think about other people's reaction to their choice. And this is indeed the case. Kitayama, Snibbe, Markus, and Suzuki (2004) asked Japanese and Canadian participants to choose between two CDs. In one condition (the standard condition used by investigators for the past forty years), participants were asked, after ranking a large number of CDs, to choose between two of the middle-ranked CDs. In the other condition, participants were also asked to rank the presumed preferences of the "average college student." In this way, the researchers "primed" or made salient a "meaningful social other" (see Box 8.1). This manipulation made no difference for the Canadians, but it made a great deal of difference for the Japanese. The Japanese showed almost no dissonance effect in the standard condition, but they showed an even larger dissonance effect than Canadians in the socially primed condition. Hoshino-Browne, Zanna, Spencer, and Zanna (2004) showed a similar effect of social priming when they asked participants to choose a CD either for themselves or for a friend. Euro-Canadians, as well as Asian-Canadians who only weakly identified themselves as Asians, showed much larger dissonance effects when choosing for themselves than when choosing for a friend, but Asian-Canadians who strongly identified themselves as Asians showed much larger dissonance effects for the friend than for themselves.

So at this point it appears that dissonance may indeed be universal. But the conditions that prompt it may be very different for different peoples. For independent Westerners, it may be prompted by a concern about the ability of the self to make an adequate choice that reflects well on one's decisiveness; for Easterners and perhaps other interdependent peoples, it may be prompted by a concern about the ability of the self to make choices that would be approved by others.

Box 8.1    FOCUS ON CULTURE

# Culture and Priming Effects of "Social" Stimuli in the Free-Choice Paradigm

The priming of social cues has very different effects on Japanese and American participants in free-choice situations. Kitayama, Snibbe, Markus, and Suzuki (2004) asked participants to choose between two CDs. For some participants, hanging right in front of them at eye level was the poster below. The poster was simply a figure from another, unrelated experiment, and the investigators' intention was to see whether the schematic faces in it might prime the concept of other people and hence prompt the Japanese participants to show a strong dissonance effect. That was exactly what was found. In the standard free-choice condition, the Japanese showed no evidence of dissonance reduction, but in the poster condition they did. American participants actually showed slightly less dissonance reduction in the "social poster" condition than in the standard condition.

| | Semantic Dimension | | |
|---|---|---|---|
| Impression | Activity | Negative Valence | Potency |
| High | | | |
| Low | | | |

**LOOKING BACK,** we have seen that behavior can have a powerful impact on our attitudes, largely because people like their attitudes to be consistent with one another and their attitudes to be consistent with their behavior. When there is inconsistency among cognitions, beliefs, or actions, dissonance is likely to be aroused. We can reduce dissonance by changing our attitudes to be in line with our behavior. Dissonance is more pronounced when the inconsistency implicates the self to a greater degree. Therefore, when people can affirm the self in some way, they are less susceptible to dissonance. Finally, different cultures find different circumstances dissonance-arousing.

# SELF-PERCEPTION THEORY

Like all prominent theories that have been around for a long time, dissonance theory has faced many theoretical challenges and has had to withstand numerous critiques. One critique, however, stands out above all others in its impact: Daryl Bem's self-perception theory (Bem, 1967, 1972). The theory began as an alternative account of all of the dissonance findings, but it has broad and important implications for self-understanding more generally, and offers novel explanations for many real-life choices and behaviors.

## INFERRING ATTITUDES

According to Bem's **self-perception theory**, people come to know their own attitudes not, as one would expect, by "looking inward" and discerning what they think or how they feel about the issue at hand. Rather, they look outward, at their behavior and the context in which it occurred, and *infer* what their attitudes must be. Self-perception works just like social perception. People come to understand themselves and their attitudes in the same way that they come to understand others and their attitudes.

At first glance, this seems bizarre—as implausible as the old joke about two behaviorists who've just finished having sex: One turns to the other and says, "That was great for you, how was it for me?" The theory feels wrong on a gut level because we're convinced there are times when we "just know" how we feel about something, and we don't need to engage in any process of inference to find out. On closer inspection, however, self-perception theory makes much more sense, in part because Bem concedes that sometimes we can just introspect and "read off" our attitudes. It is only when our prior attitudes are " . . . weak, ambiguous, and uninterpretable," he argues, that "the individual is functionally in the same position as an outside observer. . . ." The caveat is helpful. We would all agree with Bem, certainly, that there are times when we figure out how we feel about something by examining our behavior. "I guess I was hungrier than I thought," we might say after downing a second Double Whopper with cheese. The key question for Bem's analysis, then, is whether the inference process that constitutes the core of self-perception theory applies only to such trivial matters as these, or whether such processes are engaged when we grapple with attitudes of substance—for example, about volunteering to fight in Iraq or to work in a political campaign or to help underprivileged children.

By offering self-perception theory as an alternative account of the findings from the cognitive dissonance experiments, Bem was certainly laying claim to the idea that self-perception processes are responsible for much more than trivial attitudes. His account of the dissonance effects is quite simple. He argues that people in these studies are not troubled by any unpleasant state of arousal like dissonance; they merely engage in a dispassionate inference process. They do not *change* their attitudes in these studies. Rather, they infer what their attitudes must be. People value what they have chosen more after having chosen it because they infer that, "if I chose this, I must like it." People form tight bonds to groups that have taxing initiation rituals because they reason that, "if I suffered to get this, I must have felt it was worth it." And people who are offered little incentive to tell someone that a task was interesting come to view the task more favorably because they conclude that, "there's no other reason I would say this is interesting, so it really must be."

**self-perception theory** A theory that people come to know their own attitudes by looking at their behavior and the context in which it occurred and *inferring* what their attitudes must be.

"How do I know what I think until I hear what I say?"

—ANON

# EVIDENCE OF SELF-DIRECTED INFERENCE

How can we decide whether participants' responses in the dissonance experiments are the product of such dispassionate reasoning? Bem offered two main types of evidence. First, he argued that if these were the processes that participants in those experiments went through—that is, if participants took note of their behavior and the context in which it occurred to infer their true attitudes—it stands to reason that if we give *anyone* the same information about a participant's behavior and the context in which it occurred, that person should be able to infer the participant's true attitudes. Accordingly, Bem conducted a number of what he called **interpersonal simulations**. In an interpersonal simulation, an "observer-participant" is given a detailed description of one condition of a dissonance experiment, is told how a participant behaved in that situation, and is asked to predict the attitude of the participant on the basis of that behavior. The results of these studies have tended to support the self-perception account: the predictions of the observer-participants tend to mirror the actual responses observed in the original studies. Those told about someone who was paid $1 in the Festinger-Carlsmith experiment, for example, predict that the participant's attitude toward the task would be more favorable than the attitude of someone who had been paid $20. Because these observer-participants, with only their powers of inference to work with, can anticipate the true participants' attitudes, perhaps the true participants themselves are relying solely on *their* powers of inference.

But why infer one's own attitude? Why not simply remember and report it? Bem argues that surprisingly often there is no stored attitude to recall and report. To support this element of self-perception theory, Bem conducted a standard induced-compliance experiment, but with a twist. Participants were either given a choice or no choice to write an essay stating that students should have no control over the courses offered at their university. The participants had indicated earlier in the semester that (not surprisingly) they disagreed with this position. After writing these essays, half the participants were asked to indicate their current attitude on the issue. The standard dissonance effect was obtained: those who freely chose to write these counter-attitudinal essays reported being less in favor of student input into the curriculum than those required to write the essays. The other half of the participants, however, were not asked about their current attitudes; instead, they were asked to report what their old attitudes had been earlier in the semester. They knew, furthermore, that the experimenters had their earlier attitude surveys and could therefore check the accuracy of their responses. Despite this incentive to report their earlier attitudes as accurately as possible, participants' memories were biased by their experience of having written a counter-attitudinal essay. Those who had been in the condition in which they freely chose to write such essays misrecalled their earlier attitudes, thinking they had been less in favor of student input into the curriculum than they actually had been (Bem & McConnell, 1970).

These memory findings, along with the results of the interpersonal simulations, force us to take the postulates of self-perception theory seriously. So, too, do related phenomena (see Box 8.2), such as those we have discussed in other chapters. For example, the foot-in-the-door compliance technique (see Chapter 6) appears to result from people looking at their behavior (their compliance with a small request) and the context in which it occurred (no strong incentive to do so) and inferring that they must be the type of person who agrees to contribute to pro-social requests (which then makes them more likely to agree to subsequent requests). Similarly, people's emotional reactions are often strengthened or weak-

---

**interpersonal simulations**
Experiments in which an "observer-participant" is given a detailed description of one condition of a dissonance experiment, is told how a participant behaved in that situation, and is asked to predict the attitude of that participant.

Box 8.2 FOCUS ON EDUCATION

# The Overjustification Effect and Superfluous Rewards

If you dropped in on a family dinner in a foreign land and heard a parent tell a child that he had to eat his *pfunst* before he could eat his *pfeffatorst*, you would immediately conclude that the child did not like the *pfunst* but loved *pfeffatorst*. Things that people do in order to get something else are typically things they do not particularly like. But what happens when the child actually likes *pfunst*? Because the parents are making the child eat *pfunst* in order to have the privilege of eating *pfeffatorst*, the child may conclude that maybe *pfunst* isn't so great after all.

Self-perception theory makes just such a prediction. It maintains that we look at our behavior (I did X) and the context in which it occurs (in order to get Y) to draw conclusions about our underlying attitudes (I don't really like X in and of itself). This tendency to devalue those activities that we perform in order to get something else is known as the overjustification effect (Lepper, Greene, & Nisbett, 1973). The justification for performing the activity is overly sufficient: one would do it because it's inherently rewarding (or, more generally, for "intrinsic" reasons), but also because there is an external payoff for doing so ("extrinsic" reasons). Because the extrinsic reasons would be sufficient to produce the behavior, the person might discount the intrinsic reasons for performing it, and conclude that she doesn't much like the activity for its own sake.

Particularly intriguing evidence for the overjustification effect comes from a study of children's choice of activities in school. Elementary school children were shown two attractive drawing activities. In one condition, the kids were told they could first do one drawing activity and then the other. In a second condition, they were told they *had to* first do one activity *in order to* get to do the other (in both conditions, the experimenters counterbalanced which activity came first). For several days after this initial drawing session, the experimenters put out both drawing activities during the school's free-play period and covertly observed how long the children played with each. Those kids who earlier had simply drawn first with one and then the other played with both equally often. But those who earlier had done one *in order to* get to the other tended to avoid the former (Lepper, Sagotsky, Dafoe, & Greene, 1982). Their intrinsic interest in the first drawing activity had been undermined.

The overjustification effect has important implications for how rewards should be used in education and child rearing. It is common practice, for example, to reward children for reading books, getting good grades, or practicing the piano. That's fine if the child wouldn't otherwise read, study, or practice. But if the child has some interest in these activities to begin with, the rewards might put that interest

in jeopardy. In one powerful demonstration of this danger, researchers introduced a set of novel math games into the free-play portion of an elementary school curriculum. As the figure below indicates, the children initially found them interesting, as indicated by the amount of time the children chose to play with them at the outset of the experiment (baseline phase). Then, for several days afterwards, the investigators instituted a "token-economy" program whereby the children could earn points redeemable for prizes by playing with the math games. The more they played with the math games, the more points they earned. The token-economy program was effective in increasing how much the children played the games (see the bar in the treatment phase). But what happened when the token-economy program was terminated and the children no longer earned points for playing with the games? Would they still play with them? As the right bar in the figure indicates, they did not. Having once received rewards for these activities, the children came to see them as something only done to get a reward, and their original interest was diminished (Greene, Sternberg, & Lepper, 1976).

Note that this does not imply that giving out rewards is always a bad thing. People are not always intrinsically motivated and, when they are not, rewards are often the best way to get them to do something they would not otherwise do. Rewards can also be administered in ways that minimize their negative impact. For instance, there can be performance-contingent rewards—that is, those that are based on how well one performs. These have been shown to be less likely to decrease interest in an activity than task-contingent rewards, which are simply based on doing a task or not (Deci & Ryan, 1985; Harackiewicz, Manderlink, & Sansone, 1984; Sansone & Harackiewicz, 2000).

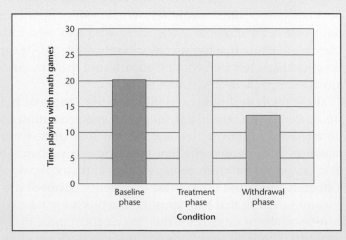

Source: Greene, Sternberg, & Lepper, 1976.

ened when they observe the surrounding context and infer how emotional they must be (see Chapter 12). For example, people who are anxious about their performance on an upcoming task calm down and become more confident if they are led to believe that their symptoms of anxiety are the product of white noise delivered over headphones (Savitsky, Medvec, Charlton, & Gilovich, 1998).

But these results, however supportive of self-perception theory they might be, do not tell us anything about whether the results of all the dissonance experiments are really the result of self-perception processes rather than efforts to reduce dissonance. To decide that issue, a very different type of experiment is required. To settle a theoretical dispute like this one, it is necessary to identify the conditions under which the two theories make different predictions. One then experimentally creates just those conditions and observes which prediction is confirmed. That is more difficult than usual in this case because the two theories make the *same* prediction in nearly all circumstances. This is not surprising, given that self-perception theory was offered specifically to account for all of the phenomena previously explained by the theory of cognitive dissonance.

## TESTING FOR AROUSAL

The one critical difference between the two theories, and hence the necessary focus of any decisive test, is whether people experience arousal in all of the standard dissonance paradigms (for example, the induced-compliance paradigm) and their everyday life analogues. Dissonance theory posits that the inconsistency between one's behavior and one's prior attitudes or values produces an unpleasant physiological state that motivates efforts to reduce the inconsistency. No arousal, no attitude change. Self-perception theory, in contrast, contends that there is no arousal involved: people coolly and rationally infer what their attitudes must be in light of their behavior and the context in which it occurred.

So how do we determine if people are indeed aroused after making difficult choices, exerting great effort for minimal benefit, and behaving in ways at variance with their earlier attitudes? In one clever early test, participants were asked to write an essay in which they argued against the position they truly believed and then were immediately put in a situation that assessed their performance on a simple task and on a difficult task. The logic was that if counter-attitudinal behavior truly does produce arousal, then, as research on social facilitation (see Chapter 2) indicates, performance on the easy task should be enhanced and performance on the difficult task should worsen. That is just what happened. Compared to those who had just written an essay consistent with their prior attitudes, those who had written a counter-attitudinal essay performed better on the easy task and worse on the difficult task (Waterman, 1969). As dissonance theory predicts, it seems that acting at variance with one's true beliefs does indeed generate arousal (Elliot & Devine, 1994; Galinsky, Stone, & Cooper, 2000; Harmon-Jones, 2000; Norton, Monin, Cooper, & Hogg, 2003).

If arousal is indeed generated, it should be possible to influence the impact of the arousal—that is, if it will lead to attitude change or not—by altering how it is interpreted (Cooper, Zanna, & Taves, 1978; Losch & Cacioppo, 1990). This has been done in experiments using "misattribution" manipulations (see Chapter 12). In one study, participants were given a drug (in reality a placebo) and told either that it would have no effect, that it would make them feel tense, or that it would make them feel relaxed (Zanna & Cooper, 1974). The participants then wrote, under free-choice or no-choice conditions, an essay arguing that inflammatory speakers should be barred from college campuses, a position with which

**Figure 8. 7  Does Arguing against One's Prior Attitude Produce Arousal?** The amount of attitude change in the direction of a previously objectionable proposition on the part of participants who wrote essays—under free-choice and no-choice conditions—in support of that proposition. Before writing these essays, participants were given a pill and told either that it would make them tense, have no effect, or make them relaxed. (Source: Zanna & Cooper, 1974)

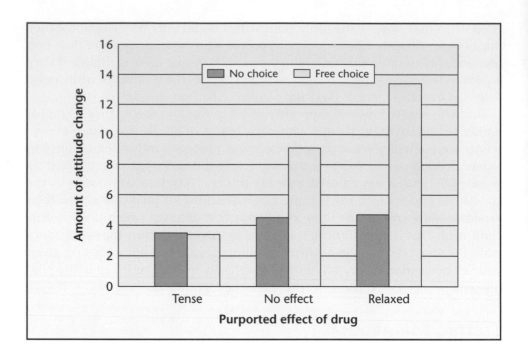

they strongly disagreed. The investigators expected to find the standard dissonance effect among participants who were told that the drug would have no effect—greater attitude change in favor of banning inflammatory speakers on the part of those who freely chose to write the essay as opposed to those in the no-choice condition. As the middle bars in Figure 8.7 show, that is precisely what happened.

But the results from the other conditions are more telling. The authors predicted that this effect would disappear when participants were told (incorrectly) that the drug would make them tense. Those who freely chose to write the essay would experience the arousal state of dissonance, but they would attribute it to the drug and thus feel no compulsion to do something (change their attitude) to get rid of their unpleasant physiological state—it would go away, they were led to believe, as soon as the drug wore off. As the leftmost bars in Figure 8.7 show, that prediction, too, was confirmed. What about the participants who were told that the drug would relax them? Those who freely chose to write the essay would experience arousal, an internal state inconsistent with the experimenter's earlier statement that the drug would make them feel relaxed. The researchers predicted that this would make them think, however implicitly, that "I must *really* have done something wrong if I am this upset"—thoughts that should set in motion particularly powerful efforts at dissonance reduction. This prediction was also confirmed. As the rightmost bars in Figure 8.7 reveal, the greatest difference between participants in the free-choice and no-choice conditions—that is, the biggest dissonance effect—was observed among participants who had been told that the drug would make them feel relaxed.

## RECONCILING THE DISSONANCE AND SELF-PERCEPTION ACCOUNTS

The experiment just described speaks volumes about the relative merits of dissonance theory and self-perception theory. It is clear that behavior that is inconsistent with one's prior attitudes does indeed generate arousal (Croyle & Cooper, 1983; Elkin & Leippe, 1986), and that it is the effort to dispel that arousal that motivates the types of attitude change found in the various dissonance experiments (Harmon-Jones, Brehm, Greenberg, Simon, & Nelson, 1996). In that sense, Festinger was right. Dissonance theory is the proper account of the phenomena observed in these experiments (and their real-world counterparts), not self-perception theory.

But note the irony here: the experiment that most powerfully supports the cognitive dissonance interpretation depends upon the very processes of inference that lie at the core of self-perception theory. When participants in that experiment implicitly reasoned, "I'm aroused, but the experimenter told me the drug would make me anxious so therefore . . .", they were—just as self-perception theory predicts—making inferences about what was going on inside of them. Self-perception theory may not provide an accurate account of what happens when one behaves in a way that challenges one's sense of oneself as a moral and rational person, but it does capture some very important aspects of how the mind works.

A consensus has thus emerged among social psychologists that both dissonance-reduction processes and self-perception processes occur and influence people's attitudes and broader views of themselves. Dissonance-reduction processes are invoked when people act in ways that are inconsistent with preexisting attitudes that are clear-cut and of some importance. Self-perception processes, in contrast, are invoked when behavior "clashes" with attitudes that are relatively vague or of little import (Chaiken & Baldwin, 1981).

This revised view makes sense from at least three perspectives. First, and most important, it is consistent with the pertinent empirical tests, such as the studies just described. Second, it is consistent with most people's everyday experience with the rationalizations that are provoked by psychological inconsistency, rationalizations that *feel* like they are motivated by a desire to reduce dissonance (Gilbert, Lieberman, Morewedge, & Wilson, 2004; Gilbert, Morewedge, Risen, & Wilson, 2004; Gilbert, Pinel, Wilson, Blumberg, & Wheatley, 1998). When a fabulously wealthy individual sees a hard-working person living in a hovel and barely getting by, he does not coolly observe his behavior (failing to help the poor) and decide, "I must think the income disparity is justified." Instead, the other person's poverty—and failure to do anything about it—is troubling, and the tension this produces sets in motion the wealthy person's very active attempts to feel better about not doing anything to help ("I've worked hard for my money"; "If she keeps working hard, things will get better for her because, in our society, hard work and talent always win out in the end"). Finally, the revised view fits with Bem's original statement of self-perception theory: that it is only when a person's attitudes are "weak, ambiguous, and uninterpretable" that "the individual is functionally in the same position as an outside observer . . ." Bem's only error, then, was to assert that the attitudes being tapped in the various cognitive dissonance experiments were the weak, ambiguous sort that engage self-perception processes rather than the strong, clear-cut, and salient sort that produce dissonance.

But before getting too comfortable with this revised view, it is important to take note of what it leaves out. Specifically, although it is true that self-perception processes are engaged primarily when one's prior attitudes are weak or unclear, a considerable body of research has made it abundantly clear that a surprising proportion of our attitudes *are* rather weak and ambiguous. Although self-perception processes may less often influence important attitudes than unimportant ones, they nevertheless do at times influence important attitudes—and important subsequent behavior. Self-perception manipulations, for example, have been shown to influence such significant phenomena as whether one is likely to contribute to the public good (Freedman & Fraser, 1966; Uranowitz, 1975), whether one is likely to cheat to reach a goal (Dienstbier & Munter, 1971; Lepper, 1973), the precise emotion one is feeling and how strongly one feels it (Dutton & Aron, 1974; Schachter & Singer, 1962; White & Kight, 1984), one's assessment of one's own personality traits (Schwarz et al., 1991; Tice, 1993), and whether one truly enjoys an activity one has engaged in all one's life (Lepper & Greene, 1978). Thus, the revised view might make it seem as if self-perception processes are relegated to the trivial fringe of social life. They are not.

In fact, the basic postulates of self-perception theory are consistent with neuroscientific evidence concerning how the mind is structured. There is increasing evidence that the brain is organized into numerous semidiscrete modules, each performing its own specified function. The clearest example of this is language. There appear to be universal aspects of grammar that are shared by everyone in the world (Chomsky, 1975, 1988; see Chapter 1), and the brain regions involved in language use and learning are well known. There is also increasing evidence that at least one brain module functions as something of an interpreter, registering the output of all other modules, including information about one's actions, and making sense of them (Gazzaniga, 1985; see Box 8.3). Particularly intriguing evidence for this proposition comes from research on "split-brain" patients (see Figure 8.8), who—unlike the rest of us—do not have a functioning corpus callo-

**Figure 8.8 Interpretation of Behavior by Split-Brain Patients**   Split-brain patients are presented with different stimuli to their left and right hemispheres (a picture of a snow scene is presented to the right hemisphere, and a picture of a bird's claw is presented to the left hemisphere). They are then asked to point (using both hands) to a picture from a series of pictures to fit what they have been shown. Each hand, controlled by different hemispheres, selects an appropriate picture. But because the patients do not have a functioning corpus callosum, the real reason that the right hemisphere chose the picture that it did cannot be communicated to the verbal centers in the left hemisphere. You might think that this would cause some confusion when these patients are then asked to explain their choices. It doesn't. Consistent with self-perception theory, the verbal left hemisphere, which is charged with crafting an explanation quickly and easily, notes the two items that have been selected and crafts a sensible (but only half-valid) account. (Source: Gazzaniga & Heatherton, 2003, p. 116)

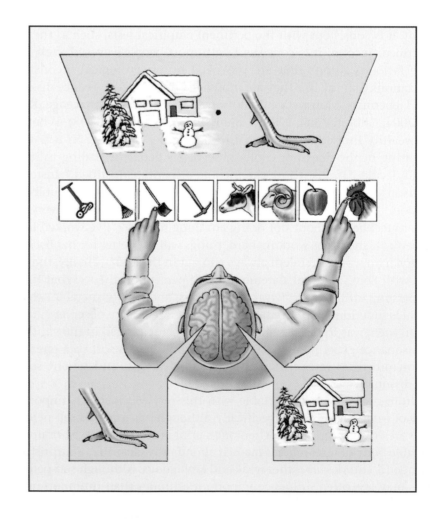

Box 8.3    FOCUS ON DAILY LIFE

# Body over Mind

Recent research has yielded evidence for a rather radical extension of self-perception theory's core thesis that our attitudes are influenced by our actions. It appears that the physical movements we engage in while evaluating stimuli have a significant effect on how favorably those stimuli are evaluated. Thus, engaging in movements that typically accompany positive reactions leads us to evaluate stimuli more favorably, even when the stimuli are not particularly desirable to begin with (see Chapter 1). The opposite is true of movements that typically accompany negative reactions. In one early demonstration of this effect, Gary Wells and Richard Petty (1980) had students ostensibly test a set of headphones by moving their heads up and down or side to side while listening to music and radio editorials. When later asked about the viewpoints advocated in the editorials, the students indicated that they agreed with them more if they had listened to them while nodding their heads up and down than if they had listened to them while shaking their heads from side to side. We nod our heads at things we approve of, and this lifelong association leads us to view more favorably those things we encounter while nodding (Epley & Gilovich, 2001; Forster & Strack, 1996).

Similar effects result from other movements associated with positive and negative reactions. Fritz Strack and his colleagues had some students hold a marker with their teeth, which creates a smiling expression (try it!). Others were asked to hold the marker with their lips, which yields an expression akin to a frown. While holding the marker in one of these ways, the participants were asked to rate how amused they were by a number of cartoons. As you can probably anticipate, students who held the marker in their teeth (the smilers) thought the cartoons were more amusing than did students in a control condition, and those who held the marker with their lips (the frowners) thought the cartoons were less amusing (Strack, Martin, & Stepper, 1988).

Other researchers have explored the implications of our tendency to push away that which we find aversive and pull inward that which we find appealing, as we saw in Chapter 1. Thus, arm extension is associated with negative stimuli and arm flexion is associated with positive stimuli. These bodily movements also have predictable effects on attitudes. In one study, John Cacioppo, Joseph Priester, and Gary Bernston (1993) showed Ohio State University students a series of twenty-four Chinese ideographs while they were either pressing down on a table (arm extension) or lifting up on a table from underneath (arm flexion). The students evaluated the ideographs presented during arm flexion more favorably. Other studies using this procedure have shown that arm flexion fosters creative insight on various problem-solving tasks (Friedman & Forster, 2000) and makes people more inclined to accept their initial stab at estimating unknown values (Epley & Gilovich, 2004).

---

sum that allows the two cerebral hemispheres to communicate with each other. Imagine, then, that two pictures are presented to the two hemispheres of a split-brain patient: (1) a picture of a snow scene to the nonverbal right hemisphere (by presenting it to the left visual field), and (2) a picture of a bird's claw to the verbal left hemisphere (by presenting it to the right visual field). The patient is then asked to select from an array of pictures the one that fits the stimuli she has just seen. She is told to point with both hands to the picture she has selected.

What happens? Typically, the patient selects two pictures: (1) with the left hand (controlled by the right hemisphere), she might select a picture of a shovel to go with the snow scene presented to the right hemisphere, and (2) with the right hand (controlled by the left hemisphere), she might select a picture of a chicken head to go with the claw presented to the left hemisphere. Both responses fit the relevant stimulus because the response mode—pointing—is one that is controlled by each hemisphere. But what happens when the patient is asked to explain the choices she has made? Even though the reason for selecting the shovel (by the nonverbal right hemisphere) is not accessible to the verbal "explanation module" in the left hemisphere, the response is typically immediate and involves such answers as, "Oh, that's simple. The chicken claw goes with the chicken, and you need a shovel to clean out the chicken shed" (Gazzaniga, 1985). Such a response fits nicely with the postulates of self-perception theory. Behavior (selecting the two pictures) is observed, and what it must mean is instantly computed by a module in the brain dedicated to sense-making or explanation.

## A FINAL CAUTION

There is a powerful tendency to believe that only *other people* think in anything less than a fully rational and appropriate manner, and that this is rarely true of our own thinking (Pronin, Gilovich, & Ross, 2004). It may be tempting, then, to believe that dissonance reduction is something in which others engage, not ourselves. But there is good reason to doubt whether there are any people who do not rationalize, and it is important to recognize this tendency in ourselves. If you think you might be immune from engaging in dissonance reduction, consider your attitudes and behavior with regard to certain issues with potentially enormous consequences for the future. For example, although you are probably concerned about the future consequences of global warming, chances are that you have done little to prevent it. This inconsistency between your attitudes and behavior is likely to produce both some tension and some effort to dispel that tension. You might say to yourself, for example, "It isn't really happening" or "it's all alarmist," or "there is nothing I can do about it," or "if it gets really bad, I'm sure something will be done about it." Only time will tell whether any of these statements will be seen to have merit. In the meantime, it is worth noting that these very same statements were uttered by many a German in the 1930s, just as the awful events that swept that country, and the world, were taking hold.

**LOOKING BACK,** we have seen that self-perception theory maintains that people infer their attitudes from their behavior, thus providing an alternate explanation for why people often change their attitudes when they conflict with their actions. Experimental evidence, however, has shown that arousal is indeed generated when behavior is not consistent with attitudes and that this arousal does indeed often motivate attitude change. Nevertheless, researchers have reconciled the dissonance and self-perception theories, showing that dissonance theory best explains attitude change for preexisting clear-cut attitudes, but that self-perception theory best explains attitude change for less clear-cut attitudes.

# SUMMARY

1. The *theory of reasoned action* maintains that attitudes guide behavior through a deliberation process that takes into account conscious attitudes toward an object and subjective norms. The *theory of planned behavior* maintains that the influence of conscious attitudes and subjective norms on behavior depends on people's beliefs that they can perform a given behavior and that the behavior will have the desired effects.

2. It can be surprisingly difficult at times to predict behavior from attitudes because (a) attitudes are sometimes *ambiguous* or *inconsistent,* (b) attitudes sometimes *conflict* with other powerful determinants of behavior, (c) attitudes are sometimes based on *secondhand information* about the object, (d) attitudes (for example, toward the environment) and the attitude targets we actually confront (for example, whether to donate to Greenpeace) may be at different *levels of generality* and may be "about" very different things, and (e) some of our behavior is *automatic* and can bypass our conscious attitudes altogether.

3. Behavior can have very substantial effects on attitudes. Most of the research showing such effects grew out of *cognitive consistency theories,* which stress how important consistency of attitudes and behavior is to most people.

4. *Balance theory* was the earliest consistency theory. It specifies that people desire balance among their beliefs and sentiments, and thus prefer to hold attitudes that "follow from" other attitudes ("my enemy's enemy is my friend"), and prefer to behave in ways that align with their attitudes.

5. *Cognitive dissonance theory* is based on the idea that people experience *dissonance,* or discomfort, when attitudes and behavior are inconsistent. People therefore often try to reduce the dissonance they are feeling by bringing their attitudes in line with their behavior.

6. People engage in dissonance reduction when making decisions. After making a choice between two objects or courses of action they find "hidden attractions" in the chosen alternative and previously undetected flaws in the unchosen alternative. This reduces the dissonance aroused by having to give up some desired object or action.

7. People engage in *effort justification* when they exert effort toward some goal and the goal turns out to be disappointing. They justify their expenditure of energy by deciding that the goal is truly worthwhile.

8. People attempt to reduce dissonance in *induced-compliance* situations—that is, in situations in which other people prompt them to do or say something that is contrary to their beliefs. For example, when induced by another person to argue for a position at variance with their true attitudes with the promise of some sort of compensation for doing so, people who are undercompensated feel that they must justify their behavior and typically do so by changing their attitudes to better align with their behavior.

9. Dissonance resulting from inconsistency between attitudes and behavior should be felt only when (a) there is *free choice* (or the illusion of it) to engage in the behavior, (b) there is *insufficient justification* for the behavior, (c) the behavior has *negative consequences* either for the self or for another, and (d) the *consequences* of the behavior were *foreseeable.*

10. The effects of inconsistency can be reduced if the individual has just had some *self-affirming* experience that obviates the need to protect the ego from the unpleasant consequences of foreseeable action.

11. Dissonance is apparently universal, but there are cultural differences in the conditions that prompt people to experience it. For example, the Japanese tend to experience post-decision dissonance only when asked to think about how another person would choose.

12. *Self-perception theory* originated as an alternative explanation for the results obtained in dissonance experiments. It is based on the premise that people do not move their attitudes into line with their behavior because they are motivated to justify them; they do so merely because they observe their behavior and the circumstances in which it occurs and infer, just as an observer might, what their attitudes must be.

13. Whereas self-perception may well play a role in generating the effects in many dissonance experiments, some evidence clearly indicates that there is often a motivational component as well. "Mere" self-perception appears to account for attitude change in situations in which attitudes are weak or unclear to begin with, whereas more motivated, dissonance-reduction processes are invoked when attitudes are more strongly held to begin with.

# CRITICAL THINKING ABOUT BASIC PRINCIPLES

1. The effects of body movements on cognition that we discussed in Box 8.3 strike many people as implausible. But you can try it yourself and see. First, try nodding your head up and down while saying to yourself "human beings will land on Mars sometime during my lifetime." Does that proposition sound plausible? Now try shaking your head back and forth while saying "eating an apple a day helps to ward off cancer." Does that sound plausible? The key question: Does the first proposition seem more plausible to you than the second? (It will help our case if you nod your head while considering this one.)

2. Benjamin Franklin was apparently fond of quoting an adage to the effect that, "He that has once done you a kindness will be more ready to do you another than he whom you yourself have obliged." How would a dissonance theorist make sense of this adage? A self-perception theorist?

3. In the induced-compliance experiments such as Festinger and Carlsmith's $1/$20 experiment, all participants agree to say or write something that is at variance with their true, initial beliefs. The typical result is an *inverse relationship* between what they are paid and their subsequent belief in what they were induced to say or write: those who were paid more believe what they said less. But what do you think the relationship between the amount paid and the final attitude would be if the incentives were *not* sufficient to get participants to say or write something they didn't believe? If everyone turned down payment to express a belief that is counter to their true attitudes, with some turning down more money than others, what do you think the relationship would be between the amount offered and final attitudes?

## KEY TERMS

balance theory (p. 309)

cognitive dissonance theory (p. 310)

effort justification (p. 312)

induced (forced) compliance (p. 315)

interpersonal simulations (p. 325)

prime (p. 307)

self-affirmation (p. 321)

self-perception theory (p. 324)

subjective norms (p. 301)

theory of planned behavior (p. 302)

theory of reasoned action (p. 301)

## FURTHER READING

Bargh, J. A., & Chen, M., & Burrows, L. (1996). Automaticity of social behavior: Direct effects of trait construct and stereotype activation on action. *Journal of Personality and Social Psychology, 71*, 230–244.

Dijksterhuis, A., Spears, R., Postmes, T., Stapel, D.A., Koomen, W., van Knippenberg, A., & Scheepers, D. (1998). Seeing one thing and doing another: Contrast effects in automatic behavior. *Journal of Personality and Social Psychology, 75*, 862–871.

Festinger, L. (1957). *A theory of cognitive dissonance*. Stanford, CA: Stanford University Press.

Wilson, T. D. (2002). *Strangers to ourselves: Discovering the adaptive unconscious*. Cambridge, MA: Harvard University Press.

# PART THREE

# Social Thought

HOW WE ACT AROUND OTHERS AND HOW WE FEEL AS A RESULT OF our interactions are powerfully influenced by how we think about them. This section of the book deals with social cognition, or how we process information about others and the effects our thoughts have on how we act and feel. In Chapter 9, we examine a particular type of judgment that we all make many times a day— determining the causes of one another's behavior. Whether a smile is seen as kind or manipulative has considerable impact on how it makes us feel and how we act toward a person, and we explore how such judgments are made. In Chapter 10, we examine judgment more broadly. How do people understand others, comprehend the past, and predict the future? We also discuss some of the most common sources of error in people's judgments, and we explore why people sometimes draw erroneous conclusions, form dubious beliefs, and choose to embark on questionable courses of action. In Chapter 11, we focus on a particularly important type of faulty thinking, the psychological processes that give rise to stereotypes of dubious validity. This chapter illustrates with particular clarity cognition's link with feeling and action, as stereotypes are intimately connected to prejudice (feeling) and discrimination (action).

# Chapter Outline

# CHAPTER 9

# Causal Attribution

O
n April 28, 1967, when U.S. involvement in the war in Vietnam was nearing its peak, twenty-six young men reported to the U.S. Armed Forces Examination and Entrance Station at 701 San Jacinto Street in Houston, Texas. After undergoing physical examinations, the men were lined up and told to take one step forward when their names were called, an action that would constitute induction into the U.S. military. Twenty-five of the twenty-six men stepped forward. The twenty-sixth was Muhammad Ali.

Citing his work as a minister for the Nation of Islam, Ali sought to be recognized by the government as a conscientious objector. He argued with characteristic directness that he "ain't got no quarrel with them Viet Cong." At the time, many young men sought to be recognized as conscientious objectors, and their cases were typically settled—win or lose—in anonymity. Not so with Ali. His stature guaranteed that his refusal to serve would draw enormous press coverage and generate tremendous controversy.

After all, Ali has been described as someone with "Babe Ruth's charisma, Jackie Robinson's courage, Bill Russell's agenda, Arthur Ashe's sense of priority, Michael Jordan's fame, and Charles Barkley's mouth" (Herzog, 1995, p. 10). That combination made him, according to *Sports Illustrated*, the most significant person in sports history. Nor was the interest in Ali hurt by the fact that he was uncommonly handsome, or that he had won an Olympic Gold Medal in boxing just a few weeks after graduating from high school, and then, less than four years later, had become the heavyweight champion of the world, a title he held until it was taken from him as a result of his refusal to join the military service. During those three years as champion, Ali dazzled boxing audiences with his remarkable speed and grace, and he delighted—or infuriated—the entire country with his braggadocio ("I am the greatest!") and his penchant for poetically predicting his fights' outcomes ("This boy likes to mix, he must fall in six."). Ali's association with Black Muslim leader Elijah Muhammad intensified the controversy surrounding him.

Ali's refusal to fight in Vietnam increased the noise level of the debate about him still higher. As he said, "I've left the sports pages. I've gone to the front pages" (Herzog, 1995, p. 13). At the core of the controversy was an important psychological question: Why did Ali act as he did? Ali's answer was religious: "I have searched my conscience, and find I cannot be true to my belief in my religion by accepting such a call" (Hauser, 1991, p. 170). Many people in America thought otherwise, particularly those who supported the war in Vietnam. They discounted Ali's claim of religious devotion and argued that it was just a pretext for saving his skin, asserting that "Anyone who makes a living by trying to beat another person's brains out can't be much of a pacifist."

Others argued precisely the opposite view. They thought that Ali must truly believe what he was saying because he was willing to pay such a heavy price to

**Attribution and Judgment**  Assigning causes to peoples' actions affects how we judge them. Muhammad Ali made his living as a fighter, but he was also a devout Muslim (he had converted to the Nation of Islam and changed his name from Cassius Clay in 1964). When he refused to be drafted to fight in Vietnam, some people attributed his stand to his religious principles and judged him positively, while others attributed it to a lack of patriotism and judged him negatively. He is pictured here (A) in a heavyweight fight with Doug Jones at Madison Square Garden in 1963, and (B) addressing the Black Muslim Annual Convention in Chicago in 1968.

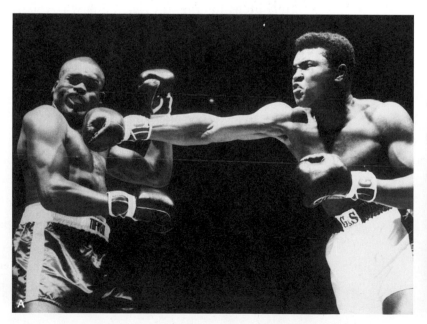

say it. His heavyweight crown was immediately taken from him, no state boxing commission in the country would sanction any kind of fight involving Ali, and the government seized his passport, depriving him of the opportunity to fight in other countries. Beyond being deprived of his livelihood, he was sentenced to five years in prison. Those who believed in Ali's religious devotion contended that "Any person willing to subject himself to the perils of prison over a stand on principle must really believe in those principles." Besides, his defenders argued, it could hardly be said that Ali was trying to save his skin because, like most celebrities, he would almost certainly have spent the war out of harm's way entertaining the troops.

Ultimately, the tide of public opinion turned in Ali's favor. Many of those who hated Ali for refusing to serve his country came to the view that the Vietnam War was not the proper test of a person's patriotism. Most of America came to revere Ali as much for his courageous stance against the draft as for his skills and personality in the ring. In fact, even his stature in the ring improved. When the Supreme Court of the United States reversed his conviction, Ali resumed his boxing career after a three-and-a-half-year absence. The intervening years had robbed his legs of their surpassing speed, and so boxing fans were treated to sides of Ali they did not know existed. He demonstrated tremendous stamina, a keen intelligence, and an ability and willingness to take punishment in a series of epic fights against the likes of Ken Norton, George Foreman, and Joe Frazier. Even Ali's most hardened critics came to admire his skill and his courage. *Ring* magazine had no qualms about anointing him the greatest heavyweight boxer of all time (Herzog, 1995, p. 9).

The controversy surrounding Muhammad Ali's refusal to enter the armed services nicely captures some of the most important elements of the topic of this chapter—causal attribution. **Attribution theory** deals with how people assign causes to the events around them and the effects that these attributions have. In Ali's case, the two sides had no quarrel about the facts. Muhammad Ali refused to serve in the U.S. military. That much was beyond dispute. But the significance of his actions depended less on what than on why. *Why* had Ali declined to serve? Was it a selfish act of self-preservation or a selfless manifestation of religious conviction? The view one had of Ali depended heavily on the answer to that question.

In this chapter, we will examine how people answer such questions. We will discuss how people explain the behavior they witness (or hear about) in others and what effect their explanations have on the judgments they make about others. We will also examine how people understand the causes of their own behavior, and the implications of their understandings for both their immediate emotional experience and their subsequent behavior. We will then discuss errors and biases in attribution, as well as how culture affects attribution. Finally, we will talk about the role of intentions in the attribution process.

> **attribution theory** An umbrella term used to describe the set of theoretical accounts of how people assign causes to the events around them and the effects that people's causal assessments have.

# WHY SOCIAL PSYCHOLOGISTS STUDY CAUSAL ATTRIBUTION

On a bright fall day in 2001, two jet planes bound from Boston to California went off course and streaked toward downtown Manhattan. Those on board the planes and in the air control towers searched for explanations of what was happening. Were the pilots trying to avoid turbulence? Were there mechanical problems? Had the planes been hijacked? And when the gruesome reality of the events that day became apparent, the search for explanations continued. "Why do they hate us?" asked President Bush in a speech to the United States Congress two weeks after the attacks on the Pentagon and World Trade Center.

**Attribution** is the process by which people explain both their own behavior and that of other people. There are two important points about causal attribution that should be made clear at the outset because they help to explain why an understanding of people's attributions is crucial to an adequate understanding of so much of their everyday social behavior: (1) we all make causal attributions many times a day, and (2) our attributions are important.

**attribution** Linking a cause to an instance of behavior—one's own or that of other people.

## THE PERVASIVENESS AND IMPORTANCE OF ATTRIBUTION

When you get back an exam, you are not simply happy or sad about the grade you received. You make an attribution. You decide that you are smart and hardworking, or that the test was unfair. Or when you ask someone out for a date but are rebuffed ("No thanks, I have a cold"), you do not simply take the response at face value. You ask why. "Does she really have a cold or am I getting the brush-off?" Attributions, in other words, are a constant part of mental life. You may ask yourself such questions as: "Did George W. Bush really believe that Saddam Hussein possessed weapons of mass destruction, or was he simply looking for an excuse to invade Iraq?" "Why did my interview take so little time? Did the interviewers conclude that I obviously have what it takes, or were they just not interested?" "Why does everything work out so well for my roommate while I have to struggle to get by?"

The second crucial point to note about causal attribution is that the causes people cite have tremendous significance. They matter. The belief that Muhammad Ali's refusal to enter the service was a principled act of self-sacrifice leads inexorably to certain thoughts and feelings about him, as well as about the government that prosecuted him, the boxing commissions that banned him, and the editorial writers who condemned him. The belief that his actions were opportunistic, on the other hand, leads to a very different set of reactions.

Likewise, concluding that someone won't go out with you because she's sick leads to an entirely different set of emotional reactions than concluding that she does not find you appealing. Attributing a bad grade on an exam to a lack of ability leads to unhappiness and withdrawal, whereas attributing failure to a lack of effort often leads to more vigorous attempts to study harder and more effectively in the future.

Systematic research on attribution has shown that people's attributions have tremendous implications in a number of domains, with the most widely studied being health and education, as we will see. In the educational sphere, setbacks are experienced by even the best students (a lost set of notes, a mystifying lecture, a failed quiz), and the attributions made about these setbacks are related to how well a student tends to perform in school.

"Happy are they who have been able to perceive the causes of things."

—VIRGIL

# EXPLANATORY STYLE AND ATTRIBUTION

One group of investigators, led by Chris Peterson and Martin Seligman, has examined the impact of attributions on academic success by relating a person's explanatory style to long-term academic performance. **Explanatory style** refers to a person's habitual way of explaining events, and it is assessed along three dimensions: internality/externality, stability/instability, and globality/specificity. To assess explanatory style, respondents are asked to imagine six different good events that might happen to them ("you do a project that is highly praised") and six bad events ("you meet a friend who acts hostilely toward you") and to provide a likely cause for each. Respondents are then asked if each cause (1) is due to something about them or something about other people or circumstances (internal/external), (2) will be present again in the future or not (stable/unstable), and (3) is something that influences other areas of their lives or just this situation (global/specific). An explanation that cites an *internal* cause implicates the self ("There I go again"), but an *external* cause does not ("That was the pickiest set of questions I've ever seen"). A *stable* cause implies that things will never change ("I'm just no good"), whereas an *unstable* cause implies that things may improve ("The cold medicine I was taking made me groggy"). Finally, a *global* cause is something that affects many areas of life ("I'm stupid"), whereas a *specific* cause applies to only a few ("I'm not good with names").

In the research by Seligman and Peterson and their colleagues, the three dimensions of internality/externality, stability/instability, and globality/specificity were combined to form an overall explanatory style index, which was then correlated with the students' GPAs. A tendency to explain negative events in terms of stable, global, and internal causes is considered a "pessimistic" explanatory style and, as anticipated, those with the most pessimistic explanatory style tended to earn lower grades than those with a more optimistic style (Peterson & Barrett, 1987).

The characteristic ways that different people explain events in their lives have also been shown to have a considerable impact on physical health. One study, for example, examined whether a person's explanatory tendencies as a young adult could predict physical health later in life (Peterson, Seligman, & Vaillant, 1988; see also Peterson, 2000). The study took advantage of the fact that members of Harvard's graduating classes from 1942 to 1944 took part in a longitudinal study that required them to complete a questionnaire every year and submit medical records of periodic physical examinations. Each person's physical health was assessed by having judges score the medical records on a 5-point scale, with "1" meaning the person was in good health and "5" meaning the person was deceased. This was done for all participants when they reached the ages of twenty-five, thirty, thirty-five, and so on.

Their physical health at each of these ages was then correlated with their explanatory style as young men, which was assessed by having judges score their descriptions of their most difficult experiences during World War II—a question they had been asked in 1946 when they were all recent college graduates. These correlations, after statistically controlling for the respondents' initial physical condition at age twenty-five, are reported in Table 9.1. As a quick glance at Table 9.1 indicates, explanatory style during young adulthood is a significant predictor of physical health in later life. (The fact that it does not correlate with health at ages thirty to forty is most likely due to the fact that nearly all of the respondents were in generally good health at those ages, and so there was nothing to predict. In similar fashion, explanatory style—or anything else for that matter—is

> **explanatory style** A person's habitual way of explaining events, typically assessed along three dimensions: internality/externality, stability/instability, and globality/specificity.

> "A pessimist sees the difficulty in every opportunity; an optimist sees the opportunity in every difficulty."
> —SIR WINSTON CHURCHILL

**Table 9.1   Does Explanatory Style Early in Life Predict Later Physical Health?**

The correlation, *r*, between explanatory style and physical health at seven points in life, with earlier physical health controlled statistically.

| AGE | CORRELATION |
| --- | --- |
| 30 | .04 |
| 35 | .03 |
| 40 | .13 |
| 45 | .37* |
| 50 | .18 |
| 55 | .22* |
| 60 | .25* |

*Denotes statistically significant correlation.

Source: Peterson, Seligman, & Vaillant, 1988.

unlikely to be related to physical health at age one hundred because at that age nearly everyone, regardless of explanatory style, is dead.) So in terms of one of the most important outcomes there can be—whether we are alive or dead, vigorous or frail—our causal attributions matter.

A second group of researchers, led by Bernard Weiner and Craig Anderson, has also conducted research that reinforces the idea that people's attributional tendencies have a powerful effect on their long-term outcomes, but these investigators emphasize whether an attribution implies that an outcome is controllable, not whether its consequences are global or specific. Attributions for failure that imply controllability—for example, a lack of effort or a poor strategy—make perseverance easier because one can always increase one's effort or try a new strategy (C. Anderson, 1991; Anderson & Deuser, 1993, Anderson, Krull, & Weiner, 1996). If outcomes are viewed as beyond one's control, on the other hand, it's tempting to simply give up—indeed, it's often rational to do so. The importance of controllability is also apparent in the impact of a person's attributions in judging someone else's behavior. People who are opposed to a gay lifestyle, for example, express more sympathetic attitudes toward gays if they consider homosexuality to be an inescapable result of a person's biology rather than a lifestyle choice (Whitely, 1990). And when a person offers an excuse for problematic behavior, it typically yields more pity and forgiveness if it involves something out of the person's control ("someone slashed my tires") than if it involves something controllable ("I wanted to go out and enjoy the sunshine") (Weiner, 1986).

Research inspired by these findings on the impact of attributional style has shown that people can be trained to adopt more productive attributional tendencies (especially to attribute failure to a lack of effort) and that doing so has beneficial effects on subsequent academic performance (Dweck, 1975; Forsterling, 1985). The effects are both substantial and touching. Blackwell, Dweck, and Trzesniewski (2004) report tough junior high school boys crying when made to realize that their grades were due to a lack of effort rather than a lack of brains. Making people believe that they can exert control over events that were formerly thought to be outside of their control serves to restore hope and unleash the kind of productive energy that makes future success more likely (Crandall, Katkovsky, & Crandall, 1965; Dweck & Reppucci, 1973; Peterson, Maier, & Seligman, 1993; Seligman, Maier, & Geer, 1968).

These sorts of training efforts might be put to good use, we should note, to undo some inadvertent attributional training that takes place in elementary school classrooms across the United States, a type that appears to give rise to a troubling gender difference in attribu-

**Attribution and Control**    Christopher Reeve was paralyzed in a riding accident, but he continued to believe that his efforts mattered and that he could control some aspects of his life. He did what he could to exercise his muscles, to campaign for further research on spinal cord injuries, and to help other disabled people. He is pictured here with his wife, Dana Reeve, and with Meryl Streep after accepting an award from an association of disabled people.

tional style. That is, boys are more likely than girls to attribute their failures to lack of effort, and girls are more likely than boys to attribute their failure to lack of ability. Carol Dweck and her colleagues have found that this difference results in part from boys and girls being subtly taught different ways to interpret both their successes and their failures (Dweck, Davidson, Nelson, & Enna, 1978). They observed teachers' feedback patterns in fourth- and fifth-grade classrooms and found that negative evaluations of girls' performance were almost exclusively restricted to intellectual inadequacies ("this is not right, Lisa"). In contrast, 45 percent of the criticism of boys' work referred to nonintellectual factors ("this is messy, Bill"). Positive evaluation of girls' performance was related to the intellectual quality of their performance less than 80 percent of the time; for boys, it was 94 percent of the time. Dweck and her colleagues argue from these data that girls learn that criticism means they lack ability, whereas boys learn that criticism likely refers to nonintellectual aspects of their behavior.

To nail this down, Dweck and her colleagues performed an experiment in which they gave students feedback of the kind girls typically receive in the class or the kind boys typically receive. They found that both boys and girls receiving the comments typically given to girls were more likely to view subsequent failure feedback as reflecting their ability. So, whatever self-presentational reasons there may be for boys crowing about their successes and dismissing their failures, they are aided in this pattern by the treatment they receive in the classroom. And whatever motivational factors operate for girls, their more modest attributions are shaped by the feedback they receive in school.

**LOOKING BACK,** we have noted that causal attribution goes on all the time in our lives and that there are substantial individual differences in explanatory style. That is, people differ in whether they tend to make attributions that are external or internal, stable or unstable, global or specific. Attributional style has been shown to predict academic success, as well as health and longevity. Belief in the controllability of one's outcomes is important, and beliefs about the controllability of academic outcomes can be altered by training. Boys and girls learn different attributional beliefs about academic outcomes, with boys receiving feedback indicating that success is due to ability and failure is due to incidental factors, and girls receiving feedback indicating the reverse.

## THE PROCESSES OF CAUSAL ATTRIBUTION

Does she really like me, or is she just acting that way because I'm rich and famous? Does that candidate really believe what she is saying, or is she just saying that to win votes? Is he really a jerk, or is he just under a lot of pressure? These types of questions run through our heads on a daily basis. Before we begin to explore how people might answer these types of questions, we should note that people's assessments of the causes of observed or reported behavior are not capricious. Rather, they follow rules that render them predictable. Much of this chapter is devoted to examining the most important of these rules, which have evolved to serve multiple functions—namely, to understand the past, illuminate the present, and predict the future. It is only by knowing the cause of a given event that we can grasp the true meaning of what has happened and anticipate what is likely to happen in the future. Toward this end, a particularly important focus of people's attributional analysis is determining whether an outcome is the product of something internal to the person (that is, an internal or "dispositional" cause) or a reflection of something about the existing context or circumstances (that is, an external or "situational" cause). Ever since Kurt Lewin (see Chapter 1) pointed out that behavior is a function of the person and the situation, all theories of attribution have been concerned with people's assessments of the relative contributions of these two types of causes (Heider, 1958; Hilton & Slugoski, 1986; Hilton, Smith, & Kim, 1995; Jones & Davis, 1965; Kelley, 1967; Medcoff, 1990). If behavior is a function of both the person and the situation, how does one figure out how much of the action came from the person and how much from the situation?

*"If we're being honest, it was your decision to follow my recommendations that cost you money."*

### ATTRIBUTION AND SINGLE-INSTANCE OBSERVATION

Sometimes we are called upon to make judgments about people after observing them on a single occasion. Someone interviews for a job and seems quite personable. Is that the way she really is, or is she just putting on a good face for the interview? Someone we do not know yells at his kids at the grocery store. Is he a bad dad, or have his kids been unusually difficult? How do we resolve these questions?

In situations such as these, in which we do not have the luxury of observing someone over time and across different circumstances, we tend to employ a simple schema that has come to be known as the **discounting principle** (Kel-

**discounting principle** The idea that we should assign reduced weight to a particular cause of behavior if there are other plausible causes that might have produced it.

ley, 1973). By this logic, our confidence that a particular cause is responsible for a given outcome is reduced (discounted) if there are other plausible causes that might have produced it. Most often what this means is that we cannot be sure that someone's actions are a reflection of the person's true self if the circumstances are such that those actions were likely anyway. For example, you cannot believe what someone says under the threat of torture because the threat is sufficient to get most people to say almost anything. In such circumstances, you discount the internal cause (the person really believes the confession or accusation) because the external cause (the threat of punishment) is sufficient to explain the behavior.

Extending the logic just a bit leads to a complementary **augmentation principle**, by which we can have great (augmented) confidence that a particular cause is responsible for a given outcome if there are other causes present that normally produce the *opposite* outcome. Once again, this typically means that we can be sure that a person's actions reflect what that person is really like if the circumstances would seem to discourage such actions. If someone advocates a position despite being threatened with torture for doing so, we can safely conclude that the person really and truly believes in that position.

> **augmentation principle** The idea that we should assign greater weight to a particular cause of behavior if there are other causes present that normally would produce the opposite outcome.

One important derivation of the discounting and augmentation principles is that it can be difficult to know what to conclude about someone who behaves "in role," but easy to figure out what to think about someone who acts "out of role." One of the earliest attribution studies makes this point quite clearly (Jones, Davis, & Gergen, 1961). The participants in this study witnessed another person present himself in either an extraverted or introverted manner during an interview. Half of the participants were led to believe he was interviewing for a job as a submariner, a position that required close contact with many people over a long period of time and thus favored extraverted personalities. The other participants thought he was interviewing for a job as an astronaut, which involved long periods of solitude and thus favored an introverted personality. (Note that this study was published in 1961, when space flight involved a single astronaut in a tiny capsule.)

In short, half the participants witnessed behavior that conformed to the dictates of the situation—someone who exhibited extraversion for the submariner job, or appeared introverted for the astronaut job. Because the behavior fit the situation in these instances, it was difficult to judge whether the behavior was a true reflection of the person being interviewed. In contrast, the other participants witnessed behavior that defied the dictates of the situation—someone who appeared introverted for the submariner assignment, or exhibited extraversion for the astronaut job. Because the behavior was at variance with what is called for in the situation, it should be seen as a clear reflection of the interviewee's true self.

When the participants subsequently rated the interviewee on a host of trait dimensions dealing with introversion/extraversion, their judgments followed the logic of the discounting and augmentation principles quite closely. As shown in Figure 9.1, in-role behavior prompted rather mild inferences (see the middle two bars), whereas out-of-role behavior prompted more extreme judgments (see the two outer bars). Someone who acts outgoing when he "should" be subdued is assumed to be a real extravert; likewise, someone who acts withdrawn when he should be outgoing is assumed to be a real introvert. A person's traits are discounted as a likely cause of behavior if the behavior goes with the flow of the situation. In contrast, a person's traits are augmented as a likely cause if the behavior goes against the flow of the situation.

To employ the discounting and augmentation principles properly, you need to

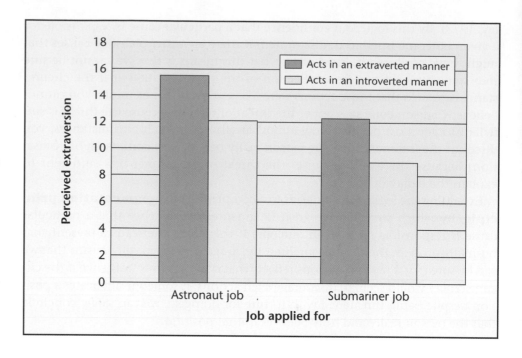

**Figure 9.1  Discounting and Augmentation**   Out-of-role behavior is seen as more informative of a person's true self than is in-role behavior. The figure shows the perceived extraversion of people who acted in an introverted or extraverted manner while interviewing for a position that favored introversion (astronaut) or extraversion (submariner). (Source: Adapted from Jones, Davis, & Gergen, 1961)

be something of a psychologist (Kelley, 1973). You must be able to comprehend the likely impact that various situational elements may have on a person. You must recognize, for example, that people tend to seek pleasure and avoid pain, that people are embarrassed if attention is called to their shortcomings, that people typically try to "fit in" to the situations in which they find themselves, and so on. After all, the causal force of many potential causes is not given; it must be inferred. Thus, people can take the same facts and come to different conclusions about what causal conclusions to draw.

This is precisely what happened when people judged the cause of Muhammad Ali's behavior. Some people thought that his refusal to join the military service cried out for the logic of discounting. One could not be sure whether he really had strong religious objections to the war because many people said this in order to avoid being sent to Vietnam. Others, in perfect contrast, thought that his situation called for invoking the augmentation principle: he sacrificed so much for his stance that he must have really believed in it. Thus, knowing exactly when to use the discounting and augmentation principles is not a given, and being able to apply them correctly requires a little knowledge about human nature, a little psychology. To employ them properly, one must be a good everyday, or "intuitive," psychologist (Kelley, 1973).

## ATTRIBUTION AND COVARIATION

There are times when the logic of discounting and augmentation is simply not helpful in answering the causal question at hand. If a friend of yours announces that she likes her statistics class, you do not ask yourself whether she really likes it or whether she was coerced into saying so. Instead, you typically take the statement at face value and wonder why she likes it. Is it something about her? (Is she a math nut?) Or is it something about her statistics class? (Is it taught by a truly gifted teacher?) To answer these questions, you might ponder your friend's reactions to other math classes, and other students' reactions to the statistics course she is taking.

This highlights the fact that we need not always base our causal judgments on a single observation. Sometimes we have the luxury of observing how a person behaves on a number of occasions, or how numerous people behave in a given situation. In these cases, we can go beyond the logic of discounting and augmentation and employ what we have learned from these multiple observations. We can employ what attribution theorists have dubbed the **covariation principle** (Kelley, 1973). We can examine whether the presence or absence of a potential cause makes a difference in producing an effect. Does the effect covary with the cause—that is, does the effect occur when the supposed cause is present, and does the effect fail to occur when the supposed cause is absent. If so, then our confidence that the true cause has been identified is increased (Cheng & Novick, 1990; Fiedler, Walther, & Nickel, 1999; Forsterling, 1989; Hewstone & Jaspers, 1987; White, 2002).

Note that the logic behind the covariation principle is the logic behind scientific experimentation. If you think ulcers are caused by a bacterium, you would want to see if individuals who are given the bacterium develop the ulcer, and whether ulcerated individuals who are given an effective antibiotic find that their condition improves.

There are three types of covariation information that psychologists believe are particularly significant for people's efforts to understand the causes of everyday social behavior. **Consensus** information refers to what most people would do in a given situation—that is, does everyone behave the same way in that situation, or do few or no other people behave that way? Is your friend one of a precious few who likes her statistics class, or do most students in the class like it? All else being equal, the more an individual's reaction is shared by others (that is, when consensus is high), the less it says about that individual and the more it says about the situation. **Distinctiveness** information refers to what an individual does in different situations—that is, whether a behavior is unique to a particular situation or occurs in all situations. Does your friend claim to like all math classes, or even all classes in general, or does she just like her statistics class? The more someone's reaction is confined to a particular situation (that is, when distinctiveness is high), the less it says about that individual and the more it says about the specific situation. **Consistency** information refers to what an individual does in a given situation on different occasions—that is, whether the behavior is the same the next time, or whether it varies. Did your friend have favorable things to say about her statistics course today only, or has she extolled its virtues all semester? The more an individual's reaction is specific to a given occasion (that is, when consistency is low), the harder it is to make a definite attribution either to the person or the situation. The effect is likely due to some less predictable combination of circumstances.

Putting the three sources of information together, a situational attribution is called for when consensus, distinctiveness, and consistency are all high (see Table 9.2). When everyone likes your friend's statistics course, when she claims to like no other math class, and when she has raved about the course all semester, there must be something special about that class. In contrast, a dispositional attribution is called for when consensus and distinctiveness are low, but consistency is high. When few other students like her class, when she claims to like all math classes, and when she has raved about the course all semester, her fondness for the course must reflect something about her.

To verify that people do indeed use covariation information in these ways, Leslie McArthur (1972) conducted an experiment in which she presented her participants with statements such as, "John laughed at the comedian. Almost every-

"The whole of science is nothing more than refinement of everyday thinking."

—ALBERT EINSTEIN

**covariation principle** The idea that we should attribute behavior to potential causes that co-occur with the behavior.

**consensus** Refers to what most people would do in a given situation—that is, whether most people would behave the same way or few or no other people would behave that way.

**distinctiveness** Refers to what an individual does in different situations—that is, whether the behavior is unique to a particular situation or occurs in all situations.

**consistency** Refers to what an individual does in a given situation on different occasions—that is, whether next time the behavior under the same circumstances would be the same or would differ.

## Table 9.2 Covariation Information

Putting covariation information to work by using consensus, distinctiveness, and consistency information. How do we explain a friend's enthusiastic comments about her statistics course? Does she have idiosyncratic tastes or is the class a gem?

| ATTRIBUTION | CONSENSUS | DISTINCTIVENESS | CONSISTENCY |
|---|---|---|---|
| An **external attribution** is likely if the behavior is: | High in **consensus**: Everyone raves about the course. | High in **distinctiveness**: Your friend does not rave about many other courses. | High in **consistency**: Your friend has raved about the course on many occasions. |
| An **internal attribution** is likely if the behavior is: | Low in **consensus**: Hardly anyone raves about the class. | Low in **distinctiveness**: Your friend raves about all math classes. | High in **consistency**: Your friend has raved about the course on many occasions. |

**Covariation and Attribution**  A person in the audience watching Robin Williams perform a comedy routine, as here, may be laughing because of his own disposition or the situation. If we can observe the person on a number of occasions at comedy clubs and find that he always laughs (high consistency) at Robin Williams's routines, that he rarely laughs (high distinctiveness) at other comedians' jokes, and that most people laugh (high consensus) when Williams performs, covariation principles will lead us to attribute the person's laughter to the situation rather than to his disposition.

one who hears the comedian laughs at him [indicating consensus]. John does not laugh at almost any other comedian [indicating distinctiveness]. In the past, John has almost always laughed at the same comedian [indicating consistency]." The participants were then asked to indicate whether they thought the event (John's laughing) was due to the person (John), the situation (the comedian), the circumstances (the details surrounding the performance that particular day), or some combination of these factors.

The results revealed consistent use of the logic of covariation. Participants tended to make situational attributions when consensus, distinctiveness, and consistency were high, and to make dispositional attributions when consensus and distinctiveness were low, but consistency was high. The only surprising finding was that the participants were only weakly influenced by the consensus information. They responded to whether or not everyone laughed at the comedian, but rather mildly. As we shall see, this reflects a common tendency to focus more on information about the person (here, distinctiveness and consistency, or what this person has done on other occasions and in other contexts) at the expense of information that speaks to the influence of the surrounding context (here, consensus, or what other people have done in this situation).

To employ the logic of covariation requires that one keep track of a lot of data about what various people have done in a variety of different circumstances. As a consequence, it has been argued that the proper use of the principle requires less of the skills of an "intuitive psychologist" and more of the skills of an "intuitive statistician" (Kelley, 1973).

## ATTRIBUTION AND IMAGINING AN ALTERNATE CHAIN OF EVENTS

The "observations" that serve as grist for the attributional mill are not limited to what we know actually happened; sometimes they are derived from what we *imagine* would happen under different situations. A person's causal analysis, in other words, can be based on the outcomes of thought experiments conducted entirely in the head. For example, in trying to fathom the high rates of obedience in Milgram's experiments (see Chapters 1 and 6), people imagine what they would do if they were one of the participants in the experiment. Because people have difficulty imagining that they themselves would administer much electric shock to the victim, they believe that a change in the person involved (in this case, oneself instead of the typical Milgram participant) would lead to a change in the outcome, and hence they conclude that it must have been the person, not the situation, that was responsible for the behavior.

**The Influence of What Almost Happened**   In one experiment that examined the role of imagined outcomes in causal attribution, participants read about a woman who went to lunch with her boss to celebrate her promotion (Wells & Gavanski, 1989). The woman's boss ordered for her, but not knowing she suffered from a rare allergy to wine, he ordered a dish made with a wine sauce. The woman fell ill shortly after the meal, went into convulsions, and died en route to the hospital. Some participants read a version of this story in which the boss had considered ordering a different dish that did not contain wine. The others read a version in which the alternative dish her boss had considered also contained wine. The participants were then asked several questions about the cause of the woman's death.

The investigators reasoned that the participants' attributions would be influenced not only by what happened in the scenario but by what *almost* happened. Those who read that the woman's boss almost ordered a dish without wine could readily imagine a chain of events in which she was just fine, and thus they would come to view the boss's choice of meals as causally significant. In contrast, when the dish the boss almost ordered also contained wine, the participants could not readily imagine a chain of events in which a different order would produce a different outcome, and so they would likely see the boss's choice of meals as less causally significant. As Figure 9.2 indicates, that is exactly what happened.

People's attributions are thus influenced not only by their knowledge of what has actually happened in the past but also by their **counterfactual thoughts** (or thoughts *counter* to the facts) of what might have, could have, or should have

**counterfactual thoughts**
Thoughts of what might have, could have, or should have happened "if only" something had been done differently.

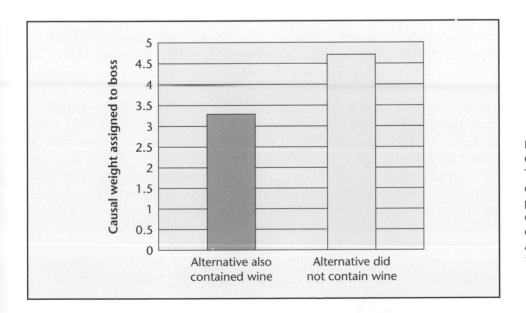

**Figure 9.2 The Role of Imagined Outcomes in Causal Attribution**
The causal significance of the boss's choice of meals as seen by participants who read that the boss almost ordered a different dish that did or did not also contain wine. (Source: Adapted from Wells & Gavanski, 1989)

**emotional amplification** A ratcheting up of an emotional reaction to an event that is proportional to how easy it is to imagine the event not happening.

**Emotional Amplification**   If you are watching a film and an appealing character utters something like, "I'm quitting the force" or "This is my last mission," you had better emotionally disinvest in that character or break out a tissue because the character has been handed a death sentence. Steven Spielberg used this phenomenon of emotional amplification in his film *Saving Private Ryan,* in which the death of Captain Miller (played by Tom Hanks as shown here) at the end of the film is made to feel even more painful because it almost did not happen—he was scheduled to go home at the end of the mission.

happened "if only" a few minor things were done differently (J. Johnson, 1986; Kahneman & Tversky, 1982; Roese, 1997; Roese & Olson, 1995; Sanna, 2000). And because people's attributions influence their emotional reactions to events, it stands to reason that their counterfactual thoughts do as well. In particular, the pain or joy people derive from any event tends to be proportional to how easy it is to imagine the event not happening. This is known as **emotional amplification**: a person's emotional reaction to an event is amplified if it almost did not happen.

Consider a news account of a father who took his young daughter to Detroit's Metropolitan Airport for a flight to visit her grandparents in Arizona. As the father tried to say goodbye near the boarding area, his daughter began to cry and say she did not want to go. The father did what most parents would do under the circumstances. He tried to reassure her that everything would be all right ("Don't worry, the flight attendants will look after you the whole way and grandma and grandpa will be there at the gate to meet you."). But he nevertheless insisted that she go. She did, and the plane crashed en route, ending her brief life (cited in Sherman & McConnell, 1995). It is impossible to consider that story without experiencing tremendous compassion for the father. Besides his agonizing grief at losing a child, the father may be tormented by the thought that he caused his daughter's death—that is, if he had only listened to his daughter she would still be alive. Because it is so easy to imagine how her fate could have been avoided, his pain is bound to be all the more intense.

Given that people's thoughts about "what might have been" exert a powerful influence on their reactions and attributions, a key question becomes what determines whether a counterfactual event seems like it "almost" happened. The most common determinants, certainly, are simple metrics of time and distance. Suppose, for example, that someone survives a plane crash in a remote area and then tries to hike to safety. Suppose he hikes to within seventy-five miles of safety before dying of exposure. How much should the airline pay his relatives in compensation? Would your estimate of the proper compensation change if you thought the individual had made it to within a quarter mile of safety? It would for most people. Those led to believe he died a quarter mile from safety recommended an average of $162,000 more in compensation than those who thought he died seventy-five miles away (Miller & McFarland, 1986). Because he almost made it (within a quarter mile), his death seems more tragic and thus more worthy of compensation.

This psychology of coming close leads to something of a paradoxical result in Olympic athletes' emotional reactions to winning a silver or bronze medal. An analysis of the smiles and grimaces that athletes exhibited on the medal stand at the 1992 Summer Olympics in Barcelona, Spain, revealed that silver medalists, who finished second, seem to be less happy than the bronze medalists, or third-place finishers, they had outperformed (Medvec, Madey, & Gilovich, 1995; see Figure 9.3). This appears to result from silver medalists being consumed by what they did not receive, the coveted gold medal, whereas bronze medalists focus on what they did receive—a medal. (Those who finish fourth in Olympic competition receive no medal at all.) Indeed, further analyses of the athletes' comments during post-event interviews confirmed the suspected difference in their counterfactual thoughts. Silver medalists were more focused on how they could have done better "if only" a few things had gone differently, whereas bronze medalists were more inclined to state that "at least" they received a medal. Second place can thus be a mixed blessing. The triumph over many can get lost in the defeat by one.

**Counterfactual Thoughts**    Pictured on the podium at the 2004 Olympics are the gold, silver, and bronze medallists in the women's under 48 kg weightlifting category. The silver medalist (on the left) looks less happy than the bronze medalist (on the right), which may be because the silver medalist keeps thinking about what she might have done to win, while the bronze medalist is just happy to be on the podium at all.

*The Influence of Exceptions versus Routines*    Another determinant of whether it is easy to imagine an event not happening is whether it resulted from a routine action or a departure from the norm. Would you feel worse, for example, if your beloved died in a plane crash after switching her assigned flight at the last minute, or after sticking with her regularly assigned flight? Most people say that a last-minute switch would make everything harder to bear because of the thought that it "almost" did not happen. In one study that examined this idea, participants read about a man who had been severely injured when a store he happened to be in was robbed. In one version of the story, the robbery took place in the store in which he most often shopped. In another version, the robbery took place in a store he decided to visit for "a change of pace." When asked how much the victim should be compensated for his injuries, those who thought they were sustained in an unusual setting recommended over $100,000 more in compensation than did those who thought they were sustained in the victim's

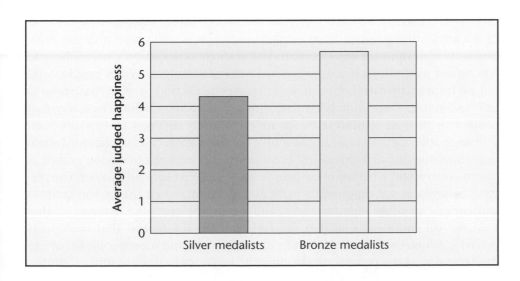

**Figure 9.3  Counterfactual Thinking among Olympic Medalists**    Ratings of how happy bronze and silver medalists appeared while on the medal stand during the 1992 Summer Olympic games in Barcelona, Spain. (Source: Adapted from Medvec, Madey, & Gilovich, 1995)

**The Anguish of What Might Have
Been** It is especially upsetting when
someone dies who was not supposed
to be in a particular situation. (A) The
bullfighter José Cubero, known as
Yiyo, died in the bullring after substi-
tuting at the last minute for another
bullfighter. (B) In the Israeli army, soldiers like this one are forbidden to
trade missions, no matter how compelling the circumstances. This is
because if a soldier died on a mission
that he was not supposed to go on,
the family would feel even greater
anguish at his "needless death," and
the soldier who should have gone
would feel great guilt at still being
alive.

usual store (Miller & McFarland, 1986). The injuries were presumably more tragic
because it is so easy to see how they could have been avoided.

This reasoning helps explain why those who perform in considerable danger,
like bullfighters and fighter pilots, often have informal rules against changing
places with someone else. Changing places is thought to be asking for trouble.
The death some years ago of the Spanish matador "Yiyo" was accompanied by
unusual anguish, in part because he violated the unwritten code of his profession
and served as a last-minute replacement for another matador (cited in Miller &
Taylor, 1995). The extra anguish that accompanies such tragedies may make
them particularly memorable and therefore lead to the superstition that switching spots somehow increases the chances of disaster—that by doing so one is
"tempting fate." In less ominous circumstances, we see the same processes at
work in the belief that you should never change lines at the grocery store or
depart from your initial hunch on a multiple-choice test. Because we "kick ourselves" when our new line slows to a crawl or when our initial hunch was right,
such occasions may be particularly memorable, and we may overestimate how
often a change of heart leads to a bad outcome (Miller & Taylor, 1995).

**LOOKING BACK,** we have seen that one of the most important elements of
causal attribution involves an assessment of how much the person or the situation was responsible for a given event. In the single-observation case, we have to
rely on our psychological acumen to make that assessment. When people stand
to gain from a particular behavior, we attribute their action to what they stood to
gain and not to their underlying dispositions; when they behave in a way that
conflicts with their self-interests, we are particularly inclined to attribute their
actions to their dispositions. In the multiple-observation case, we have information about the distinctiveness and consistency of a person's behavior, as well as
information about whether other people have behaved similarly. When the person's behavior is not unique to a particular situation, when the person behaves
consistently in those circumstances, and when not everyone behaves in that
way, we feel confident that it is something about the person that caused the
behavior. When behavior is distinctive and consistent and most people behave in
the same way as the person, we attribute the behavior to the situation. Counter-

factual thoughts about events that "almost" occurred influence our causal attributions and our emotional reactions to events that did occur.

# ERRORS AND BIASES IN ATTRIBUTION

If a student won a coveted prize, do you think you'd make the same attribution for the accomplishment if it were your best friend or your most hated enemy who had won the prize? Do you tend to make the same attributions for your own performances as you do for the performances of others? These questions highlight the possibility that the attributions we make may sometimes be less than fully rational. People's hopes and fears sometimes color their judgment, they sometimes reason from faulty premises, and they are occasionally seduced by information of questionable value and validity. Thus, one might expect people's causal attributions to reveal occasional errors and biases. Indeed, since the initial development of attribution theory in the late 1960s and early 1970s, social psychologists have expended considerable effort trying to understand some of the problems and pitfalls of everyday causal analysis.

**self-serving bias** The tendency to attribute failure and other bad events to external circumstances, but to attribute success and other good events to oneself.

## THE SELF-SERVING BIAS

One of the most consistent biases in people's everyday causal assessments is one you have doubtless noticed time and time again: people are inclined to attribute failure and other bad events to external circumstances, but to attribute success and other good events to themselves—that is, they are subject to a **self-serving bias** (Carver, DeGregorio, & Gillis, 1980; Greenberg, Pyszczynski, & Solomon, 1982; Mullen & Riordan, 1988). Think for a moment about two of your classes, the one in which you've received your highest grade and the one in which you've received your lowest. In which class would you say the exams were the most "fair" and constituted the most accurate assessment of your knowledge? If you're like most people, you'll find yourself thinking that the exam on which you performed well was the better test of your knowledge (Arkin & Maruyama, 1979; Davis & Stephan, 1980; Gilmour & Reid, 1979). Students tend to make external attributions for their failures ("The professor is a sadist," "The questions were ambiguous") and internal attributions for success ("Man, did I study hard," "I'm smart"). Research has shown that professors do the very same thing when their manuscripts are rejected for publication (Wiley, Crittenden, & Birg, 1979).

*"There might have been some carelessness on my part, but it was mostly just good police work."*

Or consider your favorite athletes and their coaches (or, for that matter, your fellow fans). How do they explain their wins and losses, their triumphs and setbacks? Richard Lau and Dan Russell (1980) examined newspaper accounts of the postgame attributions of professional athletes and coaches and found that attributions to something about one's own team were much more common for victories than for defeats. In contrast, attributions to external elements (bad calls, bad luck, and so on) were much more common for defeats than for victories. Overall, 80 percent of all attributions for victories were to aspects of one's own team, but only 53 percent of all attributions for defeats were to one's own team. Only 20 percent of attributions for victories were to external elements, whereas

"We permit all things to ourselves, and that which we call sin in others, is experience for us."

—RALPH WALDO EMERSON, *EXPERIENCE*

**Self-Serving Bias** Athletes often attribute victory to their own skills, and defeat to external factors.
(A) When the Boston Red Sox were defeated by the New York Yankees, they may have attributed their defeat to external factors like bad calls or even the "Curse of the Bambino" (Babe Ruth's revenge after the Red Sox sold his contract to the Yankees).
(B) When the Red Sox defeated the Yankees in Game 7 of the American League Championship in 2004 and went on to win the World Series that year, they most likely attributed their victories to their personal qualities and skills.

"Success has a hundred fathers; failure is an orphan."

—OLD SAYING

47 percent of attributions for defeats were to external elements (see also Roesch & Amirkhan, 1997).

We trust that you have observed this tendency to attribute success internally and failure externally (see Box 9.1). We trust as well that you can readily explain this pattern: people exhibit a self-serving bias in their attributions because doing so makes them feel good about themselves (or at least prevents them from feeling bad about themselves). The self-serving attribution bias, then, is a motivational bias. What could be simpler?

Actually, things are not so simple. Although attributing success to oneself but blaming failure on someone or something else *may* result from a desire to feel good about oneself, it could also result from more dispassionate processes. Even a perfectly rational person might very well make the same pattern of attributions, and be perfectly justified in doing so (Wetzel, 1982). After all, if someone tries to succeed at something, any success is at least partly due to the person's efforts, and thus warrants some internal attribution credit. Failure, on the other hand, usually occurs *in spite of* one's efforts, and therefore requires looking elsewhere, perhaps externally, for its cause. A fully rational individual, then, might exhibit a self-serving pattern of attribution because success is generally so much more tightly connected than failure to one's intentions and effort.

To see this more clearly, consider an experimental paradigm that reliably elicits the self-serving attributional bias (Beckman, 1970). Participants in such studies are required to tutor a student having difficulty mastering some material. (The participants in some of these studies are real teachers and in others they are college students.) After an initial round of tutoring, the child is assessed and found to have done poorly. A second round of tutoring ensues, and then an additional assessment is made. For half the participants, the child's performance on the second assessment remains poor; for the other half, the child shows marked improvement. What is typically observed in such studies is that the teachers tend to take credit if the student improves from session to session, but they tend to blame the student if the student continues to perform poorly. In other words, people make an internal attribution for success (improvement) but an external attribution for failure (continued poor performance).

It may seem as if the teachers are trying to feel good about themselves and are

Box 9.1 FOCUS ON DAILY LIFE

# Self-Serving Attributions

The magnitude of the self-serving bias can be seen in various public documents. When corporations send end-of-year letters to their shareholders, how do you think they account for their corporation's triumphs and tribulations? One study found that Chief Executive Officers claimed credit for 83 percent of all positive events and accepted blame for only 19 percent of all negative events (Salancik & Meindl, 1984). Or consider the accident reports motorists file with their insurance companies after being involved in an auto accident. The externalizing here can be downright comic. "The telephone pole was approaching; I was attempting to swerve out of its way when it struck my car," was how one motorist explained his mishap. "A pedestrian hit me and went under my car" stated another (MacCoun, 1993). These data, of course, require a disclaimer. Unlike the more controlled laboratory studies of the self-serving bias, the corporate reports and insurance forms are for public consumption. It may be, then, that the authors of these reports don't really believe what they are saying; they're just hoping others will swallow it. These examples should thus be taken as illustrations of the self-serving bias, not as solid evidence for it. The real evidence comes from the more carefully controlled studies we have described in the text.

behaving less than rationally in the process. But that is not necessarily the case. Suppose we programmed a computer, devoid of any feelings and hence having no need to feel good about itself, with software that allowed it to employ the covariation principle. What kind of attributions would it make? It would receive as inputs: (1) the child did poorly initially, (2) the teacher redoubled his or her efforts or changed teaching strategy (as anyone would do after an initial failure), and (3) the child did well or poorly in the second session. The computer would then look for a pattern of covariation between the outcome and the potential causes that would tell it what sort of attribution to make. When the child failed both times, there would no correlation between the teacher's efforts and the child's performance (some effort at Time 1 and poor performance on the part of the child; increased effort at Time 2 and continued poor performance). Because an attribution to the teacher could not be justified, the attribution would be made to the child. When the child succeeded the second time, however, there would be an association between the teacher's efforts and the child's performance (some effort at Time 1 and poor performance; increased effort at Time 2 and improved performance). An attribution to the teacher would therefore be fully justified.

This example indicates that we shouldn't be too quick to accuse others of letting the desire to feel good about themselves get in the way of sound attributional reasoning. It can be difficult to tell from the pattern of attributions alone whether someone has made an attribution to protect self-esteem. Such a pattern could be the result of a purely rational analysis, as we have just seen.

Does that mean that the self-serving bias is always rational—that it is not the result of people trying to feel good about themselves? Not at all. More extensive research has shown that such motives often are at work, showing that the self-serving bias is particularly strong when people's motivation to feel good about themselves is particularly high (Klein & Kunda, 1992; Miller, 1976; Mullen & Riordan, 1988).

As a final thought about the self-serving bias in attributions, consider how it might play out in the attributions people make about their most intimate partners. Do married couples make attributions about each other's behavior that resemble the attributions they make about themselves? They do, and they don't. That is, those in happy marriages attribute their partner's behavior in the same way they attribute their own behavior, but those in unhappy marriages do not. As you will recall from Chapter 4, happy couples explain each other's positive actions internally ("That's just the way he is"), and negative actions externally ("He's just so busy providing for all of us that he doesn't have the time"). Unhappy couples tend to do the opposite. They attribute their partner's positive behavior externally ("He just wanted to look good in front of our guests"), but they blame their partner's negative behavior on internal causes ("He just doesn't care"). Whatever betrayals or disappointments unhappy couples might have suffered, such a pattern of attributions can only poison the atmosphere further and make things worse (Fincham, 1985; Fincham, Bradbury, Arias, Byrne, & Karney, 1997; Karney & Bradbury, 2000; Miller & Rempel, 2004).

## THE FUNDAMENTAL ATTRIBUTION ERROR

Try to recall your initial thoughts about the individuals who delivered the maximum level of shock in Stanley Milgram's studies of obedience (see Chapters 1 and 6). The participants were asked to deliver more than 400 volts of electricity to another person, over the victim's protests, as part of a learning experiment. Nearly two-thirds of all participants did so. If you are like most people, you formed rather harsh opinions of these participants, thinking of them as unusually cruel and callous, perhaps, or as unusually weak. And in doing so, your judgments reflect a second way in which everyday causal attributions often depart from the general principles of attributional analysis. There seems to be a pervasive tendency to see people's behavior as a reflection of the kind of people they are, rather than as a result of the situation in which they find themselves. Note that a straightforward application of the covariation principle would lead to a situational attribution in this case, and not an inference about the participants' character or personalities. Because virtually all of these participants gave huge amounts of shock in the face of protests by the "learner," and nearly two-thirds were willing to deliver everything the machine could produce, their behavior doesn't say much about the individual people involved, but rather it speaks to something about the situation that made their behavior (surprisingly) common.

The tendency to locate the causes of behavior in elements of the person's character or personality is so common that social psychologists have given it two names: the **correspondence bias** (Jones, 1979, 1990) and the **fundamental attribution error** (Ross, 1977). It is called the "correspondence bias" because it involves drawing an inference about the person that "corresponds" to the behavior observed. The apparently less-than-compassionate behavior on the part of Milgram's participants is attributed to their being less-than-compassionate people, not to the surprisingly powerful forces operating in that setting. It is called the "fundamental attribution error" both because the problem people are trying to solve (figuring out what someone is like from a sample of behavior) is so basic and essential and because the tendency to think dispositionally—to attribute behavior to the person while ignoring important situational factors—is so common and pervasive.

**correspondence bias** The tendency to draw an inference about a person that "corresponds" to the behavior observed; also referred to as the fundamental attribution error.

**fundamental attribution error** A tendency to believe mistakenly that a behavior is due to a person's disposition rather than the situation in which the person finds himself.

*Experimental Demonstrations of the Fundamental Attribution Error*   Social psychologists have devised a number of experimental paradigms to examine the fundamental attribution error more closely (Gawronski, 2003; Gilbert & Malone, 1995; Lord, Scott, Pugh, & Desforges, 1997; Miller, Ashton, & Mishal, 1990; Miller, Jones, & Hinkle, 1981; Vonk, 1999). In one of the earliest studies, students at Duke University were asked to read an essay about Fidel Castro and his government in Cuba (Jones & Harris, 1967). Half of the participants read a pro-Castro essay and half read an anti-Castro essay, supposedly written in response to a directive to " . . . write a short, cogent essay either defending or criticizing Castro's Cuba as if you were giving the opening statement in a debate." Afterwards, the participants were asked to rate the essayist's general attitude toward Castro's Cuba. Because the essayist was thought to have been free to write an essay that was either supportive or critical of Castro's Cuba, it is not surprising that those who read a pro-Castro essay rated the writer's attitude as much more favorable toward Cuba than those who read an anti-Castro essay (see Figure 9.4).

There is nothing noteworthy in these results. But the results from another half of the participants in this "attitude attribution paradigm" are surprising. These participants read the same essays, but they were told that the stance taken in the essays (pro- or anti-Castro) had been assigned, not freely chosen. When these participants rated the essayists' true attitudes, their judgments were less extreme. But they did draw correspondent inferences: those who read a pro-Castro essay thought the author was relatively pro-Castro; those who read an anti-Castro essay thought the author was relatively anti-Castro (see the rightmost portion of Figure 9.4). From a purely logical perspective, you might say that these inferences are unwarranted. If individuals were assigned to write on a given topic, what they wrote could not be taken as an indication of what they really believed. That participants nonetheless thought the essays were informative of what the authors were like is thus a reflection of the fundamental attribution error.

You might object to this conclusion and question how much support such studies provide for the fundamental attribution error. After all, participants were given essays to read, and they were asked to infer what the essayist was like. If the experimenter is to maintain that nothing can be inferred, why did the experimenter ask for an inference? In addition, normally when people are compelled to say something that is inconsistent with their beliefs, they "distance" themselves from their statements by subtly indicating that they do not truly believe what

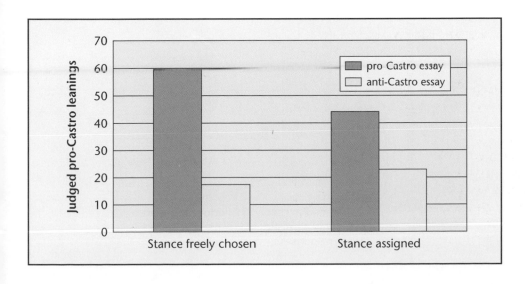

**Figure 9.4 The Fundamental Attribution Error**   Participants' ratings of the essayist's true attitude toward Castro's Cuba, with higher numbers indicating more of an assumed pro-Castro attitude. (Source: Adapted from Jones & Harris, 1967)

they are saying (Fleming & Darley, 1989). Here there were no distancing cues present in the essays, and so participants may have legitimately inferred that the essays reflected something of the essayists' true attitudes.

Another demonstration of the fundamental attribution error gets around these problems by allowing plenty of room for such distancing behaviors. In this "perceiver-induced constraint" paradigm, participants are randomly assigned to one of two roles: questioner or responder (Gilbert & Jones, 1986; Van Boven, Kamada, & Gilovich, 1999). The questioner's job is to read a series of questions over an intercom to the responder, who then answers with one of two entirely scripted responses. Thus, the responders' answers are not their own and should not be considered informative of their true personalities. The added twist in this study is that, after reading each question, the questioners themselves—with instructions from the experimenter—indicate to the responder which of the two responses he or she is to make. Thus, the questioners themselves constrain the responder's behavior. For example, in response to the question, "Do you consider yourself to be sensitive to other people's feelings?," the questioner signals to the responder to answer either with "I try to be sensitive to others' feelings all the time. I know it is important to have people one can turn to for sympathy and understanding. I try to be that person whenever possible" (altruistic response), or "I think there are too many sensitive, 'touchy-feely' people in the world already. I see no point in trying to be understanding of another if there is nothing in it for me" (selfish response).

After reading a list of these questions to the responder and eliciting a particular response, the questioners in one such study were asked to rate the responder on a set of personality traits (trustworthiness, greediness, kindheartedness). What the investigators found was that questioners drew correspondent inferences about the responders even though they had directed the responders to answer as they did! Responders led to recite mainly altruistic responses were rated more favorably than those led to recite mainly selfish responses (see Figure 9.5). Note also that this occurred even though the responders could have (and may have) tried through tone of voice to distance themselves from the responses they were asked to give (Van Boven, Kamada, & Gilovich, 1999).

**Figure 9.5 The Perceiver-Induced Constraint Paradigm** Participants' average trait ratings of individuals that *they themselves* had directed to respond in an altruistic or selfish manner. Higher numbers indicate greater assumed altruism. (Source: Adapted from Van Boven, Kamada, & Gilovich, 1999)

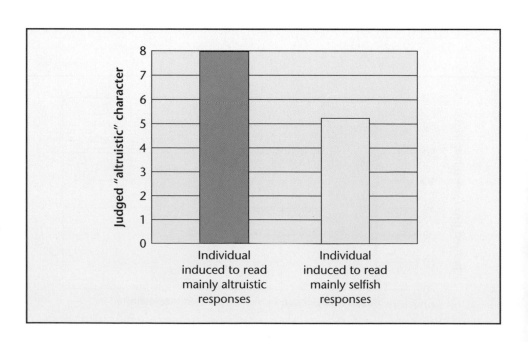

### The Fundamental Attribution Error and Perceptions of the Disadvantaged

An important inferential problem we all face in our daily lives is deciding how much credit to give to those who have been successful in life and how much blame to direct at those who have been unsuccessful. How much praise and respect should be directed at successful entrepreneurs, film stars, and artists? And to what degree should the impoverished among us be held accountable for their condition? What we have seen thus far about the fundamental attribution error suggests that we will tend to err by assigning too much responsibility to the individual for great accomplishments and not enough responsibility to the situation the person is in, broader societal forces, or pure dumb luck.

An ingenious laboratory experiment captures the essence of this inferential problem (Ross, Amabile, & Steinmetz, 1977). The study shows that people are indeed quick to commit the fundamental attribution error. From a broader perspective, it also suggests that we often fail to see the inherent advantages that some people enjoy in life and the inherent disadvantages that others must overcome. In the study, participants took part in a quiz-game competition much like the television show *Jeopardy*. One participant was assigned the role of questioner and the other the role of contestant. The questioner's job was to think of challenging but not impossible general-knowledge questions ("Who were the two co-inventors of calculus?" "Who played the role of Victor Laslo in the film *Casablanca*?"), and the contestant was to answer the questions (see answers on p. 160).

*"'No Brainers' for a thousand, Alex."*

From a self-presentation standpoint, the questioners had a tremendous advantage. It was relatively easy for the questioners to come off well because they could focus on whatever idiosyncratic knowledge they happened to have and could ignore their various pockets of ignorance. Everybody has *some* expertise, and the questioners could focus on theirs. The contestants, however, had no such luxury. They suffered from the disadvantage of having to field questions about the questioners' store of arcane knowledge, which typically did not match their own.

If people were not so dispositionist in their thinking, they would correct appropriately for the relative advantages and disadvantages enjoyed by the questioners and contestants, respectively. Thus, if asked to rate the questioners' and contestants' general knowledge and overall intelligence, they would be reluctant to make any distinction between the participants in these two roles—any difference in their *apparent* knowledge and intelligence could so easily be explained by their roles. But that was not what happened. Predictably, the unfortunate contestants did not answer many of the questions correctly. The contestants came away quite impressed by the questioners' abilities, rating them more highly than their own. When the quiz game was later re-enacted for a separate group of observers, they too rated the questioners' general knowledge more highly than that of the contestants (see Figure 9.6). Notice that the only people not fooled by the questioners' performance were the questioners themselves, who rated their own general knowledge and intelligence as roughly equal to the

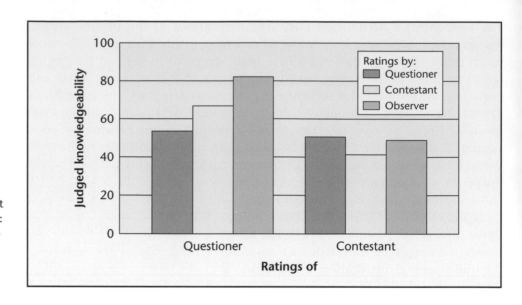

**Figure 9.6 Role-Conferred Advantage and Disadvantage** The bars show ratings of the general knowledge of the questioner and contestant in the quiz-show experiment. (Source: Adapted from Ross, Amabile, & Steinmetz, 1977)

ANSWERS TO QUIZ-SHOW GAME QUESTIONS: Isaac Newton and Gottfried von Leibnitz; Paul Henreid

**just world hypothesis** The belief that people get what they deserve in life and deserve what they get.

average of the student body. This aspect of the results is almost certainly due to the fact that the questioners knew they had skipped over yawning gaps in their knowledge base in order to come up with whatever challenging questions they could offer.

The experiment serves as a vivid, easy-to-remember caution about drawing inferences in our everyday lives. On average, the very successful among us have worked harder and exercised more talent and skill than the unsuccessful. The successful thus deserve our admiration—on average. But this experiment teaches us not to lose sight of the invisible advantages that some people enjoy and the equally invisible disadvantages that others must struggle to overcome. By dint of birth and connections, for example, some people start out in life with considerable financial resources, and for them making even more money is not terribly difficult because they already have a sizable stake. Conversely, few things are as challenging as making money when one must start from scratch and make it entirely on one's own. Thus, our attributions for success and failure in life, and the traits we infer as a result, should reflect the relative advantages and disadvantages to which different individuals have been subject (see Box 9.2).

*Causes of the Fundamental Attribution Error* Why are people so quick to see someone's actions as reflective of the person's inner traits and enduring character? Precisely because this tendency is so strong and so pervasive, it's a good bet that it is not due to one single cause. It is more likely the result of several causes acting jointly. Indeed, social psychologists have identified several psychological processes that appear to be responsible for the correspondence bias.

One reason that people are likely to attribute behavior to people's traits and dispositions is that dispositional inferences can be comforting. The twists and turns a life can take can be unsettling. A superbly qualified job candidate may be passed over in favor of a mediocre applicant with the right connections. A selfless Good Samaritan may be stricken with cancer and experience a gruesome death. A well-loved valedictorian may be murdered by a complete stranger a week after graduation. The anxiety that these events produce tempts us to think that it couldn't happen to us. There are a number of ways we can minimize the perceived threat to ourselves, and one of them is to attribute people's outcomes to something about them rather than fate, chance, or pure dumb luck (Burger,

Box 9.2 FOCUS ON POPULAR CULTURE

# I Am/Am Not Spock

The quiz-game paradigm nicely illustrates how difficult it can be to separate the person from the person's role when trying to assess what someone is like. This implies that we may have similar difficulty in trying to fathom the true character of actors who are cast in the same type of role in film after film. It may be hard to resist thinking, for example, that Dennis Hopper and Christopher Walken might be a little nuts in their daily lives, not just in their films. And is the real Tom Hanks the "good guy" we think he is from his good guy roles? The tendency to confuse actors and characters is sufficiently common that actors have been known to complain about this very error. Leonard Nimoy, who played the super-rational Mr. Spock in the original *Star Trek* television show, was so often treated as devoid of emotion by people he encountered in daily life that he felt it necessary to title his autobiography *I Am Not Spock*. The error is so fundamental and persistent, however, that Nimoy eventually gave up trying to persuade people he was not like Spock, and entitled his second autobiography *I Am Spock*.

**Separating the Person from the Role** (A) Leonard Nimoy in costume as Spock in *Star Trek*, and (B) Nimoy out of costume and at a business roundtable.

1981; Walster, 1966). More broadly, by thinking that people "get what they deserve," that "what goes around comes around," or that "good things happen to good people and bad things happen to bad people," we can reassure ourselves that nothing bad will happen to us if we are the right kind of person living the right kind of life. Part of the reason people tend to attribute behavior to dispositions, in other words, is that they are *motivated* to do so.

Social psychologists have studied this impulse as part of their examination of the **just world hypothesis**—that is, the belief that people get what they deserve in life and deserve what they get (Lambert, Burroughs, & Nguyen, 1999; Lerner, 1980; Lipkus, Dalbert, & Siegler, 1996). Victims of rape, for example, are often viewed as responsible for their fate (Abrams, Viki, Masser, & Bohner, 2003; Bell, Kuriloff, & Lottes, 1994), as are victims of domestic abuse (Summers & Feldman, 1984). This insidious tendency reaches its zenith in the claim that, if no defect in a victim's manifest character or past actions can be found, the tragic affliction must be due to some flaw or transgression

*"The employees have to assume a share of the blame for allowing the pension fund to become so big and tempting."*

in a "past life." Thus, for example, it has been argued that children who have been sexually abused must have been sex offenders themselves in a past life (Woolger, 1988). Such beliefs show the extent to which people will go to find justification, however far-fetched, for their belief in a just world. Research in this area has also shown that people tend to "derogate the victim"—that is, they rate unfavorably the character of those who suffer unfortunate outcomes that are completely beyond the victims' control (Jones & Aronson, 1973; Lerner & Simmons, 1966; Lerner & Miller, 1978).

Another reason that people are likely to make dispositional attributions is that people are more salient causes than situations. An outcome can only be attributed to those causes that spring to mind as possible causal candidates. Causes never considered cannot receive any attributional weight. But what influences whether or not a potential cause springs to mind, or how readily it springs to mind? One important determinant is how much it stands out perceptually, or how salient it is (Lassiter, Geers, Munhall, Ploutz-Snyder, & Breitenbecher, 2002; Robinson & McArthur, 1982; Smith & Miller, 1979). Those elements of the environment that more readily capture our attention are more likely to be seen as potential causes of an observed effect. And because people are so dynamic, they tend to capture our attention much more readily than the environment. Situations, if attended to at all, may be seen as mere background to the person and his or her actions. This is particularly true of various social determinants of a person's behavior (customs, social norms) that are largely invisible. Attributions to the person, then, have an edge over situational attributions in everyday causal analysis.

The importance of perceptual salience in people's attributions has been demonstrated in many ways. In one study, participants watched a videotape of a conversation between two people. Some participants saw a version of the tape that allowed them a view of only one of the individuals; others saw a tape that allowed them to see both individuals equally well. When asked to assign responsibility for the thrust of the interaction, those who could see only one individual assigned more responsibility to that individual than did those who could see both equally well (Taylor & Fiske, 1975). In another set of studies, one person in a videotaped conversation was made highly salient by being brightly lit on camera or by wearing a dramatically striped shirt. Those who witnessed the videotaped conversation made more dispositional attributions for the behavior of the salient individual than they did for the behavior of the nonsalient individual (McArthur & Post, 1977).

Perceptual salience explains some instances of the fundamental attribution error better than others. It explains the results of the quiz-show study, for example, because there the decisive situational influence—the questioner can avoid areas of ignorance but the contestant cannot—is invisible and therefore has little impact on people's judgments. But what about the attitude attribution studies in which the situational constraints are anything but invisible? In those studies, participants are acutely aware that the position the target person has advocated was assigned by the experimenter. Why don't they discount appropriately and

**Perceptual Salience and Attribution**
The fundamental attribution error is made in part because people are more salient than situations. If the people in this photo were to engage in a particular behavior—say, break out in song, tell embarrassing anecdotes, or complain about the weather—observers would be likely to assume that the behavior in question reflects the disposition of the woman in the center more than it reflects the others' dispositions because her red clothing and her uncovered face make her stand out.

363 ←

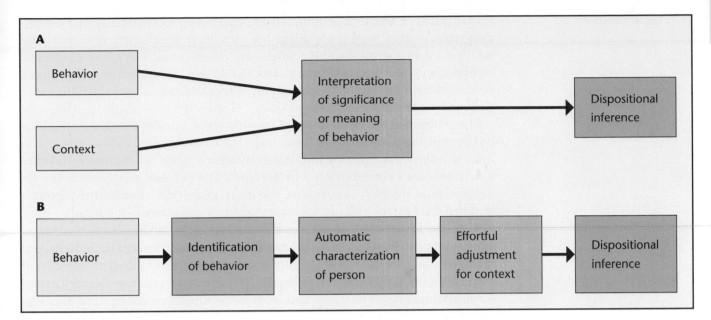

**Figure 9.7 The Discounting Principle** The discounting principle entails that a potential cause is discounted as a possible cause of a particular outcome if other causes might have produced the outcome. (A) In principle, we should simultaneously weigh both the person's behavior and the surrounding context to arrive at an explanation of a behavior. (B) In actuality, we first automatically characterize the person in terms of the behavior, and then sometimes make an effortful adjustment for the context to arrive at an explanation of the behavior.

decide that the target person's behavior is perfectly well accounted for by the prevailing situational constraints and thus refrain from making any inference about the person at all? The answer is that the cognitive machinery we draw upon when using the discounting principle doesn't work that way.

Let's review the logic of the discounting principle, depicted in Figure 9.7A. By that logic, we should simultaneously weigh what we've seen (or heard or read) about the person's behavior and the context of that behavior, or what we know (or can infer) about what might have influenced that behavior, to figure out what kind of person we're dealing with—that is, to draw a dispositional inference. What is puzzling about the fundamental attribution error, then, is why people don't weigh the situational information heavily enough when they know perfectly well (as they do in the attitude attribution paradigm) that it is sufficient to produce the observed behavior.

That would indeed be a puzzle if, in fact, people reasoned along the lines depicted in Figure 9.7A. But a sustained program of research by Daniel Gilbert makes it clear that we don't reason that way at all. Instead, we reason in the manner depicted in Figure 9.7B and, by that reasoning, people's failure to discount sufficiently for situational influences is not so puzzling after all (Gilbert, 2002). Gilbert has shown that we do not weigh behavioral and situational information simultaneously to figure out how to characterize what the actor is like. Instead, we observe the behavior in question, and we initially identify what that behavior is and what it means. For example, we see a certain pattern of gaze, a certain constriction of the muscles around the eyes, and a certain upturn of the corners of the mouth, and we must identify whether we're seeing nervousness or bemusement (Trope, 1986). We see one person in the arms of another, and we must decide whether the latter is carrying, helping, or kidnapping the other (Vallacher & Wegner, 1985).

Once we've identified what we've seen, we immediately—and automatically—characterize the person in terms of the behavior observed (Carlston & Skowronski, 1994; Moskowitz, 1993; Newman, 1993; Uleman, 1987; Winter & Uleman, 1984). Someone who acts in a hostile manner is seen as hostile regardless of what prompted the hostility; someone who acts in a compassionate manner is seen as compassionate, again, regardless of what may have prompted the compassion.

Initially, that is. Then, only upon reflection, do people consciously and deliberately take in what they know about the prevailing situational constraints and adjust their initial dispositional inference if warranted. Thus, the situational information is not weighed simultaneously along with the behavioral information; it is taken into account sequentially, after an initial dispositional inference has been made (see Figure 9.7B).

The primacy of the behavioral information gives it one of its advantages. That is, the situational information is not taken into account on its own terms, but is used to adjust the initial dispositional inference. Such adjustments, unfortunately, by their very nature tend to be insufficient (see Box 9.3). Because the situational adjustment is insufficient, the initial characterization of the person is weighed too heavily, and the fundamental attribution error is the result.

A second advantage that the initial characterization of the person has is that, since it happens automatically, it does not require much energy to perform, and it cannot easily be dampened or eliminated. It is incorruptible. The adjustment stage, however, is effortful and deliberate. It requires attention and energy to perform, and thus it can be dampened or short-circuited. It is corruptible. This suggests that when people are tired, unmotivated, or distracted, they are more likely to commit the fundamental attribution error (or to make a bigger error) because the second stage is shortened or skipped altogether.

## Box 9.3   FOCUS ON COGNITIVE PROCESSES

# Anchors Away!

We often estimate uncertain quantities by tinkering with some value we know is not quite right. For example, we might estimate the number of lives likely to be lost in an act of terrorism by adjusting from the number known to have been lost in the last terrorist act. Or we might estimate the number of layoffs in a looming recession by modifying the number in a previous recession.

Research indicates that when people estimate uncertain quantities, the adjustments they make tend to be insufficient and their estimates tend to fall short of the true value. Suppose you find yourself a contestant in the quiz-show experiment described earlier, and you are asked when George Washington was first elected president. Chances are you don't know, but you reason that it has to be after 1776, the year the United States declared its independence from Great Britain—and so you adjust up. The adjustment you would make is unlikely to be sufficient, as the estimates

people make on average (1780) fall short of the actual year (1789) (Epley & Gilovich, 2001).

You might be thinking that this is a disturbing result because it means that your judgments are at the mercy of, say, a clever salesperson who might get you to seize on one anchor value or another and, without your awareness, influence your behavior. Such fears are justified. In one marketing study, for example, "end of the aisle" products were listed on sale either as "50¢ each" or "4 cans for $2" in order to anchor people's thoughts about "how many should I buy?" on either 1 or 4, respectively. Sure enough, customers bought 36 percent more cans when the products were advertised as 4 for $2. In another study, a sign in the candy section read either "Snickers Bars—buy them for your freezer" or "Snickers Bars—buy 18 for your freezer." Anchored on 18, those who confronted the latter sign bought 38 percent more (Wansink, Kent, & Hoch, 1998).

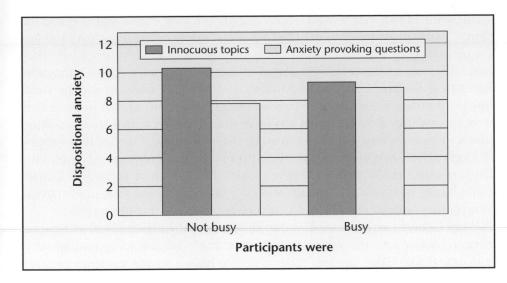

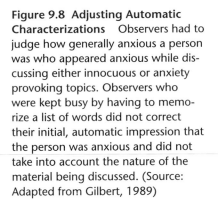

**Figure 9.8 Adjusting Automatic Characterizations** Observers had to judge how generally anxious a person was who appeared anxious while discussing either innocuous or anxiety provoking topics. Observers who were kept busy by having to memorize a list of words did not correct their initial, automatic impression that the person was anxious and did not take into account the nature of the material being discussed. (Source: Adapted from Gilbert, 1989)

Gilbert has conducted a number of ingenious experiments that demonstrate this. In one study, participants were shown a videotape, with the sound removed, of a young woman engaged in a conversation with another person. The woman appeared anxious throughout: "She bit her nails, twirled her hair, tapped her fingers, and shifted in her chair from cheek to cheek" (Gilbert, 1989, p. 194). Half the participants were told something that could explain her anxious demeanor—namely, that she was responding to a number of anxiety inducing questions (about her sexual fantasies or personal failings, for example). The other participants were told that she was responding to questions about innocuous topics (world travel or great books, for example). Gilbert reasoned that all participants, regardless of what they were told about the content of the discussion, would witness the woman's anxious demeanor and immediately and automatically assume that she was an anxious person. Those told that she was discussing anxiety producing topics, however, would then deliberatively adjust their initial characterization and conclude that maybe she was not such an anxious person after all. Those told that she was discussing a series of bland topics would not make such an adjustment. As Figure 9.8 indicates, that is just what happened. Those told she was discussing a series of innocuous topics thought she was more dispositionally anxious than those told she was discussing a series of anxiety producing topics.

So far, this is just a standard attribution experiment. But Gilbert added a wrinkle. He gave another two groups of participants the same information he gave the first two, but he had these groups perform another task simultaneously. Specifically, participants in these latter two groups were asked to memorize a list of words while watching the videotape. Gilbert reasoned that this extra demand on their attention would make them less able to carry out the deliberative stage of the attribution process in which the initial characterization of the person is adjusted to take account of any situational constraints. If so, this should lead those who knew that she was discussing anxiety provoking topics to nevertheless rate her as being just as anxious as those in the innocuous topics condition. As Figure 9.8 indicates, that is just what happened. When participants were busy memorizing a list of words, they did not have the cognitive resources necessary to adjust their initial impression, and so they rated the woman as just as anxious when they were told she was discussing anxiety provoking topics as when they were told she was discussing innocuous topics.

But some of you may remain unconvinced. You may object that *of course* the "busy" participants failed to use the situational information (the topics she was discussing) to adjust their initial, overly dispositional impression of her. They may have been so distracted by the need to memorize their list of words that they failed to notice the situational information. Thus, they failed to use the situational information, not because they were too busy to do so, but because they were so busy they didn't notice it was there to use! Gilbert anticipated this objection and incorporated a clever element of his experimental design to overcome it. The words he had his "busy" participants memorize were the words specifying the very topics the woman was being asked to discuss! These participants, then, could hardly be unaware of the situational influences on the woman's behavior, and yet they were so preoccupied that they failed to use this information.

What Gilbert's work shows us is that the seeds of the fundamental attribution error are sown into the very cognitive machinery we use to determine what someone is like. There are two reasons people have a strong tendency to make overly dispositional attributions. First, information about situational influence is used to adjust an immediate dispositional characterization and such adjustments, like adjustments of all sorts, tend to be insufficient. Second, the adjustment phase requires energy and attention, and therefore it can be disrupted by anything that tires or distracts. Because social life is so busy and complicated, and people are so often preoccupied with planning their own actions and self-presentations, all the resources necessary to do justice to the correction phase of a comprehensive attributional analysis are often not present (Geeraert, Yzerbyt, Corneille, & Wigboldus, 2004).

It stands to reason that we would focus initially on the person and his or her behavior, and only subsequently adjust to take account of the situation, because people are compelling stimuli of considerable potential importance to us. But what about those occasions in which it is the situation that is of greatest importance to us? What happens, for example, when we see someone react to a new ride at an amusement park, and we want to know whether the ride is scary or not? Do we immediately and automatically characterize the situation (the ride is terrifying) in terms of the behavior we've seen (these people are terrified), and only subsequently correct this initial situational inference in light of what we know about the individuals involved (they're rookies who've never been to a first-rate amusement park)? Research suggests that we do indeed. When people are primarily interested in finding out about the situation in which they observe someone behave (and are less interested in the person engaged in the behavior), the attributional sequence that Gilbert so carefully revealed is reversed. In such cases, people will automatically and effortlessly draw strong inferences about the situation (Krull, 1993; Krull & Dill, 1996; Krull & Erickson, 1995).

## THE ACTOR-OBSERVER DIFFERENCE IN CAUSAL ATTRIBUTIONS

It may have occurred to you that exactly how oriented one is toward either the person or the situation is quite different for two different sorts of people—the individual engaged in the action and anyone who observes the person engaged in the action. The "actor" is often primarily interested in determining "what kind of situation am I dealing with?" The observer, in contrast, is often interested in determining "what kind of person am I dealing with?" Given what we've just learned about the attribution process, this should have predictable effects on the causal attributions made by actors and observers. In particular, actors should be more likely than observers to make situational attributions for their behavior. Indeed, there is considerable research evidence for just such a difference (Jones & Nisbett, 1972; Pronin, Lin, & Ross, 2002; Saulnier & Perlman, 1981; Schoeneman & Rubanowitz, 1985; Watson, 1982).

In one of the most straightforward demonstrations of this **actor-observer difference** in attribution, participants were asked to explain why they chose the college major that they did, or why their best friends chose the major that they did. When the investigators scored the participants' explanations, they found that participants more often referred to characteristics of the person when explaining someone else's choice than when explaining their own choice, and they referred more often to the specifics of the major when explaining their own choice than when explaining someone else's choice. You might attribute your own decision to major in psychology, for instance, to the fact that the material is fascinating, the textbooks beautifully written, and the professors dynamic and accessible. In contrast, you might attribute your friend's decision to major in psychology to "issues" he needs to work out (Nisbett, Caputo, Legant, & Maracek, 1973).

> **actor-observer difference** Differences in attribution based on who is making the causal assessment: the actor (who is relatively disposed to make situational attributions) or the observer (who is relatively disposed to make dispositional attributions).

This phenomenon has significant implications for human conflict, both between individuals and between nations. Married couples, for example, often squabble over attributional differences. A husband may cite a late meeting or unusually heavy traffic to explain why an errand did not get done, whereas his wife may be more inclined to argue that he is lazy, inattentive, or "just doesn't care." Similarly, at the national level, the United States is likely to explain the stationing of its troops in so many locations across the globe as a necessary defense against immediate and future threats. Other countries may be more inclined to see it as a manifestation of U.S. "imperialism."

Like the fundamental attribution error, there is no single cause of the actor-observer difference. Several processes give rise to it. First, assumptions about what it is that needs explaining can vary for actors and observers. When asked, "why did you choose the particular college major that you did?" a person might reasonably interpret the question to mean "given that you are who you are, why did you choose the particular college major that you did?," The person is taken as a given, and therefore need not be referenced as part of the explanation. This is much like Willie Sutton's explanation of why he robbed banks: "Because that's where the money is." He takes it as given that he's a crook and thus interprets the question as one about why he robs *banks* rather than why he's a robber. Notice, in contrast, that when asked about another person ("Why did your roommate choose his or her particular college major?") the nature of the person cannot be taken as given and is thus "fair game" in offering an explanation (Kahneman & Miller, 1986; McGill, 1989).

Second, the perceptual salience of the actor and the surrounding situation is different for the actor and the observer (Storms, 1973). The actor is typically oriented outward, toward situational opportunities and constraints. Observers, in contrast, are typically focused on the actor and the actor's behavior. Because, as we saw earlier, people tend to make attributions to potential causes that are perceptually salient, it stands to reason that actors will tend to attribute their behavior to the situation and observers will tend to attribute behavior to the actor.

**The Actor-Observer Difference**
People often explain their own actions in terms of the situation, and the actions of others in terms of the person. This Palestinian hurls a petrol bomb after an Israeli missile strike killed eight Palestinians. He would probably see his actions as a response to an untenable situation, while others might see him as an aggressive and criminal hooligan.

Third, note that actors and observers differ in the amount and kind of information they have about the actor and the actor's behavior (Andersen & Ross, 1984; Jones & Nisbett, 1972; Prentice, 1990; Pronin, Gilovich, & Ross, 2004). Actors know what their intentions were in behaving a certain way; observers can only guess at those intentions. Actors are also much more likely to know whether a particular action is typical of them or not. An observer may see someone slam a door and conclude that he's an angry person. The actor, in contrast, may know that this is an unprecedented outburst and hence that it does not warrant such a sweeping conclusion. (In the attribution language used earlier, the actor is in a much better position to know if the behavior is *distinctive* and thus merits a situational rather than a dispositional attribution.)

A fourth contributor to the actor-observer difference is a rather interesting phenomenon in its own right, and thus warrants its own name and an extensive discussion. Observers sometimes witness behavior that differs from how they would behave themselves. Thus, if there is any reason that observers might tend to think that their *own* behavior is relatively common, any behavior that differs from their own will be seen as relatively rare and in line for a dispositional attribution. (In the attribution language used earlier, uncommon behavior is low in *consensus* and thus warrants an attribution to the person.)

It turns out that people do tend to think that their behavior (as well as their attitudes, preferences, or responses more generally) is relatively common, a phenomenon known as the **false consensus effect**. If asked, "what percentage of the student body is majoring in psychology?," psychology majors are likely to provide a higher estimate than economics majors, for example. Note that the false consensus effect is a *relative* phenomenon. People do not believe that whatever they do is something most people do. Vegans would not claim that most people are vegans. Nonetheless, people who believe something tend to estimate that a higher percentage of the general population shares that belief than do people with a different belief. Vegans can be counted on to give higher estimates of the prevalence of veganism than nonvegans would give.

This phenomenon was memorably demonstrated in an experiment in which Stanford University students who showed up for an experiment were asked if they would be willing to walk around campus wearing a large sandwich-board sign bearing the word "Repent" and to note other students' reactions. Or, if they preferred, they could choose to perform a more standard experimental task in the

**false consensus effect** The tendency for people to think that their behavior (as well as their attitudes, preferences, or responses more generally) is relatively common.

**False Consensus** People on different sides of controversial issues are prone to a false consensus effect. Each side tends to believe that it has more support in the general public than the other side is willing to acknowledge. At the end of a prolonged legal battle between Terri Schiavo's husband and her parents, the courts ruled that her feeding tube should be removed. These demonstrators believed that she was not brain dead and wanted the government to intervene so that she would continue to receive nourishment. In thinking that their views were relatively common among the population at large, the demonstrators, as well as many political figures, showed a false consensus effect.

lab. Approximately half the participants were willing to walk around campus wearing the sign. All participants—those who agreed to the request and those who refused—were asked to estimate the percentage of students who would be willing to wear the sign. Consistent with the investigators' expectations that people tend to anticipate a "false consensus" for their own choices, those who agreed to wear the sign estimated that 64 percent would do so, whereas those who refused to wear it thought that only 23 percent would agree to the request (Ross, Greene, & House, 1977; see also Krueger & Clement, 1994).

The false consensus effect, like the actor-observer difference and the fundamental attribution error, is the result of several causes. Self-serving motives may play a role—that is, it is often comforting to believe that others respond as we do, and so we convince ourselves that our preferences, beliefs, and actions are shared by a great many others (Marks & Miller, 1982). It is also the case that we tend to associate with people who are like us—that's one of the reasons we associate with them. Thus, if we ask ourselves, "I wonder what Ian would do?" or "Would Leticia do this too?," we are likely to consider the behavior of people who tend to be like us, and this "biased sampling" leads to the conviction that our own responses are fairly common (Ross, Greene, & House, 1977).

Finally, the way that we construe the meaning of different choice dilemmas contributes to the false consensus effect as well. Suppose you received an e-mail invitation to attend a party at your professor's house. Would you go? What percentage of the students in the class do you think would go? Your answers to both questions would depend on what you imagine the party would be like. If you imagine a sunny barbeque scene with appealing music playing and well-fed students gamboling back and forth between the swimming pool and hot tub, you might respond "count me in," and estimate that most of your classmates would respond similarly. But suppose you imagine a group of students sitting uncomfortably in your professor's living room, juggling teacups and saucers in their laps while discussing the fundamental attribution error. It's less likely that you would opt to attend and unlikely that you would think that many of your classmates would attend either. The way we construe what a given choice entails, then, creates a correlation between our own choices and our estimates of the commonness of our choices, which is the crux of the false consensus effect (Gilovich, 1990; Ross, Greene, & House, 1977).

**LOOKING BACK,** we have seen that people's attributions are subject to predictable errors and biases. People often exhibit a self-serving bias, attributing success to the self and failure to the situation. People exhibit the correspondence bias (also known as the fundamental attribution error) when they attribute behavior to people's dispositions rather than to the situation, even when there are powerful situational factors operating that they ought to take into consideration. There is a systematic actor-observer difference in attribution whereby actors are more likely than observers to attribute behavior to the situation, whereas observers are more likely than actors to attribute behavior to the dispositions of the actors. The false consensus effect leads people to think that their own behavior is relatively common. We now turn to a discussion of the role of culture in people's causal attributions and ask whether the same attribution tendencies are exhibited by people from more interdependent cultures.

# CULTURE AND THE FUNDAMENTAL ATTRIBUTION ERROR

One might expect the fundamental attribution error to be found in all cultures. After all, nearly everyone wishes to live in a just world, other people and their dispositions are everywhere more salient and capture attention more readily than the situation, and all people have the same basic cognitive machinery. Indeed, the error does appear to be widespread. For example, the classic Jones and Harris (1967) demonstration that people assume that a speech or essay presented by another person represents that person's own opinion on the topic, despite the presence of obvious situational demands, has been demonstrated in many societies, including China (Krull et al., 1996), Korea (Choi & Nisbett, 1998), and Japan (Kitayama & Masuda, 1997). Despite these findings, cultural differences have been found in what people in different cultures pay attention to and in their attributions for certain behaviors and outcomes.

## CULTURAL DIFFERENCES IN ATTENDING TO CONTEXT

We have suggested that most of the world's people tend to pay more attention to social situations and the people who comprise them than do Westerners. If this is indeed so, we might guess that Westerners would be particularly susceptible to the fundamental attribution error, while people from collectivist cultures would be less so. And in fact the kinds of social factors that are background for North Americans appear to be more salient to people from other cultures (Hedden et al., 2000; Ji, Schwarz, & Nisbett, 2000). In a particularly telling experiment, Takahiko Masuda and his colleagues showed Japanese and American participants cartoon figures having various expressions on their faces (Masuda, Ellsworth, Mesquita, Leu, & van de Veerdonk, 2004; see Figure 9.9). The central, target face was always surrounded by smaller, less salient faces, with expressions that were dissimilar to those of the target. For example, the target might appear to be happy, whereas

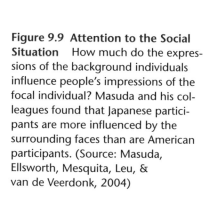

**Figure 9.9 Attention to the Social Situation** How much do the expressions of the background individuals influence people's impressions of the focal individual? Masuda and his colleagues found that Japanese participants are more influenced by the surrounding faces than are American participants. (Source: Masuda, Ellsworth, Mesquita, Leu, & van de Veerdonk, 2004)

**Figure 9.10 Noticing the Context**
What do you see? Japanese and American participants differ in their answers to this question. Americans are more likely than Japanese participants to make reference to the focal objects (that is, the fish) whereas the Japanese are more likely than the Americans to make reference to the context (that is, the rocks and plants). (Source: Masuda & Nisbett, 2001)

most of the surrounding faces might appear to be sad. The Japanese judgments about the facial expressions of the target were more influenced by the surrounding faces than were the judgments of the Americans. A happy face surrounded by sad faces was judged less happy by Japanese participants than by American participants, and a sad face surrounded by happy faces was judged less sad.

Westerners are less likely to pay attention to contexts even of a nonsocial kind. Masuda and Nisbett (2001) showed Japanese and American university students animated cartoons of underwater scenes, asking them afterward what they had seen (see Figure 9.10). The first thing the Americans reported was likely to be something about the "focal objects"—the most salient, rapidly moving, brightly colored things in the environment ("I saw three fish, maybe trout, moving off to the left"). The first thing the Japanese tended to report was information about the context ("It looked like a stream, there were some rocks and plants on the bottom"). In all, although Japanese and Americans reported similar amounts of information about the focal objects, the Japanese students reported 60 percent more information about the environment. Moreover, when asked after they had viewed all the scenes whether they had seen particular objects before, the Japanese were thrown off if the object wasn't shown in its original surroundings. Whether it was shown in the original surroundings or in novel surroundings made no difference to American students. Thus, for the Japanese, the object was "bound" to the environment in memory, and probably in initial perception as well, but for the Americans, the objects seem to have been detached from their surroundings (Chalfonte & Johnson, 1996).

Asians and Westerners also differ in the degree to which they attend to context even when they are perceiving inanimate, static objects. In a task called the Rod and Frame test, researchers asked participants to look into a long box, at the end of which was a rod and a frame (Witkin et al., 1954). The rod and frame could be tilted independently of each other, and participants were asked to ignore the frame and make judgments about the verticality of the rod. Chinese participants' judgments about the verticality of the rod were more influenced by the position of the frame (that is, the context) than were the judgments of American participants (Ji, Peng, & Nisbett, 2000). In a particularly elegant demonstration of West-

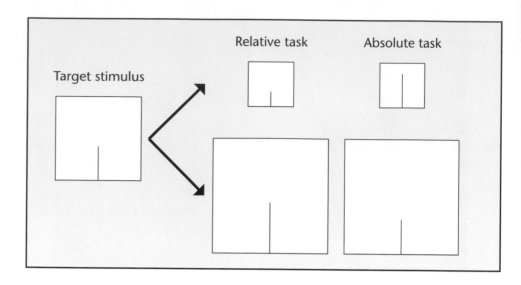

**Figure 9.11 Sensitivity to Context and the Framed Line Task** Participants are shown the target stimulus and then, after a brief interval, are asked to draw a vertical line at the bottom of an empty box. In the relative task, the line must be drawn in the same *proportion* to the box as it was originally. In the absolute task, the new line must be the exact same length as the original line. Japanese participants are better at the relative task and American participants are better at the absolute task. (Source: Kitayama, Duffy, Kawamura, & Larsen 2002)

ern insensitivity to context, and a complementary sensitivity to the properties of a focal target object, Kitayama, Duffy, Kawamura, and Larsen (2002) asked Japanese and American participants to examine a square with a line drawn at the bottom (see Figure 9.11). They then led their participants to another part of the room and showed them a square of a different size, asking them either to draw a line of the same length as the original or to draw a line having the same length *in relation to* the original square. Americans were better at the absolute judgment, which required ignoring the context, whereas Japanese were better at the relative judgment, which required paying attention to the context.

## CAUSAL ATTRIBUTION FOR INDEPENDENT AND INTERDEPENDENT PEOPLES

Given the pronounced difference between Asians' and Westerners' focus on context, it should come as no surprise to learn that Asians are inclined to attribute behavior to the situation whereas Westerners tend to attribute the same behavior to the actor.

Joan Miller (1984) compared the attributions of Hindu East Indians and Americans. She asked her participants, all of whom were middle-aged and middle class, to describe an acquaintance's behavior that they "considered a wrong thing to have done" and an acquaintance's behavior that they "considered good for someone else." She then asked her participants to explain why these events had occurred. American explanations called on twice as many presumed personality traits and other dispositions of the actor: "Jane is unselfish and likes to help other people." In contrast, the East Indians were twice as likely to explain behavior in terms of situational factors: "It was dark and there was no one else around to help." Miller also showed that children in the two cultures didn't differ in the sorts of explanations they gave. Not until adolescence did Hindu East Indians and Americans begin to diverge in their explanations. Conveniently, for Miller's purposes, some of her East Indian respondents had grown up in rather Westernized environments, speaking English and studying European culture. The attributions of these "Anglo-Indians" were midway between those of East Indians and Americans.

Differences in attribution tendencies show up for many types of events. For example, attributions for the outcomes of sports events are not the same for independent cultures as for interdependent cultures. Soccer coaches and players in the United States tend to see outcomes as the result of the abilities of individual players and the actions of coaches ("We've got a very good keeper in Bo Oshoniyi, who was defensive MVP of the finals last year"). In contrast, the attributions of Hong Kong coaches and players are more likely to refer to the other team and the context ("I guess South China was a bit tired after having played in a quadrangular tournament") (Lee, Hallahan, & Herzog, 1996).

Much other work shows that Asians see dispositions and internal causes where Westerners see situations and contexts. Morris and Peng (1994) showed that Americans are more likely than Chinese to see even the behavior of fish as being more dispositionally determined. They showed participants animated cartoons of an individual fish swimming in front of a group of fish. In some scenes, the individual fish scooted off from the approaching group; in other scenes, the fish was joined by the group and they swam off together; in still other scenes, the individual fish joined the group. Participants were asked why these events occurred. Americans tended to see the behavior of the individual fish as internally caused, and Chinese were more likely to see the behavior of the individual fish as externally caused (see also Kashima, Siegal, Tanaka, & Kashima, 1992; Rhee, Uleman, Lee, & Roman, 1995; Shweder & Bourne, 1984).

These differences in causal perception are likely due to differences in cultural outlook that in turn result in differences in what is attended to. As Markus and Kitayama (1991) put it, "If [like Asians] one perceives oneself as embedded within a larger context of which one is an interdependent part, it is likely that other objects or events will be perceived in a similar way." Westerners, in contrast, are more likely to see themselves as independent agents, and consequently they are more inclined to see people, animals, and even objects as behaving in ways that have relatively little to do with context.

It is not just Asians who differ from Westerners in explanatory tendencies. Al-Zahrani and Kaplowitz (1993) found that Saudi Arabian students were more collectivistic in orientation than Americans. We would therefore expect them to be less likely to show the correspondence bias in their causal explanations. The researchers gave brief vignettes describing morally positive and negative behaviors involving success or failure to Saudi Arabian students and American students and asked them to indicate the degree to which they thought the behaviors were caused by something internal to the person versus something external. They found that American attributions were more internal than were those of Saudis.

There are also differences in attributional tendencies among American subcultures. This has been measured by determining how often people mention traits in their descriptions. Puerto Rican children use fewer traits when describing themselves than do Anglo children (Hart, Lucca-Irizarry, & Damon, 1986) and are less likely to use traits to describe other people's behavior (Newman, 1991). Zarate, Uleman, and Voils (2001) also found that Mexican Americans and Mexicans were less likely to make trait inferences than were Anglos.

## PRIMING CULTURE

In today's world of highly mobile populations, many people have spent significant parts of their lives in both independent and interdependent societies. Such people offer psychologists an opportunity to better understand cultural influences on attribution. For example, the City of Hong Kong has been the location for several fruitful cultural studies because the British governed Hong Kong for 100 years. The culture there is substantially Westernized, and children learn English when they are quite young. People in Hong Kong, it turns out, can be

**Priming Culture** To prime Western associations and individualistic attributions, investigators might show participants a photo of (A) the U.S. Capitol building, or (B) an American cowboy roping a steer. To prime Asian associations and collectivist attributions, the investigators might show participants a photo of (C) a Chinese temple, or (D) a Laotian dragon.

encouraged to think in either an interdependent way or an independent way by presenting them with images that suggest one culture or the other. Hong, Chiu, and Kung (1997) showed some participants the U.S. Capitol building, a cowboy on horseback, and Mickey Mouse. They showed other participants a Chinese dragon, a temple, and men writing Chinese characters using a brush. They also showed a control group of participants neutral pictures of landscapes. Next the investigators showed all participants the animated cartoons of an individual fish swimming in front of a group of other fish, devised by Morris and Peng (1994), and asked them why they thought this was happening. Participants who initially saw the American pictures gave more reasons having to do with motivations of the individual fish and fewer explanations having to do with the other fish or the context than did participants who initially saw the Chinese pictures. Participants who initially saw the neutral pictures gave explanations that were in between those of the other two groups.

Other natural experiments are made possible by the fact that many people living in North America are of Asian descent and feel themselves to be partly Asian and partly Western. In one study, researchers asked Asian-American participants either to recall an experience that made their identity as an American apparent to them or to recall an experience that made their Asian identity salient. They then showed the students a battery of highly abstract cartoon vignettes suggestive of physical movements, such as an object falling to the bottom of a container of liquid, and asked them to rate the extent to which the object's movement was due to dispositional factors (for example, shape, weight) versus contextual factors (for example, gravity, friction). Participants who had had their American identity primed rated causes internal to the object as more important than did participants who had had their Asian identity primed (Peng & Knowles, 2003; see also Benet-Martinez, Leu, Lee, & Morris, 2002).

## DISPOSITIONS: FIXED OR FLEXIBLE?

So do Asians think like "social psychologists," putting great emphasis on situational determinants of behavior, whereas Westerners think like "personality psychologists," putting more emphasis on dispositional determinants? Not quite. It may be more accurate to say that Asians think like both. We European-American social psychologists find that we have no trouble gossiping about other people with our Asian friends. We understand people using the same dimensions of judgment—which are essentially the "Big Five" personality dimensions of extraversion, neuroticism, agreeableness, conscientiousness, and openness to experience. And the evidence shows that these dimensions play almost as much of a role in judging people's personalities, including one's own, for Asians as they do for Westerners (Cheung et al., 2001; McCrae, Costa, & Yik, 1996; Piedmont & Chase, 1997; Yang & Bond, 1990). Norenzayan, Choi, and Nisbett (1999) asked Korean and American college students a number of questions intended to tap their theories about the causes of behavior and found that, whereas Koreans and Americans rated the importance of personality the same, the Koreans reported situations to be more important than did the Americans.

Ara Norenzayan and his colleagues asked participants several questions about their beliefs regarding the malleability of personality—whether it is something about them that can't be altered much or whether it is subject to change. The Koreans thought that personalities are more malleable than the Americans did. The belief that personality is malleable, of course, is consistent with the view that behavior is substantially influenced by external factors.

The view that personality is changeable is also consistent with the view—much more characteristic of interdependent peoples than of independent peoples— that abilities are malleable through environmental factors and through effort (Dweck, 1999; Dweck, Chiu, & Hong, 1995; Dweck, Hong, & Chiu, 1993). Americans report placing a greater value on education than Asians do, but American students spend much less time studying than do Asian students (Stevenson & Stigler, 1992). The belief in the value of effort to overcome inadequacy is deeply rooted in the cultures of China, Korea, and Japan. In an experiment that makes this point well, Heine and his colleagues (2001) asked Japanese and Canadian university students to perform a task said to be reflective of their "creativity." They gave false feedback to the participants, telling some they had done well and others that they had done badly. The experimenters then gave the participants the opportunity to continue to work on the task. Canadian students worked more at the task if they had succeeded, savoring their newfound confidence in their creativity. Japanese students, seeing an opportunity for self-improvement, worked more on the task if they had failed. The experiment has a fascinating implication: Westerners will tend to get better on the things they already do well; Easterners seem likely to become Jacks and Jills of all trades.

Thus, much of social psychology's most valuable and hardest-won knowledge turns out to require substantial modification in light of systematic research on people other than North Americans. Asians and other interdependent peoples live in more interconnected social worlds than do Westerners. And probably as a consequence, they are attuned to more of their environment. Embedded in a social web themselves, they are inclined to see the contexts in which other people, and even other animals and objects, operate (see Box 9.4). Asians, like Westerners, do tend to make the fundamental attribution error. Nevertheless, they err to a lesser degree, presumably because they are more attuned to situational contexts, and they are more likely to correct their judgments when the context is highlighted in some way (Choi & Nisbett, 1998).

**LOOKING BACK,** we have seen that the fundamental attribution error is made by people in non-Western cultures, but that Westerners are more susceptible to it. People in collectivist cultures pay more attention to social situations and the people within these situations than do Westerners. With individuals reared in both interdependent and dependent cultures, it is possible to prime the different ways of perceiving and attributing behavior.

Box 9.4  FOCUS ON DIPLOMACY

# One Cause or Many?

An international conflict influenced by differing conceptions of causality occurred between China and the United States when a Chinese fighter plane collided with a U.S. surveillance plane in 2001 and the surveillance plane was forced to land on a Chinese island without receiving permission from the ground. The Chinese held captive the crew of the surveillance plane, demanding an apology for the incident from the United States. The Americans, asserting that the cause of the accident was the recklessness of the Chinese fighter pilot, refused. Political scientist Peter Hays Gries and social psychologist Kaiping Peng (Gries & Peng, 2002) have observed that, to the Chinese, an insistence that there was such a thing as *the* cause of the accident was hopelessly limited in its perspective. Relevant to the accident were a host of considerations, including the fact that the United States was after all spying on China, there was a history of interaction between the particular surveillance plane and the particular fighter pilot, and so on. Given the complexity and ambiguity of causality, the Chinese believed that the very least the United States could do would be to express its regrets that the incident had occurred. The presumed ambiguity of causality may lie behind Eastern insistence on apology for any action that results in harm to someone else, no matter how unintentionally and indirectly. Ultimately, the "regret" formula was the one that the two countries hit upon to resolve the impasse, but it is not likely that many people on either side understood the role played in the conflict by the differing conceptions of causality that Gries and Peng identified.

## BEYOND THE INTERNAL/EXTERNAL DIMENSION

The question of whether a given action was mainly due to something about the person involved or the situational context in which it took place is an important part of the story of everyday causal analysis. But this person/situation question is not the only one we ask, and it is not the whole story of everyday causal analysis. We often ask ourselves additional questions about people's behavior to arrive at a more nuanced understanding and to enable us to make more refined predictions about future behavior. In particular, we're often interested in understanding a person's intentions (Malle, 1999).

Think of it this way: We engage in causal analysis to make the world more predictable—to find the "glue" that holds all sorts of varying instances of behavior together. Sometimes that glue is a trait in the person—for example, her kindness explains her long hours at the soup kitchen, her unfailing politeness to everyone in the residence hall, and her willingness to share her notes with others in the class. Other times the glue is in the situation itself—for example, some people walk out of a horror film, some hold on tight to the arms of their seats, and others squeal with delight because the film is so terribly scary. Still another type of glue is provided by knowing someone's intentions—for example, the long hours in the library, the ingratiating behavior toward the professor, and the theft of another student's notes all come together and are rendered sensible by knowing that the individual has the intention of getting a good grade (Malle, Moses, & Baldwin, 2001; Searle, 1983).

Empirical studies of everyday explanations of freely chosen behavior attest to the significance people attach to understanding the reasons for a given behavior. Roughly 80 percent of the time, for example, people explain intentional actions with reference to the actor's reasons (Malle, 2001). Reasons for action, of course, are many and varied, but the overwhelming majority of the reasons offered to explain behavior fall into two classes: desires and beliefs. Why did the senator endorse an amendment banning the burning of the American flag? Because she *wants* to be reelected, and she *believes* she needs to appease her constituents. Why does he put up with his wife's abusive insults? Because he doesn't *want* to be alone, and he *believes* no one else would be interested in him. Beliefs and wants are what give rise to intentional action, and so it stands to reason that when we want to understand the behavior of others, we have to understand what they're seeking and what they believe will allow them (or not allow them) to get it.

**LOOKING BACK,** we have seen that when we want to understand a person's intentions, the attributional question we are most inclined to ask concerns the *reason* for the person's behavior. With respect to Muhammed Ali's refusal to be inducted into the U.S. armed services, the pressing question was not whether it reflected something about Ali or something about the situation, but *what* part of Ali did it reflect? What was his intention in refusing induction? Was he concerned with adhering to his Islamic beliefs or was he just trying to get out of the war?

## SUMMARY

1. People constantly search for the causes of events, and their attributions are important for their behavior. People have chronically different *explanatory styles*. Some people have a pessimistic style, attributing good outcomes to external, unstable, and local causes and bad outcomes to internal, stable, and global causes. This style is associated with poor health, poor performance, and depression.

2. Some attributions are made after witnessing a single instance of behavior, and to make an attribution based on a single observation we make use of the *discounting* and *augmentation principles*. If situational constraints could plausibly have caused an observed behavior, we discount the role of the person's dispositions. If there were strong forces that would typically inhibit the behavior, we augment its implications, and assume that the actor's dispositions were particularly powerful.

3. In the multiple-observation case, we have much more information about the person, the situation, and other people's behavior. When we have made multiple observations of a behavior, we can use the *covariation principle* to analyze that behavior. When we know that a person engages in a given behavior across many situations, and that other people tend not to engage in the behavior, we are likely to attribute the behavior to the person. When we know that the person only engages in the behavior in a particular situation, and that most people in that situation also engage in the behavior, we tend to attribute the behavior to the situation.

4. *Counterfactual thoughts* can powerfully affect attribution. We often perform mental simulations, adding or subtracting elements about the person or the situation and using these simulations to guide our attributed outcomes. Joy or pain in response to an event is *amplified* when it is easy to see how things might have turned out differently.

5. Our attributions are not always fully rational. We sometimes attribute events to causes that flatter us

beyond what the evidence calls for—revealing *self-serving attributions*.

6. The *fundamental attribution error (also known as the correspondence bias)* is the tendency to attribute behavior to real or imagined dispositions of the person and to neglect influential aspects of the situation confronting the person. Even when it ought to be obvious that the situation is a powerful influence on behavior, we often attribute behavior to presumed traits, abilities, and motivations.

7. One of the reasons we make such erroneous attributions is due to the *just world hypothesis*. We like to think that people get what they deserve and that bad outcomes are produced by bad or incompetent people.

8. Another reason for the fundamental attribution error is that people and their behavior tend to be more salient than situations.

9. A final reason for the fundamental attribution error is that attribution appears to be a two-step process. People are initially and automatically characterized in terms consistent with their behavior, and this initial characterization is only later adjusted to take account of the impact of prevailing situational forces.

10. There are *actor-observer differences* in attributions. In general, actors tend to attribute their behavior much more to situations than do observers. This is partly due to the fact that actors can usually see the situations they confront better than observers can.

11. There are marked cultural differences in susceptibility to the fundamental attribution error. Interdependent peoples are less likely to make the error than independent peoples, in part because their tendency to pay attention to context encourages them to look to the situation confronting the actor. For bicultural people, it is possible to prime one culture or the other and get very different causal attributions.

12. Much of the time we are concerned with more than whether to attribute behavior to the situation versus the person, and are interested in discerning the intentions and reasons that underlie a person's behavior.

## CRITICAL THINKING ABOUT BASIC PRINCIPLES

1. Can you think of any current events that seem to illustrate the actor-observer difference in attribution? That is, are there any events, controversies, or conflicts being covered in the news in which one "side" is offering situational explanations of its behavior and the other side is offering a dispositional account of that very same behavior?

2. Tell yourself a dispositional tale of your life—that is, how you got to where and who you are right now by virtue of your personal characteristics, traits, and decisions. Try to describe, in other words, the ways in which, if you weren't just the kind of person you are, you would not be where you are today, doing the kinds of things you are doing. After telling yourself that tale and letting it sink in, now tell a situational tale of your life—that is, how you got to where and who you are by virtue of the intervention of others, external circumstances, or simple chance. Which tale is more compelling or are they equally compelling? What does this tell you about the causes of human behavior?

3. From what you've read, either in the newspapers, for one of your classes, or from your general reading, who would you say were the most and least liked U.S. presidents in recent times? What would you say were their "attributional styles"? Does there appear to be any relationship between attributional style and popularity?

4. In what ways do the "role conferred self-presentational advantages" explored in the quiz-game study help to boost the impressions made by the professors in your university? What *specific* self-presentational advantages do they enjoy?

## KEY TERMS

actor-observer difference (p. 367)

attribution (p. 340)

attribution theory (p. 339)

augmentation principle (p. 345)

consensus (p. 347)

consistency (p. 347)

counterfactual thoughts (p. 349)

correspondence bias (p. 356)

covariation principle (p. 347)

discounting principle (p. 344)

distinctiveness (p. 347)

emotional amplification (p. 350)

explanatory style (p. 341)

false consensus effect (p. 368)

fundamental attribution error (p. 356)

just world hypothesis (p. 361)

self-serving bias (p. 353)

## FURTHER READING

Gilbert, D. T. (1995). Attribution and interpersonal perception. In A. Tesser (Ed.), *Advanced social psychology* (pp. 99–147). New York: McGraw-Hill.

Malle, B. F., Moses, L. J., & Baldwin, D. A. (2001). *Intentions and intentionality: Foundations of social cognition.* Cambridge, MA: MIT Press.

McEwan, I. (1998). *Enduring love.* New York: Anchor Books. A gripping novel showing how relationships can be shattered by a single random incident—with help from the fundamental attribution error.

Roese, N. J., & Olson, J. M. (1995). *What might have been: The social psychology of counterfactual thinking.* Mahwah, NJ: Lawrence Erlbaum Associates.

Ross, L., & Nisbett, R. E. (1991). *The person and the situation: Perspectives of social psychology.* New York: McGraw-Hill.

# Chapter Outline

CHAPTER 10

# Social Judgment

On October 18, 1992, Bonnie Peairs heard her doorbell ring and went to respond. Upon opening the door, she saw two boisterous teenagers dressed rather strangely—one with an ace bandage around his head and the other wearing a white dinner jacket à la John Travolta in *Saturday Night Fever*. Startled by the strange visitors, Mrs. Peairs slammed the door and yelled to her husband, "Get your gun!" Rodney Peairs did so, and when he went to the door, the two teenagers were still in his driveway. He told them to "freeze," but one nonetheless approached Mr. Peairs rather rapidly. Mr. Peairs then fired a single bullet from his .44 caliber revolver, killing the boy—an exchange student from Japan. Afterwards it became clear that the two boys had been looking for a Halloween costume party and had had the misfortune of knocking on the wrong door.

This story makes clear that social judgments can have substantial consequences. Effective action requires sound judgment about the world around us. "How would she react if I told her she was wrong?" "Would he be a good father to my children?" "Is it worth the investment?"

Our presentation of research on social judgment—and on the sources of error in judgment—proceeds in four parts.

Each focuses on a critical component of the process of social judgment. First, we note that judgments are only as effective as the quality of the information on which they are based, and we discuss some of the sources of bias in the information presented to a person in everyday life. Second, the way a given body of information is presented can affect the judgments that are made about it, including the order in which it is presented and the frame of reference in which it is embedded. Third, we examine what tools people bring to the task of judgment. In particular, we examine how a person's preexisting knowledge, expectations, and mental habits can influence the construal of new information, and thus substantially influence judgment. Finally, we discuss the two mental systems—intuition and reflective reasoning—that people employ in making complex judgments.

**Errors in Social Judgment** Rodney Peairs was indicted on a manslaughter charge after he mistook a boy in costume for an intruder and killed him. His error in judgment was based on a misperception of the situation before him and had grave consequences.

## WHY STUDY SOCIAL JUDGMENT?

The last chapter discussed one particular type of judgment—judgments about the causes of events. Here we examine social judgment more generally, exploring how people arrive at judgments (causal and otherwise) that help them interpret the past, understand the present, and predict the future. The field of social psychology has always been concerned with judgment because social psychology has always been a very cognitively oriented branch of psychology. Indeed, one of the earliest and most fundamental principles of social psychology is that if we want to know how a person will react in a given situation, we must understand how the situation is experienced by that person. Social stimuli rarely influence people's behavior directly; they do so indirectly through the way they are interpreted and construed.

The example that began this chapter does more than testify to the ubiquity and importance of judgment in everyday life. It also highlights the fact that our judgments are not always flawless. We trust some people we shouldn't. We make some investments that turn out to be unwise. Some of our mistakes are harmless, and others have important consequences, but all of them are potentially informative. They are informative to the individuals involved and to others who learn about their judgments because they suggest how to do better next time. They are informative to psychologists because they provide particularly helpful clues about how people go about the business of making judgments. They give psychologists hints about the strategies or rules people follow to make judgments—both those that turn out to be successful and those that lead to disaster.

The strategy of scrutinizing mistakes has a long tradition in psychology. Perceptual psychologists study illusions to illuminate general principles of perception. Psycholinguists learn about speech production by studying speech errors. Personality psychologists gain insights into healthy functioning by examining different types of psychopathology. Whether rare or common, mistakes often tell a lot about how a system works by showing its limitations. Thus, researchers interested in social judgment have often explored the limitations of everyday judgment.

But that is not the only reason that social psychologists have been interested in the errors and biases of judgment. One of the reasons that psychology as a whole is so interesting to so many people is that it holds the promise of betterment. Individually or collectively we may be doing fine, but the possibility of improvement nonetheless exists. And, as we shall see, social psychologists have coupled the study of the most common mistakes of judgment with the examination of sound judgment and effective functioning.

> *"Many complain about their memory; few about their judgment."*
>
> —La Rochefoucauld

## THE INFORMATION AVAILABLE FOR JUDGMENT

A tennis tournament has 125 contestants. On losing a match, a contestant drops out. The winner must win all the matches she plays. How many matches (involving *all* players) are needed to complete the tournament? (Answer is on p. 385)

Although many people find "word problems" like this one annoying, they do have one very appealing feature: all the information necessary for the solution is provided, and that fact is known in advance. Such is not always the case for many real-world problems. Often a person may not have—or may not know if she has—all the information needed to render an accurate judgment. Furthermore, some of the information that is available may be inaccurate. These limitations place something of a ceiling on the accuracy of judgments that are made. (But note that judgments can be perfectly "sound" or "rational" even if invalid information is used as input—and no matter how unhappy the outcome may be. The standard by which the quality of judgments should be assessed is not how well they turn out, but how sensibly they were made in light of the information available.)

Because of the strong link between information quality and judgmental accuracy, it is important to be aware of when information is likely to be accurate, and when it is likely to be misleading. We discuss some of the most common sources of distortion next.

### BIASES IN INFORMATION PRESENTED FIRSTHAND

Some of the information we have about the world comes to us firsthand, through direct experience. The rest comes to us secondhand, through gossip, news accounts, biographies, textbooks, and so on. In many cases, the information collected firsthand is more accurate. Firsthand information has the advantage of not having been filtered by someone else, who might slant things in a particular direction. But firsthand experiences can also be deceptive, as when we are inattentive toward, or misconstrue, events that happen before our eyes. Our own experience can also be unrepresentative, as when we judge the "national character" of people in a foreign land on the basis of the few individuals we encounter at hotels, restaurants, or museums. Finally, some of the firsthand information we acquire is information we extract from other people's behavior—behavior that is often strategic and thus not reflective of the true state of affairs. People's behavior often departs from their private beliefs, and this discrepancy gives rise to predictable judgmental errors.

*Pluralistic Ignorance*    One common class of situations in which other people's overt behavior can give rise to erroneous conclusions is exemplified by the following familiar scenario (Miller & McFarland, 1991): A professor finishes a discussion of a difficult topic by asking, "Are there any questions?" Numerous students are completely mystified, but no hands are raised. The befuddled students conclude that everyone else understands the material and that they alone are somehow deficient.

This is just one example of a phenomenon known as **pluralistic ignorance**. The phenomenon arises whenever people act at variance with their private beliefs because of a concern for the social consequences. The result is that everyone misperceives the group norm. It is embarrassing to admit that you did not understand a lecture when you suspect that everyone else has grasped the essential points just fine. When everyone follows that logic, however, a social "reality" exists that differs from everyone's true feelings. People conclude from the illusory group consensus that they are deviant (which only reinforces the difficulty of acting in accordance with what they really believe).

> **pluralistic ignorance** Misperception of a group norm that results from observing people who are acting at variance with their private beliefs out of a concern for the social consequences—behavior that reinforces the erroneous group norm.

Pluralistic ignorance is particularly common in situations in which "toughness" is valued, leading people to be afraid to show their kinder, gentler impulses. Gang members, for example, have been known privately to confess their objections to brutal initiation procedures and the lack of concern for human life, but they are afraid to say so out of fear of being ridiculed by their peers. The result is that few realize how many of their fellow gang members share their private reservations. Prison guards likewise think they are alone in their sympathy for inmates because the prevailing norm of being tough deters everyone from revealing whatever sympathetic feelings they have for the prisoners (Kauffman, 1981; Klofas & Toch, 1982).

Another example of pluralistic ignorance that is close to home for many college students involves attitudes toward alcohol consumption. Deborah Prentice and Dale Miller (1993) examined the discrepancy between private attitudes and public norms about alcohol at Princeton University. They thought there might be a discrepancy between the two for the following reasons:

**Pluralistic Ignorance**    University students believe that drinking alcohol is more popular among their peers than it really is. Because of this belief, they censor their own reservations about drinking, thus furthering the illusion that alcohol is so popular.

> The alcohol situation at Princeton is exacerbated by the central role of alcohol in many of the university's institutions and traditions. For example, at the eating clubs, the center of social life on campus, alcohol is on tap 24 hours a day, 7 days a week. Princeton reunions boast the second highest level of alcohol consumption for any event in the country after the Indianapolis 500. The social norms for drinking at the university are clear: Students must be comfortable with alcohol use to partake of Princeton social life.
>
> In the face of these strong norms promoting alcohol use, we suspected that students' private attitudes would reveal substantial misgivings about drinking.

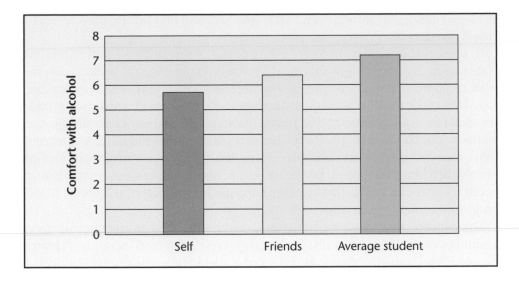

**Figure 10.1 Pluralistic Ignorance**
Princeton University students' ratings of their own and other students' comfort with campus drinking habits at Princeton. (Source: Adapted from Prentice & Miller, 1993)

Within their first few months at college, students are exposed to vivid and irrefutable evidence of the negative consequences of excessive alcohol consumption: They nurse sick roommates, overlook inappropriate behavior and memory losses, and hear about serious injuries and even deaths that result from drinking. They may have negative experiences with alcohol themselves and may notice its effects on their academic performance. This accumulating evidence of the ill effects of alcohol is likely to affect their private attitudes but not the social norm: Indeed, believing that others are still comfortable with alcohol, students will perpetuate that norm by continuing to adopt a nonchalant demeanor that masks their growing concerns (Prentice & Miller, 1993, pp. 244–245).

To find out if their hunch was correct, Prentice and Miller asked Princeton undergraduates how comfortable they felt about drinking habits at Princeton, as well as how comfortable they thought both the *average undergraduate* and their *friends* were about campus drinking habits. If the students were suffering from pluralistic ignorance on this issue, they should have indicated that they were less comfortable with drinking than they supposed most students were. The results, shown in Figure 10.1, indicate that that is exactly what happened. Hidden discomfort with alcohol existed side-by-side with perceived popular support.

What would happen if students were made aware of their misperceptions? Would they then drink less? A study by Schroeder and Prentice (1998) indicates that accurate knowledge of peers' opinions does indeed produce less drinking. They had students join in a discussion with their peers about drinking, and six months later they found that these students reported drinking less than did control participants.

*Memory Biases*    Memory was once believed to be a passive registry of information a person had encountered. We now know that this is not so, and that memory is an active, constructive process in which inferences about "what must have been" guide memories of "what was." This is not an intuitively obvious notion. Certain features of memory make it seem rather like a passive recording device. The clarity of memory seems to decay gradually over time, too much simultane-

ANSWER TO TENNIS TOURNAMENT PROBLEM: The tournament has one winner and 124 losers, each of whom loses once and only once. Thus, there are 124 matches in all. (Don't feel bad if you couldn't solve this problem; the solution wasn't obvious to us at first either.)

ous input garbles the information that is retained, and new information seems to crowd out the old.

If memory did function like a recording device, we would have only one complaint about our memories—that we do not remember enough. Information we wish to retain might simply not be available. But given that memories are not passively recorded and subsequently retrieved, but instead are actively constructed from clearly remembered fragments and general theories about how the world works, the door is open to further complaints about memory. A constructivist memory system, for example, is one that might construct memories of events that never happened. Of course, either shortcoming—not remembering enough or "remembering" what never happened—can distort judgments based on information retrieved from memory.

The concern about false memories achieved prominence in the popular press a number of years ago with the controversy over "recovered memories." Many people have claimed that they experienced a traumatic event during childhood that they had forgotten or repressed, but then recovered much later in life—often in the process of undergoing psychotherapy. The most commonly reported recovered memory is one of childhood sexual abuse. In one of the most striking examples, Eileen Franklin accused her father of having molested and murdered her close friend when the two of them were eight years old. Eileen made the accusation twenty years after her friend's murder, during which time she had no memory of the event. The memory came back to her one day while she was playing with her own children. Based almost exclusively on his daughter's testimony, George Franklin was convicted of murder and served six years in prison before his conviction was overturned.

**Recovered Memories**   (A) Eileen Franklin (center) believed that she had repressed and then recovered memories of her father, George Franklin, Sr., molesting and murdering her childhood friend twenty years earlier. (B) Based on his daughter's testimony about her recovered memories, George Franklin was found guilty and imprisoned until new evidence emerged showing that he could not have committed the crime.

We cannot say whether recovered memories such as Eileen Franklin's are real or not. If evidence were obtained establishing that one such memory was confabulated (made up and not based on actual experience), that would not imply that all of them are. Likewise, evidence indicating that one such case did in fact occur does not attest to the reality of all of them. Given what is known about the fallibility of human memory, however, it is irresponsible to insist, as some psychotherapists have, that all such accounts are valid. One reason for caution in interpreting claims about vividly remembered events is that even the most vivid memories can be inaccurate. For instance, California Angels baseball pitcher Jack

**Flashbulb Memories** People have vivid (although not always accurate) memories of where they were and what they were doing when they learned some dramatic news, such as (A) the explosion of the *Challenger* space shuttle, and (B) the collapse of the World Trade Center towers in New York City as a result of the 9/11 terrorist attacks.

Hamilton ruined the promising career of Boston's Tony Conigliaro with a fastball that crushed the left side of Conigliaro's face. That is the kind of stunning event you might think would lead to accurate recall. Nevertheless, Hamilton vividly remembered the event as having occurred during a day game when in fact it happened at night (Anderson, 1990; cited in Loftus, 1993). Both John Adams and Thomas Jefferson wrote late in their lives that they remembered signing the Declaration of Independence on July 4 but it is a matter of historical record that they did not sign it (nor did anyone else) until August 2.

**Flashbulb memories** are vivid recollections of the moment one learned some dramatic, emotionally charged news. "I know exactly where I was and what I was doing when I heard about the 9/11 attacks on the World Trade Center," would be an example. Such memories were once thought to be unusually accurate (Brown & Kulik, 1977). Though they are undoubtedly frequently both indelible and correct, subsequent research shows that they are not always accurate. In one study, people were asked about their memories of the explosion of the space shuttle *Challenger,* both the day after it happened and two and a half years later. Although the respondents described their later memories as vivid, most of these memories nonetheless had various discrepancies from their earlier memories, and more than a third of the later memories were wildly discrepant from the original ones (Neisser & Harsch, 1992). Consider the recollections of one person in this study who remembered the event as follows at the two different points in time:

> TWENTY-FOUR HOURS AFTER THE EXPLOSION: When I first heard about the explosion I was sitting in my freshman dorm room with my roommate and we were watching TV. It came on a news flash and we were both totally shocked. I was really upset and I went upstairs to talk to a friend of mine and then I called my parents.

> TWO AND A HALF YEARS AFTER THE EXPLOSION: I was in my religion class and some people walked in and started talking about [it]. I didn't know any details except that it had exploded and the schoolteacher's students had all been

**flashbulb memories** Vivid recollections of the moment one learned some dramatic, emotionally charged news.

watching which I thought was so sad. Then after class I went to my room and watched the TV program talking about it and I got all the details from that. (Reported in Neisser & Harsch, 1992)

One aspect of the fallibility of human memory that has particular significance for judgment is how people's theories of the way things *should be* can influence their memories of the way they *were*. For instance, people have theories (sometimes conscious and explicit and sometimes merely implicit) that some things in life tend to stay the same whereas others change. People tend to think that their political attitudes are stable, but that they get wiser with age. Such theories of stability and change might distort people's memories when these theories conflict with what actually happened (Ross, 1989).

One study that examined the impact of such theories on individuals' memories focused on attitudes about busing to achieve racial integration (Goethals & Reckman, 1973). Massachusetts high school students filled out a questionnaire assessing their attitudes toward numerous political and social issues, including the desirability of busing for purposes of racial integration. Four to fourteen days later, they participated in a group discussion as part of an investigation of high school students' thoughts about controversial issues. The topic of the discussion was busing. The discussion groups were composed of an experimental confederate and students who were either all opposed to busing or all in favor of it. The confederate was a "ringer" from the same high school who had been armed by the experimenters with forceful arguments in favor of both perspectives. His task was to change the students' opinions, which he did with great success. A questionnaire administered after the discussion indicated that anti-busing students became substantially more pro-busing, and pro-busing students became substantially more anti-busing. Most important, when students were asked to recall what their original attitudes had been, their recollections of their previous attitudes were distorted to fit their new opinions. Those with newly formed anti-busing attitudes recalled having always been anti-busing, and vice versa.

You might object that the students were merely *presenting* themselves as consistent. They may have felt some pressure to appear consistent (nobody wants to come across as "wishy-washy"), and so they knowingly provided incorrect "recollections" of their past attitudes that were more consistent with their current thoughts on the matter. The experimenters anticipated this objection and, to rule it out, they instructed the students to complete the attitude measures exactly as they had done before and informed them that the accuracy of their memories would be evaluated by comparing their responses to those they had made on the original questionnaire. Despite this strong encouragement for accurate recall, the students' memories were substantially biased in the direction of their current attitudes.

What about the flip side of this phenomenon? Are there times when people have implicit theories of change that lead them to recall changes that have not, in fact, taken place? Conway and Ross (1984) argued that such memory distortions are common among participants in various "self-help" programs such as diet regimens, speed-reading courses, and self-confidence seminars. Many of these programs have been found to be ineffective (or even harmful), and yet their effectiveness is acclaimed by satisfied participants. What's going on? Conway and Ross argued that people begin such programs with the expectation of success. (Why participate otherwise?) Participants then apply this general theory of improvement to their knowledge of what they are like at the end of the program, and they infer that they must have been *really* bad off beforehand. In other words, they get what they want out of the program (improvement) by unknowingly revising their assessment of where they stood initially.

To investigate their thesis, Conway and Ross interviewed students who had participated in a college "study skills" program. As predicted, the students who completed the program thought their initial study skills had been worse than they actually were. This led them to think that their skills had improved (which they hadn't), and to anticipate receiving higher grades (which they didn't).

These results indicate that we often retrieve—or construct—personal memories by assessing what we are like now, and then inferring what we must have been like earlier based on our presuppositions about whether we are *likely* to have changed or remained the same. When our presuppositions about stability or change are correct, they can facilitate accurate recollections of what we were like in the past. When they are incorrect, however, they can create memory distortion. Misguided assumptions of stability, for example, can make it hard to notice and appreciate important changes that have occurred (Goethals & Reckman, 1973; Niemi, Katz, & Newman, 1980). Perhaps this explains why each generation of professors complains that students do not seem as industrious as the professors were when they were students (Ross, 1989). Disciplined adults may have difficulty recollecting what they were really like when they were younger and less disciplined.

One word of caution before we leave the subject of memory distortions. The research indicating that memory is prone to certain systematic errors does not mean that our memories are hopelessly unreliable. Our memories are undoubtedly much more often right than wrong, and they serve us just fine most of the time. We remember where we parked the car, what we ordered the last time we visited our favorite restaurant, whether we made love last night, and so on. What the research on memory errors shows is that our memories are not recording machines; they are perhaps better thought of as devices for construing the past.

> "It is all too common for caterpillars to become butterflies and then to maintain that in their youth they had been little butterflies. Maturation makes liars of us all."
>
> —GEORGE VAILLANT

## BIASES IN INFORMATION PRESENTED SECONDHAND

Do you believe the current welfare system creates a "culture of poverty"? That Michael Jackson is a child molester? That your roommate's father is a good parent? Different people will have different answers to such questions, of course. But their different responses are alike in one important respect: All are based to a large extent on secondhand information. Few of us have any firsthand knowledge of the workings and effectiveness of the U.S. welfare system. None of us knows firsthand what Michael Jackson does or wants to do in his private moments. Similarly, for most people, knowledge of their roommate's father is restricted to whatever stories the roommate has told about him.

Because so many of our judgments are based on secondhand information, we must come to grips with the question of how accurate the information we receive from others is likely to be. What are some of the variables that influence the accuracy of secondhand information? What factors reduce the reliability of secondhand information, and when are these factors likely to come into play?

*Sharpening and Leveling*   One source of inaccuracy lies in the need for secondhand accounts to summarize what happened, since listeners are typically not patient enough, nor speakers motivated enough, to provide a full account of everything that happened. In summarizing, important elements are emphasized,

Box 10.1  FOCUS ON DAILY LIFE

# The Survival of the Most Disgusting?

Secondhand accounts of events are sharpened and leveled to make a good story, one that is likely to register with listeners and perhaps be passed on. As the paleontologist Stephen Jay Gould noted, "Stories are subject to a kind of natural selection. As they propagate in the retelling and mutate by embellishment, most eventually fall by the wayside to extinction from public consciousness. The few survivors hang tough because they speak to deeper themes that stir our souls or tickle our funny bones" (Gould, 1991, p. 244).

But what determines whether a story is likely to suffer extinction or survive in the broader marketplace of ideas? To find out, Chip Heath and his colleagues conducted a study of "urban legends"—fabricated accounts of events that circulate as "true" stories (Heath, Bell, & Sternberg, 2001). In the 1970s, for example, it was widely rumored that McDonald's supplemented its beef patties with ground earthworms. Heath and his colleagues offered an "emotional selection" account of stories' survivability and extinction. People tend to pass on stories that elicit a common emotional experience on the part of most listeners.

To test their emotional selection account, the investigators focused on one particular emotion: disgust. They first gathered examples of disgusting urban legends posted on various Web sites, and they created both less and more disgusting versions of each (see table below). Different participants read different versions of each of these stories and rated how likely they would be to pass them on to someone else. As predicted, participants were most likely to retell the most disgusting version of each urban legend. In another study, the investigators coded whether various stories posted on urban legend Web sites contained any of seven different disgust motifs (Does it involve the ingestion of an inappropriate food item? Does it involve sex? Does it involve inappropriate contact with an animal?). They then correlated the number of disgust motifs that each story contained with the number of Web sites reporting that legend—that is, with the legend's popularity. What they found supported their emotional selection account: The more disgusting the story, the more Web sites on which it was posted. Stories that stir our souls or tickle our funny bones do indeed hang tough in the marketplace of ideas, as do those that make us gag.

| STORY | LOW DISGUST | MEDIUM DISGUST | HIGH DISGUST |
|---|---|---|---|
| Rat in a soda bottle | Before he drank anything he saw there was a dead rat inside. | About halfway through he saw there was a dead rat inside. | He swallowed something lumpy and saw that there were pieces of a dead rat inside. |
| Wedding video | He forgot to erase from the tape scenes of himself masturbating. | He forgot to erase from the tape scenes of himself in sex acts with a plastic dummy. | He forgot to erase from the tape scenes of himself in sex acts with a neighbor's terrier named Ronnie. |

**sharpening** Emphasizing important or more interesting elements in telling a story to someone else.

**leveling** Eliminating or deemphasizing seemingly less important details when telling a story to someone else.

which is called **sharpening**; irrelevant details are eliminated, which is called **leveling**. To tell a story that allows a person to see the forest and not just the trees, essential elements are sharpened and extraneous features are leveled (see Box 10.1).

A telling example comes from the early history of psychology: the story of the classical conditioning of "Little Albert." As most introductory psychology textbooks proclaim, a nine-month-old child by the name of Albert once participated in an experiment in which he was greeted by the frightening sound of a hammer

**Sharpening and Leveling in Second-hand Accounts** "Little Albert" was conditioned to fear white rats, but the details of the experiment were simplified and distorted to make a more compelling story.

striking a metal bar every time he went near a white rat. Not surprisingly, Albert developed a fear of white rats, a fear that was maintained long after the experimenters stopped striking the metal bar each time he encountered a rat. Albert is also said to have developed a fear of objects that shared some of the features of the white rat, such as a rabbit, cotton balls, and a white beard.

Many of the elements of the customary story about Little Albert are true. Nevertheless, the original research report has been sharpened and leveled in order to make a simpler, more compelling story about how people develop phobias about seemingly harmless objects, and how acquired fears can generalize to other, similar objects. For example, the experimenters also made a loud noise next to Albert's head when he was near the rabbit, thereby calling into question the claim that Albert's fear of the rat "generalized" to the rabbit. Furthermore, when Albert's fear of the rat seemed to diminish after five days without hearing the threatening sound, the experimenters decided to "freshen" Albert's reaction by reintroducing the loud noise. These details cloud the central theme of the story, and so they have been leveled out of it. In addition, some of the most memorable aspects of the story of Little Albert were simply made up. A number of textbooks, for example, have invented a happy ending—one in which Albert's fear is eliminated through "reconditioning" (Harris, 1979).

> " . . . almost every canonical tale is false in the same way—a less interesting reality converted to a simple story with a message."
>
> —STEPHEN JAY GOULD

*Secondhand Impressions of Other People*   To a social psychologist, a particularly interesting class of judgments based on secondhand information involves judgments about other people. It is not at all uncommon for people to have impressions, sometimes strong impressions, about people they have never met. Many of us think we have a sense of what, say, Mike Myers, Toni Morrison, or Hillary Rodham Clinton is "really like"—without ever having made their acquaintance. Likewise, we might have strong impressions of our partner's former boyfriend or girlfriend—even when we are lucky enough to have avoided the person entirely.

How might such secondhand impressions differ from those formed firsthand? Stated differently, might secondhand accounts of a person's actions be sharpened and leveled in systematic ways? Perhaps. As we saw in the previous chapter, behavior tends to be attributed to people more than to situations, and so secondhand accounts of another person's actions may tend to be organized around the person rather than the context in which the actions took place. After all, it is the person who is typically the focus of the story (although there are exceptions). Thus, information about the person and the person's actions tends to be sharpened, whereas information about the surrounding context tends to be leveled.

(Recall that there is evidence that this is less true for interdependent peoples; see Chapter 9.)

The net result of this selective sharpening and leveling is that secondhand impressions of other people may be relatively unaffected by knowledge of how their actions were influenced by extenuating circumstances. Secondhand impressions may therefore tend to be relatively extreme. This hypothesis receives informal support from the experience many of us have had of finally meeting someone described as charming and wonderful. It is often a disappointing experience.

More systematic evidence is provided by experiments in which "first-generation" participants watch a videotape of a person describing a number of autobiographical events. These participants rate the person on a number of trait dimensions and then provide a tape-recorded account of what they have seen. "Second-generation" participants then listen to these accounts and also make trait ratings. As the analysis of selective sharpening and leveling would suggest, the second-generation participants tend to make more extreme trait ratings than their first-generation counterparts (Gilovich, 1987; Inman, Reichl, & Baron, 1993). Thus, these experiments suggest that the processes of sharpening and leveling are ubiquitous. They are invoked even when there is no motivation to provide a slanted account.

*"Here it is—the plain, unvarnished truth. Varnish it."*

*Ideological Distortions*    Of course, the biasing effects of sharpening and leveling are accentuated when there is a motivation to slant the story in a particular direction. Transmitters of information often have an ideological axe to grind, and that leads them to accentuate some elements of a story and to suppress others in order to foster certain beliefs or behaviors. Sometimes such motivated distortion is relatively "innocent." The person fervently believes in the message; it is just that certain details that might detract from the core message have been dropped. For example, when prepping Harry Truman for his 1947 speech on the containment of the Soviet Union, Undersecretary of State Dean Acheson remarked that it was necessary to be "clearer than the truth." Or consider the parent who accompanies the warning "Don't get into a car driven by a stranger," with the embellishment, "A little girl down the street did that, and her parents never heard from her again." The concern about driving with strangers is a legitimate one, and so it is accentuated by an innocent fib about a missing child down the street.

Of course, not all distortions are so innocent. People often knowingly provide highly misleading accounts for the express purpose of misleading. Republicans trumpet all manner of misleading statistics to make the Democrats look bad, and the Democrats do likewise to the Republicans. In areas of intense ethnic strife such as Kashmir, Rwanda, Aceh, and the former Yugoslavia, all sides wildly exaggerate their own rectitude and shamelessly inflate tales of atrocities committed against them (even though the reality is bad enough).

*Distortion in the Media*    One of the most pervasive sources of distortion in secondhand accounts is the desire to entertain. On a small scale, this happens in the stories we swap with one another. We often exaggerate a tale to make it more interesting. Being trapped in an elevator with twenty people for an hour is more interesting than being trapped with a dozen people for thirty-five minutes. So we round up. Or we make an event more interesting by enhancing our proximity to it. We describe something that happened to someone we barely know as happening to a "friend of mine." We tell the story of an event we only heard about as if we had actually been there.

On a larger scale, the need to entertain distorts the messages people receive through the mass media. Over the years, we have seen the steady erosion of standards in the news media, as thoughtful analyses of national and international events have given way to fluff. *Time* and *Newsweek*, for example, have fewer and fewer cover stories about world leaders and geopolitical affairs, and more and more stories about rock musicians, film stars, and athletes. The network news shows likewise devote more and more time to stories that would once have seemed appropriate only for the tabloids.

To be fair, this increase in fluff probably does little to distort people's conceptions of current events. It just deprives weighty issues of the attention they deserve. But there is one aspect of the market forces governing the news media that does have a distorting influence—the overreporting of negative, violent, and sensational events. Bad news tends to be more newsworthy than good news. Thus, the mantra of local newscasts: "If it bleeds, it leads."

The most frequently voiced concern about this bad news bias is that it distorts people's judgments of the dangers present in everyday life. Without doubt, the media provide a distorted view of reality. In the world as seen through the media, 80 percent of all crime is violent; but in the real world, only 20 percent is violent (Marsh, 1991; Sheley & Askins, 1981). In addition, news coverage of crime does not correlate with the rise and fall of the crime rate. There is just as much coverage during the best of times as there is during the worst of times (Garofalo, 1981; Windhauser, Seiter, & Winfree, 1991). The world as presented in motion pictures and television dramas is even more violent (Gerbner, Gross, Morgan, & Signorielli, 1980).

Perhaps because of constant exposure to this distorted view of reality, many people believe they are more at risk of victimization than may actually be the case. Most people are surprised to learn, for example, that the murder rate in the United States dropped by a third from 1990 to 1998, a period during which homicide coverage in the network news increased by 473 percent (Center for Media and Public Affairs, 2000).

**Media Distortion and Fear of Victimization** There is a positive correlation between watching television crime shows such as *CSI: Miami,* as seen here, and the belief that the world is a dangerous place.

Is the belief that the world is a dangerous place due in part to exposure to the world presented in the mass media? Investigators have tried to answer this question by conducting surveys in which people indicate how much television they watch and then answer questions about the prevalence of crime (for example, "How likely do you think it is that you or one of your close friends will have their house broken into during the next year?" or "If a child were to play alone in a park each day for a month, what do you think the chances are that he would be the victim of a violent crime?").

Such studies have consistently found a positive correlation between the amount of

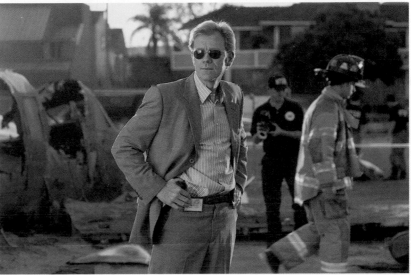

time spent watching television and the fear of victimization (Doob & MacDonald, 1979; Gerbner, Gross, Morgan, & Signorielli, 1980). As with all correlational studies, however, this finding by itself is difficult to interpret. Perhaps there is something about the kind of people who watch a lot of television—besides their television habits—that makes them feel so vulnerable. To address this problem, researchers have collected a variety of other measures (income, gender, race, residential location) and examined whether the finding holds up when these other variables are statistically controlled. When this is done, an interesting pattern emerges. The correlation between television viewing habits and perceived vulnerability is substantially reduced among people living in low-crime neighborhoods, but remains strong among those living in high-crime areas (Doob & MacDonald, 1979; Gerbner, Gross, Morgan, & Signorielli, 1980). People who live in dangerous areas and do not watch much television feel safer than their neighbors who watch a lot. Thus, the violence depicted on television can make the world appear to be a dangerous place, especially among people for whom the televised images resonate with certain aspects of their environment.

*Perceptual Vigilance and the Asymmetry between Positive and Negative Information*    The tendency on the part of the news media to hype bad news raises a more fundamental psychological question of why it's in the media's interest to do so. This translates to the question of why audiences are more interested in, titillated by, or receptive to negative information. There are doubtless many reasons, one of which implies that even if positive and negative information were presented evenhandedly, they would not have symmetrical effects.

Consider the following situation: You have just delivered a speech in a class on rhetoric. Seven of your classmates compliment you on your presentation; one comments that your introduction lacked punch. If you are like most people, you will find yourself obsessed with the one negative comment, even though it was outnumbered by the complimentary remarks.

This all-too-common reaction is one manifestation of a pervasive human tendency that has implications for our very survival. That is, we may be more attentive to negative information than positive information because the former may have more implications for our well-being. Some negative events constitute threats to survival, and thus they need to be attended to quickly. Organisms that fail to do so put themselves at risk. To be sure, many positive events such as eating also have survival implications, but they are usually not as urgent. A morsel of food not eaten now can be eaten later; a predator that is not avoided now never will be. The net result is that people may be more vigilant for potential threats than for potential benefits (Pratto & John, 1991; see also Forgas, 1992; Rozin & Royzman, 2001).

**Positive and Negative Information in the Media**    The media are more likely to report on negative than positive information, as the public seems more interested in negative information, perhaps as an evolutionary outgrowth of survival concerns. We saw and heard a great deal in the media about the devastation left by the 2005 tsunami in South Asia, but much less about relief efforts to help the victims, including U.S. marines' distribution of humanitarian aid to victims in Indonesia, as shown in this photo of a tsunami victim thanking a U.S. marine.

**LOOKING BACK,** we have seen that there are many sources of potential bias in the information available to us—and on which we base our judgments. Even firsthand information can be biased, as for example when people behave in ways that do not reflect their true attitudes or when firsthand information must be recalled from our occasionally suspect memories. There are also several sources of error in secondhand information. When people provide us with secondhand accounts of events, they typically sharpen some elements and level others. Communicators also sometimes distort information because of ideological or market reasons. Finally, perceptual vigilance inclines us to attend more to threatening stimuli than to unthreatening stimuli, which may account for why the media overreport negative, violent, and sensational stories. In the next section, we will focus on how our reactions to the information available to us can be powerfully influenced by structural aspects of the way information is presented.

## HOW INFORMATION IS PRESENTED

As an example of the power of how information is presented, consider the marketing and advertising of products in an economy of abundance. Producers can easily produce enough to satisfy the needs of society, but they find it useful to stimulate sufficient "need" so that there will be enough demand for what can be readily produced in abundance. By manipulating the messages people receive about various products through marketing, producers hope that consumers' buying impulses will be affected. The key to successful marketing, in turn, is not simply the selection of *what* information to present, but *how* to present it. It is an article of faith among advertisers that the way information is presented has a powerful influence on what people think and do.

We will examine that article of faith, but not in the domain of advertising. Instead, we will examine what social psychologists have discovered about the presentation of information and how it affects judgment more broadly. As we shall see, slight variations in the presentation of information can have a profound effect on people's judgments.

### ORDER EFFECTS

During the height of the cold war, a group of American citizens was asked the following two questions:

1. "Do you think the United States should let communist newspaper reporters from other countries come here and send back to their papers the news as they see it?"

2. "Do you think a communist country like Russia should let American newspaper reporters come in and send back to America the news as they see it?"

Thirty-six percent answered yes to the first question and 66 percent answered yes to the second—when the questions were asked in that order. A second group was asked the two questions in the reverse order, and their responses were quite different. When asked first whether American reporters should be given free reign in Russia, 90 percent said yes. Then, when asked about communist reporters in the United States, an implicit pressure to be consistent led 73 percent to say even they should be given free reign. Thus, merely changing the order of the two questions more than doubled the percentage of respondents (from 36 to 73 percent) willing to allow communist reporters into the country to report back what they wished (Hyman & Sheatsley, 1950).

In a similar vein, Schwarz, Strack, and Mai (1991) asked respondents to report on their marital satisfaction and their general life satisfaction (see also Tourangeau, Rasinski, & Bradburn, 1991; Haberstroh, Oyserman, Schwarz, Kühnen, & Ji, 2002). Some were asked the marital satisfaction question first. For these respondents, the correlation between the two questions was .67. This order made marital satisfaction quite salient for respondents, and thus it was very much in their minds when they came to answer the general life satisfaction question. In contrast, when it was the general life satisfaction question that was asked first, the correlation was only .32. Life satisfaction was seen by those participants as something broader than marital satisfaction, and so the relationship between the two was diminished. But what is the true correlation between life satisfaction and marital satisfaction? *Is* there a "true" correlation?

These results provide striking confirmation of something many people suspect—namely, that the order in which items are presented can have a powerful influence on judgment. That is why we all worry so much about whether we should go on first or last in any kind of performance. Sometimes the information presented first exerts the most influence, a phenomenon known as a **primacy effect**. On other occasions, it is the information presented last that has the most impact, a phenomenon known as a **recency effect**.

Order effects are not limited to public performances and opinion polls, of course, but are pervasive in everyday life. In one study that is particularly germane to everyday social life, Solomon Asch (1946) once asked people to evaluate a hypothetical individual described in the following terms: intelligent, industrious, impulsive, critical, stubborn, and envious. The individual was rated favorably, no doubt because of the influence of the two very positive terms that began the list—intelligent and industrious. A second group read the same trait adjectives in the opposite order and formed a much less favorable impression. Thus, there was a substantial primacy effect. Traits presented at the beginning of the list had more impact than those presented later on. Etiquette books (and your parents) are right: First impressions matter a lot.

Order effects arise for a number of reasons. Some, like the survey on the rights of newspaper reporters discussed above, are due to the pressure to be consistent. An initial response can constrain the way a person responds later on. After stating that U.S. reporters should be allowed to report what they want, it is hard to turn around and state that reporters from communist countries should not have the same right.

Other order effects arise because of information-processing limitations. Primacy effects, for example, often result from a tendency to pay great attention to stimuli presented early on, but then to lose focus during the presentation of later items. In Asch's experiment, for example, it is impossible to miss that the person described in the first list is intelligent and industrious, but once an initial positive impression is formed, it is easy to gloss over the person's stubbornness and envy. Recency effects, in contrast, typically result when the last items are easiest to recall. Information remembered obviously receives greater weight than information forgotten, and so later items sometimes exert more influence on judgment than information presented earlier.

Still other order effects arise because the initial information affects how later information is construed. All the traits in Asch's experiment have different shades of meaning, and how each is construed depends on the information already

**primacy effect** The disproportionate influence on judgment of information presented first in a body of evidence.

**recency effect** The disproportionate influence on judgment of information presented last in a body of evidence.

encountered. Take the word "stubborn." When it follows positive traits such as intelligent and industrious, one interprets it charitably, as steadfast or determined. In contrast, when it follows "envious," it is seen more negatively, as closed-minded or rigid (Asch & Zuckier, 1984; Biernat, Manis, & Kobrynowicz, 1997; Hamilton & Zanna, 1974; Higgins & Rholes, 1976).

## FRAMING EFFECTS

Order effects like those we have just discussed are a type of **framing effect**. That is, the order in which information is presented can "frame" the way it is processed and understood. Asking survey respondents first whether communist reporters should be allowed free reign in the U.S. invites them to consider the possible risks of doing so. But asking first about whether U.S. reporters should be allowed in communist countries subtly shifts the relevant frame of reference to one of "fair play."

Order effects like this are a type of "pure" framing effect. The frame of reference is changed even though the content of the information is exactly the same in the two versions—only the order is different. Consider the (probably apocryphal) story of the monk whose request to smoke while he prayed was met with a disapproving stare by his superior. When he mentioned this to a friend, he was told: "Ask a different question. Ask if you can pray while you smoke." The request is the same in both versions. But there is a subtle difference in the frame of reference. One presupposes smoking, and the other presupposes prayer.

*Spin Framing*    Framing effects are not limited to the order in which information is presented. Advertisers, for example, try to induce consumers to frame a buying decision in terms favorable to the product being advertised. They do so by utilizing what might be called spin framing, a less "pure" form of framing that varies the *content*, not just the order, of what is presented. A company with a competitive edge in quality will introduce information that frames the issue as one of quality. Another company with an edge in price will feature information that frames the issue as one of savings.

Participants in political debates likewise try to frame the discussion by "spinning," or highlighting some aspects of the relevant information and not others. Thus, we hear advocates of different positions talk of "anti-abortion" versus "the

> **framing effect** The influence on judgment resulting from the way information is presented, including the order of presentation.

*"It's not just compared to the table, damn it. This is a small portion."*

right to life," "welfare" versus "the safety net," "terrorists" versus "freedom fight-ers," "occupying army" versus "peacekeeping forces," "illegal aliens" versus "undocumented workers," and so on. The power of such terms to frame the rel-evant issues is what led the United States in 1947 to change the name of the *War* Department to the more benign-sounding *Defense* Department.

**Spin Framing**　Is this U.S. soldier in Iraq a "peacekeeper" or a member of an "occupying army"? The words used to describe him highlight differ-ent information, which affects how people react to him.

Politicians (and some polling organizations with a political mission) also engage in spin framing when they collect opinion polls to gather support for their positions. Thus, when Ross Perot asked voters in 1992, "Should the President have the line item veto to eliminate waste?," 97 percent said yes. When the ques-tion was asked in more neutral terms—"Should the President have the line item veto, or not?"—only 57 percent agreed (Crossen, 1994). Shading the question in a particular way has been shown to dramatically influence public opinion on abortion, the death penalty, and a host of other policy issues. Because it is so easy to slant public-opinion questions in a particular direction, it is important to know who sponsored a particular poll, as well as the exact wording of the questions. Without these details, one would be wise to adopt the same attitude toward polls as that of former Israeli Foreign Minister Shimon Peres, who treats them ". . . like perfume—nice to smell, dangerous to swallow."

*Gains and Losses*　Although spin framing is pervasive in marketing and poli-tics, psychologists tend to be more intrigued by pure framing—that is, how the same information can evoke different responses depending on how it is pre-sented. But besides order effects, what else qualifies as pure framing? To find out, we must digress briefly and consider some fundamental properties of perception, often referred to as the Weber-Fechner laws. Ernst Weber and Gustav Fechner were among the first to demonstrate systematically that our perception of the intensity of a sensation does not increase in direct proportion to the intensity of the stimulus that produced it. Instead, the sensation increases more and more slowly as the intensity of the stimulus increases. For example, if the illumination in your room were to double, it would seem brighter, but not twice as bright. Sim-ilarly, a twenty-pound weight seems heavier than one that weighs five pounds, but not four times heavier. The impact of a given change in stimulus intensity declines as the absolute magnitude of the stimulus increases.

The Weber-Fechner laws have important implications for the amount of hap-piness, or "utility," you derive from life events. The first dollar you earn generates more happiness than any other single dollar you will ever earn. Increasing your bank account from $1,000 to $2,000 will probably make you happier than increasing it from $11,000 to $12,000. This phenomenon of "decreasing mar-ginal utility," or each additional dollar yielding less utility the more dollars you already own, tends to make people risk averse when it comes to their assets. Most people, for example, would prefer to keep $20 in their pocket rather than risk it on a double-or-nothing bet decided by a coin flip. That makes sense. The joy you would derive from the extra $20 does not match the pain you would experience by losing your initial $20 stake—that is, the difference between $20 and $40 is not as great as the difference between $20 and $0. People tend to be conservative when it comes to taking chances on increasing their assets, in keeping with the Weber-Fechner laws.

The same laws apply when we lose money. The difference between losing $100 and losing nothing has more psychological impact than the difference between losing $1,100 and losing $1,000. In this case, according to the Weber-Fechner laws, people should be risk seeking. If I have already lost $100 and you offer me a "double or nothing" proposition, I will be inclined to take the bet. After all, the difference between losing $100 or $200 does not seem as great as the difference between losing $100 and breaking even. As a result, although people tend to be risk averse when it comes to "gains," or additions to the status quo, they tend to be risk seeking when it comes to "losses," or subtractions from the status quo.

Now back to framing. Because the status quo is not always rigidly defined, it is often possible to frame an outcome as *either* a loss or a gain. People should make different judgments and decisions as a result. Consider the following example:

> Imagine that the U.S. is preparing for the outbreak of a rare disease, which is expected to kill 600 people. Two alternative programs to combat the disease have been proposed. Assume that the exact scientific estimates of the consequences of the programs are as follows:
>
> If Program A is adopted, 200 people will be saved.
>
> If Program B is adopted, there is a 1/3 probability that 600 will be saved and a 2/3 probability that no people will be saved.

Amos Tversky and Daniel Kahneman found that when students in the United States and Canada were given this problem, 72 percent preferred Program A, the "safe" option (Tversky & Kahneman, 1981). Saving 200 people "for sure" is more appealing than trying to save all 600 lives at the risk of saving none. Other students, however, were given the same introduction as before, but with the following options:

> If Program C is adopted, 400 people will die.
>
> If Program D is adopted, there is a 1/3 probability that nobody will die, and a 2/3 probability that 600 people will die.

In this case, 78 percent preferred Program D, the risky option. A one-third probability that no one will die is preferable to the certain death of 400 people. Note, however, that Program A in the first version is identical to Program C in the second (200 people saved is equivalent to 400 people who die). Similarly, Program B is identical to Program D (a one-third probability that 600 people will be saved is equivalent to a one-third probability that nobody will die). In other words, people's judgments were dramatically affected by how the options were framed. When framed as lives saved, a large majority was risk averse; when framed as lives lost, an equally large majority was risk seeking. This is just one example of how people's judgments and behavior can be influenced by simply varying the presentation of information, thereby violating the principle of "invariance" laid out in models of rational choice (von Neumann & Morgenstern, 1947).

Results like those of Kahneman and Tversky make one wish that information was always presented in a "neutral" way. No one wants to make the wrong decision for such a trivial reason as whether the options were described as losses or gains. Unfortunately, there is often no neutral way of framing different options. One frame is picked, deliberately or not, and people's judgments and decisions are thereby slanted in a particular direction. The implications for everyday decisions are enormous. For instance, many years ago it was illegal for commercial establishments to charge two different prices for their products—a higher price for a credit-card transaction and a lower price for those who paid cash. Because companies pay a fee to the relevant credit-card institution (a fee they pass on to the customer in the form of higher prices), a single-price system could be considered unfair to those who pay cash. Cash customers end up subsidizing the credit transactions of others. As a result, Congress agreed to change the laws to permit a two-tiered pricing system. Credit-card companies lobbied vigorously to control how the two-tiered system would be labeled. They preferred that it be called a "cash discount" rather than a "credit-card surcharge." They wisely reasoned that people would be less inclined to use their credit cards if they had to pay a surcharge to do so. Paying a surcharge is experienced as a direct cost, or loss, whereas declining a cash discount is experienced as a foregone *gain.* Because losses have greater psychological impact than gains, the credit-card companies have a huge financial stake in having the price difference labeled a cash discount.

The asymmetry in people's reactions to outright losses versus foregone gains also makes it easier for government to pay for programs by granting tax breaks rather than by making cash payments. Paying for something (for example, a tax to pay for public housing) is experienced as a cost, or a loss. Granting a tax break (for example, to companies that invest in public housing) is experienced as a foregone gain—tax revenue that would have been collected, but is not. This may help explain why populist reformers have made little headway in attacking "corporate welfare." Much of the voting public is easily riled by welfare to the poor because it involves direct payments from government coffers. In contrast, it is harder to get the public as upset over corporate welfare because it typically comes in the form of tax deductions rather than direct payments. It is thus construed as a foregone gain.

Framing effects such as these can also be used as potent manipulations of "channel factors" (that is, interventions that serve to guide behavior in a particular direction; see Chapter 1). The cash discount versus credit-card surcharge frame is an important channel factor controlling attitudes and behavior. Other real-world framing effects—or channel-factor manipulations—include those governing decisions to be an organ donor (Johnson & Goldstein, 2003) or to sign up for full-coverage or limited-coverage auto insurance plans (Johnson, Hershey, Meszaros, & Kunreuther, 1993). Here the crucial frame or channel factor is whether the individual is asked to "opt in" or to "opt out." In many European countries, for example, a person is assumed to be an organ donor and must take steps not to be. In these countries, well over 90 percent of the population remain potential organ donors. In other European countries (in which popular sentiment toward organ donation is just as positive), the person is not assumed to be an organ donor and must take steps to become one. In those countries, typically less than 20 percent become potential donors.

**LOOKING BACK,** we have seen that the way information is presented, including the order in which it is presented, can affect judgment. Primacy effects occur when information presented first has more impact than information presented later, often because the initial information influences the construal of later information. Recency effects occur when later-presented information has more impact, typically because later information is more accessible to memory than early information. We are susceptible to many framing effects in information presentation. Sometimes communicators spin information so as to influence our judgment, deliberately changing the frame of reference, but sometimes framing effects are unintended. One of the most powerful framing effects concerns whether outcomes are presented as gains or losses. In general, we are risk averse when it comes to potential gains and risk seeking when it comes to potential losses. In the next section, we will consider the effect of prior knowledge on judgment.

# PRIOR KNOWLEDGE AND KNOWLEDGE STRUCTURES

What is being described in the following paragraph?

> The procedure is quite simple. First you arrange things into different groups. Of course, one pile may be sufficient, depending on how much there is to do. If you have to go somewhere else due to lack of facilities, that is the next step; otherwise you are pretty well set. (Bransford & Johnson, 1973, p. 400)

Not so easy to figure out, is it? *What* is arranged into different groups? *What* facilities might be lacking? Most people find it difficult to discern what the paragraph is about. But suppose it had the title, "Washing Clothes." Now re-read the paragraph. Suddenly it is no longer inscrutable. Each sentence makes perfect sense when construed from the perspective of doing the laundry.

That this paragraph is so easy to understand in the proper context and yet so incomprehensible outside it is a powerful testimonial to how our stored knowledge—what we already know—helps us properly construe new events. What we know about doing laundry helps us comprehend what it means to "arrange things into different groups" and to "go somewhere else due to lack of facilities." Understanding involves bringing together new information with what we already know. What we know about human nature and about surrounding context allows us to determine whether another person's tears are the product of joy or sadness. What we know about custom enables us to decide whether a gesture is hostile or friendly.

Perceiving and understanding the world inevitably involves the simultaneous operation of **bottom-up** and **top-down processes**. Bottom-up processes consist of taking in relevant stimuli from the outside world—text on a page, gestures in an interaction, sound patterns at a cocktail party, and so on. At the same time, top-down processes filter and interpret bottom-up stimuli in light of preexisting knowledge and expectations. The meaning of stimuli is not passively recorded; it is actively construed.

Preexisting knowledge is necessary for understanding, and it is surely required for judgment. Indeed, as the laundry example makes clear, judgment and understanding are inextricably linked. They both involve going beyond currently avail-

**bottom-up processes** "Data-driven" mental processing in which one takes in and forms conclusions on the basis of the stimuli encountered in one's experience.

**top-down processes** "Theory-driven" mental processing in which one filters and interprets new information in light of preexisting knowledge and expectations.

able information and making extrapolations from it. Psychologists who study judgment, then, have been interested in how people use their stored knowledge to make a variety of everyday judgments.

One principle that psychologists have discovered is that people's stored information is not filed away bit by bit. Instead, information is stored in coherent configurations, or **knowledge structures**, in which related information is stored together. Information about George W. Bush, President, is tightly connected to information about George W. Bush, born-again Christian, George W. Bush, former oilman, and George W. Bush, son of former President George H. W. Bush. Different theorists have given such knowledge structures different names, such as schemas, scripts, frames, prototypes, or personae (Bartlett, 1932; Markus, 1977; Nisbett & Ross, 1980; Schank & Abelson, 1977; Smith & Zarate, 1990). As **schema** is the most generic of these terms, we will use it as our primary term to refer to any organized body of prior knowledge (see Chapter 1). Thus, for example, you no doubt have schemas for a "fast food restaurant" (chain, so-so food, bright primary colors for décor, limited choices, cheap), a "party animal" (boisterous, drinks to excess, exuberant but none-too-graceful dancer), and "action film" (good guy establishes good guy credentials, bad guy gains the upper hand, good guy triumphs and bad guy perishes in eye-popping pyrotechnical finale).

**knowledge structures** Coherent configurations (known as schemas, scripts, frames, prototypes, or personae) in which related information is stored together.

**schema** A knowledge structure consisting of any organized body of stored information.

## How Do Schemas Influence Judgment?

The myriad schemas we all possess can affect our judgments in many ways: by directing our attention, influencing our construals, and structuring our memories (Brewer & Nakamura, 1984; Hastie, 1981; Taylor & Crocker, 1981). Without schemas, our lives would be a buzzing confusion. On the other hand, as we will see, schemas can sometimes lead us to mischaracterize the world.

*Attention* Attention is selective. We cannot focus on everything, and the knowledge we bring to bear on a given situation allows us to allocate our attention to the most important elements and to ignore the rest. The extent to which our schemas and expectations guide our attention was powerfully demonstrated by an experiment in which participants watched a videotape of two "teams" of three people each—with the members of one team wearing white shirts, and the members of the other team wearing black shirts—passing a basketball among one another. Each participant was asked to count the number of passes made by the members of one of the teams. Forty-five seconds into the action, a person wearing a gorilla costume strolled into the middle of the action. Despite the fact that this was about as noticeable a stimulus as one can imagine, only half the participants noticed it! The participants' schemas about what is likely to happen in a game of catch of this sort directed their attention so intently to some parts of the videotape that they failed to see a rather dramatic stimulus that they did not expect to see (Simons & Chabris, 1999).

**Selective Attention** It may seem hard to believe, but many participants who were engaged in counting the number of passes made by members of one of the two teams on this videotape failed to notice the gorilla when he walked into the midst of the players.

*Inference and Construal*   Meet "Donald," who may seem to you like a contestant in an "xtreme" sports competition. In actuality, Donald is a fictitious person who has been used as a stimulus in numerous experiments on the effect of prior knowledge on social judgment.

> Donald spent a great amount of his time in search of what he liked to call excitement. He had already climbed Mt. McKinley, shot the Colorado rapids in a kayak, driven in a demolition derby, and piloted a jet-powered boat—without knowing very much about boats. He had risked injury, and even death, a number of times. Now he was in search of new excitement. He was thinking, perhaps, he would do some skydiving or maybe cross the Atlantic in a sailboat. By the way he acted one could readily guess that Donald was well aware of his ability to do many things well. Other than business engagements, Donald's contacts with people were rather limited. He felt he didn't really need to rely on anyone. Once Donald made up his mind to do something it was as good as done no matter how long it might take or how difficult the going might be. Only rarely did he change his mind even when it might well have been better if he had. (Higgins, Rholes, & Jones, 1977, p. 145)

In one early study in which Donald was the featured stimulus, students participated in what they thought were two unrelated experiments (Higgins, Rholes, & Jones, 1977). In the first, they were shown a number of trait words projected on a screen as part of a perception experiment. Half of the participants were shown the words *adventurous, self-confident, independent,* and *persistent* embedded in a set of ten traits. The other half were shown the words *reckless, conceited, aloof,* and *stubborn.* After completion of the "perception" experiment, the participants moved on to the second, "reading comprehension" study in which they read the short paragraph about Donald and rated him on a number of trait scales. The investigators were interested in whether the words the participants encountered in the first experiment, having just been primed (mentally activated) and therefore being at the "top of the head," might affect their evaluation of Donald. The description of Donald, of course, had been constructed to be ambiguous with respect to whether he was a rather adventurous, appealing sort, or whether he was a reckless, unappealing person. The trait categories that the participants had at the top of their heads might shade their interpretations of what Donald was like.

The results indicated that this was exactly what happened. Those who had previously been exposed to the words *adventurous, self-confident, independent,* and *persistent* formed more favorable impressions of Donald than did those who had been exposed to the less flattering words. Thus, the trait categories that had recently been primed influenced the kind of inferences the participants made about Donald (Wyer & Srull, 1981).

The broader point, of course, is that information stored in the brain—in this case information that had just been primed—can influence how we construe new information. This is most likely to occur when the stimulus, like many of Donald's actions, is ambiguous (Trope, 1986). When this is the case, we must rely more heavily on top-down processes to compensate for the inadequacies of the information obtained from the bottom up.

*Memory*   Because schemas influence attention, they also influence memory. Indeed, *New York Times* science writer Daniel Goleman has referred to memory as "attention in the past tense" (Goleman, 1985). It is difficult to remember stimuli to which one has devoted scant attention. The influence of schemas on memory is also important for judgment. After all, many judgments are not made immediately; rather, they are made later on the basis of information retrieved from memory. Schematic influences on memory therefore have a reverberating impact on judgment.

The impact of schemas on memory has been documented in numerous experiments (Fiske & Taylor, 1991; Hastie, 1981; Stangor & McMillan, 1992). A particularly straightforward study was one in which students were asked to watch a videotape of a husband and wife having dinner together (Cohen, 1981). Half the students were told that the woman in the tape was a librarian; the other half that she was a waitress. The students were later given a quiz that assessed their memory of various features of what they had witnessed. The central question was whether the students' memories were influenced by their stereotypes (or schemas) of librarians and waitresses. They were asked, for example, whether the woman was drinking wine (librarian stereotype) or beer (waitress stereotype) and whether she had received a history book (librarian) or romance novel (waitress) as a gift. The tape had been constructed to contain an equal number of items consistent and inconsistent with each stereotype.

Did thinking that the person was a librarian make it easier to recall librarian-consistent details? It did indeed. Students who thought that the woman was a librarian recalled librarian-consistent information more accurately than librarian-inconsistent information; those who thought she was a waitress recalled waitress-consistent information more accurately than waitress-inconsistent information. Information that fits a preexisting expectation or schema often enjoys an advantage in recall (Carli, 1999; Zadny & Gerard, 1974).

Cohen's study shows that schemas might influence memory by affecting the **encoding** of information—how information is filed away in memory—in that schemas might affect what information a person attends to and how that information is initially interpreted. But schemas might also influence the **retrieval** of information, or how information is extracted from a storehouse of knowledge.

Because we know that schemas direct attention, we have good reason to believe that they influence encoding. One way to find out whether schemas influence retrieval as well would be to provide people with a schema or expectation *after* they have been exposed to the relevant information, when it obviously cannot influence encoding. Any effect of the schema on memory would thus have to be due to retrieval. Numerous experiments have utilized this tactic. The typical result is that providing a schema after the relevant information has been encountered does not affect memory as much as providing it beforehand (Bransford & Johnson, 1973; Howard & Rothbart, 1980; Rothbart, Evans, & Fulero, 1979; Wyer, Srull, Gordon, & Hartwick, 1982; Zadny & Gerard, 1974). Nonetheless, occasionally, it does have a substantial effect (Anderson & Pichert, 1978; Carli, 1999; Cohen, 1981; Hirt, 1990). Thus, the appropriate conclusion seems to be that schemas influence memory through their effect on both encoding and retrieval, but the effect on encoding is typically much stronger.

## How Is Incoming Information Mapped onto Preexisting Schemas?

In the librarian/waitress experiment just described, there is little doubt about which schema participants will apply to the information they encounter in the

**encoding** Filing information away in memory based on what is attended to and the initial interpretation of information.

**retrieval** The extraction of information from memory.

videotape. The experimenter informs them that the woman is a librarian (or waitress), and they know nothing else about her. It stands to reason, then, that they would view the videotape through the "lens" of the librarian (or waitress) schema. In real life, however, the situation is often more complicated. For instance, one might know that besides being a librarian, the woman is a triathlete, a Republican, and a gourmet cook. Which schema (or combination of schemas) is likely to be thought of, or "activated," and then used to evaluate the information presented?

For a schema to guide the interpretation of new information, an association must be made between it and the incoming information. Thus, the central question becomes what determines whether a given schema will be associated with incoming information?

***Similarity or Feature Matching*** The most common determinant of whether a particular schema will be activated and brought to bear in interpreting new information is the degree of similarity, or "fit," between critical features of the schema and the incoming stimulus (Andersen, Glassman, Chen, & Cole, 1995; Higgins & Brendl, 1995). Suppose you are taking a drive through the countryside, and you see a rather large, formally dressed group of people assembled on a hill. Whether you apply a wedding or a funeral schema to help you interpret the scene will surely depend on whether they are wearing black or more festive attire, whether a supply of champagne is packed in ice, and so on. The features of the situation tell you what kind of situation it is, and then the relevant schema is applied to assist with further interpretation of what you encounter (Holyoak & Thagard, 1995; Read, 1984, 1987; Spellman & Holyoak, 1992).

This feature-matching process ensures that the "right" schema will typically be recruited to encode a given situation. Applying a wedding schema to what is, in reality, a funeral would create too much of a mismatch between the features of the schema and the event—with the result that the wedding schema would soon be abandoned. Still, the process of applying what is stored in the head to newly encountered events leaves open the possibility of occasional misapplication. The wrong schema, in other words, might sometimes be applied to a given situation. When (as described in the opening to this chapter) Rodney Peairs shot and killed

*"But, seriously . . ."*

the individual who came to his house, one might say that he did so because he applied the wrong, "under attack," schema to what he saw of the two teenagers in his driveway.

A particularly interesting circumstance that can give rise to schema misapplication is when the schema shares certain irrelevant, superficial features of the stimulus being evaluated. The close match on such features can sometimes lead one to apply a given schema, even though the schema and stimulus are not well matched on more important dimensions. This was demonstrated in an experiment that examined the impact of the schemas we have (knowingly or not) regarding U.S. intervention in military conflicts overseas. Specifically, during the last thirty-five years, the debate about U.S. military intervention has often taken the form of "dueling metaphors." Those who favor intervention argue that we cannot sit by like the Allies did before World War II and let aggression triumph unchecked. "We should have stood up to Hitler" is how it is often put. On the other hand, those who oppose intervention tend to invoke the specter of Vietnam. "We don't want another Vietnam, a quagmire from which the United States had difficulty extricating itself." The clear implication of this battle of metaphors is that viewing a given conflict through a World War II lens is more likely to lead to intervention than viewing it through a Vietnam schema. One study investigated whether certain irrelevant similarities between aspects of a scenario and a given conflict and one of these schemas might affect policy recommendations.

Students in a course on international relations were presented with a hypothetical crisis and asked for their recommendations on how to solve it. The crisis involved a small democratic country, Country B, that was threatened by its aggressive, totalitarian neighbor, Country A (see Figure 10.2). Country A had initially confined its efforts to subversive activity in Country B, but now there were reports that it was also massing troops on the border for a possible invasion. Country B requested assistance from the United States. What to do?

The description of this crisis contained various features that were designed in one version to remind the reader of Vietnam and in another of World War II. For example, the area to the east of Countries A and B was depicted as a body of water in the Vietnam version in order to suggest the Indochina peninsula, and ethnic minorities who were fleeing Country A were described as doing so via small boats along the coast (reminiscent of the exodus of the "boat people"). In the World War II version, the people were described as leaving the country via box cars in freight trains (one of the most salient images of human suffering caused by the Nazi regime). All other variations between the two versions were similar in that they had no defensible implications for the best policy to pursue, but they nevertheless triggered strong associations to either World War II or Vietnam. And these associations had a significant impact on the policy recommendations the students made. Despite the fact that the features that triggered the association to World War II were irrelevant to the issues at hand, those who read the World War II version of the crisis recommended stronger U.S. military intervention than did those who read the Vietnam version (Gilovich, 1981).

**Figure 10.2 Applying Schemas**
The figure shows a map of countries involved in a hypothetical conflict. In the "Vietnam" version, the area to the right of Country B was shaded in and labeled "Gulf of C" to facilitate associations to the Gulf of Tonkin off the coast of Vietnam. In the "World War II" version, the same area was labeled "Country C" to facilitate associations to the landlocked conflict at the beginning of World War II. (Source: Adapted from Gilovich, 1981)

*Expectations*    Sometimes a schema is applied because of a preexisting expectation about what one will encounter. The expectation activates the schema, and the schema is then readily applied (see Box 10.2). If the expectation is warranted, this saves considerable mental energy. For example, applying a "haggling"

Box 10.2   FOCUS ON DAILY LIFE

# Self-Fulfilling Prophecies

Expectations often do more than guide how we interpret information. They also affect our behavior, which then influences the very interaction we are observing. Often the result is a self-fulfilling prophecy, whereby our expectations lead us to behave in ways that elicit the very behavior we expect from others. The most famous demonstration of the impact of self-fulfilling prophecies is a study in which elementary school teachers were told that aptitude tests indicated that several of their students could be expected to "bloom" intellectually in the coming year (Rosenthal & Jacobson, 1968). In reality, the students so described were chosen randomly. Nevertheless, the expectation that certain students would undergo an intellectual growth spurt set in motion a pattern of student-teacher interaction that led those students to score higher on IQ tests administered at the end of the year. People often unknowingly engineer the very behavior they expected all along (Jussim, 1986; Smith, Jussim, & Eccles, 1999).

Self-fulfilling prophecies have generated so much attention that it is important to note that not all prophecies are self-fulfilling. There must be some mechanism that translates a given expectation into confirmatory action. In the study of teachers' expectations, the mechanism was the teachers' behavior. In particular, the teachers tended to challenge the students they thought were about to "bloom," giving them more material, and more difficult material, to learn. Not all prophecies have that link. Someone might think that you are rich, but it is hard to imagine how that belief would help to make it so. In fact, some prophecies can even be self-negating, such as when a driver believes "nothing bad can happen to me" and therefore drives recklessly (Dawes, 1988).

schema to a given commercial transaction allows one to dismiss the stated price without much thought or anxiety, and it frees one to make a counteroffer. Misapplying the haggling schema, on the other hand, can lead to the embarrassment of making a counteroffer when it is not appropriate.

Numerous studies have demonstrated how expectations can activate specific schemas and guide subsequent information processing (Hirt, MacDonald, & Erikson, 1995; Sherman, Mackie, & Driscoll, 1990; Stangor & McMillan, 1992). This was true, for example, in the study by Cohen that we discussed earlier, in which participants thought they were seeing either a waitress or a librarian (see p. 405).

*Recent Activation*   Expectations, as we saw earlier, influence information processing by lowering the threshold for the application of a given schema. The expectation essentially pre-activates or primes the schema, and the schema is readily applied at the slightest hint that it is applicable. Schemas can be pre-activated (or partly activated) in other ways as well. Recent activation is one of the most common and important examples. If a schema has been used recently, it tends to be more accessible for re-use (Ford & Kruglanski, 1995; Herr, 1986; Sherman, Mackie, & Driscoll, 1990; Srull & Wyer, 1979, 1980; Stapel & Koomen, 2000, 2001; Todorov & Bargh, 2002).

We have already discussed the influence of recent activation in the priming study conducted by Tory Higgins and his colleagues (Higgins, Rholes, & Jones, 1977). Recall that participants in that study who had previously been exposed to rather appealing trait adjectives such as *adventurous* formed more favorable impressions of "Donald" than did those who had been exposed to adjectives such as *reckless* (see p. 403). This semantic priming effect has been demonstrated in hundreds of experiments over the past twenty-five years (Higgins, 1996).

***Consciousness of Activation: Necessary or Not?*** Carefully conducted interviews with participants at the end of many of these semantic priming experiments have found that very few (and, in many cases, none) of them suspected that there was any connection between the two parts of the study—the initial priming phase and the subsequent judgment phase. This raises the question of how conscious a person must be of a stimulus for it to effectively prime a given schema. Recent research suggests a clear-cut answer: Not at all. A great many studies have shown that stimuli presented outside of conscious awareness can prime a schema sufficiently to influence subsequent information processing (Bargh, 1996; Debner & Jacoby, 1994; Devine, 1989b; Draine & Greenwald, 1998; Ferguson, Bargh, & Nayak, 2005; Greenwald, Klinger, & Liu, 1989; Klinger, Burton, & Pitts, 2000; Lepore & Brown, 1997; Neuberg, 1988).

In one such study, researchers showed a set of words to participants on a computer screen so quickly that it was impossible to discern what the words were (Bargh & Pietromonaco, 1982). The researchers asked participants in a control condition to simply guess the identity of each word. They were unable to do so (guessing fewer than 1 percent of the words correctly), which established that the words were indeed presented too quickly to be consciously perceived. Participants in the other conditions were shown either mainly hostile words (for example, *hate, whip, stab, hostile*) or mainly nonhostile words (for example, *water, long, together, every*). Immediately afterwards, the researchers asked them to read a short paragraph about an individual who had committed a number of moderately hostile acts, and then to rate that person on a number of trait dimensions. The participants who had previously been exposed to predominantly hostile words rated the target person more negatively than did those exposed to predominantly nonhostile words. They did so, mind you, even though they were not consciously aware of the words to which they had been exposed. Thus, schemas can be primed through prior activation, even when the presentation of the activating stimuli is **subliminal**—that is, below the threshold of conscious awareness.

**subliminal** Below the threshold of conscious awareness.

**LOOKING BACK,** we have seen that knowledge structures or schemas play a role in judgment. Schemas influence judgment by guiding attention, aiding in the construal of information, and affecting memory at both the encoding and retrieval stages. Schemas are particularly likely to influence the evaluation of current information if they are habitually used or have been recently activated by other information. It is not necessary that the person be aware of the activation of a schema in order for it to exert its effects. Schemas normally allow us to make judgments with accuracy and dispatch, but they can also mislead. Next we will consider the role of intuition and heuristic processes in everyday judgment and problem solving.

# REASON, INTUITION, AND HEURISTICS

Suppose you were offered a chance to win a dollar by drawing, without looking, a red marble from a bowl containing a mixture of red and white marbles. Suppose further that you have a choice of bowls from which you can select: a small bowl with one red marble and nine white marbles, or a large bowl containing nine red marbles and ninety-one white marbles. Which bowl would you choose?

If you are like most people, you might experience some conflict here. The rational thing to do is to select the small bowl because it offers better odds: 10 percent versus 9 percent. But there are nine potential winning marbles in the large bowl, and only one in the other. The greater number of winning marbles gives many people a "gut feeling" that they should select from the large bowl, regardless of the objective odds. Indeed, in one experiment 61 percent of those who faced this decision chose the larger bowl, the one with the lower odds of winning (Denes-Raj & Epstein, 1994).

> "I know too well the weakness and uncertainty of human reason to wonder at its different results."
>
> —THOMAS JEFFERSON

These results indicate that we are often "of two minds" about certain problems. Indeed, a great deal of research suggests that our responses to stimuli are guided by two "systems" of thought, analogous to "intuition" and "reason" (Epstein, 1991; Kahneman & Frederick, 2002; Sloman, 2002; Stanovich & West, 2002). The intuitive system operates quickly and automatically, is based on associations, and performs many of its operations simultaneously—"in parallel." The rational system is slower and more controlled, is based on rules and deduction, and performs its operations one at a time—"serially."

The rapid, parallel nature of the intuitive system means that it will virtually always produce some output—an "answer" to the prevailing problem. That output or answer will then sometimes be overridden by the output of the slower, more deliberate rational system. For instance, if you had to predict the outcome of the next coin flip after witnessing five heads in a row, your intuitive system would perform a quick analysis that would tell you that six heads in a row is rare and that you should therefore bet on tails. But then your rational system would remind you of a critical feature of coin flips (that you may have learned in a statistics or probability course): the outcomes of consecutive flips are independent, so you should ignore what happened on the earlier flips.

Note that several things can happen with the output of these two systems: (1) They can agree. For example, you might have a good feeling about one job candidate over another, and the former's qualifications might fit your rule to "always go with the person with more experience." (2) As in the coin flip example, they can disagree, and the message from the rational system can override the message from the intuitive system. (3) Finally, the intuitive system can produce a response that "seems right," and do so with such speed that the rational system is never engaged. One can simply go with the flow—that is, with the quick output of the intuitive system.

We will focus on this latter pattern in the balance of this chapter in order to discuss Tversky and Kahneman's work on the "heuristics" of judgment, work that has had great impact not only in psychology, but also in economics, management, law, medicine, political science, and statistics (Gilovich, Griffin, & Kahneman, 2002; Kahneman, Slovic, & Tversky, 1982; Tversky & Kahneman, 1974). Tversky and Kahneman argued that there are mental operations that the intuitive system automatically performs—assessments of how easily something comes to mind or of how similar two entities are—that powerfully influence judgment.

**Intuitive Processing and Mistaken Judgment** Nicola Calipari, an Italian intelligence officer, was mistakenly shot and killed by a U.S. patrol in Iraq while protecting an Italian journalist whom he had just helped to free from her captors. Their car was speeding along the dangerous road to the Baghdad airport when it approached a temporary checkpoint, and the U.S. patrol, fearing that the car contained insurgents, reacted intuitively and opened fire.

They referred to these mental operations as **heuristics**—mental "shortcuts" that provide serviceable, but inexact, answers to common judgmental problems.

Tversky and Kahneman drew an analogy between our use of heuristics and our use of perceptual cues. In judging how far away an object is, for example, we can't help but notice how clear it looks, and we use that assessment of clarity to help estimate its distance. All else being equal, the farther away something is, the less distinct it appears. But all else is not always equal, and so an overreliance on clarity can give rise to misperception and illusion. On a clear day, objects appear closer than they really are; on hazy days, they appear farther away. Thus, unless one's rational system steps in and says, "Wait. It's hazy out; adjust estimate accordingly," the "clarity heuristic" will be misleading.

Tversky and Kahneman have argued that we are similarly misled in many of our everyday, nonperceptual judgments. Our intuitive system generates an assessment that relates to the task at hand and suggests what may seem like a perfectly acceptable answer to the problem. When this initial intuitive assessment is not modified or overridden by a more considered analysis, important considerations may be ignored, and our judgments may be systematically biased. Let's examine how this works in the context of two of the most general and extensively researched heuristics: the availability heuristic and the representativeness heuristic. People rely on the **availability heuristic** when they judge the frequency or probability of some event by the readiness with which similar events come to mind. People use the **representativeness heuristic** when they try to categorize something by judging how similar the object is to their conception of the typical member of the category.

## THE AVAILABILITY HEURISTIC

Which state experiences more tornadoes per year: Nebraska or Kansas? Even though the two states average the same number, you, like most people, may have experienced an urge to say "Kansas." If so, then you were guided by the availability heuristic. Examples of tornadoes in Kansas spring to mind more readily than examples of tornadoes in Nebraska. (Never mind that the example you thought of never actually happened—the storybook twister that whisked Dorothy Gale and her little dog, Toto, to the Land of Oz.)

We can't prevent ourselves from assessing the ease with which examples from

**heuristics** Intuitive mental operations that allow us to make a variety of judgments quickly and efficiently.

**availability heuristic** The process whereby judgments of frequency or probability are based on the ease with which pertinent instances are brought to mind.

**representativeness heuristic** The process whereby judgments of likelihood are based on assessments of similarity between individuals and group prototypes, or between cause and effect.

**The Availability Heuristic** People often judge the likelihood of an event based on how readily pertinent examples come to mind. (A) While tornados are equally common in Kansas and Nebraska, people tend to think that they are more common in Kansas because tornados in Kansas come more readily to mind thanks to our familiarity with (B) *The Wizard of Oz*, in which a tornado in Kansas whisks Dorothy and Toto to the land of Oz.

both Nebraska and Kansas come to mind, and, once we've made such assessments, they seem to give us our answer. It was easier to think of a tornado in Kansas than one in Nebraska, so we conclude that there are probably more tornadoes in Kansas. The implicit logic seems compelling. If examples can be quickly brought to mind, one assumes that there must be many of them. Most often, that is true. It is easier to think of male presidents of Fortune 500 companies than female presidents, easier to think of successful Russian novelists than successful Norwegian novelists, and easier to think of instances of German military aggression than Swiss military aggression precisely because there are more male presidents, more successful Russian novelists, and more instances of German military aggression, respectively. The availability heuristic, therefore, normally serves its user well. The ease with which relevant examples can be brought to mind (that is, the extent to which they are "available") is indeed a reasonably accurate guide to overall frequency or probability.

But the availability heuristic is not an infallible guide. Certain events may simply be more memorable or retrievable than others, making availability a poor guide to true number or probability. Nebraska has as many tornadoes as Kansas, but none of them are as memorable as the one in *The Wizard of Oz*. In an early demonstration of the availability heuristic, Kahneman and Tversky (1973a) asked people whether there are more words that begin with the letter "r," or more words with "r" in the third position. A large majority thought there are more words that begin with "r," but, in fact, there are more words that have "r" in the third position. Because words are stored in memory in some rough alphabetical fashion, words that begin with "r" (*rain, rowdy, redemption*) are easier to recall than those with "r" as the third letter (*nerd, north, barrister*). The latter words, although more plentiful, are harder to locate.

### Disentangling Ease of Retrieval from the Amount of Information Retrieved

As we have seen, the availability heuristic involves judging the frequency of an event, the size of a category, or the probability of an outcome by the *ease with which* relevant instances can be brought to mind (Schwarz & Vaughn, 2002). Note that it is not simply an assessment of the *number* of instances that are retrieved. But how do we know that? After all, not only do people have an easier time thinking of words that begin with "r," they also can think of many more of them. How do we know that people arrive at their answers by consulting their experience of how easy it is to think of examples rather than by simply comparing the number of examples they are able to generate? It is difficult to distinguish between these two explanations because they are so tightly intertwined. If it is easier to think of examples of one category, one will probably also think of more of them.

An ingenious experiment by Norbert Schwarz and his colleagues managed to untangle the two interpretations (Schwarz et al., 1991). In the guise of gathering material for a relaxation-training program, students were asked to review their lives for experiences relevant to assertiveness. There were four conditions in the experiment. One group was asked to list six occasions when they had acted assertively, and another was asked to list twelve such examples. A third group was asked to list six occasions when they had acted unassertively, and the final group was asked to list twelve such examples. The requirement to generate six or twelve examples of either behavior was carefully chosen so that thinking of six examples would be easy for nearly everyone, but thinking of twelve would be extremely difficult.

Notice how this disentangles the *ease* of generating examples and the *number*

## Table 10.1   The Availability Heuristic

The table shows average ratings of participants' own assertiveness. Participants were asked to think of six or twelve examples of their own assertiveness or unassertiveness.

| NUMBER OF EXAMPLES | TYPE OF BEHAVIOR | |
| --- | --- | --- |
| | ASSERTIVE | UNASSERTIVE |
| 6 | 6.3 | 5.2 |
| 12 | 5.2 | 6.2 |

Source: Schwarz et al., 1991.

of examples generated. Those who have to think of twelve examples of either assertiveness or unassertiveness will think of more examples, but they will find it hard to do so. What, then, has a greater effect on judgment? To find out, the investigators asked the participants to rate themselves in terms of how assertive they are. As Kahneman and Tversky would have predicted, the results indicated that it is the ease of generating examples that seems to guide people's judgments (see Table 10.1). Those who provided six examples of their assertiveness subsequently rated themselves as more assertive than those who provided twelve examples, even though (obviously) the latter thought of more examples. Similarly, those who provided six examples of their failure to be assertive subsequently rated themselves as less assertive than those who provided twelve examples. Indeed, the effect of ease of generation was so strong that those who thought of twelve examples of unassertiveness rated themselves as more assertive than those who thought of twelve examples of assertiveness!

*Biased Assessments of Risk*   One area in which the availability heuristic rears its head in everyday life harks back to our earlier discussion of negative information being overreported in the news. As we saw, this has the unfortunate effect of making some people more fearful than might be appropriate. But not all hazards are equally overreported. Some receive more news coverage than others. As a result, if people assess risk by the ease with which they can bring relevant episodes to mind, their assessments should be predictable from how much press attention various hazards receive (Slovic, Fischoff, & Lichtenstein, 1982).

Press attention does in fact affect the availability of information, as the following examples make clear. Do more people die each year by homicide or suicide? As you have surely noticed, homicides receive much more press coverage, and so most people think they are more common. In reality, however, suicides outnumber homicides in the United States by a 3 to 2 margin. Are people more likely to die by accident or disease? Statistics indicate that disease claims over sixteen times as many lives as accidents, but because accidents (being more dramatic) receive disproportionate press coverage, most people erroneously consider them to be as lethal as disease. Finally, do more people die each year in fires or by drownings? Again, the drama of fires garners disproportionate media attention, so most people think that fires claim more lives than drownings. In reality, there tend to be more drownings each year than deaths by fire.

## Table 10.2   Biased Assessments

The table shows biases in the perceived commonness of causes of death.

| MOST OVERESTIMATED | MOST UNDERESTIMATED |
| --- | --- |
| All accidents | Smallpox vaccination |
| Motor vehicle accidents | Diabetes |
| Tornadoes | Lightning |
| Flood | Stroke |
| All cancers | Asthma |
| Fire | Emphysema |
| Homicide | Tuberculosis |

Source: Adapted from Slovic, Fischoff, & Lichtenstein, 1982.

The common theme running through each of these examples is that people overestimate the frequency of "dramatic" deaths that claim the lives of many people at once. Deaths due to plane crashes, earthquakes, and tornadoes are good examples. In contrast, people underestimate the commonness of "silent" deaths that quietly claim individual lives, such as deaths resulting from emphysema and strokes. People also underestimate the lethality of maladies they frequently encounter in nonfatal form—deaths from vaccinations, diabetes, and asthma. Because everyone knows healthy asthmatics and healthy diabetics, it is easy to lose sight of the number of lives that have been lost to these afflictions. Lists of the most over- and underestimated hazards are provided in Table 10.2, where it can be seen that death from accidents tends to be overestimated and death from disease underestimated.

*Biased Estimates of Contributions to Joint Projects*   Another example of how the availability heuristic can distort everyday judgment involves the dynamics of joint projects. People sometimes work together on a project and then afterwards decide who gets "the credit." You work with someone on a class project and turn in a single paper. Whose name is listed first? You and an acquaintance are hired to write a computer program for a lump-sum payment. How do you split the money?

With the availability heuristic in mind, social psychologist Michael Ross predicted that people would tend to overestimate their own contributions to such projects. After all, because we devote so much energy and attention to our own contributions, they should tend to be more available than the contributions of everyone else. He and Fiore Sicoly conducted several studies that verified this prediction (Ross & Sicoly, 1979). In one study, pairs of individuals who were conversing in various places around campus were asked (separately) how much they thought each had contributed to the conversation. Respondents tended to give themselves more credit than their partners did. In another study, married couples were asked to apportion responsibility for various tasks or outcomes in everyday life—how much did each contribute to keeping the house clean, maintaining the social calendar, starting arguments, and so on. Once again, the respondents tended to give themselves too much credit. In most cases, when the estimates made by the two participants were summed, they exceeded 100 percent, or the total amount there was to divide. (Our favorite example concerns a couple asked to estimate their relative contributions to making breakfast. The wife stated that her share was 100 percent on the reasonable grounds that she bought the food, prepared it, set the table, cleared the table, and washed the dishes. The husband estimated his contribution to be 25 percent—because he fed the cat!)

It is important to note that the overestimation of one's own contribution held for negative outcomes (for example, starting arguments) as well as positive outcomes (for example, taking care of the house). This shows that it is the availability heuristic rather than self-enhancement that gives rise to this phenomenon. If the effect only held true for positive items, one would be tempted to conclude that it arose from egocentric motivations because people want to see themselves, and have others see them, in the most favorable light.

Knowing how the availability heuristic affects the interpretation of contributions to joint projects can also provide a helpful perspective on potential sources of conflict. The use of this heuristic can lead to discord if people feel that their efforts are not sufficiently acknowledged. Furthermore, because people believe there is only one reality, and they overlook the role of the other person's construal of events, they often assume that the other person's failure to acknowledge their efforts is a deliberate slight. They assume that the other person is making a selfish grab for credit. Accusations fly and ill will builds. An awareness of how the availability heuristic operates can short-circuit such conflict.

## THE REPRESENTATIVENESS HEURISTIC

We sometimes have to assess whether someone is a member of a particular category. Is he gay? Is she Jewish? Is the host a Republican? In making such assessments, we automatically assess the extent to which the person in question *seems* gay, Jewish, or Republican. In so doing, we rely on what Kahneman and Tversky (1972) have dubbed the representativeness heuristic. Assessments of similarity substitute for the assessment of likelihood. "Is this person likely to be Jewish?" becomes "Does this person seem Jewish?" or "Is this person similar to my prototype of a Jew?" The use of the representativeness heuristic thus reflects an implicit assumption that "like goes with like." A member of a given category ought to resemble the category prototype; an effect ought to resemble its cause.

The representativeness heuristic is generally useful in making judgments about people and events. Members of certain groups often resemble the group proto-

**The Representativeness Heuristic** Neither (A) Ted Bundy, who was convicted of committing multiple murders of young women, nor (B) Scott Peterson, who was convicted of killing his pregnant wife, fits our prototype of a murderer (because they are clean-cut, educated professionals, which is not part of our prototype). Because of the representativeness heuristic, people are surprised to learn that they were, in fact, the perpetrators.

type (the prototype must come from somewhere), and effects often resemble their causes. The degree of resemblance between person and group, or between cause and effect, is thus often a helpful guide to group membership and causal status. So assessing whether or not someone is gay by how much he resembles a prototypically gay man is perfectly fine—as far as it goes. The strategy is effective to the extent that there is some validity to the prototype and the members of the category cluster around the prototype.

But even when the prototype is valid, the representativeness heuristic can create difficulties if we rely on it exclusively. The problem with the representativeness heuristic is that a strong sense of resemblance can blind us to other potentially useful sources of information. One such source of useful information, known as **base-rate information**, concerns information you have about relative frequency. How many members of the category in question are there relative to the complete set of relevant categories? The individual in question is more likely to be a Republican if there are a lot of Republicans in the local population. But, as we shall see, there are times when a strong sense of representativeness leads people to ignore base-rate likelihood, which could (and should) be put to good use.

> **base-rate information** Information about the relative frequency of events or of members of different categories in the population.

*The Resemblance between Members and Categories: Base-Rate Neglect*   In one of the earliest studies of the representativeness heuristic, Kahneman and Tversky (1973b) asked participants to consider the following description of "Tom W.," which was supposedly written during Tom's senior year in high school by a psychologist who based his assessment on Tom's responses to projective tests. The participants were also told that Tom is now in graduate school.

> Tom W. is of high intelligence, although lacking in true creativity. He has a need for order and clarity, and for neat and tidy systems in which every detail finds its appropriate place. His writing is rather dull and mechanical, occasionally enlivened by somewhat corny puns and by flashes of imagination of the sci-fi type. He has a strong drive for competence. He seems to have little feel and little sympathy for other people and does not enjoy interacting with others. Self-centered, he nonetheless has a deep moral sense. (Kahneman & Tversky, 1973b, p. 238)

One group of participants was asked to rank nine academic disciplines (for example, law, computer science, social work) in terms of how similar they thought Tom was to the typical student in each discipline. A second group was asked to rank the nine disciplines in terms of how likely it is that Tom *actually chose* them for graduate study. A final group was never shown the description of Tom; these participants merely estimated the percentage of all graduate students in the United States who were enrolled in each of the nine disciplines.

Consider the participants trying to assess the likelihood that Tom would choose each discipline for graduate study. What should they do? They should certainly assess how similar Tom is to the type of person who pursues each field of study—that is, they should consider how representative Tom is of the people in each discipline. But representativeness will not be a perfect guide. Some of the least "lawyerly" people study law, and some of the least "people-oriented" individuals pursue social work. Because representativeness is not a perfect guide in this context, any additional useful information should also be considered, such as how many graduate students there are in each field compared to all graduate students—that is, base-rate information. Clearly, Tom W. is more likely to belong

## Table 10.3 The Representativeness Heuristic

Participants ranked nine academic disciplines in terms of: (1) likelihood that Tom W. chose that graduate field, (2) perceived similarity between the description of Tom W. and the prototypical student in that field, and (3) number of graduate students enrolled in each field.

| DISCIPLINE | LIKELIHOOD | SIMILARITY | BASE RATE |
| --- | --- | --- | --- |
| Business Administration | 3 | 3 | 3 |
| Computer Science | 1 | 1 | 8 |
| Engineering | 2 | 2 | 5 |
| Humanities & Education | 8 | 8 | 1 |
| Law | 6 | 6 | 6 |
| Library Science | 5 | 4 | 9 |
| Medicine | 7 | 7 | 7 |
| Physical & Life Sciences | 4 | 5 | 4 |
| Social Science & Social Work | 9 | 9 | 2 |

Source: Adapted from Kahneman & Tversky, 1973b.

to a discipline that has a thousand members on campus than one that has ten. A savvy judgment, then, would somehow combine representativeness with an assessment of the popularity of each field.

What did the participants actually do? Table 10.3 provides the rankings of the nine disciplines by each of the three groups of participants—those asked to assess likelihood, similarity, and base rate. The first thing to note is that the rankings of the likelihood that Tom chose to *study* each of the disciplines is virtually identical to the rankings of how *similar* Tom is to the students in each discipline. In other words, the participants' responses were based entirely on how much the description of Tom resembled the "typical" student in each field. This is unfortunate, because by basing their responses exclusively on representativeness, the participants failed to consider the other source of useful information—base-rate frequency. As you can see from Table 10.3, the likelihood rankings did not correspond at all to what the participants knew about the overall popularity of each of the fields. Useful information was ignored.

Numerous studies have documented this tendency for people to ignore, or "underutilize," base-rate information when assessing whether someone belongs to a particular category (Ajzen, 1977; Bar-Hillel, 1980; Ginosar & Trope, 1980; Kahneman & Tversky, 1973b; Tversky & Kahneman, 1982). The automatic assessment of the "fit" between the person and the category often blinds people to the usefulness of additional sources of information.

It should be pointed out, however, that although base-rate neglect is often observed, it is not inevitable or universal (Bar-Hillel & Fischhoff, 1981). Certain circumstances encourage the use of base-rate frequency. Two circumstances stand out as having the greatest impact. The first is whether the base-rate information has some causal significance to the task at hand (Ajzen, 1977; Tversky & Kahneman, 1982). For example, if you were given a description of an individual's academic strengths and weaknesses and were asked to predict whether the person passed an exam, you would not be indifferent to the fact that 70 percent of the students who took the exam failed (that is, that the base rate of failure was 70 percent). Note that the base rate has causal significance in this case: the fact that 70 percent of the students failed means the exam was difficult, and the difficulty of the exam is what *causes* a person to fail. People use the base rate in such contexts because its relevance is obvious. When the base rate is not causally relevant, as in the Tom W. experiment, its relevance is less obvious. If twice as many people major in business as in the physical sciences, it would make it *more likely* that Tom W. is a business major, but it would not *cause* him to be a business major. The relevance of the base rate is thus less apparent, and it is less often taken into consideration.

Another way to improve people's use of base-rate information is to change their fundamental approach to the problem. People typically try to assess whether someone belongs to a particular category by taking an "inside" view of the task. Who is this person, and what "type" does the person resemble? Notice that it is the details of the particular case at hand that are the focus of attention. But it is possible to take an "outside" view of the problem. Suppose, for example, that you are asked to predict the undergraduate majors of a large number of students, not just Tom W. The details about each individual person might now loom less large in importance, and the significance of other, purely "statistical" considerations, such as base-rate frequency, might become more apparent. In the extreme case, if everyone in a sample of twenty seemed like a pre-law student, most people would nevertheless hesitate to guess that all were pre-law students. Indeed, circumstances that encourage an outside perspective have been shown to reduce base-rate neglect and other biases of human judgment (Gigerenzer, 1991; Griffin & Tversky, 1992; Kahneman & Lovallo, 1993; Kahneman & Tversky, 1982, 1995).

*The Planning Fallacy*　A common pitfall that arises from adopting an inside view of a problem is the tendency for people to be unrealistically optimistic about how quickly they can complete a project. This tendency, known as the **planning fallacy**, is something of a paradox because people's overly optimistic assessments about their ability to finish a current project exist side-by-side with the knowledge that the amount of time needed to complete such tasks in the past has typically exceeded their original estimates. Students, for example, often confidently assert that they will have all assignments done well in advance of an exam so that they can calmly and thoroughly review the material beforehand. As students well know, however, it is distressingly common for calm review to give way to feverish cramming. Students are not the sole victims of the planning fallacy. It's doubtful that any of us is immune. The error is illustrated most dramatically by setbacks in large scale building projects. When the people of Sydney, Australia, decided in 1957 to build their now iconic opera house, the original estimates were that it would be completed by 1963 and cost $7 million. It opened in 1973 at a cost of $102 million. Similarly, when Montreal was named host of the 1976 summer Olympics, the mayor announced that the entire Olympiad would cost $120 million, and that many events would take place in a stadium with a first-of-its-kind retractable roof. The Olympics, of course, went on as planned in 1976, but the stadium did not get its roof until 1989. Moreover, the final cost of the stadium was $120 million, the amount budgeted for the entire Olympics!

To shed light on the planning fallacy, psychologists Roger Buehler, Dale Griffin, and Michael Ross (1994) have conducted a number of experiments on people's estimates of completion times. In one study, students enrolled in an honors

> **planning fallacy** The tendency for people to be unrealistically optimistic about how quickly they can complete a project.

**The Planning Fallacy** People typically estimate that all sorts of projects, from homework assignments to large-scale public works efforts, will be completed sooner than they actually are—even when they are aware of past efforts that took much longer than originally estimated to complete. (A) It took ten years longer than estimated to complete construction of the Sydney Opera House. (B) The Central Artery/Tunnel Project (the "Big Dig") in Boston was designed to replace an aging, elevated highway with a modern underground expressway. The Big Dig has been plagued with unforeseen problems that have delayed the completion of the project.

program were asked to predict as accurately as possible when they would turn in their theses. They were also asked to estimate what the completion date would be "if everything went as poorly as it possibly could." Fewer than a third of the students finished by the time they had estimated. More remarkably, fewer than half finished by the time they had estimated under the assumption that "everything went as poorly as it possibly could."

Follow-up experiments laid the blame for people's optimistic forecasts on the tendency to approach the task from an exclusively inside perspective (see Box 10.3). In one study, participants were asked to verbalize their thoughts as they were trying to estimate how long a task would take. Nearly all of their thoughts were about various plans and scenarios whereby the project would be finished. Only a precious few dealt with the participants' track record on previous tasks. Thus, the inside perspective (What are the steps by which *this* project will be completed?) crowds out the potentially informative outside perspective (How often do I get such things done on time?). Note that people have personal histories that would be helpful in accurately estimating completion times. They just don't use them. When Buehler and his colleagues asked people how often they completed tasks by the time they initially expected, the average response was only a third of the time. We don't want to depress you, but none of us has managed to regularly avoid the planning fallacy when estimating how long it would take to write an article. And don't even ask how long we thought it would take to finish this textbook!

*The Resemblance between Cause and Effect* The representativeness heuristic also affects people's assessments of cause and effect (Downing, Sternberg, & Ross, 1985; Gilovich & Savitsky, 2002). In particular, people are predisposed to look for and accept causal relationships in which "like" goes with "like." Big effects are thought to have big causes, small effects to have small causes, complicated effects to have complicated causes, and so on. This assumption is often validated by everyday experience. Being hit with a small mallet typically produces a smaller bruise than being hit with a large mallet. Resolving the complicated mess in the Middle East will probably require complex, sustained negotiation, not some sim-

Box 10.3 FOCUS ON CULTURE

# Predictions East and West

The philosopher Ludwig Wittgenstein had this to say about the direction of the future, "When we think about the future of the world, we always have in mind its being where it would be if it continued to move as we see it moving now. We do not realize that it moves not in a straight line . . . and that its direction changes constantly."

As it turns out, Wittgenstein was a little too ready to say "we." Whereas Westerners, or at any rate Americans, are indeed inclined to predict that the world will move in whatever direction it now moves, East Asians are likely to expect the world to reverse field. Ji, Nisbett, and Su (2001) pointed out that there is a tradition in the East that is thousands of years old that emphasizes change. The *Tao* (the Way) envisions the world as existing in one of two states at any given time—*yin* and *yang* (light and dark, male and female, and so on)—which alternate with one another. The fact that the world is in one state is a strong indication that it is about to be in the other state. This preparation for change is indicated by the dark dot inside the white swirl and the white dot inside the dark swirl of the *Tao* symbol.

Ji and her colleagues reasoned that the tradition of the *Tao* would cause East Asians to judge events as being likely to reverse course rather than to continue moving in their current direction. They tested this in several ways. In one study, they asked participants to read brief stories and predict how they would turn out. For example, participants read about a dating couple and were asked if they would be likely to continue to date. Americans thought this was likely; Chinese thought it was less likely. Participants also read about a poor young man and were asked how likely it was that he would become rich. Americans thought this was not so likely; Chinese thought it was more likely. In another study, Ji and her colleagues showed various time trends to participants. The graphs were alleged to be recent movements in a variety of indicators that participants would be likely to know nothing about—for example, world economic growth rate and world cancer death rate. Trends were shown as either decidedly increasing or decidedly decreasing. Americans were overwhelmingly likely to predict that, at the next time step, the trends would continue—up if they had been up to that point, down if they had been down to that point. Chinese were much more likely than Americans to predict that the trends would reverse course—to move down if they had been going up and to move up if they had been going down.

**The Tao symbol**

ple suggestion that has yet to be made. Large effects often do have large causes, small effects often have small causes, and complicated effects often have complicated causes. But not always. Tiny viruses give rise to devastating diseases like malaria or AIDS; splitting the nucleus of the atom releases an awesome amount of energy. Sometimes small causes create big effects and vice versa. Let's consider some examples of representativeness-based thinking and judgment in various walks of life (see Box 10.4).

## Box 10.4 FOCUS ON SPORTS

# Hot Hands and Cold Statistics

The belief that effects ought to resemble their causes can be thought of more broadly as the belief that outcomes should resemble the processes that produced them. This belief helps to account for a misconception known as the clustering illusion. Consider coin flips. The most salient feature of a coin flip is that it is a 50–50 proposition—there is an equal chance of heads and tails. Thus, following the representativeness heuristic, people expect a sequence of coin flips to consist of roughly 50 percent heads and 50 percent tails. In the long run, they will not be disappointed, as the "law of averages" guarantees that with a large number of flips, there will be close to 50 percent heads and tails.

In the short term, however, all bets are off. In a short sequence of, say, five or ten flips, it is not at all uncommon to observe a marked departure from a 50–50 split. Random sequences, such as those produced by flipping a coin, tend to be more clustered than people expect. As a result, truly random sequences often do not "look" random. Thus, HTTHTH seems random, whereas HTTTTT does not, although both patterns are equally likely.

This helps explain why gamblers often think they are "on a roll" when playing craps, roulette, and a host of other casino games. Although the nature of the dice and roulette wheel precludes the possibility that gamblers' chances are better during some periods than others, it is easy to see why gamblers might nevertheless be fooled into thinking they are. "Streaks" of consecutive wins (or losses) are more common than people tend to think, and thus they appear more meaningful and mysterious than they really are. But the important point is that riding such a streak—having won four, five, or six times in row—means nothing about what is likely to happen next.

There are other walks of life in which people tend to see too much order, meaning, and significance in random sequences. One of the most interesting can be found in the game of basketball. Anyone who has ever played or watched the game of basketball "knows" that players occasionally get a "hot hand"—they go through periods in which their game is elevated to a higher level, and they feel they "can't miss." Thus, the hot hand represents a belief that success breeds success—that making several shots in a row will make a player feel relaxed and confident, which will make the player more likely to continue to do well in the immediate future.

But this belief just isn't true (Gilovich, Vallone, & Tversky, 1985). As the table here indicates, basketball players—even the stars of the NBA—are not more likely to make a basket after having made their previous shot than after having missed their previous shot. Additional analyses indicate that this is true when their shooting percentages after having made several consecutive shots are compared to their shooting percentages after having missed several consecutive shots. In perhaps the most telling analysis, college basketball players who took 100 shots from a set distance were asked to indicate when they felt hot. It turns out that they did no better than average when they said they were hot.

This does not mean that performance in basketball is "random." It is certainly not random that Iverson, O'Neal, and Nowitzki are in the NBA, and Gilovich, Keltner, and Nisbett only dream of being there. It is only the *distribution* of hits and misses in a player's performance record that is "random"—and even that is random only in the sense that the outcome of a given shot is unaffected by the outcome of previous shots. There are many nonrandom determinants of whether a player makes a given shot, such as the skill of the player, the spot on the floor from which the shot is taken, and the amount of defensive pressure. But the research on the hot hand demonstrates that the player's recent history of hits and misses actually has no impact. Thus, the belief that basketball shooting is "streakier" than flipping coins is, astonishingly, an illusion.

Probability of a player making a shot given a hit or miss on the previous shot (data from 1986–1987 season).

|  | P(HIT\|HIT) | P(HIT\|MISS) |
|---|---|---|
| Michael Jordan | .56 | .53 |
| Magic Johnson | .39 | .45 |
| Larry Bird | .49 | .38 |
| Isaiah Thomas | .44 | .44 |
| Kevin McHale | .53 | .61 |
| Dominique Wilkins | .42 | .51 |
| K. Abdul Jabbar | .49 | .49 |
| Joe Dumars | .41 | .47 |
| Vinnie Johnson | .49 | .44 |
| Dennis Rodman | .55 | .63 |
| Danny Ainge | .44 | .43 |

Source: Larkey, Smith, & Kadane, 1989.

One area in which the impact of representativeness on causal judgments is particularly striking is in the domain of health and medicine. Historically, people have often assumed that the symptoms of a disease should resemble either its cause or its cure (or both). In ancient Chinese medicine, people with vision problems were fed ground bat in the mistaken belief that bats had particularly keen vision and that some of this ability might be transferred to the recipient (Deutsch, 1977). Preliterate peoples have been known to feed liver (thought to be the locus of mercy) to the mean-spirited. Others have prescribed the ground-up skull of the red bush monkey for epilepsy, noting that the herky-jerky movements of that animal resemble the violent movements of an epileptic seizure, and so some ingredient of the former is thought to be an effective cure for the latter.

Western medical practice has likewise been guided at times by the representativeness heuristic. For instance, early Western medicine was strongly influenced by what was known as the "doctrine of signatures," or the belief that " . . . every natural substance which possesses any medicinal virtue indicates by an obvious and well-marked external character the disease for which it is a remedy, or the object for which it should be employed" (cited in Nisbett & Ross, 1980, p. 116). Thus, physicians prescribed the lungs of a fox (known for its endurance) for asthmatics and the yellow spice turmeric for jaundice.

The representativeness heuristic continues to influence people's beliefs about bodily states to this day. People think that you should avoid milk if you have a cold and potato chips if you suffer from acne. Why? Because milk seems so representative of phlegm, and the greasiness of potato chips so representative of the oily skin that often accompanies acne. Sometimes this belief that "you are what you eat" is taken to almost magical extremes. In one experiment, for example, college students were asked to make inferences about the attributes of members of (hypothetical) tribes (Nemeroff & Rozin, 1989). One group was told about a tribe that ate wild boar and hunted sea turtles for their shells; a second group was told about a tribe that ate sea turtles and hunted wild boars for their tusks. The students' responses indicated that they assumed that the characteristics of the food would "rub off" on the tribe members. Members of the turtle-eating tribe were considered to be better swimmers and more generous; those who ate boar were thought to be more aggressive and more likely to have beards. To be sure, people are affected by what they eat—people gain weight by eating lots of fat and can develop an orange tint to the skin by eating too much carotene. But becoming a better swimmer by eating sea turtles is a bit of a stretch.

Another area in which representativeness affects causal judgments is in the realm of pseudoscientific belief systems. Consider, for example, the case of astrological signs and representative personality traits. A central tenet of astrology is that an individual's personality is influenced by the astrological sign under which the person was born. The personalities associated with specific astrological signs are listed in Table 10.4. Notice the resemblance between the features we associate with each animal namesake and those that supposedly characterize individuals born under each astrological sign. Were you born under the sign of the lion (Leo)? Then you are likely to be a proud, forceful leader. Born under the sign of the ram (Aries)? Then you tend, ram-like, to be headstrong and quick tempered. Born under the sign of the virgin (Virgo)? Then you are inclined to be modest and retiring.

The personality profiles that supposedly accompany various astrological signs have been shown time and again to have absolutely no validity (Abell, 1981; Schick & Vaughn, 1995; Zusne & Jones, 1982). Why, then, is astrology so popu-

> "Men will cease to commit atrocities only when they cease to believe absurdities."
> —VOLTAIRE

## Table 10.4  Representativeness and Astrological Signs

The table shows personality traits that are supposedly characteristic of people born under nine of the twelve astrological signs.

| ASTROLOGICAL SIGN | PERSONALITY CHARACTERISTICS |
| --- | --- |
| Aries (The Ram) | Quick tempered; headstrong |
| Taurus (The Bull) | Plodding; prone to rage |
| Gemini (The Twins) | Vacillating; split personality |
| Cancer (The Crab) | Attached to their homes |
| Leo (The Lion) | Proud; leader |
| Virgo (The Virgin) | Modest; retiring |
| Libra (The Scales) | Well balanced; fair |
| Scorpio (The Scorpion) | Sharp; secretive |
| Capricorn (The Goat) | Hard-working; down to earth |

Source: Huntley, 1990; Read et al., 1978.

lar? Part of the reason is that astrology takes advantage of people's use of the representativeness heuristic. Each of the personality profiles has some superficial appeal because each draws upon the intuition that like goes with like. Who is more inclined to be vacillating than a Gemini (a twin)? Who is more likely to be fair and well balanced than a Libra (the scales)?

Consider another elaborate system designed to assess the "secrets" of an individual's personality: graphology, or handwriting analysis. Corporations pay graphologists sizable fees to help screen job applicants. Most French companies will not hire someone at a senior level without a graphology report. Graphologists are also called upon to provide "expert" testimony in trial proceedings, and to help the Secret Service determine if any real danger is posed by threatening letters to government officials. How much stock can we put in handwriting analysis?

Graphology, unlike astrology, is not completely worthless. It has been, and continues to be, the subject of rigorous empirical investigation (Nevo, 1986), and it has been shown that people's handwriting can reveal certain things about them. For example, very shaky writing can be a clue that an individual suffers from some neurological disorder that causes hand tremors; whether a person is male or female can be determined with beyond-chance accuracy from a sample of handwriting. Yet, in general, what handwriting analysis can determine most reliably tends to be what can be even more reliably ascertained through other means. As for the "secrets" of an individual's personality, graphology has yet to

"For what it's worth, next week all your stars and planets will be in good aspect for you to launch an invasion of England."

show that it is any better than astrology. But that has not done much to diminish the popularity of graphology.

Part of the reason that handwriting analysis remains so popular is that, like astrology, it gains some surface plausibility by taking advantage of people's tendency to employ the representativeness heuristic. The claims about handwriting and personality have a superficial "sensible" quality, rarely violating the intuition that like goes with like. For example, some graphologists divide a person's handwriting into the top, middle, and bottom portions of each line (Basil, 1989). The three regions are said to correspond respectively to the person's instinctual, intellectual, and practical selves. Can you guess which is which? The top region, not surprisingly, corresponds to the "higher" mental faculties. The bottom region corresponds to our "lower" instincts. That leaves the middle section for our practical selves.

Other graphologists make a distinction between writing that slants to the left or to the right. One style is thought to characterize people oriented to "the past, the self, and mother"; the other to people oriented to "the future, others, and father." Again, which is which? Because Westerners write from left to right, it comes as no surprise that someone whose handwriting slants "back" to the left is considered to be oriented to the past, and someone whose handwriting slants "forward" to the right is considered to be oriented to the future.

The allure of representativeness-based associations may also be responsible for the popularity of various "New Age" beliefs. The ideas that count as "New Age" are too numerous and varied for any single, overarching assessment. Some New Age ideas doubtless have merit, but others are highly dubious. Consider the practice of "rebirthing," in which individuals reenact their own births (often through hypnosis or by immersion in a pool of water) in an effort to correct personality defects caused by having been born in an "unnatural" fashion. Not surprisingly, the defects supposedly caused by particular unnatural births are never established empirically. Instead, the claims arise from their intuitive fit—that is, from the representativeness between each defect and style of birth. One individual who was born breech (that is, feet first) underwent rebirthing to cure his sense that his life was always going in the wrong direction. Another person, born Caesarean, sought the treatment because of a lifelong difficulty in seeing things to completion, and relying on others to finish tasks for her. As one author quipped, "God knows what damage forceps might inflict . . . a lifelong neurosis that you're being dragged where you don't want to go?" (Ward, 1994).

## THE JOINT OPERATION OF AVAILABILITY AND REPRESENTATIVENESS

The availability and representativeness heuristics sometimes operate in tandem. For example, a judgment that two things belong together—that one is representative of the other—can make an instance in which they do indeed co-occur particularly available. The joint effect of these two heuristics can thus create an **illusory correlation** between two variables, or the belief that they are correlated when in fact they are not. A judgment of representativeness leads us to expect an association between the two entities, and this expectation in turn makes instances in which they are paired unusually memorable.

A classic set of experiments by Loren and Jean Chapman illustrates this point nicely (Chapman & Chapman, 1967). The Chapmans were struck by a paradox

**illusory correlation** The belief that two variables are correlated when in fact they are not.

observed in the practice of clinical psychology. Clinicians often claim that they find various projective personality tests helpful in making clinical diagnoses, but systematic research on these tests has shown many of them to be completely lacking in validity. Why would intelligent, conscientious, and well-trained clinicians believe such tests can diagnose psychopathologies when they cannot? Why, in other words, did the clinicians perceive an illusory correlation between their clients' pathologies and their responses on such tests?

To find out, the Chapmans first asked numerous clinicians about which specific test responses on the part of their clients were indicative of which specific pathological conditions. Much of their work focused on the Draw-a-Person test, in which the client simply draws a picture of a person, and the therapist interprets the picture for signs of various psychopathologies. The clinicians reported that they observed numerous connections between particular drawings and specific pathological conditions—drawings and pathologies that seem, intuitively, to belong together. People suffering from paranoia, for example, were thought to be inclined to draw unusually large or small eyes. People insecure about their intelligence were thought to be inclined to draw a large (or small) head.

To investigate these illusory correlations further, the Chapmans gathered a sample of forty-five Draw-a-Person pictures—thirty-five drawn by psychotic patients in a nearby hospital and ten drawn by graduate students in clinical psychology. They then attached a phony statement to each picture that supposedly described the pathological condition of the person who drew it. Some came with the description, "is suspicious of other people," others with the description, "has had problems of sexual impotence," and so on. The Chapmans were careful to attach descriptions to pictures so that there was absolutely no correlation between the nature of the drawings and the pathological condition attached to each. For example, "is suspicious of other people" appeared just as often on pictures with unremarkable eyes as on pictures with large or small eyes.

These pictures (with accompanying pathological conditions) were then shown to college students who had never heard of the Draw-a-Person test. Although the study was carefully designed so that there was no connection between the pictures and pathological conditions, the students nonetheless "saw" the same relationships reported earlier by the clinical psychologists. To the students, too, it seemed that prominent eyes were likely to have been drawn by individuals who were suspicious of others. This suggests, of course, that the clinical psychologists were not detecting any real correlations between pathological conditions and responses on the Draw-a-Person test. Instead, they were "detecting" the same illusory correlations that the undergraduate students were detecting—illusory correlations produced by the joint operation of availability and representativeness. Certain pictures are representative of specific pathologies (for example, prominent eyes and paranoia), and this ensures that instances in which the two are observed together (for example, a paranoid individual drawing a person with large eyes) will be particularly noteworthy and memorable.

In a final study, the Chapmans simply asked students to indicate the extent to which various conditions (suspiciousness, impotence, dependence) "called to mind" different parts of the body (eyes, sexual organs, mouth). Tellingly, their responses matched the correlations reported by the earlier groups of clinicians and students.

The Chapman and Chapman studies and a great many investigations of intuitive judgment make it clear that the intuitive system produces many errors—some of them far from trivial in their consequences. Is it possible to increase the sway of the rational system at the expense of the intuitive one? The answer is yes, and you are doing it now in your studies at your university. Many of the errors we have discussed can be reduced by training in statistics and research methods (Nisbett, Fong, Lehman, & Cheng, 1987). Moreover, some of the framing effects we discussed earlier can be reduced by training in economics (Larrick, Morgan, & Nisbett, 1990). All of these kinds of training increase the scope and sophistication of our rational and deliberate judgment tools, and the likelihood that they will intervene to override or offset a mistake spawned by the intuitive system. So, although our errors may be disconcerting, they can be reduced markedly by training.

**LOOKING BACK,** we have seen that two mental systems appear to guide our judgments and decisions: one akin to intuition and the other akin to reason. The intuitive system operates quickly and automatically, while the rational system tends to be more deliberate and controlled. These systems can lead to the same judgments; they can lead to opposite judgments; or the intuitive system may produce a satisfying judgment so quickly that the rational system is never engaged. The intuitive system uses heuristics to make its quick assessments, which can sometimes bias judgment. One heuristic is the availability heuristic, which may lead to biased assessments of risk and biased estimates of people's contributions to joint projects. Another heuristic is the representativeness heuristic, which may result in base-rate neglect and mistaken assessments of cause and effect. When these two heuristics operate together, they can lead to an illusory correlation between two variables.

## SUMMARY

1. By focusing on errors in judgment and decision making, we can come to understand the way people make judgments and learn to avoid mistakes.

2. Sometimes our judgments are biased because they are based on misleading information, which can occur even when the information is encountered firsthand.

3. One bias that can taint information experienced firsthand is that of *pluralistic ignorance,* which tends to arise in situations in which people are reluctant to express their misgivings about a perceived group norm, with their reluctance reinforcing the false norm.

4. Although people tend to believe that their memories are the product of automatic recording devices, in

actuality they are reconstructions based on general knowledge, abstract theories, and fragments of truly remembered events. The reconstructive nature of memory occasionally gives rise to recollections of events that never occurred.

5. *Flashbulb memories* are powerful images of the moment when one learned of some dramatic news, but they too are subject to error, despite the sense of certainty and vividness attached to them.

6. Information received secondhand can also be biased, as speakers often do not provide a full account of what happened or may be motivated (because of ideology or the desire to entertain) to stress certain elements at the expense of others.

7. When people describe events, they tend to *sharpen* some elements—that is, emphasize points that are salient to them and that they think will interest us—and to *level* or deemphasize other elements.

8. There is evidence that people who watch local newscasts, with their steady drumbeat of dangerous events, exaggerate the dangers in their lives.

9. How information is presented can also affect judgment. For example, the *order* in which information is presented can be quite important. When the information presented first is more influential, we say there is a *primacy effect*, usually due to the fact that initial information can affect the way subsequent information is interpreted. When information presented last is more influential, we say there is a *recency effect*, usually due to the fact that such information is more likely to be available in memory.

10. Order effects are a type of *framing effect*. Others include the "spinning" of information by varying the structure of the information that is presented to produce a desired effect in an audience. More subtle framing effects include whether information is presented as a potential gain versus a potential loss.

11. *Knowledge structures*, including *schemas*, influence our interpretation of information. Knowledge structures are the *top-down* tools we use to understand the world, as opposed to the *bottom-up* tools of perception and memory.

12. Schemas influence what we attend to, they guide our inferences and construal of information, and they direct our memories to recover what seems relevant.

13. The likelihood that a given schema will be applied to incoming information is a function of the degree to which information matches the critical features of the schema. Unfortunately, sometimes the information available increases the similarity to a schema but not the appropriateness of applying it.

14. Other things being equal, the more recently a schema has been "activated," the more likely it is to be applied to new information. It is not at all necessary that we be consciously aware of a schema in order to be influenced by it.

15. We seem to have two different systems for processing information: an *intuitive*, automatic one and a *rational*, analytic one. Intuitive responses are based on rapid, associative processes, whereas rational processes are based on slower, rule-based reasoning.

16. Intuitive *heuristics*, or mental shortcuts, are useful and seem to provide us with sound judgments most of the time, but it is possible to identify several heuristics that sometimes lead us into errors of judgment.

17. People use the *availability heuristic* when they judge the frequency or probability of some event by the readiness with which relevant instances come to mind. This can encourage us to overestimate how much we have contributed to group projects, and it can lead us to overestimate the risks posed by salient, memorable hazards like earthquakes and homicide and to underestimate the likelihood of silent killers like asthma and stroke.

18. People use the *representativeness heuristic* when they try to categorize something by judging how similar it is to their conception of the typical member of the category, or when they try to make causal attributions by assessing how similar an effect is to a possible cause. The strategy is fine as far as it goes. The problem is that we often overlook highly relevant considerations such as *base-rate information*—how many members of the category there are in a population.

19. The "inside" perspective for making judgments causes us to make errors such as the *planning fallacy*, which could be avoided if the individual took an "outside" perspective, attending to the history of finishing related tasks in a given time.

20. When availability and representativeness operate together they can produce potent *illusory correlations*, which result when people think that two variables are correlated, both because they resemble one another and because the co-occurrence of two similar events is more memorable than the co-occurrence of two dissimilar events.

# CRITICAL THINKING ABOUT BASIC PRINCIPLES

1. How successful do you think the United States is in getting people to be organ donors? What is the waiting period, in other words, for patients who urgently need crucial organs such as kidneys or livers? Do you think the United States has an "opt in" or an "opt out" policy?

2. Perhaps the most successful government intervention to increase savings in the United States and in other countries has been the introduction of payroll deduction plans in which a portion of an employee's salary goes directly into an investment account. What ideas introduced in this chapter help to explain why people find it so easy to save through such plans and so difficult to save otherwise?

3. Suppose you've had a long run of good luck when a friend asks you, "How are things going?" As soon as you respond, "Great; life has really been treating me well," you feel a compulsion to say "knock on wood," even though you don't believe in jinxes. Why, according to ideas discussed in this chapter, would someone feel such a compulsion?

# KEY TERMS

availability heuristic (p. 410)
base-rate information (p. 415)
bottom-up processes (p. 401)
encoding (p. 404)
flashbulb memories (p. 387)
framing effect (p. 397)
heuristics (p. 410)

illusory correlation (p. 423)
knowledge structures (p. 402)
leveling (p. 390)
planning fallacy (p. 417)
pluralistic influence (p. 384)
primacy effect (p. 396)
recency effect (p. 396)

representativeness heuristic (p. 410)
retrieval (p. 404)
schema (p. 402)
sharpening (p. 390)
subliminal (p. 408)
top-down processes (p. 401)

# FURTHER READING

Chapman, L. J., & Chapman, J. (1967). Genesis of popular but erroneous diagnostic observations. *Journal of Abnormal Psychology, 72,* 193–204.

Gilovich, T., (1991). *How we know what isn't so: The fallibility of human judgment in everyday life.* New York: Free Press.

Hastie, R., & Dawes, R. (2001). *Rational choice in an uncertain world: The psychology of judgment and decision making.* Thousand Oaks, CA: Sage.

Tversky, A., & Kahneman, D. (1974). Judgment under uncertainty: Heuristics and biases. *Science, 185,* 1124–1131.

# Chapter Outline

CHAPTER 11

# Stereotyping, Prejudice, and Discrimination

Cristobal Colón, known to most of us as Christopher Columbus, was no doubt in an exceptionally good mood on the morning of October 12, 1492, when he went ashore in the Bahamas on Guanahani Island, which he promptly renamed San Salvador. It had been eleven weeks since he set sail from Spain in his effort to find a western route to Japan, China, and the East Indies. Although he began his voyage with confidence (based—oddly—as much on a prophecy from the book of Isaiah as on sound knowledge of geography), he could not be certain his plan had merit. But now, after having spotted land, his long quest for personal glory was assured, as was his appointment as viceroy and governor-general of all territories he might discover—an appointment that would be passed on to his heirs in perpetuity.

It is understandable, then, that Colon was rather expansive in his journal that day. His good mood was reflected in his description of the inhabitants of San Salvador (Columbus, 1492/1990):

. . . they swam out to the ships' boats where we were and brought parrots and balls of cotton thread and spears and

**Stereotyping Outgroups** Upon landing on an island in the Bahamas, Christopher Columbus was greeted by the natives and offered gifts of welcome, as shown in this German engraving. Yet, Columbus was prejudiced against the indigenous people because they differed from Europeans, and he stereotyped them as a group that would make good slaves.

many other things, and they bartered with us for other things which we gave them, like glass beads and hawks' bells. In fact they took and gave everything they had with good will. . . . They were well built, with handsome bodies and fine features. Their hair is thick, almost like a horse's tail. . . . They do not carry arms and do not know of them because I showed them some swords and they grasped them by the blade and cut themselves . . . They are all fairly tall, good looking and well proportioned . . .

They ought to make good slaves . . .

Colón's journal on that day captures a great deal of the material in this chapter—stereotyping, prejudice, and discrimination. He was well on his way toward developing a stereotype of those he encountered, characterizing the islanders as a whole on the basis of those individuals he happened to meet that day. He was immediately prejudiced against the islanders, whose appearance and customs differed from those of his own people. And he felt no need to treat them as he would treat his crew or other Europeans, as his chilling statement "they ought to make good slaves" makes clear.

It is tempting to dismiss Colón's reactions as part of an outdated, pre-Columbian mindset. It would be nice to think that people are more enlightened today. In some ways, they are. Slavery still exists, but no longer as a sanctioned, state-sponsored enterprise. Genocide also still exists, but now perpetrators must (sometimes) answer to an international tribunal. Moreover, the world is now more truly multicultural than it has ever been, with members of different races, ethnicities, and religions living and working alongside one another more peacefully and productively than ever before.

Despite such progress, however, it is abundantly clear that the human tendencies to stereotype, harbor prejudice, and engage in discrimination are still with us. One only has to note the awful events in such places as Rwanda, Bosnia, East Timor, and Somalia, or to acknowledge the intractable conflicts in the Middle East, Kashmir, or Northern Ireland to recognize that intergroup enmity and conflict continue to be a distressingly common element of the human condition. And lest one think that such problems are confined to these other, more troubled parts of the world, one need only recall the torture of Haitian immigrant Abner Louima at the hands of New York City police, the murder of gay student Matthew Shepard by two of his peers who were "offended" by his lifestyle, and countless occasions in which members of minority groups are passed over by cab drivers and potential employers, or pulled over by police for no cause, to realize that stereotyping, prejudice, and discrimination are continuing problems. They are part of the fabric of everyday life the world over.

The continued existence of ethnic, religious, and racial animosity challenges us to understand the underlying causes of intergroup tension. Where do stereotypes, prejudice, and discrimination come from? Why do they persist? What can be done to eliminate or reduce their impact?

Any serious attempt to address these questions must begin with the fact that there is unlikely to ever be a single, comprehensive "theory" of stereotyping, prejudice, or discrimination. The causes of each are surely many and varied, and so any satisfactory account of these phenomena must incorporate numerous elements. Our discussion will therefore focus on several different perspectives that shed light on these issues. These different perspectives should not be seen as competing accounts, but as complementary elements of a more complete analysis. We will first consider the *economic perspective*, which identifies the roots of much intergroup hostility in the competing interests that set many groups apart from one another. Next we will examine the *motivational perspective*, which emphasizes the psychological needs and wishes that lead to intergroup conflict. We will then turn to the *cognitive perspective*, which traces the origin of stereotyping to the same cognitive processes that allow us to categorize, say, items of furniture into distinct classes of chairs, couches, and tables. As part of this perspective, we will examine the frequent conflict between people's consciously held beliefs and values, and their quick, unelaborated reactions to others based on membership in specific racial, ethnic, occupational, or other demographic groups. Finally, we will examine some of the psychological effects on the victims of stereotyping, prejudice, and discrimination. Before considering these different perspectives and effects, however, let us examine some of the different forms of intergroup bias.

**Violence against Outsiders** In September 1997, police arrested Haitian immigrant Abner Louima and brutally beat and tortured him. The police officers claimed that Louima had punched one of the officers, but the extreme brutality of their actions strongly suggests that anti-black prejudice was responsible for the officers' hideous actions.

# CHARACTERIZING INTERGROUP BIAS

Do you believe that Asians are industrious, that Italians are temperamental, or that Californians are "laid back"? Such beliefs are **stereotypes**—that is, beliefs about attributes that are thought to be characteristic of members of particular groups. They can be positive or negative, true or false, and, whether valid or not, they are a way of categorizing people. Stereotyping involves thinking about a person, not as an individual, but as a member of a group, and thereby bringing to bear what (you think) you know about the group onto your expectations about the individual.

Some stereotypes are grounded in fact. Consider the old joke that heaven is a place where you have an American house, a German car, French food, British police, an Italian lover, and everything is run by the Swiss. Hell, on the other hand, is a place where you have a Japanese house, a French car, British food, German police, a Swiss lover, and everything is run by the Italians. American housing stock is indeed superior to that found in Japan, and towns are rarely abuzz with talk about how hard it is to get reservations at a new British restaurant. Some stereotypes are accurate. On the other hand, is there any reason to be especially wary of German police? There certainly was during the 1930s and 1940s, but has German law enforcement been particularly likely to encroach on civil liberties since then? Maybe, maybe not. Are Italian lovers to be preferred to Swiss? You make the call.

But stereotypes about German police work or British cooking or Italian lovers are not the type that have aroused the most interest among social psychologists in the causes and consequences of stereotypes (Judd & Park, 1993). Instead, most of the concern with stereotyping has focused on beliefs characterized by some degree of inaccuracy, particularly those inaccurate beliefs that are likely to lead to prejudice and discrimination.

**Prejudice** refers to a negative attitude and affective response toward a certain group and its individual members. It involves *prejudgment* of others because they belong to a specific category. **Discrimination** corresponds to negative or pernicious behavior directed toward members of particular groups. It involves unfair treatment of others, treatment based not on the content of their character, but on their membership in a group.

Roughly speaking, stereotyping, prejudice, and discrimination refer to the belief, attitudinal, and behavioral components of problematic between-group relations. Stereotyping, prejudice, and discrimination often go together. People are more inclined to injure those they hold in low regard. But the components of intergroup bias need not be in synch. A person can discriminate without prejudice, for example. Jewish parents sometimes say they do not want their children to marry outside the faith, not because they have a low opinion of other groups, but because they are concerned about assimilation and its implications for the future of Judaism. Members of nearly all ethnic groups have harbored similar sentiments out of the same concern about preserving a cultural identity or way of life. Sometimes, of course, statements that "I have nothing against them, but . . ." are merely cover-ups of underlying bigotry. At other times, they are surely sincere.

It is also possible to be prejudiced and yet not discriminate. This is particularly likely when the culture frowns on discrimination. Civil rights laws in the United States are specifically designed to uncouple prejudiced attitudes and discriminatory actions. The threat of punishment is intended to keep people's discriminatory impulses in check.

**stereotypes** Beliefs about attributes that are thought to be characteristic of members of particular groups.

**prejudice** A negative attitude or affective response toward a certain group and its individual members.

**discrimination** Unfair treatment of members of a particular group based on their membership in that group.

# MODERN RACISM AND SEXISM

Throughout most of the world, the norms about how different groups of people are to be viewed and treated have changed. It is not legally acceptable to engage in many forms of discrimination that were common a half century ago, nor is it socially acceptable to express the sorts of prejudices and stereotypes that were common until relatively recently. This change has created conflict in many people between what they think and feel inside, and what they believe it's prudent to say or do publicly. For others, it has created a conflict between competing beliefs and values (for example, the belief in equal treatment and the desire to make up for past injustice through affirmative action) or between competing abstract beliefs and gut-level reactions (for example, the belief that one ought to feel the same toward members of all groups and some hard-to-shake resistance to that belief). These sorts of conflicts have inspired social psychologists to develop new theoretical accounts to explain this modern, more constrained or ambivalent sort of prejudice.

> **modern racism** Prejudice directed at other racial groups that exists alongside a rejection of explicitly racist beliefs.

This shift of theoretical emphasis is particularly noteworthy with respect to accounts of race relations in the United States. Some have argued that old-fashioned racism has largely disappeared in the United States, but that it has been supplanted by a subtler, more modern counterpart (Kinder & Sears, 1981; McConahay, 1986; Sears, 1988; Sears & Kinder, 1985; see Haddock, Zanna, & Esses, 1993, and Swim, Aiken, Hall, & Hunter, 1995, for similar accounts of homophobia and sexism, respectively). **Modern racism** (sometimes called **symbolic racism**) in the United States involves a rejection of explicitly racist beliefs (for example, that there are genetic differences between racial groups in intelligence) that coexists with an enduring suspicion and animosity toward African Americans fueled by the belief that blacks are undermining cherished principles of justice and equality (McConahay & Hough, 1976). Among these threatened values are self-reliance (considered to be undermined by affirmative-action policies) and "family values" (considered to be undermined by a disproportionate number of black welfare recipients, unwed mothers, and violent criminals). Whether these beliefs are correct or not, they fuel modern racism.

Gaertner and Dovidio (1986) have offered a similar account, maintaining that many Americans hold strong egalitarian values that lead them to reject prejudice and discrimination. Yet, many white Americans harbor unacknowledged negative feelings and attitudes toward minority groups that stem from ingroup favoritism and a desire to defend the status quo (Sidanius & Pratto, 1999). Thus, whether or not such a person will act in a prejudiced or discriminatory manner will very much depend on the details of the situation. If the situation offers no justification or "disguise" for discriminatory action, people's responses will conform to their egalitarian values. But if a suitable rationalization is readily available, the modern racist's prejudices will emerge.

Consider an experiment in which participants were in a position to aid a white or black individual in need of medical assistance (Gaertner & Dovidio, 1977). If the participants thought they were the only one who could help, they came to the aid of the black victim somewhat more often (94 percent of the time) than they did for the white victim (81 percent). But when they thought that other people were present so their inaction could be justified on nonracial grounds ("I thought somebody else with more expertise would intervene"), they helped the black victim much less often than the white victim (38 percent versus 75 percent). In situations such as this, the prejudice or discrimination is "masked," and the individual remains comfortably unaware of being racist. Modern racism thus only shows itself in the subtlest ways. This sort of racist would never join the Ku Klux Klan, but might consistently give black passersby a wider berth. Such a person might never utter a racist word, but might also never support a single social policy designed to aid black Americans.

Or consider a study in which white participants evaluated black and white applicants to college (Hodson, Dovidio, & Gaertner, 2002). Both prejudiced and unprejudiced participants rated white and black applicants (identified by photos attached to their applications) the same when the applicants excelled on all pertinent dimensions or were below par on all dimensions. But when the applicants excelled on certain dimensions and were below average on others, the ratings of prejudiced and unprejudiced participants diverged: the prejudiced participants rated the black applicants less favorably than did the unprejudiced participants. In these latter cases, prejudiced participants' discriminatory responses could be defended as nondiscriminatory—that is, they could be hidden—by claiming that the dimensions on which the black applicants fell short were more important than those on which they excelled. Note that the desire to appear unprejudiced is sometimes sufficiently strong to produce the *opposite* result—that is, white participants rating black applicants who were strong on some dimensions and weak on others *more* favorably than they rated white applicants who were strong on some dimensions but weak on others by judiciously choosing which dimensions of accomplishment should receive more weight (Norton, Vandello, & Darley, 2004).

## BENEVOLENT RACISM AND SEXISM

Phrases like "some of my best friends are . . . (fill in the blank)" or "I'm not sexist, I love women!" illustrate a common conviction that stereotypes must be negative to be harmful. In fact, however, many of our "isms"(racism, sexism, ageism) are ambivalent, containing both negative and positive features. A person might believe, for example, that blacks are lazier and more prone to criminality than whites, and at the same time believe they are more musically and athletically talented. Similarly, one might believe that women are less competent and intelligent than men, and at the same time believe that they are warmer and more interpersonally skilled.

In their work on ambivalent sexism, Steve Glick and Susan Fiske (2001) have interviewed 15,000 men and women in nineteen nations and found that benevolent sexism (a subjectively favorable, chivalrous ideology that offers protection and affection to women who embrace conventional roles) often coexists with hostile sexism (antipathy toward women who are viewed as usurping men's power). So what's the trouble with this? Glick and Fiske argue that such partly positive stereotypes aren't necessarily benign. Ambivalent sexist or racist attitudes may be particularly resistant to change. The favorable features of such belief structures enable the stereotype holder to deny any prejudice. Think of the trucker who romanticizes women so much he decorates his mudflaps with their likeness. Also, when we idealize only certain members of outgroups—those who meet our positive expectations (for example, the athletically talented black person, the happy housewife, or the *Playboy* centerfold)—we are likely to disparage those who don't fulfill that positive stereotype. By rewarding women for conforming to a patriarchal status quo, or blacks for conforming to a racist status quo, benevolent sexism and racism inhibit equality. In other words, those who hold ambivalent attitudes tend to act positively toward members of outgroups only if they fulfill their idealized image of what such people should be like. Those who deviate tend to be treated with hostility.

## MEASURES TO ASSESS TRUE ATTITUDES

The existence of conflict between what is felt inside and what is publicly stated, or between competing beliefs and values, has inspired social psychologists to develop new methods of assessing people's stereotypes and prejudices. Surveys of people's attitudes toward certain groups cannot be fully trusted because respondents may not think it's acceptable to express what they really feel, or people may not fully know how they feel. Given that so many forms of prejudice are ambivalent, uncertain, or hidden, they are not likely to be revealed through self-report. Social psychologists have therefore developed a number of indirect measures, two of which we discuss here.

*The Implicit Association Test (IAT)* Anthony Greenwald and Mazarin Banaji (1995) have pioneered a technique called the **implicit association test (IAT)**, for revealing the nonconscious prejudices of even those who advocate universal equality and high regard for all groups. The technique works like this: a series of words and pictures are presented on a computer screen and the respondent is told to press a key with the left hand if the picture or word conforms to one rule, and another key with the right hand if it conforms to another rule (see Figure 11.1). The rule might be to press the left-hand key for either a black face or positive word (*honor, gift, happy*), and the right-hand key for either a white face or negative word (*poison, evil, bomb*). Greenwald and Banaji argued that respondents would react faster when they were to press one key for both positive words and people in groups they regard positively, and another key for both negative words and people in groups they regard negatively. Thus, if one has a prejudice toward

> **implicit association test (IAT)**
> A technique for revealing nonconscious prejudices toward particular groups.

**Figure 11.1 The Structure of the Implicit Association Test (IAT)**
Several rounds with different stimulus/hand press rules are completed. Two are shown here.

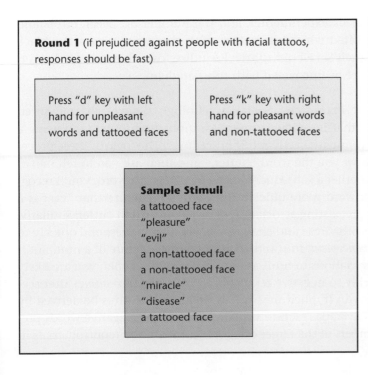

**Round 1** (if prejudiced against people with facial tattoos, responses should be fast)

Press "d" key with left hand for unpleasant words and tattooed faces

Press "k" key with right hand for pleasant words and non-tattooed faces

**Sample Stimuli**
a tattooed face
"pleasure"
"evil"
a non-tattooed face
a non-tattooed face
"miracle"
"disease"
a tattooed face

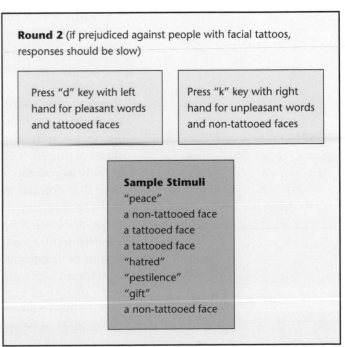

**Round 2** (if prejudiced against people with facial tattoos, responses should be slow)

Press "d" key with left hand for pleasant words and tattooed faces

Press "k" key with right hand for unpleasant words and non-tattooed faces

**Sample Stimuli**
"peace"
a non-tattooed face
a tattooed face
a tattooed face
"hatred"
"pestilence"
"gift"
a non-tattooed face

an identifiable group of people (skinheads, old people), one should be faster to press the appropriate key if that key is the same one used for negative words (because that type of person is viewed negatively), and slower to press the appropriate key if it is the one used for positive words. The pairing of the positive/negative words and the two groups of faces (black/white) are switched on different rounds, so that positive words and white faces are to be responded to the same on one round, and negative words and white faces are to be responded to the same on another round. One's nonconscious prejudice toward black people, for example, is measured by the difference between the average time it takes to respond to black faces with the same key as the positive words and the average time it takes to respond to black faces with the same key as negative words.

As we write this, well over a million people have taken the Web version of the IAT. Among other results, researchers have found that both young and older individuals show a pronounced prejudice for the young over the old, and about two-thirds of white respondents show a strong or moderate prejudice for white over black (Nosek, Banaji, & Greenwald, 2002). Interestingly, about half of all black respondents show some prejudice in favor of white faces (Southern Poverty Law Center Web site).

An important question, however, is whether a person's responses on the IAT are predictive of behavior that is more significant than pressing computer keys (Brendl, Markman, & Messner, 2001; Karpinski & Hilton, 2001). There is some evidence that they are. In one study, participants in a brain-imaging machine were shown pictures of black and white faces. The participants' earlier IAT responses were significantly correlated with differential activation of the amygdala (a brain center associated with emotional learning and evaluation; see Chapter 7) in response to two different types of faces, whereas their scores on a more traditional, conscious measure of prejudice, the Modern Racism Scale, were not, indicating that the IAT assessed an important component of their real attitudes (Phelps et al., 2000). In another study, participants first interacted with a white experimenter, took the IAT, and then interacted with a black experimenter. Their IAT scores, it turns out, were predictive of the discrepancy between how much they spoke to the white versus the black experimenter, how often they smiled at the white versus the black experimenter, and the number of speech errors and hesitations they exhibited when interacting with the white versus the black experimenter (McConnell & Leibold, 2001). Prejudice toward members of different groups can therefore be uncovered with this paradigm.

### Priming and Implicit Prejudice

Social psychologists have also measured underlying prejudices that individuals might be motivated to deny by using a number of **priming** (or mental activation) procedures. The logic of these procedures is simple: If I show you the word "butter," and then ask you to tell me, as quickly as you can, whether a subsequent string of letters is a word, you'll recognize that "bread" is a word more quickly than you'll recognize that "car" is a word because of your preexisting association between bread and butter. Similarly, if you associate nuns with virtue and charity, you are likely to respond quickly to positive terms (*good, benevolent, trustworthy*) after seeing a picture of a nun. But if you have negative associations to nuns as, say, strict, rigid, or cold, you are likely to respond more quickly to negative terms (*mean, unhappy, unbending*) after seeing a picture of a nun. An implicit measure of prejudice can thus be derived by comparing a person's average reaction time to positive and negative words preceded by faces of members of the target category (compared to "control" trials in

**priming** A procedure used to increase the accessibility of a concept or schema (for example, a stereotype).

which positive and negative words are preceded by faces of non-category members). As we will discuss later in this chapter, numerous studies using these priming methods have shown that people often have subtle prejudices against various target groups that they would steadfastly deny having (Banaji, Hardin, & Rothman, 1993; Bessenoff & Sherman, 2000; Dijksterhuis, Aarts, Bargh, & van Knippenberg, 2000; Dovidio, Kawakami, & Gaertner, 2002; Fazio & Hilden, 2001).

**LOOKING BACK,** we have seen that in much of today's Western world, prejudice and discrimination are frowned upon. This has driven them underground, so to speak, resulting in a rejection of prejudiced attitudes that exists side-by-side with subtly discriminatory behavior when it can be covered up or rationalized. The schism between what people consciously maintain—or are willing to state— and how they sometimes feel or act has led to the development of various indirect measures of attitudes toward different groups. These include priming procedures and the implicit association test, which measure the degree to which different groups trigger positive or negative associations. We will next consider some of the underlying bases of prejudice and discrimination, beginning with economic factors.

# THE ECONOMIC PERSPECTIVE

We can understand the economic approach to prejudice and discrimination through the story of Cain and Abel, the biblical account of the world's first murder, one inspired by rivalry. The Bible says, "And the Lord had regard for Abel and his offering [a lamb] but for Cain and his offering [fruit] he had no regard. So Cain was very angry . . ." Cain presumably felt jealous that his brother had the Lord's attention and affection, and he did not. So he "rose up against his brother Abel and killed him." The battle for a limited resource—in this case, the Lord's good favor—led Cain to try to win the competition by eliminating his rival. Cain is not unique in that regard. Like most biblical characters, Cain's impulses represent those of all humankind. Ethically, people do not tend to shine when engaged in competition over scarce resources.

The economic view of prejudice and discrimination makes the same claim about groups. Groups develop prejudices about one another and discriminate against one another when they compete for material resources. Religious groups, racial groups, and cultural groups all have the capacity, like Cain, to protect and promote their own interests by lashing out at those they perceive to be threatening them.

## REALISTIC GROUP CONFLICT THEORY

One version of the economic perspective has been dubbed **realistic group conflict theory** because it acknowledges that groups sometimes confront real conflict over what are essentially economic issues (Levine & Campbell, 1972). According to this theory, prejudice and discrimination often arise from competition over limited desired resources. The theory predicts, correctly, that prejudice and discrimination should increase under conditions of economic difficulty.

**realistic group conflict theory**
A theory that group conflict, prejudice, and discrimination are likely to arise over competition between groups for limited desired resources.

**ethnocentrism** Glorifying one's own group while vilifying other groups.

"Without knowledge of the roots of hostility we cannot hope to employ our intelligence effectively in controlling its destructiveness."

—GORDON ALLPORT

When there is less to go around, or when people are afraid of losing what they have, competition intensifies. The theory also predicts that prejudice and discrimination should be strongest among groups that stand to lose the most from another group's economic advance. For example, people in the working class in the United States exhibited the most anti-black prejudice in the wake of the civil rights movement (Simpson & Yinger, 1985; Vanneman & Pettigrew, 1972). Working-class jobs were most at risk once millions of black Americans were allowed to compete more freely for entry-level manufacturing jobs in companies from which they had previously been excluded.

Realistic group conflict theory also specifies some of the ways that conflict between groups is likely to be played out. First of all, a pronounced **ethnocentrism** develops—that is, the other group is vilified, and one's own group is glorified. Anyone who has ever played pick-up basketball knows this phenomenon well. An opponent whose antics seem intolerable instantly seems more likable once that person becomes a teammate. More generally, people in the outgroup are often thought of in stereotyped ways and are treated in a manner normally forbidden by one's moral code. At the same time, loyalty to the ingroup intensifies. A "circle the wagons" mentality develops. Many of these elements of ethnocentrism that are brought about by intergroup competition were very effectively studied in one of social psychology's classic experiments, one that took place at a summer camp for boys.

## THE ROBBERS CAVE EXPERIMENT

In 1954, Muzafer Sherif and his colleagues carried out a very ambitious experiment far from the confines of the psychological laboratory (Sherif, Harvey, White, Hood, & Sherif, 1961). Twenty-two fifth grade boys were taken to Robbers Cave State Park (so named because the outlaws Belle Star and Jesse James were thought to have hidden there) in southeastern Oklahoma. The boys had signed up for a two-and-a-half week summer camp experience that, unbeknownst to them, was also a study of intergroup relations. The research team spent over 300 hours screening boys from the Oklahoma City area to find twenty-two who were "average" in nearly every respect—none were from broken homes, none had had problems in school, all were from middle-class families, and there were no notable ethnic group differences among them. The boys, none of whom knew each other beforehand, were divided into two groups of eleven and taken to the park on two successive days.

*Competition and Intergroup Conflict*    In the first phase of the experiment, the two groups independently engaged in activities designed to foster group unity (for example, pitching tents, preparing meals), and contented themselves with common camp activities such as playing baseball, swimming, and putting on skits. Neither group even knew of the other's existence. Considerable cohesion developed within each group, and each chose to give itself a name—the Eagles and the Rattlers, respectively. A consistent hierarchical structure also emerged within each group, with "effective initiators"—or the boys who made suggestions that the others accepted—being rated most popular.

In the second phase, the Eagles and Rattlers were brought together for a tournament. The boys were told that each member of the winning team would receive a medal and a highly coveted pocket knife (a form of participant compensation unlikely to be given out in today's litigious climate), but that members of the losing team would not get anything. The tournament lasted five days and consisted of such activities as baseball, touch football, tug-of-war, cabin inspections, and a treasure hunt. The competitive nature of the tournament was designed to encourage each group to see the other as an impediment to the fulfillment of its own goals, and hence as a foe.

Numerous events suggest that that is exactly what happened. From the very first competitive encounter, and with steadily increasing frequency throughout the tournament, the two groups hurled insults at one another, calling those in the other group "bums," "cowards," "stinkers," and so on. Although such terms may be tame by today's trash-talking standards, they are clearly not terms of endearment, and they differ markedly from how the boys referred to members of their own group, primarily making self-glorifying and congratulatory comments about fellow group members. The expression of intergroup hostility, moreover, was not limited to words. Numerous provocations were directed at the opposing group. The Eagles captured and burned the Rattlers' flag, which of course brought about a retaliatory theft of the Eagles' flag. Food fights broke out in the dining area, raids were conducted on each other's cabins, and numerous challenges to engage in physical fights were issued.

It is particularly interesting to note how the internal dynamics of the two groups changed as they became locked into this competitive struggle. Boys who were either athletically gifted or who advocated a more aggressive stance toward the outgroup tended to gain in popularity. The initial leader of the Eagles, for example, had neither of these characteristics, and so he was essentially deposed by someone who was more athletic and more of a firebrand.

In addition to diligently recording episodes of hostility, the investigators conducted a number of more tightly controlled assessments of the degree to which the boys tended to look favorably on members of their own group while derogating members of the other group. In one assessment, the investigators scattered a large quantity of beans around a field and asked the two groups to pick up as many as they could in a one-minute period. The group collecting the most would receive $5. When the contest was over, but before the winner was announced, each boy's collection of beans was briefly projected on a wall via an opaque projector, and everyone was asked to estimate the number of beans that the boy had collected. In reality, the same quantity of beans (thirty-five) was always shown, but this was impossible to discern because of the brief duration of the projection and the large quantity of beans shown. The boys' estimates revealed clear ingroup favoritism: each group estimated that boys who were members of *their* group had collected more beans than boys who were members of the other group.

### Reducing Intergroup Conflict through Superordinate Goals

The third and final part of the experiment is in many ways the most important. It was devoted to assessing ways to reduce the conflict between the two groups. First, on seven occasions over the next two days, the two groups were simply brought together in various noncompetitive settings to ascertain whether their hostility would dissipate. It did not. Simple contact between the two groups just led to more name-calling, jeering, food fights, and insults directed at members of the other group.

Given that simple noncompetitive contact did not reduce intergroup friction, the investigators contrived to confront the boys with a number of crises that could only be resolved through the cooperative efforts of both groups. For example, the water supply to the camp was disrupted, and the entire length of pipe

**The Robbers Cave Experiment**
Muzafer Sherif divided ten-year-old boys into two groups to observe how the groups would relate to each other. (A) Initially, the two groups kept their distance and reacted hostilely toward each other. (B) When a truck carrying supplies broke down, however, they worked together to get it moving. (C) The boys in the two groups set aside their differences and became friends after accomplishing the superordinate goal.

**superordinate goals** Goals that transcend the interests of one individual group, and that can be achieved more readily by two or more groups working together.

from the reservoir to the campgrounds had to be inspected to find the source of the problem—a task made much more manageable if all the boys in both groups were assigned to inspect a given segment of the line. Also, a truck carrying supplies for a campout at a distant area of the park mysteriously "broke down." How to get it running again? The investigators had left a large section of rope near the truck in the hope that the boys might try to pull the truck to get it started. One of the boys said, "Let's get our tug-of-war rope and have a tug-of-war against the truck." They did so, with members of both groups intermingled throughout the length of rope and pulling it together.

Relations between the two groups quickly showed effects of these **superordinate goals**—that is, goals that could not be achieved by either group alone but could be accomplished by both working in concert. Name-calling abruptly dropped off, and friendships between members of the two groups appeared to germinate. When the study was completed and it was time to return to Oklahoma City, the boys insisted that everyone return on the same bus rather than on the separate buses by which they had arrived. In fact, a rather touching incident took place during the trip home. When the bus pulled over at a roadside diner, the group—the Rattlers—that had won $5 in the bean collection contest decided to spend their money on malted milks for everyone—Eagles included. The hostility produced by five days of competition was erased by the joint pursuit of common goals, resulting in a happy ending.

The Robbers Cave experiment offers several important lessons. One is that neither differences in background, nor differences in appearance, nor prior histories of conflict are necessary for intergroup hostility to develop. All that is required is that two groups enter into competition for goals that only one can achieve. Another lesson is that competition against "outsiders" often increases group cohesion. This is often used by political demagogues who invoke the specter of outside enemies to try to stamp out dissension or to distract attention from problems or conflict within the group itself. The final lesson points to how intergroup conflict can be diminished. If we want to reduce the hostility that exists between certain groups, we should think of ways to get them to work together to fulfill common goals. Simply putting adversaries together "to get to know one another better" is usually not enough (Bettencourt, Brewer, Croak, & Miller, 1992; Brewer & Miller, 1988; Stephan & Stephan, 1996; Wilder, 1986). It is the pursuit of superordinate goals that keeps everyone's eyes on the prize and away from meddlesome subgroup distinctions (see Box 11.1).

Box 11.1 FOCUS ON EDUCATION

# The "Jigsaw" Classroom

If the competitive atmosphere of most classrooms undermines curiosity for many students and exacerbates racial tensions in integrated schools, what would happen if the classroom were made less competitive? Might a more cooperative learning environment improve academic performance and race relations in integrated settings?

Social psychologist Elliot Aronson developed a cooperative learning procedure to find out. When the public school system in Austin, Texas, was integrated in 1971, the transition was not smooth. A disturbing number of physical confrontations took place between black, Hispanic, and white children, and the atmosphere in the classrooms was not what proponents of integration had hoped it would be. Aronson was invited by the superintendent of schools to do something to improve matters. Mindful of the lessons of the Robbers Cave experiment, Aronson wanted to institute procedures that would unite students in the common goal of mastering a body of material, rather than competing for the highest grades and the attention of the teacher. What he and his colleagues came up with was something called the "jigsaw" classroom (Aronson, Stephan, Sikes, Blaney, & Snapp, 1978; Aronson & Thibodeau, 1992).

In the jigsaw classroom, students are divided into small groups of roughly six students each. Every effort is made to balance the groups in terms of ethnicity, gender, ability level, leadership, and so on. The material on a given topic is then divided into six parts, and each student is required to master one part (and only one part) and to teach it to the others. For a lesson on Bill Clinton, for example, one student might be responsible for his early years, another for his governorship of Arkansas, a third for the Monica Lewinsky and other scandals, a fourth for his foreign-policy accomplishments as President, a fifth for his domestic accomplishments, and a sixth for his post–White House years. By dividing the material in this way, no student can learn the entire lesson without help from peers. Each student's material must, like the pieces of a jigsaw puzzle, fit together with all the others for everyone in the group to learn the whole lesson.

The jigsaw classroom has two things going for it that should serve to improve both ethnic relations and academic performance. Each student's dependence on the others in the group dampens the usual competitive atmosphere and encourages the students to work cooperatively toward a common goal. To the extent that the groups are ethnically heterogeneous, members of different ethnic groups should gain the experience of working productively with one another as individuals rather than as representatives of particular ethnic groups. In addition, students typically learn material best when they are required to teach it.

The effectiveness of the jigsaw classroom has been assessed in field experiments that compare students in classrooms that use the jigsaw procedure with those in classrooms that teach the same material in the usual fashion. These studies have typically found that students in the jigsaw classrooms like school more and develop more positive attitudes toward different ethnic groups than do students in traditional classrooms.

The lessons learned from the Robbers Cave experiment, that intergroup hostility can be diminished by cooperative activity directed at a superordinate goal, have profound practical significance. A simple classroom procedure derived from these lessons—one that can be used in conjunction with traditional, more individualistic classroom exercises—can both boost academic performance and facilitate positive ethnic relations.

## EVALUATING THE ECONOMIC PERSPECTIVE

The economic perspective "works" in the sense that it fits nicely with what we see around us as the successes and failures of intergroup relations. Consider race relations in the United States and the effort to build harmonious relations between two groups with a difficult history of conflict and suspicion forged in the institution of slavery. Where have efforts toward integration been most suc-

**Integration of the Military** Successful integration of blacks and whites has occurred in the U.S. military forces, where soldiers cooperate to accomplish the shared goal of defending the nation.

cessful? Many analysts cite the integration of blacks and whites in the military. The success of integration in the military makes perfect sense in light of the lessons learned from the Robbers Cave experiment. Blacks and whites in the military are in the equivalent of Phase 3 of the Robbers Cave experiment. Their whole purpose is to be ready to defend the United States against a common outside enemy. They must therefore engage in cooperative, interdependent action to accomplish shared goals—precisely the set of circumstances that brought about healthy intergroup functioning in the Robbers Cave experiment. In such circumstances, the group or category to which a person belongs recedes in importance, and what he or she can contribute to the joint effort becomes more prominent (Gaertner, Mann, Dovidio, Murrell, & Pomare, 1990; Gaertner, Murrell, & Dovidio, 1989; Miller & Brewer, 1986). Group members stand out as individuals, not as representatives of a particular subgroup.

What implications does this have for race relations on college campuses? For many students, both black and white, their college years are the first time they have had close and sustained contact with members of the other race. How well does it work? The first thing to note is that the conditions of intergroup contact are not as favorable in the classroom as they are on the battlefield. Although students will assist their close friends to help them achieve higher grades, rarely do students feel a strong cooperative bond with their classmates in general. Few students ask themselves, "Is there anything I can do to increase the mean grade of everyone else in the class?" Rather, the common reliance on curved grading encourages a highly competitive struggle of all against all in which another student's triumph is seen as a threat to one's own grade.

This implies that the integration effort on college campuses may be less successful than it has been in the military. This may indeed be the case. Students, faculty, and administrators on countless college campuses are discussing what, if anything, ought to be done about the tendency for students of different races or ethnic origins to inhabit entirely different niches in the university. Many students segregate themselves almost exclusively with other members of their own race or ethnic group in their choice of residence, dining hall, and even fields of study. To be sure, many students—perhaps most—of many ethnic groups do mix on college campuses, and the effort to integrate college campuses on the whole has been a great success. We have no wish to claim otherwise. What we do wish to suggest, however, is that the integration effort at the university may be lagging behind that in the military—a result that a close look at the Robbers Cave experiment would lead one to expect.

A fundamental weakness of the economic perspective is that it does not identify *which* groupings will serve as the basis of perceived economic competition. The economic perspective could be readily applied to the behavior of the Eagles and Rattlers because they were members of explicit teams. Life often is not like that. The authors of this textbook are white, but we are not members of any white "team." If we land lucrative jobs, for example, it is not a victory for the white team and a defeat for any other race. Ultimately, any competition is among individuals; it is individuals who land jobs or fail to land jobs, individuals who win or lose.

And individuals are members of many groups. We are white, it is true, but we are also men, teachers, researchers, environmentalists, cinephiles, sports nuts (well, two of us anyway), and many other things. Some of these categories are vested with tremendous importance and serve as the basis of perceived economic competition among groups; others rarely serve as the source of much contention. The economic perspective is largely silent on the question of which groupings are likely to be the ones around which battle lines are drawn. To come to grips with *that* question, we must consider other perspectives on stereotyping, prejudice, and discrimination.

**LOOKING BACK,** we have seen that prejudice can arise from realistic conflict between groups over scarce resources. The Robbers Cave experiment serves as an instructive model of this sort of conflict, showing how otherwise friendly boys could turn into enemies when placed in groups competing for limited resources. The enmity between the groups evaporated when they had to cooperate to achieve superordinate goals of value to both groups, a result with considerable implications for managing potentially troublesome intergroup relations around the globe. We will now consider other sources of intergroup hostility.

## THE MOTIVATIONAL PERSPECTIVE

Intergroup hostility, it turns out, can develop even in the absence of competition. This was apparent in the Robbers Cave experiment, as there were signs of increased ingroup solidarity when the two groups first learned of each others' existence—*before* they were engaged in, or even knew about, the organized competition. Midway through Phase 1 of the experiment, when the two groups were still being kept apart, they were allowed to get within hearing distance of one another. The mere fact that another group existed made each set of boys take their group membership much more seriously. The Eagles, for example, had not found it necessary to have a group name until they learned about the other boys, at which time they promptly settled on the name Eagles. Furthermore, when they learned about each other's existence, both groups' first impulse was to "run them off" and "challenge them." Both groups also became quite territorial, referring to the baseball field as "*our* diamond," and a favorite swimming spot as "*our* swimming hole."

Since all of this took place before any competition had been arranged, it indicates that intergroup hostility can develop because of the mere fact that another group exists. Imposing group boundaries on a collection of individuals, then, can be sufficient to initiate group discrimination.

### THE MINIMAL GROUP PARADIGM

People's readiness to adopt an "us/them" mentality has been extensively documented in experiments employing the **minimal group paradigm** pioneered by Henri Tajfel (Tajfel, Billig, Bundy, & Flament, 1971; Tajfel & Billig, 1974; see also Ashburn-Nardo, Voils, & Monteith, 2001; Brewer, 1979). This is an experimental setup in which researchers create groups based on arbitrary and seemingly meaningless criteria, and then examine how the members of these "minimal

**minimal group paradigm** An experimental paradigm in which researchers create groups based on arbitrary and seemingly meaningless criteria, and then examine how the members of these "minimal groups" are inclined to behave toward one another.

groups" are inclined to behave toward one another. The participants first perform a rather trivial task and are then divided into two groups, ostensibly on the basis of their responses. In one type of task, for example, participants estimate the number of dots projected on a screen. Some participants are told they belong to a group of "overestimators," and others are told they belong to a group of "underestimators." In reality, the participants are randomly assigned to the groups, and they only learn about the group to which they themselves belong—they never learn who else is in their group or who is in the other group. Thus, what it means to be part of a "group" is boiled down to the bare minimum.

In the second part of the experiment, the participants are taken individually to different cubicles and asked to assign points redeemable for money to successive pairs of their fellow participants. They do not know the identity of those to whom they are awarding points; they only know their "code number" and group membership. Participants are asked to assign points to, say, "Number 4 of the overestimator group" and "Number 2 of the underestimator group." Some of the choices provide relatively equal outcomes for members of both groups but with slightly more for the member of the outgroup; some choices offer to maximize what the ingroup member can receive but still result in more points for the members of the outgroup; and some maximize the relative ingroup advantage over the outgroup but don't provide much in the way of absolute reward for members of the ingroup.

Numerous experiments have shown that a majority of participants are interested more in maximizing the *relative* gain for members of their ingroup than in maximizing the absolute gain for their ingroup. A moment's reflection reveals just how extraordinary this is. The participants do not know who the ingroup and outgroup members are; the choices are never for themselves; and, of course, the ostensible basis for establishing the two groups is utterly trivial. Yet, they still exhibit a tendency to favor their minimal ingroup! Moreover, they are willing to do so at a cost to the ingroup, which gets less than it would if the focus were on absolute gain rather than "beating" the other group. That ingroup favoritism emerges in this context is a powerful testimonial to how easily we slip into thinking in terms of "us" versus "them" (Brewer & Brown, 1998). And if history has taught us anything, it is that the us/them distinction, once formed, can have enormous—and enormously *unfortunate*—implications.

> "Cruelty and intolerance to those who do not belong to it are natural to every religion."
> —SIGMUND FREUD

## SOCIAL IDENTITY THEORY

An astute reader might now be thinking, "Yes, yes, I understand the pervasiveness and tenacity of ingroup favoritism, but what does it have to do with the *motivational* perspective on prejudice? Might it not reflect a purely cognitive tendency to divide the world into categories of 'us' and 'them'? Just as all children quickly learn to distinguish the self from all others, might we not all learn to distinguish 'my side' from the 'other side'?"

Good point. Much of the psychology behind ingroup favoritism might very well reflect cognitive influences. The us/them distinction may be one of the basic cuts we make in dividing up and organizing the world. Yet, the ingroup favoritism observed in the minimal group situation cannot be the product of cognition alone. People's cognitive processes might lead them to make the us/them distinction, but cognitive processes alone cannot lead to one group being favored over the other. For that, we need a motivational theory. We need such a theory to explain why, once the us/them distinction is made, "we" are treated better than "they" are. The most widely recognized theory that attempts to explain this

is Henri Tajfel and John Turner's **social identity theory**, which posits the undeniable fact that a person's self-concept and self-esteem derive not only from personal identity and accomplishments, but from the status and accomplishments of the various groups to which the person belongs (Tajfel & Turner, 1979). Being "an American" is an element of the self-concept of most Americans, and with it comes the pride associated with, say, the Bill of Rights, U.S. economic and military muscle, and the accomplishments of American scientists, industrialists, and athletes. With it, too, comes the shame associated with American slavery and treatment of Indians. Similarly, being a gang member, a professor, a film buff, or a surfer means that one's identity and esteem are intimately tied up with the triumphs and tribulations of fellow gang members, academics, film buffs, and surfers.

*Boosting the Status of One's Ingroup*    Because our self-esteem is based in part on the status of the various groups to which we belong, we might be tempted to do what we can to boost the status and fortunes of these groups and their members. Therein lies a powerful cause of ingroup favoritism. By giving advantage to fellow members of an ingroup, we boost the group's standing and thereby potentially elevate our own self-esteem. Thus, feeling better about the group leads us to feel better about ourselves. Evidence in support of this thesis comes from studies that have assessed participants' self-esteem after they have had an opportunity to exhibit ingroup favoritism in the minimal group situation. As expected, those who had been allowed to engage in intergroup discrimination had higher self-esteem than those who had not been given the opportunity to discriminate (Lemyre & Smith, 1985; Oakes & Turner, 1980). Other research has shown that people who take particularly strong pride in their group affiliations are more prone to ingroup favoritism when placed in a minimal group situation (Crocker & Luhtanen, 1990). And people who are highly identified with a particular group react to criticism of the group as if it were criticism of the self (McCoy & Major, 2003).

*Basking in Reflected Glory*    Social identity theory also receives support from the everyday observation that people go to great lengths to announce their affiliation with a certain group when that group is doing well. Sports fans, for example, often chant "We're number 1!" after a team victory. But what does "We're number 1" mean? It is a rare fan indeed who throws a block, sets a screen, or does anything other than heckle referees and opposing players. Yet, countless fans

**Social Identity Theory**    People derive their sense of identity not only from their individual accomplishments but also from those of the groups to which they belong. (A) These delegates at the Democratic National Convention identify with the Democratic party. (B) These children sitting on a fence at a ranch identify with cowboys.

> **social identity theory**  A theory that a person's self-concept and self-esteem not only derive from personal identity and accomplishments, but from the status and accomplishments of the various groups to which the person belongs.

**Basking in Reflected Glory** Sports fans identify with their team and feel happiness when the team wins and dejection when it loses. To connect themselves to the team, fans often wear team shirts to the game—and to class or work the next day if the team wins. West Point cadets must wear their uniforms to games, but they show their identification by wearing foam Number 1 hands and chanting "We're Number 1."

want to be connected to the effort when the outcome is a victory. Not so after a loss. As one person put it, "Victory finds a hundred fathers but defeat is an orphan" (Ciano, 1945, p. 521).

Robert Cialdini called this tendency to identify with a winning team **basking in reflected glory**. He investigated the tendency by recording how often students wore their school sweatshirts and T-shirts to class after their football team had just won or lost a game. As expected, students wore the school colors significantly more often following victory than after defeat. Cialdini and his colleagues also tabulated students' use of first-person ("We won") and third-person pronouns ("They lost") following victory and defeat. The inclusive "we" was used significantly more often after a win, and the more restrictive "they" more often after a loss (Cialdini et al., 1976). The desire to bask in the reflected glory of those with whom we have the slightest connections may help explain why so many people paid such vast sums for items from the Kennedy estate: $772,500 for a set of golf clubs, $211,500 for an imitation pearl necklace, and $48,875 for a tape measure (*New York Times*, April 24, 1996, p. 1; April 26, 1996, p. 1)! Those who bought these items may have thought that having something from the Kennedy family would lend them some of the Camelot cachet.

## FRUSTRATION-AGGRESSION THEORY

Anyone who has ever been stuck in traffic en route to an important meeting is familiar with one of the most consistent and powerful laws of psychology, a law captured in **frustration-aggression theory**. Simply put, frustration leads to aggression. The probability of blaring the horn or swearing at a nearby motorist is much higher when the smooth transit to one's destination is blocked. This idea has been incorporated into a motivational account of prejudice and discrimination that holds that people are particularly likely to vilify outgroups under conditions of hardship. The theory predicts that frustrating times will be marked by increased aggression.

*From Generalized to Targeted Aggression*   By itself, the link between frustration and aggression cannot explain the origins of prejudice and discrimination because frustration leads to *generalized* aggression. As we all know from experience, we sometimes lash out at the ones we love. The link between frustration and aggression therefore does not explain why hard times should lead to aggression targeted at specific groups.

Another fact from everyday experience provides the rest of the explanation. Often we cannot lash out at the true source of our frustration without getting into further difficulty, so we displace our aggression onto a safer target. The person who is denied a raise at work takes it out on the kids at home. Thus, frustration-aggression theory predicts that hardship will generate malevolence directed at minority groups who, by virtue of being outnumbered and in a weaker position, constitute particularly safe and vulnerable targets (Miller & Bugelski, 1948). The classic example is anti-Semitism. Throughout history, Jews have been welcomed and accepted into numerous societies that, when times got tough, made an abrupt turnaround, targeting Jews as scapegoats and directing their anger at the Jewish community.

In one of the most frequently cited tests of this idea, Carl Hovland and Robert Sears (1940) examined the relationship between the price of cotton and the number of lynchings of blacks in the South between 1882 and 1930. Cotton was enormously important to the Southern economy during this period, and so it was assumed that times were good and frustrations low when the price was high, and times were tough and frustrations high when the price was low. Sure enough, Hovland and Sears observed a strong negative correlation between the price of cotton in a given year and the number of lynchings that took place that year. Lean times saw numerous lynchings; good times relatively few.

A reanalysis of Hovland and Sears' data that used more modern statistical techniques in some ways provides even stronger support for the frustration-aggression account (Hepworth & West, 1988). The investigators found the same

> **basking in reflected glory**  The tendency to take pride in the accomplishments of those with whom we are in some way associated (even if it is only weakly), as when fans identify with a winning team.
>
> **frustration-aggression theory**  The theory that frustration leads to aggression.

**Displaced Aggression**   Four white police officers were charged with using excessive force in the racially motivated beating of Rodney King, a black man, after they stopped him for a traffic violation. After the officers were acquitted in April 1992 by an all-white jury, the black community erupted with violence. Unable to lash out at the police or the jury, however, they took out their anger and frustration by rioting and looting stores in predominantly black neighborhoods.

negative correlation reported previously, but, unlike Hovland and Sears, they also found a similar—though weaker—negative correlation between economic conditions in the South and the number of lynchings of *whites*. This fits with the frustration-aggression account because frustration increases generalized aggression. But the fact that the relationship is stronger for blacks than for whites is also consistent with the idea that frustration leads to aggression that tends to be displaced toward relatively powerless groups. Indeed, without this element of displacement, the frustration-aggression account is not really a theory of discrimination at all, just a theory of unguided aggression.

*Bolstering Self-Esteem*   Social identity theory stipulates that derogating outgroups can enhance an individual's self-esteem, and frustration-aggression theory specifies the direction of hostility toward outgroups during difficult times. It is a small step from these theories to the prediction that people will tend to stereotype others and give in to their prejudices when they are feeling insecure or their self-esteem is threatened. Several studies have documented this self-esteem maintenance function of stereotypes and prejudice. In one study, half the participants had their self-esteem threatened by being told that they had just performed poorly on a test of intelligence; the other half were told they had done well (Fein & Spencer, 1997). The participants then watched a videotaped interview of a job applicant. The content of the videotape made it clear to half the participants that the applicant was Jewish, but not to the other half. When later asked to rate the job applicant, those who thought she was Jewish rated her more negatively than did those who were not told she was Jewish, but only if they had earlier been told they had performed poorly on a test of intelligence (see Figure 11.2A). In addition, the participants who had had their self-esteem threatened and had "taken it out" on the Jewish applicant experienced an increase in their self-esteem from the beginning of the experiment to the end (see Figure 11.2B). Stereotyping and derogating members of outgroups, it appears, serve to bolster self-esteem.

A rather stunning demonstration of this tendency was reported by Lisa Sinclair and Ziva Kunda (1999). In their study, participants were either praised or criti-

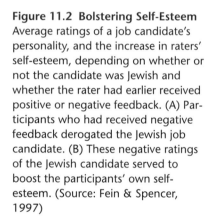

**Figure 11.2 Bolstering Self-Esteem**
Average ratings of a job candidate's personality, and the increase in raters' self-esteem, depending on whether or not the candidate was Jewish and whether the rater had earlier received positive or negative feedback. (A) Participants who had received negative feedback derogated the Jewish job candidate. (B) These negative ratings of the Jewish candidate served to boost the participants' own self-esteem. (Source: Fein & Spencer, 1997)

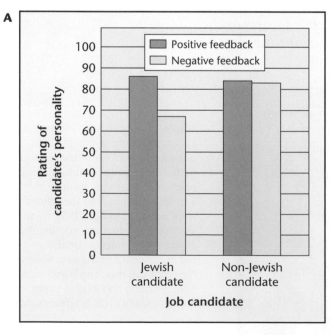

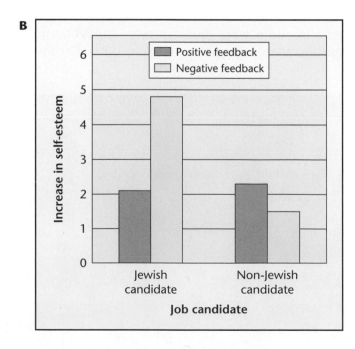

A

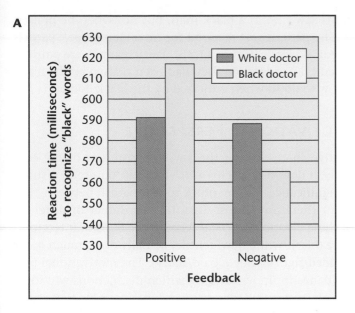

B

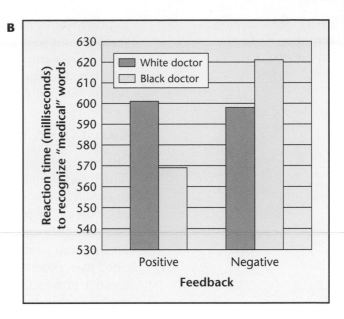

**Figure 11.3 Self-Esteem and Racial Prejudice** Participants were either praised or criticized by a white or black doctor. Reaction times to both black words and to medical words after criticism or praise by white doctors were virtually the same. But this was not true for reaction times after criticism or praise by black doctors. (A) Reaction times to recognize "black" words: When they received criticism (negative feedback) from the black doctor, the participants thought of him primarily as a black person and were therefore faster at subsequently recognizing words related to the African-American stereotype (indicated by quicker reaction time, and hence a lower bar). (B) Reaction times to recognize "medical" words: When they received praise (positive feedback) from the black doctor, however, they thought of him primarily as a doctor and were therefore subsequently faster at recognizing words related to medicine (indicated by quicker reaction time, and hence a lower bar). (Source: Sinclair & Kunda, 1999)

cized by a white or black doctor. Sinclair and Kunda predicted that the participants would be motivated to cling to the praise they received but to challenge the criticism, and that they would use the race of their evaluator to help them do so. In particular, they thought that individuals who received praise from a black doctor would tend to think of him more as a doctor (a prestigious occupation) than as a black man, whereas those who were criticized by a black doctor would tend to think of him more as a black man than as a doctor.

To test their predictions, Sinclair and Kunda had their participants perform a lexical decision task right after receiving their feedback from the doctor. That is, the researchers flashed a series of words and nonwords on a computer screen and asked the participants to indicate, as fast as they could, whether each string of letters was a word. Some of the words were associated with the medical profession (for example, *hospital, prescription*) and some were associated with common stereotypes of blacks (for example, *rap, jazz*). Sinclair and Kunda reasoned that if the participants were thinking of their evaluator primarily as a doctor, they would recognize the medical words faster; if they were thinking of their evaluator primarily as a black man, they would recognize the words associated with the black stereotype faster.

Figure 11.3 shows that that is exactly what happened. Participants were particularly fast at recognizing words associated with the black stereotype when they had been criticized by the black doctor, and particularly slow to recognize those words when praised by the black doctor (Figure 11.3A). When he criticized them, in other words, participants saw him as a black man, but not when he praised them (or not so readily). The pattern was reversed for how long it took participants to recognize the medical words (Figure 11.3B). Participants were particularly fast at recognizing medical words when they had been praised by the black doctor, and particularly slow to do so when criticized by the black doctor.

### EVALUATING THE MOTIVATIONAL PERSPECTIVE

The motivational perspective shares one of the key shortcomings of the economic perspective—namely, it does not specify *which* ingroup/outgroup distinctions will be vested with significance. We are quick to distinguish between "us" and "them," it is true, but there are almost an infinite number of different "thems." Although all of these distinctions *could* serve as the basis of intergroup hostility and conflict, some (black/white, Jew/gentile) actually do so much more often than others (left-handed/right-handed, bald/hairy). The motivational perspective provides little guidance in understanding which distinctions will form the basis of conflict, although frustration-aggression theory does hold that much hostility is directed at the relatively powerless.

The strength of the motivational perspective, on the other hand, is that it builds on two undeniably important elements of the human condition. First, people do readily draw the us/them distinction, and the various groups to which they belong are intimately connected to the motive to enhance self-esteem. Second, people tend to aggress when frustrated, often at the expense of the "safest" and least powerful targets. Social psychologist Roger Brown once likened conflict between groups to "a sturdy three-legged stool" because it rests on the pervasive and enduring human tendencies to stereotype, to glorify the ingroup, and to form societies in which there are unequal distributions of resources (Brown, 1986, p. 533). Both the motivational and economic perspectives have shown us how readily we will reward our own and penalize outsiders—leg number 2. The motivational perspective also speaks to how an unequal distribution of resources can produce the type of frustration that gives rise to intergroup hostility—leg number 3. To examine leg number 1 of Brown's stool—stereotyping—we will need to turn to the cognitive perspective.

**LOOKING BACK,** we have seen that people are inclined to favor ingroups over outgroups—even when the basis of group membership is trivial—in part because people identify with their groups and feel good about themselves when they feel good about their groups. A variant of frustration-aggression theory tells us that frustration is more likely to result in aggression toward the relatively powerless. Self-esteem threat also results in aggression toward, or at least denigration of, outgroup members. In the next section, we will examine the nature of stereotyping and the potential role it plays in prejudice and discrimination.

## THE COGNITIVE PERSPECTIVE

From the cognitive perspective, stereotyping is inevitable. It stems from the ubiquity and necessity of categorization. We categorize nearly everything, both natural (bodies of water—creek, stream, river) and artificial (cars—sports car, sedan,

SUV). Even color, which arises from continuous variation in electromagnetic wavelength, is perceived as distinct categories.

All of this categorizing has a purpose: it simplifies the task of taking in and processing the incredible volume of stimuli that confronts us. The person who is thought to have given us the term "stereotype," the American journalist Walter Lippmann, stated that "the real environment is altogether too big, too complex, and too fleeting, for direct acquaintance. We are not equipped to deal with so much subtlety, so much variety, so many permutations and combinations . . . We have to reconstruct it on a simpler model before we can manage with it" (Lippmann, 1922, p. 16). Stereotypes provide us with those simpler models that allow us to deal with the "great blooming, buzzing confusion of reality" (Lippmann, 1922, p. 96).

## STEREOTYPES AND CONSERVATION OF MENTAL RESERVES

According to the cognitive perspective, stereotypes are useful cognitive categories that allow us to process information efficiently (Macrae & Bodenhausen, 2000). If so, we should be particularly inclined to use them when we are overloaded, tired, or mentally taxed in some way—that is, when we are in need of a shortcut. Several experiments have demonstrated exactly that (Kim & Baron, 1988; Macrae, Hewstone, & Griffiths, 1993; Pratto & Bargh, 1991; Stangor & Duan, 1991). In one intriguing demonstration, students were shown to be more likely to invoke stereotypes when tested at the low point of their circadian rhythm. "Morning people" were more likely to invoke a common stereotype and conclude, for example, that a person charged with cheating on an exam was guilty if he was an athlete—but only when they were tested at night. "Night people" were more likely to conclude that a person charged with dealing drugs was guilty if he was black—but only when they were tested in the morning (Bodenhausen, 1990). Thus, people are most likely to fall back on mindless stereotypes when they lack mental energy.

If the use of stereotypes conserves intellectual energy, then encoding information in terms of relevant stereotypes should furnish extra cognitive resources that can be applied to other tasks. Resources not used on one task can be applied to another. In one test of this idea, students were asked to perform two tasks simultaneously. One required them to form an impression of a (hypothetical) person described by a number of trait terms presented on a computer screen (for example, *rebellious, dangerous, aggressive*). The other task involved monitoring a tape-recorded lecture on the economy and geography of Indonesia. For half of the students, the presentation of the trait terms was accompanied by an applicable stereotype (for example, skinhead); for the remaining students, the trait terms were presented alone. The key questions were whether the applicable stereotype would facilitate the students' later recall of the trait terms they had seen, and, more important, whether it would also release extra cognitive resources that could be devoted to the lecture on Indonesia. To find out, the students were given a brief quiz on the contents of the lecture ("What is Indonesia's official religion?" "Jakarta is found on which coast of Java?").

As the experimenters anticipated, the use of stereotypes eased the students' burden in the first task, and thereby facilitated their performance on the second (see Figure 11.4). Students who were provided with a stereotype not only remembered the relevant trait information better, they also performed better on the surprise multiple-choice test on Indonesia (Macrae, Milne, & Bodenhausen, 1994).

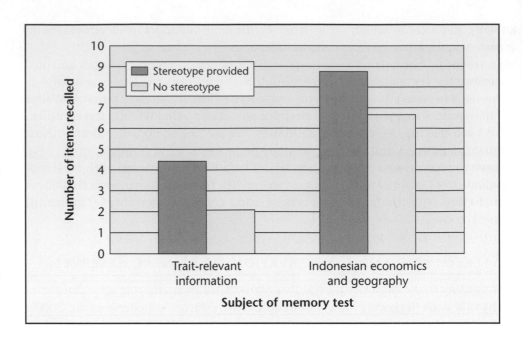

**Figure 11.4 Stereotypes and Conservation of Cognitive Resources**
Do stereotypes facilitate recall of stereotype-consistent information and furnish additional cognitive resources that can be used to aid performance on an additional task? Average performance on a test of memory for material on one subject by students with or without an applicable stereotype that could be applied to material on another, simultaneous task. (Source: Macrae, Milne, & Bodenhausen, 1994)

## CONSTRUAL PROCESSES AND BIASED ASSESSMENTS

The use of stereotypes conserves cognitive resources. That is their up side. But as is often the case, the benefit comes at a cost. What is gained in efficiency is paid for by occasional inaccuracy and error. In particular, not all category members are well captured by the stereotype. Invoking the stereotype may save time and effort, but it can lead to mistaken impressions and unfair judgments about individuals. In addition, biased information processing can help explain why even stereotypes completely lacking in validity nevertheless develop and endure. If one suspects—because of what one was told, or the implications of a joke one heard, or a hard-to-interpret performance difference—that a particular group of people might differ from the mainstream in some way, it is shockingly easy to construe pertinent information in such a way that the suspicion is confirmed, solidified, and elaborated.

The cognitive perspective on stereotyping does more than point out the obvious fact that stereotypes can distort our perceptions of others. Cognitively oriented social psychologists also seek to identify the precise construal processes that give rise to such distortions. What kind of faulty reasoning processes give rise to inaccurate stereotypes? How, in other words, might a well-meaning person, lacking any malice, nonetheless come to hold the kind of troublesome and inaccurate convictions that we tend to think about when we think of the term *stereotype*? How might such beliefs arise from pure cognitive processing? To answer these questions, we must consider the kinds of construal processes that are invoked once individuals are perceived as belonging to different groups.

*"Why is it we never focus on the things that unite us, like falafel?"*

*Accentuation of Ingroup Similarity and Outgroup Difference*    There is an apocryphal story about a man who owned a farm near the Russian-Polish border. European history being what it is, the farm had gone back and forth under the rule of each country numerous times. Indeed, with the establishment of the most recent boundaries, the farmer was uncertain whether he lived in Poland or Russia. To settle the issue, the farmer saved up to have a proper survey conducted and his national identity established. The surveyor worked long and hard making the most careful measurements. When he had finished, the farmer could scarcely contain his anticipation: "Well, do I live in Russia or Poland?" The surveyor replied that although remarkably near the border, the entire farm was located in Poland. "Good," the farmer stated, "I don't think I could take those harsh Russian winters."

The point of the story, of course, is that although an arbitrary national border cannot affect the weather at a fixed location, arbitrary categorical boundaries can have significant effects on the human mind. Although few people would make an error like that depicted in this story, research has shown that merely dividing a continuous distribution into two groups leads people to see less variability within each group and more variability between the two. In one early experiment, participants were shown a series of lines, with adjacent lines in the series varying from one another in length by a constant amount (Tajfel & Wilkes, 1963). When the series was split in half to create two groups, the participants tended to underestimate the differences between adjacent lines within each group, and to overestimate the difference between the adjacent lines that formed the intergroup border. In more social tests of this idea, participants are divided into two "minimal" groups. They then fill out an attitude questionnaire twice—once to record their own attitudes, and once to record how they think another ingroup or outgroup member might respond. Participants consistently assume that their beliefs are more similar to those of a fellow ingroup member than to those of an outgroup member—even when group membership is arbitrary (Allen & Wilder, 1979; Wilder, 1984).

What is remarkable here is *not* that people assume more similarity between members within a group than across groups. That only makes sense. After all, why categorize members into groups in the first place if the members of each group are not, on average, more similar to one another than they are to the members of the other group? What *is* remarkable, and potentially troubling, is that people make such assumptions even when the groups are formed arbitrarily, or when they are formed on the basis of a dimension (for example, skin color) that may have no bearing on the particular attitude or behavior under consideration. In these circumstances, the pure act of categorization distorts our judgment.

*The Outgroup Homogeneity Effect*    Think of a group to which you do not belong: Islamic fundamentalists, stamp collectors, heroin addicts, Winnebago owners. It is tempting to think of such groups as a unitary "they." We tend to call to mind an image of such groups in which all members think alike, act alike,

**Overcoming the Outgroup Homogeneity Effect**    We often think of outgroups as having members who all think, dress, and act alike. We might expect that all Hasidic bands would be alike, but we would soon realize that this Hasidic reggae band differs from other Hasidic bands, as well as from mainstream bands, and that individual differences also exist within the band. We see lead singer Matisyahu dressed in traditional Hasidic garb while the other members of his band are not.

even look alike. What this indicates is that the tendency to assume within-group similarity is much stronger for outgroups than for ingroups. *They* all think, act, and look alike. *We* don't. This is the **outgroup homogeneity effect**.

One study examined the outgroup homogeneity effect by showing Princeton and Rutgers students a videotape of other students making a decision, such as whether to listen to rock or classical music or whether to wait alone or with other participants during a break in an experiment. Half of the Princeton and Rutgers students were told that the students shown on the tape were from Princeton; half were told they were from Rutgers. After watching the tape, the participants estimated the percentage of students at the same university who would make the same choices as those they had seen on the tape. The results indicated that the participants assumed more similarity among outgroup members than among ingroup members. Princeton students who thought they had witnessed the behavior of a Rutgers student were willing to generalize that behavior to other Rutgers students. In contrast, Princeton students who thought they had witnessed the behavior of a *Princeton* student were less willing to generalize. The opposite was true for Rutgers students. People see more variability of habit and opinion among members of the ingroup than they do among members of the outgroup (Quattrone & Jones, 1980; see also Linville, 1982; Linville, Fischer, & Salovey, 1989; Ostrom & Sedikides, 1992; Park & Judd, 1990; Park & Rothbart, 1982).

It is easy to understand why this might be so. For one thing, we typically have much more contact with fellow members of an ingroup than with members of an outgroup, giving us greater opportunity to encounter evidence of divergent opinions and discrepant habits among ingroup members. Indeed, sometimes all we know about outgroup members is what their stereotypic characteristics are reputed to be. But differences in the number of interactions make up only half the story: the nature of the interactions we have with ingroup and outgroup members is likely to be different as well. Interactions with a fellow ingroup member typically take place on an individual-to-individual basis. Because we share the same group membership, we do not treat an ingroup member as a representative of a group. It is the person's idiosyncratic likes, dislikes, talents, and shortcomings that are front and center in the interaction. Not so with outgroup members. We often treat an outgroup member as a representative of a group, and the person's unique characteristics recede to the background.

***Biased Information Processing***   As we have just seen, people are more likely to assume that an individual action is typical of a group if the group in question is not their own. But regardless of the group under consideration, people do not generalize equally from everything they see. Some acts (an epileptic seizure, for example) discourage generalization no matter who the actor is; other acts (rudeness, for example) invite it. In general, people are more likely to extrapolate from behaviors they already suspect may be typical of an individual's fellow group members. Stereotypes can therefore be self-reinforcing. Actions that are consistent with an existing stereotype are noticed, imbued with significance, and remembered, whereas those at variance with the stereotype may be ignored, dismissed, or quickly forgotten (Bodenhausen, 1988; Kunda & Thagard, 1996; von Hippel, Sekaquaptewa, & Vargas, 1995).

Imagine, for example, that a newspaper reports that "Reggie Jefferson" stole a woman's Lexus at gunpoint while she waited at a stoplight. If, based on his name, he is thought to be African American, his race and the perceived race-relatedness of the crime are likely to command attention. The event will then feed the stereo-

---

**outgroup homogeneity effect**
The tendency to assume that within-group similarity is much stronger for outgroups than for ingroups.

---

"Stereotypic beliefs about women's roles, for example, may enable one to see correctly that a woman in a dark room is threading a needle rather than tying a fishing lure, but they may also cause one to mistakenly assume that her goal is embroidery rather than cardiac surgery."

—Dan Gilbert

type that blacks commit more than their share of violent crimes. But if, say, "Tom Gilovich" committed the same crime, the event would strike most people (most whites, at any rate) as simply a crime, not a race-related crime, and the mental record of the number of whites who commit such crimes would not be adjusted. And failing to register the instances in which whites commit violent crimes only serves to strengthen the stereotype about black criminality. Stereotypes thus influence what is noticed.

Stereotypes also influence how events are interpreted. In one striking demonstration of this effect (Duncan, 1976; see also Sagar & Schofield, 1980), white participants watched a videotape of a heated discussion between two men and were asked, periodically, to code the behavior they were watching into one of several categories (for example, "gives information," "playing around," "aggressive behavior"). At one point in the video, one of the individuals shoved the other. For half the participants, it was a black man doing the shoving; for the other half, it was a white man. The race of the person made a difference in how the action was seen. When perpetrated by a white man, the incident tended to be coded as more benign (as "playing around," for example). When perpetrated by a black man, in contrast, it was coded as a more serious action (as "aggressive behavior," for example).

The results of this study are remarkable because the shove was a perceptual fact presented in front of the participants' eyes. The influence of stereotypes is likely to be even bigger when the episode in question is presented to people second-hand and therefore is more amenable to differential construal. In one study, for example, participants listened to a play-by-play account of a college basketball game and were told to focus on the exploits of one player in particular, Mark Flick. Half the participants saw a picture of Mark that made it clear he was African American, and half saw a picture that made it clear he was white. When participants afterwards rated Mark's performance during the game, their assessments reflected commonly held stereotypes about black and white basketball players. Those who thought Mark was African American rated him as more athletic and as having played better; those who thought he was white rated him as having exhibited greater hustle and as having played a more savvy game (Stone, Perry, & Darley, 1997).

Studies such as these make it clear that people do not evaluate information evenhandedly. Instead, information that is consistent with a group stereotype typically has more impact than information that is inconsistent with it.

*Self-Fulfilling Prophecies*   Sometimes our stereotypic beliefs can further this tendency by creating a **self-fulfilling prophecy**—that is, we act toward members of certain groups in ways that encourage the very behavior we expect. Thinking that members of a particular group are hostile, we may act toward them in a guarded manner, thereby eliciting a coldness that we see as proof of their hostility. A teacher who thinks that members of a particular group lack intellectual ability may fail to offer them adequate instruction, increasing the chances that they will indeed fall behind their classmates. As Robert Merton, who coined the term "self-fulfilling prophecy," once said, "the specious validity of the self-fulfilling prophecy perpetuates a reign of error. For the prophet will cite the actual course of events as proof that he was right from the very beginning" (Merton, 1957, p. 423).

The role of self-fulfilling prophecies in the maintenance of stereotypes was powerfully illustrated in an experiment in which white Princeton students interviewed black and white men pretending to be job applicants (Word, Zanna, &

**self-fulfilling prophecy** Acting on a belief in a way that tends to support the original belief, as when we act toward members of certain groups in ways that encourage the very behavior we expect from them.

Cooper, 1974). The interviews were monitored, and it was discovered that the students (the white interviewers) unwittingly treated black and white applicants differently. When the applicant was black, the interviewer tended to sit farther away, to hem and haw throughout the session, and to terminate the proceedings earlier than when the applicant was white. This is not the type of environment to inspire self-possession and smooth interview performance.

Sure enough, the second phase of the experiment showed just how difficult it had been for the black applicants. Interviewers were trained to treat *new* applicants, all of whom were white, the way that either the white or the black applicants had been treated earlier. These interviews were tape-recorded and later rated by independent judges. Those applicants who had been interviewed in the way the black applicants had been interviewed earlier were evaluated more negatively than those who had been interviewed the way the white applicants had been interviewed. In other words, the white interviewers' negative stereotypes of blacks were likely to be confirmed by placing black applicants at a disadvantage (see Hebl, Foster, Mannix, & Dovidio, 2002, for an analogous study of reactions to homosexual job applicants).

***Distinctiveness and Illusory Correlations***   Although the cognitive perspective emphasizes the role of pure cognition in the formation and maintenance of stereotypes, it is not always clear where impartial information processing leaves off, and passions, motives, and self-interest begin. We do not wish to suggest that all of the biases we have just reviewed are solely the product of flaws in our cognitive machinery. Some doubtless reflect motivational influences as well. But there is at least one class of stereotyping bias that does arise from cognitive processes alone, one that derives from the way we react to statistically anomalous events. This is a class of **illusory correlation**, wherein people "see" correlations (or relationships) between events, characteristics, or categories that are not actually related (Fiedler, 2000; Garcia-Marques & Hamilton, 1996; Hamilton & Sherman, 1989; Hamilton, Stroessner, & Mackie, 1993; Shavitt, Sanbonmatsu, Smittipatana, & Posavac, 1999; Stangor & Lange, 1994).

Distinctive events capture attention. We would notice if a classmate were to attend a lecture wearing a clown outfit or nothing at all. Because we attend more closely to distinctive events, we are also likely to remember them better, with the result that they may become overrepresented in our memories. This has important implications for the kinds of stereotypes that are commonly associated with minority groups. By definition, minority groups are distinctive to most members of the majority, and so minority group members stand out. Note also that negative behaviors—robbing, assaulting, murdering—are (fortunately) much less common than positive behaviors—lawn mowing, saying thank you, obeying traffic signs—and so negative behaviors are distinctive as well. This means that negative behavior on the part of members of minority groups is doubly distinctive and doubly memorable. And because negative behavior by the majority or positive behavior by the minority is not as memorable, negative actions by the minority are likely to seem more common than they really are. Minority groups are therefore likely to be charged with more problematic behavior than they actually engage in.

An experiment by David Hamilton and Robert Gifford (1976) quite clearly demonstrates the impact of **paired distinctiveness**—that is, the pairing of two distinctive events that stand out even more because they co-occur. Participants were shown a series of thirty-nine slides, each of which described a positive or negative action initiated by a member of "Group A" or "Group B." ("John, a

> "Oppression has no logic—just a self-fulfilling prophecy, justified by a self-perpetuating system."
> —GLORIA STEINEM

**illusory correlation**   An erroneous belief about a connection between events, characteristics, or categories that are not, in fact, related.

**paired distinctiveness**   The pairing of two distinctive events that stand out even more because they co-occur.

member of Group A, visited a sick friend in the hospital." "Bill, a member of Group B, always talks about himself and his problems.") The groups were completely mythical, and so any judgments made about them could not be the result of any preexisting knowledge or experience on the part of the participants. Two-thirds of the actions were attributed to Group A, making A the majority group. Most of the actions attributed to each group were positive, and this was equally true of both groups: nine of thirteen, or 69 percent of the actions attributed to Group B were positive, as were eighteen of twenty-six, or 69 percent of the actions attributed to Group A. There was thus no correlation between group membership and the likelihood of positive or negative behavior.

After viewing the entire series of slides, the participants were shown just the behaviors they had seen earlier—that is, with no names or groups attached—and were asked to indicate the group membership of the person who had performed each one. They were also asked to rate the members of the two groups on a variety of trait scales. Both measures indicated that the participants had formed a distinctiveness-based illusory correlation. They overestimated how often a negative behavior was performed by a member of Group B (the smaller group), and they underestimated how often such a behavior was performed by a member of Group A (the larger group) (see Figure 11.5A). As a result, they also rated members of the larger group more favorably (see Figure 11.5B).

To show that it was paired distinctiveness, rather than something about negative behavior, that produced their results, Hamilton and Gifford showed that an

**Paired Distinctiveness**   The pairing of two distinctive events makes them stand out even more and become associated in our minds. When we see two overweight black men and a thin Japanese man (distinctive person) eating hot dogs in a hot dog eating contest (distinctive event) and learn that the Japanese man won the contest the previous year and will win again this year, we may associate the two and wonder whether the Japanese are particularly fond of hot dogs.

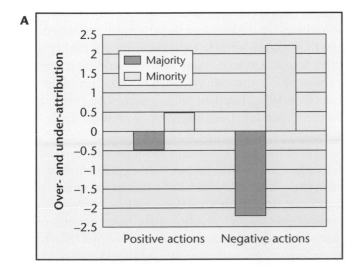

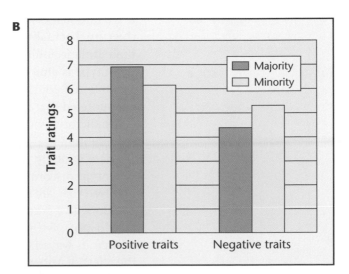

**Figure 11.5 Distinctiveness and Illusory Correlation**   Jointly distinctive events stand out and form the basis of illusory correlations. As a result, (A) members of the minority group were thought to be responsible for more of the negative behaviors than members of the majority group, and (B) members of the minority group were rated more highly on negative traits and less highly on positive traits than members of the majority group. (Source: Hamilton & Gifford, 1976)

illusory correlation was also obtained when it was positive behaviors that were in the minority. Under these circumstances, participants overestimated how often a *positive* behavior was associated with the smaller group.

In thinking about generalizing Hamilton and Gifford's results to the types of full-bodied stereotypes that exist in the everyday world, two important points should be kept in mind. The first is that their results are particularly impressive because they were obtained in a barren context that excluded elements that might accentuate the formation of such illusory correlations in everyday life. In particular, when members of different ethnic groups come together, they are often acutely aware of one another's ethnicity. And when you are especially aware of a person's ethnicity and that person proceeds to do something unusual, ethnicity is often the first thing you think of in trying to account for the action. If you have seen few Polynesians in your life, for instance, but you see a Polynesian curse out the bank teller who is serving your line, you will be sorely tempted to conclude that something about being Polynesian was at least partly responsible for the incident. ("I guess that's just the way they are.") Of course, if the same action were to be displayed by a member of your own ethnic group, you would be unlikely to consider the person's ethnicity as a possible explanation.

But one feature of Hamilton and Gifford's work does not fit real-world stereotyping so well. Their analysis predicts that people should be prone to develop illusory correlations between any two variables that are jointly distinctive. But that does not happen. Being left-handed and being a vegetarian are both relatively rare, but our culture has no stereotype of southpaws being particularly averse to eating meat. Nor are Latinos thought to be particularly likely to be gay, or Asians thought to be particularly likely to snowboard. Thus, although Hamilton and Gifford's provocative analysis captures something real and important about some illusory correlations, it overpredicts. Where their analysis falls short, then, is in specifying *which* jointly distinctive pairings are likely to form the core of commonly held stereotypes, and which are not.

## IMMUNITY TO DISCONFIRMATION

It is a rare stereotype that escapes occasional disconfirmation. Groups known for their intellectual talents nonetheless include a few dolts. Those renowned for their athletic abilities are sure to include a klutz or two. Evidence contradicting a stereotype is almost certain to be encountered, even if the stereotype is largely accurate. Of course, if the stereotype is invalid, evidence of disconfirmation is encountered that much more often. What happens when people encounter such contradictory evidence? Do they abandon their stereotypes or hold them less confidently?

There is surely no single answer to these questions. How people respond to stereotype disconfirmation doubtless varies with factors such as how emotionally involved they are in the stereotype, whether they hold the stereotype in isolation or belong to a group that preaches it, and so on. One thing is clear, however: people do not give up their stereotypes easily. Psychologists have documented numerous ways in which people evaluate apparent disconfirmations that have the effect of undermining their impact. An understanding of these processes provides some insight into one of the most vexing questions about stereotypes—namely, why they so often persist in the face of evidence that would seem to contradict them.

The first thing to note is that no stereotype contains an expectation of perfectly invariant behavior. Groups thought to be dishonest, lazy, or carefree are thought to be dishonest, lazy, or carefree *on average*, or more dishonest, lazy, or carefree than other groups. It is not expected that all of their members behave in those ways all the time. This enables people to remain unmoved by apparent disconfirmations of their stereotypes because anyone who acts at variance with the stereotype is simply walled off into a category of "exceptions." Sexists who believe that women are passive and dependent and should stay home to raise children are likely to subcategorize assertive, independent women who choose not to have children as "militant" or "strident" feminists, thereby leaving their stereotype of women largely intact. Similarly, racists who maintain that blacks are not fit to excel outside of sports and entertainment are unlikely to be much troubled by the likes of, say, Colin Powell, Vernon Jordan, or Condoleeza Rice. To the racist mind, they are merely the "exceptions that prove the rule."

This reiterates the more general truth discussed above: evidence that supports a stereotype is treated differently from evidence that refutes it. Supportive evidence tends to be accepted at face value, whereas contradictory evidence is often critically analyzed and discounted. One way this is done is by attributing behavior consistent with a stereotype to the dispositions of the people involved, and attributing inconsistent behavior to external causes (Crocker, Hannah, & Weber, 1983; Deaux & Emswiller, 1974; Kulik, 1983; Swim & Sanna, 1996; Taylor & Jaggi, 1975). An anti-Semite is likely to dismiss a Jew's acts of philanthropy as due to a desire for social acceptance, but to attribute any pursuit of self-interest as a reflection of some "true" Jewish character. Thus, episodes consistent with a stereotype reinforce its perceived validity; those that are inconsistent with it are deemed insignificant (Pettigrew, 1979).

A more subtle but equally powerful way this is done is by varying how abstractly we encode the actions of people from different groups. Almost any action can be construed at a variety of different levels of abstraction (Vallacher & Wegner, 1987). If you see someone lifting an individual who has fallen, you could describe the action as exactly that—an act of lifting. Alternatively, you could say the person was "helping" the individual. More broadly still, you might see the person as "helpful" or "altruistic." These different levels of abstraction carry different connotations. The more concrete the description, the less it says about the individual involved. Nearly anyone can lift, but not everyone is altruistic. Thus, if people's evaluations are guided by their preexisting stereotypes, we might expect them to describe actions that are consistent with a stereotype in broad terms (thus reinforcing the stereotype), but to describe actions that are inconsistent with it in concrete terms (thus averting a potential challenge to the stereotype). Stereotypes may insulate themselves from disconfirmation, in other words, by influencing the level at which relevant actions are encoded (von Hippel, Sekaquaptewa, & Vargas, 1995).

This prediction was tested in a delightful study that took place during the annual *palio* competition in Ferrara, Italy (Maass, Salvi, Arcuri, & Semin, 1989). The *palio* are horse-racing competitions that have taken place in various Italian towns since the thirteenth century (with a brief interruption only during the time of the Black Plague). The races pit different teams, or *contrade*, against one another and take place in the context of an elaborate festival in which supporters of each *contrada* root for their team. In the weeks leading up to the *palio*, feelings of intergroup competition run high.

Before one such *palio* competition, the supporters of two *contrade*, San Giorgio and San Giacomo, were recruited to participate in an experiment. Each partici-

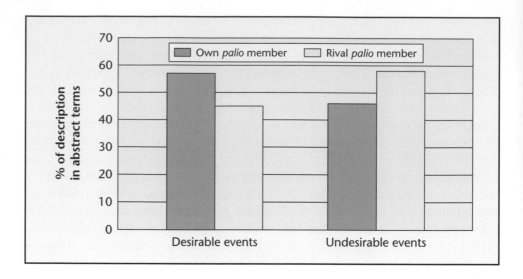

**Figure 11.6 Stereotypes and the Encoding of Behavior** Events that are consistent with preexisting stereotypes are encoded at a broader, and therefore more meaningful, level of abstraction than events that are inconsistent with preexisting stereotypes. The figure depicts the percentage of abstract versus concrete terms used to describe desirable and undesirable actions by members of the ingroup and outgroup. Abstract terms consist of state verbs or trait terms (for example, *hates, hateful*), and concrete terms consist of descriptive and interpretative action verbs (for example, *hits, hurts*). Abstract terms are used more to describe stereotype-consistent actions, and concrete terms are used more to describe stereotype-inconsistent actions. (Source: Maass, Salvi, Arcuri, & Semin, 1989)

pant was shown a number of sketches depicting a member of their own *contrada* or of the rival *contrada* engaged in an action. The *contrada* membership of the person depicted was established simply by matching the color of the protagonist's shirt with that of the relevant *contrada*. Some of the sketches portrayed desirable actions (for example, helping someone), and some portrayed undesirable actions (for example, littering). After inspecting each sketch, the participants were simply asked to describe what it depicted, and their responses were scored for level of abstraction.

The results revealed a clear bias (see Figure 11.6). Actions that were consistent with a participant's preexisting orientation (that is, positive actions by a member of one's own *contrada*; negative actions by a member of the rival *contrada*) were described at a more abstract level than actions at variance with a participant's preexisting orientation (that is, negative actions by a member of one's own *contrada*; positive actions by a member of the rival *contrada*). This asymmetry feeds the tendency to perceive the ingroup in a favorable light. Encoding events that are inconsistent with one's predilections at a concrete level renders them less consequential; encoding those that fit one's predilections at an abstract level lends them greater import. "Cheating" someone is more significant than "taking" something from them, "helping" someone is more significant than "lifting" them, and "showing concern" about someone is more significant than "visiting" them.

## AUTOMATIC AND CONTROLLED PROCESSING

Some of the cognitive processes that give rise to stereotyping and prejudice are rather deliberate, elaborate, and (literally, at any rate) "thoughtful." This is likely to be the case, for example, when people observe a member of a stigmatized group behave in a counter-stereotypic fashion and quickly invent a subcategory of, say, "professional" African Americans, or "environmental" lawyers that preserves their preexisting stereotype (Devine & Baker, 1991; Kunda & Oleson, 1995; Weber & Crocker, 1983). Other cognitive processes, in contrast, give rise to stereotyping and prejudice rapidly and automatically, without much conscious attention and elaboration. This is likely to be the case, for example, for distinctiveness-based illusory correlations and the outgroup homogeneity effect.

In the past fifteen years, researchers have explored the interplay between automatic and controlled processes and how together they give rise to the ways in which people think about and react to members of different groups (Bodenhausen, Macrae, & Sherman, 1999; Devine & Monteith, 1999). This research has shown that our reactions to different groups of people are to a surprising degree guided by quick and automatic mental processes that we can override, but not eliminate. This research has also highlighted the common rift that exists between our immediate, reflexive reactions to outgroup members and our more reflective responses.

Patricia Devine (1989b) helped spark the examination of the joint operation of automatic and controlled processes by investigating the schism that exists for many people between their knowledge of racial stereotypes and their own personal beliefs and attitudes toward those same groups. More specifically, Devine sought to demonstrate that what separates prejudiced and non-prejudiced people is not their knowledge of derogatory stereotypes, but whether or not they resist the stereotypes. To do so, she relied on the distinction between **automatic processes**, which we do not consciously control (like the use of binocular disparity to judge distance), and **controlled processes**, which, as the name suggests, we direct more consciously. The activation of stereotypes is typically automatically controlled, and thus stereotypes can be triggered even if one does not want them to be. Even a non-prejudiced person will, under the right circumstances, access an association between Muslims and fanaticism, blacks and criminality, and WASPs and emotional repression, because those associations—valid or not—are present in our culture. Whereas a bigot will endorse or employ such stereotypes, a non-prejudiced person will employ more controlled cognitive processes to suppress them—or at least try to.

> **automatic processes** Processes that occur outside of our awareness, without conscious control.
>
> **controlled processes** Processes that occur with conscious direction and deliberate thought.

To test these ideas, Devine selected groups of high- and low-prejudiced participants on the basis of their scores on the Modern Racism Scale (McConahay, Hardee, & Batts, 1981). To show that these two groups do not differ in their automatic processing of stereotypic information, she presented to each participant a set of words, one at a time, so briefly that they could not be consciously identified. She showed some of the participants neutral words (*number, animal, remember*), and other participants words stereotypically associated with blacks (*welfare, jazz, busing*). Devine hypothesized that although the stereotypic words were presented too briefly to be consciously recognized, they would nonetheless prime the participants' stereotypes of blacks. To find out if this indeed happened, she next presented the participants with a written description of an individual who acted in an ambiguously hostile manner (this description highlighted a trait—hostility—characteristic of the African-American stereotype). In one incident, for example, the target individual refused to pay his rent until his apartment was repaired. Was he being needlessly belligerent or appropriately assertive? The results indicated that he was seen as more hostile—and more negative overall—by participants who had earlier been primed by words designed to activate their stereotypes of blacks (words, it is important to note, that were not otherwise connected to the concept of hostility). Most important, this was equally true of prejudiced and non-prejudiced participants. Because the stimulus words unconsciously activated their stereotypes, the non-prejudiced participants were caught off guard and were unable to suppress the automatic processing of stereotypical information.

To demonstrate that prejudiced and non-prejudiced individuals differ primarily in their *controlled* cognitive processes, Devine next asked her participants to list characteristics of black Americans. As predicted, the two groups differed substantially in the output of this consciously controlled procedure: prejudiced participants listed many more pejorative characteristics stereotypically associated with blacks than did non-prejudiced participants. Thus, even though both prejudiced and non-prejudiced individuals have stored in their minds the same negative stereotypes of black Americans (as shown in part 1 of Devine's study), prejudiced individuals believe them, and are willing to voice these beliefs, whereas non-prejudiced individuals reject and consciously suppress them (as shown in part 2).

Subsequent investigations have qualified one element of Devine's research: automatic, negative associations to members of various stigmatized groups appear to be more easily activated among prejudiced individuals than among non-prejudiced individuals (Fazio, Jackson, Dunton, & Williams, 1995; Lepore & Brown, 1997; Wittenbrink, Judd, & Park, 1997). Nevertheless, even among non-prejudiced individuals, there is often a rift between the beliefs and sentiments elicited by automatic processes and those elicited by more controlled processes. This was shown in a recent study that examined the areas of the brain that were activated when white participants were shown pictures of black faces and white faces (Cunningham et al., 2004). When shown the faces for only 30 milliseconds, the participants exhibited greater activation in the amygdala (which registers and responds to the emotional implications of a stimulus) after exposure to black than to white faces. Furthermore, the amount of amygdala activation at this point was related to participants' implicit prejudice as measured by the IAT. But when the faces were shown for 525 milliseconds, there was no difference in amygdala activation when exposed to black versus white faces, suggesting that these participants—all of whom had expressed a strong desire to avoid prejudice—initially had an automatic response to black versus white faces that they then exerted effort to control. Indeed, at 525 milliseconds, black faces caused more activity in the prefrontal cortex—an area of the brain associated with cognitive and behavioral regulation—than did white faces.

The implications of the rift between people's automatic and controlled reactions to members of a different racial group were further investigated in a study by Dovidio, Kawakami, and Gaertner (2002). The researchers first used a priming procedure like that described on pp. 435–436 to assess white participants' implicit prejudice toward blacks and also measured their explicit attitudes with the Attitudes toward Blacks Scale (Brigham, 1993). They then had the participants engage in two three-minute conversations, one with a white student and one with a black student. They videotaped and later scored these conversations, once with the sound removed and once with all channels included, for the amount of friendliness exhibited by the participant.

Dovidio and colleagues predicted that the explicit measure of prejudice would predict ratings of the participants' friendliness made from the full videotape because those ratings would be primarily determined by what participants said, and people can readily control what they say. But they expected that the implicit measure of prejudice would predict participants' nonverbal friendliness—that is, the ratings of participants' friendliness made from the video channel only—because nonverbal behavior is harder to control. And that is just what they found. Participants' scores on the Attitudes toward Blacks Scale predicted how differentially friendly they were to the white and black students as assessed from the full videotape. These scores were also related to how differentially friendly the participants' themselves thought they were. But it was their scores on the implicit measure of prejudice (their reaction times) that predicted how differentially friendly they were to the white and black students as assessed from the video-only ratings. These scores were also related to how friendly their conversation partners thought they had been. Explicit measures of prejudice, it seems, can predict controlled behavior, but implicit measures may do a better job of predicting automatic behavior.

Another study of people's automatic reactions to members of stigmatized groups has chilling implications for everyday life. Payne (2001) had participants decide as quickly as possible whether an object depicted in a photo was either a handgun or a hand tool (for example, pliers). Each photograph was immediately preceded by a picture of either an African-American or a white face. Payne found that the (white) participants were faster to identify a weapon as a weapon when it was preceded by an African-American face and faster to identify a hand tool as a hand tool when it was preceded by a white face (see also Payne, Lambert, & Jacoby, 2002).

Is this pattern the result of automatic prejudice toward African Americans on the part of white participants? That is, is the recognition of handguns facilitated by African-American faces because both handguns and African Americans are evaluated negatively by white participants? Or, is this effect due to automatic stereotyping? That is, is the facilitation caused by a stereotypic association between handguns and African Americans that exerts its effect even among non-prejudiced individuals?

The good news (limited good news, we admit, but good news nonetheless) is that it appears to be the latter. Charles Judd, Irene Blair, and Kristine Chapleau (2004) replicated Payne's experiment with four types of target stimuli that varied in whether they were viewed positively or negatively and whether they were stereotypically associated with African Americans. Specifically, the stimuli associated with African Americans consisted of pictures of handguns (negative) and sports equipment (positive), and the stimuli not associated with African Americans consisted of pictures of insects (negative) and fruit (positive). Judd and his colleagues found that African-American faces facilitated the recognition of both positive and negative stereotypic items (handguns and sports equipment), but not the non-stereotypic items (insects and fruits), regardless of whether they were positive or negative.

A similar conclusion emerges from a study with even more chilling implications for the everyday lives of African Americans. This research was inspired by the tragic death of Amadou Diallo, a black African immigrant who in 1999 was riddled with nineteen bullets by police officers who said afterwards that they thought, incorrectly, that he was reaching for a gun. In this study, participants watched a video game in which, at unpredictable moments, a target individual—sometimes white, sometimes African American—popped up out of nowhere holding either a gun or some other object (Correll, Park, Judd, & Wittenbrink, 2002). Participants were instructed to "shoot" if the target individual was holding a gun and to press a different response key if he was not. Participants were instructed to respond as quickly as possible, which guaranteed there would be occasional mistakes. The pattern of mistakes is shown in Figure 11.7, and it is clear that participants treated African-American and white targets differently. They made both types of mistakes—shooting an unarmed target and not shooting an armed target—equally often when the target individual was white. But for African-American targets, they were much more likely to make the mistake of shooting if the target was unarmed than failing to shoot if the target was armed.

**Automatic Reactions and Stereotyping** White police officers in New York City attempted to question Amadou Diallo, a black West African immigrant who had gone outside his apartment building to get some air and who seemed to fit the description of the serial rapist they were looking for. Diallo ran up the steps of his building and then reached inside his jacket for what police believed was a gun but was actually his wallet. Reacting out of fear that Diallo was about to start firing a weapon, the four police officers fired forty-one shots, striking the innocent Diallo nineteen times and killing him.

**Figure 11.7 Automatic Stereotyping** Average number of mistakes (per twenty trials) made when images of an armed or unarmed individual suddenly appeared on the screen and participants had to respond as quickly as possible by pressing one button to "shoot" an armed individual and pressing another button if the individual was unarmed. A mistake on an armed trial involved failing to shoot when one should have, and a mistake on an unarmed trial involved shooting when one should not have. (Source: Correll, Park, Judd, & Wittenbrink, 2002)

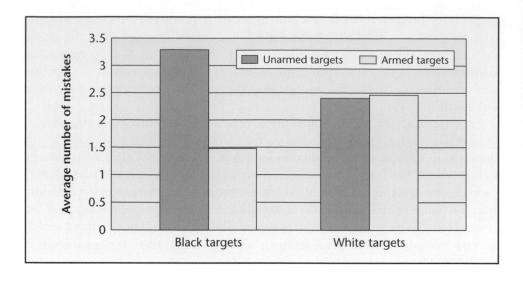

The same effect, it is important to note, was obtained in a follow-up experiment with African-American participants.

## EVALUATING THE COGNITIVE PERSPECTIVE

Critics of the cognitive perspective have said that although the approach has made some strides in advancing our knowledge of intergroup conflict, the recent emphasis on reaction-time methods and brief, reflexive phenomena may cause us to lose sight of the causes of the truly disturbing manifestations of prejudice and discrimination that are all-too-common elements of real-world experience. Indeed, when ethnic groups in Indonesia, the Balkans, Africa, the former Soviet Union, and the Middle East are bent on subjugating or exterminating one another, and when police officers in countries the world over brutalize minorities with alarming frequency, reaction-time assessments of subtle prejudices can seem rather removed from the heart of the matter. Critics have also noted that many of the effects documented in this literature are very short-lived. Seeing a person who belongs to a particular ethnic group may automatically activate one's stereotypical associations to that group, but the activation is typically brief. One team of investigators reported that they could find no trace of stereotype activation after a mere ten minutes of interaction with a member of a minority group (Kunda, Davies, Adams, & Spencer, 2002).

As important as it is to keep these concerns in mind, it also important to note that a great deal of damage can be done on the basis of people's initial, quick responses, as the shooting studies we just reviewed make so abundantly clear. It is surely no consolation to Amadou Diallo's family to know that the cognitive operations that made the police officers think Diallo was reaching for a gun rather than a wallet would shortly have been overridden by more level-headed processes. It is also important to note that, however brief these initial, automatic processes might be, they can get the ball rolling in an unfortunate direction. They can be the seeds from which deeper sorts of prejudice and discrimination are sown.

History has taught us that it is alarmingly easy for people to assign some individuals—sometimes reflexively, sometimes with considerable thought—to a category that earns them all the rights and compassion that every human being deserves, and other individuals to a category that deprives them of those rights

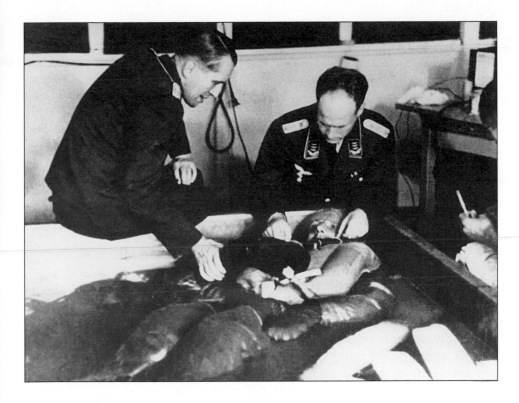

**Dehumanizing a Victim**   By assigning their victims to a category that stripped them of their humanity, Nazi officials and doctors tortured and killed without compunction victims like this man immersed in freezing water.

and compassion—indeed, that deprives them of their humanity. Consider the picture shown on this page. The Nazi officials are but inches away from the individual immersed in freezing water, a condition that brings with it unspeakable agony. Being that close to genuine human suffering—when one is not under attack oneself—typically elicits a host of emotions that lead to helping the victim (or, at the very least, to fleeing the situation to avoid the unpleasantness of another's pain).

But there is no emotion on the part of the Nazi officials. They are inches away in Euclidean space, but a universe apart in psychological space. A cognitive wall separates them from their unfortunate subject. They have assigned their victim to a cognitive category that strips him of his humanity—and therefore his suffering does not call forth the usual suite of compassionate emotions.

Note that it is a cognitive act that is decisive here. It is a thought—a categorization—that strips some groups of their full humanity and makes possible this kind of detached barbarity against them. The cognitive approach has made some progress in understanding the processes by which such categorizations are made. The ultimate verdict on this approach will rest on whatever further progress is made toward this understanding, and whether that understanding yields concrete steps to overcome the processes by which members of some groups come to be seen as something other than people with dreams, aspirations, sweethearts, and children.

**LOOKING BACK,** we have seen that stereotypes help us to make sense of the world and to process information efficiently, freeing us to use cognitive resources for other work. Nonetheless, they can also cause us to make many errors, such as seeing outgroup members as more homogeneous than they actually are. They can also lead to self-fulfilling prophecies, in which our expectations of what a group of people is like lead us to behave in ways that elicit behaviors consistent with our expectations. This can make stereotypes resistant to disconfirmation, as does the tendency to explain away information that violates a stereotype or to subcategorize those who don't fit the stereotype. Stereotypes can reflect both automatic and controlled processing, and even people who do not express prejudicial views may reflexively respond to individuals on the basis of stereotypes and prejudices of which they are unaware. We will next consider some of the consequences of knowing that other people hold stereotypes about your group.

## BEING A MEMBER OF A STIGMATIZED GROUP

To this point, the chapter has been concerned with the perpetrators of prejudice (who, it should be abundantly clear by now, can include all of us). What about the victims of prejudice? They, of course, pay an obvious and unfair price in terms of numerous indicators of material and psychological well-being—health, wealth, employment prospects, and longevity among them. But members of stereotyped or stigmatized groups are also typically aware of the stereotypes that others hold about them, and this awareness also can have negative effects on them (Crocker, Major, & Steele, 1998; Herek, 1998; Jones et al., 1984). Social psychologists have focused on two burdens that come with knowing that others may be prejudiced against one's group: attributional ambiguity and stereotype threat.

### ATTRIBUTIONAL AMBIGUITY

As we saw in Chapter 9, people want to know the causes of events around them in order to achieve a sense that they live in an ordered, predictable world. But this sense is threatened for members of stigmatized groups because they cannot tell whether many of their experiences have the same origins as those of everyone else or whether they are the result of prejudice. "Did my officemate get the promotion instead of me because I'm so overweight?" "Would the state trooper have pulled me over if I were white?" "Did I get that fellowship because I'm Latino?"

These sorts of questions may be particularly vexing with respect to negative outcomes, but they are also disconcerting in the context of positive outcomes. When one must wonder whether an accomplishment is the product of, say, an affirmative-action policy, one cannot completely "own" it and reap the full measure of pride and accomplishment it would ordinarily afford.

In one study that examined this sort of attributional predicament, African-American and white students received flattering or unflattering feedback from a white student in an adjacent room (Crocker, Voelkl, Testa, & Major, 1991). Half the participants were led to believe that this other student could see them through a one-way mirror, and half were led to believe they could not be seen (because a blind covered the mirror). Whether or not they could be seen had no effect on how white students reacted to the feedback. But it did affect how black students reacted. When black students thought the other person could not see them—and therefore didn't know their race—their self-esteem went down from the unflattering feedback and was boosted by the positive feedback. When they thought the other person could see them, in contrast, their self-esteem was not injured by the bad news, nor was it enhanced by the good news. Thus, this study indicates that members of stigmatized groups quite literally live in a less certain world, not knowing whether to attribute positive feedback to their own skill or to others' condescension nor whether to attribute negative feedback to their own error or to others' prejudice.

## STEREOTYPE THREAT

An extensive program of research initiated by Claude Steele and his colleagues speaks dramatically to a second difficulty confronting members of stigmatized groups. In particular, this research has shown that the performance of members of stigmatized groups can be impaired by **stereotype threat**—that is, the fear that one will confirm the stereotypes that others have regarding some salient group of which one is a member. In one study, Steven Spencer, Steele, and Diane Quinn (1999) looked at the effect on women's math test scores of making salient the stereotype that women do not perform well in mathematics. In one condition, participants were told there was no gender difference on a particular test they were about to take. Other participants were told that there was a gender difference in favor of men. As can be seen in Figure 11.8, men and women performed equivalently when told there was no gender difference on the test, but women performed worse than men when they were told that there was a gender difference.

It's not necessary to be so blatant in the manipulation of stereotype threat in order to have an effect. Michael Inzlicht and Talia Ben-Zeev (2000) had university women take a math test either in the company of two other women or two men. Those who took the test with other women got 70 percent of the problems right on average. Those who took the test with men got 55 percent right on average.

Steele and Joshua Aronson (1995) examined the sensitivity to stereotype threat on the part of African-American students. Playing on the stereotype that questions blacks' intellectual ability, they gave black and white Stanford University students a difficult verbal test taken from the Graduate Record Exam. Half of the students were led to believe that the test was capable of measuring their intellectual ability, and half were told that the investigators were in the early stages of

> **stereotype threat**  The fear that one will confirm the stereotypes that others have regarding some salient group of which one is a member.

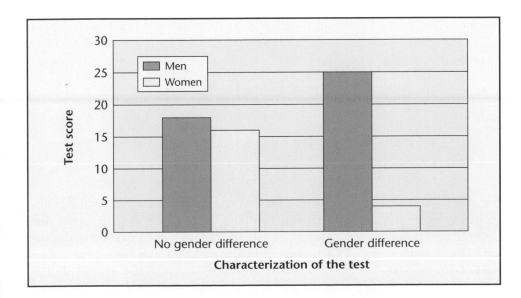

**Figure 11.8 Stereotype Threat and Performance**   Math test performance by men and women when the test is described as one that yields gender differences (and hence arouses stereotype threat among women) or is described as one that does not yield gender differences. (Source: Spencer, Steele, & Quinn, 1999)

trying to develop the test and that nothing could be learned about actual intellectual ability from their scores. This manipulation had no effect on the performance of white students. African-American students did as well as white students when they thought it was the test that was being tested, but they performed much worse than white students when they thought their intellectual ability was being tested. Moreover, a blatant manipulation was not required to produce a significant effect on the performance of African Americans. It was enough simply to have them indicate their race at the top of the page to cause their performance to be worse than in a control condition in which they did not indicate their race (Steele & Aronson, 1995).

It seems that no one is safe from stereotype threat. Joshua Aronson and his colleagues (1999) showed that the math performance of white males deteriorated when they were reminded of Asian proficiency in math. And in a particularly clever experiment, Jeff Stone and his colleagues had college students perform a laboratory golf task that was described as a measure of "natural athletic ability," "sports intelligence," or "sports psychology" (Stone, Lynch, Sjomeling, & Darley, 1999). White and black students performed equally well in the "sports psychology" condition. But black students performed significantly worse when it was described as a test of "sports intelligence," and white students performed worse when it was described as a test of "natural athletic ability."

Although everyone is vulnerable by dint of group membership to some type of stereotype threat, Steele (1997) maintains that the vulnerability of African Americans has particular potential for damage. Stereotype threat can result in poorer overall academic performance, which undermines confidence, rendering the individual still more susceptible to stereotype threat. This vicious cycle can result in "disidentification" from academic pursuits, as students who feel the threat most acutely opt out of academics altogether and identify other areas in which to invest their talent and energy and from which to derive their self-esteem.

**LOOKING BACK,** we have seen how victims of stereotyping can suffer attributional ambiguity, not knowing whether performance feedback is genuine or based on their group membership. We also discussed how they can suffer from stereotype threat, performing worse because they are afraid of affirming some stereotype that exists about their group.

# SUMMARY

1. *Stereotypes* are generalizations about groups that are often applied to individual group members. *Prejudice* involves a negative attitude and emotional response to members of a group. *Discrimination* involves negative behavior toward an individual because of the person's membership in a group.

2. Blatant, explicit racism in much of the world is now relatively rare. But more subtle *modern racism* does exist, whereby people may hold overtly egalitarian attitudes and values while at the same time unconsciously having negative attitudes and exhibiting more subtle forms of prejudice toward members of

certain groups. *Benevolent racism and sexism* consist of attitudes the individual thinks of as favorable toward a group but that have the effect of supporting traditional, subservient roles for members of oppressed groups.

3. In recent years, there have been successful efforts to measure people's true attitudes with measures that are not easy to fake. One of these is the *implicit association test,* which compares reaction times when grouping outgroup pictures (or words) and positive items together, with reaction times when grouping outgroup pictures (or words) and negative items together. Another implicit measure involves *priming* with a picture of a member of some group. If the prime increases the time it takes to recognize subsequently presented positive words, and decreases the time it takes to recognize subsequently presented negative words, this is an indication of prejudice toward the group.

4. We discussed three different approaches to prejudice and discrimination: the economic perspective, the motivational perspective, and the cognitive perspective.

5. One version of the *economic perspective* on prejudice and discrimination is *realistic group conflict theory,* which reflects the fact that groups are sometimes in competition for scarce resources and that this can lead to prejudice and discrimination. The classic Robbers Cave experiment put two groups of boys in competition at a camp. Soon the boys were expressing open hostility toward one another. When the boys were brought together in noncompetitive situations where they had to cooperate to achieve *superordinate goals*—that is, goals that could only be achieved when the two groups worked together—the hostility dissipated.

6. The *motivational perspective* on prejudice and discrimination reflects the sad fact that sometimes poor relations between groups occur simply because there *are* two groups and a we/they opposition results. This occurs even in the *minimal group paradigm,* wherein people find out they are members of one of two groups that have been defined in a trivial and arbitrary way. They will favor members of their own group over members of the other group, even when it actually costs their group something to "beat" the opposition.

7. *Social identity theory* attempts to explain ingroup favoritism, maintaining that self-esteem is derived from group membership and group success.

8. *Frustration-aggression theory* accounts for some of the most dangerous behavior toward outgroups. When people are frustrated in their attempt to reach some goal—for example, the goal of economic prosperity—they often lash out at less powerful individuals or groups. Challenges to a person's self-esteem can have similar effects, and experiments have shown that people express more antagonism toward outgroup members when they have suffered a blow to their self-esteem.

9. The *cognitive perspective* on prejudice and discrimination focuses on stereotypes, which are a form of categorization. People rely on them all the time, but especially when they are tired or overloaded.

10. Several construal processes lead to inaccurate stereotypes. Because we know our own groups best, we tend to assume that outgroups are more *homogeneous* than ours are, leading to the *outgroup homogeneity effect*. We also often engage in *biased information processing*, seeing those aspects of other groups that confirm our stereotypes and failing to see facts that are inconsistent with them. Moreover, we often unknowingly create *self-fulfilling prophecies*—applying stereotypes to members of outgroups and then behaving toward them in such a way as to bring out the very behaviors that fit our stereotypes.

11. Distinctive groups (because they are in the minority) are often associated with distinctive (because they are rare) behaviors. This sort of *paired distinctiveness* results in our attributing illusory properties to such groups.

12. Encountering contradictory evidence about groups may not change our ideas about them because we treat the evidence as if it were merely an exception that proves the rule. We tend to code favorable evidence about ingroup members at high levels of generality and the same sort of evidence about outgroup members at low levels of generality. The converse is true for unfavorable evidence. Moreover, behavior consistent with a stereotype is often attributed to the dispositions of the group members, whereas behavior that is inconsistent with a stereotype is often attributed to the situation.

13. We sometimes respond to outgroup members reflexively, relying on *automatic processes* wherein prejudice is unleashed outside of our awareness. Sometimes these automatic negative reactions can be corrected by conscious, *controlled processes*.

14. Members of stigmatized groups suffer not just from prejudice and discrimination but also from *attribu-*

*tional ambiguity*. They have to ask whether others' negative or positive behavior toward them is due to prejudice or to some factor having nothing to do with their group membership.

15. The performance of members of stigmatized groups can also be impaired by *stereotype threat*—that is, the fear that one will confirm the stereotypes that others have regarding some salient group of which one is a member.

## CRITICAL THINKING ABOUT BASIC PRINCIPLES

1. Anthony Greenwald and Mazarin Banaji have made the implicit association test (IAT) available on the Web for anyone to try—and you should try it. It's illuminating. Web versions of the IAT are available to assess your implicit prejudice toward blacks and whites, young and old, men and women, and even George W. Bush versus Franklin Delano Roosevelt! Go to https://implicit.harvard.edu/implicit/

2. It has been said (in this chapter, in fact) that race relations have progressed more smoothly in the U.S. military than on college campuses, and that this pattern fits with the findings of the Robbers Cave experiment. In what other areas might we expect (and you might have observed) race relations to progress rather smoothly? Do these examples also fit with the lessons of the Robbers Cave study? In what other areas might we expect (and you might have observed) race relations to progress less smoothly?

3. Close your eyes and try to picture in detail an aggressive act on the part of a construction worker. Briefly write down what you imagined. Now close your eyes and try to picture an aggressive act on the part of a housewife. Write down that as well. Are there any differences between the two episodes you imagined? If so, why are they different, and does this have anything to say about your stereotypes of construction workers and housewives?

## KEY TERMS

automatic processes (p. 461)
basking in reflected glory (p. 446)
controlled processes (p. 461)
discrimination (p. 432)
ethnocentrism (p. 438)
frustration-aggression theory (p. 446)
illusory correlation (p. 456)

implicit association test (p. 435)
minimal group paradigm (p. 443)
modern racism (p. 433)
outgroup homogeneity effect (p. 454)
paired distinctiveness (p. 456)
prejudice (p. 432)
priming (p. 436)

realistic group conflict theory (p. 437)
self-fulfilling prophecy (p. 455)
social identity theory (p. 445)
stereotypes (p. 432)
stereotype threat (p. 467)
superordinate goals (p. 440)

## FURTHER READING

Allport, G. (1954). *The nature of prejudice*. Reading, MA: Addison-Wesley.

Cose, E. (1993). *The rage of a privileged class*. New York: HarperCollins.

Herek, G. M. (1998). *Stigma and sexual orientation: Understanding prejudice against lesbians, gay men, and bisexuals*. Thousand Oaks, CA: Sage Publications.

Sidanius, J., & Pratto, F. (1999). *Social dominance: An intergroup theory of social hierarchy and oppression*. New York: Cambridge University Press.

Vallacher, R. R., & Wegner, D. (1985). *A theory of action identification*. Mahwah, NJ: Lawrence Erlbaum Associates.

# PART FOUR

# Social Sentiments

THE PREVIOUS SECTION EXAMINED THE IMPORTANT ROLE OF COGNItion in everyday social behavior. But we are not purely cognitive creatures. Much of our behavior is inspired and guided by moral sentiments and strong passions, and this group of chapters deals with the emotional side of everyday life. In Chapter 12, we discuss what emotions are and the important role they play in regulating social behavior. In Chapter 13, we explore the extremes to which emotions and sentiments can take us, examining our altruistic sentiments and our impulses to help others, as well as the determinants of aggression and our impulses to hurt others. In Chapter 14, we discuss our moral sentiments and our assessments of right and wrong, the determinants of our sense of justice and injustice, and the thoughts, feelings, and social structures that can bring about cooperation.

# Chapter Outline

# Emotion

Eadweard Muybridge was born in England in 1830, and in 1852 he emigrated to San Francisco, California, where he ran a successful bookshop. On July 2, 1860, Muybridge boarded a stagecoach bound for St. Louis, Missouri, where he was to catch a train and then make his way to Europe in search of rare books. In northeastern Texas, the driver of the stagecoach lost control of the horses, and the coach careened down a mountainside and crashed. Muybridge was thrown headfirst into a tree. Miraculously, he survived, and made the trip to England, where he spent six years recuperating and became a photographer.

Muybridge returned to California in 1866, but he was not the same man. He was prone to emotional outbursts and inappropriate, uncensored behavior. His photography was eery and had an obsessive quality. He took many photos of himself, naked, brow furrowed, glaring into the camera. In 1872, he married Flora Shallcross Stone, twenty-one years his junior. While Muybridge was away on assignment, Flora had an affair with the dashing Major Harry Larkyns, and soon produced a baby boy, more the source of uneasy suspicion than joy for Muybridge. Muybridge found a photo of the baby, with the inscription "Little Harry." When the baby's nurse confirmed Muybridge's suspicions—that Harry Larkyns was actually the father of his baby—Muybridge became distraught and exhibited uncontrolled agitation.

Muybridge took a train to Calistoga in Napa Valley, California, where Larkyns was working on a ranch. Finding Larkyns with a group of friends, Muybridge stated in matter-of-fact fashion: "Good evening, Major, my name is Muybridge, and here is the answer to the letter you sent my wife," at which time he raised his Smith & Wesson six-shooter, shot, and killed Larkyns.

At Muybridge's highly publicized trial, several witnesses spoke of the changes the stagecoach accident had produced in Muybridge. After the accident, he seemed like a different man—eccentric, remote, and cold. Present-day researchers speculate that Muybridge had damaged his orbitofrontal cortex, a part of the frontal lobes that lies behind the eyes and is richly connected to other areas of the brain that are involved in emotion, including the amygdala (see Chapter 7). Injury to this region can result in loss of emotional and social control due to a lack of self-censorship. The jury rejected the insanity plea but nonetheless acquitted Muybridge on the grounds of "justifiable homicide." Although emotionally damaged by the accident, Muybridge continued to excel as a photographer—perhaps as a result of the disinhibition of self-censorship produced by the accident—and to pioneer techniques in motion photography.

Our emotions may sometimes seem disruptive, maladaptive, and the source of our most unsettling difficulties, as shown by the tragic life of Eadweard Muybridge. Yet, as can also be seen from Muybridge's emotional deficits, emotions are crucial to our social functioning. In this chapter, we will seek answers to five enduring questions about emotions: To what extent are emotions universal, and to what extent do they vary across cultures? How much of emotion is in the mind, and how much in the body? What are the unconscious and conscious

**Eadweard Muybridge** (A) After suffering an accident that may have injured his orbitofrontal cortex, Eadweard Muybridge was prone to emotional outbursts and inappropriate behavior. (B) Muybridge (also known as Helios) was an innovative photographer who took a series of photographs of Yosemite, including this photo of himself perched on a thin rock ledge 2,000 feet above the river below.

construal processes that give rise to emotion? Are emotions rational? And finally: What is happiness? Before we tackle these questions, let's first define emotion, which as we'll see, is no simple task.

# CHARACTERIZING EMOTION

In 1884, William James asked in a well-known essay: "What is an emotion?" What are the butterflies in the stomach, the light-headedness, the dry cotton mouth, that beset you just before a public presentation? What is the dizzying warmth that overtakes you when longing for a romantic partner? What happens when a stranger's anonymous kindness moves you to tears? And more generally, how do emotions, such as anger or sadness, differ from moods, such as feeling irritated or blue?

## DEFINING EMOTION

A common understanding of emotion is found in Merriam-Webster's Collegiate Dictionary's definition: an **emotion** is "the affective aspect of consciousness . . . a state of feeling." We will expand on this definition, treating emotions as brief, adaptive responses, involving physiological and cognitive reactions to objects, people, or situations. Starting from this definition, researchers agree upon several things. First, emotions are *brief*. Facial expressions of emotion typically last between one and five seconds (Ekman, 1992a). The autonomic responses that accompany emotion—the elevated heart rate and changes in breathing, for example—last dozens of seconds. When we recall emotional experiences, we often recall experiences that last a few minutes. In contrast, the moods that we experience—for example, when we feel irritable or blue—last for hours and even days.

Emotions are *specific*. We feel emotions about specific people and events. Philosophers call the focus of an emotional experience its "intentional object," and here again there is a difference between emotions and moods. When you are angry, you have a very clear sense of what you are angry about (for example, your roommate's snoring or the embarrassing story your dad told about your first date). In contrast, when you are in an irritable mood, it is not so obvious why you feel as you do, and the intentional object may not be clear (although it might be all too clear to other people!).

Most typically, emotions help individuals with their *goals*. Emotions motivate behaviors to achieve certain objectives (Frijda & Mesquita, 1994; Keltner & Gross, 1999; Oatley & Jenkins, 1992; Parrott, 2001). Anger motivates people to redress injustice. Fear prompts protective action or flight. Not every episode of emotion, we hasten to note, is beneficial. Some of our experiences of anger, for example, produce maladaptive outcomes (for example, throwing a piece of toast on the floor in protest; making sarcastic comments to a traffic cop). But, in general, emotions motivate goal-directed behavior that most typically helps the individual navigate the social environment.

Finally, most emotions are profoundly *social*. Emotions promote and preserve adaptive functioning within momentary social interactions (DeSteno & Salovey, 1996; Frijda & Mesquita, 1994; Keltner & Haidt, 1999; McCullough, Kilpatrick, Emmons, & Larson, 2001; Salovey & Rodin, 1989; Salovey & Rothman, 1991). To take one example, many emotions are critical to the formation and maintenance

> **emotions** Brief psychological and physiological responses that are subjectively experienced as feelings and that prepare a person for action.

of friendships (Nesse, 1990; Trivers, 1971). Gratitude rewards others for their cooperative actions. Love motivates us to provide rewards to others. Anger punishes those who have violated the rules governing friendship—namely, to be cooperative and kind. When we violate the rules of a bond, guilt motivates us to make amends. Let's now consider in greater depth the different components of emotion.

## THE COMPONENTS OF EMOTION

Part of the difficulty in defining emotions is that they have many components (Lang, Greenwald, Bradley, & Hamm, 1993; Levenson, 1999). First of all, emotions involve physiological responses, which William James argued were the basis of the experience of emotion (see p. 487). Present-day researchers are studying how emotions involve different central nervous system processes (Davidson, Pizzagalli, Nitzschke, & Kalin, 2003), with recent studies beginning to reveal which brain regions and neurotransmitters are involved in different emotions. For example, as we know from Chapter 7, the amygdala plays a central role in our evaluative reactions. We have already seen how probable damage to the orbitofrontal cortex affected Eadweard Muybridge's emotional reactions, but we will also discuss how this region may be involved in our experience of pleasure, and how it may affect the emotional reactions that guide our judgments.

Emotions are also associated with changes in the **autonomic nervous system (ANS)**, which includes glands, organs, muscles, arteries, and veins throughout the body that are controlled by nerve cells originating in the spinal cord (see Figure 12.1).

The sympathetic autonomic nervous system (SANS) prepares the body for action—for example, during emergencies, when we engage in fight or flight responses. The SANS increases heart rate, blood pressure, and cardiac output, dilates the bronchioles and pupils, increases sweating (which cools the body and enables grasping behavior), constricts blood vessels supplying the skin (thus directing blood flow to large muscle groups), and inhibits digestive and sexual responses. The parasympathetic autonomic nervous system (PANS) restores the body's resources by decreasing heart rate and blood pressure, constricting the bronchioles and pupils, and increasing digestive processes. Later we will discuss an intense debate that concerns whether different emotions are associated with specific ANS responses (see pp. 490–492).

Emotions also involve a variety of cognitive processes. We use language to label our emotions. What we think is happening can have a strong effect on what emotion we are experiencing—from the sadness we experience when we suffer what we perceive as a setback or a loss to the happiness we experience when we realize that our loved one is not hurt or that we have not done poorly on the exam or the job interview after all. Emotions shape our memories, our judgments, and what we attend to, as we shall see.

Emotions also involve expressive behaviors, enabling us to communicate what we are feeling and our reactions to people and events. We express our emotions with our facial expressions, our voice (Scherer, Johnstone, & Klasmeyer, 2003), our posture, our physical touch (Hertenstein, 2002), and even our art, poetry, and music (Oatley, 2003). Most studies of emotional expression have focused on the face. Of the thousands of possible configurations of the forty-three sets of muscles in the face, only a limited number convey emotion. These emotional expressions tend to be brief, symmetrical (equally intense on both sides of the face), and involve specific, "reliable" muscle actions that cannot easily be produced volun-

**autonomic nervous system (ANS)** The glands, organs, muscles, arteries, and veins throughout the body that are controlled by nerve cells originating in the spinal cord, and that help the individual deal with emergency situations.

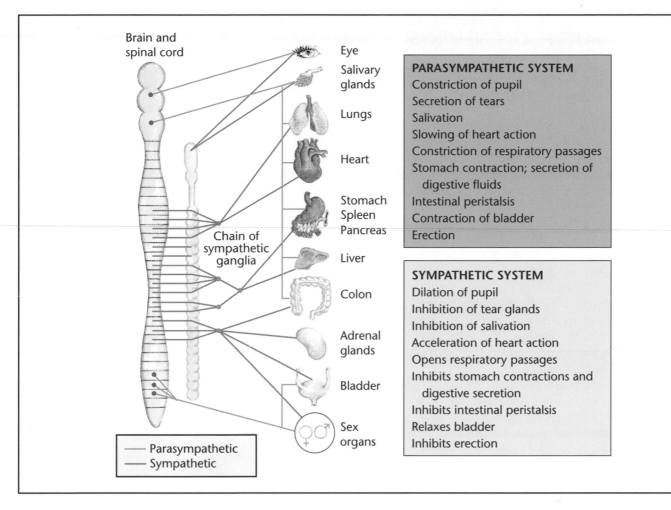

Brain and spinal cord

Eye
Salivary glands
Lungs
Heart
Stomach
Spleen
Pancreas
Liver
Colon
Adrenal glands
Bladder
Sex organs

Chain of sympathetic ganglia

—— Parasympathetic
—— Sympathetic

**PARASYMPATHETIC SYSTEM**
Constriction of pupil
Secretion of tears
Salivation
Slowing of heart action
Constriction of respiratory passages
Stomach contraction; secretion of digestive fluids
Intestinal peristalsis
Contraction of bladder
Erection

**SYMPATHETIC SYSTEM**
Dilation of pupil
Inhibition of tear glands
Inhibition of salivation
Acceleration of heart action
Opens respiratory passages
Inhibits stomach contractions and digestive secretion
Inhibits intestinal peristalsis
Relaxes bladder
Inhibits erection

**Figure 12.1 The Autonomic Nervous System** The autonomic nervous system's most general function is to maintain the internal milieu, or condition, of the body, to enable adaptive response to varying environmental events. The parasympathetic branch helps with restorative processes, reducing heart rate and blood pressure and increasing digestive processes. The sympathetic branch increases heart rate, blood pressure, and cardiac output and shuts down digestive processes, to allow the individual to engage in physically demanding actions. (Source: Gleitman, Fridlund, & Reisberg, 2004, p. 102)

tarily. Sincere, loving smiles, for example, have these characteristics. False smiles, which may be concealing negative emotion, do not (see Box 12.1).

Having a rudimentary knowledge of the emotional landscape, we are ready to tackle our first big question: In what ways are emotions universal, and in what ways do they vary across cultures?

## UNIVERSALITY AND CULTURAL SPECIFICITY OF EMOTION

At the heart of the study of emotion is a fascinating tension between theorists who offer evolutionary approaches to emotion and theorists who offer cultural approaches. The evolutionary approach contends that emotions are biologically based adaptations that increase the likelihood that our genes will be passed on to the next generation (Ekman, 1992a; Nesse, 1990; Ohman, 1986; Tooby & Cosmides, 1992). This is because emotions like fear help you respond quickly and effectively to threats related to survival. In contrast, the cultural approach assumes that emotions are strongly influenced by values, roles, institutions, socialization practices, and construal processes, and that these vary in different cultures (Ellsworth, 1994; Markus & Kitayama, 1991; Mesquita, 2003; Oatley,

Box 12.1   FOCUS ON NEUROSCIENCE

# Felt and False Smiles

Are smiles emotional or not? This seemingly modest question has been the subject of intense debate among emotion theorists. How can the smile be the primary signal of positive emotion, as Ekman (1993) asserts, and at the same time occur during anger, disgust, or grief? Answers to these kinds of questions can be found in *The Mechanism of Human Facial Expression*, published in 1862 by a French physician named Duchenne de Boulogne. In this book, Duchenne detailed the results of his research on stimulating the facial muscles with electric stimulation. He identified the actions of two muscles: (1) the *zygomatic major* muscle, which pulls the lip corners upwards; and (2) the *orbicularis oculi*, which surrounds the eye, and in contracting causes crow's-feet to form, the upper cheek to raise, and a pouch to form under the lower eyelid.

Based on this anatomical distinction, Ekman has coined the term the *Duchenne smile*, which is the smile that involves the action of the *orbicularis oculi* and tends to be associated with the experience of positive emotion. Research has shown that the Duchenne smile differs in many ways from smiles that do not involve the same muscle action. Duchenne smiles tend to last between one and five seconds, and the lip corners tend to be raised to equal degrees on both sides (Frank, Ekman, & Friesen, 1993). Duchenne smiles tend to be associated with activity in the left anterior portion of the brain, whereas non-Duchenne smiles are associated with activity in the right anterior por-

tion of the brain (Ekman & Davidson, 1993; Ekman, Davidson, & Friesen, 1990). This is consistent with a rich literature showing that positive emotions are more strongly associated with activation in the left side of the brain (Davidson, Pizzagalli, Nitzschke, & Kalin, 2003). Duchenne smiles are associated with pleasure, whereas in some studies non-Duchenne smiles have been shown to be associated with negative emotion (Hess, Banse, & Kappas, 1995; Keltner & Bonanno, 1997; Ruch, 1995).

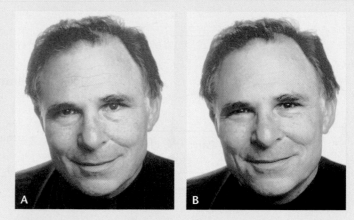

**Different Kinds of Smiles.** (A) A polite, non-Duchenne smile, and (B) a Duchenne or enjoyment smile, as demonstrated by Paul Ekman.

1993). Whereas evolutionary approaches make strong claims about the universality of emotion, cultural approaches predict significant cultural variation in emotion. Let's see the ways in which emotion is universal, and the ways in which it is culturally variable, starting with emotional expression, a topic of keen interest to Charles Darwin.

## DARWIN AND EMOTIONAL EXPRESSION

In 1872, Charles Darwin published *The Expression of Emotions in Man and Animals*, a book that he wrote feverishly in four months. This lively book would become a best seller in its day, would be reprinted in several languages, and would be ardently discussed by scientists and laypeople alike during the Victorian era.

In Darwin's time, creationists held that God had given humans special facial muscles that allowed them to express uniquely human sentiments unknown to

**Signaling Intentions** Darwin
believed that animals signal their
intentions through displays such as
(A) this dog signaling his hostile
intentions toward another dog, and
(B) this dog signaling submission to
another dog.

"lower" species. This did not sit well with Darwin. A central tenet of Darwin's theory of evolution was that humans descended from other species. To demonstrate phylogenetic continuity (the claim that humans evolved from other species), Darwin drew fascinating parallels between human expressions and the expressions of other species. For example, he juxtaposed the play faces of chimpanzees with the faces of laughing humans; he compared the threatening expressions of dogs baring their teeth with the expressions of humans in the grip of anger. Thus, Darwin linked human expressions of emotion to animal displays—that is, expressions that signaled attitudes or intentions.

Darwin sought to document the universality of emotional expression. He queried English missionaries living in other cultures about whether they had observed expressions not seen in Victorian England. The result? They had not. Of course, his question was rather biased, and may have encouraged the answer he sought. Nevertheless, Darwin was one of the first scientists to use cross-cultural methods, and his work served as inspiration for an important series of studies approximately 100 years after the publication of his book on expression.

**Charles Darwin** Not only did
Charles Darwin formulate the theory
of evolution, he also studied emotional expressions in animals and in
humans and sought to document that
human emotional expressions have
their parallels in other species and are
universal to people of all cultures.

## STUDIES OF THE UNIVERSALITY OF FACIAL EXPRESSION

Sylvan Tomkins, Paul Ekman, and Carroll Izard distilled Darwin's writings to two simple points (Ekman, Sorenson, & Friesen, 1969; Izard, 1971; Tomkins, 1962, 1963): (1) They hypothesized that if emotions were universal, across cultures the experience of different emotions would be associated with the same distinct facial expressions; this is the **encoding hypothesis**. (2) They hypothesized that if there were universal emotions, people of different cultures should interpret these expressions in the same ways; this is the **decoding hypothesis**.

Ekman and Wallace Friesen initially took more than 3,000 photos of various people (usually people well trained in expression, such as actors), as they portrayed six different emotions—anger, disgust, fear, happiness (a Duchenne smile), sadness, and surprise—according to Darwin's descriptions of the muscle configurations. Ekman and Friesen then took the most easily identified examples of each emotion, and in a first set of studies presented these photos to people in Japan, Brazil, Argentina, Chile, and the United States. Each emotion was represented by a different person. The participant's task was to select from six emotion terms the single term that best matched the feeling the person was showing in each photo. The results? A home run for Darwin. Across these five cultures, accuracy rates were typically between 80 and 90 percent for the six emotions, when chance guessing (randomly selecting one term out of six that actually matched the emotion in the photo) would be 16.6 percent (Ekman, Sorenson, & Friesen, 1969). The critics,

**encoding hypothesis** The
hypothesis that the experience of
different emotions is associated
with the same distinct facial
expressions across cultures.

**decoding hypothesis** The
hypothesis that people of different cultures can interpret distinct
facial expressions for different
emotions in the same ways.

**Facial Expressions** Groundbreaking studies by Ekman, Friesen, and Izard identified these six facial expressions as universal: (A) happiness, (B) surprise, (C) sadness, (D) anger, (E) disgust, and (F) fear.

however, were unconvinced. They noted a fundamental flaw to this first wave of research: participants in these different cultures had all seen Western media, and they may have learned how to identify the expressions via exposure to U.S. actors portraying those emotions. The universality in judging emotion that Ekman and Friesen documented may have been produced only by the media that these cultures share.

Ekman and Friesen now faced a surprisingly difficult challenge: to find a culture that had little or no exposure to Westerners or to Western media. In light of these concerns, Ekman went to Papua, New Guinea, to study a hill tribe from the Fore (pronounced foray) language group that lived in Stone Age conditions. Ekman lived with the tribe for six months and studied their emotional expressions. The Fore who participated in Ekman's study had seen no movies or magazines, they did not speak English or Pidgin (a combination of English and a native language), they had not lived in Western settlements, nor had they worked for Westerners.

In this study, Ekman used a different judgment paradigm known as the Dashiell method (Ekman & Friesen, 1971). Specifically, he devised an emotion-appropriate story for each of the six emotions. For example, the sadness story was: "the person's child had died, and he felt sad." He then presented photos of three different expressions along with a story that matched one of the expressions, and asked participants, both adults and children in this study, to match the story to an expression. Here chance guessing would have yielded identification rates of 33 percent. In another task, he asked Fore participants to show how their faces would appear if they were the individual in the emotion-specific story. Ekman videotaped these posed expressions and presented unedited clips of these expressions to Western college students, who selected from six emotion terms the one that best matched the Fore's pose in each clip.

The results would certainly have pleased Darwin. The Fore participants inter-

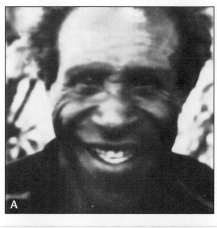
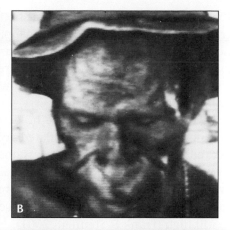
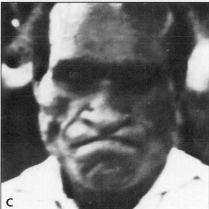
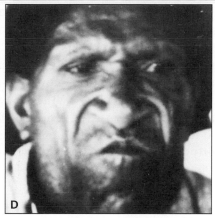

**Universality of Facial Expressions**
Paul Ekman asked members of the isolated and preliterate Fore tribe in New Guinea to show how their faces would appear if they were reacting to the following stories: (A) "Your friend has come and you are happy." (B) "Your child has died and you are sad." (C) "You are angry and about to fight." (D) "You see a dead pig that has been lying here for a long time."

preted the facial expressions of emotion he so carefully described in the same way that you would, achieving accuracy rates between 80 and 90 percent. U.S. college students correctly interpreted the posed expressions of the Fore, with the exception of fear. Subsequent studies in dozens of cultures have replicated this pattern of results, finding that people from cultures that differ in their religion, political structure, development, and self-construals nevertheless agree in how they label the photos depicting anger, disgust, fear, happiness, sadness, and surprise (Ekman, 1984, 1993; Elfenbein & Ambady, 2002b, 2003; Izard, 1971, 1994).

These results became some of the most cited findings in psychology, inspiring great interest and further research on emotion, evolution, and culture. In discussions of human nature, facial expression of emotion, along with things like incest avoidance and color perception, are considered universal to all people (Brown, 1991).

## CRITIQUES OF THE UNIVERSALITY STUDIES

How strong are Ekman and Friesen's results? What are the pitfalls of this often-cited study? Before jumping on the universality bandwagon, how might you have done the study differently had you made the arduous trip to the highland hills of New Guinea and conducted the study yourself?

As people have mulled over these findings, they have arrived at a few central critiques. One is the **free-response critique**: in Ekman's study, and almost all other judgment studies, researchers provided the terms with which participants labeled the facial expressions. If given the chance to label the faces in their own words (with free responses), perhaps people from different cultures would choose

**free-response critique** A critique of Ekman and Friesen's emotion studies based on the fact that researchers provided the terms with which participants labeled facial expressions rather than allowing the participants to label the expressions with their own words.

different terms that reflect culture-specific concepts. They might label a smile "gratitude" or "pride" rather than "happiness," or label it with some concept that does not map onto Western conceptions of emotion. Relevant studies, however, have found that participants from different cultures use similar concepts to label facial expressions of emotion when allowed to use their own words (Haidt & Keltner, 1999; Izard, 1971).

The **forced-choice critique** holds that the response format of the Ekman and Friesen study may have inflated accuracy rates by allowing participants to make educated guesses about expressions they may not have known how to label (Fridlund, 1992; Russell, 1994). Here again the critique has been answered: when participants are given additional response options such as "none of the above" that reduce the chances of guessing, accuracy rates in judging the Ekman faces are still high (Frank & Stennett, 2001).

Finally, Ekman and Friesen studied only *limited emotions*—namely anger, disgust, fear, happiness, sadness, and surprise. One might conclude that these are the only universal emotions, but that would be a mistake. For example, more recent research has documented a distinct display of embarrassment: gaze aversion, controlled smile, head movements down and to the left (which expose the neck), and face touching (Keltner, 1995). Observers are able to distinguish this display from other displays, including that of shame, which is shown by gaze and head movements down (Haidt & Keltner, 1999). Sympathy also appears to have a fairly distinct display—namely, the inner corners of the eyebrows are pulled up and in and the lips are pressed together slightly (Eisenberg et al., 1989). And, as we will see later, even love has a distinct display.

Taken together, these studies suggest that facial expressions of emotion, at least the more prototypical examples, are universal, as Darwin long ago surmised (Ekman, Friesen & Ellsworth, 1982a, 1982b; Elfenbein & Ambady, 2002b, 2003; Mesquita & Frijda, 1992). Let's now consider how emotion varies across different cultures.

## CULTURAL SPECIFICITY OF EMOTION

How do emotions vary according to culture? Recall that the cultural approach assumes that emotions are strongly influenced by culture-specific self-construals, values, practices, and institutions. Empirical studies have documented five different ways that members of different cultures vary in their emotional response.

*Cultural Variation in Emotional Expression*    Early cultural researchers argued to great effect that cultures vary profoundly in how they express emotion. This view found support in various observations. For example, the Inuit of Alaska (colloquially referred to as Eskimos) do not express anger (Briggs, 1960). Seventeenth-century Japanese wives of Samurai soldiers would smile upon receipt of the news that their husbands had died nobly in battle. In much of Southeast Asia, people express embarrassment by shrugging their shoulders and biting their protruding tongue. How do we account for differences in facial expressions across cultures?

One answer is based on Paul Ekman's analysis of **display rules**, which refer to culturally specific rules that govern how and when and to whom we express emotion. People can *de-intensify* their emotional expression—for example, suppressing the urge to laugh at a friend's fumbling on a romantic quest. People can *intensify* their expression—for example, smiling more appreciatively upon receiving yet another unfashionable sweater from Grandma. They can *mask* their neg-

---

**forced-choice critique** A critique of Ekman and Friesen's emotion study that holds that accuracy rates in judgments of emotional expressions may have been inflated by allowing participants to make educated guesses about expressions they may not have known how to label.

**display rules** Culturally specific rules that govern how and when and to whom we express emotion.

ative emotion with a polite smile. And they can *neutralize* their expression with a poker-faced demeanor.

Across cultures, people are likely to vary in how they regulate their expression of emotion according to culture-specific display rules. For example, in many Asian cultures it is inappropriate to speak of personal accomplishments, and in these cultures individuals may de-intensify their expressions of pleasure at personal success. To study display rules, Ekman (1992b) and Friesen (1972) videotaped American and Japanese college students watching a disturbing film clip of a circumcision ritual, both in the dark (the videotaping was done with infrared cameras), and in an illuminated room in the presence of an authority figure. Participants showed almost exactly the same sequence of facial expressions in the dark (primarily disgust). In the presence of the authority figure, however, American college students intensified their expressions of disgust, consistent with prevailing norms of self-expression. In contrast, Japanese college students masked their disgust with polite smiles, perhaps due to the belief that the expression of negative emotion disrupts social harmony (Markus & Kitayama, 1991; Shweder, 1994). Consistent with this view, Japanese college students attribute more intense emotion to the same facial expressions than do American college students (Matsumoto & Ekman, 1989). It appears that the Japanese assume that the individual feels more than what he or she is willing to express publicly.

Cultures also develop **ritualized displays** of emotion—that is, highly stylized ways of expressing particular emotions. In a study conducted in India and the United States, the researchers presented participants with two expressions of embarrassment, which are shown in Figure 12.2, along with the rates at which members identified the two expressions as embarrassment (Haidt & Keltner, 1999). As you can see, members of both cultures interpreted the expression to the left as embarrassment. Indian participants also readily perceived the expressions that included the tongue bite as embarrassment. In contrast, U.S. college students were bewildered by this expression, and saw little embarrassment in it.

*Culture and the Language of Emotion* Not only do cultures differ in certain emotional displays, but they also differ in their emotion vocabulary. To figure out how, James Russell read hundreds of ethnographies written by anthropologists who had lived in different cultures and were familiar with the language and life of that culture (Russell, 1991). After observing that almost all languages have terms for anger, fear, happiness, sadness, and disgust, Russell painted a fascinating picture of how cultures vary in the language of emotion.

Cultures vary in the *number of words* that represent emotion. Researchers have identified 2,000 emotion-related words in English, 750 in Taiwanese, 58 in the Ifaluk of Polynesia, and 8 in the Chewong of Malaysia. Cultures also vary in *which states* they rep-

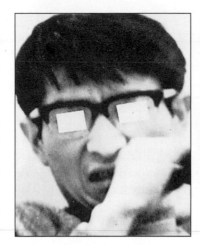 

**Culture-Specific Display Rules** When watching a stressful film, Japanese (left) and American (right) students spontaneously react with the same expression of disgust. But in the presence of an authority figure, the Japanese student will attempt to hide the expression with his hand or with a polite smile, while the American student will feel free to show his disgust and even intensify it.

**ritualized displays** Highly stylized ways of expressing particular emotions.

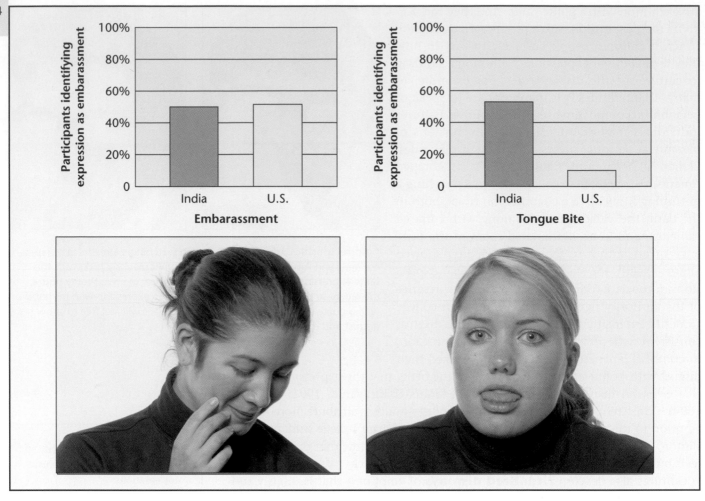

**Figure 12.2 Universality and Cultural Variation in Emotional Expression** People in the United States and India agree in their judgments of a prototypical embarrassment display, but only people in India recognize the ritualized tongue bite as a display of embarrassment. (Source: Haidt & Keltner, 1999)

**hypercognize** To represent a particular emotion with numerous words and concepts.

resent with emotion terms. In the Gifjingali language of the aborigines of Australia, fear and shame are captured by the same word, *gurakadj*. The distinction between shame and embarrassment is not made by the Japanese, Tahitians, Indonesians, or Newars of Nepal. There are states represented by a single word in other languages that are not represented by single English terms. For example, in Czech, one finds *litost*, which means the sudden realization of life's tragic circumstances. In German, there is the well-known word *Schadenfreude*, which refers to the pleasure a person experiences in seeing the failure or suffering of another person. In Japanese, there is *amae*, which refers to the feeling of pleasurable dependence upon another.

Finally, cultures vary according to whether they **hypercognize** a particular emotion—that is, represent it with numerous words and concepts. For example, in Tahiti there are forty-six separate terms that refer to anger. It has been claimed that in the United States, guilt and love are hypercognized. It seems probable that, with hypercognized emotions, people may be more likely to experience the emotion, and to experience many shadings of that emotion.

*Cultural Similarities and Differences in the Elicitors of Emotion* The elicitors, or triggers, of emotion can be quite similar across cultures. Boucher and Brandt (1981) asked American college students and young Malaysians who were not college students to describe some event from their lives in which someone had caused another person to feel a number of different emotions, such as fear, disgust, and joy. A pool of situations was chosen randomly from the ones generated by participants, an equal number from those generated by Americans and Malaysians. Participants were then asked to identify which emotion would be elicited by these situations. Members of both cultures were highly capable of identifying the emotion that would be triggered by the event and, remarkably, each group was just as accurate in predicting emotions for situations listed by the other group as for situations listed by their own group. This implied great commonality in the triggers for emotions across very different cultures (Mesquita & Frijda, 1992).

Cultures differ with respect to whether the elicitors of emotion are socially "engaging"—that is, whether they involve other people—or "disengaging"—that is, whether they primarily involve the self. Kitayama, Karasawa, Mesquita, and their colleagues showed that members of interdependent cultures—for example, Japanese, Surinamese, and Turkish cultures—tended to experience positive emotions (calm, elation) in relatively socially engaged situations—for example, in casual interactions with friends (Kitayama, Karasawa, & Mesquita, 2004; Kitayama, Markus, & Kurokawa, 2000; Kitayama, Mesquita, & Karasawa, 2005; see also Mesquita, 2001; Mesquita & Karasawa, 2002). In contrast, Americans and the Dutch tended to experience positive emotions in relatively disengaged situations—for example, in activities oriented toward personal accomplishments. Thus, while people from different cultures can reliably identify which emotions will occur in common emotion-eliciting situations in other cultures, they differ in which kinds of situations, engaging or disengaging, are the actual sources of their positive emotions.

*Cultural Differences in the Construal of Events*   Although people from different cultures seem remarkably similar in the construal *process* (Mauro, Sato, & Tucker, 1992; Mesquita & Ellsworth, 2001; Scherer, 1997), members of different cultures can differ greatly in their construal of *particular* events. As a result, the same event can produce different emotions in different cultures. Consider the example of being alone. Middle-class Europeans are likely to construe being alone as an occasion for private reflection and thus to experience pleasant emotions when alone. In contrast, Utku Inuits and many other interdependent peoples construe being alone as an experience of isolation, which prompts feelings of sadness (Mesquita & Ellsworth, 2001).

In different cultures, being dependent on others triggers quite different construals, which result in different emotions. For example, among the Awlad'Ali, a nomadic tribe living in Egypt, it is considered shameful to encounter people more powerful than oneself, because such situations are reminders that one is dependent on those people (Abu-Lughod, 1986). Such situations are occasions for the emotion called *hasham*, or the feeling of embarrassment or shame. In contrast, as we mentioned earlier, the Japanese are said to have a highly distinctive set of pleasurable emotions called *amae*, which center on the relations between people of greater and lesser power (Lebra, 1983). This is the comforting sense of dependence that a less powerful person feels vis-à-vis a more powerful person, which permits the less powerful person to engage in passive or helpless behavior in the satisfying knowledge that it will not be judged negatively. For people in European cultures, shame vis-à-vis more powerful individuals seems to be a relatively rare experience. Thus, schemas for shame, which always involve relations with other people, are more accessible for highly interdependent people like the Awlad'Ali and the Japanese, but less salient and accessible for independent people like those of European cultures (Lebra, 1983).

In short, it seems clear that there is a basic set of emotions that are experienced and recognized in every culture. It is equally clear that members of different cultures experience these emotions differently—in terms of what kinds of events trigger these emotions, how intensely they are felt, which cognitive structures and schemas they are typically filtered through, and how appropriate it is to experience the emotion (Ellsworth, 1994; Mesquita & Ellsworth, 2001; Scherer, 1997).

*Cultural Differences in Attentiveness to Emotional Cues*    Before we leave the topic of cultural influences on emotion, let's examine a particularly clever experiment that establishes that cultures differ with respect to how attentive they are to emotional cues. Keiko Ishii, Jose Alberto Reyes, and Shinobu Kitayama (2003) presented spoken words to Japanese and American participants. The words were either pleasant or unpleasant in meaning, and they were read in either a pleasant or an unpleasant tone. Participants were asked either to say whether the words were pleasant or unpleasant in meaning, or whether they were pleasant or unpleasant in tone. The time it took them to give a response was the dependent variable (see Figure 12.3).

The authors reasoned that for cultures for which emotion is important for the maintenance of harmony, attentiveness to emotional cues (in this case, vocal tone) would be very important. Hence their judgments of pleasantness of word meanings would be impaired by vocal tone that was contrary to the verbal content (for example, pleasant words read in an unpleasant tone). And indeed that was what they found: Japanese participants required more time to

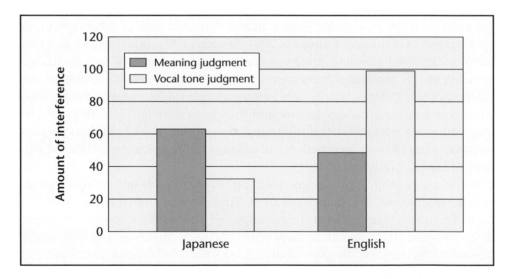

**Figure 12.3 Cultural Differences in the Importance of Emotional Cues**    Being sensitive to emotional cues is an important part of maintaining interpersonal harmony, which is prioritized in interdependent cultures. To test this hypothesis, Ishii and colleagues had Japanese and American participants listen and judge the meaning of pleasant or unpleasant words delivered in a pleasant or unpleasant voice. For the Japanese, the contradictory tone of voice interfered with their ability to judge the meaning of the words more than the meaning of the words interfered with their judgments of vocal tone, suggesting they were more sensitive to emotional tone of voice. In contrast, the meaning of the word produced greater interference in the judgments of vocal tone for American participants, suggesting they were less attuned to vocal cues of emotion. The index of interference was computed by subtracting mean response time in milliseconds for congruous stimuli (for example, positive meaning, positive tone) from mean response time for incongruous stimuli (for example, positive meaning, negative tone). (Source: Adapted from Ishii, Reyes, & Kitayama, 2003)

make a judgment of verbal content when the verbal content was contradicted by the vocal tone than when making a judgment of the vocal tone that was contradicted by the verbal meaning. Americans showed the opposite effect: they were more thrown off by verbal content when trying to judge vocal tone than they were by vocal tone when trying to judge verbal content. The results thus give strong support to the view that for people in interdependent cultures attention to emotional cues is greater than it is for people in independent cultures.

**LOOKING BACK,** we have seen that certain facets of emotion are universal, including certain facial expressions and certain elicitors or triggers of emotion. We have also seen, however, that some aspects of the expression of emotion can vary in different cultures. Thus, different cultures can vary in their display rules—that is, the rules governing how and when to express emotions—and in when to de-intensify, intensify, mask, or neutralize emotional expression, as well as in their ritualized displays of such emotions as embarrassment. Different cultures also vary in the language of emotion, including which emotional states are represented and with how many different words. Moreover, the elicitors of emotion can vary across cultures, along with the construal of particular events and the attentiveness to emotional cues. Let's now try to answer a question that has long puzzled psychologists and philosophers alike: Where does our emotional experience come from?

## EMOTION IN THE MIND AND BODY

René Descartes, no stranger to discussions about the mind and body, offered a paradoxical analysis of emotion. He said that our emotional experience is both a bodily experience and a reflection of the activity of our soul, or in contemporary terms, our mind. How much of our experience of emotion rests on construal processes in the mind? How much is based on physiological responses in the body? These questions have generated two different research traditions, which paint a complex picture of how mind and body interact to produce our emotional experience.

### WILLIAM JAMES AND EMOTION-SPECIFIC PHYSIOLOGY

In 1884, William James turned the field of emotion on its head, so to speak. Most theorists up until that time had argued that the experience of emotion follows the perception of an emotionally exciting stimulus, which causes emotion-related physiology and behavior. Emotion originates in the mind. James altered this sequence in a now-famous formulation: he argued that an emotionally exciting stimulus generates a physiological response, the perception of which is the experience of emotion. The body—in this case, activity in the autonomic nervous system—is the emotion (James, 1890). James argued that each and every emotion, from lust to sympathy to the rapture you might feel upon entering a European cathedral, involves a distinct "bodily reverberation" (what we now know as a response in the autonomic nervous system). James's evidence was largely in the form of thought experiments, such as the following: What would be left of fear, or any emotion, for that matter, if you took away the heart palpitations, muscle tension, feelings of warmth or coldness in the skin, stomach sensations, and other ANS-produced responses from the experience of those emotions? James argued that you would be left with a purely intellectual state.

James's thesis raises two questions: (1) To what extent does emotion reside in the body, in particular in the activity of the ANS, and to what extent does emotion originate in the mind, as part of our complex interpretation of the social environment?, and (2) Are there distinct ANS patterns for the different emotions? To answer these questions, we will first discuss an influential two-factor theory that takes a much different approach to emotional experience from that offered by James.

## SCHACHTER AND SINGER'S TWO-FACTOR THEORY OF EMOTION

> **two-factor theory of emotion**
> A theory that says that there are two components to emotional experience: undifferentiated physiological arousal and a person's construal of that state of undifferentiated arousal.

In 1962, Stanley Schachter and Jerome Singer proposed a **two-factor theory of emotion** (Schachter & Singer, 1962; see also Reisenzein, 1983). The theory assumed that there were two components to emotional experience: (1) undifferentiated physiological arousal, and (2) construal of the state of undifferentiated arousal, which would determine which emotion would be experienced. In other words, the specific emotion the individual experiences—for example, anger, guilt, or shame—depends largely on the meaning of the situation to which the person attributes the arousal. For example, drinking too much coffee in the morning will make you tense and jittery at lunch. If you've forgotten that the coffee is the source of your tension, you might experience your jitteriness from the coffee as anger toward your roommate who is sleeping in late after keeping you up the night before. Or, as another example, take the situation of picking up your date at her parents' house. You arrive at your date's home, are grilled by her imposing parents, and in this heightened state of arousal and confusion fall madly in love with your date as she descends the stairs. In short, the two-factor theory says that for an emotion to be experienced, the person must both be in a state of general physiological arousal and attribute that arousal to an emotional stimulus.

In the classic study testing the two-factor theory, participants arrived at the laboratory, where the experimenter told them that the experiment concerned the effects of a vitamin compound, "Suproxin," on vision. The experimenter then put some participants into a state of arousal—specifically, a medical doctor gave participants a shot, either of epinephrine (adrenaline), which elevates SANS activity (increasing blood pressure, heart rate, and so on), or a placebo saline solution, which should have no reliable effects upon SANS activity. Those given a shot of epinephrine experienced arousal and were divided into two groups. Those in the *epinephrine-informed* condition were told the actual effects they would be likely to experience from the epinephrine. They were informed that the shot would likely make their hands shake, their hearts pound, and their faces feel flushed and warm. Those in the *epinephrine-ignorant* condition were not informed of any likely effects of the shot. Thus, some the participants were physiologically aroused and some were not. For those who were aroused, some were given an explanation of that arousal in nonemotional terms and some were given no explanation.

We now turn to the manipulation of the situation, which, according to Schachter and Singer, should most affect those participants experiencing unexplained arousal. After the doctor had departed, the experimenter returned with a participant, actually a confederate, who allegedly had also received the shot of "Suproxin" and was to wait with the participant for twenty minutes before the vision tasks were to begin. The experimenter then left, apologizing for the rather disheveled condition of the laboratory. In the *euphoria condition*, the confederate carried out a variety of exhilarating activities. He first crumpled up sheets of paper and attempted jump shots into the trash can. After announcing "I feel like a kid again," he made a paper airplane, and launched it into the air. He shot pieces of paper with a rubber-band slingshot, built a tower out of manila folders, and, at the peak of euphoria, began playing with hoola hoops left behind a portable blackboard.

In the *anger condition*, the experimenter asked the confederate and the participant, sitting across a table from each other, to complete the same five-page questionnaire. The confederate first commented on the excessive length of the questionnaire. Then at Question 9 ("Do you ever hear bells?"), he blurted out: "Look at Question 9. How ridiculous can you get? I hear bells every time I change classes." After questions about his childhood diseases, his father's annual income, and psychiatric symptoms family members had shown, the confederate exploded. When asked how often he had sexual intercourse each week, and "With how many men (other than your father), has your mother had extramarital relationships?" (for which the lowest response category was "4 and under"!), the confederate erupted and stomped out of the lab room.

Schachter and Singer gathered two kinds of measures. They coded the extent to which the participant showed euphoric or angry behaviors like those of the confederate, and they had participants report how angry and happy they felt on a questionnaire administered after the experiment.

According to Schachter and Singer's two-factor theory, participants should feel especially happy when: (1) they were physiologically aroused but did not expect to be aroused by the shot, and (2) they were then placed in the euphoria condition, which would lead to a positive construal of their arousal. In contrast, participants should feel particularly angry when they were physiologically aroused from the shot of epinephrine but did not expect to be aroused by the shot, and when they were placed in the anger condition, which would provide an anger-related interpretation of their arousal. This turned out to be the case, both in terms of self-ratings of emotional state (happiness versus anger) and in terms of behavioral ratings. A surprise finding, however, was that informed participants, who knew that the shock would produce arousal, were actually less emotional than placebo subjects who received no injection. This suggests a particularly interesting cognitive twist: perhaps the informed subjects "overattributed" their arousal to the drug, discounting any arousal symptoms because they thought they knew how the symptoms had originated.

Schachter and Singer's experiment provided an initial glimpse into the importance of cognition in the experience of emotion. Their theory would later provide impetus for theories of attribution and self-perception. In the field of emotion, the idea that arousal could be misattributed to different causes generated a wave of interesting studies. The **misattribution of arousal** has been pursued in dozens of experiments exploring how arousal from one source (for example, difficulties at work), can be attributed to some other, salient source in the environment (the proverbial dog the frustrated person kicks). One major finding is that participants who engage in arousing physical exercise have greater emotional responses to stimuli presented a few moments later when they think their arousal has subsided (Zillman, 1988, 1989). Thus, people who are presented with car-

**misattribution of arousal**
Attributing arousal produced by one cause (for example, exercise) to another stimulus in the environment.

toons or erotica after exercising find the cartoons to be funnier and the erotica to be more arousing than do those who have not first engaged in the arousing exercise (Zillman, 1978). Perhaps most dramatically, individuals who complain of insomnia actually fall asleep more quickly when given a pill that was described as a stimulant (Storms & Nisbett, 1970). This allows them to attribute their anxieties produced by daily life to the pill rather than to the actual causes of their insomnia. Relieved, they fall asleep.

## EMOTION IN THE BODY: EVIDENCE FOR ANS SPECIFICITY IN EMOTION

Let's now return to William James's original claim, that each emotion has a distinct ANS pattern. Schachter and Singer asserted that this was not true, and the field largely took this as gospel for the ensuing twenty years. Yet, Paul Ekman noticed something in his studies of facial expression that suggested otherwise. Ekman and Friesen developed an anatomically based system that allows researchers to code facial muscle actions according to how they change the appearance of the face (Ekman & Rosenberg, 1997). To develop this system, Ekman and Friesen spent thousands of hours moving their facial muscles, taking careful notes about how these movements created new creases, wrinkles, dimples, bulges of skin, and changes to the shape of the eyes or lips. In the course of this endeavor, Ekman observed that moving his facial muscles seemed to change how he felt. When he furrowed his brow, his heart rate and blood pressure seemed to increase. This raised an interesting possibility: Might moving facial muscles into emotion configurations produce specific ANS activity?

To answer this question, Robert Levenson, Paul Ekman, and Wallace Friesen (1990) conducted a study using the Directed Facial Action (DFA) task. They had participants follow muscle-by-muscle instructions to configure their faces into the expressions of the six basic emotions that Ekman had studied in his cross-cultural studies. For example, for the anger expression, participants were instructed to:

1. Pull your eyebrows down and together.

2. Raise your upper eyelid.

3. Push your lower lip up and press your lips together.

Participants held these expressions for ten seconds, during which time the researchers continually took measures of ANS activity and then compared them to the measures from a neutral baseline.

Let's look closely at autonomic activation associated with four different negative emotions (see Table 12.1). When you look closely, you will see results that support James's physiological specificity hypothesis. First, heart rate is greater for fear, anger, and sadness than for disgust, suggesting, as one might expect, that the gastrointestinal processes involved in disgust reduce heart rate. Second, skin conductance, the measure of sweat activity in the hands, is greater for fear and disgust than for anger and sadness. Third, finger temperature is greater for anger than for fear, suggesting that when someone is angry blood flows freely to the hands (perhaps to aid in combat), whereas when someone is fearful blood remains near the chest to support flight-related locomo-

**The Facial Expression of Anger**   In this photograph, Winston Churchill looks like an angry bulldog, having just had his ever-present cigar taken away from him by the photographer. His eyebrows are drawn together and down, his upper eyelid is raised, his lower lip is pushed up and his lips are pressed together.

## Table 12.1 Facial Expressions of Emotion Generate Emotion-Specific ANS Physiology

To address whether emotions are associated with specific ANS responses, as William James had claimed, Levenson, Ekman, and Friesen had participants move their facial muscles in ways that would express different emotions while the researchers measured changes in ANS physiology. Three findings suggest some specificity for negative emotions: (1) disgust produced lower heart rate than the other negative emotions, (2) both fear and disgust elicited higher skin conductance responses, and (3) anger led to higher finger temperature than fear. Thus, the researchers showed that posing facial expressions associated with different negative emotions activates specific autonomic physiology.

| | ANGER | FEAR | SADNESS | DISGUST |
|---|---|---|---|---|
| Heart rate* | 5.0 | 5.5 | 4.2 | 0.7 |
| Skin conductance | .41 | .58 | .43 | .52 |
| Finger temperature | .20 | −.05 | .07 | .07 |

*Heart rate refers to increases in number of heartbeats per minute compared to a neutral baseline.

Source: Adapted from Levenson, Ekman, & Friesen, 1990.

tion. Thus, four different negative emotions have different autonomic profiles (but see Cacioppo, Klein, Berntson, & Hatfield, 1993, for a critique). Subsequent studies have replicated these emotion-specific ANS patterns in elderly adults (those aged sixty-five and older), although elderly adults show weaker ANS responses (Levenson, Carstensen, Friesen, & Ekman, 1991). Similar emotion-specific ANS activity was also observed in the Minangkabau, a matrilineal, Muslim people in West Sumatra, Indonesia, suggesting these emotion-specific ANS responses may be universal (Levenson, Ekman, Heider, & Friesen, 1992).

Are there other emotion-specific ANS responses? One obvious candidate is the blush, about which Mark Twain once observed: "humans are the only species who blush, and the only one that needs to." As it turns out, Twain was not entirely correct: some nonhuman primates show reddening in the face as an appeasement gesture (an indication to another primate that one acknowledges its higher status and power; Hauser, 1996). Darwin devoted a chapter to the blush, noting that it is associated with embarrassment, shyness, and shame. Why do we blush? Darwin suggested that the blush is produced when we direct our attention to our appearance. More recently, researchers have pinpointed a more specific cause of the blush: negative, self-focused attention (Leary, Britt, Cutlip, & Templeton, 1992).

What about the autonomic physiology of the blush? In studying self-conscious emotion, researchers have been particularly mischievous, setting up situations in which participants break an experimenter's camera, knock over a confederate's coke (which spills into the confederate's backpack), or suck on pacifiers (Buck & Parke, 1972). A study by Donald Shearn and colleagues may be the most mortifying (Shearn, Bergman, Hill, Abel, & Hinds, 1990). In the blush condition, participants first sang "The Star Spangled Banner" (which is not the simplest song to sing with correct pitch) while being videotaped. As if that were not bad enough, in the second phase of the study, participants watched the videotape of their own rendition of "The Star Spangled Banner" with a group of people. Researchers compared the participants' ANS activity in this condition with that of participants who were about to give a prepared speech, a powerful elicitor of anxiety. Embarrassment involved increased vasodilation and blood flow to the cheeks, the blush. This blush response was not observed in the anxiety condition, suggesting that the blush is unique to self-conscious emotions, such as embarrassment and shame. Here is yet another way in which emotion involves distinct ANS patterning (see also Gross, Fredrickson, & Levenson, 1994; Levenson, 2003; Porges, 1995; Schwartz, Weinberger, & Singer, 1981; Stemmler, 1989, 2003).

**LOOKING BACK,** we have reviewed evidence indicating that emotion resides both in body and mind. Schachter and Singer's two-factor theory and the studies it inspired suggest that, once aroused, our emotional experience will be shaped by the causes to which we attribute our arousal. At the same time, Levenson and others have conducted studies that have produced evidence for ANS specificity for various emotions, lending credence to James's assertion that different emotions are associated with different physiological responses in the body. Having examined the role of the body and the mind in emotional experience, we now turn to the question of how emotions arise in the first place.

## UNCONSCIOUS AND CONSCIOUS ELICITATION OF EMOTION

Our lives are filled with powerful gut feelings. We feel comforting familiarity when we're talking with a new acquaintance. A passing stranger makes our skin crawl. A lake we encounter for the first time reminds us of our childhood and brings tears to our eyes. Our emotions seem to arise automatically, and appear suddenly, beyond our volition. But many of our emotions also seem to engage our deepest, or most systematic, thought processes. For example, in the sting of a cutting remark made by a friend, we determinedly seek answers as to why our friend would humiliate us. Thus, we seem to have both automatic, unconscious emotional responses to events, as well as thoughts about the causes of why we feel as we do, and what course of action may be most appropriate.

**appraisal processes** The ways whereby we evaluate events and objects in our environment according to their relation to our current goals.

These observations concern the **appraisal processes** that give rise to emotion. By *appraisal* we mean how we evaluate events and objects in our environment according to their relation to our current goals (Lazarus, 1991; Smith & Ellsworth, 1985). We will now see that part of emotion-related appraisal is unconscious and automatic, whereas another part is conscious and complex. In this section, we will first discuss the early studies that led researchers to suspect that there were two kinds of appraisal processes. We will then look at three aspects of processing emotion, organizing our discussion around three questions: (1) How can we study automatic, unconscious emotional responses to stimuli? (2) How do we appraise the environment in ways that give rise to specific emotions? (3) Once we have experienced an emotion, what are the consequences of reflecting upon it in different ways?

# UNCONSCIOUS PROCESSING IN SPLIT-BRAIN PATIENTS

In the 1960s, Michael Gazzaniga and Roger Sperry began studying split-brain patients. These were patients who suffered from epilepsy and had undergone a last-resort treatment in which their corpus callosum, a bundle of tissues that connects the left and right cerebral cortexes of the brain, had been cut (Gazzaniga, 1985). This treatment reduced or eliminated epileptic seizures. Yet, astonishingly, it had little effect upon patients' IQ, personality, or ability to engage in meaningful social interactions.

These split-brain patients presented a remarkable opportunity for the study of the right and left hemispheres of the brain. Using controlled procedures, researchers could present information to just the right visual field, which would be recognized and processed only by the left hemisphere, or to the left visual field, which would be recognized and processed only by the right hemisphere (see Figure 12.4). This kind of research led Gazzaniga and others to conclude that the right hemisphere responds more readily than the left to emotional stimuli, such as faces, nonverbal cues, and emotion-laden images (Borod, 1992). In contrast, the left hemisphere seems designed to interpret experience with language (Gazzaniga, Ivry, & Mangun, 2002).

In one case, Gazzaniga showed a female split-brain patient a scary film about fire safety. The film was only shown to the patient's left visual field, which meant that the information was processed only by the right hemisphere. Because the images were not accessible to the language center in the left hemisphere of the brain, she was not consciously aware of having seen the film. Gazzaniga (G) then conducted the following interview with his patient (P):

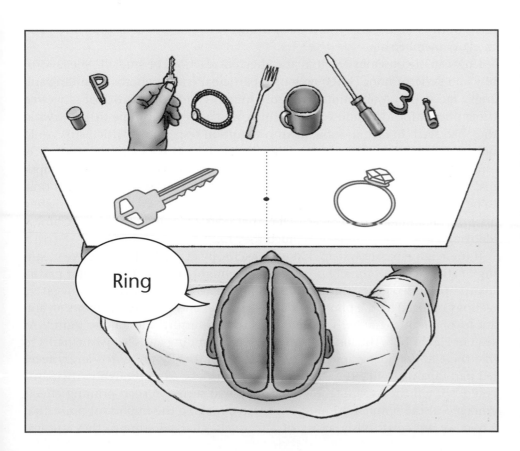

**Figure 12.4 Split-Brain Patients and Stimulus Processing** This drawing portrays an experiment with a split-brain patient, in which the participant is told to stare at a dot in the center of the screen while the researcher quickly and simultaneously flashes two images, one to the right and one to the left. The visual pathways are connected in such a way that images seen in the left visual field are processed in the right hemisphere and images seen in the right visual field are processed in the left hemisphere. Thus, the image to the left (the key) goes to the right hemisphere, and the image to the right (the ring) goes to the left hemisphere. When asked to say what has just been presented, the participant only says "ring," because the language and speech centers are in the left hemisphere. But when asked to pick out with the left hand (which is controlled by the right hemisphere) the object just presented, the participant will pick out the key and not the ring, suggesting that the right hemisphere registers what has been seen in the left visual field, despite an inability to say what was seen. (Source: Gazzaniga & Heatherton, 2003, p. 114)

G: What did you see?

P: I don't really know what I saw. I think just a white flash.

G: Were there people in it?

P: I don't think so. Maybe just some trees, red trees like in the fall.

G: Did it make you feel any emotion?

P: I don't really know why but I'm kind of scared. I feel jumpy. I think maybe I don't like this room, or maybe it's you. You're getting me nervous.

In this remarkable exchange, the patient feels fear, but does not consciously know why, because the fearful stimulus has been processed in the right hemisphere. She therefore makes up a story about how Dr. Gazzaniga makes her feel uneasy. This may remind you of Schachter and Singer's two-factor theory of emotion and its misattribution variations, which we just reviewed. This exchange also illustrates the complex ways in which we construct the meaning of emotional events.

## AUTOMATIC PROCESSING AND THE GENERATION OF EMOTION

Robert Zajonc (1980) has proposed that we process stimuli in several ways. One system provides an immediate, unconscious evaluation of whether the stimulus is good or bad (LeDoux, 1993; Mischel & Shoda, 1995). This system gives rise to automatic, unconscious emotional reactions to stimuli that call for quick responses—for example, avoiding a hissing snake in your path or approaching a crying child who has just fallen. As you learned in the chapter on attitudes and persuasion, this system likely involves a portion of the brain known as the amygdala (see Chapter 7). Other systems provide a more deliberate, complex assessment of the stimulus in terms of such things as its size, aesthetic properties, and category membership.

How can unconscious or automatic affective reactions be studied? Sheila Murphy and Robert Zajonc (1993) presented participants with photos of smiling and angry faces. In a "suboptimal" (or subliminal) condition, participants viewed these photos for four milliseconds, which was not enough time to know what they had seen. In fact, in subsequent recognition tests, these participants could not reliably tell the experimenter whether they had seen a happy or angry face, establishing that the faces had indeed been processed unconsciously. In an "optimal" condition, participants viewed the same faces for one second, plenty of time to be aware of and to identify the type of faces they were viewing. Immediately after the presentation of each face, all participants were presented with a Chinese ideograph and asked to rate how much they liked it.

If there is a separate system that unconsciously evaluates the affective meaning of stimuli, suboptimally presented faces might be expected to color participants' ratings of the Chinese ideographs. The initial positive or negative feelings induced by the photos should carry over and color participants' evaluations of the ideographs. This indeed is what Murphy and Zajonc found. As seen in Figure 12.5, the suboptimally presented smiling faces led participants to like the Chinese ideographs, whereas the suboptimally presented angry faces led participants to like the Chinese ideographs less, even though participants could not tell the experimenter what they had seen. No such priming effects emerged in the optimal priming conditions, making the important point that when we are consciously aware of affectively charged stimuli, they are less

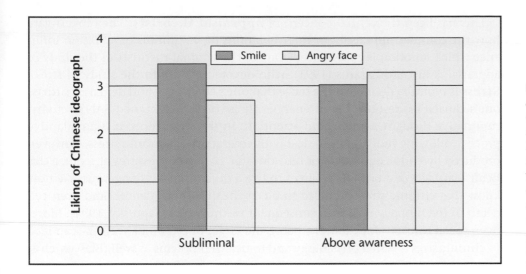

**Figure 12.5  Unconscious Appraisal and Emotion**    To explore whether evaluations can be produced unconsciously, Sheila Murphy and Robert Zajonc presented participants with slides of a smiling face or an angry face, either at subliminal (suboptimal) or above awareness (optimal) levels, and then had participants rate how much they liked Chinese ideographs presented immediately afterwards. People liked the Chinese ideographs more after they had first been presented with a subliminally presented smile, suggesting that that smile had activated positive feeling at an unconscious level. When presented with a smiling face long enough to be consciously aware of it, the smile did not lead participants to evaluate the Chinese ideographs more positively. (Source: Murphy & Zajonc, 1993)

likely to sway our judgments of other stimuli (Clore, Gasper, & Garvin, 2001; Gasper & Clore, 2000).

To the extent that unconscious processing is largely attuned to the emotional content of the stimulus, these sorts of automatic priming effects would probably not be triggered by other features of stimuli. Consistent with this assertion, in subsequent studies, researchers found that subliminally priming participants with small or large circles did not lead them to perceive the size of the ideographs differently, nor did exposing them subliminally to symmetrical or asymmetrical objects lead them to view the symmetrical nature of the ideographs differently. In short, priming size or shape information did not affect participants' reactions to the stimuli the way that priming their emotions did. Thus, we seem particularly tuned to pick up affectively relevant information about the world.

Does the unconscious processing of stimuli shape our emotional experience as well? This would be a remarkable finding, and it would lend credence to Freud's claims about the role of the unconscious in our emotional lives. Research by Ulf Dimberg and Arne Öhman (1996) suggests that Freud may not have been too far off in ascribing great importance to the unconscious causes of our emotions. These researchers presented participants with slides of angry and happy faces very briefly, and then quickly presented other stimuli. Again, participants were not aware of having seen the angry or happy face. Remarkably, suboptimally presented smiles prompted participants to smile, whereas angry faces prompted participants to furrow their brow and to show elevated physiological arousal.

## COMPLEX APPRAISAL AND THE GENERATION OF EMOTION

Thus far, we have seen that people seem to have unconscious or automatic evaluations of stimuli in the environment, evaluations centered on simple positive or negative assessments (Feldman-Barrett & Russell, 1999; see Chapter 7). But, although reacting positively or negatively to objects is no doubt a fundamental response, such things as a warm embrace from a friend, ice cream, and a sunny day at the ballpark are all equally good in many people's eyes. Much more is needed to account for the richness of emotional experience, going beyond generally positive and negative emotions to more specific emotional reactions. In particular, what is needed is a more precise theory of the construal processes that give rise to specific emotions, such as anger, guilt, gratitude, and love.

This has been the central concern of **appraisal theorists**. They investigate how the complex appraisals, or interpretations of, a stimulus or situation influence which emotion is experienced. One of the seminal theorists in the study of appraisal is Richard Lazarus (1991), who devoted his life to the study of stress. **Stress** is typically defined as the sense that one's challenges and demands surpass one's capacities, resources, and energies. It involves heightened SANS activity, ruminative thought, and vigilant attention. In the short term, it is an adaptive process, allowing individuals to deal with emergencies. Chronic stress, however, produced by enduring sources of tension—for example, pressures at work, a difficult marriage, or a lack of resources to live a decent life—is dangerous. We now know that chronic stress can lead to ulcers, heart disease, cancer, and even cell death in the hippocampus and consequent memory loss (Sapolsky, 1994). Moreover, social threats—for example, being the target of racism or sexism—can lead to chronic stress-related physiology and to health problems as well (Blascovich & Mendes, 2000; Blascovich, Spencer, Quinn, & Steele, 2001).

Lazarus noted a problem with the concept of stress—namely, that there seem to be many qualitatively different kinds of stress. The distress associated with losing a spouse is different in myriad ways from the stress associated with racial discrimination or the trials and tribulations of a rocky period in a marriage. What could account for these different kinds of stress? Lazarus's answer is that they involve different emotions, which are produced by different appraisal processes.

Lazarus proposed that there are two stages to the appraisal process. In the **primary appraisal stage**, the person evaluates ongoing events in terms of the extent to which they are congruent or incongruent with the person's goals. Goal-congruent events will tend to produce positive emotions. Goal-incongruent events will tend to produce negative emotions. In the **secondary appraisal stage**, the individual arrives at a causal attribution for the event, considers different ways of responding to the event, and assesses future consequences of different courses of action. It is at this stage that people figure out why they feel as they do and what they should do about it. The sum of these appraisal processes is a **core-relational theme**, which defines the essential meaning for each emotion (see also Ellsworth & Scherer, 2003; Roseman, 1991; Smith & Ellsworth, 1985). For example, fear is defined by the theme that one is in danger. Anger is felt when one's self or sense of "mine" is offended. Sympathy is defined by the theme that a vulnerable individual is in need of help.

**Complex Appraisal and Emotions** How we interpret what is happening affects our emotional reactions to an event. If we feel threatened or not in control, we may experience stress, as in the case of this woman who may have been cut off by someone in another car. Appraisal of a situation in terms of whether it is congruent or incongruent with a person's goals (in this case, whether the woman will get to where she is heading in a timely fashion) leads to positive or negative emotions (in this case, anger).

## DEALING WITH EMOTIONS

We have discussed how emotions can be automatic and unconscious responses to events and how the construal of events can lead in complex ways to specific emotions, but how do we deal with emotions once we become aware of them? What is the best way to respond to our emotions? Should we talk about them? Should we suppress them? Should we "go with the flow" for pleasant emotions but suppress unpleasant ones? These kinds of questions have motivated researchers who study the consequences of how we respond to our emotions.

One piece of wisdom we can offer is that during trying times it is helpful to write about your emotions. James Pennebaker and his colleagues have conducted dozens of studies in which they have had participants write about their emotions associated with traumas they have experienced (Pennebaker, 1989, 1993; Pennebaker, Hughes, & O'Heeron, 1987; Smyth, 1998). Researchers have used this procedure with people who are bereaved or divorced, who have experienced devastating earthquakes, who are Holocaust survivors, and more recently, who were directly affected by the September 11, 2001, terrorist attacks on the United States. People who write about the most difficult emotions associated with the trauma, compared with people who write in more factual fashion about the same trauma, benefit in myriad ways. They are less likely to visit the doctor, they experience elevated life satisfaction, they show enhanced immune function, they report fewer absentee days at work or school, and college students do better in school (Pennebaker, 1993).

Why does putting your emotions into words help? There are several reasons. First, people who give narrative structure to their emotions gain insight into their interior life, which should enhance their efforts to deal with their troubles and difficulties (Pennebaker, Mayne, & Francis, 1997). Pennebaker and his colleagues laboriously coded participants' written narratives, and they found that the increased use of insight words, such as "I now see" or "perspective," correlate with increased benefits. Second, putting emotions into words reduces the distress associated with not expressing your emotions. Inhibiting the expression of emotion has been shown to heighten SANS activity (Gross, 1998), and we know that chronically heightened SANS activity—for example, elevated blood pressure—can produce health problems (Sapolsky, 1994). Expressing emotions should help to bring SANS activity back to normal. Finally, labeling emotions also identifies what our emotions are about, thus reducing the extent to which they color our judgments of irrelevant domains (Keltner, Locke, & Audrain, 1993; Wilson & Brekke, 1994; Wilson, Centerbar, & Brekke, 2002). If you know that your frustration is due to a prima donna at work, it is less likely to influence your view of other facets of your life. The message is to keep writing those diaries and poems, even if they never bring you accolades or six-figure book contracts. It even appears that writing about more positive life themes, such as your most important goals or the things you feel grateful for, has similar salutary effects (Emmons, McCullough, & Tsang, 2003; King & Miner, 2000).

A second piece of wisdom might at first glance seem to contradict the benefits of writing—namely, to avoid dwelling on your negative emotions. Susan Nolen-Hoeksema (1987) has studied a process called **rumination**, which refers to the tendency to think about some event over and over again, to think of all of its ramifications, causes, and implications. It differs from what people accomplish in writing about trauma in that it does not actively lead to insight, perspective, and change. When it comes to the sources of distress in our lives, it is best not to ruminate about them. Depressed people are more likely than nondepressed individuals to ruminate about the stresses of their lives. In laboratory studies, people who are instructed to ruminate about a negative event experience prolonged negative emotion associated with that initial event, whereas people who distract themselves from the event return to a more positive baseline more quickly (Lyubomirsky & Nolen-Hoeksema, 1995; Morrow & Nolen-Hoeksema, 1990). Thus, we leave you with a rather subtle message: Find meaning in the negative events of your lives, but don't dwell on those events or the negative emotions they generate. Get them out on the page, rather than having them reverberating around and around in your head.

**primary appraisal stage** An initial, quick positive or negative evaluation of ongoing events based on whether they are congruent or incongruent with the person's goals.

**secondary appraisal stage** A subsequent evaluation in which people determine why they feel the way they do about an event, possible ways of responding to the event, and future consequences of different courses of action.

**core-relational theme** Distinct themes like danger or offense or fairness that define the essential meaning for each emotion.

**rumination** The tendency to think about some event over and over again, including thinking of all of its ramifications, causes, and implications.

**LOOKING BACK,** we have seen that appraisal processes give rise to emotion that can be unconscious and automatic, or conscious and complex. People can automatically react to stimuli outside of their awareness, as shown by responses of split-brain patients. People can be subliminally primed with emotional stimuli, which will affect their judgment of other stimuli. Their construal of the causes of events can lead them beyond primary (positive or negative) appraisals to more complex appraisals and emotions. Writing about traumatic events can have positive effects, but ruminating over negative events can lead to depression.

## THE RATIONALITY OF EMOTIONS

For centuries, philosophers have portrayed passion and reason as antagonistic forces vying for control over the human psyche. And most philosophers have sided with reason, assuming that emotions are dysfunctional, disruptive, dangerous, and need to be kept in check by reason, social norms, and morals. Yet, the literature on emotion-related appraisal that we reviewed in the previous section suggests that emotions are in one sense rational. They are based on how we construe the environment. Let's consider a second kind of rationality and ask: Do emotions help individuals respond adaptively? Are emotions rational or reasonable in this sense of the word? When you ride your bike past your romantic partner's apartment in a jealous state to try to catch a glimpse of the affair you have long suspected, are you being reasonable? Do emotions disrupt or maintain healthy social bonds?

While it is commonplace to view emotions as irrational and disruptive, they may actually be rational and serve important functions. One way to assess the rationality of emotions is to ascertain whether emotions actually contribute to or disrupt harmonious social bonds. As it turns out, many emotions that are painful or upsetting to experience in the moment actually benefit social relations in the long run.

> "We all know that emotions are useless and bad for our peace of mind and our blood pressure."
> —B. F. SKINNER

### EMOTIONS AND THE MAINTENANCE OF SOCIAL BONDS

Embarrassment provides a classic example of the social function of emotion. People avoid many realms of social life, from dancing to public speaking, out of a fear of embarrassing themselves (R. Miller, 1992, 1996; Miller & Leary, 1992; Miller & Tangney, 1994; Parrott & Smith, 1991). Researchers have conducted studies in which participants forgo making money so that they don't have to embarrass themselves by sucking on pacifiers in front of their friends. For most people, the experience of embarrassment is profoundly negative.

> "Embarrassment is not an irrational impulse breaking through socially proscribed behavior but part of this orderly behavior itself."
> —ERVING GOFFMAN

Yet, a closer analysis reveals a very rational side to embarrassment, one that serves social relations quite well. Embarrassment serves a vital social function: it signals remorse for social transgressions, prompting forgiveness and reconciliation when people violate the rules of the social contract (Miller & Leary, 1992). How do we know this? First, nonverbal displays of embarrassment—for example, gaze aversion, smile-like behavior, face touching, and head movements that reveal the neck—resemble appeasement displays in other species (Keltner & Buswell, 1997). And empirical studies have shown that such displays prompt forgiveness and reconciliation (Keltner, Young, & Buswell, 1997). In one study, par-

**Embarrassment and Appeasement and the Maintenance of Social Bonds** To maintain harmonious social relations, humans may exhibit displays that remind us of appeasement displays in animals. (A) This little boy would rather be elsewhere, but instead of running away, he averts his gaze from the little girl and exhibits a pained smile of embarrassment. (B) This prairie dog lies on its back and extends its arms and legs toward the other animal in a sign of appeasement.

ticipants observed an individual knocking over a supermarket display (Semin & Manstead, 1982). In one condition, he seemed visibly embarrassed; in the other condition, he was unperturbed. Participants had more favorable evaluations of the person who showed embarrassment. Thus, although embarrassment feels unpleasant for the individual, it is good for social relationships.

This appeasement function of embarrassment may help explain many everyday social phenomena. When people are just getting to know one another, they often embarrass themselves with self-deprecating stories as a way of demonstrating commitment to the social contract. When defendants first appear in a courtroom, there is often considerable concern about the degree to which they show remorse, a self-conscious emotion related to embarrassment.

Let's look at another example in which the apparent irrationality of emotion may actually promote harmonious bonds—love. In many well-known ways, love seems irrational. It can drive you to obsessive and even superstitious thought. People in love often lose touch with their friends and family for a considerable time. These all seem like very irrational outcomes. Or are they?

The economist Robert Frank hypothesized that love serves a vital social function (Frank, 1988). He reasoned that people in long-term intimate relationships must remain committed to each other in the face of attractive alternatives and self-interested courses of action that may harm the relationship. Long-term romantic bonds encounter many threats to commitment, ranging from financial difficulties to infidelity to chronic health problems. Love countervails against these kinds of threats to commitment. In so doing, love makes long-term commitments more viable.

This analysis suggests that romantic partners should be able to quickly convey their love to each other with expressive behaviors that are difficult to feign—namely, through using nonverbal signals (for example, facial expressions that last between one and five seconds, that are symmetrical, and that involve particular facial muscles, as well as mirrored glances and laughter and actions; see Box 12.2). Indeed, love has a distinct display, marked by a pleasurable smile, mutual gaze, approach-related posture, and friendly gestures, which is hard to produce voluntarily and readily communicates love to others (Gonzaga, Keltner, Londahl, & Smith, 2001). Love should promote commitment in relationship-threatening contexts (Diamond, 2003; Hatfield, 1988; Hatfield & Rapson, 1993a, 1993b). Consistent with this assertion, romantic partners who displayed and experienced love in one interaction engaged in more commitment-related behav-

"Reason is and ought to be the slave of passion."
—DAVID HUME

Box 12.2   FOCUS ON CULTURE

# Flirtation and the Five Kinds of Nonverbal Display

Flirting is the pattern of behavior, both verbal and nonverbal, conscious and at times out of awareness, that communicates our attraction to a potential romantic partner.

Givens (1983) and Perper (1985) spent hundreds of hours in singles bars, charting the flirtatious behaviors that predict romantic encounters. They found that in the initial attention-getting phase, men roll their shoulders and engage in exaggerated motions to show off their resource potential, raising their arms to let others admire their well-developed pecs and washboard abs, or ordering a drink in a way that lets others see their flashy Rolex watch. Women smile coyly, preen, flick their hair, and walk with arched back and swaying hips. In the recognition phase, the potential romantic partners lock their gaze upon one another, expressing interest by raised eyebrows, sing-song voices, and laughter. In the touching phase, the potential romantic partners move close, and they create opportunities to touch with provocative brushes of the arm, pats on the shoulder, or not-so-accidental bumps against one another. Finally, in the keeping-time phase, the potential partners express and assess each other's interest by lining up their actions. When they are interested in one another, their faces and hair touch, their glances and laughter mirror each other, and their shoulders and faces are aligned.

**Flirting**

What is the nonverbal language of flirtation, or of other interactions, for that matter? Paul Ekman and Wallace Friesen (1969) have organized the rich language of nonverbal behavior, so evident in flirtation, into five categories. The first is *affective displays*, or emotional expressions, which we have seen are universal. The four other categories of nonverbal behavior are more likely to vary across cultures. There are *emblems*, which are nonverbal gestures that directly translate to a word. Well-known emblems in English include the peace sign, the thumbs-up sign, the rubbing of one forefinger with the other to say "shame on you," and in the late 1960s, the raised, clenched fist for Black Power. Researchers have analyzed over 800 emblems throughout the world, and surely there are many more. It is wise not to assume that emblems have the same meaning in different cultures. For example, the gesture in which you form a circle with your thumb and forefinger means "OK" in the United States, "money" in Japan, "zero" in France, and "let's have sex" in parts of Mediterranean Europe. When accepting an invitation to dinner in Greece, be careful not to give this gesture.

American athletes at the 1968 Olympics in Mexico City raise their fists and display the emblem for Black Power.

*Illustrators* are nonverbal behaviors that we use to make our speech vivid, engaging, and easy to visualize. We rotate our hands in the air and use dramatic fist shakes to indicate the power of our convictions. We raise our eyebrows when uttering important phrases, we nod our head, and we move our torso to show empathy. When Bill Clinton was president, one of his characteristic illustrators was a fist with a partially exposed thumb, which he hoped would signify that he was optimistic and strong.

*Regulators* are nonverbal expressions we use to coordinate conversation. People look and point at people to whom they want to speak. They look and turn their bodies away from those they wish would stop speaking.

Finally, there are *self-adaptors*, which are the nervous, seemingly random behaviors people engage in when tense, as if to release nervous energy. People touch their noses, twirl their hair, jiggle their legs, and rub their chins. The author Joseph Conrad suggested that people always touch their faces when entering into public places. Try the experiment yourself. See how frequently people touch their faces when entering a restaurant or bar. Be sure to include an appropriate baseline of comparison.

iors, such as reassurance and kindness, in a conflict discussion that posed an obvious threat to the couple's bond (Gonzaga, Keltner, Londahl, & Smith, 2001). Finally, the nonverbal display of love has been shown to correlate with levels of oxytocin, a neuropeptide that promotes monogamous, affiliative behavior (Carter, 1998; Gonzaga, Turner, Keltner, Altemus, & Campos, 2005; Insel, 1993; Insel, Young, & Zuoxin, 1997; Taylor et al., 2000; Williams, Insel, Harbaugh, & Carter, 1994).

## THE EFFECTS OF EMOTION ON SOCIAL COGNITION

We have found that emotions are rational in the sense of promoting harmonious social bonds. But rationality also refers to a reasonable assessment of the evidence and the facts of any particular situation. Are emotions rational in this sense? As we have noted, for centuries philosophers contrasted reason with the passions, suggesting that the emotions are lower or more primitive ways of perceiving the world (Haidt, 2001). It is no doubt true that at extreme levels emotions can get the best of us, causing us to see events in a biased fashion. Our anger may get in the way of seeing the effective actions of an ideological opponent or the benevolence of a romantic partner. Nonetheless, twenty years of research suggest that emotions generally have principled, systematic effects upon cognitive processes, and that emotions lead to reasonable judgments of the world (Clore & Parrott, 1991; Clore, Gasper, & Garvin, 2001; Forgas, 1995, 2003; Isen, 1987; Lerner & Keltner, 2001; Loewenstein & Lerner, 2003; Rozin, 1996).

Take fear as an example. Fear is associated with an attentional bias: fearful people are more sensitive to potential threats in the environment and pay more attention to them (Mathews & MacLeod, 1994; Mineka, Rafaeli, & Yovel, 2003). When people are asked to participate in a dichotic listening task, in which different messages are fed into the right ear and the left ear, they are particularly likely to have their attention drawn away from the message they are supposed to be tracking in one ear to words presented in the other ear if they are in a fearful state and the words presented to the other ear are threatening—for example, "death" or "blood" (Mathews & MacLeod, 1994). Fear is also associated with a memory bias: fearful people are more likely to recall threatening stimuli. And fear is also associated with a judgmental bias: fearful people believe that negative events are more likely to happen to them than do people in neutral moods. When given ambiguous homophones (for example, "dye/die"), fearful individuals are more likely to select the one that has the threatening meaning. Of course, the heightened sensitivity that phobic individuals have for stimuli inappropriately seen as threatening—for example, going outside or encountering small animals—is dysfunctional. Nonetheless, when we are in truly dangerous contexts, it is beneficial to be vigilant to threat.

**Neuropeptides and Monogamy**
The neuropeptide oxytocin plays a role in sexual, parenting, and affiliative behavior in females, as does the neuropeptide vasopressin in males. (A) When the female prairie vole mates, oxytocin receptor sites in brain regions associated with reward and reinforcement are activated, leading to monogamous behavior. (B) Montane voles do not have the same distribution of oxytocin receptors in the brain and are not monogamous.

## ACCOUNTS OF THE INFLUENCE OF EMOTION ON COGNITION

So how does emotion affect cognition? According to the **emotion-congruence perspective**, moods and emotions are connected nodes, or areas, in the associative networks of the mind (Bower, 1981; Mayer, Gaschke, Braverman, & Evans, 1992). In memory, there are pathways devoted to each emotion, in which past experiences, images, related concepts, labels, and interpretations of sensations are all interconnected in a semantic network. When you experience a particular emotion, everything associated with that emotion should be more accessible and ready to guide judgment. For example, if you go home for vacation and are feel-

**emotion-congruence perspective** A theory that maintains that moods and emotions are connected nodes, or areas, in the associative networks of the mind, and that the content of the mood or emotion influences judgments of other events or objects.

ing shy and anxious around your old high school friends, all sorts of experiences and ideas related to feelings of shyness and anxiety will more readily come to mind, and will likely guide how you interpret the event.

According to the emotion-congruence account, we should be better able to learn material that is congruent with our current emotion, because that material is more readily integrated into active memory structures, and more easily retrieved at the time of recall. In one test of this hypothesis, participants were hypnotized to feel happy or sad; they then read a brief story about two college students, one doing really well, and the other doing poorly (Bower, Gilligan, & Monteiro, 1981). In a memory test the next day, the participants who were happy when reading the story remembered more facts about the student doing well, whereas the sad participants remembered more about the student doing poorly.

Specific emotions also influence social judgment in emotion-congruent fashion. For example, anger leads people to blame others for various actions, and to be acutely sensitive to unfair actions, whereas sadness leads people to attribute events to impersonal, situational causes (Feigenson, Park, & Salovey, 2001; Keltner, Ellsworth, & Edwards, 1993; Lerner, Goldberg, & Tetlock, 1998; Quigley & Tedeschi, 1996). Anger leads people to judge unfair events to be more likely in the future, whereas sadness makes loss seem more likely (DeSteno, Petty, Wegener, & Rucker, 2000). Fear leads people to be overly pessimistic and to overestimate risk in the environment (Lerner & Keltner, 2001).

A second approach to the effects of emotion on cognition is the **feelings-as-information perspective** (Clore, 1992; Clore & Parrott, 1991; Schwarz, 1990; Schwarz & Clore, 1983). This account rests on two assumptions. The first is that emotions provide us with rapid, reliable information about events and conditions within our current social environment—for example, anger signals that a state of injustice exists and needs to be changed. A second assumption is that many judgments that we routinely make—for example, deciding how happy we are, or how satisfied we are with the government—are often too complex for us to thoroughly review all the relevant evidence. For instance, a thorough answer to a question about your own personal satisfaction might lead you to think about whether you're meeting your goals, whether your health is good, whether your finances will ever be in order, whether the government will pass a bill to increase funding for college students, how serious global warming is, and so on. Given this complexity, we often rely on a simpler assessment that is based on our current feelings, asking ourselves, "How do I currently feel about it?"

To test this feelings-as-information perspective, Norbert Schwarz and Jerry Clore (1983) studied the potent effects that bright sunny days and gloomy, overcast days have on the emotional lives of people in the Midwest. They telephoned people in Illinois either on a cloudy or sunny day. They asked participants, "All things considered, how satisfied or dissatisfied are you with your life as a whole these days?" Participants had to indicate satisfaction based on a 10-point scale with 10 being "completely satisfied with life." In one condition, researchers simply asked participants about their mood and life satisfaction on that day. The researchers predicted that participants who were called on a sunny day would be happier and would report greater life satisfaction than participants who were called on a gloomy day. In a second condition, before being asked about mood and life satisfaction, other participants were asked, "How's the weather down there?" Schwarz and Clore reasoned that this question would lead those participants to attribute their current mood and life satisfaction to the weather and not to use their feelings in evaluating their life satisfaction (see Table 12.2). Finally, at the end of this brief survey, participants indicated how happy they felt at that moment.

**feelings-as-information perspective** A theory that assumes that, since many judgments are often too complex for us to thoroughly review all the relevant evidence, we rely on our emotions to provide us with rapid, reliable information about events and conditions within our social environment.

## Table 12.2   Feelings as Information

People often use their current feelings to make complex social judgments. In a study of the feelings-as-information hypothesis, Schwarz and Clore asked people to indicate how happy they were with life on either a rainy or a sunny day. People reported feeling less happy and less satisfied with life on overcast days, revealing that people use the gloomy feelings of gray days to judge their happiness and life satisfaction. This was not true, however, for people who consciously attributed their feelings to the weather, because these people no longer judged their weather-related feelings to be relevant to their overall happiness and life satisfaction.

| | NO ATTRIBUTION OF FEELINGS TO THE WEATHER | ATTRIBUTE FEELINGS TO THE WEATHER |
| --- | --- | --- |
| Happiness | | |
| Sunny | 7.43 | 7.29 |
| Overcast | 5.00 | 7.00 |
| Life Satisfaction | | |
| Sunny | 6.57 | 6.79 |
| Overcast | 4.58 | 6.71 |

Source: Adapted from Schwarz & Clore, 1983.

When asked only about their mood and life satisfaction, the participants' responses confirmed Schwarz and Clore's hypothesis about the informative value of feelings: people were happier when called on sunny than overcast, gray days, and they also indicated greater life satisfaction. In contrast, when participants were initially asked about the weather, they tended to discount the relevance of their feelings related to the weather, and thus they reported equivalent levels of life satisfaction whether it was a sunny or gloomy day.

Thus far, we have seen that the emotion-congruence perspective suggests that current moods and emotions activate memories, concepts, and feelings, which feed into cognitive processes like attention and memory. The feelings-as-information perspective proposes that people rely more directly on their feelings to make complex judgments. A third perspective, the **processing style perspective**, holds that different emotions actually lead people to reason in different ways. Most studies in this tradition have compared the effects of positive and negative moods. These studies suggest that positive moods facilitate use of already existing knowledge structures, such as heuristics and stereotypes, whereas negative moods, in particular sadness, facilitate more careful attention to situational details (Bless et al., 1996; Bless, Mackie & Schwarz, 1992; Bless, Schwarz & Wieland, 1996; Bodenhausen, Kramer, & Süsser, 1994; Fiedler, 2001; Forgas, 1998a, 1998b, 1998c; Lambert, Khan, Lickel, & Fricke, 1997). Moreover, Bodenhausen has found that people induced to experience sadness are less likely to stereotype others than are people feeling anger (Bodenhausen, Sheppard, & Kramer, 1994). Stereotypes are automatic, effort-saving tools for judging others, and they are more likely to be used when one is experiencing moods and emotions—for example, happiness or anger—that make one less systematic.

Let's take a more in-depth look at a research program motivated by a process-

**processing style perspective**
A theory that holds that different emotions lead people to reason in different ways—for example, that positive moods facilitate use of preexisting heuristics and stereotypes, whereas negative moods facilitate more careful attention to situational details.

504

ing style perspective that might actually change your views of happiness. Most people believe that happiness makes people relaxed, light-hearted, and contented. Think of a creative genius, a Monet, Woolf, Beethoven, or Darwin, and odds are that you'll imagine their creative acts as having been produced during moments of struggle, tension, somberness, and even despair.

Research by Alice Isen (1987, 1993) suggests that this view of positive emotion is wrong. Instead, she contends that happiness prompts people to think in ways that are flexible, creative, and integrative. In her studies, Isen induces positive emotion with mundane events. She gives participants little bags of candy. Participants find a dime. They give associations for positive words. They watch an amusing film clip. These subtle ways of making participants feel good produce striking changes in their thinking. When given one word (for example, "carpet") and asked to generate a related word, people feeling positive moods generated more novel associations (for example, "fresh" or "texture") than people in a neutral state, who produced more common responses (for example, "rug"). People feeling positive moods categorized objects in more inclusive ways, rating fringe members of categories (for example, "cane" or "purse" as an example of clothing) as better members of that category than people in a neutral state, whose categories were more narrowly defined. These effects of happiness have important social consequences. Negotiators in a positive mood are more likely to reach an optimal agreement that incorporates the interests of both sides, because positive moods allow opponents to think flexibly about the positions and interests of the other side (Carnevale & Isen, 1986; Forgas, 1998b).

Why might positive moods prompt us to think in more flexible, creative ways? Barbara Fredrickson (1998) has argued that the overarching function of positive emotions is to broaden and build our resources. Thus, the creativity associated with positive emotion that Isen has consistently documented builds intellectual resources by enhancing our perspective taking, our novel ideas, and our learning. Positive emotions also help us build interpersonal resources, by motivating us to approach others, to cooperate, to express affection, and to build bonds. These findings suggest we should not look upon happiness and pleasure so skeptically.

**LOOKING BACK,** we have seen that emotions are rational, helping individuals respond adaptively to situations and maintain social bonds. They also help people to assess evidence and facts about given situations, generally leading to reasonable judgments of the world. People are often better able to learn material associated with their current mood. Moreover, their feelings often enable them to make quick judgments when they don't have the time to carefully review all the facets of a particular situation. Finally, positive moods facilitate the use of preexisting heuristics and stereotypes and may also contribute to creativity, while negative moods can lead to more attention to details.

# HAPPINESS

It is only fitting that we conclude this chapter by asking a question that has long preoccupied philosophers and laypeople alike: What is happiness? The Declaration of Independence refers to inalienable rights, among which are "life, liberty, and the pursuit of happiness." Various philosophers have considered happiness to be one of the highest aims of living and a metric for assessing the moral quality of human action. What exactly is happiness? There are many ways to break down this question: What determines if we will experience pleasure? Can we predict what will make us happy? What actually brings us lasting happiness?

## THE DETERMINANTS OF PLEASURE

Pleasure is a core element of many experiences of happiness. Therefore, to study happiness, we first can ask: What makes for a pleasurable experience? Barbara Fredrickson (1998) and Daniel Kahneman (1999) have found some surprising answers to this question. In their research, they have had people experience pleasure in different ways. For example, in one study, participants watched pleasurable films, such as a comedy routine or a puppy playing with a flower (Fredrickson & Kahneman, 1993). While participants watched these clips, they rated their second-by-second pleasure using a dial. These second-by-second ratings were then correlated with their ratings of their overall pleasure at the end of the clip. The question of interest was: How do participants' immediate reports of pleasure predict their overall recollections of pleasure?

This study and others like it have documented three determinants of people's overall assessments of pleasure. First, the *peak moment* of pleasure associated with an event—for example, that burst of joy as you eat an ice-cream sundae—strongly predicts how much pleasure you will associate with the event. Second, how you feel at the *end* of the event also strongly predicts your overall reports of pleasure. If you are planning a backpacking trip through Europe or a first date, make sure that last day (or the last five minutes) is really pleasurable. Finally, and somewhat surprisingly, the length of the pleasurable experience is unrelated to overall reports of pleasure, a bias deemed **duration neglect**. Whether the neck massage lasts twenty or sixty minutes, whether a first date lasts one hour or ten, seems to have little sway over our experience of pleasure. What matters is whether the peak moment and ending are good. The same principle of the importance of peak and end moments, as well as duration neglect, holds for negative experiences. Remembered pain is predicted by peak and end discomfort, but not by its duration (Kahneman, 1999).

> **duration neglect** The relative unimportance of the length of an emotional experience, be it pleasurable or unpleasant, in judging the overall experience.

# KNOWING WHAT MAKES US HAPPY

A second question we can ask about happiness is: Do we know what makes us happy? Can we reliably predict what will make us happy, and what will bring us despair? These kinds of predictions are profoundly important. We burn the midnight oil at work on the assumption that career success will bring lasting joy. We choose graduate schools, careers, vacations, and marriage partners based on the sense that one option will bring more happiness than others. In deciding what career or romantic partner to choose, we may begin with practical questions, but we are very likely to come back to the basic question: What will make us happy? Is the answer simple? Regrettably, it is not as simple as we would like it to be.

In their research on **affective forecasting**, Daniel Gilbert and Timothy Wilson have documented a variety of biases that undermine our attempts to predict what will make us happy (Gilbert, Brown, Pinel, & Wilson, 2000). Take one study that examined the expected and actual impact of breaking up with a romantic partner (Gilbert, Pinel, Wilson, Blumberg, & Wheatley, 1998). People who had not experienced a romantic breakup, called "luckies," reported on their own overall happiness and then predicted how happy (or unhappy in this case) they would be two months after a romantic breakup. This estimate was compared with the happiness of people who had recently broken up, labeled "leftovers." As seen in Figure 12.6, leftovers were just as happy as luckies, but luckies predicted that they would be much less happy two months after a breakup than leftovers actually were. People overestimated how much a romantic breakup would diminish their life satisfaction.

A related study looked at the predicted and actual effects of getting tenure (Gilbert, Pinel, Wilson, Blumberg, & Wheatley, 1998). As you may know, professors are evaluated around six years into their job, and either given tenure, which means they have a permanent position at the university, or they are sent packing. The tenure process is fraught with anxiety, awakening young professors in cold sweats at all hours of the night, and it is the source of a host of soothing rationalizations and jokes ("Did you hear why Jesus didn't get tenure? He was a great teacher, but he didn't publish much.").

As it turns out, many of these tenure-related anxieties and aspirations may be misguided. Professors who did not get tenure were not significantly less happy

> **affective forecasting** Predicting our future emotions—for example, whether an event will make us happy or angry or sad, or for how long.

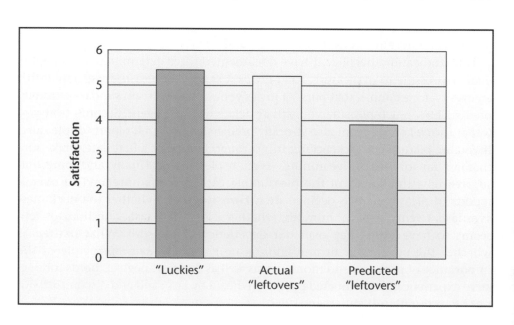

**Figure 12.6 Do We Know What Makes Us Happy?** Daniel Gilbert and his colleagues asked whether people are accurate in their judgments of how happy they will be following a romantic breakup. Consistent with their claims about biased affective forecasting, people predicted that a romantic breakup would make them less happy (predicted "leftovers") than was actually the case (actual "leftovers"). (Source: Adapted from Gilbert, Pinel, Wilson, Blumberg, & Wheatley, 1998)

than those who did. Once again, predictions differed from reality. Young assistant professors predicted a level of happiness after a favorable decision that was far above what was actually observed in professors who did get tenure. Assistant professors expected a level of happiness after a denial of tenure that was far below what was actually observed in professors who had been denied tenure.

A variety of biases interfere with our attempts to predict the level of our future happiness. One is **immune neglect** (Gilbert, Pinel, Wilson, Blumberg, & Wheatley, 1998). We are often remarkably resilient in responding to painful setbacks, in large part because of what Gilbert and Wilson deem the "psychological immune system," which allows us to rise above the effects of negative experience and trauma. We find the silver lining, the humor, the potential for growth, insight, and positive change in the face of painful setbacks and traumatic experiences, and these "immune-related" processes allow us to return to satisfying lives in the face of negative experiences. The problem in predicting happiness, however, is that we fail to consider these processes when estimating the effects of traumatic events like breakups or failures at work. We assume that we will be devastated by traumatic negative events, but in fact we often respond in resilient fashion. As a consequence, we have difficulties predicting our future happiness.

Another bias is **focalism**: we focus too much on the main elements of significant events, such as the initial despair after learning that one has been denied tenure, neglecting to consider how other aspects of our lives will also shape our satisfaction (Wilson, Wheatley, Meyers, Gilbert, & Axson, 2000). As we move through life, it is common for us to assume that once one event happens—for example, once we ace our GREs, get married, or have children—we will be truly happy. What we forget to consider is that often after those exam scores arrive, after our wedding, or after the arrival of our children, many other events—for example, problems on our job, conflicts with our spouse, or difficulties with our children—will impinge on our happiness. Or as another example, we imagine a trip to the tropics and focus on sunny relaxation, avocado shrimp cocktails, swimming amidst brilliantly colored fish, and dancing in the sand. We fail to think of the sunburn, the funky rent-a-car, the daily hassles of exchanging money and finding lodging, and squabbling with family members over the right place to eat.

**immune neglect** The tendency to underestimate our capacity to be resilient in responding to difficult life events, which leads us to overestimate the extent to which life's difficulties will reduce our personal well-being.

**focalism** A tendency to focus too much on a central aspect of an event, while neglecting to consider the impact of ancillary aspects of the event or the impact of other events.

## THE HAPPY LIFE

Our final question concerning happiness may be the most important of all: What brings people happiness in their lives? In an integration of studies that involved 1.1 million people, Ed Diener and his colleagues discovered that most people are happy (Diener, Oishi, & Lucas, 2003). The modal response on a 10-point scale, with 10 defined as very happy, was 7 (Myers, 2000a, 2000b). Although depression and generalized anxiety understandably attract a lot of attention, most people seem to be fairly happy with how life is going.

What, then, are the sources of general satisfaction with life? Let's begin our answer to this question with a classic study. What would your life be like if you won the lottery, or you lost the use of your legs? You might predict that you'd rather die than lose the use of your legs for the rest of your life, and that if you won the lottery, you'd quit your job and live a blissful life free of worry. To the contrary, Philip Brickman and his colleagues found that lottery winners were only slightly more happy than a control group, and that people who had lost the use of their legs in an accident were only modestly less satisfied with their lives than were control participants (Brickman, Coates, & Janoff-Bulman, 1978; see

**Figure 12.7 Satisfaction with Life and Adaptation to Life Events**   Do significant life events radically shift our well-being? Perhaps not as much as we might expect, or as much as we would posit to account for the frenzies surrounding the sales of lottery tickets. In this study, winning the lottery did not make people more happy compared to a control group of participants, and becoming paraplegic only modestly reduced personal happiness. (Source: Adapted from Brickman, Coates, & Janoff-Bulman, 1978)

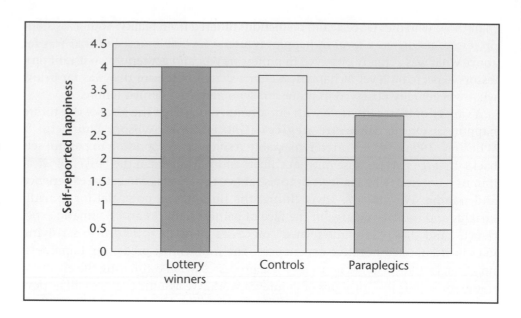

"Nothing's either good or bad but thinking makes it so."
—WILLIAM SHAKESPEARE, HAMLET

Figure 12.7). This may be because we find ways to accept whatever happens to us, employing all the tools in our psychological immune system. We adapt rapidly to life circumstances. It often seems that our personal satisfaction rests more on how we interpret what life presents us than on the actual events themselves.

What about other determinants of life satisfaction? Do you have any intuitions about who is happier: women or men? It turns out that gender matters little in the realm of happiness: women are about as happy as men. The same is true for age: although people become a bit happier as they age, in general age has a weak effect on happiness. So much for midlife crises.

What about money? Here the story is a bit complicated, and not what one might expect. In wealthier countries, money has little relationship with life satisfaction. College undergraduates now state that earning a lot of money is the primary reason for going to college (74 percent reported this in one recent survey, up from 24 percent twenty years ago), and yet for these individuals more money is not likely to lead to more satisfaction (Myers, 2000b). But money does affect life satisfaction for people who have little. People from poorer nations are less happy than those in rich nations. This may be because they often suffer from a lack of jobs, poor nutrition, and diseases that are correlated with poverty.

What about relationships? Are they a source of happiness? Relationships do matter, it turns out, a great deal. In the 1970s and 1980s in the United States, married people were twice as likely to say that they are "very happy" (48 percent) than were unmarried people (24 percent). Moreover, contact with friends consistently correlates strongly with levels of life satisfaction (Myers, 1999). We are social beings, and having strong social bonds brings great satisfaction.

Broader cultural factors matter as well. In surveys of individuals from different countries, people are happier in individualistic cultures, in cultures where individuals have rights—for example, the right to vote—and in countries where there is more rather than less economic equality (Diener, 2000).

**LOOKING BACK,** we have seen that people's retrospective experiences of happiness are based on peak and end pleasures, but not on the duration of the pleasurable experience. People have difficulty predicting whether they will be happy in the future, as they are often more resilient than they realize they will be, and they may tend to focus on certain aspects of future events while neglecting other aspects that will actually be important in the future. Most people are happy because they are able to adapt rapidly to life's circumstances. In wealthy countries, money, age, and gender do not seem to affect life satisfaction, but relationships with family and friends are important sources of happiness for people throughout the world.

## SUMMARY

1. *Emotions* can be defined as multi-component, brief, goal-based responses that help us respond to problems and opportunities, especially social ones.

2. The experience of emotion is generally *brief,* lasting on the order of seconds or minutes, as opposed to the experience of moods, which often last for hours and days.

3. Emotions are generally felt about *specific* people and events, motivating individuals to achieve specific *goals*, such as redressing injustice or fleeing from a dangerous situation, or promoting and *preserving social bonds.*

4. Emotions involve physiological processes, including changes in the *autonomic nervous system*. The sympathetic nervous system (SANS) prepares the body for action by increasing heart rate, blood pressure, and cardiac output, among other effects, while the parasympathetic nervous system (PANS) restores the body's resources by decreasing heart rate and blood pressure, among other effects.

5. Emotions involve expressive processes, enabling us to communicate our feelings and reactions through configurations of muscles in the face, as well as through touch, the voice, and art.

6. Emotions involve cognitive processes. Language enables us to label our emotions. At the same time, emotion shapes our memories and judgments as well as what we pay attention to.

7. There are universal aspects to emotion based on evolutionary factors, not surprising given that emotions enable us to respond quickly and effectively to threats and opportunities related to survival.

8. Paul Ekman's studies revealed that people in dramatically different cultures judge expressions of anger, disgust, fear, happiness, sadness, and surprise in highly similar fashion.

9. There are cultural differences in when and which emotions are expressed based on culturally specific *display rules* and *ritualized displays*.

10. There is cultural variation as to the number of words used to represent various emotions, as well as in what triggers various emotions. Cultures vary as to whether elicitors of emotion are socially "engaging" or "disengaging." In different cultures, similar construal processes give rise to the experience of emotion, but people from different cultures vary in their construal of *particular events* and in which *emotional cues* they pay attention to.

11. William James believed that an emotionally exciting stimulus generated a physiological response, the perception of which is the emotion, and that each emotion had a distinct bodily response.

12. Stanley Schachter and Jerome Singer proposed a *two-factor theory of emotion* in which the two components are undifferentiated physiological arousal and the construal of the state of undifferentiated arousal. Their studies showed the importance of cognition in the experience of emotion, as participants often made a *misattribution of arousal*.

13. Paul Ekman and Wallace Friesen found distinct patterns of facial expression for different emotions. Using the Directed Facial Action (DFA) task, Ekman and Friesen, along with Robert Levenson, directed participants to make faces of the sort that would be

produced by various emotions. They found that different expressions resulted in different autonomic patterns for anger, disgust, and fear.

14. There is both conscious and unconscious elicitation of emotion. Some emotion-related appraisal is unconscious and automatic, as shown by studies using subliminal priming, and some is conscious and complex.

15. Robert Zajonc and others demonstrated that unconscious perception of anger and happiness can change the evaluations of subsequently presented stimuli, the individual's emotional response.

16. Appraisal theorists such as Richard Lazarus study *primary* and *secondary appraisal*. In the primary appraisal stage, people evaluate whether ongoing events are congruent with their goals, experiencing positive emotions for goal-congruent events and negative emotions for goal-incongruent events. In the secondary appraisal stage, people determine why they feel as they do and what to do about it, considering different ways of responding and possible future consequences of different responses.

17. There are different ways of dealing with emotions once we become aware of what we are feeling. There are benefits to writing about negative emotions and perils to ruminating on them.

18. Emotions are rational in that they can help people respond adaptively in different situations. Emotions tend to promote order in social relations. Contrary to intuition, emotions like embarrassment and love, while experienced as chaotic and irrational, actually promote more stable social bonds.

19. Emotions can help us to make rational assessments of complex situations. According to the *emotion-congruence account*, emotions can influence thinking by making anything associated with a particular emotion more accessible and ready to guide judgment.

20. The *feelings-as-information account* says that emotions provide rapid and reliable information for different judgments when we don't have enough time to evaluate detailed and complex information.

21. The *processing style account* says that different emotions lead us to process information in different ways, with positive emotions leading to the use of heuristics and stereotypes, and negative emotions leading to more systematic and detailed assessments.

22. People's overall assessments of pleasure seems closely tied to the peak and end of the pleasurable stimulus, and surprisingly, have little to do with its duration. Our ability to predict the sources of happiness turns out to be suspect, in part due to two biases: *immune neglect* and *focalism*.

23. Many objective factors, such as gender, age, and money, have surprisingly small effects on our happiness. In contrast, social-cultural factors, such as relationships with friends and family, and social equality, have substantial effects upon our happiness.

## CRITICAL THINKING ABOUT BASIC PRINCIPLES

1. Knowing what you now know about emotion, if you were to redo the Ekman study of facial expression in a culture that had had no contact with Western culture, how would you redo the study? What methodological pitfalls of Ekman's study would you avoid? Where would you expect to document universality of expression? And where would you expect to find cultural variation?

2. Are emotions rational? Define what you mean by rational, and provide evidence arguing for the claim that emotions are rational.

3. Do we know what makes us happy? Why is it that we often seem to have little knowledge about what will make us happy or not? In a related vein, what insights did you glean from this chapter regarding living a more satisfying life?

## KEY TERMS

affective forcasting (p. 506)

appraisal processes (p. 492)

appraisal theorists (p. 496)

autonomic nervous system (p. 476)

core-relational theme (p. 496)

decoding hypothesis (p. 479)

display rules (p. 482)

duration neglect (p. 505)

emotion-congruence perspective
(p. 501)

emotions (p. 475)

encoding hypothesis (p. 479)

feelings-as-information perspective
(p. 502)

focalism (p. 507)

forced-choice critique (p. 482)

free-response critique (p. 481)

hypercognize (p. 484)

immune neglect (p. 507)

misattribution of arousal (p. 489)

primary appraisal stage (p. 496)

processing style perspective (p. 503)

ritualized displays (p. 483)

rumination (p. 497)

secondary appraisal stage (p. 496)

stress (p. 496)

two-factor theory of emotion
(p. 488)

## FURTHER READING

Damasio, A. R. (1994). *Descartes' error: Emotion, reason, and the human brain*. New York: Free Press.

Darwin, C. (1872/1998). *The expression of emotions in man and animals* (3rd ed.). New York: Oxford University Press.

Forgas, J. P. (1995). Mood and judgment: The affect infusion model (AIM). *Psychological Bulletin, 117*(1), 39–66.

Keltner, D., & Haidt, J. (2001). Social functions of emotions. In T. Mayne & G. Bonanno (Eds.), *Emotions: Current issues and future directions* (pp. 192–213). New York: Guilford Press.

Mesquita, B., & Frijda, N. H. (1992). Cultural variations in emotions: A review. *Psychological Bulletin, 112*, 179–204.

# Chapter Outline

# CHAPTER 13

# Aggression and Altruism

On the evening of April 6, 1994, Odette and Jean-Baptiste, Rwandan physicians who were married to each other, were enjoying a drink with a friend while listening to the radio. Just after eight o'clock, they heard that the plane carrying President Juvenal Habyarimana of Rwanda and President Cyprien Ntaryamira of Burundi, both of whom were Hutus, had been struck by a missile and crashed outside the airport of Kigali, the capital of Rwanda. Odette knew there was going to be trouble. Unlike the Hutu president or her husband, Odette was a Tutsi, and she had witnessed several massacres of her people at the hands of the Hutus, a people with whom they shared a language, religion, and history of living together. She was worried that the incident would be used to fuel anti-Tutsi sentiment among the majority Hutus.

Tragically, she proved to be right. In the 100 days that followed, Hutus would massacre approximately 800,000 Tutsis and moderate Hutus. The violence was incited by a small coterie of Hutus and a manifesto known as "The Hutu Ten Commandments" published in a widely read newspaper, the *Kangura*. Much as Nazi laws set the stage for the extermination of 6 million Jews, these commandments warned of the dangers of the Tutsis, insisting that Tutsi women were secret agents bent on Hutu demise, that Hutu men who married or employed Tutsi women were traitors, that Hutus who did business with a Tutsi were enemies of the Hutu people, and that the country should be purified of the Tutsis.

Many of the massacres were carried out by militiamen, known as the *interahamwe*. Often drunk on beer, they set up roadblocks throughout Rwanda, pulled Tutsis from their cars, and killed them. Thousands of other massacres were carried out in small Rwandan towns. Hutus turned on their Tutsi neighbors, brutally killing them with machetes. Hutu schoolteachers massacred their Tutsi students. Even Tutsis taking sanctuary in churches were massacred. Hutus were encouraged to disembowel pregnant Tutsis. In some parts of Rwanda, Hutus were given a small monetary reward for bringing in the heads of Tutsis. Throughout the rolling hills of Rwanda, flocks of crows and buzzards signaled where massacres had taken place.

Amidst this unthinkable violence, pockets of altruism arose. Bonaventure Nyibizi, a Tutsi economist who had worked for the U.S. Agency for International Development, escaped with his family to a Catholic cathedral, a sanctuary for hundreds of Tutsis. The *interahamwe* arrived at the church, intent on killing many Tutsis who had taken shelter there. Nyibizi and his family hid in a small room as the *interahamwe* read a list of names of men, including Mr. Nyibizi, who were to be killed. Nyibizi evaded the roundup, and afterward a Hutu priest hid him in a small office. There he remained for several months, cramped but safe, until the massacres had ended.

Paul Rusesabagina, a Hutu, was the acting manager of the most prestigious hotel in Kigali, the Mille Collines. During the massacres he hid over a thousand people (both Tutsis and moderate Hutus) at the hotel. Each day, the Hutu *interahamwe* would arrive and demand to take some of the Tutsis away. Rusesabagina would ply them with beer and sometimes money and would frantically call and fax influential contacts, appealing for their help. Often risking his own life, he argued time and time again for the survival of his guests.

Rusesabagina and other altruistic Hutus saved Odette and Jean-Baptiste and their children. Upon hearing of the president's assassination, the couple decided to flee to southern Rwanda, where Tutsis were in the majority and where the killing had yet to begin. They first attempted to escape by crossing the Nyabarongo River just south of Kigali. They were pounced upon by *interahamwe*, and they would have died, were it not for $300 given to them by a Hutu nun a few hours earlier, which they used to buy their safety. They then fled through the corpse-strewn streets of Kigali to the Mille Collines. Odette made it past the phalanx of Hutu army officers surrounding the hotel by saying she had been summoned to treat the manager's children. Her children and

**Altruism in Rwanda** Paul Rusesabagina, acting manager of the Mille Collines Hotel in Kigali, Rwanda, saved over a thousand people from massacre by sheltering them at the hotel, bribing the *interahamwe,* and appealing to influential contacts.

**Mass Murder** Genocide did not end with the Nazi murder of millions, it has also occurred in the former Yugoslavia, in Cambodia, in Rwanda, and in Sudan, among other places. (A) An open grave of 10,000 naked bodies was found at the Bergen-Belsen Concentration Camp when the British liberated the camp in April 1945. (B) A church in Nitarama, Rwanda, holding the remains of 400 Tutsis killed by the Hutu *interahamwe* was discovered by a United Nations team in September 1994.

Jean-Baptiste were being taken to the hotel separately and were not so fortunate. The children were stopped at a roadblock and, after a two-hour negotiation, were set to be executed. At that very moment, the vice president of the *interahamwe* happened to arrive and, recognizing the children as friends of his own children, lied to save their lives. Finally, the children and later Jean-Baptiste made it to the hotel (Gourevitch, 1998).

In reading about massacres like the one in Rwanda or the Nazi Holocaust or the political murders of 10 to 15 million of his own people by Joseph Stalin or the mass murder of hundreds of thousands of their fellow Cambodians by the Khmer Rouge, we cannot help but feel despair about human nature and the prospects of humankind. We cannot help but wonder how such violence arises and why it repeats itself in such senseless and mind-numbing fashion. At the same time, we are heartened by something just as striking—how common it is for people to risk their lives for others, even strangers or ideological opponents. We are each potentially capable of aggression and acts of cruelty, just as we are each also capable of generosity and self-sacrifice. These are two of the basic tendencies that define us as human beings, and in this chapter we will explore how these phenomena become manifest in our daily lives.

In discussing aggression and altruism, we will rely on four of the central ideas of social psychology that we have examined in this book. We will consider different situational factors that produce aggression and altruism, from the influence of the media to the effects of subtle time pressures. We will consider how people's construal of complex situations can give rise to violence in some cases and to charitable action in others. We will also turn to recent studies of evolution and of culture to understand how aggression and altruism are universal tendencies and how particular instances can vary by geographical region, gender, and kinship ties. Finally, we will ask whether it is possible for humans to act out of pure compassion.

# AGGRESSION

In terms of the sheer number of people killed by their fellow human beings, the last century was the most violent in history. How can we account for such wanton acts of destruction? Why, after so many years of civilization, are we still killing one another in such alarming numbers? To address these questions, we will examine various situational, cultural, and biological determinants of aggression, and we will explore how construal processes make aggression more or less likely.

Explanations for why aggression occurs vary according to whether it is hostile or instrumental aggression. **Hostile aggression** refers to behavior motivated by feelings of anger and hostility and whose primary aim is to harm another, either physically or psychologically. **Instrumental aggression**, in contrast, refers to behavior that is intended to harm another in the service of motives other than pure hostility. People harm others, for example, to gain status, to attract attention, to acquire wealth, and to advance political and ideological causes. Many acts of aggression are likely to involve a mix of hostile and instrumental motives. A football player who intentionally harms another might do so out of aggressive emotion (hostile aggression), or for a variety of instrumental reasons—for example, to foster a fearless reputation, to help his team win, or to make the kind of plays that secure a place on the team or that earn lucrative contracts.

**hostile aggression** Behavior intended to harm another, either physically or psychologically, and motivated by feelings of anger and hostility.

**instrumental aggression** Behavior intended to harm another in the service of motives other than pure hostility (for example, to attract attention, to acquire wealth, or to advance political and ideological causes).

## GENDER AND AGGRESSION

The aggression part of this chapter focuses on men because violence and aggression are heavily gendered. As Michael Kimmel (2004) has written, when we think about "teen violence" or "inner-city crime" or "urban gangs" we rarely consider that whether white or black, urban or suburban, marauding "youths" are virtually all young men. News reports simply don't mention that nearly all the violence in the world today is committed by men, perhaps because this is experienced as normal. Physical aggression is, in fact, from early childhood to old age, the most marked and stubborn gender difference. Ninety-nine percent of all people arrested for rape, 88 percent of all arrested for murder, 92 percent arrested for robbery, and 87 percent arrested for aggravated assault are men. Men are also overwhelmingly the victims of violence. Therefore, most studies of the situational determinants of aggression focus on boys and men.

Women are, of course, also aggressive, but in different ways. New research is exploring the "relational aggression" in which girls and women excel—that is, through the use of gossip, alliance formation, and exclusion (Dodge & Schwartz, 1997). Many female readers will remember with a wince the vicious ways girls can behave toward one another in middle school. Obviously, this kind of aggression can be extremely hurtful emotionally.

The question of why such an overwhelming gender difference exists (and why we rarely question it) is important, but difficult to answer. Are men biologically predisposed to higher levels of aggression? Have evolutionary forces shaped more aggression in males of the species than in females? Does our socialization of boys into masculinity, with violent toys, video games, books and movies, and our "boys will be boys" attitude toward male violence encourage aggressive men? Undoubtedly, all of these forces are operating, and the gender difference in aggression is multiply determined.

We will consider several factors underlying the gender difference in this chapter, but it would be well to start by noting that evolutionary considerations would lead us to expect that men would be more aggressive, at least in the instrumental sense. During the period of evolutionary adaptation in early human history, women were gatherers and nurturers of infants and children, and men were hunters and protectors. Both of men's primary tasks involved instrumental aggression. Men have also, in various historical and cultural circumstances, employed aggression in the service of obtaining mates. Raids on other tribes and communities often involved raping the women and killing their male protectors. Though the upsetting proposal has been made that such behavior had survival value (Thornhill & Thornhill, 1983), increasing the **inclusive fitness** (survival of one's own and one's relatives' genes) of the perpetrators, it is comforting to know that, like almost all human tendencies, the behavior is highly subject to modification and is rare in some societies, including most modern ones.

> **inclusive fitness** An evolutionary tendency to look out for oneself, one's offspring, and one's close relatives together with their offspring so that one's genes will survive.

## SITUATIONAL DETERMINANTS OF AGGRESSION

Many factors make people more aggressive. These include chemical factors such as alcohol, even among people not generally prone to aggression (White, 1997; Yudko, Blanchard, Henne, & Blanchard, 1997). They also include biochemical factors such as testosterone, with delinquents having higher levels than college students (Banks & Dabbs, 1996), and members of rowdier fraternities having higher levels than members of more responsible fraternities (Dabbs, 2000). Moreover, certain genetic factors predispose individuals to greater aggression (see Chapter 5), as does growing up in a violent, abusive household (Caspi et al., 2002). But, as you might expect by this point, many of the most important variables influencing aggression are largely situational in character. Thus, we will begin our discussion by examining some of the better-documented situational determinants of violence.

*Media Violence*    The average American child watches three to four hours of television a day, and many of the programs children watch are violent. Prime-time television programs on average have about five to six violent acts per hour, and about 90 percent of the programs that children watch portray at least some violence (Gerbner, Gross, Morgan, & Signorielli, 1986). By the age of twelve, the average viewer of American television has seen about 100,000 acts of violence, from car crashes on reality police shows to murders and beatings on weekly crime or courtroom dramatic series to dead bodies on the nightly news. Some estimates

**Copycat Violence**    Violence in the media sometimes is imitated in real life, as demonstrated in the attempted assassination of President Ronald Reagan in imitation of an attempted assassination of a politician in the film *Taxi Driver*. (A) Robert De Niro played the would-be assassin in the film. (B) John Hinckley, Jr., attempted to assassinate the president after seeing the film.

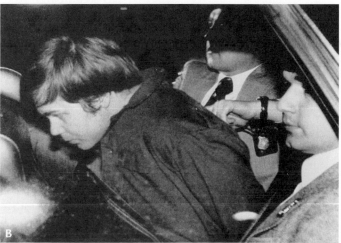

Box 13.1   FOCUS ON THE MEDIA

# Copycat Violence

David Phillips (1986) has marshaled evidence that indicates that one type of copycat violence, namely suicide—which is the ultimate form of violence against the self—is a very real phenomenon. In a first study, Phillips identified thirty-five suicides reported in the U.S. media from 1947 to 1968, and asked whether suicide rates rose in the following months. He compared the suicide rates of those months with the rates observed during the same months the year prior to each suicide, as well as during the same months the year after. This allowed him to control for the effects of weather and season on aggressive behavior (which, as we shall see in an ensuing section, are significant).

In twenty-six of the thirty-five widely reported suicides, the suicide rate rose substantially more in the month following the suicide than in the two comparison months. For example, Marilyn Monroe's widely publicized overdose in August 1962 was followed by a 12 percent increase in suicides in the United States and a 10 percent increase in Great Britain. Phillips also observed a strong positive correlation between the amount of media coverage the suicide received and the increase in the suicide rate. That is, the greater the amount of newspaper space devoted to a suicide, the greater the increase in copycat suicides. And more detailed analyses suggested that people were not engaging in copycat suicides out of grief; people even imitated the suicides of despised individuals—for example, the suicide of a leader of the Ku Klux Klan.

You might be wondering about the effect of a number of variables that Phillips could not measure. For example, were particularly depressive or aggressive people—that is, those more inclined initially to harm self or others—most likely to imitate the publicized acts of violence and commit suicide? Phillips's data do not allow us to tell. But even if people who were depressed or aggressive were more likely to commit copycat suicide, this would not undermine Phillips's claim about imitative suicide; it would just indicate that the effect is particularly pronounced among certain segments of the population.

are that the average high school graduate in America has seen 13,000 killings on TV, not to mention those seen in the movies and in video games.

Does the violence portrayed in the media make people more aggressive? Every year, concerned citizens urge the entertainment industry to curtail its depiction of violence. For example, Tipper Gore, the wife of former Vice President Al Gore, led a campaign to reduce the violent imagery and language in the music industry. Journalists routinely decry the violence on television and in the movies. Are these movements founded on an empirically established link between violent media and aggressive behavior?

Several strands of evidence suggest that people who campaign against media violence are correct in their basic assumption—that exposure to media violence increases aggressive behavior. Let's start with copycat violence—that is, the imitation of specific violent acts depicted in the media (see Box 13.1). In March 1981, John Hinckley, Jr., attempted to assassinate President Ronald Reagan, shooting him in the chest and, by many accounts, severely impairing Reagan's ability to lead the country in the months afterward. What investigators soon discovered was unnerving evidence about the nature of copycat violence. Hinckley had seen Martin Scorsese's movie *Taxi Driver*, which starred Robert DeNiro as a sociopathic, violent man who attempts to kill a politician to win the love of a young prostitute played by Jodi Foster. In Hinckley's own hotel room, there was a letter addressed to Jodi Foster, in which he declared that he was going to kill President Reagan for her.

How prevalent is copycat violence? We know the answer for media violence, not only for the short term, but over much of the life span as well. The work of people like Rowell Huesmann and Leonard Eron and their colleagues in many different countries has led to a clear verdict on the question of whether early exposure to media violence leads to aggressive behavior later in life. Consider one illustrative study in which Eron and Huesmann followed children from the age of eight to thirty (Huesmann, Moise-Titus, Podolski, & Eron, 2003). They assessed the television viewing habits of 211 boys in Columbia County in upstate New York, from childhood to adulthood. They then asked whether the boy's preference for watching violent TV at age eight would predict how much criminal activity he would engage in by age thirty. Importantly, they controlled for how aggressive the child was at age eight—that is, they looked separately at men who had been especially aggressive at age eight. As you can see in Figure 13.1, men who had liked watching a lot of violent TV at age eight engaged in substantially more serious criminal activity by age thirty than men who had not liked watching violent TV at age eight.

The conclusions that Huesmann and Eron have drawn from this research have been reinforced by the results of laboratory studies on the effects of exposure to media violence on aggression immediately afterward (Geen, 1998). In these studies, participants typically view aggressive films and then are given an opportunity to act in an aggressive fashion—for example, by shocking a confrontational confederate (for review, see Berkowitz, 1993). The results of these studies indicate that watching aggressive films does indeed make people more aggressive. For example, one study showed that watching aggressive films compared to control films made juvenile delinquents staying at a minimum security penal institution more aggressive (Leyens, Camino, Parke, & Berkowitz, 1975). Another study indicated that male college students behaved more aggressively toward a female when they were angered (Donnerstein, 1980; Donnerstein & Berkowitz, 1981).

By controlling the specific kinds of violent media participants view, these experimental studies have uncovered the sorts of media violence that are most likely to lead to aggression. People tend to be more aggressive, for example, after seeing films in which they identify with the perpetrator of the violent act (Leyens

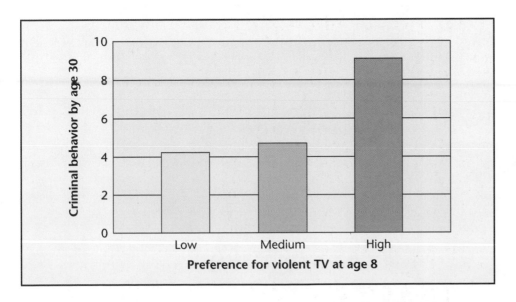

**Figure 13.1 Preference for Media Violence and Aggressiveness**  Men who liked to watch violent TV at age eight, holding constant how aggressive they were at that age, were more likely to commit serious criminal acts, such as assault or robbery, at age thirty than were men who had had little or moderate liking for violent TV at age eight. The y-axis scale for criminal behavior reflects two measures: number of criminal convictions and seriousness of each crime. (Source: Huesmann,1986)

& Picus, 1973). People are also more likely to be aggressive after watching violent films that portray justified violence—that is, violence perpetrated against "bad people" (Berkowitz, 1965). When participants are led to direct their attention away from the aggressive content of the violent film—for example, by focusing on the aesthetic features of the film—they are less likely to be aggressive (Leyens, Cisneros, & Hossay, 1976).

*Violent Video Games*    About 85 percent of American teens play video games regularly (Anderson & Bushman, 2001). Among eight- to thirteen-year-old boys, the average is more than 7.5 hours per week (Roberts, Foehr, Rideout, & Brodie, 1999). And as with anything, there are the extremes—in this case, video game addicts. Two percent of college-age males in America play video games twenty hours or more a week.

Two such aficionados of video games were Eric Harris and Dylan Klebold. They played violent video games habitually, their favorite being the game Doom. Harris himself created a custom version of Doom in which two shooters, armed with extra weapons and unlimited ammunition, would gun down an array of helpless victims who could not fight back. A short time later, on April 20, 1999, reality mirrored their video game world. Harris and Klebold planted bombs and took several guns and massive amounts of ammunition to their school, Columbine High School in Littleton, Colorado, where they killed twelve of their classmates and one teacher, as well as injuring twenty-three students, before killing themselves.

Are video games the cause of this and other kinds of violence? Certainly not the only cause, and many representatives of the video game industry strongly claim that there is *no* relationship between playing video games and violence. For example, in a May 12, 2000, interview on CNN, Doug Lowenstein, president of the Interactive Digital Software Association, stated, "There is absolutely no evidence, none, that playing a violent video game leads to aggressive behavior." Yet, research by Craig Anderson and Brad Bushman and their colleagues indicates otherwise, and suggests that we have reason to worry about the prevalence of video games in youth culture today (Anderson & Bushman, 2001; Anderson & Dill, 2000).

In one illustrative study, forty-three undergraduate women and men with an

**Video Games and the Columbine Massacre**    The correlation between playing violent video games and aggressive thoughts and behavior documented in the laboratory may play out in real life. (A) Eric Harris and (B) Dylan Klebold spent hours playing the violent video game Doom in which two shooters gun down help-less victims, and some observers have speculated that this may have con-tributed to their decision to plant bombs and shoot their classmates at Columbine High School in Littleton, Colorado. (C) Cameras in the school cafeteria on April 20, 1999, showed them armed with guns and getting ready to shoot their fellow students who were huddled beneath the tables. They killed twelve students and one teacher before killing themselves.

average amount of experience playing video games were randomly assigned to play one of two video games. Some played Mortal Kombat, a video game in which the player chooses one character and attempts to kill six other characters. The more killings, and the more violent the deaths, the more points the participant wins. Others played PGA Tournament Golf, a video game in which they completed eighteen holes of simulated golf, choosing appropriate clubs and shots best suited to the simulated wind conditions, sand traps, and trees. All participants then played a competitive game with a confederate. When participants lost, they were punished by the confederate with a burst of white noise. When participants won, they punished the confederate with a burst of white noise. The finding of note: Participants who had played Mortal Kombat gave longer and more intense bursts of white noise to their competitor than those who had played the golf game.

In a review of thirty-five studies like the one just described, Anderson and Bushman documented five disturbing effects of playing violent video games (Anderson & Bushman, 2001): (1) playing such games increases aggressive behavior; (2) it reduces pro-social behavior, like helping or altruism; (3) it increases aggressive thoughts; (4) it increases aggressive emotions; and (5) it increases blood pressure and heart rate, physiological responses associated with fighting and fleeing. These effects were observed in children and adult women as well as in men.

*Heat* The first line of Spike Lee's movie *Do the Right Thing* comes from a radio newscaster who says, "It's hot out there folks." It's early in the morning, and the main characters, clad in T-shirts and shorts, are already uncomfortable and sweating profusely. By the end of the day, tensions between African Americans and Italian Americans escalate, and a race riot ensues.

People have long believed that moods and actions are closely tied to the weather. Perhaps the most widely assumed connection between weather and human behavior is that between heat and aggression. We metaphorically think of angry people as boiling over, "steamed," and "hot under the collar." This is in part due to what anger does to the body: it literally raises temperature in the hands. The connection between anger and heat may also have to do with what the ambient temperature does to people's emotions and actions.

Are people more aggressive when it's hot? As early as the nineteenth century, social theorists noted that violent crime rates were higher in southern France and southern Italy, where the temperatures are hotter, than in northern France and northern Italy. Of course, other factors—such as levels of unemployment, per capita income, ethnic composition, or average age—might also have produced these regional differences in aggression.

Craig Anderson has provided evidence indicating that higher than normal temperatures are associated with increased aggression (Anderson, 1987, 1989). First, there are higher rates of violent crimes in hotter regions. Anderson examined the crime rates of 260 cities throughout the United States. For each city, he identified the number of days in which the temperature exceeded 90 degrees Fahrenheit. The number of hot days (above 90 degrees) was a strong predictor of elevated violent crime rates but not nonviolent crime rates. This was true even when Anderson

**Violent Video Games and Aggressiveness** Playing violent video games like Mortal Kombat may prime aggressive thoughts and feelings, leading to aggressive behaviors.

"I pray thee good Mercutio, let's retire;
The day is hot, the Capulets abroad.
And, if we meet, we shall not 'scape a brawl,
For now, these hot days, is the mad blood stirring."
—SHAKESPEARE, *ROMEO AND JULIET*

**Heat and Violence** People are more likely to become aggressive when the temperatures are especially high. In the film *Do the Right Thing,* racial tensions exploded into violence on a sweltering summer day.

**Figure 13.2. Effects of Season on Violent Behavior.** Do the hot months of summer make people more aggressive? Various studies of aggressive behaviors throughout different months of the year indicate that they do. As shown in the graph, violent crimes such as murder and rape are more likely to occur during the hot summer season than during the other three seasons. (Source: Adapted from Anderson, 1989, p. 82)

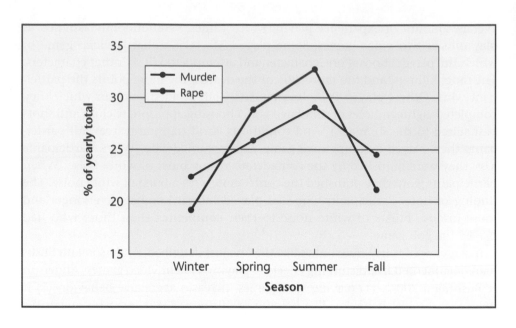

**Construal and Aggression**   Construal processes play an important role in whether there is aggression. If a batter thinks that the pitcher has deliberately thrown the ball to hit him, he may attempt to charge the mound to punch the pitcher. (A) New York Mets batter Jay Payton was hit by a pitch by Houston Astros pitcher Jose Lima. (B) After being hit by a ball pitched by Red Sox pitcher Derek Lowe, Baltimore Orioles batter Gary Matthews tried to go after Lowe but was held back by others.

controlled for the city's level of unemployment, per capita income, and average age of its citizens (Anderson, 1987).

People are also more violent during hot months, such as July and August, than during cooler months like January and February (the one exception to this rule is December, during which time violent crime rates also rise). For example, in Figure 13.2, you can see that murder and rape rise during the summer months compared to the other three seasons. Moreover, in one of the cleverest of the "heat" studies, it was found that major league baseball pitchers are more likely to hit batters as the weather gets hotter and hotter (Reifman, Larrick, & Fein, 1991). This is not due to reduced competence; neither wild pitches nor bases on balls go up with the temperature (see also Kenrick & MacFarlane, 1984).

What is it about high temperatures that might make people more aggressive? One possible explanation involves attributional processes. According to the misattribution perspective, people are aroused by the heat, but they are largely unaware of their arousal. When they encounter circumstances that prompt anger—say, a frustrating driver or an irritating romantic partner—they attribute

their arousal to that person, and their anger and aggression mount. Another possibility is that heat (or other aversive stimuli) triggers a variety of feelings and ideas that potentiate (make more likely) aggressive behavior. It is to this explanation, and its historical precedents, that we now turn.

## CONSTRUAL PROCESSES AND AGGRESSION

Thus far, we have seen that several situational factors—media violence, violent video games, and excessive heat—make people more aggressive. Of course, as we have emphasized throughout this book, situations do nothing by themselves. Rather, they require construal by the individual confronting them. We will describe several efforts to show how construal of some situations can lead to aggression.

*The Frustration-Aggression Hypothesis*   In the late 1930s and 1940s, Neal Miller and John Dollard offered a simple account of aggression based largely on laboratory studies of rats (Dollard, Doob, Miller, Mowrer, & Sears, 1939; N. Miller, 1941). Miller and Dollard argued that *the* determinant of aggression is **frustration**, the thwarting of an individual's attempts to achieve some goal (see Chapter 11). All acts of aggression follow thwarted attempts to reach some goal, and all frustrations lead to aggression—or at any rate, the desire to commit it.

In refined versions of this influential theory, the researchers offered more specific ideas about the determinants of aggression. They proposed that aggression increases in direct proportion to: (1) the amount of satisfaction the person anticipates before a goal is blocked, (2) the more completely the person is prevented from achieving the goal, (3) the more frequently the person is blocked from achieving the goal, and (4) the closer the individual is to achieving the goal (N. Miller, 1941). In a study that illustrates some of these principles, a confederate cut in front of individuals waiting patiently in line to see a movie. In one condition the target was twelfth in line; in the second condition, the target was second in line, about to purchase a ticket and therefore close to two hours of anticipated pleasure. As predicted by the frustration-aggression account, the target who was second in line was much more aggressive in response to the confederate who cut in line than the person who was twelfth in line (Harris, 1974).

*Critiques of the Frustration-Aggression Account*   As compelling as the frustration-aggression account may be, it has been subject to numerous critiques over the years (Berkowitz, 1993). One line of criticism has called into question the assertion that all aggressive behaviors follow from frustration, or the thwarting of goal-directed activity. Consider again the relationship between heat and aggression. How is it that heat blocks an individual's goals? Other findings also suggest that aggression often follows stimuli that do not directly block goal-directed behavior. When animals are shocked, for example, they often aggress against others in their vicinity (Berkowitz, 1993). When people are exposed to extreme levels of pollution, crowding, or pain, they are also more likely to act in violent fashion (Rotton & Frey, 1985). And some forms of instrumental aggression, such as bullying, are not the direct product of the blocking of goals (Olweus, 1979, 1980). For example, bullies often act aggressively against weaker opponents out of an interest in raising their status or showing off—a form of instrumental aggression. In each of these cases, it appears that the stimulus that produces aggression does not have to do with blocking an individual's goals.

The frustration-aggression hypothesis presupposes that frustration necessarily leads to aggression, and not to other responses. This assumption has been called

**frustration** The internal state that accompanies the thwarting of an individual's attempts to achieve some goal.

**learned helplessness** Passive and depressed responses that individuals show when their goals are blocked and they feel that they have no control over their outcomes.

into question as well. Frustration can lead to responses other than aggression. The best example here comes from the literature on **learned helplessness**, or the passivity and depressive responses people show when their goals are blocked and they believe that they have no control over their outcomes (Seligman, 1975). In a series of frequently cited studies, dogs were shocked and prevented from escaping. The dogs did not show aggression; instead, they collapsed into a pitiable state of helplessness and resignation.

*A Neo-Associationistic Account of Aggression* The two critiques of the frustration-aggression hypothesis bring into focus the importance of construal processes in the initiation of aggressive behavior. It is not just having our goals blocked that leads to aggression, it is how we interpret the actions that seem to have caused it. Acts that we construe as having been intentionally harmful, for example, are more likely to make us aggressive than acts seen to be accidental that produce equivalent harm (Worchel, 1974). Observations such as these set the stage for Leonard Berkowitz's neo-associationistic account of aggression, which gets its name because it presupposes that anger-related thoughts and feelings associated with different aversive stimuli are what give rise to aggression.

Berkowitz (1989) argued that any aversive event can elicit an aggressive response—pain, hunger, fatigue, humiliation, anxiety, insults, you name it. The critical determinant is whether the event produces anger. As you learned in Chapter 12, anger is associated with thoughts about the perpetrator's responsibility, fight-flight physiology, and feelings of injustice and revenge. Once activated, this constellation of thoughts, feelings, and physiological reactions makes intentional harm against another—aggression—more likely (see Figure 13.3).

Berkowitz's account helps make sense of why certain stimuli produce aggression without explicitly blocking an individual's goal-directed activity. When heat, pollution, physical pain, and so on, trigger anger, they can lead to aggressive behavior. Berkowitz and his colleagues have shown that simply making people experience pain—for example, by having them raise their arms horizontally for six minutes—can make them judge other people in more aggressive fashion (Berkowitz & Troccoli, 1990). Other aversive events can also cause aggression. For example, the experience of shame often triggers anger and aggression (Tangney, Burggraf, & Wagner, 1995).

*Weapons and Violence* We live in an era in which weapons are pervasive. Worldwide, there are over 638 million guns in the hands of nonmilitary citizens (United Nations, 2002). In the United States, there are over 200 million guns in private hands. Gun control is one of the most divisive political issues in the United States today. Opponents of gun control see the possession of firearms as a constitutionally guaranteed right to bear arms. Advocates of gun control believe that restricting the purchase and use of guns would reduce the number of acts of aggression—especially lethal aggression.

Berkowitz has gathered data that might be used by advocates of gun control.

**Figure 13.3 The Neo-Association-istic Account of Aggression** This theory holds that aggression occurs following aversive events that make people angry. (Source: Adapted from Berkowitz, 1989)

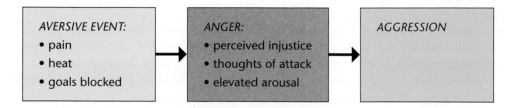

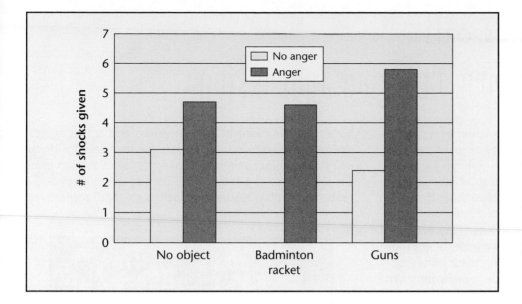

**Figure 13.4 Priming of Anger-Related Aggression** Participants who were angered by shocks they received from a confederate were more likely to retaliate with shocks when there were violent weapons as opposed to harmless objects near the shock machine. (Source: Adapted from Berkowitz & LePage, 1967)

According to Berkowitz, guns serve as a powerful cue that primes anger-related associations, and thus make aggression more likely (see Box 13.2). To test his hypothesis, Berkowitz had male participants engage in an experiment with a male confederate on "the effects of physiological stress upon work" (Berkowitz & LePage, 1967). The participant and a confederate worked on a series of problems, and they took turns "evaluating each other's performance." They did so by delivering between one and ten shocks—with the instruction to deliver more shocks for performances that most needed improvement.

The researchers had the participants work on the problems first. Unknown to the participants, the confederate delivered shocks based on whether the participants had been assigned to a neutral or anger condition (not based on their actual performance). The participants were the first to receive the shocks from the confederates. The confederate shocked those assigned to the neutral condition one time, and those assigned to the anger condition seven times. The participant then watched the confederate work on the problems and gave his evaluation of the confederate's performance in the form of shocks, under one of three conditions. In a "no object" condition, there were no objects near the shock machine. In a "neutral object" condition, there were badminton rackets and shuttlecocks near the shock machine. In a "gun" condition, there was a revolver and a shotgun sitting near the shock machine—a rather unusual experimental circumstance, to say the least! According to the neo-associationistic account of aggression, participants who were angry and primed to think aggressive thoughts by the presence of the guns should be particularly aggressive toward the confederate. As you can see in Figure 13.4, that is what Berkowitz found. It's important to note that the aggression-priming effect of the guns was observed only in the condition in which subjects were made angry; the guns had no effect if participants were not angry (see also Frodi, 1975; Turner & Leyens, 1992).

## CULTURE AND AGGRESSION

In his Oscar-winning documentary *Bowling for Columbine*, Michael Moore pointed out that Canada and the United States have similar numbers of guns per capita, and yet the rate of homicide in the United States is many times higher than that of Canada (United Nations, 2002). Is there something about the culture

Box 13.2   FOCUS ON SPORTS

# The Effect of Uniform Color on Aggression

The tendency to act more aggressively when a weapon is nearby reinforces one of the core lessons of social psychology—the situationist message that seemingly small changes in the environment can have a substantial impact on behavior. It also raises the question of whether there are other environmental cues that might foster or inhibit aggression. Thus, the clothes people wear may exert an impact on how they behave, including whether or not they behave aggressively. Might the menacing black shirts worn by Hitler's S.S. (*Schutzstaffel*) have made it easier for them to brutalize the populace of conquered lands?

Support for such a possibility comes from research on the effect of uniform color on aggressiveness in professional sports (Frank & Gilovich, 1988). The investigators began by examining the penalty records of all teams in professional football (the NFL) and ice hockey (the NHL) from 1970 to 1985. As shown in the accompanying figure, the black uniformed teams consistently ranked near the top in penalties every year. As pronounced as this tendency might be, however, it cannot tell us whether wearing black actually causes players to be more aggressive. There are two other possibilities. First, because of some rather negative stereotypes involving the color black (for example, cinematic villains typically dress in black), players in black uniforms may look more malevolent even if they play no differently than do players on other teams. Thus, players in black uniforms may be more likely than others to be penalized for marginal infractions. Second, the finding may simply be a selection effect—that is, the management of certain teams may believe that aggressiveness pays off in victories, and therefore they may recruit particularly aggressive players and, incidentally, give them black uniforms to foster an image.

The latter interpretation can be ruled out. By a convenient twist of fate, several teams switched uniforms from non-black to black during the period under investigation, and all experienced a corresponding increase in penalties. One team, the NHL's Pittsburgh Penguins, changed uniform colors in the middle of a season, meaning the switch was not accompanied by any changes in players, coaches, or front-office personnel. Nevertheless, the Penguins averaged eight penalty minutes in the blue uniforms they wore before the switch and twelve penalty minutes in the black uniforms they wore after—a 50 percent increase.

Follow-up laboratory experiments have obtained support

both for perceptions of aggressiveness and actual aggressiveness of players in black. Thus, the tendency for black-uniformed teams to accrue so many penalties appears to be the joint effect of a bias on the part of the referees and a tendency for players wearing black to act more aggressively (Frank & Gilovich, 1988).

**Aggressiveness of Pittsburgh Steelers**   The Pittsburgh Steelers, wearing black uniforms, were known for their aggressive play.

But does wearing black always make people more aggressive? Probably not. The effect seems to be limited to contexts that are already associated with confrontation and aggression. Thus, the black clothing worn by Catholic clerics and Hasidic Jews may not make them any more aggressive, but the black shirts worn by Hitler's S.S. might very well have contributed to their brutality.

**Uniform Color and Aggression**   Penalty records of black uniformed teams in the NFL and NHL from 1970 to 1985 (note that the hockey season always stretches across two calendar years; thus, "1985" corresponds to the 1985–1986 season). Points on the graph represent the difference between the average ranking of the black uniformed teams and the average to be expected on the basis of chance alone (represented by the green horizontal line at 0). (Source: Adapted from Frank & Gilovich, 1988)

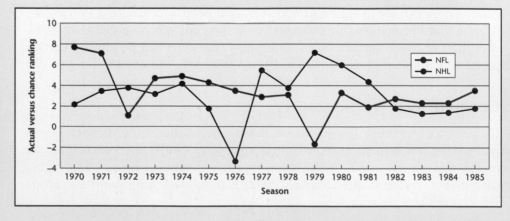

of the United States that makes it so violent—the most violent of any Western industrialized nation except for Russia (United Nations, 2002)? Anthropologists have long noted dramatic cultural variation in levels of aggression. People in certain cultures have been observed to be kind, peaceful, and cooperative. Alaskan Inuits, for example, have been described as rarely expressing anger or aggression. People in other cultures have been portrayed as violent, belligerent, and aggressive. Among the Yanomamo, aggression is encouraged in children, intra-tribal fighting with spears and knives is a weekly source of injury and death, and rape and war are considered an intrinsic part of human nature (Chagnon, 1997).

On the other hand, before we jump to the conclusion that Americans are plain nastier than Canadians, it should be noted that the difference between homicide rates in Canada and in the United States might lie in some factor that is more societal and situational than grounded in national character. And this is what has been proposed by Martin Daly, Margot Wilson, & Shawn Vasdev (2001), who, we hasten to say, are Canadians themselves. They observe that homicide rates at every population level—from neighborhoods to nations—are very sensitive to income inequality. They believe that this is the case because inequality throws males into competition for economic resources and for females—two sources of conflict that often lie behind murder and other crimes. Income inequality in the United States is far greater than that in Canada (and in fact the United States has pulled drastically away from Canada and most other Western countries in terms of income inequality in the past couple of decades; see Chapter 14). The investigators believe that the income inequality difference is sufficiently great to account for the differences in the homicide rate between the two countries.

Furthermore, the cultural perspective on aggression holds that there are certain values, as well as habitual ways of construing the self and others, that make members of one culture more aggressive and violent than others, or more prone to specific kinds of aggression. Let's look at two distinct lines of research that illustrate the cultural approach to aggression.

**The Culture of Honor**    Richard Nisbett and Dov Cohen have explored regional differences in violence in the U.S. South and North (Cohen, Nisbett, Bowdle, & Schwarz, 1996; Cohen & Nisbett, 1997; Nisbett, 1993; Nisbett & Cohen, 1996). Nisbett and Cohen argue that in the South many people feel part of a **culture of honor**, which is defined by concerns over one's reputation for toughness, machismo, and the willingness and ability to avenge a wrong or insult. These

> **culture of honor** A culture that is defined by strong concerns about one's own and others' reputations, leading to sensitivity to slights and insults and a willingness to use violence to avenge any perceived wrong or insult.

**Culture and Aggression** There are cultural, as well as individual differences in the expression of aggression. (A) The Alaskan Inuits rarely express anger or aggression. (B) The Yanomamo encourage aggression in their children and are known for their violent raids against their enemies.

concerns give rise to firm rules of politeness and other means by which people recognize the honor of others, thus lending stability to social relations and reducing the risk of violence. The downside of the concern with honor is that it makes people particularly sensitive to slights and insults, and it gives rise to an obligation to respond with violence to protect or reestablish one's honor.

Several lines of evidence indicate that Southerners are more sensitive to threats against their honor and more inclined to respond with violence to defend it than those from other parts of the United States (Nisbett & Cohen, 1996; see Box 13.3). In archival research, Nisbett, Polly, and Lang (1995) looked at the prevalence of two kinds of homicides: argument-related homicides that involve threats to honor (for example, a lovers' triangle), and felony-related homicides that do not explicitly involve threats to honor (for example, murders in the context of a store robbery). In this study, as in all their research, they examined data only for white males—whites because the various regions of the country differ greatly in the percentage of nonwhites, and males because it is males who commit the great majority of homicides and other violent acts. Nisbett and his colleagues found that murders in the context of a felony were about equally common in the North as in the South and Southwest, but that honor-related homicides were far more common in the South and Southwest than in the North (see Figure 13.5).

These correlational findings, of course, call for experimental research. To examine participants' sensitivity to slights and insults, Cohen and his colleagues set up situations in the laboratory in which confederates insulted participants so that the researchers could see how the participants reacted (Cohen, Nisbett, Bowdle, & Schwarz, 1996). In the insult paradigm, the experimenter asked the participant to deposit a questionnaire on a table at the end of a narrow hallway. In doing so, the participant had to pass a confederate who was looking into a file drawer, which he had to close to let the participant get by. When the participant passed the confederate a second time on his way back, the confederate bumped into the participant and muttered under his breath, "asshole" (and then briskly retreated behind a locked door!). The authors expected Southerners to react more aggressively than Northerners to this insult, which threatened their honor, and they did.

In one study of this type, insulted students from Southern states showed more anger in their facial expressions than did students from the North (Cohen, Nisbett, Bowdle, & Schwarz, 1996). In a second study, insulted Southerners, but not

**Figure 13. 5  The Culture of Honor and Homicide**   The rates of felony-related murders are similar in different regions of the United States, but argument-related murders are much more common in the U.S. South and Southwest than in other regions in the United States, pointing to a sensitivity to slights and insults that characterizes a culture of honor in the South and Southwest. (Source: Nisbett & Cohen, 1996, p. 21; based on data from Fox & Pierce, 1987)

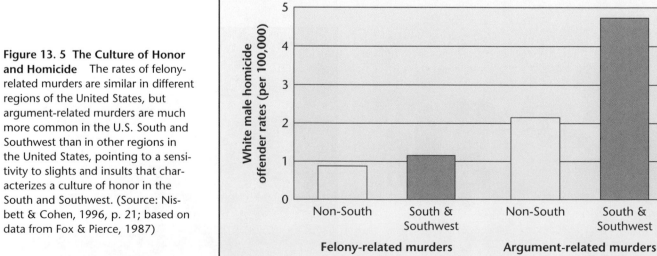

Box 13.3    FOCUS ON CULTURE

# Forgiveness North and South

Social psychologists sometimes employ field experiments to examine the effects of particular manipulations. Such research takes place in real-world settings making use of realistic procedures and materials. One such field experiment concerning honor was conducted by Cohen and Nisbett (1997). They created a job application letter and sent it to several hundred retail businesses across the country. The letter allegedly was from a twenty-seven-year-old man who was qualified to be an assistant manager. In one version of the letter, there was a paragraph stating that the man wanted to be up front about his past:

> I have been convicted of a felony, namely motor vehicle theft. . . . I have no excuse for my behavior. I was young and I needed money. I had a wife and kids . . . and I was able to pay off bills that I owed. . . . I was sentenced to grand theft auto and am very sorry for my crime. I was desperate but now I realize that this is no excuse. I realize that what I did was wrong.

In another version of the letter, the man wrote about a crime of honor:

> I have been convicted of a felony, namely manslaughter. . . . I got into a fight with someone who was having an affair with my fiancée . . . one night this person confronted me in front of my friends at the bar. He told everyone that he and my fiancée were sleeping together. He laughed at me to my face and asked me to step outside if I was man enough. I was young and didn't want to back down from a challenge. . . . As we went into the alley, he started to attack me. He knocked me down and he picked up a bottle. I could have run away and the judge said I should have, but my pride wouldn't let me. Instead I picked up a pipe that was laying in the alley and hit him with it. I didn't mean to kill him, but he died a few hours later in the hospital. I realize that what I did was wrong.

The responses from the businesses to which the letters were sent were coded as to their compliance with requests in the letters: Did they send an application form? Did they suggest hours to stop by? Did they give the name of a contact person? The responses were also coded with respect to the warmth of their tone: How encouraging was the letter? How personal was the letter?

There was no difference in compliance or tone between Northerners on the one hand and Southerners and Westerners on the other for the "theft" letter. For the "manslaughter" letter, Northerners complied less than Southerners or Westerners, and Northerners wrote letters that were coded as being less warm. Indeed, Southern and Western employers could sometimes be quite warm toward the applicant in the manslaughter condition. No Northerner was coded as responding in the warmest possible way, but fully a quarter of the Southern and Western letters got the highest score on the warmth index. An example may convey this difference better than numbers. One Southern store owner wrote back that though she had no jobs, she was sympathetic to the man's plight:

> As for your problem of the past, anyone could probably be in the situation you were in. It was just an unfortunate incident that shouldn't be held against you. Your honesty shows that you are sincere. . . .
>
> I wish you the best of luck for your future. You have a positive attitude and a willingness to work. Those are the qualities that businesses look for in an employee. Once you get settled, if you are near here, please stop in and see us.

No Northern employer wrote a letter that even approached the warmth and encouragement shown by the Southern employer toward the man who had killed to defend his honor.

insulted Northerners, showed elevated testosterone, a hormone associated with aggression and status concerns. Insulted Southerners, but not insulted Northerners, also showed increased levels of cortisol, a hormone that indicates the presence of stress and is involved in fight-flight responses. After being insulted, Southerners shook another person's hand more firmly than Northerners, presumably to reestablish their strength, honor, and machismo. And in another study, the just-insulted participant walked down a narrow hallway toward another person, a confederate of the experimenters, who was 6' 3" tall and 250 lbs. This confederate was instructed not to step out of the way of the participant, no matter what happened. Non-insulted Southerners moved out of the way of this imposing confederate at about nine feet; insulted Southerners waited until they were less than three feet away! Northerners turned aside at about five feet, regardless of whether they had been insulted or not. Thus, non-insulted Southerners actually stepped out of the way sooner than non-insulted Northerners—perhaps displaying some fabled Southern politeness.

Why is honor-related homicide more common in the South? Could it just be the higher temperatures there? It's not likely, because honor-related homicides are more common in the relatively cool mountain regions of the South than in the relatively hot lowlands. Could it be the brutal history of slavery? Again, it's not likely, and for the same geographic reason. Homicide is more common in the highlands, where slavery was relatively uncommon, than in the lowlands, where slavery was ubiquitous.

Why are Southerners more obsessed with honor than Northerners? And why is it that the highlands of the South are more violence-prone than the lowlands?

These questions are intimately related. Nisbett and Cohen (1996) argue that the culture of honor in the South is a variant of one found worldwide in which people earn their living by herding animals. Herders are susceptible to loss of their entire wealth in an instant if someone steals their cows, pigs, or sheep. Farmers, in contrast, are susceptible to no such rapid and catastrophic loss—at least not at the hands of another person. The vulnerability of the herder means that he has to develop a tough exterior and make it clear that he is willing to take a stand against the slightest threat, even an insult or a joke at his expense. This difference fits the pattern of violence in the United States because the North was founded primarily by farmers from England, Germany, and the Netherlands, whereas the South was founded primarily by Scottish and Irish settlers—Celtic peoples who had herded, rather than farmed, since prehistorical times. Thus, the people in the Southern highlands, where the herding culture continued to be a major economic activity until quite recently, were more likely to be violent than the people in the lowlands, where settlers had taken advantage of the rich soil to become farmers.

***Rape-Prone Cultures***  Rape, the coercive forcing of sex by one person (overwhelmingly male) upon another (typically female), is one of the most disturbing acts of violence. The consequences of rape can be cataclysmic, deep, and lasting. Many rape victims are scarred for years. They can suffer post-traumatic stress, generalized anxiety, and fearfulness in open places and toward strange men. Many suffer eating disorders and develop problems in their romantic relations.

What makes rape more prevalent in one culture than another? And how would you tackle this question empirically? Peggy Reeves-Sanday (1981, 1997) relied upon archival records to address the cultural determinants of rape. She read rich descriptions provided by historians and anthropologists of 156 cultures dating back to 1750 BC and continuing to the 1960s. She looked carefully for references to rape in these accounts, and identified what she called **rape-prone cultures**. She defined such cultures according to whether they used rape as: (1) an act of war against enemy women; (2) a ritual act—for example, as part of a wedding ceremony or of an adolescent male's rite of passage to adulthood; and (3) a threat against women so that they would remain subservient to the men.

Of the 156 cultures Reeves-Sanday studied, 47 percent were classified as rape-free, 18 percent as rape-prone, and 35 percent as rape-present, where rape occurs but not as a ritual, threat, or act of war. You should be skeptical of these percentages, of course. They are based largely on anthropologists' observations, and rape is one of the most difficult acts to observe and is a taboo subject in many cultures. It would not be surprising if these figures underestimated the prevalence of rape-proneness across cultures, and worse, from the standpoint of getting accurate information, the figures might differentially underestimate the incidence in some cultures compared to others.

Putting these concerns aside, let's look at what Reeves-Sanday found. One question she addressed is the following: What sexual attitudes predict the prevalence of rape across the 156 cultures? One might theorize that in more sexually repressed cultures individuals would resort to rape to gratify their sexual desire. But she did not find that to be so. She assessed the extent of each culture's sexual repressiveness according to the prevalence of postpartum and premarital sex taboos. The prevalence of rape in each culture was unrelated to these sexually restrictive beliefs or practices.

What about the general level of violence in the culture? If rape at its core is an act of violence, then it should be more likely in more aggressive, violent cultures. This would fit with Berkowitz's account of aggression—that is, members of highly aggressive, hostile cultures should be more prone to feelings of anger, and this should generalize to a greater incidence of all kinds of violence, including rape. This indeed proved to be the case. Rape-prone cultures were more likely to have high levels of violence, a history of frequent warfare, and an emphasis on machismo and male toughness.

Finally, many scholars have treated rape as an act of dominance, a means of subordinating women, relegating them to lower-status positions. This suggests that rape may be more prevalent in cultures in which women have lower status. This too proved to be true. In rape-prone cultures, women were less likely to participate in education and political decision making than were women in rape-free cultures. Women in rape-free cultures were likely to be granted equal status with men.

Consider the Mbuti Pygmies as an illustration of these findings (Turnbull, 1965). In this (reportedly) nearly rape-free society, there is minimal interpersonal violence and fighting. Great prestige is attached to the raising of children, and women's contribution to society is valued. Women and men assume different duties, but they have equal standing. And women and men participate equally in political decision making.

**rape-prone cultures** Cultures in which rape tends to be used as an act of war against enemy women, as a ritual act, and as a threat against women so that they will remain subservient to men.

## EVOLUTION AND VIOLENCE

Throughout the world, literature is full of tales of wicked stepparents who abuse their children and enraged husbands who murder their wives. In the animal kingdom, "step-relations" seem similarly prone to violence. To take one example, when male lions acquire a new mate, they routinely kill all of that mate's cubs from prior relations. Evolutionary psychologists Margo Wilson and Martin Daly suggest that these propensities in our animal forebears have left their trace in human nature as well (Daly & Wilson, 1996; Wilson, Daly, & Weghorst, 1980).

Consider violence against stepchildren among humans. Natural selection, Daly and Wilson reason, has rewarded those parents who devote resources to their own offspring. All the behaviors related to parental care—from filial love to breast-feeding—help to ensure the survival of one's own offspring, thereby increasing one's inclusive fitness—that is, one's own survival plus that of individuals carrying one's genes. Parental care, however, is costly, as any parent of a newborn will tell you, requiring time, effort, and the commitment of resources. In evolutionary terms, these expenditures are offset by the gains enjoyed by having offspring—namely, assuring the survival of one's genes. Stepparents, on the other hand, incur the same costs with no enhancement of their inclusive fitness, since they do not share genes with their stepchildren.

Survey research consistently finds that relations between stepparents and stepchildren tend to be more distant and conflict-laden, and less committed and satisfying, than relations between parents and their genetic offspring (Hobart, 1991). The story gets even worse. Daly and Wilson (1996) found that in the United States children who are less than two years of age are 100 times more likely to suffer lethal abuse at the hands of stepparents than of genetic parents, and in Canada they are 70 times more likely to suffer lethal abuse from stepparents than from genetic parents. These findings hold, it is important to note, even when researchers control for a variety of likely contributing causes, such as poverty, youth of the mother, duration of co-residency, number of children in the house, or reporting biases. In a study of a South American foraging people, 43 percent of children raised by a mother and stepfather died before their fifteenth birthday, more than twice the rate of death (19 percent) of children raised by two genetic parents. (This does not imply that the stepchildren were killed, but at the least that they were more likely to be denied resources—for example, food and health care—that are made available to genetic offspring.)

Let's turn to an evolutionary account of another kind of family violence, uxoricide, or murder of a wife by her husband. The logic of evolutionary theory provides some insight into why males would commit such an act of violence. In a monogamous union, the genetic interests of women and men merge. They both devote resources to their offspring. The problems arise with the possibility of infidelity, which affects women and men differently. A man can be cuckolded (that is, his wife can have sexual relations with another man and consequently bear the child of her lover while passing the child off as that of her husband). When

**Violence against Stepchildren**
Literature and fairy tales in particular abound with tales of stepchildren treated badly by their stepmothers, as illustrated in (A) Cinderella, who becomes the scullery maid for her stepmother and stepsisters, and (B) Hansel and Gretel, who are sent out to die in the forest at the urging of their stepmother.

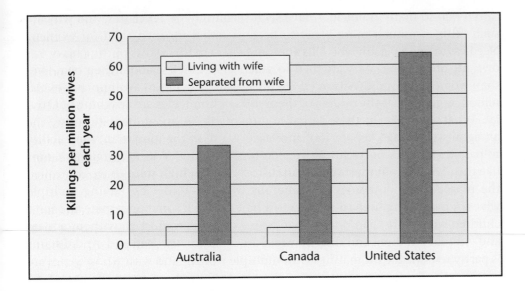

**Figure 13.6 Concerns about Infidelity and Violence**   Husbands are two to five times more likely to kill their wives when they do not live with them. According to Wilson and Daly, this is due to the husband's overpowering jealousy about the possibility that his wife might have children with another man. (Source: Adapted from Wilson & Daly, 1996)

this happens, the husband is led to invest resources in an offspring that is not his—which is why the maternal grandparents go to such great pains to assert that a newborn looks so much like the father (Daly & Wilson, 1982)! This is not only costly in terms of money and resources, but it is likely to reduce his chances of being able to reproduce (since his wife's pregnancy lasts nine months, during which time she does not become pregnant by her husband). It also reduces the resources that will be available for his own offspring, since some of his resources will be going to the other man's child. As a result, one would expect sexual infidelity to be more likely to trigger distress and aggression in men against women than vice versa.

Indeed, Wilson and Daly (1996) contend that concern over infidelity does motivate violent acts perpetrated by men against their wives. They point out that lethal violence against wives in Australia, Canada, and the United States is two to five times higher when the couple is separated than when they are together (see Figure 13.6). When the wife is separated, she has more opportunities, the reasoning goes, to reproduce with other men—an unbearable prospect to her mate. In a similar vein, lethal violence is eight times more likely in de facto marriages—that is, those that have not attained official legal status—than in registered unions (Wilson, Johnson, & Daly, 1995). Again, this may be due to jealousy and suspicions of infidelity, as well as to actual occurrences of infidelity.

An even more remarkable facet of the link between gender and homicide is the relative likelihood of men killing men versus women killing women. Worldwide, across cultures ranging from modern postindustrial societies to traditional hunter-gatherer societies, men are about twenty times as likely to kill other men as women are to kill other women (Daly & Wilson, 1988). Because men as a group are much more likely than women to engage in physical aggression of nearly all sorts, this difference in homicide rates may not be terribly surprising to you. What may be surprising, however, is the precise nature of so many male-male homicides. Extensive studies of the subject have shown that by far the most common type of homicide results from relatively minor skirmishes getting out of hand and escalating to lethal violence. President Lyndon Johnson's National Commission on the Causes and Prevention of Violence put it this way: "Altercations appeared to be the primary motivating forces. . . . Ostensible reasons for disagreements are usually trivial, indicating that many homicides are spontaneous acts of passion, not products of a single determination to kill" (Mulvihill, Tumin, & Curtis, 1969, p. 230).

Why do so many homicides have such seemingly trivial causes, and why are such "tiffs" so much more likely to become lethal for men than for women? Needless to say, a person who kills another person in this way is putting his or her own life on the line. Why are men so much more careless about their own lives than women? Daly and Wilson (1988) once again provide an evolutionary explanation, arguing that the origins of these sorts of homicides are anything but trivial. What's at stake in these lethal arguments is, in an immediate sense, the antagonists' prestige, reputation, and "face," and, in the long term, their ability to pass their genes on to future generations. Daly and Wilson's argument runs like this: Throughout most of human history, men of high status have controlled the reproductive outcomes of numerous women—either by having multiple wives or overseeing something akin to a harem. But if some men mate and have children with more than one woman, some other men must go without a mate and without children, and thus they face an evolutionary dead end. And if status is partly responsible for matings with multiple women and with whose genes are passed on and whose die out, men will compete bitterly to avoid the latter fate. So, although many of these altercations might seem trivial on the surface, Daly and Wilson argue that their roots lie in a capacity for violence that helps to maintain a man's status and, ultimately, his access to a mate (or mates). Those who lack this capacity for violence, and who do not defend their status with sufficient vigor, run the risk of being shut out of the ultimate evolutionary prize—passing on their genes to future generations.

And why are men so much more likely than women to worry about passing on their genes? Daly and Wilson argue that it's because there is so much more variability in "reproductive success" for men than for women (some men have children with several women, whereas historically the opposite rarely happened). Throughout history, reproductively healthy women who wanted to pass on their genes were, almost without exception, able to do so. Not so for men. When Moulay Ismail the Bloodthirsty, the Moroccan emperor during the early eighteenth century, maintained his harem of 500 concubines, that meant there were not enough women for a large number of other Moroccan men, and so some simply did not reproduce. (Genghis Khan was far more successful. It has been estimated that more than 32 million people alive today are his descendants.) Studies of mating practices and heredity in various hunter-gatherer societies also confirm the greater variability of male reproductive success. Among the Xavante Indians of Brazil, for example, 40 percent of the men had more than one wife. Some men, but not a single woman, thus remained unmarried for life. And by the age of twenty, only 1 out of 195 women had yet to give birth, whereas 6 percent of the men were still childless by the age of forty (Salzano, Neel, & Maybury-Lewis, 1967).

**LOOKING BACK,** we have seen that several situational factors—violent television, violent video games, and excessive heat—can make people more aggressive. We have also seen that construal processes matter. In particular, when we blame others for their actions, and experience anger, we are more likely to act in an aggressive fashion. We have also discussed how aggression may vary from one society to another, exploring how people who adhere to a culture of honor are more prone to certain kinds of violence, and how violent cultures that do not give women equality and power are more prone to rape. Finally, we have looked at evolutionary accounts of aggression, which provide compelling explanations of the elevated violence perpetrated against stepchildren and romantic partners. We now turn to the second major topic of this chapter: altruism.

# ALTRUISM

In the early morning hours of March 13, 1964, Winston Moseley stalked a young woman as she walked home in Queens, New York. He tackled her in front of a bookstore near her apartment and stabbed her in the chest. As she screamed for help, lights went on and several windows opened in the surrounding apartments. From his seventh floor window, one neighbor yelled, "Let that girl alone!"

Moseley left the woman, only to return a short while later. He stalked his screaming victim to a stairwell in her apartment house, stabbed her eight more times, and sexually assaulted her. New York police received their first call about the incident at 3:50 a.m., thirty minutes after the cries of distress first awakened neighbors. By the time they arrived, Kitty Genovese was beyond help.

Thirty-eight of the neighbors admitted to having heard her screams. No one intervened aside from the neighbor who yelled from afar. As she struggled and screamed for help, not a single person called the police. Kitty Genovese's life could have been saved. Instead, investigators heard explanations such as "I was tired"; "We thought it was a lover's quarrel"; "We were afraid." One couple simply watched the assault from behind curtains in their dimly lit apartment.

The Kitty Genovese incident shocked the American public. It also moved several social psychologists to attempt to understand the reasons why people fail to intervene during emergencies. Like the Milgram studies of obedience to authority (see Chapters 1 and 6), the Kitty Genovese incident also raises fundamental questions about what we are like as a species. People may not have helped Kitty directly because they feared that direct intervention would expose them to obvious dangers and risks. But why didn't anyone call the police immediately? Are we simply that callous in response to others' suffering?

The Kitty Genovese incident, and the studies we are about to review, reveal a more complicated story about pro-social behavior. At issue is the study of **altruism**—that is, unselfish behavior that benefits others without regard to consequences for the self. There are clearly feelings of compassion and altruistic inclinations that act as forces leading the individual to pro-social, often noble acts. Near the end of this section, we'll discuss the scientific study of how compassion motivates pro-social behavior and altruism. Yet, there are also numerous forces inhibiting altruistic action, including the fear of being hurt and the simple embarrassment one risks by misinterpreting a mundane interaction as an emergency. It seems likely that such concerns were swirling around in the minds of the people who witnessed the Kitty Genovese incident. These sorts of constraints on altruistic action have received the attention of social psychologists; we will examine them as we discuss the situational determinants of pro-social behavior.

**Failure to Intervene in an Emergency**  Kitty Genovese was a young woman who was stalked and killed in Queens in front of her apartment as her neighbors watched from their windows and failed to intervene.

> **altruism** Unselfish behavior that benefits others without regard to the consequences for the self.

## SITUATIONAL DETERMINANTS OF ALTRUISM

No research better reveals the powerful situational determinants of altruism than a classic study by John Darley and Daniel Batson from 1973 that we discussed briefly in Chapter 1. Their study was modeled on the timeless tale of the Good Samaritan, which talks about different reactions to a man who has been robbed, stripped, and left in a ditch. In the Bible story, a busy priest first walks by. Despite being a religious leader and ostensibly concerned with those in need, he fails to stop and help the man. Next a Levite, another religious functionary, arrives and also avoids the man. Finally, a resident of Samaria, a member of a group that followed different religious customs and was despised by mainstream society, sees the half-dead man. The Samaritan stops, helps the man, takes him to an inn, and provides money for clothes and food, which restores the victim's strength.

Darley and Batson's study, which was inspired by the Good Samaritan parable, makes for an even better story than the classic tale itself. The lesson is that subtle situational factors, such as whether or not you are late, powerfully determine whether you will help someone in need.

Darley and Batson (1973) asked Princeton seminary students to give a talk to undergraduate students on another part of the Princeton campus. In one condition, the seminary students were told that the topic of the talk would be the jobs that seminary students typically can find upon graduating. In a second condition, they were to give a talk on the tale of the Good Samaritan. The experimenter then gave them a map of the Princeton campus, and showed them the building in which they were to give their talk. In one condition, the no hurry condition, participants were told they had plenty of time to get to the designated room. In a moderate hurry condition, it was clear that the seminary students would have to hustle a bit to be on time. In the high hurry condition, the seminarians were told that they were already a bit late for the students waiting to hear their words of wisdom.

As the seminarians crossed the Princeton campus, their path led them past a man (actually a confederate) who was slumped over and groaning in a passageway. When the seminary students got within earshot, he complained that he was having trouble breathing. The man was clearly, visibly and audibly, in distress. The question was: What proportion of seminary students in the various conditions would stop to help the man?

The topic of the talk had no statistically significant effect upon the seminary students, though the tendency was for those who were to talk about the Good Samaritan to be more likely to help than those who thought they were to talk about jobs. The big effect was produced by the most subtle of variables: whether or not the students were late. Seminary students who were not in a hurry were more than six times as likely to stop and attend to the suffering man than were the seminary students who were in a hurry to give a talk. Only 10 percent of the students who were in a hurry stopped to help (see Figure 1.1 on p. 12).

Like so many of the classic studies in social psychology, this one offers lasting lessons about human nature. It illustrates how powerful situations can be. Being late made it unlikely that the very people we would expect to exhibit altruism—students studying to be spiritual leaders—would do so. We don't like to discover that we are so susceptible to such minor situational factors. The study itself has many compelling features: the use of seminary students as participants, the naturalistic setting, the assessment of real behavior as the dependent measure. Let's now look at other kinds of situational factors that affect the likelihood of altruistic behavior.

*Audience Effects* One extremely important factor influencing helping is whether other people are present. Researchers who have studied **bystander intervention**—that is, how likely it is for people to intervene in an emergency—have found that people are less likely to help when other people are around (Latané & Nida, 1981). In part, the presence of other bystanders at emergencies reduces the likelihood of helping due to a **diffusion of responsibility**. Knowing that others have seen the emergency, each individual is likely to assume that others will intervene, and thus each

THE FAR SIDE® BY GARY LARSON

Crossing the village, Mowaka is overpowered by army ants. (Later, bystanders were all quoted as saying they were horrified, but "didn't want to get involved.")

feels less responsibility for helping the victim. The witnesses of the Kitty Genovese murder may have seen other apartment dwellers' lights go on, or they may have seen others in the windows, and they may have assumed that others would help. The end result is a disturbing lack of action.

Consider one of the most well known of the studies of audience constraints on helping, a study by John Darley and Bibb Latané inspired by the Kitty Genovese tragedy (Darley & Latané, 1968). College students sat in separate cubicles discussing the problems associated with living in an urban environment. They engaged in this conversation over an intercom system, which allowed only one participant to talk at a time. In one condition, participants were led to believe that their discussion group consisted of two people (the participant and the future victim). In another condition, the conversation was among three people (the participant, the future victim, and another person). And in a final condition, the audience was the largest: the conversation apparently involved six people (the participant, the future victim, and four other people). A confederate (one of the authors of this book as it happens) played the role of the victim.

In the first round of comments, the future victim described his difficulties adjusting to urban life and mentioned that he had problems with seizures from time to time, especially when under stress. After the first round of comments, the victim took his second turn. As he did so, he became increasingly loud and incoherent; he choked and gasped. Before falling silent, he uttered the following words:

> If someone could help me out it would it would er er s-s-sure be sure be good . . . because er there er er a cause I er I uh I've got a a one of the er sei-er-er things coming on and and and I could really er use some help so if somebody would er give me a little h-help uh er-er-er-er-er c-could somebody er er help er uh uh uh (choking sounds) . . . I'm gonna die er er I'm gonna die er help er er seizure er (chokes, then quiet). (Darley & Latané, 1968, p. 379)

The question, of course, was whether the other students would leave their cubicles to help the victim, who was presumably suffering from a potentially lethal epileptic seizure.

The presence of others had a strong effect on helping rates. Eighty-five percent of the participants who were in the two-person condition, and hence the only witness of the victim's seizure, left their cubicles to help. In contrast, 62 percent of the participants who were in the three-person condition and 31 percent of the participants in the six-person condition attempted to help the victim (see Box 13.4). The presence of other people, at least of strangers, strongly inhibits helping behavior (Latané & Nida, 1981).

Several different types of studies have pursued this question of whether we are more or less likely to help when other people are around or when we are alone (for review, see Latané & Nida, 1981). In some studies, people witnessed a victim who was in danger or in pain. For example, participants might witness a person who had passed out in a subway. In other studies, participants might witness a staged theft in a liquor store or on the beach. Across these kinds of studies, 75 percent of people helped when they were alone compared to 53 percent who helped when they were in the presence of others.

**Victim Characteristics**   Needless to say, altruism is not blind. One powerful determinant of helping is whether there is anything about the victim that suggests it might be costly to render assistance. In one study, carried out on a subway train in Philadelphia, a victim (actually a confederate) staggered across the car,

## Box 13.4 FOCUS ON DAILY LIFE

# Likelihood of Being Helped

A given bystander is less likely to help in an emergency situation if there are other bystanders around. But the chances of your receiving help are the chances of your receiving help from *any* of the bystanders, and when there are more bystanders there are more people who might help. Consider the "seizure" study described in the text. When participants thought they were alone, they helped 85 percent of the time. When they thought there was one other person who might help, they intervened 62 percent of the time. If there really had been two bystanders, each of whom had a 62 percent chance of intervening, the victim would have received help 86 percent of the time—virtually identical to the rate of receiving help with one bystander (probability of receiving help = $1 - .38^2 = .86$). When participants thought there were four other people who might render assistance, they intervened 31 percent of the time. Again, had there really been five bystanders, each of whom had a 31 percent chance of intervening, the victim would have received help 85 percent of the time (probability of receiving help = $1 - .69^5 = .85$)! Does this mean that it doesn't matter whether there are many or few people around? Not so fast. These studies have also measured how quickly people come to the aid of someone in distress, and they have consistently found that single bystanders act more quickly than the *quickest* person to react in a group of bystanders. And when you're in an emergency situation, a lack of speed can kill.

collapsed to the floor, and then stared up at the ceiling (Piliavin & Piliavin, 1972). In one condition, a trickle of blood was seen to flow from the victim's chin. In the other condition, there was no blood on the victim. The researchers believed that bystanders would find it more costly to help the bleeding victim, who would likely expose the helper to greater trauma and might require greater medical care. The influence of such anticipated costs was reflected in the results of this study. The victim was less likely to get help when he was bleeding (65 percent of the time) than when he had no blood trickling from his mouth (95 percent of the time). Even though the bleeding victim's need was more apparent, the likely costs of helping inhibited altruistic intervention.

More enduring characteristics of the victim also powerfully influence rates of helping. People are more likely to help similar others (Dovidio, 1984; Dovidio & Gaertner, 1981), including being more likely to help others from their own racial or ethnic groups (Latané & Nida, 1981). The effect of similarity is seen in other species as well. Several nonhuman primates will give up the opportunity to eat, and partially starve themselves, if their action will terminate a shock that is being administered to a member of their own species, something they will not do for members of other species (Preston & de Waal, 2002). Moreover, interpersonal attraction, which is enhanced by similarity (see Chapter 3), is also likely to increase helping behavior.

When harm to the victim is clear and the need is unambiguous, helping is more likely (Clark & Word, 1972; Gaertner & Dovidio, 1977). Researchers have studied altruistic intervention by having conditions in which a person in need either screams or remains silent. Bystanders help victims who scream and make their needs known between 75 and 100 percent of the time compared to helping silent victims between 25 and 40 percent of the time.

The gender of the victim also matters. In general, women tend to receive more help than men (Latané & Nida, 1981). But this varies according to the appearance of the female confederate. More attractive and femininely dressed women tend to receive more help from passersby (Piliavin & Unger, 1985). One can readily think of several explanations of this finding. Women in feminine attire fit the gender stereotype that women are more dependent and helpless and thus may be seen to be in greater need of help. Male passersby may view their intervention as a foot-in-the-door for a possible romantic involvement with the attractive woman in need.

As we have discussed the findings pertaining to the situational determinants of helping, we hope you have been putting yourself in the participant's position. What would go through your mind if you encountered a person slumped over in a hallway while on your way to a talk, or when seeing someone pass out on the subway? What is it about being late, or hearing unambiguous cries of distress, or being in the presence of others, that influences our predilection to help? We now turn to an integrative answer to these questions, which focuses on the construal processes that influence whether we help or not.

## CONSTRUAL PROCESSES AND ALTRUISM

In their theorizing about the determinants of bystander intervention, Latané and Darley (1969) have highlighted how construal processes make helping more or less likely. Many instances of distress are surprisingly ambiguous. A loud apparent dispute between a man and a woman overheard on the street might be careening toward violence and require intervention. Or perhaps it's a nonthreatening lovers' spat. A large group of adolescent boys may be mercilessly pummeling a smaller boy, or perhaps they're just playfully wrestling.

Given the ambiguity of many emergencies, helping requires first that the potential helper perceive that a person is suffering and that there is a need for intervention. The details of the victim's behavior contribute to the inference that help is needed. When a victim's distress is not salient, the victim is less likely to receive help. As we have seen, when people in need vocalize their distress with loud cries, they are much more likely to be helped (Clark & Word, 1972; Schroeder, Penner, Dovidio, & Piliavin, 1995). In a similar vein, another study found that people are more likely to help when they are aware of the events leading up to the victim's distress (Piliavin, Piliavin, & Broll, 1976). When the situation is vivid and dramatic, the bystander is more likely to notice what is happening and to understand what is going on. In one condition, participants saw another person, a confederate, faint and slowly regain consciousness. In the less vivid condition, the participant only saw the aftermath of the accident—a confederate just regaining consciousness. Participants were much more likely to come to the individual's aid (89 percent versus 13 percent) when they saw the entire drama unfold, which led them to notice the full nature of the problem.

The surrounding social context also plays an important role in determining whether bystanders conclude that assistance is called for or not. A form of pluralistic ignorance occurs when

**Pluralistic Ignorance** Bystanders may do nothing if they are not sure what is happening and don't see anyone else responding. We may look at these two men and wonder if they are just having a conversation after a heated basketball game or if they are about to start fighting. If we think that nothing is wrong, we will not try to intervene.

people are uncertain about what is happening and assume that nothing is wrong because no one else is responding or appears concerned. When everyone in some potentially dangerous situation is behaving as if nothing is amiss, there will be a tendency for people to mistake each other's calm demeanor as a sign that no emergency is actually taking place (Latané & Darley, 1968). There are strong norms that we maintain a cool, calm, and collected demeanor in public, especially during emergencies. It is somewhat embarrassing, after all, to be the one who loses composure when no danger actually exists. During emergencies we can collectively lead one another to the inference, shaped by our calm demeanor, that there is in fact no serious problem, no person in need.

In one study that examined the role of pluralistic ignorance in bystander intervention, researchers asked participants to fill out a stack of questionnaires in a laboratory room (Latané & Darley, 1968). The participants did so in one of three conditions: alone, in a room with two passive confederates exhibiting the calm demeanor that was intended to produce pluralistic ignorance, or with two other real participants. As participants in these three conditions filled out their questionnaires, a rather strange and unnerving thing happened that, one would think, would serve as a fairly clear signal of likely danger: smoke started to filter into the room underneath a door, filling the laboratory room.

*"I said, 'I'm not on duty! I just came back to get my flip-flops.'"*

When participants were alone, and they had no input from other participants as to what was happening, they were quite likely to take action. Seventy-five percent of the participants in this condition left the room and reported the smoke to the experimenter (one wonders what the other 25 percent of the participants were thinking!). In the two other conditions, pluralistic ignorance took hold, and participants were less likely to assume that an emergency was occurring. With three real participants, only 38 percent of the participants left to report the smoke. And quite remarkably, with two passive confederates showing no signs of concern, only 10 percent of the participants reported the smoke to the experimenter. Apparently, people prefer the risk of physical danger to the prospect of embarrassing themselves in front of strangers. Anecdotal evidence from this study suggests that participants construed the smoke much differently in the three conditions. Participants who did not report the smoke to the experimenter consistently told the experimenter that they did not feel it was dangerous. One participant ventured the hypothesis that it was truth gas! The students who did report the smoke construed it much differently, as a sign of imminent danger.

Bystanders seem to be less likely to fall prey to pluralistic ignorance when they can clearly see someone else's expressions of concern. This hypothesis was tested in an interesting study in which participants were led through a construction-filled hallway to a lab (Darley, Teger, & Lewis, 1973). As they walked to the experimental room, they passed several stacks of wooden frames used in construction, and a workman who seemed to be doing repairs. Once in the lab room, they began the ostensible task of the experiment—they were to do their best drawing of a model horse. Darley and his colleagues varied the degree to which participants would be able to see others' nonverbal expressions, those reliable signals of concern about a possible emergency. In the control condition, the participant was alone. In another condition, the two participants were seated facing each other as they drew the model horse. With this alignment, they would see each other's immediate, spontaneous expressions of emotion when the emergency occurred. In a final condition, participants were seated back-to-back. Here they had no visual access to each other's immediate reactions.

As the participants labored over their drawings, they suddenly heard a loud crash and the workman crying out in obvious pain, "Oh, my leg!" The results of this study clearly indicate that seeing others' spontaneous emotional expressions reduces the effects of pluralistic ignorance. Ninety percent of the participants who were alone left the room to help the workman. Eighty percent of the participants who were seated face-to-face did so. Only 20 percent of the participants who were seated back-to-back left to help. Not having others' reactions to help interpret the incident, these participants collectively assumed that nothing was wrong.

So how do you improve the chances of getting help when you need it? According to John Darley, who studied the factors affecting bystander intervention for more than a decade, there are two things you can do that are likely to be effective: (1) make your need clear—"I've twisted my ankle and I can't walk; I need help," and (2) select a specific person—"You there, can you help me?" By doing so, you overcome the two biggest obstacles to intervention: You prevent people from concluding there is no real emergency (thereby eliminating the effect of pluralistic ignorance), and you prevent them from thinking that someone else will help (thereby overcoming diffusion of responsibility).

## EVOLUTIONARY APPROACHES TO ALTRUISM

There is no human behavior more problematic from an evolutionary perspective than altruism. Natural selection, you'll recall, favors behaviors that increase the likelihood of survival and reproduction. Altruistic behavior, by its very nature, is costly; it devotes precious resources to others that could be used for oneself or one's genetic relatives. The costs of altruism can include the ultimate sacrifice. Consider the fates of four college-aged friends who took a day off from their jobs at a summer camp in upstate New York to relax at a swimming hole formed from waterfalls. Walking down a steep path to get there, one of them slipped and fell into a whirlpool. When he was sucked down under the raging, foamy water, each of his three friends was moved by altruistic concerns and, in succession, jumped into the river to save the others. They all died. Individuals guided by unbounded altruism, it would seem, would not have fared well in evolutionary history.

How, then, have evolutionary theorists accounted for altruistic behavior, which surely exists? Three evolutionary explanations have been offered: kin selection, reciprocity, and reputational advantage or social rewards.

*Kin Selection*   One evolutionary explanation for altruism is based on the concept of **kin selection**, which refers to the tendency for natural selection to favor behaviors that increase the chances of survival of genetic relatives (Hamilton, 1964). This derives from an individual's inclusive fitness, which as we have noted is an evolutionary tendency to look out for oneself, one's offspring, and one's close relatives together with their offspring, so that one's genes will survive. Thus, from the perspective of kin selection, people should be more likely to help those who share more of their genes, helping siblings more than first cousins, first cousins more than second cousins, and so on. Much altruism, therefore, is not really selfless, for it is designed to help individuals who share their own genes. By helping relatives survive, people help their own genes survive so that they can be passed on to future generations.

**kin selection** The tendency for natural selection to favor behaviors that increase the chances of survival of genetic relatives.

> "A chicken is only an egg's way
> of making another egg."
> —SAMUEL BUTLER, *LIFE AND HABIT*
>
> "An organism is a gene's way of
> making another gene."
> —RICHARD DAWKINS

**Riciprocal Altruism**  Vampire bats will regurgitate blood to feed starving bats that have given blood to them in the past, but they will not give blood to bats that have not helped them in the past.

**reciprocal altruism**  The tendency to help other individuals with the expectation that they will be likely to help in return at some other time.

A first prediction guided by the kin selection thesis is that we should have a highly developed capacity to recognize kin. This would help us with the important task of determining whom to help and whom to ignore. Indeed, there is evidence that at least some nonhuman animals reared apart can recognize their kin through specific visual cues and smells (Rushton, Russell, & Wells, 1984). Human mothers can recognize their new babies from photographs, even when they have had very little contact with the baby (Porter, Cernoch, & Balogh, 1984), and from smells left by the baby on T-shirts (Porter, Cernoch, & McLaughlin, 1983). (Though to our knowledge there is no evidence that fathers are equally capable of identifying their own offspring. If there were, the issue of cuckoldry would likely not be the enormous concern that it is.)

The more obvious prediction from kin selection theory is that we should direct more of our helping behavior toward kin than toward nonkin. There is support for this hypothesis. Take two cases in the animal world. Mockingbirds have been observed to be more likely to feed hungry, closely related nestlings that are not their own but that are more closely related than other hungry nestlings (Curry, 1988). Ground squirrels, when sensing that a predatory coyote or weasel is in the vicinity, will be more likely to emit an alarm call, which puts themselves in danger by alerting the predator as to where they are, in order to warn a genetic relative or a squirrel with which they have lived than to warn unrelated squirrels or squirrels from other areas (Sherman, 1985).

In humans, genetic relatedness seems to influence helping as well. Across numerous cultures, people report receiving more help from close kin than from more distal relatives or nonrelatives (Essock-Vitale & McGuire, 1985). When hypothetical situations are described to them, people report being more willing to help closely related individuals (especially those young enough to still have children) than more distantly related individuals or strangers (Burnstein, Crandall, & Kitayama, 1994). In a study of kidney donors, donors were about three times as likely to engage in this altruistic act for a relative (73 percent) than for nonrelatives (27 percent) (Borgida, Conner, & Manteufel, 1992). In a puzzle task that required cooperation, identical twins, who share all their genes, were found to cooperate about twice as often (94 percent) than fraternal twins (46 percent), who share only half of their genes (Segal, 1984; see also Burnstein, 2005).

*Reciprocity*    Genetic relatedness, then, is a powerful determinant of our helping behavior. But what about helping nonkin? We sometimes go to great lengths to help our friends. We give them money, let them sleep at our apartments and eat out of our refrigerators, help them move, and so on. And sometimes we put our lives on the line to help them, as we saw in the story of the friends who died trying to save their friend from drowning. Even more compelling, perhaps, is the frequency with which we help total strangers. People will dive into icy waters to save strangers, give money anonymously to charities, and engage in all sorts of more ordinary, less costly behaviors, such as taking the time to help someone cross a street. Such actions can be accounted for in part by reciprocity and cooperation, which form the basis of the second major evolutionary explanation for altruism.

In traditional, preliterate societies, individuals living in groups were best able to survive when they cooperated with each other. To explain how cooperation evolved, evolutionary theorists most commonly invoke the concept of **reciprocal altruism**, or the tendency to help other individuals with the expectation that they will be likely to help in return at some other time (Trivers, 1971). Cooperation among nonkin provides many benefits that increase the chances of survival and reproduction for both parties. Reciprocal altruism reduces the

**Reciprocal Grooming among Mammals** Reciprocity helps to promote group living and to reduce aggression, as evidenced by grooming in (A) macaques, and (B) lionesses.

likelihood of dangerous conflict, it helps overcome the problems arising from scarce resources, and it offers a basis for individuals to form alliances and to constrain more dominant individuals (Preston & de Waal, 2002).

There is select evidence for the mutual helping that is at the core of the reciprocal altruism thesis. Vampire bats need blood meals to survive and may starve to death if they do not have a blood meal after sixty hours. Researchers have found that satiated bats will regurgitate blood to feed bats that have given to them in the past, but will not make a donation to a bat that has not been a donor itself (Wilkinson, 1990). In his observations of chimpanzees and bonobos, Frans de Waal (1996) has observed several forms of reciprocity. In observations of over 5,000 instances of food sharing, symmetrical trades predominate: primates are disposed to share with other primates who share with them. The same is true of looking after each other's offspring: bonobos trade babysitting for each other's offspring. Moreover, social grooming, in which individuals remove insects and parasites from each other's fur, has also been shown to be reciprocal, helping to reduce aggression and to cement alliances (de Waal, 1996).

In humans, reciprocity is one of the most powerful principles governing social interaction, and the impulse to return favors appears to be a human universal (Gouldner, 1960). Consider the following experiment. Researchers mailed Christmas cards to numerous complete strangers. About 20 percent reciprocated by sending their own Christmas cards back to the senders, whom they had never met (Kunz & Woolcott, 1976). Either the participants had too few friends to accommodate the stacks of Christmas cards they bought, or they felt compelled by the norm of reciprocity to respond with a Christmas card to the sender. Once primed, reciprocity also generalizes to other people: participants who receive favors from a confederate are more helpful to others in an ensuing interaction (Berkowitz & Daniels, 1964). Thus, altruistic behavior directed toward nonkin appears to follow rules related to reciprocity, and is an important part of the social contract.

*Reputational Advantages and Social Rewards* Another type of altruism may be related to gaining **social rewards**—that is, improving one's image by showing a willingness to deliver benefits to others (Campbell, 1975; Nowak & Sigmund, 1998; Nowak, Page, & Sigmund, 2000). In this case, we help because of the likely rewards we will receive for helping. Helping is a highly valued behavior, and it generates all forms of praise, positive attention, tangible rewards,

**social rewards** Benefits like praise, positive attention, tangible rewards, honors, and gratitude that may be gained from helping others.

544

honors, and gratitude. These social rewards are a strong incentive. Charitable contributions are sometimes given less to improve the plight of others than to enhance others' perception of the power of the donor to deliver benefits. It should be noted that the desire for reputational advantage need not be a conscious one on the part of the donor. Indeed, it seems likely both that our hunter-gatherer forebears engaged in giving and aiding in order to gain stature and power and that they would not have done so by calculating costs and benefits of their actions in a conscious way.

## EMPATHY-BASED ALTRUISM: A CASE OF PURE ALTRUISM?

To this point, you may have developed the nagging sense that the field has abandoned the notion of pure altruism—that is, helping others for completely selfless motives, solely out of a concern for enhancing the welfare of others, even at our own expense. Our three evolutionary accounts highlight the "selfish" benefits of altruistic behavior. In kin selection theory, altruism benefits those individuals who share our genes. In reciprocal altruism, we help with the clear expectation that we will be helped in return. In social rewards altruism, we help to attain greater power and influence. None of these forms of helping seems to reflect selfless behavior.

What about feelings of compassion prompted by strangers in need, or by a passerby in distress? During the peak of the Los Angeles riots of 1992, Reginald Denny, a white truck driver, was being beaten severely by four black youths. Several black residents who lived near the area saw the beating live on television, and rushed to the scene to save Denny's life, risking their own lives in the process. What motivates this kind of action?

In an important line of research, Daniel Batson has made a persuasive case for

**Compassion by Strangers** Sometimes even strangers will respond to an individual's distress and offer aid without thought of rewards or danger. (A) During the riots in Los Angeles in 1992, Reginald Denny was pulled from his car and severely beaten. (B) Upon seeing the incident on television, Bobby Green (pictured here) and several other local residents rushed to the scene to rescue him.

a selfless, other-oriented state that motivates altruistic behavior (Batson & Shaw, 1991). Batson begins by making a series of distinctions, proposing that there are several motives that are likely to be in play in producing altruistic action. Two of these motives are at base selfish; a third is more purely oriented toward unselfishly benefiting another person.

The first selfish motive is one that we have just discussed: the social rewards motive. Those motivated by social rewards and a desire for enhanced reputation help others to order to elevate how they are esteemed by others. The second egoistic motive for helping is the **experienced distress** motive. People are motivated to help others in need to reduce their *own* distress (Cialdini & Fultz, 1990; Cialdini & Kenrick, 1976). The most direct way to alleviate their own distress is to reduce the distress of the other person, and helping behavior is one way to accomplish that aim.

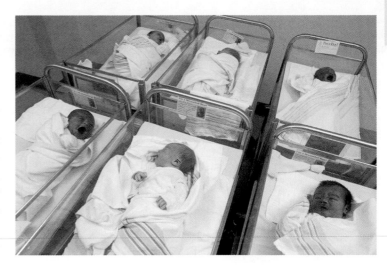

**Empathy among Newborns** When newborns hear another newborn cry, they feel the distress of the other baby and will also begin to cry, as seen in this photo of newborns in a hospital nursery.

Finally, there is **empathy**, identifying with another person and feeling and understanding what that person is experiencing. When we encounter another person in need or distress, we often imagine what their experience is like. From the first moments of life, we respond to others' distress with our own distress. For example, in one study, one-day-old infants either heard a tape recording of their own crying, the crying of another one-day-old, or the crying of an eleven-month-old (Martin & Clark, 1982). One-day-olds actually cried the most in response to the cries of distress of another one-day-old. We are wired to feel distress when witnessing others in need. As we grow older, when we take the other's perspective, we feel an empathic state of concern for that person, and we are motivated to have that person's needs addressed, to enhance that person's welfare, even at our own expense. Thus, empathy produces a selfless, or other-oriented altruism.

Now comes the tricky part. How can one demonstrate that behavior can be motivated by empathy-based altruism? Batson and his colleagues have taken an imaginative approach to this question in experiments in which participants are exposed to another person in distress. The experiments are set up such that egoistic motives—to reduce personal distress or to gain social rewards—would lead to little helping behavior. At the same time, the participant is led to empathize with the person in need. If an empathic focus produces helping, even in the face of egoistic opportunities to avoid it, one can confidently infer that there is an empathy-based form of helping that is not selfishly motivated. Let's see how this empirical strategy plays out in two studies.

A first study pitted the experienced distress and empathy motives against one another by allowing participants to escape their aversive arousal by simply leaving the experiment. The researchers anticipated that if they still helped, it must be due to empathy-based motives (Batson, O'Quin, Fultz, Vanderplas, & Isen, 1983). Participants were told that they would interact with another participant of the same sex. The other participant was to complete several trials of a digit recall task, and to receive a shock after each mistake. In the easy-escape condition, the participant was only required to watch the confederate receive two of the ten shocks, and the participant was then free to leave the experiment while the confederate finished the study. In this condition, if participants were guided primarily by the egoistic motive to reduce personal distress, one should see relatively

**experienced distress** A motive for helping that may arise from a need to reduce one's *own* distress.

**empathy** Identifying with another person and feeling and understanding what that person is experiencing.

little helping behavior, for the participant could simply leave. In the difficult-to-escape condition, the participant was told it would be necessary to watch the other person take all ten shocks.

After the first two trials, the confederate, made to look a little pale, asked for a glass of water, mentioned feelings of discomfort, and recounted a traumatic shock experience from childhood. At this time, the participant provided self-reports of distress-related emotions (for example, feeling upset, worried, perturbed) and empathy-related emotions (for example, feeling sympathetic, compassionate, tender). Batson and his colleagues used the self-reports to divide participants into those who were feeling egoistic distress and those who were feeling empathy. In the next phase of the experiment, the experimenter turned to the participant to ask whether he or she would sit in for the confederate, taking some of this person's shocks. If there is such a thing as empathy-based, other-oriented altruism, Batson and colleagues reasoned one should see substantial levels of altruism (agreeing to sit in for the confederate) on the part of participants who felt empathic concern for the confederate, even when they could simply leave the experiment and escape their empathic distress. That is just what Batson and his colleagues observed. Those participants who mostly felt distress and could escape the situation took few shocks on behalf of the confederate. Those participants who felt empathy, on the other hand, volunteered to take more shocks, even when they could simply leave the study.

For those still skeptical of the possibility of empathy-based altruism, you might have a few concerns about this study. First of all, empathy was not manipulated; instead, Batson and his colleagues identified empathic participants according to their self-reports. Perhaps there was a selection bias in this study—namely, the high-empathy participants might just be more helpful in general, for reasons other than a selfless response to the confederate in need. Second, the experimenter knew of the participant's actions, so a social rewards account of this study cannot be eliminated. Perhaps participants who took more shocks on behalf of the confederate hoped to impress the experimenter, or wanted to avoid embarrassing themselves by leaving a person in obvious need. It would be much more telling to document substantial rates of helping when volunteering to do so is completely anonymous. That notion motivated Batson's next study.

In this study, female participants engaged in an impression-formation task while seated at separate cubicles (Fultz, Batson, Fortenbach, McCarthy, & Varney, 1986). The communicator (a confederate), supposedly a student named Janet Arnold, wrote two notes to the participant, expressing honest information about herself. The task of the listener (the actual participant) was to form as accurate an impression of the communicator as possible. This time empathy was manipulated. In the low-empathy condition, the participant was told to be as objective as possible when reading the notes, to concentrate on the facts at hand. In the high-empathy condition, the participant was told to imagine as vividly as possible how the communicator—the other person—felt. In the first note to the participant, Janet confessed to feeling out of place at her new home at the university. In the second note, Janet expressed a strong need for a friend, and she rather forthrightly asked the participant if she'd like to pal around a bit. At the end of the sec-

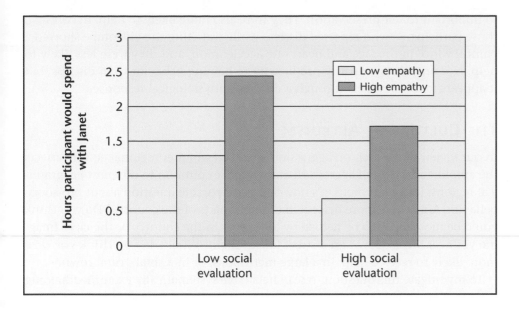

**Figure 13.7 Empathy and Altruism**
Participants who were encouraged to feel empathy for another student, Janet, who reports feeling lonely, volunteer to spend more time with her, even in the low-social-evaluation condition, where their volunteering is anonymous. (Source: Fultz, Batson, Fortenbach, McCarthy, & Varney, 1986)

ond note, the participant was told that Janet had finished and left the study. At this point, the experimenter gave the participant a form that described another "long-term relationship study" and asked whether the participant would like to spend time with the other communicator, our lonely Janet Arnold. In the low-social-evaluation condition, Janet's notes were delivered in sealed envelopes, and not read or known by the experimenter. Similarly, the participant indicated how much time she would spend with Janet on a form that she enclosed in a sealed envelope that would be sent to the professor conducting the study (who was never to meet the participant). Neither the experimenter nor Janet would know of the participant's response. In the high-social-evaluation condition, things were much different. The experimenter and the participant read Janet's notes, and Janet and the experimenter were privy to the participant's indication of how much time she would spend with Janet. The critical dependent measure was the number of hours the participant volunteered to spend with Janet. As you can see in Figure 13.7, participants instructed to empathize with Janet volunteered to spend more time with her, even when no one would know of their action.

Let's review one final study that is especially helpful in assessing whether there is some kind of selfless state, as Batson supposes, that motivates altruistic behavior. Particularly strong evidence for such a motive would be to show that empathy or compassion has a distinct physiological signature that predicts whether or not a person will act altruistically. Nancy Eisenberg and her colleagues have conducted such a study (Eisenberg et al., 1989). In this experiment, participants, either second-graders or fifth-graders or college students, watched a videotape of a woman and her children who had recently been in an accident. Her children were forced to miss school while they recovered from their injuries in the hospital. As the participants watched this moving videotape, their facial expressions were recorded on videotape and continuous measures of heart rate were taken. After watching the videotape, the participants were given the opportunity to help by taking homework to the recovering children during their recess (and thus sacrificing their playtime, which was highly valued by the younger participants). What Eisenberg and her colleagues found was that people who felt sympathy and concern in response to the accident victims, or empathy in Batson's terms, showed oblique eyebrows and concerned gaze, and heart rate deceleration—a physiological response that is the opposite of fight-or-flight physiology, which is so important to self-preservation. They were also more likely to help. In contrast, those participants who reported distress while watching the videotape showed a painful wince in the face and heart rate acceleration, and they were less likely to help. Not only does empathy produce more helping behavior than distress, but it appears to do so in part through a different physiological response.

## THE CULTURE OF ALTRUISM

In our review of research on aggression we asked whether regional culture affects the amount and kind of aggression and violence common to different geographical regions. Indeed, it did. Let's now ask a comparable question about pro-social behavior. Are people more helpful in different parts of the country? Do you think you'd be more likely to be helped by a stranger in the country or the city? Imagine your car breaks down on a street late at night. Where do you think you'd be more likely to receive help: in a large metropolis, or in a small, rural town?

To investigate this question, researchers have systematically examined helping rates in rural and urban environments. Nancy Steblay (1987) reviewed thirty-five different studies that permitted comparisons of helping rates in rural and urban environments. She looked at the helping rates in communities of different sizes, ranging from fewer than 1,000 to more than one million. In all, seventeen different kinds of helping behaviors were created experimentally, typically in naturalistic settings. Researchers examined whether people would grant simple requests (for example, give the time of day), whether they would intervene to stop a crime, and whether they would help people in need (for example, an injured pedestrian).

Steblay's analysis showed that strangers are significantly more likely to be helped in rural communities than in urban areas. The effect of population size was particularly pronounced in towns with populations between 1,000 and 50,000. Thus, you're much more likely to be helped in a town of 1,000 than of 5,000, in a town of 5,000 than of 10,000, and so on. Once the population rises above 50,000, however, there is little effect of increasing population. To get a better picture of these results, consider a few more specific findings presented in Figure 13.8. As you can see, people are more likely to engage in a variety of helping behaviors—for example, correcting an overpayment, helping a lost child, giving a donation—in rural environments.

**Figure 13.8 Helping in Rural versus Urban Environments** People are more likely to engage in a variety of helpful acts in rural as opposed to urban settings. (Source: Steblay, 1987)

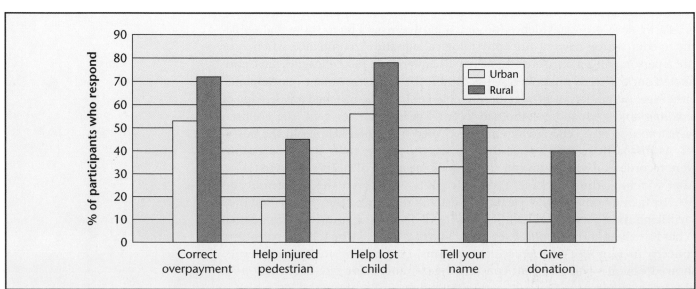

Let's dissect this finding a bit. One question you might ask is whether it is the context a person is currently in that matters, or the context in which the person was brought up. For example, if you were brought up in a small rural town but currently live in a big city, which is more likely to influence whether you will engage in helping behavior? Is it the current situation or your background and upbringing? As it turns out, it is the current situation. In analyzing these thirty-five studies, the participant's current context, rural or urban, was a much stronger predictor of helping behavior than the person's rural or urban background. This is another nod to the power of the current situation. And, incidentally, it is a finding that makes it less likely that the rural-urban differences are merely due to self-selection as opposed to a real difference between rural and urban environments.

**Helping in the Country** People living in rural settings are more likely to help others than people in the city, as shown here by volunteers in the process of searching for survivors along the tree line of the forest.

What accounts for this rural-urban difference in helping rates? Researchers have offered two explanations. Stanley Milgram (1970) attributed it to stimulus overload. The amount of stimulation in modern urban environments is so great that you cannot attend to all of it. There are simply too many inputs, and so you shut down a bit and are less likely to attend to and orient toward others. This means that the ordinary ways you notice and interpret emergencies are interfered with, inhibiting your impulses to help. As you walk down a city street, for example, the traffic, the construction, the swarms of people, are, in combination, too much to take in fully. You narrow your focus, both attentionally and in terms of what circumstances you recognize as having a claim on your thoughts, feelings, and actions. This limits your responsiveness to people in need. A second explanation might be labeled the diversity hypothesis. Earlier we noted that people are more likely to help others who are similar to themselves. Urban areas, of course, are made up of more diverse populations. Thus, on average, you're more likely to encounter someone similar to yourself in a rural environment than in an urban environment. This may contribute to the observed urban-rural difference in helping rates. Finally, there are likely to be more people around to help in urban areas than in more rural environments, and so a "diffusion of responsibility" may discourage people from helping.

**LOOKING BACK,** we have examined altruism, unselfish behavior that benefits others. We have shown how there are powerful situational determinants of whether people help others or not. We have considered how the presence of other bystanders may lead to a diffusion of responsibility in which everyone assumes someone else will help. We have discussed how characteristics of the victim also affect whether people will help, with people being more likely to help similar others. Moreover, we have discussed how construal processes influence helping, showing how pluralistic ignorance leads people to be less likely to help. We have also discussed selfish motives for helping, including kin selection, reciprocity, social rewards, and a reduction of experienced distress, and how they contrast with a pure form of altruism based on empathy. Finally, we have seen how culture can affect helping, with people in rural settings being more likely to help others than people in urban settings.

# SUMMARY

1. *Hostile aggression* is motivated by anger and hostility, with the primary aim of harming others, either physically or psychologically. *Instrumental aggression* is behavior that is intended to achieve some goal that just happens to require aggression.

2. Violent and aggressive acts are more likely to be committed by men than by women. Women are likely to be aggressive in different ways than men, using relational violence such as gossip and ostracism to hurt others emotionally.

3. *Media violence* has been shown to cause violence and aggression in real life. When a media-publicized suicide occurs, copycat suicides follow. Longitudinal studies show that children who watch lots of violence on TV commit more serious crimes as adults than children who watch less violence. Watching violence on TV also causes more violent behavior in the short run. Violent video games also increase the likelihood of violence.

4. *Heat* affects levels of violence. There are higher rates of violent crime in hotter cities and more violence during hot months than during cool months.

5. According to the *frustration-aggression hypothesis,* aggression results from thwarted needs, and thwarted needs result in aggression.

6. Construal processes affect both anger and aggression. Acts that seem to be intentional are more likely to cause aggression than identical acts that do not seem intentional.

7. People in many parts of the world, including many people in the U.S. South, adhere to a *culture of honor,* meaning that they are inclined to respond to insults and actions that convey malicious intentions with violence or threats of violence. Such cultures can be found wherever there is a history of herding, with its great attendant risks of loss of all wealth.

8. Rape-prone cultures have high levels of violence in general and use rape as a weapon in battle. They also use rape as a ritual act and as a threat to keep women subservient to men. Relatively rape-free cultures tend to grant women equal status.

9. Evolutionary theory provides a useful perspective on *family violence.* Stepchildren are more subject to abuse than genetic offspring who can carry on one's genetic line. Men, who have more to gain by eliminating romantic rivals, are vastly more likely to kill other men than women are to kill other women.

10. Situational determinants of altruism can be far stronger than our intuitions tell us they should be. Being late reduced the likelihood of a seminary student's helping a victim from 60 percent to 10 percent.

11. Whether someone offers help to a victim or not (*bystander intervention*) also depends greatly on the number of people who observe some incident. The presence of others leads to a *diffusion of responsibility,* in which no one individual takes responsibility for helping the victim.

12. *Pluralistic ignorance* occurs when people are uncertain about what is happening and do nothing, often out of fear of embarrassment in case nothing is really wrong. Their reaction reinforces everyone's erroneous conclusion that the events are innocuous.

13. *Victim characteristics* that increase the likelihood of being helped include whether the victim is similar to the target, whether the victim screams and makes known the situation, and whether the victim is female.

14. Evolutionary approaches to altruism lead initially to a puzzle as to why it would exist at all. From the standpoint of evolution, all our actions should serve to increase the likelihood of survival and reproduction. The *kin selection* hypothesis explains, however, that people will help others to preserve the genes of close kin so as to benefit their own gene pool.

15. Another kind of helping behavior, *reciprocal altruism,* also arises out of selfish motives. The reciprocity motive entails that people grant others favor or help others in the belief that those whom they have helped will at some future time grant them favors of similar value.

16. People may help others out of another selfish motive—to enhance their reputation or to obtain *social rewards.* People may help others to gain praise, attention, rewards, honor, or gratitude. They may make charitable contributions to improve their image and to gain the approbation of others.

17. Another form of altruism that is actually based on a selfish motive is the reduction of *experienced distress* —one person helps another simply to avoid feeling distress at the other's pain.

18. A form of pure, undiluted altruism is based on *empathy*—the feeling of concern for another person after observing and being moved by that person's needs.

Experimenters have found clever ways to distinguish between people who help for empathic and nonempathic reasons. Those who help for egoistic distress-avoidance reasons actually show different physiological patterns than those who help for empathic reasons.

19. People who live in rural settings are more likely to help others than people who live in urban settings.

## CRITICAL THINKING ABOUT BASIC PRINCIPLES

1. Think of a situation in which aggression is likely to be both hostile and instrumental. Do you think people would be more likely to perceive the hostile motives or the instrumental ones?

2. Do you think that knowing about the Darley and Latané findings on bystander intervention would affect bystanders' behavior when they see someone who suddenly appears to be seriously ill or is involved in an accident? (To find out if it really does, see Beaman, Barnes, Kleentz, & McQuirk, 1978.)

3. Who would be more likely to give altruistic aid—a member of an independent culture or a member of an interdependent culture? Would it make a difference whether the victim was a member of an ingroup or an outgroup?

4. Think of some ways you might reduce hostile aggression in some setting. Think of some ways you might increase altruism in some setting.

## KEY TERMS

altruism (p. 535)
bystander intervention (p. 536)
culture of honor (p. 527)
diffusion of responsibility (p. 536)
empathy (p. 545)

experienced distress (p. 545)
frustration (p. 523)
hostile aggression (p. 516)
inclusive fitness (p. 517)
instrumental aggression (p. 516)

kin selection (p. 541)
learned helplessness (p. 524)
rape-prone cultures (p. 531)
reciprocal altruism (p. 542)
social rewards (p. 543)

## FURTHER READING

Batson, C. D. (1991). *The altruism question: Toward a social-psychological answer.* Hillsdale, NJ: Lawrence Erlbaum.

Berkowitz, L. (1993). *Aggression.* New York: McGraw-Hill.

Nisbett, R. E., & Cohen, D. (1996). *Culture of honor: The psychology of violence in the South.* Boulder, CO: Westview Press.

Schroeder, D. A., Penner, L. A., Dovidio, J. F., & Piliavin, J. A. (1995). *The psychology of helping and altruism.* New York: McGraw-Hill.

Sober, E., & Wilson, D. S. (1998). *Unto others: The evolution and psychology of unselfish behavior.* Cambridge, MA: Harvard University Press.

# Chapter Outline

C H A P T E R   1 4

# Morality, Justice, and Cooperation

I n November 1943, S. L. A. "Slam" Marshall, a U.S. Army lieutenant colonel, arrived with American troops on the beaches of Makin Island to fight the Japanese. After four days of intense combat, the Americans secured the island. What took place next would put Marshall at the center of a dispute that would change how wars are fought. Marshall was asked to interview different soldiers about whether a private named Schwartz, machine gun in hands, had held off eleven Japanese attacks entirely on his own, or whether he had done so by following the orders of his lieutenant. Each soldier he interviewed added a piece to the confusing puzzle, which eventually painted an irrefutably clear picture of the heroism of Private Schwartz.

Marshall subsequently interviewed hundreds of soldiers who fought in Europe and the Pacific during World War II, often immediately after they had engaged in battle. In 1947, he published the results from these interviews in *Men Against Fire: The Problem of Battle Command*. His interviews yielded startling findings. Only 15 percent of World War II riflemen had fired at the enemy during combat (Marshall, 1947/2000). Often soldiers refused to fire, even in the heat of deadly battle with superior officers barking orders right

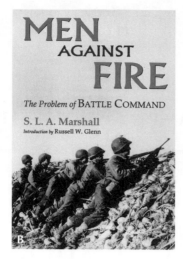

**Morality and Killing** Almost all people are reluctant to kill and often must be trained to overcome their moral scruples to do so, even in times of war. (A) S.L.A. Marshall interviewed soldiers who had fought during World War II to find out why many of them did not fire their weapons, and (B) published the surprising results in *Men Against Fire: The Problem of Battle Command.*

next to them. In the wake of this revelation, the army radically changed how it prepared soldiers to carry out their combat duties. Infantry training exercises played down the notion that shooting kills humans. The effects were dramatic. According to army estimates, 90 percent of soldiers in the Vietnam War fired at their opponents.

You might be surprised by Marshall's findings on the low killing rates during World War II. You might ask: How can such a powerful situation as war produce such "unwarlike" behavior—the refusal to kill other human beings? One answer is that at the core of human nature is a capacity to be good to others, even mortal enemies who might be shooting at us in the heat of battle. Although humans have an undeniable capacity for cruelty and aggression (see Chapters 2, 11, and 13), people also want to avoid harming others, and have deep concerns about right and wrong, good and evil, fairness and justice. These concerns are the very bedrock of strong communities and ultimately of our own ability to survive. Thus, in this chapter, we examine the different domains of morality, considering where our moral judgments come from and how moral judgment varies and is similar across cultures. We also look into the basis of justice, focusing on three kinds of justice: judgments of fair or just rewards, judgments of the fairness with which appropriate procedures have been followed in meting out justice, and the restoration of just relations in the face of wrongdoing and injustice. Finally, in the last section of the chapter, we examine the tendency to cooperate. But before we begin these discussions of morality, justice, and cooperation, we first ask: What lies at the heart of people's inclination toward kindness and benevolence? To start our inquiry into this question, let's consider how fair and cooperative behavior might have arisen in the course of evolution.

## THE EVOLUTION OF MORALITY, JUSTICE, AND COOPERATION

Is our capacity for cooperation a biologically based adaptation? This question has intrigued evolutionary theorists for more than 150 years. Intuitively, it seems that moral, just, and cooperative individuals would be easily exploited by amoral, unjust, competitive individuals, and thus they would be less likely to reproduce or propagate their genes. Survival of the most selfish seems the most obvious prediction to make from evolutionary theory.

But Darwin himself reasoned that we are good to others because we expect them to be good in return, and we benefit from such an exchange (Cronin, 1991;

Wright, 1995). In Chapter 13, we explored this concept, known today as reciprocal altruism, in some detail. Darwin also speculated that we are good to others because such behavior makes our group more effective in competition against other groups.

Darwin's most ardent supporters, however, had different ideas about human nature (Cronin, 1991). Alfred Russel Wallace, a co-discoverer of the theory of natural selection, argued that while the body was developed through natural selection, our mental faculties, and most notably our capacity for goodness, were created by spiritual forces. T. H. Huxley posited a different source of human goodness: culture and learning. Human nature, in Huxley's eyes, is forged by evolution in a violent, selfish struggle for existence. Tendencies toward selfless conduct must be cultivated by education, training, and culture to counteract our more base instincts—greed, aggression, and desire.

More recently, evolutionary theorists have arrived at the view that our capacity for treating others decently, much like other mental faculties, has been produced by specific selection pressures in the course of human evolution (Buss & Kenrick, 1998; Cosmides, 1989; Cronin, 1991; de Waal, 1996; Eibl-Eibesfeldt, 1989; Sober & Wilson, 1998). This new approach proceeds as follows: Some of the most important selection pressures that have shaped human nature are social. We reproduce, raise offspring, avoid predation, gather food, and stay warm, all in the context of relationships with other people. We are more likely to succeed at these endeavors when we behave in a cooperative fashion, mindful of others' needs, not just our own.

In more specific terms, our capacity for selfless behavior appears to have four elements, with evolutionary roots in the behaviors of closely related species (de Waal, 1996). One of these is compassion. In his studies of different primates, Frans de Waal has catalogued remarkable acts of compassion. Chimpanzees, baboons, and macaques become wildly distressed when witnessing harm to other group members. Primates take care of vulnerable individuals. For example, monkeys, like humans, are sometimes born blind, which exposes the blind monkey to numerous dangers, ranging from falling out of trees to straying from the group. Several researchers have found that other monkeys in the group will take on the burden of protecting the blind monkey and helping with such activities as feeding. In Chapter 13, we explored how compassion is a powerful source of altruistic behavior, and is rightly considered a central part of our capacity for goodness.

A second element of our capacity for cooperative, even selfless, behavior is our tendency to act on moral principles, rules for being a person of virtue and character. When our actions are guided by moral principles, we feel a sense of virtue. People who embody important moral principles—for example, the saints, tireless community leaders, and everyday heroes—inspire us. The rudiments of character and virtue can be seen in the actions of other species. For example, the position a chimpanzee achieves in the social hierarchy depends on the ability to act in a "moral" fashion (de Waal, 1996). High-status chimpanzees do not monopolize all of the food; instead, they share continuously, and they take great pains to ensure that group members have food. They spend a good part of their day breaking up conflicts between lower-status chimps. Their elevated status depends on their exemplary character in relation to the rest of the group.

A third element of our capacity for selfless behavior is our sense of justice, which affects how we allocate resources and what we do about individuals who violate rules regarding the allocation of resources. Again we see the predecessors of our sense of justice in the actions of our primate relatives, particularly in how

> "To know the good is to do the good."
>
> —PLATO, *THE REPUBLIC*

> "At the most fundamental level our nature is compassionate. . . . Cooperation, not conflict, lies at the heart of the basic principles that govern our human existence."
>
> —THE DALAI LAMA

**Cooperation among Chimpanzees**
Chimpanzees live in groups in which alpha males assure cooperative behavior among the group members. (A) The alpha male shares food with lower-status chimpanzees, and (B) the alpha male mediates disputes and breaks up conflicts to promote more cooperative groups.

they share food (Boesch & Boesch, 1989; de Waal, 1996). Social species like chimpanzees hunt in cooperative groups, and they have developed sophisticated rules for sharing food. When chimpanzees share the meat of a kill, they give it to other chimps who were helpful on the hunt, but they do not give it to chimps who contributed little. Chimpanzees trade and reciprocate. In his observations of over 5,000 incidents of food sharing, de Waal found that chimps systematically shared with other chimps who had shared with them previously, as well as with chimps who had groomed them earlier in the day! Moreover, chimps punish other chimps who steal food from others. Chimpanzees, it is quite clear, rely upon a complex set of principles to make sure that their group members contribute as they should and receive a fair piece of the pie.

A final aspect of our capacity for selfless behavior may be the most subtle, but also the most pervasive. This is our capacity to cooperate. Conflict is an inevitable part of group living, and it can readily escalate into dangerous, even life-threatening, fighting. Group-living species such as humans are well served by traits or behaviors that prevent or reduce conflict and aggression. Through careful studies of chimpanzees and bonobos, de Waal has illuminated the numerous ways that these primates avoid conflict and aggression, or defuse it once it is underway (de Waal, 1986, 1996; Keltner & Potegal, 1997). They display submissive gestures, they offer food, they groom, and third parties intervene on others' behalf, all to bring about more cooperative relations between conflicting parties. Humans likewise have a multifaceted capacity to cooperate, which is an essential part of our capacity for moral behavior.

> "Life is mostly froth and bubble, but two things stand as stone: Kindness in another's troubles and courage in your own."
> —ANDREW BARTON ("BANJO") PATERSON

## MORALITY

We offer the advanced student of moral history the following summary:

Roman era: anything goes
Medieval era: nothing goes
Renaissance: anything goes
17th century Spain: nothing goes
18th century France: anything goes
19th century England: nothing goes

1920s America: anything goes
1950s America: nothing goes
1990s America: anything goes

— Steve Martin, actor, comedian, writer, from "The Third Millennium:
So far, so good," January 2, 2000

Like most humor, Steve Martin's parody of a history of morality contains a fundamental truth. People seem to live according to very different moral principles in different cultures and during different historical eras. Some eras seem relatively lawless and hedonistic. For many, the 1990s will be remembered as a time of exuberant and sometimes corrupt financial markets, violent video games, gas-guzzling SUVs, and school shootings. Other eras seem oppressively upright and constrained. For many, the 1950s were a time of conformity in which people lived in similar suburban houses, women stayed home with the children, men dressed and worked in lockstep with their corporate identity, and everyone had an unquestioning respect for authority.

What are your moral principles? Do not kill? But what if killing prevents the kind of genocide that occurred in Rwanda, which you read about in Chapter 13? Do not lie? Honor freedom of expression? Counterexamples and problems with each readily come to mind. Even what might appear to be the most unobjectionable moral rules—for example, do not harm young children—are problematic under some circumstances. Children have been allowed to serve as suicide bombers in the Palestinian-Israeli conflict, and have been celebrated as martyrs. Moreover, when food is extremely scarce, human infanticide can occur (Hrdy, 1999). This might seem inconceivable, but a parent might rationally choose infanticide rather than a slow, miserable death from malnutrition for the infant and compromised lives for other offspring. So how do we define morality?

## DEFINING MORALITY AND MORAL JUDGMENT

**Morality** is a system of principles and ideals that people use as obligatory guides to making evaluative judgments (good versus bad) of the actions or character of a person (Haidt, 2001). Although exactly what is considered moral can vary across time and culture, as we shall soon see, scholars do agree upon general characteristics of actions that are judged as morally right or wrong. First, morality includes *obligation*—that is, a sense that the rule is supposed to be followed. If you consider being benevolent toward others a moral principle, you will have the sense that you are obliged to act in accordance with that principle. You are likely to say to yourself, "I should be kind," even when you feel like behaving otherwise.

Second, moral principles are *inclusive*. Moral rules should apply to all people, and ideally in all contexts. Returning to our last example, if benevolence is a moral principle for you, then you may believe that people in different cultures and contexts should be benevolent. It should be noted, however, that this requirement is not regarded as universally binding by everyone. For many peoples, moral principles are inclusive only for "our kind"—our nation, our religion, our tribe, or even our family.

Finally, moral principles involve *sanctions*—that is, punishments for violations and praise for adherence to moral standards. We have legal systems that mete out punishment for moral violations, and we have honorific systems—from the Nobel Peace Prize to Boy Scout badges—that reward moral virtue. Having characterized morality in terms of obligation, inclusiveness, and sanctions, let's examine the content of moral judgment in terms of universality and cultural variation.

> **morality** A system of principles and ideals that people use as a guide to making evaluative judgments of the actions or character of a person.

**Rewards for Moral Virtue** People who have worked to bring peace to the world have been rewarded with the Nobel Prize, including (A) Martin Luther King, Jr., in 1954, and (B) Tenzin Gyatso, the Dalai Lama, in 1989.

## UNIVERSALITY AND CULTURAL VARIATION IN MORAL JUDGMENT

If you have traveled abroad, or read much about other cultures, you cannot help but be struck by two things. The first is the apparent similarity in many of our moral judgments. People in radically different cultures seem similarly appalled by harm to children, genocide, incest, and the like. And in an important line of work, Elliot Turiel and his colleagues have found that, starting at about age ten, children in different cultures, such as Israel, Nigeria, and South Korea, agree in identifying harm and violations of important rights as immoral (Turiel, 2002). These findings may be explained by evolution. As a species, humans have evolved biologically based emotions that are attuned to harm (for example, horror at the killing or maiming of others) and violations of basic rights (for example, the taking of someone's property) to enable people to live together in groups. Thus, as part of our evolutionary heritage, moral judgments related to harm and violations of basic rights are likely to be universal.

At the same time, one cannot help but be amazed by the cultural variation in moral judgment. What is accepted in one culture—polygamy, public beheadings, dancing—is morally outrageous in others. People in India think it's immoral for people of different social positions to come into contact with one another, a judgment that might strike you as a bit odd (though one doesn't have to go terribly far back in U.S. history to find similar proscriptions against contact between blacks and whites). One way to think about cultural variation in moral judgment is to draw an analogy to language acquisition. Early in life, the infant is capable of producing all phonemes. Cultures then select certain phonemes and not others to constitute a given culture's language. The same may be true of morality. Our minds are equipped with the ability to take on any number of emotion-based moral intuitions. In becoming a member of a particular culture, however, certain intuitions are emphasized and others are de-emphasized, due to that culture's history, institutions, practices, and general understanding of the social world.

*Moral Transgressions and Transgressions of Social Conventions* In thinking about moral principles, people from Western cultures are likely to think about concepts like "rights," "freedom," and "equality." For decades, these concepts were a central focus in the study of moral judgment (Darley & Schultz, 1990;

> "This, then, is the appropriate region of human liberty. It comprises, first, the inward domain of consciousness, demanding liberty of conscience . . . thought, and feeling, absolute freedom of opinion and sentiment on all subjects. . . . Secondly, the principle requires liberty of tastes and pursuits, of doing as we like, subject to such consequences as may follow, without impediment from our fellow creatures, so long as what we do does not harm them."
>
> —J. S. MILL, *ON LIBERTY*

Kohlberg, 1976; Turiel, 2002). Treating these concepts as core elements of moral judgment was consistent with the long-standing emphasis in Western cultures on the sanctity of individual rights, the equality of people, and personal freedom.

You might be tempted to conclude that rights, equality, and freedom, and the avoidance of harm, are universal moral principles. A series of studies of people in India, Japan, the Philippines, and Brazil, however, suggests that we need to define morality more broadly, and in a way that includes ideas about duty and obligation, as well as about bodily and spiritual purity (Jensen, 1997; Rozin, Lowery, Imada, & Haidt, 1999; Shweder, Much, Mahapatra, & Park, 1997; Vasquez, Keltner, Ebenbach, & Banaszynski, 2001). To this end, researchers have studied both **moral transgressions**—that is, violations of rights or harm to others, such as beating up someone else or taking a toy or money—as well as **social convention transgressions**—that is, violations of agreed-upon rules that govern how we greet each other, whom we associate with, how we eat, the gender-based roles and identities we assume, and sexual behavior. Consider Richard Shweder's research on the moral beliefs of individuals in Bhubaneshwar, a medium-sized city in eastern India. In one study, Shweder and his colleagues presented Indian participants from Bhubaneshwar and American participants from Hyde Park in Chicago with scenarios of thirty-nine different inappropriate actions to determine whether the participants believed that moral rules or social conventions had been violated (Shweder, Much, Mahapatra, & Park, 1997). The researchers asked the participants to answer three questions about each violation: How serious was the action? Was it right or wrong? Would the action be acceptable in other contexts, or should it be condemned in all circumstances? Morally inappropriate actions included physical harm, violations of promises, physical assaults, and incest, to name a few examples. Violations of social conventions included transgressions of rules related to attire, manners of addressing others, food, and sex roles.

The Indian participants, much as their American counterparts, judged harmful acts to be serious, wrong, and worthy of condemnation. Avoidance of harm to others is a universal moral concept. But marked cultural differences emerged in the judgments of behaviors that Westerners would define as mere violations of social convention. The Indian participants judged these transgressions as more serious, wrong, and worthy of condemnation than did the American participants. For example, Indian participants indicated that it was morally wrong for a child to cut his hair after the death of his father, for a woman to eat with her hus-

**Cultural Variation in Moral Judgment** Customs and behaviors that may be accepted in some cultures may be frowned on in others and judged to be morally unacceptable. (A) Polygamy is against the law in the United States, but still practiced by some Mormons in Utah and by many Muslims throughout the world. Tom Green has five wives and at least twenty-nine children. (B) Some cultures do not allow men and women to dance together, although most see nothing wrong with the practice.

> **moral transgressions** Violations of others' rights, or harm to others.
>
> **social convention transgressions** Violations of agreed-upon rules that govern such things as how we greet each other, how we eat, and the gender-based roles and identities we assume.

band's elder brother, for a husband to cook for his wife or to massage her legs, and for upper-caste individuals to come into physical contact with lower-caste individuals.

*Ethics of Moral Reasoning*    In light of the findings on moral transgressions and transgressions of social conventions, Richard Shweder has offered a theory of three broad ethics, or frameworks, of moral reasoning that specify the content of moral judgment (Shweder, Much, Mahapatra, & Park, 1997). The **ethic of autonomy** is centered on rights and equality, and is focused on protecting individuals' freedom to pursue their own interests. The U.S. Constitution revolves around the ethic of autonomy, describing inalienable rights and freedoms, such as freedom of expression and freedom of religious belief.

The **ethic of community** revolves around the themes of duty, status, hierarchy, and interdependence. The goal is to protect the network of relationships and roles that define a family, company, community, or any other social entity. Within this framework, the individual is defined by the appropriate roles and identities to be assumed within the social entity. For example, in Confucianism, an ethical philosophy that guides the lives of hundreds of millions of people in China and elsewhere, a central moral concept is *li*, which refers to finding one's place in a community.

Finally, the **ethic of divinity** is defined by a concern for purity, sanctity, pollution, and sin. The goal is to protect the individual from degradation, impurity, and contamination. This perspective assumes that the individual, both in body and spirit, is to be kept pure. When former President Jimmy Carter expressed remorse for having had adulterous thoughts, he surprised many Americans, and he revealed his commitment to the morality of pure thoughts. To Westerners the ethic of divinity may seem the least relevant to morality because in many Western cultures bodily and spiritual purity are thought to be matters of personal choice rather than moral obligation. Nonetheless, in many ways, Westerners do care a great deal about the purity of mind and body (Cohen & Rozin, 2001; Tetlock, Kristel, Elson, Green, & Lerner, 2000). For example, homeless people and AIDS victims are often condemned because they are seen as dirty or "contaminated." People speak of "washing their sins away." And an old saying from Western Europe exhorts us to believe that "cleanliness is next to godliness." Clearly, purity is an important, albeit implicit, theme of many moral judgments, even in the West.

We have emphasized that people in Western cultures give priority to the ethic of autonomy in their moral judgments. Members of some other cultures are more likely to rely on concepts related to the ethics of community and divinity in their moral judgment. A study that illustrates this contention compared the moral concepts of college students from the Philippines and from the United States (Vasquez, Keltner, Ebenbach, & Banaszynski, 2001). In part due to their Asian background, people in the Philippines attach great importance to community-related values, including family, social harmony, and deference. As Catholics (due to the colonial Spanish presence in the Philippines), Filipinos also consider purity to be an important moral virtue. For example, if young romantic partners in the Philippines are seen exhibiting a public display of affection, such as kissing or embracing, they are subject to moral condemnation.

In the study by Vasquez and her colleagues, Filipino and U.S. college students were asked to list moral rules, which were then classified as corresponding to one of the three Shweder ethics. The U.S. students most often listed rules that were examples of the ethic of autonomy (see Figure 14.1). For example, the two most frequently cited moral rules for U.S. students were: "People should have the right

**ethic of autonomy** A framework of moral reasoning that is centered on rights and equality, and is focused on protecting individuals' freedom to pursue their own interests.

**ethic of community** A framework of moral reasoning that revolves around duty, status, hierarchy, and interdependence whose goal is to protect relationships and roles within social groups to which one belongs.

**ethic of divinity** A framework of moral reasoning that is defined by a concern for purity, sanctity, pollution, and sin.

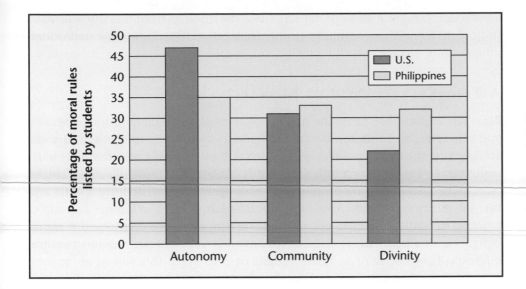

**Figure 14.1 Moral Rules in the United States and the Philippines** The ethic of autonomy is a more prominent moral reality for U.S. college students compared with students in the Philippines, who consider the ethics of community and divinity to be just as central to their moral concerns. In this study, students listed the rules that they thought were moral. U.S. college students were more likely to list rules related to individual rights and freedom, whereas Filipino college students were more likely to list rules concerning bodily and mental purity (divinity). (Source: Adapted from Vasquez , Keltner, Ebenbach, & Banaszynski, 2001)

to act and think as they like" and "People should not have the right to look down on others." In contrast, the Filipino students drew equally from all three ethics in stating their important moral rules. Their two top rules were: "People should be loyal and respectful members of their group and community" and "People should act with restraint and avoid harming others." In the United States, people seem to construe moral events more consistently in terms of rights and equality; in the Philippines, people think of morality more broadly, in the language and concepts of all three ethics.

*Reciprocity and Moral Reasoning* Another example of cultural differences in moral reasoning involves the commitment to the principle of reciprocity (Miller & Bersoff, 1994). Reciprocity is perhaps the most basic social obligation, the very foundation of communities. You give to others what they have given to you (Gouldner, 1960). At the same time, reciprocity constrains others' actions, and in this sense potentially impinges upon the individual's rights and freedom. This analysis might lead one to expect members of cultures that give priority to community to attach greater moral significance to violations of reciprocity than do members of cultures that prioritize individual rights and freedom.

To test this hypothesis, Joan Miller and David Bersoff asked U.S. and Hindu Indian college students to evaluate the following scenario:

> One day John was riding home when he noticed that Bill, a man who lived in his area, was planting a new flower garden. John had considerable spare time on weekends. So John offered to help the man complete the planting of the new garden. Several weeks later, Bill, the man whom John had helped previously, was riding through the neighborhood when he saw John was painting the fence around his house a new color. Bill had plenty of free time after work. So Bill offered to help John paint his fence a new color. (Miller & Bersoff, 1994)

Participants were asked to indicate whether Bill's reciprocity was a moral issue or a matter of personal choice. Seventy-eight percent of the Indian students thought Bill's reciprocity was a moral matter, and 22 percent thought it was a matter of personal choice. The results were almost reversed for the American students: 89 percent thought Bill's reciprocity was a matter of personal choice, and

11 percent thought it was a moral act. Thus, the findings from this study seem to indicate a clear difference in how people from different cultures view their moral obligation to engage in reciprocity.

## A Two-System View of Morality

Thus far, we have seen that the moral realm involves obligation, inclusiveness, and sanctions, and that some moral judgments seem to be universal and some are based on the social conventions of one's culture. We have seen that the moral realm can be broken down into three kinds of concerns: those related to autonomy (rights, freedom), community (duties, obligations), and divinity (bodily and mental purity). Moreover, we have discussed how such concerns can affect whether certain behaviors—for example, reciprocity—are considered a moral obligation or a personal choice. But we have not yet answered the most central question: How do we make moral judgments? To begin to arrive at an answer, read the following scenario, and decide whether you think the action described is right or wrong:

> Mark and Julie are brother and sister. They are traveling together in France on a summer vacation from college. One night they are staying alone in a cabin near the beach. They decide that it would be interesting and fun if they tried making love. At the very least it would be a new experience for each of them. Julie was already taking birth control pills, but Mark uses a condom, too, just to be safe. They both enjoy making love, but they decide not to do it again. They keep that night as a special secret, which makes them feel even closer to each other.

When asked whether such a situation is wrong, nearly all college students immediately say yes, typically with pronounced disgust and immovable certainty (Haidt, 2001). They're in good company. All cultures around the world view incest as immoral (D. Brown, 1991). When pressed to explain why Julie and Mark's encounter is wrong, people may reason that it is dangerous to inbreed, only to remember that Julie and Mark are using birth control. They may contend that each would be hurt emotionally, but recall that it was clearly specified that Julie and Mark were not harmed in any way by the event. Eventually, when all of their possible reasons have been refuted, people may simply say, "I can't explain why, I just know this is wrong."

This scenario illustrates how people make moral judgments, according to Jonathan Haidt's two-system account of moral judgment (Haidt, 2001). Throughout this book, we have talked about two systems of judgment: one that is quicker, intuitive, and often emotional in nature; another that is slower, controlled, deliberate, and that engages higher-order reasoning processes. Haidt proposes that our moral judgments likewise involve two different systems.

***When Each System Is Used***    The first system of moral judgment is fast, effortless, and automatic, and it gives us moral intuitions, or gut feelings, about right and wrong. Moral intuitions appear suddenly in consciousness, and they are emotional in nature (Batson, Engel, & Fridell, 1999; Greene & Haidt, 2002; Haidt, 2003). *Harm-related* emotions like sympathy and concern motivate pro-social responding to people who suffer or are vulnerable (Batson & Shaw, 1991; Eisenberg et al., 1989). *Self-critical* emotions, such as shame, embarrassment, and guilt, arise when we have violated moral codes or ideas about virtue and character, and they motivate moral behavior (Baumeister, Stillwell, & Heatherton, 1994; Higgins, 1987; Keltner & Anderson, 2000; Keltner & Buswell, 1997; Tangney, Miller, Flicker, & Barlow, 1996). *Other-praising* emotions, most notably gratitude and "elevation" or awe, signal our approval of others' moral virtues (Haidt, 2003; Keltner & Haidt, 2003; McCullough, Kilpatrick, Emmons, & Larson, 2001). And *other-condemning* emotions, such as anger, disgust, or contempt, underlie our condemnation of others' immoral actions, and as we shall soon see, are important to a sense of justice (Lerner, Goldberg, & Tetlock, 1998). These emotion-based moral intuitions arise quickly and automatically, and they direct our attention to harm and suffering, our own transgressions, others' virtues, and injustice and impurity.

The second system of moral judgment is slow and effortful, and it uses controlled reasoning processes to determine the morality of various actions. When we encounter morally relevant events, we contemplate the evidence, we consider logical and ethical principles, and we debate the consequences of different actions. One kind of reasoning that is central to moral judgment is perspective taking (Kohlberg, 1976). Young children tend to view moral actions from their own egocentric perspective. At about age ten, children start evaluating the moral content of specific actions from society's perspective. And at the highest level of moral judgment, people look upon actions from a prior-to-society perspective, considering what actions and principles and rules they consider to be right regardless of what position (for example, socioeconomic status) people occupy in society (Kohlberg, 1976; Rawls, 1971). For example, this perspective would consider slavery to be wrong because no one would choose to enter such a society without knowing whether he or she would occupy the position of slave or master. This last kind of perspective taking requires considerable cognitive sophistication, and in fact, may be achieved by only a small percentage of people.

***Studies of the Two Systems of Moral Judgment***    Our moral judgments are the product of fast, emotion-based intuitions, as well as more complex and conscious reasoning processes. How do the systems interact in shaping our moral judgment? Let's look at some specific studies of moral judgment that suggest that these two systems are indeed separate, and that our moral reasoning is often merely a post-hoc rationalization of our emotion-based moral intuitions.

In one study, participants in Brazil and Philadelphia read a number of scenarios and had to say whether they thought the people in the scenarios should be punished for their actions (Haidt, Koller, & Dias, 1993). Some of these situations involved harm: a boy pushes a girl off a swing that he wants to use. Others involved violations of a social convention: a man eats food with his hands, both in public and private, after washing them. Still others depicted harmless but offensive actions: a family eats the family dog that had been hit by a car. In another scenario, a woman finds an old flag in her closet, cuts it up, and uses it to clean her bathroom. In perhaps the most shocking story, a man goes to the supermarket once a week, buys a dead chicken, has sex with it, and then cooks and eats it. In each case, participants indicated whether they thought the person should be punished. As an indication of their emotional responses, participants indicated whether witnessing such an act would bother them. As an indication of their more controlled reasoning about the event, participants reported whether they thought that such an act would have harmful social consequences and therefore should be punished.

As you can see in Table 14.1, members of both cultures were strongly inclined to punish perpetrators of harmful acts (that is, pushing someone off the swings), but much less inclined to punish violators of social conventions (that is, eating

## Table 14.1 Punishment for Inappropriate Actions

People in Brazil and the United States were asked whether they would punish people who have engaged in moral infractions, who have violated a social convention, and who have done impure things that cause no harm. People in both cultures and from different class backgrounds were inclined to punish people who have violated moral rules. People in both cultures are less likely to punish people who have violated a social convention. Members of the different cultures diverge, however, in their responses to the harmless but offensive acts. Numbers in the table refer to the percentages of participants in each culture that would punish the perpetrator described in the scenario.

|  | BRAZIL | | UNITED STATES | |
| --- | --- | --- | --- | --- |
|  | Low SES | High SES | Low SES | High SES |
| **Moral Violation** | | | | |
| Boy pushes girl off swings. | 82 | 87 | 100 | 100 |
| **Violation of Social Convention** | | | | |
| Person eats with hands. | 38 | 32 | 53 | 13 |
| **Harmless but Offensive Act** | | | | |
| Person cleans toilet with flag. | 58 | 20 | 50 | 0 |
| Family eats their dog run over by car. | 53 | 38 | 80 | 10 |
| Man eats chicken he's had sex with. | 83 | 57 | 80 | 27 |

Source: Adapted from Haidt, Koller, & Dias, 1993.

with hands). Members of different cultures diverged in their responses to the harmless but offensive actions. Moreover, socioeconomic status (SES) also sometimes affected participants' responses. For example, low SES respondents, both Brazilian and American, and high SES Brazilian participants tended to think that punishment was warranted for such actions, but most high SES Americans (in this study, they were students at the University of Pennsylvania) did not think punishment was warranted, although the numbers varied, depending on the particular action.

Haidt explains the observed cultural differences in the reaction to harmless but offensive acts as follows: In Brazil and in lower SES communities in the United States, people have broader definitions of morality and feel that violations of social conventions and impure acts are morally wrong. Among high SES individuals in the United States, in contrast, morality is defined more narrowly in terms of individual rights and harm. As a result, high SES University of Pennsylvania students probably felt disgusted by the harmless but offensive acts but were able to put those feelings aside and let their considerations of individual rights and avoidance of harm guide their moral judgment. Consistent with this analysis, for Brazilian participants, affective reactions to the stories—that is, whether they were bothered by them—were strong predictors of their inclination to punish. In contrast, the punitive judgments of high SES American participants were driven by a more deliberate analysis of who might actually be harmed by the harmless but offensive acts and what societal costs might result.

Haidt's study of harmless but offensive acts thus provides suggestive evidence for two distinct systems that guide moral judgment. A more recent study suggests that these two systems may involve different central nervous system structures (Greene, Sommerville, Nystrom, Darley, & Cohen, 2001). Participants judged different moral and non-moral dilemmas in terms of whether they considered the action to be appropriate or not. Some of the moral dilemmas were likely to engage mainly rational calculation. For example, in the "trolley dilemma" the participant imagines a runaway trolley headed for five people who will be killed if it proceeds on its present course. The only way to save them is to hit a switch that will turn the trolley onto an alternate set of tracks where it will kill one person instead of five. The participant is asked whether it is appropriate to hit that switch and save five lives. Most participants answer yes with only a little hesitation.

In the more emotionally evocative "footbridge dilemma," again five people's lives are threatened by a trolley, but in this case the participant is asked to imagine standing next to a very heavy stranger on a footbridge over the trolley tracks. The participant is told that pushing the stranger off the bridge and onto the tracks would kill the stranger, but his dead body would cause the train to veer off its course and thus would save the lives of the five other individuals. (The participant's own weight, it is explained, is insufficient to send the trolley off the track.) Is it appropriate to push the stranger off the footbridge? The same two options are presented in the trolley dilemma—one death or five deaths—but in the footbridge dilemma the action is highly personal. The participant must imagine using his or her own hands to push the stranger to his gruesome death.

As participants responded to several different dilemmas of this sort, functional magnetic resonance imaging techniques ascertained which parts of the participant's brain were active. Consistent with Haidt's two-system theory, the personal moral dilemmas activated regions of the brain that previous research had found to be involved in emotion. The impersonal moral dilemmas and the non-moral dilemmas activated brain regions associated with working memory, regions centrally involved in more deliberative reasoning (see Box 14.1).

The interaction between the intuitive and rational systems involved in these moral judgments was evident in other findings. Greene and colleagues assessed how long it took participants to answer "appropriate" or "inappropriate" to the moral dilemmas (Greene, Sommerville, Nystrom, Darley, & Cohen, 2001). Of particular interest was how long it took participants to respond "appropriate" to actions taken in the personal moral dilemmas (for example, whether it's appropriate to push the man off the footbridge to save the other five individuals' lives). In these instances, emotional moral intuitions (it's horrible to physically push someone to his death) contradict more deliberate, cost-benefit reasoning (it's worth one person's life to save the lives of five people), which presumably would lead to a long delay between question and response. Indeed, in such personal moral dilemmas, people were the slowest to say "appropriate." Deliberate moral reasoning had to override emotion-based moral intuitions.

**LOOKING BACK,** we have seen that morality is a system of principles involving obligation, inclusiveness, and sanctions. Certain actions—namely, those that involve harm and violations of rights—are good candidates for moral universals, yet at the same time cultures vary dramatically in terms of which moral intuitions are most salient. Our moral judgments concern matters of autonomy (specifically, rights and freedom), community (fulfilling obligations and duties),

# Box 14.1 FOCUS ON NEUROSCIENCE

# The Moral Brain?

Phineas Gage was a likable foreman working on the construction of the Rutland and Burlington Railroad in Vermont. On September 13, 1848, he and some of his fellow workers were about to blast a rock with dynamite. Gage himself rammed the powder down with an iron rod that was three and a half feet long, an inch in diameter, and thirteen pounds in weight. As he did this, the iron struck up a spark, igniting a deafening explosion. The rod blasted through Gage's skull just beneath the left eyebrow and exited from a hole in the top of his head, landing 80 feet away. Gage bled terribly, but remarkably he survived, or at least his body did.

After the accident, Gage's character, his comportment, his soul, were different; he was "no longer Gage" in the words of his friends. Once amiable, courteous, and pleasant, he now was impatient, irreverent, and irritable. Once a reliable worker, he no longer could hold down a job. He eventually drifted around the United States, exhibiting himself at fairgrounds, accompanied by the iron bar that changed his life. The medical doctor who cared for Gage, John Harlow, offered one of the few recorded observations about Gage: "He is fitful, irreverent, indulging at times in the grossest profanity (which was not previously his custom), manifesting but little deference for his fellows, impatient of restraint or advice when it conflicts with his desires."

Reconstructions of Gage's injury indicate that it damaged Gage's orbitofrontal cortex, a part of the frontal lobes that is adjacent to the jagged, bony ridges of the skull's openings for the eyes. The orbitofrontal cortex is richly connected to other areas of the brain that have a rightful claim to being called parts of our moral brain. It receives information from the amygdala, a small almond-shaped part of the midbrain, which, as you will recall, provides extremely fast, unconscious assessment of whether objects are good or bad. Remarkably, damage to the orbitofrontal region of the frontal lobes does not impair language, memory, or sensory processing. But orbitofrontal damage does seem to knock out people's moral sense, as seen in Phineas Gage (Damasio, Tranel, & Damasio, 1990).

It is not unusual for orbitofrontal patients to greet strangers by kissing them, to tell inappropriate jokes to strangers, or to disclose their sexual preferences to people they have just met (Beer, Heerey, Keltner, Scabini, & Knight, 2003). One orbitofrontal patient, upon initially being hospitalized, rode gurneys down the halls and abused nurses. Hannah and Antonio Damasio have done well-known studies with a gambling task showing that orbitofrontal patients cannot avoid gambles that offer unlikely large gains but potentially devastating losses (Bechera, Damasio, & Damasio, 2000). They appear not to integrate the pain of loss into future decision making. And in another study, orbitofrontal patients teased an attractive confederate whom they did not know in inappropriate, often lewd fashion, but instead of feeling embarrassed about this inappropriate behavior, as did control participants, the orbitofrontal patients actually felt pride (Beer, Heerey, Keltner, Scabini, & Knight, 2003). The Damasios have argued that the orbitofrontal cortex integrates our moral intuitions into judgment and decision making. Consistent with Jonathan Haidt's two-system view of moral judgment, it appears that orbitofrontal patients do not have access to the emotion-based moral intuitions—for example, being embarrassed about untoward behavior, or caring what other people think or feel—to guide their judgments and actions.

**Phineas Gage**  A computer-generated image of Phineas Gage's skull shows how the iron rod pierced the skull, damaging his frontal cortex.

and divinity (matters of purity in mind and body). Moreover, our moral judgments involve fast, emotion-based intuitions, as well as more complex reasoning processes about moral intuitions—for example, by taking different perspectives on morally relevant actions.

## JUSTICE

L. Dennis Kozlowski rose to the top of Tyco Corporation thanks to an astounding work ethic and aggressive takeovers. He was lauded with numerous business awards and was a favorite on the lecture circuit. What most employees at Tyco's modest New Hampshire headquarters did not know was the extent of Kozlowski's greed, and his misuse of Tyco funds. With company money, he built himself a 20,000-square-foot house in Florida, and in Manhattan he lived in a luxury penthouse whose walls were decorated with expensive paintings on which he had avoided paying $1 million in state sales taxes. Eventually, he and the company's chief financial officer, Mark Swartz, were accused of looting the company of $600 million by awarding themselves unauthorized bonuses, illegally writing off personal loans from the company, and fraudulently inflating the value of company stock. Their first trial ended in a hung jury, but in June 2005 they were found guilty at the conclusion of their retrial.

Reading about Kozlowski's greed is likely to have stirred your sense of justice. Moral judgments and emotions like those described in the last section are often tied to our sense of justice—that is, our sense of what is fair. We care about whether we are being treated fairly or unfairly and about whether other people are being treated fairly or unfairly by other individuals, society, and the government. For example, our sense of justice tracks the allocation of collective resources, and how we deal with violators of rules and norms. In a dog-eat-dog world of pure selfishness, only the strong would obtain resources and mete out punishment. Group living would be rife with injustice. Our sense of justice, however, is a safeguard against the unchecked pursuit of self-interest; it promotes the fair allocation of resources to group members, which is so vital to cooperation.

**Justice**  At the turn of the century, several high-powered corporate executives were found guilty of corporate malfeasance, including L. Dennis Kozlowski, who was convicted of fraud, conspiracy, and grand larceny.

Our sense of justice can be broken down into three more specific concerns. A first goes by the label of **distributive justice**, which refers to whether people feel that the *outcomes* they receive—for example, their workload and salary—are fair or unfair. In reading about Dennis Kozlowski, you might ask: Why do people like Kozlowski take so much of the pie, when others go hungry? This is a question that concerns distributive justice.

A second kind of justice, **procedural justice**, concerns whether authority figures, such as Kozlowski, are meting out rewards and punishments in an unbiased, trustworthy, and legitimate fashion (Jost & Major, 2001). Odds are most employees at Tyco, upon discovering Kozlowski's means of satisfying his greed, were likely to feel a deep sense of procedural *injustice*.

And finally, how do we punish people for such excesses and other transgressions? This is a question of **restorative justice**, which refers to the actions peo-

**distributive justice**  A type of justice that is based on whether people feel that the outcomes they receive are fair or unfair.

**procedural justice**  A type of justice that is based on whether the processes by which rewards and punishments are distributed are considered fair.

**restorative justice**  The actions people take, from apologies to punishment, to restore justice.

ple take, from apologies to punishment, to restore justice. For Kozlowski it was a date in court, two trials, and ultimately conviction for fraud, conspiracy, and grand larceny.

As we now look at these three forms of justice in more detail, we will return to a theme we developed earlier: Our sense of justice, much like our moral intuitions, limits the selfish side of human nature. It keeps self-interested motives from being the sole motivators of behavior.

## DISTRIBUTIVE JUSTICE

At its core, distributive justice has to do with whether you believe that the rewards you receive correspond to the contributions you make. In the language of theorists in the field, do your inputs match your outputs (Walster, Walster, & Berscheid, 1978)? You are likely to believe that a distribution of resources is fair when the resources you gain match your contributions. Thus, you are likely to believe there is distributive justice when your salary matches your contribution at work and when the affection you enjoy in a relationship corresponds to the affection you give.

*Self-Interest and Distributive Justice* What determines how we allocate resources, and whether we think that distribution is fair? One determinant is self-interest. We tend to allocate resources in ways that favor the self, and yet find a way to think that this is fair. Others, of course, may not agree. Consider what has happened to the salaries of CEOs and ordinary workers over the past thirty-five years (see Figure 14.2). The average annual salary in America, expressed in 1998 dollars, rose from $32,522 in 1970 to $35,864 in 1999, a 10 percent increase. Over the same period, the average annual compensation of the top hundred CEOs went from $1.3 million, thirty-nine times the annual pay of the average worker, to $37.5 million, more than one thousand times the pay of the average worker. This increase at the top yields some rather stunning facts to mull over: In 1999, for example, the 13,000 richest families in America had an income equal to that of the poorest 20 million families (Krugman, 2002). When Jack Welch stepped down as the CEO of General Electric, his retirement package included an $80,000-a-month (yes, month) Central Park apartment, lifetime use of a company jet, maid service at his multiple homes, membership at an array of country clubs, flowers, limousine service, computers, furniture, and prime tickets to Wimbledon, the opera, the U.S. Open, and every New York Knicks home game. Quite a package for a person already worth hundreds of millions of dollars! When given the chance, CEOs let self-interest guide their sense of distributive justice. What about ordinary people?

*Egocentric Construals and Distributive Justice* CEOs are not alone in allocating resources in ways that favor their self-interest. People in more ordinary circumstances also let self-interest guide their sense of distributive justice. People may be aided in this by the common assumption that one's own contributions exceed those of others. For example, in a simple study by David Messick and his colleagues, participants listed examples of recent fair and unfair acts that either they or others had engaged in (Messick, Bloom, Boldizar, & Samuelson, 1985). As you can see in Figure 14.3, participants felt that they were the more common source of fair actions, and that other people were the more common source of unfair actions. In another example, thirty-nine married couples were asked to list specific examples of their own and their partner's contributions to twenty house-

**Figure 14.2 Income Disparities**
Changes in annual income (in inflation-adjusted dollars) between 1970 and 1999 for the top 100 CEOs and average workers in the United States. (Source: Adapted from Phillips, 2002)

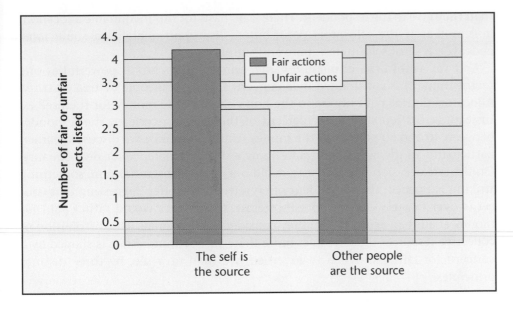

**Figure 14.3 Egocentric Judgment of Fairness**    When asked to list fair and unfair events that have recently happened, participants show evidence of egocentric conceptions of fairness. They felt that they themselves were the more frequent source of fair actions in their lives, and that other people were the more common source of unfair actions. (Source: Adapted from Messick, Bloom, Boldizar, & Samuelson, 1985)

hold activities, including doing the dishes, shopping for groceries, washing clothes, taking out the garbage, taking care of the children, choosing friends, and keeping in touch with relatives. The partners indicated that they had consistently contributed more than their partners had (Ross & Sicoly, 1979; see Chapter 10).

If people assume that they act in fairer ways than others do or that they contribute more than others, then they should expect greater rewards than other people for efforts that in fact are fully comparable to those of others. A study by Messick and Sentis (1979) supports this unsettling claim. Participants were asked to choose fair payments for themselves and another individual. In one scenario, participants were told to imagine that they had worked ten hours on a job and that their partner had worked seven hours. After being told that their partner had been paid $25, participants decided that it would be fair if they were paid $35.24 on average. In a different condition, participants were told to imagine that they had worked seven hours for $25 and their partner had worked ten hours. In this case, they thought it would be fair if their partner were paid $30.29. Thus, participants thought they deserved $5 more than another individual for the same work!

*Self-Interest in the Ultimatum Game*    Thus far, we have seen that CEOs and college students alike prioritize their own self-interest when allocating resources. Research by economists makes a similar point. In the ultimatum game, an *allocator* is given a certain amount of money, say $10, and told to keep a certain amount and allocate the rest to a second participant, a *responder*. The responder is then given the choice to either accept or reject the allocator's offer. If rejection is the choice, neither player receives anything.

In studies conducted in several different countries (Fehr & Schmidt, 1999), self-interest prevails. Allocators most typically give themselves more of the money

**Distributive Justice and CEOs**    Jack Welch, the former CEO of General Electric, earned millions of dollars as head of the company and retired with a package that included a $9 million annual pension, free use of an expensive Central Park apartment, a corporate jet, a helicopter, a limo, and other perks that many felt were an unfair distribution of the assets of General Electric. After the details came out during his divorce, he agreed to pay the company $2.5 million a year for the use of the apartment, jet, helicopter, and limo.

than they give to the respondent. There is no basis for this inequitable allocation; it is not as if the allocators contributed disproportionately to some joint endeavor. It's just self-interest, pure and simple.

And yet, within the ultimatum game, self-interest is not as powerful as one might think. It is constrained by a concern that other people be treated fairly. Allocators do not typically claim the lion's share of the money for themselves. Instead, across ten studies, 71 percent of the allocators offered the responder between 40 and 50 percent of the money. Unlike the CEOs we discussed earlier, participants in the ultimatum game show a strong preference for near equality. On the rare occasion when allocators did not offer a substantial sum, something striking happened: the respondent often rejected the offer, suggesting that concerns over fairness can trump self-interest. Responders would rather gain no money at all than accept a sum they consider unfairly small. The distribution of collective resources thus involves more than pure self-interest; it is shaped by a concern for fairness, which is governed, we shall now see, by three distinct principles.

*Relationship-Specific Principles of Distributive Justice*    In Chapter 4, we learned that people keep track of rewards and needs to different degrees in communal versus exchange relationships. Does our sense of distributive justice likewise vary in different relationships? Are you more willing to be on the short end of the stick with family members, say, than with people at work? Indeed this is the case. Three distinct principles of distributive justice appear to govern how we allocate resources in different relationships (Deutsch, 1975).

The principle of **equity** is based on the concept of *ratio equivalence,* according to which individuals should receive rewards that directly correspond to their contributions. If you write 70 percent of a screenplay, you should receive 70 percent of the royalties. The principle of equity seems most relevant in work relationships (Fiske, 1992). You might not be surprised to learn that people with power and wealth tend to prefer the principle of equity (Cook & Hegtvedt, 1986), as do more conservative and more materialistic individuals (Rasinski, 1987). People in power prefer the equity principle, partly because the alternative principles of need and equality, which we describe below, would compel them to reallocate more of their resources to others. The principle of equity is the most likely to guarantee that individuals with resources will keep them.

The principle of **equality** dictates that all individuals making contributions to some endeavor—for example, scientists working on an experiment together or basketball players on a team—should receive equal rewards. The principle of equality tends to govern the distribution of resources in friendships—cookies are split evenly, everyone gets the same amount of time on the trampoline, and everyone is expected to do a roughly equal share of the work. When teams win the World Series or Super Bowl, all players, MVPs and benchwarmers alike, receive the same bonus. But the data we presented earlier clearly suggest that at least in terms of worker compensation, the United States is moving further away than ever from the principle of equality when it comes to workplace compensation (Phillips, 2002).

Finally, according to the principle of **need**, those individuals with the greatest needs should be given priority for resources. The principle of need tends to prevail in families (Tyler & Smith, 1998). Resources are preferentially allocated to those in need—a newborn, a sick child, or a struggling parent. Young children do not generally make contributions to family income, yet they often absorb a great deal of the family's resources. This provokes little consternation on the

**equity** A principle of distributive justice according to which individuals should receive rewards that directly correspond to their contributions.

**equality** A principle of distributive justice that dictates that all individuals making contributions to some endeavor should receive equal rewards.

**need** A principle of distributive justice that dictates that individuals with the greatest needs should be given priority for resources.

"From each according to his abilities, to each according to his needs."

—Karl Marx

part of the parents (and none at all on the part of the kids!), for parents feel moved by the compelling needs of their children. Our sense of what is fair, then, strongly depends on our relationship with those with whom we are sharing resources.

*Social Comparison and Distributive Justice*    Consider the following puzzle: In the United States, lower SES individuals receive fewer resources, and they are more likely to have babies born with low birth weights, to be exposed to environmental hazards like toxic waste, to receive less adequate health care, and to live shorter lives (Adler et al., 1994; Yu & Williams, 1999). But low SES individuals are about as satisfied with their lives as individuals who live on vast estates, dine on the best of foods, and travel the world at the drop of a hat (Myers, 2000a).

One explanation of these findings is that low SES individuals think their lives are fair because they compare themselves with similar individuals who live nearby (Major, 1994), namely other low SES individuals, and even those individuals who are less well off than they are. People tend to only become dissatisfied with their lot when they experience what psychologists refer to as **relative deprivation**—that is, when their comparison with relevant others indicates that they are doing poorly (Crosby, 1976; Walker & Pettigrew, 1984).

> **relative deprivation** A feeling of deprivation based on comparisons with relevant others who are seen as doing better than oneself.

In one of the first demonstrations of relative deprivation, Stouffer and colleagues asked African-American soldiers right after World War II how happy they were with their life circumstances (Stouffer, Suchman, DeVinney, Star, & Williams, 1949). What they found was that African-American soldiers stationed in the South were more satisfied than those stationed in the North, even though Jim Crow laws still prevailed in the South and blacks were not treated well. The source of this disparity between objective circumstances and subjective well-being was that African-American soldiers in the South compared their life in the military with the typical life of southern blacks, and the black soldiers saw that they fared well by comparison. In contrast, African-American soldiers in the North did not fare so well in the analogous social comparison; the successes that their nearby African-American civilian peers were enjoying led the black soldiers to look less favorably upon their own life circumstances.

Findings such as these raise the intriguing question: When might we expect the disadvantaged to feel that life is unfair and to rise up and protest? The literature on relative deprivation indicates that they are most likely to do so when the social comparisons they make yield unfavorable assessments about their lot in life. Thus, it is typically the relatively *advantaged* members of disadvantaged groups who engage in collective action, such as protests. These individuals are more likely to come into contact with members of advantaged groups at elite universities, for example, and compare their lives with those of members of such groups. In so doing, they experience a sense of injustice (Gurin & Epps, 1975; Pettigrew, 1972). It is also after experiencing economic and political gains that members of disadvantaged groups are most likely to feel a sense of injustice, and thus more likely to engage in collective action (Gurr, 1970). Their improved life situation leads them to adopt new standards and expec-

**Social Comparison and Distributive Justice**    The slums of Caracas, Venezuela, are next to posh neighborhoods containing modern high-rise buildings and mansions. Yet, those who live in the slums generally do not compare their lives to those of the wealthy. Rather, they compare themselves to other poor people who live close by, and they are likely to feel relative deprivation if they think they are not doing as well as their neighbors are.

tations about still greater improvement. When this improvement slows, or doesn't proceed as quickly as expected or desired, protest and collective action become more likely.

In this discussion of distributive justice, we have seen that one part of whether we think the allocation of resources is fair or not is our self-interest. The more resources we receive, the fairer we are likely to think things are. If the only basis of our sense of distributive justice were self-interest, however, groups would be torn apart by competing claims of what is fair. As constraints upon self-interest and greed, we factor other concerns into our sense of distributive justice. For example, relationships matter. Thus, we are likely to want resources to be allocated based on equity at the workplace, equality with friends, and need with family members, often subordinating our own interests to enhance the welfare of others. We also decide what is fair by comparing our lot to others. And we will now see that our sense of fairness is also shaped by how authority figures allocate the outcomes that we receive.

## PROCEDURAL JUSTICE

Procedural justice refers to assessments of whether the manner in which rewards and punishments are distributed is fair. Our concern about procedural justice is salient, for example, when we mull over whether employers use consistent criteria to give out bonuses, or when there are conflicts about which criteria to use to admit students to colleges and universities.

Three factors shape our sense of procedural justice, according to social psychologist Tom Tyler (1994). First, there is a concern for the *neutrality* of the authority figure. For example, when Olympic judges give substantially higher ratings to figure skaters from their own country, their neutrality is clearly in question, and the sense of procedural justice is jeopardized. Second, there must be *trust* in the system. We must have confidence that authority figures will be fair, that they will treat others according to similar principles and standards. And finally, the individual must feel that he or she is treated with *respect*. It is interesting to note how often authority figures meting out justice—police officers giving out traffic tickets or judges delivering sentences, for example—treat those they are punishing politely. (Judge Judy is perhaps the rare exception to this!)

Tyler and his colleagues contend that these three facets of procedural justice have as much to do with our sense that outcomes are fair as the actual content, good or bad, of the outcome itself. In survey research, they have contacted people who have had recent experiences with authority figures. In one study, participants had recently received sentences for crimes they had committed (Tyler, 1987; Tyler & Caine, 1981). In another, Tyler surveyed people regarding their experiences with their supervisors at work (Tyler, 1994). Participants indicated what reward or punishment they had received—for example, how long they had been sentenced to prison or the size of the promotion they had received—matters that tap into the very substance of distributive justice. Participants also indicated the extent to which they believed that the authority figure had been neutral, trustworthy, and had treated them with respect. The dependent measure of interest was the participant's feelings about the authority figure's fairness.

Two findings stand out. First, the magnitude of rewards and punishments people received, whether prison sentences or promotions, was *not* correlated with their sense of procedural justice. Our concerns about dis-

*"Don't worry about it. One day you're feeling down and you dish out twenty years to some poor devil. The next day you feel great and everybody gets a suspended sentence. It all evens out in the end."*

tributive and procedural justice are distinct (Brockner & Weisenfeld, 1994; Folger, 1977). Second, and perhaps more striking, people's ratings of neutrality, trust, and respect were stronger determinants of their belief in the fairness of the authority figure than the actual reward or punishment they received! Even if a judge gives you a harsh sentence, or your boss passes you over for a promotion, you will conclude that the judge or boss is fair as long as he or she seems neutral and trustworthy and treats you with respect.

Our sense of justice thus revolves around more than personal gains or losses. We care profoundly about the neutrality of authority figures, the trustworthiness of the system, and the respect we receive from others. On the one hand, you might take heart from these results. We can build a prevailing sense of justice in groups and communities by being neutral, trustworthy, and respectful, and we can do this without changing the allocation of material resources. On the other hand, there is potentially a more sinister implication to Tyler's findings: Authority figures can hand out all sorts of outcomes, from job layoffs to unwarranted prison sentences, without people protesting, as long as they deliver them in a neutral, trustworthy, and respectful fashion.

## RESTORATIVE JUSTICE

Thus far, we have focused on the elements of our sense of justice: our self-interest, concerns over equality, equity, and need, and our sense of whether authority figures use fair procedures. When these important principles are honored, we maintain a **belief in a just world,** the cherished conviction that people get what they deserve in life, and that their outcomes match their actions and character (Furnham, 1993; Lerner, 1980; Lerner & Miller, 1978; see Chapter 9). The alternative, that the world is unjust and that rewards and punishments are randomly distributed in some grand lottery of life, is a possibility simply too unpleasant for most people to entertain. We do not like to think that a child's physical health or disability, lucky breaks and freak accidents, occur randomly, flowing from the whim of fate alone. Instead, we hold fast to beliefs that life is fair, that people get what they deserve, and, for many of those with faith, that "God balances the scales" in the afterlife.

Because our belief in a just world is so cherished, injustice is especially repugnant, and motivates restorative action (Adams, 1965; Greenberg, 1990; Hafer & Olson, 1993; Walster, Walster, & Berscheid, 1978). Consider one simple example: When people are overcompensated for their efforts, they may actually increase how hard they work (Tyler & Smith, 1998). Again we return to this theme: We will sacrifice our own self-interest to make sure that things are fair.

Of course, fate can be profoundly unfair. Random genetic defects, violent crimes, company layoffs, and the simple fact of being born into poverty can shift the course of life dramatically, at times threatening the belief in a just world. People restore their belief in a just world in several ways.

*Shifting Perceptions of Perpetrators and Victims* One way to restore a belief in a just world in the face of injustice is to shift your beliefs about the perpetrators and victims of injustice (see Chapter 9). We can convince ourselves that victims deserve their lot through some flaw in their character or foolish action. Evidence of this regrettable tendency is commonplace. People tend to stigmatize those with mental disorders (Hinshaw & Cicchetti, 2000), individuals living in poverty, and rape victims (Jones & Aronson, 1973), in ways that suggest that victims of these fates deserve what they get.

**belief in a just world** The conviction that people get what they deserve in life, that their outcomes match their actions and character.

**system justification** The tendency to justify differences in wealth and opportunity with beliefs that imply that such inequalities are deserved, just, and even natural and inevitable.

**retributive punishment** Punishment based on eye-for-an-eye justice in which the goal is to avenge a prior evil deed rather than prevent future ones.

**utilitarian punishment** Punishment in which the goal is reducing the likelihood of future crimes committed by the criminal through such means as rehabilitation or isolation of the criminal.

**Punishment** Utilitarian punishment seeks to reduce the likelihood of future crimes. (A) Convicts in Georgia were placed in stocks for infractions while working on the chain gang. (B) People were forced to wear shame masks in medieval times for behavior that offended public decency. This mask in the shape of a pig was used for people who displayed "piggish behavior."

People exhibit a similar tendency to rationalize society-wide injustices. As we have seen in this chapter, there is a widening gap between the rich and poor. This creates dramatic inequalities in opportunities. To reduce the dissonance created by this societal fact, John Jost claims we engage in **system justification**, which refers to the tendency to justify preexisting differences in wealth and opportunity with beliefs that imply that such inequalities are deserved, just, and even natural and inevitable (Jost & Banaji, 1994; Jost, Banaji, & Nosek, 2004).

Empirical studies point to two primary ways that society-wide inequalities are justified. First, we maintain more positive stereotypes about high-status individuals—for example, as being intelligent or hard working—and more negative stereotypes about working-class individuals—as being lazy or irresponsible—which thereby explain differences in wealth and opportunity. Quite strikingly, members of low-status groups, including U.S. minorities and students at less prestigious universities, consistently show very positive evaluations of high-status groups compared to their own (Conway, Pizzamiglio, & Mount, 1996; Glick & Fiske, 2001; Jost, Pelham, & Carvallo, 2002). Second, we espouse ideologies, like the ideology of meritocracy, which at its core assumes that people get what they deserve, that the lower classes could rise in status if only they chose to do so and applied themselves (Kluegel & Smith, 1986).

*Punishment*    Of course, we can do more to restore a sense of justice than shifting our beliefs; we can also punish. Punishment has been a central, at times horrifying part of human culture across time. Scholars differentiate between two kinds of punishment (Carlsmith, Darley, & Robinson, 2002; Weiner, Graham, & Reyna, 1997). **Retributive punishment** matches the pain inflicted by the wrongdoing. This is an eye-for-an-eye justice; the goal is to avenge a prior evil deed rather than prevent future ones. For example, your brother pinches you on the shoulder, and as punishment, you pinch him back on the very same spot and to the same extent (or perhaps a bit harder for good measure). **Utilitarian punishment** has the goal of reducing the likelihood of future crimes committed by the criminal. This might be accomplished by efforts at rehabilitation or by isolating the criminal from society.

As in the domain of moral judgment, fast, emotion-based intuitions guide punitive judgments (Weiner, Graham, & Reyna, 1997). If you believe the perpetrator is responsible for the crime, and that the action reflects a stable part of his character, you will likely feel anger. When people feel anger and can act on that

anger, the region of their brain known to promote goal-directed, situation-changing behavior—the left side of the frontal cortex—is activated, and they are more likely to take restorative action (Harmon-Jones, Sigelman, Bohlig, & Harmon-Jones, 2003). Angered individuals should prefer the most vengeful form of punishment—retributive punishment (Lerner, Goldberg, & Tetlock, 1998). In contrast, if you attribute the criminal act to the situation, and assume it does not reflect a stable part of the defendant's character, you will probably feel sympathy. Feeling sympathy increases forgiveness, and makes people prefer forms of punishment that protect the criminal and society, namely utilitarian punishment (Weiner, Graham, & Reyna, 1997).

*Reconciliation*    A final means by which we can restore justice is to reconcile, which involves two important elements: apologies and forgiveness. Insight into the nature of reconciliation among primates comes from Frans de Waal, who spent thousands of hours observing what different primates—macaques and chimpanzees—do following aggressive encounters. The prevailing wisdom had been that after an aggressive encounter, the two aggressors would move away from each other as far as possible—the dispersal hypothesis. Much as humans often put distance between themselves and their enemies with walls, boundaries, and restraining orders, animals were believed to gravitate to physical spaces that made aggression less likely.

This view might make sense for solitary species, such as golden hamsters, who flee upon attack, or territorial species, such as many birds, who rely on territorial arrangements to avoid deadly conflicts. But social mammals, like chimpanzees and humans, need to stay in groups to survive, and thus they need to restore cooperative relations following unjust acts. De Waal discovered that pairs of chimps who had just engaged in aggressive conflict were more likely to show friendly contact behavior than the same pairs during less strife-ridden times (de Waal & van Roosmalen, 1979). Either party, winner or loser of the conflict, could initiate such acts of reconciliation, which would eventually lead to affiliative grooming, physical contact, and even embraces that would reconcile the warring parties, thereby renewing their bond.

In humans, reconciliation involves *apologies*, in which the infringing party takes responsibility for the wrongdoing and expresses remorse; such apologies reduce the anger in the victims of the injustice (Keltner, Young, & Buswell, 1997; Tedeschi & Reiss, 1981). A study by Ohbuchi, Kameda, and Agarie (1989) suggests that we may be wise to say "I'm sorry" more than we might be inclined. In this study, a confederate made a series of errors that led participants, students at a Japanese university, to fail on intellectual tasks. Participants liked and trusted the mistake-prone confederate more when he apologized than when he did not. Other studies have shown that apologies that involve sincere remorse and some restitution are especially likely to lead victims of injustice to forgive the perpetrator of the wrongdoing (Worthington, 1998). When we apologize, we feel distress, we can lose face, and we acknowledge our culpability, but apologies help maintain harmonious social bonds.

**Reconciliation**    Justice can be restored through gestures of reconciliation, including apologies and forgiveness, which enable humans and many other animal species to live more cooperatively in groups. Ten minutes after an aggressive encounter between two adult male chimpanzees, the challenged male reached out his hand to his opponent to bring about reconciliation.

A second component of reconciliation is *forgiveness*. Forgiveness involves the release of negative feelings and increased compassion and empathy toward the perpetrator of injustice (McCullough, 2000; McCullough, Sandage, & Worthington, 1997; Worthington, 1998). Forgiveness has been shown to be an important factor in restoring justice, and one with important salutary effects. In one study, participants were asked to imagine a grudge they held against someone (whom they had not forgiven) or forgiving someone who had harmed them (Witvliet, Ludwig, & Vander Laan, 2001). Participants who imagined being harmed unjustly but who also forgave showed lower blood pressure, less stress-related heart rate increase and skin conductance response in the hands, and reduced brow furrowing associated with anger (see also Lawler et al., 2003).

**LOOKING BACK**, we have seen that justice has many facets. Distributive justice refers to our concern over the fair distribution of resources, which is determined by our self-interest, by the relationships of the people involved, and by social comparison. Procedural justice refers to our sense that the manner in which outcomes are distributed is fair. And restorative justice concerns what we do when people have acted in unjust fashion: shift our attitudes toward victims, punish, or apologize, forgive, and reconcile. These facets of justice are all essential to our capability to live in cooperative groups. We now turn to a discussion of cooperation itself.

## COOPERATION

In the last hundred years, the world has become substantially more interconnected (Wright, 2000). Businesses are multinational, many college campuses draw students from all over the world, and we communicate with people from distant lands over the Internet. How are we doing in our more interconnected world? One answer is not so great. Tensions between Islamic and Western countries, Israelis and Palestinians, Pakistan and India, to name a few examples, are extreme, and darkened by the specter of weapons of mass destruction. Within the United States, "culture wars" surrounding affirmative action, abortion, the environment, and gay marriage divide the nation (Hunter, 1991). The country is split into two opposed camps: the red states and the blue states. In such a polarizing time, one is tempted to say that conflict might be the natural state of affairs for humans.

But cooperation can emerge in the most improbable places. In the trenches of World War I, British and French soldiers were separated from their enemies, the Germans, by a few hundred yards of no man's land (Axelrod, 1984). Brutal assaults by one side were typically met with equally fierce resistance by the other. And, yet, even here cooperation frequently emerged, allowing soldiers to eat meals peacefully, to enjoy long periods of nonconfrontation, and even to fraternize with one another. The two sides would fly special flags, make verbal agreements, and fire symbolic yet misguided shots, all to signal and maintain peaceful cooperation in between episodes of attack in which each side was bent on the extermination of the other.

The tendency to cooperate, we argued earlier, is part of our evolutionary heritage. It is required of a social species such as ours. To survive and reproduce in groups, we must cooperate. In our examination of cooperation we rely on an

**Cooperation**    During World War I, there were instances of cooperation among the enemy soldiers, including during this informal Christmas truce in 1914, when soldiers from both sides emerged from their trenches and fraternized in no man's land, as shown in this lithograph that was published in 1915.

experimental paradigm known as the prisoner's dilemma game to identify processes that prevent cooperation and those that promote it. We discussed this game briefly in Chapter 1, and we will deal with it more fully here.

## THE PRISONER'S DILEMMA GAME

Imagine being in an experiment in which you are ushered into a small cubicle by the experimenter, who informs you that there is another participant (whom you will never meet) in a cubicle nearby. What is required of each of you is to make a simple decision: you must independently choose to "cooperate" with each other (do what will benefit both of you) or "defect" (do what will disproportionately benefit yourself). You will be paid for your participation, and your compensation will depend on the choices you make. If both of you cooperate, you will each receive $5. If both of you defect, you will each get $2. If one cooperates and the other defects, the defector will receive $8, and the cooperator will not receive anything. The experimenter says that you will be paid as soon as each of you makes your choice, and reiterates that you and the other subject will never meet. What do you do?

From the perspective of maximizing your own outcomes, the best or "rational" thing to do is to defect. Whatever your partner does, you make more money by defecting than by cooperating. To see this, consult the summary of payoffs presented in Table 14.2. If your partner cooperates, you receive $8 by defecting but only $5 by cooperating. If your partner defects, you receive $2 by defecting and nothing by cooperating. Defection thus "dominates" cooperation. So why not defect?

Here's the catch: the payoffs are the same for both players, and so if both reason this way and choose to defect, they receive only $2 rather than the $5 that would be theirs through mutual cooperation. The "best" choice for each individual (defection) is a terrible choice from the standpoint of the two subjects as a whole.

Countless individuals have participated in over two thousand experiments of just this type, involving what is known as the prisoner's dilemma game. The name derives from a problem in game theory: Two suspects are arrested and held in separate cells on suspicion that they have committed a crime. They are both guilty, but there is no evidence, and they cannot be convicted unless they confess. If nei-

## Table 14.2   Payoff Matrix for Prisoner's Dilemma Game

Your payoffs are represented by the numbers on the left in each cell, and those of your partner are represented by the numbers on the right in each of the cells.

|  |  | YOUR PARTNER | |
|---|---|---|---|
|  |  | Cooperate | Defect |
| YOU | Cooperate | $5      $5 | 0      $8 |
|  | Defect | $8      0 | $2      $2 |

ther confesses, neither of them can be convicted. Thus, it is in the best interests of both to cooperate by not confessing. But if one of them cooperates (not confessing to the crime) and the other defects (confessing to the crime), the defector will get a light sentence (say, one year) and the cooperator will get a heavy sentence (say, ten years). If both defect and confess the crime, both will get heavy sentences that are lightened a bit (say, eight years) because of their admission of guilt.

On the surface, the prisoner's dilemma game seems to hold little promise for teaching us anything significant about real human interaction. Unlike many real-world situations, there is not a range of cooperative to competitive behaviors from which to choose; there are only two—cooperate or defect. In addition, participants are not allowed to discuss the choices beforehand, and they are never permitted to explain or justify them afterward. It all seems too limited, too artificial, to tell us anything significant about "real world" cooperation and competition.

Looks may be deceiving in this case, however. As simple as the prisoner's dilemma might seem, it nevertheless captures the essential features of many significant real-world situations (Dawes, 1980; Schelling, 1978). Consider a real-world analogue: India and Pakistan have been engaged in an arms race for decades. Like nearly all such struggles, the contest is ultimately futile because its structure is that of the prisoner's dilemma. Each country must decide whether to spend more on armaments or to stop spending money on more arms and enjoy a significant economic "peace dividend" as the United States did following the breakup of the Soviet Union. Regardless of what the other does, it is "better" to acquire more arms. (If India freezes its acquisition of weapons, Pakistan can achieve an edge by spending more. If India builds up its arsenal, Pakistan has to spend more to avoid vulnerability.) Nonetheless, because the new weapons systems developed by one side are quickly matched by the other, the net effect is waste. The two countries pay dearly for a military balance that was attainable for less expense. The thousands of studies using the prisoner's dilemma game provide some excellent insights regarding conflict and cooperation, since they illuminate why people or groups or countries would be likely to defect or cooperate, and suggest what might be done.

***Primed to Cooperate or Defect***   We are often unduly influenced by what happens to be "on the top of our heads." If someone yells at us in traffic, we sometimes take it out on an undeserving store clerk. Having just seen a film biography of Mother Teresa, we may be temporarily more inclined to act kindly toward others.

Our recent experience, then, may be an important determinant of whether we cooperate or compete. In a compelling demonstration of this notion, Steve Neuberg (1988) had male undergraduates participate in a standard prisoner's dilemma experiment. Before doing so, however, the participants were subliminally "primed" with one of two different sets of stimulus words, ostensibly as part of another experiment. For one group, Neuberg flashed twenty-two hostile words (for example, *competitive, hostile, unfriendly*) for sixty milliseconds—too fast for anyone to "see" them and consciously register what they were, but also long enough, research has shown, for them to leave a subconscious impression. He showed another group a list of neutral words (for example, *house, looked, always*) for an equally brief period. The question was whether exposure to the hostile words would lead participants to think "it's a dog-eat-dog world out there" in which a person has to look out for his own interests because no one else will.

Exposure to the hostile words did affect the actions of the participants. Eighty-four percent of the participants exposed to the hostile words defected on a majority of the trials in the subsequent prisoner's dilemma game; only 55 percent of the participants exposed to the neutral words did so. This study gives reason for concern about the kinds of stimuli to which people are commonly exposed. The ideas in the air—the competitive and aggressive images we see in the media, in video games, in films—are likely to foster a more competitive society.

***Cooperation on Wall Street and Main Street***    Based on the results from Neuberg's study, one might expect that the way we explicitly label different situations might influence levels of competition and cooperation. If we think of international crises as buildups to war, diplomatic solutions may become less likely. When lawyers treat divorce settlements as adversarial and as opportunities to get their client the best outcome at the expense of the estranged spouse, entrenched bitterness seems inevitable. If we believe that most people are competitive and self-interested, we ourselves, we shall soon see, are more likely to act in competitive fashion (see Box 14.2).

In a striking demonstration of the power of labels, Liberman, Samuels, and Ross (2002) conducted a study with students at Stanford University in which they labeled the prisoner's dilemma game in one of two ways (see Chapter 1). Half of the participants were told they were going to play the Wall Street game; the others were told it was the community game. Everything else about the experiment was the same for the two groups.

What might seem to be a trivial change of labels had a dramatic effect on the subjects' behavior. As you will recall from Chapter 1, those playing the community game cooperated on the opening round twice as often as those playing the Wall Street game. Moreover, these initial differences were maintained throughout the subsequent rounds of the experiment. The Wall Street label doubtless made the subjects adopt a perspective in which maximizing their own profits was paramount. In contrast, the community label no doubt conjured up a different set of images and motives that increased the appeal of maximizing the participants' joint outcomes.

***Competition Begets Competition***    The results we have reviewed thus far on the effect that competitive primes, labels, and ideologies can have in promoting competition should lead us to expect that some people would be chronically inclined

> " . . . every individual, therefore, endeavors as much as he can . . . to employ his capital in the support of domestic industry, and so to direct that industry that its produce may be of greatest value; every individual necessarily labours to render the annual revenue of the society as great as he can. He . . . neither intends to promote the public interest, nor knows how much he is promoting it. By . . . directing that industry in such a manner as its produce may be of greatest value, he intends only his own gain, and he is in this, as in many other cases, led by an invisible hand to promote an end which was no part of his intention."
>
> —ADAM SMITH (1776)

Box 14.2   FOCUS ON BUSINESS/EDUCATION

# Do Economists Make Bad Citizens?

Priming and labeling represent rather localized influences on cooperation and competition. Priming effects decay quickly; labeling effects are specific to the stimuli labeled in a particular way. Other influences are more global and enduring. Foremost among these is the general culture or subculture to which you belong.

Within universities, consider the subculture of the discipline of economics, typically one of the most popular majors on campus. Economic theory assumes that people are rational actors who always act in self-interested fashion, attempting to maximize their own gains. This sounds bad to many people, but following eighteenth-century philosopher Adam Smith, economists have assumed that individuals and society are best served if individuals are allowed to selfishly pursue their own ends. The storekeeper and restaurateur will succeed to the extent that they serve their patrons well, simultaneously improving the lot of their customers and doing well themselves by charging as much as a competitive market will allow.

Does training in the discipline of economics encourage people to act in more competitive fashion? The results of several studies indicate that it does (Carter & Irons, 1991; Frank, Gilovich, & Regan, 1993b; Marwell & Ames, 1981).

In one study, Cornell undergraduates who were majoring in economics and in a variety of other disciplines participated in a single-trial prisoner's dilemma game in which great pains were taken to ensure that each person's response would remain anonymous (Frank, Gilovich, & Regan, 1993b). Seventy-two percent of the economics majors defected on their partners, whereas only 47 percent of those majoring in other disciplines did so.

You may also be interested to learn that academic economists contribute proportionately less to charity than professors in other academic disciplines. In a random sample of over a thousand professors in twenty-three different disciplines, participants were asked how much money they gave annually to public television, the United Way, and to other charitable causes. The economists were twice as likely as the members of all the other academic disciplines to "free ride" on the contributions of their fellow citizens—that is, to give nothing at all to charity while presumably enjoying services such as public television to the same extent as everyone else. The subculture in which one is immersed appears to have a powerful influence on one's inclination to cooperate with others or look after the self.

to interpret situations as occasions for competition rather than cooperation. A fascinating study by Kelley and Stahelski (1970) using the prisoner's dilemma game tested this hypothesis, as well as the more intriguing idea that competitive people create more competitive interactions and thus come to construe their counterparts as also being competitive—which in turn justifies their own competitive behavior.

Upon arriving at the laboratory, participants were shown the game and its payoff matrix. Was the goal to beat the other person or to maximize mutual gain? Some participants made it clear that they thought that competition was the goal; others indicated they thought cooperation was the goal. The experimenters paired off cooperators with cooperators, cooperators with competitors, and competitors with competitors, and they had the participants play a number of rounds of the prisoner's dilemma game. After a certain number of trials, the players had to judge whether their partners were competitors or cooperators, as originally assessed prior to the prisoner's dilemma game.

What happened with these various combinations? A revealing tale emerged about how competition begets increased competition. First, the competitors made everyone, including the cooperators, more competitive. Wouldn't you be competitive if your partner consistently defected on you, enjoying high rewards at your expense? Second, whereas cooperators were pretty accurate in their judgments of whether they were interacting with a cooperator or competitor, competitors were not. Competitive participants, who made others more competitive, mistakenly assumed everyone was competitive! This study provides insight into how readily competition can spread. It evokes escalating competitive responses in others, and prompts perceptions that justify competition. The competitive apple spoils the barrel, when, as in the prisoner's dilemma game, competition lowers the outcomes obtained by all.

## FAILURE TO PERCEIVE COMMON GROUNDS FOR COOPERATION

Thus far, we have seen that competitive expectations lead to greater competition in the prisoner's dilemma game. Do these findings generalize to the ideological conflicts that polarize so much of the world today? Regrettably, the answer is a resounding yes. Outside of the laboratory, we all too readily construe our opponents as enemies, often failing to see opportunities for agreement, common ground, and cooperation.

There are many facets of the tendency for ideological opponents to construe each other as enemies. People tend to view their own group as moral, good, principled, and reasonable, and other groups as amoral or guided by strange and often dangerous or politically motivated moral precepts (Bar-Tal, 1990; Brewer & Kramer, 1985; LeVine & Campbell, 1972; see Chapter 2). People construe opponents' more general interests as hostile and antithetical to their own (Plous, 1985). These construal tendencies can have several regrettable consequences that amplify social conflict.

First, people often overlook areas of agreement with their ideological opponents. In a series of studies, researchers have examined the attitudes of opposing partisans to the conflicts over abortion, affirmative action, criminal justice, government budget cuts, and the content of the liberal arts curriculum (Keltner & Robinson, 1996; Robinson, Keltner, Ward, & Ross, 1995; Robinson & Keltner, 1996). For example, in the study of abortion, pro-choice and pro-life partisans indicated their beliefs about such issues as when life begins, the proportion of abortions that are done for health-related causes, and the effects of outlawing abortion. Partisans also estimated the attitudes of typical members of the "other" side and their "own" side. This allowed a comparison between opposing partisans' actual differences with the differences they perceived to exist between themselves and their ideological opponents.

The opposing partisans certainly disagreed about the basic issues related to the conflict. But opponents greatly exaggerated their differences, typically overestimating the differences between the two sides by a substantial amount. In studies of negotiations, a similar tendency is seen: negotiators typically underestimate the amount of common ground in their attitudes and preferences and tend to settle for outcomes that are less desirable than others that are available (Thompson & Hrebec, 1996).

Being inclined to construe opponents as extremists, opposing partisans could be expected to be quite suspicious of their opponent's offers or concessions, presuming that these are insincere or less cooperative than they appear on the sur-

**Figure 14.4 Reactive Devaluation**
During the apartheid era in South Africa, U.S. college students demanded that their universities divest from firms with ties to South Africa. In this study, Stanford students evaluated a particular plan before and after their opponents, the university administration, actually adopted the plan. As one can see, students reactively devalued the plan. They found it less favorable after the plan had actually been adopted by the administration than before. (Source: Adapted from Ross & Stillinger, 1991)

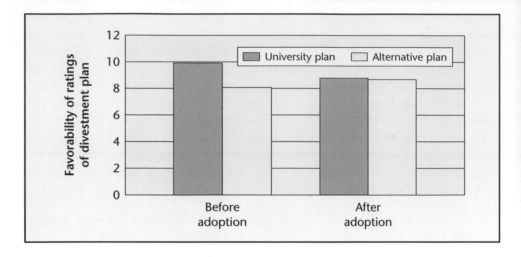

**reactive devaluation** Reduced attractiveness of an offer from an opposing side just because the other side made it.

face. There is such a tendency, and it is known as **reactive devaluation**—that is, the mere fact that the other side has offered a concession is enough to reduce its attractiveness (Ross & Stillinger, 1991). Adversaries are likely to reason that "if my extremist opponent is offering this, it can't be good for me." To study this phenomenon, Lee Ross and his colleagues examined ongoing tensions between university students and administrators regarding their university's investments in companies in South Africa in the 1980s. At the time, an apartheid system legally segregated whites and "coloreds" in South Africa. Although they were a small proportion of the population, whites held positions of power and lived relatively comfortable lives. Most coloreds lived in impoverished townships, had little if any political power, and were terrorized by a secret branch of the South African police. Many U.S. college students demanded that their universities sell their investments in companies that had South African operations.

In response to this kind of protest, administrators at Stanford University were considering, and in fact were about to adopt, a partial divestment plan from companies that had operations in South Africa. They were going to propose that Stanford divest from companies that did not meet certain standards regarding opportunities for coloreds in South Africa. Ross and Stillinger anticipated this imminent announcement, and they were able to measure students' evaluations of the partial divestment plan, both prior to and after the university administration had put forward the plan. What one sees in Figure 14.4 is strong evidence of reactive devaluation. Before the university adopted the partial divestment plan, students felt it was a significant and positive move, particularly compared with an alternate plan. But after Stanford adopted the partial divestment plan, students evaluated it less favorably.

If there is a lesson in this section it is the perils of construal processes as they operate in situations of social conflict (see Box 14.3). When we approach interactions with a competitive mind-set, we are more likely to compete, often at our own and others' expense. We stereotype our opponents as immoral, extremists, and hostile (see Chapter 11). The risks are numerous. We often underestimate our common ground with our opponents and the prospects for cooperation. We construe their disagreements as non-negotiable matters of absolute right and wrong, battles between clashing cultures or civilizations. Fortunately, the very same paradigm, the prisoner's dilemma game, has yielded other results that point to specific principles that make cooperation more likely.

Box 14.3   FOCUS ON POLITICS

# The Complex Mind of Cooperation

A general theme of this section is that simplistic thinking about opponents exacerbates social conflicts. Is the complement also true? Does more complex thinking lead opponents to navigate differences of opinion and preference more effectively? Philip Tetlock's work on "integrative complexity" suggests that it does.

Positions on complex issues such as globalization, tax policy, or affirmative action involve a variety of specific beliefs. For example, your position on globalization is likely to reflect your beliefs about the extent to which multinational corporations generate wealth for average citizens, pollute or preserve the environment, are accountable to the laws of the countries in which they operate, and so on. Integrative complexity is defined by two properties. The first is differentiation, or the extent to which the individual considers several different principles and issues in arriving at a judgment. The second is integration, or the number of connections that the individual makes between the different facts, principles, and arguments related to an issue. People hold more complex attitudes when they incorporate many facts and principles, even opposing ones, into their position, and when they draw many connections between these different kinds of information.

Tetlock and his colleagues have coded the integrative complexity of politicians' reasoning from records of their speeches and interviews. Who do you think engages in more complex rhetoric: incumbents or people seeking re-election? Tetlock coded the integrative complexity of ten randomly selected paragraphs from papers and speeches of ten presidents, from McKinley to Carter (Tetlock, 1981). Only one of the ten candidates was more complex while on the campaign trail than while speaking as an elected president: Herbert Hoover. In general, presidents were less complex, and in effect more simplistic and extremist, while wooing potential voters on the campaign trail. When speaking as an elected president, and having to deal with the complexities and give-and-take of the real world, presidents employed more complex rhetoric.

Who do you think is more complex: liberals or conservatives? (Your answer, of course, probably depends on your own political persuasion.) It turns out that extremists on both sides are less complex in

their public rhetoric than moderate liberals and moderate conservatives. In one study, Tetlock coded the interviews of eighty-nine members of the British House of Commons, and found that extreme socialists and extreme conservatives were less complex than moderate socialists or moderate conservatives (Tetlock, 1984). He also found evidence that integrative complexity can prevent conflict. More complex politicians, both on the right and left of the political spectrum, tended to de-emphasize differences between the two parties, to express tolerance of their opponents' views, and to resist blaming their opponents for England's woes at that time.

Does complexity actually help during situations of growing conflict? One would think that it would help, for there is correlational evidence linking the complexity of British politicians with their tendency to be less dogmatic, to see issues from multiple perspectives, and to refrain from blaming others or thinking in polarized terms. Further evidence comes from a study that examined the complexity of political leaders' rhetoric during two different crises: the disastrous buildup to World War I in 1914, and the 1962 Cuban Missile Crisis, in which U.S. President John F. Kennedy and Soviet Premier Nikita Khrushchev averted a nuclear encounter (Suedfeld & Tetlock, 1977; see Chapter 2). As one can see in the figure below, in the crisis that was successfully resolved, there was an increase in the complexity of the leaders' rhetoric.

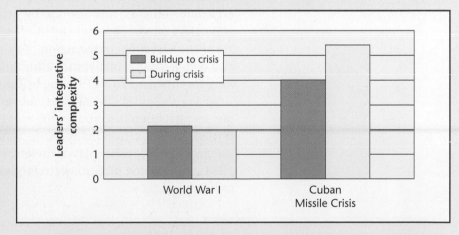

**Complex Thought and International Crises**   Leaders engaged in more complex rhetoric during the most critical times of the Cuban Missile Crisis, using language that incorporated different perspectives, including that of the opposition. While it is impossible to know whether this rhetoric accounts for the successful resolution of the crisis, the data support this possibility. (Source: Adapted from Suedfeld & Tetlock, 1977)

## TIT FOR TAT AND THE ELEMENTS OF COOPERATION

Let's examine these principles by looking at a study by Robert Axelrod that, although simple in design, yields rather profound lessons. Axelrod, a seminal figure in the prisoner's dilemma game tradition, ran a tournament in which players—academics, prize-winning mathematicians, computer hackers, and common folk—were invited to submit computer programs that specified what choice to make on a certain round of the prisoner's dilemma game, given what had happened on previous rounds (Axelrod, 1984). In Axelrod's first tournament, fourteen different strategies were submitted. Each strategy played 200 rounds of the prisoner's dilemma game with each other strategy. The points were tallied, and an overall winner was declared. The winner? It was a so-called "tit-for-tat" strategy, which was submitted by Anatol Rapaport.

The **tit-for-tat strategy** is disarmingly simple: It cooperates on the first round with every opponent and then reciprocates whatever the opponent did on the previous round. An opponent's cooperation was rewarded with immediate cooperation; defection was punished with immediate defection. In other words, start out cooperatively, and reciprocate your partner's previous move. Axelrod held a second tournament that attracted the submission of sixty-two strategies. All of the entrants knew the results of the first round, namely that the tit-for-tat strategy had won. In the second tournament, the tit-for-tat strategy again prevailed. It is important to note that the tit-for-tat strategy did not win every round when pitted against different strategies. Instead, it did better overall against the diversity of strategies. What makes the tit-for-tat strategy special, and why might it be relevant to your own life?

Axelrod contends that the tit-for-tat strategy is based on a set of principles that we would all be well advised to follow. As we form friendships, deal with the occasional difficult personality at work, negotiate with bosses, persevere in long-term romantic bonds, and raise children, the tit-for-tat strategy might be a good framework by which to abide. Five factors make it an especially compelling strategy: First, it is *cooperative*, and thus it encourages mutually supportive action toward a shared goal. Second, it is *not envious*. A partner using this strategy can do extremely well without resorting to competitive behavior. Third, it is *not exploitable*—that is, it is not blindly pro-social. If you defect on the tit for tat, it will defect on you. Fourth, the tit for tat *forgives*—that is, it is willing to cooperate at the first cooperative action of its partner, even after long runs of defection and competition. Finally, the tit for tat is *easy to read*—that is, it should not take long for others to know that the tit-for-tat strategy is being played.

As Axelrod put it, "Its niceness prevents it from getting into unnecessary trouble. Its retaliation discourages the other side from persisting whenever defection is tried. Its forgiveness helps restore mutual cooperation. And its clarity makes it intelligible to the other player, thereby eliciting long-term cooperation" (Axelrod, 1984, p. 54). Being nice, stalwart, forgiving, and clear—not a bad set of principles to live by.

> **tit-for-tat strategy**  A strategy in which one cooperates with one's opponent on the first round and then reciprocates whatever the opponent did on the previous round, meeting cooperation with cooperation, and defection with defection

**LOOKING BACK,** we have seen that cooperation is part of our evolutionary heritage, as it facilitates living in groups. The prisoner's dilemma game models the many situations in everyday life in which defection is the best solution for each individual, but cooperation benefits the two as a whole. People can be primed to cooperate or to defect. Competition leads to more competition, and reactive devaluation may lead opponents to reject concessions that are actually to their benefit. The tit-for-tat strategy involves initial cooperation and then reciprocation of whatever one's opponent has done in the previous round. It is a useful strategy to follow, as it encourages cooperation and does not blindly permit an opponent to take advantage.

# SUMMARY

1. Humans are a social species, and to survive and reproduce they must often behave in cooperative fashion, at least to those in face-to-face groups. Evolutionary theorists have argued that there are four aspects of benign human behavior: compassion, a sense of morality, a desire for justice, and the capacity to cooperate.

2. *Morality* is a system of principles people use as guides to making evaluative judgments about their own and others' actions and character. It involves obligation, inclusiveness, and sanctions.

3. The moral realm encompasses the *ethic of autonomy*, concerning rights and freedom, the *ethic of community*, concerning obligations and duties, and the *ethic of divinity*, concerning ideas about purity and sin.

4. Moral judgment is similar across different cultures in that most people condemn such moral transgressions as harm to children, incest, and genocide. But moral judgment can also differ across cultures, with some cultures favoring one or more of the three aspects of morality more than the others.

5. Our moral judgments involve two systems—fast, *emotion-based intuitions,* and more *complex reasoning processes* about moral intuitions.

6. *Distributive justice* involves the assessment of whether resources have been allocated fairly or unfairly. Self-interest and egocentric construals can distort people's sense of distributive justice.

7. Three different principles affect people's reactions to how resources are allocated in different relationships: *equity, equality,* and *need*. Different domains (family versus work) and different cultures rely on different principles in establishing distributive justice. *Relative deprivation* also affects people's sense of distributive justice.

8. The manner in which authority figures allocate resources and punishments goes by the label of *procedural justice*. There is a sense of procedural justice when authority figures are seen to be *neutral, trustworthy*, and *respectful* of others.

9. *Restorative justice* refers to the actions people take to restore just conditions in the face of injustice. This includes maintaining a *belief in a just world* by finding victims to be at fault. It also includes *retributive punishment,* or revenge, as well as *utilitarian punishment,* which is designed to lessen the likelihood of further damage by the perpetrator.

10. Another form of restorative justice is *reconciliation,* which reestablishes a bond between opponents through apologies and forgiveness.

11. *Cooperation* is part of our evolutionary heritage and is necessary for living together peacefully in groups.

12. The *prisoner's dilemma* game is used to study cooperation. It tempts participants to maximize their own outcomes at the expense of another person by defecting. This strategy backfires if the other person also defects. The optimum outcome is for both to settle for something less than the theoretical maximum by cooperating.

13. Cooperators tend to recognize that some people are cooperators and others are competitors, whereas competitors behave in such a way as to confirm their mistaken hypothesis that everyone is a competitor.

14. The *tit-for-tat* strategy in the prisoner's dilemma game is a reciprocal strategy that is cooperative, not envious, not exploitable, forgives, and is easy to read. This strategy helps maximize outcomes in potentially competitive situations that occur in real life.

# CRITICAL THINKING ABOUT BASIC PRINCIPLES

1. Use Shweder's three ethics of morality—autonomy, community, and divinity—to illuminate the views of individuals who oppose gay marriage, and those who support it.

2. Imagine that your professor decides to give A's only to those students who weigh between 135 and 156 pounds. What form of injustice are you most likely to experience?

3. What psychological principles that you have learned about in this course help explain the reactive devaluation phenomenon?

4. Can you think of situations in which the tit-for-tat strategy might not actually be the best strategy for negotiating with others?

# KEY TERMS

belief in a just world (p. 573)

distributive justice (p. 567)

equality (p. 570)

equity (p. 570)

ethic of autonomy (p. 560)

ethic of community (p. 560)

ethic of divinity (p. 560)

morality (p. 557)

moral transgressions (p. 559)

need (p. 570)

procedural justice (p. 567)

reactive devaluation (p. 582)

relative deprivation (p. 571)

retributive punishment (p. 574)

restorative justice (p. 567)

social convention transgressions (p. 559)

system justification (p. 574)

tit-for-tit strategy (p. 584)

utilitarian punishment (p. 574)

# FURTHER READING

Axelrod, R. (1984). *The evolution of cooperation*. New York: Basic Books.

de Waal, F. (1996). *Good natured: The origins of right and wrong in humans and other animals*. Cambridge, MA: Harvard University Press.

Haidt, J. (2001). The emotional dog and its rational tail: A social intuitionist approach to moral judgment. *Psychological Review, 108*, 814–834.

Turiel, E. (2002). *The culture of morality*. New York: Cambridge University Press.

# Glossary

**actor-observer difference** Differences in attribution based on who is making the causal assessment: the actor (who is relatively disposed to make situational attributions) or the observer (who is relatively disposed to make dispositional attributions).

**actual self** The self we truly believe ourselves to be.

**affective forecasting** Predicting our future emotions—for example, whether an event will make us happy or angry or sad, or for how long.

**agenda control** Efforts of the media to select certain events and topics to emphasize, and thereby shape what issues and events we think of as important.

**altruism** Unselfish behavior that benefits others without regard to the consequences for the self.

**anxious attachment style** An attachment style characterized by feelings of insecurity in relationships; individuals with this style compulsively seek closeness, express continual worries about relationships, and during situations of threat and uncertainty excessively try to get closer to others.

**appraisal processes** The ways whereby we evaluate events and objects in our environment according to their relation to our current goals.

**appraisal theorists** Researchers who investigate how the complex appraisals of a stimulus or situation influence which emotion is experienced.

**attachment theory** A theory about how our early attachments with our parents shape our relationships for the remainder of our lives.

**attitude** An evaluation of an object in a positive or negative fashion that includes the three elements of affect, cognitions, and behavior.

**attitude inoculation** Small attacks upon our beliefs that engage our attitudes, prior commitments, and knowledge structures, enabling us to counteract a subsequent larger attack and be resistant to persuasion.

**attribution** Linking a cause to an instance of behavior—one's own or that of other people.

**attribution theory** An umbrella term used to describe the set of theoretical accounts of how people assign causes to the events around them and the effects that people's causal assessments have.

**augmentation principle** The idea that we should assign greater weight to a particular cause of behavior if there are other causes present that normally would produce the opposite outcome.

**authority** Power that derives from institutionalized roles or arrangements.

**authority ranking relationship** A relationship based on hierarchy, status, and a linear ordering of people within a group.

**autokinetic illusion** The apparent motion of a stationary point of light in a completely darkened environment.

**automatic processes** Processes that occur outside of our awareness, without conscious control.

**autonomic nervous system (ANS)** The glands, organs, muscles, arteries, and veins throughout the body that are controlled by nerve cells originating in the spinal cord, and that help the individual deal with emergency situations.

**availability heuristic**   The process whereby judgments of frequency or probability are based on the ease with which pertinent instances are brought to mind.

**avoidant attachment style**   An attachment style characterized by feelings of insecurity in relationships; individuals with this style are prone to exhibit compulsive self-reliance, prefer distance from others, and during conditions of threat and uncertainty are dismissive and detached.

**balance theory**   A theory that people try to maintain balance among their beliefs, cognitions, and sentiments.

**base-rate information**   Information about the relative frequency of events or of members of different categories in the population.

**basking in reflected glory**   The tendency to take pride in the accomplishments of those with whom we are in some way associated (even if it is only weakly), as when fans identify with a winning team.

**belief in a just world**   The conviction that people get what they deserve in life, that their outcomes match their actions and character.

**Big Five Model**   Five personality traits (openness, conscientiousness, extraversion, agreeableness, and neuroticism) that psychologists believe are the basic building blocks of personality. Also known as the five-factor model.

**bottom-up processes**   "Data-driven" mental processing in which one takes in and forms conclusions on the basis of the stimuli encountered in one's experience.

**bystander intervention**   Helping a victim of an emergency by those who have observed what is happening; it is generally reduced as the number of observers increases, as each individual feels that someone else will be likely to help.

**central route of persuasion**   A persuasive route wherein people think carefully and deliberately about the content of a message, attending to its logic, cogency, and arguments, as well as to related evidence and principles. Also known as the systematic route of persuasion.

**chameleon effect**   The nonconscious mimicry of the expressions, mannerisms, movements, and other behaviors of those with whom one is interacting.

**channel factors**   Certain situational circumstances that appear unimportant on the surface but that can have great consequences for behavior, either facilitating or blocking it, or guiding behavior in a particular direction.

**cognitive dissonance theory**   The theory that inconsistencies among a person's thoughts, sentiments, and actions create an aversive emotional state (dissonance) that leads to efforts to restore consistency.

**collectivistic cultures**   Cultures in which people tend to define themselves as part of a collective, inextricably tied to others in their group, and in which they have relatively little individual freedom or personal control over their lives but do not necessarily want or need these things. Also known as interdependent cultures.

**communal relationships**   Relationships in which the individuals feel a special responsibility for one another and give according to the principle of ability and receive according to the principle of need; such relationships are often long term.

**communal sharing relationship**   A relationship based on a sense of sameness and kinship. Resources are generated by those in the group capable of doing so, and resources go to those in need.

**compliance**   Responding favorably to an explicit request by another person.

**complementarity**   The tendency for people to seek out others with characteristics that are different from and that complement their own.

**conformity**   Changing one's behavior or beliefs in response to explicit or implicit (whether real or imagined) pressure from others.

**consensus**   Refers to what most people would do in a given situation—that is, whether most people would behave the same way or few or no other people would behave that way.

**consistency**   Refers to what an individual does in a given situation on different occasions—that is, whether next time the behavior under the same circumstances would be the same or would differ.

**construal**   Interpretation and inference about the stimuli or situations we confront.

**contingencies of self-worth**   An account of self-esteem maintaining that self-esteem is contingent on successes and failures in domains upon which a person has based his or her self-worth.

**control group**   The group of participants that does not receive the experimental manipulation.

**controlled processes**   Processes that occur with conscious direction and deliberate thought.

**core-relational theme**   Distinct themes like danger or offense or fairness that define the essential meaning for each emotion.

**correlational research**   Research in which there is not random assignment to different situations or conditions, and from which psychologists can just see whether or not there is a relationship between the variables.

**correspondence bias**   The tendency to draw an inference about a person that "corresponds" to the behavior observed. Also known as the fundamental attribution error.

**counterbalancing**   A methodological procedure whereby an investigator makes sure that any extraneous variable (for example, a stimulus person's name) that might influence the dependent measure (for example, liking) is distributed equally often across the different levels of the independent variable (for example, the stimulus person a participant expects to meet and the stimulus person the participant does not expect to meet).

**counterfactual thoughts**   Thoughts of what might have, could have, or should have happened "if only" something had been done differently.

**covariation principle**   The idea that we should attribute behavior to potential causes that co-occur with the behavior.

**culture of honor**   A culture that is defined by strong concerns about one's own and others' reputations, leading to sensitivity to slights and insults and a willingness to use violence to avenge any perceived wrong or insult.

**decoding hypothesis**   The hypothesis that people of different cultures can interpret distinct facial expressions for different emotions in the same ways.

**deindividuation**   The reduced sense of individual identity accompanied by diminished self-regulation that comes over a person when he or she is in a large group.

**dependent variable**   The variable that is presumed to be affected by the independent variable manipulation and that is measured in experimental research.

**demonstrations**   Research in which no variable is correlated with any other variable and in which nothing is manipulated.

**diffusion of responsibility**   A reduction of a sense of urgency to help someone involved in an emergency or dangerous situation under the assumption that others who are also observing the situation will help.

**discounting principle**   The idea that we should assign reduced weight to a particular cause of behavior if there are other plausible causes that might have produced it.

**discrimination**   Unfair treatment of members of a particular group based on their membership in that group.

**display rules**   Culturally specific rules that govern how and when and to whom we express emotion.

**dispositions**   Internal factors, such as beliefs, values, personality traits, or abilities that guide a person's behavior.

**distinctiveness**   Refers to what an individual does in different situations—that is, whether the behavior is unique to a particular situation or occurs in all situations.

**distinctiveness hypothesis**   The hypothesis that we identify what makes us unique in each particular context, and we highlight that in our self-definition.

**distraction-conflict theory**   A theory based on the idea that being aware of another person's presence creates a conflict between attending to that person and attending to the task at hand, and that it is this attentional conflict that is arousing and that produces social facilitation effects.

**distributive justice**   A type of justice that is based on whether people feel that the outcomes they receive are fair or unfair.

**diversification**   A principle that maintains that siblings develop into quite different people so that they can peacefully occupy different niches within the family environment.

**dizygotic twins**   Twins who originate from two different eggs fertilized by different sperm cells; like ordinary siblings, they share on average half of their genes. Also known as fraternal twins.

**dominance**   Behavior that has the acquisition or demonstration of power as its goal.

**dominant response**   In a hierarchy of responses, the response you are most likely to make.

**door-in-the-face technique**   Asking someone for a very large favor that he or she will certainly refuse, and then following that request with one for a more modest favor (that tends to be seen as a concession that the target will feel compelled to honor). Also known as the reciprocal concessions technique.

**duration neglect**   The relative unimportance of the length of an emotional experience, be it pleasurable or unpleasant, in judging the overall experience.

**effort justification**   The tendency to reduce dissonance by finding reasons for why a person has devoted time, effort, or money for something that turned out to be unpleasant or disappointing to the person.

**ego-defensive function**   An attitudinal function that enables us to maintain cherished beliefs about ourselves by protecting us from awareness of our negative attributes and impulses or from facts that contradict our cherished beliefs or desires.

**ethnocentrism**   Glorifying one's own group while vilifying other groups.

**Elaboration Likelihood Model**   A model of persuasion that maintains that there are two different routes of persuasion: the central route and the peripheral route.

**emergent properties of groups**   Those behaviors that only surface ("emerge") when people are in groups.

**emotional amplification**   A ratcheting up of an emotional reaction to an event that is proportional to how easy it is to imagine the event not happening.

**emotion-congruence perspective**   A theory that maintains that moods and emotions are connected nodes, or areas, in the associative networks of the mind, and that the content of the mood or emotion influences judgments of other events or objects.

**emotions**   Brief psychological and physiological responses that are subjectively experienced as feelings and that prepare a person for action.

**empathy**   Identifying with another person and feeling and understanding what that person is experiencing.

**encoding**   Filing information away in memory based on what is attended to and the initial interpretation of information.

**encoding hypothesis**   The hypothesis that the experience of different emotions is associated with the same distinct facial expressions across cultures.

**equality**   A principle of distributive justice that dictates that all individuals making contributions to some endeavor should receive equal rewards.

**equality matching relationship**   A relationship based on equality, reciprocity, and balance.

**equity**   A principle of distributive justice according to which individuals should receive rewards that directly correspond to their contributions.

**equity theory**   A theory that maintains that people are motivated to pursue fairness, or equity, in their relationships, with rewards and costs shared roughly equally among individuals.

**ethic of autonomy**   A framework of moral reasoning that is centered on rights and equality, and that is focused on protecting individuals' freedom to pursue their own interests.

**ethic of community**   A framework of moral reasoning that revolves around duty, status, hierarchy, and interdependence and whose goal is to protect relationships and roles within social groups to which one belongs.

**ethic of divinity**   A framework of moral reasoning that is defined by a concern for purity, sanctity, pollution, and sin.

**evaluation apprehension**   A concern about how one appears in the eyes of others—that is, about being evaluated.

**exchange relationships**   Relationships in which the individuals feel little responsibility toward one another and in which giving and receiving are governed by concerns about equity and reciprocity; such relationships are often short term.

**experienced distress**   A motive for helping that may arise from a need to reduce one's *own* distress.

**experience-sampling studies**   Studies in which researchers provide participants with beepers and randomly signal them throughout the day so that the participants will provide information about what they are doing and how they are feeling at that precise moment.

**experimental research**  Research in which people are randomly assigned to different situations (or conditions), and from which it is possible to make very strong inferences about how these different situations or conditions affect people's behavior.

**explanatory style**  A person's habitual way of explaining events, typically assessed along three dimensions: internality/externality, stability/instability, and globality/specificity.

**external validity**  An experimental setup that closely resembles real-life situations.

**face**  Who we want others to think we are.

**false consensus effect**  The tendency for people to think that their behavior (as well as their attitudes, preferences, or responses more generally) is relatively common.

**feelings-as-information perspective**  A theory that assumes that, since many judgments are often too complex for us to thoroughly review all the relevant evidence, we rely on our emotions to provide us with rapid, reliable information about events and conditions within our social environment.

**field experiments**  Experiments that are set up in the real world, usually under circumstances in which participants are not aware that they are in a study of any kind.

**five-factor model**  Five personality traits (openness, conscientiousness, extraversion, agreeableness, and neuroticism) that psychologists believe are the basic building blocks of personality. Also known as the Big Five Model.

**flashbulb memories**  Vivid recollections of the moment one learned some dramatic, emotionally charged news.

**focalism**  A tendency to focus too much on a central aspect of an event, while neglecting to consider the impact of ancillary aspects of the event or the impact of other events.

**foot-in-the-door technique**  A compliance technique in which one makes an initial small request to which nearly everyone complies, followed by a larger request involving the real behavior of interest.

**forced-choice critique**  A critique of Ekman and Friesen's emotion study that holds that accuracy rates in judgments of emotional expressions may have been inflated by allowing participants to make educated guesses about expressions they may not have known how to label.

**forced compliance**  Subtly compelling individuals to behave in a manner that is inconsistent with their beliefs, attitudes, or values, which typically leads to dissonance and often to a change in their original attitudes or values in order to reduce their dissonance. Also known as induced compliance.

**framing effect**  The influence on judgment resulting from the way information is presented, including the order of presentation.

**fraternal twins**  Twins who originate from two different eggs fertilized by different sperm cells; like ordinary siblings, they share on average half of their genes. Also known as dizygotic twins.

**free-response critique**  A critique of Ekman and Friesen's emotion studies based on the fact that researchers provided the terms with which participants labeled facial expressions rather than allowing the participants to label the expressions with their own words.

**frustration**  The internal state that accompanies the thwarting of an individual's attempts to achieve some goal.

**frustration-aggression theory**  The theory that frustration leads to aggression.

**fundamental attribution error**  A tendency to believe mistakenly that a behavior is due to a person's disposition rather than the situation in which the person finds himself. Also known as the correspondence bias.

**functional distance**  An architectural layout's propensity to encourage or inhibit certain activities, like contact between people.

**Gestalt psychology**  Based on the German word, *Gestalt*, meaning "form" or "figure," this approach stresses the fact that objects are perceived not by means of some automatic registering device but by active, usually unconscious, interpretation of what the object represents as a whole.

**group polarization**  The tendency for group decisions to be more extreme than those made by individuals; whatever way the individuals are leaning, group discussion tends to make them lean further in that direction.

**groupthink**  A kind of faulty thinking on the part of highly cohesive groups in which the critical scrutiny that should be devoted to the issues at hand is subverted by social pressures to reach consensus.

**halo effect**  The common belief—accurate or not—that attractive individuals possess a host of positive qualities beyond their physical appearance.

**heritability**  The degree to which traits or physical characteristics are determined by genes, and hence inherited from parents.

**heuristic route of persuasion**  A persuasive route wherein people attend to relatively simple, superficial cues related to the message, such as the length of the message or the expertise or attractiveness of the communicator. Also known as the peripheral route of persuasion.

**heuristics**  Intuitive mental operations that allow us to make a variety of judgments quickly and efficiently.

**heuristic-systematic model of persuasion**  A model of persuasion that maintains that there are two different routes of persuasion: the systematic route and the heuristic route.

**hostile aggression**  Behavior intended to harm another, either physically or psychologically, and motivated by feelings of anger and hostility.

**hypercognize**  To represent a particular emotion with numerous words and concepts.

**ideal self**  The self that embodies the wishes and aspirations we and other people maintain about ourselves.

**identical twins**  Twins who originate from a single fertilized egg that splits into two exact replicas that then develop into two genetically identical individuals. Also known as monozygotic twins.

**identifiable victim effect**  The tendency to be more moved by the plight of a single, vivid individual than by a more abstract aggregate of individuals.

**identity cues**  Customary facial expressions, posture, gait, clothes, haircuts, and bodily decorations, which signal to others important facets of our identity, and by implication, how we are to be treated and construed by others.

**ideomotor action**  The phenomenon whereby merely thinking about a behavior makes its actual performance more likely.

**illusory correlation** An erroneous belief about a connection between events, characteristics, or categories that are not, in fact, related.

**immune neglect** The tendency to underestimate our capacity to be resilient in responding to difficult life events, which leads us to overestimate the extent to which life's difficulties will reduce our personal well-being.

**implicit association test (IAT)** A technique for revealing nonconscious prejudices toward particular groups.

**impression management** Attempting to control the beliefs other people have of us.

**inclusive fitness** An evolutionary tendency to look out for oneself, one's offspring, and one's close relatives, together with their offspring, so that one's genes will survive.

**independent cultures** Cultures in which people tend to think of themselves as distinct social entities, tied to each other by voluntary bonds of affection and organizational memberships but essentially separate from other people and having attributes that exist in the absence of any connection to others. Also known as individualistic cultures.

**independent variable** The variable about which a prediction is made, and which is manipulated in experimental research.

**individualistic cultures** Cultures in which people tend to think of themselves as distinct social entities, tied to each other by voluntary bonds of affection and organizational memberships but essentially separate from other people and having attributes that exist in the absence of any connection to others. Also known as independent cultures.

**individuation** Emphasizing individual identity by focusing attention on the self, which will generally lead a person to act carefully and deliberately and in accordance with his or her sense of propriety and values.

**induced compliance** Subtly compelling individuals to behave in a manner that is inconsistent with their beliefs, attitudes, or values, which typically leads to dissonance and often to a change in their original attitudes or values in order to reduce their dissonance. Also known as forced compliance.

**informational social influence** The influence of other people that results from taking their comments or actions as a source of information as to what is correct, proper, or efficacious.

**instrumental aggression** Behavior intended to harm another in the service of motives other than pure hostility (for example, to attract attention, to acquire wealth, or to advance political and ideological causes).

**interaction dynamics approach** A methodological approach to the study of the behaviors and conversations of couples, with a focus on negative behaviors such as anger, criticism, defensiveness, contempt, sadness, and fear, and positive behaviors such as affection, enthusiasm, interest, and humor.

**interdependent cultures** Cultures in which people tend to define themselves as part of a collective, inextricably tied to others in their group, and in which they have relatively little individual freedom or personal control over their lives but do not necessarily want or need these things. Also known as collectivistic cultures.

**internalization** Private acceptance of a proposition, orientation, or ideology.

**interpersonal relationships** Attachments in which bonds of family or friendship or love or respect or hierarchy tie together two or more individuals over an extended period of time.

**interpersonal simulations** Experiments in which an "observer-participant" is given a detailed description of one condition of a dissonance experiment, is told how a participant behaved in that situation, and is asked to predict the attitude of that participant.

**intersex attraction** The interest in and attraction toward a member of one sex on the part of a member of the opposite sex.

**intrasex competition** Direct competition among two or more males or among two or more females for access to members of the opposite sex.

**investment model of interpersonal relationships** A model of interpersonal relationships that maintains that three things make partners more committed to one another: rewards, alternatives, and investments in the relationship.

**just world hypothesis** The belief that people get what they deserve in life and deserve what they get.

**kin selection** The tendency for natural selection to favor behaviors that increase the chances of survival of genetic relatives.

**knowledge function** An attitudinal function whereby attitudes help organize our understanding of the world, guiding how we attend to, store, and retrieve information.

**knowledge structures** Coherent configurations (known as schemas, scripts, frames, prototypes, or personae) in which related information is stored together.

**learned helplessness** Passive and depressed responses that individuals show when their goals are blocked and they feel that they have no control over their outcomes.

**leveling** Eliminating or deemphasizing seemingly less important details when telling a story to someone else.

**Likert scale** A scale used to assess people's attitudes that includes a set of possible answers and that has anchors on each extreme.

**longitudinal studies** Studies conducted over a long period of time with the same population, which is periodically assessed regarding particular behaviors.

**market pricing relationship** A relationship based on a sense of proportion, trade, and equity, in which people are concerned with ensuring that their inputs to a relationship correspond to what they get out of the relationship.

**mere exposure effect** The finding that repeated exposure to a stimulus (for example, an object or person) leads to greater liking of the stimulus.

**message characteristics** Aspects of the message itself, including the quality of the evidence and the explicitness of its conclusions.

**minimal group paradigm** An experimental paradigm in which researchers create groups based on arbitrary and seemingly meaningless criteria, and then examine how the members of these "minimal groups" are inclined to behave toward one another.

**misattribution of arousal** Attributing arousal produced by one cause (for example, exercise) to another stimulus in the environment.

**modern racism** Prejudice directed at other racial groups that exists alongside a rejection of explicitly racist beliefs.

**monozygotic twins** Twins who originate from a single fertilized egg that splits into two exact replicas that then develop into two genetically identical individuals. Also known as identical twins.

**morality** A system of principles and ideals that people use as a guide to making evaluative judgments of the actions or character of a person.

**moral transgressions** Violations of others' rights, or harm to others.

**natural experiments** Naturally occurring events or phenomena having somewhat different conditions that can be compared with almost as much rigor as in experiments where the investigator manipulates the conditions.

**naturalistic fallacy** The claim that the way things *are* is the way they *should be*.

**natural selection** An evolutionary process that operates to mold animals and plants such that traits that enhance the probability of survival and reproduction are passed on to subsequent generations.

**need** A principle of distributive justice that dictates that individuals with the greatest needs should be given priority for resources.

**negative state relief hypothesis** The idea that people engage in certain actions, such as agreeing to a request, in order to relieve negative feelings and to feel better about themselves.

**normative social influence** The influence of other people that comes from the desire to avoid their disapproval, harsh judgments, and other social sanctions (for example, barbs, ostracism).

**norm of reciprocity** A norm dictating that people should provide benefits to those who benefit them.

**obedience** Social influence in which the less powerful person in an unequal power relationship submits to the demands of the more powerful person.

**observational studies** Research involving observation of and often participation in the lives of people in some group or situation with the intention of studying aspects of group beliefs, values, or behavior.

**off-record communication** Indirect and ambiguous communication that allows you to hint at ideas and meanings that are not explicit in the words you utter.

**on-record communication** The statements we make that we intend to be taken literally.

**ought self** The self that is concerned with the duties, obligations, and external demands we feel we are compelled to honor.

**outgroup homogeneity effect** The tendency to assume that within-group similarity is much stronger for outgroups than for ingroups.

**paired distinctiveness** The pairing of two distinctive events that stand out even more because they co-occur.

**parental investment** The evolutionary principle that since males and females have different costs and benefits associated with reproduction and the nurturing of offspring, one sex will value and invest more in each child than will the other.

**peripheral route of persuasion** A persuasive route wherein people attend to relatively simple, superficial cues related to the message, such as the length of the message or the expertise or attractiveness of the communicator. Also known as the heuristic route of persuasion.

**planning fallacy** The tendency for people to be unrealistically optimistic about how quickly they can complete a project.

**pluralistic ignorance** Misperception of a group norm that results from observing people who are acting at variance with their private beliefs out of a concern for the social consequences—behavior that reinforces the erroneous group norm.

**power** The ability to control one's own outcomes and those of others, and the freedom to act.

**prejudice** A negative attitude or affective response toward a certain group and its individual members.

**prevention focus** A sensitivity to negative outcomes often motivated by a desire to live up to our ought self and to avoid the guilt or anxiety that results when we fail to live up to our sense of what we ought to do.

**primacy effect** The disproportionate influence on judgment of information presented first in a body of evidence.

**primary appraisal stage** An initial, quick positive or negative evaluation of ongoing events based on whether they are congruent or incongruent with the person's goals.

**prime** A stimulus (typically a word or image) presented to mentally activate a concept, and hence, make it accessible.

**priming** A procedure used to increase the accessibility of a concept or schema (for example, a stereotype).

**prisoner's dilemma** A situation involving payoffs to two people in which trust and cooperation lead to higher joint payoffs than mistrust and defection. The game gets its name from the dilemma that would confront two criminals who were together involved in a crime and who are being held and questioned separately. Each must decide whether to "cooperate" and stick with a prearranged alibi, or "defect" and confess to the crime in hope of lenient treatment.

**private self-consciousness** Our awareness of our interior lives—our private thoughts, feelings, and sensations.

**procedural justice** A type of justice that is based on whether the processes by which rewards and punishments are distributed are considered fair.

**processing style perspective** A theory that holds that different emotions lead people to reason in different ways—for example, that positive moods facilitate use of preexisting heuristics and stereotypes, whereas negative moods facilitate more careful attention to situational details.

**promotion focus** A focus on positive outcomes, approach-related behavior, and cheerful emotions that help us live up to our ideals and aspirations.

**propinquity** Physical proximity.

**public compliance** Agreeing with someone or advancing a position in public but continuing to believe something else in private.

**public self-consciousness** Our awareness of what other people think about us—our public identity.

**random assignment** Assigning participants in experimental research to different groups randomly, such that they are as likely to be assigned to one condition as to another.

**rape-prone cultures** Cultures in which rape tends to be used as an act of war against enemy women, as a ritual act, and as a threat against women so that they will remain subservient to men.

**reactance theory** Reasserting prerogatives in response to the unpleasant state of arousal experienced by people when they believe their freedoms are threatened.

**reactive devaluation**   Reduced attractiveness of an offer from an opposing side just because the other side made it.

**realistic group conflict theory**   A theory that group conflict, prejudice, and discrimination are likely to arise over competition between groups for limited desired resources.

**receiver characteristics**   Characteristics of the person who receives the message, including age, mood, and motivation to attend to the message.

**recency effect**   The disproportionate influence on judgment of information presented last in a body of evidence.

**reciprocal altruism**   The tendency to help other individuals with the expectation that they will be likely to help in return at some other time.

**reciprocal concessions technique**   Asking someone for a very large favor that he or she will certainly refuse, and then following that request with one for a more modest favor (that tends to be seen as a concession that the target will feel compelled to honor). Also known as the door-in-the-face technique.

**reference groups**   Groups whose opinions matter to us and that affect our opinions and beliefs.

**relational models theory**   A theory that there are four qualitatively different kinds of relationships (communal sharing, authority ranking, equality matching, and market pricing), each characterized by highly distinct ways of defining the self and others, allocating resources and work, making moral judgments, and punishing transgressions.

**relational self**   The beliefs, feelings, and expectations about our selves that derive from our relationships with significant others in our lives.

**relational self-beliefs**   Beliefs about our identities in specific relationships.

**relational self theory**   A theory that examines how prior relationships shape our current beliefs, feelings, and interactions vis-à-vis people who remind us of significant others from our past.

**relative deprivation**   A feeling of deprivation based on comparisons with relevant others who are seen as doing better than oneself.

**reliability**   The degree to which the particular way one measures a given variable is likely to yield consistent results.

**representativeness heuristic**   The process whereby judgments of likelihood are based on assessments of similarity between individuals and group prototypes, or between cause and effect.

**reproductive fitness**   The capacity to get one's genes passed on to subsequent generations.

**response latency**   The time it takes an individual to respond to a stimulus such as an attitude question.

**restorative justice**   The actions people take, from apologies to punishment, to restore justice.

**retributive punishment**   Punishment based on eye-for-an-eye justice in which the goal is to avenge a prior evil deed rather than prevent future ones.

**retrieval**   The extraction of information from memory.

**risky shift**   The tendency for groups to make riskier decisions than individuals.

**ritualized displays**   Highly stylized ways of expressing particular emotions.

**rumination**   The tendency to think about some event over and over again, including thinking of all of its ramifications, causes, and implications.

**schemas**   Generalized knowledge about the physical and social world and how to behave in particular situations and with different kinds of people.

**secondary appraisal stage**   A subsequent evaluation in which people determine why they feel the way they do about an event, possible ways of responding to the event, and future consequences of different courses of action.

**secure attachment style**   An attachment style that is characterized by feelings of security in relationships; individuals with this style are comfortable with intimacy, and they desire to be close to others during times of threat and uncertainty.

**self-affirmation**   Taking stock of one's good qualities and core values, which can help a person cope with threats to self-esteem.

**self-awareness theory**   A theory that predicts that when people focus their attention inward on themselves, they become concerned with self-evaluation and how their current behavior conforms to their internal standards and values.

**self-censorship**   The decision to withhold information or opinions in group discussions.

**self-concept**   An understanding of the existence and properties of a separate self and its characteristics.

**self-esteem**   The positive or negative overall evaluation you have of yourself.

**self-evaluation maintenance model**   A model that says that we are motivated to view ourselves in a favorable light, and that we do so through two processes: reflection and social comparison.

**self-expansion account of relationships**   A theory that holds that people enter into and remain in close relationships to expand the self by including resources, perspectives, experiences, and characteristics of the other as part of their own self-concept.

**self-discrepancy theory**   A theory that appropriate behavior is motivated by cultural and moral standards regarding the ideal self and the ought self. Violations of those standards produce emotions like guilt and shame when they are not adhered to.

**self-fulfilling prophecy**   Acting on a belief in a way that tends to support the original belief, as when we act toward members of certain groups in ways that encourage the very behavior we expect from them.

**self-handicapping**   The tendency to engage in self-defeating behaviors in order to prevent others from drawing unwanted attributions about the self as a result of poor performance.

**self-image bias**   The tendency to judge others' personalities according to their similarity or dissimilarity to our own personality.

**self-monitoring**   The tendency for people to monitor their behavior in such a way that it fits the demands of the current situation.

**self-perception theory**   A theory that people come to know their own attitudes by looking at their behavior and the context in which it occurred and *inferring* what their attitudes must be.

**self-presentation**   Presenting who we actually are, or who we would like others to believe we are.

**self-reference effect**   The tendency to elaborate upon and recall information that is integrated into our self-knowledge.

**self-schemas**   Knowledge-based summaries of our feelings and actions and how we understand others' views about the self.

**self-selection**   A problem that arises when the participant, rather than the investigator, selects his or her own level on each variable, bringing with this value unknown other properties that make causal interpretation of a relationship difficult.

**self-serving bias**   The tendency to attribute failure and other bad events to external circumstances, but to attribute success and other good events to oneself.

**self-verification theory**   A theory that maintains that we strive for stable, accurate beliefs about the self because such beliefs give us a sense of coherence.

**sharpening**   Emphasizing important or more interesting elements in telling a story to someone else.

**sleeper effect**   An effect that occurs when messages from unreliable sources initially exert little influence but later cause individuals' attitudes to shift.

**social beliefs**   Beliefs about the roles, duties, and obligations we assume in groups.

**social comparison theory**   A theory that maintains that when there is not an objective standard of evaluation or comprehension, people evaluate their opinions and abilities and internal states by comparing themselves to others.

**social convention transgressions**   Violations of agreed-upon rules that govern such things as how we greet each other, how we eat, and the gender-based roles and identities we assume.

**social dominance orientation**   The desire to see one's own group dominate other groups.

**social exchange theory**   A theory based on the fact that there are costs and rewards in all relationships, and that how people feel about a relationship depends on their assessments of its costs and rewards, and the costs and rewards available to them in other relationships.

**social facilitation**   Initially a term for enhanced performance in the presence of others; now a broader term for the effect—positive or negative—of the presence of others on performance.

**social identity theory**   A theory that a person's self-concept and self-esteem not only derive from personal identity and accomplishments, but from the status and accomplishments of the various groups to which the person belongs.

**social influence**   The myriad ways that people impact one another, including changes in attitudes, beliefs, feelings, and behavior that result from the comments, actions, or even the mere presence of others.

**social loafing**   The tendency to exert less effort when working on a group task in which individual contributions cannot be monitored.

**social psychology**   The scientific study of the feelings, thoughts, and behaviors of individuals in social situations.

**social rewards**   Benefits like praise, positive attention, tangible rewards, honors, and gratitude that may be gained from helping others.

**sociometer hypothesis**   A hypothesis that maintains that self-esteem is an internal, subjective index or marker of the extent to which we are included or looked on favorably by others.

**sociometric survey**   A survey that attempts to measure the interpersonal relationships in a group of people.

**source characteristics**   Characteristics of the person who delivers the message, including the person's attractiveness, credibility, and expertise.

**spotlight effect**   People's conviction that other people are attending to them—to their appearance and behavior—more than is actually the case.

**state self-esteem**   The dynamic, changeable self-evaluations that are experienced as momentary feelings about the self.

**statistical significance**   A measure of the probability of a given result occurring by chance.

**status**   The outcome of an evaluation of attributes that produces differences in respect and prominence, which in part determines an individual's power within a group.

**stereotypes**   Schemas that we have for people of various kinds that can be applied and misapplied so as to facilitate, and sometimes derail, the course of interaction. These include beliefs about attributes that are thought to be characteristic of members of particular groups.

**stereotype threat**   The fear that one will confirm the stereotypes that others have regarding some salient group of which one is a member.

**strange situation**   An experimental situation designed to assess attachment to caregivers: an infant is observed after her caregiver has left her alone in an unfamiliar room with a stranger and then reacts to reunion with the caregiver upon her return to the room.

**stress**   Heightened sympathetic autonomic nervous system activity, ruminative thought, and vigilant attention based on a sense that one's challenges and demands surpass one's capacities, resources, and energies.

**subjective norms**   People's beliefs about whether others are likely to approve of a course of action.

**subliminal**   Below the threshold of conscious awareness.

**suicide baiting**   Urging a person who is on the verge of committing suicide to end his life.

**superordinate goals**   Goals that transcend the interests of one individual group, and that can be achieved more readily by two or more groups working together.

**surveys**   A series of questions asked of people, sometimes students in laboratories and sometimes citizens in the community, to ascertain their attitudes or beliefs.

**systematic route of persuasion**   A persuasive route wherein people think carefully and deliberately about the content of a message, attending to its logic, cogency, and arguments, as well as to related evidence and principles. Also known as the central route of persuasion.

**system justification**   The tendency to justify differences in wealth and opportunity with beliefs that imply that such inequalities are deserved, just, and even natural and inevitable.

**terror management theory**   A theory positing that to ward off the anxiety we feel when contemplating our own demise, we cling to cultural worldviews and strongly held values out of a belief that by doing so part of us will survive death.

**that's-not-all technique**    Adding something to an original offer, which is likely to create some pressure to reciprocate.

**theory of mind**    The understanding that other people have beliefs and desires.

**theory of planned behavior**    The successor to the theory of reasoned action that maintains that the best predictors of deliberate behavior are people's attitudes toward specific behaviors, their subjective norms, and their beliefs about whether they can successfully perform the behavior in question.

**theory of reasoned action**    A theory that maintains that people's deliberate behavior can be accurately predicted by knowing their attitudes toward specific behaviors and their subjective norms.

**third-person effect**    The assumption by most people that "other people" are more prone to being influenced by persuasive messages (such as those in media campaigns) than they themselves are.

**thought polarization hypothesis**    The hypothesis that more extended thought about a particular issue tends to produce more extreme, entrenched attitudes.

**tit-for-tat strategy**    A strategy in which one cooperates with one's opponent on the first round and then reciprocates whatever the opponent did on the previous round, meeting cooperation with cooperation and defection with defection.

**top-down processes**    "Theory-driven" mental processing in which one filters and interprets new information in light of preexisting knowledge and expectations.

**traits**    Consistent ways that people think, feel, and act across classes of situations.

**trait self-esteem**    The enduring level of confidence and affection that people have for their defining abilities and characteristics across time.

**transactive memory**    The tendency for people in relationships to share information processing of events based on their knowledge of their partner's encoding, storage, and retrieval of information.

**triangular theory of love**    A theory that states that there are three major components of love—intimacy, passion, and commitment—which can be combined in different ways.

**two-factor theory of emotion**    A theory that says that there are two components to emotional experience: undifferentiated physiological arousal and a person's construal of that state of undifferentiated arousal.

**utilitarian function**    An attitudinal function that serves to alert us to rewarding objects and situations we should approach, and costly or punishing objects or situations we should avoid.

**utilitarian punishment**    Punishment in which the goal is reducing the likelihood of future crimes committed by the criminal through such means as rehabilitation or isolation of the criminal.

**value-expressive function**    An attitudinal function whereby attitudes help us express our most cherished values—usually in groups in which they can be supported and reinforced.

**working models of relationships**    Conceptual models of relationships with current others based on the other person's availability, warmth, and ability to provide security as derived from children's experience with how available and how warm their parents were.

# References

Abell, G. O. (1981). Astrology. In G. O. Abell & B. Singer (Eds.), *Science and the paranormal: Probing the existence of supernatural*. New York: Charles Scribner's Sons.

Abrams, D., Viki, G. T., Masser, B., & Bohner, G. (2003). Perceptions of stranger and acquaintance rape: The role of benevolent and hostile sexism in victim blame and rape proclivity. *Journal of Personality and Social Psychology, 84,* 111–125.

Abramson, L. Y., Metalsky, G. I., & Alloy, L. B. (1989). Hopelessness depression: A theory-based subtype of depression. *Psychological Review, 96,* 358–372.

Abu-Lughod, L. (1986). *Veiled sentiments.* Berkeley, CA: University of California Press.

Adams, G. R. (1978). Racial membership and physical attractiveness effects on teachers' expectations. *Child Study Journal, 8,* 29–41.

Adams, G. R., & Crane, P. (1980). An assessment of parents' and teachers' expectations of preschool children's social preference for attractive or unattractive children and adults. *Child Development, 51,* 224–231.

Adams, J. S. (1965). Inequity in social exchange. In L. Berkowitz (Ed.), *Advances in experimental social psychology* (Vol. 2, pp. 267–299). New York: Academic Press.

Adler, J. (1994, November 7). Beyond the bell curve. *Newsweek,* p. 56.

Adler, N. E., Boyce, T., Chesney, M. A., Cohen, S., Folkman, S., Kahn, R. L., et al. (1994). Socioeconomic status and health: The challenge of the gradient. *American Psychologist, 49,* 15–24.

Agnew, C. R., Van Lange, P. A. M., Rusbult, C. E., & Langston, C. A. (1998). Cognitive interdependence: Commitment and the mental representation of close relationships. *Journal of Personality and Social Psychology, 74,* 939–954.

Ainsworth, M. D. S. (1993). Attachment as related to mother-infant interaction. *Advances in Infancy Research, 8,* 1–50.

Ainsworth, M. D. S., Blehar, M., Waters, E., & Wall, S. (1978). *Patterns of attachment.* Hilldale, NJ: Lawrence Erlbaum Associates.

Ajzen, I. (1977). Intuitive theories of events and the effects of base-rate information on prediction. *Journal of Personality and Social Psychology, 35,* 303–314.

Ajzen, I. (1985). From intentions to actions: A theory of planned behavior. In J. Kuhl & J. Beckman (Eds.), *Action-control: From cognition to behavior.* Heidelberg, Germany: Springer-Verlag.

Ajzen, I. (1987). Attitudes, traits, and actions: Dispositional prediction of behavior in personality and social psychology. In L. Berkowitz (Ed.), *Advances in experimental social psychology* (Vol. 20, pp. 1–63). San Diego, CA: Academic Press.

Ajzen, I. (1996). The directive influence of attitudes on behavior. In P. M. Gollwitzer & J. A. Bargh (Eds.), *The psychology of action: Linking cognition and motivation to behavior* (pp. 385–403). New York: Guilford Press.

Ajzen, I., & Fishbein, M. (1980). *Understanding attitudes and predicting social behavior.* Englewood Cliffs, NJ: Prentice-Hall.

Ajzen, I., & Madden, T. J. (1986). Prediction of goal-directed behavior: Attitudes, intentions, and perceived behavioral control. *Journal of Experimental Social Psychology, 22,* 453–474.

Aldag, R. J., & Fuller, S. R. (1993). Beyond fiasco: A reappraisal of the groupthink phenomenon and a new model of group decision processes. *Psychological Bulletin, 113*, 533–552.

Allee, W. C., & Masure, R. H. (1936). A comparison of maze behavior in paired and isolated shell-parakeets (*Melopsittacus undulatus Shaw*) in a two-alley problem box. *Journal of Comparative Psychology, 3*, 159–182.

Allen, V. L. (1965). Situational factors in conformity. In L. Berkowitz (Ed.), *Advances in experimental social psychology* (Vol. 2, pp. 133–175). New York: Academic Press.

Allen, V. L., & Wilder, D. A. (1979). Group categorization and attribution of belief similarity. *Small Group Behavior, 10*, 73–80.

Allport, F. H. (1920). The influence of the group upon association and thought. *Journal of Experimental Psychology, 3*, 159–182.

Allport, G. (1935). Attitudes. In C. Murchison (Ed.), *Handbook of social psychology* (pp. 798–884). Worcester, MA: Clark University Press.

Allport, G. (1954). *The nature of prejudice*. Cambridge: Addison-Wesley.

Alluisi, E. A., & Adams, O. S. (1962). Predicting letter preferences: Aesthetics and filtering in man. *Perceptual and Motor Skills, 14*, 123–131.

Al-Zahrani, S. S. A., & Kaplowitz, S. A. (1993). Attributional biases in individualistic and collectivistic cultures: A comparison of Americans with Saudis. *Social Psychology Quarterly, 56*, 223–233.

Amato, P. R., & Keith, B. (1991). Parental divorce and well-being of children. *Psychological Bulletin, 110*, 26–46.

Ambady, N., Hallahan, M., & Rosenthal, R. (1995). On judging and being judged in zero-acquaintance situations. *Journal of Personality and Social Psychology, 69*, 518–529.

American Society of Plastic and Reconstructive Surgeons. (1990). *Report of the estimated number of aesthetic surgery procedures*. Arlington Heights, IL

Amoto, P. R., & Keith, B. (1991). Parental divorce and the well-being of children. *Psychological Bulletin, 110*, 26–46.

Andersen, S. M., & Chen, S. (2002). The relational self: An interpersonal social-cognitive theory. *Psychological Review, 109*, 619–645.

Andersen, S. M., Glassman, N. S., Chen, S., & Cole, S. W. (1995). Transference in social perception: The role of chronic accessibility in significant-other representations. *Journal of Personality and Social Psychology, 69*, 41–57.

Andersen, S. M., Reznik, I., & Manzella, L. M. (1996). Eliciting facial affect, motivation, and expectancies in transference: Significant-other representations in social relations. *Journal of Personality and Social Psychology, 71*, 1108–1129.

Andersen, S. M., & Ross, L. (1984). Self knowledge and social influence I: The impact of cognitive/affective and behavioral data. *Journal of Personality and Social Psychology, 46*, 280–293.

Anderson, C. A. (1987). Temperature and aggression: Effects on quarterly, yearly, and city rates of violent and nonviolent crime. *Journal of Personality and Social Psychology, 52*, 1161–1173.

Anderson, C. A. (1989). Temperature and aggression: Ubiquitous effects of heat on occurrences of human violence. *Psychological Bulletin, 106*, 74–96.

Anderson, C. A. (1991). How people think about causes: Examination of the typical phenomenal organization of attributions for success and failure. *Social Cognition, 9*, 295–329.

Anderson, C. A., & Bushman, B. J. (2001). Effects of violent video games on aggressive behavior, aggressive cognition, aggressive affect, physiological arousal, and prosocial behavior: A meta-analytic review of the scientific literature. *Psychological Science, 12*, 353–359.

Anderson, C. A., & Dill, K. E. (2000). Video games and aggressive thoughts, feelings, and behavior in the laboratory and in life. *Journal of Personality and Social Psychology, 78*, 772–790.

Anderson, C. A., & Deuser, W. E. (1993). The primacy of control in causal thinking and attributional style: An attributional functionalism perspective. In G. Weary, F. Gleicher, & K. L. Marsh (Eds.), *Control motivation and social cognition* (pp. 94–121). New York: Springer-Verlag.

Anderson, C., John, O. P., Keltner, D., & Kring, A. (2001). Social status in naturalistic face-to-face groups: Effects of personality and physical attractiveness in men and women. *Journal of Personality and Social Psychology, 81*, 1108–1129.

Anderson, C., Keltner, D., & John, O. P. (2003). Emotional convergence between people over time. *Journal of Personality and Social Psychology, 84*, 1054–1068.

Anderson, C. A., Krull, D. S., & Weiner, B. (1996). Explanations: Processes and consequences. In E. T. Higgins & A. W. Kruglanski (Eds.), *Social psychology: Handbook of basic principles* (pp. 271–296). New York: Guilford Press.

Anderson, D. (1990, February 27). Handcuffed in history to Tony C. *New York Times*, p. B9.

Anderson, J. L., Crawford, C. B., Nadeau, J., & Lindberg, T. (1992). Was the duchess of Windsor right? A cross-cultural review of the socioecology of ideals of female body shape. *Ethology and Sociobiology, 13*, 197–227.

Anderson, R., & Nida, S. A. (1978). Effect of physical attractiveness on opposite- and same-sex evaluations. *Journal of Personality, 46*, 401–413.

Anderson, R. C., & Pichert, J. W. (1978). Recall of previously unrecallable information following a shift in perspective. *Journal of Verbal Learning and Verbal Behavior, 17*, 1–12.

Ansolabehere, S., & Iyengar, S. (1995). *Going negative: How political ads shrink and polarize the electorate*. New York: Free Press.

Antill, J. K. (1983). Sex role complementarity versus similarity in married couples. *Journal of Personality and Social Psychology, 45*, 145–155.

Argyle, M. (1999). Causes and correlates of happiness. In D. Kahneman, E. Diener, & N. Schwarz (Eds.), *Well-being. The foundations of hedonic psychology* (pp. 353–373). New York: Russell Sage.

Arkin, R. M., & Baumgardner, A. H. (1985). Basic issues in attribution theory and research. In J. H. Harvey & G. Weary (Eds.), *Self handicapping* (pp. 169–202). New York: Academic Press.

Arkin, R. M., & Maruyama, G. M. (1979). Attribution, affect and college exam performance. *Journal of Educational Psychology, 71*, 85–93.

Arndt, J., Greenberg, J., & Cook, A. (2002). Mortality salience and the spreading activation of worldview-relevant constructs: Exploring the cognitive architecture of terror management. *Journal of Experimental Psychology: General, 131*, 307–324.

Aron, A., & Aron, E. N. (1997). Self-expansion motivation and including the other in self. In S. Duck (Ed.), *Handbook of personal relationships: Theory, research, and interventions* (2nd ed., pp. 251–270). Chichester, England: Wiley.

Aron, A., Aron, E. N., & Allen, J. (1989). *The motivation for unrequited love: A self-expansion perspective*. Paper presented at the International Conference on Personal Relationships, Iowa City, IA.

Aron, A., Aron, E. N., Tudor, M., & Nelson, G. (1991). Close relationships as including other in self. *Journal of Personality and Social Psychology, 60*, 241–253.

Aron, A., & Fraley, B. (1999). Relationship closeness as including other in the self: Cognitive underpinnings and measures. *Social Cognition 17*, 140–160.

Aron, A., Norman, C. C., Aron, E. N., McKenna, C., & Heyman, R. E. (2000). Couples' shared participation in novel and arousing activities and experienced relationship quality. *Journal of Personality and Social Psychology, 78*, 273–284.

Aronson, E. (1969). The theory of cognitive dissonance: A current perspective. In L. Berkowitz (Ed.), *Advances in experimental social psychology* (Vol. 4, pp. 1–34). New York: Academic Press.

Aronson, E., & Carlsmith, J. M. (1963). Effect of severity of threat in the devaluation of forbidden behavior. *Journal of Abnormal and Social Psychology, 66*, 584–588.

Aronson, E., Ellsworth, P. C., Carlsmith, J. M., & Gonzalez, M. H. (1990). *Methods of research in social psychology* (2nd ed.). New York: McGraw-HIll.

Aronson, E., Fried, C., & Stone, J. (1991). Overcoming denial and increasing the intention to use condoms through the induction of hypocrisy. *American Journal of Public Health, 81*, 1636–1638.

Aronson, E., & Linder, D. (1965). Gain and loss of esteem as determinants of interpersonal attractiveness. *Journal of Experimental Social Psychology, 1*, 156–171.

Aronson, E., & Mills, J. (1959). The effect of severity of initiation on liking for a group. *Journal of Abnormal and Social Psychology, 59*, 177–181.

Aronson, E., Stephan, C., Sikes, J., Blaney, N., & Snapp, M. (1978). *The jigsaw classroom*. Beverly Hills, CA: Sage.

Aronson, E., & Thibodeau, R. (1992). The jigsaw classroom: A cooperative strategy for reducing prejudice. In J. Lynch, C. Modgil, & S. Modgil (Eds.), *Cultural diversity in the schools* (pp. 110–118). London: Falmer Press.

Aronson, J. M., Lustina, M. J., Good, C., Keough, K., Steele, C. M., & Brown, J. (1999). When white men can't do math: Necessary and sufficient factors in stereotype threat. *Journal of Experimental Social Psychology, 35*, 29–46.

Asch, S. E. (1940). Studies in the principles of judgments and attitudes: II. Determination of judgments by group and by ego standards. *Journal of Social Psychology, 12*, 584–588.

Asch, S. E. (1946). Forming impressions on personality. *Journal of Abnormal and Social Psychology, 41*, 258–290.

Asch, S. (1951). Effects of group pressure upon the modification and distortion of judgments. In G. Guetzkow (Ed.), *Groups, leadership, and men* (pp. 177–190). Pittsburgh, PA: Carnegie Press.

Asch, S. (1952). *Social psychology*. Englewood Cliffs, NJ: Prentice-Hall.

Asch, S. (1956). Studies of independence and conformity: A minority of one against a unanimous majority. *Psychological Monographs, 70* (Whole No. 416).

Asch, S. E., & Zuckier, H. (1984). Thinking about person. *Journal of Personality and Social Psychology, 46*, 1230–1240.

Ashburn-Nardo, L., Voils, C. I., & Monteith, M. J. (2001). Implicit associations as the seeds of intergroup bias: How easily do they take root? *Journal of Personality and Social Psychology, 81*, 789–799.

Aspinwall, L. G., & Brunhart, S. M. (1996). Distinguishing optimism from denial: Optimistic beliefs predict attention to health threats. *Personality and Social Psychology Bulletin, 22*, 993–1003.

Aspinwall, L. G., & Taylor, S. E. (1993). Effects of social comparison direction, threat and self-esteem on affect, evaluation and expected success. *Journal of Personality and Social Psychology, 64*, 708–722.

Averill, J. R. (1980). A constructivist view of emotion. In R. Plutchik & H. Kellerman (Eds.), *Emotion: Theory, research, and experience* (pp. 205–339). New York: Academic Press.

Avis, J., & Harris, P. L. (1991). Belief-desire reasoning among Baka children: Evidence for a universal conception of mind. *Child Development, 62*, 460–467.

Axelrod, R. (1984). *The evolution of cooperation*. New York: Basic Books.

Ayduk, O., Downey, G., Testa, A., Yen, Y., & Shoda, Y. (1999). Does rejection elicit hostility in high rejection sensitive women? *Social Cognition, 17*, 245–271.

Bain, L. L., Wilson, T., & Chaikind, E. (1989). Participant perceptions of exercise programs for overweight women. *Research Quarterly for Exercise and Sport, 60*, 134–143.

Baldwin, M. W. (1992). Relational schemas and the processing of social information. *Psychological Bulletin, 112*, 461–484.

Baldwin, M. W. (1994). Primed relational schemas as a source of self-evaluative reactions. *Journal of Social and Clinical Psychology, 13*, 380–403.

Baldwin, M. W. (1999). *Relational schemas: Research into social cognitive aspects of interpersonal experience*. New York: Guilford Press.

Baldwin, M. W., Carrell, S., & Lopez, D. F. (1990). Priming relationship schemas: My advisor and the Pope are watching me from the back of my mind. *Journal of Experimental Psychology, 26*, 435–454.

Baldwin, M. W., & Fehr, B. (1995). On the instability of attachment style ratings. *Personal Relationships, 2*, 247–261.

Baldwin, M. W., & Holmes, J. G. (1987). Salient private audiences and awareness of the self. *Journal of Personality and Social Psychology, 53*, 1087–1098.

Baldwin, M. W., Keelan, J. P. R., Fehr, B., Enns, V., & Koh-Rangarajoo, E. (1996). Social-cognitive conceptualizations of attachment working models: Availability and accessibility effects. *Journal of Personality and Social Psychology, 71*, 94–109.

Banaji, M., Hardin, C. C., & Rothman, A. J. (1993). Implicit stereotyping in person judgement. *Journal of Personality and Social Psychology, 65*, 272–281.

Banaji, M. R., & Steele, C. M. (1989). Alcohol and self-evaluation: Is a social cognitive approach beneficial? *Social Cognition, 7*, 139–153.

Banks, T., & Dabbs, J. M., Jr. (1996). Salivary testosterone and cortisol in delinquents and violent urban culture. *Journal of Social Psychology, 136*, 49–56.

Bargh, J. A. (1996). Automaticity in social psychology. In E. T. Higgins & A. W. Kruglanski (Eds.), *Social psychology: Handbook of basic principles* (Vol. 1, pp. 1–40). New York: Guilford Press.

Bargh, J. A., Bond, R. N., Lombardi, W. J., & Tota, M. E. (1986). The additive nature of chronic and temporary sources of construct accessibility. *Journal of Personality and Social Psychology, 50,* 869–878.

Bargh, J. A., Chaiken, S., Raymond, P., & Hymes, C. (1996). The automatic evaluation effect: Unconditional automatic activation with a pronunciation task. *Journal of Experimental Social Psychology, 31,* 104–128.

Bargh, J. A., Chen, M., & Burrows, L. (1996). Automaticity of social behavior: Direct effects of trait construct and stereotype activation on action. *Journal of Personality and Social Psychology, 1,* 1–40.

Bargh, J. A., Gollwitzer, P. M., Lee-Chai, A., Barndollar, K., & Trotschel, R. (2001). The automated will: Nonconscious activation and pursuit of behavioral goals. *Journal of Personality and Social Psychology, 81,* 1014–1027.

Bargh, J. A., & Pietromonaco, P. (1982). Automatic information processing and social perception: The influence of trait information presented outside of conscious awareness on impression formation. *Journal of Personality and Social Psychology, 43,* 437–449.

Bargh, J. A., Raymond, P., Pryor, J. B., & Strack, F. (1995). Attractiveness of the underling: An automatic power-sex association and its consequences for sexual harassment and aggression. *Journal of Personality and Social Psychology, 68*(5), 768–781.

Bar-Hillel, M. (1980). The base-rate fallacy in probability judgments. *Acta Psychologica, 44,* 211–233.

Bar-Hillel, M., & Fischhoff, B. (1981). When do base-rates affect predictions? *Journal of Personality and Social Psychology, 41,* 671–680.

Barnett, P. A., & Gotlib, I. H. (1988). Psychosocial functioning and depression: Distinguishing among antecedents, concomitants, and consequences. *Psychological Bulletin, 104,* 97–126.

Baron, R. S. (1986). Distraction-conflict theory: Progress and problems. In L. Berkowitz (Ed.), *Advances in experimental social psychology* (Vol. 19, pp. 1–40). New York: Academic Press.

Baron, R. S., Moore, D., & Sanders, G. S. (1978). Distraction as a source of drive in social facilitation research. *Journal of Personality and Social Psychology, 36,* 816–824.

Baron, R. S., Vandello, J. A., & Brunsman, B. (1996). The forgotten variable in conformity research: Impact of task importance on social influence. *Journal of Personality and Social Psychology, 71,* 915–927.

Baron-Cohen, S., Leslie, A. M., & Frith, U. (1985). Does the child have a "theory of mind"? *Cognition, 21,* 37–46.

Bar-Tal, D. (1990). Causes and consequences of delegitimization: Models of conflict and ethnocentrism. *Journal of Social Issues, 46,* 65–81.

Bar-Tal, D., & Saxe, L. (1976). Perceptions of similarly and dissimilarly attractive couples and individuals. *Journal of Personality and Social Psychology, 33,* 772–781.

Bartholomew, K., & Horowitz, L. M. (1991). Attachment styles among young adults: A test for a four-category model. *Journal of Personality and Social Psychology, 61,* 226–244.

Bartlett, F. A. (1932). *Remembering: A study in experimental psychology.* Cambridge: Cambridge University Press.

Basil, R. (1989). Graphology and personality: "Let the buyer beware." *Skeptical Inquirer, 13,* 241–243.

Batson, C. D., Engel, C. L., & Fridell, S. R. (1999). Value judgments: Testing the somatic-marker hypothesis using false physiological feedback. *Personality and Social Psychology Bulletin, 25,* 1021–1032.

Batson, C. D., O'Quin, K., Fultz, J., Vanderplas, M., & Isen, A. (1983). Self-reported distress and empathy and egoistic versus altruistic motivation for helping. *Journal of Personality and Social Psychology, 45,* 706–718.

Batson, C. D., & Shaw, L. L. (1991). Evidence for altruism: Toward a pluralism of prosocial motives. *Psychological Inquiry, 2,* 107–122.

Baumeister, R. F. (1982). A self-presentational view of social interaction. *Psychological Bulletin, 91,* 3–26.

Baumeister, R. F. (1987). How the self became a problem: A psychological review of historical research. *Journal of Personality and Social Psychology, 52,* 163–176.

Baumeister, R. F. (1991). *Escaping the self: Alcoholism, spirituality, masochism, and other flights from the burden of selfhood.* New York: Basic Books.

Baumeister, R. F., Bratslavsky, E., Finkenauer, C., & Vohs, K. D. (2001). Bad is stronger than good. *Review of General Psychology, 5,* 323–370.

Baumeister, R. F., & Leary, M. R. (1995). The need to belong: Desire for interpersonal attachments as a fundamental human motivation. *Psychological Bulletin, 117,* 497–529.

Baumeister, R. F., Smart, L., & Boden, J. M. (1996). Relation of threatened egotism to violence and aggression: The dark side to high self-esteem. *Psychological Review, 103,* 5–33.

Baumeister, R. F., Stillwell, A. M., & Heatherton, T. F. (1994). Guilt: An interpersonal approach. *Psychological Bulletin, 115,* 243–267.

Baumeister, R. F., Twenge, J. M., & Nuss, C. (2002). Effects of social exclusion on cognitive processes: Anticipated aloneness reduces intelligent thought. *Journal of Personality and Social Psychology, 83,* 817–827.

Baumgardner, A. H., & Brownlee, E. A. (1987). Strategic failure in social interaction: Evidence for expectancy confirmation effects. *Journal of Personality and Social Psychology, 52,* 525–535.

Beaman, A. L., Barnes, P. J., Kleentz, B., & McQuirk, B. (1978). Increasing helping rates through informational dissemination: Teaching pays. *Personality and Social Psychology Bulletin, 4,* 406–411.

Beaman, A. L., Klentz, B., Diener, E., & Svanum, S. (1979). Self-awareness and transgression in children: Two field studies. *Journal of Personality and Social Psychology, 37,* 1835–1946.

Bechera, A., Damasio, H., & Damasio, A. R. (2000). Emotion, decision making, and the orbitofrontal cortex. *Cerebral Cortex, 10,* 295–307.

Beck, S. P., Ward-Hull, C. I., & McLear, P. M. (1976). Variables related to women's somatic preferences of the male and female body. *Journal of Personality and Social Psychology, 34,* 1200–1210.

Becker, M. H., & Josephs, J. G. (1988). Aids and behavioral change to reduce risk: A review. *American Journal of Public Health, 78,* 394–410.

Beckman, L. (1970). Effects of students' performance on teachers' and observers' attributions of causality. *Journal of Educational Psychology, 61,* 76–82.

Beer, J., Heerey, E. A., Keltner, D., Scabini, D, & Knight, R. (2003). The regulatory function of self-conscious emotion: Insights from patients with orbitofrontal damage. *Journal of Personality and Social Psychology, 85,* 594–604.

Bell, S. T., Kuriloff, P.J., & Lottes, I. (1994). Understanding attributions of blame in stranger-rape and date-rape situations: An examinations of gender, race, identification, and students' social perceptions of rape victims. *Journal of Applied Social Psychology, 24*, 1719–1734.

Bem, D. J. (1967). Self-perception: An alternative interpretation of cognitive dissonance phenomena. *Psychological Review, 74*, 183–200.

Bem, D. J. (1972). Self-perception theory. In L. Berkowitz (Ed.), *Advances in experimental social psychology* (Vol. 6, pp. 1–62). New York: Academic Press.

Bem, D. J., & McConnell, H. K. (1970). Testing the self-perception explanation of dissonance phenomena: On the salience of pre-manipulation attitudes. *Journal of Personality and Social Psychology, 14*, 23–31.

Bem, S. L. (1993). *The lenses of gender: Transforming the debate on sexual inequality.* New Haven: Yale University Press.

Benet-Martinez, V., Leu, J., Lee, F., & Morris, M. W. (2002). Negotiating biculturalism: Cultural frame switching in biculturals with oppositional versus compatible cultural identities. *Journal of Cross-Cultural Psychology, 33*, 492–516.

Berg, J. H., & McQuinn, R. D. (1986). Attraction and exchange in continuing and noncontinuing dating relationships. *Journal of Personality and Social Psychology, 50*, 942–952.

Berglas, S., & Jones, E. E. (1978). Drug choice as a self-handicapping strategy in response to non-contingent success. *Journal of Personality and Social Psychology, 36*, 405–417.

Berk, M. S., & Andersen, S. M. (2000). The impact of past relationships on interpersonal behavior: Behavioral confirmation in the social-cognitive process of transference. *Journal of Personality and Social Psychology, 79*, 546–562.

Berkman, L. F. (1995). The role of social relations in health promotion. *Psychosomatic Medicine, 57*, 245–254.

Berkman, L. F., & Syme, S. L. (1979). Social networks, host resistance, and mortality: A nine year follow-up study of Alameda County residents. *American Journal of Epidemiology, 100*, 186–204.

Berkowitz, L. (1965). Some aspects of observed aggression. *Journal of Personality and Social Psychology, 2*, 359–369.

Berkowitz, L. (1989). The frustration-aggression hypothesis: An examination and reformulation. *Psychological Bulletin, 106*, 59–73.

Berkowitz, L. (1993). *Aggression.* New York: McGraw-Hill.

Berkowitz, L., & Daniels, L. R. (1964). Affecting the salience of the social responsibility norm: Effect of past help on the responses to dependency relationships. *Journal of Abnormal and Social Psychology, 68*, 275–281.

Berkowitz, L., & LePage, A. (1967). Weapons as aggression-eliciting stimuli. *Journal of Personality and Social Psychology, 7*, 202–207.

Berkowitz, L., & Troccoli, B. T. (1990). Feelings, direction of attention, and expressed evaluation of others. *Cognition and Emotion, 4*, 305–325.

Bernieri, F. J., Zuckerman, M., Koestner, R., & Rosenthal, R. (1994). Measuring person perception accuracy: Another look at self-other agreement. *Personality and Social Psychology Bulletin, 20*, 367–378.

Bernstein, I. H., Lin, T., & McClellan, P. (1982). Cross- vs. within-racial judgments of attractiveness. *Perception and Psychophysics, 32*, 495–503.

Bernstein, W. M., Stephenson, B. O., Snyder, M. L., & Wicklund, R. A. (1983). Causal ambiguity and heterosexual affiliation. *Journal of Experimental Social Psychology, 19*, 78–92.

Berry, D. S., & McArthur, L. Z. (1986). Perceiving character in faces: The impact of age-related craniofacial changes in social perception. *Psychological Bulletin, 100*, 3–18.

Berscheid, E., Brothen, T., & Graziano, W. (1976). Gain-loss theory and the "law of infidelity": Mr. Doting versus the admiring stranger. *Journal of Personality and Social Psychology, 33*, 709–718.

Berscheid, E., Dion, K., Walster, E., & Walster, G. W. (1971). Physical attractiveness and dating choice: A test of the matching hypothesis. *Journal of Experimental Social Psychology, 7*, 173–189.

Berscheid, E., & Reis, H. T. (1998). Attraction and close relationships. In D. T. Gilbert, S. T. Fiske, & G. Lindzey (Eds.), *The handbook of social psychology* (4th ed, Vol. 2, pp. 193–281). New York: McGraw-Hill.

Bessenoff, G. R., & Sherman, J. W. (2000). Automatic and controlled components of prejudice toward fat people: Evaluation versus stereotype activation. *Social Cognition, 18*, 329–353.

Bettencourt, B. A., Brewer, M. B., Croak, M. R., & Miller, N. (1992). Cooperation and the reduction of intergroup bias: The role of reward structure and social orientation. *Journal of Experimental Psychology, 28*, 301–319.

Biernat, M., Manis, M., & Kobrynowicz, D. (1997). Simultaneous assimilation and contrast effects in judgments of self and others. *Journal of Personality and Social Psychology, 73*, 254–269.

Bird, K. (2002). Advertise or die: Advertising and market share dynamics revisited. *Applied Economic Letters, 9*, 763–767.

Blackwell, L. S., Dweck, C. S., & Trzesniewski, K. (2004). *Implicit theories of intelligence predict achievement across an adolescent transition: A longitudinal study and an intervention.* Unpublished manuscript, Columbia University.

Blair, I. V., Judd, C. M., & Fallman, J. L. (2004). The automaticity of race and Afrocentric facial features in social judgments. *Journal of Personality and Social Psychology, 87*, 763–778.

Blanton, H., Pelham, B. W., De Hart, T., & Kuyper, H. (1999). When better-than-others compare upward: Choice of comparison and comparative evaluation as independent predictors of academic performance. *Journal of Personality and Social Psychology, 76*, 420–430.

Blascovich, J., & Mendes, W. B. (2000). Challenge and threat appraisals: The role of affective cues. In J. Forgas (Ed.), *Feeling and thinking: The role of affect in social cognition* (pp. 59–82). Cambridge, England: Cambridge University Press.

Blascovich, J., Mendes, W. B., Hunter, S. B., & Salomon, K. (1999). Social "facilitation" as challenge and threat. *Journal of Personality and Social Psychology, 77*, 68–77.

Blascovich, J., Spencer, S., Quinn, D., & Steele, C. (2001). African-Americans and high blood pressure: The role of stereotype threat. *Psychological Science, 12*, 225–229.

Blass, T. (1999). The Milgram paradigm after 35 years: Some things we now know about obedience to authority. *Journal of Applied Social Psychology, 29*, 955–978.

Blass, T. (2000). *Obedience to authority: Current perspectives on the Milgram paradigm.* Mahwah, NJ: Lawrence Erlbaum Associates.

Blass, T. (2004). *The man who shocked the world: The life and legacy of Stanley Milgram.* New York: Basic Books.

Bless, H., Clore, G. L., Schwarz, N., Golisano, V., Rabe, C., & Wölk, M. (1996). Mood and the use of scripts: Does a happy mood really lead to mindlessness? *Journal of Personality and Social Psychology, 71(4),* 665–679.

Bless, H., & Fiedler, K. (1995). Affective states and the influence of general activated knowledge. *Personality and Social Psychology Bulletin, 21(7),* 766–778.

Bless, H., Hamilton, D. L., & Mackie, D. M. (1992). Mood effects on the organization of person information. *European Journal of Social Psychology, 22,* 497–509.

Bless, H., Mackie, D. M., & Schwarz, N. (1992). Mood effects on attitude judgments: Independent effects of mood before and after message elaboration. *Journal of Personality and Social Psychology, 63(4),* 585–595.

Bless, H., Schwarz, N., & Wieland, R. (1996). Mood and the impact of category membership and individuating information. *European Journal of Social Psychology, 26,* 935–959.

Block, J., & Robins, R. W. (1993). A longitudinal study of consistency and change in self-esteem from early adolescence to early adulthood. *Child Development, 64,* 909–923.

Block, J. D., Weiss, S., & Thorne, A. (1979). How relevant is a semantic similarity interpretation of personality ratings? *Journal of Personality and Social Psychology, 37,* 1055–1074.

Bloom, B. L., White, S. W., & Asher, S. J. (1979). Marital disruption as a stressful life event. In G. Levinger & O. C. Moles (Eds.), *Divorce and separation: Context, causes, and consequences* (pp. 184–200). New York: Basic Books.

Blumberg, H. H. (1972). Communication of interpersonal intentions. *Journal of Personality and Social Psychology, 23,* 157–162.

Bochner, S. (1994). Cross-cultural differences in the self-concept. *Journal of Cross-Cultural Psychology, 25,* 273–283.

Bodenhausen, G. V. (1988). Stereotypic biases in social decision making and memory: Testing process models of stereotype use. *Journal of Personality and Social Psychology, 55,* 726–737.

Bodenhausen, G. V. (1990). Stereotypes as judgmental heuristics: Evidence of circadian variations in discrimination. *Psychological Science, 1,* 319–322.

Bodenhausen, G. V., Kramer, G. P., & Susser, K. (1994). Happiness and stereotypic thinking in social judgment. *Journal of Personality and Social Psychology, 66,* 621–632.

Bodenhausen, G. V., Macrae, C. N., & Sherman, J. W. (1999). On the dialectics of discrimination: Dual processes in social stereotyping. In S. Chaiken & Y. Trope (Eds.), *Dual process theories in social psychology* (pp. 271–290). New York: Guilford Press.

Bodenhausen, G., Sheppard, L., & Kramer, G. (1994). Negative affect and social judgment: The different impact of anger and sadness. *European Journal of Social Psychology, 24,* 45–62.

Boesch, C., & Boesch, H. (1989). Hunting behavior of wild chimpanzees in the Tai National Park. *American Journal of Physical Anthropology, 78,* 547–573.

Boice, R., Quanty, C. B., & Williams, R. C. (1974). Competition and possible dominance in turtles, toads, and frogs. *Journal of Comparative and Physiological Psychology, 86,* 1116–1131.

Bolger, N., Davis, A., & Rafaeli, E. (2003). Diary methods: Capturing life as it is lived. *Annual Review of Psychology, 54,* 579–616.

Bolger, N., & Schilling, E. A. (1991). Personality and the problems of everyday life: The role of neuroticism in exposure and reactivity to daily stressors. *Journal of Personality, 59,* 355–386.

Bonanno, G. A., & Kaltman, S. (1999). Toward an integrative perspective on bereavement. *Psychological Bulletin, 125,* 760–776.

Bond, M. H., & Cheung, T. (1983). College students' spontaneous self-concept. *Journal of Cross-Cultural Psychology, 14,* 154–171.

Bond, R., & Smith, P. B. (1996). Culture and conformity: A meta-analysis of studies using Asch's line judgment task. *Psychological Bulletin, 119,* 111–137.

Borgida, E., Conner, C., & Manteufel, L. (1992). Understanding living kidney donations: A behavioral decision-making perspective. In S. Spacapan & S. Oskamp (Eds.), *Helping and being helped.* Newbury Park, CA: Sage.

Bornstein, R. F. (1989). Exposure and affect: Overview and meta-analysis of research, 1968–1987. *Psychological Bulletin, 106,* 265–289.

Borod, J. C. (1992). Interhemispheric and intrahemispheric control of emotion: A focus on unilateral brain damage. *Journal of Consulting and Clinical Psychology, 60,* 339–348.

Boster, F. J., & Mongeau, P. (1984). Fear-arousing persuasive messages. In R. N. Bostrom (Ed.), *Communication yearbook* (Vol. 8, pp. 330–375). Beverly Hills, CA: Sage.

Boucher, J. D., & Brandt, M. E. (1981). Judgment of emotion: American and Malay antecedents. *Journal of Cross-Cultural Psychology, 12,* 272–283.

Bower, G. H. (1981). Mood and memory. *American Psychologist, 36,* 129–148.

Bower, G. H., Gilligan, S. G., & Monteiro, K. P. (1981). Selectivity of learning caused by affective states. *Journal of Experimental Psychology: General, 110,* 451–473.

Bowlby, J. (1982). *Attachment and loss* (2nd ed., Vol. 1). New York: Basic Books.

Boyd, R., & Richardson, P. J. (1985). Frequency-dependent bias and the evolution of cooperation. In R. Boyd & P. J. Richardson (Eds.), *Culture and the evolutionary process* (pp. 204–240). Chicago: University of Chicago Press.

Boyden, T., Carroll, J. S., & Maier, R. A. (1984). Similarity and attraction in homosexual males: The effects of age and masculinity-femininity. *Sex Roles, 10,* 939–948.

Bradbury, T. N. (1998). *The developmental course of marital dysfunction.* New York: Cambridge University Press.

Bradbury, T. N., & Fincham, F. D. (1990). Attributions in marriage: Review and critique. *Psychological Bulletin, 107,* 3–33.

Bradbury, T. N., & Karney, B. R. (1993). Longitudinal study of marital interaction and dysfunction. *Clinical Psychology Review, 13,* 15–27.

Bransford, J. D., & Johnson, M. K. (1973). Considerations of some problems of comprehension. In W. G. Chase (Ed.), *Visual information processing* (pp. 383–438). New York: Academic Press.

Brauer, M., Chambres, P., Niedenthal, P. M., & Chatard-Pannetier, A. (2004). The relationship between expertise and evaluative extremity: The moderating role of experts' task characteristics. *Journal of Personality and Social Psychology, 86,* 5–18.

Breckler, S. J. (1984). Empirical validation of affect, behavior, and cognition as distinct components of attitude. *Journal of Personality and Social Psychology, 47,* 1191–1205.

Brehm, J. W. (1956). Post-decision changes in desirability of alternatives. *Journal of Abnormal and Social Psychology, 52,* 384–389.

Brendl, C. M., Higgins, E. T., & Lemm, K. M. (1995). Sensitivity to varying gains and losses: The role of self-discrepancies and event framing. *Journal of Personality and Social Psychology, 69,* 1028–1051.

Brendl, C. M., Markman, A. B., & Messner, C. (2001). How do indirect measures of evaluation work? Evaluating the inference of prejudice in the implicit association test. *Journal of Personality and Social Psychology, 81,* 760–773.

Brennan, K. A., Clark, C. L., & Shaver, P. R. (1998). Self-report measurement of adult attachment: An integrative overview. In J. A. Simpson & W. S. Rholes (Eds.), *Attachment theory and close relationships* (pp. 46–76). New York: Guilford Press.

Brennan, K. A., & Shaver, P. R. (1993). Attachment styles and parental divorce. *Journal of Divorce and Remarriage, 21,* 161–175.

Brewer, M. B. (1979). In-group bias in the minimal intergroup situation: A cognitive-motivational analysis. *Psychological Bulletin, 86,* 307–324.

Brewer, M. B. (1988). A dual process model of impression formation. In T. K. Srull & R. S. Wyer (Eds.), *Advances in social cognition.* Hillsdale, NJ: Lawrence Erlbaum Associates.

Brewer, M. B., & Brown, R. J. (1998). Intergroup relations. In D. T. Gilbert, S. T. Fiske, & G. Lindzey (Eds.), *The handbook of social psychology* (4th ed., Vol. 2, pp. 554–594). New York: McGraw-Hill.

Brewer, M. B., & Gardner, W. (1996). Who is the "we"? Levels of collective identity and self-representations. *Journal of Personality and Social Psychology, 71,* 83–93.

Brewer, M. B., & Kramer, R. M. (1985). The psychology of intergroup attitudes and behavior. *Annual Review of Psychology, 36,* 219–243.

Brewer, M. B., & Miller, N. (1988). Contact and cooperation: When do they work? In P. Katz & D. Taylor (Eds.), *Eliminating racism: Profiles in controversy* (pp. 315–326). New York: Plenum Press.

Brewer, M. B., & Nakamura, G. V. (1984). The nature and functions of schemas. In R. S. Wyer & T. K. Srull (Eds.), *The handbook of social cognition* (Vol. 1). Hillsdale, NJ: Lawrence Erlbaum Associates.

Brickman, P., & Campbell, D. T. (1971). Hedonic relativism and planning the good society. In M. H. Appley (Ed.), *Adaptation level theory: A symposium* (pp. 287–302). New York: Academic Press.

Brickman, P., Coates, D., & Janoff-Bulman, R. J. (1978). Lottery winners and accident victims: Is happiness relative? *Journal of Personality and Social Psychology, 36,* 917–927.

Briggs, J. L. (1960). *Never in anger: Portrait of an Eskimo family.* Cambridge, MA: Harvard University Press.

Brigham, J. C. (1993). College students' racial attitudes. *Journal of Applied Social Psychology, 23,* 1933–1967.

Brislin, R. W., & Lewis, S. A. (1968). Dating and physical attractiveness: Replication. *Psychological Reports, 22,* 976.

Brockner, J. (1979). The effects of self-esteem, success-failure, and self-consciousness on task performance. *Journal of Personality and Social Psychology, 37,* 1732–1741.

Brockner, J., Guzzi, B., Kane, J., Levine, E., & Shaplen, K. (1984). Organizational fundraising: Further evidence on the effects of legitimizing small donations. *Journal of Consumer Research, 11,* 611–614.

Brockner, J., & Weisenfeld, B. M. (1994). The interactive impact of procedural and outcome fairness on reactions to a decision: The effects of what you do depend on how you do it. *Psychological Bulletin, 120,* 189–208.

Brown, D. E. (1991). *Human universals.* New York: McGraw-Hill.

Brown, D. E. (2000). Human universals and their implications. In N. Roughley (Ed.), *Being humans: Anthropological universality and particularity in transdisciplinary perspectives.* New York: Walter de Gruyter.

Brown, J. D. (1998). *The self.* New York: McGraw-Hill.

Brown, J. D., & Dutton, K. A. (1995). The thrill of victory, the complexity of defeat: Self-esteem and people's emotional reactions to success and failure. *Journal of Personality and Social Psychology, 68,* 712–722.

Brown, P., & Levinson, S. C. (1987). *Politeness: Some universals in language usage.* Cambridge, England: Cambridge University Press.

Brown, R. (1986). *Social psychology* (2nd ed.). New York: Free Press.

Brown, R., & Kulik, J. (1977). Flashbulb memories. *Cognition, 5,* 73–99.

Browning, C. R. (1992). *Ordinary men: Reserve police battalion 101 and the final solution in Poland.* New York: Aaron Asher.

Brownstein, A. L. (2003). Biased predecision processing. *Psychological Bulletin, 129,* 545–568.

Brumberg, J. J. (1997). *The body project: An intimate history of American girls.* New York: Random House.

Buck, R. W., & Parke, R. D. (1972). Behavioral and physiological response to the presence of a friendly or neutral person in two types of stressful situations. *Journal of Personality and Social Psychology, 24,* 143–153.

Buehler, R., Griffin, D., & Ross, M. (1994). Exploring the "planning fallacy": Why people underestimate their task completion times. *Journal of Personality and Social Psychology, 67,* 366–381.

Bugental, D. B., & Lewis, J. C. (1999). The paradoxical misuse of power by those who see themselves as powerless: How does it happen? *Journal of Social Issues, 55,* 51–64.

Burger, J. M. (1981). Motivational biases in the attribution of responsibility for an accident: A meta-analysis of the defensive-attribution hypothesis. *Psychological Bulletin, 90,* 496–512.

Burger, J. M. (1986). Increasing compliance by improving the deal: The that's-not-all technique. *Journal of Personality and Social Psychology, 51,* 277–283.

Burger, J. M. (1999). The foot in the door compliance procedure: A multiple process analysis and review. *Personality and Social Psychology Review, 3,* 303–325.

Burger, J. M., Reed, M., DeCesare, K., Rauner, S., & Rozolis, J. (1999). The effects of initial request size on compliance: More about the that's-not-all technique. *Basic and Applied Social Psychology, 21,* 243–249.

Burgess, E. W., & Wallin, P. (1953). *Engagement and marriage.* Philadelphia: Lippincott.

Burkhart, K. (1973). *Women in prison.* Garden City, NY: Doubleday.

Burnstein, E. (2005). Kin altruism: The morality of biological systems. In D. M. Buss (Ed.), *The handbook of evolutionary psychology* (pp. 528–551). New York: Wiley.

Burnstein, E., Crandall, C., & Kitayama, S. (1994). Some neo-Darwinian decision rules for altruism: Weighing cues for inclusive fitness as a function of the biological importance of the decision. *Journal of Personality and Social Psychology, 67,* 773–789.

Burnstein, E., & Vinokur, A. (1973). Testing two classes of theories about group induced shifts in individual choice. *Journal of Experimental Social Psychology, 9,* 123–137.

Burnstein, E., Vinokur, A., & Trope, Y. (1973). Interpersonal comparison versus persuasive argumentation: A more direct test of alternative explanations for group-induced shifts in individual choice. *Journal of Experimental Social Psychology, 9,* 236–245.

Buss, D. M. (1984). Toward a psychology of person-environment (PE) correlation: The role of spouse selection. *Journal of Personality and Social Psychology, 47,* 361–377.

Buss, D. M. (1989). Sex differences in human mate preference: Evolutionary hypothesis tested in 37 cultures. *Behavioral and Brain Sciences, 12,* 1–49.

Buss, D. (1992). Mate preference mechanisms: Consequences for partner choice and intrasexual competition. In J. H. Barkow, L. Cosmides, & J. Tooby (Eds.), *The adapted mind* (pp. 267–288). New York: Oxford University Press.

Buss, D. M. (1994a). *The evolution of desire: Strategies of human mating.* New York: Basic Books.

Buss, D. M. (1994b). The strategies of human mating. *American Scientist, 82,* 238–249.

Buss, D. M. (1999). Human nature and individual differences: The evolution of human personality. In L. A. Pervin & O. P. John (Eds.), *Handbook of personality: Theory and research* (2nd ed., pp. 31–56). New York: Guilford Press.

Buss, D. M., & Kenrick, D. T. (1998). Evolutionary social psychology. In D. T. Gilbert, S. T. Fiske, & G. Lindzey (Eds.), *The handbook of social psychology* (4th ed., Vol. 2, pp. 982–1026). New York: McGraw-Hill.

Buss, D. M., Larsen, R., Westen, D., & Semmelroth, J. (1992). Sex differences in jealousy: Evolution, physiology, and psychology. *Psychological Science, 3,* 251–255.

Byrne, D. (1961). Interpersonal attraction and attitude similarity. *Journal of Abnormal and Social Psychology, 62,* 713–715.

Byrne, D., Clore, G. L., & Smeaton, G. (1986). The attraction hypothesis: Do similar attitudes predict anything? *Journal of Personality and Social Psychology, 51,* 1167–1170.

Byrne, D., Griffitt, W., & Stefaniak, D. (1967). Attraction and similarity of personality characteristics. *Journal of Personality and Social Psychology, 5,* 82–90.

Byrne, D., & Nelson, D. (1965). Attraction as a linear function of proportion of positive reinforcements. *Journal of Abnormal and Social Psychology, 1,* 659–663.

Cacioppo, J. T., & Bernston, G. G. (1994). Relationship between attitudes and evaluative space: A critical review with emphasis on the separability of positive and negative substrates. *Psychological Bulletin, 115,* 401–423.

Cacioppo, J. T., & Gardner, W. L. (1999). Emotion. *Annual Review of Psychology, 50,* 191–214.

Cacioppo, J. T., Klein, D. J., Berntson, G. G., & Hatfield, E. T. (1993). The psychophysiology of emotion. In M. Lewis & J. M. Haviland (Eds.), *Handbook of emotions* (pp. 119–142). New York: Guilford Press.

Cacioppo, J. T., Petty, R. E., Feinstein, J., & Jarvis, B. (1996). Individual differences in cognitive motivation: The life and times of people varying in need for cognition. *Psychological Bulletin, 119,* 197–253.

Cacioppo, J. T., Petty, R. E., & Morris, K. J. (1983). Effects of need for cognition on message evaluation, recall, and persuasion. *Journal of Personality and Social Psychology, 45,* 805–818.

Cacioppo, J. T., Petty, R. E., & Sidera, J. (1982). The effects of salient self-schema on the evaluation of proattitudinal editorials: Top-down versus bottom-up message processing. *Journal of Experimental Social Psychology, 18,* 324–338.

Cacioppo, J. T., Priester, J. R., & Berntson, G. G. (1993). Rudimentary determinants of attitude. II. Arm flexion and extension have differential effects on attitudes. *Journal of Personality and Social Psychology, 65,* 5–17.

Campbell, D. T. (1975). On the conflicts between biological and social evolution and between psychology and moral tradition. *American Psychologist, 30,* 1103–1126.

Campbell, J. D., & Fairey, P. J. (1989). Informational and normative routes to conformity: The effect of faction size as a function of norm extremity and attention to the stimulus. *Journal of Personality and Social Psychology, 57,* 457–468.

Carli, L. L. (1999). Cognitive reconstruction, hindsight, and reactions to victims and perpetrators. *Personality and Social Psychology Bulletin, 25,* 966–979.

Carlsmith, J. M., & Gross, A. E. (1969). Some effects of guilt on compliance. *Journal of Personality and Social Psychology, 11,* 232–239.

Carlsmith, K. M., Darley, J. M., & Robinson, P. H. (2002). Why do we punish? Deterrence and just deserts as motives for punishment. *Journal of Personality and Social Psychology, 83,* 284–299.

Carlson, J. A., & Davis, C. M. (1971). Cultural values and the risky shift: A cross-cultural test in Uganda and the United States. *Journal of Personality and Social Psychology, 20,* 236–245.

Carlson, M., Charlin, V., & Miller, N. (1988). Positive mood and helping behavior: A test of six hypotheses. *Journal of Personality and Social Psychology, 55,* 211–229.

Carlston, D. E., & Skowronski, J. J. (1986). Trait memory and behavior memory: The effects of alternative pathways on impression judgment response times. *Journal of Personality and Social Psychology, 50,* 5–13.

Carlston, D. E., & Skowronski, J. J. (1994). Savings in the relearning of trait information as evidence for spontaneous inference generation. *Journal of Personality and Social Psychology, 66,* 840–880.

Carnevale, P. J., & Isen, A. M. (1986). The influence of positive affect and visual access on the discovery of integrative solutions in bilateral negotiation. *Organizational Behavior and Human Decision Processes, 37,* 1–13.

Carter, C. S. (1998). Neuroendocrine perspectives on social attachment and love. *Psychoneuroendocrinology, 23(8),* 779–818.

Carter, J., & Irons, M. (1991). Are economists different, and if so, why? *Journal of Economic Perspectives, 5,* 171–177.

Cartwright, D., & Zander, A. (1968). *Group dynamics: Research and theory.* New York: Harper & Row.

Carver, C. S. (1974). Facilitation of physical aggression through objective self-awareness. *Journal of Experimental Social Psychology, 10,* 365–370.

Carver, C. S., DeGregorio, E., & Gillis, R. (1980). Ego-defensive attribution among two categories of observers. *Personality and Social Psychology Bulletin, 6,* 4–50.

Carver, C. S., & Scheier, M. F. (1981). The self-attention-induced feedback loop and social facilitation. *Journal of Experimental Social Psychology, 17,* 545–568.

Carver, C. S., & Scheier, M. F. (1982). Control theory: A useful conceptual framework for personality-social, clinical, and health psychology. *Psychological Bulletin, 92,* 111–135.

Cash, T. F., & Derlaga, V. J. (1978). The matching hypothesis: Physical attractiveness among same-sexed friends. *Personality and Social Psychology Bulletin, 4,* 240–243.

Cash, T. F., & Duncan, N. C. (1984). Physical attractiveness stereotyping among black American college students. *Journal of Social Psychology, 122,* 71–77.

Cash, T. F., & Kilcullen, R. N. (1985). The eye of the beholder: Susceptibility to sexism and beautyism in the evaluation of managerial applicants. *Journal of Applied Social Psychology, 15,* 591–605.

Cash, T. F., & Trimer, C. A. (1984). Sexism and beautyism in women's evaluations of peer performance. *Sex Roles, 10,* 87–98.

Caspi, A. (1998). Personality development across the life course. In W. Damon (Ser. Ed.) & N. Eisenberg (Vol. Ed.), *Handbook of child psychology. Vol. 3: Social, emotional, and personality development* (pp. 311–388). New York: Wiley.

Caspi, A., Elder, G. H., Jr., & Bem, D. J. (1987). Moving against the world: Life-course patterns of explosive children. *Developmental Psychology, 23(2),* 308–313.

Caspi, A., Elder, G. H., Jr., & Bem, D. J. (1988). Moving away from the world: Life-course patterns of shy children. *Developmental Psychology, 24,* 824–831.

Caspi, A., & Herbener, E.S. (1990). Continuity and change: Assortative marriage and the consistency of personality in adulthood. *Journal of Personality and Social Psychology, 58,* 250–258.

Caspi, A., McClay, J., Moffitt, T. E., Mill, J., Martin, J., Craig, I. W., et al. (2002). Role of genotype in the cycle of violence in maltreated children. *Science, 297,* 851–854.

Caspi, A., & Roberts, B. W. (2001). Personality development across the life course: The argument for change and continuity. *Psychological Inquiry, 12,* 49–66.

Cate, R. M., Lloyd, S. A., Henton, J. M., & Larson, J. H. (1982). Fairness and reward level as predictors of relationship satisfaction. *Social Psychology Quarterly, 45,* 177–181.

Center for Media and Public Affairs. (July-August 2000). The media at the millennium: The networks' top topics, trends, and joke targets of the 1990s. *Media Monitor, 14,* 1–6.

Chagnon, N. (1997). *Yanamamo.* New York: Harcourt, Brace, Jovanovich.

Chaiken, S. (1980). Heuristic versus systematic information processing in the use of source versus message cues in persuasion. *Journal of Personality and Social Psychology, 39,* 752–766.

Chaiken, S., & Baldwin, M. W. (1981). Affective-cognitive consistency and the effect of salient behavioral information on the self-perception of attitudes. *Journal of Personality and Social Psychology, 41,* 1–12.

Chaiken, S., & Eagly, A. H. (1976). Communication modality as a determinant of persuasion: The role of communicator salience. *Journal of Personality and Social Psychology, 45,* 241–256.

Chaiken, S., Liberman, A., & Eagly, A. H. (1989). Heuristic and systematic processing within and beyond the persuasion context. In J. S. Uleman & J. A. Bargh (Eds.), *Unintended thought* (pp. 212–252). New York: Guilford Press..

Chalfonte, B. L., & Johnson, M. K. (1996). Feature memory and binding in young and older adults. *Memory and Cognition, 24,* 403–416.

Champagne, A. B., Klopfer, L. E., & Anderson, J. H. (1980). Factors influencing the learning of classical mechanics. *American Journal of Physics, 48,* 1074–1079.

Chan, W.-T. (1967). Chinese theory and practice, with special reference to humanism. In C. A. Moore (Ed.), *The Chinese mind: Essentials of Chinese philosophy and culture.* Honolulu: East-West Center Press.

Chapman, L. J., & Chapman, J. (1967). Genesis of popular but erroneous diagnostic observations. *Journal of Abnormal Psychology, 72,* 193–204.

Chartrand, T. L., & Bargh, J. A. (1999). The chameleon effect: The perception-behavior link and social interaction. *Journal of Personality and Social Psychology, 76,* 893–910.

Chen, S., Lee-Chai, A. Y., & Bargh, J. A. (2001). Relationship orientation as moderator of the effects of social power. *Journal of Personality and Social Psychology, 80,* 183–187.

Chen, S. C. (1937). Social modification of the activity of ants in nest-building. *Physiological Zoology, 10,* 420–436.

Cheng, P. W., & Novick, L.R. (1990). A probabilistic contrast model of causal induction. *Journal of Personality and Social Psychology, 58,* 545–567.

Cheung, F. M., Leung, K., Zhang, J. X., Sun, H. F., Gan, Y. Q., Song, W. Z., & Dong, X. (2001). Indigenous Chinese personality constructs: Is the five-factor model complete? *Journal of Cross-Cultural Psychology, 32,* 407–433.

Choi, I., & Nisbett, R. E. (1998). Situational salience and cultural differences in the correspondence bias and in the actor-observer bias. *Personality and Social Psychology Bulletin, 24,* 949–960.

Choi, I., Nisbett, R. E., & Smith, E. E. (1997). Culture, category salience and inductive reasoning. *Cognition, 65,* 15–32.

Chomsky, N. (1975). *Reflections on language.* New York: Pantheon.

Chomsky, N. (1988). *Language and problems of knowledge: The Managua lectures.* Cambridge, MA: MIT Press.

Chua, H., Leu, J., & Nisbett, R. E. (2005). Culture and the diverging views of social events. *Personality and Social Psychology Bulletin, 31,* 925–934.

Cialdini, R. B. (1984). *Influence: How and why people agree to things.* New York: Quill.

Cialdini, R. B., Borden, R. J., Thorne, A., Walker, M. R., Freeman, S., & Sloan, L. R. (1976). Basking in reflected glory: Three (football) field studies. *Journal of Personality and Social Psychology, 34,* 366–375.

Cialdini, R. B., Darby, B. L., & Vincent, J. E. (1973). Transgression and altruism: A case for hedonism. *Journal of Experimental Social Psychology, 9,* 502–516.

Cialdini, R. B., & Fultz, J. (1990). Interpreting the negative mood-helping literature via "mega" analysis: A contrarian view. *Psychological Bulletin, 107,* 210–214.

Cialdini, R. B., Kallgren, C. A., & Reno, R. R. (1991). A focus theory of normative conduct: A theoretical refinement and reevaluation of the role of norms in human behavior. In M. P. Zanna (Ed.), *Advances in experimental social psychology* (Vol. 24, pp. 201–234). San Diego, CA: Academic Press.

Cialdini, R. B., & Kenrick, D. T. (1976). Altruism as hedonism: A social development perspective on the relationship of negative mood state and helping. *Journal of Personality and Social Psychology, 34*, 907–914.

Cialdini, R. B., Schaller, M., Houlihan, D., Arps, K., Fultz, J., & Beaman, A. L. (1987). Empathy-based helping: Is it selflessly or selfishly motivated? *Journal of Personality and Social Psychology, 52*, 749–758.

Cialdini, R. B., & Schroeder, D. A. (1976). Increasing compliance by legitimizing paltry contributions: When even a penny helps. *Journal of Personality and Social Psychology, 34*, 599–604.

Cialdini, R. B., & Trost, M. R. (1998). Social influence: Social norms, conformity, and compliance. In D. T. Gilbert, S. T. Fiske, & G. Lindzey (Eds.), *The handbook of social psychology* (4th ed., Vol. 2, pp. 151–192). New York: McGraw-Hill.

Cialdini, R. B., Vincent, J. E., Lewis, S. K., Catalan, J., Wheeler, D., & Darby, B. L. (1975). Reciprocal concessions procedure for inducing compliance: The door-in-the-face technique. *Journal of Personality and Social Psychology, 31*, 206–215.

Ciano, G. (1945). *The Ciano diaries.* Garden City, NY: Doubleday.

Clancy, S. M., & Dollinger, S. J. (1993). Photographic depictions of the self: Gender and age differences in social connectedness. *Sex Roles, 15*, 145–158.

Clark, H. H. (1996). *Using language.* Cambridge: Cambridge University Press.

Clark, M., & Isen, A. M. (1982). Toward understanding the relationship between feeling states and social behavior. In A. H. Hastorf & A. M. Isen (Eds.), *Cognitive social psychology* (pp. 73–108). New York: Elsevier.

Clark, M. S. (1984). Record keeping in two types of relationships. *Journal of Personality and Social Psychology, 47*, 549–557.

Clark, M. S. (1992). Research on communal and exchange relationships viewed from a functionalist perspective. In D. A. Owens & M. Wagner (Eds.), *Progress in modern psychology: The legacy of American functionalism* (pp. 241–258). Westport, CT: Praeger.

Clark, M. S., & Mills, J. (1979). Interpersonal attraction in exchange and communal relationships. *Journal of Personality and Social Psychology, 37*, 12–24.

Clark, M. S., & Mills, J. (1993). The difference between communal and exchange relationships: What is and is not. *Personality and Social Psychology Bulletin, 19*, 684–691.

Clark, M. S., Mills, J., & Powell, M. C. (1986). Keeping track of needs in communal and exchange relationships. *Journal of Personality and Social Psychology, 51*, 333–338.

Clark, M. S., Ouellette, R., Powell, M. C., & Milberg, S. (1987). Recipient's mood, relationship type, and helping. *Journal of Personality and Social Psychology, 53*, 94–103.

Clark, M. S., & Taraban, C. (1991). Reactions to and willingness to express emotion in communal and exchange relationships. *Journal of Experimental Social Psychology, 27*, 324–336.

Clark, R., Crockett, W., & Archer, R. (1971). Risk-as-value hypothesis: The relationship between perception of self, others, and the risky shift. *Journal of Personality and Social Psychology, 20*, 425–429.

Clark, R. D., & Hatfield, E. (1989). Gender differences in receptivity to sexual offers. *Journal of Psychology and Human Sexuality, 2*, 39–55.

Clark, R. D. I., & Word, L. E. (1972). Why don't bystanders help? Because of ambiguity? *Journal of Personality and Social Psychology, 24*, 392–400.

Clifford, M. M., & Walster, E. (1973). The effect of physical attractiveness on teacher expectations. *Sociology of Education, 46*, 248–258.

Clore, G. L. (1992). Cognitive phenomenology: Feelings and the construction of judgment. In L. L. Martin & A. Tesser (Eds.), *The construction of social judgments* (pp. 133–163). Hillsdale, NJ: Lawrence Erlbaum Associates.

Clore, G. L., & Byrne, D. (1974). A reinforcement-effect model of attraction. In T. L. Huston (Ed.), *Foundations of interpersonal attraction* (pp. 143–170). New York: Academic Press.

Clore, G. L., Gasper, K., & Garvin, E. (2001). Affect as information. In J. P. Forgas (Ed.), *Handbook of affect and social cognition* (pp. 121–144). Mahwah, NJ: Lawrence Erlbaum Associates.

Clore, G. L., & Gormly, J. B. (1974). Knowing, feeling, and liking: A psychophysical study of attraction. *Journal of Research in Personality, 8*, 218–230.

Clore, G. L., & Parrott, W. G. (1991). Moods and their vicissitudes: The informational properties of affective thoughts and feelings. In J. Forgas (Ed.), *Emotion and social judgments* (pp. 107–123). Elmsford, NY: Pergamon Press.

Coats, E. J., & Feldman, R. S. (1996). Gender differences in nonverbal correlates of social status. *Personality and Social Psychology Bulletin, 22*, 1014–1022.

Cohen, A. B., & Rozin, P. (2001). Religion and the morality of mentality. *Journal of Personality and Social Psychology, 81*, 697–710.

Cohen, C. E. (1981). Person categories and social perception: Testing some boundaries of the processing effects of prior knowledge. *Journal of Personality and Social Psychology, 40*, 441–452.

Cohen, D., & Gunz, A. (2002). *As seen by the other...: The self from the "outside in" and the "inside out" in the memories and emotional perceptions of Easterners and Westerners.* Unpublished manuscript, University of Waterloo.

Cohen, D., & Nisbett, R. E. (1997). Field experiments examining the culture of honor: The role of institutions in perpetuating norms about violence. *Personality and Social Psychology Bulletin, 23*, 1188–1199.

Cohen, D., Nisbett, R. E., Bowdle, B., & Schwarz, N. (1996). Insult, aggression, and the Southern culture of honor: An "experimental ethnography." *Journal of Personality and Social Psychology, 70*, 945–960.

Coleman, M., Campbell, E. O., Hobson, C. V., McPartland, J. M., Mood, A. M., Weinfeld, F. D., et al. (1966). *Equality of educational opportunity.* Washington, DC: U.S. Government Printing Office.

Collins, N. L. (1996). Working models of attachment: Implications for explanation, emotion, and behavior. *Journal of Personality and Social Psychology, 71*, 810–832.

Collins, N. L., & Feeney, B. C. (2000). A safe haven: An attachment theory perspective on support seeking and caregiving in intimate relationships. *Journal of Personality and Social Psychology, 78*, 1053–1073.

Collins, N. L., & Miller, L. C. (1994). Self-disclosure and liking: A meta-analytic review. *Psychological Bulletin, 116*, 457–475.

Collins, N. L., & Read, S. J. (1994). Cognitive representations of attachment: The structure and function of working models.

In K. Bartholomew & D. Perlman (Eds.), *Attachment processes in adulthood: Advances in personal relationships* (Vol. 5, pp. 53–90). London: Kingsley.

Collins, R. L., Taylor, S. E., Wood, J. V., & Thompson, S. C. (1988). The vividness effect: Elusive or illusory? *Journal of Experimental Social Psychology, 24*, 1–18.

Colman, A. M. (1982). Experimental games. In A. Colman (Ed.), *Cooperation and competition in humans and animals* (pp. 113–140). Berkshire, England: Van Nostrand Reinhold.

Columbus, C. (1492/1990). *Journal of the first voyage*. Warmister, England: Aris and Phillips Ltd.

Colvin, C. R., & Block, J. (1994). Do positive illusions foster mental health? An examination of the Taylor and Brown formulation. *Psychological Bulletin, 116*, 3–20.

Colvin, C. R., Block, J., & Funder, D. C. (1995). Overly positive self-evaluations and personality: Negative implications for mental health. *Journal of Personality and Social Psychology, 68*, 1152–1162.

Condon, J. W., & Crano, W. D. (1988). Inferred evaluation and the relation between attitude and interpersonal attraction. *Journal of Personality and Social Psychology, 54*, 789–797.

Connolly, K. (1968). The social facilitation of preening behavior of Drosophila melanogaster. *Animal Behavior, 16*, 385–391.

Conway, M., Pizzamiglio, M. T., & Mount, L. (1996). Status, communality, and agency: Implications for stereotypes of gender and other groups. *Journal of Personality and Social Psychology, 71*, 25–38.

Conway, M., & Ross, M. (1984). Getting what you want by revising what you had. *Journal of Personality and Social Psychology, 47*, 738–748.

Cook, K. S., & Hegtvedt, K. A. (1986). Justice and power: An exchange analysis. In H. W. Bierhoff, R. L. Cohen, & J. Greenberg (Eds.), *Justice in social relations* (pp. 19–43). New York: Plenum Press.

Cooley, C. H. (1902). *Human nature and the social order*. New York: Charles Scribner's Sons.

Cooper, H. M. (1979). Statistically combining independent studies: Meta-analysis of sex differences in conformity research. *Journal of Personality and Social Psychology, 37*, 131–146.

Cooper, J. (1971). Personal responsibility and dissonance: The role and foreseen consequences. *Journal of Personality and Social Psychology, 18*, 354–363.

Cooper, J. (1980). Reducing fears and increasing assertiveness: The role of dissonance reduction. *Journal of Experimental Social Psychology, 16*, 199–213.

Cooper, J., & Worchel, S. (1970). Role of undesired consequences in arousing cognitive dissonance. *Journal of Personality and Social Psychology, 16*, 199–206.

Cooper, J., Zanna, M. P., & Goethals, G. R. (1974). Mistreatment of an esteemed other as a consequence affecting dissonance reduction. *Journal of Experimental Social Psychology, 10*, 224–233.

Cooper, J., Zanna, M. P., & Taves, T. A. (1978). Arousal as a necessary condition for attitude change following induced compliance. *Journal of Personality and Social Psychology, 36*, 1101–1106.

Cooper, M. L., Shaver, P., & Collins, N. L. (1998). Attachment styles, emotion regulation, and adjustment in adolescence. *Journal of Personality and Social Psychology, 74*, 1380–1397.

Correll, J., Park, B., Judd, C. M., & Wittenbrink, B. (2002). The police officer's dilemma: Using ethnicity to disambiguate potentially threatening individuals. *Journal of Personality and Social Psychology, 83*, 1314–1329.

Cosmides, L. (1989). The logic of social exchange: Has natural selection shaped how humans reason? Studies with the Wason selection task. *Cognition, 31*, 187–276.

Cosmides, L., & Tooby, J. (1987). From evolution to behavior: Evolutionary psychology as the missing link. In J. Dupre (Ed.), *The latest on the best: Essays on evolution and optimality*. Cambridge, MA: MIT Press.

Costa, P. T., Jr., & McCrae, R. R. (1988). Personality in adulthood: A six year longitudinal study of self-reports and spouse ratings on the NEO Personality Inventory. *Journal of Personality and Social Psychology, 54*, 853–863.

Costa, P. T., & McCrae, R. R. (1995). Domains and facets: Hierarchical personality assessment using the Revised NEO Personality Inventory. *Journal of Personality Assessment, 64*, 21–50.

Cota, A. A., & Dion, K. L. (1986). Salience of gender and sex composition of ad hoc groups: An experimental test of the distinctiveness theory. *Journal of Personality and Social Psychology, 50*, 770–776.

Cotterell, N., Eisenberger, R., & Speicher, H. (1992). Inhibiting effects of reciprocation wariness on interpersonal relationships. *Journal of Personality and Social Psychology, 62*, 658–668.

Cottrell, N. B., Wack, D. L., Sekerak, G. J., & Rittle, R. H. (1968). Social facilitation of dominant responses by the presence of an audience and the mere presence of others. *Journal of Personality and Social Psychology, 9*, 245–250.

Cousins, S. D. (1989). Culture and self-perception in Japan and the United States. *Journal of Personality and Social Psychology, 56*, 124–131.

Crandall, C. S. (1988). Social contagion of binge eating. *Journal of Personality and Social Psychology, 55*, 588–598.

Crandall, V. C., Katkovsky, W., & Crandall, V. J. (1965). Children's beliefs in their own control of reinforcements in intellectual-academic achievement situations. *Child Development. 36*, 91–109.

Crano, W. D. (1970). Effects of sex, response order, and expertise in conformity: A dispositional approach. *Sociometry, 33*, 239–252.

Crocker, J., Hannah, D. B., & Weber, R. (1983). Person memory and causal attributions. *Journal of Personality and Social Psychology, 44*, 55–66.

Crocker, J., & Luhtanen, R. (1990). Collective self-esteem and ingroup bias. *Journal of Personality and Social Psychology, 58*, 60–67.

Crocker, J., Luhtanen, R. K., Cooper, M. L., & Bouvrette, A. (2003). Contingencies of self-worth in college students: Theory and measurement. *Journal of Personality and Social Psychology, 85*, 894–908.

Crocker, J., Major, B., & Steele, C. (1998). Social stigma. In D. T. Gilbert, S. T. Fiske, & G. Lindzey (Eds.), *The handbook of social psychology* (4th ed., Vol. 2, pp. 504–553). New York: McGraw-Hill.

Crocker, J., & Park, L. E. (2003). Seeking self-esteem: Construction, maintenance, and protection of self-worth. In M. R. Leary & J. P. Tangney (Eds.), *Handbook of self and identity* (pp. 291–313). New York: Guilford Press.

Crocker, J., & Park, L. E. (2004). The costly pursuit of self-esteem. *Psychological Bulletin, 130*, 392–414.

Crocker, J., Sommers, S. R., & Luhtanen, R. K. (2002). Hopes dashed and dreams fulfilled: Contingencies of self-worth and graduate school admissions. *Personality and Social Psychology Bulletin, 28*, 1275–1286.

Crocker, J., Voelkl, K., Testa, M., & Major, B. (1991). Social stigma: The affective consequences of attributional ambiguity. *Journal of Personality and Social Psychology, 60*, 218–228.

Crocker, J., & Wolfe, C. T. (2001). Contingencies of self-worth. *Psychological Review, 108*, 593–623.

Cronbach, L. J. (1955). Processes affecting scores on "understanding of others" and "assumed similarity." *Psychological Bulletin, 52*, 177–193.

Cronin, H. (1991). *The ant and the peacock.* New York: Cambridge University Press.

Crosby, F. (1976). A model of egoistical relative deprivation. *Psychological Review, 83*, 85–113.

Cross, H. A., Halcomb, C. G., & Matter, W. W. (1967). Imprinting or exposure learning in rats given early auditory stimulation. *Psychonomic Science, 7*, 233–234.

Cross, J. F., & Cross, J. (1971). Age, sex, race, and the perception of facial beauty. *Developmental Psychology, 5*, 433–459.

Cross, S., & Markus, H. (1991). Possible selves across the life span. *Human Development, 34*, 230–255.

Cross, S. E., & Madson, L. (1997). Models of the self: Self-construals and gender. *Psychological Bulletin, 122*, 5–37.

Crossen, C. (1994). *Tainted truth: The manipulation of fact in America.* New York: Simon and Schuster.

Croyle, R. T., & Cooper, J. (1983). Dissonance arousal: Physiological evidence. *Journal of Personality and Social Psychology, 45*, 782–791.

Cunningham, M. R. (1986). Levites and brother's keepers: A sociobiological perspective on prosocial behavior. *Humboldt Journal of Social Relations, 13*, 35–67.

Cunningham, M. R., Roberts, A. R., Barbee, A. P., Druen, P. B., & Wu, C. (1995). "Their ideas of beauty are, on the whole, the same as ours": Consistency and variability in the cross-cultural perception of female physical attractiveness. *Journal of Personality and Social Psychology, 68*, 261–279.

Cunningham, W. A., Johnson, M. K., Raye, C. L., Gatenby, J. C., Gore, J. C., & Banaji, M. R. (2004). Separable neural components in the processing of black and white faces. *Psychological Science, 15*, 806–813.

Curran, J. P., & Lippold, S. (1975). The effects of physical attractiveness and attitude similarity on attraction in dating dyads. *Journal of Personality, 43*, 528–539.

Curry, R. L. (1988). Influence of kinship on helping behavior in Galapagos mockingbirds. *Behavioral Ecology and Sociobiology, 38*, 181–192.

Curtis, R., & Miller, K. (1986). Believing another likes or dislikes you: Behaviors making the beliefs come true. *Journal of Personality and Social Psychology, 51*, 284–290.

Cutrona, C. E. (1982). Transition to college: Loneliness and the process of social adjustment. In L. A. Peplau & D. Perlman (Eds.), *Loneliness: A sourcebook of current theory, research, and therapy* (pp. 291–309). New York: Wiley.

Dabbs, J. M., Jr. (2000). *Heroes, rogues and lovers.* New York: McGraw-Hill.

Daly, M., Salmon, C., & Wilson, M. (1997). The conceptual hole in psychological studies of social cognition and close relationships. In J. A. Simpson & D. T. Kenrick (Eds.), *Evolutionary social psychology* (pp. 265–296). Hillsdale, NJ: Lawrence Erlbaum Associates.

Daly, M., & Wilson, M. I. (1982). Whom are newborn babies said to resemble? *Ethology and Sociobiology, 3*, 69–78.

Daly, M., & Wilson, M. (1983). *Sex, evolution, and behavior* (2nd ed.). Belmont, CA: Wadsworth.

Daly, M., & Wilson, M. (1988). *Homicide.* New York: De Gruyter.

Daly, M., & Wilson, M. I. (1996). Violence against stepchildren. *Current Directions in Psychological Science, 5*, 77–81.

Daly, M., Wilson, M., & Vasdev, S. (2001). Income inequality and homicide rates in Canada and the United States. *Canadian Journal of Criminology*, 219–236.

Damasio, A. R. (1994). *Descartes' error: Emotion, reason, and the human brain.* New York: Free Press.

Damasio, A. R., Tranel, D., & Damasio, H. (1990). Individuals with sociopathic behavior caused by frontal damage fail to respond autonomically to social stimuli. *Behavioral Brain Research, 41*, 81–94.

D'Andrade, R. G. (1965). Trait psychology and componential analysis. *American Anthropologist, 67*, 215–228.

Darley, J. M., & Batson, C. D. (1973). From Jerusalem to Jericho: A study of situational and dispositional variables in helping behavior. *Journal of Personality and Social Psychology, 27*, 100–119.

Darley, J. M., & Berscheid, E. (1967). Increased liking as a result of the anticipation of personal contact. *Human Relations, 20*, 29–40.

Darley, J. M., & Latané, B. (1968). Bystander intervention in emergencies: Diffusion of responsibility. *Journal of Personality and Social Psychology, 8*, 377–383.

Darley, J., & Schultz, T. (1990). Moral rules: Their content and acquisition. *Annual Review of Psychology, 41*, 525–556.

Darley, J. M., Teger, A. I., & Lewis, L. D. (1973). Do groups always inhibit individuals' responses to potential emergencies? *Journal of Personality and Social Psychology, 26*, 395–399.

Darlington, R. B., & Macker, C. E. (1966). Displacement of guilt-produced altruistic behavior. *Journal of Personality and Social Psychology, 4*, 442–443.

Darwin, C. (1871). *The descent of man, and selection in relation to sex.* London: John Murray.

Darwin, C. (1872/1998). *The expression of emotions in man and animals* (3rd ed.). New York: Oxford University Press.

Dashiell, J. F. (1930). An experimental analysis of some group effects. *Journal of Abnormal and Social Psychology, 25*, 190–199.

Davidson, A. R., & Jaccard, J. J. (1979). Variables that moderate the attitude-behavior relation: Results of a longitudinal survey. *Journal of Personality and Social Psychology, 37*, 1364–1376.

Davidson, A. R., Yantis, S., Norwood, M., & Montano, D. E. (1985). Amount of information about the attitude object and attitude-behavior consistency. *Journal of Personality and Social Psychology, 49*, 1184–1198.

Davidson, R. J., Pizzagalli, D., Nitzschke, J. B., & Kalin, N. H. (2003). Parsing the subcomponents of emotion and disorders: Perspectives from affective neuroscience. In R. J. Davidson, K. Scherer, & H. H. Goldsmith (Eds.), *Handbook of affective science* (pp. 8–24). New York: Oxford University Press.

Davis, D. (1981). Implications for interaction versus effectance as mediators of the similarity-attraction relationship. *Journal of Experimental Social Psychology, 17,* 96–116.

Davis, J. H. (1973). Group decision and social interaction: A theory of social decision schemes. *Psychological Review, 80,* 97–125.

Davis, M. H. (1980). A multidimensional approach to individual differences in empathy. *JSAS Catalog of Selected Documents in Psychology, 10,* 85.

Davis, M. H., & Franzoi, S. L. (1991). Stability and change in adolescent self-consciousness and empathy. *Journal of Research in Personality, 25,* 70–87.

Davis, M. H., & Stephan, W. G. (1980). Attributions for exam performance. *Journal of Applied Social Psychology, 10,* 235–248.

Dawes, R. M. (1980). Social dilemmas. *Annual Review of Psychology, 31,* 169–193.

Dawes, R. M. (1988). *Rational choice in an uncertain world.* San Diego: Harcourt, Brace, Jovanovich.

Dawkins, R. (1976). *The selfish gene.* Oxford, England: Oxford University Press.

Dearing, J. W., & Rogers, E. M. (1996). *Agenda-setting.* Thousand Oaks, CA: Sage.

Deaux, K., & Emswiller, T. (1974). Explanations of successful performance on sex-linked tasks: What is skill for the male is luck for the female. *Journal of Personality and Social Psychology, 29,* 80–85.

Deaux, K., Reid, A., Mizrahi, K., & Ethier, K. A. (1995). Parameters of social identity. *Journal of Personality and Social Psychology, 68,* 280–291.

Debner, J. A., & Jacoby, L. L. (1994). Unconscious perception: Attention, awareness, and control. *Journal of Experimental Psychology: Learning, Memory and Cognition, 20,* 304–317.

Deci, E. L., & Ryan, R. M. (1985). *Intrinsic motivation and self-determination in human behavior.* New York: Plenum Press.

Delespaul, P., Reis, H. T., & DeVries, P. (1996). *Comparison of event-based and experience sampling diaries.* Rijksuniversiteit Limburg, The Netherlands: Department of Social Psychiatry.

Denes-Raj, V., & Epstein, S. (1994). Conflict between intuitive and rational processing: When people behave against their better judgment. *Journal of Personality and Social Psychology, 66,* 819–829.

DePaulo, B. M., & Friedman, H. S. (1998). Nonverbal communication. In D. T. Gilbert, S. T. Fiske, & G. Lindzey (Eds.), *Handbook of social psychology* (4th ed., Vol. 2, pp. 3–40). New York: McGraw-Hill.

DePaulo, B. M., Lanier, K., & Davis, T. (1983). Detecting the deceit of the motivated liar. *Journal of Personality and Social Psychology, 43,* 1096–1103.

Deppe, R. K., & Harackiewicz, J. M. (1996). Self-handicapping and intrinsic motivation: Buffering intrinsic motivation from the threat of failure. *Journal of Personality and Social Psychology, 70,* 868–876.

DePue, R. A. (1995). Neurobiological factors in personality and depression. *European Journal of Personality, 9,* 413–439.

Dermer, M., & Theil, D. (1975). When beauty may fail. *Journal of Personality and Social Psychology, 31,* 1168–1177.

DeSteno, D., Petty, R., Wegener, D., & Rucker, D. (2000). Beyond valence in the perception of likelihood: The role of emotion specificity. *Journal of Personality and Social Psychology, 78,* 397–416.

DeSteno, D. A., & Salovey, P. (1996). Jealousy and the characteristics of one's rival: A self-evaluation maintenance perspective. *Personality and Social Psychology, 22,* 920–932.

Deutsch, M. (1975). Equity, equality, and need: What determines which value will be used as a basis for distributive justice? *Journal of Social Issues, 31,* 137–149.

Deutsch, M., & Gerard, H. B. (1955). A study of normative and informational social influence upon individual judgment. *Journal of Abnormal and Social Psychology, 51,* 629–636.

Deutsch, R. M. (1977). *The new nuts among the berries: How nutrition nonsense captured America.* Palo Alto, CA: Ball Publishing.

Devine, P. G. (1989a). Automatic and controlled processes in prejudice: The roles of stereotypes and personal beliefs. In A. R. Pratkanis, S. J. Breckler, & A. G. Greenwald (Eds.), *Attitude structure and function.* Hillsdale, NJ: Lawrence Erlbaum Associates.

Devine, P. G. (1989b). Stereotypes and prejudice: Their automatic and controlled components. *Journal of Personality and Social Psychology, 56,* 5–18.

Devine, P. G., & Baker, S. M. (1991). Measurement of racial stereotype subtyping. *Personality and Social Psychology Bulletin, 17,* 44–50.

Devine, P. G., & Monteith, M. J. (1999). Automaticity and control in stereotyping. In S. Chaiken & Y. Trope (Eds.), *Dual process theories in social psychology* (pp. 339–360). New York: Guilford Press.

Devine, P. G., Monteith, M. J., Zuwerink, J. R., & Elliot, A. J. (1991). Prejudice with and without compunction. *Journal of Personality and Social Psychology, 60,* 817–830.

Devine, P. G., Plant, E. A., Amodio, D. M., Harmon-Jones, E., & Vance, S. L. (2002). Exploring the relationship between implicit and explicit prejudice: The role of motivations to respond without prejudice. *Journal of Personality and Social Psychology, 82,* 835–848.

de Waal, F. B. M. (1986). The integration of dominance and social bonding in primates. *Quarterly Review of Biology, 61,* 459–479.

de Waal, F. B. M. (1996). *Good natured: The origins of right and wrong in humans and other animals.* Cambridge, MA: Harvard University Press.

de Waal, F. B. M., & van Roosmalen, A. (1979). Reconciliation and consolation among chimpanzees. *Behavioral Ecology and Sociobiology, 5,* 55–66.

Dhawan, N., Roseman, I. J., Naidu, R. K., Thapa, K., & Rettek, S. I. (1995). Self-concepts across two cultures: India and the United States. *Journal of Cross-Cultural Psychology, 26,* 606–621.

Diamond, L. M. (2003). What does sexual orientation orient? A biobehavioral model distinguishing romantic love and sexual desire. *Psychological Review, 110,* 173–192.

Diener, E. (1980). Deindividuation: The absence of self-awareness and self-regulation in group members. In P. Paulus (Ed.), *The psychology of group influence* (pp. 209–242). Hillsdale, NJ: Lawrence Erlbaum Associates.

Diener, E. (1984). Subjective well-being. *Psychological Bulletin, 95,* 542–575.

Diener, E. (2000). Subjective well-being: The science of happiness, and some policy implications. *American Psychologist, 55,* 34–43.

Diener, E., Fraser, S. C., Beaman, A. L., & Kelem, R. T. (1976).

Effects of deindividuation variables on stealing among Halloween trick-or-treaters. *Journal of Personality and Social Psychology, 33,* 178–183.

Diener, E., Larsen, R. J., & Emmons, R. A. (1984). Person X situation interactions: Choice of situations and congruence response models. *Journal of Personality and Social Psychology, 47,* 580–592.

Diener, E., Oishi, S., & Lucas, R. E. (2003). Personality, culture, and subjective well-being: Emotional and cognitive evaluations of life. *Annual Review of Psychology, 54,* 403–425.

Diener, E., & Wallbom, M. (1976). Effects of self-awareness on antinormative behavior. *Journal of Research in Personality, 10,* 107–111.

Diener, E., Wolsic, B., & Fujita, F. (1995). Physical attractiveness and subjective well-being. *Journal of Personality and Social Psychology, 69,* 207–213.

Dienstbier, R. A., & Munter, P. O. (1971). Cheating as a function of the labeling of natural arousal. *Journal of Personality and Social Psychology, 17,* 208–213.

Dijksterhuis, A., Aarts, H., Bargh, J. A., & Van Knippenberg, A. (2000). On the relation between associative strength and automatic behavior. *Journal of Experimental Social Psychology, 36,* 531–544.

Dijksterhuis, A., Aarts, H., & Smith, P. K. (2005). The power of the subliminal: On subliminal persuasion and other potential applications. In R. R. Hassin, J. S. Uleman, & J. A. Bargh (Eds.), *The new unconscious.* New York: Oxford University Press.

Dijksterhuis, A., Spears, R., Postmes, T., Stapel, D. A., Koomen, W., van Knippenberg, A., et al. (1998). Seeing one thing and doing another: Contrast effects in automatic behavior. *Journal of Personality and Social Psychology, 75,* 862–871.

Dijksterhuis, A., & van Knippenberg, A. (1998). The relation between perception and behavior, or how to win a game of Trivial Pursuit. *Journal of Personality and Social Psychology, 74,* 865–877.

Dimberg, U., & Öhman, A. (1996). Behold the wrath: Psychophysiological responses to facial stimuli. *Motivation and Emotion, 20,* 149–182.

Dion, K. K. (1972). Physical attractiveness and evaluation of children's transgressions. *Journal of Personality and Social Psychology, 24,* 207–213.

Dion, K. K. (1973). Young children's stereotyping of facial attractiveness. *Developmental Psychology, 9,* 183–188.

Dion, K. K., & Berscheid, E. (1974). Physical attractiveness and peer perception among children. *Sociometry, 37,* 1–12.

Dion, K. K., Berscheid, E., & Walster, E. (1972). What is a beautiful good. *Journal of Personality and Social Psychology, 24,* 285–290.

Ditto, P. H., Jemmott, J. B., & Darley, J. M. (1988). Appraising the threat of illness: A mental representational approach. *Health Psychology, 7,* 183–200.

Ditto, P. H., & Lopez, D. F. (1992). Motivated skepticism: Use of differential decision criteria for preferred and nonpreferred conclusions. *Journal of Personality and Social Psychology, 63,* 568–584.

Dodge, K. A., & Schwartz, D. (1997). Social information mechanisms in aggressive behavior. In D. M. Stoff & J. Breiling (Eds.), *Handbook of antisocial behavior* (pp. 171–180). New York: Wiley.

Dollard, J., Doob, L. W., Miller, N. E., Mowrer, H. H., & Sears, R. (1939). *Frustration and aggression.* New Haven: Yale University Press.

Domhoff, G. W. (1998). *Who rules America.* Mountain View, CA: Mayfield Publishing.

Donnellan, M. B., Trzesniewski, K. H., Robins, R. W., Moffitt, T. E., & Caspi, A. (2005). Low self-esteem is related to aggression, antisocial behavior, and delinquency. *Psychological Science, 16,* 328–335.

Donnerstein, E. (1980). Aggressive erotica and violence against women. *Journal of Personality and Social Psychology, 39,* 269–277.

Donnerstein, E., & Berkowitz, L. (1981). Victim reactions in aggressive erotic films as a factor in violence against women. *Journal of Personality and Social Psychology, 41,* 710–724.

Doob, A. N., & MacDonald, G. E. (1979). Television and fear of victimization: Is the relationship causal? *Journal of Personality and Social Psychology, 37,* 170–179.

Doris, J. M. (2002). *Lack of character: Personality and moral behavior.* New York: Cambridge University Press.

Dornbusch, S. M., Hastorff, A. H., Richardson, S. A., Muzzy, R. E., & Vreeland, R. S. (1965). The perceiver and the perceived: Their relative influence on the categories of interpersonal cognition. *Journal of Personality and Social Psychology, 1,* 434–440.

Dovidio, J. F. (1984). Helping behavior and altruism: An empirical and conceptual overview. In L. Berkowitz (Ed.), *Advances in experimental social psychology* (pp. 361–427). New York: Academic Press.

Dovidio, J. F., Brown, C. E., Heltman, K., Ellyson, S. L., & Keating, C. F. (1988). Power displays between women and men in discussions of gender-linked tasks: A multichannel study. *Journal of Personality and Social Psychology, 55,* 580–587.

Dovidio, J. F., Ellyson, S. L., Keating, C. F., Heltman, K., & Brown, C. E. (1988). The relationship of social power to visual displays of dominance between men and women. *Journal of Personality and Social Psychology, 54,* 233–242.

Dovidio, J. F., & Gaertner, S. L. (1981). The effects of race, status, ability on helping behavior. *Social Psychology Quarterly, 44,* 192–203.

Dovidio, J. F., Kawakami, K., & Gaertner, S. L. (2002). Implicit and explicit prejudice and interracial interaction. *Journal of Personality and Social Psychology, 82,* 62–68.

Downey, G., & Feldman, S. (1996). Implications of rejection sensitivity for intimate relationships. *Journal of Personality and Social Psychology, 70,* 1327–1343.

Downey, G., Feldman, S., & Ayduk, O. (2000). Rejection sensitivity and male violence in romantic relationships. *Personal Relationships, 7,* 45–61.

Downey, G., Freitas, A. L., Michaelis, B., & Khouri, H. (1998). The self-fulfilling prophecy in close relationships: Rejection sensitivity and rejection by romantic partners. *Journal of Personality and Social Psychology, 75,* 545–560.

Downey, G., Lebolt, A., Rincon, C., & Freitas, A. L. (1998). Rejection sensitivity and children's interpersonal difficulties. *Child Development, 69,* 1072–1089.

Downing, C. J., Sternberg, R. J., & Ross, B. H. (1985). Multicausal inference: Evaluation of evidence in causally complex situations. *Journal of Experimental Psychology: General, 114,* 239–263.

Downing, J. W., Judd, C. M., & Brauer, M. (1992). Effects of repeated expression of attitudes on attitude extremity. *Journal of Personality and Social Psychology, 63,* 17–29.

Draine, S. C., & Greenwald, A. G. (1998). Replicable unconscious semantic priming. *Journal of Experimental Psychology: General, 127,* 286–303.

Druckman, D. (1967). Dogmatism, prenegotiation experience, and simulated group representation as determinants of dyadic behavior in a bargaining situation. *Journal of Personality and Social Psychology, 6,* 276–290.

Duck, J. M., & Mullin, B. (1995). The perceived impact of the mass media: Reconsidering the third-person effect. *European Journal of Social Psychology, 25,* 77–93.

Duck, S. (1997). *Handbook of personal relationships: Theory, research, and interventions* (2nd ed.). Chichester, England: Wiley.

Duncan, B. L. (1976). Differential social perception and attribution on intergroup violence: Testing the lower limits of stereotyping of blacks. *Journal of Personality and Social Psychology, 34,* 590–598.

Dunn, J., & Herrera, C. (1997). Conflict resolution with friends, siblings and mothers: A developmental perspective. *Aggressive Behavior, 23,* 343–357.

Dunn, J., & Munn, P. (1985). Becoming a family member: Family conflict and the development of social understanding in the second year. *Child Development, 56,* 480–492.

Dunning, D., & Cohen, G. L. (1992). Egocentric definitions of traits and abilities in social judgment. *Journal of Personality and Social Psychology, 63,* 341–355.

Dunning, D., Meyerowitz, J. A., & Holzberg, A. (1989). Ambiguity and self-evaluation: The role of idiosyncratic trait definitions in self-serving assessments of ability. *Journal of Personality and Social Psychology, 57,* 1082–1090.

Dunning, D., Perie, M., & Story, A. L. (1991). Self-serving prototypes of social categories. *Journal of Personality and Social Psychology, 61,* 957–968.

Dutton, D. G., & Aron, A. P. (1974). Some evidence for heightened sexual attraction under conditions of high anxiety. *Journal of Personality and Social Psychology, 30,* 510–517.

Duval, T. S., & Lalwani, N. (1999). Objective self-awareness and causal attributions for self-standard discrepancies: Changing self or changing standards of correctness. *Personality and Social Psychology Bulletin, 25,* 1220–1229.

Duval, T. S., & Wicklund, R. A. (1972). *A theory of objective self-awareness.* New York: Academic Press.

Dweck, C. S. (1975). The role of expectations and attributions in the alleviation of learned helplessness. *Journal of Personality and Social Psychology, 31,* 674–685.

Dweck, C. S. (1999). *Self-theories: Their role in motivation, personality and development.* Philadelphia: Taylor and Francis/Psychology Press.

Dweck, C. S., Chiu, C., & Hong, Y. (1995). Implicit theories and their role in judgments and reactions: A world from two perspectives. *Psychological Inquiry, 6,* 267–285.

Dweck, C. S., Davidson, W., Nelson, S., & Enna, B. (1978). Sex differences in learned helplessness: (II) The contingencies of evaluative feedback in the classroom and (III) An experimental analysis. *Developmental Psychology, 14,* 268–276.

Dweck, C. S., Hong, Y.Y., & Chiu, C.Y. (1993). Implicit theories and individual differences in the likelihood and meaning of dispositional inference. *Personality and Social Psychology Bulletin, 19,* 644–656.

Dweck, C. S., & Reppucci, N. D. (1973). Learned helplessness and reinforcement responsibility in children. *Journal of Personality and Social Psychology, 25,* 109–116.

Eagly, A. H. (1978). Sex differences influenceability. *Psychological Bulletin, 85,* 86–116.

Eagly, A. H. (1987). *Sex differences in social behavior: A social-role interpretation.* Hillsdale, NJ: Lawrence Erlbaum Associates.

Eagly, A. H., Ashmore, R. D., Makhijani, M. G., & Longo, L. C. (1991). What is beautiful is good, but ... : A meta-analytic review of research on the physical attractiveness stereotype. *Psychological Bulletin, 110,* 109–128.

Eagly, A. H., & Carli, L. L. (1981). Sex of researchers and sex-typed communications as determinants of sex differences in influenceability: A meta-analysis of social influence studies. *Psychological Bulletin, 110,* 109–128.

Eagly, A. H., & Chaiken, S. (1993). *The psychology of attitudes.* Fort Worth, TX: Harcourt Brace & Company.

Eagly, A. H., & Chaiken, S. (1998). Attitude structure and function. In D. T. Gilbert, S. T. Fiske, & G. Lindzey (Eds.), *Handbook of social psychology* (4th ed., Vol. 1, pp. 269–322). New York: McGraw-Hill.

Eagly, A. H., & Wood, W. (1999). The origins of sex differences in human behavior: Evolved dispositions vs. social roles. *American Psychologist, 54,* 408–423.

Ebbesen, E. B., Kjos, G. L., & Konecni, V. (1976). Spatial ecology: Its effects on the choice of friends and enemies. *Journal of Experimental Social Psychology, 12,* 505–518.

Eckland, B. (1968). Theories of mate selection. *Social Biology, 15,* 71–84.

Efran, M. G. (1974). The effect of physical appearance on judgments of guilt, interpersonal attractiveness, and severity of recommended punishment in a simulated jury task. *Journal of Research in Personality, 8,* 45–54.

Eibach, R. P., Libby, L. K., & Gilovich, T. (2003). When change in the self is mistaken for change in the world. *Journal of Personality and Social Psychology, 84,* 917–931.

Eibl-Eibesfeldt, I. (1989). *Human ethology.* New York: Aldine de Gruyter Press.

Eisenberg, N., Fabes, R. A., Miller, P. A., Fultz, J., Shell, R., Mathy, R. M., et al. (1989). Relation of sympathy and distress to prosocial behavior: A multimethod study. *Journal of Personality and Social Psychology, 57,* 55–66.

Eisenberg, N., & Lennon, R. (1983). Sex differences in empathy and related capacities. *Psychological Bulletin, 94,* 100–131.

Ekman, P. (1984). Expression and the nature of emotion. In K. Scherer & P. Ekman (Eds.), *Approaches to emotion.* Hillsdale, NJ: Lawrence Erlbaum Associates.

Ekman, P. (1992a). An argument for basic emotions. *Cognition and Emotion, 6,* 169–200.

Ekman, P. (1992b). *Telling lies: Clues to deceit in the marketplace, marriage, and politics* (reissue ed.). New York: Norton.

Ekman, P. (1993). Facial expression and emotion. *American Psychologist, 48,* 384–392.

Ekman, P. (2001). *Telling lies: Clues to deceit in the marketplace, marriage, and politics* (2nd rev. ed.). New York: Norton.

Ekman, P., & Davidson, R. J. (1993). Voluntary smiling changes regional brain activity. *Psychological Science, 4,* 342–345.

Ekman, P., Davidson, R. J., & Friesen, W. V. (1990). The Duchenne smile: Emotional expression and brain physiology II. *Journal of Personality and Social Psychology, 58,* 342–353.

Ekman, P., & Friesen, W. V. (1969). The repertoire of nonverbal behavior: Categories, origins, usage, and coding. *Semiotica, 1*, 49–98.

Ekman, P., & Friesen, W. V. (1971). Constants across cultures in the face and emotion. *Journal of Personality and Social Psychology, 17*, 124–129.

Ekman, P., & Friesen, W. V. (1982). Felt, false, and miserable smiles. *Journal of Nonverbal Behavior, 6*, 238–252.

Ekman, P., Friesen, W. V., & Ellsworth, P. C. (1982a). *Emotion in the human face.* Cambridge, England: Cambridge University Press.

Ekman, P., Friesen, W. V., & Ellsworth, P. C. (1982b). What are the similarities and differences in facial behavior across cultures? In P. Ekman (Ed.), *Emotion in the human face.* Cambridge, England: Cambridge University Press.

Ekman, P., & O'Sullivan, M. (1991). Who can catch a liar? *American Psychologist, 46*, 913–920.

Ekman, P., O'Sullivan, M., & Matsumoto, D. (1991). Contradictions in the study of contempt: What's it all about? *Motivation and Emotion, 15*, 293–296.

Ekman, P., & Rosenberg, E. L. (1997). *What the face reveals.* New York: Oxford University Press.

Ekman, P., Sorenson, E. R., & Friesen, W. V. (1969). Pan cultural elements in facial displays of emotions. *Science, 164*, 86–88.

Elfenbein, H. A., & Ambady, N. (2002a). Is there an ingroup advantage in emotion recognition. *Psychological Bulletin, 128*, 243–249.

Elfenbein, H. A., & Ambady, N. (2002b). On the universality and cultural specificity of emotion recognition: A meta-analysis. *Psychological Bulletin, 128*, 203–235.

Elfenbein, H. A., & Ambady, N. (2003). Universals and cultural differences in recognizing emotions. *Current Directions in Psychological Science, 12*, 159–164.

Elkin, R. A., & Leippe, M. R. (1986). Physiological arousal, dissonance, and attitude change: Evidence for a dissonance-arousal link and a "don't remind me" effect. *Journal of Personality and Social Psychology, 51*, 55–65.

Elliot, A. J., & Devine, P. G. (1994). On the motivational nature of cognitive dissonance: Dissonance as psychological discomfort. *Journal of Personality and Social Psychology, 67*, 382–394.

Ellis, B. (1992). The evolution of sexual attraction: Evaluative mechanisms in women. In J. H. Barkow, L. Cosmides, & J. Tooby (Eds.), *The adapted mind* (pp. 267–288). New York: Oxford University Press.

Ellis, B. J., & Malamuth, N. M. (2000). Love and anger in romantic relationships: A discrete systems model. *Journal of Personality, 68*, 525–556.

Ellsworth, P. C. (1994). Sense, culture and sensibility. In S. Kitayama & H. R. Markus (Eds.), *Emotion and culture.* Washington, DC: American Psychological Association.

Ellsworth, P. C., & Scherer, K. (2003). Appraisal processes in emotion. In R. J. Davidson, K. Scherer, & H. H. Goldsmith (Eds.), *Handbook of affective science* (pp. 572–595). New York: Oxford University Press.

Ellyson, S. L., & Dovidio, J. F. (Eds.). (1985). *Power, dominance, and nonverbal behavior.* New York: Springer-Verlag.

Elms, A. C., & Milgram, S. (1966). Personality characteristics associated with obedience and defiance toward authoritative command. *Journal of Experimental Research in Personality, 1*, 282–289.

Emlen, S. T. (1997). The evolutionary study of human family systems. *Social Science Information, 36*, 563–589.

Emmons, R. A., McCullough, M. E., & Tsang, J. (2003). Counting blessings versus burdens: An experimental investigation of gratitude and subjective well-being in daily life. *Journal of Personality and Social Psychology, 84*, 377–389.

Epley, N., & Gilovich, T. (2001). Putting adjustment back in the anchoring and adjustment heuristic: Divergent processing of self-generated and experimenter-provided anchors. *Psychological Science, 12*, 391–396.

Epley, N., & Gilovich, T. (2004). Are adjustments insufficient? *Personality and Social Psychology Bulletin, 30*, 447–460.

Epley, N., Savitsky, K., & Gilovich, T. (2002). Empathy neglect: Reconciling the spotlight effect and the correspondence bias. *Journal of Personality and Social Psychology, 83*, 300–312.

Epstein, S. (1991). Cognitive-experiential self-theory: An integrative theory of personality. In R. Curtis (Ed.), *The self with others: Convergences in psychoanalytic, social, and personality psychology* (pp. 111–137). New York: Guilford Press.

Esser, J. K. (1998). Alive and well after 25 years: A review of groupthink research. *Organizational Behavior and Human Decision Processes, 73*, 116–141.

Esser, J. K., & Lindoerfer, J. S. (1989). Groupthink and the space shuttle *Challenger* accident: Toward a quantitative case analysis. *Journal of Behavioral Decision Making, 2*, 167–177.

Essock-Vitale, S. M., & McGuire, M. T. (1985). Women's lives viewed from an evolutionary perspective II. Patterns of helping. *Ethology and Sociobiology, 6*, 155–173.

Ettinger, R. F., Marino, C. J., Endler, N. S., Geller, S. H., & Natziuk, T. (1971). Effects of agreement and correctness on relative competence and conformity. *Journal of Personality and Social Psychology, 19*, 204–212.

Evans, R. (1980). *The making of social psychology.* New York: Gardner Press.

Eysenck, H. J. (1987). Arousal and personality: The origins of a theory. In J. Strelau & H. J. Eysenck (Eds.), *Personality dimensions and arousal* (pp. 1–13). New York: Plenum Press.

Fallon, A. (1990). Culture in the mirror: Sociocultural determinants of body image. In T. F. Cash & T. Pruzinsky (Eds.), *Body images: Development, deviance, and change* (pp. 80–109). New York: Guilford Press.

Fallon, A. E., & Rozin, P. (1985). Sex differences in perceptions of desirable body shape. *Journal of Abnormal Psychology, 94*, 102–105.

Farber, P. D., Khavari, K. A., & Douglass, F. M., IV. (1980). A factor analytic study of reasons for drinking: Empirical validation of positive and negative reinforcement dimensions. *Journal of Consulting and Clinical Psychology, 48*, 780–781.

Farley, F. (1986, May). The big T in personality. *Psychology Today*, pp. 44–52.

Fazio, R. H. (1995). Attitudes as object-evaluation associations: Determinants, consequences, and correlates of attitude accessibility. In R. E. Petty & J. A. Krosnick (Eds.), *Attitude strength: Antecedents and consequences* (pp. 247–282). Mahway, NJ: Lawrence Erlbaum Associates.

Fazio, R. H., & Hilden, L. E. (2001). Emotional reactions to a seemingly prejudiced response: The role of automatically-activated racial attitudes and motivation to control prejudiced reactions. *Personality and Social Psychology Bulletin, 27*, 538–549.

Fazio, R. H., Jackson, J. R., Dunton, B. C., & Williams, C. J. (1995). Variability in automatic activation as an unobtrusive measure of racial attitudes: A bona fide pipeline? *Journal of Personality and Social Psychology, 69,* 1013–1027.

Fazio, R. H., Sanbonmatsu, D. M., Powell, M. C., & Kardes, F. R. (1986). On the automatic activation of attitudes. *Journal of Personality and Social Psychology, 50,* 229–238.

Fazio, R. H., & Williams, C. J. (1986). Attitude accessibility as a moderator of the attitude-perception and attitude-behavior relations: An investigation of the 1984 presidential election. *Journal of Personality and Social Psychology, 51,* 505–514.

Fazio, R. H., & Zanna, M. P. (1978). Attitudinal qualities relating to the strength of the attitude-behavior relationship. *Journal of Experimental Social Psychology, 14,* 398–408.

Feeney, B. C., & Collins, N. L. (2001). Predictors of caregiving in adult intimate relationships: An attachment theoretical perspective. *Journal of Personality and Social Psychology, 80,* 972–994.

Fehr, B. (1994). Prototype based assessment of laypeoples' views of love. *Personal Relationships, 1,* 309–331.

Fehr, B. (1996). *Friendship processes.* Thousand Oaks, CA: Sage.

Fehr, B., & Russell, J. A. (1991). The concept of love viewed from a prototype perspective. *Journal of Personality & Social Psychology, 60,* 425–438.

Fehr, E., & Schmidt, K. M. (1999). A theory of fairness, competition, and cooperation. *Quarterly Journal of Economics, 114,* 817–868.

Feigenson, N., Park, J., & Salovey, P. (2001). The role of emotions in comparative negligence judgments. *Journal of Applied Social Psychology, 31,* 576–603.

Fein, S., & Spencer, S. (1997). Prejudice as a self-esteem maintenance: Affirming the self through derogating others. *Journal of Personality and Social Psychology, 73,* 31–44.

Feingold, A. (1984). Correlates of physical attractiveness among college students. *Journal of Social Psychology, 122,* 139–140.

Feingold, A. (1990). Gender differences in effects of physical attractiveness on romantic attraction: A comparison across five research paradigms. *Journal of Personality and Social Psychology, 59,* 981–993.

Feingold, A. (1992a). Gender differences in mate selection preferences: A test of the parental investment model. *Psychological Bulletin, 112,* 125–139.

Feingold, A. (1992b). Good looking people are not what we think. *Psychological Bulletin, 111,* 304–341.

Feldman-Barrett, L., & Russell, J. A. (1999). Structure of current affect. *Current Directions in Psychological Science, 8,* 10–14.

Fenigstein, A. (1984). Self-consciousness and the overperception of self as target. *Journal of Personality and Social Psychology, 47,* 860–870.

Fenigstein, A., Scheier, M. F., & Buss, A. H. (1975). Public and private self-consciousness: Assessment and theory. *Journal of Consulting and Clinical Psychology, 43,* 522–527.

Ferguson, M. J., Bargh, J. A., & Nayak, D. (2005). After-affects: How automatic evaluations influence the interpretation of subsequent, unrelated stimuli. *Journal of Experimental Social Psychology, 41,* 182–191.

Festinger, L. (1954). A theory of social comparison processes. *Human Relations, 7,* 117–140.

Festinger, L. (1957). *A theory of cognitive dissonance.* Stanford: Stanford University Press.

Festinger, L. (1964). *Conflict, decision, and dissonance.* Stanford: Stanford University Press.

Festinger, L., & Carlsmith, J. M. (1959). Cognitive consequences of forced compliance. *Journal of Abnormal and Social Psychology, 47,* 382–389.

Festinger, L., Pepitone, A., & Newcomb, T. (1952). Some consequences of deindividuation in a group. *Journal of Abnormal and Social Psychology, 47,* 382–389.

Festinger, L., Riecken, H. W., & Schachter, S. (1956). *When prophecy fails.* Minneapolis: University of Minnesota Press.

Festinger, L., Schachter, S., & Back, K. (1950). *Social pressures in informal groups.* Stanford: Stanford University Press.

Fiedler, K. (2000). Illusory correlations: A simple associative algorithm provides a convergent account of seemingly divergent paradigms. *Review of General Psychology, 4,* 25–58.

Fiedler, K. (2001). Affective states trigger processes of assimilation and accommodation. In L. L. Martin & G. L. Clore (Eds.), *Theories of mood and cognition: A user's guidebook.* Mahwah, NJ: Lawrence Erlbaum Associates.

Fiedler, K., Walther, E., & Nickel, S. (1999). Covariation-based attribution: On the ability to assess multiple covariations of an effect. *Personality and Social Psychology Bulletin, 25,* 607–622.

Field, T. (1995). Infants of depressed mothers. *Infant Behavior and Development, 18,* 1–13.

Fincham, F. D. (1985). Attribution processes in distressed and nondistressed couples: 2. Responsibility for marital problems. *Journal of Abnormal Psychology, 94,* 183–190.

Fincham, F. D. (2003). Marital conflict: Correlates, structure, and context. *Current Directions in Psychological Science, 12,* 23–27.

Fincham, F. D., & Bradbury, T. N. (1993). Marital satisfaction, depression, and attributions: A longitudinal analysis. *Journal of Personality and Social Psychology, 64,* 442–452.

Fincham, F. D., Bradbury, T. N., Arias, I., Byrne, C. A., & Karney, B. R. (1997). Marital violence, marital distress, and attributions. *Journal of Family Psychology, 11,* 367–372.

Finkel, E. J., Rusbult, C. E., Kumashiro, M., & Hannon, P. A. (2002). Dealing with betrayal in close relationships: Does commitment promote forgiveness? *Journal of Personality and Social Psychology, 82,* 956–974.

Fishbein, M., & Ajzen, I. (1975). *Belief, attitude, intention, and behavior: An introduction to theory and research.* Reading, MA: Addison-Wesley.

Fisher, H. (1992). *Anatomy of love.* New York: Fawcett Columbine.

Fiske, A. P. (1991a). *Cultural relativity of selfish individualism: Anthropological evidence that humans are inherently sociable.* Beverly Hills: Sage.

Fiske, A. P. (1991b). *Structures of social life: The four elementary forms of human relations.* New York: Free Press.

Fiske, A. P. (1992). The four elementary forms of sociality: Framework for a unified theory of social relations. *Psychological Review, 99,* 689–723.

Fiske, A. P. (1993). Social errors in four cultures: Evidence about the universal forms of social relations. *Journal of Cross-Cultural Psychology, 24,* 463–494.

Fiske, A. P., Kitayama, S., Markus, H. R., & Nisbett, R. E. (1998). The cultural matrix of social psychology. In D. T. Gilbert, S. T. Fiske, & G. Lindzey (Eds.), *Handbook of social psychology* (4th ed., pp. 915–981). New York: McGraw-Hill.

Fiske, S. T. (1993). Controlling other people: The impact of power on stereotyping. *American Psychologist, 48(6),* 621–628.

Fiske, S. T., & Neuberg, S. E. (1990). A continuum of impression formation, from category-based to individuating processes: Influences of information and motivation on attention and interpretation. In M. P. Zanna (Ed.), *Advances in experimental social psychology* (Vol. 23, pp. 1–74). San Diego: Academic Press.

Fiske, S. T., & Taylor, S. E. (1991). *Social cognition.* New York: McGraw-Hill.

Fivush, R. (1989). Exploring sex differences in the emotional content of mother-child conversations about the past. *Sex Roles, 20,* 675–691.

Fivush, R. (1992). Gender differences in parent-child conversations about past emotions. *Sex Roles, 27,* 683–698.

Fleming, J. H., & Darley, J. M. (1989). Perceiving choice and constraint: The effects of contextual and behavioral cues on attitude attribution. *Journal of Personality and Social Psychology, 56,* 27–40.

Florian, V., Mikulincer, M., & Bucholtz, I. (1995). Effects of adult attachment style on the perception and search for social support. *Journal of Psychology, 126,* 665–676.

Fodor, J. (1983). *The modularity of mind.* Cambridge, MA: MIT Press.

Folger, R. (1977). Distributive and procedural justice: Combined impact of "voice" and improvement on experienced inequity. *Journal of Personality and Social Psychology, 35,* 108–119.

Folkes, V. S. (1982). Forming relationships and the matching hypothesis. *Personality and Social Psychology Bulletin, 8,* 631–636.

Ford, C. S., & Beach, F. A. (1951). *Patterns of sexual behavior.* New York: Harper & Row.

Ford, T. E., & Kruglanski, A. (1995). Effects of epistemic motivations on the use of momentarily accessible constructs in social judgment. *Personality and Social Psychology Bulletin, 21,* 950–962.

Ford, T. E., & Thompson, E. P. (2000). Preconscious and postconscious processes underlying construct accessibility effects: An extended search model. *Personality and Social Psychology Review, 4,* 317–336.

Forgas, J. P. (1992). Mood and the perception of unusual people: Affective asymmetry in memory and social judgments. *European Journal of Social Psychology, 22,* 531–547.

Forgas, J. P. (1995). Mood and judgment: The affect infusion model (AIM). *Psychological Bulletin, 117(1),* 39–66.

Forgas, J. P. (1998a). Asking nicely? Mood effects on responding to more or less polite requests. *Personality and Social Psychology Bulletin, 24,* 173–185.

Forgas, J. P. (1998b). On being happy and mistaken: Mood effects on the fundamental attribution error. *Journal of Personality and Social Psychology, 75(2),* 318–331.

Forgas, J. P. (1998c). On feeling good and getting your way: Mood effects on negotiation strategies and outcomes. *Journal of Personality and Social Psychology, 74,* 565–574.

Forgas, J. P. (2003). Affective influences on attitudes and judgments. In R. J. Davidson, K. R. Scherer, & H. H. Goldsmith (Eds.), *Handbook of affective sciences* (pp. 596–618). New York: Oxford University Press.

Forgas, J. P., & Bower, G. H. (1987). Mood effects on person perception judgments. *Journal of Personality and Social Psychology, 53,* 53–60.

Forster, J., & Strack, F. (1996). Influence of overt head movements on memory for valenced words: A case of conceptual-motor compatibility. *Journal of Personality and Social Psychology, 71,* 421–430.

Forsterling, F. (1985). Attributional retraining: A review. *Psychological Bulletin, 98,* 495–512.

Forsterling, F. (1989). Models of covariation and attribution: How do they relate to the analogy of analysis of variance? *Journal of Personality and Social Psychology, 57,* 615–625.

Foushee, M. C. (1984). Dyads and triads at 35,000 feet. *American Psychologist, 39,* 885–893.

Fox, J. A., & Pierce, G. L. (1987). *Supplementary homicide reports 1976–1986 (machine-readable data file).* Ann Arbor, Michigan.

Fraley, R. C., & Shaver, P. R. (1998). Airport separations: A naturalistic study of adult attachment dynamics in separating couples. *Journal of Personality and Social Psychology, 75,* 1198–1212.

Fraley, R. C., & Spieker, S. J. (2003). Are infant attachment patterns continuously or categorically distributed? A taxometric analysis of strange situation behavior. *Developmental Psychology, 34,* 387–404.

Frank, M. G., & Ekman, P. (1997). The ability to detect deceit generalizes across different types of high stake lies. *Journal of Personality and Social Psychology, 72,* 1429–1439.

Frank, M. G., Ekman, P., & Friesen, W. V. (1993). Behavioral markers and recognizability of the smile of enjoyment. *Journal of Personality and Social Psychology, 64,* 83–93.

Frank, M. G., & Gilovich, T. (1988). The dark side of self and social perception: Black uniforms and aggression in professional sports. *Journal of Personality and Social Psychology, 54,* 74–85.

Frank, M. G., & Stennett, J. (2001). The forced-choice paradigm and the perception of facial expressions of emotion. *Journal of Personality and Social Psychology, 80,* 75–85.

Frank, R. H. (1988). *Passions within reason.* New York: Norton.

Frank, R. H., Gilovich, T., & Regan, D. T. (1993a). The evolution of one-shot cooperation: An experiment. *Ethology and Sociobiology, 14,* 247–256.

Frank, R. H., Gilovich, T., & Regan, D. T. (1993b). Does studying economics inhibit cooperation? *Journal of Economic Perspectives, 7,* 159–171.

Fredrickson, B. L., & Roberts, T. (1997). Objectification theory: Toward understanding women's lived experiences and mental health risks. *Psychology of Women Quarterly, 21,* 173–206.

Fredrickson, B. L. (1998). What good are positive emotions? *Review of General Psychology, 2,* 300–319.

Fredrickson, B. L., & Kahneman, D. (1993). Duration neglect in retrospective evaluations of affective episodes. *Journal of Personality and Social Psychology, 65,* 45–55.

Freedman, J. L. (1965). Long-term behavioral effects of cognitive dissonance. *Journal of Experimental Social Psychology, 1,* 145–155.

Freedman, J. L., & Fraser, S. C. (1966). Compliance without pressure: The foot-in-the-door-technique. *Journal of Personality and Social Psychology, 4,* 195–203.

French, H. W. (2001, August 7). Hypothesis: A scientific gap. Conclusion: Japanese custom. *New York Times,* p. A1.

French, J., & Raven, B. (1959). The bases of social power. In D. Cartwright (Ed.), *Studies of social power* (pp. 150–167). Ann Arbor, MI: Institute for Social Research.

Frenkel, O. J., & Doob, A. N. (1976). Post-decision dissonance at the polling booth. *Canadian Journal of Behavioral Science, 8*, 347–350.

Frenkel-Brunswik, E., Levinson, D. J., & Sanford, R. N. (1958). The anti-democratic personality. In E. E. Maccoby, T. M. Newcomb, & E. L. Hartley (Eds.), *Readings in social psychology* (3rd ed.). New York: Holt, Rinehart & Winston.

Freud, A., & Dann, S. (1951). An experiment in group upbringing. *Psychoanalytic Study of the Child, 6*, 127–168.

Fridlund, A. J. (1991). Sociality of solitary smiling: Potentiation by and implicit audience. *Journal of Personality and Social Psychology, 60*, 229–240.

Fridlund, A. J. (1992). The behavioral ecology and sociality of human faces. *Review of Personality and Social Psychology, 13*, 90–121.

Friedman, R. S., & Forster, J. (2000). The effects of approach and avoidance motor actions on the elements of creative thought. *Journal of Personality and Social Psychology, 79*, 477–492.

Friesen, W. V. (1972). *Cultural differences in facial expressions in a social situation: An experimental test of the concept of display rules.* Unpublished doctoral dissertation, University of California, San Francisco.

Frieze, I. H., Olson, J. E., & Russell, J. (1991). Attractiveness and income for men and women in management. *Journal of Applied Social Psychology, 21*, 1039–1057.

Frijda, N. H. (1986). *The emotions.* Cambridge, England: Cambridge University Press.

Frijda, N. H., & Mesquita, B. (1994). The social roles and functions of emotions. In S. Kitayama & H. Markus (Eds.), *Emotion and culture: Empirical studies of mutual influence* (pp. 51–87). Washington, DC: American Psychological Association.

Frodi, A. (1975). The effect of exposure to weapons on aggressive behavior from a cross-cultural perspective. *International Journal of Psychology, 10*, 283–292.

Froming, W. J., Walker, G. R., & Lopyan, K. J. (1982). Public and private self-awareness: When personal attitudes conflict with societal expectations. *Journal of Experimental Social Psychology, 18*, 476–487.

Fromm, E. (1955). *The sane society.* New York: Henry Holt.

Fultz, J., Batson, C. D., Fortenbach, V. A., McCarthy, P. M., & Varney, L. (1986). Social evaluation and the empathy-altruism hypothesis. *Journal of Personality and Social Psychology, 50*, 761–769.

Funder, D. C. (1995). On the accuracy of personality judgment: A realistic approach. *Psychological Review, 102*, 652–670.

Funder, D. C., & Colvin, C. R. (1988). Friends and strangers: Acquaintanceship, agreement, and the accuracy of personality judgment. *Journal of Personality and Social Psychology, 55*, 149–158.

Furnham, A. (1993). Just world beliefs in twelve societies. *Journal of Social Psychology, 133*, 317–329.

Gable, S. L., Reis, H. T., Impett, E. A., & Asher, E. R. (2004). What do you do when things go right? The intrapersonal and interpersonal benefits of sharing positive events. *Journal of Personality and Social Psychology, 87*, 228–245.

Gaertner, S. L., & Dovidio, J. F. (1977). The subtlety of white racism, arousal, and helping behavior. *Journal of Personality and Social Psychology, 35*, 691–707.

Gaertner, S. L., & Dovidio, J. F. (1986). The aversive form of racism. In J. F. Dovidio & S. L. Gaertner (Eds.), *Prejudice, discrimination, and racism* (pp. 61–89). Orlando, FL: Academic Press.

Gaertner, S. L., Mann, J., Dovidio, J. F., Murrell, A., & Pomare, M. (1990). How does cooperation reduce intergroup bias? *Journal of Personality and Social Psychology, 59*, 692–704.

Gaertner, S. L., Murrell, A., & Dovidio, J. F. (1989). Reducing intergroup bias: The benefits of recategorization. *Journal of Personality and Social Psychology, 57*, 239–249.

Galanter, H. (1989). *Cults: Faith, healing, and coercion.* New York: Oxford University Press.

Galinsky, A. D., Gruenfeld, D. H., & Magee, J. C. (2003). From power to action. *Journal of Personality and Social Psychology, 85*, 453–466.

Galinsky, A. D., Stone, J., & Cooper, J. (2000). The reinstatement of dissonance and psychological discomfort following failed affirmations. *European Journal of Social Psychology, 30*, 123–147.

Galton, F. (1878). Composite portraits. *Journal of the Anthropological Institute of Great Britain and Ireland, 8*, 132–142.

Gangestad, S. W., & Buss, D. M. (1993). Pathogen prevalence and human mate preference. *Ethology and Sociobiology, 14*, 89–96.

Gangestad, S. W., Simpson, J. A., Cousins, A. J., Garver-Apgar, C. E., & Christensen, P. N. (2004). Women's preferences for male behavioral displays change across the menstrual cycle. *Psychological Science, 15*, 203–207.

Gangestad, S. W., & Snyder, M. (2000). Self-monitoring: Appraisal and reappraisal. *Psychological Bulletin, 126*, 530–555.

Gangestad, S. W., & Thornhill, R. (1998). Menstrual cycle variation in women's preference for the scent of symmetrical men. *Proceedings of the Royal Society of London B, 265*, 727–733.

Garcia-Marques, L., & Hamilton, D. L. (1996). Resolving the apparent discrepancy between the incongruency effect and the expectancy-based illusory correlation effect: The TRAP mode. *Journal of Personality and Social Psychology, 71*, 845–860.

Gardner, W. L., Gabriel, S., & Lee, A. Y. (1999). "I" value freedom, but "we" value relationships: Self-construal priming mirrors cultural differences in judgment. *Psychological Science, 10*, 321–326.

Garner, D. M., Garfinkel, P. E., Schwartz, D., & Thompson, M. (1980). Cultural expectations of thinness in women. *Psychological Reports, 47*, 483–491.

Garofalo, J. (1981). Crime and the mass media: A selective review of research. *Journal of Research in Crime and Delinquency, 18*, 319–350.

Gasper, K., & Clore, G. L. (1998). The persistent use of negative affect by anxious individuals to estimate risk. *Journal of Personality and Social Psychology, 74*, 1350–1363.

Gasper, K., & Clore, G. L. (2000). Do you have to pay attention to your feelings in order to be influenced by them? *Personality and Social Psychology Bulletin, 26*, 698–711.

Gates, G. S. (1924). The effects of an audience upon performance. *Journal of Abnormal and Social Psychology, 18*, 334–342.

Gawronski, B. (2003). Implicational schemata and the correspondence bias: On the diagnostic value of situationally constrained behavior. *Journal of Personality and Social Psychology, 84*, 1154–1171.

Gazzaniga, M. S. (1985). *The social brain*. New York: Basic Books.

Gazzaniga, M. S., & Heatherton, T. F. (2003). *Psychological science: Mind, brain, and behavior*. New York: Norton.

Gazzaniga, M. S., Ivry, R. B., & Mangun, G. R. (2002). *Cognitive neuroscience*. New York: Norton.

Geen, R. G. (1989). Alternative conceptions of social facilitation. In P. B. Paulus (Ed.), *Psychology of group influence* (2nd ed., pp. 15–51). Hillsdale, NJ: Lawrence Erlbaum Associates.

Geen, R. G. (1998). Aggression and antisocial behavior. In D. T. Gilbert, S. T. Fiske, & G. Lindzey (Eds.), *The handbook of social psychology* (4th ed., Vol. 2, pp. 317–356). New York: McGraw-Hill.

Geeraert, N. Y., Yzerbyt, V. Y., Corneille, O., & Wigboldus, D. (2004). The return of dispositionalism: On the linguistic consequences of dispositional suppression. *Journal of Experimental Social Psychology, 40*, 264–272.

Gentner, D., Holyoak, K. J., & Kokinov, B. N. (Ed.). (2001). *The analogical mind: Perspectives from cognitive science*. Cambridge, MA: MIT Press.

Georgeson, J. C., Harris, M., Milich, R., & Young, J. (1999). "Just teasing ...": Personality effects on perception and life narratives of childhood teasing. *Personality and Social Psychology Bulletin, 10*, 1254–1267.

Gerard, H. B., Whilhelmy, R. A., & Conolley, E. S. (1968). Conformity and group size. *Journal of Personality and Social Psychology, 8*, 79–82.

Gerbner, G., Gross, L., Morgan, M., & Signorielli, N. (1980). The "mainstreaming" of America: Violence profile no. 11. *Journal of Communication, 30*, 10–29.

Gerbner, G., Gross, L., Morgan, M., & Signorielli, N. (1986). Living with television: The dynamics of the cultivation process. In J. Bryant & D. Zillman (Eds.), *Perspectives on media effects* (pp. 17–40). Hillsdale, NJ: Lawrence Erlbaum Associates.

Gibbons, F. X. (1978). Sexual standards and reactions to pornography: Enhancing behavioral consistency through self-focused attention. *Journal of Personality and Social Psychology, 36*, 976–987.

Gigerenzer, G. (1991). How to make cognitive illusions disappear: Beyond "Heuristics and biases." In W. Stroche & M. Hewstone (Eds.), *European review of social psychology* (Vol. 2, pp. 83–115). Chichester, England: Wiley.

Gilbert, D. T. (1989). Thinking lightly about others: Automatic components of the social inference process. In J. S. Uleman & J. A. Bargh (Eds.), *Unintended thought*. New York: Guilford Press.

Gilbert, D. T. (2002). Inferential correction. In T. Gilovich, D. W. Griffin, & D. Kahneman (Eds.), *Heuristics and biases: The psychology of intuitive judgment*. New York: Cambridge University Press.

Gilbert, D. T., Brown, R. P., Pinel, E. E., & Wilson, T. D. (2000). The illusion of external agency. *Journal of Personality and Social Psychology, 79*, 690–700.

Gilbert, D. T., & Hixon, J. G. (1991). The trouble of thinking: Activation and application of stereotypic beliefs. *Journal of Personality and Social Psychology, 60*, 509–517.

Gilbert, D. T., & Jones, E. E. (1986). Perceiver-induced constraint: Interpretations of self-generated reality. *Journal of Personality and Social Psychology, 50*, 269–280.

Gilbert, D. T., Lieberman, M. D., Morewedge, C. K., & Wilson, T. D. (2004). The peculiar longevity of things not so bad. *Psychological Science, 15*, 14–19.

Gilbert, D. T., & Malone, P. S. (1995). The correspondence bias. *Psychological Bulletin, 117*, 21–38.

Gilbert, D. T., Morewedge, C. K., Risen, J. L., & Wilson, T. D. (2004). Looking forward to looking backward: The misprediction of regret. *Psychological Science, 15*, 346–350.

Gilbert, D. T., Pinel, E. C., Wilson, T. D., Blumberg, S. J., & Wheatley, T. (1998). Immune neglect: A source of durability bias in affective forecasting. *Journal of Personality and Social Psychology, 75*, 617–638.

Gilbert, S. J. (1981). Another look at the Milgram obedience studies: The role of the gradated series of shocks. *Personality and Social Psychology Bulletin, 4*, 690–695.

Gilmour, T. M., & Reid, D. W. (1979). Locus of control and causal attribution for positive and negative outcomes on university examinations. *Journal of Research in Personality, 13*, 154–160.

Gilovich, T. (1981). Seeing the past in the present: The effect of associations to familiar events on judgments and decisions. *Journal of Personality and Social Psychology, 40*, 797–808.

Gilovich, T. (1987). Secondhand information and social judgment. *Journal of Experimental Social Psychology, 23*, 59–74.

Gilovich, T. (1990). Differential construal and the false consensus effect. *Journal of Personality and Social Psychology, 59*, 623–634.

Gilovich, T., Griffin, D. W., & Kahneman, D. (Eds.). (2002). *Heuristics and biases: The psychology of intuitive judgment*. New York: Cambridge University Press.

Gilovich, T., Kruger, J., & Medvec, V. H. (2002). The spotlight effect revisited: Overestimating the manifest variability in our actions and appearance. *Journal of Experimental Social Psychology, 38*, 93–99.

Gilovich, T., Medvec, V. H., & Savitsky, K. (2000). The spotlight effect in social judgment: An egocentric bias in estimates of the salience of one's own actions and appearance. *Journal of Personality and Social Psychology, 79*, 211–222.

Gilovich, T., & Savitsky, K. (1999). The spotlight effect and the illusion of transparency: Egocentric assessments of how we're seen by others. *Current Directions in Psychological Science, 8*, 165–168.

Gilovich, T., & Savitsky, K. (2002). Like goes with like: The role of representativeness in erroneous and pseudo-scientific beliefs. In T. Gilovich, D. W. Griffin, & D. Kahneman (Eds.), *Heuristics and biases: The psychology of intuitive judgment* (pp. 617–624). New York: Cambridge University Press.

Gilovich, T., Vallone, R., & Tversky, A. (1985). The hot hand in basketball: On the misperception of random sequences. *Cognitive Personality, 17*, 295–314.

Ginosar, Z., & Trope, Y. (1980). The effects of base rates and individuating information on judgments about another person. *Journal of Experimental Social Psychology, 16*, 228–242.

Givens, D. B. (1983). *Love signals: How to attract a mate*. New York: Crown.

Gladwell, M. (2000). *The tipping point: How little things can make a big difference*. Boston: Little, Brown and Co.

Gleitman, H., Fridlund, A. J., & Reisberg, D. (2004). *Psychology* (6th ed.). New York: Norton.

Glenn, N. D. (1991). The recent trend in marital success in the United States. *Journal of Marriage and the Family, 53*, 261–270.

Glick, P., & Fiske, S. T. (2001a). Ambivalent sexism. In M. P. Zanna (Ed.), *Advances in experimental social psychology* (Vol. 33, pp. 115–188). Thousand Oaks, CA: Academic Press.

Glick, P., & Fiske, S. T. (2001b). An ambivalent alliance: Hostile and benevolent sexism as complementary justifications of gender inequality. *American Psychologist, 56*, 109–118.

Goethals, G. R., Cooper, J., & Naficy, A. (1979). Role of foreseen, foreseeable, and unforeseeable behavioral consequences in the arousal of cognitive dissonance. *Journal of Personality and Social Psychology, 37*, 1179–1185.

Goethals, G. R., & Reckman, R. F. (1973). The perception of consistency in attitudes. *Journal of Experimental Social Psychology, 9*, 491–501.

Goffman, E. (1959). *The presentation of self in everyday life.* Garden City, NY: Doubleday.

Goffman, E. (1961). *Encounters: Two studies in the sociology of interaction.* New York: Penguin.

Goffman, E. (1966). *Behavior in public places.* New York: Free Press.

Goffman, E. (1967). *Interaction ritual: Essays on face-to-face behavior.* New York: Doubleday.

Goldberg, J., Lerner, J., & Tetlock, P. (1999). Rage and reason: The psychology of the intuitive prosecutor. *European Journal of Social Psychology, 29*, 781–795.

Goldman, W., & Lewis, P. (1977). Beautiful is good: Evidence that the physically attractive are more socially skillful. *Journal of Experimental Social Psychology, 13*, 125–130.

Goleman, D. (1985). *Vital lies, simple truths: The psychology of self-deception.* New York: Simon and Schuster.

Gologor, E. (1977). Group polarization in a non-risk taking culture. *Journal of Cross-Cultural Psychology, 8*, 331–346.

Gonzaga, G. C., Keltner, D., Londahl, E. A., & Smith, M. (2001). Love and the commitment problem in romantic relations and friendship. *Journal of Personality and Social Psychology, 81*, 247–262.

Gonzaga, G. G., Keltner, D., & Ward, D. A. (2003). *Power and flirtation.* Unpublished manuscript, University of California, Berkeley.

Gonzaga, G. C., Turner, R. A., Keltner, D., Altemus, M., & Campos, B. (2005). *Romantic love and sexual desire in close relationships.* Unpublished manuscript, University of California, Los Angeles.

Gonzalez, R., & Griffin, D. (1997). On the statistics of interdependence: Treating dyadic data with respect. In S. Duck (Ed.), *Handbook of personal relationships: Theory, research, and interventions* (2nd ed., pp. 271–302). Chichester, England: Wiley.

Goodwin, S. A., Gubin, A., Fiske, S. T., & Yzerby, V. Y. (2000). Power can bias impression processes: Stereotyping subordinates by default and by design. *Group Processes and Intergroup Relations, 3*, 227–256.

Gosling, S. D., Ko, S. J., Mannarelli, T., & Morris, M. E. (2002). A room with a cue: Judgments of personality based on offices and bedrooms. *Journal of Personality and Social Psychology, 82*, 379–398.

Gotlib, I. H. (1992). Interpersonal and cognitive aspects of depression. *Current Directions in Psychological Science, 1*, 149–154.

Gottman, J. M., & Levenson, R. W. (1992). Marital processes predictive of later dissolution: Behavior, physiology, and health. *Journal of Personality and Social Psychology, 63*, 221–233.

Gottman, J. M., & Levenson, R. W. (1999). Rebound from marital conflict and divorce prediction. *Family Processes, 38*, 287–292.

Gottman, J. M., & Levenson, R. W. (2000). The timing of divorce: Predicting when a couple will divorce over a 14–year period. *Journal of Marriage and the Family, 62*, 737–745.

Gottman, J., Notarius, C., Markman, H., Bank, S., Yoppi, B., & Rubin, M. E. (1976). Behavioral exchange theory and marital decision making. *Journal of Personality and Social Psychology, 34*, 14–23.

Gould, S. J. (1991). *Bully for brontosaurus: Reflections in natural history.* New York: Norton.

Gouldner, A. W. (1960). The norm of reciprocity: A preliminary statement. *American Sociological Review, 25*, 161–178.

Gourevitch, P. (1998). *We wish to inform you that tomorrow we will be killed with our families.* New York: Picador Press.

Grammer, K. (1990). Strangers meet: Laughter and nonverbal signs of interest in opposite-sex encounters. *Journal of Nonverbal Behavior, 14*, 209–236.

Green, D. P., Wong, J., & Strolovitch, D. (1996). *The effects of demographic change on hate crime.* New Haven: Institution for Social and Policy Studies, Yale University.

Greenberg, J. (1990). Employee theft as a reaction to underpayment inequity: The hidden cost of pay cuts. *Journal of Applied Psychology, 75*, 561–568.

Greenberg, J., Pyszczynski, T., & Solomon, S. (1982). The self-serving attributional bias: Beyond self-presentation. *Journal of Experimental Social Psychology, 18*, 56–67.

Greenberg, J., Pyszczynski, T., Solomon, S., Rosenblatt, A., Veeder, M., Kirkland, S., et al. (1990). Evidence for terror management theory II: The effects of mortality salience on reactions to those who threaten or bolster the cultural worldview. *Journal of Personality and Social Psychology, 58*, 308–318.

Greenberg, J., Pyszczynski, T., Solomon, S., Simon, L., & Breus, M. (1994). Role of consciousness and accessibility of death-related thoughts in mortality salience effects. *Journal of Personality and Social Psychology, 67*, 627–637.

Greene, D., Sternberg, B., & Lepper, M. R. (1976). Overjustification in a token economy. *Journal of Personality and Social Psychology, 34*, 1219–1234.

Greene, J. D., & Haidt, J. (2002). How (and where) does moral judgment work? *Trends in Cognitive Sciences, 6*, 517–523.

Greene, J. D., Sommerville, R. B., Nystrom, L. E., Darley, J. M., & Cohen, J. D. (2001). An fMRI investigation of emotional engagement in moral judgment. *Science, 293*, 2105–2108.

Greenwald, A. G. (1980). The totalitarian ego: Fabrication and revision of personal history. *American Psychologist, 35*, 603–618.

Greenwald, A. G., & Banaji, M. R. (1995). Implicit social cognition: Attitudes, self-esteem, and stereotypes. *Psychological Review, 102*, 4–27.

Greenwald, A. G., Klinger, M. R., & Liu, T. J. (1989). Unconscious processing of dichotically masked words. *Memory and Cognition, 17*, 35–47.

Greenwald, A. G., McGhee, D. E., & Schwartz, D. L. K. (1998). Measuring individual differences in implicit cognition: The Implicit Association Test. *Journal of Personality and Social Psychology, 74*, 1464–1480.

Greenwald, A. G., Spangenberg, E. R., Pratkanis, A. R., & Eskenazi, J. (1991). Double-blind tests of subliminal self-help audiotapes. *Psychological Science, 2*, 119–122.

Gresham, L. G., & Shimp, T. A. (1985). Attitude toward advertisement and brand attitude: A classical conditioning perspective. *Journal of Advertising, 14*, 10–17.

Grice, H. P. (1975). *Logic and conversation.* New York: Academic Press.

Gries, P. H., & Peng, K. (2002). Culture clash? Apologies East and West. *Journal of Contemporary China, 11*, 173–178.

Griffin, D., & Ross, L. (1991). Subjective construal, social inference, and human misunderstanding. *Advances in Experimental Social Psychology, 24*, 319–359.

Griffin, D., & Tversky, A. (1992). The weighing of evidence and the determinants of confidence. *Cognitive Psychology, 24*, 411–435.

Griffitt, W., & Veitch, R. (1971). Hot and crowded: Influences of population density and temperature on interpersonal affective behavior. *Journal of Personality and Social Psychology, 17*, 92–98.

Griffitt, W., & Veitch, R. (1974). Preacquaintance attitude similarity and attraction revisited: Ten days in a fall-out shelter. *Sociometry, 37*, 163–173.

Groff, B. D., Baron, R. S., & Moore, D. L. (1983). Distraction, attentional conflict, and drivelike behavior. *Journal of Experimental Social Psychology, 19*, 359–380.

Gross, J. J. (1998). Antecedent-and-response-focused emotion regulation: Divergent consequences for experience, expression, and physiology. *Journal of Personality and Social Psychology, 74*, 224–237.

Gross, J. J., Fredrickson, B. L., & Levenson, R. W. (1994). The psychophysiology of crying. *Psychophysiology, 31*, 460–468.

Gruenfeld, D. H. (1995). Status, ideology, and integrative complexity on the U.S. Supreme Court: Rethinking the politics of political decision making. *Journal of Personality and Social Psychology, 68*(1), 5–20.

Gruenfeld, D. H., & Kim, P. H. (1998). *Dissent and decision making on the U.S. Supreme Court: Conflict with a minority predicts cognitive complexity in the majority.* J. L. Kellogg Graduate School of Management, Northwestern University.

Grush, J. E. (1980). Impact of candidate expenditures, regionality, and prior outcomes on the 1976 presidential primaries. *Journal of Personality and Social Psychology, 38*, 337–347.

Guerin, B. (1993). *Social facilitation.* New York: Cambridge University Press.

Guinote, A., Judd, C. M., & Brauer, M. (2002). Effects of power on perceived and objective group variability: Evidence that more powerful groups are more powerful. *Journal of Personality and Social Psychology, 82*, 708–721.

Gurin, P., & Epps, E. (1975). *Black consciousness, identity and achievement: A study of students in historically black colleges.* New York: Wiley.

Gurr, T. T. (1970). *Why men rebel.* Princeton: Princeton University Press.

Haberstroh, S., Oyserman, D., Schwarz, N., Kühnen, U., & Ji, L.-J. (2002). Is the interdependent self more sensitive to question context than the independent self? Self-construal and the observation of conversational norms. *Journal of Experimental Social Psychology, 38*, 323–329.

Haddock, G., Zanna, M. P., & Esses, V. M. (1993). Assessing the structure of prejudicial attitudes: The case of attitudes toward homosexuals. *Journal of Personality and Social Psychology, 65*, 1105–1118.

Hafer, C. L., & Olson, J. M. (1993). Beliefs in a just world, discontent, and assertive actions by working women. *Personality and Social Psychology Bulletin, 19*, 30–38.

Haidt, J. (2001). The emotional dog and its rational tail: A social intuitionist approach to moral judgment. *Psychological Review, 108*, 814–834.

Haidt, J. (2003). The moral emotions. In R. J. Davidson, K. R. Scherer, & H. H. Goldsmith (Eds.), *Handbook of affective sciences* (pp. 852–870). Oxford, England: Oxford University Press.

Haidt, J., & Keltner, D. (1999). Culture and facial expression: Open ended methods find more faces and a gradient of universality. *Cognition and Emotion, 13*, 225–266.

Haidt, J., Koller, S. H., & Dias, M. G. (1993). Affect, culture, and morality, or Is it wrong to eat your dog? *Journal of Personality and Social Psychology, 65*, 613–628.

Halberstam, D. (1969). *The best and the brightest.* New York: Random House.

Hall, E. T. (1976). *Beyond culture.* New York: Anchor Books.

Hall, J. A. (1984). *Nonverbal gender differences: Accuracy of communication and expressive style.* Baltimore: Johns Hopkins University Press.

Hall, J. A., & Halberstadt, A. G. (1994). "Subordination" and sensitivity to nonverbal cues: A study of married working women. *Sex Roles, 31*, 149–165.

Hamill, R., Wilson, T. D., & Nisbett, R. E. (1980). Insensitivity to sample bias: Generalizing from atypical cases. *Journal of Personality and Social Psychology, 39*, 578–589.

Hamilton, D. L., & Gifford, R. K. (1976). Illusory correlation in interpersonal perception: A cognitive basis of stereotypic judgments. *Journal of Experimental Social Psychology, 12*, 392–407.

Hamilton, D. L., & Sherman, S. J. (1989). Illusory correlations: Implications for stereotype theory and research. In D. Bar-Tal, C. F. Graumann, A. W. Kruglanski, & W. Stroebe (Eds.), *Stereotypes and prejudice: Changing conceptions* (pp. 59–82). New York: Springer-Verlag.

Hamilton, D. L., Stroessner, S., & Mackie, D. M. (1993). The influence of affect on stereotyping: The case of illusory correlations. In D. M. Mackie & D. L. Hamilton (Eds.), *Affect, cognition, and stereotyping: Interactive processes in group perception* (pp. 39–61). San Diego, CA: Academic Press.

Hamilton, D. L., & Trolier, T. K. (1986). Stereotypes and stereotyping: An overview of the cognitive approach. In J. F. Dovidio & S. L. Gaertner (Eds.), *Prejudice, discrimination and racism* (pp. 127–163). Orlando, FL: Academic Press.

Hamilton, D. L., & Zanna, M. P. (1974). Context effects in impression formation: Changes in connotative meaning. *Journal of Personality and Social Psychology, 29*, 649–654.

Hamilton, W. D. (1963). The evolution of altruistic behavior. *American Naturalist, 97*, 354–356.

Hamilton, W. D. (1964). The genetical evolution of social behavior. *Journal of Theoretical Biology, 7*, 1–52.

Hammill, R., Wilson, T. D., & Nisbett, R. E. (1980). Insensitivity to sample bias: Generalizing from atypical cases. *Journal of Personality and Social Psychology, 39*, 578–589.

Hampden-Turner, C., & Trompenaars, A. (1993). *The seven cultures of capitalism: Value systems for creating wealth in the United States, Japan, Germany, France, Britain, Sweden, and the Netherlands.* New York: Doubleday.

Han, S., & Shavitt, S. (1994). Persuasion and culture: Advertising appeals in individualistic and collectivistic societies. *Journal of Experimental Social Psychology, 30,* 326–350.

Haney, C., Banks, C., & Zimbardo, P. G. (1973). Interpersonal dynamics in a simulated prison. *International Journal of Criminology and Penology, 1,* 69–97.

Hanna, J. (1989, September 25). Sexual abandon: The condom is unpopular on the campus. *Macleans,* p. 48.

Harackiewicz, J. M., Manderlink, G., & Sansone, C. (1984). Rewarding pinball wizardry: Effects of evaluation and cue value on intrinsic interest. *Journal of Personality and Social Psychology, 47,* 287–300.

Harari, H., Mohr, D., & Hosey, K. (1980). Faculty helpfulness to students: A comparison of compliance techniques. *Personality and Social Psychology Bulletin, 6,* 373–377.

Harcourt, A. H., Harvey, P. H., Larson, S. G., & Short, R. V. (1980). Testis weight, body weight and breeding system in primates. *Nature, 293,* 55–57.

Hare, R. D. (1993). *Without conscience: The disturbing world of the psychopaths among us.* New York: Simon & Schuster/Pocket.

Harlow, H. F. (1959). Love in infant monkeys. *Scientific American, 200,* 68–86.

Harmon-Jones, E. (2000). Cognitive dissonance and experienced negative affect: Evidence that dissonance increases experienced negative affect even in the absence of aversive consequences. *Personality and Social Psychology Bulletin, 26,* 1490–1501.

Harmon-Jones, E., Brehm, J. W., Greenberg, J., Simon, L., & Nelson, D. E. (1996). Evidence that the production of aversive consequences is not necessary to create cognitive dissonance. *Journal of Personality and Social Psychology, 70,* 5–16.

Harmon-Jones, E., & Mills, J. (1999). *Cognitive dissonance: Progress on a pivotal theory in social psychology.* Paper presented at the American Psychological Association, Washington, DC.

Harmon-Jones, E., Sigelman, J. D., Bohlig, A., & Harmon-Jones, C. (2003). Anger, coping, and frontal cortical activity: The effect of coping potential on anger-induced left frontal activity. *Cognition and Emotion, 17,* 1–24.

Harris, B. (1979). Whatever happened to little Albert? *American Psychologist, 34,* 151–160.

Harris, M. B. (1974). Mediators between frustration and aggression in a field experiment. *Journal of Experimental Social Psychology, 10,* 561–571.

Harris, R. J., Benson, S. M., & Hall, C. L. (1975). The effects of confession on altruism. *Journal of Social Psychology, 96,* 187–192.

Harrison, A. A., & Saeed, L. (1977). Let's make a deal: An analysis of revelations and stipulations in lonely hearts advertisements. *Journal of Personality and Social Psychology, 35,* 257–264.

Hart, D., Lucca-Irizarry, N., & Damon, W. (1986). The development of self-understanding in Puerto Rico and the United States. *Journal of Early Adolescence, 6,* 293–304.

Harter, S. (1983). Developmental perspectives on the self-system. In M. Hetherington (Ed.), *Handbook of child psychology: Social and personality development* (Vol. 4, pp. 275–385). New York: Wiley.

Hartup, W. W., & Stevens, N. (1997). Friendships and adaptation in the life course. *Psychological Bulletin, 121,* 355–370.

Haslam, N. (1994). Categories of social relationships. *Cognition and Emotion, 53,* 59–90.

Haslam, N., & Fiske, A. P. (1992). Implicit relationship prototypes: Investigating five theories of the cognitive organization of social relationships. *Journal of Experimental Social Psychology, 28,* 441–474.

Hass, R. G., & Linder, D. E. (1972). Counterargument availability and the effects of message structure on persuasion. *Journal of Personality and Social Psychology, 23,* 219–233.

Hastie, R. (1981). Schematic principles in human memory. In E. T. Higgins, C. P. Herman, & M. P. Zanna (Eds.), *Social cognition: The Ontario Symposium* (Vol. 1, pp. 39–88). Hillsdale, NJ: Lawrence Erlbaum Associates.

Hatfield, E. (1988). Passionate and companionate love. In R. J. Sternberg & M. L. Barnes (Eds.), *The psychology of love* (pp. 191–217). New Haven: Yale University Press.

Hatfield, E., Greenberger, D., Traupmann, J., & Lambert, P. (1982). Equity and sexual satisfaction in recently married couples. *Journal of Sex Research, 18,* 18–32.

Hatfield, E., & Rapson, R. (1993a). Love and attachment processes. In M. Lewis & J. M. Haviland-Jones (Eds.), *Handbook of emotions* (pp. 595–604). New York: Guilford Press.

Hatfield, E., & Rapson, R. L. (1993b). *Love, sex, and intimacy.* New York: HarperCollins.

Hatfield, E., & Sprecher, S. (1986). Measuring passionate love in intimate relationships. *Journal of Adolescence, 9,* 383–410.

Hatfield, E., & Walster, G. W. (1978). *A new look at love.* Lantham, MA: University Press of America.

Haugtvedt, C. P., & Petty, R. E. (1992). Personality and persuasion: Need for cognition moderates the persistence and resistance of attitude changes. *Journal of Personality and Social Psychology, 63,* 308–319.

Hauser, C. (2004, May 6). Many Iraqis are skeptical of Bush TV appeal. *New York Times,* p. 13.

Hauser, M. D. (1996). *The evolution of communication.* Cambridge, MA: MIT Press.

Hauser, T. (1991). *Muhammad Ali: His life and times.* New York: Simon and Schuster.

Hawkins, M. W., Carrere, S., & Gottman, J. M. (2002). Marital sentiment override: Does it influence couples' perceptions? *Journal of Marriage and the Family, 64,* 193–201.

Hays, R. B. (1984). The development and maintenance of friendship. *Journal of Social and Personal Relationships, 1,* 75–98.

Hazan, C., & Shaver, P. (1987). Romantic love conceptualized as an attachment process. *Journal of Personality and Social Psychology, 52,* 511–524.

Hazan, C., & Shaver, P. (1994). Attachment as an organizational framework for research on close relationships. *Psychological Inquiry, 5,* 1–22.

Heath, C., Bell, C., & Sternberg, E. (2001). Emotional selection in memes: The case of urban legends. *Journal of Personality and Social Psychology, 81,* 1028–1041.

Heatherton, T. F., & Polivy, J. (1991). Development and validation of a scale for measuring state self-esteem. *Journal of Personality and Social Psychology, 60,* 895–910.

Hebl, M. R., Foster, J. B., Mannix, L. M., & Dovidio, J. F. (2002).

Formal and interpersonal discrimination: A field study of bias toward homosexual applicants. *Personality and Social Psychology Bulletin, 28*, 815–825.

Hebl, M., & Heatherton, T. F. (1997). The stigma of obesity in women: The difference is black and white. *Personality and Social Psychology Bulletin, 24*, 417–426.

Hebl, M., & Mannix, L. (2003). The weight of obesity in evaluating others: A mere proximity effect. *Personality and Social Psychology Bulletin, 29*, 28–38.

Hedden, T., Ji, L., Jing, Q., Jiao, S., Yao, C., Nisbett, R. E., et al. (2000). *Culture and age differences in recognition memory for social dimensions.* Paper presented at the Cognitive Aging Conference, Atlanta.

Heider, F. (1946). Attitudes and cognitive organization. *Journal of Psychology, 21*, 107–112.

Heider, F. (1958). *The psychology of interpersonal relations.* New York: Wiley.

Heine, S. J. (2005). Constructing good selves in Japan and North America. In *Culture and social behavior: The tenth Ontario Symposium* (pp. 115–143). Hillsdale, NJ: Lawrence Erlbaum Associates.

Heine, S. J., Kitayama, S., Lehman, D. R., Takata, T., Ide, E., Leung, C., & Matsumoto, H. (2001). Divergent consequences of success and failure in Japan and North America: An investigation of self-improving motivations and malleable selves. *Journal of Personality and Social Psychology, 81*, 599–615.

Heine, S. J., & Lehman, D. R. (1995). Cultural variation in unrealistic optimism: Does the West feel more invulnerable than the East? *Journal of Personality and Social Psychology, 68*, 595–607.

Heine, S. J., & Lehman, D. R. (1997). Culture, dissonance, and self-affirmation. *Personality and Social Psychology Bulletin, 23*, 389–400.

Heine, S. J., & Lehman, D. R. (2003). Move the body, change the self: Acculturative effects on the self-concept. In M. Schaller & C. S. Crandall (Eds.), *Psychological foundations of culture* (pp. 305–331). Mahwah, NJ: Lawrence Erlbaum Associates.

Heine, S. J., Lehman, D. R., Markus, H. R., & Kitayama, S. (1999). Is there a universal need for positive self-regard. *Psychological Review, 106*, 766–794.

Heine, S. J., Lehman, D. R., Peng, K., & Greenholtz, J. (2002). What's wrong with cross-cultural comparisons of subjective Likert scales: The reference group problem. *Journal of Personality and Social Psychology, 82*, 903–918.

Helgeson, V. S., & Mickelson, K. D. (1995). Motives for social comparison. *Personality and Social Psychology Bulletin, 21*, 1200–1209.

Helson, H. (1964). *Adaptation level theory.* New York: Harper & Row.

Henley, N. (1977). *Body politics: Power, sex, and nonverbal communication.* Englewood Cliffs, NJ: Prentice-Hall.

Henley, N. M., & LaFrance, M. (1984). Gender as culture: Difference and dominance in nonverbal behavior. In A. Wolfgang (Ed.), *Nonverbal behavior: Perspectives, applications, intercultural insights.* Lewiston, NY: C. J. Hogrefe.

Henrich, J., & Boyd, R. (1998). The evolution of conformist transmission and the emergence of between-group differences. *Evolution and Human Behavior, 19*, 215–242.

Hepworth, J. T., & West, S. G. (1988). Lynchings and the economy: A time-series reanalysis of Hovland and Sears (1940). *Journal of Personality and Social Psychology, 55*, 239–247.

Herek, G. M. (1998). *Stigma and sexual orientation: Understanding prejudice against lesbians, gay men, and bisexuals.* Thousand Oaks, CA: Sage.

Herr, P. M. (1986). Consequences of priming: Judgment and behavior. *Journal of Personality and Social Psychology, 51*, 1106–1115.

Hertenstein, M. J. (2002). Touch: Its communicative functions in infancy. *Human Development, 45*, 70–94..

Herzog, B. (1995). *The sports 100: The 100 most important people in American sports history.* New York: Macmillan.

Heslin, R., & Boss, D. (1980). Nonverbal intimacy in airport arrival and departure. *Personality and Social Psychology Bulletin, 6*, 248–252.

Hess, U., Banse, R., & Kappas, A. (1995). The intensity of facial expression is determined by underlying affective states and social situations. *Journal of Personality and Social Psychology, 69*, 280–288.

Hewstone, M., & Jaspers, J. (1987). Covariation and causal attribution: A logical model of the intuitive analysis of variance. *Journal of Personality and Social Psychology, 53*, 663–672.

Higgins, E. T. (1987). Self discrepancy: A theory relating self and affect. *Psychological Review, 94*, 319–340.

Higgins, E. T. (1989). Self-discrepancy theory: What patterns of self-beliefs cause people to suffer? In L. Berkowitz (Ed.), *Advances in experimental social psychology* (Vol. 22, pp. 93–136). New York: Academic Press.

Higgins, E. T. (1996). Knowledge application: Accessibility, applicability, and salience. In E. T. Higgins & A. R. Kruglanski (Eds.), *Social psychology: Handbook of basic principles* (pp. 133–168). New York: Guilford Press.

Higgins, E. T. (1997). Beyond pleasure and pain. *American Psychologist, 52*, 1280–1300.

Higgins, E. T. (1999). Promotion and prevention as motivational duality: Implications for evaluative processes. In S. Chaiken & Y. Trope (Eds.), *Dual-process theories in social psychology.* New York: Guilford Press.

Higgins, E. T., & Brendl, M. (1995). Accessibility and applicability: Some "activation rules" influencing judgment. *Journal of Experimental Social Psychology, 31*, 218–243.

Higgins, E. T., King, G. A., & Mavin, G. H. (1982). Individual construct accessibility and subjective impressions and recall. *Journal of Personality and Social Psychology, 43*, 35–47.

Higgins, E. T., Klein, R., & Strauman, T. J. (1985). Self-concept discrepancy theory: A psychological model for distinguishing among different aspects of depression and anxiety. *Social Cognition, 3*, 51–76.

Higgins, E. T., & Rholes, W. S. (1976). Impression formation and role fulfillment: A "holistic reference" approach. *Journal of Experimental Social Psychology, 12*, 422–435.

Higgins, E. T., Rholes, W. S., & Jones, C. R. (1977). Category accessibility and impression formation. *Journal of Experimental Social Psychology, 13*, 141–154.

Higgins, E. T., Shah, J., & Friedman, R. (1997). Emotional responses to goal attainment: Strength of regulatory focus as a moderator. *Journal of Personality and Social Psychology, 72*, 515–525.

Hill, C. T., & Peplau, L. A. (1998). Premarital predictors of relationship outcomes: A 15–year follow-up of the Boston Couples Study. In T. N. Bradbury (Ed.), *The developmental course of marital dysfunction.* New York: Cambridge University Press.

Hill, C. T., Rubin, Z., & Peplau, L. A. (1976). Breakups before marriage: The end of 103 affairs. *Journal of Social Issues, 32,* 147–168.

Hilton, D. J., & Slugoski, B. R. (1986). Knowledge-based causal attribution: The abnormal conditions focus model. *Psychological Review, 93,* 75–88.

Hilton, D. J., Smith, R. H., & Kim, S. H. (1995). Process of causal explanation and dispositional attribution. *Journal of Personality and Social Psychology, 68,* 377–387.

Hinkley, K., & Andersen, S. M. (1996). The working self-concept in transference: Significant-other activation and self change. *Journal of Personality and Social Psychology, 71,* 1279–1295.

Hinshaw, S. P., & Cicchetti, D. (2000). Stigma and mental disorder: Conceptions of illness, public attitudes, personal disclosure, and social policy. *Development and Psychopathology, 12,* 555–598.

Hinsz, V. B. (1989). Facial resemblance in engaged and married couples. *Journal of Social and Personal Relationships, 6,* 223–229.

Hinsz, V. B., Tindale, R. S., & Vollrath, D. A. (1997). The emerging conceptualization of groups as information processors. *Psychological Bulletin, 121,* 43–64.

Hirt, E. R. (1990). Do I see only what I expect? Evidence for an expectancy-guided retrieval model. *Journal of Personality and Social Psychology, 58,* 937–951.

Hirt, E. R., MacDonald, H. E., & Erikson, G. A. (1995). How do I remember thee? The role of encoding set and delay in reconstructive memory processes. *Journal of Experimental Social Psychology, 31,* 379–409.

Hirt, E. R., Zillman, D., Erickson, G. A., & Kennedy, C. (1992). Costs and benefits of allegiance: Changes in fans' self-ascribed competence after team victory versus defeat. *Journal of Personality and Social Psychology, 63,* 724–738.

Hobart, C. (1991). Conflict in remarriages. *Journal of Divorce and Remarriage, 15,* 69–86.

Hoch, S. J. (1985). Counterfactual reasoning and accuracy in predicting personal events. *Journal of Experimental Psychology: Learning, Memory and Cognition, 11,* 719–731.

Hodson, G., Dovidio, J. F., & Gaertner, S. L. (2002). Processes in racial discrimination: Differential weighting of conflicting information. *Personality and Social Psychology Bulletin, 28,* 460–471.

Hoeksema-van Orden, C. Y. D., Gaillard, A. W. K., & Buunk, B. P. (1998). Social loafing under fatigue. *Journal of Personality and Social Psychology, 75,* 1179–1190.

Hofstede, G. (1980). *Culture's consequences: International differences in work-related values.* Beverly Hills: Sage.

Holmberg, D., Markus, H., Herzog, A. R., & Franks, M. (1997). *Self-making in American adults: Content, structure and function.* Ann Arbor: University of Michigan.

Holtgraves, T., & Lasky, B. (1999). Linguistic power and persuasion. *Journal of Language and Social Psychology, 18,* 196–205.

Holyoak, K. J., & Thagard, P. (1995). *Mental leaps: Analogy in creative thought.* Cambridge, MA: MIT Press.

Homans, G. C. (1961). *Social behavior: Its elementary forms.* New York: Harcourt, Brace, and World.

Homans, G. C. (1965). Group factors in worker productivity. In H. Proshansky & L. Seidenberg (Eds.), *Basic studies in social psychology.* New York: Holt.

Hong, Y., Chiu, C., & Kung, T. (1997). Bringing culture out in front: Effects of cultural meaning system activation on social cognition. In K. Leung, U. Kim, S. Yamaguchi, & Y. Kashima (Eds.), *Progress in Asian social psychology* (Vol. 1, pp. 135–146). Singapore: Wiley.

Hoorens, V., Nuttin, J. M, Herman, I. E., & Pavakanun, U. (1990). Mastery pleasure versus mere ownership: A quasi-experimental cross-cultural and cross-alphabetical test of the name letter effect. *European Journal of Social Psychology, 20,* 181–205.

Hoorens, V., & Ruiter, S. (1996). The optimal impact phenomenon: Beyond the third person effect. *European Journal of Social Psychology, 26,* 599–610.

Hosey, G. R., Wood, M., Thompson, R. J., & Druck, P. L. (1985). Social facilitation in a non-social animal, the centipede *Lithobius forficatus. Behavioral Processes, 10,* 123–130.

Hoshino-Browne, E., Zanna, A. S., Spencer, S. J., & Zanna, M. P. (2004). Investigating attitudes cross-culturally: A case of cognitive dissonance among East Asians and North Americans. In G. Haddock & G. R. Maio (Eds.), *Contemporary perspectives on the psychology of attitudes* (pp. 375–397). East Sussex, England: Psychology Press.

Hosman, L. A. (1989). The evaluative consequences of hedges, hesitations, and intensifiers: Powerful and powerless speech styles. *Human Communication Research, 15,* 383–406.

Hovland, C. I., Janis, I. L., & Kelley, H. H. (1953). *Communication and persuasion: Psychological studies of opinion change.* New Haven: Yale University Press.

Hovland, C. J., Lumsdaine, A. A., & Sheffield, F. D. (1949). *Experiments on mass communication.* Princeton: Princeton University Press.

Hovland, C. J., & Sears, R. R. (1940). Minor studies in aggression: VI. Correlation of lynchings with economic indices. *Journal of Abnormal and Social Psychology, 9,* 301–310.

Hovland, C. J., & Weiss, W. (1951). The influence of source credibility on communication effectiveness. *Public Opinion Quarterly, 15,* 635–660.

Howard, J. W., & Rothbart, M. (1980). Social categorization and memory for ingroup and outgroup behavior. *Journal of Personality and Social Psychology, 38,* 301–310.

Hrdy, S. B. (1999). *Mother nature: A history of mothers, infants, and natural selection.* New York: Pantheon.

Hsu, F. L. K. (1953). *Americans and Chinese: Two ways of life.* New York: Schuman.

Hubschman, J. H., & Stack, M. A. (1992). Parasite-induced changes in chironomus decorus (Diperta: Chironomidae). *Journal of Parasitology, 78,* 872–875.

Huesmann, L. R. (1986). Psychological processes promoting the relations between exposure to media violence and aggressive behavior by the viewer. *Journal of Social Issues, 42,* 125–139.

Huesmann, L. R., Moise-Titus, J., Podolski, C.-L., & Eron, L. D. (2003). Longitudinal relations between children's exposure to TV violence and their aggressive and violent behavior in young adulthood: 1977–1992. *Developmental Psychology, 39,* 201–221.

Huguet, P., Galvaing, M. P., Monteil, J. M., & Dumas, F. (1999). Social presence effects in the Stroop task: Further evidence for an attentional view of social facilitation. *Journal of Personality and Social Psychology, 77,* 1011–1025.

Hull, J. G., Levenson, R. W., Young, R. D., & Sher, K. J. (1983). Self-awareness reducing effects of alcohol consumption. *Journal of Personality and Social Psychology, 44,* 461–473.

Hull, J. G., & Young, R. D. (1983). Self-consciousness, self-esteem, and success-failure as determinants of alcohol consumption in male social drinkers. *Journal of Personality and Social Psychology, 44,* 1097–1109.

Hull, J. G., Young, R. D., & Jouriles, E. (1986). Applications of the self-awareness model of alcohol consumption: Predicting patterns of use and abuse. *Journal of Personality and Social Psychology, 51,* 790–796.

Hummert, M. L., Crockett, W. H., & Kemper, S. (1990). Processing mechanisms underlying use of the balance schema. *Journal of Personality and Social Psychology, 58,* 5–21.

Hunter, J. D. (1991). *Culture wars.* New York: Basic Books.

Huntley, J. (1990). *The elements of astrology.* Shaftesbury, Dorset, England: Element Books Unlimited.

Hyman, H. H., & Sheatsley, P. B. (1950). The current status of American public opinion. In J. C. Payne (Ed.), *The teaching of contemporary affairs: Twenty-first yearbook of National Council of Social Studies* (pp. 11–34). Washington, DC: National Council for the Social Studies.

Ickes, W., Robertson, E., Tooke, W., & Teng, G. (1986). Naturalistic social cognition: Methodology, assessment, and validation. *Journal of Personality and Social Psychology, 51,* 66–82.

Iliffe, A. H. (1960). A study of preferences in feminine beauty. *British Journal of Psychology, 51,* 267–273.

Inman, M. L., Reichl, A. J., & Baron, R. S. (1993). Do we tell less than we know or hear less than we are told? Exploring the teller-listener extremity effect. *Journal of Experimental Social Psychology, 29,* 528–550.

Innes, J. M., & Zeitz, H. (1988). The public's view of the impact of the mass media: A test of the "third person" effect. *European Journal of Social Psychology, 18,* 457–463.

Insel, T. R. (1993). Oxytocin and the neuroendocrine basis of affiliation. In J. Schulkin (Ed.), *Hormonally induced changes in mind and brain* (pp. 225–251). San Diego: Academic Press.

Insel, T. R., Young, L., & Zuoxin, W. (1997). Molecular aspects of monogamy. In C. S. Carter & I. I. Lederhendler (Eds.), *Annals of the New York Academy of Sciences* (Vol. 807, pp. 302–316). New York: New York Academy of Sciences.

Insko, C. A. (1984). Balance theory, the Jordan paradigm, and the Wiest tetrahedron. In L. Berkowitz (Ed.), *Advances in experimental social psychology* (Vol. 18, pp. 89–140). San Diego, CA: Academic Press.

Insko, C. A., Smith, R. H., Alicke, M. D., Wade, J., & Taylor, S. (1985). Conformity and group size: The concern with being right and the concern with being liked. *Personality and Social Psychology Bulletin, 11,* 41–50.

Insko, C. A., & Wilson, M. (1977). Interpersonal attraction as a function of social interaction. *Journal of Personality and Social Psychology, 35,* 903–911.

Inzlicht, M., & Ben-Zeev, T. (2000). A threatening intellectual environment: Why females are susceptible to experiencing problem-solving deficits in the presences of males. *Psychological Science, 11,* 365–371.

Ip, G. W. M., & Bond, M. H. (1995). Culture, values, and the spontaneous self-concept. *Asian Journal of Psychology, 1,* 29–35.

Isen, A. M. (1987). Positive affect, cognitive processes, and social behavior. In L. Berkowitz (Ed.), *Advances in experimental social psychology* (pp. 203–253). New York: Academic Press.

Isen, A. M. (1993). Positive affect and decision making. In M.

Lewis & J. M. Haviland-Jones (Eds.), *Handbook of emotions* (pp. 261–278). New York: Guilford Press.

Isen, A. M. (1999). Positive affect. In T. Dalgleish & M. J. Power (Eds.), *Handbook of cognition and emotion* (pp. 521–539). Chichester, England: Wiley.

Isen, A. M., Clark, M., & Schwartz, M. F. (1976). Duration of the effect of good mood on helping: Footprints on the sands of time. *Journal of Personality and Social Psychology, 34,* 385–393.

Isen, A. M., & Levin, P. F. (1972). Effect of feeling good on helping: Cookies and kindness. *Journal of Personality and Social Psychology, 21,* 384–388.

Ishii, K., Reyes, J. A., & Kitayama, S. (2003). Spontaneous attention to word content versus emotional tone: Differences among three cultures. *Psychological Science, 14,* 39–46.

Itard, J. M. G. (1962). *The wild boy of Aveyron* (G. Humphrey & M. Humphrey, Trans.). New York: Appleton-Century-Crofts (original work published 1801).

Ito, T. A., Larsen, J. T., Smith, N. K., & Cacioppo, J. T. (1998). Negative information weighs more heavily on the brain: The negativity bias in evaluative categorizations. *Journal of Personality and Social Psychology, 75,* 887–900.

Iyengar, S. (2004). Engineering consent: The renaissance of mass communications research in politics. In J. T. Jost, M. R. Banaji, & D. Prentice (Eds.), *Perspectives in social psychology: The yin and the yang of scientific progress: Perspectives on the social psychology of thought systems.* Washington, DC: APA Press.

Iyengar, S., & Kinder, D. (1987). *News that matters: Television and American opinion.* Chicago: University of Chicago Press.

Iyengar, S., Kinder, D. R., Peters, M. D., & Krosnick, J. A. (1984). The evening news and presidential evaluations. *Journal of Personality and Social Psychology, 46,* 778–787.

Izard, C. E. (1971). *The face of emotion.* New York: Appleton-Century-Crofts.

Izard, C. E. (1994). Innate and universal facial expressions: Evidence from developmental and cross-cultural research. *Psychological Bulletin, 115,* 288–299.

Jackson, D. N., Chau, D. W., & Stricker, L. J. (1979). Implicit personality theory: Is it illusory? *Journal of Personality, 47,* 1–10.

Jacobson, G. C. (1978). The effects of campaign spending in house elections. *American Political Science Review, 72,* 469–1191.

James, W. (1890). *Principles of psychology.* New York: Holt.

James, W. (1892/1948). *Psychology.* Cleveland: World Publishing Company.

Janes, L. M., & Olson, J. M. (2000). Jeer pressure: The behavioral effects of observing ridicule of others. *Personality and Social Psychology Bulletin, 26,* 474–485.

Janis, I. L. (1972). *Victims of groupthink.* Boston: Houghton Mifflin.

Janis, I. L. (1982). *Groupthink: Psychological studies of policy decisions and fiascos* (2nd ed.). Boston: Houghton Mifflin.

Janis, I. L., Kaye, D., & Kirschner, P. (1965). Facilitating effects of eating while reading on responsiveness to persuasive communications. *Journal of Personality and Social Psychology, 1,* 181–186.

Janis, I. L., & Mann, L. (1977). *Decision making.* New York: Free Press.

Janis, I., & Mann, L. (1991). Cognitive complexity in international decision making. In P. Suedfeld & P. E. Tetlock (Eds.), *Psychology and social policy* (pp. 33–49). New York: Hemisphere.

Jellison, J. M., & Riskind, J. (1970). A social comparison of abilities interpretation of risk-taking behavior. *Journal of Personality and Social Psychology, 15,* 375–390.

Jemmott, J. B. I., Jemmott, L. S., Braverman, P. K., & Fong, G. T. (2005). HIV/STD risk reduction interventions for African American and Latino adolescent girls at an inner-city adolescent medicine clinic: A randomized controlled trial. *Archives of Pediatrics and Adolescent Medicine, 159,* 440–449.

Jemmott, J. B., III, Jemmott, L. S., & Fong, G. T. (1998). Abstinence and safer sex: A randomized controlled trial of HIV sexual risk-reduction interventions for young African American adolescents. *Journal of the American Medical Association, 279,* 1529–1536.

Jenkins, J. M., & Asington, J. W. (1996). Cognitive factors and family structure associated with theory of mind in young children. *Developmental Psychology, 32,* 70–78.

Jensen, L. A. (1997). Different worldviews, different morals: America's culture war divide. *Human Development, 40,* 325–344.

Ji, L.J., Nisbett, R. E., & Su, Y. (2001). Culture, change, and prediction. *Psychological Science, 12,* 450–456.

Ji, L., Peng, K., & Nisbett, R. E. (2000). Culture, control, and perception of relationships in the environment. *Journal of Personality and Social Psychology, 78,* 943–955.

Ji, L., Schwarz, N., & Nisbett, R. E. (2000). Culture, autobiographical memory, and social comparison: Measurement issues in cross-cultural studies. *Personality and Social Psychology Bulletin, 26,* 585–593.

Job, R. F. S. (1988). Effective and ineffective use of fear in health promotion campaigns. *American Journal of Public Health, 78,* 163–167.

John, O. P. (1990). The "big five" factor taxonomy: Dimensions of personality in the natural language and in questionnaires. In L. A. Pervin (Ed.), *Handbook of personality: Theory and research* (pp. 66–100). New York: Guilford Press.

John, O. P., & Robins, R. W. (1993). Determinants of interjudge agreement on personality traits: The big five domains, observability, evaluativeness, and the unique perspective of the self. *Journal of Personality, 61,* 521–551.

John, O. P., & Robins, R. W. (1994). Accuracy and bias in self-perception: Individual differences in self-enhancement and the role of narcissism. *Journal of Personality & Social Psychology, 66*(1), 206–219.

John, O. P., & Srivastava, S. (1999). The big five trait taxonomy: History, measurement, and theoretical perspectives. In L. A. Pervin & O. P. John (Eds.), *Handbook of personality: Theory and research* (2nd ed., pp. 102–138). New York: Guilford Press.

Johnson, E. J., & Goldstein, D. (2003). Do defaults save lives? *Science, 302,* 1338–1339.

Johnson, E. J., Hershey, J., Meszaros, J., & Kunreuther, H. (1993). Framing, probability distortions, and insurance decisions. *Journal of Risk and Uncertainty, 7,* 35–51.

Johnson, J. T. (1986). The knowledge of what might have been: Affective and attributional consequences of near outcomes. *Personality and Social Psychology Bulletin, 12,* 51–62.

Johnson, R. D., & Downing, L. L. (1979). Deindividuation and

valence of cues: Effects on prosocial and antisocial behavior. *Journal of Personality and Social Psychology, 37,* 1532–1538.

Jones, C., & Aronson, E. (1973). Attribution of fault to a rape victim as a function of the respectability of the victim. *Journal of Personality and Social Psychology, 26,* 415–419.

Jones, E. E. (1964). *Ingratiation.* New York: Appleton-Century-Crofts.

Jones, E. E. (1979). The rocky road from acts to dispositions. *American Psychologist, 34,* 107–117.

Jones, E. E. (1990). *Interpersonal perception.* New York: Freeman.

Jones, E. E., & Berglas, S. C. (1978). Control of attributions about the self through self-handicapping strategies: The appeal of alcohol and the role of underachievement. *Personality and Social Psychology Bulletin, 4,* 200–206.

Jones, E. E., & Davis, K. E. (1965). From acts to dispositions: The attribution process in person perception. In L. Berkowitz (Ed.), *Advances in experimental social psychology* (Vol. 2, pp. 219–266). New York: Academic Press.

Jones, E. E., Davis, K. E., & Gergen, K. J. (1961). Role playing variations and their informational value for person perception. *Journal of Abnormal and Social Psychology, 63,* 302–310.

Jones, E. E., Farina, A., Hastorf, A. H., Markus, H., Miller, D. T., & Scott, R. A. (1984). *Social stigma: The psychology of marked relationships.* New York: Freeman.

Jones, E. E., & Harris, V. A. (1967). The attribution of attitudes. *Journal of Experimental Social Psychology, 3,* 1–24.

Jones, E. E., & Nisbett, R. E. (1972). The actor and the observer: Divergent perceptions of the causes of behavior. In E. E. Jones, D. E. Kanouse, H. H. Kelley, R. E. Nisbett, S. Valins, & B. Weiner (Eds.), *Attribution: Perceiving the causes of behavior.* Morristown, NJ: General Learning Press.

Jost, J. T. (1998). Fairness norms and the potential for mutual agreements involving majority and minority groups. In M. A. Neale, E. A. Mannix, & R. Wageman (Eds.), *Research on managing groups and teams: Context* (Vol. 2). Greenwich, CT: JAI Press.

Jost, J. T., & Banaji, M. R. (1994). The role of stereotyping in system justification and the production of false consciousness. *British Journal of Social Psychology, 33,* 1–27.

Jost, J. T., Banaji, M. R., & Nosek, B. A. (2004). A decade of system justification theory and unconscious bolstering of the status quo. *Political Psychology, 25,* 881–919.

Jost, J. T., & Major, B. (2001). *The psychology of legitimacy: Emerging perspectives on ideology, justice, and intergroup relations.* New York: Cambridge University Press.

Jost, J. T., Pelham, B. W., & Carvallo, M. (2002). Non-conscious forms of system justification and behavioral preferences for higher status groups. *Journal of Experimental Social Psychology, 38,* 586–602.

Judd, C. M., Blair, I. V., & Chapleau, K. M. (2004). Automatic stereotypes vs. automatic prejudice: Sorting out the possibilities in the Payne (2001) weapon paradigm. *Journal of Experimental Social Psychology, 40,* 75–81.

Judd, C. M., Drake, R. A., Downing, J. W., & Krosnick, J. A. (1991). Some dynamic properties of attitude structures: Context induced responses facilitation and polarization. *Journal of Personality and Social Psychology, 60,* 193–202.

Judd, C. M., Kenny, D. A., & Krosnick, J. A. (1983). Judging the positions of political candidates: Models of assimilation and contrast. *Journal of Personality and Social Psychology, 46,* 1193–1207.

Judd, C. M., & Lusk, C. M. (1984). Knowledge structures and evaluative judgments: Effects of structural variables on judgment extremity. *Journal of Personality and Social Psychology, 46*, 1193–1207.

Judd, C. M., & Park, B. (1993a). Definition and assessment of accuracy of social stereotypes. *Psychological Review, 100*, 109–128.

Judd, C. M., & Park, B. (1993b). The assessment of accuracy of social stereotypes. *Psychological Review, 100*, 109–128.

Jussim, L. (1986). Self-fulfilling prophecies: A theoretical and integrative review. *Psychological Review, 93*, 429–445.

Kagan, J. (1989). Temperamental contributions to social behavior. *American Psychologist, 44*, 668–674.

Kahneman, D. (1999). Objective happiness. In D. Kahneman, E. Diener, & N. Schwarz (Eds.), *Hedonic psychology*. New York: Cambridge University Press.

Kahneman, D., & Frederick, S. (2002). Representativeness revisited: Attribute substitution in intuitive judgment. In T. Gilovich, D. W. Griffin, & D. Kahneman (Eds.), *Heuristics and biases: The psychology of intuitive judgment* (pp. 49–81). New York: Cambridge University Press.

Kahneman, D., & Lovallo, D. (1993). Timid choices and bold forecasts: A cognitive perspective on risk taking. *Management Science, 39*, 17–31.

Kahneman, D., & Miller, D. T. (1986). Norm theory: Comparing reality to its alternatives. *Psychological Review, 93*, 136–153.

Kahneman, D., Slovic, P., & Tversky, A. (1982). *Judgment under uncertainty: Heuristics and biases*. New York: Cambridge University Press.

Kahneman, D., & Tversky, A. (1972). Subjective probability: A judgment of representativeness. *Cognitive Psychology, 3*, 430–454.

Kahneman, D., & Tversky, A. (1973a). Availability: A heuristic for judging frequency and probability. *Cognitive Psychology, 4*, 207–232.

Kahneman, D., & Tversky, A. (1973b). On the psychology of prediction. *Psychological Review, 80*, 237–251.

Kahneman, D., & Tversky, A. (1982a). The simulation heuristic. In D. Kahneman, P. Slovic, & A. Tversky (Eds.), *Judgment under certainty: Heuristics and biases* (pp. 201–208). New York: Cambridge University Press.

Kahneman, D., & Tversky, A. (1982b). Variants of uncertainty. *Cognition, 11*, 143–157.

Kahneman, D., & Tversky, A. (1995). On the reality of cognitive illusions. *Psychological Review, 103*, 582–591.

Kaid, L. L. (1981). Political advertising. In D. D. Nimmo & K. R. Sanders (Eds.), *Handbook of political communication*. Beverly Hills, CA: Sage.

Kaplan, H. I., Sadock, B. J., & Grebb, J. A. (1994). *Synopsis of psychiatry* (7th ed.). Baltimore, MD: Williams and Wilkins.

Karau, S. J., & Williams, K. D. (1995). Social loafing: Research findings, implications, and future directions. *Current Directions in Psychological Science, 4*, 134–140.

Karney, B. R., & Bradbury, T. N. (1995). The longitudinal course of marital quality and stability: A review of theory, method, and research. *Psychological Bulletin, 118*, 3–34.

Karney, B. R., & Bradbury, T. N. (1997). Neuroticism, marital interaction, and the trajectory of marital satisfaction. *Journal of Personality and Social Psychology, 72*, 1075–1092.

Karney, B. R., & Bradbury, T. N. (2000). Attributions in marriage: State or trait? A growth curve analysis. *Journal of Personality and Social Psychology, 78*, 295–309.

Karney, B. R., Bradbury, T. N., Fincham, F. D., & Sullivan, K. T. (1994). The role of negative affectivity in the association between attributions and marital satisfaction. *Journal of Personality and Social Psychology, 66*, 413–424.

Karney, B. R., & Coombs, R. H. (2000). Memory bias in long-term relationships: Consistency or improvement? *Personality and Social Psychology Bulletin, 26*, 959–970.

Karpinski, A., & HIlton, J. L. (2001). Attitudes and the Implicit Association Test. *Journal of Personality and Social Psychology, 81*, 774–788.

Kashima, Y., Siegal, M., Tanaka, K., & Kashima, E. S. (1992). Do people believe behaviours are consistent with attitudes? Towards a cultural psychology of attribution processes. *British Journal of Social Psychology, 37*, 111–124.

Kashima, Y., Yamaguchi, S., Kim, U., Choi, S.-C., Gelfand, M. J., & Yuki, M. (1995). Culture, gender, and self: A perspective from individualism-collectivism research. *Journal of Personality and Social Psychology, 69*, 925–937.

Katz, I., Glucksberg, S., & Krauss, R. (1960). Need satisfaction and Edwards PPS scores in married couples. *Journal of Consulting Psychology, 24*, 205–208.

Kauffman, K. (1981). Prison officer attitudes and perceptions of attitudes. *Journal of Research in Crime Delinquency, 18*, 272–294.

Kelley, H. H. (1967). Attribution theory in social psychology. In D. Levine (Ed.), *Nebraska Symposium on Motivation* (Vol. 15, pp. 192–238). Lincoln: University of Nebraska Press.

Kelley, H. H. (1973). The processes of causal attribution. *American Psychologist, 28*, 107–128.

Kelley, H. H., & Stahelski, A. J. (1970). The social interaction basis of cooperators' and competitors' beliefs about others. *Journal of Personality and Social Psychology, 16*, 66–91.

Kelley, H. H., & Thibaut, J. W. (1978). *Interpersonal relations: A theory of interdependence*. New York: Wiley.

Kellman, P. J., & Spelke, E. S. (1983). Perception of partially occluded objects in infancy. *Cognitive Psychology, 15*, 483–524.

Kelly, G. A. (1955). *The psychology of personal constructs*. New York: Norton.

Kelly, J. R., & Karau, S. J. (1999). Group decision making: The effects of initial preference and time pressure. *Personality and Social Psychology Bulletin, 25*, 1342–1354.

Kelman, H. C. (1958). Compliance, identification, and internalization: Three processes of attitude change. *Journal of Conflict Resolution, 2*, 51–60.

Keltner, D. (1995). The signs of appeasement: Evidence for the distinct displays of embarrassment, amusement, and shame. *Journal of Personality and Social Psychology, 68*, 441–454.

Keltner, D., & Anderson, C. (2000). Saving face for Darwin: Functions and uses of embarrassment. *Current Directions in Psychological Science, 9*, 187–191.

Keltner, D., & Bonanno, G. A. (1997). A study of laughter and dissociation: The distinct correlates of laughter and smiling during bereavement. *Journal of Personality and Social Psychology, 73*, 687–702.

Keltner, D., & Buswell, B. N. (1997). Embarrassment: Its distinct form and appeasement functions. *Psychological Bulletin, 122*, 250–270.

Keltner, D., Capps, L. M., Kring, A. M., Young, R. C., & Heerey,

E. A. (2001). Just teasing: A conceptual analysis and empirical review. *Psychological Bulletin, 127*, 229–248.

Keltner, D., Ellsworth, P. C., & Edwards, K. (1993). Beyond simple pessimism: Effects of sadness and anger on social perception. *Journal of Personality and Social Psychology, 64*, 740–752.

Keltner, D., & Gross, J. J. (1999). Functional accounts of emotion. *Cognition and Emotion, 13*, 467–480.

Keltner, D., Gruenfeld, D. H., & Anderson, C. A. (2003). Power, approach, and inhibition. *Psychological Review, 110*, 265–284.

Keltner, D., & Haidt, J. (1999). Social functions of emotions at four levels of analysis. *Cognition and Emotion, 13*, 505–521.

Keltner, D., & Haidt, J. (2001). Social functions of emotions. In T. Mayne & G. Bonanno (Eds.), *Emotions: Current issues and future directions* (pp. 192–213). New York: Guilford Press.

Keltner, D., & Haidt, J. (2003). Approaching awe, a moral, spiritual, and aesthetic emotion. *Cognition and Emotion, 17*, 297–314.

Keltner, D., Locke, K. D., & Audrain, P. C. (1993). The influence of attributions on the relevance of negative feelings to personal satisfaction. *Personality and Social Psychology Bulletin, 19*, 21–29.

Keltner, D., & Potegal, M. (1997). Appeasement and reconciliation: Introduction to an *Aggressive Behavior* special issue. *Aggressive Behavior, 23*, 309–314.

Keltner, D., & Robinson, R. J. (1996). Extremism, power, and the imagined basis of social conflict. *Current Directions in Psychological Science, 5*, 101–105.

Keltner, D., & Robinson, R. J. (1997). Defending the status quo: Power and bias in social conflict. *Personality and Social Psychology Bulletin, 23*(10), 1066–1077.

Keltner, D., Young, R., & Buswell, B. N. (1997). Appeasement in human emotion, personality, and social practice. *Aggressive Behavior, 23*, 359–374.

Keltner, D., Young, R. C., Heerey, E. A., Oemig, C., & Monarch, N. D. (1998). Teasing in hierarchial and intimate relations. *Journal of Personality and Social Psychology, 75*, 1231–1247.

Kemper, T. D. (1991). Predicting emotions from social relations. *Social Psychology Quarterly, 54*, 330–342.

Kenny, D. (1991). A general model of consensus and accuracy in interpersonal perception. *Psychological Review, 98*, 155–163.

Kenny, D. A., & LaVoie, L. (1982). Reciprocity of interpersonal attraction: A confirmed hypothesis. *Social Psychology Quarterly, 45*, 54–58.

Kenny, D. A., & Nasby, W. (1980). Splitting the reciprocity correlation. *Journal of Personality and Social Psychology, 38*, 249–256.

Kenrick, D. T., & Keefe, R. C. (1992). Age preferences in mates reflect sex differences in reproductive strategies. *Behavioral and Brain Sciences, 15*, 75–133.

Kenrick, D. T., & MacFarlane, S. W. (1984). Ambient temperature and horn-honking: A field study of the heat/aggression relationship. *Environment and Behavior, 18*, 179–191.

Kenrick, D. T., Sadalla, E. K., Groth, G., & Trost, M. R. (1990). Evolution, traits, and the stages of human courtship: Qualifying the parental investment model. *Journal of Personality, 58*, 97–116.

Kenyatta, J. (1938). *Facing Mt. Kenya*. Nairobi, Kenya: Heinemann.

Kerr, N. L., & Kaufman-Gilliland, C. M. (1994). Communication, commitment, and cooperation in social dilemmas. *Journal of Personality and Social Psychology, 66*, 513–529.

Kerr, N. L., MacCoun, R. J., & Kramer, G. P. (1996). Bias in judgment: Comparing individuals and groups. *Psychological Review, 103*, 687–719.

Kiecolt-Glaser, J. K., Malarkey, W. B., Cacioppo, J. T., & Glaser, R. (1994). Stressful personal relationships: Immune and endocrine function. In R. Glaser & Kiecolt-Glaser (Eds.), *Handbook of human stress and immunity* (pp. 321–339). San Diego, CA: Academic Press.

Kiesler, S. B. (1971). *The psychology of commitment: Experiments linking behavior to belief*. New York: Academic Press.

Kiesler, S. B., & Mathog, R. (1968). The distraction hypothesis in attitude change. *Psychological Reports, 23*, 1123–1133.

Kihlstrom, J. F., & Cantor, N. (1984). Mental representations of the self. In L. Berkowitz (Ed.), *Advances in experimental social psychology* (Vol. 17, pp. 1–47). New York: Academic Press.

Kim, H., & Baron, R. S. (1988). Exercise and illusory correlation: Does arousal heighten stereotypic processes? *Journal of Experimental Social Psychology, 24*, 366–380.

Kim, H., & Markus, H. R. (1999). Deviance or uniqueness, harmony or conformity?: A cultural analysis. *Journal of Personality and Social Psychology, 77*, 785–800.

Kimmel, M. S. (2004). *The gendered society* (2nd ed.). New York: Oxford University Press.

Kinder, D. R., & Sears, D. O. (1981). Prejudice and politics: Symbolic racism versus racial threats to the good life. *Journal of Personality and Social Psychology, 40*, 414–431.

King, L. A., & Miner, K. N. (2000). Writing about the perceived benefits of traumatic events: Implications for physical health. *Personality and Social Psychology Bulletin, 26*, 220–230.

Kinsey, A. C., Pomeroy, W. B., & Martin, C. E. (1948). *Sexual behavior in the human male*. Philadelphia: Saunders.

Kinsey, A. C., Pomeroy, W. B., Martin, C. E., & Gebhard, P. H. (1953). *Sexual behavior in the human female*. Philadelphia: Saunders.

Kirkpatrick, L. A., & Hazan, C. (1994). Attachment styles and close relationships: A four-year prospective study. *Personal Relationships, 1*, 123–142.

Kitayama, S., Duffy, S., Kawamura, T., & Larsen, J. T. (2002). Perceiving an object in its context in different cultures: A cultural look at the New Look. *Psychological Science, 14*, 201–206.

Kitayama, S., Karasawa, M., & Mesquita, B. (2004). Collective and personal processes in regulating emotions: Emotion and self in Japan and the United States. In P. Philipot & R. S. Feldman (Eds.), *The regulation of emotion* (pp. 251–273). Hillsdale, NJ: Lawrence Erlbaum Associates.

Kitayama, S., Markus, H. R., & Kurokawa, M. (2000). Culture, emotion, and well-being: Good feelings in Japan and the United States. *Cognition and Emotion, 14*, 93–124.

Kitayama, S., Markus, H. R., Matsumoto, H., & Norasakkunkit, V. (1997). Individual and collective processes in the construction of the self: Self-enhancement in the United States and self-depreciation in Japan. *Journal of Personality and Social Psychology, 72*, 1245–1267.

Kitayama, S., & Masuda, T. (1997). Shaiaiteki ninshiki no bunkateki baikai model: taiousei bias no bunkashinrigakuteki kentou. (Cultural psychology of social inference: The correspondence bias in Japan.). In K. Kashiwagi, S.

Kitayama, & H. Azuma (Eds.), *Bunkashinrigaku: riron to jisho. (Cultural psychology: Theory and evidence)*. Tokyo: University of Tokyo Press.

Kitayama, S., Mesquita, B., & Karasawa, M. (2005). *Culture and emotional experience: Socially engaging and disengaging emotions in Japan and the United States*. Unpublished manuscript.

Kitayama, S., Snibbe, A. C., Markus, H. R., & Suzuki, T. (2004). Is there any "free" choice? Self and dissonance in two cultures. *Psychological Science, 15*, 527–533.

Klein, S. B., & Kihlstrom, J. F. (1986). Elaboration, organization, and the self-reference effect in memory. *Journal of Experimental Psychology: General, 115*, 26–38.

Klein, S. B., & Loftus, J. (1988). The nature of self-referent encoding: The contributions of elaborative and organizational processes. *Journal of Personality and Social Psychology, 55*, 5–11.

Klein, W. M., & Kunda, Z. (1992). Motivated person perception: Constructing justifications for desired beliefs. *Journal of Experimental Social Psychology, 28*, 145–168.

Kleinhesselink, R. R., & Edwards, R. E. (1975). Seeking and avoiding belief-discrepant information as a function of its perceived refutability. *Journal of Personality and Social Psychology, 31*, 787–790.

Klinger, M. R., Burton, P. C., & Pitts, G. S. (2000). Mechanisms of unconscious priming I: Response competition, not spreading activation. *Journal of Experimental Psychology: Learning, Memory, and Cognition, 26*, 441–455.

Klofas, J., & Toch, H. (1982). The guard subculture myth. *Journal of Research in Crime Delinquency, 19*, 238–254.

Klohnen, E. C., & Bera, S. J. (1998). Behavioral and experiential patterns of avoidantly and securely attached women across adulthood: A 30–year longitudinal perspective. *Journal of Personality and Social Psychology, 74*, 211–223.

Kluegel, J. R., & Smith, E. R. (1986). *Beliefs about inequality: Americans' views of what is and what ought to be*. Hawthorne, NY: Aldine de Gruyter.

Kniffin, K. M., & Wilson, D. S. (2004). The effect of nonphysical traits on the perception of physical attractiveness: Three naturalistic studies. *Evolution and Human Behavior, 25*, 88–101.

Knight, N., Varnum, M. E. W., & Nisbett, R. E. (2005). *Culture and class effects on categorization*. Ann Arbor, MI: University of Michigan.

Knox, R. E., & Inkster, J. A. (1968). Postdecision dissonance at post-time. *Journal of Personality and Social Psychology, 8*, 319–323.

Kohlberg, L. (1976). Moral stages and moralization: The cognitive-developmental approach. In T. Lickona (Ed.), *Moral development and behavior: Theory, research, and social issues* (pp. 31–53). New York: Holt, Rinehart, & Winston.

Krosnick, J. A. (1988). The role of attitude importance in social evaluation: A study of policy preferences, presidential candidate evaluations, and voting behavior. *Journal of Personality and Social Psychology, 55*, 196–210.

Krosnick, J. A., Betz, A. L., Jussim, L. J., & Lynn, A. R. (1992). Subliminal conditioning of attitudes. *Personality and Social Psychology Bulletin, 18*, 152–162.

Krosnick, J. A., & Petty, R. E. (1995). Attitude strength: An overview. In R. E. Petty & J. A. Krosnick (Eds.), *Attitude strength: Antecedents and consequences* (pp. 1–24). Mahwah, NJ: Lawrence Erlbaum Associates.

Krueger, J., & Clement, R. W. (1994). The truly false consensus effect: An ineradicable and egocentric bias in social perception. *Journal of Personality and Social Psychology, 67*, 596–610.

Kruger, J., & Burrus, J. (2004). Egocentrism and focalism in unrealistic optimism (and pessimism). *Journal of Experimental Social Psychology, 40(3)*, 332–340.

Kruglanski, A. W., & Webster, D. M. (1991). Group members' reactions to opinion deviates and conformists at varying degrees of proximity to decision deadline and of environmental noise. *Journal of Personality and Social Psychology, 61*, 212–225.

Krugman, P. (2002, October 20). For richer. *New York Times*.

Krull, D. S. (1993). Does the grist change the mill? The effect of the perceiver's inferential goal on the process of social inference. *Personality and Social Psychology Bulletin, 19*, 340–348.

Krull, D. S., & Dill, J. C. (1996). On thinking first and responding fast: Flexibility in social inference processes. *Personality and Social Psychology Bulletin, 22*, 949–959.

Krull, D. S., & Erickson, D. J. (1995). Inferential hopscotch: How people draw social inferences from behavior. *Current Directions in Psychological Science, 4*, 35–38.

Krull, D. S., Loy, M., Lin, J., Wang, C.-F., Chen, S., & Zhao, X. (1996). *The fundamental attribution error: Correspondence bias in independent and interdependent cultures*. Paper presented at the 13th Congress of the International Association for Cross-Cultural Psychology, Montreal, Quebec, Canada.

Kuhlmeier, V., Wynn, K., & Bloom, P. (2003). Attribution of dispositional states by 12–month-olds. *Psychological Science, 5*, 402–408.

Kuhn, M. H., & McPartland, T. S. (1954). An empirical investigation of self-attitudes. *American Sociological Review, 19*, 68–76.

Kühnen, U., & Oyserman, D. (2002). *Thinking about the self influences thinking in general: Cognitive consequences of salient self-concept*. Ann Arbor: University of Michigan.

Kulik, J. A. (1983). Confirmatory attribution and the perpetuation of social beliefs. *Journal of Personality and Social Psychology, 44*, 1171–1181.

Kunda, Z. (1990). The case for motivated reasoning. *Psychological Bulletin, 108*, 480–496.

Kunda, Z., Davies, P. G., Adams, B., & Spencer, S. J. (2002). The dynamic time course of stereotype activation: Activation, dissipation, and resurrection. *Journal of Personality and Social Psychology, 82*, 283–299.

Kunda, Z., & Nisbett, R. E. (1986). Prediction and the partial understanding of the law of large numbers. *Journal of Experimental Social Psychology, 22*, 339–354.

Kunda, Z., & Oleson, K. C. (1995). Maintaining stereotypes in the face of disconfirmation: Constructing grounds for subtyping deviants. *Journal of Personality and Social Psychology, 68*, 565–579.

Kunda, Z., & Spencer, S. J. (2003). When do stereotypes come to mind and when do they color judgement? A global-based theory of stereotype activation and application. *Psychological Bulletin, 129*, 522–544.

Kunda, Z., & Thagard, P. (1996). Forming impressions from stereotypes, traits, and behaviors: A parallel-constraint-satisfaction theory. *Psychological Review, 103*, 646–657.

Kunz, P. R., & Woolcott, M. (1976). Seasons greetings: From my status to yours. *Social Research, 5*, 269–278.

Kurdek, L. A. (1993). Predicting marital dissolution: A 5 year prospective longitudinal study of newlywed couples. *Journal of Personality and Social Psychology, 64*, 221–242.

LaFrance, M., & Banaji, M. (1992). Toward a reconsideration of the gender-emotion relationship. In M. S. Clark (Ed.), *Emotion and social behavior* (pp. 178–201). Newbury Park, CA: Sage.

LaFrance, M., Henley, N. M., Hall, J. A., & Halberstadt, A. G. (1997). Nonverbal behavior: Are women's superior skills caused by their oppression? In M. R. Walsh (Ed.), *Women, men and gender: Ongoing debates*. New Haven: Yale University Press.

Lakin, J. L., & Chartrand, T. L. (2003). Using nonconscious behavioral mimicry to create affiliation and rapport. *Psychological Science, 14*, 334–339.

Lakoff, G. (1987). *Women, fire and dangerous things*. Chicago: University of Chicago Press.

Lamal, P. A. (1979). College students' common beliefs about psychology. *Teaching of Psychology, 6*, 155–158.

Lambert, A. J., Burroughs, T., & Nguyen, T. (1999). Perceptions of risk and the buffering hypothesis: The role of just world beliefs and right-wing authoritarianism. *Personality and Social Psychology Bulletin, 25*, 643–656.

Lambert, A. J., Khan, S. R., Lickel, B. A., & Fricke, K. (1997). Mood and the correction of positive versus negative stereotypes. *Journal of Personality and Social Psychology, 72*, 1002–1016.

Lambert, A. J., Payne, B. K., Jacoby, L. L., Shaffer, L. M., Chasteen, A. L., & Khan, S. R. (2003). Stereotypes as dominant responses: On the "social facilitation" of prejudice in anticipated public contexts. *Journal of Personality and Social Psychology, 84*, 277–295.

Landes, E. M., & Rosenfield, A. M. (1994). Durability of advertising revisited. *Journal of Industrial Economics, 43*, 263–277.

Landy, D., & Sigall, H. (1974). Beauty is talent: Task evaluation as a function of the performer's physical attractiveness. *Journal of Personality and Social Psychology, 29*, 299–304.

Lang, P. J., Greenwald, M. K., Bradley, M. M., & Hamm, A. O. (1993). Looking at pictures: Affective, facial, visceral, and behavioral reactions. *Psychophysiology, 30*, 261–273.

Langer, E. (1975). The illusion of control. *Journal of Personality and Social Psychology, 32*, 311–328.

Langer, E., Blank, A., & Chanowitz, B. (1978). The mindlessness of ostensibly thoughtful action: The role of "placebic" information in interpersonal interaction. *Journal of Personality and Social Psychology, 36*, 635–642.

Langlois, J. H., Kalakanis, L., Rubenstein, A. J., Larson, A., Hallam, M., & Smoot, M. (2000). Maxims or myths of beauty? A meta-analytic review and theoretical review. *Psychological Bulletin, 126*, 390–423.

Langlois, J. H., Ritter, J. M., Casey, R. J., & Sawin, D. B. (1995). Infant attractiveness predicts maternal behaviors and attitudes. *Developmental Psychology, 31*, 464–472.

Langlois, J. H., Ritter, J. M., Roggman, L. A., & Vaughn, L. S. (1991). Facial diversity and infant preferences for attractive faces. *Developmental Psychology, 27*, 79–84.

Langlois, J. H., & Roggman, L. A. (1990). Attractive faces are only average. *Psychological Science, 1*, 115–121.

Langlois, J. H., Roggman, L. A., Casey, R. J., Ritter, J. M., Rieser-Danner, L. A., & Jenkins, V. Y. (1987). Infant preferences for attractive faces: Rudiments of a stereotype. *Developmental Psychology, 23*, 363–369.

Langlois, J. H., Roggman, L. A., & Rieser-Danner, L. A. (1990). Infants' differential social responses to attractive and unattractive faces. *Developmental Psychology, 26*, 153–159.

LaPiere, R. T. (1934). Attitudes versus actions. *Social Forces, 13*, 230–237.

Larkey, P. D., Smith, R. A., & Kadane, J. B. (1989). It's okay to believe in the hot hand. *Chance, 2*, 22–30.

Larrick, R. P., Morgan, J. N., & Nisbett, R. E. (1990). Teaching the use of cost-benefit reasoning in everyday life. *Psychological Science, 1*, 362–370.

Lassiter, G. D., Geers, A. L., Munhall, P. J., Ploutz-Snyder, R. J., & Breitenbecher, D. L. (2002). Illusory causation: Why it occurs. *Psychological Science, 13*, 299–305.

Latané, B., & Darley, J. M. (1968). Group inhibition of bystander intervention in emergencies. *Journal of Personality and Social Psychology, 10*, 215–221.

Latané, B., & Darley, J. M. (1969). Bystander "apathy." *American Scientist, 57*, 218–250.

Latané, B., & Nida, S. (1981). Ten years of research on group size and helping. *Psychological Bulletin, 89*, 308–324.

Latané, B., Williams, K., & Harkins, S. (1979). Many hands make the work light: The causes and consequences of social loafing. *Journal of Personality and Social Psychology, 37*, 822–832.

Lau, R. R., & Russell, D. (1980). Attributions in the sports pages: A field test of some current hypotheses about attribution research. *Journal of Personality and Social Psychology, 39*, 29–38.

Laughlin, P. R. (1988). Collective induction: Group performance, social combination processes, and mutual majority and minority influence. *Journal of Personality and Social Psychology, 54*, 254–267.

Laughlin, P. R., & Ellis, A. L. (1986). Demonstrability and social combination processes on mathematical intellective tasks. *Journal of Experimental Social Psychology, 22*, 177–189.

Lawler, K. A., Younger, J. W., Piferi, R. L., Billington, E., Jobe, R., Edmondson, K., et al. (2003). A change of heart: Cardiovascular correlates of forgiveness in response to interpersonal conflict. *Journal of Behavioral Medicine, 26*, 373–393.

Lawson, A. (1988). *Adultery: An analysis of love and betrayal*. New York: Basic Books.

Lazarus, R. S. (1991). *Emotion and adaptation*. New York: Oxford University Press.

Lea, M., Spears, R., & de Groot, D. (2001). Knowing me, knowing you: Anonymity effects on social identity processes within groups. *Personality and Social Psychology Bulletin, 27*, 526–537.

Leary, M. R., Britt, T. W., Cutlip, W. D. I., & Templeton, J. L. (1992). Social blushing. *Psychological Bulletin, 112*, 446–460.

Leary, M. R., & Jones, J. L. (1993). The social psychology of tanning and sunscreen use: Self-presentational motives as a predictor of health risk. *Journal of Applied Social Psychology, 23*, 1390–1406.

Leary, M. R., & Kowalski, R. M. (1990). Impression management: A literature review and two-component model. *Psychological Bulletin, 107*, 34–47.

Leary, M. R., Tambor, E. S., Terdal, S. K., & Downs, D. L. (1995). Self-esteem as an interpersonal monitor: The sociometer hypothesis. *Journal of Personality and Social Psychology, 68*, 518–530.

Leary, M. R., Tchividjian, L. R., & Kraxberger, B. E. (1994). Self-presentation can be hazardous to your health: Impression management and health risk. *Health Psychology, 13,* 451–470.

LeBon, G. (1895). *The crowd.* London: Unwin.

Lebra, T. S. (1983). Shame and guilt: A psychocultural view of the Japanese self. *Ethos, 11,* 192–209.

LeDoux, J. E. (1989). Cognitive-emotional interactions in the brain. *Cognition and Emotion, 3,* 267–289.

LeDoux, J. E. (1993). Emotional networks in the brain. In M. Lewis & J. M. Haviland (Eds.), *Handbook of emotions* (pp. 109–118). New York: Guilford Press.

LeDoux, J. E. (1996). *The emotional brain.* New York: Simon and Schuster.

Lee, F., Hallahan, M., & Herzog, T. (1996). Explaining real life events: How culture and domain shape attributions. *Personality and Social Psychology Bulletin, 22,* 732–741.

Lee-Chai, A. Y., & Bargh, J. A. (2001). *The use and abuse of power: Multiple perspectives on the causes of corruption.* Philadelphia: Psychology Press.

Leik, R., & Leik, S. (1976). Transition to interpersonal commitment. In R. L. Hamblin & J. H. Kunkel (Eds.), *Behavioral theory in sociology* (Vol. 61, pp. 299–322). New Brunswick, NJ: Transaction.

Leippe, M. R., & Elkin, R. A. (1987). When motives clash: Issue involvement and response involvement as determinants of persuasion. *Journal of Personality and Social Psychology, 52,* 269–278.

Lemyre, L., & Smith, P. M. (1985). Intergroup discrimination and self-esteem in the minimal group paradigm. *Journal of Personality and Social Psychology, 49,* 660–670.

Lepore, L., & Brown, R. (1997). Category and stereotype activation: Is prejudice inevitable? *Journal of Personality and Social Psychology, 72,* 275–287.

Lepper, M. R. (1973). Dissonance, self-perception, and honesty in children. *Journal of Personality and Social Psychology, 23,* 65–74.

Lepper, M. R., & Greene, D. (1978). *The hidden costs of reward.* Hillsdale, NJ: Lawrence Erlbaum Associates.

Lepper, M. R., Greene, D., & Nisbett, R. E. (1973). Undermining children's intrinsic interest with extrinsic reward: A test of the overjustification hypothesis. *Journal of Personality and Social Psychology, 28,* 129–137.

Lepper, M. R., Ross, L., Vallone, R., & Keavney, M. (unpublished data). Biased perceptions of victory and media hostility in network coverage of presidential debates.

Lepper, M. R., Sagotsky, G., Dafoe, J., & Greene, D. (1982). Consequences of superfluous social constraints: Effect on young children's social inferences and subsequent intrinsic interest. *Journal of Personality and Social Psychology, 42,* 51–65.

Lerner, J. S., Goldberg, J. H., & Tetlock, P. E. (1998). Sober second thoughts: The effects of accountability, anger, and authoritarianism on attributions of responsibility. *Personality and Social Psychology Bulletin, 24,* 563–574.

Lerner, J. S., Gonzalez, R. M., Small, D. A., & Fischhoff, B. (2003). Effects of fear and anger on perceived risks of terrorism: A national field experiment. *Psychological Science, 14,* 144–150.

Lerner, J. S., & Keltner, D. (2001). Fear, anger, and risk. *Journal of Personality and Social Psychology, 81,* 146–159.

Lerner, J. S., Small, D. A., & Loewenstein, G. (2004). Heart strings and purse strings: Carryover effects of emotions on economic decisions. *Psychological Science, 15,* 337–341.

Lerner, M. J. (1980). *The belief in a just world: A fundamental delusion.* New York: Plenum Press.

Lerner, M. J., & Miller, D. T. (1978). Just world research and the attribution process: Looking back and ahead. *Psychological Bulletin, 85,* 1030–1051.

Lerner, M. J., & Simmons, C. H. (1966). Observer's reactions to the "innocent victim": Compassion or rejection? *Journal of Personality and Social Psychology, 4,* 203–210.

Leslie, A. M. (1994). ToMM, ToBY, and agency: Core architecture and domain specificity. In L. A. Hirschfeld & S. A. Gelman (Eds.), *Mapping the mind: Domain specificity in cognition and culture.* Cambridge: Cambridge University Press.

Leslie, A. (2000). "Theory of mind" as a mechanism of selective attention. In M. S. Gazzaniga (Ed.), *The new cognitive neurosciences* (pp. 1235–1247). Cambridge, MA: MIT Press.

Leung, K., Cheung, F. M., Zhang, J. X., Song, W. Z., & Dong, X. (1998). The five- factor model of personality in China. In K. Leung, U. Kim, S. Yamaguchi, & Y. Kashima (Eds.), *Progress in Asian social psychology* (Vol. 1). Singapore: Wiley.

Levenson, R. W. (1999). The intrapersonal functions of emotion. *Cognition and Emotion, 13,* 481–504.

Levenson, R. W. (2003). Autonomic specificity and emotion. In R. J. Davidson, K. R. Scherer, & H. H. Goldsmith (Eds.), *Handbook of affective sciences* (pp. 212–224). New York: Oxford University Press.

Levenson, R. W., Carstensen, L. L., Friesen, W. V., & Ekman, P. (1991). Emotion, physiology, and expression in old age. *Psychology and Aging, 6(1),* 28–35.

Levenson, R. W., Ekman, P., & Friesen, W. V. (1990). Voluntary facial action generates emotion-specific autonomic nervous system activity. *Psychophysiology, 27 (4),* 363–384.

Levenson, R. W., Ekman, P., Heider, K., & Friesen, W. V. (1992). Emotion and autonomic nervous system activity in the Minangkabau of West Sumatra. *Journal of Personality and Social Psychology, 62 (6),* 972–988.

Levenson, R. W., & Gottman, J. M. (1983). Marital interaction: Physiological linkage and affective exchange. *Journal of Personality and Social Psychology, 45,* 587–597.

Leventhal, H. (Ed.). (1970). *Findings and theory in the study of fear communications.* New York: Academic Press.

Leventhal, H., Singer, R. P., & Jones, S. H. (1965). The effects of fear and specificity of recommendation upon attitudes and behavior. *Journal of Personality and Social Psychology, 2,* 20–29.

Leventhal, H., Watts, J. C., & Pagano, F. (1967). Effects of fear and instructions on how to cope with danger. *Journal of Personality and Social Psychology, 6,* 313–321.

Levine, J. M. (1989). Reaction to opinion deviance in small groups. In P. B. Paulus (Ed.), *Psychology of group influence* (2nd ed, pp. 187–231). Hillsdale, NJ: Lawrence Erlbaum Associates.

Levine, J. M., Higgins, E. T., & Choi, H. S. (2000). Development of strategic norms in groups. *Organizational Behavior and Human Decision Processes, 82,* 88–101.

Levine, J. M., & Moreland, R. L. (1990). Progress in small group research. *Annual Review of Psychology, 41,* 585–634.

Levine, J. M., & Moreland, R. L. (1998). Small groups. In D. T. Gilbert, S. T. Fiske, & G. Lindzey (Eds.), *The handbook of social psychology* (4th ed., Vol. 2, pp. 415–469). New York: McGraw-Hill.

LeVine, R. A., & Campbell, D. T. (1972). *Ethnocentrism*. New York: Wiley.

Levinger, G. (1964). Note on need complementarity in marriage. *Psychological Bulletin, 61*, 153–157.

Levinger, G., & Schneider, D. J. (1969). Test of the "risk as a value" hypothesis. *Journal of Personality and Social Psychology, 11*, 165–169.

Levinger, G., Senn, D. J., & Jorgensen, B. W. (1970). Progress toward permanence in courtship: A test of the Kerckhoff-Davis hypothesis. *Sociometry, 33*, 427–433.

Levitt, S. D. (1994). Using repeat challengers to estimate the effect of campaign spending on election outcomes in the U.S. House. *Journal of Political Economy, 102*, 777–798.

Lewicki, P. W. (1983). Self-image bias in person perception. *Journal of Personality and Social Psychology, 45*, 384–393.

Lewin, K. (1935). The conflict between Aristotelian and Galilean modes of thought in contemporary psychology. *Journal of General Psychology, 5*, 141–177.

Lewin, K. (1952). Group decision and social change. In G. E. Swanson, T. M. Newcomb, & E. L. Hartley (Eds.), *Readings in social psychology*. New York: Henry Holt.

Leyens, J. P., Camino, L., Parke, R. D., & Berkowitz, L. (1975). Effects of movie violence on aggression in a field setting as a function of group dominance and cohesion. *Journal of Personality and Social Psychology, 32*, 346–360.

Leyens, J. P., Cisneros, T., & Hossay, J. F. (1976). Decentration as a means of reducing aggression after exposure to violent stimuli. *European Journal of Social Psychology, 6*, 459–473.

Leyens, J. P., & Picus, S. (1973). Identification with the winner of a fight and name mediation: Their differential effects upon subsequent aggressive behavior. *British Journal of Social and Clinical Psychology, 12*, 374–377.

Liberman, V., Samuels, S. M., & Ross, L. (2002). The name of the game: Predictive power of reputations vs. situational labels in determining Prisoner's Dilemma game moves. *Personality and Social Psychology Bulletin, 30*, 1175–1185.

Lin, Y. (1936). *My country and my people*. London: William Heinemann.

Linder, D. E., Cooper, J., & Jones, E. E. (1967). Decision freedom as a determinant of the role of incentive magnitude in attitude change. *Journal of Personality and Social Psychology, 6*, 245–254.

Linville, P. W. (1982). The complexity-extremity effect and age-based stereotyping. *Journal of Personality and Social Psychology, 42*, 193–211.

Linville, P. W. (1987). Self-complexity as a cognitive bugger against stress-related illness and depression. *Journal of Personality and Social Psychology, 52*, 663–676.

Linville, P. W., Fischer, G. W., & Salovey, P. (1989). Perceived distributions of the characteristics of in-group and out-group members: Empirical evidence and a computer simulation. *Journal of Personality and Social Psychology, 57*, 165–188.

Lipkus, I. M., Dalbert, C., & Siegler, I. C. (1996). The importance of distinguishing the belief in a just world for self versus for others: Implications for psychological well-being. *Personality and Social Psychology Bulletin, 22*, 666–677.

Lippmann, W. (1922). *Public opinion*. New York: Harcourt Brace.

Livshits, G., & Kobyliansky, E. (1991). Fluctuating asymmetry as a possible measure of developmental homeostasis in humans: A review. *Human Biology, 63*, 441–466.

Locke, K. D., & Horowitz, L. M. (1990). Satisfaction in interpersonal interactions as a function of similarity in level of dysphoria. *Journal of Personality and Social Psychology, 58*, 823–831.

Lockwood, P. (2002). Could it happen to you? Predicting the impact of downward social comparisons on the self. *Journal of Personality and Social Psychology, 82*, 343–358.

Loehlin, J. C. (1992). *Genes and environment in personality development*. Newbury Park, CA: Sage.

Loewenstein, G., & Lerner, J. S. (2003). The role of affect in decision making. In R. J. Davidson, K. R. Scherer, & H. H. Goldsmith (Eds.), *Handbook of affective sciences* (pp. 619–642). New York: Oxford University Press.

Loftus, E. F. (1979). *Eyewitness testimony*. Cambridge, MA: Harvard University Press.

Loftus, E. F. (1993). The reality of repressed memories. *American Psychologist, 48*, 518–537.

Loftus, E. F. (2003). The dangers of memory. In R. J. Sternberg (Ed.), *Psychologists defying the crowd: Stories of those who battled the establishment and won* (pp. 105–117). Washington, DC: American Psychological Association.

Longley, J., & Pruitt, D. G. (1980). Groupthink: A critique of Janis' theory. In L. Wheeler (Ed.), *Review of personality and social psychology*. Beverly Hills, CA: Sage.

Lord, C. G., Desforges, D. M., Ramsey, S. L., Trezza, G. R., & Lepper, M. R. (1991). Typicality effects in attitude-behavior consistency: Effects of category discrimination and category knowledge. *Journal of Experimental Social Psychology, 27*, 550–575.

Lord, C. G., Lepper, M. R., & Mackie, D. (1984). Attitude prototypes as determinants of attitude-behavior consistency. *Journal of Personality and Social Psychology, 46*, 1254–1266.

Lord, C., Ross, L., & Lepper, M. (1979). Biased assimilation and attitude polarization: The effects of prior theories on subsequently considered evidence. *Journal of Personality and Social Psychology, 37*, 2098–2109.

Lord, C. G., Scott, K. O, Pugh, M. A., & Desforges, D. M. (1997). Leakage beliefs and the correspondence bias. *Personality and Social Psychology Bulletin, 23*, 824–836.

Losch, M. E., & Cacioppo, J. T. (1990). Cognitive dissonance may enhance sympathetic tonus, but attitudes are changed to reduce negative affect rather than arousal. *Journal of Experimental Social Psychology, 26*, 289–304.

Lott, A. J., & Lott, B. E. (1961). Group cohesiveness, communication level, and conformity. *Journal of Abnormal and Social Psychology, 62*, 408–412.

Lott, A. J., & Lott, B. E. (1974). The role of reward in formation of positive interpersonal attitudes. In T. L. Huston (Ed.), *Foundations of interpersonal attraction* (pp. 171–189). New York: Academic Press.

Luker, K. (1984). *Abortion and the politics of motherhood*. Los Angeles, CA: University of California Press.

Lutz, C. (1990). Engendered emotion: Gender, power, and the rhetoric of emotional control in American discourse. In C. A. Lutz & L. Abu-Lughod (Eds.), *Language and the politics of emotions* (pp. 69–91). New York: Cambridge University Press.

Lydon, J., Zanna, M. P., & Ross, M. (1988). Bolstering attitudes by autobiographical recall: Attitude persistence and selective memory. *Personality and Social Psychology Bulletin, 14*, 78–86.

Lynam, D. R., Milich, R., Zimmerman, R., Novak, S. P., Logan,

T. K., Martin, C. E., et al. (1999). Project DARE: No effects at 10–year follow-up. *Journal of Consulting and Clinical Psychology, 67,* 590–593.

Lynch, J. J. (1979). *The broken heart: The medical consequences of loneliness.* New York: Basic Books.

Lyubomirsky, S., & Nolen-Hoeksema, S. (1995). Effects of self-focused rumination on negative thinking and interpersonal problem solving. *Journal of Personality and Social Psychology, 69,* 176–190.

Ma, V., & Schoeneman, T. J. (1997). Individualism versus collectivism: A comparison of Kenyan and American self-concepts. *Basic and Applied Social Psychology, 19,* 261–273.

Maass, A., & Clark, R. D. III. (1983). Internalization versus compliance: Different processes underlying minority influence and conformity. *European Journal of Social Psychology, 13,* 197–215.

Maass, A., Salvi, D., Arcuri, L., & Semin, G. (1989). Language use in intergroup contexts: The linguistic intergroup bias. *Journal of Personality and Social Psychology, 57,* 981–993.

Maccoby, E. E. (1990). Gender and relationships: A developmental account. *American Psychologist, 45,* 513–520.

Maccoby, E. E., & Jacklin, C. N. (1974). *The psychology of sex differences.* Stanford: Stanford University Press.

MacCoun, R. (1993). Blaming others to a fault. *Chance, 6,* 31–33.

Mackie, D. M. (1987). Systematic and nonsystematic processing of majority and minority persuasive communications. *Journal of Personality and Social Psychology, 53,* 41–52.

Mackie, D. M., & Worth, L. T. (1989). Cognitive deficits and the mediation of positive affect in persuasion. *Journal of Personality and Social Psychology, 57,* 27–40.

MacLeod, C., & Matthew, A. (1988). Anxiety and the allocation of attention to threat. *Quarterly Journal of Experimental Psychology, 40,* 653–670.

Macrae, C. N., Alnwick, K. A., Milne, A. B., & Schloerscheidt, A. M. (2002). Person perception across the menstrual cycle: Hormonal influences on social-cognitive functioning. *Psychological Science, 13,* 532–536.

Macrae, C. N., & Bodenhausen, G. V. (2000). Social cognition: Thinking categorically about others. *Annual Review of Psychology, 51,* 93–120.

Macrae, C. N., Hewstone, M., & Griffiths, R. J. (1993). Processing load and memory for stereotype-based information. *European Journal of Social Psychology, 23,* 77–87.

Macrae, C. N., Milne, A. B., & Bodenhausen, G. V. (1994). Stereotypes as energy-saving devices: A peek inside the cognitive toolbox. *Journal of Personality and Social Psychology, 66,* 37–47.

Macrae, C. N., Stangor, C., & Milne, A. B. (1994). Activating social stereotypes: A functional analysis. *Journal of Experimental Social Psychology, 30,* 370–389.

Madden, T. J., Ellen, P. S., & Ajzen, I. (1992). A comparison of the theory of planned behavior and the theory of reasoned action. *Personality and Social Psychology Bulletin, 18,* 3–9.

Major, B. (1994). From social inequality to personal entitlement: The role of social comparisons, legitimacy appraisals, and group membership. *Advances in Experimental Social Psychology, 26,* 293–355.

Malamuth, N. M., & Check, J. V. P. (1985). The effects of aggressive pornography in beliefs in rape myths: Individual differences. *Journal of Research in Personality, 19,* 299–320.

Malatesta, C. Z. (1990). The role of emotions in the development and organization of personality. In R. A. Thompson (Ed.), *Socioemotional development: Nebraska Symposium on Motivation* (pp. 1–56). Lincoln: University of Nebraska Press.

Malle, B. F. (1999). How people explain behavior: A new theoretical framework. *Personality and Social Psychology Review, 3,* 23–48.

Malle, B. F. (2001). Folk explanations of intentional actions. In B. F. Malle, L. J. Moses, & D. A. Baldwin (Eds.), *Intentions and intentionality: Foundations of social cognition.* Cambridge, MA: MIT Press.

Malle, B. F., Moses, L. J., & Baldwin, D. A. (2001). *Intentions and intentionality: Foundations of social cognition.* Cambridge, MA: MIT Press.

Mann, L. (1981). The baiting crowd in episodes of threatened suicide. *Journal of Personality and Social Psychology, 41,* 703–709.

Manning, J. T., & Hartley, M. A. (1991). Symmetry and ornamentation are correlated in the peacock's train. *Animal Behavior, 42,* 1020–1021.

Manstead, A. S. R., Profitt, C., & Smart, J. L. (1983). Predicting and understanding mothers' infant-feeding intentions and behavior: Testing the theory of reasoned action. *Journal of Personality and Social Psychology, 44,* 657–671.

Maret, S. M. (1983). Attractiveness ratings of photographs of blacks by Cruzans and Americans. *The Journal of Psychology, 115,* 113–116.

Maret, S. M., & Harling, G. A. (1985). Cross cultural perceptions of physical attractiveness: Ratings of photos of whites by Cruzans and Americans. *Perceptual and Motor Skills, 60,* 163–166.

Margolin, L., & White, L. (1987). The continuing role of physical attractiveness in marriage. *Journal of Marriage and the Family, 49,* 21–27.

Markow, T. A., & Ricker, J. P. (1992). Male size, developmental stability and mating success in natural populations on three Drosophilia species. *Heredity, 69,* 122–127.

Marks, G., & Miller, N. (1982). Target attractiveness as a mediator of assumed attitude similarity. *Personality and Social Psychology Bulletin, 8,* 728–735.

Markus, H. (1977). Self-schemata and processing information about the self. *Journal of Personality and Social Psychology, 35,* 63–78.

Markus, H. (1978). The effect of mere presence on social facilitation. An unobtrusive test. *Journal of Experimental Social Psychology, 14,* 389–397.

Markus, H. R., & Kitayama, S. (1991). Culture and the self: Implications for cognition, emotion, and motivation. *Psychological Review, 98,* 224–253.

Markus, H., & Nurius, P. S. (1986). Possible selves. *American Psychologist, 41,* 954–969.

Marsh, H. L. (1991). A comparative analysis of crime coverage in newspapers in the United States and other countries from 1960–1989: A review of the literature. *Journal of Criminal Justice, 19,* 67–79.

Marsh, H. W., & Parker, J. W. (1984). Determinants of student self-concept: Is it better to be a relatively large fish in a small pond even if you don't learn to swim as well? *Journal of Personality and Social Psychology, 47,* 213–231.

Marshall, S. L. A. (1947/2000). *Men against fire: The problem of battle command*. Norman, OK: University of Oklahoma Press.

Martin, G. G., & Clark, R. D. I. (1982). Distress crying in infants: Species and peer specificity. *Developmental Psychology, 18*, 3–9.

Martin, T., & Bumpass, L. (1989). Recent trends in marital disruption. *Demography, 26*, 37–52.

Martinek, T. J. (1981). Physical attractiveness: Effects on teacher expectations and dyadic interactions in elementary age children. *Journal of Sports Psychology, 3*, 196–205.

Maruyama, G., & Miller, N. (1980). Physical attractiveness, race, and essay evaluation. *Personality and Social Psychology Bulletin, 6*, 384–390.

Marwell, G., & Ames, R. (1981). Economists free ride, does anyone else: Experiments on the provision of public goods, IV. *Journal of Public Economics, 15*, 295–310.

Masuda, T., Ellsworth, P. C., Mesquita, B., Leu, J., & van de Veerdonk, E. (2004). *A face in the crowd or a crowd in the face: Japanese and American perceptions of others' emotions.* Unpublished manuscript, Hokkaido University.

Masuda, T., & Nisbett, R. E. (2001). Attending holistically vs. analytically: Comparing the context sensitivity of Japanese and Americans. *Journal of Personality and Social Psychology, 81*, 922–934.

Mathews, A., & MacLeod, C. (1994). Cognitive approaches to emotion and emotional disorders. *Annual Review of Psychology, 45*, 25–50.

Matsumoto, D. (2002). Methodological requirements to test a possible in-group advantage in judging emotions across cultures: Comment on Elfenbein and Ambady (2002) and evidence. *Psychological Bulletin, 128*, 236–242.

Matsumoto, D., & Ekman, P. (1989). American-Japanese cultural differences in intensity ratings of facial expressions of emotion. *Motivation and Emotion, 13*, 143–157.

Matsumoto, D., & Kudoh, T. (1993). American-Japanese cultural differences in attributions of personality based on smiles. *Journal of Nonverbal Behavior, 17*, 231–243.

Mauro, R., Sato, K., & Tucker, J. (1992). The role of appraisal in human emotions: A cross-cultural study. *Journal of Personality and Social Psychology, 62*, 301–317.

Mayer, J. D., Gaschke, Y. N., Braverman, D. L., & Evans, T. W. (1992). Mood-congruent judgment is a general effect. *Journal of Personality and Social Psychology, 63*, 119–132.

McAdams, D. P. (1996). Personality, modernity, and the storied self: A contemporary framework for studying persons. *Psychological Inquiry, 7*, 295–321.

McArthur, L. Z. (1972). The how and what of why: Some determinants and consequences of causal attribution. *Journal of Personality and Social Psychology, 13*, 733–742.

McArthur, L. Z., & Baron, R. M. (1983). Toward an ecological theory of social perception. *Psychological Review, 90*, 215–238.

McArthur, L. Z., & Post, D. L. (1977). Figural emphasis and person perception. *Journal of Experimental Social Psychology, 13*, 520–533.

McCain, J. (1999). *The faith of my fathers.* New York: Random House.

McCain, J. (2003). *Personal communication.*

McCaul, K. D., Sandgren, A. K., O'Neill, H., & Hinsz, V. B. (1993). The value of the theory of planned behavior, perceived control, and self-efficacy for predicting health-protective behaviors. *Basic and Applied Social Psychology, 14*, 231–252.

McCauley, C. (1989). The nature of social influence in groupthink: Compliance and internalization. *Journal of Personality and Social Psychology, 57*, 250–260.

McCauley, C. (1998). Group dynamics in Janis's theory of groupthink: Backward and forward. *Organizational Behavior and Human Decision Processes, 73*, 142–162.

McConahay, J. B. (1986). Modern racism, ambivalence, and the modern racism scale. In J. F. Dovidio & S. L. Gaertner (Eds.), *Prejudice, discrimination, and racism* (pp. 91–126). Orlando, FL: Academic Press.

McConahay, J. B., Hardee, B. B., & Batts, V. (1981). Has racism declined in America? It depends upon who is asking and what is asked. *Journal of Conflict Resolution, 25*, 563–579.

McConahay, J. B., & Hough, J. C. J. (1976). Symbolic racism. *Journal of Social Issues, 32*, 23–45.

McConnell, A. R., & Leibold, J. M. (2001). Relations among the implicit association test, discriminatory behavior, and explicit measures of racial attitudes. *Journal of Experimental Social Psychology, 37*, 435–442.

McCord, W., & McCord, J. (1959). *Origins of crime.* New York: Columbia.

McCoy, S. K., & Major, B. (2003). Group identification moderates emotional responses to perceived prejudice. *Personality and Social Psychology Bulletin, 29*, 1005–1017.

McCrae, R. R. (1982). Consensual validation of personality traits: Evidence from self-reports and ratings. *Journal of Personality and Social Psychology, 43*, 293–303.

McCrae, R. R., Costa, P. T., & Yik, M. S. M. (1996). Universal aspects of Chinese personality structure. In M. H. Bond (Ed.), *The handbook of Chinese psychology* (pp. 189–207). Hong Kong: Oxford University Press.

McCullough, M. C., Kilpatrick, S. D., Emmons, R. A., & Larson, D. B. (2001). Is gratitude a moral affect? *Psychological Bulletin, 127*, 249–266.

McCullough, M. E. (2000). Forgiveness as human strength: Theory, measurement, and links to well-being. *Journal of Social and Clinical Psychology, 19*, 43–55.

McCullough, M. E., Sandage, S. J., & Worthington, E. L. J. (1997). *To forgive is human.* Downers Grove, NJ: InterVarsity.

McGill, A. L. (1989). Context effects in judgements of causation. *Journal of Personality and Social Psychology, 57*, 189–200.

McGrath, J. (1984). *Groups: Interaction and performance.* Englewood Cliffs, NJ: Prentice-Hall.

McGuire, W. J. (1985). Attitudes and attitude change. In G. Lindzey & E. Aronson (Eds.), *Handbook of social psychology* (3rd ed., Vol. 2, pp. 233–346). New York: Random House.

McGuire, W. J. (1986). The myth of massive media impact: Savagings and salvagings. *Public Communication and Behavior, 1*, 173–257.

McGuire, W. J., & Padawer-Singer, A. (1978). Trait salience in the spontaneous self-concept. *Journal of Personality and Social Psychology, 33*, 743–754.

McGuire, W. J., & Papageorgis, D. (1961). The relative efficacy of various types of prior belief-defense in producing immunity against persuasion. *Journal of Abnormal and Social Psychology, 62*, 327–337.

McKenna, K. Y. A., & Bargh, J. A. (1998). Coming out in the age of the Internet: Identity demarginalization through virtual group participation. *Journal of Personality and Social Psychology, 75,* 681–694.

McNulty, J. K., & Karney, B. R. (2001). Attributions in marriage: Integrating specific and global evaluations of a relationship. *Personality and Social Psychology Bulletin, 27,* 943–955.

McPherson, K. (1983). Opinion-related information seeking: Personal and situational variables. *Personality and Social Psychology Bulletin, 9,* 116–124.

McPherson, M., Smith-Lovin, L., & Cook, J. M. (2001). Birds of a feather: Homophily in social networks. *Annual Review of Sociology, 27,* 415–444.

Mead, G. H. (1934). *Mind, self, and society.* Chicago: University of Chicago Press.

Medcoff, J. W. (1990). PEAT: An integrative model of attribution processes. In M. P. Zanna (Ed.), *Advances in experimental social psychology* (Vol. 23, pp. 111–209). New York: Academic Press.

Medvec, V. H., Madey, S. F., & Gilovich, T. (1995). When less is more: Counterfactual thinking and satisfaction among Olympic medalists. *Journal of Personality and Social Psychology, 69,* 603–610.

Mehrabian, A., & Williams, M. (1969). Nonverbal concomitants of perceived and intended persuasiveness. *Journal of Personality and Social Psychology, 13,* 37–58.

Merton, R. (1948). The self-fulfilling prophecy. *Antioch Review, 8,* 193–210.

Merton, R. (1957). *Social theory and social structure.* Glencoe, IL: Free Press.

Mesquita, B. (2001). Emotions in collectivist and individualist contexts. *Journal of Personality and Social Psychology, 80,* 68–74.

Mesquita, B. (2003). Emotions as dynamic cultural phenomena. In R. J. Davidson, K. R. Scherer, & H. H. Goldsmith (Eds.), *Handbook of affective sciences* (pp. 871–890). New York: Oxford University Press.

Mesquita, B., & Ellsworth, P. C. (2001). The role of culture in appraisal. In K. R. Scherer & A. Schorr (Eds.), *Appraisal processes in emotion. Theory, methods, research.* New York: Oxford University Press.

Mesquita, B., & Frijda, N. H. (1992). Cultural variations in emotions: A review. *Psychological Bulletin, 112,* 179–204.

Mesquita, B., & Karasawa, M. (2002). Different emotional lives. *Cognition and Emotion, 16,* 127–141.

Messick, D. M., Bloom, S., Boldizar, J. P., & Samuelson, C. (1985). Why we are fairer than others. *Journal of Experimental Social Psychology, 21,* 480–500.

Messick, D. M., & Sentis, K. P. (1979). Fairness and preference. *Journal of Experimental Social Psychology, 15,* 418–434.

Mettee, D., Taylor, S. E., & Friedman, H. (1973). Affect conversion and the gain-loss effect. *Sociometry, 36,* 505–519.

Meyer, J. P., & Pepper, S. (1977). Need compatibility and marital adjustment in young married couples. *Journal of Personality and Social Psychology, 35,* 331–342.

Michaels, J. W., Blommel, J. M., Brocato, R. M., Linkous, R. A., & Rowe, J. S. (1982). Social facilitation and inhibition in a natural setting. *Replications in Social Psychology, 2,* 21–24.

Michaels, J. W., Edwards, J. N., & Acock, A. C. (1984). Satisfaction in intimate relationships as a function of inequality, inequity, and outcomes. *Social Psychology Quarterly, 47,* 347–357.

Mikulincer, M., & Florian, V. (2000). Exploring individual differences in reactions to mortality salience: Does attachment style regulate terror management mechanisms. *Journal of Personality and Social Psychology, 79,* 260–273.

Mikulincer, M., Gillath, O., & Shaver, P. R. (2002). Activation of the attachment system in adulthood: Threat-related primes increase the accessibility of mental representations of attachment figures. *Journal of Personality and Social Psychology, 83,* 881–895.

Mikulincer, M., & Shaver, P. R. (2003). The attachment behavioral system in adulthood: Activation, psychodynamics, and interpersonal processes. In M. P. Zanna (Ed.), *Advances in experimental social psychology* (Vol. 35, pp. 53–152). New York: Academic Press.

Milbank, D., & Deane, C. (2003, September 7). Poll: 70% think Hussein, 9/11 linked. *Washington Post.*

Milgram, S. (1961). Nationality and conformity. *Scientific American, 205,* 45–51.

Milgram, S. (1963). Behavioral study of obedience. *Journal of Abnormal and Social Psychology, 67,* 371–378.

Milgram, S. (1965). Some conditions of obedience and disobedience to authority. *Human Relations, 18,* 57–75.

Milgram, S. (1970). The experience of living in cities. *Science, 167,* 1461–1468.

Milgram, S. (1974). *Obedience to authority: An experimental view.* New York: Harper & Row.

Mill, J. S. (1872/1843). *A system of logic ratiocinative and inductive* (8th ed.). London: Longmans, Green and Reader.

Millar, M., & Tesser, A. (1986). Effects of affective and cognitive focus on the attitude-behavior relation. *Journal of Personality and Social Psychology, 51,* 270–276.

Miller, A. G. (1986). *The obedience experiments: A case study of controversy in social science.* New York: Praeger.

Miller, A. G., Ashton, W., & Mishal, M. (1990). Beliefs concerning the features of constrained behavior: A basis for the fundamental attribution error. *Journal of Personality and Social Psychology, 59,* 635–650.

Miller, A. G., Gillen, B., Schenker, C., & Radlove, S. (1974). The prediction and perception of obedience to authority. *Journal of Personality, 42,* 23–42.

Miller, A. G., Jones, E. E., & Hinkle, S. (1981). A robust attribution error in the personality domain. *Journal of Experimental Social Psychology, 17,* 587–600.

Miller, D. T. (1976). Ego involvement and attributions for success and failure. *Journal of Personality and Social Psychology, 34,* 901–906.

Miller, D. T., & Gunasegaram, S. (1990). Temporal order and the perceived mutability of events: Implications for blame assignment. *Journal of Personality and Social Psychology, 59,* 1111–1118.

Miller, D. T., & McFarland, C. (1986). Counterfactual thinking and victim compensation: A test of norm theory. *Personality and Social Psychology Bulletin, 12,* 513–519.

Miller, D. T., & McFarland, C. (1991). When social comparison goes awry: The case of pluralistic ignorance. In J. M. Suls & T. A. Wills (Eds.), *Social comparison: Contemporary theory and research* (pp. 287–313). Hillsdale, NJ: Lawrence Erlbaum Associates.

Miller, D. T., & Taylor, B. R. (1995). Counterfactual thought, regret, and superstition: How to avoid kicking yourself. In N. J. Roese & J. M. Olson (Eds.), *What might have been: The social psychology of counterfactual thinking.* Mahwah, NJ: Lawrence Erlbaum Associates.

Miller, D. T., Turnbull, W., & McFarland, C. (1990). Counterfactual thinking and social perception: Thinking about what might have been. In M. P. Zanna (Ed.), *Advances in experimental social psychology* (Vol. 23, pp. 305–331). San Diego, CA: Academic Press.

Miller, J. G. (1984). Culture and the development of everyday social explanation. *Journal of Personality and Social Psychology, 46*, 961–978.

Miller, J. G. (1994). Cultural psychology: Bridging disciplinary boundaries in understanding the cultural grounding of self. In P. K. Bock (Ed.), *Psychological anthropology* (pp. 139–170). Westport: Praeger.

Miller, J. G., & Bersoff, D. M. (1994). Cultural influences on the moral status of reciprocity and the discounting of endogenous motivation. *Personality and Social Psychology Bulletin, 20*, 592–602.

Miller, N., & Brewer, M. B. (1986). Categorization effects on ingroup and outgroup perception. In J. F. Dovidio & S. L. Gaertner (Eds.), *Prejudice, discrimination, and racism* (pp. 209–230). Orlando, FL: Academic Press.

Miller, N. E. (1941). The frustration-aggression hypothesis. *Psychological Review, 48*, 337–342.

Miller, N. E., & Bugelski, R. (1948). Minor studies of aggression: II. The influence of frustrations imposed by the ingroup on attitudes expressed toward out-groups. *Journal of Psychology, 25*, 437–442.

Miller, P. J. E., & Rempel, J. K. (2004). Trust and partner-enhancing attributions in close relationships. *Personality and Social Psychology Bulletin, 30*, 695–705.

Miller, R. S. (1992). The nature and severity of self-reported embarrassing circumstances. *Personality and Social Psychology Bulletin, 18*, 190–198.

Miller, R. S. (1996). *Embarrassment: Poise and peril in everyday life*. New York: Guilford Press.

Miller, R. S., & Leary, M. R. (1992). Social sources and interactive functions of embarrassment. In M. Clark (Ed.), *Emotion and social behavior*. New York: Sage.

Miller, R. S., & Tangney, J. P. (1994). Differentiating embarrassment from shame. *Journal of Social and Clinical Psychology, 13*, 273–287.

Mineka, S., Rafaeli, E., & Yovel, I. (2003). Cognitive biases in emotional disorders: Information processing and social-cognitive perspectives. In R. J. Davidson, K. R. Scherer, & H. H. Goldsmith (Eds.), *Handbook of affective sciences* (pp. 976–1009). New York: Oxford University Press.

Mischel, W. (1968). *Personality and assessment*. New York: Wiley.

Mischel, W. (2004). Toward an integrated science of the person. *Annual Reviews of Psychology, 55*, 1–22.

Mischel, W., & Shoda, Y. (1995). A cognitive-affective system theory of personality: Reconceptualizing situations, dispositions, dynamics, and invariance in personality structures. *Psychological Review, 102*, 246–268.

Mischel, W., Shoda, Y., & Mendoza-Denton, R. (2002). Situation-behavioral profiles as a locus of consistency in personality. *Current Directions in Psychological Science, 11*, 50–54.

Mita, T. H., Dermer, M., & Knight, J. (1977). Reversed facial images and the mere-exposure hypothesis. *Journal of Personality and Social Psychology, 35*, 597–601.

Miyamoto, Y., & Kitayama, S. (2002). Cultural variation in correspondence bias: The critical role of attitude diagnosticity of socially constrained behavior. *Journal of Personality and Social Psychology, 83*, 1239–1248.

Moller, A. P. (1992a). Female swallow preference for symmetrical male sexual ornaments. *Nature, 357*, 238–240.

Moller, A. P. (1992b). Parasites differentially increase the degree of fluctuating asymmetry in secondary sexual characteristics. *Journal of Evolutionary Biology, 5*, 691–699.

Mook, D. G. (1983). In defense of external validity. *American Psychologist, 38*, 379–387.

Moore, J. S., Graziano, W. G., & Millar, M. G. (1987). Physical attractiveness, sex role orientation, and the evaluation of adults and children. *Personality and Social Psychology Bulletin, 13*, 95–102.

Moore, M. M. (1985). Nonverbal courtship patterns in women: Context and consequences. *Ethology and Sociobiology, 6*, 237–247.

Moreland, R. L., & Beach, S.R. (1992). Exposure effects in the classroom: The development of affinity among students. *Journal of Experimental Social Psychology, 28*, 255–276.

Moreland, R. L., & Levine, J. M. (1989). Newcomers and old-timers in small groups. In P. Paulus (Ed.), *Psychology of group influence* (2nd ed., pp. 143–186). Hillsdale, NJ: Lawrence Erlbaum Associates.

Morling, B. (1997). *Controlling the environments and controlling the self in the United States and Japan*. Paper presented at the Second Conference of the Asian Association of Social Psychology, Kyoto.

Morling, B., Kitayama, S., & Miyamoto, Y. (2002). Cultural practices emphasize influence in the U.S. and adjustment in Japan. *Personality and Social Psychology Bulletin, 28*, 311–323.

Morris, M. W., & Peng, K. (1994). Culture and cause: American and Chinese attributions for social and physical events. *Journal of Personality and Social Psychology, 67*, 949–971.

Morrow, J., & Nolen-Hoeksema, S. (1990). Effects of responses to depression on the remediation of depressive affect. *Journal of Personality and Social Psychology, 58*, 519–527.

Moscovici, S. (1985). Social influence and conformity. In G. Lindzey & E. Aronson (Eds.), *The handbook of social psychology* (3rd ed., Vol. 2, pp. 347–412). New York: Random House.

Moscovici, S., Lage, E., & Naffrechoux, M. (1969). Influences of a consistent minority on the responses of a majority in a color perception task. *Sociometry, 32*, 365–380.

Moscovici, S., & Zavalloni, M. (1969). The group as a polarizer of attitudes. *Journal of Personality and Social Psychology, 12*, 125–135.

Moskowitz, D. S. (1994). Cross-situational generality and the interpersonal circumplex. *Journal of Personality and Social Psychology, 66*, 921–933.

Moskowitz, G. B. (1993). Individual differences in social categorization: The influence of personal need for structure on spontaneous trait inferences. *Journal of Personality and Social Psychology, 65*, 132–142.

Mueller, U., & Mazur, A. (1997). Facial dominance in Homo Sapiens as honest signaling of male quality. *Behavioral Ecology, 8*, 569–579.

Mullen, B. (1991). Group composition, salience, and cognitive representations: The phenomenology of being in a group. *Journal of Experimental Social Psychology, 27*, 297–323.

Mullen, B., & Riordan, C. A. (1988). Self-serving attributions for performance in naturalistic settings: A meta-analytic review. *Journal of Applied Social Psychology, 18*, 3–22.

Mulvihill, D. J., Tumin, M. M., & Curtis, L. A. (1969). *Crimes of violence* (Vol. 11). Washington, DC: U.S. Government Printing Office.

Munro, D. (1985). Introduction. In D. Munro (Ed.), *Individualism and holism: Studies in Confucian and Taoist Values* (pp. 1–34). Ann Arbor: Center for Chinese Studies, University of Michigan.

Murdock, G. P. (1967). *Ethnographic atlas*. Pittsburgh: University of Pittsburgh Press.

Murphy, S. T., & Zajonc, R. B. (1993). Affect, cognition, and awareness: Affective priming with optimal and suboptimal stimulus exposures. *Journal of Personality and Social Psychology, 64*, 723–739.

Murray, S. L., & Holmes, J. G. (1993). Seeing virtues in faults: Negativity and the transformation of interpersonal narratives in close relationships. *Journal of Personality and Social Psychology, 65*, 707–723.

Murray, S. L., & Holmes, J. G. (1997). A leap of faith? Positive illusions in romantic relationships. *Personality and Social Psychology Bulletin, 23*, 586–604.

Murray, S. L., & Holmes, J. G. (1999). The (mental) ties that bind: Cognitive structures that predict relationship resilience. *Journal of Personality and Social Psychology, 77*, 1228–1244.

Murray, S. L., Holmes, J. G., Dolderman, D., & Griffin, D. W. (2000). What the motivated mind sees: Comparing friends' perspectives to married partners' views of each other. *Journal of Experimental Social Psychology, 36*, 600–620.

Murray, S. L., Holmes, J. G., & Griffin, D. W. (1996). The benefits of positive illusions: Idealization and the construction of satisfaction in close relationships. *Journal of Personality and Social Psychology, 70*, 79–98.

Murray, S. L., Holmes, J. G., MacDonald, G., & Ellsworth, P. C. (1998). Through the looking glass darkly? When self-doubts turn into relationship insecurities. *Journal of Personality and Social Psychology, 75*, 1459–1480.

Murstein, B. I. (1972). Physical attractiveness and marital choice. *Journal of Personality and Social Psychology, 22*, 8–12.

Mwaniki, M. K. (1973). *The relationship between self-concept and academic achievement in Kenyan pupils*. Unpublished doctoral dissertation, Stanford University, California.

Myers, D. G. (1999). Close relationships and quality of life. In K. Kahneman, E. Diener, & N. Schwarz (Eds.), *Well-being: The foundations of hedonic psychology* (pp. 374–391). New York: Sage.

Myers, D. G. (2000a). *The American paradox*. New Haven: Yale University Press.

Myers, D. G. (2000b). The funds, friends, and faith of happy people. *American Psychologist, 55*, 56–67.

Myers, D. G., & Bishop, G. D. (1971). Enhancement of dominant attitudes in group discussion discussion. *Journal of Personality and Social Psychology, 20*, 386–391.

Nahemow, L., & Lawton, M. P. (1975). Similarity and propinquity in friendship formation. *Journal of Personality and Social Psychology, 32*, 205–213.

Neff, L. A., & Karney, B. R. (2002). Judgments of a relationship partner: Specific accuracy but global enhancement. *Journal of Personality, 70*, 1079–1112.

Neimeyer, R. A., & Mitchell, K. A. (1988). Similarity and attraction: A longitudinal study. *Journal of Social and Personal Relationships, 5*, 131–148.

Neisser, U., & Harsch, N. (1992). Phantom flashbulbs: False recollections of hearing the news about *Challenger*. In E. Winograd & U. Neisser (Eds.), *Affect and accuracy in recall: Studies of "flashbulb" memories* (pp. 9–13). New York: Cambridge University Press.

Nel, E., Helmreich, R., & Aronson, E. (1969). Opinion change in the advocate as a function of the persuasibility of his audience: A clarification on the meaning of dissonance. *Journal of Personality and Social Psychology, 12*, 117–124.

Nelson, L. D., & Morrison, E. L. (2005). Judgments of food and finances influence preferences for potential partners. *Psychological Science, 16*, 167–173.

Nemeroff, C., & Rozin, P. (1989). "You are what you eat": Applying the demand-free "impressions" technique to an unacknowledged belief. *Ethos, 17*, 50–69.

Nemeth, C. (1986). Differential contributions of majority and minority influence. *Psychological Review, 93*, 23–32.

Nesse, R. (1990). Evolutionary explanations of emotions. *Human Nature, 1*, 261–289.

Neuberg, S. L. (1988). Behavioral implications of information presented outside of conscious awareness: The effect of subliminal presentation of trait information on behavior in the Prisoner's Dilemma game. *Social Cognition, 6*, 207–230.

Neuberg, S. L., & Fiske, S. T. (1987). Motivational influences on impression formation: Outcome dependency, accuracy-driven attention, and individuating processes. *Journal of Personality and Social Psychology, 53*, 431–444.

Nevo, B. (Ed.). (1986). *Scientific aspects of graphology: A handbook*. Springfield, IL: Charles C. Thomas.

Newcomb, T. M. (1956). The prediction of interpersonal attraction. *American Psychologist, 1*, 575–586.

Newcomb, T. M. (1958). Attitude development as a function of reference groups. In E. E. Maccoby, T. M. Newcomb, & E. L. Hartley (Eds.), *Readings in social psychology* (3rd ed.). New York: Holt, Rinehart and Winston.

Newcomb, T. M. (1961). *The acquaintance process*. New York: Holt, Rinehart and Winston.

Newman, L. S. (1991). Why are traits inferred spontaneously? A developmental approach. *Social Cognition, 9*, 221–253.

Newman, L. S. (1993). How individualists interpret behavior: Idiocentrism and spontaneous trait inference. *Social Cognition, 11*, 243–269.

Newman, L. S. (1996). Trait impressions as heuristics for predicting future behavior. *Personality and Social Psychology Bulletin, 22*, 395–411.

Ng, S. H. (1980). *The social psychology of power*. San Diego, CA: Academic Press.

Niemi, G., Katz, R. S., & Newman, D. (1980). Reconstructing past partisanship: The failure of party identification recall questions. *American Journal of Political Science, 24*, 633–651.

Niemi, R. G., & Jennings, M. K. (1991). Issues and inheritance in the formation of party identification. *American Journal of Political Science, 35*, 970–988.

Nisbett, R. E. (1993). Violence and U.S. regional culture. *American Psychologist, 48*, 441–449.

Nisbett, R. E. (2003). *The geography of thought: Why we think the way we do*. New York: Free Press.

Nisbett, R. E., Caputo, C., Legant, P., & Maracek, J. (1973). Behavior as seen by the actor and as seen by the observer. *Journal of Personality and Social Psychology, 27*, 154–164.

Nisbett, R. E., & Cohen, D. (1996). *Culture of honor: The psychology of violence in the South.* Boulder: Westview Press.

Nisbett, R. E., Fong, G. T., Lehman, D. R., & Cheng, P. W. (1987). Teaching reasoning. *Science, 238,* 625–631.

Nisbett, R. E., & Masuda, T. (2003). Culture and point of view. *Proceedings of the National Academy of Sciences of the United States of America, 100,* 11163–11175.

Nisbett, R. E., Polly, G., & Lang, S. (1995). Homicide and U. S. regional culture. In B. Ruback & N. Weiner (Eds.), *Interpersonal violent behavior: Social and cultural aspects.* New York: Springer-Verlag.

Nisbett, R. E., & Ross, L. (1980). *Human inference: Strategies and shortcomings of social judgment.* Englewood Cliffs, NJ: Prentice-Hall.

Nisbett, R. E., & Wilson, T. D. (1977). Telling more than we can know: Verbal reports on mental processes. *Psychological Review, 84,* 231–259.

Nobel gene biz bombs—moms opt for lookers. (1985, October 20). *Chicago Sun-Times.*

Nolen-Hoeksema, S. (1987). Sex differences in unipolar depression: Evidence and theory. *Psychological Bulletin, 101,* 259–282.

Norenzayan, A., Choi, I., & Nisbett, R. E. (1999). Eastern and Western perceptions of causality for social behavior: Lay theories about personalities and social situations. In D. Prentice & D. Miller (Eds.), *Cultural divides: Understanding and overcoming group conflict* (pp. 239–272). New York: Sage.

Norenzayan, A., & Heine, S. J. (2004). *Psychological universals: What are they and how can we know?* Vancouver: University of British Columbia.

Norenzayan, A., Smith, E. E., Kim, B. J., & Nisbett, R. E. (2002). Cultural preferences for formal versus intuitive reasoning. *Cognitive Science, 26,* 653–684.

Norman, R. (1975). Affective-cognitive consistency, attitudes, conformity, and behavior. *Journal of Personality and Social Psychology, 32,* 83–91.

Norton, M. I., Monin, B., Cooper, J., & Hogg, M. (2003). Vicarious dissonance: Attitude change from the inconsistency of others. *Journal of Personality and Social Psychology, 85,* 47–62.

Norton, M. I., Vandello, J. A., & Darley, J. M. (2004). Casuistry and social category bias. *Journal of Personality and Social Psychology, 87,* 817–831.

Nosek, B. A., Banaji, M. R., & Greenwald, A. G. (2002). Harvesting implicit group attitudes and beliefs from demonstration web site. *Group Dynamics: Theory, Research, and Practice, 6,* 101–115.

Nowak, M. A., Page, K. M., & Sigmund, K. (2000). Fairness versus reason in the ultimatum game. *Science, 289,* 1773–1775.

Nowak, M. A., & Sigmund, K. (1998). Evolution of indirect reciprocity by image scoring. *Nature, 393,* 573–576.

Nuttin, J. M. (1987). Affective consequences of mere ownership: The name letter effect in 12 European languages. *European Journal of Social Psychology, 17,* 381–402.

Oakes, P. J., & Turner, J. C. (1980). Social categorization and intergroup behavior: Does minimal intergroup discrimination make social identity more positive? *European Journal of Social Psychology, 10,* 295–301.

Oatley, K. (1993). Social construction in emotion. In M. Lewis & J. Haviland (Eds.), *Handbook of emotions* (pp. 342–352). New York: Guilford Press.

Oatley, K. (2003). Creative expression and communication of emotions in the visual and narrative arts. In R. J. Davidson, K. R. Scherer, & H. H. Goldsmith (Eds.), *Handbook of affective sciences* (pp. 481–502). New York: Oxford University Press.

Oatley, K., & Jenkins, J. M. (1992). Human emotions: Function and dysfunction. *Annual Review of Psychology, 43,* 55–85.

Ogbu, J. U. (1991). Low performance as an adaptation: The case of Blacks in Stockton California. In M. A. Gibson & J. U. Ogbu (Eds.), *Minority status and schooling* (pp. 249–285). New York: Grand.

Ogbu, J. U., & Davis, A. (2003). *Black American students in an affluent suburb: A study of academic disengagement.* New York: Lawrence Erlbaum Associates.

Ohbuchi, K., Kameda, N., & Agarie, M. (1989). Apology as aggression control: Its role in mediating appraisal of and response to harm. *Journal of Personality and Social Psychology, 56,* 219–227.

Ohman, A. (1986). Face the beast and fear the face: Animal and social fears as prototypes for evolutionary analysis of emotions. *Psychophysiology, 23,* 123–145.

Olweus, D. (1979). Stability of aggressive reaction patterns in males: A review. *Psychological Bulletin, 86,* 852–875.

Olweus, D. (1980). Familial and temperamental determinants of aggressive behavior in adolescent boys: A causal analysis. *Developmental Psychology, 16,* 644–660.

Orians, G. H., & Heerwagen, J. H. (1992). Evolved responses to landscapes. In J. H. Barlow, L. Cosmides, & J. Tooby (Eds.), *The adapted mind* (pp. 555–580). New York: Oxford University Press.

Ortony, A., Clore, G., & Collins, A. (1988). *The cognitive structure of emotions.* New York: Cambridge University Press.

Ostrom, T. M., & Sedikides, C. (1992). Out-group homogeneity effects in natural and minimal groups. *Psychological Bulletin, 112,* 536–552.

Oxman, T. E., & Hull, J. G. (1997). Social support, depression, and activities of daily living in older heart surgery patients. *Journal of Gerontology: Psychological Sciences, 52,* 1–14.

Pagel, M., & Mace, R. (2004). The cultural wealth of nations. *Nature, 428,* 275–278.

Pallak, M. S., Mueller, M., Dollar, K., & Pallak, J. (1972). Effects of commitment on responsiveness to an extreme consonant communication. *Journal of Personality and Social Psychology, 23,* 429–436.

Palmer, J. F., & Smardon, R. C. (1989). Measuring human values associated with wetlands. In L. Kriesberg, T. A. Northrup, & S. J. Thorson (Eds.), *Intractable conflicts and their transformation* (pp. 156–179). Syracuse, NY: Syracuse University Press.

Palombit, R., Seyfarth, R. M., & Cheney, D. L. (1997). The adaptive value of "friendships" to female baboons: Experimental and observational evidence. *Animal Behavior, 54,* 599–614.

Park, B., & Judd, C. M. (1990). Measures and models of perceived group variability. *Journal of Personality and Social Psychology, 59,* 173–191.

Park, B., & Rothbart, M. (1982). Perception of out-group homogeneity and levels of social categorization: Memory for the subordinate attributes of in-group and out-group members. *Journal of Personality and Social Psychology, 42,* 1051–1068.

Parkinson, B., & Manstead, A. S. R. (1992). Appraisal as a cause of emotion. In M. S. Clark (Ed.), *Emotion.* Newbury Park, CA: Sage.

Parrott, W. G. (2001). Implications of dysfunctional emotions for understanding how emotions function. *Review of General Psychology, 5*, 180–186.

Parrott, W. G., & Smith, S. F. (1991). Embarrassment: Actual vs. typical cases, classical vs. prototypical representations. *Cognition and Emotion, 5*, 467–488.

Paulhus, D. L. (1998). Interpersonal adaptiveness of trait self-enhancement: A mixed blessing? *Journal of Personality and Social Psychology, 74*, 1197–1208.

Payne, B. K. (2001). Prejudice and perception: The role of automatic and controlled processes in misperceiving a weapon. *Journal of Personality and Social Psychology, 81*, 181–192.

Payne, B. K., Lambert, A. J., & Jacoby, L. L. (2002). Best laid plans: Effect of goals on accessibility bias and cognitive control in race-based misperceptions of weapons. *Journal of Experimental Social Psychology, 38*, 384–396.

Pearson, C. M., & Porath, C. L. (1999). *Workplace incivility: The target's eye view.* Paper presented at the Annual Meeting of the Academy of Management, Chicago.

Peng, K., & Knowles, E. (2003). Culture, ethnicity and the attribution of physical causality. *Personality and Social Psychology Bulletin, 29*, 1272–1284.

Peng, K., & Nisbett, R. E. (2000). *Cross-cultural similarities and differences in the understanding of physical causality.* Berkeley: University of California.

Pennebaker, J. W. (1989). Confession, inhibition, and disease. In L. Berkowitz (Ed.), *Advances in experimental social psychology* (Vol. 22, pp. 211–244). New York: Academic Press.

Pennebaker, J. W. (1993). Putting stress into words: Health, linguistic and therapeutic implications. *Behavioral Research and Therapy, 31*, 539–548.

Pennebaker, J. W., Hughes, C. F., & O'Heeron, R. C. (1987). The psychophysiology of confession: Linking inhibitory and psychosomatic processes. *Journal of Personality and Social Psychology, 52*, 781–793.

Pennebaker, J. W., Mayne, T. J., & Francis, M. (1997). Linguistic predictors of adaptive bereavement. *Journal of Personality and Social Psychology, 72*, 863–871.

Pennebaker, J. W., & Roberts, T. A. (1992). Toward a his and hers theory of emotion: Gender differences in visceral perception. *Journal of Social and Clinical Psychology, 11*, 199–212.

Penton-Voak, I. S., Perrett, D. I., Castles, D. L., Kobayashi, T., Burt, D. M., Murray, L. K., et al. (1999). Menstrual cycle alters face preference. *Nature, 399*, 741–742.

Peplau, L. A., & Perlman, D. (1982). Perspectives on loneliness. In L. A. Peplau & D. Perlman (Eds.), *Loneliness: A sourcebook of current theory, research, and therapy* (pp. 1–18). New York: Wiley.

Perloff, L. S., & Fetzer, B. K. (1986). Self-other judgments and perceived vulnerability of victimization. *Journal of Personality and Social Psychology, 50*, 502–510.

Perloff, R. M. (1993). Third-person effect research 1983–1992: A review and synthesis. *International Journal of Public Opinion Research, 5*, 167–184.

Perner, J., Frith, U., Leslie, A. M., & Leekam, S. R. (1989). Exploration of the autistic child's theory of mind: Knowledge, belief and communication. *Child Development, 60*, 689–700.

Perner, J., Leekam, S. R., & Wimmer, H. (1987). Three-year olds' difficulty with false belief: The case for a conceptual deficit. *British Journal of Developmental Psychology, 5*, 125–137.

Perner, J., Ruffman, T., & Leekam, S. R. (1994). Theory of mind is contagious: You catch it from your sibs. *Child Development, 65*, 1228–1238.

Perper, T. (1985). *Sex signals: The biology of love.* Philadelphia: ISI Press.

Perrett, D. I., Lee, K., Penton-Voak, I., Burt, D. M., Rowland, D., Yoshikawa, S., et al. (1998). Sexual dimorphism and facial attractiveness. *Nature, 394*, 884–886.

Perrett, D. I., May, K. A., & Yoshikawa, S. (1994). Facial shape and judgments of female attractiveness. *Nature, 368*, 239–242.

Perrin, S., & Spencer, C. (1981). Independence of conformity in the Asch experiment as a reflection of cultural or situational factors. *British Journal of Social Psychology, 20*, 205–209.

Pessin, J. (1933). The comparative effects of social and mechanical stimulation on memorizing. *American Journal of Psychology, 45*, 263–270.

Pessin, J., & Husband, R. W. (1933). Effect of social stimulation on human maze learning. *Journal of Abnormal and Social Psychology, 28*, 148–154.

Peterson, C. (1993). *Learned helplessness: A theory for the age of personal control.* New York: Oxford University Press.

Peterson, C. (2000). The future of optimism. *American Psychologist, 55*, 44–55.

Peterson, C., & Barrett, L. C. (1987). Explanatory style and academic performance among university freshmen. *Journal of Personality and Social Psychology, 53*, 603–607.

Peterson, C., Maier, S., & Seligman, M. E. P. (1993). *Learned helplessness.* New York: Oxford University Press.

Peterson, C., & Seligman, M. E. P. (1984). Causal explanations as a risk factor for depression: Theory and evidence. *Psychological Review, 91*, 347–374.

Peterson, C., Seligman, M. E. P., & Vaillant, G. E. (1988). Pessimistic explanatory style is a risk factor for physical illness: A thirty-five-year longitudinal study. *Journal of Personality and Social Psychology, 55*, 23–27.

Pettigrew, T. F. (1972). *Racially separate or together.* New York: McGraw-Hill.

Pettigrew, T. (1979). The ultimate attribution error: Extending Allport's cognitive analysis to prejudice. *Personality and Social Psychology Bulletin, 5*, 461–476.

Petty, R. E., & Cacioppo, J. T. (1979). Issue involvement can increase or decrease persuasion by enhancing message-relevant cognitive responses. *Journal of Personality and Social Psychology, 37*, 1915–1926.

Petty, R. E., & Cacioppo, J. T. (1984). The effects of involvement on responses to argument quantity and quality: Central and peripheral routes to persuasion. *Journal of Personality and Social Psychology, 46*, 69–81.

Petty, R. E., & Cacioppo, J. T. (1986). The elaboration likelihood model of persuasion. In L. Berkowitz (Ed.), *Advances in experimental social psychology* (Vol. 19, pp. 123–205). New York: Academic Press.

Petty, R. E., Cacioppo, J. T., & Goldman, R. (1981). Personal involvement as a determinant of argument-based persuasion. *Journal of Personality and Social Psychology, 41*, 847–855.

Petty, R. E., Cacioppo, J. T., & Schumann, D. W. (1983). Central and peripheral routes to advertising effectiveness: The moderating role of involvement. *Journal of Consumer Research, 10*, 135–146.

Petty, R. E., Haugtvedt, C. P., & Smith, S. M. (1995). Elaboration as a determinant of attitude strength. In R. E. Petty & J. A.

Krosnick (Eds.), *Attitude strength: Antecedents and consequences* (pp. 93–130). Mahwah, NJ: Lawrence Erlbaum Associates.

Petty, R. E., & Wegener, D. (1998). Attitude change: Multiple roles for persuasion variables. In D. T. Gilbert, S. T. Fiske, & G. Lindzey (Eds.), *Handbook of social psychology* (4th ed., pp. 323–390). New York: McGraw-Hill.

Phelps, E. A., O'Connor, K. J., Cunningham, W. A., Funayama, E. S., Gatenby, J. C., Gore, J. C., et al. (2000). Performance on indirect measure of race evaluation predicts amygdala activation. *Journal of Cognitive Neuroscience, 12,* 729–738.

Phillips, D. P. (1986). Natural experiments on the effects of mass media violence on fatal aggression: Strengths and weakness of a new approach. In L. Berkowitz (Ed.), *Advances in experimental social psychology* (Vol. 19, pp. 207–250). Orlando, FL: Academic Press.

Phillips, K. (2002). *Wealth and democracy*. New York: Broadway Books.

Piedmont, R. L., & Chase, J. H. (1997). Cross-cultural generality of the five-factor model of personality: Development and validation of the NEO-PI-R for Koreans. *Journal of Cross-Cultural Psychology, 28,* 131–155.

Pietromonaco, P. R., & Feldman-Barrett, L. (2000). Internal working models: What do we know about knowing the self in relation to others. *Review of General Psychology, 4,* 155–175.

Pietromonaco, P. R., & Nisbett, R. E. (1982). Swimming upstream against the fundamental attribution error: Subjects' weak generalizations from the Darley and Batson study. *Social Behavior and Personality, 10,* 1–4.

Piliavin, J. A., & Piliavin, I. M. (1972). The effects of blood on reactions to a victim. *Journal of Personality and Social Psychology, 23,* 253–261.

Piliavin, J. A., Piliavin, I. M., & Broll, L. (1976). Time of arousal at an emergency and likelihood of helping. *Personality and Social Psychology Bulletin, 2,* 273–276.

Piliavin, J. A., & Unger, R. K. (1985). The helpful but helpless female: Myth or reality? In V. O'Leary, R. K. Unger, & B. S. Wallston (Eds.), *Women, gender and social psychology* (pp. 149–186). Hillsdale, NJ: Lawrence Erlbaum Associates.

Pinker, S. (1994). *The language instinct*. New York: Harper-Collins.

Pinker, S. (2002). *The blank slate: The modern denial of human nature*. New York: Viking.

Pinker, S., & Bloom, P. (1990). Natural language and natural selection. *Behavioral and Brain Sciences, 13,* 703–784.

Plant, E. A., & Devine, P. G. (1998). Internal and external motivation to respond without prejudice. *Journal of Personality and Social Psychology, 75,* 811–832.

Platt, J. J., & James, W. T. (1966). Social facilitation of eating behavior in young opossums: I. Group vs. solitary feeding. *Psychonomic Science, 6,* 421–422.

Platt, J. J., Yaksh, T., & Darby, C. L. (1967). Social facilitation of eating behavior in armadillos. *Psychological Reports, 20,* 1136.

Plomin, R., & Caspi, A. (1998). DNA and personality. *European Journal of Personality, 12,* 387–407.

Plomin, R., & Caspi, A. (1999). Behavioral genetics and personality. In L. A. Pervin & O. P. John (Eds.), *Handbook of personality: Theory and research* (2nd ed., pp. 251–276). New York: Guilford Press.

Plous, S. (1985). Perceptual illusions and military realities. *Journal of Conflict Resolution, 29,* 363–389.

Podratz, K. E., Halverson, S. K., & Dipboye, R. L. (2004). Physical attractiveness biases in ratings of employment suitability: Tracking down the "beauty is beastly." Manuscript submitted for publication.

Polak, M. (1993). Parasitic infection increases fluctuating asymmetry of male Drosophila Nigrospiracula: Implications for sexual selection. *Genetica, 89,* 255–265.

Porges, S. P. (1995). Orienting in a defensive world: Mammalian modifications of our evolutionary heritage. A polyvagal theory. *Psychophysiology,* 301–317.

Porter, R. H., Cernoch, J. M., & Balogh, R. D. (1984). Recognition of neonates by facial-visual characteristics. *Pediatrics, 74,* 501–504.

Porter, R. H., Cernoch, J. M., & McLauglin, F. J. (1983). Maternal recognition of neonates through olfactory cues. *Physiology and Behavior, 30,* 151–154.

Postmes, T., & Spears, R. (1998). Deindividuation and antinormative behavior: A meta-analysis. *Psychological Bulletin, 123,* 238–259.

Postmes, T., Spears, R., & Cihangir, S. (2001). Quality of decision making and group norms. *Journal of Personality and Social Psychology, 80,* 918–930.

Pratkanis, A. R., & Aaronson, E. (2000). *Age of propaganda*. New York: Freeman.

Pratkanis, A. R., Breckler, S. J., & Greenwald, A. G. (Eds.). (1989). *Attitude structure and function*. Hillsdale, NJ: Lawrence Erlbaum Associates.

Pratkanis, A. R., Eskenazi, J., & Greenwald, A. G. (1994). What you expect is what you believe (but not necessarily what you get): A test of the effectiveness of subliminal self-help audiotapes. *Basic and Applied Social Psychology, 15,* 251–276.

Pratkanis, A. R., Greenwald, A. G., Leippe, M. R., & Baumgardner, M. H. (1988). In search of reliable persuasion effects: III. The sleeper effect is dead. Long live the sleeper effect. *Journal of Personality and Social Psychology, 54,* 203–218.

Pratto, F. (1996). Sexual politics: The gender gap in the bedroom, the cupboard, and the cabinet. In D. M. Buss & N. M. Malamuth (Eds.), *Sex, power, and conflict: Evolutionary and feminist perspectives* (pp. 179–230). New York: Oxford University Press.

Pratto, F., & Bargh, J. A. (1991). Stereotyping based upon apparently individuating information: Trait and global components of sex stereotypes under attention overload. *Journal of Experimental Psychology, 27,* 26–47.

Pratto, F., & John, O. P. (1991). Automatic vigilance: The attention-grabbing power of negative social information. *Journal of Personality and Social Psychology, 61,* 380–391.

Prentice, D. A. (1990). Familiarity and differences in self- and other-representations. *Journal of Personality and Social Psychology,* 369–383.

Prentice, D. A., & Miller, D. T. (1993). Pluralistic ignorance and alcohol use on campus: Some consequences of misperceiving the social norm. *Journal of Personality and Social Psychology, 64,* 243–256.

Prentice-Dunn, S., & Rogers, R. W. (1989). Deindividuation and self regulation of behavior. In P. Paulus (Ed.), *The psychology of group influence* (2nd ed., pp. 87–109). Hillsdale, NJ: Lawrence Erlbaum Associates.

Preston, S. D., & de Waal, F. B. M. (2002). Empathy: Its ultimate and proximate bases. *Behavioral and Brain Sciences, 25*, 1–72.

Profet, M. (1992). Pregnancy sickness as adaptation: A deterrent to maternal ingestion of teratogens. In J. H. Barlow, L. Cosmides, & J. Tooby (Eds.), *The adapted mind* (pp. 327–366). New York: Oxford University Press.

Pronin, E., Gilovich, T., & Ross, L. (2004). Objectivity in the eye of the beholder: Divergent perceptions of bias in self versus others. *Psychological Review, 111*, 781–799.

Pronin, E., Lin, D.Y., & Ross, L. (2002). The bias blind spot: Perceptions of bias in self versus others. *Personality and Social Psychology Bulletin*, 369–381.

Ptacek, J. T., & Dodge, K. L. (1995). Coping strategies and relationship satisfaction in couples. *Personality and Social Psychology Bulletin, 21*, 76–84.

Pyszczynski, T., Greenberg, J., Solomon, S., Arndt, J., & Schimel, J. (2004). Why do people need self-esteem: A theoretical and empirical review. *Psychological Bulletin, 130*, 435–468.

Quattrone, G. A., & Jones, E. E. (1980). The perception of variability within in-groups and out-groups: Implications for the law of small numbers. *Journal of Personality and Social Psychology, 38*, 141–152.

Quigley, B., & Tedeschi, J. (1996). Mediating effects of blame attributions on feelings of anger. *Personality and Social Psychology Bulletin, 22*, 1280–1288.

Rajecki, D. W., Bledsoe, S. B., & Rasmussen, J. L. (1991). Successful personal ads: Gender differences and similarities in offers, stipulations, and outcomes. *Basic and Applied Psychology, 12*, 457–469.

Rajecki, D. W., Ickes, W., Corcoran, C., & Lenerz, K. (1977). Social facilitation of human performance: Mere presence effects. *Journal of Social Psychology, 102*, 297–310.

Rasinski, K. (1987). What's fair is fair...or is it? Value differences underlying public views of social justice. *Journal of Personality and Social Psychology, 53*, 201–211.

Raskin, R., & Terry, H. (1988). A principal-components analysis of the Narcissistic Personality Inventory and further evidence of its construct validity. *Journal of Personality and Social Psychology, 54*, 890–902.

Rawls, J. (1971). *A theory of justice.* Cambridge, MA: Harvard University Press.

Razran, G. H. S. (1940). Conditioned response changes in rating and appraising sociopolitical slogans. *Psychological Bulletin, 37*, 481.

Read, A. W., et al. (1978). *Funk and Wagnalls new comprehensive international dictionary of the English language.* New York: Publisher's Guild Press.

Read, S. J. (1984). Analogical reasoning social judgment: The importance of causal theories. *Journal of Personality and Social Psychology, 46*, 14–25.

Read, S. J. (1987). Similarity and causality in the use of social analogies. *Journal of Experimental Social Psychology, 23*, 189–207.

Reed, J. S. (1990). Billy, the fabulous moolah, and me. In J. S. Reed (Ed.), *Whistling Dixie* (pp. 119–122). San Diego: Harcourt Brace Jovanovich.

Reeder, G. D., & Brewer, M. B. (1979). A schematic model of dispositional attribution in interpersonal perception. *Psychological Review, 86*, 61–79.

Reeves, R. A., Baker, G. A., Boyd, J. G., & Cialdini, R. B. (1991). The door-in-the-face technique: Reciprocal concessions vs. self-presentational explanations. *Journal of Social Behavior and Personality, 6*, 645–658.

Reeves, R. A., Macolini, R. M., & Martin, R. C. (1987). Legitimizing paltry contributions: On-the-spot vs. mail-in requests. *Journal of Applied Social Psychology, 7*, 731–738.

Reeves-Sanday, P. (1981). The socio-cultural context of rape: A cross-cultural study. *Journal of Social Issues, 37*, 5–27.

Reeves-Sanday, P. (1997). The socio-cultural context of rape: A cross-cultural study. In L. L. O'Toole (Ed.), *Gender violence: Interdisciplinary perspectives.* New York: New York University Press.

Regan, D. T. (1971). Effects of a favor and liking on compliance. *Journal of Experimental Social Psychology, 7*, 627–639.

Regan, D. T., & Fazio, R. (1977). On the consistency between attitudes and behavior: Look to the method of attitude formation. *Journal of Experimental Social Psychology, 13*, 28–45.

Regan, D. T., & Kilduff, M. (1988). Optimism about elections: Dissonance reduction at the ballot box. *Political Psychology, 9*, 101–107.

Regan, D. T., Williams, M., & Sparling, S. (1972). Voluntary expiation of guilt: A field experiment. *Journal of Personality and Social Psychology, 24*, 42–45.

Regan, J. W. (1971). Guilt, perceived injustice, and altruistic behavior. *Journal of Personality and Social Psychology, 18*, 124–132.

Reifman, A. S., Larrick, R. P., & Fein, S. (1991). Temper and temperature on the diamond: The heat-aggression relationship in major league baseball. *Personality and Social Psychology Bulletin, 17*, 580–585.

Reis, H. T., & Downey, G. (1999). Social cognition in relationships: Building essential bridges between two literatures. *Social Cognition, 17*, 97–117.

Reis, H. T., Nezlek, J., & Wheeler, L. (1980). Physical attractiveness in social interaction. *Journal of Personality and Social Psychology, 38*, 604–617.

Reis, H. T., Wheeler, L., Speigel, N., Kernis, M. H., Nezleck, J., & Perri, M. (1982). Physical attractiveness in social interaction: 2. Why does appearance affect social experience? *Journal of Personality and Social Psychology, 43*, 979–996.

Reisenzein, R. (1983). The Schachter theory of emotion: Two decades later. *Psychological Bulletin, 94(2)*, 239–264.

Remley, A. (1988, October). From obedience to independence. *Psychology Today*, pp. 56–59.

Rest, J. (1979). *Development in judging moral issues.* Minneapolis: University of Minnesota Press.

Rhee, E., Uleman, J. S., Lee, H. K., & Roman, R. J. (1995). Spontaneous self-descriptions and ethnic identities in individualistic and collectivist cultures. *Journal of Personality and Social Psychology, 69*, 142–152.

Rhine, R. J., & Severance, L. J. (1970). Ego-involvement, discrepancy, source credibility, and attitude change. *Journal of Personality and Social Psychology, 16*, 175–190.

Rhodes, G., Yoshikawa, S., Clark, A., Lee, K., McKay, R., & Akamatsu, S. (2001). Attractiveness of facial averageness and symmetry in non-Western cultures: In search of biologically based standards of beauty. *Perception, 30*, 611–625.

Rholes, W. S., Simpson, J. A., & Orina, M. M. (1999). Attachment and anger in an anxiety-provoking situation. *Journal of Personality and Social Psychology, 76*, 940–957.

Riggio, R. E., & Friedman, H. S. (1983). Individual differences and cues to deception. *Journal of Personality and Social Psychology, 45*, 899–915.

Riggio, R. E., & Woll, S. B. (1984). The role of nonverbal cues and physical attractiveness in the selection of dating partners. *Journal of Social and Personal Relationships, 1*, 347–357.

Robberson, M. R., & Rogers, R. W. (1988). Beyond fear appeals: Negative and positive persuasive appeals to health and self-esteem. *Journal of Applied Social Psychology, 18*, 277–287.

Roberts, B. W., & DelVecchio, W. F. (2000). The rank-order consistency of personality traits from childhood to old age: A quantitative review of longitudinal studies. *Psychological Bulletin, 126*, 3–25.

Roberts, D. F., Foehr, U. G., Rideout, V. G., & Brodie, M. (1999). *Kids & Media @ The new millennium.* Menlo Park, CA: Kaiser Family Foundation.

Roberts, T. A., & Pennebaker, J. W. (1995). Gender differences in perceiving internal state: Toward a his-and-hers model of perceptual cue use. In M. Zanna (Ed.), *Advances in experimental social psychology* (Vol. 27, pp. 143–176). New York: Academic Press.

Robins, R. W., & Beer, J. S. (2001). Positive illusions about the self: Short-term benefits and long-term costs. *Journal of Personality and Social Psychology, 80*, 340–352.

Robinson, E. A., & Price, M. G. (1980). Pleasurable behavior in marital interaction: An observational study. *Journal of Consulting and Clinical Psychology, 48*, 117–118.

Robinson, J., & McArthur, L. Z. (1982). Impact of salient vocal qualities on causal attribution for a speaker's behavior. *Journal of Personality and Social Psychology, 43*, 236–247.

Robinson, R., & Keltner, D. (1996). Much ado about nothing? Revisionists and traditionalists choose an English syllabus. *Psychological Science, 7*, 18–24.

Robinson, R., Keltner, D., Ward, A., & Ross, L. (1995). Actual versus assumed differences in construal: "Naive realism" in intergroup perception and conflict. *Journal of Personality and Social Psychology, 68*, 404–417.

Roesch, S. C., & Amirkhan, J. H. (1997). Boundary conditions for self-serving attributions. Another look at the sports pages. *Journal of Applied Social Psychology, 27*, 245–261.

Roese, N. J. (1997). Counterfactual thinking. *Psychological Bulletin, 121*, 133–148.

Roese, N. J., & Olson, J. M. (Eds.). (1995). *What might have been: The social psychology of counterfactual thinking.* Mahwah, NJ: Lawrence Erlbaum Associates.

Rogers, R. W. (1985). Attitude change and information integration in fear appeals. *Psychological Reports, 56*, 179–182.

Rogers, R. W., & Mewborn, C. R. (1976). Fear appeals and attitude change: Effects of a threat's noxiousness, probability of occurrence and the efficacy of coping responses. *Journal of Personality and Social Psychology, 34*, 54–61.

Rogers, T. B., Kuiper, N. A., & Kirker, W. S. (1977). Self-reference and the encoding of personal information. *Journal of Personality and Social Psychology, 35*, 677–688.

Rohrer, J. H., Baron, S. H., Hoffman, E. L., & Swander, D. V. (1954). The stability of autokinetic judgments. *Journal of Abnormal and Social Psychology, 49*, 595–597.

Roseman, I. J. (1984). Cognitive determinants of emotion: A structural theory. In P. Shaver (Ed.), *Review of personality and social psychology: Vol. 5 Emotions, relationships and health* (pp. 11–36). Beverly Hills, CA: Sage.

Roseman, I. J. (1991). Appraisal determinants of discrete emotions. *Cognition and Emotion, 5*, 161–200.

Rosenberg, L. A. (1961). Group size, prior experience, and conformity. *Journal of Abnormal and Social Psychology, 63*, 436–437.

Rosenberg, M. (1965). *Society and the adolescent self-image.* Princeton: Princeton University Press.

Rosenblatt, A., & Greenberg, J. (1988). Depression and interpersonal attraction: The role of perceived similarity. *Journal of Personality and Social Psychology, 55*, 112–119.

Rosenthal, R., & Jacobson, L. (1968). *Pygmalion in the classroom: Teacher expectation and student intellectual development.* New York: Holt, Rinehart and Winston.

Ross, L. (1977). The intuitive psychologist and his shortcomings. In L. Berkowitz (Ed.), *Advances in experimental social psychology* (Vol. 10, pp. 173–220). New York: Academic Press.

Ross, L. (1988). Situationist perspectives on the obedience experiments. *Contemporary Psychology, 33*, 101–104.

Ross, L., Amabile, T. M., & Steinmetz, J. L. (1977). Social roles, social control, and biases on social-perception processes. *Journal of Personality and Social Psychology, 35*, 485–494.

Ross, L., Bierbrauer, G., & Hoffman, S. (1976). The role of attribution process in conformity and dissent: Revisiting the Asch situation. *American Psychologist, 31*, 148–157.

Ross, L., Greene, D., & House, P. (1977). The "false consensus effect": An egocentric bias in social perception and attribution processes. *Journal of Experimental Social Psychology, 13*, 279–301.

Ross, L., Lepper, M. R., & Hubbard, M. (1975). Perseverance in self perception and social perception: Biased attribution processes in the debriefing paradigm. *Journal of Personality and Social Psychology, 32*, 888–892.

Ross, L., & Nisbett, R. E. (1991). *The person and the situation: Perspectives of social psychology.* New York: McGraw-Hill.

Ross, L., & Stillinger, C. (1991). Barriers to conflict resolution. *Negotiation Journal, 8*, 389–404.

Ross, L., & Ward, A. (1995). Psychological barriers to dispute resolution. In M. P. Zanna (Ed.), *Advances in experimental social psychology* (Vol. 27, pp. 255–304). San Diego, CA: Academic Press.

Ross, L., & Ward, A. (1996). Naive realism: Implications for social conflict and misunderstanding. In T. Brown, E. Reed, & E. Turiel (Eds.), *Values and knowledge* (pp. 103–135). Hillsdale, NJ: Lawrence Erlbaum Associates.

Ross, M. (1989). Relation of implicit theories to the construction of personal histories. *Psychological Review, 96*, 341–357.

Ross, M., & Sicoly, F. (1979). Egocentric biases in availability and attribution. *Journal of Personality and Social Psychology, 32*, 880–892.

Ross, S., & Ross, J. G. (1949). Social facilitation of feeding behavior in dogs: I. Group and solitary feeding. *Journal of Genetic Psychology, 74*, 97–108.

Roszell, P., Kennedy, D., & Grabb, E. (1989). Physical attractiveness and income attainment among Canadians. *Journal of Psychology, 123*, 547–559.

Rothbart, M., Evans, M., & Fulero, S. (1979). Recall for confirming events: Memory processes and the maintenance of social stereotyping. *Journal of Experimental Social Psychology, 15*, 343–355.

Rothberg, J. M., & Jones, F. D. (1987). Suicide in the U.S. Army:

Epidemiological and periodic aspects. *Suicide and Life-Threatening Behavior, 17*, 119–132.

Rotton, J., & Frey, J. (1985). Air pollution, weather, and violent crime: Concomitant time-series analysis of archival data. *Journal of Personality and Social Psychology, 49*, 1207–1220.

Rozin, P. (1996). Towards a psychology of food and eating: From motivation to module to model to marker, morality, meaning, and metaphor. *Current Directions in Psychological Science, 5*, 18–24.

Rozin, P., & Kalat, J. (1971). Specific hungers and poison avoidance as adaptive specialization of learning. *Psychological Review, 78*, 459–486.

Rozin, P., Lowery, L., Imada, S., & Haidt, J. (1999). The CAD triad hypothesis: A mapping between three moral emotions (contempt, anger, and disgust), and three moral codes (community, autonomy, divinity). *Journal of Personality and Social Psychology, 66*, 870–881.

Rozin, P., & Royzman, E. B. (2001). Negativity bias, negativity dominance, and contagion. *Personality and Social Psychology Review, 5*, 296–320.

Rubin, Z. (1973). *Liking and loving: An invitation to social psychology*. New York: Holt, Rinehart, and Winston.

Ruch, W. (1995). Will the real relationship between facial expression and affective experience please stand up: The case of exhilaration. *Cognition and Emotion, 9*, 33–58.

Rudman, L. A., & Borgida, E. (1995). The afterglow of construct accessibility: The behavioral consequences of priming men to view women as sexual objects. *Journal of Experimental Social Psychology, 31*, 493–517.

Rusbult, C. E. (1980). Commitment and satisfaction in romantic associations: A test of the investment model. *Journal of Experimental Social Psychology, 17*, 172–186.

Rusbult, C. E. (1983). A longitudinal test of the investment model: The development (and deterioration) of satisfaction and commitment in heterosexual involvements. *Journal of Personality and Social Psychology, 45*, 101–117.

Rusbult, C. E., & Martz, J. M. (1995). Remaining in an abusive relationship: An investment model analysis of nonvoluntary commitment. *Personality and Social Psychology Bulletin, 21*, 558–571.

Rushton, J. P., Russell, R. J. H., & Wells, P. A. (1984). Genetic similarity theory: Beyond kin selection altruism. *Behavioral Genetics, 14*, 179–193.

Russell, J. A. (1991). Culture and categorization of emotion. *Psychological Bulletin, 110*, 426–450.

Russell, J. A. (1994). Is there universal recognition of emotion from facial expression? A review of cross-cultural studies. *Psychological Bulletin, 115*, 102–141.

Russo, J. E., Medvec, V. H., & Meloy, M. G. (1996). The distortion of information during decisions. *Organizational Behavior and Human Decision Processes, 66*, 102–110.

Russo, J. E., Meloy, M. G., & Medvec, V. H. (1998). Predecisional distortion of product information. *Journal of Marketing Research, 35*, 438–452.

Sabini, J. (1995). *Social psychology* (2nd ed.). New York: Norton.

Sacks, O. (1985). *The man who mistook his wife for a hat and other clinical tales.* New York: Summit Books.

Saegert, S., Swap, W., & Zajonc, R. B. (1973). Exposure, context, and interpersonal attraction. *Journal of Personality and Social Psychology, 25*, 234–242.

Sagar, H. A., & Schofield, J. W. (1980). Racial and behavioral cues in black and white children's perceptions of ambiguously aggressive acts. *Journal of Personality and Social Psychology, 39*, 590–598.

Sakai, H. (1981). Induced compliance and opinion change. *Japanese Psychological Research, 23*, 1–8.

Salancik, G., & Meindl, J. R. (1984). Corporate attributions as strategic illusions of management control. *Administrative Science Quarterly, 29*, 238–254.

Sally, D. F. (1995). Conversation and cooperation in social dilemmas: Experimental evidence from 1958 to 1992. *Rationality and Society, 7*, 58–92.

Salovey, P., & Rodin, J. (1989). Envy and jealousy in close relationships. *Review of Personality and Social Psychology, 10*, 221–246.

Salovey, P., & Rothman, A. J. (1991). Jealousy and envy: Self and society. In P. Salovey (Ed.), *The psychology of jealousy and envy* (pp. 271–286). New York: Guilford Press.

Salzano, F. M., Neel, J. V., & Maybury-Lewis, D. (1967). Further studies on the Xavante Indians. I. Demographic data on two additional villages: Genetic structure of the tribe. *American Journal of Human Genetics, 19*, 463–489.

Samuels, C. A., & Ewy, R. (1985). Aesthetic perception of faces during infancy. *British Journal of Developmental Psychology, 3*, 221–228.

Samuelson, R. J. (1994, May 9). The triumph of the psycho-fact. *Newsweek*, p. 73.

Sanchez-Burks, J. (2002). Protestant relational ideology and (in)attention to relational cues in work settings. *Journal of Personality and Social Psychology, 83*(4), 919–929.

Sanders, G. S. (1981). Driven by distraction: An integrative review of social facilitation theory and research. *Journal of Experimental Social Psychology, 17*, 227–251.

Sanders, G. S., & Baron, R. S. (1975). The motivating effects of distraction on task performance. *Journal of Personality and Social Psychology, 32*, 956–963.

Sanna, L. J. (1992). Self-efficacy theory: Implications for social facilitation and social loafing. *Journal of Personality and Social Psychology, 62*, 774–786.

Sanna, L. J. (2000). Mental simulation, affect, and personality: A conceptual framework. *Current Directions in Psychological Science, 9*, 168–173.

Sansone, C., & Harackiewicz, J. M. (Eds.). (2000). *Intrinsic and extrinsic motivation: The search for optimal motivation and performance.* San Diego, CA: Academic Press.

Sapolsky, R. M. (1994). *Why zebras don't get ulcers.* New York: Freeman.

Sastry, J., & Ross, C. E. (1998). Asian ethnicity and the sense of personal control. *Social Psychology Quarterly, 61*, 101–120.

Satterwhite, R., Feldman, J., Catrambone, R., & Dai, L.-Y. (2000). Culture and perceptions of self-other similarity. *International Journal of Psychology, 35*, 287–293.

Saulnier, K., & Perlman, D. (1981). The actor-observer bias is alive and well in prison: A sequel to Wells. *Personality and Social Psychology Bulletin, 7*, 559–564.

Savin-Williams, R. C. (1977). Dominance in a human adolescent group. *Animal Behavior, 25*, 400–406.

Savitsky, K., Epley, N., & Gilovich, T. (2001). Is it as bad as we fear? Overestimating the extremity of others' judgments. *Journal of Personality and Social Psychology, 81*, 44–56.

Savitsky, K., Medvec, V. H., Charlton, A., & Gilovich, T. (1998). "What, me worry?": Arousal, misattribution, and the effect of temporal distance on confidence. *Personality and Social Psychology Bulletin, 24*, 529–536.

Schachter, S. (1951). Deviation, rejection and communication. *Journal of Abnormal and Social Psychology, 46*, 190–207.

Schachter, S., & Singer, J. E. (1962). Cognitive, social and psychological determinants of emotional state. *Psychological Review, 69*, 379–399.

Schanie, C. F., & Sundel, M. (1978). A community mental health innovation in mass media preventive education: The alternative project. *American Journal of Community Psychology, 6(6)*, 573–581.

Schank, R., & Abelson, R. P. (1977). *Scripts, plans, goals, and understanding: An inquiry into human knowledge structures.* Hillsdale, NJ: Lawrence Erlbaum Associates.

Schavitt, S., Sanbonmatsu, D. M., Smittipatana, S., & Posavac, S. S. (1999). Broadening the conditions for illusory correlation formation: Implications for judging minority groups. *Basic and Applied Social Psychology, 21*, 263–279.

Scheier, M. F., & Carver, C. S. (1977). Self-focused attention and the experience of emotion: Attraction, repulsion, elation, and depression. *Journal of Personality and Social Psychology, 35*, 625–636.

Scheier, M. F., & Carver, C. S. (1987). Dispositional optimism and physical well-being: The influence of generalized outcome expectancies on health. *Journal of Personality, 55*, 169–210.

Scheier, M. F., Fenigstein, A., & Buss, A. H. (1974). Self-awareness and physical aggression. *Journal of Experimental Social Psychology, 10*, 264–273.

Schelling, T. C. (1978). *Micromotives and macrobehavior.* New York: Norton.

Scherer, K. R. (1984). On the nature and function of emotion: A component process approach. In P. Ekman & K. R. Scherer (Eds.), *Approaches to emotion* (pp. 293–317). Hillsdale, NJ: Lawrence Erlbaum Associates.

Scherer, K. R. (1997). The role of culture in emotion-antecedent appraisal. *Journal of Personality and Social Psychology, 73*, 902–922.

Scherer, K. R., Johnstone, T., & Klasmeyer, G. (2003). Vocal expression of emotion. In R. J. Davidson, K. R. Scherer, & H. H. Goldsmith (Eds.), *Handbook of affective science* (pp. 433–456). New York: Oxford University Press.

Scherer, K. R., & Wallbott, H. G. (1994). Evidence for universality and cultural variation of differential emotion response patterning. *Journal of Personality and Social Psychology, 66*, 310–328.

Schick, T., & Vaughn, L. (1995). *How to think about weird things: Critical thinking for a new age.* Mountain View, CA: Mayfield Publishing Co.

Schifter, D. B., & Ajzen, I. (1985). Intention, perceived control, and weight loss: An application of the theory of planned behavior. *Journal of Personality and Social Psychology, 49*, 843–851.

Schkade, D. A., & Kahneman, D. (1998). Does living in California make people happy? A focusing illusion in judgments of life satisfaction. *Psychological Science, 9*, 340–346.

Schlenker, B. R. (1980). *Impression management: The self-concept, social identity, and interpersonal relations.* Monterey, CA: Brooks/Cole.

Schlenker, B. R., & Leary, M. R. (1982). Social anxiety and self-presentation: A conceptualization and a model. *Psychological Bulletin, 92*, 641–669.

Schmitt, B. H., Gilovich, T., Goore, N., & Joseph, L. (1986). Mere presence and social facilitation: One more time. *Journal of Experimental Social Psychology, 22*, 242–248.

Schmitt, D. P. (2003). Universal sex differences in the desire for sexual variety: Tests from 52 nations, 6 continents, and 13 islands. *Journal of Personality and Social Psychology, 85*, 85–104.

Schoeneman, T. J., & Rubanowitz, D. E. (1985). Attributions in the advice columns: Actors and observers, causes and reasons. *Personality and Social Psychology Bulletin, 11*, 315–325.

Schroeder, C. M., & Prentice, D. A. (1998). Exposing pluralistic ignorance to reduce alcohol use among college students. *Journal of Applied Social Psychology, 28*, 2150–2180.

Schroeder, D. A., Penner, L. A., Dovidio, J. F., & Piliavin, J. A. (1995). *The psychology of helping and altruism.* New York: McGraw-Hill.

Schulman, G. I., & Hoskins, M. (1986). Perceiving the male vs the female face. *Psychology of Women Quarterly, 10*, 141–153.

Schulz-Hardt, S., Frey, D., Luthgens, C., & Moscovici, S. (2000). Biased information search in group decision making. *Journal of Personality and Social Psychology, 78*, 655–669.

Schwartz, G. E., Weinberger, D. A., & Singer, J. A. (1981). Cardiovascular differentiation of happiness, sadness, anger, and fear following imagery and exercise. *Psychosomatic Medicine, 43*, 343–364.

Schwartz, J. (2004, May 6). Simulated prison in '71 showed a fine line between "normal" and "monster." *New York Times,* p. A14.

Schwartzwald, J., Bizman, A., & Raz, M. (1983). The foot-in-the-door paradigm: Effects of second request size on donation probability and donor generosity. *Personality and Social Psychology Bulletin, 9*, 443–450.

Schwarz, N. (1990). Feelings as information: Informational and motivational functions of affective states. In E. T. Higgins & R. M. Sorrentino (Eds.), *Handbook of motivation and cognition* (Vol. 2, pp. 527–561). New York: Guilford Press.

Schwarz, N., & Bless, H. (1992). Constructing reality and its alternatives: An inclusion/exclusion model of assimilation and contrast in social judgment. In L. L. Martin & A. Tesser (Eds.), *The construction of social judgments* (pp. 217–245). Hillsdale, NJ: Lawrence Erlbaum Associates.

Schwarz, N., Bless, H., Strack, F., Klumpp, G., Rittenauer-Schatka, & Simons, A. (1991). Ease of retrieval as information: Another look at the availability heuristic. *Journal of Personality and Social Psychology, 61*, 195–202.

Schwarz, N., & Clore, G. L. (1983). Mood, misattribution, and judgments of well-being: Informative and directive functions of affective states. *Journal of Personality and Social Psychology, 45*, 513–523.

Schwarz, N., Strack, F., & Mai, H. P. (1991). Assimilation-contrast effects in part-whole question sequences: A conversational logic analysis. *Public Opinion Quarterly, 55*, 3–23.

Schwarz, N., & Vaughn, L. A. (2002). The availability heuristic revisited: Ease of recall and content of recall as distinct sources of information. In T. Gilovich, D. W. Griffin, & D. Kahneman (Eds.), *Heuristics and biases: The psychology of intuitive judgment* (pp. 103–119). New York: Cambridge University Press.

Searle, J. R. (1983). *Intentionality: An essay in the philosophy of mind*. Cambridge, England: Cambridge University Press.

Sears, D. O. (1986). College students in the laboratory: Influences of a narrow data base on social psychology's view of human nature. *Journal of Personality and Social Psychology, 51*, 515–530.

Sears, D. O. (1988). Symbolic racism. In P. A. Katz & D. A. Taylor (Eds.), *Eliminating racism: Profiles in controversy* (pp. 53–84). New York: Plenum Press.

Sears, D. O., & Kinder, D. R. (1985). Whites' opposition to busing: On conceptualizing and operationalizing group conflict. *Journal of Personality and Social Psychology, 48*, 1141–1147.

Sedikides, C. (1995). Central and peripheral self-conceptions are differentially influenced by mood: Tests of the differential sensitivity hypothesis. *Journal of Personality and Social Psychology, 69*, 759–777.

Sedikides, C., Gaertner, L., & Toguchi, T. (2003). Pancultural self-enhancement. *Journal of Personality and Social Psychology, 84*, 60–79.

Sedikides, C., Olsen, N., & Reis, H. T. (1993). Relationships as natural categories. *Journal of Personality and Social Psychology, 64*, 71–82.

Sedikides, C., & Skowronski, J. J. (1997). The symbolic self in evolutionary context. *Personality and Social Psychology Review, 1*, 80–102.

Segal, M. W. (1974). Alphabet and attraction: An unobtrusive measure of the effect of propinquity in a field setting. *Journal of Personality and Social Psychology, 30*, 654–657.

Segal, N. L. (1984). Cooperation, competition, and altruism within twin sets: A reappraisal. *Ethology and Sociobiology, 5*, 163–177.

Seligman, M. E. P. (1975). *Helplessness: On depression, development, and death*. San Francisco: Freeman.

Seligman, M. E. P. (1988). Boomer blues. *Psychology Today, 22*, 50–53.

Seligman, M. E. P. (1991). *Learned optimism*. New York: Knopf.

Seligman, M. E. P., Maier, S. F., & Geer, J. H. (1968). Alleviation of learned helplessness in the dog. *Journal of Abnormal Psychology, 73*, 256–262.

Seligman, M. E. P., & Schulman, P. (1986). Explanatory style as a predictor of productivity and quitting among life insurance agents. *Journal of Personality and Social Psychology, 50*, 832–838.

Semin, G. R., & Manstead, A. S. R. (1982). The social implications of embarrassment displays and restitution behavior. *European Journal of Social Psychology, 12*, 367–377.

Semin, G. R., & Rubini, M. (1990). Unfolding the concept of person by verbal abuse. *European Journal of Social Psychology, 20,* 463–474.

Seta, C. E., & Seta, J. J. (1992). Increments and decrements in mean arterial pressure levels as a function of audience composition: An averaging and summation analysis. *Personality and Social Psychology Bulletin, 18*, 173–181.

Shah, J., & Higgins, E. T. (2001). Regulatory concerns and appraisal efficiency: The general impact of promotion and prevention. *Journal of Personality and Social Psychology, 80*, 693–705.

Shaver, P. R., & Brennan, K. A. (1992). Attachment style and the "big five" of personality traits: Their connections with each other and with romantic relationship outcomes. *Personality and Social Psychology Bulletin, 18*, 536–545.

Shavitt, S., Sanbonmatsu, D. M., Smittipatana, S., & Posavac, S. S. (1999). Broadening the conditions for illusory correlation formation: Implications for judging minority groups. *Basic and Applied Social Psychology, 21*, 263–279.

Shearn, D., Bergman, E., Hill, K., Abel, A., & Hinds, L. (1990). Facial coloration and temperature responses in blushing. *Psychophysiology, 27*, 687–693.

Shedler, L., & Manis, M. (1986). Can the availability heuristic explain vividness effects? *Journal of Personality and Social Psychology, 51*, 26–36.

Sheeran, P., & Taylor, S. (1999). Predicting intentions to use condoms: A meta-analysis of comparison of the theories of reasoned action and planned behavior. *Journal of Applied Social Psychology, 29*, 1624–1675.

Sheley, J. F., & Askins, C. D. (1981). Crime, crime news, and crime views. *Public Opinion Quarterly, 45*, 492–506.

Shelley, H. P. (1965). Eating behavior: Social facilitation or social inhibition. *Psychonomic Science, 3*, 521–522.

Shepperd, J. A. (1995). Remedying motivation and productivity loss in collective settings. *Current Directions in Psychological Science, 4*, 131–134.

Shepperd, J. A., Ouellette, J. A., & Fernandez, J. K. (1996). Abandoning unrealistic optimism: Performance estimates and the temporal proximity of self-relevant feedback. *Journal of Personality and Social Psychology, 70*, 844–855.

Shepperd, J. A., & Taylor, K. M. (1999). Social loafing and expectancy-value theory. *Personality and Social Psychology Bulletin, 25*, 1147–1158.

Sherif, M. (1936). *The psychology of social norms*. New York: Harper.

Sherif, M., Harvey, O. J., White, B. J., Hood, W., & Sherif, C. (1961). *Intergroup conflict and cooperation: The Robbers Cave experiment*. Norman, OK: University of Oklahoma Institute of Group Relations.

Sherman, P. W. (1985). Alarm calls of Belding's ground squirrels to aerial predators: Nepotism or self-preservation? *Behavioral Ecology and Sociobiology, 17*, 313–323.

Sherman, S. J., & Gorkin, L. (1980). Attitude bolstering when behavior is inconsistent with central attitudes. *Journal of Experimental Social Psychology, 16*, 388–403.

Sherman, S. J., Mackie, D. M., & Driscoll, D. M. (1990). Priming and the differential use of dimensions in evaluation. *Personality and Social Psychology Bulletin, 16*, 405–418.

Sherman, S. J., & McConnell, A. R. (1995). Dysfunctional implications of counterfactual thinking: When alternatives to reality fail us. In N. J. Roese & J. M. Olson (Eds.), *What might have been: The social psychology of counterfactual thinking*. Mahwah, NJ: Lawrence Erlbaum Associates.

Short, R. V. (1979). Sexual selection and its component parts, somatic and genital selection, as illustrated by man and the great apes. *Advances in the Study of Behavior, 9*, 131–158.

Showers, C. (1992). Compartmentalization of positive and negative self-knowledge: Keeping bad apples out of the bunch. *Journal of Personality and Social Psychology, 62*, 1036–1049.

Shrauger, J. S., & Shoeneman, T. J. (1979). Symbolic interactionist view of self-concept: Through the looking glass darkly. *Psychological Bulletin, 86*, 549–573.

Shweder, R. A. (1982). Fact and artifact in trait perception: The systematic distortion hypothesis. In B. A. Maher (Ed.), *Progress in experimental personality research* (Vol. 11, pp. 65–100). New York: Academic Press.

Shweder, R. A. (1994). You're not sick, you're just in love: Emotion as an interpretive system. In P. Ekman & R. J. Davidson (Eds.), *The nature of emotion: Fundamental questions* (pp. 32–44). New York: Oxford University Press.

Shweder, R. A., & Bourne, E. J. (1984). Does the concept of the person vary cross-culturally? In R. A. Shweder & R. A. Levine (Eds.), *Culture theory: Essays on mind, self, and emotion* (pp. 158–199). Cambridge, England: Cambridge University Press.

Shweder, R. A., & D'Andrade, R. G. (1979). Accurate reflection or systematic distortion? A reply to Block, Weiss and Thorne. *Journal of Personality and Social Psychology, 37,* 1075–1084.

Shweder, R. A., Jensen, L. A., & Goldstein, W. M. (1995). Who sleeps by whom revisited: A method for extracting moral goods implicit in practice. *New Directions in Child Development, 67,* 21–39.

Shweder, R. A., Much, N. C., Mahapatra, M., & Park, L. (1997). The "big three" of morality (autonomy, community, divinity), and the "big three" explanations of suffering. In A. Brandt & P. Rozin (Eds.), *Morality and health* (pp. 119–169). New York: Routledge.

Sidanius, J. (1993). The psychology of group conflict and the dynamics of oppression: A social dominance perspective. In S. S. Iyengar (Ed.), *Explorations in political psychology*. Durham, NC: Duke University Press.

Sidanius, J., & Pratto, F. (1999). *Social dominance: An intergroup theory of social hierarchy and oppression*. New York: Cambridge University Press.

Sigall, H., & Landy, D. (1973). Radiating beauty: Effects of having a physically attractive partner on person perception. *Journal of Personality and Social Psychology, 31,* 218–224.

Sigall, H., & Ostrove, N. (1975). Beautiful but dangerous: Effects of offender attractiveness and nature of the crime on juridic judgment. *Journal of Personality and Social Psychology, 31,* 410–414.

Silverstein, B., Perdue, L., Peterson, L., & Kelly, E. (1986). The role of the mass media in promoting a thin standard of bodily attractiveness for women. *Sex Roles, 14,* 519–532.

Simon, D., Krawczyk, D. C., & Holyoak, K. J. (2004). Construction of preferences by constraint satisfaction. *Psychological Science, 15,* 331–336.

Simon, D., Pham, L. B., Le, Q. A., & Holyoak, K. J. (2001). The emergence of coherence over the course of decision making. *Journal of Experimental Psychology: Learning, Memory and Cognition, 27,* 1250–1260.

Simons, D. J., & Chabris, C. F. (1999). Gorillas in our midst: Sustained inattentional blindness for dynamic events. *Perception, 28,* 1059–1074.

Simpson, G. E., & Yinger, J. M. (1985). *Racial and cultural minorities: An analysis of prejudice and discrimination*. New York: Plenum Press.

Simpson, J. A. (1987). The dissolution of romantic relationships: Factors involved in relationship stability and emotional distress. *Journal of Personality and Social Psychology, 53,* 683–692.

Simpson, J. A., Ickes, W., & Grich, J. (1999). When accuracy hurts: Reactions of anxious-ambivalent dating partners to a relationship-threatening situation. *Journal of Personality and Social Psychology, 76,* 754–769.

Simpson, J. A., & Kenrick, D. T. (1998). *Evolutionary social psychology*. Hillsdale, NJ: Lawrence Erlbaum Associates.

Simpson, J. A., & Rholes, W. S. (1998). *Attachment theory and close relationships*. New York: Guilford Press.

Simpson, J. A., Rholes, W. S., & Phillips, D. (1996). Conflict in close relationships: An attachment perspective. *Journal of Personality and Social Psychology, 71,* 899–914.

Sinclair, L., & Kunda, Z. (1999). Reactions to a black professional: Motivated inhibition and activation of conflicting stereotypes. *Journal of Personality and Social Psychology, 77,* 885–904.

Singer, J. E., Brush, C. A., & Lublin, S. C. (1965). Some aspects of deindividuation: Identification and conformity. *Journal of Experimental Social Psychology, 1,* 356–378.

Singh, D. (1993). Adaptive significance of female physical attractiveness: Role of waist-to-hip ratio. *Journal of Personality and Social Psychology, 65,* 293–307.

Sistrunk, F., & McDavid, J. W. (1971). Sex variable in conforming behavior. *Journal of Personality and Social Psychology, 17,* 200–207.

Sloman, S. A. (2002). Two systems of reasoning. In T. Gilovich, D. W. Griffin, & D. Kahneman (Eds.), *Heuristics and biases: The psychology of intuitive judgement* (pp. 379–396). New York: Cambridge University Press.

Slovic, P., Fischoff, B., & Lichtenstein, S. (1982). Facts versus fears: Understanding perceived risk. In D. Kahneman, P. Slovic, & A. Tversky (Eds.), *Judgment under uncertainty: Heuristics and biases* (pp. 463–489). New York: Cambridge University Press.

Smith, A. (1776/1998). *The wealth of nations*. Washington, DC: Regnery Publishing.

Smith, A. E., Jussim, L., & Eccles, J. S. (1999). Do self-fulfilling prophecies accumulate, dissipate, or remain stable over time? *Journal of Personality and Social Psychology, 77,* 548–565.

Smith, C., & Ellsworth, P. (1985). Patterns of cognitive appraisal in emotion. *Journal of Personality and Social Psychology, 48,* 813–838.

Smith, E. R., & Miller, F. D. (1979). Salience and the cognitive mediation of attribution. *Journal of Personality and Social Psychology, 37,* 2240–2252.

Smith, E. R., & Zarate, M. A. (1990). Exemplar and prototype use in social categorization. *Social Cognition, 8,* 243–262.

Smoski, M. J., & Bachorowski, J.-A. (2003). Antiphonal laughter between friends and strangers. *Cognition and Emotion, 17,* 327–340.

Smuts, B. B. (1985). *Sex and friendship in baboons*. Hawthorne, NY: Aldine Publishing Co.

Smyth, J. M. (1998). Written emotional expression: Effect sizes, outcome types, and moderating variables. *Journal of Consulting and Clinical Psychology, 66,* 174–184.

Snyder, M. (1974). Self-monitoring of expressive behavior. *Journal of Personality and Social Psychology, 30,* 526–537.

Snyder, M. (1979). Self-monitoring processes. In L. Berkowitz (Ed.), *Advances in experimental social psychology* (Vol. 12, pp. 85–128). New York: Academic Press.

Snyder, M., Tanke, E. D., & Berscheid, E. (1977). Social perception and interpersonal behavior: On the self-fulfilling nature of social stereotypes. *Journal of Personality and Social Psychology, 35,* 656–666.

Sober, E., & Wilson, D. S. (1998). *Unto others: The evolution and psychology of unselfish behavior*. Cambridge, MA: Harvard University Press.

Sparacino, J., & Hansell, S. (1979). Physical attractiveness and academic performance: Beauty is not always talent. *Journal of Personality, 47*, 449–469.

Spears, R., Gordijn, E., Dijksterhuis, A., & Stapel, D. A. (2004). Reaction in action: Intergroup contrast in automatic behavior. *Personality and Social Psychology Bulletin, 30*, 605–616.

Spellman, B. A., & Holyoak, K. J. (1992). If Saddam is Hitler then who is George Bush?: Analogical mapping between systems of social roles. *Journal of Personality and Social Psychology, 62*, 913–933.

Spencer, S. J., Steele, C. M., & Quinn, D. M. (1999). Stereotype threat and women's math performance. *Journal of Experimental Social Psychology, 3*, 4–28.

Sperber, D. (1996). *Explaining culture: A naturalistic approach.* Oxford, England: Blackwell.

Spiegel, D., Bloom, J. R., Kraemer, H. C., & Gottheil, E. (1989). Effect of psychosocial treatment on survival of patients with metastatic breast cancer. *Lancet, 2*, 888–891.

Spivey, C. B., & Prentice-Dunn, S. (1990). Assessing the directionality of deindividuated behavior: Effects of deindividuation, modeling, and private self-consciousness on aggressive and pro-social responses. *Basic and Applied Psychology, 11*, 387–403.

Srull, T. K., & Wyer, R. S. (1979). The role of category accessibility in the interpretation of information about persons: Some determinants and implications. *Journal of Personality and Social Psychology, 37*, 1660–1672.

Srull, T. K., & Wyer, R. S. (1980). Category accessibility and social perception: Some implications for the study of person memory and interpersonal judgments. *Journal of Personality and Social Psychology, 38*, 841–856.

Staats, A. W., & Staats, C. K. (1958). Attitudes established by classical conditioning. *Journal of Abnormal and Social Psychology, 57*, 37–40.

Stangor, C., & Duan, C. (1991). Effects of multiple task demands upon memory for information about social groups. *Journal of Experimental Social Psychology, 27*, 357–378.

Stangor, C., & Lange, J. E. (1994). Mental representation of social groups: Advances in understanding stereotypes and stereotyping. In M. P. Zanna (Ed.), *Advances in experimental social psychology* (Vol. 26). San Diego, CA: Academic Press.

Stangor, C., & McMillan, D. (1992). Memory for expectancy-congruent and expectancy-incongruent information: A review of the social and social developmental literatures. *Psychological Bulletin, 111*, 42–61.

Stanovich, K. E., & West, R. F. (2002). Individual differences in reasoning: Implications for the rationality debate. In T. Gilovich, D. W. Griffin, & D. Kahneman (Eds.), *Heuristics and biases: The psychology of intuitive judgment* (pp. 421–440). New York: Cambridge University Press.

Stapel, D. A., & Blanton, H. (2004). From seeing to being: Subliminal social comparisons affect implicit and explicit self-evaluations. *Journal of Personality and Social Psychology, 87*, 468–481.

Stapel, D. A., & Koomen, W. (2000). How far do we go beyond the information given? The impact of knowledge activation on interpretation and inference. *Journal of Personality and Social Psychology, 78*, 19–37.

Stapel, D., & Koomen, W. (2001). Let's not forget the past when we go to the future: On our knowledge of knowledge accessibility effects. In G. Moskowitz (Ed.), *Cognitive social psychology: The Princeton symposium on the legacy and future of social cognition* (pp. 229–246). Mahwah, NJ: Lawrence Erlbaum Associates.

Stapel, D. A., Koomen, W., & van der Plight, J. (1997). Categories of category accessibility: The impact of trait versus exemplar priming on person judgments. *Journal of Experimental Social Psychology, 33*, 44–76.

Stasser, G. (1999). The uncertain role of unshared information in collective choice. In L. L. Thomson, J. M. Levine, & D. M. Messick (Eds.), *Shared cognition in organizations: The management of knowledge* (pp. 46–69). Mahwah, NJ: Lawrence Erlbaum Associates.

Stasser, G., & Titus, W. (1985). Pooling of unshared information in group decision making: Biased information sampling during discussion. *Journal of Personality and Social Psychology, 48*, 1467–1478.

Staub, E. (1989). *The roots of evil: The origins of genocide and other group violence.* Cambridge, England: Cambridge University Press.

Stayman, D. M., & Kardes, F. R. (1992). Spontaneous influence processes in advertising: Effects of need for cognition and self-monitoring on inference generation and utilization. *Journal of Consumer Psychology, 1*, 125–142.

Steblay, N. M. (1987). Helping behavior in rural and urban environments: A meta-analysis. *Psychological Bulletin, 102*, 346–356.

Steele, C. M. (1988). The psychology of self-affirmation: Sustaining the integrity of the self. In L. Berkowitz (Ed.), *Advances in experimental social psychology* (Vol. 21). Orlando, FL: Academic Press.

Steele, C. M. (1997). A threat in the air: How stereotypes shape intellectual identity and performance. *American Psychologist, 52*, 613–629.

Steele, C. M., & Aronson, J. (1995). Stereotype threat and the intellectual test performance of African Americans. *Journal of Personality and Social Psychology, 69*, 797–811.

Stein, N., & Levine, L. L. (1987). Thinking about feelings: The development and organization of emotional knowledge. In R. E. Snow & M. Farr (Eds.), *Aptitude, learning, and instruction: Cognition, conation, and affect* (Vol. 3, pp. 165–197). Hillsdale, NJ: Lawrence Erlbaum Associates.

Stemmler, G. (1989). The autonomic differentiation of emotions revisited: Convergent and discriminant validation. *Psychophysiology, 26(6)*, 617–632.

Stemmler, G. (2003). Methodological considerations in the psychophysiological study of emotion. In R. J. Davidson, K. R. Scherer, & H. H. Goldsmith (Eds.), *Handbook of affective sciences* (pp. 225–255). New York: Oxford University Press.

Stephan, W. G., & Stephan, C. W. (1996). *Intergroup relations.* Madison, WI: Brown & Benchmark.

Sternberg, R. J. (1986). A triangular theory of love. *Psychological Review, 93*, 119–135.

Stevenson, H. W., & Stigler, J. W. (1992). *The learning gap: Why our schools are failing and what we can learn from Japanese and Chinese education.* New York: Summit Books.

Stewart, D. (1988). Fleece chief. *Omni, 10(4)*, 56–61.

Stewart, J. E. (1980). Defendant's attractiveness as a factor in the outcome of criminal trials: An observational study. *Journal of Applied Social Psychology, 10,* 348–361.

Stone, J., Lynch, C. I., Sjomeling, M., & Darley, J. M. (1999). Stereotype threat effects on Black and White athletic performance. *Journal of Personality and Social Psychology, 77,* 1213–1227.

Stone, J., Perry, Z., & Darley, J. (1997). "White men can't jump": Evidence for perceptual confirmation of racial stereotypes following a basketball game. *Basic and Applied Social Psychology, 19,* 291–306.

Stoner, J. A. F. (1961). *A comparison of individual and group decisions involving risk.* Unpublished master's thesis, MIT, Cambridge, Massachusetts.

Storms, M. D. (1973). Videotape and the attribution process: Reversing actors' and observers' points of view. *Journal of Personality and Social Psychology, 27,* 165–175.

Storms, M. D., & Nisbett, R. E. (1970). Insomnia and the attribution process. *Journal of Personality and Social Psychology, 16,* 319–328.

Stouffer, S. A., Suchman, E. A., DeVinney, L. C., Star, S. A., & Williams, R. A., Jr. (1949). *The American soldier: Adjustments during army life* (Vol. 1). Princeton: Princeton University Press.

Strack, F., Martin, L. L., & Stepper, S. (1988). Inhibiting and facilitating conditions of the human smile: A nonobtrusive test of the facial feedback hypothesis. *Journal of Personality and Social Psychology, 53,* 768–777.

Strahan, E. J., Spencer, S. J., & Zanna, M. P. (2002). Subliminal priming and persuasion: Striking while the iron is hot. *Journal of Experimental Social Psychology, 38,* 556–568.

Strauman, T. J., & Higgins, E. T. (1987). Automatic activation of self-discrepancies and emotional syndromes: When cognitive structures influence affect. *Journal of Personality and Social Psychology, 53,* 1004–1014.

Strobel, M. G. (1972). Social facilitation of operant behavior in satiated rats. *Journal of Comparative Physiological Psychology, 80,* 502–508.

Strohmetz, D., Rind, B., Fisher, R. & Lynn, M. (2002). Sweetening the til: The use of candy to increase restaurant tipping. *Journal of Applied Social Psychology, 32,* 300–329.

Studd, M. V. (1996). Sexual harassment. In D. M. Buss & N. M. Malamuth (Eds.), *Sex, power, and conflict: Evolutionary and feminist perspectives.* New York: Oxford University Press.

Suedfeld, P., & Tetlock, P. E. (1977). Integrative complexity of communications in international crises. *Journal of Conflict Resolution, 21,* 169–184.

Suh, E., Diener, E., Oishi, S., & Triandis, H. C. (1998). The shifting basis of life satisfaction judgments across cultures: Emotions versus norms. *Journal of Personality and Social Psychology, 74,* 482–493.

Sulloway, F. J. (1996). *Born to rebel: Birth order, family dynamics, and creative lives.* New York: Pantheon Books.

Sulloway, F. J. (2001). Birth order, sibling competition, and human behavior. In H. R. Halcomb III (Ed.), *Conceptual challenges in evolutionary psychology: Innovative research strategie: Studies in cognitive systems* (Vol. 27, pp. 39–83). Dordrecht, The Netherlands: Kluwer Academic Publishers.

Suls, J. M., & Wheeler, L. (2000). *Handbook of social comparison: Theory and research.* New York: Kluwer Academic/Plenum.

Summers, G., & Feldman, N.S. (1984). Blaming the victim versus blaming the perpetrator: An attributional analysis of spouse abuse. *Journal of Applied Social and Clinical Psychology, 2,* 339–347.

Swann, W. B., Jr. (1984). Quest for accuracy in person perception: A matter of pragmatics. *Psychological Review, 91,* 457–477.

Swann, W. B., Jr. (1992). Seeking "truth," finding despair: Some unhappy consequences of a negative self-concept. *Current Directions in Psychological Science, 1,* 15–18.

Swann, W. B., Jr., De La Ronde, C., & Hixon, J. G. (1994). Authenticity and positivity strivings in marriage and courtship. *Journal of Personality and Social Psychology, 66,* 857–869.

Swann, W. B., Griffin, J. J., Predmore, S. C., & Gaines, B. (1987). The cognitive-affective cross: When self-consistency confronts self-enhancement. *Journal of Personality and Social Psychology, 52,* 881–889.

Swann, W. B., Hixon, J. G., & De La Ronde, C. (1992). Embracing the bitter "truth": Negative self-conceptions and marital commitment. *Psychological Science, 3,* 118–121.

Swann, W. B., Jr., & Read, S. J. (1981). Self-verification processes: How we sustain our self-conceptions. *Journal of Experimental Social Psychology, 17,* 351–372.

Swann, W. B., Jr., Wenzlaff, R. M., Krull, D. S., & Pelham, B. W. (1992). The allure of negative feedback: Self-verification strivings among depressed persons. *Journal of Abnormal Psychology, 101,* 293–306.

Sweeney, P. D., & Gruber, K. L. (1984). Selective exposure: Voter information preferences and the Watergate affair. *Journal of Personality and Social Psychology, 46,* 1208–1221.

Swim, J. K., Aikin, K. J., Hall, W. S., & Hunter, B. A. (1995). Sexism and racism: Old-fashioned and modern prejudices. *Journal of Personality and Social Psychology, 68,* 199–214.

Swim, J. K., & Sanna, L. (1996). He's skilled, she's lucky: A meta-analysis of observers' attributions for women's and men's successes and failures. *Personality and Social Psychology Bulletin, 22,* 507–519.

Tajfel, H., & Billig, M. G. (1974). Familiarity and categorization in intergroup behavior. *Journal of Experimental Social Psychology, 10,* 159–170.

Tajfel, H., Billig, M. G., Bundy, R. P., & Flament, C. (1971). Social categorization and intergroup behavior. *European Journal of Social Psychology, 1,* 149–177.

Tajfel, H., & Turner, J. (1979). An integrative theory of intergroup conflict. In W. G. Austin & S. Worchel (Eds.), *The social psychology of intergroup relations.* Monterey, CA.: Brooks/Cole.

Tajfel, H., & Wilkes, A. (1963). Classifications and quantitative judgment. *British Journal of Social Psychology, 54,* 101–114.

Tan, D. T. Y., & Singh, R. (1995). Attitudes and attraction: A developmental study of the similarity-attraction dissimilarity-repulsion hypotheses. *Personality and Social Psychology Bulletin, 21,* 975–986.

Tangney, J. P., Burggraf, S. A., & Wagner, P. E. (1995). Shame-proneness, guilt-proneness, and psychological symptoms. In J. P. Tangney & K. W. Fischer (Eds.), *Self-conscious emotion* (pp. 343–367). New York: Guilford Press.

Tangney, J. P., Miller, R. S., Flicker, L., & Barlow, D. H. (1996). Are shame, guilt, and embarrassment distinct emotions? *Journal of Personality and Social Psychology, 70,* 1256–1264.

Taylor, D. M., & Jaggi, V. (1974). Ethnocentrism and causal

attribution in a South Indian context. *Journal of Cross-Cultural Psychology, 5,* 162–171.

Taylor, S. E. (1989). *Positive illusions: Creative self-deception and the healthy mind.* New York: Basic Books.

Taylor, S. E. (1991). Asymmetrical effects of positive and negative events: The mobilization-minimization hypothesis. *Psychological Bulletin, 110,* 67–85.

Taylor, S. E., & Brown, J. D. (1988). Illusion and well-being: A social psychological perspective on mental health. *Psychological Bulletin, 103,* 193–210.

Taylor, S. E., & Brown, J. D. (1994). Positive illusions and well-being revisited: Separating fact from fiction. *Psychological Bulletin, 116,* 21–27.

Taylor, S. E., & Crocker, J. (1981). Schematic bases of social information processing. In E. T. Higgins, C. P. Herman, & M. P. Zanna (Eds.), *Social cognition: The Ontario Symposium* (Vol. 1, pp. 89–134). Hillsdale, NJ: Lawrence Erlbaum Associates.

Taylor, S. E., & Fiske, S. T. (1975). Point of view and perceptions of causality. *Journal of Personality and Social Psychology, 32,* 439–445.

Taylor, S. E., Klein, L. C., Lewis, B. P., Gruenewal, T. L., Gurung, R. A. R., & Updegraff, J. A. (2000). Biobehavioral responses to stress in females: Tend-and-befriend, not fight-or-flight. *Psychological Review, 107,* 411–429.

Taylor, S. E., & Thompson, S. C. (1982). Stalking the elusive "vividness" effect. *Psychological Review, 89,* 155–181.

Tec, N. (1986). *When light pierced the darkness.* New York: Oxford University Press.

Tedeschi, J. T., & Reiss, M. (1981). Identities, the phenomenal self, and laboratory research. In J. T. Tedeschi (Ed.), *Impression management theory and social psychological research* (pp. 3–22). New York: Academic Press.

Teger, A. I., & Pruitt, D. G. (1967). Components of group risk taking. *Journal of Experimental Social Psychology, 3,* 189–205.

Tesser, A. (1980). Self-esteem maintenance in family dynamics. *Journal of Personality and Social Psychology, 39,* 77–91.

Tesser, A. (1988). Toward a self-evaluation maintenance model of social behavior. In L. Berkowitz (Ed.), *Advances in experimental social psychology* (Vol. 21, pp. 181–227). San Diego, CA: Academic Press.

Tesser, A. (1993). The importance of heritability in psychological research: The case of attitudes. *Psychological Review, 100,* 129–142.

Tesser, A., Campbell, J. D., & Mickler, S. (1983). The role of social pressure, attention to the stimulus, and self-doubt in conformity. *European Journal of Social Psychology, 13,* 217–233.

Tesser, A., Campbell, J., & Smith, M. (1984). Friendship choice and performance: Self-evaluation maintenance in children. *Journal of Personality and Social Psychology, 46,* 561–574.

Tesser, A., & Conlee, M. C. (1975). Some effects of time and thought on attitude polarization. *Journal of Personality and Social Psychology, 31,* 262–270.

Tesser, A., Martin, L., & Mendolia, M. (1995). The impact of thought on attitude extremity and attitude-behavior consistency. In R. E. Petty & J. Krosnick (Eds.), *Attitude strength: Antecedents and consequences.* Mahwah, NJ: Lawrence Erlbaum Associates.

Tesser, A., & Smith, J. (1980). Some effects of friendship and task relevance on helping: You don't always help the one you like. *Journal of Experimental Social Psychology, 16,* 582–590.

Tetlock, P. E. (1981). Pre-to post-election shifts in presidential rhetoric: Impression management or cognitive adjustment. *Journal of Personality and Social Psychology, 41,* 207–212.

Tetlock, P. E. (1984). Cognitive style and political belief systems in the British House of Commons. *Journal of Personality and Social Psychology, 41,* 365–375.

Tetlock, P. E., Hannum, K. A., & Micheletti, P. M. (1984). Stability and change in the complexity of senatorial debate: Testing the cognitive versus rhetorical style hypotheses. *Journal of Personality and Social Psychology, 46,* 979–990.

Tetlock, P. E., Kristel, O., Elson, B., Green, M., & Lerner, J. (2000). The psychology of the unthinkable: Taboo trade-offs, forbidden base rates, and heretical counterfactuals. *Journal of Personality and Social Psychology, 78,* 853–870.

Tetlock, P. E., Peterson, R. S., McGuire, C., Chang, S., & Feld, P. (1992). Assessing political group dynamics: A test of the groupthink model. *Journal of Personality and Social Psychology, 20,* 142–146.

Thakerar, J. N., & Iwawaki, S. (1979). Cross-cultural comparisons in interpersonal attraction of females toward males. *Journal of Social Psychology, 108,* 121–122.

The price of beauty. (1992, January 11). *The Economist,* p. 25.

Thomas, S. L., Skitka, L. J., Christen, S., & Jurgena, M. (2002). Social facilitation and impression formation. *Basic and Applied Social Psychology, 24,* 67–70.

Thompson, L. (2004). *The mind and heart of the negotiator* (3rd ed.). Upper Saddle River, NJ: Prentice Hall.

Thompson, L., & Hrebec, D. (1996). Lose-lose arguments in interdependent decision making. *Psychological Bulletin, 120,* 396–409.

Thornhill, R., & Gangestad, S. W. (1993). Human facial beauty: Averageness, symmetry, and parasite resistance. *Human Nature, 4,* 237–269.

Thornhill, R., & Gangestad, S. W. (1999). The scent of symmetry: A human sex pheromone that signals fitness? *Evolution and Human Behavior, 20,* 175–201.

Thornhill, R., & Thornhill, N. W. (1983). Human rape: An evolutionary analysis. *Ethology and Sociobiology, 4,* 137–173.

Tice, D. M. (1993). Self-concept change and self-presentation: The looking glass self is also a magnifying glass. *Journal of Personality and Social Psychology, 63,* 435–451.

Tiedens, L. Z., & Linton, S. (2001). Judgment under emotional certainty and uncertainty: The effects of specific emotions on information processing. *Journal of Personality and Social Psychology, 81,* 973–988.

Todorov, A., & Bargh, J. A. (2002). Automatic sources of aggression. *Aggression and Violent Behavior, 7,* 53–68.

Tomkins, S. S. (1962). *Affect, imagery, consciousness: I. The positive affects.* New York: Springer.

Tomkins, S. S. (1963). *Affect, imagery, consciousness: II. The negative affects.* New York: Springer.

Tooby, J., & Cosmides, L. (1992). The psychological foundations of culture. In J. H. Barkow, L. Cosmides, & J. Tooby (Eds.), *The adapted mind: Evolutionary psychology and the generation of culture.* New York: Oxford University Press.

Torrance, E. P. (1955). Some consequences of power differences in decision making in permanent and temporary 3–man groups. In A. P. Hare, E. F. Bogatta, & R. F. Bales (Eds.), *Small groups: Studies in social interaction.* New York: Knopf.

Tourangeau, R., Rasinski, K., & Bradburn, N. (1991). Measuring happiness in surveys: A test of the subtraction hypothesis. *Public Opinion Quarterly, 55*, 255–266.

Trafimow, D., Triandis, H. C., & Goto, S. G. (1991). Some tests of the distinction between the private self and the collective self. *Journal of Personality and Social Psychology, 60*, 649–655.

Traupmann, J., Petersen, R., Utne, M., & Hatfield, E. (1981). Measuring equity in intimate relations. *Applied Psychological Measurement, 5*, 467–480.

Travis, L. E. (1925). The effect of a small audience upon eye-hand coordination. *Journal of Abnormal and Social Psychology, 20*, 142–146.

Triandis, H. C. (1972). *The analysis of subjective culture*. New York: Wiley.

Triandis, H. C. (1989). The self and social behavior in differing cultural contexts. *Psychological Review, 96*, 269–289.

Triandis, H. C. (1994). *Culture and social behavior*. New York: McGraw-Hill.

Triandis, H. C. (1995). *Individualism and collectivism*. Boulder: Westview Press.

Triandis, H. C., McCusker, C., & Hui, C. H. (1990). Multimethod probes of individualism and collectivism. *Journal of Personality and Social Psychology, 56*, 1006–1020.

Triplett, N. (1898). The dynamogenic factors in pacemaking and competition. *American Journal of Psychology, 9*, 507–533.

Trivers, R. L. (1971). The evolution of reciprocal altruism. *Quarterly Review of Biology, 46*, 35–57.

Trivers, R. L. (1985). *Social evolution*. Menlo Park, CA: Benjamin/Cummngs.

Trope, Y. (1986). Identification and inferential processes in dispositional attribution. *Psychological Review, 93*, 239–257.

Turiel, E. (1983). *The development of social knowledge: Morality and convention*. Cambridge, England: Cambridge University Press.

Turiel, E. (2002). *The culture of morality*. Cambridge, England: Cambridge University Press.

Turiel, E., Killen, M., & Helwig, C. (1987). Morality: Its structure, functions, and vagaries. In J. Kagan & S. Lamb (Eds.), *The emergence of morality in children* (pp. 155–243). Chicago: University of Chicago Press.

Turnbull, C. (1965). *Wayward servants*. New York: Natural History Press.

Turner, C., & Leyens, J. (1992). The weapons effect revisited: The effects of firearms on aggressive behavior. In P. Suedfeld & P. E. Tetlock (Eds.), *Psychology and social policy* (pp. 201–221). New York: Hemisphere.

Turner, M. E., & Pratkanis, A. R. (1998). Twenty-five years of groupthink theory and research: Lessons from the evaluation of a theory. *Organizational Behavior and Human Decision Processes, 73*, 105–115.

Tversky, A. (1977). Features of similarity. *Psychological Review, 84*, 327–352.

Tversky, A., & Kahneman, D. (1974). Judgment under uncertainty: Heuristics and biases. *Science, 185*, 1124–1131.

Tversky, A., & Kahneman, D. (1981). The framing of decisions and the psychology of choice. *Science, 21*, 453–458.

Tversky, A., & Kahneman, D. (1982). Evidential impact of base rates. In D. Kahneman, P. Slovic, & A. Tversky (Eds.), *Judgment under uncertainty: Heuristics and biases* (pp. 153–160). New York: Cambridge University Press.

Tversky, A., & Kahneman, D. (1983). Extensional versus intuitive reasoning: The conjunction fallacy in probability judgment. *Psychological Review, 90*, 293–315.

Tversky, A., & Simonson, I. (1993). Context-dependent preferences. *Management Science, 39*, 1179–1189.

Twenge, J. M. (2002). Birth cohort, social change, and personality: The interplay of dysphoria and individualism in the 20th century. In D. Cervone & W. Mischel (Eds.), *Advances in personality science*. New York: Guilford Press.

Twenge, J. M., & Campbell, W. K. (2001). Age and birth cohort differences in self-esteem: A cross-temporal analysis. *Personality and Social Psychology Review, 5*, 321–344.

Tyler, T. R. (1984). Assessing the risk of crime victimization: The integration of personal victimization experience and socially transmitted information. *Journal of Social Issues, 40*, 27–38.

Tyler, T. R. (1987). Conditions leading to value-expressive effects in judgments of procedural justice: A test of four models. *Journal of Personality and Social Psychology, 52*, 333–344.

Tyler, T. R. (1994). Psychological models of the justice motive: Antecedents of distributive and procedural justice. *Journal of Personality and Social Psychology, 67*, 850–863.

Tyler, T. R., & Caine, A. (1981). The influence of outcomes and procedures on satisfaction with formal leaders. *Journal of Personality and Social Psychology, 41*, 642–655.

Tyler, T. R., & Smith, H. J. (1998). Social justice and social movements. In D. T. Gilbert, S. T. Fiske, & G. Lindzey (Eds.), *The handbook of social psychology* (4th ed., Vol. 2, pp. 595–629). New York: McGraw-Hill.

Uchino, B. N., Cacioppo, J. T., & Kiecolt-Glaser, J. K. (1996). The relationship between social support and physiological process: A review with emphasis on underlying mechanisms and implications for health. *Psychological Bulletin, 119*, 88–531.

Uematsu, T. (1970). Social facilitation of feeding behavior in fresh-water fish. I. rhodeus, acheilognathus and rhinogobius. *Annual of Animal Psychology, 20*, 87–95.

Uleman, J. S. (1987). Consciousness and control: The case of spontaneous trait inferences. *Personality and Social Psychology Bulletin, 13*, 337–354.

Umberson, D., & Hughes, M. (1987). The impact of physical attractiveness on achievement and psychological well-being. *Social Psychology Quarterly, 50*, 227–236.

United Nations. (2002a). *Small arms survey*. New York: United Nations.

United Nations. (2002b). 2000 demographic yearbook. New York: United Nations.

Uranowitz, S. W. (1975). Helping and self-attributions: A field experiment. *Journal of Personality and Social Psychology, 31*, 852–854.

Valenti, A. C., & Downing, L. L. (1975). Differential effects of jury size on verdicts following deliberations as a function of the apparent guilt of a defendant. *Journal of Personality and Social Psychology, 32*, 655–663.

Vallacher, R. R., & Wegner, D. M. (1985). *A theory of action identification*. Hillsdale, NJ: Lawrence Erlbaum Associates.

Vallacher, R. R., & Wegner, D. M. (1987). What do people think they're doing? Action identification and human behavior. *Psychological Review, 94*, 3–15.

Vallone, R. P., Ross, L., & Lepper, M. R. (1985). The hostile media phenomenon: Biased perception and perceptions of media bias in coverage of the Beirut massacre. *Journal of Personality and Social Psychology, 49*, 577–585.

Van Baaren, R. B., Holland, R. W., Kawakami, K., & van Knippenberg, A. (2004). Mimicry and pro-social behavior. *Psychological Science, 15*, 71–74.

Van Baaren, R. B., Holland, R. W., Steenaert, B., & van Knippenberg, A. (2003). Mimicry for money: Behavioral consequences of imitation. *Journal of Experimental Social Psychology, 39*, 393–398.

Van Boven, L., Kamada, A., & Gilovich, T. (1999). The perceiver as perceived: Everyday intuitions about the correspondence bias. *Journal of Personality and Social Psychology, 77*, 1188–1199.

Van Dort, B. E., & Moos, R. H. (1976). Distance and the utilization of a student health center. *Journal of the American College Health Association, 24*, 159–162.

Van Lange, P. A. M., Rusbult, C. E., Drigotas, S. M., Arriaga, X. B., Witcher, B. S., & Cox, C. L. (1997). Willingness to sacrifice in close relationships. *Journal of Personality and Social Psychology, 72*, 1373–1395.

Vandals ignite 400 fires in Detroit. (1984). *Washington Post*, p. A18.

Vandello, J., & Cohen, D. (1999). Patterns of individualism and collectivism across the United States. *Journal of Personality and Social Psychology, 77*, 279–292.

Vanneman, R. D., & Pettigrew, T. F. (1972). Race and relative deprivation in the urban United States. *Race, 13*, 461–486.

Varey, C., & Kahneman, D. (1992). Experiences extended across time: Evaluation of moments and episodes. *Journal of Behavioral Decision Making, 5*, 169–186.

Vasquez, K., Keltner, D., Ebenbach, D. H., & Banaszynski, T. L. (2001). Cultural variation and similarity in moral rhetorics: Voices from the Philippines and United States. *Journal of Cross-Cultural Psychology, 32*, 93–120.

Vescio, T. K., Snyder, M., & Butz, D. (2003). Power in stereotypically masculine domains: A social influence strategy X stereotype match model. *Journal of Personality and Social Psychology, 85*, 1062–1078.

von Hippel, W., Sekaquaptewa, D., & Vargas, P. (1995). On the role of encoding processes in stereotype maintenance. In M. P. Zanna (Ed.), *Advances in experimental social psychology* (Vol. 27, pp. 177–254). San Diego, CA: Academic Press.

von Hippel, W., Sekaquaptewa, D., & Vargas, P. (1997). The linguistic intergroup bias as an implicit indicator of prejudice. *Journal of Experimental Social Psychology, 33*, 490–509.

Von Neumann, J., & Morgenstern, O. (1947). *Theory of games and economic behavior*. Princeton: Princeton University Press.

Vonk, R. (1999). Effects of outcome dependency on the correspondence bias. *Personality and Social Psychology Bulletin, 25*, 382–389.

Vonk, R. (2002). Self-serving interpretations of flattery: Why ingratiation works. *Journal of Personality and Social Psychology, 82*, 515–526.

Wagner, H. L., MacDonald, C. J., & Manstead, A. S. R. (1986). Communication of individual emotions by spontaneous facial expression. *Journal of Personality and Social Psychology, 50*, 737–743.

Wagner, R. C. (1975). Complementary needs, role expectations, interpersonal attraction and the stability of work relationships. *Journal of Personality and Social Psychology, 32*, 116–124.

Walker, I., & Pettigrew, T. F. (1984). Relative deprivation theory: An overview and conceptual critique. *British Journal of Social Psychology, 23*, 300–310.

Wallach, M. A., Kogan, N., & Bem, D. J. (1962). Group influences on individual risk taking. *Journal of Abnormal and Social Psychology, 65*, 75–86.

Wallerstein, J. S., Lewis, J., & Blakeslee, S. (2000). *The unexpected legacy of divorce: The 25–year landmark study*. New York: Hyperion.

Walster, E. (1966). Assignment of responsibility for an accident. *Journal of Personality and Social Psychology, 3*, 73–79.

Walster, E., Aronson, E., & Abrahams, D. (1966). On increasing the persuasiveness of a low prestige communicator. *Journal of Experimental Social Psychology, 2*, 325–342.

Walster, E., Aronson, V., Abrahams, D., & Rottman, L. (1966). Importance of physical attractiveness in dating behavior. *Journal of Personality and Social Psychology, 4*, 508–516.

Walster, E., Walster, G. W., & Berscheid, E. (1978). *Equity theory and research*. Boston: Allyn and Bacon.

Wansink , B., Kent, R. J., & Hoch, S. J. (1998). An anchoring and adjustment model of purchase quantity decisions. *Journal of Marketing Research, 35*, 71–81.

Ward, R. (1994). Maternity ward. *Mirabella*, pp. 89–90.

Waterman, C. K. (1969). The facilitating and interfering effects of cognitive dissonance on simple and complex paired associates learning tasks. *Journal of Experimental Social Psychology, 5*, 31–42.

Watson, D. (1982). The actor and the observer: How are their perceptions of causality divergent? *Psychological Bulletin, 92*, 682–700.

Watson, D. (1989). Strangers' ratings of the five robust personality factors: Evidence for a surprising convergence with self-report. *Journal of Personality and Social Psychology, 57*, 120–128.

Watson, D., & Pennebaker, J. W. (1989). Health complaints, stress, and distress: Exploring the central role of negative affectivity. *Psychological Review, 96*, 234–254.

Watson, R. I. (1973). Investigation into deindividuation using a cross-cultural survey technique. *Journal of Personality and Social Psychology, 25*, 342–345.

Weber, M. (1947). *The theory of social and economic organization* (A. M. Henderson & T. Parsons, Trans.). New York: Oxford University Press.

Weber, R., & Crocker, J. (1983). Cognitive processes in the revision of stereotypic beliefs. *Journal of Personality and Social Psychology, 45*, 961–977.

Wegener, D. T., & Petty, R. E. (1994). Mood management across affective states: The hedonic contingency hypothesis. *Journal of Personality and Social Psychology, 66*, 1034–1048.

Wegener, D. T., Petty, R. E., & Smith, S. M. (1995). Positive mood can increase or decrease message scrutiny: The hedonic contingency view of mood and message processing. *Journal of Personality and Social Psychology, 69*, 5–15.

Wegner, D. M. (1986). Transactive memory: A contemporary analysis of the group mind. In B. Mullen & G. R. Goethals (Eds.), *Theories of group behavior* (pp. 185–208). New York: Springer-Verlag.

Wegner, D. M., & Bargh, J. A. (1998). Control and automaticity in everyday life. In D. T. Gilbert, S. T. Fiske, & G. Lindzey (Eds.), *The handbook of social psychology*. New York: McGraw-Hill.

Wegner, D. M., Erber, R., & Raymond, P. (1991). Transactive memory in close relationships. *Journal of Personality and Social Psychology, 61,* 923–929.

Weiner, B. (1980). A cognitive (attribution)-emotion-action model of judgments of help-giving. *Journal of Personality and Social Psychology, 39,* 186–200.

Weiner, B. (1985). An attributional theory of achievement motivation and emotion. *Psychological Review, 92,* 548–573.

Weiner, B. (1986). *An attributional theory of achievement and motivation.* New York: Springer-Verlag.

Weiner, B., Graham, S., & Reyna, C. (1997). An attributional examination of retributive versus utilitarian philosophies of punishment. *Social Justice Research, 10,* 431–452.

Weinstein, N. D. (1980). Unrealistic optimism about future life events. *Journal of Personality and Social Psychology, 39,* 806–820.

Wellman, H. M. (1990). *The child's theory of mind.* Cambridge, MA: MIT Press.

Wells, G. L., & Gavanski, I. (1989). Mental simulation of causality. *Journal of Personality and Social Psychology, 56,* 161–169.

Wells, G. L., & Petty, R. E. (1980). The effects of overt head movements on persuasion: Compatibility and incompatibility of responses. *Basic and Applied Social Psychology, 1,* 219–230.

Wenzlaff, R. M., & Prohaska, M. L. (1989). When misery prefers company: Depression, attributions, and responses to others' moods. *Journal of Experimental Social Psychology, 25,* 220–233.

West, S. G., & Brown, T. J. (1975). Physical attractiveness, the severity of the emergency and helping: A field experiment and interpersonal simulation. *Journal of Experimental Social Psychology, 11,* 531–538.

Wetzel, C. G. (1982). Self-serving biases in attribution: A Bayesian analysis. *Journal of Personality and Social Psychology, 43,* 197–209.

Weyant, J. M. (1984). Applying social psychology to induce charitable donations. *Journal of Applied Social Psychology, 14,* 441–447.

Whatley, M. A., Webster, J. M., Smith, R. H., & Rhodes, A. (1999). The effect of a favor on public and private compliance: How internalized is the norm of reciprocity? *Basic and Applied Social Psychology, 21,* 251–259.

Wheeler, L., & Kim, Y. (1997). What is beautiful is culturally good: The physical attractiveness stereotype has different content in collectivistic cultures. *Personality and Social Psychology Bulletin, 23,* 795–800.

Wheeler, L., & Nezlek, J. (1977). Sex differences in social participation. *Journal of Personality and Social Psychology, 35,* 742–754.

White, G. L. (1980). Physical attractiveness and courtship progress. *Journal of Personality and Social Psychology, 39,* 660–668.

White, G. L., & Kight, T. D. (1984). Misattribution of arousal and attraction: Effects of salience of explanations of arousal. *Journal of Experimental Social Psychology, 20,* 55–64.

White, H. (1997). Longitudinal perspective on alcohol and aggression during adolescence. In M. Galanter (Ed.), *Recent developments in alcoholism: Alcohol and violence: Epidemiology, neurobiology, psychology, and family issues* (Vol. 13, pp. 81–103). New York: Plenum Press.

White, L. K., & Booth, A. (1991). Divorce over the life course: The role of marital happiness. *Review of Personality and Social Psychology, 12,* 265–289.

White, P. A. (2002). Causal attribution from covariation information: The evidential evaluation model. *European Journal of Social Psychology, 32,* 667–684.

Whitely, B. E. (1990). The relationship of heterosexuals' attributions for the causes of homosexuality to attitudes towards lesbians and gay men. *Personality and Social Psychology Bulletin, 16,* 369–377.

Whyte, W. H. (1956). *The organization man.* New York: Simon and Schuster.

Wichman, H. (1972). Effects of isolation and communication on cooperation in a two-person game. In J. Wrightsman, J. O'Connor, & N. J. Baker (Eds.), *Cooperation and competition: Readings on mixed motive games* (pp. 197–205). Belmont: Brooks-Cole.

Wicker, A. W. (1969). Attitudes versus actions: The relationship of verbal and overt behavioral responses to attitude objects. *Journal of Social Issues, 25,* 41–78.

Wicklund, R. A. (1975). Objective self-awareness. In L. Berkowitz (Ed.), *Advances in experimental social psychology* (Vol. 8, pp. 233–275). New York: Academic Press.

Wieselquist, J., Rusbult, C. E., Agnew, C. R., & Foster, C. A. (1999). Commitment, pro-relationship behavior, and trust in close relationships. *Journal of Personality and Social Psychology, 77,* 942–966.

Wiggins, J. S., Wiggins, N., & Conger, J. C. (1968). Correlates of heterosexual somatic preference. *Journal of Personality and Social Psychology, 10,* 82–90.

Wilder, D. A. (1984). Predictions of belief homogeneity and similarity following social categorization. *British Journal of Social Psychology, 23,* 323–333.

Wilder, D. A. (1986). Social categorization: Implications for creation and reduction of intergroup bias. In L. Berkowitz (Ed.), *Advances in experimental social psychology* (Vol. 19, pp. 291–355). San Diego, CA: Academic Press.

Wiley, M. G., Crittenden, K. S., & Birg, L. D. (1979). Why a rejection? Causal attribution of a career achievement event. *Social Psychology Quarterly, 42,* 214–222.

Wilkinson, G. (1990, February). Food sharing in vampire bats. *Scientific American,* pp. 76–82.

Williams, D. R., & Collins, C. (1995). U.S. socioeconomic and racial differences in health: Patterns and explanations. *Annual Review of Sociology, 21,* 349–386.

Williams, G. C. (1966). *Adaptation and natural selection.* Princeton: Princeton University Press.

Williams, J. R., Insel, T. R., Harbaugh, C. R., & Carter, C. S. (1994). Oxytocin administered centrally facilitates formation of a partner preference in female prairie voles (Microtus Ochrogaster). *Journal of Neuroendocrinology, 6,* 247–250.

Williams, K. D., Harkins, S., & Latané, B. (1981). Identifiability as a deterrent to social loafing: Two cheering experiments. *Journal of Personality and Social Psychology, 40,* 303–311.

Wilson, M. I., & Daly, M. (1996). Male sexual proprietariness and violence against wives. *Current Directions in Psychological Science, 5,* 2–7.

Wilson, M. I., Daly, M., & Weghorst, S. J. (1980). Household composition and the risk of child abuse and neglect. *Journal of Biological Science, 12,* 333–340.

Wilson, M. I., Johnson, H., & Daly, M. (1995). Lethal and non-lethal violence against wives. *Canadian Journal of Criminology, 37*, 331–361.

Wilson, T. D. (2002). *Strangers to ourselves: Discovering the adaptive unconscious.* Cambridge, MA: Belknap Press of Harvard University Press.

Wilson, T., & Brekke, N. (1994). Mental contamination and mental correction: Unwanted influences on judgments and evaluations. *Psychological Bulletin, 116*, 117–142.

Wilson, T., Centerbar, D., & Brekke, N. (2002). Mental contamination and the debiasing problem. In T. Gilovich, D. W. Griffin, & D. Kahneman (Eds.), *Heuristics and biases: The psychology of intuitive judgment* (pp. 185–200). New York: Cambridge University Press.

Wilson, T. D., & Dunn, D. S. (1986). Effects of introspection on attitude-behavior consistency: Analyzing reasons versus focusing on feelings. *Journal of Experimental Social Psychology, 22*, 249–263.

Wilson, T. D., Dunn, D. S., Bybee, J. A., Hyman, D. B., & Rotondo, J. A. (1984). Effects of analyzing reasons on attitude-behavior consistency. *Journal of Personality and Social Psychology, 47*, 5–16.

Wilson, T. D., Lisle, D., Schooler, J. W., Hodges, S. D., Klaaren, K. J., & LaFleur, S. J. (1993). Introspecting about reasons can reduce post-choice satisfaction. *Personality and Social Psychology Bulletin, 19*, 331–339.

Wilson, T. D., & Schooler, J. W. (1991). Thinking too much: Introspection can reduce the quality of preferences and decisions. *Journal of Personality and Social Psychology, 60*, 181–192.

Wilson, T. D., Wheatley, T., Kurtz, J., Dunn, & Gilbert, D. T. (2004). When to fire: Anticipatory versus postevent reconstrual of uncontrollable events. *Personality and Social Psychology Bulletin, 30*, 1–12.

Wilson, T. D., Wheatley, T., Meyers, J. M., Gilbert, D. T., & Axson, D. (2000). Focalism: A source of durability bias in affective forecasting. *Journal of Personality and Social Psychology, 78*, 821–836.

Winch, R. F. (1955). The theory of complementary needs in mate selection: A test of one kind of complementariness. *American Sociological Review, 20*, 52–56.

Winch, R. F., Ktanes, T., & Ktanes, V. (1954). The theory of complementary needs in mate-selection: An analytic and descriptive study. *American Sociological Review, 19*, 241–249.

Winch, R. F., Ktanes, T., & Ktanes, V. (1955). Empirical elaboration of the theory of complementary needs in mate selection. *Journal of Abnormal and Social Psychology, 51*, 508–513.

Windhauser, J., Seiter, J., & Winfree, T. (1991). Crime news in the Louisiana press. *Journalism Quarterly, 45*, 72–78.

Wink, P. (1991). Two faces of narcissism. *Journal of Personality and Social Psychology, 61*, 590–597.

Winter, D. G. (1973). *The power motive.* New York: Free Press.

Winter, D. G. (1988). The power motive in women and men. *Journal of Personality and Social Psychology, 54*, 510–519.

Winter, D. G., & Barenbaum, N. B. (1985). Responsibility and the power motive in women and men. *Journal of Personality, 53*, 335–355.

Winter, L., & Uleman, J. S. (1984). When are social judgments made? Evidence for the spontaneousness of trait inferences. *Journal of Personality and Social Psychology, 47*, 237–252.

Wiselquist, J., Rusbult, C. E., Foster, C. A., & Agnew, C. R. (1999). Commitment and pro-relationship behavior, and

trust in close relationships. *Journal of Personality and Social Psychology, 77*, 942–966.

Wiseman, C. V., Gray, J. J., Mosimann, J. E., & Ahrens, A. H. (1992). Cultural expectations of thinness in women: An update. *International Journal of Eating Disorders, 11*, 85–89.

Witkin, H. A., Lewis, H. B., Hertzman, M., Machover, K., Meissner, P. B., & Karp, S. A. (1954). *Personality through perception.* New York: Harper.

Wittenbrink, B., Judd, C. M., & Park, B. (1997). Evidence for racial prejudice at the implicit level and its relationship with questionnaire measures. *Journal of Personality and Social Psychology, 72*, 262–274.

Witvliet, C., Ludwig, T. E., & Vander Laan, K. L. (2001). Granting forgiveness or harboring grudges: Implications for emotion, physiology, and health. *Psychological Science, 12*, 117–123.

Wolf, S. (1985). Manifest and latent influence on majorities and minorities. *Journal of Personality and Social Psychology, 48*, 899–908.

Wolfe, T. (1979). *The right stuff.* New York: Farrar, Strauss, Giroux.

Woll, S. (1986). So many to choose from: Decision strategies in videodating. *Journal of Social and Personal Relationships, 3*, 43–52.

Wood, J. V. (1989). Theory and research concerning social comparisons of personal attributes. *Psychological Bulletin, 106*, 231–248.

Wood, J. V. (1996). What is social comparison and how should we study it? *Personality and Social Psychology Bulletin, 22*, 520–537.

Wood, W. (1982). Retrieval of attitude relevant information from memory: Effects of susceptibility to persuasion and on intrinsic motivation. *Journal of Personality and Social Psychology, 42*, 798–810.

Wood, W., & Eagly, A. H. (2002). A cross-cultural analysis of the behavior of women and men: Implications for the origin of sex differences. *Psychological Bulletin, 126*, 699–727.

Wood, W., & Kallgren, C. A. (1988). Communicator attributes and persuasion: Recipients access to attitude-relevant information in memory. *Personality and Social Psychology Bulletin, 14*, 172–182.

Wood, W., Lundgren, S., Ouellette, J. A., Busceme, S., & Blackstone, T. (1994). Minority influence: A meta-analytic review of social influence processes. *Psychological Bulletin, 115*, 323–345.

Wooley, S. C., & Wooley, O. W. (1980). Eating disorders: Obesity and anorexia. In A. M. Brodsky & R. T. Hare-Mustin (Eds.), *Women and psychotherapy: An assessment of research and practice* (pp. 135–158). New York: Guilford Press.

Woolger, R. J. (1988). *Other lives, other selves: A Jungian psychotherapist discovers past lives.* New York: Bantam.

Worchel, S. (1974). The effects of three types of arbitrary thwarting on the instigation to aggression. *Journal of Personality, 42*, 301–318.

Word, C. O., Zanna, M. P., & Cooper, J. (1974). The nonverbal mediation of self-fulfilling prophecies in interracial interaction. *Journal of Experimental Social Psychology, 10*, 109–120.

Worthington, E. L. J. (1998). Empirical research in forgiveness: Looking backward, looking forward. In J. E. L. Worthington

(Ed.), *Dimensions of forgiveness* (pp. 321–339). Philadelphia: Templeton Foundation Press.

Wright, R. (1995, March 13). The biology of violence. *New Yorker,* pp. 68–77.

Wright, R. (2000). *Nonzero: The logic of human destiny.* New York: Pantheon Books.

Wyer, R. S., & Srull, T. K. (1981). Category accessibility: Some theoretical and empirical issues concerning the processing of social stimulus information. In E. T. Higgins, C. P. Herman, & M. P. Zanna (Eds.), *Social cognition: The Ontario symposium* (pp. 161–197). Hillsdale, NJ: Lawrence Erlbaum Associates.

Wyer, R. S., Srull, T. K., Gordon, S. E., & Hartwick, J. (1982). Effects of processing objectives on the recall of prose material. *Journal of Personality and Social Psychology, 43,* 674–688.

Yang, M. H., & Bond, M. H. (1990). Exploring implicit personality theories with indigenous or imported constructs: The Chinese case. *Journal of Personality and Social Psychology, 58,* 1087–1095.

Yu, Y., & Williams, D. R. (1999). Socioeconomic status and mental health. In C. S. Aneshensel & J. C. Phelan (Eds.), *Handbook of sociology and mental health* (pp. 151–166). New York: Plenum Press.

Yudko, E., Blanchard, D., Henne, J., & Blanchard, R. (1997). Emerging themes in preclinical research on alcohol and aggression. In M. Galanter (Ed.), *Recent developments in alcoholism: Alcohol and violence: Epidemiology, neurobiology, psychology, and family issues* (Vol. 13, pp. 123–138). New York: Plenum Press.

Zadny, J., & Gerard, H. B. (1974). Attributed intentions and informational selectivity. *Journal of Experimental Social Psychology, 10,* 34–52.

Zahavi, A., & Zahavi, A. (1997). *The handicap principle.* New York: Oxford University Press.

Zajonc, R. B. (1965). Social facilitation. *Science, 149,* 269–274.

Zajonc, R. B. (1968). The attitudinal effects of mere exposure. *Journal of Personality and Social Psychology, 9* (monographs), 1–27.

Zajonc, R. B. (1980). Feeling and thinking: Preferences need no inferences. *American Psychologist, 35,* 151–175.

Zajonc, R. B. (2001). Mere exposure: A gateway to the subliminal. *Current Directions in Psychological Science, 10,* 224–228.

Zajonc, R. B. (2002). The zoomorphism of human collective violence. In L. S. Newman & R. Erber (Eds.), *Understanding genocide: The social psychology of the Holocaust* (pp. 222–240). New York: Oxford University Press.

Zajonc, R. B., Adelmann, P. K., Murphy, S. T., & Niedenthal, P. M (1987). Convergence in the physical appearance of spouses. *Motivation and Emotion, 11,* 335–346.

Zajonc, R. B., Heingartner, A., & Herman, E. M. (1969). Social enhancement and impairment of performance in the cockroach. *Journal of Personality and Social Psychology, 13,* 83–92.

Zanna, M. P., & Cooper, J. (1974). Dissonance and the pill: An attribution approach to studying the arousal properties of dissonance. *Journal of Personality and Social Psychology, 29,* 703–709.

Zanna, M. P., Kiesler, C. A., & Pilkonis, P. A. (1970). Positive and negative attitudinal affect established by classical conditioning. *Journal of Personality and Social Psychology, 14,* 321–328.

Zanna, M. P., & Rempel, J. K. (1988). Attitudes: A new look at an old concept. In D. Bar-Tal & A. W. Kruglanski (Eds.), *The social psychology of knowledge* (pp. 315–334). Cambridge, England: Cambridge University Press.

Zarate, M. A., Uleman, J. S., & Voils, C. I. (2001). Effects of culture and processing goals on the activation and binding of trait concepts. *Social Cognition, 19,* 295–323.

Zebrowitz, L. (1997). *Reading faces: Window to the soul?* Boulder, CO: Westview Press.

Zebrowitz, L. A., Olson, K., & Hoffman, K. (1993). Stability of babyfaceness and attractiveness across the life span. *Journal of Personality and Social Psychology, 64,* 453–466.

Zillman, D. (1978). Attribution and misattribution of excitatory reactions. In J. H. Harvey, W. J. Ickes, & R. F. Kidd (Eds.), *New directions in attribution research* (Vol. 2, pp. 335–368). Hillsdale, NJ: Lawrence Erlbaum Associates.

Zillman, D. (1988). Cognitive excitation interdependencies in aggressive behavior. *Aggressive Behavior, 14,* 51–64.

Zillman, D. (1989). Effects of prolonged consumption of pornography. In D. Zillman & J. Bryand (Eds.), *Pornography: Research advances and early policy considerations.* Hillsdale, NJ: Lawrence Erlbaum Associates.

Zimbardo, P. G. (1970). *The human choice: Individuation, reason and order versus deindividuation, impulse and chaos.* Paper presented at the Nebraska Symposium on Motivation (1969), Lincoln, Nebraska.

Zimbardo, P. G., & Leippe, M. R. (1991). *The psychology of attitude change and social influence.* New York: McGraw-Hill.

Zuber, J. A., Crott, H. W., & Werner, J. (1992). Choice shift and group polarization: An analysis of the status of arguments and social decision schemes. *Journal of Personality and Social Psychology, 62,* 50–61.

Zuckerman, M. (1996). The psychobiological model for impulsive unsocialized sensation seeking: A comparative approach. *Neuropsychobiology, 34,* 125–129.

Zuckerman, M. (1998). Psychobiological theories of personality. In D. F. Barone, M. Hersen, & V. B. V. Hasselt (Eds.), *Advanced personality* (pp. 123–154). New York: Plenum Press.

Zusne, L., & Jones, W. H. (1982). *Anomalistic psychology.* Hillsdale, NJ: Lawrence Erlbaum Associates.

Zuwerink, J. R., & Devine, P. G. (1996). Attitude importance and resistance to persuasion: It's not just the thought that counts. *Journal of Personality and Social Psychology, 70,* 931–944.

# Credits and Acknowledgments

## FIGURES

**Figure 1.1** Adapted from Darley, J. M., & Batson, C. D. (1973). From Jerusalem to Jericho: A study of situational and dispositional variables in helping behavior. *Journal of Personality and Social Psychology, 27*, 100–119. **Figure 1.2** From Kanizsa, G. (1976). Subjective contours. *Scientific American, 234*, 48–52. Used by permission of Jerome Kuhl. **Figure 1.3** *Slave Market with the Disappearing Bust of Voltaire* (1940). Oil on canvas, 18 1/4 x 25 3/8 inches. Collection of The Salvador Dali Museum, St. Petersburg, Florida. © 2005 Salvador Dali, Gala-Salvador Dali Foundation/Artists Rights Society (ARS), New York. Photo © 2005 Salvador Dali Museum, Inc. **Figure 1.4** From Liberman, V., Samuels, S. M., & Ross, L. (2002). The name of the game: Predictive power of reputations vs. situational labels in determining Prisoner's Dilemma game moves. *Personality and Social Psychology Bulletin, 30*, 1175–1185. **Figure 1.5** From Nisbett, R. E. (2003). *The geography of thought: Why we think the way we do*. New York: Free Press. **Figure 1.6** From Sabini, J. (1995). *Social psychology* (2nd ed.), p. 261. New York: Norton. Copyright © 1995 W. W. Norton & Company. **Figure 1.7** From Ma, V., & Schoeneman, T. J. (1997). Individualism versus collectivism: A comparison of Kenyan and American self-concepts. *Basic and Applied Social Psychology, 19*, 261–273.

**Figure 2.2** From Zajonc, R. B., Heingartner, A., & Herman, E. M. (1969). Social enhancement and impairment of performance in the cockroach. *Journal of Personality and Social Psychology, 13*, 83–92. Copyright © 1969 by the American Psychological Association. Reprinted with permission. **Figure 2.3** From Cottrell, N. B., Wack, D. L., Sekerak, G. J., & Rittle, R. H. (1968). Social facilitation of dominant responses by the presence of an audience and the mere presence of others. *Journal of Personality and Social Psychology, 9*, 245–250. **Figure 2.4** From Zimbardo, P. G. (1970). *The human choice: Individuation, reason and order versus deindividuation, impulse and chaos*. Paper presented at the Nebraska Symposium on Motivation (1969), Lincoln, Nebraska. **Figure 2.5** Adapted from Mann, L. (1981). The baiting crowd in episodes of threatened suicide. *Journal of Personality and Social Psychology, 41*, 703–709. **Figure 2.6** Adapted from Janis, I. L., & Mann, L. (1977). *Decision making*, p. 132. New York: Free Press.

**Figure 3.1** From Festinger, L., Schachter, S., & Back, K. (1950). *Social pressures in informal groups*. Stanford: Stanford University Press. **Figure 3.2** From Segal, M. W. (1974). Alphabet and attraction: An unobtrusive measure of the effect of propinquity in a field setting. *Journal of Personality and Social Psychology, 30*, 654–657. **Figure 3.3** From Zajonc, R. B. (1968). The attitudinal effects of mere exposure. *Journal of Personality and Social Psychology, 9* (monographs), 1–27. **Figure 3.4** From Cross, H. A., Halcomb, C. G., & Matter, W. W. (1967). Imprinting or exposure learning in rats given early auditory stimulation. *Psychonomic Science, 7*, 233–234. **Figure 3.5** Adapted from Whyte, W. H. (1956). *The organization man*. New York: Simon and Schuster. Copyright © 1956 Simon and Schuster. **Figure 3.6** From Buss, D. M. (1989). Sex differences in human mate preference. Evolutionary hypothesis tested in 37 cultures. *Behavioral and Brain Sciences, 12*, 1–49.

Figure 4.1: Adapted from Berk, M. S., & Andersen, S. M. (2000). The impact of past relationships on interpersonal behavior: Behavioral confirmation in the social-cognitive process of transference. *Journal of Personality and Social Psychology, 79,* 546–562. **Figure 4.2** Adapted from Aron, A., Aron, E. N., Tudor, M., & Nelson, G. (1991). Close relationships as including other in self. *Journal of Personality and Social Psychology, 60,* 241–253. **Figure 4.3** Adapted from Wegner, D. M., Erber, R., & Raymond, P. (1991). Transactive memory in close relationships. *Journal of Personality and Social Psychology, 61,* 923–929. **Figure 4.4** From Clark, M. S., Mills, J., & Powell, M. C. (1986). Keeping track of needs in communal and exchange relationships. *Journal of Personality and Social Psychology, 51,* 333–338. **Figure 4.5** From Keltner, D., Young, R. C., Heerey, E. A., Oemig, C., & Monarch, N. D. (1998). Teasing in hierarchial and intimate relations. *Journal of Personality and Social Psychology, 75,* 1231–1247. **Figure 4.6** From Gottman, J. M., & Levenson, R. W. (1999). Rebound from marital conflict and divorce prediction. *Family Processes, 38,* 287–292.

**Figure 5.1** Adapted from Loehlin, J. C. (1992). *Genes and environment in personality development.* Newbury Park, CA: Sage. **Figure 5.2** Adapted from McGuire, W. J., & Padawer-Singer, A. (1978). Trait salience in the spontaneous self-concept. *Journal of Personality and Social Psychology, 33,* 743–754. **Figure 5.3** From Markus, H. R., & Kitayama, S. (1991). Culture and the self: Implications for cognition, emotion, and motivation. *Psychological Review, 98,* p. 226. Copyright 1991 by the American Psychological Association. Reprinted with permission. **Figure 5.4** Adapted from Rogers, T. B., Kuiper, N. A., & Kirker, W. S. (1977). Self-reference and the encoding of personal information. *Journal of Personality and Social Psychology, 35,* 677–688. **Figure 5.5** Adapted from Tesser, A., & Smith, J. (1980). Some effects of friendship and task relevance on helping: You don't always help the one you like. *Journal of Experimental Social Psychology, 16,* 582–590. **Figure 5.6** Adapted from Heine, S. J., & Lehman, D. R. (2003). Move the body, change the self: Acculturative effects on the self-concept. In M. Schaller & C. S. Crandall (Eds.), *Psychological foundations of culture* (pp. 305–331). Mahwah, NJ: Lawrence Erlbaum Associates.

**Figure 6.1** Chartrand, T. L., & Bargh, J. A. (1999). The chameleon effect: The perception-behavior link and social interaction. *Journal of Personality and Social Psychology, 76,* 893–910. **Figure 6.3** From Sherif, M. (1936). *The psychology of social norms.* New York: Harper. **Figure 6.4** From Asch, S. (1956). Studies of independence and conformity: A minority of one against a unanimous majority. *Psychological Monographs, 70* (Whole No. 416). **Figure 6.5** From Asch, S. (1951). Effects of group pressure upon the modification and distortion of judgments. In G. Guetzkow (Ed.), *Groups, leadership, and men* (pp. 177–190). Pittsburgh, PA: Carnegie Press. **Figure 6.6** From Ross, L., Bierbrauer, G., & Hoffman, S. (1976). The role of attribution process in conformity and dissent: Revisiting the Asch situation. *American Psychologist, 31,* 148–157. **Figure 6.7** From Milgram, S. (1965). Some conditions of obedience and disobedience to authority. *Human Relations, 18,* 57–75. **Figure 6.8** From Milgram, S. (1965). Some conditions of obedience and disobedience to authority. *Human Relations, 18,* 57–75. **Figure 6.9** From Isen, A. M., Clark, M., & Schwartz, M. F. (1976). Duration of the effect of good mood on helping: Footprints on the sands of time. *Journal of*

*Personality and Social Psychology, 34,* 385–393. **Figure 6.10** From Cialdini, R. B., Darby, B. L., & Vincent, J. E. (1973). Transgression and altruism: A case for hedonism. *Journal of Experimental Social Psychology, 9,* 502–516.

**Figure 7.1** From Newcomb, T. M. (1958). Attitude development as a function of reference groups. In E. E. Maccoby, T. M. Newcomb, & E. L. Hartley (Eds.), *Readings in social psychology* (3rd ed.). New York: Holt, Rinehart and Winston. **Figure 7.2** From Lepper, M. R., Ross, L., Vallone, R., & Keavney, M. (unpublished data). Biased perceptions of victory and media hostility in network coverage of presidential debates. **Figure 7.4** Adapted from Petty, R. E., & Cacioppo, J. T. (1986). The elaboration likelihood model of persuasion. In L. Berkowitz (Ed.), *Advances in experimental social psychology,* p. 154. New York: Academic Press. **Figure 7.5** From Leventhal, H., Watts, J. C., & Pagano, F. (1967). Effects of fear and instructions on how to cope with danger. *Journal of Personality and Social Psychology, 6,* 313–321. **Figure 7.6** From Kunda, Z. (1990). The case for motivated reasoning. *Psychological Bulletin, 108,* 480–496. **Figure 7.7** From McGuire, W. J., & Papageorgis, D. (1961). The relative efficacy of various types of prior belief-defense in producing immunity against persuasion. *Journal of Abnormal and Social Psychology, 62,* 327–337.

**Figure 8.1** From Madden, T. J., Ellen, P. S., & Ajzen, I. (1992). A comparison of the theory of planned behavior and the theory of reasoned action. *Personality and Social Psychology Bulletin, 18,* 3–9. **Figure 8.2** From Davidson, A. R., & Jaccard, J. J. (1979). Variables that moderate the attitude-behavior relation: Results of a longitudinal survey. *Journal of Personality and Social Psychology, 37,* 1364–1376. **Figure 8.3** Adapted from Aronson, E., & Mills, J. (1959). The effect of severity of initiation on liking for a group. *Journal of Abnormal and Social Psychology, 59,* 177–181. **Figure 8.4** From Cooper, J. (1980). Reducing fears and increasing assertiveness: The role of dissonance reduction. *Journal of Experimental Social Psychology, 16,* 199–213. **Figure 8.5** From Festinger, L., & Carlsmith, J. M. (1959). Cognitive consequences of forced compliance. *Journal of Abnormal and Social Psychology, 47,* 382–389. **Figure 8.6** From Aronson, E., & Carlsmith, J. M. (1963). Effect of severity of threat in the devaluation of forbidden behavior. *Journal of Abnormal and Social Psychology, 66,* 584–588. **Figure 8.7** From Zanna, M. P., & Cooper, J. (1974). Dissonance and the pill: An attribution approach to studying the arousal properties of dissonance. *Journal of Personality and Social Psychology, 29,* 703–709. **Figure 8.8** From Gazzaniga, M. S., & Heatherton, T. F. (2003). *Psychological science: Mind, brain, and behavior,* p. 116. New York: Norton. Copyright © 2003 by W. W. Norton & Company. **Figure in Box 8.1 (p. 323)** From Kitayama, S., Snibbe, A. C., Markus, H. R., & Suzuki, T. (2004). Is there any "free" choice? Self and dissonance in two cultures. *Psychological Science, 15,* 527–533. Reprinted by permission of Blackwell Publishers, Ltd. **Figure in Box 8.2 (p. 326)** From Greene, D., Sternberg, B., & Lepper, M. R. (1976). Overjustification in a token economy. *Journal of Personality and Social Psychology, 34,* 1219–1234.

**Figure 9.1** Adapted from Jones, E. E., Davis, K. E., & Gergen, K. J. (1961). Role playing variations and their informational value for person perception. *Journal of Abnormal and Social Psychology, 63,* 302–310. **Figure 9.2** Adapted from Wells, G. L., & Gavanski,

I. (1989). Mental simulation of causality. *Journal of Personality and Social Psychology, 56,* 161–169. **Figure 9.3** Adapted from Medvec, V. H., Madey, S. F., & Gilovich, T. (1995). When less is more: Counterfactual thinking and satisfaction among Olympic medalists. *Journal of Personality and Social Psychology, 69,* 603–610. **Figure 9.4** Adapted from Jones, E. E., & Harris, V. A. (1967). The attribution of attitudes. *Journal of Experimental Social Psychology, 3,* 1–24. **Figure 9.5** Adapted from Van Boven, L., Kamada, A., & Gilovich, T. (1999). The perceiver as perceived: Everyday intuitions about the correspondence bias. *Journal of Personality and Social Psychology, 77,* 1188–1199. **Figure 9.6** Adapted from Ross, L., Amabile, T. M., & Steinmetz, J. L. (1977). Social roles, social control, and biases on social-perception processes. *Journal of Personality and Social Psychology, 35,* 485–494. **Figure 9.8** Adapted from Gilbert, D. T. (1989). Thinking lightly about others: Automatic components of the social inference process. In J. S. Uleman & J. A. Bargh (Eds.), *Unintended thought.* New York: Guilford Press. **Figure 9.9** From Masuda, T., Ellsworth, P. C., Mesquita, B., Leu, J., & van de Veerdonk, E. (2004). *A face in the crowd or a crowd in the face: Japanese and American perceptions of others' emotions.* Unpublished manuscript, Hokkaido University. Courtesy Professor Taka Masuda, Hokkaido University. **Figure 9.10** From Masuda, T., & Nisbett, R. E. (2001). Attending holistically vs. analytically: Comparing the context sensitivity of Japanese and Americans. *Journal of Personality and Social Psychology, 81,* 922–934. Courtesy Professor Taka Masuda, Hokkaido University. **Figure 9.11** From Kitayama, S., Duffy, S., Kawamura, T., & Larsen, J. T. (2002). Perceiving an object in its context in different cultures: A cultural look at the New Look. *Psychological Science, 14,* 201–206.

**Figure 10.1** Adapted from Prentice, D. A., & Miller, D. T. (1993). Pluralistic ignorance and alcohol use on campus: Some consequences of misperceiving the social norm. *Journal of Personality and Social Psychology, 64,* 243–256. **Figure 10.2** Adapted from Gilovich, T. (1981). Seeing the past in the present: The effect of associations to familiar events on judgments and decisions. *Journal of Personality and Social Psychology, 40,* 797–808.

**Figure 11.2** From Fein, S., & Spencer, S. (1997). Prejudice as a self-esteem maintenance: Affirming the self through derogating others. *Journal of Personality and Social Psychology, 73,* 31–44. **Figure 11.3** Adapted from Sinclair, L., & Kunda, Z. (1999). Reactions to a black professional: Motivated inhibition and activation of conflicting stereotypes. *Journal of Personality and Social Psychology, 77,* 885–904. **Figure 11.4** From Macrae, C. N., Milne, A. B., & Bodenhausen, G. V. (1994). Stereotypes as energy-saving devices: A peek inside the cognitive toolbox. *Journal of Personality and Social Psychology, 66,* 37–47. **Figure 11.5** From Hamilton, D. L., & Gifford, R. K. (1976). Illusory correlation in interpersonal perception: A cognitive basis of stereotypic judgments. *Journal of Experimental Social Psychology, 12,* 392–407. **From 11.6** From Maass, A., Salvi, D., Arcuri, L., & Semin, G. (1989). Language use in intergroup contexts: The linguistic intergroup bias. *Journal of Personality and Social Psychology, 57,* 981–993. **Figure 11.7** From Correll, J., Park, B., Judd, C. M., & Wittenbrink, B. (2002). The police officer's dilemma: Using ethnicity to disambiguate potentially threatening individuals. *Journal of Personality and Social Psychology, 83,* 1314–1329. **Figure 11.8** From Spencer, S. J., Steele, C. M., &

Quinn, D. M. (1999). Stereotype threat and women's math performance. *Journal of Experimental Social Psychology, 3,* 4–28.

**Figure 12.1** Gleitman, H., Fridlund, A. J., & Reisberg, D. (2004). *Psychology* (6th ed.), p. 102. New York: Norton. Copyright © 2004 W. W. Norton & Company. **Figure 12.2** From Haidt, J., & Keltner, D. (1999). Culture and facial expression: Open ended methods find more faces and a gradient of universality. *Cognition and Emotion, 13,* 225–266. Photos courtesy Professor Dacher Keltner. **Figure 12.3** Adapted from Ishii, K., Reyes, J. A., & Kitayama, S. (2003). Spontaneous attention to word content versus emotional tone: Differences among three cultures. *Psychological Science, 14,* 39–46. **Figure 12.4** Gazzaniga, M. S., & Heatherton, T. F. (2003). *Psychological science: Mind, brain, and behavior.* New York: Norton. Based on Figure 9.9 in Gazzaniga, M. S., Ivry, R. B., & Mangun, G. R. (1998). *Cognitive neuroscience: The biology of the mind,* p. 331. New York: Norton. Copyright © 1998 W. W. Norton & Company. **Figure 12.5** From Murphy, S. T., & Zajonc, R. B. (1993). Affect, cognition, and awareness: Affective priming with optimal and suboptimal stimulus exposures. *Journal of Personality and Social Psychology, 64,* 723–739. **Figure 9.5** Adapted from Gilbert, D. T., Pinel, E. C., Wilson, T. D., Blumberg, S. J., & Wheatley, T. (1998). Immune neglect: A source of durability bias in affective forecasting. *Journal of Personality and Social Psychology, 75,* 617–638. **Figure 12.7** Adapted from Brickman, P., Coates, D., & Janoff-Bulman, R. J. (1978). Lottery winners and accident victims: Is happiness relative? *Journal of Personality and Social Psychology, 36,* 917–927.

**Figure 13.1** From Huesmann, L. R. (1986). Psychological processes promoting the relations between exposure to media violence and aggressive behavior by the viewer. *Journal of Social Issues, 42,* 125–139. **Figure 13.2** Adapted from Anderson, C. A. (1989). Temperature and aggression: Ubiquitous effects of heat on occurrences of human violence. *Psychological Bulletin, 106,* p. 82. **Figure 13.3** Adapted from Berkowitz, L. (1989). The frustration-aggression hypothesis: An examination and reformulation. *Psychological Bulletin, 106,* 59–73. **Figure 13.4** Adapted from Berkowitz, L., & LePage, A. (1967). Weapons as aggression-eliciting stimuli. *Journal of Personality and Social Psychology, 7,* 202–207. **Figure 13.5** From Nisbett, R. E., & Cohen, D. (1996). *Culture of honor: The psychology of violence in the South,* p. 21. Boulder, CO: Westview Press. **Figure 13.6** Adapted from Wilson, M. I., & Daly, M. (1996). Male sexual proprietariness and violence against wives. *Current Directions in Psychological Science, 5,* 2–7. **Figure 13.7** From Fultz, J., Batson, C. D., Fortenbach, V. A., McCarthy, P. M., & Varney, L. (1986). Social evaluation and the empathy-altruism hypothesis. *Journal of Personality and Social Psychology, 50,* 761–769. **Figure 13.8** From Steblay, N. M. (1987). Helping behavior in rural and urban environments: A meta-analysis. *Psychological Bulletin, 102,* 346–356. **Figure in Box 13.2 (p. 526)** Adapted from Frank, M. G., & Gilovich, T. (1988). The dark side of self and social perception: Black uniforms and aggression in professional sports. *Journal of Personality and Social Psychology, 54,* 74–85.

**Figure 14.1** Adapted from Vasquez, K., Keltner, D., Ebenbach, D. H., & Banaszynski, T. L. (2001). Cultural variation and similarity in moral rhetorics: Voices from the Philippines and United States. *Journal of Cross-Cultural Psychology, 32,* 93–120. **Figure 14.2** Adapted from Phillips, K. (2002). *Wealth and* *democracy.* New York: Broadway Books. **Figure 14.3** Adapted from Messick, D. M., Bloom, S., Boldizar, J. P., & Samuelson, C. (1985). Why we are fairer than others. *Journal of Experimental Social Psychology, 21,* 480–500. **Figure 14.4** Adapted from Ross, L., & Stillinger, C. (1991). Barriers to conflict resolution. *Negotiation Journal, 8,* 389–404. **Figure in Box 14.3 (p. 583)** Adapted from Suedfeld, P., & Tetlock, P. E. (1977). Integrative complexity of communications in international crises. *Journal of Conflict Resolution, 21,* 169–184.

## TABLES

**Table 1.2** Compiled by Brown, D. E. (1991). *Human universals.* New York: McGraw-Hill, appearing in S. Pinker (2002), *The blank slate: The modern denial of human nature.* New York: Viking. **Table 1.4** From Hofstede, G. (1980). *Culture's consequences: International differences in work-related values.* Beverly Hills: Sage Publications. **Table 2.1** From Markus, H. (1978). The effect of mere presence on social facilitation. An unobtrusive test. *Journal of Experimental Social Psychology, 14,* 389–397. **Table 2.2** From Diener, E., Fraser, S. C., Beaman, A. L., & Kelem, R. T. (1976). Effects of deindividuation variables on stealing among Halloween trick-or-treaters. *Journal of Personality and Social Psychology, 33,* 178–183. **Table 4.1** Adapted from Hazan, C., & Shaver, P. (1987). Romantic love conceptualized as an attachment process. *Journal of Personality and Social Psychology, 52,* 511–524. **Table 4.2** Adapted from Rusbult, C. E. (1980). Commitment and satisfaction in romantic associations: A test of the investment model. *Journal of Experimental Social Psychology, 17,* 172–186. **Table 5.2** From Semin, G. R., & Rubini, M. (1990). Unfolding the concept of person by verbal abuse. *European Journal of Social Psychology, 20,* 463–474. Copyright © 1990 John Wiley & Sons Limited. Reproduced with permission. **Table 5.3** From Weinstein, N. D. (1980). Unrealistic optimism about future life events. *Journal of Personality and Social Psychology, 39,* 806–820. **Table 5.4** Rosenberg, M. (1965). *Society and the adolescent self-image.* Princeton: Princeton University Press. **Table 6.1** From Ross, L., Bierbrauer, G., & Hoffman, S. (1976). The role of attribution process in conformity and dissent: Revisiting the Asch situation. *American Psychologist, 31,* 148–157. **Table 9.1** From Peterson, C., Seligman, M. E. P., & Vaillant, G. E. (1988). Pessimistic explanatory style is a risk factor for physical illness: A thirty-five-year longitudinal study. *Journal of Personality and Social Psychology, 55,* 23–27. **Table 10.1** From Schwarz, N., Bless, H., Strack, F., Klumpp, G., Rittenauer-Schatka, & Simons, A. (1991). Ease of retrieval as information: Another look at the availability heuristic. *Journal of Personality and Social Psychology, 61,* 195–202. **Table 10.2** Adapted from Slovic, P., Fischoff, B., & Lichtenstein, S. (1982). Facts versus fears: Understanding perceived risk. In D. Kahneman, P. Slovic, & A. Tversky (Eds.), *Judgment under uncertainty: Heuristics and biases* (pp. 463–489). New York: Cambridge University Press. **Table 10.3** Adapted from Kahneman, D., & Tversky, A. (1973). On the psychology of prediction. *Psychological Review, 80,* 237–251. **Table 10.4** From Huntley, J. (1990). *The elements of astrology.* Shaftesbury, Dorset, England: Element Books Unlimited. Also from Read, A. W., et al. (1978). *Funk and Wagnalls new comprehensive international dictionary of the English language.* New York: Publisher's Guild Press. **Table in Box 10.4 (p. 420)** Larkey, P. D., Smith, R. A., & Kadane, J. B. (1989). It's okay to believe in the hot hand. *Chance, 2,* 22–30. **Table 12.1** Adapted from Levenson, R. W., Ekman, P., & Friesen, W. V. (1990). Voluntary facial action generates emotion-specific autonomic nervous system activity. *Psychophysiology, 27* (4), 363–384. **Table 12.2** Adapted from Schwarz, N., & Clore, G. L. (1983). Mood, misattribution, and judgments of well-being: Informative and directive functions of affective states. *Journal of Personality and Social Psychology, 45,* 513–523. **Table 14.1** Adapted from Haidt, J., Koller, S. H., & Dias, M. G. (1993). Affect, culture, and morality, or Is it wrong to eat your dog? *Journal of Personality and Social Psychology, 65,* 613–628.

## PHOTOS AND CARTOONS

### CHAPTER 1

**Page 2:** John S. Dykes. **p. 4:** *(left)* Corbis; *(right)* Photo from the Zimbardo Simulated Prison Study, August 15–20, 1971, Stanford University. Reproduced by permission of Professor Philip G. Zimbardo. **p. 6:** Corbis. **p. 9:** *(top)* Bettmann/Corbis; *(right)* Archives of the History of American Psychology, University of Akron. **p. 10:** *(left and right)* From the film *Obedience,* © 1965 by Stanley Milgram and distributed by Penn State Media Sales. **p. 15:** *Slave Market with the Disappearing Bust of Voltaire* (1940). Oil on canvas, 18 1/4 x 25 3/8 inches. Collection of The Salvador Dali Museum, St. Petersburg, Florida. © 2005 Salvador Dali, Gala-Salvador Dali Foundation/Artists Rights Society (ARS), New York. Photo: © 2005 Salvador Dali Museum, Inc. **p. 18:** *(left)* Mark L. Stephenson/Corbis; *(right)* Steve Prezant/Corbis. **p. 19:** Ali Jasim/Reuters/Corbis. **p. 20:** *(top)* Stone/Getty Images; *(bottom)* Bettmann/Corbis. **p. 22:** © The New Yorker Collection, 2001 Mort Gerberg, from cartoonbank.com. All Rights Reserved. **p. 23:** *(left)* Tom Brakefield/Corbis; *(right)* Reuters/Corbis. **p. 26:** Will & Demi McIntyre/Photo Researchers, Inc. 7F7243. **p. 29:** *(left)* Tom Wagner/Corbis Saba; *(right)* James Marshall/Corbis. **p. 34:** *(left)* McCain Library and Archives, University of Southern Mississippi; *(right)* Hong Kong Educational Publishing Co. **p. 40:** © The New Yorker Collection, 1982 Dana Fradon, from cartoonbank.com. All Rights Reserved.

### CHAPTER 2

**Page 46:** John S. Dykes. **p. 48:** *(left)* Courtesy Press Office of John McCain; *(right)* AFP/Getty Image. **p. 51:** Tim de Waele/Corbis. **p. 55:** Rubes cartoon by permission of Leigh Rubin and Creators Syndicate, Inc. **p. 60:** Charles Gupton/Corbis. **p. 62:** *(left)* Roger Ressmeyer/Corbis; *(right)* Bettmann/Corbis. **p. 63:** Reuters/Corbis. **p. 64:** Peter Turnley/Corbis. **p. 65:** Kevin Fleming/Corbis. **p. 67:** Eugene Delacroix. *A Fight Between Knights.* The Louvre, Paris, France. Photo: Erich Lessing/Art Resource, NY/Corbis. **p. 68:** *The Dying Gaul.* Roman copy of Greek original, ca. 230–220 BCE. Musei Capitolini, Rome, Italy. Photo: Scala/Art Resource, NY. **p. 70:** Royalty-Free/Corbis. **p. 76:** AP/Wide World Photos. **p. 78:** © The New Yorker Collection, 1994 Mike Twohy, from cartoonbank.com. All Rights Reserved.

### CHAPTER 3

**Page 86:** John S. Dykes. **p. 88:** Dave Allocca/Time Life Pictures/Getty Images. **p. 92:** The Far Side by Gary Larson, © 1984 FarWorks, Inc. All rights reserved. Used by permission. Distributed by Creators Syndicate. **p. 94:** *(left)* Natalie Fobes/Corbis; *(right)* Craig Lovell/Corbis; **p. 96:** (left) Brooks Kraft/Corbis; **p.**

Sygma. **p. 309:** Hunter Martin/Corbis. **p. 310:** *(top)* David Turnley/Corbis; *(bottom)* © 1982 Karen Zebuion, Courtesy New School Public Relations Department. **p. 311:** *(top)* Rob Rogers, © 1994 The Pittsburgh Post-Gazette/Distributed by United Feature Syndicate, Inc.; *(bottom)* Kevin R. Morris/Corbis. **p. 312:** Bettmann/Corbis. **p. 314:** Gabe Palmer/Corbis. **p. 321:** DILBERT, © 1999 Scott Adams/Distributed by United Feature Syndicate, Inc.

CHAPTER **9**

**Page 336:** John S. Dykes. **p. 338:** *(left and right)* Bettmann/Corbis. **p. 343:** Mitchell Gerber/Corbis. **p. 344:** © The New Yorker Collection, 1999 Leo Cullum, from cartoonbank.com. All Rights Reserved. **p. 348:** Ethan Miller/Reuters/Corbis. **p. 350:** Corbis Sygma. **p. 351:** Andrea Comas/Reuters/Corbis. **p. 352:** *(left)* From Yiyo y Sanchez Cubero. Photo: Nuñez; *(right)* Reuters/Corbis. **p. 353:** © The New Yorker Collection, 2002 Frank Cotham, from cartoonbank.com. All Rights Reserved. **p. 354:** *(left)* AP/Wide World Photos; *(right)* Mike Segar/Reuters/Corbis. **p. 359:** © The New Yorker Collection, 1994 Robert Mankoff, from cartoonbank.com. All Rights Reserved. **p. 361:** *(top left)* Underwood & Underwood/Corbis; *(top right)* Frederick M. Brown/Getty Images; *(bottom)* © The New Yorker Collection, 1997 Leo Cullum, from cartoonbank.com. All Rights Reserved. **p. 362:** Reuters/Corbis. **p. 367:** Reuters/Corbis; **p. 368:** Bob Croslin/Corbis; **p. 374:** *(left)* Wes Thompson Photography/Corbis; *(2nd from left)* Dale C. Spartas/Corbis; *(2nd from right)* Imagemore Co., Ltd./Corbis; *(right)* Chris Heller/Corbis.

CHAPTER **10**

**Page 380:** John S. Dykes. **p. 382:** Thom Scott/AFP/Getty Images. **p. 384:** Chuck Savage/Corbis. **p. 386:** *(left and right)* AP/Wide World Photos. **p. 387:** *(left)* NASA/AP/Wide World Photos; *(right)* AP/Wide World Photos. **p. 391:** Courtesy Professor Benjamin Harris, University of New Hampshire. **p. 392:** © The New Yorker Collection, 1999 Richard Cline, from cartoonbank.com. All Rights Reserved. **p. 393:** Gary M. Adler/CBS Photo Archive via Getty Images. **p. 394:** AP/Wide World Photos. **p. 397:** © The New Yorker Collection, 2001 J. C. Duffy, from cartoonbank.com. All Rights Reserved. **p. 398:** AP/Wide World Photos. **p. 402:** Pion Press; figure provided by Daniel J. Simons. **p . 405:** © The New Yorker Collection, 1996 John Jonik, from cartoonbank.com. All Rights Reserved. **p. 409:** AP/Wide World Photos/Il Messaggero. **p. 410:** *(left)* Eric Nguyen/Jim Reed Photography/Corbis; *(right)* MGM/Photofest. **p. 414:** *(left)* Bettmann/Corbis; *(right)* AP/Wide World Photos/Al Golub, Pool, The Modesto Bee. **p. 418:** *(left)* Charles & Josette Lenars/Corbis; *(right)* Ed Quinn/Corbis. **p. 419:** Blank Archives/Getty Images. **p. 422:** © The New Yorker Collection, 1977 Dana Fradon, from cartoonbank.com. All Rights Reserved.

CHAPTER **11**

**Page 428:** John S. Dykes. **p. 430:** Stapleton Collection/Corbis. **p. 431:** Reuters/Corbis. **p. 433:** © The New Yorker Collection, 1996 Roz Chast, from cartoonbank.com. All Rights Reserved. **p. 440:** *(all)* Archives of the History of American Psychology, University of Akron; The Carolyn and Muzafer Sherif Papers. **p. 442:** Kevin Fleming/Corbis. **p. 445:** *(left)* Wally McNamee/Corbis; *(right)* David Stoecklein/Corbis. **p. 446:** *(top)* Duomo/Corbis; *(bottom)* © The New Yorker Collection, 1996 Roz Chast, from cartoonbank.com. All Rights Reserved. **p. 447:** Steve Grayson/WireImage.com. **p. 452:** © The New Yorker Collection, 2000 David Sipress, from cartoonbank.com. All Rights Reserved. **p. 453:** Photo by Jesse Grant/WireImage.com/ABC. **p. 457:** AP/Wide World Photos. **p. 463:** Corbis Sygma. **p. 465:** Keystone/Gamma.

CHAPTER **12**

**Page 472:** John S. Dykes. **p. 474:** *(left)* Corbis; *(right)* Detail from Eadweard Muybridge's photograph of Falls of the Yosemite. From Glacier Rock (Great Grizzly Bear) 2000 feet fall, No. 36. Courtesy of The Bancroft Library, University of California, Berkeley. **p. 478:** *(left and right)* ©Ekman 1975–2004. **p. 479:** *(top left)* From *The Expression of the Emotions in Man and Animals* by Charles Darwin, fig. 5; *(top right)*: From *The Expression of the Emotions in Man and Animals* by Charles Darwin, fig. 6; *(bottom)* Bettmann/Corbis. **p. 480:** *(all)* Photographs courtesy Professor Dacher Keltner. **p. 481:** *(all)* © Ekman 1972–2004. **p. 483:** *(top)* © Ekman 2004; *(bottom)* © The New Yorker Collection, 2003 Roz Chast, from cartoonbank.com. All Rights Reserved. **p. 484:** *(left and right)* Photographs courtesy Dacher Keltner. **p. 490:** Courtesy Library and Archives, Canada. Photograph by Yousef Karsh. **p. 496:** Jose Luis Palaez, Inc./Corbis. **p. 499:** *(left)* Digital Vision/Getty Images; *(right)* George D. Lepp/Corbis; **p. 500:** *(left)* Peter M. Fisher/Corbis; *(right)* Bettmann/Corbis; **p. 501:** *(top)* Courtesy Larry J. Young, PhD, Yerkes National Primate Research Center, Emory University;*(bottom)* © Tom McHugh/Photo Researchers, Inc. **p. 504:** Courtesy Huguette Martel.

CHAPTER **13**

**Page 512:** John S. Dykes. **p. 514:** Carlo Allegri/Getty Images. **p. 515:** *(left)* Bettmann/Corbis; *(right)* Scott Peterson/Getty Images. **p. 517:** *(left)* Sunset Boulevard/Corbis Sygma; *(right)* AFP/Getty Images. **p. 520:** *(top left and bottom left)* AP/Wide World Photos; *(right)* Reuters/Corbis. **p. 521:** *(top)* Getty Images; *(bottom)* Universal Pictures/Photofest. **p. 522:** *(left)* Ray Stubblebine/Reuters/Corbis; *(right)* Brian Snyder/Reuters/Corbis, **p. 526:** Focus on Sport/Getty Images. **p. 527:** *(left)* Robert van der Hilst/Corbis; *(right)* Photo by Dr. Napoleon A. Chagnon. **p. 530:** © The New Yorker Collection, 2003 Frank Cotham, from cartoonbank.com. All Rights Reserved. **p. 532:** *(left)* Leonard de Selva/Corbis; *(right)* Bettmann/Corbis; **p. 535:** Courtesy The New York Times Picture Archives. **p. 536:** The Far Side by Gary Larson, © 1992 FarWorks, Inc. All Rights Reserved. Used with permission of Creators Syndicate. **p. 539:** Gabe Palmer/Corbis. **p. 540:** © The New Yorker Collection, 2004 Michael Crawford, from cartoonbank.com. All Rights Reserved. **p. 542:** Michael and Patricia Fogden/Corbis. **p. 543:** *(left)* Royalty-Free/Corbis; *(right)* Tom Brakefield/Corbis. **p. 544:** *(top)* © the New Yorker Collection, 1988 Ed Fisher, from cartoonbank.com. All Rights Reserved. **p. 544:** *(bottom left)* Alan Levenson/Time Life Pictures/Getty Images; *(bottom right)* Courtesy Debra DiPaolo. **p. 545:** Blaine Harrington III/Corbis. **p. 546:** © The New Yorker Collection, 1989 Danny Shanahan, from cartoonbank.com. All Rights Reserved. **p. 549:** Michael Mulvey/Dallas Morning News/Corbis.

CHAPTER **14**

**Page 552:** John S. Dykes. **p. 554:** *(left)* Courtesy of the S.L.A. Marshall Collection, Archives at St. Bonaventure University; *(right)* Courtesy of the University of Oklahoma Press. **p. 556:** *(left and right)* Frans de Waal, Yerkes Primate Research Center,

# Name Index

Page numbers in *italics* refer to figures, illustrations, and tables.

# Subject Index

Page numbers in *italics* refer to figures, illustrations, and tables.

guilt, compliance and, 247–51

Halloween study, of deindividuation, 68–69
halo effect, 106–7
*Hamlet* (Shakespeare), 508
happiness, 479, *480, 481,* 505–9
  determinants of pleasure in, 505, 508
  predicting levels of, 506–7, *506,* 508–9
  sources of, 507–8, *508, 509*
Harlow's deprivation studies with monkeys, 131–32, *132*
*Harry Potter and the Sorceror's Stone* (Rowling), 223
hate crimes, 155
heat, violence and, 521–23, *521, 522,* 534
heritability, 172–74, *173*
heterosexuality, 101
heuristic route to persuasion, *see* peripheral route to persuasion
heuristics, 409–25
  availability, 410–14, *410, 412, 413*
  base-rate neglect, 415–17
  biased assessments of risk, 412–13
  biased estimates of contributions, 413–14
  definition of, 410
  judgment and, 409–25
  planning fallacy, 417–18
  representativeness, 410, 414–23, *414, 416, 422*
  statistics and, 420, *420*
heuristic-systematic model, 270, *271*
hierarchical relationships, 151–56
  *see also* power
high-context cultures, 179–80
  *see also* individualistic cultures
Holocaust, 130, 214, 235, 236, 238–40, 252, 515
homicide, gender and, 523–24, *533*
hostile aggression, 516
hostile media phenomenon, 286
*How to Win Friends and Influence People* (Carnegie), 123
human universals, 23–25, *23, 24,* 28, 171–72, *173–74,* 330
  critiques of studies of, 481–82
  emotion as, 477–82, *479,* 484–85, *484*
  facial expressions as, 479–81, *480, 481,* 487
  morality and, 558–62
Hush Puppies, 216, *216*
Hutus, 513–14
"Hutu Ten Commandments, The," 513–14
hypercognize, 484
hypothesis, defining of, 37, 41

ideal self, 186, 191
identifiable victim effect, 277–78, *278*

identity cues, 197–98, *197*
ideomotor action, 216–17, *217*
illusions and idealization, in romantic relationships, 164–65
illusory correlation, 423–25, 456–58, *457*
illustrators, 500
immune neglect, 507
implicit association test (IAT), 435–36, *435,* 437
impression management, 202–3
  *see also* self-presentation
impulsive behavior, deindividuation and, 65, *65*
"incestuous amplification," 73
inclusive fitness, 517, 532
independent cultures, 29–31, *29, 30, 31, 34,* 35–36, 37, 179–80, *179, 180,* 182–83, 199
  causal attribution in, 372–73, 376
  conformity in, 225, 230
  dispositions as fixed in, 374–75
  persuasive messages in, 279, *280*
  vs. collectivism in the workplace, 32–33, *32*
  *see also* cultural differences
independent variable, 39
individualistic cultures, *see* independent cultures
individuation, 70–71, *70*
induced (forced) compliance, 315–18, *316*
information:
  biases in, 383–95
  firsthand biases in, 383–89, 394–95
  framing effects and, 397–401
  as mapped onto preexisting schemas, 404–8, *406*
  order effects and, 395–97, 400–401
  presentation of, 395–401
  secondhand biases in, 389–95
informational social influence, 219, 227, 230
ingroups, *30*
  accentuation of outgroup similarity and difference of, 453
  boosting status of, 445
  *see also* intergroup hostility
instrumental aggression, 516
integration, 441–42, *442*
integrative complexity, 583
interaction, anticipating, 92–93
interaction dynamics approach, 159–61
*interahamwe,* 514–15
interdependent cultures, *29,* 30–31, *30, 31,* 35–36, 37, 179–81, *179, 180,* 183, 186, 199
  causal attribution in, 372–73, 376
  conformity in, 225, 230
  dispositions as malleable in, 374–75
  emotional cues in, 486–87, *486*
  persuasive messages in, 279, *280*

vs. individualism in the workplace, 32–33, *32*
  *see also* cultural differences
intergroup hostility, 437–43
  characterization of bias and, 432–37
  cognitive perspective on, 450–66
  construal processes and biased assessments in, 452–58
  economic perspective on, 437–43
  frustration-aggression theory on, 446–50, *447*
  immunity to disconfirmation and, 458–60, 466
  minimal group paradigm and, 443–44, 450
  motivational perspective on, 443–50
  realistic group conflict theory on, 437–38, 443
  reduction of, 439–40, *440,* 441–42
  Robbers Cave experiment on, 438–40, *440,* 441, 442, 443
  social identity theory on, 444–46, *445*
internalization, 226
interpersonal attraction, *see* attraction
interpersonal relationships, 131
  investment model of, *158,* 162–64, *162,* 166
  *see also* relationships
interpersonal simulations, 325
interpretative context of disagreement, 227–29, *228*
intersex attraction, 116
intrasex competition, 116
introversion, 7, 173, 185
intuitive processing, 409, *409,* 425
  *see also* heuristics
investment model of interpersonal relationships, *158,* 162–64, *162,* 166
  battered women and, 163
Iraq, invasion of, 73

James's theory of emotion-specific physiology, 487–88, 490, *491*
*Jane's Defense Weekly,* 73
"jigsaw" classroom, 441
Johnson administration, 72
justice, 553–56, 567–76, *567*
  distributive, 567, 568–72, *569, 571,* 576
  evolution of, 554–56
  procedural, 567, 572–73, 576
  restorative, 567–68, 573–76, *574, 575*
just world hypothesis, 360, 361–62, 573

Kahneman and the heuristics of judgment, 399, 409–10, 411, 412, 414, 415
*Kangura,* 513
Kanisza triangle, *14*
Kennedy administration, 72, 74–75, *76*
Khmer Rouge, 515

HALF PRICE BOOKS
2036 Shattuck Ave.
Berkeley, CA  94704-1117
510-526-6080

08/22/07 08:45 PM
#00037/BE0037/00001

CUSTOMER: 000000000
SALE: 0000631679

| 1 | @7.98 | UN | 7.98 |
| | 5799-(Used books at low prices) | | |
| 1 | @29.98 | UN | 29.98 |
| | 5799-(Used books at low prices) | | |

| SHIP/HAND | 0.00 |
| TAX (8.75% on $37.96) | 3.32 |
| TOTAL | 41.28 |

### PAYMENT TYPE
MC (**5449/REF:4084184)          41.28
AUTH CODE:045347

| PAYMENT TOTAL | $ | 41.28 |
| CHANGE DUE | $ | 0.00 |

### THANK YOU!

We buy books, music, movies and more!

### END OF TRANSACTION